SPARKNOTES 101

Women's Literature

SPARK PUBLISHING

Spark Publishing
120 Fifth Avenue
New York, NY 10011
www.sparknotes.com

ISBN-10: 1-4114-0338-X
ISBN-13: 978-1-4114-0338-3

Please submit comments and questions or report errors to www.sparknotes.com/errors

Printed and bound in the United States.

Library of Congress Cataloging-in-Publication Data

Sparknotes 101 : women's literature.
p. cm.
Includes bibliographical references.
ISBN-13: 978-1-4114-0338-3
1. English literature—Women authors—Examinations—Study guides.
2. American literature—Women authors—Examinations—Study guides.
3. Women and literature—English-speaking countries—Examinations—Study guides.
I. Title: Sparknotes one hundred one. II. Title: Sparknotes one hundred and one.

PR111.S73 2006
820.9'9287—dc22

2005021274

Contents

Acknowledgments

SparkNotes would like to thank the following writers and contributors:

Joshua Adams
Amy Alexander
Adrien Ardoin
Etienne Benson
Rebecca Benson
Somer Bingham
Annie Bourneuf
Juliana Castedo
Jim Cocola
Michael Cohen
Amanda David
Ross Douthat
Katherine Flanagan-Hyde
Deborah Forbes
Brendan Gibbon
Lina Goldberg
Debra Grossman
Juliette Guilbert
Alexa Gutheil
Kyle Hawkins
David Hopson
Pelagia Horgan
Kadi Hughes
Mike Lew
Meghan Lydon
Melissa Martin
Amanda McCormick
Kate McGovern
Dinaw Mengestu
Erin Moncada
Brenna Moore
Jon Natchez
Heather Otrando
Geoffrey Owens
Brian Phillips
Irena Pochop
Alexandra Price
Megan Ryan
Doug Sanders
Matilda Santos
Katherine Schweighofer
Caroline Smith
Sarah Spain
Sasha Stiles
Keja Valens
Emily Von
Joel Walsh
Selena Ward
Jen Wardell
Anna Weinberg
Jennifer Wortman
Amanda Zafian

A Note from SparkNotes

Welcome to the *SparkNotes 101* series! This book will help you succeed in your introductory college course on Women's Literature. *Women's Literature 101* gives you notes on the sixty-five books you're most likely to encounter when you're studying women's lit, and we've compressed the notes to give you *exactly* what you need to know. Here's what you'll find in this *101*:

INTRODUCTION

Before delving into the notes, you may want to get a view of women's literature in general. The Introduction will discuss the evolution of women's literature, the historical contexts of women writers, and the most important themes that works of women's literature have in common.

THE NOTES

To make navigation easy, the sixty-five entries are arranged alphabetically by title. If you want to see the works listed by author, turn to page 629 and consult the Appendix. Each note contains the following sections:

- **Context:** An overview that traces the author's biographical details and explores the work's historical, ideological, and biographical circumstance. It also discusses how the work fits into the field of women's literature.
- **Plot Overview:** A concise summary of the book to refresh your memory and help you understand major plot points.
- **Character List:** A sketch of the work's cast of characters in order of importance, along with a brief explanation of the role each character plays.
- **Analysis of Major Characters:** In-depth studies of what makes the principal characters tick.
- **Themes, Motifs, and Symbols:** The most important ideas of the work, all in one place. Themes are the fundamental and often universal ideas explored in a literary work. Motifs are recurring structures, contrasts, or literary devices that can help to develop and inform the plot and thematic development. Symbols are objects, characters, figures, or colors used to represent abstract concepts.
- **Important Quotations Explained:** The most important lines from the work with explanations of why they're significant.

A+ STUDENT ESSAYS

We give you ten essays of A+ quality so you can see how students have responded to prompts similar to what you would find on an exam. We've based our essays on ten of the most popular works in women's literature.

We hope *SparkNotes 101: Women's Literature* helps you, gives you confidence, and occasionally saves your grade! Your input makes us better. Let us know what you think or how we can improve this book at www.sparknotes.com/comments.

Introduction

WHAT IS WOMEN'S LITERATURE?

"Women's literature" is a deceptively simple name for something that's not easily defined. By its very nature, women's literature resists pigeonholing or narrow definition, so we can best clarify the idea of women's literature by emphasizing what it's *not.* Women's literature comprises works written by women—but not all works written by women are necessarily women's literature. Likewise, many works that comprise women's literature are about women—but not all books about women are women's literature. Perhaps most important, women's literature is not just for women. It is as important as any other category in the broad history of literature.

Women's lit isn't chick lit—*Bridget Jones's Diary* and *Bergdorf Blondes*, for example, don't make the cut. Women writers are held to the same standards as male writers in terms of language, plot, characterization, and theme, and just because a work is "women's literature" doesn't mean it's not great literature as well. The category of women's literature also exists to emphasize the idea that the female voice has historically had to struggle to be heard in the male-dominated world of writing. Though there are certainly common themes that run through women's literature, which we'll discuss in a moment, the perspectives, plots, characters, and voices differ as widely as do the works in any other literary field—and the works are just as influential, affecting, and significant.

The field of women's literature is growing as writing becomes more accessible to women with different experiences, backgrounds, and histories. Women from all over the world have overcome and continue to overcome economic and social obstacles to writing, and as a result, the field of women's literature is extremely diverse.

MAJOR HISTORICAL TIME PERIODS

Unlike general literature, which typically falls into traditional categories such as Romanticism or Victorianism, women's literature is usually classified by historical time period. There are six major categories:

1. Middle Ages/Renaissance
2. 1600–1700
3. The Nineteenth Century
4. The Turn of the Century
5. Early Twentieth Century
6. Later Twentieth Century

The literature of each of these periods usually has several unifying characteristics, most of which are determined by the historical developments taking place at the time.

MIDDLE AGES/RENAISSANCE During the Middle Ages and the Renaissance, the few samples of women's writing came from women in special circumstances, such as those who had been taught by an educated father or husband or those associated with the church or with the state. Reading and writing were reserved for the elite, and the themes focused on historical or religious subjects. The reign of England's Queen Elizabeth II, a powerful and charismatic woman, began to challenge the idea that women could not be powerful, successful, or educated, which was a new idea in a world where nearly all formal power belonged to men. Margery Kempe was one of these few women writers; her autobiography, *The Book of Margery Kempe*, was heavily influenced by her spiritual struggles and multiple pilgrimages.

1600–1700 Between 1600 and the end of the 1700s, the face of writing completely changed. With the invention of the printing press, writing became commercialized; instead of being dependent on wealthy patrons, writers could publish more easily, and works became widely available. This change allowed more women writers—even those not part of the upper class—to publish. Religious disputes between Protestants and Catholics, political debates surrounding the British empire and its breakaway colony, America, and other intellectual and economic issues provided plenty of material for emerging women writers.

THE NINETEENTH CENTURY The 1800s were dominated by the "woman question": were women equal to men? Women everywhere worked to prove they deserved equality. They lobbied for the right to vote, joined trade unions, studied medicine, and became more and more visible outside the home. Women writers produced masterpieces, often addressing themes of liberty, social class, nature, beauty, and individualism. Jane Austen, Mary Shelley, and the Brontë sisters made their mark on literature during this period.

THE TURN OF THE CENTURY The years just before and after 1900 brought a surge in the world of literature. The continuing commercialization of literature, as well as the rising literacy rates created a whole new class of cheap, low-quality publications that flooded the market. Writers and artists were already disillusioned by the artificial grandeur of the late 1800s and the rapid rise of industrialism (the increase in factories and mass-production). These writers became more critical when this new trend of mass-produced novels exploded, creating a break between "high art" and "low art" forms. Kate Chopin, Edith Wharton, and Charlotte Perkins Gilman are major woman writers from this time.

EARLY TWENTIETH CENTURY The early decades of the twentieth century were marked by economic depression, industrialization, and wartime. These forces brought with them irony, horror, depression, and helplessness. Women writers echoed these turbulent emotional shifts in their work, exploring issues of class, race, integrity, and origins. Willa Cather, Virginia Woolf, and Zora Neale Hurston built upon the now-established work of other women writers and brought their new voices and their new issues to light.

LATER TWENTIETH CENTURY The later twentieth century marked an explosion of women writers who pushed the boundaries of women's literature further than ever imagined. Toni Morrison, Maya Angelou, and Alice Walker proved black women's writing deserving of the highest praises. Sylvia Plath and other women writers created new forms of and approaches to poetry, in addition to their prose. Short stories, biographies, novellas, and other nontraditional forms of writing allowed these writers to share their ideas. To address questions of identity, women writers brought together new ideas on race, class, geography, and family. They also focused on love, desire, and sexuality and their roles in lesbian desire, female friendships, and sexual control.

MAJOR THEMES

There are no limits to the themes and topics women's literature can address. However, several major themes have proven to be significant in shaping both women's literature and literature in general. Here is a brief overview of some of these themes, along with examples of writers who deal with that theme in their work:

THE CONFLICT BETWEEN SOCIAL EXPECTATIONS AND IDENTITY

- Kate Chopin, *The Awakening*
- Virginia Woolf, *Mrs. Dalloway*

THE CONNECTION BETWEEN SEXUALITY AND IDENTITY, LOVE, ABUSE, AND DESIRE

- Jeanette Winterson, *Oranges Are Not the Only Fruit*
- Emily Brontë, *Wuthering Heights*

THE RELATIONSHIP BETWEEN MOTHERS AND DAUGHTERS

- Amy Tan, *The Joy Luck Club*
- Rita Mae Brown, *Rubyfruit Jungle*

THE CHALLENGES OF GROWING UP

- Louisa May Alcott, *Little Women*
- Charlotte Brontë, *Jane Eyre*

THE INFLUENCE OF FEMINISM AND THE WOMEN'S MOVEMENT

- Charlotte Perkins Gilman, *Herland*
- Virginia Woolf, *A Room of One's Own*

* * * * * * * *

The writers we've included in *SparkNotes 101: Women's Literature* come from a wide variety of time periods, backgrounds, and experiences, and their works address a vast spectrum of themes and ideas. All of these authors have contributed in some way to the development of women's literature—and their voices, themes, and ideas have not only shaped the canon but informed readers around the world as well.

All But My Life

Gerda Weissmann Klein
(1924–)

A

CONTEXT

All But My Life is Gerda Weissmann Klein's memoir of her experiences during World War II. Klein was born on May 8, 1924, in Bielitz (now Bielsko), Poland. She remembers her childhood as being happy, even idyllic. The Weissmanns were a Jewish family, and their town had been part of the Austro-Hungarian Empire before 1919. Like most of the residents in the area, the Weissmann family was bilingual, speaking both Polish and German, and Klein's older brother, Arthur, studied English as well. Klein's father, Julius, was a business executive who had lived in Bielitz for more than twenty years, and Helene, her mother, was born there, as were both Klein and Arthur. The family was horrified when German Nazi forces invaded Poland on September 1, 1939. Despite the fact that Britain and the United States declared war on Germany two days later, it took the Nazis only eighteen days to conquer Poland.

Soon afterward, the entire Jewish population of Bielitz was forced to register with the police, and soon, sanctions were imposed against the Jews. First, they were required to turn in all gold, automobiles, bicycles, and radios. Many Jews were forced out of their homes, and the local temple was burned down. In October of 1939, all Jewish men between the ages of sixteen and fifty were forced to register, whereupon they were sent in cattle cars to rebuild parts of Poland that had been destroyed by Allied attacks. Klein's brother was sent to the interior of Poland in one of these transports. In December, the Weissmann family was forced to move into the basement of their home, while the woman who had been their laundress took over the main house. After Christmas, the Nazis restricted the local Jewish population's food supply by stamping their ration cards with the word "JEW," entitling them to less than half the amount of food that non-Jews received. Their coal rations were also cut, and they were forced to wear blue and white armbands and, later, yellow stars that identified them as Jews.

Before the war began, Bielitz had a Jewish population of nearly 8,000 people. As news of the German treatment of Jews reached them, however, more and more Jews fled to the Russian-occupied parts of Poland that had not been claimed during the German takeover. By the spring of 1940, the Jewish population in Bielitz had dwindled to little more than three hundred people, most of them children and the elderly. Like Klein's brother, all of the young men had left in the transports. The young female population was declining as well, as more and more families left or sent their children out of the country. On April 19, 1942, all of the remaining Jews in Bielitz were ordered to move into a newly constructed Jewish ghetto. In May of 1942, shortly after Klein's eighteenth birthday, all Jews were required to register for work. Those who did not comply were sent to Auschwitz, a nearby concentration camp intended to enable the Nazis to kill those people who were deemed not useful to the German cause. Soon, the Weissmann family was told that they would be sent to camps in order to make Bielitz *Judenrein*—free of Jews. Klein's father and mother were taken to death camps, where they were killed, along with one to three million others.

Poland was the center of the Jewish Holocaust, and Auschwitz, Treblinka, Belzec, Majdanek, Sobibor, and Birkenau, the infamous concentration camps, were all located there. The survival rate for Jews living in Poland during the war was lower than in any other country. Poland's Jewish population dropped from 3,500,000 to just 50,000 by the end of the war. At the same time that her parents were taken to Auschwitz, Klein and many other young Polish people were taken to labor camps, where they became slaves forced to work for the German war effort. As it became obvious that Germany was losing the war, the Germans started dismantling the camps and forcing the prisoners onto marches that became known as "death marches" because of their extremely high mortality rate. In the winter of 1945, more than four thousand young women were forced onto a three-hundred-mile "death march" from a number of labor camps in Germany and Poland to Czechoslovakia. Among them was Gerda Weissmann Klein—one of only 120 women in her group of 2,000 who survived this march. Klein and the other women were liberated by American troops—including one soldier who eventually became Klein's husband in the spring of 1945.

All But My Life is Klein's memoir of the period from September 3, 1939, two days after the Nazi invasion of Poland, until September of 1945. In 1946, Klein moved to Buffalo, New York, with her husband, Kurt Klein, where she began working to raise awareness about the Holocaust, prevent hunger, and promote tolerance. She quickly formed ties with a number of Jewish groups and began lecturing about her experiences as a young woman during the Holocaust. First published in 1957, Klein's story was the basis for the Academy Award-winning documentary *One Survivor Remembers*. Klein also went on to write a number of other books, including a collection of her correspondence with her then-fiancé, Kurt Klein, before their marriage in 1946.

All But My Life is just one of many memoirs written in the decades immediately following the end of World War II. In 1995 the memoir was revised and re-released with an epilogue describing Klein's postwar life.

PLOT OVERVIEW

Gerda Weissmann Klein's story begins on September 3, 1939, when she is fifteen. This day, she says, was the beginning of a tragedy that lasted six years. She is living in Bielitz, Poland, the town of her birth, and she reacts with horror as she watches her neighbors greet the invading Nazis with joy. The family had been trying to hide the possibility of war from Gerda's father because he was ill and they didn't want to upset him. Once their town is invaded, though, they can no longer keep it a secret from him. Sanctions start being imposed on the Jews, and Jewish men are being abducted by the Nazis.

In October, Gerda's brother, Arthur, is forced to leave in a Nazi transport with all of the other young men in town. Gerda never sees him again, although she receives letters from him throughout much of the war. The situation becomes more and more dire for the Jews, as their Aryan neighbors take advantage of the situation as much as they can, buying their possessions for a fraction of their worth and taking over the factories they own. The Weissmanns are forced to switch homes with their laundress, who has been living in their basement, and not long after, they are told they will soon be forced to move into a Jewish ghetto. Gerda travels with her childhood friend Ilse to visit a camp for young Jewish men and meets Abek Feigenblatt, who quickly falls in love with her, although his feelings are not reciprocated. Gerda thinks of Abek is a friend and nothing more.

Gerda becomes increasingly aware of how truly horrifying the situation has gotten when she receives a letter from her friend Erika, telling her how her mother, baby brother, and boyfriend were forced to lie naked on the cobblestones of their town and were then trampled to death by Nazis on horseback.

In 1942, the family is forced into a Jewish ghetto and ordered to work for the German war effort. However, it is not long before all the Jews are told they will be moved out of town so Bielitz can be *Judenrein*—free of Jews. Gerda is separated from her parents and never sees them again.

Gerda goes to a transit camp in Sosnowitz, where Abek's family makes sacrifices to try and get her freedom. However, she chooses to not go with them because she realizes that she will be so thoroughly in their debt that she will be forced to marry Abek, which she does not want to do. Gerda and Ilse are then transported to a labor camp that specializes in weaving, which they are forced to do for the German war effort. Gerda regularly receives loving letters from Abek while in the camp.

In August of 1943, the girls are divided into groups and told they will be leaving the camp and taken to Märzdorf, another labor camp. Luckily, Gerda and Ilse are in the same group. Märzdorf is almost unbearable for Gerda once she refuses a supervisor's advances and is punished by being forced to work both the day and night shifts. Ilse manages to save her by having them both transferred to a weaving camp in Landeshut.

They discover that there is a men's camp next door, reputed to be the worst camp in all of Germany. Gerda is shocked and guilt-ridden when she hears that Abek has voluntarily transferred there to be closer to her.

On May 6, 1944, the girls find out that they are to be transferred again. Ilse and Gerda continue to mourn the loss of their families but still have hope for their own survival. The new camp, Grünberg, is brutal, but still not as bad as Märzdorf. In November, the girls are forced to strip naked and be visually inspected by the SS (stands for *Schutzstaffel*, the term for Hitler's elite group of soldiers). They hear rumors that they may be sent to provide "amusement" for wounded German soldiers. Gerda manages to buy enough poison for both herself and Ilse so that they will be able to avoid this fate.

As the war progresses and Germany begins to falter, the situation at the camp becomes worse and worse. In January 1945, they find out that Germany is being invaded by the Allies. Girls from other work camps arrive, increasing the camp population to over 4,000 young women. They are divided into two groups and told they will be marching to a concentration camp. Gerda says that her group was doomed—only 120 of them survived—but she expresses no regrets about being assigned to this group. They begin their march, and after only a few days, girls begin to die of starvation and cold. They march for weeks through bombed-out cities of Germany and, in March, finally arrive at another camp, Helmbrechts.

The next month, however, they are forced to begin marching again, and they soon cross the Czechoslovakian border. Ilse grows weaker and weaker, and Gerda tries in vain to protect her. Ilse dies on the march, as do most of the other prisoners. One night, in a town called Volary, they are locked into a factory building and left there by the SS with a bomb outside.

The bomb does not go off, however, and the Czech people unlock the doors, announcing that the war is over. The surviving girls are taken to a makeshift hospital by the Red Cross and American soldiers. One of these American soldiers is Kurt Klein, who continues to visit Gerda while she is in the hospital. Before he is forced to go back to America, he asks Gerda to come with him and be his wife. She says she knows she will never be alone again.

CHARACTER LIST

Gerda Weissmann Klein The narrator of the memoir that covers six years of her life. The title *All But My Life* refers to what the Nazis took from Gerda, and the book covers the physical and psychological journey that begins when she is just fifteen years old—a journey that she barely survives. Throughout the ordeal, Gerda remains hopeful about both her family's fate and her own, and she emphasizes the positive attributes of those around her. Gerda's character is epitomized by her brave optimism and strength in the face of the Holocaust.

Julius Weissmann Gerda's father, referred to as "Papa." Despite his illness, Julius does not complain and does what little he can to make the lives of his family better. Although he lives only through Part One of the book, Gerda constantly thinks about him and prays for his survival. She believes that he is responsible for saving her life, first by insisting that she wear her skiing boots before she left on the transport and then by making her promise that she would not kill herself.

Helene Weissmann Gerda's mother, known as "Mama." Helene tries to make the best of her situation and is willing to sacrifice anything she can for her family. Helene was born in Bielitz, and although she is shocked by the invasion and the townspeople's response, she is stoic about what is happening around her. She is separated from Gerda and the end of Part One, and although Gerda never sees her again, she reminisces about her constantly and remembers her in her prayers.

Arthur Weissmann Gerda's older brother. Losing Arthur is one of Gerda's greatest trials during the war. Witty and attractive, Arthur is a brave young man who urges Gerda to be strong for their parents. Although Arthur exists mainly in Gerda's memories, he is still a driving force in her memoir.

Ilse Kleinzähler A childhood friend of Gerda's from Bielitz. Together, Gerda and Ilse are forced into camps and onto a death march, where Ilse eventually dies. Ilse is a good friend to Gerda, sacrificing her food for her and putting herself at risk to help her. Ilse's friendship is one of Gerda's key motivators throughout their time in the camps and during the death march.

Abek Feigenblatt A suitor of Gerda's. Abek hopes that one day after the war, Gerda will marry him. He sacrifices much to be with her, despite the fact that her feelings are not reciprocated and that she regards him as more of an older brother figure than a boyfriend. Eventually, his hopes are crushed, and he loses his will to live while housed in the most horrific German labor camp.

Kurt Klein An American soldier who helps liberate Gerda and the other girls. His parents were victims of the Holocaust, so he is very empathetic to Gerda's needs and seems to know instinctively what will make her feel better. His love and compassion are vital to her recovery from the horrors she experiences during the war.

Suse and Liesel Two girls whom Gerda befriends in the camps and who end up on the death march with her. Together with Ilse, the four girls form a loving community of support for each other during their journey. Both Suse and Liesel die immediately after the march.

Erika A childhood friend of Gerda's. It is her heartbreaking letter that brings the reality of the Holocaust home to Gerda. Erika's love for her fiancé also helps Gerda explore her own feelings for Abek.

Mrs. Berger The Jewish woman in charge of the girls at Bolkenhain; a fellow prisoner at Landeshut. Although Mrs. Berger has many undesirable qualities, she also exhibits integrity and courage and makes the girls' experiences at Bolkenhain more pleasant.

Tusia A giraffe-necked girl in the camps. Tusia shares the same birthday as Gerda. Her words, before she goes mad and dies, have a prophetic quality.

Frau Kügler A worker for the SS whose appearance resembles that of a bulldog. Frau Kügler still has sympathy for some Jews, as she demonstrates when she saves Gerda's life by not allowing her to remain in the sickroom when the SS come to the camp for selections.

Peter A friend of Arthur's who visits from Krakow, bearing good news about Arthur. He later confesses to Gerda that he made up the news to bring her parents some happiness, and Gerda decides to keep it a secret.

Merin A Jewish leader who works with the SS to help them liquidate his fellow Jews. He sends Gerda's mother to her death, but despite her pleading, forces her to go with the other group, thus sparing her from Auschwitz. He is called "The King of the Jews."

Uncle Leo Gerda's mother's brother, who lives in Turkey. Leo is one of Gerda's only relatives to survive the Holocaust, and he helps her in any way he can throughout the war, sending her packages and ultimately inviting her to live with him at the end of the war.

Aunt Anna Gerda's father's sister. Anna has two children, Miriam and David. Her experiences are the first firsthand accounts that the Weissmanns hear about the horror of what is to come. After she moves to the interior of Poland to escape the Nazis, she is never heard from again.

Mr. Pipersberg Gerda's father's business partner and a family friend. Mr. Pipersberg urges Gerda to keep secret the fact that he was beaten for going to their factory once the Nazis have taken it over. He moves to the interior of Poland under an assumed identity and is never heard from again.

Hanka A girl in the camps who, on the death march, remains strong. She sneaks the girls extra food in the camps and protects them while on the march. Through her help, Gerda ultimately survives and doesn't lose her precious skiing shoes.

Niania Brenza An old Austrian who speaks only German and remains loyal to the dead emperor, Franz Josef. Niania was Gerda and Arthur's nanny and lived with the family for thirteen years. She continues to visit them, despite being warned not to by the Nazis. Gerda is annoyed by her easy security but still loves her dearly.

ANALYSIS OF MAJOR CHARACTERS

GERDA WEISSMANN KLEIN Gerda's maturation takes place gradually throughout *All But My Life*, under the shadow of the Nazi regime. At the beginning of her memoir, Gerda depicts herself as an innocent and naïve teenager. As she loses her family members one by one, she is forced to become entirely self-reliant, and only then does her resolute spirit truly become apparent. Most notable about Gerda is her ability to remain optimistic in the face of the Holocaust and despite everything, to focus on the positive aspects of her life. This optimism allows Gerda to make her memoir a tale of love and community set against the backdrop of the horrors of the Holocaust, rather than a tale that focuses on the cruelty that she has endured.

Though Gerda encounters almost unbelievable evil during her life, she also witnesses many instances of kindness, though she never becomes sentimental when she describes them. She relates the events as they happen but leaves out a certain element of emotional complexity, which keeps us from getting to know her better. However, the distance that Gerda maintains offers an insight into her character as well. Her inability to attach emotional resonance to the events that she witnesses shows just how damaged she is by the events of the Holocaust. Her insistence on paying homage to the goodness of her peers in the camps epitomizes her belief that bearing witness to what happened is more important than merely telling her own story, and this belief illustrates her unselfish character. Gerda's personality is typified by her steadfast hope, brave optimism, and willingness to help her comrades despite personal risk.

ILSE KLEINZÄHLER Ilse, one of Gerda's childhood friends, eventually becomes Gerda's only family. Ilse is a talented musician who plays the piano with emotional intensity and gives herself entirely to her music. Although Ilse is more timid than Gerda, she is intensely brave in her own way and is willing to sacrifice much to assist her friend. She is not envious of Gerda's good fortune when Gerda is given the opportunity to leave the transit camp to be with Abek's family; rather, she is genuinely happy for Gerda. They hold hands constantly throughout the memoir, both to give each other strength and to demonstrate their unbreakable friendship. They are even holding hands when Ilse dies during the last week of the death march.

Perhaps because Gerda wrote her memoir after Ilse's death, she attributes a sort of otherworldly goodness to Ilse and credits her with saving her life many times. She attaches great significance to the time that Ilse found a slightly crushed raspberry and carried it all day to give it as a gift to Gerda that night. This moment—when Ilse's only possession in the world is nothing more than a bruised raspberry, yet she chooses to give it to her friend—provides an intimate view of Ilse's character. Not only is she kind and sweet, but she is self-sacrificing and willing to do anything she can to help Gerda. Even on her deathbed, she expresses concern for her friends and her family, forcing Gerda to promise to live to see the end of the war, and asking that Gerda spare Ilse's parents the pain of hearing that Ilse died as she did. Her character is that of an admirable martyr without whom Gerda would have probably not survived the war.

ABEK FEIGENBLATT Abek is an intense and passionate young man who falls in love with Gerda at first sight and continues to love her despite her constant rejections. He is a Jewish Hebrew scholar and has a superior air about him when he speaks to people. He is intelligent and has sound judgment, and even Gerda's father respects him. Abek is convinced that Gerda's love is all he needs in order to maintain the courage required to get through the war. He is determined and forceful, yet Gerda sees his neediness toward her as a sign of weakness. She feels that were he more forceful, perhaps he could be the man she is searching for, but his weakness disillusions her.

In Gerda's life, Abek takes the role of an older brother, although he would prefer to be her lover. His love for her is intense—he forces his family to help Gerda, at great personal sacrifice, and he truly believes that one day he will be able to change her feelings toward him. Abek writes to Gerda faithfully, even when he receives no response, and eventually he voluntarily transfers to the worst camp in Germany to be closer to her. Though Abek initially functions as an older brother in Gerda's life, he eventually becomes the focus of the guilt she feels when she recognizes that he has made his life nearly unbearable in order to be closer to her. Only when he truly realizes that Gerda does not love him does he give up hope completely and begin to lose the desire to live.

KURT KLEIN Kurt is an American soldier who helps liberate the remaining girls from the death march, and Gerda believes that he is her soul mate. Kurt was born in Germany, and he moved to the United States a year after Hitler came to power, leaving his parents behind. His parents were put in a camp, and his letters to them were marked "Undeliverable." The suffering and guilt he feels regarding his parents' fate allow him to understand Gerda's feelings, and this helps the two connect more deeply. Intuitively, Kurt understands what Gerda feels and needs, and his instinctual understanding of her makes Gerda believe that they are truly destined to be together. While she is in the hospital, he does not bring her clothes and food, though she needs them, because he wants her to feel that this is a normal courtship and that he does not see her as victim. Although Gerda doesn't explore his character very thoroughly in her memoir, his deep and abiding love for Gerda, and hers for him, is clear.

THEMES, MOTIFS, AND SYMBOLS

THEMES

THE SUSTAINING POWER OF HOPE Despite all she endures, Gerda never loses hope that her life will improve and that her suffering has some greater meaning. Gerda is not strongly religious, but she has faith in humanity, nature, and the belief that no matter what happens, something good can come from it. When Gerda writes about being in the group sent on the death march from Grünberg, of which only 120 out of the 2,000 in her part of the group survived, she says of another group that was liberated earlier, "Had I been part of it my fate would have been different. Less suffering, yes, but less happiness, too, I am sure." Gerda clearly believes that the pain and hardship in her life have been more than offset by the happiness she has experienced. From her perspective, the war took her family, but it brought her a new family as well: because of the war and the Holocaust, she met the man who became her loving husband and the father of her children. The idea that one must persevere through pain in order to experience joy has helped Gerda come to terms with her experiences.

THE IMPORTANCE OF BEARING WITNESS In the epilogue, Gerda writes that she hopes her lifelong efforts to raise awareness about the Holocaust have given back some small part of what she has received. One way she does this is by bearing witness to the life and death of those who have no other voice. Gerda strives to provide as much first-hand information as she possibly can about her fellow prisoners. In the section describing her time in Bolkenhain, she describes what happens to a fellow prisoner, Lotte, saying, "I cannot help but want to tell her story, for I might be the only one left in the world who knows it." Gerda believes her duty is to be as detailed as possible when she writes about the others in her camp. Just as she does not know what her family's last days or weeks were like, she recognizes that most Holocaust victims died in obscurity, and she uses her memoir to try to right that wrong. In many instances, she includes people's full names and their fates, even if they are such minor characters that they are mentioned in only one or two sentences. For Gerda, telling the stories of others who died is just as important as telling her own story, and she does so in a way that is both respectful and deeply moving.

MORALITY IS A CHOICE No matter what their circumstances or situation, people have free will, and they always have the option to act with morality and humanity. Gerda illustrates this theme by writing about people who behave in unexpected ways, such as the decision by Frau Kügler, who works for the SS, to save Gerda's life. By giving examples of people who, while working for the Nazis, nevertheless behaved with humanity, Gerda illustrates that it was not impossible for Germans during the Nazi era to act decently toward Jews, forcing the reader to question why it was only these few specific people who chose to behave humanely. By pointing out that some people chose to show compassion, she makes the parallel point that those who behaved cruelly were making a choice as well. She also gives numerous examples of girls who helped one another in the camps, at great personal risk to themselves. Even under the harshest conditions, whether working for the Nazis or imprisoned in a slave labor camp, people are not entirely powerless or entirely unable to make a moral choice. Some become monsters, and some choose to treat others as fellow human beings and thereby reaffirm their own humanity.

MOTIFS

THE BEAUTY OF NATURE Despite the horrors that the Nazis perpetrate on the Jews, Gerda is quick to point out that there is still beauty in the world, although perhaps it exists only in nature. When the Germans first invade Bielitz, Gerda is brought to tears when her neighbor picks Gerda's mother's white roses to give to the Nazis. He drops them, however, and she watches as the soldiers' boots trample the roses in the dust. She points out the incongruousness of the Nazis' depraved behavior when set against the backdrop of the glorious natural world. Gerda describes the Grünberg labor camp as "cruelty set against a backdrop of beauty." Her surprise at seeing a camp lined with tulips in full bloom yet filled with skeletal girls underscores the horror of the scene. During the death march, a few girls stop and are unable to go on. Gerda looks around and admires the beauty of the snowy pine trees while she hears the gunshots as the girls are executed. She cannot understand how a world that is so full of beauty can also be inhabited by people who are so heartless.

HOME Throughout *All But My Life*, Gerda lovingly describes her childhood home. The day before she is moved to the ghetto, Gerda takes a serious risk, saying, "I did not care whether I was caught or not, I had to see my beloved home once more!" In the camps, Gerda often thinks of her parents and brother, always set against the backdrop of her home as it was before they were forced to sell their belongings and move out. She uses fantasies of returning home and meeting her family to help her get through the horrors of her days in the camps, and her longing for home sometimes comes close to overwhelming her while she is on the death march. The feeling of security she gets from picturing her childhood home does not diminish until she is liberated. Only then does she slowly start to realize that her home no longer exists in the way she remembers it. In her epilogue, however, Gerda recalls her first steps on American soil, with Kurt, her husband, embracing her and saying, "You have come home." Only then does Gerda realize that home is not a physical place but, rather, a set of feelings that has survived the destruction of the war and will live on through her new family.

CHANCE Rather than portraying her survival as the result of her own cunning or of divine intervention, Gerda is quick to note the many times that sheer luck determined whether she would live to see the end of the war. Gerda's brushes with death are too numerous to count, and only because of a series of close calls and coincidences does she avoid being exterminated with the rest of her family. The police officer who lets her go when she is caught studying English, her father's insistence that she wear her ski boots before she leaves their home, Merin's forcing her onto the truck to the camps instead of to Auschwitz, and Ilse's backing out of their escape plan at the last minute are all examples of the role that chance plays in her eventual survival. By accentuating these moments, Gerda makes clear that she does not believe herself to be superior to those who did not live. Rather, she portrays the wartime world as a terrifying place where matters of life and death are again and again determined completely by chance.

KINDNESS The Holocaust is one of the most dramatic instances of people behaving inhumanely and treating others with hideous cruelty, yet Gerda chooses to focus on the deep friendships she develops during the war and the acts of generosity she witnesses. Other Holocaust memoirs, such as *Night* by Elie Wiesel, detail not only the brutality of the Nazis but also the cruelty of the Jews toward one another as they are forced to struggle for their own survival. In contrast, Gerda in almost every case shows the acts of kindness among her peers in the camps and tries to act as charitably as they do. Despite the fact that she and her fellow prisoners are near starvation, Gerda gives her food away many times and, when she is weak, is given food by Ilse and Hanka. Much like Anne Frank, the author of the Holocaust memoir *Diary of a Young Girl*, Gerda is inspired by the horrors of the war to be more generous and kind rather than less so.

A

SYMBOLS

FLOWERS Gerda mentions flowers dozens of times in her memoir: roses, buttercups, daisies, lilacs, tulips, and violets. These references often point to the beauty of nature and the goodness of which the world is capable. Flowers are also important symbols for the memories of home that sustain her during her ordeal. When Kurt brings Gerda lilies-of-the-valley early in their courtship, he brings her to tears by reminding her of her childhood garden. To keep hope alive during her time in the camps, she often recalls images of flowers. She uses the beauty of these images to underscore all that she has lost in the war and to remind herself that, despite what she has endured, the world is still capable of producing beauty and inspiring hope.

SHOES In the world of the Holocaust, shoes represent the difference between life and death. Many times in her memoir, Gerda says she believes that the fact that her father insisted she wear her skiing shoes before she left for the camps saved her life. She sleeps curled around her shoes on the death march, to protect them from the shoeless girls who would otherwise steal them during the night, for those who are properly shod have the best chance of surviving. She writes of seeing a girl break off her own toes after they become thoroughly frozen, and of other girls who leave bloody trails in the snow when they walk. Gerda keeps poison in her shoe as well, to be used as a last resort. Her shoes not only have the power to assure her survival—they also contain the means of her death, if she so chooses.

IMPORTANT QUOTATIONS EXPLAINED

---

1. *He looked steadily at me and then answered my thoughts. "Whatever you are thinking now is wrong. It is cowardly." I couldn't deny it. He lifted my chin up and looked at me firmly again. "Promise me that no matter what happens you will never do it."*

In Part One, Chapter 5, when Gerda finishes selling the family's possessions to the neighbors to finalize their move to the ghetto, she recalls hearing of a family that committed suicide together. She half-heartedly wishes that her parents would suggest this. As she is considering the idea, her father walks into the room and forces her to promise to never do it—though neither he nor Gerda specify out loud what "it" is.

This scene is the first of two major events during which Gerda's father gives the impression of omniscience—he knows what she is thinking without her saying a word, and he knows what is best for her. The second instance of her father's wisdom is when he insists that she wear her ski boots despite the fact that it is summer—a request that ultimately saves her life.

Throughout the book, Gerda gives the impression of her father's impotence in the face of the Nazis—he cannot save his family or stop what is happening to them. However, this scene makes clear that no matter what the Nazis' power, Gerda's father still has the power to save her through small acts such as this one. Once Gerda is sent to the labor camps, she remembers the promise she made to her father, and it motivates her to go on. In the Märzdorf labor camp, where Gerda is working both the day and night shifts, she considers jumping onto the railroad tracks. At that moment, she gets a feeling in her neck that reminds her of how her father had held her head while making her promise to never give up. At that moment, when death seems like the only solution, the memory of this conversation, and of her father's love for her, gives Gerda the courage to stay alive.

A

2. *"I hope you will never be disillusioned. To you, life still means beauty, and that is how it should be. Continue to go through mud without dirtying your feet." She spoke without explanation or introduction and without finishing, and then she stalked away towards our quarters.*

In Part Two, Chapter 5, Tusia says this to Gerda while they are in Bolkenhain together. Tusia's words in the book have a prophetic tone, particularly when she gives a similarly worded outburst in a fit of madness immediately before her death at Helmbrechts. Despite Tusia's apparent lunacy, her words are largely accurate. The idea that cruelty can breed cruelty is reflected in Gerda's descriptions of the girls in the camp who steal one another's shoes, and the girl who betrays her fellow inmates by having an affair with an SS guard. However, these are behaviors that Gerda would never exhibit, and her reaction to the brutality she is forced to endure provokes quite the opposite reaction in her. If anything, Gerda becomes more dedicated to remaining kind and generous. The Nazis may destroy her body, but she refuses to let them consume her soul.

The slave labor camps and the death march are the mud that Gerda is going through, both literally and figuratively, yet despite the hunger and deprivation that she must suffer in order to survive, she continues to treat her peers with respect and dignity, thus not "dirtying her feet." Although Gerda recognizes the viciousness that is possible in humankind and that which she sees in the Nazis, she also stops to notice the beauty that exists in nature and in the hearts of the other girls in the camps. Her memoir focuses more on the friendships that she manages to develop in the camps than on the harsh treatment that the girls endure. Although the title of Gerda's book, *All But My Life,* describes what the Nazis have taken from her, she also succeeds at holding onto her own humanity, no matter what the circumstances.

---

3. *My eyes remained dry. I felt my features turn stony. "Now I have to live," I said to myself, "because I am alone and nothing can hurt me any more."*

Gerda's thoughts, which appear in the first chapter of Part Two immediately after she has been separated from her mother, are paradoxical, for she implies that to lose everything is a kind of liberation. The natural reaction to losing all of one's family members might tend toward becoming more self-destructive, but Gerda takes the opposite view. Thanks to Gerda's unique optimistic viewpoint, even her most morbid thoughts, such as this one, reflect her positive perspective. Gerda finds that losing her family prompts her to go on living. She sees this loss as a new kind of freedom: now she doesn't have to worry about her parents' welfare or being forced to make the "right" decisions, and she can put her own desires before her duty to her parents, which feels like a reprieve from responsibility. Knowing that her only duty is to look out for her own survival allows her the discretion to express the feelings, such as rage she shows here, that she has kept inside for fear of upsetting her parents.

The idea that all suffering comes from attachment is reflected in Gerda's thoughts: she believes that now that her family has been taken from her, she can no longer be hurt. However, this conclusion is much like her mother's belief that once the Nazis took their house they were safe, because that was the worst injustice they could place upon them. Obviously, this is a miscalculation on both of their parts, for the Nazis continue to prove that they can always commit worse injustices. In a sense, though, the freedom Gerda now feels is very real. The loss of responsibility to her parents allows her the audaciousness to behave in ways that she would not have considered before, such as barging into the commander's office at Sosnowitz, which ultimately benefits her.

---

4. *There is a watch lying on the green carpet of the living room of my childhood. The hands seem to stand motionless at 9:10, freezing time when it happened.*

The first lines of *All But My Life* reflect Gerda's belief that the Nazis stole her childhood, and that, in a way, time stopped for her when her town was invaded. Many times throughout the book, Gerda writes about feeling that her childhood ended when the Nazis first came to Bielitz, and that at that moment her life changed dramatically. From the first days of the invasion, the burden of responsibility in her family was placed on her shoulders. Jewish adults who freely walked the streets were often abducted or assaulted, so Gerda is the only member of her family who can come and go from their house unchallenged, forcing her to assume responsibility for many important decisions. Her role with her parents switches after the invasion, for she becomes the caregiver in many respects, causing her to feel that she must behave as an adult at all costs.

The idea that time stops for Gerda when the invasion occurs is a notion that she visits again in her epilogue. She says she experienced a break in her social development because she was not allowed to participate in ordinary adolescent activities during the six years of war. Her normal emotional growth was slowed. Although she had more horrifying experiences in her teenage years than most people see in a lifetime, she also had a huge gap in her social development. In a sense, time did stop for Gerda when the war started, for after she was liberated she was still a girl of fifteen in many respects. She writes that, at the age of twenty-one, she was afraid that Kurt would attempt to kiss her, much as she feared Abek's romantic attempts as a teenager.

A

---

5. *I had reached the summit, as I had dreamed I would in the dark years of slavery, and there, beyond the sphere of human vision, we met and embraced. We would never be alone again.*

The last lines of the memoir summarize Gerda's feelings about life and love. She believes that no matter what happens in a person's life, there is no pain or suffering that love cannot heal. While she does not believe she will be rewarded in life just because she has suffered, she recognizes that in order to reap the rewards of a wonderful life, one must be willing to endure the pain of that life as well. Gerda has endured the suffering of the Holocaust (which she terms "the dark years of slavery"), and she now sees her love for Kurt as her reward. She believes that they are not merely engaged to be married, but that they are soul mates who connect on a level beyond what we as humans can understand—perhaps even in a place where only God makes the decisions. The idea that a power greater than either Kurt or Gerda brought them together is implied when Gerda says that they met beyond the sphere of human vision. This idea comforts Gerda, who has been through so much in the preceding years.

For a woman like Gerda, who has lost her entire family and seen how readily a person can lose everything in life, the idea that now she and Kurt will never have to be alone again is radical. Gerda knows all too well how easy it is to lose someone you love—love in itself does not protect against that loss. However, Gerda feels that her relationship with Kurt is not merely physical, but spiritual as well. Although their bodies may be taken, their souls cannot be captured, and in that sense, Gerda and Kurt will remain together forever.

Annie John

Jamaica Kincaid (1949–)

CONTEXT

Jamaica Kincaid is known for her autobiographical work, and *Annie John* is considered a fairly accurate fictionalization of her childhood. Kincaid was born Elaine Potter Richardson in Antigua in 1949, to a Dominican mother. As a child, Kincaid adored her mother, but as she grew older, their relationship became strained, a shift that influenced Kincaid to examine mother-daughter relationships in most of her works. The colonialist system under which Kincaid grew up also provided material for much of her writing. Kincaid left Antigua at the age of sixteen to work as a nanny in New York City, where she began writing interviews for a magazine. She changed her name to avoid her family's disapproval of her new career, choosing Jamaica as a reference to her Caribbean background. She began writing for *The New Yorker* when she met William Shawn, its editor at the time. Kincaid married Shawn's son, Allen, and later had two children, Annie and Harold.

"Girl," Kincaid's first short story, is a page-long list of a mother's advice and demands, all in one sentence. It became one of ten *New Yorker* stories collected in Kincaid's first book, *At the Bottom of the River* (1978), all of which concern a young girl growing up in the Caribbean. *Annie John* (1985) was Kincaid's next book. It, too, is comprised of stories published individually in *The New Yorker*, but it develops many of the themes of *At the Bottom of the River* in a more traditional plot. Kincaid continued tapping her own autobiography in *Lucy* (1990), whose protagonist goes to New York to be a nanny for a white family. *The Autobiography of My Mother* (1994) returns to the mother-daughter relationship by imagining the life of a Dominican girl whose mother dies when she's born. But before these, Kincaid published *A Small Place* (1988), an essay focused not on a young girl's angry relationship with her mother but on Kincaid's angry relationship with colonialism. Kincaid condemns white Europeans for maintaining a colonialist attitude toward blacks, and Caribbeans for accepting their role as reverent subjects of white rule, even after Antigua gained its political independence.

Annie John is set during Britain's colonial rule over Antigua, and this historical context is essential to understanding the novel. The British colonized the island in 1632, after Columbus discovered it in 1493. Most of the island's native people had already died from disease or oppression, so the British imported African slaves to work on their highly profitable sugar plantations. In 1834, slavery was abolished, and these slaves became paid workers, but British rule of the island continued until 1981, when Antigua became politically fully independent. Annie, like most Antiguans, is a descendant of the slaves who came from Africa, but she leaves Antigua before it gains its independence. Her country is governed by the British, and her daily life is influenced by British culture and tradition. Annie goes to a British school, where her British teachers instruct her in the European "discovery" of the Caribbean, as if the Caribbean didn't matter until the British found out about it. She celebrates British holidays and, as a British subject, pledges allegiance to Britain at her Brownie meetings. Although Annie is aware that her ancestors were slaves, the world around her encourages her to feel more British than Caribbean or African.

Kincaid makes clear in *A Small Place* that she has strong feelings against the British domination of Antigua, and this hatred influences her treatment of Annie's colonialist world. As a child, Kincaid was taught to respect the British unquestioningly, and her literary education included only the European classics, not any Caribbean or African ones. This narrow approach encouraged her to believe that anything of value was European, which she later defied by creating, in *Annie John* and other works, a unique and successful literary style based on her Caribbean heritage. Kincaid shows the oppressive effect of British rule whenever Annie is punished for questioning authority, such as her teachers' portrayal of Columbus as a hero, or her mother's strict rules. Under British colonialism, Kincaid believes, Antiguans such as Annie are not permitted to develop their own identities, either as individuals or as a nation. Although Kincaid is certainly interested in mother-daughter relationships themselves, she also examines Annie's mother as a symbol of colonial government, controlling and overbearing even as she expects adoration from Annie, her subject. Kincaid's two primary interests in *Annie John*, motherhood and colonialism, merge in a single argument against the dangers of domination.

PLOT OVERVIEW

Annie John is a young girl in Antigua who tells the story of her growth from a child to a young adult ready to leave her home. The novel begins when Annie is eight and unaware of the world beyond her home. Annie and her mother do everything together, from doing household chores to taking baths. Annie's mother teaches her how to do everything, and all Annie wants is to please her. Annie has a trunk filled with items from her childhood. She is happiest when her mother empties the trunk and tells her stories about all of the items, because it shows her how much her mother cares about her. But as Annie enters adolescence, her mother begins spending less time with her. Annie's mother says they cannot do many of the things they used to do together, including dressing alike and looking through the trunk. Annie is devastated. She feels that the most important part of her life has been taken from her. When Annie catches her parents in bed together, the way she views her mother changes, and she talks back to her mother for the first time, signaling the end of Annie's worship of her mother.

Soon after, Annie begins attending a new school. At first, she is nervous and envious of the intimate friendships the other girls already have. But when Annie tells a story about her fear that her mother will one day leave her, all of the other girls admire her and want to be her friend. Annie quickly establishes a reputation as one of the smartest girls in the class, and the teachers favor her even though she misbehaves outside of class. Annie becomes especially good friends with a girl named Gwen. Annie and Gwen do everything together, tell each other all their secrets, and even feel as though they are in love with each other. Annie and Gwen become part of a small group of popular girls who gather near some tombstones to tell secrets and wonder about their slowly maturing bodies. When Annie begins to menstruate, the girls are fascinated and make her show them, but Annie can't explain why she isn't very enthusiastic. She feels incredibly happy with her life and wishes she could stay by the tombstones with her friend forever, away from the rest of the world and from her mother, whom she says she no longer loves.

Annie's rebellious side emerges as she starts sneaking around, stealing, and lying. She meets a girl she calls the Red Girl, whose mother lets her do whatever she wants and who gives Annie some marbles. Annie likes the Red Girl a lot and begins meeting her secretly in an abandoned lighthouse. Annie loves it when the Red Girl pinches her until she cries and then kisses her. Annie begins neglecting her friends to play marbles all the time. She has a huge, hidden marble collection. When her mother catches Annie carrying a marble, she is furious because playing marbles is not respectable. Annie denies everything, and her mother never finds the rest of the marbles, but Annie's relationship with her mother becomes increasingly tense. Because Annie's mother starts watching her more closely, she cannot visit the Red Girl anymore. Annie also gets in trouble with her teacher, Miss Edward, when she writes a disrespectful caption under a photo of Columbus in her history book. Miss Edward already doesn't like Annie because she once caught a group of girls, clearly led by Annie, showing off their legs and their fancy underwear to each other by the tombstones.

Annie's relationship with her mother gets even worse when her mother tricks her into eating some breadfruit, her least favorite food. From then on, Annie does everything she can to spite her mother. Annie feels inexplicably depressed and dreams of a new life. She skips a few grades and is no longer the center of attention at school, and she doesn't feel as close to her friends as she used to, not even Gwen. Gwen suggests that Annie should marry her brother, and Annie realizes that Gwen doesn't understand her—but she also worries that she doesn't understand herself. When Annie talks to some boys who have been mocking her on the street, her mother calls her a slut. Annie snaps at her mother but immediately regrets doing so when her mother tells her that she used to be her favorite person.

Annie's depression becomes a physical ailment when she develops an inexplicable illness. She stays in bed for months, feverish and hallucinating about her childhood. The doctor and the mystical obeah woman both treat her, but nothing seems to help. At the same time, it is raining nonstop in Antigua. When Annie gets better and the rain stops, she decides she never wants to see anything in Antigua again. She soon leaves for England, where she eventually becomes a nurse, and she vows never to return to her family or Antigua again.

CHARACTER LIST

Annie John A young girl growing up in Antigua and the protagonist and narrator of the novel, which covers her life from age ten to seventeen. Annie is smart, but adults dislike her because she is rebellious and tough. She is very generous to the people she likes and popular with her peers, and both her peers and her superiors see her as a leader. Annie, initially worshipful of her mother, eventually becomes fiercely independent.

Annie's Mother The major source of conflict in the novel, also named Annie John. Annie's mother can be extremely loving or terribly cruel. She is beautiful and highly respected, but she is also strict, controlling, stubborn, and willing to trick Annie in order to get what she wants. Annie's mother is superstitious and cares greatly about maintaining socially acceptable appearances.

Gwen Annie's first and closest friend, whom she meets on the first day at her new school. Gwen adores Annie and shares her most intimate secrets with her. She is kind, thoughtful, and loyal, but she can also be aloof and ditzy. She has nine siblings.

Annie's Father A carpenter who is much older than Annie's mother. Annie's father is relatively quiet, but he likes to complain about his business. His parents abandoned him when he was a child. He had many lovers before Annie's mother.

The Red Girl A girl of Annie's age who isn't socially accepted. The Red Girl, as Annie calls her, is dirty and wild, and her parents let her do whatever she wants. She climbs trees and plays marbles with boys.

Ma Chess Annie's maternal grandmother. Ma Chess mysteriously appears toward the end of the novel when Annie gets sick. She has a strong, unpleasant odor and is superstitious but knowledgeable. She insists on taking care of Annie as she sees fit.

Miss Edward Annie's teacher at the school she attends. Miss Edward is strict and nasty and takes pleasure in scolding dumb or misbehaving students. She is especially oppressive toward Annie, whom she strongly dislikes.

Sonia An early friend of Annie's. Sonia is older than Annie but smaller, meeker, and quite dumb. She is unpopular and covered in dark body hair.

Miss Herbert Annie's Brownie troop leader. Miss Herbert claims to be egalitarian, treating all the Brownies equally, but she doesn't particularly like Annie. She works in the hardware department of a store.

Mr. Oatie Annie's father's business partner. Annie's father complains that Mr. Oatie is cheap and stupid.

Pa Chess Annie's maternal grandfather. Pa Chess is stubborn and authoritarian, but he becomes physically crippled in his old age.

Ma Jolie A Dominican obeah woman. Ma Jolie is the local authority for mystical advice and healing treatment.

Dr. Stephens Annie's British doctor. Dr. Stephens is highly concerned with germs and provides medicinal treatment for Annie when she is sick.

Uncle Johnnie Annie's mother's brother. Johnnie died when he was twenty-three. He was a playful trickster who was adored by his family.

Mr. Nigel A local fishermen. Mr. Nigel shares a home and a wife with Mr. Earl, another fisherman. He is generally quiet but has a huge laugh, and he reminds Annie of her father.

Miss Nelson Annie's first teacher at her new school. Miss Nelson has a pleasant appearance and is not very strict. Her students like her.

Miss Moore The headmistress at Annie's new school. Miss Moore is British, and her throat wobbles as if there were a fish in it.

Hilarene A prissy but smart classmate of Annie's. Hilarene vies with Annie for first place in the class and likes setting the standard for good behavior in the classroom.

Ruth The least intelligent member of Annie's class. Ruth is a British minister's daughter, and she frequently blushes with embarrassment.

Mineu A boy with whom Annie played when she was little. Mineu was a cruel tormentor then, and as a teenager he mocks her with his friends, unaware of who she is.

Rowan Gwen's brother. Rowan thinks highly of Annie, and Gwen hopes they will get married.

Miss Catherine The two fishermen's wife, who does not live with them. Miss Catherine can't have children, has a slight handicap, and spits a lot.

ANALYSIS OF MAJOR CHARACTERS

ANNIE JOHN As the protagonist in a coming-of-age novel, Annie John loses her childhood identity as she gains experience in her search for a real sense of self. Everything in the novel is seen through Annie's eyes, not just because she is the narrator but because she is unusually self-absorbed. She is interested in people and events only as they relate to her, and everything in the novel is unreliably portrayed according to Annie's often-emotional interpretations. However, Annie's powerful emotions make her a strong character even though her qualities change as she grows older. When Annie is a child, everything she does is meant to make her mother happy, and all of her own happiness comes from her mother's attention. As she grows older and her daily life begins to change, Annie becomes bewildered and disillusioned. She doesn't understand why she cannot always be with her mother or why she must start behaving like a "young lady." She questions and protests the changes in her life. As she gets older, Annie feels out of control, and she doesn't like it.

When Annie goes to a new school, she has a chance to assert her independence. She likes being the center of attention, and her intelligence and confidence earn her praise from her teachers and classmates, filling the void left by her mother's inattention. Annie is smart about keeping her popularity. She misbehaves only outside of the classroom so her teachers will like her. She is kind to her classmates when she wants them to like her, and cruel when she wants to assert her power. She becomes independent to the point of rebelliousness. Annie is passionate, and when she cares about something or someone, such as her best friend Gwen, she throws herself into her love for them. But she also has a sense that she is better than others, so her love eventually fades. When Annie realizes that she isn't satisfied with anything in her life, not even herself, she plunges into a serious depression. When she emerges, all that remains of her former confidence is a determination to live her life as she sees fit, without her mother, her heritage, or her popularity controlling her actions. As she leaves Antigua, she's not really sure who she is, but she's ready to find out.

ANNIE'S MOTHER Annie's mother expects Annie to become just as strong-willed as she is, but at the same time, she doesn't want to relinquish her power over her. Annie's mother left her home in Dominica as a teenager because she fought with her father, who didn't want her to live on her own. When she married Annie's father, he had had many other lovers, but her beauty and charm won him over. In fact, Annie's mother wins everyone over. She doesn't question her ways, and she expects Annie to live by her standards. For example, she doesn't let Annie play marbles because that's socially unacceptable in her view. Annie's mother has strong opinions about what other people do and is quick to brand those people as unrespectable. Like Annie, she thinks she is better than everyone. In Annie's view, this feeling of superiority gives her mother's actions an edge of cruelty. Annie's mother doesn't feel bad tricking her daughter into eating food she hates, for example, and Annie finds this deceit more malicious than well-intentioned.

In a way, Annie's mother is no different from most mothers, who make their children do things they think are best for them. But Annie's mother seems to actually take pleasure in deceiving her and manipulating her into do what she wants. While it seems to Annie that this trickery in her mother develops as she gets older, it's really Annie who becomes more resistant to her mother's control. When Annie is a child, she's happy to do whatever her mother wants, so her mother doesn't seem controlling, but as Annie begins to disobey her mother's commands, she views her mother as more of a tyrant. Annie's mother loves her, but she's so stubborn and sure of herself that she can't give Annie the independence she once demanded for herself. In this way, Annie's relationship with her mother serves as an allegory for Antigua's relationship with England. The influence of Annie's cultural heritage, which is more British than Caribbean, is strong. However, in the novel this influence is mostly expressed through Annie's mother, who represents England's tight control of Antigua, rather than discussed explicitly.

GWEN When Gwen kindly tries to befriend Annie on the first day of school, Annie is so grateful for the attention and so envious of the closeness she sees in the other girls that she instantly falls in love with Gwen. During their friendship, Annie idealizes Gwen, whose neat, girlish appearance seems perfect to Annie. Without boys around, Gwen and Annie use each other for the physical closeness they're beginning to desire as they enter puberty, and they are excited to tell each other all of their secrets. Gwen happily goes along with all of Annie's ideas and plans, but she never suggests any of her own. Annie likes that Gwen is submissive because it gives her control over their friendship. Annie can abandon Gwen for a while and know that she can have Gwen's friendship back when she wants it.

Eventually, Gwen begins to seem too accepting of the life that is expected of her and Annie, such as when she suggests that Annie marry her brother. Gwen hasn't really changed, but Annie's perception of her has. The submissive nature that Annie used to like in Gwen bothers her when Gwen doesn't share her resistance to marriage, and Annie is no longer interested in the things that used to fascinate them both, such as breasts. Gwen represents the extremely strong sense of self that Annie has as an adolescent, when she's sure she could be eternally happy if her life would never change, but that fades simply because she grows older and more mature.

THEMES, MOTIFS, AND SYMBOLS

THEMES

THE STRUGGLE BETWEEN MOTHERS AND DAUGHTERS *Annie John* depicts the relationship between mothers and daughters as a power struggle fueled by both love and authority. Annie's relationship with her mother shows how the contradiction of loving someone you must obey creates this struggle. Annie resents her mother's authority whenever she tries to dictate Annie's behavior, but Annie also remembers a time when she used to love her mother unconditionally, which complicates her feelings toward her. For example, Annie doesn't understand how she can find her mother as beautiful as she used to, now that she doesn't love her anymore. Annie wishes she could love her mother as before and resents her more for changing. She resolves the conflict by rebelling against her mother, refusing to either love or obey her. But this solution doesn't work for her mother, who tries to control Annie because she loves her. For Annie's mother, making Annie eat breadfruit, for example, is part of loving Annie. Annie and her mother disagree on the relationship between love and authority because they see it from different perspectives, and the result is an endless struggle as each asserts her own independence or authority at the expense of the love they share.

THE IMPERMANENCE OF CHILDHOOD IDENTITY As Annie enters adolescence, she must give up her childhood identity to figure out who she really is. She develops from adoring daughter to popular teenager to independent woman. Part of Annie's identity change is involuntary: as the circumstances of her life change, she must adapt to them. For example, when she is too old to spend all of her time with her mother, she must find other ways to entertain herself. Annie's first menstruation also represents an involuntary change, and she isn't excited about it because she knows it makes her a different person, closer to a woman than a child. Part of growing up is accepting and adapting to these changes. Annie creates new identities for herself several times, such as when she goes to a new school and when she recovers from her illness. She begins to rely on herself to determine her identity, rather than on external forces such as her mother or her classmates. This independent approach to identity turns an adolescent into an adult, which Annie has become when she finally sets off to see the world on her own.

THE OPPRESSIVENESS OF AUTHORITY Several authority figures assert control over Annie, and each one demonstrates the oppressive effect that authority has on individuality. When Annie's mother enforces strict rules about Annie's behavior, she discourages Annie from developing her own personality, with her own tastes and ways of doing things. Annie finds her talent as a marbles player, for example, only by defying her mother's authority, but when her mother finds out, Annie is forced to stop playing. Annie's teachers are just as oppressive, but in a more intellectual sense. Teachers such as Miss Edward enforce a European way of seeing the world and punish Annie when she defies it by insulting Columbus in her textbook. Annie is not encouraged to consider the world from her own perspective—to question and criticize it—which inhibits Annie's ability to develop her own identity. On a larger scale, Miss Edward represents the British government, which has oppressively imposed its culture on Antigua. Thus, Antigua does not have a strong, independent identity, and Annie's upbringing is more British than Antiguan. Authority in this novel serves only to oppress individuality, encouraging a bland conformity.

MOTIFS

LEAVING The act of leaving frequently marks independence and the permanence of change in *Annie John*. Early in the novel, Annie views leaving as a negative change because she worries that her parents, upon whom she depends, could easily leave her since they are not dependent upon her. Because leaving is an individual decision that separates a person from others, it embodies the independence that Annie initially lacks. Once she attains it, however, this independence is permanent, so almost every trip in the novel is one way, from Annie's mother leaving Dominica to the Red Girl moving away to Annie's final departure from Antigua. These trips represent major life changes, which often require Annie to break entirely with the past. Once Annie changes, she cannot revert to the person she used to be, just as the travelers in the novel can't go back to the places they've left. When Annie leaves Antigua, she not only leaves the island permanently but also severs her relationship with her mother forever. Annie, who was once afraid to be left, asserts her new independence and solidifies her new identity by becoming the person who leaves.

CONFRONTATION Annie and her mother oppose each other over various issues, and these confrontations structure Annie's change in attitude toward her mother. Early in the novel, Annie is so unaccustomed to being at odds with her mother that their first confrontations, such as when her mother refuses to go through Annie's trunk, simply stun her. Annie accepts her mother's decisions only because she is too bewildered to protest. But as Annie grows frustrated by and angry with her mother's frequent opposition, she herself becomes confrontational. The first time Annie talks back to her mother, she reveals that she is unwilling to play a submissive role in their relationship. Gradually, these confrontations become more aggressive, culminating in the scene where Annie's mother calls her a slut. However, in addition to revealing the increasing animosity between Annie and her mother, these confrontations reveal Annie's increasing likeness to her mother. She is just as treacherous, defiant, and manipulative as her mother is when they argue. The confrontations exemplify the struggle between mother and daughter as well as their increasing equality in that struggle.

DREAMS Annie has many dreams that reveal her true emotional state in a way that her narration cannot. As the narrator, Annie can present her thoughts and actions however she wants, but when she describes her dreams, she gives the reader a more accurate, honest glimpse into her subconscious self. Because Annie doesn't always understand her dreams, they are open to the reader's interpretation without her interference. Some of Annie's dreams highlight the things that bother her most, such as the possibility of her mother leaving her. Others highlight Annie's hopes and desires, such as the dream in which she and the Red Girl live on an island together. This dream also reveals the dark undercurrent to Annie's desires, since in it she takes pleasure in shipwrecks. In a similarly disturbing dream, Annie thinks that she and her mother would kill each other if they could. Because Annie's dreams are out of her control, her strong feelings against her mother seem more genuine and powerful when they surface in them. Thus, dreams provide an essential, though often cryptic, key to understanding Annie's feelings about the world around her.

SYMBOLS

WATER Water repeatedly appears as a symbol of the forces that overwhelm and constrain Annie. As an island, Antigua is surrounded by water, so water defines Annie's physical world. In Annie's essay about swimming with her mother, the ocean separates Annie from her past in the form of her mother, and the ocean also separates her from her future until she crosses it by boat at the end of the novel. Sometimes, water also represents the connection between Annie and her mother, such as the baths they take together. In this context, water symbolizes the blood that unites Annie and her mother, as well as the fluids of the womb, in which Annie was literally attached to her mother. Later, the long rain, coinciding with Annie's illness, suggests that all of the pressures of Annie's world come down around her. Only when these pressures are released can Annie finally defy all the constraints that the water symbolizes and set off for another life.

ANNIE'S MOTHER'S MOUTH Annie's mother's mouth, which Annie frequently notices, represents the affection she longs for as well as the authority she resents. Early in the novel, Annie's mother uses her mouth to kiss or praise Annie or to laugh with her. As their relationship changes, Annie's mother uses her mouth to scold Annie or laugh at her. Annie often gets jealous of her father because he makes her mother laugh, which shows how much she loves him. When Annie imagines her mother at her age, she pictures a person so shy that she never showed her teeth. This description shows how closely Annie associates her mother's identity with her mouth, because before she developed her identity as caregiver and authoritarian, her mouth wasn't as expressive. Annie's mother's mouth provides the ultimate symbol for the change in Annie's perception of her when she laughs at Annie after tricking her into eating breadfruit. At this moment, her teeth, which Annie once found so beautiful, remind Annie of a dangerous crocodile. As Annie comes to see her mother differently, her mother's mouth symbolizes different aspects of her mother's role in her life.

ANNIE'S TRUNK Annie's trunk suggests her connection to her past as well as to her mother's past. The trunk previously belonged to Annie's mother, who used it to leave her childhood home, as Annie does at the end of the novel. The fact that Annie inherited the trunk from her mother symbolizes all of the other things that Annie inherited from her mother, especially the determination and independence that lead them both to leave their homes. But Annie's mother keeps all of Annie's childhood belongings in the trunk, preventing Annie from using the trunk to enter the future by filling it up with the past. The trunk binds Annie to her mother, not just because they will both use it to leave but because it contains all of the items that represent a time when Annie didn't want to leave her mother. Annie needs her father to make her a new trunk that will allow her to unload the weight of her past and to travel into her own future. In this way, Annie's two trunks symbolize both her attachment to her mother and her eventual break from her.

IMPORTANT QUOTATIONS EXPLAINED

---

1. *How terrible it must be for all the people who had no one to love them so and no one whom they loved so, I thought.*

This observation is made in Chapter Two, when Annie's mother tells her stories about the items in her trunk and shows how essential Annie's relationship with her mother is to her at the time. Annie is still young, and the tension between her and her mother has not yet begun. The observation emphasizes the mutual adoration and attachment Annie and her mother feel for each other at the time. Their love keeps them together all the time, and they turn basic household chores into opportunities to show their affection for each other. Moments like this one show Annie how much her mother loves her, and Annie loves her mother so much that the undivided attention she showers on Annie makes her feel special. For Annie, her mother's attention is the definition of happiness, and it seems to Annie that she is the source of her mother's happiness as well.

The observation also reveals how important it is for Annie to feel loved. The quotation doesn't specify a mother's love, although that is clearly what Annie intends at the time, and later, Annie will replace her mother's love with the affection of Gwen, the Red Girl, and her teachers. Loving attention provides Annie with a sense of self-validation. She feels worthwhile only when others think of her that way. In fact, love is so important to Annie that when she has it, she uses it to feel better than everyone else. In this case, Annie's relationship with her mother encourages Annie's already-emerging sense of superiority, as she declares how much worse life must be for other people, who do not have the love she shares with her mother. Her reaction is one of pity, not contempt: she feels bad for people who don't have mothers as loving as hers, not happy at their misfortune. Later, Annie's popularity will give her a haughtier sense of superiority, but for now she simply feels lucky to have something so special and rare in the form of her mother's love.

2. *When I looked at them sitting around me, the church in the distance, beyond that our school, with throngs of girls crossing back and forth in the schoolyard, beyond that the world, how I wished that everything would fall away, so that suddenly we'd be sitting in some different atmosphere, with no future full of ridiculous demands, no need for any sustenance save our love for each other, with no hindrance to any of our desires, which would, of course, be simple desires—nothing, nothing, just sitting on our tombstones forever. But that could never be, as the tolling of the school bell testified.*

This phrase, which is situated in the novel after Annie has just started menstruating and is sitting by the tombstones with her friends at the end of Chapter Three, shows how vital and consuming Annie's adolescent friendships are for her. She is so happy with her friends and their time alone together that she feels that nothing else in the world matters. They all share the meaningful bonds that come from having the same fears and desires, and Annie considers their love for each other as essential as food, or "sustenance." Annie even wishes that their moments together could last forever without anything changing. These sentiments are almost exactly the same as Annie's earlier desire to spend the rest of her life alone with her mother, which highlights the fact that Annie's school friends have filled the void her mother left when she stopped spending so much time with her. Whereas Annie's mother once determined her world and her happiness, her friends now provide her with a separate world in which she can be utterly carefree and happy.

This phrase also reveals Annie's anxiety about growing up. Annie knows that the sense of security her friends offer is false and that she cannot really stay alone with them forever. She fears the future, with its "ridiculous demands" and "hindrance" to her desires. She has already seen her relationship with her mother disrupted by time and its demand that she become a young lady, and she fears that the same fate will befall her relationships with her friends. Annie sees the world as a complicated place that will come between her and the "simple" but happy life she wants to lead. The sheer length of this phrase shows how overwhelmed Annie is by it all. She wants to avoid entering that world, but it already forces itself on her in the form of church and school. The sound of the school bell reminds Annie that she has no choice but to grow up.

3. *Of course, sometimes, what with our teachers and our books, it was hard for us to tell on which side we now belonged—with the masters or with the slaves—for it was all history, it was all in the past, and everybody behaved differently now; all of us celebrated Queen Victoria's birthday, even though she had been dead a long time.*

Annie has this thought in Chapter Five when her class is studying Columbus's discovery of Dominica, and it shows her ambivalent feelings toward her country's slaveholding past and colonialist present. On one hand, Annie feels she has inherited the innocence of her ancestors in relation to slavery. Since they were the slaves, Annie associates with the victims and has nothing to be ashamed of, unlike her British classmates, such as Ruth, who are associated with the masters and must bear some guilt for wrongs they had no hand in dealing. Ironically, Annie and her Caribbean classmates derive a sense of superiority from the fact that their ancestors were treated as inferiors. Because their ancestors were oppressed, Annie feels that they have a right to act as oppressors in making their European classmates aware of their shame. Annie feels righteousness and entitlement based on her black Caribbean heritage.

As Annie points out, the difference between the Caribbean students and British students like Ruth isn't so clear. With the abolition of slavery in Antigua, the lines between former masters and former slaves became blurred so that the descendants of former slaves act just as the former masters once did, celebrating British holidays and following British conventions. Annie's family lives comfortably in Antigua, and her mother's frequently condescending attitude toward others suggests that they belong to one of the higher social classes, putting them more in line with former masters than former slaves. Annie doesn't suffer prejudice in the novel, and there are no opportunities that are closed to her because of her race, so she isn't directly affected by her country's history of racial inequality. Because Antigua is a British colony, Annie grows up in a society that is practically more British than it is Caribbean, and she has a hard time identifying with her oppressed Caribbean ancestors.

4. *Why, I wonder, didn't I see the hypocrite in my mother when, over the years, she said that she loved me and could hardly live without me, while at the same time proposing and arranging separation after separation, including this one, which, unbeknownst to her, I have arranged to be permanent?*

This remark, which Annie makes when she is about to leave Antigua in Chapter Eight, summarizes her tense relationship with her mother, which is characterized by both extreme attachment and extreme independence throughout the novel. Because Annie and her mother love each other so much at the beginning of the novel, they are always together and express their great affection for each other by saying, for example, that they could never be apart. Annie's mother, as an adult, knows that this is simply an exaggeration of love, but for young Annie, this sentiment feels very real. So, when their relationship begins to change and Annie's mother makes it clear that they have to be apart, Annie is shocked. For her, love means a refusal to be apart, but for her mother, part of a mother's love is knowing how to let go. This remark makes clear that this difference between Annie's view and her mother's view of love has fueled much of their struggle against each other. Annie simply cannot reconcile her mother's love for her with her mother's desire that Annie be independent.

Annie's final reaction to this conflict is to give up altogether on her mother's love in favor of her own independence. Annie cannot love someone passionately and leave them willingly, so, since her mother wants her to leave, Annie can no longer love her mother. When Annie leaves, she leaves for good, permanently ending her relationship with her mother. In a way, this is Annie's revenge on her mother for not loving Annie as much as Annie wanted her to, but it is also Annie's acceptance of and cooperation with her mother's decision. In finalizing the separation her mother has encouraged, Annie does exactly what her mother wants, even if she does it in an extreme way. Annie also, in a sense, becomes her mother, as she breaks from her past with the understanding that a daughter must make her own way in the world, independent of her family. Annie has suffered so much from the contradictions of a mother's love that she abandons her relationship with her mother forever.

5. *I don't know why seeing that struck me so, but suddenly a wave of strong feeling came over me, and my heart swelled with a great gladness as the words "I shall never see this again" spilled out inside me. But then, just as quickly, my heart shriveled up and the words "I shall never see this again" stabbed at me.*

This comment, which is relayed in Chapter Eight when Annie arrives at the jetty to leave for England, shows her mixed emotions about leaving Antigua. She is determined to leave and keeps saying that she never wants to see anything in Antigua again, but it also pains her to go. As tired as Annie is of her life and as ready as she is to move on to something new, she is giving up her entire world. All of her experiences have been in Antigua, so a major part of her sense of identity depends on the place. Annie is leaving behind part of her identity, and even though the point of leaving is to find a new identity, she still feels empty. A part of her life is ending, and she is excited for a new one to begin, but she cannot help but mourn the life she is losing. This contradiction applies to most of Annie's struggles throughout the novel, such as her relationship with her mother and her friendship with Gwen. With her final departure, Annie breaks with the part of herself that wants to hold on to the past, enabling her to boldly embrace her independence.

The Awakening

Kate Chopin (1850–1904)

A

CONTEXT

Kate Chopin was born Catherine O'Flaherty on February 8, 1850, in St. Louis, Missouri. She was one of five children, but both her sisters died in infancy and her brothers died in their twenties. When she was five years old, Chopin was sent to a Catholic boarding school named The Sacred Heart Academy. Just months later, however, her father died in a train accident, and she was sent home to live with her mother, grandmother, and great-grandmother, all widowed. After two years in their care, she returned to Sacred Heart, where she excelled in French and English, finishing at the top of her class.

Both at home with family and at school with the nuns, Kate grew up surrounded by intelligent and independent women. Her childhood lacked male role models; thus, she was rarely witness to the tradition of female submission and male domination that defined most late nineteenth-century marriages. The themes of female freedom and sexual awareness that dominated Chopin's adult writings were undoubtedly a result of the atmosphere in which she was raised.

After graduating from Sacred Heart, Chopin became part of the St. Louis social scene. In 1870 she married Oscar Chopin, the son of a prominent Creole family from Louisiana. Fulfilling the social responsibilities expected of her, Chopin bore six children in the first ten years of her marriage to Oscar. Unlike many women of her time, however, she also enjoyed a wide range of unconventional freedoms. While Chopin was known to be a good wife and mother, she often grew tired of domestic life and escaped to smoke cigarettes or take solitary walks through New Orleans. She took strong, often-controversial positions on the issues of the day. Chopin's husband loved her very deeply and supported and admired her independence and intelligence. She and her family lived happily in New Orleans for nine years.

When Oscar Chopin's cotton brokerage failed in 1879, he moved his family to Cloutierville, Louisiana, where he owned some land. Chopin adjusted her habits easily to the smaller provincial lifestyle of Cloutierville and became the subject of much gossip. While other women in town were completing their household chores, Chopin would stroll or ride horseback down the town's main street, earning the attention and admiration of any man who passed her. In 1882, her husband died suddenly of swamp fever, leaving Chopin devastated. However, she would soon learn to enjoy the pleasures of independence and was rumored to have had an affair with a married neighbor, Albert Sampite, in the year following her husband's death. After spending a year managing her late husband's general store and plantation, Chopin moved back to Missouri with her children to be with her mother and family, a move that may have coincided with the end of her affair with Sampite. Sadly, Chopin's mother died shortly after her return, another in the series of tragic deaths that marked Chopin's life.

In 1889 Chopin began writing fiction, an activity that enabled her to develop and express her strong views on women, sex, and marriage while simultaneously supporting her family. Chopin enjoyed immediate success with her writings about the French Creoles and Cajuns she had met and observed during her New Orleans and Cloutierville years. She sold dozens of short stories and essays exploring themes of love, independence, passion, and freedom. By setting her stories in a specific region and community and by basing her characters on real people, Chopin was able to publish controversial stories in a socially acceptable format. Readers could choose to see the passions she described as curiosities of a localized culture rather than universalities in human nature. Chopin was often asked to attend conferences and give speeches and was widely celebrated for the majority of her short but prolific career.

Chopin's second and final novel, *The Awakening,* was published in 1899 at the height of her popularity. Ironically, this work, now regarded as a classic, essentially marked the end of Chopin's writing career. Many of Chopin's earlier works had been accepted despite their controversial subject matter because they appeared to contain narrative reporting rather than critical commentary. An underlying sense of support invaded the generally objective tone of *The Awakening*, however, and the reading public was shocked by such a sympathetic view toward the actions and emotions of the sexually aware and independent female protagonist.

The feminist movement, just beginning to emerge in other parts of America, was almost entirely absent in the conservative state of Louisiana. In fact, under Louisiana law, a woman was still considered the property of her husband. Chopin's novel was scorned and ostracized for its open discussion of the emotional and sexual needs of women. Surprised and deeply hurt by the negative reaction to *The Awakening*, Chopin published only three more short stories before she died in 1904 of a brain hemorrhage.

After her death, Chopin was remembered for her "local color" works about the people of New Orleans but was never acknowledged as a true literary talent until the rediscovery of *The Awakening* some fifty years later. New generations, more accepting of the notions of female sexuality and equality, praise the novel's candid and realistic views and have found it to be informative about early American feminism. Modern critics have noted the book's rich detail and imagery and find that its ironic narrative voice is a rich source for analysis. *The Awakening* has now earned a place in the literary canon for the way it uses these formal and structural techniques to explore themes of patriarchy, marriage and motherhood, woman's independence, desire, and sexuality both honestly and artistically.

PLOT OVERVIEW

The Awakening opens in the late 1800s in Grand Isle, a summer holiday resort popular with the wealthy inhabitants of nearby New Orleans. Edna Pontellier is vacationing with her husband, Léonce, and their two sons at Madame Lebrun's cottages, which house affluent Creoles from the French Quarter. Léonce is kind and loving but preoccupied with his work. His frequent business-related absences mar his domestic life with Edna. Consequently, Edna spends most of her time with her friend Adèle Ratignolle, a married Creole who epitomizes womanly elegance and charm. Through her relationship with Adèle, Edna learns a great deal about freedom of expression. Because Creole women were expected and assumed to be chaste, they could behave in a forthright and unreserved manner. Exposure to such openness liberates Edna from her previously prudish behavior and repressed emotions and desires.

Edna's relationship with Adèle begins Edna's process of "awakening" and self-discovery, which constitutes the focus of the book. The process accelerates as Edna comes to know Robert Lebrun, the elder, single son of Madame Lebrun. Robert is known among the Grand Isle vacationers as a man who chooses one woman each year—often a married woman—to whom he then plays "attendant" all summer long. This summer, he devotes himself to Edna, and the two spend their days together lounging and talking by the shore. Adèle Ratignolle often accompanies them.

At first, the relationship between Robert and Edna is innocent. They mostly bathe in the sea or engage in idle talk. As the summer progresses, however, Edna and Robert grow closer, and Robert's affections and attention inspire in Edna several internal revelations. She feels more alive than ever before, and she starts to paint again as she did in her youth. She also learns to swim and becomes aware of her independence and sexuality. Edna and Robert never openly discuss their love for one another, but the time they spend alone together kindles memories in Edna of the dreams and desires of her youth. She becomes inexplicably depressed at night with her husband and profoundly joyful during her moments of freedom, whether alone or with Robert. Recognizing how intense the relationship between him and Edna has become, Robert honorably removes himself from Grand Isle to avoid consummating his forbidden love. Edna returns to New Orleans a changed woman.

Back in New Orleans, Edna actively pursues her painting and ignores all of her social responsibilities. Worried about the changing attitude and increasing disobedience of his wife, Léonce seeks the guidance of the family physician, Doctor Mandelet. A wise and enlightened man, Doctor Mandelet suspects that Edna's transformation is the result of an affair, but he hides his suspicions from Léonce. Instead, Doctor Mandelet suggests that Léonce let Edna's defiance run its course, since attempts to control her would only fuel her rebellion. Léonce heeds the doctor's advice, allowing Edna to remain home alone while he is away on business. With her husband gone and her children away as well, Edna wholly rejects her former lifestyle. She moves into a home of her own and declares herself independent—the possession of no one. Her love for Robert still intense, Edna pursues an affair with the town seducer, Alcée Arobin, who is able to satisfy her sexual needs. Never emotionally attached to Arobin, Edna maintains control throughout their affair, satisfying her animalistic urges but retaining her freedom from male domination.

At this point, the self-sufficient and unconventional old pianist Mademoiselle Reisz adopts Edna as a sort of protégé, warning Edna of the sacrifices required of an artist. Edna is moved by Mademoiselle Reisz's piano playing and visits her often. She is also eager to read the letters from abroad that Robert sends the woman. A woman who devotes her life entirely to her art, Mademoiselle Reisz serves as an inspiration and model to Edna, who continues her process of awakening and independence. Mademoiselle Reisz is the only person who knows of Robert and Edna's secret love for one another and she encourages Edna to admit to, and act upon, her feelings.

Unable to stay away, Robert returns to New Orleans, finally openly expressing his feelings for Edna. He admits his love but reminds her that they cannot possibly be together, since she is the wife of another man. Edna explains to him her newly established independence, denying the rights of her husband over her and explaining how she and Robert can live together happily, ignoring everything extraneous to their relationship. But despite his love for Edna, Robert feels unable to enter into the adulterous affair.

When Adèle undergoes a difficult and dangerous childbirth, Edna leaves Robert's arms to go to her friend. She pleads with him to wait for her return. From the time she spends with Edna, Adèle senses that Edna is becoming increasingly distant, and she understands that Edna's relationship with Robert has intensified. She reminds Edna to think of her children and advocates the socially acceptable lifestyle Edna abandoned so long ago. Doctor Mandelet, while walking Edna home from Adèle's, urges her to come see him because he is worried about the outcome of her passionate but confused actions. Already reeling under the weight of Adèle's admonition, Edna begins to perceive herself as having acted selfishly.

Edna returns to her house to find Robert gone, a note of farewell left in his place. Robert's inability to escape the ties of society now prompts Edna's most devastating awakening. Haunted by thoughts of her children and realizing that she would have eventually found even Robert unable to fulfill her desires and dreams, Edna feels an overwhelming sense of solitude. Alone in a world in which she has found no feeling of belonging, she can find only one answer to the inescapable and heartbreaking limitations of society. She returns to Grand Isle, the site of her first moments of emotional, sexual, and intellectual awareness, and, in a final escape, gives herself to the sea. As she swims through the soft, embracing water, she thinks about her freedom from her husband and children, as well as Robert's failure to understand her, Doctor Mandelet's words of wisdom, and Mademoiselle Reisz's courage. The text leaves open the question of whether the suicide constitutes a cowardly surrender or a liberating triumph.

CHARACTER LIST

Edna Pontellier The protagonist of the novel. The "awakening" to which the title refers is Edna's. The twenty-eight-year-old wife of a New Orleans businessman, Edna suddenly finds herself dissatisfied with her marriage and the limited, conservative lifestyle that it allows. She emerges from her semiconscious state of devoted wife and mother to a state of total awareness, in which she discovers her own identity and acts on her desires for emotional and sexual satisfaction. Through a series of experiences, or "awakenings," Edna becomes a shockingly independent woman, who lives apart from her husband and children and is responsible only to her own urges and passions. Tragically, Edna's awakenings isolate her from others and ultimately lead her to a state of total solitude.

Mademoiselle Reisz The most influential character in Edna's awakening. Mademoiselle Reisz is unmarried and childless, and she devotes her life to her passion: music. A talented pianist and somewhat of a recluse, she represents independence and freedom and serves as a sort of muse for Edna. When Edna begins to actively pursue personal independence, she seeks Mademoiselle Reisz's companionship. Mademoiselle Reisz warns Edna that she must be brave if she wishes to be an artist—that an artist must have a courageous and defiant soul. Mademoiselle Reisz is the only character in the novel who knows of the love between Robert and Edna, and she, thus, serves as a true confidante for Edna despite their considerably different personalities. Mademoiselle Reisz is also a foil for Edna's other close female friend, Adèle Ratignolle, who epitomizes the conventional and socially acceptable woman of the late nineteenth century.

Adèle Ratignolle Edna's close friend. Adèle represents the Victorian feminine ideal. She idolizes her children and worships her husband, centering her life around caring for them and performing her domestic duties. While her lifestyle and attitude contrast with Edna's increasing independence, Adèle unwittingly helps facilitate her friend's transformation. Her free manner of discourse and expression, typical of Creole women of the time, acts as a catalyst for Edna's abandonment of her former reserved and introverted nature. Adele is also a foil for Mademoiselle Reisz, whose independent and unconventional lifestyle inspires Edna's transgressions.

Robert Lebrun The twenty-six-year-old single man with whom Edna falls in love. Dramatic and passionate, Robert has a history of becoming the devoted attendant to a different woman each summer at Grand Isle. Robert offers his affections comically and in an over-exaggerated manner, and thus is never taken seriously. As the friendship between Robert and Edna becomes more intimate and complex, however, he realizes that he has genuinely fallen in love with Edna. He is torn between his love for her and society's view that women are the possessions of their husbands.

Alcée Arobin The seductive, charming, and forthright Don Juan of the New Orleans Creole community. Arobin enjoys making conquests out of married women, and he becomes Edna's lover while her husband is on a business trip to New York. Although Robert Lebrun is the man whom Edna truly loves, Arobin satisfies Edna's physical urges while Robert is in Mexico. Throughout their passionate affair, Edna retains authority and never allows Alcée to own or control her.

Léonce Pontellier A forty-year-old, wealthy New Orleans businessman and Edna's husband. Although Léonce loves Edna and his sons, he spends little time with them because he is often away on business or with his friends. Very concerned with social appearances, Léonce wishes Edna to continue the practices expected of New Orleans women despite her obvious distaste for them. He treats Edna with love and kindness, but their relationship lacks passion and excitement, and he knows very little of his wife's true feelings and emotions.

A

Doctor Mandelet Léonce and Edna's family physician. Doctor Mandelet is a fairly enlightened man who silently recognizes Edna's dissatisfaction with the restrictions placed on her by social conventions. When Léonce consults with him about Edna's unconventional behavior, the doctor suspects that Edna is in love with another man, although he keeps his suspicions to himself because he recognizes that there is little Léonce can do if Edna is indeed in love with someone else and that any further constraints imposed on her will only intensify her revolt. Doctor Mandelet offers Edna his help and understanding and is worried about the possible consequences of her defiance and independence.

The Colonel A former Confederate officer in the Civil War and Edna's father. The Colonel is a strict Protestant and believes that husbands should manage their wives with authority and coercion. While Edna's relationship with her father is not affectionate, she is surprised by how well she gets along with her father when they are together.

Victor Lebrun Robert's wayward younger brother. He spends his time chasing women and refuses to settle down into a profession.

Madame Lebrun The widowed mother of Victor and Robert. She owns and manages the cottages on Grand Isle where the novel's characters spend their summer vacations.

The Lady in Black A vacationer at the Lebrun cottages on Grand Isle. The lady in black embodies the patient, resigned solitude that convention expects of a woman whose husband has died, but her solitude does not speak to any sort of independence or strength. Rather, it owes to a self-effacing withdrawal from life and passion out of utter respect for her husband's death. Throughout the novel, the lady in black remains silent, which contributes to her lack of individuality and to her role within the text as the symbol of the socially acceptable husbandless woman.

The Two Lovers Vacationers at the Lebrun cottages on Grand Isle. The lovers represent the form of young love accepted by society. Always appearing in conjunction with the lady in black, the lovers represent the stage of a woman's life that precedes her maternal duties.

The Farival Twins Fourteen-year-old girls who vacation at Grand Isle with their family and who frequently entertain their fellow guests by playing the piano. The Farival twins represent the destiny of adolescent Victorian girls: chaste motherhood. Having been dedicated to the Virgin Mary at birth, they wear her colors at all times. Moreover, they embody society's expectations of the way women should use art—as a way of making themselves more delightful to others, rather than as a means of self-expression.

Mrs. Highcamp A tall, worldly woman in her forties. Mrs. Highcamp spends time with many of the fashionable single men of New Orleans under the pretext of finding a husband for her daughter. Alcée Arobin is one of these young men, and the two call on Edna to attend the races and to accompany them to dinner—meetings that catalyze the affair between Edna and Arobin.

Janet Pontellier Edna's younger sister. Edna was never close to Janet and refuses to attend her wedding.

Margaret Pontellier Edna and Janet's older sister. After their mother died, Margaret took over the role of mother figure for her younger sisters.

Mariequita A young, pretty Spanish girl. Mariequita is a mischievous flirt who lives on Grand Isle. She seems to fancy both Robert and Victor Lebrun and, along with Adèle, is the picture of the self-demeaning coquetry that Edna avoids.

Madame Antoine A friendly inhabitant on the island of Chênière Caminada. When Edna feels faint at the Sunday service on the island, she and Robert go to Madame Antoine's for the day. Madame Antoine takes them in and cares for Edna, to whom she tells stories of her life.

Mr. and Mrs. Merriman, Miss Mayblunt, and Mr. Gouvernail Some of the guests present at the dinner party Edna holds to celebrate her move to the "pigeon house"

Etienne and Raoul Pontellier Edna and Léonce's two sons. Etienne and Raoul are four and five years old, respectively.

ANALYSIS OF MAJOR CHARACTERS

EDNA PONTELLIER Edna Pontellier is a respectable woman of the late 1800s who not only acknowledges her sexual desires but also has the strength and courage to act on them. Breaking through the role appointed to her by society, she discovers her own identity independent of her husband and children. At the beginning of the novel, Edna exists in a sort of semiconscious state. She is comfortable in her marriage to Léonce and unaware of her own feelings and ambitions. Edna has always been a romantic, enamored with a cavalry officer at a very young age, in love with a man visiting a neighboring plantation in her teens, and infatuated with a tragedian as a young woman. But she saw her marriage to Léonce as the end to her life of passion and the beginning of a life of responsibility. Although she expected her dreams of romance to disappear along with her youth, her fantasies and yearnings only remain latent, reemerging on Grand Isle in the form of her passion for Robert Lebrun.

The people Edna meets and the experiences she has on Grand Isle awaken desires and urges for music, sexual satisfaction, art, and freedom that she can no longer bear to keep hidden. Like a child, Edna begins to see the world around her with a fresh perspective, forgetting the behavior expected of her and ignoring the effects of her unconventional actions. Yet Edna is often childish as well as childlike: she harbors unrealistic dreams about the possibilities of a wild adulterous romance without consequences, and she fails to consider the needs and desires of anyone but herself. Her flagrant disregard for reality is revealed when she mocks Robert's apprehensions about adultery, and when she leaves her children in the care of their grandmother without a second thought. Edna's independence frequently amounts to selfishness.

Although the text never presents Edna's escape from tradition as heroic, it also never declares her actions shameful. The narrative may sometimes portray Edna as selfish in the ways she acts out her defiance of convention, but it never portrays Edna's defiance itself as intrinsically wrong. Perhaps, even, the novel portrays Edna's rebellion as intrinsically right. Given the book's ambiguity, Edna's decision to commit suicide at the end of the novel can be read either as an act of cowardice—of submission to thoughts of her sons' reputations and to a sense that life has become too difficult—or as an act of final rebellion—of refusal to sacrifice her integrity by putting her life in the hands of controlling powers.

MADEMOISELLE REISZ Mademoiselle Reisz is an unconventional and unpopular older woman who serves as an inspiration to Edna throughout her gradual awakening. A small, homely woman, Mademoiselle Reisz is distant and reserved in her interaction with the other guests on Grand Isle. Although she is often called upon to entertain people at gatherings with her expert piano playing, she realizes that Edna is the only one of the guests who is truly touched and moved by the music. Mademoiselle Reisz seeks out Edna shortly after Robert's departure to Mexico, and her exchange with Edna by the shore fosters a relationship that continues upon their return home to New Orleans. Edna is inexplicably drawn to the older woman, whose lifestyle she envies, despite finding her disagreeable and difficult. In fact, neither Edna nor Mademoiselle Reisz can claim to be particularly fond of the other, but Mademoiselle

Reisz understands Edna's passions and enjoys the company and the opportunity to share her thoughts on art and love.

Through her relationship with the pianist, Edna increases her awareness of herself as a woman capable of passionate art and passionate love. While the two capacities are interconnected, Mademoiselle Reisz serves to further each specifically. Not only is the pianist in touch with her own artistic emotions, she is, on a more pragmatic level, in touch with the traveling Robert and is the only one to whom he speaks of his love for Edna. Mademoiselle Reisz is the woman that Edna could have become, had she lived into her old age and remained independent of her husband and children. Mademoiselle Reisz functions as a sort of muse for her young companion, acting as a living example of an entirely self-sufficient woman, who is ruled by her art and her passions, rather than by the expectations of society. Mademoiselle Reisz acts as a foil for Adèle Ratignolle, who lives the socially accepted lifestyle that Mademoiselle Reisz rejected for solitude and freedom.

ADÈLE RATIGNOLLE A foil for Mademoiselle Reisz, Adèle is a devoted wife and mother, the epitome of nineteenth-century womanhood. Adèle spends her days caring for her children, performing her domestic duties, and ensuring the happiness of her husband. Ironically, while Adèle is comfortable and happy with her simple, conformist existence, she unintentionally catalyzes Edna's movement away from such a lifestyle with her manner of speech: because she and her fellow Creole women are so clearly chaste and irreproachably moral, society allows them to speak openly on such matters as pregnancy, undergarments, and romantic gossip. Adèle's conversation reminds Edna of the romantic dreams and fantasies of her youth, and Edna gradually begins to uncover the desires that had been suppressed for so many years. Although Adèle's behavior represents that which is expected of Edna, the effect of her words proves more powerful than her example.

A

Adèle is a static character—she shows no change or growth from the beginning of the novel to its end. She is also somewhat simple: when Edna reveals to Adèle that she would give up her money and her life for her children but not herself, Adèle cannot understand what more one could give than one's own life. Edna's understanding of an inner, autonomous spirit defies the belief of the time that women were simply the property of their husbands, who served a specific role as wives and mothers and devoted themselves solely to those around them at their own expense. Later in the novel, it is apparent that Adèle still views a woman's life in terms of the service she performs for her family and society. When she suspects Edna of having an affair with Alcée Arobin she reminds Edna of her duty to her children. Having just given birth to another child, Adèle still represents the ideal Victorian woman, whereas Edna ignores her responsibilities to husband and children, seeking freedom up until, or perhaps even through, her death.

ROBERT LEBRUN Although he remains away in Mexico for much of Edna's awakening, Robert Lebrun plays an invaluable role in its beginning and end. His flirtations, along with Adèle's freedom of expression, inspire Edna to forget her reserve and to begin revealing herself to others. For several summers, Robert has devoted himself to women at Grand Isle, showering them with affections rooted in admiration but lacking serious intent. Although notoriously ruled by his passions and impulses, he nevertheless cannot forget the societal conventions that both allow and limit his actions. Unlike the Creole women who play along with his flirtations, enjoying the company and attention, Edna is swept away by Robert's devotion. She sees in him a promise of the love and excitement that have been missing from her life since she married Léonce. Although he never consummates their relationship physically, Robert's tender treatment of Edna proves that his love for her extends beyond the superficial adoration he is used to showing his female companions. When Robert recognizes the intensity of his feelings for Edna, he decides to go to Mexico because he cannot bear to be near Edna and know that he may never act on his love.

Robert's courtship of Edna on Grand Isle perches precariously on the boundary between innocence and misconduct, suggesting that defiance and daring may lie beneath his reputation as a harmless flirt. Robert's sudden return from Mexico and his unrealistic plan to request that Léonce set Edna free so that Robert may make her his wife manifest a bolder side to Robert's nature. However, Robert pragmatically recognizes the difference between daydream and reality. When he returns to New Orleans, he accepts the impossibility of his intentions, and he ignores Edna's claims of independence and self-ownership. Despite his sincere love and urgent lust, Robert cannot, as Edna has, escape from or ignore the rules of society. The note he leaves when he flees her house sums up for Edna the unjust, unchangeable state of the world around her. Robert's ultimate fidelity to convention and society solidifies her disappointment with life and with the role she is expected to play. While Edna despairs over Robert's rejection of her, her suicide is not a response to her disappointment but rather to the final awakening that it affords her. When even Robert, whose love matches the sincerity and desperation of her own, will not trespass the boundaries of societal convention, Edna acknowledges the profundity of her solitude.

THEMES, MOTIFS, AND SYMBOLS

THEMES

SOLITUDE AS THE RESULT OF INDEPENDENCE For Edna Pontellier, the protagonist of *The Awakening*, independence and solitude are almost inseparable. The expectations of tradition coupled with the limitations of law gave women of the late 1800s very few opportunities for individual expression, not to mention independence. Expected to perform their domestic duties and care for the health and happiness of their families, Victorian women were prevented from seeking the satisfaction of their own wants and needs. During her gradual awakening, Edna discovers her own identity and acknowledges her emotional and sexual desires.

Initially, Edna experiences her independence as no more than an emotion. When she swims for the first time, she discovers her own strength, and through her pursuit of her painting she is reminded of the pleasure of individual creation. Yet when Edna begins to verbalize her feelings of independence, she soon meets resistance from the constraints—most notably, her husband—that weigh on her active life. And when she makes the decision to abandon her former lifestyle, Edna realizes that independent ideas cannot always translate into a simultaneously self-sufficient and socially acceptable existence. Ultimately, the passion that Robert feels for Edna is not strong enough to join the lovers in a true union of minds, since although Robert's passion is strong enough to make him feel torn between his love and his sense of moral rectitude, it is not strong enough to make him decide in favor of his love. The note Robert leaves for Edna makes clear to Edna the fact that she is ultimately alone in her awakening. Once Robert refuses to trespass the boundaries of societal convention, Edna acknowledges the profundity of her solitude.

THE IMPLICATIONS OF SELF-EXPRESSION Edna's discovery of ways to express herself leads to the revelation of her long-repressed emotions. During her awakening, Edna learns at least three new "languages." First, she learns the mode of expression of the Creole women on Grand Isle. Despite their chastity, these women speak freely and share their emotions openly. Their frankness initially shocks Edna, but she soon finds it liberating. Edna learns that she can face her emotions and sexuality directly, without fear. Once her Creole friends show her that it is okay to speak and think about one's own feelings, Edna begins to acknowledge, name, define, and articulate her emotions.

Edna also learns to express herself through art. This lesson occurs in Chapter IX, when Edna hears Mademoiselle Reisz perform on the piano. Whereas previously music had called up images to her mind, Mademoiselle Reisz's piano playing stirs her in a deeper way: "she saw no pictures of solitude, of hope, of longing, or of despair. But the very passions themselves were aroused within her soul, swaying it, lashing it, as the waves daily beat upon her splendid body." As the music ceases to conjure up images in Edna mind, it becomes for Edna a sort of call to something within herself. Additionally, Mademoiselle Reisz has felt that she and Edna have been communicating through the music: noting Edna's "agitation," she says that Edna is "the only one" at the party who is "worth playing for." Once Edna is aware of music's power to express emotion, she begins to paint as she has never painted before. Painting ceases to be a diversion and becomes instead a form of true expression.

From Robert and Alcée, Edna learns how to express the love and passion she has kept secret for so long. As with her other processes of language-learning, Edna finds that once she learns the "vocabulary" with which to express her needs and desires, she is better able to define them for herself. A pattern emerges—Edna can learn a language from a person but then surpass her teacher's use of her newfound form of expression. For example, while Adèle teaches her that they can be open with one another, Edna soon wants to apply this frankness to all areas of her life. And although Robert helps to teach her the language of sexuality, she wants to speak this language loudly, as it were, while Robert still feels social pressure to whisper.

As Edna's ability to express herself grows, the number of people who can understand her newfound languages shrinks. Ultimately, Edna's suicide is linked to a dearth of people who can truly understand and empathize with her. Especially after Robert's rejection of her in Chapter XXXVIII, Edna is convinced definitively of her essential solitude because the language of convention Robert speaks has become incomprehensible to Edna. Although Robert has taught her the language of sexuality, Edna has become too fluent. In this dilemma, Edna mirrors the parrot in Chapter I, which speaks French and "a little Spanish" but "also a language which nobody understood, unless it was the mocking-bird. . . ." The mockingbird, which merely whistles inarticulate "fluty notes" with "maddening persistence," resembles Edna's friends who seem to understand Edna but do not speak back.

MOTIFS

MUSIC Throughout *The Awakening,* the manner in which each of the characters uses and understands music gives us a sense of Edna's ideological alignment in relation to the novel's other characters. Additionally, Edna's exploration of music and her meditations upon its significance enable her own (visual) art to flourish. Edna first learns about the emotive power of music from Mademoiselle Reisz. Whereas Adèle Ratignolle's piano playing had merely conjured sentimental pictures for Edna, the older woman's playing stirs new feelings and probes unexplored emotional territories in her. Mademoiselle Reisz uses music as a form of artistic expression, not merely as a way of entertaining others. In contrast to Mademoiselle Reisz, the Farival twins play the piano purely for the sake of the gathered company. The twins' association with the Virgin Mary, and, hence, with a destiny of chaste motherliness, links them thematically with notions of how Victorian women should behave. Their piano playing—entertaining but not provocative, pleasant but not challenging—similarly serves as the model for how women *should* use art. It becomes clear that, for a Victorian woman, the use of art as a form of self-exploration and self-articulation constitutes a rebellion. Correspondingly, Mademoiselle Reisz's use of music situates her as a nonconformist and a sympathetic confidante for Edna's awakening.

The difference Edna detects between the piano-playing of Mademoiselle Reisz and Adèle Ratignolle seems also to testify to Edna's emotional growth. She reaches a point in her awakening in which she is able to hear what a piece of music says to her, rather than idly inventing random pictures to accompany the sounds. Thus, music, or Edna's changing reactions to it, also serves to help the reader locate Edna in her development.

CHILDREN Images of children, and verbal allusions to them, occur throughout the novel. Edna herself is often metaphorically related to a child. In her awakening, she is undergoing a form of rebirth as she discovers the world from a fresh, childlike, perspective. Yet Edna's childishness has a less admirable side. Edna becomes self-absorbed, she disregards others, and she fails to think realistically about the future or to meditate on the consequences of her actions. Ultimately, Edna's thoughts of her children inspire her to commit suicide, because she realizes that no matter how little she depends on others, her children's lives will always be affected by society's opinion of her. Moreover, her children represent an obligation that, unlike Edna's obligation to her husband, is irrevocable. Because children are so closely linked to Edna's suicide, her increasing allusions to "the little lives" of her children prefigure her tragic end.

HOUSES Edna stays in many houses in *The Awakening*: the cottages on Grand Isle, Madame Antoine's home on the *Chênière Caminada,* the big house in New Orleans, and her "pigeon house." Each of these houses serves as a marker of her progress as she undergoes her awakening. Edna is expected to be a "mother-woman" on Grand Isle, and to be the perfect social hostess in New Orleans. While she is living in the cottage on Grand Isle and in the big house in New Orleans, Edna maintains stays within the "walls" of these traditional roles and does not look beyond them. However, when she and Robert slip away to the *Chênière Caminada,* their temporary rest in Madame Antoine's house symbolizes the shift that Edna has undergone. Staying in the house, Edna finds herself in a new, romantic, and foreign world. It is as though the old social structures must have disappeared, and on this new island Edna can forget the other guests on Grand Isle and create a world of her own. Significantly, Madame Antoine's house serves only as a temporary shelter—it is not a "home." Edna's newfound world of liberty is not a place where she can remain.

The "pigeon house" does allow Edna to be both at "home" and independent. Once she moves to the pigeon house, Edna no longer has to look at the material objects that Léonce has purchased and with which Edna equates herself. She can behave as she likes, without regard to how others will view her actions. In the end, however, the little house will prove not to be the solution Edna expected. While it does provide her with independence and isolation, allowing her to progress in her sexual awakening and to escape the gilded cage that Léonce's house constituted, Edna finds herself cooped anew, if less extravagantly. The fact that her final house resembles those used to keep domesticated pigeons does not bode well for Edna's fate. In the end, feeling alternately an exile and a prisoner, she is "at home" nowhere. Only in death can she hope to find the things a home offers—respite, privacy, shelter, and comfort.

SYMBOLS

BIRDS In *The Awakening*, caged birds serve as reminders of Edna's entrapment and also of the entrapment of Victorian women in general. Madame Lebrun's parrot and mockingbird represent Edna and Madame Reisz, respectively. Like the birds, the women's movements are limited (by society), and they are unable to communicate with the world around them. The novel's "winged" women may only use their wings to protect and shield, never to fly.

Edna's attempts to escape her husband, children, and society manifest this arrested flight, as her efforts only land her in another cage: the pigeon house. While Edna views her new home as a sign of her independence, the pigeon house represents her inability to remove herself from her former life, as her move takes her just "two steps away." Mademoiselle Reisz instructs Edna that she must have strong wings in order to survive the difficulties she will face if she plans to act on her love for Robert. She warns: "The bird that would soar above the level plain of tradition and prejudice must have strong wings. It is a sad spectacle to see the weaklings bruised, exhausted, fluttering back to earth." Critics who argue that Edna's suicide marks defeat, both individually and for women, point out the similar wording of the novel's final example of bird imagery: "A bird with a broken wing was beating the air above, reeling, fluttering, circling disabled down, down to the water." If, however, the bird is not a symbol of Edna herself, but rather of Victorian womanhood in general, then its fall represents the fall of convention achieved by Edna's suicide.

THE SEA In *The Awakening*, the sea symbolizes freedom and escape. It is a vast expanse that Edna can brave only when she is solitary and only after she has discovered her own strength. When in the water, Edna is reminded of the depth of the universe and of her own position as a human being within that depth. The sensuous sound of the surf constantly beckons and seduces Edna throughout the novel.

Water's associations with cleansing and baptism make it a symbol of rebirth. The sea, thus, also serves as a reminder of the fact that Edna's awakening is a rebirth of sorts. Appropriately, Edna ends her life in the sea: a space of infinite potential becomes a blank and enveloping void that carries both a promise and a threat. In its sublime vastness, the sea represents the strength, glory, and lonely horror of independence.

IMPORTANT QUOTATIONS EXPLAINED

---

1. *In short, Mrs. Pontellier was beginning to realize her position in the universe as a human being, and to recognize her relations as an individual to the world within and about her. . . . [T]he beginning of things, of a world especially, is necessarily vague, tangled, chaotic, and exceedingly disturbing. How few of us ever emerge from such beginning! How many souls perish in its tumult! The voice of the sea is seductive . . . The voice of the sea speaks to the soul. The touch of the sea is sensuous, enfolding the body in its soft, close embrace.*

These lines from Chapter VI describe the beginning of Edna's process of awakening. Most of the concepts explored in the novel are mentioned in this passage: independence and solitude, self-discovery, intellectual maturation, and sexual desire and fulfillment. With the remark, "How few of us ever emerge from such beginning!" the narrator points out that Edna is unique in her willingness to embark upon her quest for autonomy, fulfillment, and self-discovery. Certainly, each new character that appears in the book only serves to highlight Edna's uniqueness. The narrator's subsequent remark, "How many souls perish in [the beginning's] tumult!" foreshadows the turmoil that will result from Edna's growing awareness. It seems to suggest that from the moment her awakening begins, Edna is marked for death. Additionally, the mention of the sea's sensual and inviting voice presages Edna's eventual suicide. The line that begins, "The voice of the sea . . ." is repeated almost verbatim just before Edna's death.

2. *She perceived that her will had blazed up, stubborn and resistant. She could not at that moment have done other than denied and resisted. She wondered if her husband had ever spoken to her like that before, and if she had submitted to his command. Of course she had; she remembered that she had. But she could not realize why or how she should have yielded, feeling as she then did.*

In this passage, from Chapter XI, Edna has just returned from her catalytic first swim and is lying on the porch hammock, refusing her husband's entreaties to come inside to bed. For the first time in her life, Edna does not, out of habit, yield to Léonce's command. Rather, she speaks against his control and does as she wishes. The narrator highlights the fact that, as Edna's thoughts and emotions begin to change, she also becomes more self-aware and begins to analyze her former behavior. Her distance from her former self is emphasized by her inability to reconnect to her former mindset; although Edna remembers having submitted to her husband's authority in the past, she cannot re-create the logic that would have led her to do such a thing, and her own past behavior seems alien and incomprehensible.

A

3. *"How many years have I slept?" she inquired. "The whole island seems changed. A new race of beings must have sprung up, leaving only you and me as past relics. How many ages ago did Madame Antoine and Tonie die? And when did our people from Grand Isle disappear from the earth?"*

These lines, which Edna speaks in Chapter XIII, reflect her desire to be isolated with Robert and, thus, free from the restrictions of the society that surrounds them. At the same time, her fantasy that she and Robert have already been left alone as "past relics" evidences the way that her new self-awareness has separated her—dangerously—from reality. Mentally, Edna is already living in her own isolated, island-like, mythical world. She has not yet fully acknowledged her feelings for Robert, nor does she understand the effect that her love for him will have on her life in the real world. Indeed, the conditions that Edna describes in this daydream are the only ones in which a relationship between Edna and Robert would be possible. As long as they live within society, their love is unable to overcome social convention and tradition.

4. *The pigeon-house pleased her. It at once assumed the intimate character of a home, while she herself invested it with a charm which it reflected like a warm glow. There was with her a feeling of having descended in the social scale, with a corresponding sense of having risen in the spiritual. Every step which she took toward relieving herself from obligations added to her strength and expansion as an individual. She began to look with her own eyes; to see and to apprehend the deeper undercurrents of life. No longer was she content to "feed upon opinion" when her own soul had invited her.*

These lines, which are found in Chapter XXXII, chart Edna's growing independence. In part, Edna's strength comes from her rejection of her social role. Her new house is more modest, and its small size disallows the entertaining that was such a part of her former life. Consequently, Edna believes that independence and social rank form an inverse relationship; she has "descended in the social scale," but she has "risen in the spiritual." Ignoring the expectations of those around allows her to act in accordance with her own impulses and opinions.

Edna's association of strength and individual expansion with a total rupture from society seems somewhat erroneous. Ultimately, Edna defines herself according to her ability to disregard, rather than interact with, others. Her belief that independence and integration within society are diametrically opposed may underlie her tragic death at the end of the book because Edna leads herself to a profound solitude just at the moment when her sense of self is most acute. Perhaps, however, the society in which Edna lives does not allow her to integrate herself and remain independent. Because her society denies women the ability to think and act as individuals, a woman who asserts her own, differing set of hopes and dreams may end in an all-or-nothing bind.

5. *"The years that are gone seem like dreams—if one might go on sleeping and dreaming—but to wake up and find—oh! well! Perhaps it is better to wake up after all, even to suffer, rather than to remain a dupe to illusions all one's life."*

This quotation, drawn from a conversation Edna has with Doctor Mandelet in Chapter XXXVIII, may be considered the overarching message, or "moral," of *The Awakening*. Even though Edna's awakening causes her to suffer from the wisdom and self-awareness it affords her, the year of joy and understanding that accompanies this suffering is worth more to Edna than a lifetime of the semi-conscious submission that defined her former existence. According to Edna, to live with self-awareness, possessed and controlled only by one's own soul, offers an existence far richer than a life lived according to the restricting "illusions" that are imposed by the expectations of others.

Describe the evolution of one of the characters in *The Awakening*. How does this character change from the beginning of the novel to the end?

Kate Chopin's *The Awakening* chronicles the story of one woman, Edna Pontellier, and her journey of self-discovery. In the beginning, Edna appears to be just another nineteenth-century woman oblivious to her oppression and undeniable subordination to men. But Edna quickly begins to challenge this seemingly predetermined fate; by the end of the novel, she has experienced an internal metamorphosis. As the novel progresses, Edna develops distinct outer and inner selves; the discrepancy between the two increases dramatically, culminating in Edna's suicide at the end of the novel.

Edna's outer self is the mask that everyone around her sees. This is the part of Edna that dutifully performs everything expected of her: her outer self obeys her husband, attends societal functions, and takes interest in her children. Her inner self, which holds Edna's true desires for life—namely, her desire for independence—is in direct conflict with this outward self. A power struggle between these selves exists throughout the book. Edna's two experiences with the sea, which bookend her story, epitomize this struggle.

Edna's first encounter with the sea leaves her overcome with terror. Many people have tried to teach Edna to swim, but her lack of progress has deterred even her most eager teacher, Robert. Edna's greatest obstacle is her intense fear of being alone in the water. Chopin writes, "A certain ungovernable dread hung about her when in the water, unless there was a hand nearby that might reach out and reassure her"(Chapter X). One night, Edna manages to swim what seems like a very far distance out into the sea. When she realizes how far she has gone, and how fatigued she is, she becomes terrified and is overcome with visions of death. Indeed, she is so dependent upon others for her survival that she nearly dies when she is briefly out of their reach. She somehow musters up the energy to return to shore, but when she breathlessly retells her terrifying experience to her husband, he shrugs

Student Essay

off her concerns. Breezily, Leonce proclaims, "You were not so very far, my dear; I was watching you" (Chapter X). He makes light of her fears, which only heightens her sense of alienation.

While many people watched Edna in the first sea scene, she is utterly alone in the final scene of the novel. The only other animate object is a bird with a broken wing, which, like Edna, is slowly meeting its death. Edna is naked and alone—but she is no longer frightened. Whereas Edna once needed a reassuring hand before she would venture into the water, she is now confident. Her actions are decisive and deliberate: "She went on and on . . . She did not look back now" (Chapter XXXIX). Though the sea is treacherous—"The foamy wavelets curled up to her white feet and coiled like serpents about her ankles"—Edna is a willing participant in her death (Chapter XXXIX).

The Awakening concludes with Edna's self-inflicted death. As this is a story about the maturation and, as the title implies, the awakening of a woman, its powerful ending raises important questions. Was this the only possible conclusion? Perhaps the disparity between Edna's inner and outer selves had grown so large that only with death could she reconcile them. She chooses to kill her external self (i.e., her body) because it can never accurately embody her inner one.

The Bell Jar

Sylvia Plath (1932–1963)

B

CONTEXT

Sylvia Plath was born to Otto and Aurelia Plath in 1932 and spent her early childhood in the seaport town of Winthrop, Massachusetts. Otto Plath died when Sylvia was eight years old, and she moved with her mother, younger brother, and maternal grandparents to Wellesley, an inland suburb of Boston. Sylvia Plath excelled in school and developed a strong interest in writing and drawing. In 1950, she won a scholarship to attend Smith College, where she majored in English. *The Bell Jar* recounts, in slightly fictionalized form, the events of the summer and autumn after Plath's junior year. Like Esther, the protagonist of *The Bell Jar*, Plath was invited to serve as guest editor for a woman's magazine in New York. After returning to Wellesley for the remainder of the summer, she had a nervous breakdown and attempted suicide.

Plath went on to complete a highly successful college career. She won the prestigious Fulbright scholarship to study at Cambridge University in England, where she met the English poet Ted Hughes. They married in 1956, and after a brief stint in the United States, where Plath taught at Smith, they moved back to England in 1959. Plath gave birth to her first child, Freda, the following year. The same year, she published *The Colossus*, her first volume of poetry. Her second child, Nicholas, was born in 1962. Hughes and Plath separated shortly afterward; her instability and his affair with another woman had placed great strain on their marriage. Plath and her children moved to an apartment in London, where she continued to write poetry. The poems she wrote at this time were later published in a collection titled *Ariel* (1965). In February 1963, she gassed herself in her kitchen, ending her life at the age of thirty-one.

Plath most likely wrote a first draft of *The Bell Jar* in the late 1950s. In 1961 she received a fellowship that allowed her to complete the novel. *The Bell Jar* was published in London in January of 1963 under the pseudonym Victoria Lucas. Plath chose to publish the work under a pseudonym in order to protect the people she portrayed in the novel and because she was uncertain of the novel's literary merit. The novel appeared posthumously in England under her own name in 1966, and in America, over the objections of her mother, in 1971. *The Bell Jar* has received moderate critical acclaim, and has long been valued not only as a glimpse into the psyche of a major poet but as a witty and harrowing American coming-of-age story. Plath is primarily known not as a novelist but as an outstanding poet. *Ariel* cemented her reputation as a great artist. Her other volumes of poetry, published posthumously, include *Crossing the Water* (1971), *Winter Trees* (1971), and *The Collected Poems* (1981), which won the Pulitzer Prize.

Plath's literary persona has always provoked extreme reactions. Onlookers tend to mythologize Plath either as a feminist martyr or a tragic heroine. The feminist martyr version of her life holds that Plath was driven over the edge by her misogynist husband, and sacrificed on the altar of prefeminist, repressive 1950s America. The tragic heroine version of her life casts Plath as a talented but doomed young woman, unable to deal with the pressures of society because of her debilitating mental illness. Although neither myth presents a wholly accurate picture, truth exists in both. *The Bell Jar* does not label its protagonist's life as either martyred or heroic. Plath does not attribute Esther's instability to men, society, or Esther herself, although she does criticize all three. Rather, she blames mental illness, which she characterizes as a mysterious and horrific disease.

PLOT OVERVIEW

Esther Greenwood, a college student from Massachusetts, travels to New York to work on a magazine for a month as a guest editor. She works for Jay Cee, a sympathetic but demanding woman. Esther and eleven other college girls live in a women's hotel. The sponsors of their trip wine and dine them and shower them with presents. Esther knows she should be having the time of her life, but she feels deadened. The execution of the Rosenbergs worries her, and she can embrace neither the rebellious attitude of her friend Doreen nor the perky conformism of her friend Betsy. Esther and the other girls suffer food poisoning after a fancy banquet. Esther attempts to lose her virginity with a UN interpreter, but he seems disinterested. She questions her abilities and worries about what she will do after college. On her last night in the city, she goes on a disastrous blind date with a man named Marco, who tries to rape her.

Esther wonders if she should marry and live a conventional domestic life or attempt to satisfy her ambition. Buddy Willard, her college boyfriend, is recovering from tuberculosis in a sanitarium and wants to marry Esther when he regains his health. To an outside observer, Buddy appears to be the ideal mate: he is handsome, gentle, intelligent, and ambitious. But he does not understand Esther's desire to write poetry, and when he confesses that he slept with a waitress while dating Esther, Esther thinks him a hypocrite and decides she cannot marry him. She sets out to lose her virginity as though in pursuit of the answer to an important mystery.

Esther returns to the Boston suburbs and discovers that she has not been accepted to a writing class she had planned to take. She will spend the summer with her mother instead. She makes vague plans to write a novel, learn shorthand, and start her senior thesis. Soon she finds the feelings of unreality she experienced in New York taking over her life. She is unable to read, write, or sleep, and she stops bathing. Her mother takes her to Dr. Gordon, a psychiatrist who prescribes electric shock therapy for Esther. Esther becomes more unstable than ever after this terrifying treatment and decides to kill herself. She tries to slit her wrists, but can bring herself only to slash her calf. She tries to hang herself but cannot find a place to tie the rope in her low-ceilinged house. At the beach with friends, she attempts to drown herself, but she keeps floating to the surface of the water. Finally, she hides in a basement crawl space and takes a large quantity of sleeping pills.

Esther awakens to find herself in the hospital. She has survived her suicide attempt with no permanent physical injuries. Once her body heals, she is sent to the psychological ward in the city hospital, where she is uncooperative, paranoid, and determined to end her life. Eventually, Philomena Guinea, a famous novelist who sponsors Esther's college scholarship, pays to move her to a private hospital. In this more enlightened environment, Esther comes to trust her new psychiatrist, a woman named Dr. Nolan. She slowly begins to improve with a combination of talk therapy, insulin injections, and properly administered electric shock therapy. She becomes friends with Joan, a woman from her hometown and college who has had experiences similar to Esther's. She is repulsed, however, when Joan makes a sexual advance toward her.

As Esther improves, the hospital officials grant her permission to leave the hospital from time to time. During one of these excursions, she finally loses her virginity with a math professor named Irwin. She begins bleeding profusely and has to go to the emergency room. One morning, Joan, who seemed to be improving, hangs herself. Buddy comes to visit Esther, and both understand that their relationship is over. Esther will leave the mental hospital in time to start winter semester at college. She believes that she has regained a tenuous grasp on sanity, but knows that the bell jar of her madness could descend again at any time.

CHARACTER LIST

Esther Greenwood The protagonist and narrator of the novel. Esther has just finished her junior year of college. She grew up in the Boston suburbs with her mother and brother. Her father died when she was nine years old. Esther is attractive, talented, and lucky, but uncertainty plagues her, and she feels a disturbing sense of unreality.

Mrs. Greenwood Esther's mother. Mrs. Greenwood has had a difficult life. She lost her husband when her children were still young. Because her husband had inadequate life insurance, she struggles to make a living by teaching typing and shorthand. Practical and traditional, she loves Esther and worries about her future but cannot understand her.

Buddy Willard Esther's college boyfriend. Buddy is an athletic, intelligent, good-looking man who graduated from Yale and went to medical school. He cares for Esther but has conventional ideas about women's roles and fails to understand Esther's interest in poetry. He represents everything that, according to society, Esther should want but does not.

Doctor Nolan Esther's psychiatrist at the private mental hospital. Esther comes to trust and love Dr. Nolan, who acts as a kind and understanding surrogate mother. Progressive and unconventional, Dr. Nolan encourages Esther's unusual thinking.

Doreen Esther's companion in New York, a blond, beautiful southern girl with a sharp tongue. Esther envies Doreen's nonchalance in social situations, and the two share a witty, cynical perspective on their position as guest editors for a fashion magazine. Doreen represents a rebellion against societal convention that Esther admires but cannot entirely embrace.

Joan Gilling Esther's companion in the mental hospital. A large, horsy woman, Joan was a year ahead of Esther in college, and Esther envied her social and athletic success. Joan once dated Buddy, Esther's boyfriend. In the mental ward, Esther comes to think of Joan as her double, someone with similar experiences to Esther's whom Esther does not particularly like, but toward whom she feels an affinity.

Jay Cee Esther's boss at the magazine, an ambitious career woman who encourages Esther to be ambitious. Jay Cee is physically unattractive but moves self-confidently in her world. She treats Esther brusquely but kindly.

Betsy A pretty, wholesome girl from Kansas who becomes Esther's friend when they both work at the magazine. Esther feels she is more like Betsy than she is like Doreen, but she cannot relate to Betsy's cheerfulness and optimism.

Constantin A UN simultaneous interpreter who takes Esther on a date. Handsome, thoughtful, and accomplished, Constantin seems sexually disinterested in Esther, who is willing to let him seduce her.

Marco A tall, dark, well-dressed Peruvian who takes Esther on a date to a country club. Marco expresses dashing self-confidence but also a hatred of women. Violent and sadistic, he believes that all women are sluts.

Irwin Esther's first lover. Irwin is a tall, intelligent, homely math professor at Harvard. He is charming and seductive but not particularly responsible or caring.

Doctor Gordon Esther's first psychiatrist, whom she distrusts. Dr. Gordon is good-looking and has an attractive family, and Esther thinks him conceited. He does not know how to help Esther and ends up doing her more harm than good.

Philomena Guinea A famous, wealthy novelist who gives Esther a scholarship to attend college and pays for Esther's stay in the private mental hospital. Philomena is elderly, generous, and successful.

Mrs. Willard A friend of Esther's mother and the mother of Esther's sometime-boyfriend, Buddy Willard. Mrs. Willard, who feels protective of her son, has traditional ideas about the roles men and women should play.

Lenny Shepherd Doreen's love interest. Lenny is a New York DJ and smooth older man. He wears cowboy-style clothes and has a cowboy-style home.

Eric A past acquaintance of Esther's with whom she had her most open conversation about sex. Eric is a southern prep school boy who lost his virginity with a prostitute and now associates love with chastity and sex with behaving like an animal.

Dodo Conway The Greenwoods' neighbor. Dodo is a Catholic woman with six children and a seventh on the way. She lives unconventionally, but everyone likes her.

Jody A friend of Esther's, with whom she is supposed to live while she takes a summer writing course. Jody is friendly and tries to be helpful but cannot reach Esther.

Valerie A friend of Esther's in the private mental hospital. Valerie has had a lobotomy and is friendly and relaxed.

ANALYSIS OF MAJOR CHARACTERS

ESTHER GREENWOOD Esther Greenwood is the protagonist and narrator of *The Bell Jar*. The plot of the novel follows her descent into and return from madness. *The Bell Jar* tells an atypical coming-of-age story: instead of undergoing a positive, progressive education in the ways of the world, culminating in a graduation into adulthood, Esther learns from madness, and graduates not from school but from a mental institution.

Esther behaves unconventionally in reaction to the society in which she lives. Society expects Esther to be constantly cheerful and peppy, but her dark, melancholy nature resists perkiness. She becomes preoccupied with the execution of the Rosenbergs and the cadavers and pickled fetuses she sees at Buddy's medical school, because her brooding nature can find no acceptable means of expression. Society expects Esther to remain a virgin until her marriage to a nice boy, but Esther sees the hypocrisy of this rule and decides that, like Buddy, she wants to lose her virginity before marriage. She embarks on a loveless sexual encounter because society does not provide her with an outlet for healthy sexual experimentation. Plath distinguishes Esther's understandably unconventional behavior from her madness. Even though society's ills disturb Esther, they do not make her mad. Rather, madness descends upon her, an illness as unpreventable and destructive as cancer.

Largely because of her mental illness, Esther behaves selfishly. She does not consider the effect her suicide attempts have on her mother, or on her friends. Her own terrifying world occupies her thoughts completely. Though inexperienced, Esther is also observant, poetic, and kind. Plath feels affection toward her protagonist, but she is unswerving in depicting Esther's self-absorption, confusion, and naïveté.

MRS. GREENWOOD Mrs. Greenwood remains in the background of the novel, for Esther makes little attempt to describe her. However, despite her relative invisibility, Mrs. Greenwood's influence pervades Esther's mind. Mrs. Greenwood subscribes to society's notions about women. She sends Esther an article emphasizing the importance of guarding one's virginity, and while she encourages Esther to pursue her ambition to write, she also encourages her to learn shorthand so that she can find work as a secretary. While Esther worries that her desire to be a poet or a professor will conflict with her probable role as wife and mother, her mother hopes that Esther's ambitions will not interfere with her domestic duties.

Mrs. Greenwood clearly loves Esther and worries about her: she runs through her money paying for Esther's stay in the hospital, and brings Esther roses on her birthday. Still, Esther partly faults her mother for her madness, and Plath represents this assigning of blame as an important breakthrough for Esther. When Esther tells Dr. Nolan that she hates her mother, Nolan reacts with satisfaction, as if this admission explains Esther's condition and marks an important step in her recovery. The doctors decide that Esther should stay in the hospital until winter term at college begins rather than go home to live with her mother. Perhaps Esther hates her mother partly because she feels guilty about inflicting such vast pain on her.

BUDDY WILLARD By the standards of the 1950s, Buddy is nearly flawless. Handsome and athletic, he attends church, loves his parents, thrives in school, and is studying to become a doctor. Esther appreciates Buddy's near-perfection, and admires him for a long time from afar. But once she gets to know him, she sees his flaws. In what was considered natural behavior in men at that time, Buddy spends a summer sleeping with a waitress while dating Esther, and does not apologize for his behavior.

Esther also realizes that while Buddy is intelligent, he is not particularly thoughtful. He does not understand Esther's desire to write poetry, telling her that poems are like dust, and that her passion for poetry will change as soon as she becomes a mother. He accepts his mother's conventional ideas about how he should organize his domestic and emotional life. Buddy's sexuality proves boring—Esther finds his kisses uninspiring, and when he undresses before her, he does so in a clinical way, telling her she should get used to seeing him naked, and explaining that he wears net underwear because his "mother says they wash easily." Finally, he seems unconsciously cruel. He tells Esther he slept with the waitress because she was "free, white, and twenty-one," acts pleased when Esther breaks her leg on a ski slope, and, in their last meeting, wonders out loud who will marry her now that she has been in a mental institution.

In some ways, Buddy and Esther endure similar experiences. They both show great promise at the beginning of the novel, and at the end of the novel they have become muted and worldly. Buddy's time in the sanitarium during his bout with tuberculosis parallels Esther's time in the mental institution. Both experiment with premarital sex. Still, they share few character traits, and Esther must reject Buddy because she rejects his way of life. She will not become a submissive wife and mother and shelve her artistic ambitions.

THEMES, MOTIFS, AND SYMBOLS

THEMES

GROWTH THROUGH PAIN AND REBIRTH *The Bell Jar* tells the story of a young woman's coming-of-age, but it does not follow the usual trajectory of adolescent development into adulthood. Instead of undergoing a progressive education in the ways of the world, culminating in an entrance into adulthood, Esther regresses into madness. Experiences intended to be life-changing in a positive sense—Esther's first time in New York City, her first marriage proposal, her success in college—are upsetting and disorienting to her. Instead of finding new meaning in living, Esther wants to die. As she slowly recovers from her suicide attempt, she aspires simply to survive.

Esther's struggles and triumphs seem more heroic than conventional achievements. Her desire to die rather than live a false life can be interpreted as noble, and the gradual steps she takes back to sanity seem dignified. Esther does not mark maturity in the traditional way of fictional heroines, by marrying and beginning a family, but by finding the strength to reject the conventional model of womanhood. Esther emerges from her trials with a clear understanding of her own mental health, the strength that she summoned to help her survive, and increased confidence in her skepticism of society's mores. She describes herself, with characteristic humor, as newly "patched, retreaded and approved for the road."

B

THE EMPTINESS OF CONVENTIONAL EXPECTATIONS Esther observes a gap between what society says she should experience and what she does experience, and this gap intensifies her madness. Society expects women of Esther's age and station to act cheerful, flexible, and confident, and Esther feels she must repress her natural gloom, cynicism, and dark humor. She feels she cannot discuss or think about the dark spots in life that plague her: personal failure, suffering, and death. She knows the world of fashion she inhabits in New York should make her feel glamorous and happy, but she finds it filled with poison, drunkenness, and violence. Her relationships with men are supposed to be romantic and meaningful, but they are marked by misunderstanding, distrust, and brutality. Esther almost continuously feels that her reactions are wrong, or that she is the only one to view the world as she does, and eventually she begins to feel a sense of unreality. This sense of unreality grows until it becomes unbearable, and attempted suicide and madness follow.

THE RESTRICTED ROLE OF WOMEN IN 1950s AMERICA Esther's sense of alienation from the world around her comes from the expectations placed upon her as a young woman living in 1950s America. Esther feels pulled between her desire to write and the pressure she feels to settle down and start a family. While Esther's intellectual talents earn her prizes, scholarships, and respect, many people assume that she most wants to become a wife and mother. The girls at her college mock her studiousness and only show her respect when she begins dating a handsome and well-liked boy. Her relationship with Buddy earns her mother's approval, and everyone expects Esther to marry him. Buddy assumes that Esther will drop her poetic ambitions as soon as she becomes a mother, and Esther also assumes that she cannot be both a mother and a poet.

Esther longs to have adventures that society denies her, particularly sexual adventures. She decides to reject Buddy for good when she realizes he represents a sexual double standard. He has an affair with a waitress while dating Esther, but expects Esther to remain a virgin until she marries him. Esther understands her first sexual experience as a crucial step toward independence and adulthood, but she seeks this experience not for her own pleasure but rather to relieve herself of her burdensome virginity. Esther feels anxiety about her future because she can see only mutually exclusive choices: virgin or whore, submissive married woman or successful but lonely career woman. She dreams of a larger life, but the stress of even dreaming such a thing worsens her madness.

THE PERILS OF PSYCHIATRIC MEDICINE *The Bell Jar* takes a critical view of the medical profession—in particular, psychiatric medicine. This critique begins with Esther's visit to Buddy's medical school, where Esther is troubled by the doctors' arrogance and lack of sympathy for the pain suffered by a woman in labor. When Esther meets her first psychiatrist, Dr. Gordon, she finds him self-satisfied and unsympathetic. He does not listen to her and prescribes a traumatic and unhelpful shock therapy treatment. Joan, Esther's acquaintance in the mental hospital, tells a similar tale of the insensitivity of male psychiatrists. Some of the hospitals in which Esther stays are frighteningly sanitized and authoritarian.

The novel does not paint an entirely negative picture of psychiatric care, however. When Esther goes to a more enlightened, luxurious institution, she begins to heal under the care of Dr. Nolan, a progressive female psychiatrist. The three methods of 1950s psychiatric treatment—talk therapy, insulin injections, and electroshock therapy—work for Esther under the proper and attentive care of Dr. Nolan. Even properly administered therapy does not receive unmitigated praise, however. Shock therapy, for example, works by clearing the mind entirely. After one treatment, Esther finds herself unable to think about knives. This inability comes as a relief, but it also suggests that the therapy works by the dubious method of blunting Esther's sharp intelligence.

MOTIFS

NEWS AND FASHION MEDIA Esther frequently reads newspaper headings and thumbs through magazines. The information that she absorbs from these sources tells us what interests her most: the papers fascinate her with their stories of the execution of the Rosenbergs and a man's suicide attempt. Periodicals also reinforce the values of mainstream 1950s America. Esther's mother sends her a pamphlet defending chastity, and in the doctor's waiting room Esther reads magazines about young motherhood. The power of magazine images to distort and alienate is most obvious when Esther sees a picture of herself in a fashion magazine in the mental hospital and feels the distance between her actual life and the image of glamour and happiness she sees in the magazine.

B

MIRRORS Esther continually confronts reflections of herself, reflections she often fails to recognize. After her evening with Doreen and Lenny, Esther fails to recognize her own reflection in the elevator doors. After her first shock treatment with Dr. Nolan, she thinks her reflection is another woman in the room. Most dramatically, after her suicide attempt Esther fails to recognize her bruised and discolored face in a mirror, and cannot even tell if the creature she sees is a man or a woman. Esther increasingly struggles to keep the outward self she presents to the world united with the inner self that she experiences. Her failure to recognize her own reflection stands for the difficulty she has understanding herself.

BLOOD The shedding of blood marks major transitions in Esther's life. When Marco attempts to rape her, she gives him a bloody nose, and he smears his blood on her like war paint. When she decides to kill herself, she slashes her calf to practice slashing her wrists. When she loses her virginity, she bleeds so copiously that she must seek medical attention. The presence of blood suggests a ritual sacrifice: Esther will sacrifice her body for peace of mind, and sacrifice her virginity for the sake of experience. The presence of blood also indicates the frightening violence of Esther's experiences. For her, transformations involve pain and suffering, not joy.

SYMBOLS

THE BELL JAR The bell jar is an inverted glass jar, generally used to display an object of scientific curiosity, contain a certain kind of gas, or maintain a vacuum. For Esther, the bell jar symbolizes madness. When gripped by insanity, she feels as if she is inside an airless jar that distorts her perspective on the world and prevents her from connecting with the people around her. At the end of the novel, the bell jar has lifted, but she can sense that it still hovers over her, waiting to drop at any moment.

THE FIG TREE Early in the novel, Esther reads a story about a Jewish man and a nun who meet under a fig tree. Their relationship is doomed, just as she feels her relationship with Buddy is doomed. Later, the tree becomes a symbol of the life choices that Esther must face. She imagines that each fig represents a different life. She can only choose one fig, but because she wants all of them, she sits paralyzed with indecision, and the figs rot and fall to the ground.

HEADLINES Chapter 16 marks one of Esther's most debilitating bouts with her illness. In this chapter, headlines are reprinted in the text of the novel. Joan gives Esther actual headlines from articles reporting Esther's disappearance and attempted suicide. These headlines symbolize Esther's exposure, her effect on others, and the gap between Esther's interpretation of her experiences and the world's interpretation of them. First, they show Esther that the public knows about her behavior—she does not act in a vacuum, but in the interested eye of the world. The headlines also demonstrate the power Esther's behavior has on people who are almost strangers to her. Joan, for example, says the headlines inspired her to move to New York and attempt suicide. Finally, the headlines represent the dissonance between Esther's experience of herself and others' experience of her. While Esther sees only pain and swallowing pills in the darkness, the world sees a sensational story of a missing girl, a hunt in the woods, and the shocking discovery of Esther in her own house.

THE BEATING HEART When Esther tries to kill herself, she finds that her body seems determined to live. Esther remarks that if it were up to her, she could kill herself in no time, but she must outwit the tricks and ruses of her body. The beating heart symbolizes this bodily desire for life. When she tries to drown herself, her heart beats, "I am I am I am." It repeats the same phrase when Esther attends Joan's funeral.

IMPORTANT QUOTATIONS EXPLAINED

---

1. *Look what can happen in this country, they'd say. A girl lives in some out-of-the-way town for nineteen years, so poor she can't afford a magazine, and then she gets a scholarship to college and wins a prize here and a prize there and ends up steering New York like her own private car. . . . I guess I should have been excited the way most of the other girls were, but I couldn't get myself to react. I felt very still and very empty, the way the eye of a tornado must feel . . .*

B

This comment, which concludes the first section of Chapter 1, describes the disconnect that Esther feels between the way other people view her life and the way she experiences her life. By all external measures, Esther should feel happy and excited. She has overcome her middle-class, small-town background with luck, talent, and hard work, and her reward is a glamorous month in New York. Although she recognizes these objective facts, Esther feels uncertain both about her own abilities and about the rewards that these abilities have garnered her. To her own puzzlement, she does not find New York thrilling and romantic. Instead, she finds it dizzying and depressing, and she finds the fashion world she inhabits superficial and disorienting. The feeling of numbness that Esther describes here is the kernel of the madness that will soon overtake her. Eventually, the gap between societal expectations and her own feelings and experiences becomes so large that she feels she can no longer survive.

---

2. *When I was nineteen, pureness was the great issue. Instead of the world being divided up into Catholics and Protestants or Republicans and Democrats or white men and black men or even men and women, I saw the world divided into people who had slept with somebody and people who hadn't . . . I thought a spectacular change would come over me the day I crossed the boundary line.*

This observation from Chapter 7 shows that Esther inhabits a world of limited sexual choices. Convention dictates that she will remain a virgin until she marries. If she chooses to have sex before marriage, she risks pregnancy, displeasing her future husband, and ruining her own name. Esther sets out to defy conventional expectations by losing her virginity with someone she does not expect to marry. Despite this firm goal, she finds it difficult to gain an independent sexual identity. The men in her life provide little help: Buddy has traditional ideas about male and female roles even though he has mildly transgressed by having an affair with a waitress; an acquaintance named Eric thinks sex is disgusting, and will not have sex with a woman he loves; and Marco calls Esther a slut as he attempts to rape her. When Esther finally loses her virginity, she does not experience the "spectacular change" that she expects, although the experience does satisfy her in some says. Esther only partially escapes the repressive ideas about sexuality that surround her. By losing her virginity, she frees herself of the oppressive mandate to remain pure, but she fails to find sexual pleasure or independence.

3. *[W]herever I sat—on the deck of a ship or at a street café in Paris or Bangkok—I would be sitting under the same glass bell jar, stewing in my own sour air.*

This statement, from the beginning of Chapter 15, introduces the symbol of the bell jar. Esther explains that no matter where she goes, she exists in the hell of her own mind. She is trapped inside herself, and no external stimulation, no matter how new and exciting, can ameliorate this condition. The bell jar of Esther's madness separates her from the people she should care about. Esther's association of her illness with a bell jar suggests her feeling that madness descends on her without her control or assent—it is as if an unseen scientist traps her. Esther's suicidal urges come from this sense of suffocating isolation.

4. *To the person in the bell jar, blank and stopped as a dead baby, the world itself is the bad dream.*

This remark comes from the last chapter of the novel, in which Esther attempts to draw some conclusions about the experiences she has undergone. Her mother suggests that they treat Esther's madness as if it were a bad dream that can be forgotten. This quotation records Esther's inward response; she feels that madness is like being trapped in a bad dream, but it is a bad dream from which one cannot awake. Esther likens the person who suffers from mental illness to the pickled fetuses she saw at Buddy's medical school, a morbid connection that illustrates the terror of madness.

5. *How did I know that someday—at college, in Europe, somewhere, anywhere—the bell jar, with its stifling distortions, wouldn't descend again?*

This thought, also from the last chapter of the novel, provides the final word on Esther's supposed cure. The bell jar has lifted enough that Esther can function more or less normally. She has relinquished her desire to kill herself, and she begins to form tenuous connections with other people and with the outside world. But Esther still feels the bell jar hovering above her, and worries that it will trap her again. Her madness does not obey reason, and though she feels grateful to have escaped from it, she does not believe that this escape represents a fundamental or permanent change in her situation. If we read *The Bell Jar* as partly autobiographical, Plath's own life story confirms that the bell jar can descend again. Just as the pressures that culminated in her late teens drove Plath to attempt suicide, the pressures that culminated in her early thirties drove her to commit suicide.

Trace the symbol of the bell jar throughout Sylvia Plath's *The Bell Jar*.

A bell jar is a bell-shaped glass cover that has three basic uses: to hold a specimen for observation, to contain gases, and to maintain a vacuum. The bell jar appears in each of these capacities in *The Bell Jar*, Sylvia Plath's semi-autobiographical novel, and each appearance marks a different stage in Esther's mental breakdown.

Plath introduces bell jars during Esther's visit to her boyfriend's medical school lab. There she sees fetuses and other specimens under various glass covers for observation and study. The image of the specimen under observation continues as Esther watches a woman in the midst of a painful childbirth and is told she has been drugged so that she won't remember her pain. These two experiences highlight the way the bell jar is an appropriate symbol for the plight of women in the hands of male doctors. The women have become the specimens; indeed, Esther feels outside herself, as if she too is under observation, drugged, and unable to respond. "I couldn't get myself to react. I felt very still and very empty" (Chapter 1), she says. This isolation continues in New York, where she feels cut off from the city, her roommates, her friends, and her family.

A second function of bell jars is to contain gases that might otherwise disperse, and this function appears in the novel as Esther's breakdown worsens. Esther realizes she cannot escape: "[W]herever I sat—on the deck of a ship or at a street café in Paris or Bangkok—I would be sitting under the same glass bell jar, stewing in my own sour air" (Chapter 15). Now Esther is the specimen trapped within the bell jar, unable to breathe. Her mental trouble has moved from a distancing isolation to a rotting, pervasive cloud that will not break up. If Esther's bell jar were lifted, perhaps the "sour air" of her mental illness would disperse, leaving her happy, alive, and unburdened by the world's expectations, but this doesn't seem likely.

Student Essay

As Esther's mental state deteriorates, the bell jar appears yet again, this time as a vessel that can create and maintain a vacuum. A vacuum is formed when matter or air is removed, even partially, from a container. Life cannot exist within a vacuum; it is a space of emptiness, silence, and death. This morbid image corresponds to Esther's lowest point. When her mother likens Esther's breakdown to a bad dream, Esther objects: "To the person in the bell jar, blank and stopped as a dead baby, the world itself is a bad dream" (Chapter 20). The bell jar now creates the vacuum's nothingness, leaving her "blank," "stopped," and "dead." The reference to dead babies brings the image of the bell jar full circle; now Esther has been choked by the noxious fumes trapped in the jar and killed by the vacuum's deadly emptiness. She takes the place of the specimen, useful only for study.

Finally, after changing hospitals and doctors and using both talk and electroshock therapies, Esther begins to feel the bell jar lifting—she is able to feel happy again, begins to form relationships with other people, and interacts with the outside world once more. While she is not "cured," she is on her way to resuming some of her normal activities. Yet there hangs over the book the concern that this might not be the end of her problems. The bell jar imagery perfectly reflects this: "How did I know that someday—at college, in Europe, somewhere, anywhere—the bell jar, with its stifling distortions, wouldn't descend again?" (Chapter 20) she worries. The bell jar shifts and changes, but it remains a symbol of Esther's oppression in its various forms.

Beloved

Toni Morrison
(1931–)

CONTEXT

Toni Morrison was born Chloe Anthony Wofford in 1931 and spent the first years of her life in Ohio. She received an undergraduate degree in English from Howard University and a master's degree from Cornell. When many of her classmates had difficulty pronouncing her uncommon first name, she changed it to Toni (a derivative of her middle name). In 1958, she married Harold Morrison, an architect from Jamaica, and the couple had two sons. They divorced six years later. After pursuing an academic career teaching English at Howard, Morrison became an editor at Random House, where she specialized in black fiction. At the same time, she began building a body of creative work that, in 1993, would make her the first African-American woman to receive the Nobel Prize for Literature. Her 1970 novel, *The Bluest Eye*, was followed by *Sula* in 1974, which secured Morrison a nomination for the National Book Award. In 1977, Morrison won the National Book Critics Circle Award for her book *Song of Solomon*. Her other works include *Tar Baby* (1981), *Jazz* (1992), *Paradise* (1998), and, of course, *Beloved*. This novel, considered by many to be her best, won the Pulitzer Prize in 1988. Today, Morrison is the Robert F. Goheen Professor in the Council of Humanities at Princeton University, where she conducts undergraduate workshops in creative writing.

Set during the Reconstruction era in 1873, *Beloved* centers on the powers of memory and history. For the former slaves in the novel, the past is a burden that they desperately and willfully try to forget. Yet for Sethe, the protagonist of the novel, memories of slavery are inescapable. They continue to haunt her, literally, in the spirit of her deceased daughter. Eighteen years earlier, Sethe had murdered this daughter in order to save her from a life of slavery. Morrison borrowed the event from the real story of Margaret Garner, who, like Sethe, escaped from slavery in Kentucky and murdered her child when slave catchers caught up with her in Ohio. Beloved straddles the line between fiction and history; from the experiences of a single family, Morrison creates a powerful commentary on the psychological and historical legacy of slavery.

Part of Morrison's project in *Beloved* is to recuperate a history that had been lost to the ravages of forced silences and willed forgetfulness. Morrison writes Sethe's story with the voices of a people who historically have been denied the power of language. *Beloved* also contains a didactic element. From Sethe's experience, we learn that before a stable future can be created, we must confront and understand the "ghosts" of the past. Morrison suggests that, like Sethe, contemporary American readers must confront the history of slavery in order to address its legacy, which manifests itself in ongoing racial discrimination and discord.

Morrison once said that she wanted to help create a canon of black work, noting that black writers too often have to pander to a white audience when they should be able to concentrate on the business of writing instead. Many readers believe Morrison's novels go a long way toward the establishment of her envisioned tradition. The poetic, elegant style of her writing in *Beloved* panders to no one. Morrison challenges and requires the reader to accept her on her own terms.

PLOT OVERVIEW

Beloved begins in 1873 in Cincinnati, Ohio, where Sethe, a former slave, has been living with her eighteen-year-old daughter, Denver. Sethe's mother-in-law, Baby Suggs, lived with them until her death eight years earlier. Just before Baby Suggs's death, Sethe's two sons, Howard and Buglar, ran away. Sethe believes they fled because of the malevolent presence of an abusive ghost that has haunted their house at 124 Bluestone Road for years. Denver, however, likes the ghost, which everyone believes to be the spirit of her dead sister.

On the day the novel begins, Paul D, whom Sethe has not seen since they worked together on Mr. Garner's Sweet Home plantation in Kentucky approximately twenty years earlier, stops by Sethe's house. His presence resurrects memories that have been buried in Sethe's mind for almost two decades. From this point on, the story will unfold on two temporal planes. The present in Cincinnati constitutes one plane, while a series of events that took place around twenty years earlier, mostly in Kentucky, constitutes the other. This latter plane is accessed and described through the fragmented flashbacks of the major characters. Accordingly, we frequently read these flashbacks several times, sometimes from varying perspectives, with each successive narration of an event adding a little more information to the previous ones.

From these fragmented memories, the following story begins to emerge: Sethe, the protagonist, was born in the South to an African mother she never knew. When she is thirteen, she is sold to the Garners, who own Sweet Home and practice a comparatively benevolent kind of slavery. There, the other slaves, who are all men, lust after her but never touch her. Their names are Sixo, Paul D, Paul A, Paul F, and Halle. Sethe chooses to marry Halle, apparently in part because he has proven generous enough to buy his mother's freedom by hiring himself out on the weekends. Together, Sethe and Halle have two sons, Howard and Buglar, as well as a baby daughter whose name we never learn. When she leaves Sweet Home, Sethe is also pregnant with a fourth child. After the eventual death of the proprietor, Mr. Garner, the widowed Mrs. Garner asks her sadistic, vehemently racist brother-in-law to help her run the farm. He is known to the slaves as schoolteacher, and his oppressive presence makes life on the plantation even more unbearable than it had been before. The slaves decide to run.

Schoolteacher and his nephews anticipate the slaves' escape, however, and capture Paul D and Sixo. Schoolteacher kills Sixo and brings Paul D back to Sweet Home, where Paul D sees Sethe for what he believes will be the last time. She is still intent on running, having already sent her children ahead to her mother-in-law Baby Suggs's house in Cincinnati. Invigorated by the recent capture, schoolteacher's nephews seize Sethe in the barn and violate her, stealing the milk her body is storing for her infant daughter. Unbeknownst to Sethe, Halle is watching the event from a loft above her, where he lies frozen with horror. Afterward, Halle goes mad: Paul D sees him sitting by a churn with butter slathered all over his face. Paul D, meanwhile, is forced to suffer the indignity of wearing an iron bit in his mouth.

When schoolteacher finds out that Sethe has reported his and his nephews' misdeeds to Mrs. Garner, he has her whipped severely, despite the fact that she is pregnant. Swollen and scarred, Sethe nevertheless runs away, but along the way she collapses from exhaustion in a forest. A white girl, Amy Denver, finds her and nurses her back to health. When Amy later helps Sethe deliver her baby in a boat, Sethe names this second daughter Denver after the girl who helped her. Sethe receives further help from Stamp Paid, who rows her across the Ohio River to Baby Suggs's house. Baby Suggs cleans Sethe up before allowing her to see her three older children.

Sethe spends twenty-eight wonderful days in Cincinnati, where Baby Suggs serves as an unofficial preacher to the black community. On the last day, however, schoolteacher comes for Sethe to take her and her children back to Sweet Home. Rather than surrender her children to a life of dehumanizing slavery, she flees with them to the woodshed and tries to kill them. Only the third child, her older daughter, dies, her throat having been cut with a handsaw by Sethe. Sethe later arranges for the baby's headstone to be carved with the word "Beloved." The sheriff takes Sethe and Denver to jail, but a group of white abolitionists, led by the Bodwins, fights for her release. Sethe returns to the house at 124, where Baby Suggs has sunk into a deep depression. The community shuns the house, and the family continues to live in isolation.

Meanwhile, Paul D has endured torturous experiences in a chain gang in Georgia, where he was sent after trying to kill Brandywine, a slave owner to whom he was sold by schoolteacher. His traumatic experiences have caused him to lock away his memories, emotions, and ability to love in the "tin tobacco box" of his heart. One day, a fortuitous rainstorm allows Paul D and the other chain gang members to escape. He travels northward by following the blossoming spring flowers. Years later, he ends up on Sethe's porch in Cincinnati.

Paul D's arrival at 124 commences the series of events taking place in the present time frame. Prior to moving in, Paul D chases the house's resident ghost away, which makes the already lonely Denver resent him from the start. Sethe and Paul D look forward to a promising future together, until one day, on their way home from a carnival, they encounter a strange young woman sleeping near the steps of 124. Most of the characters believe that the woman—who calls herself Beloved—is the embodied spirit of Sethe's dead daughter, and the novel provides a wealth of evidence supporting this interpretation. Denver develops an obsessive attachment to Beloved, and Beloved's attachment to Sethe is equally if not more intense. Paul D and Beloved hate each other, and Beloved controls Paul D by moving him around the house like a rag doll and by seducing him against his will.

When Paul D learns the story of Sethe's "rough choice"—her infanticide—he leaves 124 and begins sleeping in the basement of the local church. In his absence, Sethe and Beloved's relationship becomes more intense and exclusive. Beloved grows increasingly abusive, manipulative, and parasitic, and Sethe is obsessed with satisfying Beloved's demands and making her understand why she murdered her. Worried by the way her mother is wasting away, Denver leaves the premises of 124 for the first time in twelve years in order to seek help from Lady Jones, her former teacher. The community provides the family with food and eventually organizes under the leadership of Ella, a woman who had worked on the Underground Railroad and helped with Sethe's escape, in order to exorcise Beloved from 124. When they arrive at Sethe's house, they see Sethe on the porch with Beloved, who stands smiling at them, naked and pregnant. Mr. Bodwin, who has come to 124 to take Denver to her new job, arrives at the house. Mistaking him for schoolteacher, Sethe runs at Mr. Bodwin with an ice pick. She is restrained, but in the confusion, Beloved disappears, never to return.

Afterward, Paul D comes back to Sethe, who has retreated to Baby Suggs's bed to die. Mourning Beloved, Sethe laments, "She was my best thing." But Paul D replies, "You your best thing, Sethe." The novel then ends with a warning that "[t]his is not a story to pass on." The town, and even the residents of 124, have forgotten Beloved "[l]ike an unpleasant dream during a troubling sleep."

CHARACTER LIST

B

Sethe The protagonist of *Beloved*, a proud and independent woman who is extremely devoted to her children. Though Sethe barely knew her own mother, her motherly instincts are her most striking characteristic. Unwilling to relinquish her children to the physical, emotional, sexual, and spiritual trauma she endured as a slave at Sweet Home, she attempts to murder them in an act of motherly love and protection. She remains haunted by this and other scarring events in her past, which she tries, in vain, to repress.

Denver Sethe's youngest child and the most dynamic character in the novel. Though intelligent, introspective, and sensitive, Denver has been stunted in her emotional growth by years of relative isolation. Beloved's increasing malevolence, however, forces Denver to overcome her fear of the world beyond 124 and seek help from the community. Her foray out into the town and her attempts to find permanent work and possibly attend college mark the beginning of her fight for independence and self-possession.

Beloved A being whose identity is mysterious. The novel provides evidence that she could be an ordinary woman traumatized by years of captivity, the ghost of Sethe's mother, or, most convincingly, the embodied spirit of Sethe's murdered daughter. On an allegorical level, Beloved represents the inescapable, horrible past of slavery returned to haunt the present. Her presence, which grows increasingly malevolent and parasitic as the novel progresses, ultimately serves as a catalyst for Sethe's, Paul D's, and Denver's respective processes of emotional growth.

Paul D A man who suffered physical and emotional brutality at Sweet Home and as part of a chain gang, which has caused him to bury his feelings in the "rusted tobacco tin" of his heart. Paul D represses his painful memories and believes that the key to survival is not becoming too attached to anything. At the same time, he seems to incite the opening up of others' hearts, and women in particular tend to confide in him. Sethe welcomes him to 124, where he becomes her lover and the object of Denver's and Beloved's jealousy. Though his union with Sethe provides him with stability and allows him to come to terms with his past, Paul D continues to doubt fundamental aspects of his identity, such as the source of his manhood and his value as a person.

Baby Suggs Halle's mother. After Halle buys Baby Suggs her freedom, she travels to Cincinnati, where she becomes a source of emotional and spiritual inspiration for the city's black residents. She holds religious gatherings at a place called the Clearing, where she teaches her followers to love their voices, bodies, and minds. However, after Sethe's act of infanticide, Baby Suggs stops preaching and retreats to a sickbed to die. Even so, Baby Suggs continues to be a source of inspiration long after her death: in Part Three her memory motivates Denver to leave 124 and find help. It is partially out of respect for Baby Suggs that the community responds to Denver's requests for support.

Stamp Paid A man whom the community considers to be a figure of salvation. Stamp is welcomed at every door in town. An agent of the Underground Railroad, he helps Sethe to freedom and later saves Denver's life. A grave sacrifice he made during his enslavement has caused him to consider his emotional and moral debts to be paid off for the rest of his life, which is why he decided to rename himself

"Stamp Paid." Yet by the end of the book he realizes that he may still owe protection and care to the residents of 124. Angered by the community's neglect of Sethe, Denver, and Paul D, Stamp begins to question the nature of a community's obligations to its members.

Schoolteacher The person who takes charge of Sweet Home following Mr. Garner's death. Cold, sadistic, and vehemently racist, schoolteacher replaces what he views as Garner's too-soft approach with an oppressive regime of rigid rules and punishment on the plantation. Schoolteacher's own habits are extremely ascetic: he eats little, sleeps less, and works hard. His most insidious form of oppression is his "scientific" scrutiny of the slaves, which involves asking questions, taking physical measurements, and teaching lessons to his white pupils on the slaves' "animal characteristics." The lower-cases of schoolteacher's appellation may have an ironic meaning: although he enjoys a position of extreme power over the slaves, they attribute no worth to him.

Halle Sethe's husband and Baby Suggs's son. Halle is generous, kind, and sincere. He is very much alert to the hypocrisies of the Garners' "benevolent" form of slaveholding. He eventually goes mad, presumably after witnessing schoolteacher's nephews' violation of Sethe.

Lady Jones A light-skinned black woman who loathes her blond hair and is convinced that everyone despises her for being a woman of mixed race. Despite Lady Jones's feelings of alienation, she maintains a strong sense of community obligation and teaches the underprivileged children of Cincinnati in her home. She is skeptical of the supernatural dimensions of Denver's plea for assistance, but she nevertheless helps organize the community's delivery of food to Sethe's plagued household.

B

Ella A woman who worked with Stamp Paid on the Underground Railroad. Traumatized by the sexual brutality of a white father and son who once held her captive, Ella believes, like Sethe, that the past is best left buried. When it surfaces in the form of Beloved, Ella organizes the women of the community to exorcise Beloved from 124.

Mr. and Mrs. Garner The comparatively benevolent owners of Sweet Home. The events at Sweet Home reveal, however, that the idea of benevolent slavery is a contradiction in terms. The Garners' paternalism and condescension are simply watered-down versions of schoolteacher's vicious racism.

Mr. and Miss Bodwin Siblings and white abolitionists who have played an active role in winning Sethe's freedom. There is something disconcerting about the Bodwins' politics. Mr. Bodwin longs a little too eagerly for the "heady days" of abolitionism, and Miss Bodwin demonstrates a condescending desire to "experiment" on Denver by sending her to Oberlin College. The distasteful figurine Denver sees in the Bodwins' house, portraying a slave and displaying the message "At Yo' Service," marks the limits and ironies of white involvement in the struggle for racial equality. Nevertheless, the siblings are motivated by good intentions, believing that "human life is holy, all of it."

Amy Denver A nurturing and compassionate girl who works as an indentured servant. Amy is young, flighty, talkative, and idealistic. She helps Sethe when she is ill during her escape from Sweet Home, and when she sees Sethe's wounds from being whipped, Amy says that they resemble a tree. She later delivers baby Denver, whom Sethe names after her.

Paul A, Paul F, and Sixo Paul A and Paul F are the brothers of Paul D. They were slaves at Sweet Home with him, Halle, Sethe, and, earlier, Baby Suggs. Sixo is another fellow slave. Sixo and Paul A die during the escape from the plantation.

ANALYSIS OF MAJOR CHARACTERS

SETHE Sethe, the protagonist of the novel, is proud and noble. She insists on sewing a proper wedding dress for the first night she spends with Halle, and she finds schoolteacher's lesson on her "animal characteristics" more debilitating than his nephews' sexual and physical abuse. Although the community's shunning of Sethe and Baby Suggs for thinking too highly of themselves is unfair, the fact that Sethe prefers to steal food from the restaurant where she works rather than wait on line with the rest of the black community shows that she does consider herself different from the rest of the blacks in her neighborhood. Yet Sethe is not too proud to accept support from others in every instance. Despite her independence (and her distrust of men), she welcomes Paul D and the companionship he offers.

Sethe's most striking characteristic is her devotion to her children. Unwilling to relinquish her children to the physical, emotional, and spiritual trauma she has endured as a slave, she tries to murder them in an act that is, in her mind, one of motherly love and protection. Her memories of this cruel act and of the brutality she herself suffered as a slave infuse her everyday life and lead her to contend that past trauma can never really be eradicated—it continues to exist in the present. She spends her life attempting to avoid encounters with her past. Perhaps Sethe's fear of the past is what leads her to ignore the overwhelming evidence that Beloved is the reincarnation of her murdered daughter. Even after she acknowledges Beloved's identity, Sethe shows herself to be still enslaved by the past, because she quickly succumbs to Beloved's demands and allows herself to be consumed by Beloved. Only when Sethe learns to confront the past head-on—to assert herself in its presence—can she extricate herself from its oppressive power and begin to live freely, peacefully, and responsibly in the present.

DENVER Sethe's daughter Denver is the most dynamic character in the novel. She is shy, intelligent, introspective, sensitive, and inclined to spend hours alone in her "emerald closet," a sylvan space formed by boxwood bushes. Her mother considers Denver a "charmed" child who has miraculously survived, and throughout the book Denver is in close contact with the supernatural. Despite Denver's abilities to cope, she has been stunted emotionally by years of relative isolation. Though eighteen years old, she acts much younger, maintaining an intense fear of the world outside 124 and a perilously fragile sense of self. Her self-conception remains so tentative that she feels slighted by the idea of a world that does not include her—even the world of slavery at Sweet Home. Denver defines her identity in relation to Sethe. She also defines herself in relation to her sister—first in the form of the baby ghost, then in the form of Beloved. When she feels that she is being excluded from her family's attentions—for example, when her mother devotes her energies to Paul D—Denver feels threatened and angry. Correspondingly, she treats Paul D coldly much of the time.

In the face of Beloved's escalating malevolence and her mother's submissiveness, Denver is forced to step outside the world of 124. Filled with a sense of duty, purpose, and courage, she enlists the help of the community and cares for her increasingly self-involved mother and sister. She enters a series of lessons with Miss Bodwin and considers attending Oberlin College someday. Her last conversation with Paul D underscores her newfound maturity: she presents herself with more civility and sincerity than in the past and asserts that she now has her own opinions.

BELOVED Beloved's elusive, complex identity is central to our understanding of the novel. She may, as Sethe originally believes, be an ordinary woman who was locked up by a white man and never let outside. Her limited linguistic ability, neediness, baby-soft skin, and emotional instability could all be explained by a lifetime spent in captivity. But these traits could also support the theory that is held by most of the characters in the novel: Beloved is the embodied spirit of Sethe's dead daughter. Beloved is the age the baby would have been had it lived, and she bears the name printed on the baby's tombstone. She first appears to Sethe soaking wet, as though newly born, and Sethe has the sensation of her water breaking when she sees her. Additionally, Beloved knows about a pair of earrings Sethe possessed long ago, she hums a song Sethe made up for her children, she has a long scar under her chin where her death-wound would have been dealt, and her breath smells like milk.

A third interpretation views Beloved as a representation of Sethe's dead mother. In Chapter 22, Beloved recounts memories that correspond to those that Sethe's mother might have had of her passage to America from Africa. Beloved has a strange manner of speaking and seems to wear a perpetual smile—traits we are told were shared by Sethe's mother. By Chapter 26, Beloved and Sethe have switched places, with Beloved acting as the mother and Sethe as the child. Their role reversal may simply mark more explicitly what has been Beloved's role all along. On a more general level, Beloved may also stand for all of the slaves who made the passage across the Atlantic. She may give voice to and embody the collective unconscious of all those oppressed by slavery's history and legacy.

Beloved is presented as an allegorical figure. Whether she is Sethe's daughter, Sethe's mother, or a representative of all of slavery's victims, Beloved represents the past returned to haunt the present.

The characters' confrontations with Beloved and, consequently, their pasts, are complex. The interaction between Beloved and Sethe is given particular attention in the book. Once Sethe reciprocates Beloved's violent passion for her, the two become locked in a destructive, exclusive, parasitic relationship. When she is with Beloved, Sethe is paralyzed in the past. She devotes all her attention to making Beloved understand why she reacted to schoolteacher's arrival the way she did. Paradoxically, Beloved's presence is enabling at the same time that it is destructive. Beloved allows and inspires Sethe to tell the stories she never tells—stories about her own feelings of abandonment by her mother, about the harshest indignities she suffered at Sweet Home, and about her motivations for murdering her daughter. By engaging with her past, Sethe begins to learn about herself and the extent of her ability to live in the present.

Beloved also inspires the growth of other characters in the novel. Though Paul D's hatred for Beloved never ceases, their strange, dreamlike sexual encounters open the lid of his "tobacco tin" heart, allowing him to remember, feel, and love again. Denver benefits the most from Beloved's presence, though indirectly. At first she feels an intense dependence on Beloved, convinced that in Beloved's absence she has no "self" of her own. Later, however, Beloved's increasingly malevolent, temperamental, self-centered actions alert Denver to the dangers of the past that Beloved represents. Ultimately, Beloved's tyranny over Sethe forces Denver to leave 124 and seek help in the community. Denver's exile from 124 marks the beginning of her social integration and of her search for independence and self-possession.

Although Beloved vanishes at the end of the book, she is never really gone—her dress and her story, forgotten by the town but preserved by the novel, remain. Beloved represents a destructive and painful past, but she also signals the possibility of a brighter future. She gives the people of 124, and eventually the entire community, a chance to engage with the memories they have suppressed. Through confrontation, the community can reclaim and learn from its forgotten and ignored memories.

THEMES, MOTIFS, AND SYMBOLS

THEMES

SLAVERY'S DESTRUCTION OF IDENTITY *Beloved* explores the physical, emotional, and spiritual devastation wrought by slavery, a devastation that continues to haunt those characters who are former slaves even in freedom. The most dangerous of slavery's effects is its negative impact on the former slaves' senses of self, and the novel contains multiple examples of self-alienation. Paul D, for instance, is so alienated from himself that at one point he cannot tell whether the screaming he hears is his own or someone else's. Slaves were told they were subhuman and were traded as commodities whose worth could be expressed in dollars. Consequently, Paul D is very insecure about whether or not he could possibly be a real "man," and he frequently wonders about his value as a person.

Sethe, also, was treated as a subhuman. She once walked in on schoolteacher giving his pupils a lesson on her "animal characteristics." She, too, seems to be alienated from herself and filled with self-loathing. She sees the best part of herself as her children. Yet her children also have volatile, unstable identities. Denver conflates her identity with Beloved's, and Beloved feels herself actually beginning to physically disintegrate. Slavery has also limited Baby Suggs's self-conception by shattering her family and denying her the opportunity to be a true wife, sister, daughter, or loving mother.

As a result of their inability to believe in their own existences, both Baby Suggs and Paul D become depressed and tired. Baby Suggs's fatigue is spiritual, while Paul D's is emotional. While a slave, Paul D developed self-defeating coping strategies to protect him from the emotional pain he was forced to endure. Any feelings he had were locked away in the rusted "tobacco tin" of his heart, and he concluded that one should love nothing too intensely.

Other slaves—Jackson Till, Aunt Phyllis, and Halle—went insane and thus suffered a complete loss of self. Sethe fears that she, too, will end her days in madness. Indeed, she does prove to be mad when she kills her own daughter. Yet Sethe's act of infanticide illuminates the perverse forces of the institution of slavery: under slavery, a mother best expresses her love for her children by murdering them and thus protecting them from the more gradual destruction wrought by slavery.

Stamp Paid muses that slavery's negative consequences are not limited to the slaves: he notes that slavery causes whites to become "changed and altered . . . made . . . bloody, silly, worse than they ever wanted to be." The insidious effects of the institution affect not only the identities of its black victims but those of the whites who perpetrate it and the collective identity of Americans. Where slavery exists, everyone suffers a loss of humanity and compassion. For this reason, Morrison suggests that our nation's identity, like the novel's characters, must be healed. America's future depends on its understanding of the past: just as Sethe must come to terms with her past before she can secure a future with Denver and Paul D, and before we can address slavery's legacy in the contemporary problems of racial discrimination and discord, we must confront the dark and hidden corners of our history. Crucially, in *Beloved,* we learn about the history and legacy of slavery not from schoolteacher's or even from the Bodwins' point of view but rather from Sethe's, Paul D's, Stamp Paid's, and Baby Suggs's. Morrison writes history with the voices of a people historically denied the power of language, and *Beloved* recuperates a history that had been lost—either due to willed forgetfulness (as in Sethe's repression of her memories) or to forced silence (as in the case of Paul D's iron bit).

THE IMPORTANCE OF COMMUNITY SOLIDARITY *Beloved* demonstrates the extent to which individuals need the support of their communities in order to survive. Sethe first begins to develop her sense of self during her twenty-eight days of freedom, when she becomes a part of the Cincinnati community. Similarly, Denver discovers herself and grows up when she leaves 124 and becomes a part of society. Paul D and his fellow prison inmates in Georgia prove able to escape only by working together. They are literally chained to one another, and Paul D recalls that "if one lost, all lost." Lastly, it is the community that saves Sethe from mistakenly killing Mr. Bodwin and casting the shadow of another sin across her and her family's life.

Cincinnati's black community plays a pivotal role in the events of 124. The community's failure to alert Sethe to schoolteacher's approach implicates it in the death of Sethe's daughter. Baby Suggs feels the slight as a grave betrayal from which she never fully recovers. At the end of the novel, the black community makes up for its past misbehavior by gathering at 124 to collectively exorcise Beloved. By driving Beloved away, the community secures Sethe's, and its own, release from the past.

THE POWERS AND LIMITS OF LANGUAGE When Sixo turns schoolteacher's reasoning around to justify having broken the rules, schoolteacher whips him to demonstrate that "definitions belong to the definers," not to the defined. The slaves eventually come to realize the illegitimacy of many of the white definitions. Mr. Garner, for example, claims to have allowed his slaves to live as "real men," but Paul D questions just how manly they actually are. So, too, does Paul D finally come to realize with bitter irony the fallacy of the name "Sweet Home." Although Sixo eventually reacts to the hypocrisy of the rhetoric of slavery by abandoning English altogether, other characters use English to redefine the world on their own terms. Baby Suggs and Stamp Paid, for example, rename themselves. Beloved may be read as Morrison's effort to transform those who have always been the defined into the definers.

While slaves, the characters manipulate language and transcend its standard limits. Their command of language allows them to adjust its meanings and to make themselves indecipherable to the white slave owners who watch them. For example, Paul D and the Georgia prison inmates sing together about their dreams and memories by "garbling . . . [and] tricking the words."

The title of the novel alludes to what is ultimately the product of a linguistic misunderstanding. At her daughter's funeral, Sethe interpreted the minister's address to the "Dearly Beloved" as referring to the dead rather than the living. All literature is indebted to this "slippery," shifting quality of language: the power of metaphor, simile, metonymy, irony, and wordplay all result from the ability of words to attach and detach themselves from various possible meanings.

MOTIFS

THE SUPERNATURAL Morrison enhances the world of *Beloved* by investing it with a supernatural dimension. While it is possible to interpret the book's paranormal phenomena within a realist framework, many events in the novel—most notably, the presence of a ghost—push the limits of ordinary understanding. Moreover, the characters in *Beloved* do not hesitate to believe in the supernatural status of these events. For them, poltergeists, premonitions, and hallucinations are ways of understanding the significance of the world around them. Such occurrences stand in marked contrast to schoolteacher's perverse hyper-"scientific" and empirical studies.

ALLUSIONS TO CHRISTIANITY *Beloved*'s epigraph, taken from Romans 9:25, bespeaks the presence that Christian ideas will have in the novel. The "four horsemen" who come for Sethe reference the description of the Apocalypse found in the Book of Revelations. Beloved is reborn into Sethe's world, drenched in a sort of baptismal water. As an infant, Denver drinks her sister's blood along with her mother's breast milk, which can be interpreted as an act of Communion that links Denver and Beloved and that highlights the sacrificial aspect of the baby's death. Sethe's act so horrifies schoolteacher that he leaves without taking her other children, allowing them to live in freedom. The baby's sacrificial death, like that of Christ, brings salvation. The book's larger discussions of sin, sacrifice, redemption, forgiveness, love, and resurrection similarly resound with biblical references.

SYMBOLS

THE COLOR RED Colors from the red part of the spectrum (including orange and pink) recur throughout *Beloved*, although the meaning of these red objects varies. Amy Denver's red velvet, for example, is an image of hope and a brighter future, while Paul D's "red heart" represents feeling and emotion. Overall, red seems to connote vitality and the visceral nature of human existence. Yet, in *Beloved*, vitality often goes hand in hand with mortality, and red images simultaneously refer to life and death, to presence and absence. For example, the red roses that line the road to the carnival serve to herald the carnival's arrival in town and announce the beginning of Sethe, Denver, and Paul D's new life together; yet they also stink of death. The red rooster signifies manhood to Paul D, but it is a manhood that Paul D himself has been denied. The story of Amy's search for carmine velvet seems especially poignant because we sense the futility of her dream. Sethe's memory is awash with the red of her daughter's blood and the pink mineral of her gravestone, both of which have been bought at a dear price.

TREES In the world of *Beloved*, trees serve primarily as sources of healing, comfort, and life. Denver's "emerald closet" of boxwood bushes functions as a place of solitude and repose for her. The beautiful trees of Sweet Home mask the true horror of the plantation in Sethe's memory. Paul D finds his freedom by following flowering trees to the North, and Sethe finds hers by escaping through a forest. By imagining the scars on Sethe's back as a "chokecherry tree," Amy Denver sublimates a site of trauma and brutality into one of beauty and growth. But as the sites of lynchings and of Sixo's death by burning, however, trees reveal a connection with a darker side of humanity as well.

THE TIN TOBACCO BOX Paul D describes his heart as a "tin tobacco box." After his traumatizing experiences at Sweet Home and, especially, at the prison camp in Alfred, Georgia, he locks away his feelings and memories in this "box," which has, by the time Paul D arrives at 124, "rusted" over completely. By alienating himself from his emotions, Paul D hopes to preserve himself from further psychological damage. In order to secure this protection, however, Paul D sacrifices much of his humanity by foregoing feeling and gives up much of his selfhood by repressing his memories. Although Paul D is convinced that nothing can pry the lid of his box open, his strange, dreamlike sexual encounter with Beloved—perhaps a symbol of an encounter with his past—causes the box to burst and his heart once again to glow red.

IMPORTANT QUOTATIONS EXPLAINED

---

1. *124 was spiteful. Full of a baby's venom.*

Each of *Beloved*'s three parts begins with an observation about 124, the house occupied by Sethe and her daughter Denver. Part One of the novel begins with this quotation, Part Two with "124 was loud," and Part Three with "124 was quiet." Their house, 124, is haunted by the abusive and malevolent spirit of Sethe's dead daughter. When the novel opens, the ghost rages with a fury that is most definitely a baby's. In Chapter 5, however, the baby ghost manifests herself in the form of Beloved, who seems to be a reincarnation of the baby Sethe murdered eighteen years ago. As the novel progresses, Beloved will become more powerful, until, in Chapter 19, she is said to wield the force of a collective "black and angry dead." The spirit will wreak havoc on 124 until the community exorcises Beloved in Chapter 26.

---

2. *White people believed that whatever the manners, under every dark skin was a jungle. Swift unnavigable waters, swinging screaming baboons, sleeping snakes, red gums ready for their sweet white blood. In a way . . . they were right. . . . But it wasn't the jungle blacks brought with them to this place. . . . It was the jungle whitefolks planted in them. And it grew. It spread . . . until it invaded the whites who had made it. . . . Made them bloody, silly, worse than even they wanted to be, so scared were they of the jungle they had made. The screaming baboon lived under their own white skin; the red gums were their own.*

In Chapter 19, at the beginning of Part Two, Stamp Paid considers the ways in which slavery corrupts and dehumanizes everyone who comes in contact with it, including the white slave owners. It makes them fearful, sadistic, and raving. For example, one could say that schoolteacher's perverse lessons and violent racism exist because they are his means of justifying the institution of slavery. In his thoughts, Stamp Paid depicts the jungle from a white person's point of view—as awesome, exotic, and thrilling. He perceives anxiety on the part of the whites about the unknown, unintelligible, "unnavigable" psyche of the slaves they steal. The sense of anxiety is emphasized by the images of wild consumption in the passage—jungles growing and spreading, red gums ready for blood. The conclusion of this passage asserts that what the whites recognize and run from is in fact their own savagery. They project this savagery onto those whom they perceive to be their opposites—"the Other." The passage derives its power from the way Morrison moves the images of the jungle around, so that, by the end, the whites are the ones who hide a jungle under their skin; they are consuming themselves.

---

3. *Saying more might push them both to a place they couldn't get back from. He would keep the rest where it belonged: in that tobacco tin buried in his chest where a red heart used to be. Its lid rusted shut.*

In Chapter 7, Paul D begins sharing his painful memories with Sethe, but he fears that revealing too much will wrench the two former slaves back into a past from which they might never escape. Both Sethe and Paul D avoid the pain of their past as best they can, and both have developed elaborate and ultimately destructive coping mechanisms to keep the past at bay. Sethe has effectively erased much of her memory, and Paul D functions by locking his memories and emotions away in his imagined "tobacco tin." The rustiness of the tin contributes to the reader's sense of the inaccessibility and corrosiveness of Paul D's memories. His separation from his emotions means he is alienated from himself, but Paul D is willing to pay the price to keep himself from his painful and turbulent past. When Paul D is forced to confront the past during his erotic encounter with Beloved, the rusted lid of his heart begins to break open. At the end of the novel, Paul D reveals that he is willing finally to risk emotional safety and open himself to another person, to love Sethe.

---

4. *. . . [I]f you go there—you who was never there—if you go there and stand in the place where it was, it will happen again; it will be there, waiting for you . . . [E]ven though it's all over—over and done with—it's going to always be there waiting for you.*

This passage is from Chapter 3. In her "emerald closet," Denver remembers what Sethe once said about the indestructible nature of the past. According to Sethe's theory of time, past traumas continue to reenact themselves indefinitely, so it is possible to stumble across someone else's unhappy memory. Accordingly, although Sethe describes for Denver what "was," she turns to the future tense and tells her that the past will "always be there waiting for you." Sethe pictures the past as a physical presence, something that is "there," that fills a space. Beloved's arrival confirms this notion of history's corporeality.

The force of the past is evident even in the difficulty Sethe has speaking about it. She stutters, backtracks, and repeats herself as though mere words cannot do justice to her subject matter. Even in this passage, as she warns Denver against the inescapability of the past, Sethe enacts and illustrates the very phenomenon she describes. She repeats her warning several times in a manner that demonstrates the recurrence of ideas and her inability to leave past thoughts behind. Sethe's warnings are the main cause of Denver's fears of leaving 124 and of the community. Only in Chapter 26 does Denver finally venture out alone. She realizes that even if she succeeds in preventing chance encounters with the past, the past may nevertheless actively begin to come after her.

5. *And if she thought anything, it was* No. No. Nono. Nonono. *Simple. She just flew. Collected every bit of life she had made, all the parts of her that were precious and fine and beautiful, and carried, pushed, dragged them through the veil, out, away, over there where no one could hurt them. Over there. Outside this place, where they would be safe.*

After Paul D learns about Sethe's crime from Stamp Paid in Chapter 18, he goes to 124 in search of an explanation. This passage, although written in the third person, records Sethe's thoughts. Sethe saw the decision she made as "simple." She wanted to secure her children's safety, to send them "over there" into the afterlife rather than let them be pulled back to Sweet Home with schoolteacher. Sethe's passion for her children, which infuses so much of the novel, shines through in this passage with particular clarity. The moment Sethe's reason reduced itself to instinct, her language broke down as well: she recalls her words as "No. No. Nono. Nonono." For her, the border between life and death is tenuous, nothing more than a screen or "veil" that she hopes to place in front of her children.

Another significant aspect of the passage is Sethe's identification of her children as "the parts of her that were precious and fine and beautiful"; for Sethe, to allow schoolteacher to take her children would be to allow him to destroy everything that is good in herself, to destroy all the "life" she had made. According to this understanding, Sethe's murder of her daughter seems a less legally and morally reprehensible crime because it becomes an act of self-defense. Yet the question of Sethe's guilt is never fully settled in the book. The characters debate the morality of her act in pointed language, but Morrison herself withholds judgment on the deed. Throughout the book, she focuses her criticisms instead on the forces of slavery that led Sethe to kill her own daughter. In this passage and elsewhere, Morrison condemns slavery as an institution so perverse that it could mutate a mother's love into murder.

Describe the differences in the ways the male and female characters in *Beloved* treat love.

In Toni Morrison's *Beloved*, the male and female characters love in two distinct ways. Women, in the way they live their lives and their attitudes about love, differ vastly from the men. The love of the women is intense. It causes them pain and demands sacrifice. Meanwhile, the love of the men in *Beloved* is loose, never binding or restrictive. This divide forces both men and women into relationships that are unsatisfying and incomplete. The novel's two main characters, Sethe and Paul D, typify these differences, but the differences exist within the minor characters as well. Only through modifying their treatments of love can each come to a happier state.

Paul D prides himself on his carefree lifestyle, which allows him the freedom to do as he pleases. When he stumbles upon Sethe's home, Paul D has no real love in his life. He believes it is better to love everything just a little bit; that way, he can minimize the disappointment in his life. Paul D's cautious, conservative attitude about love reflects the commitment-free way of life he's chosen. It also demonstrates the lingering influences of slavery on his everyday life. As a slave, he owned nothing—neither his body, nor his name, nor his freedom—so he learned not to waste too much love on anything. Paul D's treatment of love is a survival mechanism for coping with the hardships in his life.

Unlike Paul D, Sethe has a life full of intense, inescapable love. The ghost of her dead daughter, Beloved, haunts and terrorizes Sethe and her family, but Sethe resists moving: she knows Beloved's ghost will follow her wherever she goes. When Paul D suggests to Sethe that she move, she says, "No more running—from nothing. I will never run from another thing on this Earth" (Chapter 1). Yet her plan to stay put and re-earn Beloved's love nearly destroys the lives of everyone else she cares for. Later, Paul D tells Sethe, "Your love is too thick," to which she coolly responds, "Love is or it ain't. Thin love ain't love at all" (Chapter 18). Her "thick love" led her to kill Beloved: she chose to kill her children rather than subject them to a life of slavery. Yet Beloved is the only one she actually kills. This decision has haunted her ever since.

These attitudes about love remain split along gender lines in the next generation. Near the beginning of *Beloved*, Denver expresses a dire need to leave her home. During her breakdown, she sobs, "I can't live here. I don't know where to go or what to do, but I can't live here" (Chapter 1). Sethe leads her away, and after that scene, Denver never again mentions leaving. Through Sethe's example, Denver learns that she must confront the difficulties of her life, not flee them. In contrast, her brothers, Howard and Buglar, flee the house at a very young age. Morrison writes, "Each fled at once—the moment the house committed what was for him the one insult not to be born or witnessed a second time" (Chapter 1).

By the end of *Beloved*, these attitudes about love and relationships change. Denver and Paul D switch roles: Denver leaves to find work and Paul D moves in to care for Sethe. Finally, the uncommitted male finds an intense, stationary, and at times painful way of loving. The female lover is able to find a bit of freedom, learning to leave some of the loved ones behind in prioritizing personal needs. Still, when she does leave, Denver does so to alleviate a problem, not flee one. In this way, the women of the novel have learned to take care of themselves, as well as the ones they love, and the men have also learned the necessity of sacrificing something for love.

The Bluest Eye

Toni Morrison (1931–)

CONTEXT

Toni Morrison was born Chloe Anthony Wofford in 1931 in Lorain, Ohio. Her mother's family had come to Ohio from Alabama via Kentucky, and her father had migrated from Georgia. Morrison grew up with a love of literature and received her undergraduate degree from Howard University. She received a master's degree from Cornell University, completing a thesis on William Faulkner and Virginia Woolf. Afterward, she taught at Texas Southern University and then at Howard University, in Washington, D.C., where she met Harold Morrison, an architect from Jamaica. The marriage lasted six years, and Morrison gave birth to two sons. She and Harold divorced while she was pregnant with her second son, and she returned to Lorain to give birth. She then moved to New York and became an editor at Random House, specializing in black fiction. During this difficult and somewhat lonely time, she began working on her first novel, *The Bluest Eye*, which was published in 1970.

The Bluest Eye was not an immediate success, but she continued to write. *Sula*, which appeared in 1973, was more successful, earning a nomination for the National Book Award. In 1977, *Song of Solomon* launched Morrison's national reputation, winning her the National Book Critics' Circle Award. Her most well-known work, *Beloved*, was published in 1987 and won the Pulitzer Prize. Her other novels include *Tar Baby* (1981), *Jazz* (1992), and *Paradise* (1998). Meanwhile, Morrison returned to teaching and was a professor at Yale and the State University of New York at Albany. Today, she is the Robert F. Goheen Professor in the Council of Humanities at Princeton University, where she teaches creative writing. In 1993, Morrison became the first African-American woman to receive the Nobel Prize in literature.

The Bluest Eye contains a number of autobiographical elements. It is set in the town where Morrison grew up, and it is told from the point of view of a nine-year-old, the age Morrison would have been the year the novel takes place (1941). Like the MacTeer family, Morrison's family struggled to make ends meet during the Great Depression. Morrison grew up listening to her mother singing and her grandfather playing the violin, just as Claudia does. In the novel's afterword, Morrison explains that the story developed out of a conversation she had had in elementary school with a little girl who longed for blue eyes. She was still thinking about this conversation in the 1960s, when the Black is Beautiful movement was working to reclaim African-American beauty, and she began her first novel.

While its historical context is clear, the literary context of *The Bluest Eye* is more complex. Faulkner and Woolf, whose work Morrison knew well, influenced her style. She uses the modernist techniques of stream-of-consciousness, multiple perspectives, and deliberate fragmentation. But Morrison understands her work more fundamentally as part of a black cultural tradition and strives to create a distinctively black literature. Her prose is infused with black musical traditions such as the spirituals, gospel, jazz, and the blues. She writes in a black vernacular, filling her novel with turns of phrase and figures of speech unique to the community in which she grew up, with the hope that if she is true to her own particular experience, it will be universally meaningful. In this way, she attempts to create what she calls a "race-specific yet race-free prose."

In the afterword to *The Bluest Eye,* Morrison explains her goal in writing the novel. She wants to make a statement about the damage that internalized racism can do to the most vulnerable member of a community—a young girl. At the same time, she does not want to dehumanize the people who wound this girl, because that would simply repeat their mistake. Also, she wants to protect this girl from "the weight of the novel's inquiry," and thus decides to tell the story from multiple perspectives. In this way, as she puts it, she "shape[s] a silence while breaking it," keeping the girl's dignity intact.

PLOT OVERVIEW

Nine-year-old Claudia and ten-year-old Frieda MacTeer live in Lorain, Ohio, with their parents. It is the end of the Great Depression, and the girls' parents are more concerned with making ends meet than with lavishing attention upon their daughters, but there is an undercurrent of love and stability in their home. The MacTeers take in a boarder, Henry Washington, and also a young girl named Pecola. Pecola's father tried to burn down his family's house, and Claudia and Frieda feel sorry for her. Pecola loves Shirley Temple, believing that whiteness is beautiful and that she is ugly.

Pecola moves back in with her family, and her life is difficult. Her father drinks, her mother is distant, and the two of them often beat each other. Her brother, Sammy, frequently runs away. Pecola believes that if she had blue eyes, she would be loved and her life would be transformed. Meanwhile, she continually receives confirmation of her own sense of ugliness—the grocer looks right through her when she buys candy, boys make fun of her, and a light-skinned girl, Maureen, who temporarily befriends her makes fun of her too. She is wrongly blamed for killing a boy's cat and is called a "nasty little black bitch" by his mother.

We learn that Pecola's parents have both had difficult lives. Pauline, her mother, has a lame foot and has always felt isolated. She loses herself in movies, which reaffirm her belief that she is ugly and that romantic love is reserved for the beautiful. She encourages her husband's violent behavior in order to reinforce her own role as a martyr. She feels most alive when she is at work, cleaning a white woman's home. She loves this home and despises her own. Cholly, Pecola's father, was abandoned by his parents and raised by his great aunt, who died when he was a young teenager. He was humiliated by two white men who found him having sex for the first time and made him continue while they watched. He ran away to find his father but was rebuffed by him. By the time he met Pauline, he was a wild and rootless man. He feels trapped in his marriage and has lost interest in life.

Cholly returns home one day and finds Pecola washing dishes. With mixed motives of tenderness and hatred that are fueled by guilt, he rapes her. When Pecola's mother finds her unconscious on the floor, she disbelieves Pecola's story and beats her. Pecola goes to Soaphead Church, a sham mystic, and asks him for blue eyes. Instead of helping her, he uses her to kill a dog he dislikes.

Claudia and Frieda find out that Pecola has been impregnated by her father, and unlike the rest of the neighborhood, they want the baby to live. They sacrifice the money they have been saving for a bicycle and plant marigold seeds. They believe that if the flowers live, so will Pecola's baby. The flowers refuse to bloom, and Pecola's baby dies when it is born prematurely. Cholly, who rapes Pecola a second time and then runs away, dies in a workhouse. Pecola goes mad, believing that her cherished wish has been fulfilled and that she has the bluest eyes.

CHARACTER LIST

Pecola Breedlove The protagonist of the novel, an eleven-year-old black girl who believes that she is ugly and that having blue eyes would make her beautiful. Sensitive and delicate, Pecola passively suffers the abuse of her mother, father, and classmates. She is lonely and imaginative.

Claudia MacTeer The narrator of parts of the novel. An independent and strong-minded nine-year-old, Claudia is a fighter and rebels against adults' tyranny over children and against the black community's idealization of white beauty standards. She has not yet learned the self-hatred that plagues her peers.

Cholly Breedlove Pecola's father, who is impulsive and violent—free, but in a dangerous way. Having suffered early humiliations, Cholly takes out his frustration on the women in his life. He is capable of both tenderness and rage, but as the story unfolds, rage increasingly dominates.

Pauline (Polly) Breedlove Pecola's mother, who believes that she is ugly; this belief has made her lonely and cold. Polly has a deformed foot and sees herself as the martyr of a terrible marriage. She finds meaning not in her own family but in romantic movies and in her work caring for a well-to-do white family.

Frieda MacTeer Claudia's ten-year-old sister, who shares Claudia's independence and stubbornness. Because she is closer to adolescence, Frieda is more vulnerable to her community's equation of whiteness with beauty. Frieda is more knowledgeable about the adult world and sometimes braver than Claudia.

Mrs. MacTeer Claudia's mother, an authoritarian and sometimes callous woman who nonetheless steadfastly loves and protects her children. Mrs. MacTeer is given to fussing aloud and to singing the blues.

Mr. MacTeer Claudia's father, who works hard to keep the family fed and clothed. Mr. MacTeer is fiercely protective of his daughters.

Henry Washington The MacTeers' boarder, who has a reputation for being a steady worker and a quiet man. Middle-aged, Henry has never married and has a lecherous side.

Sammy Breedlove Pecola's fourteen-year-old brother, who copes with his family's problems by running away from home. Sammy's active response contrasts with Pecola's passivity.

China, Poland, Miss Marie The local whores. Miss Marie (also known as the Maginot Line) is fat and affectionate, China is skinny and sarcastic, and Poland is quiet. They live above the Breedlove apartment and befriend Pecola.

Mr. Yacobowski The local grocer, a middle-aged white immigrant. Mr. Yacobowski has a gruff manner toward little black girls.

Rosemary Villanucci A white, comparatively wealthy girl who lives next door to the MacTeers. Rosemary makes fun of Claudia and Frieda and tries to get them into trouble, and they sometimes beat her up.

B

Maureen Peal A light-skinned, wealthy black girl who is new at the local school. Maureen accepts everyone else's assumption that she is superior and is capable of both generosity and cruelty.

Geraldine A middle-class black woman who, though she keeps house flawlessly and diligently cares for the physical appearances of herself and her family (including her husband, Louis, and her son, Junior), is essentially cold. Geraldine feels real affection only for her cat.

Junior Geraldine's son, who, in the absence of genuine affection from his mother, becomes cruel and sadistic. Junior tortures the family cat and harasses children who come to the nearby playground.

Soaphead Church Born Elihue Micah Whitcomb, is a light-skinned West Indian misanthrope and self-declared "Reader, Adviser, and Interpreter of Dreams." Soaphead hates all kinds of human touch, with the exception of the bodies of young girls. He is a religious hypocrite.

Aunt Jimmy The elderly woman who raises Cholly. Aunt Jimmy is affectionate but physically deteriorated.

Samson Fuller Cholly's father, who abandoned Cholly's mother when she got pregnant. Samson lives in Macon, Georgia, and is short, balding, and mean.

Blue Jack A co-worker and friend of Cholly's during his boyhood. Blue Jack is a kind man and excellent storyteller.

M'Dear A quiet, elderly woman who serves as a doctor in the community where Cholly grows up. M'Dear is tall and impressive, and she carries a hickory stick.

Darlene The first girl that Cholly likes. Darlene is pretty, playful, and affectionate.

ANALYSIS OF MAJOR CHARACTERS

PECOLA BREEDLOVE Pecola is the protagonist of *The Bluest Eye*, but despite this central role she is passive and remains a mysterious character. Morrison explains in the afterword that she purposely tells Pecola's story from other points of view to keep Pecola's dignity and, to some extent, to preserve her mystery. She wishes to prevent us from labeling Pecola or prematurely believing that we understand her. Pecola is a fragile and delicate child when the novel begins, and by the end of the novel, she has been almost completely destroyed by violence. At the beginning of the novel, two desires form the basis of her emotional life: first, she wants to learn how to get people to love her; second, when forced to witness her parents' brutal fights, she simply wants to disappear. Neither wish is granted, and Pecola is forced further and further into her fantasy world, which is her only defense against the pain of her existence. She believes that being granted the blue eyes she wishes for would change both how others see her and what she is forced to see. At the end of the novel, she delusively believes that her wish has been granted, but only at the cost of her sanity. Pecola's fate is worse than death because she is not allowed any release from her world—she simply moves to "the edge of town, where you can see her even now."

Pecola is also a symbol of the black community's self-hatred and belief in its own ugliness. Others in the community, including her mother, father, and Geraldine, act out their own self-hatred by expressing hatred toward her. At the end of the novel, we are told that Pecola has been a scapegoat for the entire community. Her ugliness has made them feel beautiful, her suffering has made them feel comparatively lucky, and her silence has given them the opportunity for speaking. But because she continues to live after she has lost her mind, Pecola's aimless wandering at the edge of town haunts the community, reminding them of the ugliness and hatred that they have tried to repress. She becomes a reminder of human cruelty and an emblem of human suffering.

CLAUDIA MACTEER Claudia narrates parts of *The Bluest Eye*, sometimes from a child's perspective and sometimes from the perspective of an adult looking back. Like Pecola, Claudia suffers from racist beauty standards and material insecurity, but she has a loving and stable family, which makes all the difference for her. Whereas Pecola is passive when she is abused, Claudia is a fighter. When Claudia is given a white doll she does not want, she dissects and destroys it. When she finds a group of boys harassing Pecola, she attacks them. When she learns that Pecola is pregnant, she and her sister come up with a plan to save Pecola's baby from the community's rejection. Claudia explains that she is brave because she has not yet learned her limitations—most important, she has not learned the self-hatred that plagues so many adults in the community.

B

Claudia is a valuable guide to the events that unfold in Lorain because her life is stable enough to permit her to see clearly. Her vision is not blurred by the pain that eventually drives Pecola into madness. Her presence in the novel reminds us that most black families are not like Pecola's; most black families pull together in the face of hardship instead of fall apart. Claudia's perspective is also valuable because it melds the child's and the adult's points of view. Her childish viewpoint makes her uniquely qualified to register what Pecola experiences, but her adult viewpoint can correct the childish one when it is incomplete. She is a messenger of suffering but also of hope.

CHOLLY BREEDLOVE By all rights, we should hate Cholly Breedlove, given that he rapes his daughter. But Morrison explains in her afterword that she did not want to dehumanize her characters, even those who dehumanize one another, and she succeeds in making Cholly a sympathetic figure. He has experienced genuine suffering, having been abandoned in a junk heap as a baby and having suffered humiliation at the hands of white men. He is also capable of pleasure and even joy, in the experience of eating a watermelon or touching a girl for the first time. He is capable of violence, but he is also vulnerable, as when two white men violate him by forcing him to perform sexually for their amusement and when he defecates in his pants after encountering his father. Cholly represents a negative form of freedom. He is not free to love and be loved or to enjoy full dignity, but he is free to have sex and fight and even kill; he is free to be indifferent to death. He falls apart when this freedom becomes a complete lack of interest in life, and he reaches for his daughter to remind himself that he is alive.

PAULINE BREEDLOVE Like Cholly, Pauline inflicts a great deal of pain on her daughter, Pecola, but Morrison nevertheless renders her sympathetically. She experiences more subtle forms of humiliation than Cholly does—her lame foot convinces her that she is doomed to isolation, and the snobbery of the city women in Lorain condemns her to loneliness. In this state, she is especially vulnerable to the messages conveyed by white culture—that white beauty and possessions are the way to happiness. Once, at the movies, she fixes her hair like the white sex symbol Jean Harlow and loses her tooth while eating candy. Though her fantasy of being like Harlow is a failure, Pauline finds another fantasy world—the white household for which she cares. This fantasy world is more practical than her imitation of Hollywood actresses and is more socially sanctioned than the madness of Pecola's fantasy world, but it is just as effective in separating her from the people— her family—she should love. In a sense, Pauline's existence is just as haunted and delusional as her daughter's.

THEMES, MOTIFS, AND SYMBOLS

THEMES

WHITENESS AS THE STANDARD OF BEAUTY *The Bluest Eye* provides an extended depiction of the ways in which internalized white beauty standards deform the lives of black girls and women. Implicit messages that whiteness is superior are everywhere, including the white baby doll given to Claudia, the idealization of Shirley Temple, the consensus that light-skinned Maureen is cuter than the other black girls, the idealization of white beauty in the movies, and Pauline Breedlove's preference for the little white girl she works for over her daughter. Adult women, having learned to hate the blackness of their own bodies, take this hatred out on their children—Mrs. Breedlove shares the conviction that Pecola is ugly, and lighter-skinned Geraldine curses Pecola's blackness. Claudia remains free from this worship of whiteness, imagining Pecola's unborn baby as beautiful in its blackness. But it is hinted that once Claudia reaches adolescence, she too will learn to hate herself, as if racial self-loathing were a necessary part of maturation.

The person who suffers most from white beauty standards is, of course, Pecola. She connects beauty with being loved and believes that if she possesses blue eyes, the cruelty in her life will be replaced by affection and respect. This hopeless desire leads ultimately to madness, suggesting that the fulfillment of the wish for white beauty may be even more tragic than the wish impulse itself.

SEEING VERSUS BEING SEEN Pecola's desire for blue eyes, while highly unrealistic, is based on one correct insight into her world: she believes that the cruelty she witnesses and experiences is connected to how she is seen. If she had beautiful blue eyes, Pecola imagines, people would not want to do ugly things in front of her or to her. The accuracy of this insight is affirmed by her experience of being teased by the boys—when Maureen comes to her rescue, it seems that they no longer want to behave badly under Maureen's attractive gaze. In a more basic sense, Pecola and her family are mistreated in part because they happen to have black skin. By wishing for blue eyes rather than lighter skin, Pecola indicates that she wishes to see things differently as much as she wishes to be seen differently. She can only receive this wish, in effect, by blinding herself. Pecola is then able to see herself as beautiful, but only at the cost of her ability to accurately see both herself and the world around her. The connection between how one is seen and what one sees has a uniquely tragic outcome for her.

B

THE POWER OF STORIES *The Bluest Eye* is not one story, but multiple, sometimes contradictory, interlocking stories. Characters tell stories to make sense of their lives, and these stories have tremendous power for both good and evil. Claudia's stories, in particular, stand out for their affirmative power. First and foremost, she tells Pecola's story, and though she questions the accuracy and meaning of her version, to some degree her attention and care redeem the ugliness of Pecola's life. Furthermore, when the adults describe Pecola's pregnancy and hope that the baby dies, Claudia and Frieda attempt to rewrite this story as a hopeful one, casting themselves as saviors. Finally, Claudia resists the premise of white superiority, writing her own story about the beauty of blackness. Stories by other characters are often destructive to themselves and others. The story that Pauline Breedlove tells herself about her own ugliness reinforces her self-hatred, and the story she tells herself about her own martyrdom reinforces her cruelty toward her family. Soaphead Church's personal narratives about his good intentions and his special relationship with God are pure hypocrisy. Stories are as likely to distort the truth as they are to reveal it. While Morrison apparently believes that stories can be redeeming, she is no blind optimist and refuses to let us rest comfortably in any one version of what happens.

THE PERILS AND PLEASURES OF SEXUAL INITIATION To a large degree, *The Bluest Eye* is about both the pleasures and the perils of sexual initiation. Early in the novel, Pecola has her first menstrual period, and toward the end of the novel she has her first sexual experience, which is violent. Frieda knows about and anticipates menstruating, and she is initiated into sexual experience when she is fondled by Henry Washington. We are told the story of Cholly's first sexual experience, which ends when two white men force him to finish having sex while they watch. The fact that all of these experiences are humiliating and hurtful indicates that sexual coming-of-age is fraught with peril, especially in an abusive environment.

In the novel, parents carry much of the blame for their children's often traumatic sexual coming-of-age. The most blatant case is Cholly's rape of his own daughter, Pecola, which is, in a sense, a repetition of the sexual humiliation Cholly experienced under the gaze of two racist whites. Frieda's experience is less painful than Pecola's because her parents immediately come to her rescue, playing the appropriate protector and underlining, by way of contrast, the extent of Cholly's crime against his daughter. But Frieda is not given information that lets her understand what has happened to her. Instead, she lives with a vague fear of being "ruined" like the local prostitutes. The prevalence of sexual violence in the novel suggests that racism is not the only thing that distorts black girlhoods. There is also a pervasive assumption that women's bodies are available for abuse. The refusal on the part of parents to teach their girls about sexuality makes the girls' transition into sexual maturity difficult.

SATISFYING APPETITES VERSUS SUPPRESSING THEM A number of characters in *The Bluest Eye* define their lives through a denial of their bodily needs. Geraldine prefers cleanliness and order to the messiness of sex, and she is emotionally frigid as a result. Similarly, Pauline prefers cleaning and organizing the home of her white employers to expressing physical affection toward her family. Soaphead Church finds physicality distasteful, and this peculiarity leads to his preference for objects over humans and to his perverse attraction to little girls. In contrast, when characters experience happiness, it is generally in viscerally physical terms. Claudia prefers to have her senses indulged by wonderful scents, sounds, and tastes than to be given a hard white doll. Cholly's greatest moments of happinesses are eating the best part of a watermelon and touching a girl for the first time. Pauline's happiest memory is of sexual fulfillment with her husband. The novel suggests that, no matter how messy and sometimes violent human desire is, it is also the source of happiness. Denial of the body begets hatred and violence, not redemption.

MOTIFS

THE DICK-AND-JANE NARRATIVE The novel opens with a narrative from a Dick-and-Jane reading primer, a narrative that is distorted when Morrison runs its sentences and then its words together. The gap between the idealized, sanitized, upper-middle-class world of Dick and Jane (who we *assume* to be white, though we are never told so) and the often dark and ugly world of the novel is emphasized by the chapter headings excerpted from the primer. But Morrison does not mean for us to think that the Dick-and-Jane world is better—in fact, it is largely because the black characters have internalized white Dick-and-Jane values that they are unhappy. In this way, the Dick-and-Jane narrative and the novel provide ironic commentary on each other.

THE SEASONS AND NATURE The novel is divided into the four seasons, but it pointedly refuses to meet the expectations of these seasons. For example, spring, the traditional time of rebirth and renewal, reminds Claudia of being whipped with new switches, and it is the season when Pecola is raped. Pecola's baby dies in autumn, the season of harvesting. Morrison uses natural cycles to underline the unnaturalness and misery of her characters' experiences. To some degree, she also questions the benevolence of nature, as when Claudia wonders whether "the earth itself might have been unyielding" to someone like Pecola.

WHITENESS AND COLOR In the novel, whiteness is associated with beauty and cleanliness (particularly according to Geraldine and Mrs. Breedlove), but also with sterility. In contrast, color is associated with happiness, most clearly in the rainbow of yellow, green, and purple memories Pauline Breedlove sees when making love to Cholly. Morrison uses this imagery to emphasize the destructiveness of the black community's privileging of whiteness and to suggest that vibrant color, rather than the pure absence of color, is a stronger image of happiness and freedom.

EYES AND VISION Pecola is obsessed with having blue eyes because she believes that this mark of conventional white beauty will change the way that she is seen and therefore the way that she sees the world. There are continual references to other characters' eyes as well—for example, Mr. Yacobowski's hostility to Pecola resides in the blankness in his own eyes, as well as in his inability to see a black girl. This motif underlines the novel's repeated concern for the difference between how we see and how we are seen, and the difference between superficial sight and true insight.

DIRTINESS AND CLEANLINESS The black characters in the novel who have internalized white, middle-class values are obsessed with cleanliness. Geraldine and Mrs. Breedlove are excessively concerned with housecleaning—though Mrs. Breedlove cleans only the house of her white employers, as if the Breedlove apartment is beyond her help. This fixation on cleanliness extends into the women's moral and emotional quests for purity, but the obsession with domestic and moral sanitation leads them to cruel coldness. In contrast, one mark of Claudia's strength of character is her pleasure in her own dirt, a pleasure that represents self-confidence and a correct understanding of the nature of happiness.

SYMBOLS

THE HOUSE The novel begins with a sentence from a Dick-and-Jane narrative: "Here is the house." Homes not only indicate socioeconomic status in this novel, but they also symbolize the emotional situations and values of the characters who inhabit them. The Breedlove apartment is miserable and decrepit, suffering from Mrs. Breedlove's preference for her employer's home over her own and symbolizing the misery of the Breedlove family. The MacTeer house is drafty and dark, but it is carefully tended by Mrs. MacTeer and, according to Claudia, filled with love, symbolizing that family's comparative cohesion.

BLUEST EYE(S) To Pecola, blue eyes symbolize the beauty and happiness that she associates with the white, middle-class world. They also come to symbolize her own blindness, for she gains blue eyes only at the cost of her sanity. The "bluest" eye could also mean the saddest eye. Furthermore, *eye* puns on *I*, in the sense that the novel's title uses the singular form of the noun (instead of *The Bluest Eyes*) to express many of the characters' sad isolation.

THE MARIGOLDS Claudia and Frieda associate marigolds with the safety and well-being of Pecola's baby. Their ceremonial offering of money and the remaining unsold marigold seeds represents an honest sacrifice on their part. They believe that if the marigolds they have planted grow, then Pecola's baby will be all right. More generally, marigolds represent the constant renewal of nature. In Pecola's case, this cycle of renewal is perverted by her father's rape of her.

B

IMPORTANT QUOTATIONS EXPLAINED

---

1. *It never occurred to either of us that the earth itself might have been unyielding. We had dropped our seeds in our own little plot of black dirt just as Pecola's father had dropped his seeds in his own plot of black dirt. Our innocence and faith were no more productive than his lust or despair.*

This passage is from the second prologue to the novel, in which Claudia anticipates the events that the novel will recount, most notably Pecola's pregnancy by incest. Here, she remembers that she and Frieda blamed each other for the failure of the marigolds to grow one summer, but now she wonders if the earth itself was hostile to them—a darker, more radical possibility. The idea of blame is important because the book continually raises the question of who is to blame for Pecola's suffering. Are Claudia and Frieda at fault for not doing more to help Pecola? To some degree, we can blame Pecola's suffering on her parents and on racism; but Cholly and Pauline have themselves suffered, and the causes of suffering seem so diffuse and prevalent that it seems possible that life on earth itself is hostile to human happiness.

This hostility is what the earth's hostility to the marigolds represents. The complexity of the question of blame increases when Claudia makes the stunning parallel between the healing action of their planting of the marigold seeds and Cholly's hurtful action of raping Pecola. Claudia suggests that the impulse that drove her and her sister and the impulse that drove Cholly might not be so different after all. Motives of innocence and faith seem to be no more effective than motives of lust and despair in the universe of the novel.

---

2. *It had occurred to Pecola some time ago that if her eyes, those eyes that held the pictures, and knew the sights—if those eyes of hers were different, that is to say, beautiful, she herself would be different.*

These lines, which introduce Pecola's desire for blue eyes, are found in Chapter 3 of the "Autumn" section of the novel. They demonstrate the complexity of Pecola's desire—she does not want blue eyes simply because they conform to white beauty standards, but because she wishes to possess different sights and pictures, as if changing eye color will change reality. Pecola has just been forced to witness a violent fight between her parents, and the only solution she can imagine to her passive suffering is to witness something different. She believes that if she had blue eyes, their beauty would inspire beautiful and kindly behavior on the part of others. Pecola's desire has its own logic even if it is naïve. To Pecola, the color of one's skin and eyes do influence how one is treated and what one is forced to witness.

3. *We had defended ourselves since memory against everything and everybody, considered all speech a code to be broken by us, and all gestures subject to careful analysis; we had become headstrong, devious, and arrogant. Nobody paid us any attention, so we paid very good attention to ourselves. Our limitations were not known to us—not then.*

This remark is from Claudia, and it occurs in the second-to-last chapter of the novel. It can be read as a concise description of Claudia and Frieda's ethos as a whole. The MacTeer girls take an active stance against whatever they perceive threatens them, whether it is a white doll, boys making fun of Pecola, Henry's molestation of Frieda, or the community's rejection of Pecola. Their active and energetic responses contrast sharply with Pecola's passive suffering. Though Claudia and Frieda's actions are childish and often doomed to failure, they are still examples of vigorous responses to oppression. Claudia hints here, however, that this willingness to take action no matter who defies them disappears with adulthood. Frieda and Claudia are able to be active in part because they are protected by their parents, and in part because they do not confront the life-or-death problems that Pecola does. As adults, they will learn to respond to antagonism in more indirect and perhaps more self-destructive ways.

4. *The birdlike gestures are worn away to a mere picking and plucking her way between the tire rims and the sunflowers, between Coke bottles and milkweed, among all the waste and beauty of the world—which is what she herself was. All of our waste which we dumped on her and which she absorbed. And all of our beauty, which was hers first and which she gave to us.*

This phrase, from the last chapter of the novel, sums up Claudia's impressions of Pecola's madness. Here, she transforms Pecola into a symbol of the beauty and suffering that marks all human life and into a more specific symbol of the hopes and fears of her community. The community has dumped all of its "waste" on Pecola because she is a convenient scapegoat. The blackness and ugliness that the other members of the community fear reside in themselves can instead be attributed to her. But Claudia also describes Pecola as the paragon of beauty, a startling claim after all the emphasis on Pecola's ugliness. Pecola is beautiful because she is human, but this beauty is invisible to the members of the community who have identified beauty with whiteness. She gives others beauty because their assumptions about her ugliness make them feel beautiful in comparison. In this sense, Pecola's gift of beauty is ironic—she gives people beauty because they think she is ugly, not because they perceive her true beauty as a human being.

5. *Love is never any better than the lover. Wicked people love wickedly, violent people love violently, weak people love weakly, stupid people love stupidly, but the love of a free man is never safe. There is no gift for the beloved. The lover alone possesses his gift of love. The loved one is shorn, neutralized, frozen in the glare of the lover's inward eye.*

This thought is from the last chapter of the novel, in which Claudia attempts to tell us what her story means. It describes love as a potentially damaging force, following the suggestion that Cholly was the only person who loved Pecola "enough to touch her." If love and rape cannot be distinguished, then we have entered a world in which love itself is ambiguous. Against the usual idea that love is inherently healing and redemptive, Claudia suggests that love is only as good as the lover. This is why the broken, warped human beings in this novel fail to truly love one another. In fact, Claudia suggests, love may even be damaging, because it locks the loved one in a potentially destructive gaze. Romantic love creates a damaging demand for beauty—the kind of beauty that black girls, by definition, may never be able to possess because of the racist standards of their society. But the pessimism of this passage is offset by the inherent hopefulness of the idea of love. If we can understand Cholly's behavior as driven by love as well as anger (and his rape of Pecola is in fact described in these terms), then there is still some good in him, however deformed. We are left to hope for a kind of love that is a genuine gift for the beloved.

The Book of Margery Kempe

Margery Kempe (1373–1438)

CONTEXT

The Book of Margery Kempe is the earliest autobiography written in English, but for years it was known only through a book of extracts published in the sixteenth century. A copy of the original fifteenth-century manuscript finally appeared in 1934, in the collection of an English Catholic family. The document that emerged was the record, dictated to an unnamed priest, of the spiritual life of a fascinating woman—Margery Kempe of King's Lynn, the daughter of a former mayor of Lynn, and the wife of John Kempe. Aside from being one of the great literary discoveries of the twentieth century, *The Book of Margery Kempe* is an important addition to the body of English mystical writings and provides an intimate look at a remarkable medieval life.

B

Kempe narrates her story in rough chronological order, beginning with her breakdown following the birth of her first child. However, the text retains the rambling, somewhat repetitive quality of a tale told from memory, as the events reappear in the mind of the teller. Though Kempe is illiterate, her *Book* has clear literary ancestors. The genre of the Christian "spiritual autobiography" goes back to St. Augustine (354–430 A.D.), whose *Confessions* tell the story of his early life and conversion to Christianity. Following Augustine's example, spiritual autobiographies tend to be tightly focused on the author's subjective experience, relating all the events of the author's life to his or her religious development. This is clearly the case with Kempe's *Book*, which tends to deal with the external world only as it directly impinges on Kempe's inner growth—even her children go unnamed and practically unmentioned unless they somehow figure into the primary subject at hand: Kempe's devotional life and her mystical contact with Jesus.

The other major literary genre to influence Kempe (primarily through the teaching of her confessor and of her friend Master Aleyn) was the works of the Christian mystics. The medieval period was the golden age of Christian mysticism, which is a spiritual discipline aimed at a direct union with God through intense prayer and contemplation. When mystics achieve the union that they seek with God, the experience is often marked by a trancelike state, visions, and a kind of physical ecstasy or even pain.

The most famous Christian mystics with whom Kempe would have been familiar include St. Francis of Assisi (1182–1226), founder of the Franciscan order of mendicant friars (monks who travel from place to place preaching and living off the charity of others), and St. Bonaventure (1221–1274), a great theologian and philosopher, whose guide to the contemplative life is read to Kempe by one of her priestly friends. Other mystics whom Kempe cites by name include St. Bridget of Sweden (1303–1373), author of a spiritual autobiography that deeply influenced Kempe; and the Englishmen Walter Hilton (?–1396) and Richard Rolle (?–1349), whose descriptions of the raptures of mystical contact with God have much in common with Kempe's. And of course Kempe actually meets and speaks to one of the greatest English mystics, Julian of Norwich, an anchoress (a kind of hermit devoted to the religious life) and the author of her *Revelations of Divine Love*.

Although Kempe does her best to follow the examples of her great precursors and focus exclusively on her spiritual life, more mundane reality often breaks into her narrative. For example, one of the more interesting aspects of the travelogue portions of the *Book* is the glimpse we get of the practical realities of making a long journey during Kempe's era. At times the effect is homely and charming, as when Kempe describes her domestic life and her disputes with her husband. The political side of the religious life also intrudes on Kempe when she is arrested on suspicion of heresy, thanks to her idiosyncratic dress and behavior. Specifically, Kempe is accused of "Lollardy," that is, of being a Lollard, a follower of the reformer John Wycliffe (1320–1384). Wycliffe challenged the church hierarchy of his time, especially by translating the Bible into English, and his followers called for sweeping church reforms, many of which were later instituted during the English Reformation. At the time of Kempe's *Book*, however, Lollardy was illegal and punishable by death. The Archbishop of Canterbury at the time, whom Kempe meets, was particularly committed to stamping out the Lollards, and Kempe's efforts to emphasize her orthodoxy and loyalty to the church are a shaping force of the story she tells in her *Book*.

PLOT OVERVIEW

Margery Kempe is a well-off middle-class townswoman in the medieval English town of King's Lynn. After the birth of her first child, Margery has a nervous breakdown, seeing hideous devils all around her. Margery recovers after having a vision of Jesus Christ, and she decides to devote her life to holiness and contemplation of God. One of the first hurdles Margery has to overcome is convincing her husband to live a life of celibacy with her—she succeeds only after having fourteen children. After the failure of a brewing business she starts, Margery becomes certain that God wants her to turn away from the world. Margery's devotion to Jesus is highly emotional and dramatic, and she soon acquires a reputation as a religious eccentric, a potentially dangerous reputation in a time when heresy was a capital offense. Margery faces doubt and temptation, especially sexual temptation, but she perseveres and often receives guidance in her visions.

Margery makes several pilgrimages, the longest and most difficult of which is a journey to Jerusalem, with a long stopover in Rome. During the pilgrimage, Margery is shunned by her fellow travelers but is often accepted by the poor, a pattern that repeats itself throughout her life. In Jerusalem, Margery has several intense visions, and she begins to have spells in which she sobs and cries uncontrollably. These crying fits come upon her most often during religious services, but they also occur whenever she simply thinks of Jesus or sees something that reminds her of his suffering. Margery is stranded in Rome for a time after giving away her money to the poor, and she makes her way by begging. Margery's extreme behavior begins to make her notorious, and she makes enemies among the English contingent in Rome. Eventually, Margery is given enough money to return home.

Upon her return to England, Margery does her best to live a life of devotion to Christ. As a married woman, however, she is somewhat constrained, such as by the fact that she cannot become a nun. Margery travels to various churches and holy sites in England, attracting attention wherever she goes, thanks to her public weeping and her all-white wardrobe. At times, Margery is accepted as a holy woman, and her advice and blessings are solicited. More often, she is treated as an oddity or a nuisance and mocked. On occasion, the hostile attention she draws goes beyond mockery. Traveling through the north of England, Margery is arrested several times and almost burned at the stake as a heretic, though she is saved by the intervention of the church authorities. Each time she is arrested, Margery defends herself vigorously. She is respectful to authority but firm in her beliefs, none of which are heretical, as her examiners soon see.

Margery continues to have mystical visions of Jesus, the Virgin Mary, and several saints. Margery's devotion to Christ is particularly intense and is expressed in highly physical, even sexual, terms. In her visions, Margery often sees herself as a servant to Mary or Jesus, acting as an eyewitness to the events of the gospels. Jesus speaks to Margery in her visions of such subjects as the Trinity, the salvation and damnation of souls, and the meaning of the constant tears he sends her. Margery tries to spend as much time as she can in prayer or in conversation with her spiritual guides. Even so, her dramatic weeping in church and elsewhere continues to draw attention and, often, censure. Margery comes into particular conflict with a friar who moves to Lynn and refuses to allow Margery to hear him preach because of her disruptive weeping.

As time goes on, Margery's husband becomes old and infirm, and Margery returns to his household to care for him. One of Margery's sons turns from his sinful ways after much praying and beseeching by Margery, and he marries a German woman. The couple comes to England for a visit, and the son takes ill and dies, soon followed by his father. In her last extended journey, Margery accompanies her daughter-in-law (who is less than enthusiastic about being joined by her odd mother-in-law) back to Germany, only deciding to leave at the last minute. Margery's trip overland from Germany to France is her most grueling yet, and she is again scorned by other travelers from England, to whom she turns for help. Eventually, Margery makes it to London and finally back to Lynn. Home once again, Margery, now an old woman, decides to record the story of her life and her devotions, and begins the dictation of her *Book*.

CHARACTER LIST

Margery Kempe The narrator of the *Book*, which is Kempe's autobiography. Margery begins her story when she is a young wife suffering a post-partum breakdown. She then tells of her first mystical visions of Jesus and the ways her life changed afterward. Margery has an eventful life, full of travel, controversy, and confrontation. She travels across England, as well as to Jerusalem, Rome, Spain, and Germany—extraordinary for a middle-class woman of her time. Everywhere she goes, her ostentatious, highly emotional religiosity attracts attention, and her claims of receiving direct visions of Jesus arouse suspicions of heresy. Her most important experiences, however, are all spiritual, and her narrative reflects Margery's intense inward focus and her mystical raptures.

John Kempe Margery's husband. John is confused by Margery's turn away from married life and toward religious devotion, and he shows both frustration and a great deal of patience with his rather demanding wife. It takes Margery several years (and many children) before she can convince John that the two of them should live together chastely, devoting themselves to God. Eventually, Margery succeeds, and they take a vow of chastity. For many years afterward, Margery and her husband live apart, and her great travels are solo journeys. Margery returns to her husband in his old age, however, after he is injured in a fall. She speaks of John in his decrepit state sadly and tenderly, and she nurses him until his death.

B

Margery's Son The only one of Margery's children to emerge as a full-fledged character. Margery's son is described as "a tall young man" who works as a merchant in Germany. He is at first rather loose-living, and his mother warns him often of the dangers of lust and "lechery." Margery's worry causes friction between them, but when the son becomes covered in sores and pustules, apparently due to a venereal complaint, he decides to mend his ways. Margery's son eventually reforms, makes a trip to Rome, and settles down with a German woman. After the birth of their first child, the couple comes to England to visit Margery, but the son becomes sick and dies soon after.

Margery's Daughter-in-Law The German woman whom Margery's son marries. Margery's daughter-in-law stays with Margery for several months after the death of her husband. As the daughter-in-law is preparing to return home, Margery suddenly decides to accompany her back to Germany. Margery's daughter-in-law seems reluctant and is rather inhospitable to Margery when they are in Germany.

Alan of Lynn ("Master Aleyn") One of Margery's spiritual advisors and friends. Master Aleyn is a Carmelite Friar and an expert in mystical writings and theology. He befriends Margery soon after her mystical experiences begin and defends her when her unusual behavior begins to draw hostile notice. Margery learns much of the writings of such English mystics as Walter Hilton and Richard Rolle, as well as female precursors such as St. Bridget, thanks to Master Aleyn. Much later, Master Aleyn's association with Margery gets him in trouble with his superiors in the church, and the two are forbidden to meet for a time. Before Master Aleyn's death, however, the pair have a joyful reunion.

Archbishop of Canterbury ("Arundel") The most important and powerful bishop in England. Margery seeks an audience with the Archbishop on the advice of the Bishop of Lincoln. The Archbishop is curious about Margery and asks her many questions regarding her spiritual experiences and her beliefs. Margery speaks with him well into the night, and in the end, he decides to sanction her unusual choice of spiritual vocation. The Archbishop gives Margery permission to wear white clothes, and, later, he writes her a letter certifying that she is not a heretic.

The "Preaching Friar" A friar, renowned for his preaching, who comes to live in Lynn. Margery looks forward to hearing the friar preach, but he is not used to being interrupted by loud wailing during his sermons. The other religious figures in Lynn try to get him to accept Margery's eccentricities, but he cannot. He bans Margery from his church and sparks a backlash against Margery in Lynn, inspiring many who dislike her behavior to speak out against her.

Julian of Norwich ("Dame Julian") One of the greatest English mystics and best-known female writers of the Middle Ages. Julian was an anchoress (female hermit) in a convent in the city of Norwich. The author of a book of her "revelations," Julian was often sought out for guidance by political and religious authorities, as well as by common folk. Margery goes to pay her respects to Julian soon after her own mystical visions commence. The pair have a long conversation in which Julian tries to instruct

Margery how to tell a true vision from a false one. Julian also tells Margery that her tears are a blessing and a sign of God's favor.

The German Priest A priest who befriends Margery in Rome. After Margery is kicked out of the English community in Rome, she is taken in by several others, including a German priest who becomes her confessor. The priest advises Margery to give up her all-white wardrobe and care for a destitute Roman woman, and Margery obeys. Since the priest does not speak English and Margery does not speak German, the propriety of his acting as Margery's spiritual advisor is suspect. At dinner one evening, however, Margery speaks to the German priest in English, and he translates her words into Latin for some English priests, who become convinced that God approves of the relationship.

Unnamed Priest, Margery's Secretary The priest who records Margery's words, providing the text of the *Book*. This priest befriends Margery late in her life and agrees to help her tell her story. This is actually the second attempt to write down Margery's life story. The first came several years before, when Margery made the attempt with an unnamed helper (very likely her son), and the result was a nearly illegible manuscript. The priest breaks into Margery's story on occasion to verify her account or to back up her claims—for example, when Margery helps heal the young woman stricken, as Margery had been, with post-partum psychosis. The priest has a brief episode of trouble with his vision at the start of writing the *Book*, but he and Margery pray and his vision clears.

B

Richard ("The Broken-Backed Man") A poor Irishman who aids Margery on her return from Jerusalem. Before Margery leaves on her pilgrimage to the Holy Land, her confessor prophesies that she will receive help from "a broken-backed man." In Venice, on her way home from Jerusalem, Margery is abandoned by her fellow pilgrims, but she meets Richard, who has a deformed spine. Margery immediately sees Richard as the "broken-backed" man of her confessor's prophecy and hires him as an escort. Richard frequently seems bemused by his employer and is often afraid that they will attract bandits as they travel. In Rome, Margery gives some of Richard's money (which he has given her for safekeeping) to the poor, which annoys Richard. Margery promises to repay him, and does so when, by chance, she meets Richard again at Bristol, where Margery is setting off on her second pilgrimage abroad.

Margery's Confessor ("Master R," "Master Robert Spryngolde") A priest of Lynn, and Margery's primary spiritual advisor. In Margery's visions, Jesus instructs her several times to honor and obey the wisdom of Master Robert. Master Robert believes in Margery's visions and defends her several times against those who would claim that her tears are fake or inspired by the devil rather than by God. Master Robert predicts that Margery will be helped on her pilgrimage by a "broken-backed man," and the appearance of Richard in Venice seems to fulfill his prophecy. Margery's confessor helps her through many crises, including Margery's difficulty with her enemy (the preaching friar) and the great fire that endangers the church in Lynn. The greatest crisis in their relationship comes when Margery departs for Germany with her daughter-in-law, after Master Robert has advised her to stay home. On her return, Margery apologizes humbly and is forgiven. Margery's sense of profound gratitude toward her confessor is best expressed by her prayer to Jesus that Master Robert have half of any blessing that Margery may receive in heaven.

Vicar of St. Stephen's ("Richard of Caister") A priest of Norwich, well-known for his personal holiness and his great knowledge. The Vicar befriends Margery and defends her from accusations of heresy. He asks for Margery's prayers, and Margery is greatly moved to learn of his death.

Archbishop of York The spiritual leader of one of the largest towns in England, and one of Margery's inquisitors. When Margery is arrested near York, she is brought before the Archbishop, who questions her sharply about her tears. The Archbishop is soon convinced of Margery's orthodoxy but is still concerned about the rumors he hears about her. In the end, the Archbishop simply tells her to leave town as soon as she can. When Margery is arrested again soon after, she is once more brought before the Archbishop. This time, the Archbishop seems more annoyed at Margery's accusers, and he refuses to imprison her, despite the protestations of the men of the Duke of Bedford. The Archbishop appreciates Margery's homespun wisdom—he is clearly amused by certain earthy stories Margery tells, although the stories are critical of priests. The Archbishop seems to grow to like Margery the more he sees of her, but as a busy administrator, he is glad to see the troublesome woman depart.

ANALYSIS OF MAJOR CHARACTERS

MARGERY KEMPE The Margery Kempe that emerges over the course of the *Book* is perhaps not quite the figure the author intended to portray. The *Book* is clearly meant to be a sort of brief for Margery's holiness and divine inspiration—her sainthood, in fact—but the reader is left with the impression that, mystic or not, Margery could be an exasperating person to deal with: unpredictable, hyper-emotional, and rather self-obsessed. When we consider many of the routine occurrences of Margery's life (such as her loud weeping during church services and her walking up to a total stranger's child and bursting into tears because the child reminds her of Jesus), it is hard not to sympathize with her angry neighbors and frustrated fellow-pilgrims. One of the few comic moments of the *Book* occurs when Margery's husband, exhausted by her insistence that the pair be celibate, asks if she would rather see him decapitated by a murderer than have sex with him. Margery says yes, and John, thoroughly and understandably discouraged, replies, "You are no good wife."

Margery is honest about her own failings, and her attention to her shortcomings is just as important as her self-praise. Margery does brag about the ways God has singled her out, but she just as often emphasizes her weakness and *dependence* on God. For example, Margery includes the embarrassing moment when she tries to take a man up on his proposal that they begin an adulterous affair—only to find that the man had been joking. She remains conscious of others' opinions and guards her reputation, but she shows herself repeatedly humiliated and scorned, begging for food in Rome and often treated like an outcast at home. A kind of irony marks many of Margery's experiences. For example, she gives up sex with her husband but has sexually charged visions of Jesus. She says that before her mystical life began, she had been overly concerned with having fancy clothes, yet she then devotes chapters of her memoir to her all-white wardrobe. Margery is devout and respectful of the forms of the church, yet she is often disruptive in her congregation, pursuing an individualistic spiritual path and challenging the clergy when she sees fit.

B

What unifies all of the disparate elements of Margery's personality and experiences is her overwhelming urge to refer everything to the spiritual plane—to see God's will and love as immanent in every aspect of her life. Seen in this particular light, certain elements of a story such as hers which might *seem* important—a person's name, for example, or the description of a landscape—can be left out if they do not help us toward this primary understanding. What matters in any situation is the way in which it reveals to us God's will as active in the world. God's will is active in the weather and in the Mass; Jesus is present in our minds and in a child in the street. This is the main thing Margery learns from her visions. Again and again, Jesus tells her that he has chosen her personally, that he died on the cross for her personally, and that he remains concerned with the smallest events of her life.

Margery's *Book* can be seen as one woman's effort to sift through her personal history, searching for moments where God's presence can be felt and described. For all of her exotic religious experiences, Margery does not claim to be special; she does not claim to know why God has chosen to visit her, and not someone else, with tears and visions (though she dutifully records all of the praise she does receive from Jesus). Part of her point is that if these things can happen to plain, undeserving Margery Kempe of Lynn, they can happen to anyone, anywhere, who has faith and turns to God. As an example, she presents her own story of transformation, showing us how God can turn a trembling invalid into a courageous pilgrim—someone willing to stand up to hostile authority and even face down an angry mob. In the end, even if Margery fails to make the case for her own sainthood, she leaves behind a remarkable testimony of personal faith and conviction.

THEMES, MOTIFS, AND SYMBOLS

THEMES

THE IMPORTANCE OF SUFFERING FOR CHRIST'S SAKE The concept of suffering for Jesus's sake is rooted in the New Testament book of the Acts of the Apostles, where Christ informs St. Paul that he must "suffer in my name." Margery does not cite this verse directly, but the idea of undergoing suffering as a form of devotion to Jesus is central to her spirituality. The traditional form of such suffering occurs whenever a Christian believer is persecuted for his or her beliefs, and the hallmark of a Christian martyr is a willingness to turn suffering and death into a "witness" of faith ("martyr" means "witness"). Margery interprets the scorn she encounters in this light—she is being persecuted because of her devotion to

Christ, and her suffering is a reminder of the greater suffering of Jesus. Margery's visions make her a "witness" in a different but related sense—she sees the suffering of Jesus and Mary and in some sense takes part in it. Her tears become a sign of her willingness to share in Christ's suffering. They are a reaction to, and a reminder of, Christ's own redemptive anguish. Margery speaks of her tears as "saving" others, and this transformation of suffering into personal union with God places Margery firmly in the tradition of Christian mystics.

MARGERY IS VINDICATED Margery never misses an opportunity to describe an occasion when something she predicts comes to pass, one of her prayers is answered, or one of her enemies comes to grief. Margery has several motives for dwelling on such moments of vindication. First, she wants to show that her claims of direct contact with God are justified. Despite the accusations of hypocrisy or madness that are hurled at her, in the end she is revealed to be in the right. She offers evidence for her rightness by describing storms that peter out harmlessly, thanks to her prayers, and liars she is able to confound. Margery also wants to protect herself from any charges of heresy, and she makes an effort to describe any occasion that might plausibly be construed as a demonstration of God's favor. Margery also focuses on moments when she is vindicated by church authorities against those who accuse her of Lollardy. She takes care to emphasize her orthodox answers to the questions put to her by the Archbishops of Canterbury and York and to record their willingness to vouch for her. In this sense, Margery's *Book* is as much about self-defense as about self-expression.

DESIRE FOR GOD AS LIFE PURPOSE Margery is concerned with earthly suffering, but she also has an intense desire for union with God. Margery's life and life story are organized around her spiritual experiences, and some of her mystical visions receive more attention than even the birth of one of her fourteen children. Margery seeks out spiritual authorities such as Julian, and travels to holy sites as far away as Jerusalem, often at great expense and personal risk, all in order to advance her spiritual journey toward God. Along the way, she treats everyone and everything she meets as either a spiritual obstacle or a spiritual aid, and any aspect of her life that does not fit into one of these two categories generally goes unmentioned. Margery tries to make every detail of her day-to-day life, from the food she eats (or abstains from) to the clothes she wears, an act of devotion. These small devotions help make her larger moments of ecstatic devotion possible. For example, by deferring sexual pleasure on earth, Margery directs that energy into her visions, where sexual union becomes an image of heavenly contact, or "marriage," with God. In this way, Margery's mystical desire for God becomes the organizing principle of her life.

MOTIFS

USE OF THE THIRD PERSON Throughout the *Book*, Margery speaks of herself in the third person, as "this creature." On one level, doing so is a simple act of humility on Margery's part: her purpose is simply to tell her story, not to make herself famous. But this act of humility is deeply significant for Margery, who comes to see herself truly in terms of her created nature, her "creaturehood." All of the conflict in Margery's life—within her family, her society, and even herself—has its resolution in Margery's commitment to place Jesus's purposes for her life above all others', including her own. Many of the most dramatic moments of Margery's story come when she is publicly forced to honor Christ's will over the will of her husband, the secular or religious authorities, and even, in the case of her inconvenient tears, her own will. In the end, Margery gladly embraces her status as "this creature" of God.

CONVERSATIONS WITH GOD Margery has several extended conversations with Jesus (and other heavenly persons) over the course of her life. Indeed, she tends to express most of the workings of her mind in terms of a conversation with God. Where one might ordinarily say, "I became suspicious of him," Margery will typically say something to the effect of, "The Lord warned this creature in her thoughts about this man." Margery means for the reader to take these statements literally—she is reporting what are for her actual discussions with, and revelations from, God. This is especially true with the extended visions in which Margery witnesses scenes from the gospels. But Margery is also trying to teach us to see our thoughts as being in constant dialogue with God (and the devil), and to be open to prompting from above (and wary of temptation from below). Again, she is trying to emphasize—to provide an image of—the activity and presence of God in everyday life as well as in intense mystical experience.

PHYSICALITY One of the most striking elements of Margery's story is the intense physicality she ascribes to what we generally consider un-bodily, spiritual experiences. One example is Margery's tears, the most typical physical expression of her religious emotion. Margery also sees visions, hears music, smells delightful odors, and feels a pleasant warmth when she is in the midst of one of her mystic reveries. She also has a long sequence of visions in which she describes herself as embracing Jesus physically, culminating in her "marriage" to Christ. The point of this is both to make Margery's abstract, spiritual experience concrete and comprehensible and to make Margery's physical experience spiritual. Margery wants us to feel that the effects of Jesus's contact with her soul are made visible to others through her bodily reactions. Although it is impossible to know for sure, the teaching of Margery's confessor and other mentors may have guided her interpretations and descriptions of what was happening to her. As Margery is careful to say, in the very last chapter of Book One, visions are often hard to interpret, and "sometimes, what she understood physically was to be understood spiritually."

SYMBOLS

B

MARGERY'S TEARS The uncontrollable tears that flow whenever Margery worships or even thinks of God are a source of both difficulty and pride. She believes that God sends her tears, but she is initially unsure about how to interpret them. In a vision, Jesus explains the meaning of her tears. First, they are an outward sign of Margery's deep love of Christ. As a symbol of Margery's inner being, the tears show others the depth of Margery's faith. They call to mind the suffering of Christ, who, in Christian doctrine, dies to save the souls of all people. In this sense, Margery's tears are a symbolic form of prayer, worship, and teaching. But Jesus tells Margery that the tears are meaningful in another sense as well: by coming and going as unpredictably as a rainstorm, Margery's tears suggest her complete dependence on God. By making her cry at his whim, Jesus is showing Margery that she is his "creature," as Margery refers to herself. Margery is grateful for this rather difficult blessing, and her understanding of its symbolic value helps her whenever her tears draw hostile attention.

IMPORTANT QUOTATIONS EXPLAINED

---

1. *She greeted the Vicar, asking him if she could—in the afternoon, when he had eaten—speak with him for an hour or two of the love of God. He, lifting up his hands and blessing himself, said, "Bless us! How could a woman occupy one or two hours with the love of our Lord? I shan't eat a thing till I find out what you can say of our Lord God in the space of an hour."*

This is the first meeting that Margery has with the Vicar of St. Stephens, recorded in Book One, section 17 of the *Book*. Although he sounds dubious here, the Vicar soon becomes one of Margery's champions. Even from those who are disposed to believe her, such as the Vicar, Margery must contend initially with skepticism and condescension. The Vicar shows both pastoral friendliness and authoritative assertion in his response to Margery's request for an appointment, just as both humility and self-assertion exist in the request itself. Note that Margery makes it sound as if *she* will be doing the talking during the hour, not the learned Vicar. The Vicar responds with a challenge, offering Margery a chance to prove herself but expressing his doubt that she will do so. Margery is undaunted, as usual, and she makes the quizzical Vicar into a fast friend.

---

2. *Therefore I must be intimate with you, and lie in your bed with you. Daughter, you greatly desire to see me, and you may boldly, when you are in bed, take me to you as your wedded husband. . . .*

In the midst of one of Margery's extended visions in Book One, section 36, Jesus makes this remarkable statement to Margery. The sexual content of the statement is naturally the most striking part, but it soon becomes clear that he is speaking in spiritual terms—that sex is being used here as a metaphor or image of mystical union. Jesus does not merely say that he wants to be Margery's lover; he addresses her as his daughter, and says he intends to be her father, son, husband, and brother—while she is to be his wife, mother, sister, and child. In other words, Jesus intends to be all men—all things—to her, and she will be known and loved by him completely, in all aspects of her being as a woman. Margery's earthly mystical experience is meant as a foretaste of heaven itself. In effect, Margery's female experience of the male Christ is presented as the essence of what all humans, male and female, can expect from direct union with God—a bold, pro-woman statement indeed.

---

3. *When her crying was passed, she came before the Archbishop and fell down on her knees, the Archbishop saying very roughly to her, "Why do you weep so, woman?"*
   She answering said, "Sir, you shall wish some day that you had wept as sorely as I."

Margery's retort to the Archbishop of York in Book One, section 52, demonstrates her confidence in the face of aggressive questioning from a powerful figure of authority. Margery's absolute confidence in God's blessing on her, in the form of her tears, is enough to give her the courage to stand up to, and even to rebuke, a man as imposing as the Archbishop. The point of Margery's statement is also important, hinting at the symbolic value of her tears as prayer. Someday, Margery is saying, the Archbishop will wish that he had been as thoroughly attuned to the way Christ suffered for his sake as Margery is. Her tears are not a punishment, but a sign of grace, and those who are not so blessed would do well to pay attention.

---

4. *[She] many times met with men of that district who said to her, "Woman, give up this life that you lead and go and spin, and card wool, as other women do, and do not suffer so much shame and so much unhappiness. We would not suffer so much for any money on earth."*
   Then she said to them, "I do not suffer as much sorrow as I would do for our Lord's love, for I only suffer cutting words, and our merciful Lord Christ Jesus. . . . suffered hard strokes, bitter scourgings, and shameful death at the last, for me and for all mankind, blessed may he be."

When Margery is arrested for the second time in Yorkshire, in Book One, section 53, she faces ridicule for making such an unfeminine spectacle of herself and is urged to return home and take up her wifely duties once again. Margery's answer ignores the content of the men's remarks, focusing instead on the unspiritual small-mindedness revealed by their attitude toward suffering. In response to their assertion that living as she does is simply not worth the trouble, Margery invokes the crucified Jesus to ask, in effect, do you wish *he* had chosen the easy path instead of the way that leads to suffering? Seen in this light, Margery says, her own suffering is nothing, and she can even gladly accept it as part of her devotion to Christ.

---

5. *Then the lady's priest came to her, saying, "Woman, Jesus is long since dead."*
   When her crying ceased, she said to the priest, "Sir, his death is as fresh to me as if he had died this same day, and so, I think, it ought to be to you and to all Christian people."

In Book One, section 60, Margery is again being challenged by a religious figure for her emotional displays, in this case for weeping at the sight of a statue of Mary holding the dead Jesus. And again, Margery's response is forthright and unafraid. Turning the priest's question around, she shifts the issue from the impropriety of her unusual reaction to the death of Jesus to the fact that her response is, indeed, so unusual. Why, Margery wants to know, doesn't everybody cry when they think of Jesus—that's the real question. Margery's tears once again take on their symbolic, didactic value. She cries because she sees Christ's sacrifice as occurring even now, and eternally—which is in fact what Christians profess to believe. The greatest spiritual danger for a Christian is to forget about Christ, and Margery's greatest ambition is to become a living reminder of his love.

The Book of the City of Ladies

Christine de Pizan (~1364–~1430)

CONTEXT

Some critics consider Christine de Pizan, born in around 1364, to be France's, if not the world's, first professional female author. In addition, her classic work, *The Book of the City of Ladies,* is commonly held to be the first feminist text written by a Western woman. In it, she directly confronts the sexism and misogyny that characterized and plagued not only the literature of her day, fourteenth- and fifteenth-century Europe, but representations of women reaching back into antiquity.

B

Her intention was to defend unwarranted attacks on the characters of women and to provide examples of the unquestionable virtue of her sex. Though this seems like a lofty and daunting goal, it is grounded in a specific response to contemporary events surrounding her life as a writer in France. *The Book of the City of Ladies,* as a philosophical treatise, can be seen as directly answering the writer Jean de Meun, who between 1269 and 1278 wrote a more than 17,000-line continuation of Guillaume de Lorris's epic poem *The Romance of the Rose,* initially completed in the 1230s. *The Romance of the Rose* is an allegorical dream poem and treatise on courtly love, and it was one of the best-selling publications in thirteenth- and fourteenth-century France. While de Lorris's section, the shorter of the two, is more of a traditional allegorical romance in its lyrical tale of the Dreamer, de Meun's sizeable addition has a more satirical bent, focusing on social practice and the folly of women. De Pizan was familiar with the work, and in her *The Tale of the Rose* (1402) and *Letters on the Debate of the Romance of the Rose* (1403), she attacked de Meun's writing for its immoral, often vicious portrayals of women. She endured criticism for being too pointedly on the defensive.

De Pizan's writings from the early fifteenth century and her growing resistance to the irresponsible portrayal of women led directly to the composition of *The Book of the City of Ladies*, in which she casts herself as one of the main characters. Mirroring the author's passionate response to de Meun's misogyny, in the opening sections of the work, Christine the character's ire is again raised by a book by Mathéolus, most likely his *Lamentations,* as translated by Jean le Fèvre. The book, while professing to address the subject of respecting women, devolved instead into yet another attack on females and the vice that universally grips their lives. Christine takes up her pen to "unearth" the truth and lay the foundation for an accurate and morally responsible portrayal of women. Along the way, she cites and addresses certain points raised in the Italian writer Boccaccio's *De mulieribus claris* (*On Famous Women*), the first book in Western literature to talk about virtuous women. But where Boccaccio also falls into the trap of maligning women, Christine sets out to correct the gaps and lapses in his thinking and his portrayals. Using the figures of three allegorical women—Reason, Rectitude, and Justice—she seeks to construct the titular City of Ladies, a symbolic repository of all that is good and noble in women and a place of refuge that can stand in its irrefutable truth as an impregnable defense against future attacks by sharp-tongued and sexist male writers.

Christine's city offers a gallery of compelling models of womanhood. The permanent residents of the City of Ladies are united and strong. Scholars, inventors, artists, prophets, saints, warriors, pious wives, and dutiful daughters all take their place in the well-proportioned and carefully designed auspices of her city. In sampling from history, mythology, literature, and the Bible, Christine offers her own full, complete, and universal portrait of womanhood. Using approaches later championed by religion and the developing sciences, she slowly and methodically builds her case, gathering and collecting data and empirical observations as a means of arriving at the truth that supports her conclusions. In doing so, Christine repossesses and saves the reputation and good nature of women, acknowledging the moral strength and essential contributions of women, without which Western society, life, and culture would not be possible.

Her unique work offers a window into the world of medieval women and the way in which they were perceived and treated by the society of the time. It also introduces the prevailing notions about womanhood and the debates that often raged in the world of men intent on protecting their positions as the unquestioned rulers of their social and political realms. By using examples of virtue and citing achievements from the past, Christine adopts a three-pronged focus—targeting the intellectual, the spiritual, and the physical—to show that women are no more fallible or praiseworthy than the greatest or worst of men.

PLOT OVERVIEW

In her study, taking a break from her work, Christine de Pizan picks up a slim volume someone has given her. Shocked by the author's harsh and extreme portrayal of the immoral and inconstant nature of women, Christine is saddened by this state of affairs. A flash of light startles her, and three women, allegorical figures representing Reason, Rectitude, and Justice, appear to her. They tell her she is to build the City of Ladies and populate it with the noblest and most accomplished women the world has known. The city is to serve as a safeguard against the cruel accusations of men as well as a reminder of the true and laudable nature of women.

Lady Reason takes Christine to the Field of Letters, a fertile plain where the city is to be built, and encourages her to use her pen to start excavating the earth so they can lay the foundations that will support the City of Ladies. Reason narrates the lives of various women and the testament of their strength collectively helps to build the city's firm support. Reason first tells of women who have distinguished themselves in the political and military realms, individuals who have judiciously ruled vast realms as well as defended those realms from insurgents and attacks from beyond their borders. Next, she discusses learned women, like Christine, who have developed their intellectual capacities. Collectively, these women of letters have helped shape Western history and culture. Finally, Reason relates tales that demonstrate the prudence that women possess. Having completed the foundation and the walls, Reason turns over the city's completion to her two sisters.

Rectitude is the next to address Christine and help her, with the mortar of her words, to complete and enclose the palaces, mansions, and domiciles that will house the city's residents. Rectitude begins by telling of ladies of vision and prophecy who, despite the fact that few heeded their predictions, accurately foresaw the shape of the future. Rectitude then focuses on the family unit, relaying tales of faithful daughters and pious wives whose dedication to and love of their relatives superseded all. Rectitude celebrates all the good and countless benefits women have brought to the world and argues that they should be given the same access to education that is extended to men. She then tackles the importance of chastity to women and the horror and repulsion of rape, which is often insidiously characterized as something that is actively sought by women or which affects them little. Men, she claims, are the fickle ones when compared to the steadfastness of most women, especially those in love. Rectitude concludes her narration with the assertion that it is integrity, honesty, and generosity that earn a woman distinction, and not her physical attractiveness. Having completed the city's edifices and populated it with noble ladies, Rectitude turns the project over to her sister, Justice, for completion.

Justice is left with the task of putting on the city's finishing touches. Through her tales of holy women, she completes the roofs and adds doorways and gates to the City of Ladies. Most importantly, she brings the Virgin Mary to the city to serve as its guide and queen. Justice tells of various women who have been martyred for their faith. Faced with worshiping false idols and renouncing their love of Jesus Christ, they never wavered in their love of the one god. Though their physical bodies were abused, tortured, and violated, their intangible, spiritual selves remained intact, unsullied, and as strong as ever. Most of these women would go on to be declared saints. They wished to remain virginal and pure and went to their deaths in defense of their principles. Some even witnessed the torture and deaths of their children before succumbing themselves. Justice tells of several women who lived disguised as men in monasteries so they could remain free of the undesired attentions of suitors and pursue their religious devotion unhindered.

Having completed the city, the three Virtues turn it over to Christine, who rejoices in all that they have accomplished. Christine speaks to all women and declares the City of Ladies a refuge where they can find respite and safety from the sexual aggression and cruel attacks by men. She reminds the inhabitants of this community of women to stay strong and true and to uphold the noble virtues that have made the construction of the city possible. The city serves as a testament to the power and unity of women and of their own high standards and unshakeable virtue.

CHARACTER LIST

Christine de Pizan The protagonist. Christine is a successful writer and scholar who is visited by three women representing Reason, Rectitude, and Justice. They help her to counter the sexist claims popularly made by male writers of the day. They also debate and discuss the merits and accomplishments of notable women, thereby constructing the titular City of Ladies.

Reason The narrator of most of Part One. Reason helps Christine de Pizan lay the foundation for the City of Ladies and constructs the exterior walls for the city's buildings. She discusses women who have distinguished themselves intellectually, politically, and militarily. She also provides numerous examples of the prudence that women display.

Rectitude The narrator of most of Part Two. Rectitude celebrates women as prophets, wives, and daughters, defends women against the horrors of rape, and pleads the case for the constancy of her sex. She completes the various structures that make up the City of Ladies and populates it with noble and upstanding women.

Justice The narrator of most of Part Three. Justice finishes the construction of the city—roofing the structures, adding the doorways and gates, and then ushering in Mary, the Queen, and other holy women. She discusses the lives of women who have martyred themselves for their faith.

B

Artemisia The Queen of Caria. Artemisia was praised for her moral insight and wisdom and known for her strength as a leader both in the palace and on the battlefield. She conquered the Rhodians and then defeated Xerxes and the Persians to help defend Sparta. In honor of her husband, King Mausolus, she built the first mausoleum.

Blanche The Queen of France and mother of Saint Louis. After the death of her husband, Blanche kept the realm unified and ruled France until her son could come of age. Known for her goodness, wisdom, and integrity, her son's enemy became enamored of her and composed many love poems in her honor.

Saint Christine The daughter of Urban. Christine's patron and namesake, Saint Christine refused to worship her father's gold and silver idols, which she smashed and gave to the poor. Imprisoned, beaten, burned, covered in boiling oil, crushed on a torture wheel, thrown into the sea with a stone tied to her, beset with snakes, her tongue and breasts cut out, and shot with arrows, she was martyred to her faith and responsible for thousands of conversions by the example she set with her unshakeable love of God.

Dido The Queen of Carthage. Also called Elissa, Dido fled her cruel brother, Pygmalion, and founded a great city in North Africa. Known for her cunning, physical prowess, and nobility, she welcomed the warrior Aeneas and fell deeply in love with him. When he left her secretly in the night, she committed suicide.

Fredegund The Queen of France. Cruel and severe, Fredegund ruled France until her son was old enough to assume the throne. A brilliant military strategist, she brought her infant son into battle to urge the men to secure victory for their future king at all costs. She had her men camouflage their horses with branches. Then she instructed them to tie bells to their mounts, which the enemy mistook for grazing animals, allowing Fredegund's forces to penetrate the enemy camp.

Lucretia A Roman noblewoman. Lucretia was propositioned by Tarquin the Proud, son of the king. When he threatened to ruin her reputation with false accusations, she submitted to his demands, later confessing the violation to her husband, father, and family before taking out a dagger and plunging it into her breast.

Medea The daughter of the king of Colchis. Beautiful and noble, Medea had extensive knowledge of herbs and botanicals and, through her enchantments, could control the elements and provoke spontaneous combustion. She fell in love with Jason and through her spells helped him secure the Golden Fleece. Soon after, he left her for another woman.

Nicostrata A scholar also known as Carmentis. Nicostrata named the Palentine hill and in a vision predicted it would be the future site of the Roman Empire. She laid the city's first stone, instituted a system of laws for the surrounding region, and invented the Latin alphabet and language.

Sappho A Greek poet and scholar. Beautiful, intelligent, and articulate, Sappho won the praise of Greece's leading literary lights for her talents as a writer. She invented new poetic forms and was honored as one of the leading figures of her times with a bronze statue erected in the city in which she lived.

Thisbe The daughter of a nobleman. When Thisbe fell in love with Pyramus, her mother grew alarmed and locked her in her bedroom, the wall of which adjoined Pyramus's chambers. Finding a crack in the wall, Thisbe made a hole and was able to arrange to meet her lover. When Pyramus arrived, he found her handkerchief soiled with a lion's vomit. Thinking she had been mauled and eaten, he took his life. Thisbe emerged from her hiding spot, found her lover dead, and then committed suicide as well.

ANALYSIS OF MAJOR CHARACTERS

CHRISTINE DE PIZAN Christine de Pizan is both the author of and a character in her literary creation. She straddles two realms, serving as a bridge between the book's historical and contemporary references and the imaginative world of the three allegorical figures and their symbolic city. In addition, her presence accommodates and unites the various references that constitute the wealth of examples that Reason, Rectitude, and Justice cite as evidence of women's virtue. In stating her case, Christine integrates into her treatise women from history as well as fictional characters from legend and mythology. Although Christine argues that these seemingly fictionalized presences were based on actual, real women, it is her dual status as both authorial presence and literary character that allows the real and the fantastic to seamlessly fuse and to form a unified and convincing argument. Without her presence, critics may have found her scholarship flawed and her citation of fictional lives questionable, thus compromising the impact of her words.

Christine assumes another unique pose and fulfills yet another specific function in her work. Throughout, she adopts and utilizes what is known as the modesty topos, a rhetorical device in which she willfully appears to be more ignorant, naïve, or uninformed than she actually is in order to make her various points more powerful. Rather than stating that women are virtuous and talented, she instead asks the three Virtues if there is any truth to the statements that male authors make, maligning and dismissing women's accomplishments. By casting her work in the form of a dialogue (a philosophical debate utilizing a question-and-answer format), Christine avoids the charge of shrilly preaching to her readers. This approach is more effective: readers can trace her logic and see how she arrives at her conclusions rather than simply being told the direct result of her contemplations. Ultimately, this self-effacing stance stands out against the self-promotion she indulges on several different occasions. In answering Christine's questions, the three allegorical figures often acknowledge and cite some of Christine's other books in what amounts to a brief endorsement of the esteemed author's body of scholarship.

REASON Reason is the first of the three allegorical figures to step forward and announce her intention to dispel the insecurity and ignorance that clouds Christine's intellect. She is also the first to announce the figures' intention to appear to Christine and present her with her task of constructing the City of Ladies. Reason presents herself as an administrator who will oversee the construction of a flawless city. Reason helps Christine perform the initial excavation work. She encourages Christine to reassess the power of her pen as a device that can be used to unearth the truth and to remove the mud and dirt that previously sullied the good name of women. Only then can a solid foundation be established. As a symbolic presence, Reason is an important first figure to appear to Christine, as all philosophical arguments must originate and proceed with logic. Without logic, any ensuing evidence or conclusions would lack solid framework and would crumble.

In her oration and her response to Christine's various questions concerning the nature of women, Reason establishes several important patterns. She uses Christine's questions as prompts to help her develop thematic elements that are also qualities shared by all virtuous and notable women. From these initial suggestions, Reason, and subsequently the two other Virtues, provide a series of narrations as a growing body of evidence supporting the defense of women. Story by story, the argument gains strength, just as brick by brick the city grows larger and more forbidding. Reason cites examples from a variety of sources. She tells of women from the past as well as the present. By doing so, she draws parallels between past and present, suggesting a continuous and ongoing history of virtue on the part of women. In establishing this second pattern, Reason wishes to dispel any notion that venerable women were solely a thing of the past.

JUSTICE The hard work of building and partially populating the city completed, Justice comes to sanctify the proceedings. She represents herself as the daughter of God, a direct descendant and representative. In this sense, the City of Ladies and Christine's project are being given a final divine endorsement and blessing. By completing the roofs of the city, Justice symbolically links the community of women directly to the kingdom of Heaven. There is a direct correlation established in conjoining two metaphorical, abstract realms. In addition, Justice's tales assume a darker, more violent character representing women's bodies as the target of severe physical abuse and degradation. But the extremity of the aggressor's actions toward these women is met with retribution that is equally cruel and forbidding. For their sin and idolatry, men are burned to ash and set to consuming their own flesh. Justice represents the darker side of divine love and the unyielding judgment that is meted out to those whose perversions and propensity for sin win out over their capacity for love, acceptance, and forgiveness. Justice's presence serves as an absolute if not terrifying reminder of the fate awaiting those ruled by their cruelty and misogynistic acts.

RECTITUDE Rectitude serves as a transitional figure in the work. Adopting the methods and procedures established by Christine and Reason in Part One, Rectitude strengthens and expands their arguments. She takes Reason's strong foundation and sturdy walls and adds shape, character, and life to the city in the stories she relates. In doing so, Rectitude serves as a bridge between the earth, or Reason's foundation, and heaven, the holy realm that Justice will provide access to. Thus, she provides examples of women who have used virtue as a means of paving their way to heaven. She also integrates higher ideals of selfless, Christ-like conduct by introducing stories of women who follow God's will in their daily lives. Like Christine, Rectitude resides in two realms, living more in heaven than on Earth. But she arrives as a messenger of God's goodness and a symbol of the radiance and splendor of the heavenly realm in order to inspire and exhort all of humanity to right and just conduct. This intention signals one of the motivations driving Christine de Pizan's work. Model lives can serve as inspiration not just for women but for men as well, encouraging mutual respect, common courtesy, and proper conduct.

THEMES, MOTIFS, AND SYMBOLS

THEMES

MISREPRESENTATION VS. TRUTH One of this work's central concerns is countering the destructive and false testimony that male authors have supplied in their written works for centuries. Christine attempts to strip away the layers of distortion and misrepresentation to present an accurate portrait of the true and essential nature of women. Christine's approach, through her line of questioning, gives voice to the various opinions and untruths men perpetuate in society, in an effort to debunk them with the Virtues' orations and stories. Christine directly addresses the issue when Reason argues that, contrary to popular belief, man was not made in God's image, as in an exact physical likeness. Instead, Reason contends that all people, men and women, share in this replication of God's essential nature and that there is a spiritual likeness and similarity. This desire to penetrate the essential, internal nature of the good found in people by transcending the physical is yet another of Christine's central themes.

PHYSICAL VS. SPIRITUAL Women were the subject of repression in many forms, most notably in the strict regulation of their behavior and the roles they were expected to fulfill in society. In addition, as Christine's narrative attests, women were often turned into sexual subordinates, objectified and transformed into sources of desire that alternately tempted and pleased men. These attitudes led to the widespread acceptance of rape. In the concluding section, Part Three—after Rectitude's discussion of the horrors of rape in Part Two, Justice cites many cases of the martyrdom of holy women. These individuals were the subject of severe physical trials as well as sexual abuse. Women were burned, tortured, and beaten, and the foolhardy men who sought to unleash their anger and hatred of these women could find no other means of harming them than through their bodies. What remained constant and allowed the martyrs to endure these severe punishments was their highly developed spiritual life and intense bond with God. This distinction crowns Christine's arguments, in which she attests to intangible inner qualities—intelligence, generosity, virtue, constancy—that are the mark of an individual, and not the attributes, limitations, and vulnerabilities of the body.

WRITING AS REPOSSESSION Critics have often viewed de Pizan as a repossessor, setting out to wrest away the tight control men had over the lives and representations of woman. In writing her book, de Pizan attempts to reclaim and restore the image of her sex, turning common misperceptions on their heads. One popular misconception was of the helplessness and dependency of women. Both before and after her life and times, men were the predominant force shaping discourse and dictating public law, social convention, and commonly held attitudes and beliefs. De Pizan's book marks a radical departure, a lone female voice challenging this status quo. In the Virtues' long list of stories, a new picture of women emerges. Women such as Fredegund and Ops seize and assert their power. They don't need rescuing, and they themselves are a source of liberation, ensuring and extending freedom to those around them. By seizing the image of women and safely storing it in the City of Ladies, de Pizan attempts to right centuries of injustice and set the record straight once and for all.

THE UNIVERSALITY OF HUMAN EXPERIENCE Christine argues that there are no special qualities reserved for one sex and absent from the other, just as no one social role or function belongs solely to the realm of men. For those male writers who would relegate women to a traditional, domestic sphere, the Virtues offer countless examples of women as warriors, brilliant military strategists who turn the tide of battle, and shrewd political leaders. Christine is not trying to elevate women at the expense of men but is gesturing instead to the equality of the sexes. She attempts to eradicate the perceived differences between men and women to highlight the virtues all paragons of conduct share and to present a universal portrait of human experience.

MOTIFS

ALLEGORY In *The Book of the City of Ladies*, allegory functions on two primary levels. First, three of the primary characters are allegorical figures who represent abstract notions or imaginative concepts—in this case, Reason, Rectitude, and Justice. They assume the form of noblewomen but are also the embodiment of the qualities from which they take their names. Christine needs to tap into these three qualities if she is to build a powerful and convincing argument. This argument itself becomes another mode of allegory. Christine is not physically laboring to build an actual, tangible city. Instead, she is using the trowel of her pen and the mortar of her ink to symbolically construct this all-female community. The bricks with which she raises the city's walls are the various and accumulating stories the Virtues offer as evidence of the constancy and purity of the female nature. The city's building blocks are the qualities, such as goodness and righteousness, that are eternal and cannot be destroyed. In this way, the City of Ladies functions as an imaginative concept, a product of the writer's mind. It is a "place" that serves to hold and store women's best attributes and greatest accomplishments.

PHILOSOPHICAL DIALOGUE Christine adopts the form of a traditional philosophical dialogue on which to determine and arrive at the truth. She functions as the student, and the three Virtues are her teachers, using discourse and debate to lead her on the path to insight. In this way, the work functions as a cross-examination in which Christine poses tough questions to the figures of Reason, Rectitude, and Justice. Christine serves as devil's advocate, giving voice to the attitudes and accusations of the opposition, men who hold misogynistic views of women. By using a question-and-answer format, Christine is able to slowly and methodically construct her argument. The solidity of her logic is akin to the sturdy and stable city she has at the end of the book.

STORYTELLING Narration and the art of storytelling are central to *The Book of the City of Ladies*, which is essentially a collection of parables from which Christine draws various conclusions about the nature of women. The work can be viewed as many stories contained within the larger unifying tale of the city's construction. The three Virtues take on the qualities of a writer by presenting the various plotlines of the women whose lives are related. They become stand-ins for Christine, who loses her "authority," or authorial voice, when she is plagued with doubts about the nature of women. Just as Christine is assigned the task of restoring the reputation of women, the three Virtues, in turn, work to infuse Christine's vision, and, by extension, her writing, with the power and insight that such a mouthpiece on behalf of women would require.

SYMBOLS

JUSTICE'S VESSEL OF GOLD The container of gold was given to Justice from God. It represents the eternal reward and salvation that await the faithful. It also stands for a justice that is higher and superior to the justice of man practiced and measured out on Earth. From this vessel, Justice gives out each person's "rightful portion," the payment received as a reflection of how morally and forthrightly an individual lived his or her life. It is inscribed with the fleur-de-lis, or lily, which signifies the Trinity. In this way, the three Virtues appearing to Christine are symbolically linked to the Trinity of Father, Son, and Holy Ghost that constitute the cornerstone of Christian faith.

REASON'S MIRROR Encrusted with jewels, Reason's mirror is a source of wisdom, clarity, and, above all, self-knowledge. Reason brings the mirror to Christine to give her the direction and certainty she needs to pursue the truth about the virtues of women. The Virtues stress to Christine that she must do a good job of constructing the city and that the task must be performed flawlessly. The mirror aids this pursuit in unveiling to Christine the essence and inherent qualities of the subjects she will be tackling in her text.

B

RECTITUDE'S RULER Rectitude carries her "shining ruler" in her right hand, and this ruler carries several meanings. In order to build the City of Ladies, Christine must measure her words carefully and proportion them to the task at hand. The ruler is offered to her as she constructs the facades of the palaces, houses, and public buildings and lays out the city's squares and streets. Rectitude wields her ruler as a staff of judgment. It separates right from wrong and indicates the dividing line between good and evil. The ruler is a guide that, when heeded, indicates the proper path or decision. Rectitude also declares that it is a rod of peace that supports the just and punishes the unjust.

IMPORTANT QUOTATIONS EXPLAINED

---

1. *The man or the woman in whom resides greater virtue is the higher; neither the loftiness nor the lowliness of a person lies in the body according to the sex but in the perfection of conduct and virtues.*

Reason speaks these words in Part One, section 9.3. They help to capture the essence of Christine's project. While one of her intentions of writing *The Book of the City of Ladies* is to defend and restore the honor and reputation of women, her ultimate goal is not to assert the superiority of women but to argue for equality and the fair and equal treatment of all people, regardless of gender. Christine asserts that a person's sex is not a fair measure of his or her character. Rather, an individual's moral development and personal conduct are worthy of esteem. In making this statement, Reason points out the reductive thinking employed by many people of the time, who make facile distinctions and focus on the inconsequential surface qualities that define an individual's appearance. Later in her work, Christine argues that beauty is no reflection or indicator of a woman's inner beauty. In challenging the prevailing notions of the day, she is asking readers to look beneath the surface and to think about the world in new and more responsible ways. She is also calling people to serve as moral beacons and models of upstanding conduct.

---

2. *[A]nd there is nothing which so instructs a reasonable creature as the exercise and experience of many different things.*

This statement comes from Reason and is found in Part One, section 27.1. One of Christine's intentions in writing her treatise is to provide a sound and defensible argument for why women should be given the same educational opportunities as men. She argues that if men feel women are intellectually and morally inferior, despite the fact that such a generalization is untrue, one possible explanation would be their lack of exposure to things beyond the domestic realm and the lack of opportunity to develop their minds and critical-thinking skills. She believes that men withhold education from women for fear it will be revealed that their intelligence rivals if not trumps men's. Christine believes that it is every individual's right to be exposed to as many ideas and influences as possible and that such a course strengthens and expands character, experience, and rational insight.

---

3. *Rest assured, dear friend, chaste ladies who live honestly take absolutely no pleasure in being raped. Indeed, rape is the greatest possible sorrow for them.*

This passage comes from Rectitude's oration in Part Two, section 44.1. In her work, de Pizan attempts to tackle stereotypes concerning women and to demystify commonly held and erroneous assumptions. In de Pizan's day, wives were viewed as property. This belief extended to a woman's body, and many men believed they had the right to use their wives' bodies in any way they saw fit. As in all eras, rape was a shocking and violent reality for many women, who lacked access to any system that could support rape victims or advocate on their behalf. De Pizan's work takes a bold step in directly addressing this controversial topic. It was often assumed that sexual violence was something women just had to endure, and that men were born with aggressive, insatiable sexual appetites. Such attitudes were allowed to endure as long as men held the positions of power and silenced the voices of women. Some rapists justified their actions by avowing that women wanted to be raped, enjoyed it, or, in some way, "asked for it." Christine was just one of many women who spoke out against the horrors of rape and identified it as a serious crime.

---

4. *But, just as I told you before, the fool sees his neighbor's peccadillo and fails to see his own enormous crime.*

Rectitude makes this statement in Part Two, section 66.1, when she is discussing the nature of greed and whether women have more of a propensity for avarice than men. Her words take on the nature of an aphorism and resemble a Biblical phrase or the moral to an allegorical tale. They are basically a means of restating the tenet "Judge not lest ye be judged" and show the degree to which the book is intended to instruct people in proper conduct. Rectitude's observation emphasizes the heart of the critiques Christine makes throughout her work. Women would not be so maligned, she argues, if men were not so concerned with searching for and exaggerating their flaws. If men scrutinized their own failings, they could hardly match up to the shortcomings of others. *Peccadillos* are minor behavioral missteps or slight social mistakes. When compared to immoral or destructive acts, their importance is negligible. In making this statement, Rectitude is pinpointing the major source of the world's conflicts and misrepresentations. Christian teachings, and Christine's own ethic, teach acceptance and tolerance and stress individual improvement as opposed to severe criticism or self-inflation at another's expense.

---

5. *Most excellent, revered, and honored princesses of France and of all lands, and all ladies and maidens, and, indeed, all women who have loved and do love and will love virtue and morality, as well as all who have died or who are now living or who are to come, rejoice and exult in our new City which, thanks to God, is already formed and almost finished and populated.*

Christine speaks these words in Part Two, section 69.1. With this pronouncement, she is, in effect, declaring the City of Ladies open and ready to house and nurture the scores of women who will come to take up residence there. This statement is a conclusion to the book's second part as well as a transition to the final sentiments contained in Part Three. Christine is welcoming the women who have been summoned through the narration and storytelling that comprise most of the work. They represent the earthly realm of women and the numerous good works and improvements women have contributed to human life. Then, in a nod to the book's concluding section, Christine gives thanks to God, who will ordain and sanctify the city.

In her declaration, Christine establishes two important precedents that her work and the organizing principles of the City of Ladies subscribe to. First of all, although she acknowledges a hierarchy of women and women's roles from princess to ladies to maidens, she makes it clear that all women, regardless of class or social standing, have a place in her city. By doing this, Christine is erasing one of the factors that divide and separate women, in an attempt to create greater unity and sisterhood. Second, Christine establishes a historical continuum, including women from the past and present and invoking the women of the future. In this way, Christine hopes to universalize the experiences of women and not just speak to readers of her time. She attempts to unify the past and the present in order to ensure a brighter future in which women, united and strong, openly resist the abuse and misrepresentation they have suffered.

B

A Border Passage

Leila Ahmed
(1940–)

CONTEXT

Born in 1940 in Cairo, Leila Ahmed grew up during a time of major political change in Egypt. As a result, the complicated relationship between Egypt, Europe, and the Middle East is a central concern in Ahmed's memoir, *A Border Passage*, and understanding that relationship requires a closer look at Egypt's turbulent modern history. Egypt's national identity and borders have existed since ancient times, but its people were ruled by foreign invaders and empires such as Alexander the Great, the Arabs, and the Ottoman Empire, until they finally attained full national sovereignty in 1952. Situated in North Africa, Egypt shares borders with Libya, Sudan, and Israel. During the eighteenth and nineteenth centuries, Egypt developed a unique position regarding its neighbors in the Middle East through shifting alliances with the Ottoman Empire and the West. Egypt was ruled by the Turks until the British Occupation of Egypt began in 1882. Egypt was never officially a British colony, but it was nonetheless shaped by the policies of its rulers in the West.

Egypt prospered under the somewhat relaxed rule of the British through the turn of the nineteenth century, enjoying a free press and open immigration policy that encouraged the immigration of droves of newcomers from both Ottoman and European territories. Free debate contributed to a lively intellectual atmosphere in Egypt, and modern technology such as the automobile appeared in the cosmopolitan centers of Egypt at around the same time it did in Europe. This set Egypt apart from its Middle Eastern neighbors, where the forces of modernization acted at a slower pace. Fearing competition from the increasingly prosperous nation under its rule, however, the British reigned in the full modernization of Egypt well into the twentieth century. The negotiations of Egyptian officials with the British for national independence would spark the partial withdrawal of British forces after World War I and would set the stage for a new Egypt, independent of any foreign interest.

The Great Depression of the 1930s, which so shaped Europe and the United States, was also felt in Egypt, where new classes of educated young men and women were increasingly frustrated by their lack of upward mobility under British rule. Nationalist groups like the Muslim Brotherhood grew during the 1930s, advocating independence from the West and its values. Young Egyptian army officers like Abdel Nasser and Anwar al-Sadat were shaped profoundly by their experience fighting against the Israeli army in the Six Day War, the conflict that presaged the foundation of the state of Israel in 1948 and whose impact can still be felt in the region's geopolitics. They eventually saw the defeat of the Arab cause in that conflict as the failing of a corrupt political establishment in Egypt, and they located themselves at the forefront of change. Egypt's revolution of 1952 was a bloodless one, and the deposed King Farouk was saluted as he sailed to exile in Italy.

Initially, the aims of the revolutionaries in Egypt—ending corruption, injustice, and poverty through progressive social reform—seemed to represent a positive change. However, these high ideals were muted by the dictatorial rule established by Abdel Nasser, who became prime minister of Egypt in 1954. In 1956, Nasser nationalized the Suez Canal in order to both finance the construction of the High Dam, a project designed to control flooding along the Nile River, and further assert Egypt's national independence. The nationalization of the Canal rankled England and France, who had enjoyed its revenues for years. With Israel's aid, British and French forces attacked Egypt, but they were quickly forced to withdraw as a result of loud international outcry and pressure from the United States. In 1958, Egypt joined Syria to form the United Arab Republic, a pact that only lasted a few years. In 1971, the country was renamed the United Republic of Egypt.

In *A Border Passage*, Ahmed also touches on issues that are still being debated today, including whether there is a true interpretation of Islam and how non-Western women fit into the discipline of women's studies. In a post-September 11th world, some writers have pointed to violent passages in Muslim doctrine to paint Islam as a violent faith, though Ahmed convincingly argues that it is the interpretation of that doctrine and the way it is used by various political powers that make it such a pawn in religious conflicts. Ahmed notes the similarities between the oral traditions in Judaism and Islam, further reinforcing the way that major world faiths are compatible and consistent with each other, rather than at odds. In keeping with her respect for multiple interpretations, Ahmed became a part of a major movement that took shape in the 1990s to bring a renewed interest on college campuses to nonwhite and non-Western perspectives in academia. She has taught in the women's studies departments of the University of Massachusetts at Amherst and the Harvard Divinity School. In addition, Ahmed is the author of two other books: a biography of Edward William Lane, begun during her graduate study at Cambridge, and a critical study entitled *Women and Gender in Islam.*

PLOT OVERVIEW

Growing up during the last days of the British colonial presence in Egypt, Leila Ahmed's childhood is marked by a collision of cultures. Among Syrians, Lebanese, Palestinians, and other Egyptians from a similar class background in school, young Ahmed considers it quite normal to grow up speaking English or French and being called by the anglicized name "Lily" in school. Ahmed lives in Cairo, at the crossroads of spiritual hubs, ancient sites, and modern sprawl, in a beautiful house known as Ain Shams. Her father is an esteemed engineer who, as chairman of the Nile Water Control Board, had run into trouble with the government for opposing their plan to build the High Dam on ecological grounds. Though her father's concerns about the fate of the Nile River will ultimately be born out by the facts, his opposition to the government's grand improvement project will haunt him for years to come. Later, he will be harassed by authorities and have his bank account frozen.

As a young child, Ahmed is very attached to Nanny, her Croatian governess. Nanny is a deeply religious Christian and tells Ahmed stories of angels and the supernatural. Ahmed has a more conflicted relationship with her mother. Ahmed aspires to be a professional and views her mother with contempt for not working. Later, when Ahmed's father falls ill with chronic pneumonia, Ahmed will come to value her mother's dedication more, as well as the strength of the bond between her parents. One of Ahmed's closest childhood friends is Gina, a neighbor girl and the daughter of Italian parents. Gina's older brother, Freddy, subjects Ahmed to brutal and sexual games when she is around eight years old, and when Ahmed's mother finds out about it, she beats her and takes her to a doctor to be examined. In the aftermath of this event, Ahmed is forbidden to play outside, even with Gina, and is subjected to her mother's disdain, furthering the rift between mother and daughter.

Ahmed's view of Islam is shaped through the time she spends at her mother's childhood home of Zatoun, in Cairo, where Ahmed is surrounded by a rich and engaging community of women. While listening to her mother, grandmother, and other women converse, Ahmed learns about Islam as being a generous and pacifistic faith. Though she receives no direct religious instruction from these women, and her father has decided not to send her to an Islamic school, Ahmed nonetheless comes to appreciate the oral, living tradition of Islam, which, in contrast to the rigid, authoritative Islam that is handed down in texts, encompasses many interpretations. As much as she recognizes the positive force that this humane form of Islam has manifested in her family's life, she also recognizes the powerlessness of her mother and grandmother in the society they live in. Ahmed's grandmother, for instance, has for years been mourning the suicide of her son Fuad, a tragedy she blames on her husband's disapproval of Fuad. A similar fate befell Grandmother's daughter Aida, who committed suicide after being unable to secure permission for a divorce from an unhappy marriage through the stern figure of Grandfather. Because of these tragedies, the estate of Zatoun always seems to have a pall of gloom over it in young Ahmed's eyes.

Ahmed attends a British school in the suburbs of Cairo and prefers play to work, though her test scores and voracious appetite for books help her move ahead quickly in school. Jews and Muslims at the school are excused from the daily Christian prayers, and that's how Ahmed meets and befriends Joyce, a Jewish girl in her grade. Ahmed is encouraged to skip a grade, but her academic ambitions are tempered by the school's English headmaster, Mr. Price, who accuses her of plagiarizing her own well-written essays. Ahmed likewise finds her English teachers discouraging of her ambitions of pursuing science or mathematics. In school, Ahmed studies the history, geography, and flora and fauna of Europe, while learning little about that of her own country. Still, Ahmed isn't completely insulated from the politics of her day. She recognizes the growing influence of a group called the Muslim Brotherhood, which stands in opposition to colonialism and Western influence in the Middle East.

Ahmed is soon headed to Cambridge, England, to study literature, a place she reveres as an intellectual wonderland and the embodiment of all the things she remembers reading in English books as a child—forests, fog, turrets, and towers. Here, Ahmed finds a different kind of community of women in teachers like Mrs. Madge and Miss Bradbrook, and with friends like Veena, an Indian woman who shares some of Ahmed's feelings of displacement. At Cambridge, Ahmed experiences a more genteel form of racism, a feeling of being lumped together with all the people who aren't part of the white British establishment, no matter what their race or cultural background. Between her undergraduate and graduate days, Ahmed returns to Egypt to find it totally changed. Her father is gravely ill, and she can tell that her mother had suffered the burden of her father's illness as well as persecution via Nasser's increasingly repressive regime. Upon returning to Cambridge to begin graduate studies, Ahmed meets Alan, the man she will marry and eventually divorce.

During her graduate studies, Ahmed yearns for a place in the academy for the voices from the margins—blacks, women, and people from the third world. Toward the end of her graduate student days, Ahmed begins to suffer from a mysterious illness. After several frustrating visits with different doctors, Ahmed is finally diagnosed with sarcodosis, a chronic autoimmune disease. Ahmed reads Edward Said's *Orientalism* while trying to sort out her place as an Egyptian woman in the West. After leaving Cambridge, Ahmed accepts a teaching position in Abu Dhabi and joins a committee to help reform education throughout the United Arab Emirates. Recognizing the unique qualities of this "Gulf Arabic" culture helps her to re-examine the implications of her own "Egyptian Arabic" identity and her place in the larger Arab world. Ahmed moves to the United States and finds that the atmosphere in women's studies departments in the 1980s is not exactly hospitable to the viewpoints of women from other cultures. However, she does find her new environment exciting and intellectually stimulating, and even as she endeavors to make a contribution to her the world of ideas in her new home, she never turns her back on her Egyptian heritage.

CHARACTER LIST

Leila Ahmed An Egyptian woman and academic. Ahmed grew up in Cairo and attended an English school until she ultimately left Egypt to attend Cambridge University in England. Ahmed constantly finds herself in places where cultures intersect, clash, or inform each other, from her childhood in an English school in Cairo to her young adulthood in England to her experience as an academic in the United States. Chief among Ahmed's concerns is understanding the labels that are applied to her—Egyptian, Arab, black, feminist, intellectual—and unraveling the implications of being a Arab woman in the modern world.

Ahmed's Mother A Turkish woman and member of the upper class. Ahmed and her mother have a conflicted relationship, partially because of an incident that occurs when Ahmed is younger than ten. Ahmed's mother does not work, so she takes care of her husband when he becomes ill with chronic pneumonia. She draws Ahmed into a community of women that will forever influence Ahmed's view on Islamic culture.

Ahmed's Father An esteemed engineer and native Egyptian. Ahmed's father's life changes when he decides to oppose Prime Minister and President Nasser's plan to build the High Dam. Ahmed's father has legitimate environmental concerns, but his opposition costs him dearly, as he is persecuted by the government for the rest of his life. In her father, Ahmed also sees the roots of "colonial consciousness," an acceptance or even reverence for the culture of the oppressor.

Nanny The governess who looks after Ahmed. Nanny, a Croatian woman, is sixty years old when Ahmed is born. During Ahmed's childhood, Nanny is her closest companion, though Nanny seems to be in constant conflict with Ahmed's mother. From Nanny, Ahmed adopts a reverent attitude for the world of the unseen, a world of ghosts and angels drawn from Nanny's deep Christian faith.

Samia Ahmed's cousin, four years her senior. Samia visits Ain Shams, Ahmed's home in Cairo, and spends hours discussing her love life with Ahmed's mother. Ahmed is perhaps envious of this relationship, one in which her mother offers wise and even-handed advice. If Samia were her own daughter, Ahmed's mother would, Ahmed is certain, be more judgmental.

Grandmother Ahmed's mother's mother. Grandmother presides over the lively group of women friends and relatives who gather in her home, Zatoun, to discuss everything from their lives to Islam to world events. Grandmother is in perpetual mourning over her son Fuad, who committed suicide, a tragedy she blames on unending conflict with his father.

Grandfather Ahmed's mother's father. Grandfather dresses well and is very formal, and he instills fear and reverence in his many children. Ahmed points to Grandfather's sternness and religious rigidity as contributing factors in the suicides of two of his children, Aida and Fuad.

Um Said Grandmother's servant. Um Said has been Grandmother's servant since she was a girl, and, accordingly, they have a very close relationship. Grandmother arranged Um Said's marriage, and though her husband has taken another wife, Um Said is still reluctant to divorce him. Um Said is the only servant welcome in the salon of women over which Grandmother presides.

Yusef Ahmed's mother's brother. Yusef was his family's only male heir, so he is responsible for carrying on the family line. Yusef married a French woman named Colette who converted to Islam for him. Diagnosed with terminal lung cancer in his thirties, Yusef bowed to family pressure to divorce the infertile Collette and accept a new bride, only to have this arrangement end disastrously.

Gina Ahmed's childhood friend and neighbor. Gina is an Italian girl who spends long afternoons playing with Ahmed in the sprawling, beautiful garden that surrounds her house.

B

Freddy Gina's older brother. Freddy is six years older than Ahmed and subjects her to humiliating sexual games when she is eight or nine. Ahmed attempts to run away from and otherwise avoid Freddy, but he holds the threat of revealing everything about her over her head. Finally, the truth about Freddy's "games" comes out, and Ahmed is forbidden to ever play outside.

Joyce Ahmed's schoolmate and best friend. Joyce meets Ahmed when they are six at the English school they attend together. The two girls bond over the fact that they are excused from daily Christian prayers, as Joyce is Jewish and Ahmed is Muslim. Together, they share a passion for American movies. After the later conflagration with British, French, and Israeli forces over the Suez Canal, Joyce's family leaves the country, fearing persecution over their religion. Ahmed never hears from her again.

Jean Said Another schoolmate and friend of Ahmed's. Jean comes from a Christian Palestinian family and is the younger sister of Edward Said, the well-known scholar of Middle Eastern studies.

Karima Ahmed's mother's cousin. Karima was orphaned as a child and inherited enough money to live comfortably and independently. Karima represents a contrast to the fate of Aida in Ahmed's mind. Karima also found herself in an unhappy marriage, but since she had married on her own terms and knew how to invoke an Islamic law that would allow her to divorce, Karima was able to negotiate her way out of an untenable situation.

Aida Ahmed's mother's sister. Aida finds herself in a disastrous marriage, though her father won't allow her to divorce. Depressed and hopeless, Aida begins to take pills. Her husband arranged for her to get electroshock treatments, but nothing helps her. Aida finally resorts to suicide. To Ahmed, Aida's story represents a cautionary tale of what can happen to women in a rigid, patriarchal society.

Mr. Price The headmaster of Ahmed's English school. Mr. Price is doubtful that Ahmed could have written the essays she hands in. Ahmed's experience with Mr. Price opens her eyes to how people are categorized due to their culture, race, and gender.

Veena A fellow student at Cambridge. Veena, from a poor village in India, is a brilliant student of theoretical biochemistry, and a practicing Hindu and vegetarian. Veena falls in love with a Czech student, and when his family forbids their marriage, Veena has a nervous breakdown. In Veena's predicament, Ahmed discerns echoes of the circumstances of women in her family and throughout the Arab world.

Alan Ahmed's husband. Alan is an American and meets Ahmed during their graduate studies. They get married while Ahmed's mother is at Cambridge. Alan converts to Islam in order to win Ahmed's mother's approval, though the marriage lasts only a few years.

ANALYSIS OF MAJOR CHARACTERS

LEILA AHMED In *A Border Passage*, Leila Ahmed searches for the meaning of her identity as a woman, an Arab, and an Egyptian, as well as an understanding of how being in those categories shapes her place in the world. As a child, she moves unthinkingly between the imaginative realm of her home, the women's community at her grandmother's house, and an English school in which Western ideas are revered over all others, but she ultimately learns that negotiating such cultural and social borders has serious consequences. Her playmates hail from many parts of the world and from many different faiths, and Ahmed understands the implications of those cultural and religious differences only after experiencing the turmoil of her country's quest for independence and leaving Egypt to explore the larger world. While at Cambridge, Ahmed struggles to understand how her intelligent classmates can practice such a genteel form of racism, lumping together all students from the third world under the banner of "black." Ahmed's investigation of such categories becomes central to her academic pursuits.

Through her highly personal writing, Ahmed makes many connections between her own experiences and politics, showing how personal decisions and identities resonate in the larger world. Ahmed locates her political awakening in her childhood, when she first discovered the contrast between men's and women's ways of knowing and discussing Islam in her grandmother's living room. This discovery colors her further investigations into religious, race, and gender studies, as Ahmed works to unravel the diverse strands of her upbringing. In her memoir, Ahmed reveals what it means to move across the world's increasingly fluid borders, and she offers a view of history that is more powerful because it is so personal. Her identity is shaped by a feeling of cultural displacement as an Egyptian student in an English school in Cairo, and then as a minority student at Cambridge, and Ahmed applies keen insight to the question of what it means to be an Arab woman in the modern world. As an adult, Ahmed is able to embrace varying labels—Muslim feminist, intellectual, Egyptian, Arab—while bringing a nuanced understanding of how those labels both limit and define those who adopt them.

AHMED'S MOTHER Ahmed's mother is complicated and difficult regarding both her place in society and her relationship with Ahmed. Ethnically Turkish, the nationality of the ruling class of Egypt before the British took power in the late nineteenth century, Ahmed's mother is afforded many privileges by virtue of her station in life. She doesn't have to work, a fact that Ahmed looks down upon when she is a teenager. Ahmed herself vows to have a professional identity and set herself apart from her mother in whatever ways she can. The biggest rift in their relationship occurs when Ahmed is around eight or nine, when her mother finds out that a neighbor boy has been subjecting Ahmed to humiliating sexual games. Her shock and disdain are traumatic for Ahmed, who, after this discovery, is estranged from her mother for several months. Her mother's preoccupation with traditional moral values and the appearance of propriety gets in the way of her offering her daughter the support that she needs after such a traumatic event.

Despite Ahmed's conflict with her mother, she still reveres her for the influences she's brought to her life. Through her mother and grandmother, Ahmed is granted entry into a community of women, where she absorbs Islam's rich and humane oral tradition. Ahmed recognizes the challenges that face her mother's generation: while they are the keepers and transmitters of these deep religious ethics, they possess little consciousness of how their culture takes away their voices. Ahmed also knows that the class who will change the status of women in Egypt is the middle class, not her mother's class, where education and upward mobility are not chief concerns.

AHMED'S FATHER Through her father, Ahmed is able to witness the costs of the shifting political fortunes of Egypt. As the Chairman of the Hydro-Electric Power Corporation, Ahmed's father opposes Prime Minister Nasser's plan to build the Aswan High Dam on ecological grounds. The Dam is a highly important project for the Nasser regime: it will establish Egypt's ability to take on grand modernization projects, and its construction involves further establishing Egypt's independence from France and England. Nothing sways Ahmed's father from him idealistic position, and he goes on to publish books in the 1950s condemning the plan, which are confiscated by the government. Ahmed views her father as so invested in his scientific ideals that he is unable to see the political consequences of his actions. The stubborn stance he takes will haunt him for the rest of his life, as the government meddles in his financial and personal affairs and harasses his family.

Ahmed's father is the source of much of Ahmed's conflict regarding the multiple cultures that surround her. He does not send his children to an Islamic school to study the Quran, in part because of his traumatic experience there as a child, being beaten by stern teachers for small infractions. A native Egyptian, Ahmed's father earns part of his status in society by marrying a member of the Turkish upper-classes—Turks were the ruling class of the Ottoman Empire and thus enjoyed high standing in Egyptian society. Nonetheless, Ahmed's father constantly hits boundaries in his professional life. When he is a student, for instance, British authorities, fearing the expansion of the educated, skilled classes in Egypt, demand he switch majors from engineering to geography in order to receive a scholarship. Despite his setbacks, Ahmed's father never loses his reverence for British culture and ideas, an attitude that Ahmed chalks up to "colonial consciousness," or an atmosphere in which the colonized begin to internalize the ideology that oppresses them.

THEMES, MOTIFS, AND SYMBOLS

THEMES

THE EXISTENCE OF TWO ISLAMS Ahmed believes that Islam can be separated into two distinctly different, often-contradictory strands: the expansive, pacifist oral tradition, and the more rigid, authoritarian written tradition. Islam's oral tradition is one that she associates with women, and she was immersed in it as a young child at her grandmother's house in Cairo. In this tradition, she finds multiple possibilities and a humane orientation toward the world. As she examines the impact of faith on her own identity and in the larger world, Ahmed associates Islam's rigid written tradition with the rise of fundamentalism. Fundamentalism, in Ahmed's view, obscures much of the beauty and meaning she was raised to associate with her faith. She finally points to this split as being responsible for abuse of politic power, as rigid interpretations of Islam become tools in the hands of religious demagogues.

B

THE RICHNESS OF CULTURAL PLURALISM Ahmed is raised speaking English, French, and Arabic, and schooled in England, and her entire life is defined by a collision of different cultural influences. Though she recognizes the inherent problems in being caught between two worlds, for Ahmed this plurality of influences is a rich part of her identity. As she makes an intellectual home for herself in Cambridge, England, Ahmed traces the influences in books that have brought her to this place. When she accepts a teaching job in the United Arab Emirates, Ahmed notes the differences between that "Gulf Arabic" culture and her own "Egyptian Arabic" culture. Appreciating such cultural intersections allows Ahmed to better understand what it means to be Egyptian.

THE POLITICS OF LANGUAGE The very language that people use in expressing themselves has political implications—it defines identity and often limits potential according to the labels people must wear. Through speaking English as a child in a British school, Ahmed comes to see the Arabic of her parents as inferior to the languages of western Europe. Given the anglicized name "Lily" in school, Ahmed examines the implications of denying her own cultural identity to adopt a new one only in later years, when she recalls her confusion at meeting Nasser and not knowing what to say her name is. While at Cambridge, Ahmed, like any other person from a third-world country, is labeled "black," which prompts her to unravel the real implications of such labels as "Egyptian," "African," and "Arab."

THE PREVALENCE OF COLONIAL CONSCIOUSNESS Growing up in Egypt before it had attained independence from colonial influences, Ahmed draws a stark picture of the way the Egyptians internalized a "colonial consciousness" in their reverence for all things British. This is an attitude she particularly ascribes to her father, who, despite being held back professionally by British policies, still seems to see British culture as superior to his own native Egyptian culture. Ahmed traces the rapid political changes that will end the Western colonial presence in much of the Middle East and points to political writers like Frantz Fanon and Albert Memmi, who were instrumental in dismantling colonial consciousness through their influential critiques of the dynamic between the colonizer and the colonized. She also notes the positive sides of Egypt's existence under British rule: the fact that the British presence helped speed Egypt's modernization and created a somewhat free press. In exploring the complicated legacy of colonial rule, Ahmed traces the implications of politics on a more personal level.

MOTIFS

PLACE From the enchanting gardens of her Cairo home, Ain Shams, to the spires and forests of England, location figures prominently into *A Border Passage*. Ahmed's environment helps her define her place in relation to the world, and she uses the idea of place to explore the tensions of identity in a world where cultural identifications are complex and politically loaded. Ain Shams is where Ahmed develops her powers of imagination. Zatoun, her grandmother's estate, is where she discovers a community of women who shape her attitudes toward Islam. At Cambridge, Ahmed finds another type of community of women, one that will introduce her to a world of ideas.

CULTURAL DISPLACEMENT Again and again, Ahmed faces a feeling of being displaced—whether she is in Egypt, England, or the United States. She traces her consciousness of her own cultural identity to her school days, where she recognizes a subtle form of racism from her English teachers because of her status as an Egyptian. One teacher accuses her of plagiarizing her well-written papers, and others discourage her from pursuing math or science. At Cambridge, Ahmed finds herself surprised to be labeled "black" and lumped together with many other students from the third world. While in Abu Dhabi, Ahmed confronts once again what it means to be an Arab woman in an Arab culture that holds as many differences as it does similarities to the culture she knows in Egypt.

B

COMMUNITIES OF WOMEN Throughout her life, Ahmed draws strength and intellectual wealth from communities of women. The most formative of these is the group of women Ahmed interacts with at her grandmother's home, Zatoun. Here, Ahmed is steeped in the rich, multilayered tradition of Islam, and she comes to understand how the oral traditions of Arab women are different from the written, and more rigid, traditions of men. At Cambridge, Ahmed joins another important community of women, which feeds her intellectual curiosity and fosters her growth as an academic thinker. Finally, Ahmed circulates in women's studies departments in the United States in the early 1980s, finding them not exactly receptive to the input of third world women, but stimulating nonetheless.

SYMBOLS

THE HAREM In Chapter 8, Ahmed sees the community of women she is immersed in at Cambridge as a "harem perfected." Instead of belonging to the realm of male fantasy, the harem suggests for Ahmed a nurturing community of women in which the old preside over the young—and in this way is similar to the community of women that she knew as a child, at her grandmother's house. By transposing an image of great symbolic power from her own culture to a Western one, Ahmed reclaims its power to represent a haven for women. Though the harem is traditionally seen as a symbol of female subservience, Ahmed seems to be suggesting that at Cambridge it became a manifestation truer to its historical roots.

ANGELS For the young Ahmed, angels represent the magic and mysteries of the unseen world and were first introduced to her as a concept by her deeply religious nanny. Angels are a unifying symbol of both Nanny's faith and Ahmed's Islam. Ahmed recalls her grandmother telling her that during the holy month of Ramadan, God allows angels to descend freely, and one can see them if one looks hard enough. She also recalls the sense of wonder that overtook her as she stood on a Cairo rooftop, waiting for the angels to appear. As a symbol of a rich, hidden world, angels serve as a concrete manifestation of the imaginative world that Ahmed develops as a child.

MUSIC Ahmed writes of her childhood as having "its own music," a music that is symbolic of both a sense of innocence and the seemingly effortless blending of disparate cultural influences that marked her childhood. This imagery of music helps brings together the past and present, an overlapping of thousand-year-old artifacts and religious sites and a young girl's dawning political consciousness. This music also unites place, the beautiful garden of Ain Shams with the gloomy richness of Zatoun, and Ahmed's family's trips to the shore. Ahmed's childhood, characterized by a unifying music, contrasts with her later experience of displacement, as she spends time in several places where diverse cultural influences are not so easily blended together.

IMPORTANT QUOTATIONS EXPLAINED

1. *Egyptians, for instance, might, with equal accuracy, define themselves as African, Nilotic, Mediterranean, Islamic, or Coptic. Or as all, or any combination of, the above. Or, of course, as Egyptian: pertaining to the land of Egypt.*

In exploring the number of labels that can be applied to Egyptians in Chapter 1, Ahmed pinpoints a problem of identity that is uniquely Egyptian and anticipates the challenges of identification that arise for any minority group. As Ahmed shows, Egyptian identity is inextricably tied to a turbulent history under which Egyptians were ruled by, and absorbed the influences of, a number of different ruling parties, from the Arabs to the Turks to the British. The "land of Egypt" itself defies category, situated as it is between Africa and the Middle East. With that taken into account, and with all of the influences that have shaped Egypt over the millennia, is there a distinctly "Egyptian" identity? This is one of the central questions that directs Ahmed's inquiry into her past and the history of her homeland. Her investigation reveals a complex answer to this question—that yes, we are defined by our religious faith, our culture, and our national identifications, but ultimately, we are uniquely formed out of multiple influences.

B

Through the quote and the general thrust of her book, Ahmed reveals that questions of national identity cannot be answered with simple labels. To be called "Egyptian" in the world today carries the weight of thousands of years of history, not to mention the associations placed on the Islamic faith in a time of numerous world conflicts over faith exist. In describing her childhood in Cairo, where ancient ruins and modern sprawl coexist, Ahmed contemplates how complex those identifications can be. In some ways, labels are what she carries with her, categories that change shape and meaning depending on her surroundings. While in England, Ahmed will be labeled a "black," the catch-all term for any person of color, sparking a renewed interest in exactly the issue that she talks about in this quote. Are Egyptians primarily Africans? Or is their major identification with Islam? The answer that Ahmed arrives at is a complex consideration of the disparate elements that have made her: she can take ownership of labels like "Egyptian," "Muslim," and "feminist" and still assert her identity as an individual.

2. *[W]e all automatically assume that those who write and who put their knowledge down in texts have something more valuable to offer than those who simply live their knowledge and use it to inform their lives.*

In this remark from Chapter 5, Ahmed explores the inherent conflict between "written Islam" and "living Islam"—that is, the oral tradition of religious stories and teachings that she knows from her grandmother's circle. In Ahmed's eyes, written Islam has been given more authority than it deserves, partially through the Western academic world, which values texts over all other manifestations of a given faith. The contrast to the official Islam of ancient texts is the living Islam that Ahmed experiences in the company of women in Egypt. This type of Islam is welcoming and humane, yet its ethical core is often rejected by the sheiks and ayatollahs who hold sway in the Muslim world. Ahmed argues that such an oral and aural component of Islam is intrinsic to the faith and also the Arabic language. She highlights a similarity between Arabic and Hebrew: no vowels are seen in written text, and so in a sense, the text cannot fully be realized until someone literally breathes life into it through voice. In this way, she emphasizes the importance of people who "live their knowledge," as their knowledge is more alive, possessing many more dimensions than a rigid, literal interpretation.

This comment also points to the high esteem in which Ahmed holds the example set by the women around her. She indicates how much she has been shaped by absorbing their values and interpretations of Islam. She also recognizes the impact on the lives of the women around her the realities of living in a society where women's prerogatives are not honored. She witnesses the fate of her Aunt Aida, who, forbidden to leave an unhappy marriage by her strict father, commits suicide. Ahmed views with disdain her mother's traditional values and lack of a professional identity. She also feels pity for her grandmother, who is sentenced to a life of grief after the suicide of her son—a suicide that came about because of the son's conflicted relationship with the family's strict patriarch. Though she benefits greatly from the teachings and influence of the women around her, Ahmed is still critical of their refusal to see the implications of their roles in society.

3. *[T]he devastation unloosed on Muslim societies in our day by fundamentalism . . . seems to be not merely the erasure of the living, oral, ethical, and human traditions of Islam but the literal destruction of and annihilation of the Muslims who are the bearers of those traditions. In Algeria, Iran, Afghanistan, and, alas, in Egypt, this narrow, violent variant of Islam is ravaging its way through the land.*

In this passage from Chapter 5, Ahmed further explores the conflict between the way religious ethics are lived and the way they are taught, especially pertaining to our contemporary global political climate. Though some may see Islam as a violent faith, Ahmed writes that it is violent only when it falls into the hands of extremists and fundamentalists, who bend and twist ancient texts to support their fanatical world views. Such a major world faith must leave room for multiple interpretations, even for those who want to go by "the book." Ahmed writes about how Muslim scholars used to study many texts in order to understand various objections and debates and to come to an informed consensus regarding theological interpretations. More radical Muslims today, Ahmed writes, take their literal truth from one text only.

Written Islam, Ahmed points out, is not the Islam of the "book," the Quran, but the Islam of medieval texts that give rise to rigid, fundamentalist interpretation of religious doctrine. This is also what Ahmed recognizes as "official Islam," something that the Muslims she identifies with, conditioned by living under numerous authoritarian regimes that co-opt their faith, reject on principle. Her critique of this narrow view emphasizes the importance of considering multiple points of view, whether evaluating a text or examining the larger implications of the ethics that grow from faith. Ahmed sees the living manifestations of religious ethics all around her, especially in women. This is a living, expansive expression of faith, in contrast to the type of Islam she talks about in this quote, which is restrictive and often hostile.

B

4. *We lived in fact, throughout our childhoods, easily and unthinkingly crossing thresholds between one place and another—Ain Shams, Zatoun, our school—places that formed their own particular and different worlds with their own particular and different underlying beliefs, ideals, assumptions.*

In this phrase describing the landscape of her childhood from Chapter 6, Ahmed finds herself at the crossroads of influences and culture that will so often haunt her sense of identity. Ain Shams is the name of Ahmed's childhood home in Cairo, where, in the grand and sprawling garden, she develops an imaginative identity that permeates her lyrical writing about this time in her life. Zatoun is her grandparents' house, a place where Ahmed grows acquainted with a rich community of female relatives and the oral tradition through which they experience Islam. Ahmed identifies this interpretation of Islam as feminine and humane, accepting of multiple interpretations, and a rich, living manifestation of centuries-old religious ethics. Ahmed's school is British, where speaking English is second nature and ideas and values central to the Western tradition supersede those belonging to the Arab world.

Ahmed's analysis of how easily she moved between the three worlds is significant in the way it contrasts with her adult understanding of the more rigid boundaries and categories that apply to women and Arabs in the world. While at Cambridge, she finds herself lumped together with all other students from the third world and subjected to a sort of "genteel" racism that inherently devalues her non-Western perspective. She also comes to understand the implication of the "colonial consciousness" that afflicted the Egypt of her childhood, especially through her father, who revered all things British while failing to see the ways the British colonial authorities held back his career as an engineer. As an academic in the United States, she experiences difficulty getting her voice as a foreign woman heard in women's studies departments in the early 1980s. Whether in Egypt or elsewhere in the world, she comes to understand the overt and more subtle ways racism is used to marginalize the perspective of minorities.

5. *"One is not born but rather becomes a woman," goes Simone de Beauvoir's famous dictum. I obviously was not born but became black when I went to England. Similarly, of course, I was not born but became a woman of color when I went to America.*

In this quote from Chapter 10, Ahmed explores a feeling of cultural displacement that comes through being viewed as "other" by the dominant class in whatever culture she finds herself. In this passage, Ahmed details her dawning consciousness of what it means to be "marked" with a label and how such categorization is inherently limiting. Ahmed had faced this sort of discrimination before, during her school days, through British teachers who accused her of plagiarizing her papers and discouraged her from pursuing math or science, subjects that weren't considered appropriate for a young Arab girl. Ahmed's experience of this kind of labeling and subtle racism is a major factor in directing her academic interests toward advocating on behalf of minority perspectives. During the 1980s, she witnesses an academic revolution in which the fields of women's studies and cultural studies flower into vibrant disciplines with much new scholarship.

Ahmed compares the "genteel racism" she experiences at Cambridge to the feminist writer Betty Friedan's description of the "problem that has no name." Just as Friedan wrote about women who predated feminism—women who were unable to give voice to their dissatisfaction—Ahmed demonstrates how minority perspectives are undermined in a pervasive and yet subtle way. The problem runs much deeper than instantly being cast as a member of a minority group, and correcting such simple categorization is a complicated task. It begins with naming the problem and offering a wealth of minority voices that, before the 1980s, were virtually unheard within campuses in England and the United States. One of the objectives of her memoir, as well, seems to be that by grappling with such artificial categories, she can transcend them. Ahmed dedicates herself to changing the status of women and minorities in academia, and this quote traces the experiences that first galvanized her.

Bread Givers

Anzia Yezierska ([1880–1885]–1970)

CONTEXT

Anzia Yezierska was born sometime between 1880 and 1885 in a small Polish village. Her father was a Talmudic scholar, and the large family lived on the money her mother made from peddling goods, as well as on contributions from neighbors, who honored the way the family supported their studious and holy father.

Yezierska and her family immigrated to New York City in around 1890. Her brother Meyer, one of Yezierska's eight siblings, had come over several years earlier and changed his name to Max Mayer. He gave his new surname to his family, so for a time, Anzia Yezierska became Hattie Mayer. Young Hattie had a variety of jobs, first peddling homemade paper bags on Hester Street and later becoming a laundress, waitress, and sweatshop worker. Rebelling against her parents' wishes that she assume a traditional path, she left home at age seventeen to live at the Clara de Hirsch home for working girls—one of the city's charitable shelters. She continued her education and earned a four-year scholarship to study domestic science at Teachers College at Columbia University in New York City. Though bitterly disappointed that in many cases "domestic science" meant nothing more than cooking classes, she graduated and went on to hold a succession of teaching jobs before leaving for a time to room at the socialist dormitory of the Rand School, also in New York City. There, she socialized with well-known, outspoken women, such as Charlotte Perkins Gilman, and absorbed iconoclastic ideas about marriage and women's independence that expanded and strengthened her own views. During this period, Yezierska married two times: she had the first marriage annulled, and she left the second after three years. The second marriage yielded a daughter, Louise, whom Yezierska eventually left for her former husband to raise.

Yezierska published her first story in 1915, and she began receiving wide recognition for her writing in 1919. She published her first novel, *Salome of the Tenements*, in 1923. In each of her books, Yezierska worked to recreate the feelings of the immigrant girl she had once been, trying to break away from the oppressive strictures of her religion and make a place for herself in a new land. Yezierska also recalled the conditions she'd grown up in by repeatedly echoing the tumultuous relationship she had with her father, whom she respected for his holiness but resented for his complete rejection of her work. She continued to revisit the distance between her and her father in her books, even as critical response dimmed and friends begged her to find something new to write about. Yezierska's final published book, a fictionalized autobiography, *Red Ribbon on a White Horse*, was one last retelling of the story she had spent her entire life writing. She died in 1970.

Though Yezierska achieved a measure of success during her lifetime, it was always a struggle. In America, she had to overcome many obstacles that weren't so different from the obstacles Jewish women had to face in her home county—that is, she had to fight for the privilege of being independent. Usually, the only aspect of the American dream available to women was the expectation of marriage and motherhood, varied only by a factory job or, if the girl was lucky, work as a typist or a salesgirl. The highest aspiration for a Jewish girl was to become a teacher, a goal that went against many of the norms at the time. However, becoming a teacher meant the family had to support her in school until she was eighteen or nineteen, and most immigrants couldn't afford such an expense, even with the promise of future returns. If a choice had to be made between sending a daughter or a son to college, parents often chose to send the son because of both religious beliefs and economic reality. The old world and new world were in complete agreement on what a woman should be allowed to do with her life, and Yezierska had to fight to pursue a different path.

Certain factors, however, precluded the permanence of such a restricting arrangement for women. Instead of becoming shy, submissive workers, generations of Polish women became aggressive and articulate, more than capable of holding their own in the world. With the men secluded in religious study, wives and daughters assumed much of the economic burden. They brought in the wages, spotted cheats, haggled over prices, and slowly but surely learned skills that left them better able to transverse the wider world. These women then immigrated to America, full of stories of people with similar skills who had managed to shape new lives for themselves. Though it didn't happen immediately, Jewish women began to be tempted by the possibility of new lives, and they focused on education as the logical starting point for building them. Some Jewish girls, Yezierska included, left home to pursue their dreams; others persuaded their mothers to persuade their fathers to allow them to do so. Whatever the method, Jewish girls began to take the first step in finding their own identity, and by 1916, more than half of the Jewish graduates of Hunter College, one of the prominent schools in the New York City area, were women.

PLOT OVERVIEW

The Smolinsky family is on the verge of starvation. The older daughters, Bessie, Mashah, and Fania, can't find work, and Mashah spends what little money she has to make herself look more beautiful. Their father, Reb Smolinsky, doesn't work at all, spending his days reading holy books and commandeering his daughters' wages—his due as a Jewish father. When Mrs. Smolinsky despairs over the situation, the youngest daughter, Sara, promptly goes outside to sell herring and makes the family some money. Later, the older girls find jobs, and Mrs. Smolinsky rents out the second room, improving the family's financial situation.

Quiet, dutiful Bessie soon falls for a young man named Berel Berenstein and invites him home for dinner one night. The rest of the family is excited for Bessie, but when Reb Smolinsky finds out, he decides he can't live without the wages Bessie brings in. Though Berel is willing to marry Bessie without a dowry, her father says Berel must also pay for the entire wedding and set him up in business as well. Berel refuses and storms out. When he says Bessie should defy her crazy father and marry him at City Hall, Bessie says she doesn't dare. Berel promptly gets engaged to someone else, crushing Bessie's spirit.

Mashah is the next daughter to find a romance that Reb Smolinsky considers inappropriate. She falls in love with Jacob Novak, a piano player from a rich family. Mashah's father disapproves of the match and blackmails Jacob into staying away for several days, breaking Mashah's heart. When Jacob comes back to beg for forgiveness, Mashah feels defeated enough to stand by and let her father kick Jacob out for playing piano on the Sabbath. Reb Smolinsky also disapproves of Fania's sweetheart, a poor poet named Morris Lipkin, and shames him away. He then arranges marriages for all three girls, which leave them all desperately unhappy. Sara is furious with her father for what he's done to her sisters, but her age and gender leave her powerless.

Despite Mrs. Smolinsky's warning, Reb Smolinsky takes all of the money he got from Bessie's marriage and sinks it into a grocery store that the previous owner had filled with fake stock. Sara and Mrs. Smolinsky must again scramble for survival, and each day they endure increasing criticism from Reb Smolinsky. One day, Sara reaches her breaking point. She runs away from home and decides to become a teacher. She plans to live with either Bessie or Mashah, but both have been beaten down by poverty and bad marriages. Instead, she rents a small, dirty, private room of her own. To pay for it, Sara finds a day job in a laundry, using her nights to study and take classes.

The life Sara has chosen is not easy. She faces discrimination for being a woman and living alone; her fellow workers ostracize her; her mother begs her to come home more often; and her unhappy sisters nag her to find a husband of her own. On top of all this, Sara is desperately lonely, and when she is visited by an acquaintance of Fania's, Max Goldstein, she nearly marries him and gives up her dream of seeking knowledge. When she realizes Max is interested only in possessions, however, she refuses him. When Reb Smolinsky hears of this, he's so furious with Sara that he promptly disowns her.

College is another struggle against poverty and loneliness, but Sara wants so badly to be like the clean, beautiful people around her that she perseveres and graduates. She gets a job in the New York school system, buys nicer clothing, and rents a cleaner, larger apartment as a celebration of her new financial independence. Her excitement ends quickly, however, when she learns that her mother, whom she hasn't visited in six years, is dying. Though her mother's deathbed wish is that Sara take care of her father, Reb Smolinsky quickly gets remarried to Mrs. Feinstein, a widow who lives upstairs. His daughters are deeply offended by this insult to their mother, and after Mrs. Feinstein tries to extort money from her new stepchildren, all of them decide to stop speaking to their father.

Furious at her unexpected poverty, Mrs. Feinstein writes a nasty letter to Hugo Seelig, the principal of Sara's school. The letter, however, actually draws Hugo and Sara together, and their bond tightens as they talk of their shared heritage in Poland. This new relationship finally marks the end of Sara's loneliness, and in her new happiness, she decides once again to reach out to her father. Hugo does this as well, and the novel ends with the implication that Reb Smolinsky will soon escape his new wife by moving in with Hugo and Sara. Sara's life has come full circle.

CHARACTER LIST

Sara Smolinsky The youngest Smolinsky daughter and narrator of *Bread Givers*. The most fiercely independent of Reb Smolinsky's daughters, Sara wants more than any of them to create a life of her own. Though she admires her father's dedication and inner flame, she is also deeply resentful of his hypocrisy and the chances he has denied all his daughters. She develops crushes on men with similar dedication and fire, seeking a more willing and understanding role model than Reb Smolinsky, as well as a companion who will acknowledge and appreciate the identity she's struggled to build. Sara is willing to work hard to get what she wants, but her ceaseless craving for companionship and tendency to romanticize her situation sometimes distract her from her ultimate goal.

Reb Smolinsky The head of the Smolinsky family and Sara's major antagonist. Extremely dedicated in his religious beliefs, Reb Smolinsky has devoted his entire life to studying the Torah and other Jewish holy books. The spirit he gathers from these studies fills him with a holy light that leaves others in awe but causes family problems when Reb Smolinsky confuses this spiritual knowledge with more worldly wisdom. His innocence often leads him to make foolish decisions that he refuses to acknowledge, insisting that a man as learned as he could never make such mistakes. After his wife dies, he remarries quickly and forces his daughters to remain with him as long as possible because he knows he needs someone to take care of him.

Shena Smolinsky Sara's mother and Reb Smolinsky's long-suffering wife. Shena is truly in awe of her husband's holiness, though she complains bitterly about the poverty it forces on her. She also feels protective of her husband—he lives so much in his own world that it's hard for him to function in the real one. She firmly believes a woman's highest aspiration is to be a wife and mother, and despite her husband's manipulations, she genuinely wishes to see her daughters settled into good marriages. Though she doesn't understand why Sara desires a different route, she loves her enough to support her in the best way she can.

Bessie Smolinsky The oldest Smolinsky daughter. Bessie is the major financial support for the family, and even at a young age she is worn out from constant stress and work. She despises her father for using up all her good years for himself but is afraid to leave because providing for others is the only life she knows. Resentful of her status as an old maid, Bessie finds joy in her eventual marriage to Zalmon only because of the affection that her youngest stepson, Benny, feels for her. The only reason Bessie agrees to marry Zalmon is that Benny needs her.

Mashah Smolinsky One of the middle Smolinsky daughters. Mashah is extremely beautiful, and the rest of the family thinks she is vain. In fact, Mashah needs beauty to sustain her, and her own looks, as well as the music in the park, are the only resources she has. She falls in love with the music Jacob Novak makes before she even sees Jacob himself, and when he breaks her heart, he destroys her hope of finding any more beauty in the world. She wastes away to a worn, quiet shadow of her former self, and hints of her former spirit show only in her enjoyment of her children and the cleanliness of her small house.

Fania Smolinsky One of the middle Smolinsky daughters. Comfortable with speaking her mind, Fania goes further than either Bessie or Mashah in defending her sweetheart. However, Fania is also more practical than her sisters and attempts to make her father's choice of husband work for her. Ultimately unsuccessful, she complains bitterly about her marriage at every opportunity and, though she frequently derides Sara's accomplishments, appears jealous of her sisters, as well. Though she lives across the country, Fania keeps in regular contact with her mother and sisters.

Berel Berenstein The clothing cutter with whom Bessie falls in love. An ambitious young man who plans to open his own shop, Berel wants to marry Bessie because she's a sensible, competent girl who would be a great help in running his business. Somewhat sporadic in his religious observance, Berel thinks anyone who clings to the old ways is crazy and has no patience for anyone who attempts to make him follow those ways.

Hugo Seelig The school principal with whom Sara falls in love. An intelligent, well-respected man, Hugo is filled with the knowledge that Sara longs for and admires. A kind man who treats everyone with respect, Hugo puts far more value on his personal observations about people than on what others might say about them. Hugo still feels a great bond with the old country and the customs he was raised with, and he holds Reb Smolinsky's learning in awe.

Morris Lipkin The poet with whom Fania falls in love. A pale young man with a shabby coat and a desperate need for a haircut, Morris believes strongly in the power of both love and poetry. When Reb Smolinsky forces Fania away from him, however, he becomes bitter enough to crush Sara when she comes to him with her own dreams. Morris earns a living writing for newspapers and spends his free time at the library.

Jacob Novak The piano player with whom Mashah falls in love. The son of wealthy parents, Jacob has grown up with money but doesn't share his father's prejudice against those who haven't. Though he cares deeply for Mashah, Jacob loves music more than anything else and will temporarily sacrifice even Mashah in order to continue performing it.

Moe Mirsky The diamond dealer Reb Smolinsky chooses to be Mashah's husband. A charming and generous man on the surface, Moe is in fact a calculating liar who will say anything to get what he wants. Unable to hold down a regular job, he emotionally abuses Mashah and thinks nothing of dining out and wearing fancy clothes while his wife and children starve.

Zalmon The fish peddler Reb Smolinsky chooses to be Bessie's husband. A basically honest man who desperately needs help caring for his children, Zalmon genuinely means to give Bessie everything he promises her during their courtship. However, he is too conservative to bother finding out what might actually win her over—one of many concerns he feels is too "Americanized."

Abe Schmukler The cloaks-and-suits dealer Reb Smolinsky chooses to be Fania's husband. Abe substitutes expensive presents for genuine affection or attention, both during courtship and after he and Fania return to Los Angeles. A compulsive gambler, Abe uses his wife's appearance to show the world how affluent he is.

Max Goldstein Abe's partner, who comes to New York to court Sara. A self-made businessman who is derisive of the education he never had, Max is completely focused on money, possessions, and potential profit. During his time with Sara, he flaunts his wealth and worldliness instead of showing any interest in her needs.

Mrs. Feinstein Reb Smolinsky's second wife. Originally a widow who lived above the Smolinskys' place, Mrs. Feinstein pretends to be a supportive woman but truthfully cares only about financial gain. She feels life owes her a certain amount of wealth, and when she doesn't get it, she takes vengeance on everyone around her.

ANALYSIS OF MAJOR CHARACTERS

SARA SMOLINSKY The driving force in Sara's life is her desire to find her own version of the light she sees radiating from her father. As a child, she yearns for something that will inspire her, such as Morris Lipkin's poetry briefly does. As a teen, she dreams of becoming a teacher so that all eyes will be on her the way they are on her father when he preaches. Later, she finds books that fuel her from day to day. When she gives up Max Goldstein because he would have stopped her education, she comforts herself with the thought that her sacrifice is like her father's rejection of worldly success in order to study the Torah more fully. When she begins to understand what it takes to find an inner light, the first thing she wants to do is share it with him, believing he's the only one who will truly understand. Knowledge, she decides, is what she wants more than anything in the world, and she devotes the same time and energy to obtaining it that her father does to studying his holy books.

During her quest for an internal flame, Sara hones her sense of fury at the injustices committed by others. Though she has no backing, she has the courage to protest at the restaurant when the cook gives her less meat because she is a woman. She is furious with both Berel and Jacob for hurting her sisters, and her hatred for her father begins when she sees the way he denies his daughters any chance to have lives of their own choosing. This need to fight injustice, however, is also what helps her reconcile with her father, and the first steps are inspired by her mother's promise and the guilt Sara feels at returning home just as she is dying. Later, when Sara sees the way her father's new wife treats him, she considers the possibility of once again living under one roof with her father, despite the tyranny she fears will reenter her life. Her father's light is threatened, and Sara knows better than anyone the importance of keeping it lit.

REB SMOLINSKY Having spent his entire life wrapped up in the study of the Torah and other holy books, Reb Smolinsky lives in his own private world of religious study, a world that is sometimes highly incompatible with the one in which the rest of his family lives. His days and nights are focused on the promise of heaven and offering charitable contributions to others, making him unable to see that on Earth, a man needs to make sure his own children are fed before he gives to strangers. In the holy works, men are good and kind, and they value the importance of study; he attempts to translate this awareness to a world where people don't care what your excuses are for not paying them and try to cheat you on business deals. Even more damaging to himself and those around him is the fact that in his world of words, Reb Smolinsky is incredibly knowledgeable. He mistakenly believes this means that he is equally knowledgeable in the outside world, and he makes potentially foolish decisions without feeling the need to consult his much more sensible wife. If his decisions prove to have been poorly made, Reb Smolinsky refuses to admit this to himself and will allow the decision to degrade further rather than to confess that he might have been wrong.

BESSIE SMOLINSKY Bessie has been crushed for so long by the weight of responsibility and family duty that it is hard to determine any personality she might have had beyond that. She has no time for outside interests because she's forced to work all hours of the day to keep her family fed and clothed. She also has no hope of a future escape because her father needs the money she brings in too badly to ever really let her go. Though it often seems, especially to Sarah, that this treatment has crushed Bessie's spirit enough that all she's capable of is mute acceptance, Bessie does in fact plan to run away rather than marry Zalmon, the fish peddler. However, that would leave Bessie on her own, trying to create a life for herself without ever having the opportunity even to discover what she might want to be a part of that life. Being left alone with so few internal resources very reasonably terrifies her, so she resigns herself to what little light can be reflected off of the people she serves. First it was her father with his holy light, then little Benny, the fish peddler's son, whose eyes shone with something fresh and beautiful. Better to cling to the little light you have, she feels, than to risk seeking more and find you have nothing at all.

MASHAH SMOLINSKY Though her family suspects she is shallow and empty-headed, Mashah is instead simply a lover of beauty. She buys paper flowers, makes a special trip to listen to the free music in the park, and lavishes attention on her face and figure simply because they are some of the few reliable sources of beauty available to her in her impoverished life. Sara says early in the book that Mashah seems to feed off her beauty the way other people feed off food, and the time she puts into keeping herself attractive is simply a way of keeping her food supply strong. She is first drawn to her great love, Jacob Novak, through the beautiful music he produces. She responds to that love by spreading beauty as far as she can: the house becomes cleaner and more organized, the table has fresh flowers, and the joy on her face brings light to all who know her. She puts so much effort into creating beauty for Jacob's sake that when he leaves, her belief in beauty itself is crushed. Her spirit slowly drains away. She still keeps herself looking nice, but there is no longer any heart behind it.

THEMES, MOTIFS, AND SYMBOLS

THEMES

THE HAZARDS OF DEPENDENCE In *Bread Givers*, those who make someone else an integral part of realizing their dreams inevitably wind up being failed by the other person. Mrs. Smolinsky hopes that the grocery store will finally mean a steady income for her family, but her husband, who insists on making the purchase, allows the previous owner to scam him. Sara puts all of her young, romantic hopes into Morris Lipkin and the beautiful words he writes, only to have him crush her dreams with a curt rejection. Mashah puts all of her dreams of beauty and love into Jacob Novak, only to find that he is willing to sacrifice her for the sake of his music. Sara hopes to share her new dedication to knowledge with her father, but he disowns her for failing to get married. Reb Smolinsky marries Mrs. Feinstein with the hope that she'll be as wonderful and dedicated a wife as Mrs. Smolinsky had been, but he finds himself trapped with a demanding, money-grubbing shrew who wants him to die. Only Sara's dream of becoming a teacher, which depends only on Sara herself, is ever fulfilled.

THE CONFLICT BETWEEN INDEPENDENCE AND FAMILY OBLIGATIONS In *Bread Givers*, familial duty is what most often holds characters back from getting what they really want. Bessie's sense of duty to her father keeps her from accepting Berel's proposal and running away with him, and Jacob Novak's obligation to his father keeps him away from Mashah and makes him break her heart. Because of their obligations to family, both Bessie and Mashah lose the people they want to be with forever. After enduring years of her father's mistreatment, Bessie nearly works up the courage to escape, only to be held back by the feeling that she is the only person truly willing to take care of young Benny. Sara, for her part, is nearly able to escape hazardous obligations by refusing to see her family while she goes to school, lest they say or do something that will divert her from her education. However, guilt over not being there for her sick mother leads Sara to feel that she has an obligation to care for her father, and with Hugo's invitation for Reb Smolinsky to live with them, Sara will soon be living under her father's command once again.

THE ELUSIVENESS OF HAPPINESS Though several of the characters in *Bread Givers* have a goal or dream of some kind, achieving that goal isn't necessarily the magic solution they hoped it would be. Bessie desperately longs to get married, but when she does, she finds that her life is filled with more unappreciated drudgery than it was when she was alone. Fania marries Abe with the hope that she can escape her father to the dream city of Los Angeles, only to find a life full of pointlessly expensive showpieces and incredible loneliness. When Sara rents her own room, she fantasizes about how wonderful and enriching it will be finally to have some space to herself, only to find herself desperately longing for someone to talk to. When her hard work finally pays off and she gets a teaching job, Sara is surprised to find that it doesn't make her feel as complete as she hoped it would. Hugo Seelig seems to fill this hole, but his insistence that they would love to have Sara's father live with them leaves her with a nagging fear that her independent identity will suffer.

MOTIFS

INADEQUATE PROVIDERS Nearly all of the men in the novel fail to provide sufficiently for the women in their lives. Reb Smolinsky denies his family sufficient finances and wisdom, refusing to contribute any money to the household and either giving away or making foolish choices with the money his children bring in. According to Jewish faith, only men are allowed to study the Torah. Women are destined only to ease the lives of the men in their families, keeping them fed and clothed so they need to do nothing more than focus on the holy word. This service should be a woman's highest aspiration, because the Torah teaches that it is only through a man that a woman can enter heaven. The men in a woman's life define her very existence. The title of the novel, *Bread Givers*, refers to the inadequacy of the men in the Smolinsky women's lives: though the women refer to men as "bread givers," they themselves must do the largest share of the providing.

Reb Smolinsky's wisdom also fails his daughters in another way, as his authority to choose their husbands traps his three oldest into unhappy and sometimes abusive marriages. Mashah's husband fails her and his children in every way possible, denying them basic necessities while he can afford to eat out and buy himself fancy new clothing. Though Fania's husband keeps her well fed and draped in fancy clothing, he holds so much back from her emotionally that she feels more alone with him than she did when she was single. Sara's teachers at the college fail her academically, not willing to take any extra time to help her satisfy her voracious need for knowledge. None of these men give the women in the novel what they need to survive, leaving them either to perish or, as Sara did, to learn how to fulfill their own needs.

THE OPPRESSION OF WOMEN *Bread Givers* is full of men and even women oppressing other women, so much so that many women consider oppression an acceptable way of life. Reb Smolinsky constantly berates his far-wiser wife for attempting to make decisions and demands all of his daughters' wages for his own use. He denies his older daughters a chance at happiness, pushing their sweethearts away because he resents not having chosen them himself. Mashah's husband emotionally abuses her and doesn't allow her to defend herself or her children against his injustice. Max Goldstein oppresses Sara in a more subtle manner, constantly attempting to deny her the right to have her own thoughts and opinions. Women even oppress other women. One refuses to rent Sara a single room because of her gender, and the female servers at the cafeteria consider her less worthy of meat than the man standing behind her in line. Sara must fight against this oppression nearly every moment of her life, which emphasizes her struggle to gain acceptance on the strength of her own identity.

THE YEARNING FOR PLEASURE At several points in *Bread Givers*, people express a desire to get out and enjoy life, though none of them ever seem able to fulfill that wish. After Bessie meets Berel, she tells her mother that they should save less and enjoy life more—but her ability to enjoy life is crushed when Berel leaves. Sara complains that instead of geometry she wants to learn subjects that will help her truly live her life, but she is taunted for that desire for the rest of her time in school. Fania berates Sara for studying by telling her she should get out and enjoy life, but Fania herself has admitted on several occasions that her own life gives her no pleasure at all. Sara nearly rejects her studying for Max's sake because he makes her feel more fun and full of life, but she later discovers that Max's pleasure is hollow and not dependent on any interest in Sara herself. The characters' desire to live life is truly a desire to escape into a new life, a process that takes far more work than a simple wish.

SYMBOLS

B

INTERNAL LIGHT The internal light that several characters in *Bread Givers* either have or are seeking symbolizes their self-chosen purpose for living. Reb Smolinsky spends all hours of his day devoting himself to understanding the Torah and other holy works, and many people talk about the light that shines constantly from his face. This is especially true whenever he's expounding on a scripture or holy principle. Love for Jacob Novak is what finally brings light to Mashah's face, as she turns her time and energy from maintaining her own appearance to tending to Jacob's every need. Yezierska talks about the innocent light that shines from young Benny's face, and Bessie decides that caring for him will be the purpose that makes her marriage to an old fish peddler tolerable. Sara spends most of the novel struggling to get an education, hoping to find a purpose that will define her life the way religion defines her father's. She admires Hugo Seelig so much because he is lit by that purpose. The light of knowledge shines from him and touches everyone he knows.

SOLITUDE For Sara, the chance to be alone represents the achievement of her own identity. When she was growing up, her father was always allowed time and space to be alone with his books while he forced the women to crowd together in the remaining available space. After finally defying her father and running away back to New York, the first thing Sara does is eat a meal with just herself for company, reveling in her independence. She believes that a room where she can be by herself, her next goal, will give her the chance to focus on studying and be free from the pressures of her family. She prefers solitude to being with Max because, though he is fun to be with, he tries to make her into a perfect little possession instead of the teacher she wants to become. When she does become a teacher, she buys another little room of her own to celebrate the experience. It is larger and much cleaner than the first, but more important, it's even quieter and more isolated, as safe from dirt and shouting as she wants her life to be from poverty and her past.

A "REAL" PERSON Sara spends most of the book wanting to become a "real" person, an unreachable state of being that symbolizes everything she believes a successful and happy person should be and have. Early in her life, a major qualification for being successful and happy is money. According to Sara, real people also sit down for dinner at a table and go out and earn their own money. This idea urges her at a young age to sell herring on the street. Later, being real means living on her own, where she has the space and the quiet to figure out who she's supposed to be. When she finally becomes a teacher, she believes she is real for a while. However, Mr. Seelig shines with a greater internal light than she does, and she decides this light is what it takes to be real. In Sara's mind, it's impossible for her to become a real person: no matter what she does with her life, there will always be some better and more perfect thing to be.

IMPORTANT QUOTATIONS EXPLAINED

1. *This door was life. It was air. The bottom starting-point of becoming a person. I simply must have this room with the shut door.*

This phrase from Chapter X, when Sara finds the room she wants to rent, describes the bases on which Sara plans to build her new, independent life. The first of these is economic improvement, getting an education so she can later get a job that will pull her out of poverty. Practically, a private room will give her the quiet she needs to focus on her studying, which will help her get through school and on to her dreamed-of employment. Psychologically, the room helps keep Sara focused on the goal she is working so hard to achieve. Having her own room frees Sara somewhat from the pull of her family's needs and expectations, which are so different from her own. The room also gives Sara a small taste of her completed goal. As Mrs. Smolinsky says earlier in the novel, in America only the rich can afford privacy. Sara values her first cramped, dirty bit of this piece of the American dream, and the solitude she'll gain when she is a working teacher promises to be even more wonderful.

B

The room is even more important to the second base of Sara's new life, the quest for her own identity. If Sara had stayed in her parents' home, she would have remained what she had grown up being—a mere extension of her father's will. Under Reb Smolinsky's roof, his beliefs about a woman's place in the world would always hold sway, and he would always have too much influence on Sara's daily life for her ever to be able to escape those beliefs. If she had married someone like Max Goldstein, who wanted her merely as another possession, she would have become an extension of her husband's will instead of her father's. Her mother desperately worried about Sara's single status, and though Fania hated her marriage, she worked tirelessly to push Sara into a similar state. If Sara had remained with any of these people, her own opinions and ambitions never would have survived. Only on her own, in her own little room, can Sara find the silence and the freedom necessary to discover who she is.

2. *It says in the Torah: What's a woman without a man? Less than nothing—a blotted out existence. No life on earth and no hope in heaven.*

This comment is from Chapter XV, when Reb Smolinsky berates Sara for refusing Max Goldstein. Sara spends many of her formative years defying this teaching, declaring in a variety of ways that her existence is as strong and important as any man's. Women are not supposed to judge men, yet at a young age, Sara interrupts the engagement party of Bessie's former love, Berel, to curse him for hurting her sister, and she later grows to hate her father for hurting his daughters. She refuses to bow to her father's will concerning store decisions she believes are wrong and defies him in a loud shouting match. Sara then runs away from home, hoping to live the life she chooses and not the one her father dictates for her. Despite her father's strict disapproval, she also refuses to marry Max Goldstein, sensing that the marriage would stop her from fulfilling her dream. Sara pursues her goals using her own will on her own terms.

As Sara gets older, however, she begins to wonder whether her father's words might hold a grain of truth. Sara is a total outcast in school and at work, left out of all social groups because of the way she has chosen to live her life. Society believes that girls her age should be seeking husbands, and no one is willing to accept or understand that Sara would much rather be on a quest for knowledge. She develops impossible crushes, first with Morris Lipkin and then with Mr. Edman, in an attempt to find a connection with someone. She's so starved for male companionship that she nearly allows herself to be swept away by Max Goldstein, despite the fact that he can talk only about himself and belittles the education Sara is working so hard to achieve. Even the glories of a teaching job eventually begin to ring hollow, and not until Sara and Hugo Seelig become a couple do her descriptions of life regain their original glow. Though Sara is able to have a life on her own, she feels life is much richer when a man is involved.

3. *I know I'm a fool. But I cannot help it. I haven't the courage to live for myself. My own life is knocked out of me. No wonder Father called me the burden bearer.*

Bessie makes this admission near the end of Chapter III, when she explains to Berel why she can't run away with him, and it presents a complex picture of the forces that shape the lives of Bessie and many other women in *Bread Givers*. Outside forces and restrictions, rooted mainly in religion, are immeasurably influential in their lives. According to Judaism, women must dedicate their lives to men's needs. If Bessie's father chooses to call her a "burden bearer" for the family, she is then obligated to take on that role. This is the only way of life she and generations before her have ever known, and according to them and the community in which she lives, her very worth as a woman depends on this obedience and selfless dedication. Bessie must also deal with the guilt that comes from knowing that due to her family's poverty and her father's unwillingness to work, there is a distinct possibility that her family would literally starve without her.

The far more subtle and persuasive restriction, however, is Bessie's own reliance on such a system. Unlike her sisters, Bessie has spent her entire life living for others until it gets to the point that filling other people's needs is the only thing she knows how to do. Bessie stays with her father, as she explains, because he is truly helpless without her. Later, she attempts to run away from home but is called back by the needs of Zalmon's youngest child, Benny, a little boy clearly desperate for a mother, which Bessie is capable of being. Berel, on the other hand, needed Bessie so little that he attempted to push Bessie into an ultimatum, and the moment she refused, he ran off and got engaged to someone else. He refused to understand that his lack of need would force her into an entirely new way of life, one she would need time and patience to learn. Without that time, there was nothing she could do but reject him.

B

4. *I felt the shadow still there, over me. It wasn't just my father, but the generations who made my father whose weight was still upon me.*

This passage, given by Sara as the final line of the novel, suggests that despite her profession, her romantic partner, and the many gains she has made for herself, Sara's struggle for an independent identity is far from over. Her once mighty father has become frail, and despite the alternatives Sara has tried to set up, the weight of expectation is pushing her into taking him into her own home. She knows it is what she has been taught to do, and the fiancé who has already moved her closer to cultural acceptance is so aware of the proper way of doing things that he assumes Reb Smolinsky will be moving in without a word of discussion. Though Sara can see the tyranny that will reenter her life, Hugo doesn't understand, seeing only the community belief that serving their elders, particularly their male elders, brings blessings into the younger people's lives. Despite how far she has come in developing her identity, the life her culture requires and expects is still waiting for her, ready to take advantage of the slightest slip in her vigilance.

Despite her dread, Sara still feels tied to her family. Her efforts to gain an education separated her from her family for six years, and the guilt she feels about coming back when her mother is dying lead her to promise to fulfill her mother's last wish: to take care of her father. Feeling as though she failed her mother in life, Sara feels she has to sacrifice her own independence in order not to fail her mother in death. Also, Sara begins to teach herself to see her father through her mother's eyes and to see that, despite his faults, he is a lonely old man whose internal candle is flickering out. Sara remembers this flame she was once so in awe of and wants to keep it lit, but to do so would bring Reb Smolinsky under her own roof and, she fears, restore to him the power he once had over her. In a way, her love proves to be just as solid a trap as her culture.

5. *There was one in the school who was what I dreamed a teacher to be—the principal,* Mr. Hugo Seelig. *He kept that living thing, that flame, that I used to worship as a child. And yet he had none of that aloof dignity of a superior. He was just plain human. When he entered a classroom sunlight filled the place.*

Though this statement, given by Sara early in Chapter XX, is describing the man Sara falls in love with, it also goes far in explaining the love-hate relationship Sara has with her father. According to Sara, the thing that drew her most to Hugo was the living flame that drove his teaching, the light that even passersby could see shining from him. Though Sara herself fails to note the comparison, Yezierska specifically mentions several times how the light shone from Reb Smolinsky's face, even noting that this light was one of the qualities that first appealed to Sara's mother. Sara has long admired this light of her father's and seeks to find something similar for herself through her devotion to education. When she thinks she's found it, after Max leaves, the first thing she wants to do is share it with her father. Even though he refuses the connection, Sara still can't help but look for similar qualities in a potential husband.

Sara is careful to note at least one significant difference between herself and her father. Along with his light, one of the first qualities that drew Sara to Hugo was his humanity. Unlike Reb Smolinsky, who always set himself above the rest of his family and rejected his daughter's attempts to reach out to him, Hugo is careful not to be seen as either aloof from or superior to the teachers and students with whom he worked. He treats small, grubby children with the same respect as learned scholars, a quality Sara reveres. Hugo respects Sara's intelligence and ability, not taking credit for her work and not pressuring her into doing something more traditional. He understands her in a way her father never did, fulfilling the need that sent her running away from home and kept her resolve firm, even after she was disowned. Hugo might not have the same prestige as Reb Smolinsky, but in Sara's eyes, it is that very prestige that kept her father from being the support she needed him to be.

Ceremony

Leslie Marmon Silko
(1948–)

CONTEXT

Born on March 5, 1948, in Albuquerque, New Mexico, of mixed Laguna Pueblo, white, and Mexican ancestry, Leslie Marmon Silko grew up on a Laguna Pueblo reservation. She attended Bureau of Indian Affairs Schools and then the University of New Mexico. After a brief stint at law school, she pursued graduate studies in English and began the writing career that has led her to be considered the premier Native American novelist and poet of her generation. Silko has lived and taught English in New Mexico, Alaska, and Arizona.

Silko's first book was the poetry collection *Laguna Woman* (1974), followed by *Ceremony* (1977). The first novel by a Native American women to be published in the United States, *Ceremony* received immediate critical and popular acclaim. Since *Ceremony*, Silko has published numerous books, including *Storyteller* (1981), which combines poetry, tribal stories, fiction, and photographs; a collection of selected correspondence with nature poet James Wright, *The Delicacy and Strength of Lace* (1985); the novel *Almanac of the Dead* (1991); *Yellow Woman and a Beauty of the Spirit*(1996), a collection of essays on Native American life; and the novel *Gardens in the Dunes* (1999).

While one Native American author, D'Arcy McNickle, published several novels in the 1930s, it was not until the late 1960s and early 1970s, with N. Scott Momaday's *House Made of Dawn*, and then Silko's work, that Native American authors became a significant presence in the American literary scene. During this same time, works by and about a range of "ethnic" or multicultural American authors began to gain access to publication and attention across the country. This was due in large part to the increased contact between communities instigated by the demographic shifts caused by World War II and to the Harlem Renaissance and then the equal rights movements of the 1960s.

Ceremony is set on the same Laguna Pueblo reservation where Silko grew up. Pueblo Indians refers to the group of Native Americans, including Hopi, Zuni, and Laguna, from the Pueblo crescent, which runs from central New Mexico through northeastern Arizona. The Laguna Reservation lies between Albuquerque and Los Alamos, New Mexico. The Pueblos first came into contact with whites in the sixteenth century, when the Spanish settled in the area. Pueblo territory became a part of Mexico in the early 1800s, when Mexico gained independence from Spain. The United States took control of the region after the Mexican-American war, with the 1848 Treaty of Guadalupe-Hidalgo. The United States government introduced the Reservation system, originally intended to maintain racial segregation, and established the Bureau of Indian Affairs, which instituted, among other things, government-run schools for Native American children.

All of Silko's work draws on her personal experience as a Native American. As she often points out in interviews, Native American culture is passed on through a profoundly communal process of storytelling. Silko bases her work on traditional Native American stories, using narrative techniques that emphasize their communal aspects, even in books authored by one woman. The oral nature of traditional Native American storytelling ensures that each version will be slightly changed and updated. In this spirit, she affirms in interviews, Silko's works are a continuation, not a reinterpretation, of the traditional stories.

Ceremony features the three of the most important figures in Pueblo mythology, Thought Woman, Corn Mother, and Sun Father, both in their traditional stories and in updated versions. Tayo, the main character in *Ceremony*, is also a figure in traditional Laguna stories. All of Silko's works demonstrate her concern with the preservation of Native American culture, including traditions, languages, and natural resources, in combination with an awareness of the reality of cultural miscegenation (mixing).

PLOT OVERVIEW

Returning home to the Laguna Pueblo reservation from World War II, via a Veterans' Hospital, Tayo must find a way to cure himself of his mental anguish and to bring the rain back to his community. Combining prose and poetry, *Ceremony* interweaves the individual story of Tayo and the collective story of his people. As Tayo's journey unfolds, it is paralleled by poems telling old stories.

The trauma of thinking that he saw his uncle Josiah's face among a crowd of Japanese soldiers he was ordered to shoot, and then of watching his cousin Rocky die, drove Tayo out of his mind. A period of time in a Veterans' Hospital gets him well enough to return to his home, with his grandmother, his auntie, and her husband Robert. This is the family unit that raised him after his mother, who had conceived him with an unknown white man, left him for good at the age of four. In his family's home Tayo faces not only their disappointment at the loss of Rocky but also his continued grieving over Uncle Josiah's death. He also contends with his guilt over a prayer against the rain he uttered in the forests of the Philippines, which he thinks is responsible for the six-year drought on the reservation.

As he slowly recuperates, Tayo realizes he is not alone. His childhood friends Harley, Leroy, Emo, and Pinkie, who also fought in the war, contend with similar post-traumatic stress, self-medicating with alcohol. The company is little comfort. His old friends spend their drunken hours reminiscing about how great the war was and how much respect they got while they were in uniform. These stories only make Tayo think about the tremendous discrimination the Native Americans face at the hands of the whites, whom they nonetheless seem to admire, and he is even more saddened and infuriated. Just as Tayo begins to give up hope and to wish he could return to the VA hospital, his grandmother calls in the medicine man, Ku'oosh. Ku'oosh performs for Tayo a ceremony for warriors who have killed in battle, but both Ku'oosh and Tayo fear that the ancient ceremonies are not applicable to this new situation.

Tayo is helped but not cured by Ku'oosh's ceremony. It prompts him to consider his childhood, especially the summer before he left for the army. Although Auntie did her best to keep the two boys separate, Tayo and Rocky became close friends, and the summer after they graduated from high school, they enlisted in the army together. That summer, Josiah fell in love with Night Swan, a Mexican woman who lived just outside the reservation. At her urging, he invested in a herd of Mexican cattle, which Tayo helped him to care for. As so often happens, there was a drought that summer. Having heard the old stories of how droughts were ended, Tayo went to a spring and invented a rain ceremony. The following day it rained. In addition to helping the crops and the cattle, the rain kept Josiah from visiting Night Swan. He asked Tayo to bring her a note. Tayo delivered the note, and in the process was seduced by Night Swan.

Realizing that his ceremony has not been enough for Tayo, Ku'oosh sends him to the nearby town of Gallup to see another medicine man, Betonie, who knows more about the problems incurred by the contact between Native American and white cultures. Although he is skeptical of Betonie's strange ways and especially high connection with the white world, Tayo tells him what is troubling him. Betonie listens and explains that they must invent and complete a new ceremony. Tayo accepts. Betonie tells Tayo stores of the old ceremonies as he performs them. Then, Betonie tells Tayo stories of his grandfather, Descheeny, and the beginning of the creation of a new ceremony to stop the destruction the whites are wreaking on the world.

Betonie sends Tayo back home, reminding him that the ceremony is still far from complete. When he meets Harley and Leroy on the way home, Tayo slips back into their lifestyle for a moment, but he soon moves on, heeding the signs Betonie told him of as he searches for Josiah's cattle. Tayo follows the stars to a woman's house. After spending a night with the woman, Ts'eh, Tayo heads into the mountains. He finds Josiah's cattle fenced into a white man's pasture. While Tayo breaks into the pasture, the cattle run off to its far reaches, and Tayo spends all night looking for them. As dawn approaches, Tayo is about to give up when a mountain lion comes up to him. Tayo honors the mountain lion and follows its tracks to the cattle. Just as he herds the cattle out of the pasture, two white patrolmen find Tayo. Not realizing that the cattle are missing but knowing Tayo has trespassed, the patrolmen arrest Tayo. Before they can bring him to town, however, they notice the mountain lion tracks and let Tayo go in order to hunt it. As Tayo heads out, it begins to snow. Tayo knows this will cover the tracks of his cattle and of the mountain lion, making the patrolmen's efforts fruitless. On the way down the mountain, Tayo meets a hunter, who lives with Ts'eh. When they arrive back at her house, she has corralled Tayo's cattle, which she keeps until Tayo and Robert return with a cattle truck to gather them up.

Returning home with Josiah's cattle, Tayo feels cured. However, the drought persists, and Tayo knows the ceremony is not complete. He goes to the family's ranch with the cattle, where he finds Ts'eh. They spend the summer together, but as it draws to an end Robert visits and warns Tayo that Emo has been spreading rumors about him. Shortly thereafter, Ts'eh tells Tayo that Emo and the white police are coming after him. Before she leaves, she tells Tayo how to avoid capture.

Following Ts'eh's instructions, Tayo easily evades the white police. Still running from Emo, he meets Harley and Leroy. Almost too late, Tayo realizes that Harley and Leroy have joined forces with Emo. Running again, Tayo finds himself in an abandoned uranium mine. As he looks at the gaping hole left in the earth, Tayo realizes that this is the last station of his ceremony, the one where he incorporates an element of white culture, the mine. All he has to do is to spend the night there and the ceremony will be complete. Soon Emo and Pinkie arrive. From a hiding place, Tayo must watch them torture Harley to death, and restrain himself from killing Emo in order to save Harley. With the help of the wind, Tayo survives the night. He returns home and goes back to Ku'oosh. After hearing all about Tayo's ceremony, Ku'oosh pronounces that Ts'eh was in fact A'moo'ooh, who has given her blessings to Tayo and his ceremony; the drought is ended and the destruction of the whites is stopped. Tayo spends one last night in Ku'oosh's house to finish off the ceremony, and then he returns home.

CHARACTER LIST

Tayo The protagonist of the novel. Tayo struggles with a sense of belonging in his family throughout his childhood and of belonging in his community after his return from World War II. Educated in white schools, Tayo has always maintained a belief in the Native American traditions. Painfully aware of the social realities surrounding Native American life on and off the reservation—and Native American participation in World War II—Tayo is able to make use of his double consciousness (of white and Native American life) to cure himself and his community.

C

Betonie The medicine man who guides Tayo through his ceremony. Betonie lives on the edge of the Navajo reservation, on a cliff overlooking the white town of Gallup. Feared and mistrusted by many for his eccentricities and for his contact with whites, Betonie comes from a long line of medicine men and women who struggle to create a new ceremony that will answer to the needs of the contemporary world. His wisdom is a key element in Tayo's cure.

Auntie Tayo's aunt. As the eldest daughter in her family, Auntie is in charge of running the household and caring for the family. Although she performs her duties diligently, Auntie is a proud and spiteful woman. She is largely responsible for Tayo's sense of exclusion from his family. In addition to following the old Native American traditions almost blindly, Auntie is a devout Christian who thrives on martyrdom.

Josiah Tayo's uncle. Josiah is the person who teaches Tayo the Native American traditions and makes him feel most at home in the family. Although he adheres strongly to tradition, Josiah is not afraid of change, falling in love with the Mexican Night Swan and following her advice to undertake raising a herd of Mexican cattle crossbred with Herefords.

Harley Tayo's childhood friend. Harley returns from fighting in World War II apparently less troubled than Tayo but with a severe alcohol addiction. Harley tries to be a good friend to Tayo but is impeded by his alcoholism.

Rocky Tayo's cousin and adopted brother. He represents for Tayo and his family the perfect success of a Native American to integrate white society. Much to everyone's dismay, Rocky dies in the Philippines during World War II.

Grandma Tayo's grandmother and the matriarch of the family. Already old and wise when Tayo is just a child, Grandma intervenes at key moments in Tayo's life to bring him to the medicine men or to provide tidbits of advice in the form of seemingly random comments.

Night Swan Josiah's girlfriend. Night Swan is a strong, smart, sexy, self-aware woman. She is the first of two Mexican women who appear in the novel to represent an aspect of the contact between white and Native American cultures. A former cantina dancer, she also seduces Tayo in order to teach him his first lesson about miscegenation and change.

Old Ku'oosh The Laguna medicine man. A very traditional medicine man, Ku'oosh does not have the wherewithal to invent the new ceremonies needed to treat the new diseases. He does, however, possess the wisdom to send Tayo to see someone else and to embrace Tayo when he returns with the completed new ceremony.

Emo A childhood acquaintance of Tayo's. Emo has always been critical of Tayo for his mixed race and been full of an undirected rage that only increases as a result of his fighting in World War II. Like the other war veterans, he is unable to find a place for himself on his return and spends his time drinking and reliving idealized memories of his army days. When Tayo criticizes Emo's idealization of his army days, Emo's rage becomes directed at Tayo.

Robert Auntie's husband. Robert is a mild-mannered quiet man who has little power in the family. He generally minds his own business, adhering to the old traditions. Robert shows his deep caring for Tayo as he welcomes him home from the war and as he warns him of Emo's impending attack.

The woman (Ts'eh) A sacred figure in Laguna cosmology incarnated as Ts'eh to help Tayo in his ceremony. Ts'eh appears at three moments in Tayo's journey to help him with the cattle and to teach him about wild herbs, love, and evading his pursuers.

Descheeny Betonie's grandfather. Along with the Mexican woman, Descheeny, a medicine man, began the creation of the new ceremony that would be able to cure the world of the destruction of the whites. He was the first of his people to recognize the need for collaboration between Native Americans and Mexicans.

Mexican Girl Betonie's grandmother. As a Mexican woman, like Night Swan, she represents the miscegenation of white and Native American cultures. Wise even as a young girl, she begins the new ceremony along with Descheeny. She raises Betonie and ensures that he gains the tools he will need to continue the ceremony.

The Hunter An animal spirit sacred to the Native Americans. The hunter appears to Tayo in both his animal and his human forms to help him catch Josiah's cattle.

Leroy A childhood friend of Tayo's. Leroy is Harley's drinking buddy who fought in the war with him and is now Harley's sidekick.

Pinkie A childhood friend of Tayo's, and Emo's drinking buddy and sidekick. Pinkie is eventually betrayed and killed by Emo.

Laura Tayo's mother. Unable to negotiate the conflicting lessons she learned at home and at school, Laura became a victim of the contact between white and Native American cultures. Consumed by alcoholism, she conceived Tayo with an anonymous white man, and, by the time Tayo was four years old, she was completely unable to care for him.

Helen Jean A woman Harley and Leroy pick up in a bar. Helen Jean represents all of the young Native American women who went to the white towns looking for a good job and end up being dragged into prostitution and alcoholism.

ANALYSIS OF MAJOR CHARACTERS

TAYO Tayo embodies the confluence of Native American and white cultures, present in both his ancestry and his life, which brings him from the reservation, to the U.S. army, to the Philippines, to a Veteran's Hospital, and back to the reservation. Carrying the signs of the cultural mixing in his green eyes often makes Tayo bear the brunt of a whole society's confusion at the ways in which the world is changing. He never knew his father and was abandoned by his mother at the age of four, and as a result, he encounters great difficulty in negotiating his mixed identity and experience. This difficulty is exacerbated by his Auntie, who raises him with the constant reminder of his difference. Like most of his peers, Tayo is educated in white-run schools. Unlike his friends, however, he often finds the white ways of life faulty and continues to respect and to believe in the Native American traditions he learns from his family. Tayo is prepared to serve as a bridge between the older and younger generations of Native Americans.

World War II interrupts Tayo's life, as it does the lives of most Americans of his generation. He comes of age on the battlefield, amidst tremendous death and destruction. His awareness of the connections among of all people and all things makes it incredibly difficult for Tayo to kill in a war he does not understand, in a place far from his home. The majority of the Native American men who return from World War II drown their trauma in alcohol, full of confused anger. Tayo, however, is more sad than angry. Painfully aware of the ways in which Native Americans were and are mistreated by whites, Tayo is not interested in glorifying his time in the army. These characteristics allow him to respond to the help the medicine men Ku'oosh and Betonie offer.

Tayo's lifelong desperation to belong in his family and his community and his deep-seated belief in the power of the old traditions allow Tayo to take up the challenge offered by Betonie and to undertake the completion of the ceremony, which can cure both himself and his people. Although he often falters along the path, Tayo's acceptance of the Native American mythical world allows him to benefit from the aid of accidents, animals, spirits, and the elements.

BETONIE As a medicine man, Betonie bridges the real and the mythical worlds. He spends much of his time in communication with spirits and stories to which others do not have access. The story of his own childhood appears magical: he is descended from a woman who one day appears hanging in a treetop and turned out to be in search of her husband. In these ways, Betonie is like the other medicine man in the story, Ku'oosh. However, Betonie is also shockingly connected with the mundane details not only of Native American society but also of white society. Betonie attended a white-run boarding school and keeps old gas station calendars among his sacred herbs and stones. He lives not at the sacred center of the reservation but on a cliff overlooking a run-down white town. He is descended from generations of Laguna medicine men and women only on one side; the other part of his ancestry is Mexican. He is a kindred spirit to Tayo, standing at the brink of a culture clash. But while Tayo tries desperately to make sense of the world, Betonie was raised with a deep understanding of and profound tolerance for it. Where Tayo cries, Betonie laughs.

While Betonie is wise, he is not omnipotent (all-powerful). Medicine men are vehicles rather than agents; they observe, remember, and advise, but they need patients through whom to perform their ceremonies. Betonie provides Tayo with the tools and the faith Tayo needs in order to complete the ceremony. Betonie's role is that of the teacher, rather than of the hero.

AUNTIE Although *Ceremony* is clearly a Native American novel about the adverse effects that white people have on Native American culture and on the world in general, the Native Americans in the story are not idealized, nor are they wholly positive characters. Along with Emo, Auntie is one of the most negative characters in the novel. In addition to embracing some of the more destructive elements of white society, Auntie also adheres to Native American tradition in a destructive manner.

The eldest daughter of Grandma, Auntie, whose given name is Thelma, will be the next matriarch of her family. As such, she feels responsible to the community for her family and especially her younger siblings. However, Auntie is more concerned with possible rumors and how Laura and Josiah's actions will affect the community's respect for her family than she is with their welfare. Similarly, she follows the letter rather than the spirit of Native American traditions, leading her to condemn completely any relationship outside of the community. In addition to this blind adherence to Native American social mores, Auntie is a devout Christian who thrives on a narrow interpretation of the concept of martyrdom. In Auntie's understanding of martyrdom, she will gain the respect of her peers if she is seen to suffer for the sins of others. She raises Tayo in this spirit, rather than out of any love for him or any sense of the Native American concept of family, which is not limited to nuclear units (mother, father, and child).

Although Auntie is a highly problematic character who causes all sorts of unnecessary problems in Tayo's life, she is not demonized. Although she does not do it out of love, she does raise Tayo. She causes difficulty, but not ruin. Her mistreatment of Tayo is attenuated by the rest of her family. Auntie's misunderstanding of both Native American and Christian traditions is the result of the same clashing of cultures that affects everyone in the novel.

THEMES, MOTIFS, AND SYMBOLS

THEMES

THE IMPORTANCE OF STORYTELLING Storytelling in the context of *Ceremony* refers not only to the general process of telling a story but also to the particular Native American tradition of storytelling. Traditionally, Native American cultural is oral, and everything from biology to history to morality to medicine is passed on in the form of stories. While the elders in a community may be the official storytellers, storytelling is a profoundly communal event. Since stories are intended to pass on information that will be remembered, they are often rhythmic, almost sung, and contain a large amount of repetition. This mode of storytelling is presented in *Ceremony* in the form of poems, both framing the main narrative (at the beginning and end) and interspersed throughout. These stories are in fact traditional Pueblo stories, known outside of the context of the novel. Tayo's tale reflects the traditional stories but is original. Along with the arrangement of the prose and poem passages, it can be seen as Silko's personal intervention in the communal process of storytelling.

While the prose sections of *Ceremony* are primarily narrated in a third person limited voice, the poems vary between first and third person. They announce the elements of this theme that will recur throughout the novel. Stories have the power to heal: they contain the rituals and ceremonies that can cure individuals and communities. They do this primarily by reminding us of the interrelations between all people and all things. As a story is told communally or is shared by one person with another, it creates a sense of community between those people. The presence of both the first and third person in the poems reinforces this aspect. For Tayo, the stories represent the Native American understanding of the world that he grew up with but that the white schools, the army, and the doctors and the VA hospital tried to convince him were incorrect. As he remembers and reenacts the old stories, Tayo reconnects with his community, recovers from the trauma of the war, and returns the rain to his land. The stories teach Tayo that he is not alone, both because he shares stories with a whole community and also because content of the ancient stories remind him that others before him have had similar experiences—he is not alone, and there is always hope for renewal.

THE DESTRUCTIVENESS OF CONTACT BETWEEN CULTURES The contact between Native American and white cultures in *Ceremony* is largely destructive. While the novel presents its devastating effects in somber terms, it is not concerned with simply lamenting the fact that whites arrived on the American continent and established systems that prove fatal to the indigenous peoples. Rather, *Ceremony* presents an attempt to contend with the reality of a mixed cultural landscape in a way that allows Native American culture to persist, even as it changes. Tayo himself embodies the contact between Native American and white cultures, as he bears his mixed racial heritage in his green eyes. Tayo must learn to make use of the white parts of himself and of the world around him, without abandoning his primary allegiance to Native American traditions.

For many in the novel, the first contact between the cultures takes place in the white schools that the Native Americans attend. There, white teachers tell them that their stories are not true and that their understanding of the world is not valid. Most significant, the white teachers present a completely different view of science and nature, and, as a result, the younger generations of Native Americans want to abandon traditional farming practices. This creates an agricultural crisis that is exacerbated by the pollution of reservation lands by white mines and military industry. In addition, white towns attract Native Americans with the prospect of white-collar jobs and good pay, but racism denies Native Americans access to those positions, while the cash they are able to make allows them greater access to the bars and the alcoholism whites have also introduced. All of these serve as strong indictments of the effect of whites on Native American culture. However, the relationship between white and Native American cultures is completely shifted in *Ceremony* when Betonie reveals that whites are an invention of Native American witchcraft. In the revelation, although they are still a primarily destructive force, whites are shown to be a part of Native American culture and traditions.

THE NECESSITY OF TRADITION In *Ceremony*, preserving tradition is essential to saving the Native American community. Both for Tayo and in the ancient stories, forgetting tradition brings massive drought and disaster. A key role of the medicine men is to preserve tradition, as is symbolized by the crates of artifacts they store. However, in order for tradition to survive, it must change with the times. The reservation medicine man, Ku'oosh, is unable to cure Tayo because he knows only the traditional healing ceremonies, which are not applicable to contemporary illnesses. As Betonie explains, traditions must be constantly reinvented to reflect the ever-changing reality of the world. Similarly, the novel shows the dangers of blindly adhering to traditions rather than trying to follow their intent. Auntie represents those who simply follow the dictates of traditions, as she mistrusts any form of interracial relationship. Josiah, on the other hand, represents those who follow the spirit of traditions, such as when he finds a way to interbreed Mexican and Hereford cattle to create a herd that will be both hardy and productive.

THE CONSTANT THREAT OF DROUGHT Water is essential to the survival of crops and animals for the Laguna, whose primary occupation is agriculture. Without city-sponsored plumbing and irrigation systems, and not wanting to interrupt the natural flow of water with dams, the Laguna are completely dependent on natural rainfall. Living in the desert land that comprises much of the southwest of the United States, the Laguna are constantly threatened by drought. Many of the traditional stories and ceremonies revolve around ensuring adequate rainfall. The primary signal of the spirits' displeasure with something the people has done is a drought, and one of the greatest feats of a destructive spirit is the creation of a drought. However, as Josiah tells Tayo when he is a child, everything has both its good and its bad sides. While too little rainfall can be disastrous, so can too much, as Tayo learns in the Philippine jungle. Tayo commits a grievous error when he forgets this lesson and, in the midst of a flood, curses the rain. Whether or not Tayo's curse is actually responsible for the drought on the reservation, it is essential for his health as well as for that of his community that he learn through his ceremony to respect the patterns of nature. Once he does that, the rain returns.

MOTIFS

NONLINEAR NARRATIVE STRUCTURE The Native Americans of the Pueblo see time as cyclical rather than linear. Silko produces a text that emphasizes this notion by using a nonlinear narrative structure. In most of Western literature, narrative proceeds in a temporal succession from beginning to end and from earlier to later. Although features such as analepsis (shifting back in time) and prolepsis (shifting forward in time) are standard, they are generally clearly marked and take up much less of the time and space of the novel than does the primary narrative. In *Ceremony*, on the other hand, it is often difficult to distinguish between primary and secondary narratives, or between past and present. Silko switches back and forth from Tayo's childhood to his time in the Philippines to various moments after his return, following no order except the order of thematic connections between the different events. The entire novel is narrated in the past tense, so whether an event actually occurred before Tayo's birth or in the midst of the ceremony, it appears to happen at the same time. The effect of this is to recreate a Pueblo sense of time, where all things are cyclic and where their immediacy is related not to how long ago they happened but to how important they feel in the present.

THE COMBINATION OF POETRY AND PROSE Silko's use of poetry invokes the rhythmic, communal storytelling patterns of the Native Americans, while her use of prose belongs to a Western narrative tradition. By combining the two in her novel, Silko asserts that the form as well as the content of the story is about the blending of the two cultures. Thematically, white and Native American cultures clash with each other more often than they complement each other, but the prose and poetry weave together easily. In many ways, they tell the same story; "only thing is," as Grandma says at the end, "the names sound different." The entire stories sound different as well, as versification (the division of the verses), rhyming, alliteration (the repetition of the first letter of a word), and repetition give the poems a distinctive rhythm. The poem at the end of the novel completes the line on the page before the first prose section, enclosing the entire novel within a poem. In other words, just as whites are said to be an invention of Native American witchcraft, so is a Western form of storytelling shown to be contained within a Native American form of storytelling.

SYMBOLS

THE GALLUP CEREMONIAL Every year, the white mayor and council of Gallup organize a Ceremonial. The Gallup Ceremonial symbolizes the ways in which whites misunderstand Native American tradition and appropriate it for their own purposes. Dancers from a wide range of Native American groups are invited the Gallup Ceremonial and are paid for their performances. This demonstrates the whites' lack of comprehension of the differences between Native American tribes, as well as their ignorance of the specific purpose of each individual ceremony. Whereas traditional ceremonies are performed around important events or times of year, with a specific ritual meaning, the Gallup Ceremonial is intended purely for the entertainment of whites. In addition, for the rest of the year, the town of Gallup at best ignores and at worst promotes the racist mistreatment of Native Americans, symbolizing the ways in which whites are eager to praise Native American artifacts but do not want to deal with the ongoing lives of real Native Americans.

IMPORTANT QUOTATIONS EXPLAINED

---

1. *Jungle rain had no beginning or end; it grew like foliage from the sky, branching and arching to the earth, sometimes in solid thickets entangling the islands, and, other times, in tendrils of blue mist curling out of coastal clouds. The jungle breathed an eternal green that fevered men until they dripped sweat the way rubbery jungle leaves dripped the monsoon rain. It was there that Tayo began to understand what Josiah had said. Nothing was all good or all bad either; it all depended.*

One of the most important lessons Tayo learns is that everything has both its positive and its negative aspects. This moment of realization comes early in the novel, as Tayo, newly returned to the reservation, remembers the most traumatic moments of his service in World War II, which include Rocky's death, at least in part from gangrene caused by the effect of the wet conditions on his wounds. Although this lesson is stated within the first fifteen pages of the story, its wording is key. Tayo does not understand the lesson; he only begins to understand it. It will take the rest of the novel for Tayo to come to a full comprehension of the intricate interrelations of all things. Although the message is simple, almost cliché, it cannot be taken lightly nor learned easily. Not only can the rain, so desperately prayed for on the desert reservation, be as bad as it is good, so also can whites, so detrimental to the Native American customs, also be an integral element in the ceremony that cures Tayo and his community. Although Josiah dies before Tayo returns from the Philippines, his teachings are among the most important in Tayo's life. As a child, Josiah was Tayo's male role model. Josiah initiated Tayo into Native American cosmology and also into the need to adapt to the ever-changing world, with the help of simple age-old lessons such as this one.

---

2. *The word he chose to express "fragile" was filled with the intricacies of a continuing process, and with a strength inherent in spider webs woven across paths through sand hills where early in the morning the sun becomes entangled in each filament of web. It took a long time to explain the fragility and intricacy because no word exists alone, and the reason for choosing each word had to be explained with a story about why it must be said this certain way. That was the responsibility that went with being human, old Ku'oosh said, the story behind each word must be told so there could be no mistake in the meaning of what had been said; and this demanded great patience and love.*

Tayo returns home from the war both sick with malaria and deeply troubled on an emotional level. His stay at the Veteran's Hospital does little to help with the latter problem. Once home, as soon as he is well enough to get out of bed, Tayo's Grandma arranges for him to see the medicine man, Ku'oosh. Ku'oosh begins his ceremony by repeating to Tayo the names and locations of the places that are sacred to the Laguna, and the basis of their understanding of the world. With Spider Woman as one of the most important figures in Pueblo mythology, the metaphor of the web is most appropriate for describing their world-view. Throughout the novel, animals and plants serve as symbols of the deep connection the Pueblo people have with the natural world.

Although the entire novel is written in English, we have been informed that in this section Ku'oosh speaks to Tayo "using the old dialect." Although we read English words, it is insisted upon that these are only a translation of the original language in which Ku'oosh's words are uttered. In addition, in that language the particular choice of individual words is of prime importance. As this is insisted on, the reader is reminded that although we can read and understand *Ceremony*, it does not offer us complete access to every element either of the original story or, more significant, of Laguna culture.

3. *Here they were, trying to bring back that old feeling, that feeling they belonged to America the way they felt during the war. They blamed themselves for losing the new feeling; they never talked about it, but they blamed themselves just like they blamed themselves for losing the land the white people took. They never thought to blame the white people for any of it; they wanted white people for their friends. They never saw that it was the white people who gave them that feeling and it was the white people who took it away again when the war was over.*

After they return to the reservation, the young men who fought in World War II often meet at the bars on the reservation line to drink and reminisce. As Tayo accompanies Harley to the bar, shortly after his first session with Ku'oosh, he remembers the last time they went, along with Leroy and Emo, on a similar outing. Emo and Tayo have never gotten along well, however, and on that occasion, under the influence of alcohol, Tayo became so disgusted and infuriated with Emo that he stabbed him in the stomach with a broken beer bottle. This quote demonstrates the elements on Emo's vision that set Tayo off.

In this passage, Tayo, and the narrator as he (or she) is aligned with Tayo, expose Emo's reaction to Tayo's identification of internalized racism. Even in the face of Tayo's analysis of the phenomenon, Emo provides a classic example of internalized racism. He believes the point of view of the white racists. He blames himself and the other victims of racism for being its cause. For the brief period when they wore the U.S. Army uniforms, Emo and the other Native Americans were able to escape from much of the racism, which had always plagued their lives. Emo and many others who internalize racism do not see that there is a systemic problem and only wish desperately to recapture the one moment when it did not operate as usual. As a result, Emo is not able to understand that when he put on the uniform, it was not he who changed but the whites' perception of him. He does not recognize the racism that leads whites to mistreat Native Americans, be it in the form of unfair land deals or the denial of equal access to respect and jobs after the war. As Tayo and the narrator evaluate Emo's internalized racism, they show it to be almost as detrimental to Native Americans as is the racism of the whites.

C

4. *"How did you know I'd be here?" he said, still watching the cattle. She laughed and shook her head, "the way you talk!" she said. "I was here almost a week before you came. How did you know I'd be here? Tell me that first."*

After being helped by a woman on his search for Josiah's cattle, Tayo dreams of her almost constantly. Then, the following summer, Tayo goes out to the ranch to care for the cattle and the new calves. When he arrives at the ranch, he finds the woman camped nearby. From her first appearance in the novel, she has offered Tayo almost magical assistance. Here, she confirms her role as one of his teachers, reminding him of the complexity of the world. Her words underline the cyclical nature of all things. Discovering who came in search of whom is like determining whether the chicken or the egg came first. She also points to the existence of designs greater than the plans or intentions of any one person. Tayo has been dreaming of meeting her for months, since she will play an integral role in the completion of the ceremony that the medicine man Betonie has already outlined. However, without any planning or communication, their meeting cannot have been consciously or mortally organized by either of them.

5. *Old Grandma shook her head slowly, and closed her cloudy eyes again. "I guess I must be getting old," she said, "because these goings-on around Laguna don't get me excited any more." She sighed, and laid her head back on the chair. "It seems like I already heard these stories before . . . only thing is, the names sound different."*

Old Grandma's words, the last lines in the prose section of *Ceremony*, refer most directly to the information that Emo killed Pinkie, but the FBI called it an accident and simply asked Emo to leave town. However, symbolically, her statement is meant to be applied to the entire novel. It affirms the cyclic nature of Laguna cosmology. Although the world is seen to change, it does not progress in a straight line, but rather constantly curves back on itself, so that the new repeats and connects with the old to the point where even the terms past and present are only somewhat applicable. Throughout the novel, the poems and the prose sections share plot lines, so that they are also the same stories with different names. In this way, Silko shows that her book is also part of the cycle. Having Grandma comment explicitly on the phenomenon also underscores the Native American's self-awareness. Old Grandma's words are not the result of the confusion of old age but of an understanding of the way the world works.

Changes: A Love Story

Ama Ata Aidoo (1942–)

CONTEXT

Ama Ata Aidoo was born in 1942 in pre-independence Ghana. The daughter of a village chief in the town of Abeadzi Kyiakor, Aidoo was raised in a comfortable and progressive household that not only supported but also encouraged her education. Aidoo's father opened the first school in their village, and sent Aidoo to the prestigious Wesley Girls High School in Cape Coast, where she first began to consider herself a writer. She published her first short story in 1958 after winning a writing competition, which encouraged her to keep writing. Three years later, Aidoo entered the University of Ghana at Legon where she continued to write short stories, poetry, and plays. In 1964, Aidoo's first play, *The Dilemma of a Ghost*, was staged and later published. The play was one of Aidoo's earliest explorations of several prominent themes that would dominate her later works. In the play, two young college graduates, one Ghanaian and the other African-American, fall in love and marry. This sets off an exploration of cultural differences and colonial legacies. Aidoo's work led to the formation of a strong, female literary presence that would be vital to her work and to African literature as a whole.

Following Aidoo's graduation from the University of Ghana in 1964, she worked as a research fellow at the Institute for African Studies. Six years earlier, Chinua Achebe published his novel *Things Fall Apart*. Achebe's novel marked a dramatic turning point in African literature. With its incorporation of both African and Western literary traditions, *Things Fall Apart* served as a model for discussing Africa's colonial legacy while simultaneously reaffirming the traditional values of African culture. This novel offered the first and most significant example of the style of postcolonial African literature.

As Ghana and most of the rest of Africa struggled to break free from colonial rule and assert its cultural and economic independence, Aidoo was acutely aware of a woman's role in traditional African society. An ardent feminist, Aidoo wanted to incorporate into her art a representation of women that highlighted not only their place but also the changing role of women in the post-colonial Africa. For Aidoo, there was no separation between the liberation of African countries from colonial rulers and the liberation of women from traditional patriarchal authority. In addition, there remained few strong female characters within African literature. Following the publication of *The Dilemma of a Ghost*, Aidoo published another play, *Anowa*, and one novel, *Our Sister Killjoy*. Both works further developed the themes in *The Dilemma of a Ghost*, particularly the role of women in African society, and the structure of patriarchal authority.

At the same time that Aidoo continued to write increasingly influential works, she held several prominent posts as both an academic and political figure. From 1972 to 1982, Aidoo served as Coordinator of the African Literature Program at Cape Coast, while also serving at various points as the director of Ghana Broadcasting Corporation and of the Arts Council of Ghana. In 1982, Aidoo was appointed to serve as Minister of Education in Ghana. Aidoo used her position to begin campaigning for affordable, universal education for all. Aidoo's strong-minded position lead to a falling out with the Ghanaian government, and after little more than a year, she abandoned her post to move to Zimbabwe in order to write full-time.

In 1991, Aidoo published her most famous and influential work, *Changes: A Love Story*. Although the introduction states that the novel is "not meant to be a contribution to any debate, however current," it is full of characters and themes that reflect the emergence of a new, highly educated class of men and women struggling to understand their contemporary identities in conjunction with their ancient traditions. Aidoo critically examines the tensions and changing dynamic within the next generation of Africa's emerging middle class through the lives of the novel's main characters, Esi Sekyi and Ali Kondey. *Changes: A Love Story* brought international acclaim for Aidoo, winning her the Commonwealth Writers Prize Africa Division. She has since published another novel, *The Girl Who Can and Other Stories*, along with several children's books and collections of poetry.

PLOT OVERVIEW

Esi, a government official who works for the Department of Urban Statistics, drives her old car over to the offices of Linga HideAway Travel in order to make some business travel arrangements. There, she meets the head of the company, Ali Kondey, a charming and handsome man who is later described as the best advertisement for the company because of his multiple national identities. The two are immediately attracted to each another. Ali offers to drive Esi home after promising to take care of all of the necessary travel arrangements, but Esi declines because she has her own car.

One morning, Ogyaanowa, the daughter of Esi and Oko, listens to the sounds of her parents fighting while she eats her breakfast. In the bedroom, Oko and Esi instigate yet another fight about their marriage. Oko is angry that Esi refuses to have another child and that she spends so much time at work. Oko says that his friends are beginning to laugh at him. Angry, he grabs Esi and forces her to have sex with him. Rather than apologize for his actions, he grabs the bed sheet and walks out of the bedroom. At work, Esi contemplates the fact that what just happened to her could be described as marital rape, even though no such term exists. She decides that she is going to leave her husband.

Opokuya, Esi's best friend, begins a conversation with her husband, Kubi, about which of them needs the car. Opokuya, in addition to being a nurse, is also a mother. Although Kubi's needs are frequently less pressing than Opakuya's, he almost always "wins" their argument and gets use of the car. Esi runs into Opokuya in a hotel lobby. The two women have a drink and discuss Esi's recent decision to divorce her husband. As they talk, Ali coincidentally enters the hotel as well. Esi tells Opokuya about the gifts that Ali has been sending her, and Opokuya tells Esi about her children and marriage. Esi hopes that Opokuya can understand her decision to leave Oko.

Ali is already married to his childhood friend and love, Fusena. The two have known each other since they were young, and after developing a friendship, they finally married. Following their marriage, Ali moved to London to complete his education. Fusena gave up her career and education in order to become a mother at Ali's insistence. In spite of his marriage to Fusena, Ali and Esi's relationship grows, and they soon become lovers. Ali disappears for two weeks, in part because of complications with his marriage and work. Shortly after he sees Esi again, he proposes to her. After discussing the potential complications with family and Ali's wife, Ali offers Esi a wedding band. Following the proposal, Ali begins to spend more and more time at Esi's house, showering her and her family with gifts. Esi discusses with Opokuya her upcoming marriage and her thoughts on polygamy.

Ali takes one of his coworkers to visit Esi's family to discuss the marriage according to proper tradition. He is rejected because he fails to bring along a respectable member of his family. When Ali finally approaches his family and asks them to speak on his behalf, they are at first reluctant, but eventually consent. Esi's mother and grandmother are disappointed in her decision to get divorced and become a second wife, but in the end they accept her decision. Ali returns to Esi's family with his elders, and the marriage is approved. It is a simple ceremony, and afterward, Esi returns home alone.

On New Year's Eve, Ali rushes over to Esi's house before returning to his family. Shortly after, Oko appears with their daughter, and the two men begin to fight. Esi grabs Ogyaanowa and runs out of the house to Opokuya's place. She tells Opokuya and Kubi everything that happened. Kubi goes to Esi's house and finds that both men have left. He checks on Oko at Oko's mother's house and finds that he is only slightly injured.

Six months later, Ali takes Esi to Bamako, his home village, for a vacation. They have a wonderful time. Ali's family, after initially rejecting Esi, now accepts her. Their relationship begins to change, though after they return, Ali starts spending less time with Esi. Rather than spending time with her after work, he drives his new secretary, who is young and attractive, home. By the end of the year, Esi feels completely abandoned. She is alienated from her own daughter and spends Christmas alone. She takes sleeping pills to help her get through the day. Finally, on New Year's Day, Ali appears at Esi's house, driving a brand new car. The car is a present and a bribe for Esi. Immediately after giving her the car, Ali drives off. Esi drives the new car to Opokuya's house. Opokuya is so jealous and taken aback by the new car that Esi cannot begin to tell her how she really feels about the present. Esi offers Opokuya her old car.

At the start of another new year, Ali spends more time with Esi but quickly falls back into his old habits. He sends her gifts from all over the world in order to compensate for his absence. Three years into their marriage, Esi finally tells Ali that she cannot be in such a relationship with him. Three months later, Opokuya finally goes to Esi's house to take away her old car. She is too excited about owning a car to share in Esi's sadness. After Opokuya leaves, Kubi arrives and searches for his wife. Upon seeing that Esi is distraught, he hugs her and then begins to kiss her. Before Kubi can take off his clothes, Esi backs away from him, and he leaves. Esi and Ali remain close friends and occasional lovers, and they never get a divorce even though Ali continues to have affairs with other women.

CHARACTER LIST

Esi Sekyi The primary female character of the novel. Esi is a strong, well-educated, and independent woman who, at the start of the novel, lives with her husband, Oko, and their daughter, Ogyaanowa. Esi works at the Department of Urban Statistics and often brings her work home with her. After being raped by her husband, Esi decides to seek a divorce. She wants to live an independent life in which she prioritizes her career and is free from the traditional boundaries imposed by marriage. When she falls in love with Ali Kondey and agrees to become his second wife, she thinks she may have found the perfect arrangement. However, her marriage to Ali leaves her feeling terribly alone and isolated.

Ali Kondey Esi's second husband and the managing director of Linga HideAway Travel. Ali is a very handsome and well-educated man. The son of a traveling, polygamist father, Ali is the embodiment of a cosmopolitan man. He happily claims several different nationalities as his own, and he spends much of his life traveling from one part of the world to another. He grows up and marries his childhood friend and first love, Fusena. Drawn to Esi's beauty and independence, he takes her as a second wife but quickly begins to spend less and less time with her. Ali is a self-absorbed man who tries to use his money to placate Esi and his wife. He is, above all, a traveler—a man who spends his life moving from one woman and destination to the next. Ali continues his multiple affairs throughout his marriage to Esi.

C

Oko Sekyi Esi's first husband. Oko, despite his differences and difficulties with Esi, continues to love her very deeply. Raised in a traditional household, he tries to get Esi to adapt to a more standard form of marriage. He wants to have another child, and he wants to spend more time with his wife, who is constantly traveling or working. His desire for Esi to be a traditional wife eventually causes him to rape her, which leads to their divorce. He never fully accepts their divorce, even though he takes on a new young wife given to him by his mother. He becomes increasingly bitter toward Esi and her remarriage to Ali, an emotion that culminates in his violent confrontation with Esi at her house.

Ogyaanowa Sekyi The daughter of Esi and Oko. As a young child, Ogyaanowa is caught in the middle of her parents' frequent fights and eventual divorce. These experiences will clearly haunt her later in life. She is shuffled back and forth between her parents, but she is primarily raised by her father and her father's mother. Although she loves her mother, she is clearly much more comfortable spending time at her grandmother's house than in the empty home where her mother lives.

Opokuya Dakwa Esi's best friend. Opokuya is a dedicated wife and a loving mother. She works long hours as a nurse while also raising a family. She constantly fights with her husband over control of their car. During Esi's crises, she always turns to Opokuya for love, support, and understanding. Compared to Esi, Opokuya is a much more traditional female figure. Both at work and at home, Opokuya is a constant source of support and compassion—a woman who frequently sacrifices her own needs for others'.

Kubi Dakwa Opokuya's husband. Kubi is a slightly arrogant and self-absorbed. He constantly controls the car, despite his wife's legitimate need for it. He is friends with Oko, and as such, is hostile toward Esi following her divorce. At the end of the novel, he attempts to sleep with Esi, which again reveals his self-centered nature. Like Oko, Kubi is representative of a traditional patriarchal figure. His arrogance and concern only for himself causes him to slight his wife and family.

Fusena Kondey Ali's first wife. Fusena has known Ali since they were young children. Following her marriage to Ali and the birth of her first child, Fusena abandons her career and education. She longs to finish school and get her degree but is constantly held back by Ali, who insists that he can earn enough money to support the family. She tries to resist Ali's desire for a second marriage but is eventually coaxed into it by the elder women of Ali's family. She is resentful of the fact that Ali has chosen a woman with a university degree to be his second wife, given that he prevented her from completing her degree. She is a somewhat tragic figure in that she has sacrificed her independence and career for a husband who not only takes a second wife but also continues to have multiple affairs with numerous other women.

Mma Danjuma The sister of Ali's father. Following the death of Ali's mother, Mma Danjuma raises Ali as her own son. She advocates for him to be educated in the French schools and plays a critical role in arranging Ali's marriage to Fusena. Although she is initially resistant to Ali taking Esi as a second wife, she is eventually able to accept Esi (to a limited degree).

Musa Musa (Ali Baba) Ali Kondey's father. Musa Musa spent his life acquiring wealth and traveling throughout the continent. He has a fondness for young women and is continually acquiring new wives, along with his artifacts. Much like his son, he is an arrogant man who believes at least partially in his own immortality. For Musa Musa, the entire world can either be purchased or seduced by him.

Nana Esi's grandmother. Nana is a very traditional woman who has a hard time accepting her daughter's decision to divorce Oko, whom she views as a respectable and loving husband.

ANALYSIS OF MAJOR CHARACTERS

ESI SEKYI Esi Sekyi is the paradigm of the strong, independent woman. In addition to having a job that pays more than her husband's job, Esi owns the home in which she lives. She has a master's degree and genuinely enjoys her career. Advancing within her profession is as much a priority for her as her family. Given the traditional role that women were generally expected to play within the family, Esi's strong will and independent nature is unique. Esi comes to represent the emergence of a new feminine identity—one that can compete equally with men in terms of financial and personal security. At the same time that Esi may want the freedom to pursue her own career and desires, she still very much wants to love and be loved. What she sees in Ali is the potential to have both the freedom that she desires and the love that she needs. Although Esi tries very hard to live her life according to rational principles, she finds herself feeling devastated and lonely because of her relationship with Ali.

C

ALI KONDEY Ali Kondey is the male counterpart to Esi's character. Attractive, intelligent, and well-educated, Ali is a worldly man. His job as the head of a travel agency suits his wandering personality, which constantly seeks not only new experiences, but new women as well. Ali has grown up in two distinct worlds: his father's world and the Western world in which he was educated. Like his father, Ali believes he can possess as many women as he wants, on account of his charm and wealth. He takes Esi as a second wife, even though he knows that his first wife and love, Fusena, will never be able to fully accept it. He places limits on Fusena's ambitions and prevents her from completing her degree. Even after marrying two women, Ali continues to acquire new mistresses, which causes both of his wives to feel abandoned. In a traditional, male-dominated society such as the one in which Ali's father grew up, such behavior would have been accepted. But Ali lives in a different world. He knows that it may very well be impossible to maintain a marriage with two contemporary women, and yet he tries anyway, because he believes he can purchase whatever he wants.

OPOKUYA DAKWA As Esi's best friend, Opokuya Dakwa inhabits a space in between the nearly extreme independence that Esi represents and the traditional role expected of a woman in the household. Like Esi, Opokuya has her own career that is personally and financially rewarding. She is educated and clearly has the freedom to pursue her career. At the same time, Opokuya has a large family and a husband. She struggles to manage the demands of her job and family, and it is evident that the two demands take their toll on her emotional well-being. Nonetheless, Opokuya manages to fulfill all of the roles demanded of her by her life. She is at once a dedicated nurse and a dedicated mother and wife, but her life is not easy. She begins her days fighting with her husband. The fact that she rarely wins their morning dispute over the car is frustrating for Opokuya, but also clearly not enough of a problem for her to ever contemplate leaving her husband. In the end, Opokuya is able to resolve her morning disputes with her husband by obtaining her own car, thereby demonstrating her ability to be both an independent, modern woman, and a loving wife.

FUSENA KONDEY Fusena's character and identity as a women change throughout the course of the novel. Before she gets married, she is an intelligent and ambitious young woman. She wants to complete her degree and continue her teaching career. However, once Fusena marries Ali, her world is quickly restricted. She bears one child, and then another. With Ali studying abroad, Fusena is relegated to the home, where she remains until Ali purchases a kiosk for her to operate. Upon hearing of Ali's decision to remarry, she immediately asks him if the woman he is considering to be his second wife has a university degree. By asking that question, Fusena reveals the degree to which her life's ambitions have been frustrated and abandoned for the sake of her marriage and children. Despite her ambition and strong will, Fusena is relegated to the role of a dependent housewife.

OKO SEKYI Oko Sekyi is at once a sympathetic and an abhorrent character in the novel. He loves his wife Esi dearly, not only for her beauty but also for her independence and intelligence. But at the same time, Oko resents her for exactly the same reasons. He is bothered by the comments made by his friends, who are beginning to regard him as less and less of a man because of his wife's independence from him. Oko's response to his friends' ridicule is to rape his wife—an act that leads directly to Esi's decision to divorce him, given that he does not even apologize. Like all of the characters in the novel, Oko is struggling to understand his relationships in a changing world. Following his divorce, Oko's mother presents him with a gift: a young girl who can play the role of a compliant and obedient wife. Even though there may very well be some appeal to such a relationship, Oko continues to love his strong-willed ex-wife.

KUBI DAKWA A relatively minor figure in the novel, Kubi Dakwa represents a middle ground between Ali and Oko. Although he still acts as and considers himself to be the head of the house, he is able to maintain a marriage to a woman as strong-willed as Opokuya. He is a selfish character, as evidenced by his reluctance to share the car with his wife and by his attempt to sleep with Esi. At the same time, however, Kubi also clearly accepts his wife's right to disagree with him.

THEMES, MOTIFS, AND SYMBOLS

THEMES

MODERN VS. TRADITIONAL The characters of *Changes* live their lives split between two poles. They are modern, well-educated figures who nonetheless try and maintain a strong connection to their traditional cultural roots and values. Esi, the primary figure in the novel, is the best example of the tension between modern and traditional values. She is a remarkably independent woman dedicated to her career as a government official. As such, she has a hard time accepting the traditional roles defined by her culture for a woman. She places a higher value on her career and her own personal fulfillment than on playing the role of a proper wife. This tension leads directly to her divorce with her first husband, Oko, who wants her to be a traditional African wife.

At the same time, Esi is also still clearly attached to the values she learned while growing up. She allows herself to become a second wife to Ali, and she performs all of the necessary rituals that her culture dictates. Like Esi, Ali tries to bridge the gap between the world in which his elders were raised and his own modern lifestyle. The ensuing tension and unofficial divorce that surround his second marriage highlight the limited degree to which traditional values can be upheld in modern times.

THE RIPPLE EFFECT OF CHANGES The title of the novel, *Changes: A Love Story*, refers to the numerous personal and cultural transformations that lie at the heart of the narrative. The changes that occur throughout the course of the novel take place both at the character level and at the societal level. At the time of the novel, Ghana had recently achieved its political independence. The country is changing politically, economically, and culturally. Similarly, Esi achieves her own independence from her husband and marriage. Consequently, she becomes free to pursue her own ambitions without a family or a husband to restrict her. In a sense, she has transformed herself into a model of the modern woman: she is not only financially stable but also completely independent. Esi's new independence is also symbolic of a larger change occurring within African societies. As women like Esi have an increasing number of educational and professional opportunities available to them, their roles both in the home and in society inevitably change. They are no longer simply wives and mothers who are dedicated to their own ambitions.

THE POWER OF EDUCATION All of the major characters in the novel are well-educated. Their education is not only the mark of their place in society but also an ironic and elusive symbol that signifies both change and stasis at the same time. The two primary lovers in the novel, Esi and Ali, are also the most highly educated. Esi holds a master's degree, and Ali has studied in France and England. Upon hearing of Ali's second marriage, the first question that his wife, Fusena, asks him is whether or not the woman has a university degree. This question highlights the degree to which education symbolizes progress, modernity, and independence for the women of the novel.

For Esi, her education enables her to have a well-paying job that can secure her independence. It is precisely that independence that attracts Ali to her, and it is the same independence that earns Esi the scorn of her first husband's family. Esi's education sets her apart from traditional African culture, making her feel alienated from her mother and grandmother, neither of whom can understand her attitudes towards marriage and work. Ali is as educated as Esi, and like her, he struggles to balance the two worlds in which he lives. When Ali proposes to his elders that he take a second wife, they are shocked. For them, Ali's education has propelled him into a new world that does not allow for such actions.

MOTIFS

TRAVEL Throughout the novel, Ali and Esi are constantly traveling the continent and the globe. They are cosmopolitan figures, worldly in their knowledge of life and its variety of opportunities. Esi meets Ali while trying to finalize travel arrangements for work, while Ali has made a life out of traveling and assisting others in doing the same. The constant travel in Ali's and Esi's lives serves as a reminder of the degree to which each character is transient. Esi and Ali leave the country, their marriages, and, eventually, each other. From a young age, Ali has been a traveler like his merchant father. He continues this tradition in his profession and in his relationships. He travels from one woman to the next. He treats his wives much the same as he would treat any one of the destinations he frequently visits.

PROVERBS Brief statements that are written to resemble the tone and nature of African proverbs are inserted throughout the narrative. The proverbs serve several important rhetorical functions. They remind the reader of the African context in which the novel is written, and as such, serve as a bridge between African and Western literary traditions. The proverb is a traditional literary device used in African cultures to share wisdom and culture. By incorporating them into her novel, Aidoo is reasserting the value and function of African literary traditions in a genre—the fictional novel—which arose out of Western culture.

FRIENDSHIP Esi and Opokuya's friendship is the most stable and equitable relationship in the novel. The two women treat each other as equals, and it is evident that they can speak freely and openly to each other in a way that they never do with either one of their husbands. For Esi, her friendship with Opokuya is also the most stable relationship that she has with anyone outside of her family. After leaving Oko and eventually Ali, Opokuya still remains. At the end of the novel, Opokuya's husband begins to kiss Esi, and in that moment, Esi is reminded of her relationship with Opokuya. The thought is enough to draw her back into reality such that she moves away from Kubi.

SYMBOLS

THE CAR The tiny car that Esi uses to get to and from work each day is barely functional. It is so decrepit that upon seeing it, Ali says he will drive Esi home. The car serves as an initial attempt by Ali to enter Esi's life. At the same time, Esi's friend Opokuya engages in a daily struggle with her husband over who will control the car that day. In Opokuya's marriage, the car becomes symbolic of the value placed on women's work versus that of men. Despite the numerous needs of the house that Opokuya must tend to every day, her husband Kubi inevitably controls the car the majority of the time. When Ali finally buys Esi a car in order to apologize for his absence and placate Esi, he is inadvertently liberating Opokuya from having to depend on her husband.

THE WEDDING BAND When Ali proposes to Esi, he offers her a wedding band, a symbol of marriage perhaps original to Western culture that, when incorporated into Ali's cultural tradition, is only offered to the first wife of a husband. Esi is taken aback by the wedding ring, as is her entire family. By bringing the wedding band into his marriage ceremony, Ali is not only showing his ability to accept and adapt to Western customs, but he is also demonstrating his attempt to incorporate those customs into an African context. The polygamous marriage upon which Ali is about to embark is contrary to the tradition of marriage symbolized by the wedding band that Ali offers Esi. Ali's decision to take a second wife is both an embrace of traditional African marriages, and a rejection of the standards of Western marriage. As a result, the wedding band that Ali offers Esi becomes a symbolic bridge that unites the two traditions.

PROFESSIONS Each of the characters in the novel is at least partially defined by his or her career. Esi's job with the Department of Urban Statistics highlights her rational personality, while Ali's job at a travel agency reminds the reader of his tendency to move from one woman to the next. Contrary to Esi and Ali are Oko and Opokuya. Both characters work in professions that demand personal sacrifice—Oko as a teacher and Opokuya as a nurse. The fact that each character works in a field that reflects his or her personality demonstrates the substantial role that careers play in defining identity for the new generation.

IMPORTANT QUOTATIONS EXPLAINED

---

1. *Is Esi too an African woman? She not only is, but there are plenty of them around these days. . . these days. . . these days.*

Esi's husband, Oko, has these thoughts in the first few pages of the novel as he watches his wife from bed. In his mind, the fact that the house in which they live is a benefit of her job, not his. This causes him to feel insecure about their relationship and his role as a man in his household. He even wonders if, given her accomplishments and dedication to her career, she can still be considered an African woman. Compared to the women who raised Oko, Esi's independence is startling and even unthinkable. Nonetheless, Oko answers his own question regarding Esi's African identity. He knows that she is still an African woman despite gaining independence from the men in her life. There is a strong sense of nostalgia implied in Oko's thoughts by the series of ellipses surrounding the words "these days." In part, this is nostalgia for an era in which women were relegated to the household while men were responsible for earning a living. In that bygone era, Oko would not have felt so threatened and emasculated. Immediately following this thought, Oko tells Esi that his friends are beginning to mock him for not being a man, and shortly afterwards, he proceeds to rape her.

---

2. *But Opokuya wasn't having any of her self-pity. So she countered rather heavily. "Why is life so hard on the non-professional African woman? Eh? Esi, isn't life even harder for the poor rural and urban African woman?"*

In Chapter 6, shortly after Esi and her best friend Opokuya happen to run into each other in a hotel lobby, Esi tells her friend of her decision to divorce her husband Oko. The two women begin to lament the difficulties of being a working woman. Opokuya's response is not only an answer to Esi's question about why life is so difficult for the professional African woman, it is also a response by the author of this novel. Aidoo is aware that all of the characters she has chosen to depict are comfortable, well-educated Africans whose lives are troubled by only petty concerns. Opokuya's response to Esi also reminds the reader of Aidoo's preface to the novel in which she writes, "Because surely in our environment there are more important things to write about?" Opokuya's statement does not discredit the worth of writing the novel's subject matter, but it does remind the reader that this is not the only story that can and should be told. In addition, Opokuya's statement reminds her friend that their lot in life remains vastly greater than the majority of African women who continue to live poor lives. For those women, the thought of leaving a husband they no longer loved would be all but impossible. They have no rewarding jobs they could complain of, and certainly no new potential love interests who shower them with gifts.

---

3. *Esi was thinking that the whole thing sounded so absolutely lunatic and so 'contemporary African' that she would save her sanity probably by not trying to understand it. The only choice left to her was to try and enter into the spirit of it.*

After flattering Esi in Chapter 10 with compliments regarding her beauty and intelligence, Ali surprises her by asking for her hand in marriage. He follows this surprise by taking Esi's hand and slipping a wedding band over it. Esi is astonished that he would do such a thing because wedding bands, when used at all, are supposed to be given only to a man's first wife. When Esi presses Ali about the purpose and necessity for her to wear a wedding ring, he proudly proclaims that its purpose is to let other men know that she is spoken for. As Esi is well aware, there is something preposterous to Ali's statement regarding the symbolic intention of a wedding band. Missing from Ali's perspective is any sense that the wedding band symbolizes commitment and shared love. The only meaning that the wedding band has for Ali is possession. He wants Esi to wear his ring so that no other man will try to take her away from him. For Esi, Ali's ideas are not only African, they are "contemporary African." The contemporary nature of Ali's thoughts lies in his desire to break the tradition of having only one woman wear his ring. Prior to offering Esi his ring, Ali rationalizes both polygamy and the legitimacy of using wedding rings to symbolize marriage. In his willingness to break with tradition, Ali exhibits his unique contemporary African nature, which is riddled with contradictions and complications. She must either blindly accept this fact or reject Ali and his proposal.

---

4. *From the inner room Esi heard them and pain filled her chest. She could never be as close to her mother as her mother was to her grandmother. Never, never, never. And she knew why.*

In Chapter 14, after returning home one weekend, Esi overhears her mother and grandmother talking. The two women have been discussing Esi, and their discussion reveals their closeness and similarity in speech and language. Listening to the two women communicate so naturally and easily with one another fills Esi with a deep loneliness. Because of her education, she will always be somewhat separated from these two women. As Esi later notes, the cost of her education has been a high one.

Esi's disconnection from her mother and grandmother is also significant on a larger, cultural scale. The more educated and westernized Africa becomes, the more likely it is that it will lose touch with certain elements of its rich tradition and history. Each generation will be a little less connected to the past, as Esi herself has become. The loss, of course, is not without its benefits, though. By having access to a wonderful education, Esi has more personal freedom and wealth than either her mother or grandmother had. For Esi, the question remains whether or not the price she has paid for her modernity is too high.

---

5. *Ali phoned regularly to announce his imminent departures. He phoned from the different cities and towns inside and outside the country to which he traveled. He phoned to report his arrivals. In between his travels, he phoned regularly when the telephone lines permitted. He and Esi always had good telephone conversations.*

Following the conclusion of Ali and Esi's wedding and honeymoon phase in Chapter 22, the two lovers begin to see less and less of each other. Their marriage, in which Esi once placed so much hope, has been reduced to a series of phone calls. Ali phones frequently just before he leaves town; in other words, his phone calls are a means for him to say that he is unavailable. If his departure time is quickly approaching, then contacting Esi just before he leaves means that he can avoid having to see her before he leaves.

Like his father, Musa Musa, Ali has made his career by traveling around the world. He can no more settle permanently into one location than he can settle on one—or even two—women. His constant traveling and womanizing seem to be essential elements of his personality: they are so intertwined that they cannot be separated from one another. Ali uses his travel and work to maintain distance from the women in his life, thereby permitting him the space and time to pursue additional women. He has clearly become very adept at maintaining and managing that distance. Ali and Esi may no longer have a strong marriage, but they can still have good phone conversations. Those good phone conversations are all that Esi has left of what she once thought would be an ideal marriage.

Child of the Dark

Carolina Maria de Jesus (1914–1977)

CONTEXT

Carolina Maria de Jesus was born in 1914 to a single mother in a rural town outside of São Paulo. After de Jesus's father left her and her mother destitute, de Jesus's mother took the only job available—working as a housekeeper in a brothel—and endured scorn from those around her. De Jesus's childhood was marked by prejudice and ostracism for several reasons: she was black, the child of a single mother, and very outspoken, even at a young age. A benefactor's intervention allowed de Jesus to attend school at the age of seven, but she had to leave only two years later due to a family move. De Jesus continued to read and learn in her spare time, despite the fact that people accused her of being a witch.

When de Jesus was twenty-three, her mother died, and she decided to relocate to São Paulo. De Jesus did not last long working as a maid, one of the few jobs a black woman could hope for at that time—the families that employed her found de Jesus too educated, too spirited, and not docile enough. At age thirty-three, de Jesus became pregnant with João, and after being fired from another maid job, she took refuge in the favela (shantytown). The postwar economic boom had changed residential patterns in large Brazilian cities like São Paulo and Rio. As luxury buildings were going up, poor families were being pushed to the outskirts of town, and many ended up in the favelas.

Always interested in books and writing, de Jesus continued to write throughout her time in the favela, where she wrote many plays, stories, and aphorisms, as well as the diary that made her famous. In April 1958, a young reporter named Audalio Dantas decided to write a story about the favela and happened upon a scene unfolding at a playground. As a group of men made trouble, Dantas observed a tall black woman threatening to write about them in her notebook. He asked her about it, and de Jesus showed him stacks of writing she had in her hut in the favela. With his guidance and editing, de Jesus published *Quarto de Despejo* ("The Garbage Room," later published in English as *Child of the Dark*) in 1960, to national and then international acclaim. Magazines the world over wrote features about de Jesus, heralding her harrowing description of the life of the poor as one of the first accounts of poverty actually written from the inside.

Soon after the publication of her diary, de Jesus was able to realize a long-held dream of moving her family out of the favela. However, the price of fame was high. People constantly bothered her at home for autographs and money, while at the same time, de Jesus and her children were shunned by their new white neighbors. The boys found the adjustment from favela life most difficult because of their more advanced ages. De Jesus yearned to publish her poems and stories but found no assistance in Dantas, who did not have interest in anything beyond her more political writings. Dantas had also lost patience with de Jesus, whom he saw as a difficult, demanding prima donna. The press and public also viewed this prideful, outspoken woman with mixed emotions. De Jesus, for her part, embraced the fame she thought she deserved and refused to conform to any role that society imposed upon her. About a year after the publication of her first book, de Jesus published a continuation of her diary *Casa de Alvenaria* ("The Brick House"), but it was much less successful than the first installment. De Jesus continued to write until her death, but she never forgot the pain of being so quickly spurned by a fickle public.

PLOT OVERVIEW

Child of the Dark, the diary of Carolina Maria de Jesus, covers the period between July 1955 and January 1, 1960, with a gap, due to editing, between 1955 and 1958. Carolina has three children: Vera (two), José Carlos (five), and João (eight). They live in a favela, or shantytown, where living spaces consist of crude huts built of cardboard and wood scraps. Her daily life consists of collecting paper and metal scraps for food money. While looking for scraps outside a football stadium, Carolina endures taunts from white patrons. Carolina often fares no better closer to home—meddlesome favela woman like Dona Rosa and Dona Silvia pick fights with Carolina's children and try to provoke Carolina. Favela life is full of hunger, disease, violence, and alcoholism. Carolina's only consolation is writing and the occasional kindness of friends and strangers, such as when a man stops by the favela and gives Carolina's daughter, Vera, one hundred cruzieros, the equivalent of what Carolina often earns in a day.

Carolina struggles to insulate her children from bad influences, but she receives several summons from the police station regarding her boys' behavior. After a few visits there, and after a neighbor woman, Chica, levels an accusation of rape against João, Carolina briefly considers interning her children in a public shelter for their own safety and wellbeing. Carolina believes that João's accuser is lying, but she worries that her children are in danger while the matter is being investigated. After two runaways from the shelter seek refuge in Carolina's home, and she hears their stories of horrible abuse, she changes her mind about putting her children there, recognizing that the experience would likely turn them into criminals. The fact that the favela changes everyone it touches is a reality that Carolina fully understands. As she observes a new resident become increasingly argumentative and desperate as they adapt to the "dog-eat-dog" mentality that rules the favela, Carolina recognizes that a person can resist being dragged down by it only for so long.

Carolina takes every opportunity she can get to participate in Brazil's political system, but after going to Congress to observe her leaders, she feels nothing but disgust. In response to the ignorance she sees from those in power, Carolina levels many critiques against the political system that she believes contributes to the poverty and hunger of the favelados. To Carolina, Brazil's President Juscelino is a bird in a cage, and the favela dwellers are hungry cats that may someday rise up against him if given the chance. On a more day-to-day level, Carolina senses that she lives in a system that conspires against the poor. Inflation is rampant, and prices for basic necessities, such as rice and flour, can be absurd. When Carolina watches a factory owner dump rotted food near the favela, she considers it an act of blatant cruelty. Carolina also endures racial and class discrimination every time she ventures out of the favela and into the city of São Paulo. While taking a streetcar, Carolina discusses the politician Dr. Adhemar with other passengers, who blame him for the steep increases in the cost of transportation. Carolina thinks that Adehemar is angry and wants to punish the poor. In the often-brutal world she lives in, Carolina wonders how much worse conditions can get.

Carolina refuses to put her interest in marrying before her interest in her children, even when she is proposed to by a man named Manuel, who, compared to the other favelados, is fairly well off, a worker and abstainer from alcohol. Against her own better judgment, Carolina also becomes intertwined with a gypsy named Raimundo, who awakens in her a sense of romance and adventure. Ultimately, she decides that he is not the man she thought he was, but when he moves away, she is sick and broken-hearted. Through both entanglements, Carolina maintains that she is not the marrying type, her children come first, and she is unwilling to make the sacrifices that she sees other women making in order to get married.

The intervention of a journalist named Audalio Dantas helps Carolina to realize her dream of being published. When excerpts of her diary appear in a weekly magazine called O *Cruziero*, Carolina tells everyone she can about her new fame. Unfortunately, being published does not have the effect that she was hoping for. Not only do Carolina's dire daily circumstances remain unchanged, but she quickly finds success to be a bitter pill when the favela fills with disparaging talk of her motives. Even after her publication, Carolina must deal with the same challenges and frustrations: the struggle to scrape together enough money for food, the lines at the water spigot, the fights, and the racism and sexism she faces on a daily basis. Despite these daily humiliations, Carolina holds fast to her dream of finding a home far from the favela for her family.

CHARACTER LIST

Carolina Maria de Jesus The author of, and central player in, the diary. Carolina, forty-one years old and the mother of three young children, lives in a favela, or slum, in Brazil. She collects paper scraps to sell in order to buy food and writes in her diary about daily life. In contrast to the other women of the favela, Carolina does not drink, engage in fighting, or otherwise compromise the safety of her children. She has also resolved not to marry. Perceptive, critical, and sometimes dryly humorous, Carolina creates an accurate record of life in the favela.

Vera Carolina's youngest child. Vera is two when the diary begins, and her longings for nice clothes and food are particularly difficult for Carolina to cope with. At one point, Vera asks to be given to a richer family so that she might have what favela life lacks—a request that pains Carolina.

José Carlos Carolina's middle child. José Carlos is almost five when the diary begins. At one point, José Carlos is detained at the local police station for truancy. When Carolina picks him up, she is relieved to find him crying rather than acting like the hardened child-criminals who surround him.

João Carolina's oldest son. João is eight when the diary begins. When a neighbor accuses him of raping her daughter midway through the diary, he is interrogated by the local authorities, who ask prying questions in front of his brother and sister about his knowledge of sex. Nothing comes of the charges by the end of the book.

Manuel Carolina's long-time lover. Manuel appears to be better than the favelados: he doesn't drink, he works, and he dresses and behaves like a man of a much higher station. Manuel would like to marry Carolina, but her feelings about him fluctuate. On one hand, she thinks very highly of him and has obvious affection for him, though she is fundamentally resistant to the idea of marrying anyone. Manuel grows jealous of Carolina's relationship with the gypsy Raimundo, though he comes back to her, as she predicts.

Raimundo The mysterious gypsy who enters Carolina's life and sweeps her off her feet. Raimundo reverses her stereotypes about gypsies and helps awaken her to her own romantic longings for travels and freedom. Raimundo's presence reveals Carolina's more playful side. However, Raimundo is not as perfect as Carolina initially makes him out to be. He's fickle, can't be pinned down, and openly pursues other women. When Carolina sees him eyeing a fourteen-year-old girl, she resolves to have nothing more to do with him.

Audalio Dantas The reporter who helps Carolina get published in a weekly magazine, *O Cruziero*. Dantas discovers Carolina when he overhears her threatening to put some troublemakers in her "book." Dantas's aid also allows Carolina's diary to be published in book form.

Brother Luiz A clergyman from the local Catholic church. Brother Luiz comes to the favela to offer aid and religious instruction, but Carolina thinks he is blind to the needs of the poor.

Euclides A disabled beggar who lives in the favela. Euclides reacts to the publication of Carolina's diary by telling her she is now in his heart and head. He also offers to "keep" Carolina so that she can continue writing, but she turns him down.

Dona Julita A more fortunate friend of Carolina's. Dona Julita offers aid, food, and companionship to Carolina when she needs it most.

President Juscelino The president of Brazil. President Juscelino is described by Carolina as a bird in a cage, ignorant of the hungry cats (the *favelados*) who circle around him.

Chica A neighbor woman. Chica accuses Carolina's son João of raping her daughter.

Dona Rosa A neighbor in the favela. Dona Rosa picks fights with Carolina's children.

Dona Silvia A favela woman. Dona Silvia visits Carolina to complain about her children's poor education.

Orlando Lopes A man who lives and works in the favela. Orlando is sometimes helpful to Carolina, as when he helps her slaughter a pig, but he is also corrupt. In charge of electricity in the favela, he collects electrical deposits even thought the electric company abolished such deposits years ago. Orlando also reacts negatively to Carolina's publication and the fact that she accused him of being lazy in her account—he shuts off her electricity for nonpayment of the dubious fees.

Dona Elvira A quarrelsome favela woman. Dona Elvira may have had something to do with the burning of some paper that Carolina had collected to sell.

Vera's Father Identified in the diary as Senhor J. A. M. V. Vera's father is described as a businessman with many employees. Though she respects his wishes not to be identified by name in her diary, Carolina describes how he fails to provide for his daughter and rarely visits.

Antonio and Nelson The two runaways from the public children's shelter whom Carolina assists during July 1958. Antonio and Nelson tell stories about the horrors of the shelter and impress Carolina and her children. The children realize they'd better behave, and Carolina realizes that she needs to think twice about interning her children at the shelter.

C

I. and C. Two young favela women who have turned to prostitution. I. and C. are identified by their initials only, and Carolina tells their story to offer a moral about what happens to people who are not willing to try to better themselves.

Senhor Tomas A favela man who commits suicide. The fate of Senhor Tomas causes Carolina to become discouraged about her own life.

ANALYSIS OF MAJOR CHARACTERS

CAROLINA DE JESUS The self-portrait that Carolina de Jesus creates in her diary gains texture from the fact that she grants such close access to her inner thoughts, feelings, and dreams. Carolina shows herself in high spirits and low, floating on the joy of falling in love and dragged down by the desperate moments when she knows that her children will have to go hungry that day. She can by turns be critical, humorous, plaintive, strong, and poetic. As a single mother, Carolina feels ostracized, but she takes pride in the fact that she earns her own way instead of stealing from others. She has mixed emotions about relying on anyone, especially men. She cares about books, writing, and her children, and is unwilling to jeopardize any of these things for the security a husband might bring her.

Carolina keeps a diary to assert her sense of self, create a record of life in the favela, and account for the bad actions of both the people around her and the politicians who contribute to the plight of the poor. She tells those who wrong her that they'll end up in her book, and though this strategy can come across as overbearing, her task is important. She has biting and important things to say about the failure of authority to address the needs of the poor, and her chronicle of the many instances of petty fighting, criminality, racism, and sexism in the society she lives in add up to a powerful portrait. Carolina is a keen reporter, able to bring into focus the existence of a *favelado* in unexpected and moving ways. While she is often quite critical, she also has a sense of humor that leavens and illuminates aspects of what is otherwise quite a grim story.

Now, as well as then, Carolina defies a number of stereotypes about the poor. Though she has only two years of formal education, she is intelligent and educated in her own way. Her views are sophisticated, her conclusions complex. Furthermore, Carolina is not meek or docile. She takes pride in being able to earn her own way and chafes at the patronizing attitudes of the more fortunate. Throughout the diary, Carolina is a complicated and even difficult figure. By depicting the complex social and economic forces that conspire against the poor, Carolina shows that there are no quick fixes or magical solutions when dealing with poverty. By being a forceful, challenging, independent woman, Carolina reminds us that the poor are not just a group to be pitied—they are people just as individual and human as anyone else.

THEMES, MOTIFS, AND SYMBOLS

THEMES

THE SYMBIOSIS OF RICH AND POOR In *Child of the Dark*, the fates of the rich and poor are intertwined, and the rich ignore the existence and plight of the poor at their own peril. Though the rich might want to forget about the poor and push them out of sight in the favelas, the poor are as vital to the city as the rich are. When Carolina crosses the dividing line between these two worlds, she sees the contrast and connection between them more clearly. Several times, strong imagery highlights this parallel track, such as the image of the city as a beautiful woman with cheap, torn stockings underneath her ritzy clothes, and especially in terms of the image of São Paulo as a house where the favela functions as a backyard garbage dump. The rich would be lost without a place to dump their garbage, Carolina seems to be saying, and this unsettling observation provides a new perspective on the ever-present link between rich and poor.

THE VALUE OF INDEPENDENCE Carolina's pride in her own independence is the central value that determines both her identity and the way she interacts with other favelados. On one level, her independence is the main guiding force in a strong set of values that she adheres to in the face of numerous threats and temptations. Rampant theft, alcoholism, and violence surround her, and to set herself apart from these scourges, she must maintain a mental distance from them. On another level, Carolina's sense of independence grows out of her resistance to, or mistrust of, other people. Manuel repeatedly proposes marriage, and when she turns him down, Carolina refers to her closely held sense of independence. She points to the subservience that other women must endure in marriage as her reason for staying alone, and since Carolina's independence defines her sense of self, giving up her autonomy would compromise not only her social standing but also her sense of identity as a writer.

THE POWER OF WORDS Whether she is simply recording daily events or creating complex critiques of those around her, Carolina derives tremendous power and identity from the act of writing. On the most basic level, Carolina uses her diary as a weapon against those in the favela who wrong her—she threatens to put them in her book. If Carolina didn't sense that words have intrinsic power, she wouldn't bother making such a threat. There are subtler means, however, that Carolina uses to express the power of writing in her life, such as when she describes how writing makes her feel as though she lives in a golden castle. When she writes about her desire to escape the favela, she is putting words to—and therefore making more real—something she only dreams about.

THE BLINDNESS OF AUTHORITY Fighting back at figures of authority in both the church and the government through her writing, Carolina accuses those in power for being blind to the needs of the poor. She chides the president of Brazil for being like a bird in a gilded cage, ignorant of the hungry cats (the favelados) who are circling. She takes on rich business owners, who price common goods at a level that is out of the poor's reach. She castigates clergymen for preaching sermons that are not only out of touch with the favela but may in fact be harmful. For example, one sermon advised favelados to have more children. Throughout the diary, Carolina repeatedly calls attention to the responsibility that those in power have shirked. In that sense, her diary acts as a corrective to the neglect that the favela has endured for so many years.

C

MOTIFS

HUMOR Though the diary is a grim telling of the desperate existence of the favelado, humor frequently appears as well. Humor leavens some of the darkest events and gives Carolina another point of perspective from which to comment on what she observes. In explaining why she thinks that marrying Manuel would be a mistake, Carolina wonders why a man would want to marry a woman who sleeps with a pen under her pillow. Carolina's ability to poke fun at herself serves as a survival mechanism: by retaining a capacity to laugh at something, she can make it small enough to handle. Even in the midst of extremely grim circumstances, Carolina's wry observations shed light on things we wouldn't otherwise see. For example, she points out that women in the welfare office talk about their children's fathers as horses or asses, and she threatens Manuel by saying she'll begin acting like the other favela women in order to put him in line.

CAROLINA'S THREAT TO PUT PEOPLE IN HER "BOOK" Carolina's constant threat to put those who do her wrong in her "book" defines her character throughout the diary. Carolina has appointed herself an arbiter of accountability, and people will have to answer for their indiscretions. Accountability is surely lacking in the favela, and Carolina thinks she can restore it through writing. With her threats, Carolina is also reminding those around her that she is a person to be reckoned with. Her assertion is ultimately born out by the facts: her threat is responsible for her publication, as reporter Audalio Dantas becomes curious about Carolina's "book" when he overhears her threatening to write about people destroying a children's playground.

SYMBOLS

THE GOLDEN CASTLE When Carolina writes, she imagines she "lives in a golden castle that shines in the sunlight." The act of writing represents many things for Carolina. Writing offers refuge from the humiliations and setbacks she experiences on a daily basis. It is also a source of illumination—it offers Carolina a place to process her thoughts and form meaningful conclusions about what she observes.

A BIRD IN A CAGE In casting the president of Brazil as a bird in a cage, Carolina implies that he is trapped in his own ignorance and is ineffectual at making changes, especially concerning the poor. The image of the bird in a cage makes diminutive a figure of presumably great power. In this construction,

Carolina casts the president as a small and confined bird, while the favelados are wild and hungry cats. This symbol is especially interesting in terms of describing a shifting power relationship. She leaves uncertain the possibility of when the cats will get the bird, and doesn't specify whether or not the bird has anything with which to protect itself beyond the flimsy bars of a self-constructed cage.

THE BEAUTIFUL WOMAN WITH CHEAP STOCKINGS By personifying São Paulo as a beautiful woman with cheap, ragged stockings underneath her fine clothing, Carolina creates a colorful, playful representation of the favela. The rich people of São Paulo must recognize that their lives are intertwined with those of the favelados and act accordingly. The image suggests two of the major themes that define Carolina's diary: the blindness of authority and the symbiosis of the rich and poor. In this case, Carolina chides São Paulo for not seeing its cheap stockings. By putting the city of São Paulo and the favelas on the body of the same beautiful woman, Carolina reveals their inherent interconnectedness.

IMPORTANT QUOTATIONS EXPLAINED

---

1. *I can take the ups and downs of life. If I can't store up the courage to live, I've resolved to store up the patience.*

C

In her entry from July 19, 1955, Carolina's frustrations with meddling favela women and trying to earn enough money to feed her children find an outlet in this new resolution. In Carolina's hand-to-mouth existence, her biggest challenges are the daily ones: finding food and protecting her children. Necessity dictates that she must learn how to cope with innumerable challenges, and patience proves more important than courage. Possessing a laudable virtue like courage may seem luxurious to someone in Carolina's position. Patience is more practical, and it allows her to break down a problem and deal with it constructively. When so many crises threaten to overwhelm Carolina, patience helps her negotiate them with dignity and grace. Over the course of the diary, writing becomes part of Carolina's strategy to "store up the patience." It gives her life meaning and allows her to record the wrong actions of people who might be held accountable later. In this way, Carolina avoids being dragged into the senseless fights she sees all around her, and can escape the larger and subtler sense of despair that afflicts the entire favela.

---

2. *Ah, São Paulo! A queen that vainly shows her skyscrapers that are her crown of gold. All dressed up in velvet and silk but with cheap stockings underneath—the favela.*

Carolina writes this amusing metaphor in her entry of May 22, 1958. Her message is clear: São Paulo's glory is all surface, and the hidden spaces of the favela, her rotten underside, shine through. The gently chiding tone fits in with her stance during the rest of the narrative: though no one else may see what's really going on, she herself is keeping score. The image of the beautiful woman is similar to the metaphor of São Paulo being like a house where the favela is a backyard garbage dump. In both cases, Carolina recognizes that the fates of the rich and the poor are intertwined, and one cannot exist without the other. At the same time, she chides the city's rich for not being willing to see its garbage dump or cheap stockings. Underneath the prized accomplishments, the "crown of gold," a seedy underside roils with unrest.

---

3. *When I write I think I live in a golden castle that shines in the sunlight.*

On June 12, 1958, Carolina chooses an apt symbol for the function writing serves in her life. This castle is both beautiful and protective, a place where she finds the hope she needs to carry on, and a refuge from the daily struggles and humiliations of daily life. Carolina is the queen of this castle, and in writing, she potentially summons the only source of power she has in a life where things often seem out of control. Though this image seems magical and imaginary, Carolina actually builds something concrete through her words: a remembrance, evidence that she was there. Rather than being purely dreamy or ephemeral, her writing charts concrete progress toward a permanent place in the world. She may not have a home or a job, but through writing, she can establish a sense of self that outlasts the whims of fate.

4. *If the Brother saw his children eating rotten food already attacked by vultures and rats, he would stop talking about resignation and rebel, because rebellion comes from bitterness.*

In her entry from July 8, 1958, Carolina chides the Brother of the local Catholic church for being inattentive to the needs of the poor. When factory owners have spoiling food to dispose of, they often dump it near the favela, which incenses Carolina. The local church does help the favelados through visits and food donations, but when Carolina looks at the larger picture, she doubts whether the Church's intervention makes much difference. This thread points to her larger mistrust of the Church and even seems to imply that the Church may be lulling the favelados into a state of denial. In this quote, Carolina also signals her growing political consciousness, though she stops short of advocating a specific plan. Still, the question looms: when will the favelados be ready to rebel? Carolina is aware of talk on the streets, and in taking the Brother to task in this passage, she bemoans the lack of real leadership in the favela. She suggests that the favelados need figures who are in touch with their real struggles and who are willing to move past the easy platitudes and effect change.

5. *The cat is a wise one. She doesn't have any deep loves and doesn't let anyone make a slave of her.*

In her entry from December 29, 1958, Carolina writes of a cat that has killed a rat she's been trying to catch for days. In the cat, Carolina sees the value she prizes most in herself: independence. By ascribing a lack of "deep loves" to the animal, Carolina reveals one of her own survival strategies: she refuses to get married or put her love interests before the interests of her children. As she describes it, marriage resembles slavery. Having watched the women around her get beaten by their husbands, she decides that violence and subservience are givens within marriage. In a larger sense, Carolina is deeply ambivalent about putting her trust in anyone but herself. In the desperate world of the favela, every man or woman must fend for him- or herself. The cat represents the characteristic that allows Carolina to survive in the favela: self-reliance.

The Color Purple

Alice Walker (1944–)

CONTEXT

Alice Walker was born on February 9, 1944, in the small rural town of Eatonton, Georgia. She was the eighth and last child of sharecroppers Willie Lee Walker and Minnie Tallulah Grant. Walker's parents' experiences with the oppressive sharecropping system and the racism of the American South deeply influenced Walker's writing and life's work. When Walker was eight, one of her brothers accidentally shot her, permanently blinding her in one eye. Ashamed of her facial disfigurement, Walker isolated herself from other children, reading and writing to pass the time.

In 1961, on a scholarship for disabled students, Walker enrolled in Spelman College in Atlanta, where she became active in the African-American civil rights movement. Two years later, Walker transferred to Sarah Lawrence College in New York and eventually traveled to Uganda as an exchange student. When she returned for her senior year, Walker was shocked to learn that she was pregnant, and, afraid of her parents' reaction, she considered suicide. However, a classmate helped Walker obtain a safe abortion, and she graduated from Sarah Lawrence in 1965. At this time, Walker composed two early landmark pieces: "To Hell with Dying," her first published short story, and *Once: Poems*, her first volume of poetry.

Walker continued her involvement with the civil rights movement after graduation, working as a volunteer on black voter registration drives in Georgia and Mississippi in 1965 and 1966. In 1967, Walker married Melvyn Leventhal, a Jewish civil rights lawyer, and had one daughter with him before the two divorced in the mid-1970s. Walker's second novel, *Meridian* (1976), explored the controversial issue of sexism in the civil rights movement.

In 1982, Walker published her most famous novel, *The Color Purple*. Walker won the Pulitzer Prize and the American Book Award for this novel, which chronicles the struggle of several black women in rural Georgia in the first half of the twentieth century.

Upon its publication, *The Color Purple* unleashed a storm of controversy. It instigated heated debates about black cultural representation, as a number of male African-American critics complained that the novel reaffirmed old racist stereotypes about pathology in black communities and of black men in particular. Critics also charged Walker with focusing heavily on sexism at the expense of addressing notions of racism in America. Nonetheless, *The Color Purple* also had its ardent supporters, especially among black women and others who praised the novel as a feminist fable. The heated disputes surrounding *The Color Purple* are a testimony to the resounding effects the work has had on cultural and racial discourse in the United States. In 1985, a Steven Spielberg film based on the novel was released to wide audiences and significant acclaim.

Walker's 1992 novel, *Possessing the Secret of Joy*, concerns the marriage of Adam and Tashi—two characters who make their first appearance in *The Color Purple*—and the consequences of Tashi's decision to undergo the traditional African ritual of female circumcision. Walker has continued to explore the unique problems that face black women in both in the United States and Africa. Her novels, poetry, essays, and criticism have become an important part in a burgeoning tradition of talented black women writers.

PLOT OVERVIEW

Celie, the protagonist and narrator of *The Color Purple*, is a poor, uneducated fourteen-year-old black girl living in rural Georgia. Celie starts writing letters to God because her father, Alphonso, beats and rapes her. Alphonso already impregnated Celie once. Celie gave birth to a girl, whom her father stole and presumably killed in the woods. Celie has a second child, a boy, whom her father also steals. Celie's mother becomes seriously ill and dies. Alphonso brings home a new wife but continues to abuse Celie.

Celie and her bright, pretty younger sister, Nettie, learn that a man known only as Mr. ______ wants to marry Nettie. Mr. ______ has a lover named Shug Avery, a sultry lounge singer whose photograph fascinates Celie. Alphonso refuses to let Nettie marry, and instead offers Mr. ______ the "ugly" Celie as a bride. Mr. ______ eventually accepts the offer and takes Celie into a difficult and joyless married life. Nettie runs away from Alphonso and takes refuge at Celie's house. Mr. ______ still desires Nettie, and when he advances on her, she flees for her own safety. Never hearing from Nettie again, Celie assumes she is dead.

Mr. ______'s sister Kate feels sorry for Celie and tells her to fight back against Mr. ______ rather than submit to his abuses. Harpo, Mr. ______'s son, falls in love with a large, spunky girl named Sofia. Shug Avery comes to town to sing at a local bar, but Celie is not allowed to go see her. Sofia becomes pregnant and marries Harpo. Celie is amazed by Sofia's defiance in the face of Harpo's and Mr. ______'s attempts to treat Sofia as an inferior. Harpo's attempts to beat Sofia into submission consistently fail, as Sofia is by far the physically stronger of the two. Shug falls ill and Mr. ______ takes her into his house. Shug is initially rude to Celie, but the two women become friends as Celie takes charge of nursing Shug. Celie finds herself infatuated with Shug and attracted to her sexually. Frustrated with Harpo's consistent attempts to subordinate her, Sofia moves out, taking her children. Several months later, Harpo opens a juke joint where Shug sings nightly. Celie grows confused over her feelings toward Shug.

Shug decides to stay when she learns that Mr. ______ beats Celie when Shug is away. Shug and Celie's relationship grows intimate, and Shug begins to ask Celie questions about sex. Sofia returns for a visit and promptly gets into a fight with Harpo's new girlfriend, Squeak. In town one day, the mayor's wife, Miss Millie, asks Sofia to work as her maid. Sofia answers with a sassy "Hell no." When the mayor slaps Sofia for her insubordination, she returns the blow, knocking the mayor down. Sofia is sent to jail. Squeak's attempts to get Sofia freed are futile. Sofia is sentenced to work for twelve years as the mayor's maid.

C

Shug returns with a new husband, Grady. Despite her marriage, Shug instigates a sexual relationship with Celie, and the two frequently share the same bed. One night, Shug asks Celie about her sister. Celie assumes Nettie is dead because she had promised to write to Celie but never did. Shug says she has seen Mr. ______ hide away numerous mysterious letters that have arrived in the mail. Shug manages to get her hands on one of these letters, and they find that it is from Nettie. Searching through Mr. ______'s trunk, Celie and Shug find dozens of letters that Nettie has sent to Celie over the years. Overcome with emotion, Celie reads the letters in order, wondering how to keep herself from killing Mr. ______.

The letters indicate that Nettie befriended a missionary couple, Samuel and Corrine, and traveled with them to Africa to do ministry work. Samuel and Corrine have two adopted children, Olivia and Adam. Nettie and Corrine become close friends, but Corrine, noticing that her adopted children resemble Nettie, wonders if Nettie and Samuel have a secret past. Increasingly suspicious, Corrine tries to limit Nettie's role within her family.

Nettie becomes disillusioned with her missionary experience, as she finds the Africans self-centered and obstinate. Corrine becomes ill with a fever. Nettie asks Samuel to tell her how he adopted Olivia and Adam. Based on Samuel's story, Nettie realizes that the two children are actually Celie's biological children, alive after all. Nettie also learns that Alphonso is really only Nettie and Celie's step-father, not their real father. Their real father was a storeowner whom white men lynched because they resented his success. Alphonso told Celie and Nettie he was their real father because he wanted to inherit the house and property that was once their mother's.

Nettie confesses to Samuel and Corrine that she is in fact their children's biological aunt. The gravely ill Corrine refuses to believe Nettie. Corrine dies but accepts Nettie's story and feels reconciled just before her death. Meanwhile, Celie visits Alphonso, who confirms Nettie's story, admitting that he is only their stepfather. Celie begins to lose some of her faith in God, but Shug tries to get her to re-imagine God in her own way, rather than in the traditional image of the old, bearded white man.

The mayor releases Sofia from her servitude six months early. At dinner one night, Celie finally releases her pent-up rage, angrily cursing Mr. ______ for his years of abuse. Shug announces that she and Celie are moving to Tennessee, and Squeak decides to go with them. In Tennessee, Celie spends her time designing and sewing individually tailored pairs of pants, eventually turning her hobby into a business. Celie returns to Georgia for a visit, and finds that Mr. ______ has reformed his ways and that Alphonso has died. Alphonso's house and land are now hers, so she moves there.

Meanwhile, Nettie and Samuel marry and prepare to return to America. Before they leave, Samuel's son, Adam, marries Tashi, a native African girl. Following African tradition, Tashi undergoes the painful rituals of female circumcision and facial scarring. In solidarity, Adam undergoes the same facial scarring ritual.

Celie and Mr. ______ reconcile and begin to genuinely enjoy each other's company. Now independent financially, spiritually, and emotionally, Celie is no longer bothered by Shug's passing flings with younger men. Sofia remarries Harpo and now works in Celie's clothing store. Nettie finally returns to

America with Samuel and the children. Emotionally drained but exhilarated by the reunion with her sister, Celie notes that though she and Nettie are now old, she has never in her life felt younger.

CHARACTER LIST

Celie The protagonist and narrator of *The Color Purple*. Celie is a poor, uneducated black woman with a sad personal history. She survives a stepfather, who rapes her and steals her babies, and also an abusive husband. As an adult, Celie befriends and finds intimacy with a blues singer, Shug Avery, who gradually helps Celie find her voice. By the end of the novel, Celie is a happy, independent, and self-confident woman.

Nettie Celie's younger sister, whom Mr. ______ initially wanted to marry. Nettie runs from Alphonso to Mr. ______, and later runs away from Mr. ______. She meets a husband-and-wife pair of missionaries, Samuel and Corrine. With them, she moves to Africa to preach. Nettie becomes the caretaker of Samuel and Corrine's adopted children (who, Nettie later learns, are Celie's biological children, whom Celie and Nettie's stepfather stole and subsequently sold) and faithfully writes letters to Celie for decades. Nettie's experiences in Africa broaden the novel's scope, introducing issues of imperialism and pan-African struggles.

Mr. ______ Celie's husband, who abuses her for years. Mr. ______ , whose first name is Albert, pines away for Shug during his marriage to Celie and hides Nettie's letters to Celie in his trunk for decades. After Celie finally confronts Mr. ______ , denouncing him for his abuse, he undergoes a deep personal transformation, reassessing his life and eventually becoming friends with Celie.

Shug Avery A sultry blues singer who first appears as Mr. ______'s mistress. Shug becomes Celie's friend and eventually her lover, all the while remaining a gentle mentor who helps Celie evolve into an independent and assertive woman. Shug does not at first appear to be the mothering kind, yet she nurtures Celie physically, spiritually, and emotionally. Shug gives Celie the idea of sewing pants for a living.

Harpo Mr. ______'s eldest son. Many of Harpo's actions overturn stereotypical gender roles. He confesses to Celie about his love for Sofia, cries in her arms, enjoys cooking and housework, kisses his children, and marries an independent woman, Sofia. However, Mr. ______'s expectations of stereotypical male dominance convince Harpo that he needs to beat Sofia. His efforts to abuse Sofia fail, since she is much stronger than he is. At the end of the novel, Harpo reforms his ways, and he and Sofia reconcile and save their marriage.

Sofia A large, fiercely independent woman who befriends Celie and marries Harpo. Sofia refuses to submit to whites, men, or anyone else who tries to dominate her. After defying the town's mayor, Sophia is sentenced to twelve years in jail, but the sentence is later commuted to twelve years of labor as the mayor's maid. The hardship Sofia endures serves as a reminder of the costs of resistance and the difficulties of combating cultural and institutional racism.

Squeak Harpo's lover after Sofia leaves him. As a mulatto, a person of mixed black and white ancestry, Squeak highlights the complex nature of racial identification. Although abused like many of the women in the novel, Squeak eventually undergoes a transformation much like Celie's. She demands to be called by her real name, Mary Agnes, and she pursues a singing career.

Alphonso Celie and Nettie's stepfather, whom the sisters think is their real father until Nettie learns the truth years later. When Celie is young, Alphonso rapes and abuses her until she moves out of the house. Unlike Mr. ______ and Harpo, who are transformed, Alphonso remains an abuser until his death. Celie inherits her house and property after Alphonso dies.

Samuel A minister who, along with his wife, Corrine, adopts Celie's biological children, Olivia and Adam. A wise, spiritually mature black intellectual committed to "the uplift of black people everywhere," Samuel takes Corrine, Nettie, and the children to Africa for missionary work. He tells Nettie a story that makes her realize Alphonso is her stepfather rather than her biological father. After Corrine's death, Samuel marries Nettie.

Corrine Samuel's wife. After moving to Africa, Corrine grows increasingly suspicious and jealous of Nettie's role in her family, convinced that Nettie and Samuel have had an affair. While still in Africa, Corrine dies from a fever, opening up the opportunity for Nettie and Samuel to marry.

Olivia Celie and Alphonso's biological daughter, who is adopted by Samuel and Corrine. Olivia develops a close sisterly relationship with Tashi, an Olinka village girl. This friendship, which crosses cultural boundaries, serves as an example of the strength of relationships between women.

Adam Celie and Alphonso's biological son, who, like Olivia, is adopted by Samuel and Corrine. Adam falls in love with Tashi, a young Olinka girl. By marrying Tashi, Adam symbolically bridges Africa and America, and his respect for and deference to her subverts patriarchal notions that women are subordinate to men.

Tashi An Olinka village girl who befriends Olivia and marries Adam. Tashi defies white imperialist culture and embodies the struggle of traditional cultural values against colonization. She chooses to undergo two painful African traditions—facial scarring and genital mutilation—as a way to physically differentiate her culture from imperialist culture.

Miss Millie The wife of the mayor of the town where Celie lives. Miss Millie is racist and condescending, but she admires the cleanliness and good manners of Sofia's children, so she asks Sofia to be her maid. Sofia replies, "Hell no," and is sent first to jail, then to Miss Millie's, where she ends up working as her maid after all.

Eleanor Jane The mayor's daughter. Eleanor Jane develops a strong attachment to Sofia and turns to her for emotional support. However, Sofia does not reciprocate Eleanor Jane's feelings because of the years of mistreatment she suffered at the hands of Eleanor Jane's parents. Toward the end of the novel, Eleanor Jane finally begins to understand the injustices Sofia and other blacks have suffered. She attempts to atone for her part in the unjust treatment of Sofia by caring for Sofia's daughter Henrietta.

Grady Shug's husband. Grady is a loving and sweet man, but also a womanizer. He spends Shug's money flamboyantly and frequently smokes marijuana. When Grady and Squeak begin an affair, Shug seems relieved to be rid of any responsibility to her relationship with Grady.

Kate One of Mr. ______'s sisters. Kate urges Celie to stand up for herself and defy Mr. ______'s abuses.

ANALYSIS OF MAJOR CHARACTERS

CELIE As a young girl, Celie is constantly subjected to abuse and told she is ugly, so she tries to make herself silent and invisible. Celie's letters to God are her only outlet and means of self-expression. Abused into submission both verbally and physically, Celie does little to fight back against her stepfather, Alphonso. Later in life, when her husband, Mr. ______, abuses her, she reacts in a similarly passive manner. However, Celie latches on to Shug Avery, a beautiful and seemingly empowered woman, as a role model. After Shug moves into Celie and Mr. ______'s home, Celie has the opportunity to befriend the woman whom she loves and to learn, at last, how to fight back. Shug's maternal prodding helps spur Celie's development. Gradually, Celie recovers her own history, sexuality, spirituality, and voice. When Shug says Celie is "still a virgin" because she has never had a satisfying sex life, Shug demonstrates to Celie the renewing and empowering capacity of storytelling. Shug also opens Celie's eyes to new ideas about religion, empowering Celie to believe in a nontraditional, non-patriarchal form of God.

Nettie's long-lost letters, which Celie discovers (with Shug's help) hidden in Mr. ______'s trunk, fortify Celie's sense of self by informing her of her personal history and of the fate of her children. As her letters show, Celie gradually gains the ability to synthesize her thoughts and feelings into a voice that is fully her own. Celie's process of finding her own voice culminates with her enraged explosion at Mr. ______, in which she curses him for his years of abuse and abasement. Mr. ______ responds in his characteristic insulting manner, but his put-downs have no power once Celie possesses the sense of self-worth she previously lacked. The self-actualization Celie achieves transforms her into a happy, successful, independent woman. Celie takes on the act of sewing, which is traditionally thought of as a mere chore for women who are confined to a domestic role, and turns it into an outlet for creative self-expression and a profitable business. After being voiceless for so many years, she is finally content, fulfilled, and self- sufficient. When Nettie, Olivia, and Adam return to Georgia from Africa, Celie's circle of friends and family is finally reunited. Though Celie has endured many years of hardship, she says, "[D]on't think us feel old at all. . . . Matter of fact, I think this the youngest us ever felt."

SHUG AVERY Shug has a reputation as a woman of dubious morals who dresses scantily, has some sort of "nasty woman disease," and is shunned by her own parents. But Celie immediately sees something more in Shug. When Celie looks at Shug's photograph, not only does Shug's glamorous appearance amaze her, but Shug also reminds Celie of her "mama." Celie compares Shug to her mother throughout the novel. Unlike Celie's natural mother, who was oppressed by traditional gender roles, Shug refuses to allow herself to be dominated by anyone. Shug has fashioned her identity from her many experiences instead of subjecting her will to others and allowing them to impose an identity upon her.

Though Shug's sexy style, sharp tongue, and many worldly experiences make her appear jaded, Shug is actually warm and compassionate at heart. When Shug falls ill, she not only appreciates, but also reciprocates the care and attention Celie lavishes upon her. As Shug's relationship with Celie develops, Shug fills the roles of mother, confidant, lover, sister, teacher, and friend. Shug's many roles make her an unpredictable and dynamic character who moves through a whirlwind of different cities, trysts, and late-night blues clubs. Despite her unpredictable nature and shifting roles, Shug remains Celie's most constant friend and companion throughout the novel.

MR. ______ Although Mr. ______'s development is not the subject of the novel, he undergoes just as significant a transformation as Celie does. Mr. ______ initially treats Celie as nothing more than an object. He beats her like an animal and shows no human connection, even during sex. He also hides Nettie's letters to Celie from Celie for years. Mr. ______'s treatment of Celie, though harsh, also spurs her development. Celie's discovery of Nettie's letters begins her first experience with raw anger, which culminates in her angry denunciation of Mr. ______ in front of the others at dinner. Celie's newfound confidence, instilled in her by Shug, inspires her to react assertively and forcefully to Mr. ______'s abuse.

When Celie returns from Tennessee, she finds that Mr. ______ has re-evaluated his life and attempted to correct his earlier wrongs. Mr. ______ finally listens to Celie, and the two come to enjoy conversing and sewing together. Mr. ______ eventually expresses his wish to have an equal and mutually respectful marriage with Celie, but she declines.

NETTIE Though younger than her sister, Nettie often acts as Celie's protector. Nettie is highly intellectual and recognizes the value of education from an early age. However, even though Nettie is smart and ambitious, Mr. ______ effectively silences her by hiding her letters from Celie. In her letters to Celie, Nettie writes that she is lonely, showing that, like Celie, Nettie needs a sympathetic audience to listen to her thoughts and concerns.

Critics have faulted Nettie's letters for being digressive and boring in comparison to Celie's. Although Nettie's letters are indeed quite encyclopedic and contain less raw experience and emotion, they play an important role in the novel. As a black intellectual traveling the world in pursuit of "the uplift of black people everywhere," Nettie has a vastly different experience from Celie. Yet her letters, which recount the problems Nettie has encountered in Africa, broaden the novel's scope and show that oppression—of women by men, of blacks by whites, and even of blacks by blacks—is universal. The imperial, racial, and cultural conflict and oppression Nettie encounters in Africa parallel the smaller-scale abuses and hardships that Celie experiences in Georgia.

THEMES, MOTIFS, AND SYMBOLS

THEMES

THE POWER OF NARRATIVE AND VOICE Walker emphasizes throughout the novel that the ability to express one's thoughts and feelings is crucial to developing a sense of self. Initially, Celie is completely unable to resist those who abuse her. Remembering Alphonso's warning that she "better not never tell nobody but God" about his abuse of her, Celie feels that the only way to persevere is to remain silent and invisible. Celie is essentially an object, an entirely passive party who has no power to assert herself through actions or words. Her letters to God, in which she begins to pour out her story, become her only outlet. However, because she is so unaccustomed to articulating her experience, her narrative is initially muddled despite her best efforts at transparency.

In Shug and Sofia, Celie finds sympathetic ears and learns lessons that enable her to find her voice. In renaming Celie a "virgin," Shug shows Celie that she can create her own narrative, a new interpretation of herself and her history that counters the interpretations forced upon her. Gradually, Celie begins to flesh out more of her story by telling it to Shug. However, it is not until Celie and Shug discover Nettie's letters that Celie finally has enough knowledge of herself to form her own powerful narrative. Celie's forceful assertion of this newfound power, her cursing of Mr. _____ for his years of abuse, is the novel's climax. Celie's story dumbfounds and eventually humbles Mr. _____, causing him to reassess and change his own life.

Though Walker clearly wishes to emphasize the power of narrative and speech to assert selfhood and resist oppression, the novel acknowledges that such resistance can be risky. Sofia's forceful outburst in response to Miss Millie's invitation to be her maid costs her twelve years of her life. Sofia regains her freedom eventually, so she is not totally defeated, but she pays a high price for her words.

THE POWER OF STRONG FEMALE RELATIONSHIPS Throughout *The Color Purple,* Walker portrays female friendships as a means for women to summon the courage to tell stories. In turn, these stories allow women to resist oppression and dominance. Relationships among women form a refuge, providing reciprocal love in a world filled with male violence. Female ties take many forms: some are motherly or sisterly, some are in the form of mentor and pupil, some are sexual, and some are simply friendships. Sofia claims that her ability to fight comes from her strong relationships with her sisters. Nettie's relationship with Celie anchors her through years of living in the unfamiliar culture of Africa. Samuel notes that the strong relationships among Olinka women are the only thing that makes polygamy bearable for them. Most important, Celie's ties to Shug bring about Celie's gradual redemption and her attainment of a sense of self.

THE CYCLICAL NATURE OF RACISM AND SEXISM Almost none of the abusers in Walker's novel are stereotypical, one-dimensional monsters whom we can dismiss as purely evil. Those who perpetuate violence are themselves victims, often of sexism, racism, or paternalism. Harpo, for example, beats Sofia only after his father implies that Sofia's resistance makes Harpo less of a man. Mr. _____ is violent and mistreats his family, much like his own tyrantlike father treated him. Celie advises Harpo to beat Sofia because she is jealous of Sofia's strength and assertiveness.

The characters are largely aware of the cyclical nature of harmful behavior. For instance, Sofia tells Eleanor Jane that societal influence makes it almost inevitable that her baby boy will grow up to be racist. Only by forcefully talking back to the men who abuse them and showing them a new way of doing things do the women of the novel break these cycles of sexism and violence, causing the men who abused them to stop and reexamine their ways.

THE DISRUPTION OF TRADITIONAL GENDER ROLES Many characters in the novel break the boundaries of traditional male or female gender roles. Sofia's strength and sass, Shug's sexual assertiveness, and Harpo's insecurity are major examples of such disparity between a character's gender and the traits he or she displays. This blurring of gender traits and roles sometimes involves sexual ambiguity, as we see in the sexual relationship that develops between Celie and Shug.

Disruption of gender roles sometimes causes problems. Harpo's insecurity about his masculinity leads to marital problems and his attempts to beat Sofia. Likewise, Shug's confident sexuality and resistance to male domination cause her to be labeled a tramp. Throughout the novel, Walker wishes to emphasize that gender and sexuality are not as simple as we may believe. Her novel subverts and defies the traditional ways in which we understand women to be women and men to be men.

MOTIFS

LETTERS Walker uses the novel's epistolary (letter-writing) form to emphasize the power of communication. Celie writes letters to God, and Nettie writes letters to Celie. Both sisters gain strength from their letter-writing, but they are saved only when they receive responses to their letters. Therefore, although writing letters enables self-expression and confession, it requires a willing audience. When Celie never responds to Nettie's letters, Nettie feels lost because Celie is her only audience. Nettie grows disillusioned with her missionary work because the imperialists will not listen to her and because the Olinka villagers are stubborn. Only after Nettie returns home to Celie, an audience guaranteed to listen, does she feel fulfilled and freed.

THE RURAL FARM COMMUNITY Walker sets most of her novel in a rural farm community that has few visitors, and she focuses on colorful portraits of each of her characters. By focusing on the personal lives and transformations of her characters, Walker renders public events almost irrelevant. When Shug and Celie hear news of current events from the outside world, it all just sounds "crazy" to them. The unspecific time and place broaden the novel's scope, making its themes more universal.

COLORS Throughout the novel, the appearance of brighter colors indicates the liberation various characters experience. Walker uses color to signal renewals and rebirths at several points in the novel. When Kate takes Celie shopping for a new dress, the only color options are drab ones—brown, maroon, and dark blue. Later, Celie and Sofia use bright yellow fabric from Shug's dress to make a quilt. When Celie describes her religious awakening, she marvels how she never noticed the wonders that God has made, such as "the color purple." Upon Mr. ______'s transformation, he paints the entire interior of his house "fresh and white," signaling his new beginning.

SYMBOLS

SEWING AND QUILTS In general, sewing in *The Color Purple* symbolizes the power women can gain from productively channeling their creative energy. After Sofia and Celie argue about the advice Celie has given Harpo, Sofia signals a truce by suggesting they make a quilt. The quilt, composed of diverse patterns sewn together, symbolizes diverse people coming together in unity. Like a patchwork quilt, the community of love that surrounds Celie at the end of the novel incorporates men and women who are bonded by family and friendship, and who have different gender roles, sexual orientations, and talents. Another important instance of sewing in the novel is Celie's pants-sewing business. With Shug's help, Celie overturns the idea that sewing is marginal and unimportant women's labor, and she turns it into a lucrative, empowering source of economic independence.

GOD In the early parts of the novel, Celie sees God as her listener and helping hand, yet Celie does not have a clear understanding of who God is. She knows deep down that her image of God as a white patriarch "don't seem quite right," but she says it's all she has. Shug invites Celie to imagine God as something radically different, as an "it" that delights in creation and just wants human beings to love what it has created. Eventually, Celie stops thinking of God as she stops thinking of the other men in her life—she "git man off her eyeball" and tells God off, writing, "You must be sleep." But after Celie has chased her patriarchal God away and come up with a new concept of God, she writes in her last letter, "Dear God. Dear stars, dear trees, dear sky, dear peoples. Dear Everything. Dear God." This reimagining of God on her own terms symbolizes Celie's move from an object of someone else's care to an independent woman. It also indicates that her voice is now sufficiently empowered to create her own narrative.

IMPORTANT QUOTATIONS EXPLAINED

---

1. *Harpo say, I love you, Squeak. He kneel down and try to put his arms round her waist. She stand up. My name Mary Agnes, she say.*

This passage is from Celie's forty-first letter. Squeak has just returned from an unsuccessful attempt to release Sofia from prison. The prison warden raped Squeak, and she returns home battered and torn. However, Squeak is not defeated, and she makes an important act of resistance when she decides to reject the belittling nickname, Squeak, that Harpo has given her. She insists on being called by her given name, Mary Agnes. By renaming herself, Mary Agnes resists the patriarchal words and symbols that Harpo has imposed upon her. Walker repeatedly stresses the importance of language and storytelling as ways of controlling situations and as the first steps toward liberation. Just as Shug renames Celie a virgin, and just as Celie reverses Mr. ______'s words to say, "I'm pore, I'm black, I may be ugly and can't cook. . . . But I'm here," Mary Agnes renames herself to show her refusal to let the man in her life gain interpretive control over her.

2. *Us sleep like sisters, me and Shug.*

In her sixtieth letter, Celie is recovering from the shock of learning Mr. ______ has been hiding Nettie's letters to her. To help Celie overcome her anger, Shug positions herself as a very maternal or sisterly figure who protects and arranges Celie's outside environment and makes sure Celie does not act on her instinct to murder Mr. ______. Nonetheless, though Celie and Shug's relationship becomes more sisterly and familial, the intimate and sexual side does not disappear. In Shug and Celie's relationship, Walker shows sexuality to be a complex phenomenon. Celie and Shug are sexual with one another, but they are simultaneously maternal, sisterly, friendly, and loving.

3. *It must have been a pathetic exchange. Our chief never learned English beyond an occasional odd phrase he picked up from Joseph, who pronounces "English" "Yanglush."*

In the sixty-fifth letter, Nettie shares with Celie her sentiments about the Olinka villagers. After the Olinka have this "pathetic exchange" with a white man from the English rubber company, the Olinka conclude that it is a waste of breath to argue with men who cannot or will not listen. The cultural barrier between the Olinka and the English is so vast that both parties readily give up, believing no communication is possible. Samuel later mentions that the only way he and the other Americans could remain in Africa is to join the *mbeles*, the natives who have fled deep into the jungle and refuse to work for the white settlers.

With this discussion of the barrier separating the Olinka from the English, Walker emphasizes that, though narrative can be a powerful force, some differences cannot be overcome. Cultural complexities and gulfs of foreignness sometimes render communication futile. This provides a sobering counterexample to Celie's success at finding her voice and using it as the key to her discovery of self- worth. Walker admits that some cultural differences are so great that there is little hope for communication. Unfortunately, she suggests no solution to this problem.

4. *Well, us talk and talk about God, but I'm still adrift. Trying to chase that old white man out of my head. I been so busy thinking bout him I never truly notice nothing God make. Not a blade of corn (how it do that?) not the color purple (where it come from?). . . .*

In the seventy-third letter of the novel, Celie reminds Nettie about this conversation with Shug. Celie has told Shug that she has stopped writing to God altogether. In response, Shug tries to help Celie develop a new understanding of God, which involves sidelining Celie's notion of a God who is white and male and with whom she feels she has nothing in common. Shug gently suggests that instead of being mad at God for his injustice, Celie should reimagine God as a figure or entity with which she can more closely connect. Just because Celie's image of an archetypal old, bearded white man will no longer do, Shug argues, Celie does not need to reject God altogether. Shug urges Celie to be creative and to see the presence of God in everything and everyone, as a sort of disembodied "it" with no race or gender. Shug's lesson is part of a greater lesson that argues for reimagining one's oppressors rather than rejecting them. Shug shows Celie that she does not need to reject men altogether. She explains that Celie can have men as friends and that her life does not need to revolve around men exclusively. Instead of dismissing men and God, Shug changes the power dynamic by reimagining them.

5. *Shug act more manly than most men . . . he say. You know Shug will fight, he say. Just like Sofia. She bound to live her life and be herself no matter what.*

   Mr. ______ think all this is stuff men do. But Harpo not like this, I tell him. You not like this. What Shug got is womanly it seem like to me. Specially since she and Sofia the ones got it.

Celie recounts this conversation she has with Mr. ______ near the end of the novel, in her eighty-seventh letter. Their words of reconciliation concern the acceptance of differences—in gender roles, talents, and sexual orientation. *The Color Purple* concerns a universe in which traditionally masculine traits such as assertiveness, sexual gratification, and physical strength are present in female as well as male characters. Sofia's assertiveness and strength are virtually unsurpassed by any of the male characters, whereas the nurturing and care that Harpo displays toward Mr. ______ could be considered feminine.

By the end of the novel, a sort of mixing has occurred, as some characters' masculine traits have rubbed off onto more feminine characters, and vice versa. Shug, for instance, learns from and reciprocates Celie's gentleness and care, while Celie picks up some of Shug's sexual assertiveness and follows Shug's suggestion that she become owner of a business, a traditionally male role. Mr. ______ and Harpo, conversely, become somewhat feminized. Mr. ______ learns to sew and to be a good listener, and Harpo cooks, changes his baby's diaper, and kisses his children. By the end of the novel, it is clear that Walker sees fixed gender roles as meaningless and impractical.

Coming of Age in Mississippi

Anne Moody (1940–)

C

CONTEXT

Today, Anne Moody is famous for two things: being one of the students who demanded service at the famous Woolworth's lunch-counter sit-in in Jackson, Mississippi, and her autobiography, *Coming of Age in Mississippi*, which stands out as one of the classic autobiographies of American literature. Most leaders of the civil rights movement, such as Martin Luther King, Jr., and W. E. B. Dubois, were middle-class or even wealthy. Moody is unique in being the direct voice of the most oppressed rural blacks.

African Americans had won their freedom in the Civil War and were guaranteed equal rights under new amendments to the Constitution. But when the federal government stopped enforcing the rule of law in the South, whites terrorized blacks into second-class citizenship. Using the Jim Crow laws, whites effectively barred blacks from voting, and almost all public facilities were segregated. Jim Crow was in effect throughout the time period of *Coming of Age in Mississippi*. As Moody tries to register voters, their applications are denied for a variety of pretenses, among them useless voting tests and archaic requirements.

Like most African Americans in the rural South before the civil rights movement, Moody's family worked as sharecroppers. Sharecropping, also called "tenant farming," entails a farmer renting the land on which he farms. Often, the rent is paid as either a percentage or fixed amount of the crop. Before the Civil War, sharecropping was the way many rural southern whites eked out a living. With the end of slavery, most ex-slaves simply became sharecroppers, often on the same plantation on which they had worked as slaves. Academics have argued that in economic terms, sharecropping can be as exploitative as slavery, since the landowner risks nothing if there is a bad crop.

In 1968, when *Coming of Age in Mississippi* was released, critics tended to focus less on the book's value as a work of literature, looking at it instead as social commentary and an exposé of racism in the South. The civil rights movement was beginning to run out of steam. The Voting Rights Act and the repeal of numerous Jim Crow laws had already granted blacks the legal rights the movement demanded. But it became increasingly obvious that these political rights would not mean an end to the poverty and suffering of most blacks. The Vietnam War drafted many of the young black men who had helped form its base and also took away headlines and resources from the fight for civil rights. Moody and others believed that the civil rights movement's leaders, such as Martin Luther King, Jr., relied too heavily upon nonviolent demonstrations and rallies that were proving largely ineffective. The closing chapters of *Coming of Age* stress the need to reinvigorate the movement.

Moody has said publicly that when she wrote her autobiography, she considered herself an activist, not a writer. A review in *The Nation* called *Coming of Age* "crude and undeniable and, against all principles of beauty, beautiful." Today, the book is assigned in literature courses, as well as history and social science courses. Of all the tens of thousands of memoirs, social exposés, and historical narratives, *Coming of Age* is one of the few still widely taught today.

PLOT OVERVIEW

When Anne is four years old, she and her mother, Toosweet, her father, Diddly, and her younger sister, Adline, live in a two-room shack on a plantation. None of the shacks of the black plantation workers has electricity or indoor plumbing, while the Carter family's house has both. At night, when the white family's house is the only one lit up, Anne's mother says the plantation owner is counting money he made off of them. While Anne's parents are out working in the fields during the day, George Lee, Toosweet's eight-year-old brother, watches Anne and her sister inside. Resentful of having to babysit, George Lee hits the girls and one day accidentally sets the wallpaper on fire while trying to scare them with matches.

Amid anxieties over money, the fire, and the death of his best friend, Diddly eventually leaves the family for an affair with Florence, a lighter-skinned black woman. Toosweet and the children, who now include a son, Junior, eventually move to at least six different houses over the next six years. Toosweet works as a waitress at a café for blacks, and then as a maid for white families. Toosweet's family is constantly hungry, often eating only bread and beans supplemented by table scraps from Toosweet's white employers. Still, Anne does exceptionally well in school. In the fourth grade, Anne begins working part-time cleaning the houses of white families. She will continue working until her senior year of high school, spending most of her after-school hours doing menial jobs in order to put food on the family's table. Most of her employers are fairly easy to get along with. The Claibornes even encourage Anne in her studies and ask her to eat with them at their table. But Mrs. Burke, a nasty woman and a racist, makes life difficult, especially when her son Wayne grows close to Anne. Mrs. Burke finally accuses Anne's brother Junior of stealing in order to get back at her, relenting only after leaving both children shaken. Anne quits.

Meanwhile, Anne has begun to attract the attention of the boys in her high school and the men in her community. When she outgrows her school dresses, she wears jeans, which she cannot afford to replace even when they grow tight. She becomes so popular with the boys that she is elected homecoming queen. Diddly even provides Anne with a beautiful gown, making the homecoming parade one of the few joyful moments of her young life. When Anne is still very young, her mother develops a romantic relationship with Raymond Davis, with whom she has four more children. Raymond's family, especially Miss Pearl, Raymond's mother, looks down on Toosweet because she has darker skin than they do. Yet Anne enjoys their new home in Centreville, and especially Centreville Baptist Church, the upscale church Raymond's family attends. When Anne's mother wants her to attend their old, poorer church, Anne gets into the first of many serious conflicts with her mother.

In the summer of 1955, when Anne hears that Emmett Till, a 14-year-old black boy visiting from Chicago, has been brutally murdered for allegedly whistling at a white woman, she becomes acutely conscious of the racial inequality around her. As a younger child, she struggled to understand the inequity between the races, and she gains no more understanding of this fact as she grows older. She wonders if there are any real differences between blacks and whites, save for the fact that the black women clean the white women's homes.

When Anne first hears about the NAACP (the National Association for the Advancement of Colored People), a forbidden organization in rural Mississippi, she begins to contemplate how the racial inequalities around her can be overthrown. Meanwhile, however, her own struggles with her family are more pressing. Toosweet feels that Anne is starting to look down on her, especially when Anne changes her name from Essie Mae to Annie Mae because she thinks Essie Mae sounds like a name for barnyard animals. Anne's family does not understand Anne's growing interest in the civil rights movement; in fact, they are afraid of it. Anne spends her last three summers of high school in Baton Rouge and New Orleans, doing menial jobs for more money than she could earn at home. Eventually, Anne can no longer stand the family, especially Raymond, and she storms out and moves in with her father, Diddly, and his wife, Emma. Emma and her family are light skinned, but do not hold themselves above anyone, and Anne grows close to them.

Anne accepts a basketball scholarship to Natchez College, a suffocatingly conservative Baptist college in Mississippi. There, Anne has her first boyfriend. She eventually transfers to Tougaloo College for her final two years of college. At Tougaloo, she joins the NAACP, in spite of the strong protests of her mother. The local sheriff even tells Anne's mother that Anne must not attend NAACP events or it will mean trouble for her family. Nonetheless, Anne becomes active in the NAACP and the civil rights movement, despite her family's impassioned pleas for her to quit.

Anne participates in the famous sit-in at the lunch counter of the Woolworth's in Jackson, Mississippi. She later works as a CORE (Coalition for the Organization of Racial Equality) activist in rural Madison County, Mississippi, where she and the other activists are the targets of violent threats. After exhaustive work, Anne concludes that the movement has not improved the lives of people in Mississippi. It has focused too much on voter registration and even political theater, such as the Freedom Vote, a mock vote intended to protest disenfranchisement of blacks. Instead, Anne wants the movement to focus on economic issues, such as helping black farmers buy their own land. At the end of her memoir, twenty-three-year-old Anne is getting on a bus to Washington. The bus is filled with volunteers who all seem far more exuberant and younger than she. As they sing "We Shall Overcome," Anne wonders if blacks will ever really overcome racism.

CHARACTER LIST

Anne Moody The subject of the autobiography. Moody's given name is Essie Mae, though she goes by Anne.

Toosweet Davis (Mama) Anne's mother. Toosweet strives to feed and clothe her children and encourages Anne's schoolwork early on. However, she does not encourage Anne to go to college and begs Anne to get out of the civil rights movement.

Adline Moody Anne's younger sister. Adline and her mother do not support Anne's civil rights work, though Adline eventually supports Anne's decision to go to college

Diddly Moody (Dil) Anne's father. Moody deserts Toosweet for Florence. Anne goes to live with him after she leaves Toosweet.

James Moody Anne's younger brother and Raymond's son.

Junior Moody Anne's younger brother and Diddly's son.

Virginia Moody (Jennie Mae) Toosweet's daughter by Raymond.

Alberta Toosweet's sister. Alberta moves nearby after Virginia is born.

Darlene Raymond's younger sister. Darlene is Anne's age. Anne delights in outperforming her in school and church activities.

Wayne Burke Mrs. Burke's son. Wayne grows attached to Anne, enraging his mother.

Mrs. Burke Linda Mae and Wayne's mother. Mrs. Burke employs Anne as a maid. Mrs. Burke is highly unpleasant and looks down on blacks. Anne first hears about the NAACP when she overhears Mrs. Burke discussing it with a ladies' group.

The Carter Family Owners of the plantation where Anne lives at the start of the memoir. The Carter family employs Anne and her family. Anne's mother says Mr. Carter stays up at night counting money he has made off the black plantation workers.

Reverend Carson Anne's teacher at Mt. Pleasant School. Reverend Carson terrifies the children with his loud voice and his switch; he is fairly inept as a teacher.

The Claiborne Family The family that employs Anne. The Claiborne family encourages Anne in her schoolwork and shares their dinner table with her. She helps them around the house.

Aunt Cindy Toosweet's sister. Aunt Cindy hosts Anne during the first few weeks after she leaves Dil.

The Cook Family A family that is acquainted with Anne's. The Cook family rents Anne's mother her first house after Anne's father abandons her. They are kind to Anne and her family.

Raymond Davis Toosweet's second husband. Raymond Davis and Anne have a tense relationship, which prompts Anne to move out of her immediate family's house.

Doris A fellow CORE activist with Anne in Canton. Doris grows extremely nervous in the face of constant white terrorism.

Florence Exceptionally beautiful mulatto widow of Dil's best friend, Hank. Dil has an affair with her that destroys his marriage with Toosweet.

George Lee Toosweet's younger brother. Lee is forced to look after Anne and Adline—when he is only eight years old—while their parents are working. He hits the girls and accidentally sets the wallpaper on fire when he tries to scare them with matches.

Mr. Hicks Gym teacher and athletic coach. Mr. Hicks becomes infatuated with Anne.

Linda Mae Jenkins A woman who employs Anne as a maid and babysitter.

The Johnson Family Family who employs Toosweet as a maid. The Johnson family is kinder to Toosweet than her other employers. She works for them after quitting the café but before moving in with Raymond.

C

Ola Johnson Grandmother of the Johnson family. Johnson takes Anne under her wing and encourages her in all pursuits.

Keemp A basketball player at Natchez and Anne's first boyfriend.

Reverend Edward King A white southern minister and civil rights activist who befriends Anne.

Miss Pearl Raymond's mother. Miss Pearl treats Toosweet coldly because Toosweet is darker skinned.

Grandfather Moody Anne's grandfather. Grandfather Moody is regretful of his son's abandonment of Anne's family, and so he gives them money from the pouch around his waist.

Mrs. Rice Anne's teacher. Rice tells Anne about the NAACP and encourages her to learn more about the civil rights movement.

Uncle Ed Toosweet's brother. Ed is Anne's favorite uncle when she is a child.

Mr. Willis Principal of Anne's high school. Mr. Willis is considered the biggest "Uncle Tom" in Anne's town. Many believe he helped conspire to murder an NAACP activist.

Mrs. Willis Anne's eighth-grade teacher. Mrs. Willis's extraordinary skills as a fund-raiser help Anne become homecoming queen.

C

Winny Anne's grandmother. Winny is Toosweet's mother. She has thirteen children and has never married.

ANALYSIS OF MAJOR CHARACTERS

ANNE MOODY (ESSIE MAE) *Coming of Age in Mississippi* covers a span of nineteen years, from when Anne is four to twenty-three years old. Moody's own personal evolution parallels and symbolizes the development of the civil rights movement. Anne Moody was born Essie May Moody in 1940. She grew up in Wilkerson County, a rural county marked by extreme poverty and racism. Her family spent time working on plantations until her father deserted the family. Her mother worked as a maid for various white families, as did Anne, in order to supplement her family's meager income. Just as the civil rights movement was maturing in the early 1950s, Anne also was maturing as a young woman. She was also becoming increasingly conscious of racial inequalities. With the 1955 murder of Emmett Till, Anne first heard of the NAACP and began thinking of the possibility of overthrowing the institutions that oppressed African Americans.

Toosweet and the rest of the family do not understand Anne's ambitions. Around the time that Anne is graduating from high school in the late 1950s, the movement to end segregation has prompted the government to build new, better schools for black students. But Anne believes that they should not settle for anything less than complete equality as represented by integration. Even when Anne graduates from college, her family does not attend the ceremony. Anne's separation from them is symbolic of the civil rights movement's necessary break with the older, limited realities of southern blacks. It is also a very painful, personal coming of age. Anne's conflict with her family is one of the most universal aspects of *Coming of Age in Mississippi*.

TOOSWEET DAVIS (MAMA) In many ways, Toosweet represents the older generation of rural African Americans in the deep South. She is constantly struggling to survive yet terrified of risking what little she has to challenge the system of inequality. But Toosweet is not just a symbol. As Moody's mother, she is portrayed as a real person with real concerns and real fears. In many ways, as much as she symbolizes the older generation's resistance to change, she also makes that resistance seem very understandable. Toosweet's relationship with Anne becomes increasingly strained as Anne grows older and her horizons broaden. Toosweet becomes an obstacle to Anne, as she clings to her daughter and encourages her to become more like everyone else in their rural community. Toosweet does push her daughter to succeed in school, but her reason for wanting Anne to succeed is largely to prove to her new husband's family that her children are the equals of their daughters. She does not think about her daughter attending college; in fact, when Anne's gym teacher and coach pursues her romantically, Toosweet urges her to marry him.

Anne's frustration with her mother is understandable. Still, Toosweet's sadness at seeing her daughter distance herself from the family is poignant. Toosweet realizes that, in leaving behind her family's way of life, Anne is starting to look down on her family. Anne even takes the opportunity of a mistake on her birth certificate to change her name from the one her mother gave her. Toosweet resists, but ultimately she gives in to her persuasive daughter. After Anne graduates from high school, she realizes that she has ignored her mother's feelings in order to preserve her own ambition. She does not regret what she has done, but she also recognizes the pain her mother feels. Toosweet is most troubled by Anne's involvement in the civil rights movement. She receives threats from the local sheriff that Anne must not return to town or she will be killed. Soon, her son Junior is nearly lynched and her brother Buck is beaten up because of Anne's actions. Terrified, she writes letters to Anne begging her to quit the movement. Anne refuses.

MRS. BURKE Mrs. Burke is one of the numerous white women for whom Anne works as a maid. The nastiest and most blatantly racist, she is the closest portrait of prejudice in the book. Though Mrs. Burke ultimately gives Anne grudging respect, she still distrusts the majority of African Americans and remains ardently opposed to integration. Mrs. Burke demonstrates just how senseless and destructive the whites' prejudice is against blacks.

THEMES, MOTIFS, AND SYMBOLS

THEMES

THE ABSURDITY OF RACIAL DISTINCTIONS While Anne does not question that race and racism are very real facts of life, she does show how absurd and arbitrary racial distinctions are. During Anne's childhood, many whites publicly argued that blacks were genetically inferior to whites. One of the most memorable episodes of *Coming of Age* is when Anne, as a child, has her white friends undress so she can examine their genitalia for the secret of their better luck in life. Her reasoning is logical: it is not at all evident why they should be better off than blacks, and that is the only part of a white person's body or life she has not seen. The fact that so many blacks have at least some white ancestry serves to highlight how arbitrary a distinction race really is.

THE EVIL OF DISUNITY AMONG BLACKS IN THE FACE OF WHITE OPPRESSION When blacks refuse to band together to improve their situation, improvement becomes difficult if not impossible. Throughout *Coming of Age*, Anne is repeatedly frustrated by how willing blacks are to accept injustice. This includes her family, as well as numerous other blacks who work to perpetuate racial inequalities despite being black themselves. Anne is also shocked by the fact that lighter-skinned blacks try to give themselves a social distinction relative to darker-skinned blacks. They all share a common oppression at the hands of whites.

THE DESTRUCTIVE POWER OF PREJUDICE One of the most important themes of *Coming of Age in Mississippi* is the destructive power of prejudice. There is the prejudice of whites against blacks, and also the prejudice of lighter-skinned blacks toward darker-skinned blacks, and of people with money against poorer people. Anne experiences each kind of prejudice, which causes her great pain. In fact, being the victim of prejudice tends to prejudice Anne herself against whites and lighter-skinned blacks. Her prejudice is demonstrated by the fact that she nearly refuses to attend Tougaloo College, the place where she joins the civil rights movement, because she fears that it has too many light-skinned black students. She also distrusts her professors because they are white, and the Reverend Edward King, who is, worse yet, a southern white. Finally, after meeting lighter-skinned blacks and whites who do not look down on her, Anne accepts that not all members of these groups are untrustworthy. However, prejudice nearly costs her important opportunities in her life, and makes her a suspicious and pessimistic person.

MOTIFS

FOOD Moody repeatedly uses food to remind readers of the extreme poverty in which she grows up. For most of her childhood, Moody and her family live a hand-to-mouth existence. On many days, they truly eat nothing but bread and beans. In good times, they supplement their diets with table scraps and milk or peanut butter from middle-class white families. Moody rarely makes any mention of the suffering that accompanies this deprivation, but the details alone are enough to make the reader dizzy.

Food is also used to mark the powerful distinctions in status between blacks and whites. Food is representative of the difference in wealth between blacks and whites, as when the Moody family survives on

C

the white Cook family's table scraps, and Toosweet steals corn meant for the Cooks' cows. Food is also indicative of how dependent middle-class white families are on blacks: Moody notes that these families seem unable to cook for themselves, and many do not even know how to prepare food hygienically. Moody also uses food to draw attention to the low regard in which some whites hold blacks, as when a white woman lets her cats drink out of the vat of milk that she then sells to black people. Generosity with food is also a sign that a white person is kind to blacks, as when the Clairbornes invite Anne to dinner, and Mrs. Claiborne gives her candy and hot dogs.

SKIN COLOR Skin-color gradations among blacks greatly affect the characters in *Coming of Age*. Lighter-skinned blacks, whom Anne calls "mulatto" or "yellow," often try to carve out a higher social status for themselves, despite the fact that they are legally no better off than blacks relative to whites. Thus, the motif of skin color draws attention to an important theme of *Coming of Age*: the evil of disunity in the black community. The fact that so many blacks look almost like white people also highlights another important theme: that racial distinctions are ultimately absurd, since they are socially constructed and have no real basis in physical reality. Finally, the fact that some lighter-skinned blacks are prejudiced against darker-skinned blacks, and that Anne herself becomes so suspicious of lighter-skinned blacks that she herself becomes prejudiced, serves to highlight the theme of how destructive prejudice can be.

C

PREJUDICE Prejudice, while intangible, is a powerful force in *Coming of Age*. This motif appears in every chapter. There is the prejudice of whites against blacks, and also the prejudice of lighter-skinned blacks toward darker-skinned blacks, and of people with money against people who are poorer than they are. Anne experiences each kind of prejudice painfully. Anne even herself becomes prejudiced against whites and lighter-skinned blacks. Finally, after meeting lighter-skinned blacks and whites, particularly southern whites, who do not look down on her, Anne accepts that not all members of these groups are untrustworthy.

SYMBOLS

ANNE'S PERSONAL GROWTH Anne's own growth and maturation are symbolic of the concurrent growth and maturation of the civil rights movement. The symbolism is made possible by the fact that Anne's maturity coincides very closely with the 1950s civil rights era. Since she is born in 1940, she becomes a precocious young adult around the early 1950s. Earlier, as a young child, she had already found that there were no real reasons to consider whites superior to blacks, which was an argument that the earliest civil rights thinkers had made. Early in the twentieth century, there had been failed attempts to stop lynching, and also to unionize black workers. It is in the early 1950s that a new civil rights movement is born that combines lawsuits with activism. In Mississippi, the movement is kicked off when the NAACP fights for the prosecution of the murderers of Emmett Till, a black fourteen-year-old visiting Mississippi from Chicago, who was supposedly murdered because he had whistled at a white woman. The murder occurs just as Anne is starting to become exasperated with racial inequalities and the ridiculous prejudices of many white people.

Around the time that Anne is graduating from high school in the late 1950s, the movement to end segregation has prompted the government to build new, better schools for black students. But Anne, like the movement, realizes that they should not settle for anything less than complete equality as represented by integration. Once she is finally an adult, Anne realizes, as the movement must realize, that the future of the movement is in the youth, and the movement must focus on practical affairs. Symbolically, she has become an old woman, just as the civil rights movement has become mature and also faded. It is time for a younger generation, and a new version of the civil rights movement, to take over.

THE TWELVE-YEAR-OLD BOY On the bus to Washington at the very end of *Coming of Age*, Anne sits down next to a twelve-year-old boy who has unbridled energy, contrasted with Anne's exhaustion and frustration. The boy is symbolic of the younger generations who are the hope of the struggle for equality.

CLOTHING Clothing serves as an important symbol for transitions or stages of growth in Anne's life. Tight blue jeans signal her maturation. The pageantry of homecoming, with her beautiful gown, marks the end of childhood and the beginning of adulthood, though Anne is barely a teenager. As an activist, Anne buys clothing for children who have no school clothes, and she makes sure the movement distributes clothing to needy blacks in the area. She has grown from someone scraping to clothe herself and her own family to someone who can provide clothing for others.

When Anne graduates from college, clothing is once again an important symbol of transition and growth in her life: her sister Adline celebrates her college graduation by giving her a beautiful green dress. The green dress symbolizes both her attainment of a college degree and Adline's acceptance of Anne's goals. Earlier her family had not given her much support in her academic ambitions; no one had gone to her college graduation ceremony. Now Adline herself says she would like to get a college degree.

The importance of clothing as a symbol underscores Anne's earlier poverty. Adline chooses between buying Anne a graduation present or paying to travel to her graduation; she cannot do both. This symbol demonstrates the way in which Anne's growth as a person has been aligned with her basic struggle to survive.

IMPORTANT QUOTATIONS EXPLAINED

---

1. *They were Negroes and we were also Negroes. I just didn't see Negroes hating each other so much.*

This remark sums up Anne's feelings in Chapter 4. "They" are Raymond's family, especially his mother, Miss Pearl. As lighter-skinned African Americans, they look down on Anne's family members, who have darker skin. It is implied, though not actually stated, that they would prefer Raymond marry a woman with lighter skin. Before the civil rights movement, many lighter-skinned blacks aspired to a higher social status, though they were not given any special legal treatment. Lighter-skinned blacks were called by names like "yellow," "mulatto," and "high yellow," and their skin tones reflected the predominance of white ancestry. In some cases, blacks' appearance was indistinguishable from that of whites. In *Coming of Age*, the degree of intermixing among whites and blacks helps establish the absurdity of racial distinctions. The fact that blacks make such distinctions despite sharing common mistreatment by whites underscores this, and also highlights the need for unity among blacks.

After her mother is so coldly treated by Raymond's family, Anne becomes suspicious of lighter-skinned blacks. In fact, she almost does not go to Tougaloo College because she fears the students are mostly lighter-skinned and will look down on her. She eventually becomes so suspicious of the potential prejudice of lighter-skinned blacks that she is herself prejudiced, furthering the theme of the evil of prejudice.

---

2. *I had to help secure that plate of dry beans.*

In Chapter 9, this is the reason Anne decides to work for Mrs. Burke after Linda Mae moves away. Anne does not want to work for the racist and domineering Mrs. Burke, but she cannot afford to leave work, even for one week, and Mrs. Burke is offering her a job to start immediately. She has been working cleaning houses to supplement her family's income since she was nine years old. Not working would mean risking starvation. Even when she does work to supplement her family's income, her diet is painfully meager. Food is an important motif in *Coming of Age in Mississippi*. In this case, it represents Anne's constant struggle to survive, along with the difficult circumstances survival entails.

---

3. *It no longer seemed important to prove anything. I had found something outside myself that gave meaning to my life.*

In Chapter 22, while Anne is trying to decide what to do after college, she realizes that she is content with being an activist, and does not need to seek others' approval or achieve financial security. Her whole life, Anne had striven for approval and recognition, and also to make money. Now, having finally achieved her college education, Anne is broke and hungry. But she does not care whether she has a real job or not. She prefers to work in the movement, where she can act on her drive to fight racial inequality, and where she feels accepted. Anne even feels more at home among her fellow activists than among her family members. When she reunites with family in New Orleans, she does not even know how to talk with them. She feels an urge to move back to Canton with the other activists. As a memoir of a life in activism, *Coming of Age* provides an important insight into why people would take on the risks and trying lifestyle of full-time activist. For Anne, the lack of traditional rewards is made up for by intangible ones, to the point that she is willing to go hungry.

---

4. *We had "dreamers" instead of leaders leading us.*

This is the conclusion Anne reaches in Chapter 24, while listening to the speeches given by the leaders of the civil rights movement at the famous March on Washington, particularly Martin Luther King, Jr.'s famous "I Have a Dream" speech. After attending the March on Washington, Anne's uncertainty about the movement is increased. She had already felt that the leaders of the movement were out of touch with the base, as evidenced by their emphasis on voting rights for the poor rural blacks in Mississippi rather than poverty relief. At the time Moody wrote *Coming of Age*, King was still alive, and so this statement was probably in part intended to affect the ongoing debate. Ironically, at around the time the book was going to print, King was in fact pushing for a change in direction in the movement to focus more on bread-and-butter issues. He was shot while rallying striking workers in Memphis. It was 1968, the same year *Coming of Age* was published.

C

5. *I WONDER. I really WONDER.*

These are the final words in *Coming of Age in Mississippi.* The statement refers to Anne's attitude while singing the civil rights anthem "We Shall Overcome" on a bus to Washington to attend a hearing on the situation in Mississippi. She is wondering whether blacks really will overcome all of their problems. This statement reflects her severe frustration with the movement in Mississippi. After doing exhaustive work on voter registration in the small town of Canton in rural Mississippi, the situation for blacks there is arguably worse. In fact, the local man who had done the most to get the movement started in the community was now impoverished and in jail. Ultimately, Anne wishes the movement would focus on concrete economic improvements in the lives of the rural blacks, rather than on voting rights and on symbolic actions such as the Freedom Vote, a mock vote to protest the real vote in Mississippi. She works to distribute clothing to the poor of Canton, and tries to establish a program to help blacks borrow money to buy their own farms. She believes that economic security will give blacks the power and inclination to demand all their other rights. Yet Anne is not just disappointed with the movement. She is disgusted that so many whites in Mississippi are holding on so hard and so violently to racial inequality. She also is saddened by the willingness of so many blacks to compensate for the injustices rather than stick their necks out to seek change.

Distant View of a Minaret

Alifa Rifaat (1930–1996)

CONTEXT

Alifa Rifaat was born in 1930 and spent her entire life in Egypt, where she was raised in the traditions and culture of Islam. Though Rifaat wanted to attend college and pursue an education and a career in the arts, her parents arranged for her to be married instead, and she submitted. Her husband died early in her married life, leaving her to raise their three children. Rifaat, a Muslim (a follower of Islam), could read only Arabic, so her exposure to literature was limited to works written in or translated into Arabic, and the Qur'an (the text of the Islamic religion) and the Hadith (a book of sayings of the Islamic prophet Muhammad).

D

Although Rifaat did not attend college, she did receive some education at the British Institute in Cairo (1946–1949). Rifaat continued reading works of Arab fiction and religious works, and she eventually began writing in 1955. Having traveled little in her life, many of her stories are set in provincial Egypt and are untouched by Western influence. As a result, instead of taking the conventional feminist approach and looking to the Christian West for a model of how women's lives should change, Rifaat criticizes men for not fulfilling their role within the Islamic tradition. She does not question the role of women according to the Islamic faith, but rather depicts the hardships imposed on women because of men's shortcomings. Her collection of short stories, *Distant View of a Minaret* (1983), features recurring ideas of sexual frustration, pervasive cultural pressures, and death.

In Islamic society, a woman is under the protection and rule of her husband if she is married, or of her oldest brother if she is single or widowed. She often has little or no control of finances or major decisions. Though Rifaat laments the limits placed on women in Islamic society in *Distant View of a Minaret*, she never questions Islam's ultimate validity, and every story contains elements of the Islamic faith. Muslims believe there is one God, and that whatever occurs in a person's life happens through the will of Allah (the Islamic word for God). Allah has communicated to man through the Qur'an, which provides guidelines for living. Muslims are guided by the Five Pillars of Faith: the acknowledgment of Allah as the one true deity; the performance of prayer rituals at least five times a day; the giving of alms; refraining from eating, drinking, smoking, and sex from dawn until dusk during the month of Ramadan; and making at least one pilgrimage to Mecca (in modern-day Saudi Arabia) during one's lifetime. These guidelines, as well as other elements of Islam, pervade Rifaat's stories and place them firmly in the Islamic tradition.

Other works by Rifaat include *Girls of Baurdin* (1995), *Kad Lia al-Hawa* (1985), *Love Made a Trap for Me* (1991), *Leil Al-Shetaa Al-taweel* (translated as *The Long Night of Winter and Other Stories*) (1985), *Jawharah Farum* (1978), *Pharaoh's Jewel* (1991), and the short-story collection *Hawatandbi-Adam* (translated as *Eve Returns With Adam to Paradise*) (1975). Reviewers overwhelmingly praise Rifaat for the sense of raw emotion and authenticity in her writing. She died in Egypt in 1996.

PLOT OVERVIEW

Distant View of a Minaret is a collection of fifteen short stories that give readers a glimpse of what it means to be a woman in an Orthodox Muslim society in Egypt. The stories are not interconnected, but together they form a vivid portrayal of Rifaat's world.

"DISTANT VIEW OF A MINARET"

A woman and her husband are having sex. The wife thinks about her lack of sexual fulfillment—her husband always stops as soon as he climaxes. She's told him her desires, but he ignores her and makes her feel embarrassed for trying to prolong their sexual intercourse so that she, too, might have an orgasm.

The wife hears the call for the daily afternoon prayer. She gets up to wash herself after having sex, in accordance with Islamic practice. Her husband stays in bed to nap. After prayer, the wife gazes out the window of their apartment, thinking that she once had a view of the entire city of Cairo. The city has built up over the years, and now the view is limited to that of a single minaret (tower of a mosque). She had wished to have a house with a garden in the suburbs, but because of her husband's job, they got an apartment in the city. She didn't mind so much because of the wonderful view, but now it is gone.

The wife prepares the afternoon coffee and brings it into the bedroom for her husband, only to find that he has suffered an attack (about which the reader receives no other information except that these attacks have happened before) and died. She tells her son to fetch the doctor, then pours a cup of coffee for herself. She thinks to herself that she is surprisingly calm.

"BAHIYYA'S EYES"

Bahiyya, an elderly woman, tells a story to her visiting daughter. Bahiyya recently took herself to the hospital because she was losing her sight. The doctor indicates that it is too late to help her—Bahiyya will soon be blind. She tells her daughter that her blindness is a result of the tears she has cried for being born a girl rather than a boy. Bahiyya explains that she had to accept her brother's abuse because he was the man of the family. She learned about sex from watching animals. When some of the village women found that she had made mud dolls with genitalia, they castrated her. Bahiyya liked a boy in the village, but her family arranged a marriage for her with another man. Her husband died soon after they married. Bahiyya describes the loneliness of being a woman without a man and says that she feels her life and youth have been a waste.

"TELEPHONE CALL"

In the middle of the night, the narrator hears a phone ringing in another apartment. Her husband has recently died, and as she sits alone she hopes for some sort of sign from beyond the grave. Since his death, she sleeps during the day and stays up at night. Suddenly her own phone rings. She picks it up, but there is only silence. The narrator believes that this is her sign. Morning comes, and during her morning prayer she is grateful and content. The phone rings again. This time it is the phone operator, who tells the narrator that a call was accidentally directed to the wrong house last night. She returns to her prayers to ask forgiveness from Allah for having asked for so much.

"THURSDAY LUNCH"

The narrator has recently turned fifty. She thinks of how old she looks, after having borne three children, and also reflects that in old age one has fewer close friends to rely on. She has no one to whom she can talk about the poor relations between herself and her husband. She angrily sends the servant out on an errand and immediately feels very alone and starts to cry.

She must pull herself together since she is meeting her mother for their weekly Thursday lunch. She is not close to her mother and has always been afraid to be open with her. They have a very large meal, and as her mother is complaining about young people, the narrator wishes she and her mother were close and that she could speak about her marriage problems. Suddenly, her mother reveals that today is the anniversary of the death of her own husband and that she still thinks of him every day. The narrator, unsure what to do or say, notices her mother crying. Her mother then bids her goodbye, until next Thursday's lunch.

"AN INCIDENT IN THE GHOBASHI HOUSEHOLD"

Zeinet awakes to find that her unmarried daughter Ni'ma is showing signs of pregnancy. Zeinet's husband, Ghobashi, left their home to work in Libya. Ni'ma tells Zeinet she became pregnant right after Ghobashi went away. The night before he left, Ghobashi told Zeinet to watch over Ni'ma and said he hoped to bring back a wedding dress for her so that she could be married. Zeinet considers the dishonor of Ni'ma's illegitimate pregnancy and how Ghobashi might react.

Ni'ma tells Zeinet it would be best if she just slipped into the canal so that the family would not be troubled, but Zeinet rebukes her and says they will find another solution. Zeinet takes out some money she's stashed away and gives it to Ni'ma. She tells Ni'ma to go to Cairo, have the child, and come back in the middle of the night. Then Zeinet wraps some clothing under her own clothes to make it look like she is pregnant. She will tell Ghobashi, when he returns, that the baby is their son, rather than their illegitimate grandson.

"BADRIYYA AND HER HUSBAND"

Badriyya sees her husband, Omar, walking down the street with a group of men. They are celebrating Omar's release from prison. Badriyya's mother comments that Omar was a fool for stealing a couple of worthless tires, and she clearly disapproves of Badriyya's choice of a husband. Omar comes home late, and he is drunk. He is glad that Badriyya's mother has gone to bed so that he doesn't have to endure her snide remarks.

Badriyya remembers their romance. Omar followed her into a movie theater and sat beside her. He asked her out for the next week. Omar talked of his plans to open his own café. Badriyya felt that Omar, like a hero in the movies, would rescue her from a life that seemed like a long, dark tunnel. Badriyya's uncle told her that Omar was "all talk," but allowed her to marry him. A month later, Omar was arrested. Badriyya's uncle and mother then tried to convince Badriyya to divorce Omar, for they believed he was a good-for-nothing who was simply looking for a woman to support him. Badriyya refused.

The morning after Omar's return, Badriyya comes home from work to find her mother and Omar laughing and playing cards. Badriyya thinks that she has never seen her mother in such a good mood, and her mother says that Omar has turned out to be a nice fellow. Omar tells them about the people he met in prison, especially a contractor/vendor who has promised to help Omar. Omar is to meet him that evening, but Badriyya is disappointed that he's leaving because she has made them a nice dinner.

From then on, Omar stays out late and comes home tired from drinking and drugs. He says that at night he's scouting for a location for his café. They have not had sex, and when Badriyya hints at it, Omar replies that there's plenty of time for that in the future. When Badriyya's mother asks when she can expect a grandchild, Omar implies that Badriyya never wants to have sex. Badriyya is upset and thinks she is unattractive to Omar or that he is having an affair. She goes to the store to buy Omar a pack of cigarettes on her own credit account. The store's owner tells her Omar is no good, and everyone knows that he sleeps around every night. Badriyya finally understands and hopes she will have the strength to turn him away when he tries to come home that night.

"ME AND MY SISTER"

The narrator is a little girl. Her older sister, Dalal, tells their mother she wants to go to a party that evening and that she will take the narrator so their mother won't worry about her going out alone after dark. Dalal is often mean to the narrator, sometimes hitting her and causing their father to believe that she has been bad.

When they go out, they don't go to a party. Instead, Dalal meets a boy named Mahmoud. He picks them up in a car, and Dalal and Mahmoud speak in French so the narrator doesn't understand. Dalal threatens the narrator and makes her swear to Allah that she won't tell anyone where they have gone. Mahmoud buys perfume for Dalal and chocolates for the narrator, then drives them to a kiosk where he buys some hashish. Mahmoud and Dalal get into the backseat together.

They repeat the secret meetings many times, and eventually Dalal tells Mahmoud that though her father has arranged for her to marry someone else, she loves Mahmoud and wants to marry him. Mahmoud tells her he does not want to marry her. The next time they meet, Dalal tells the narrator to go on without her and tell Mahmoud that she will meet them in an hour. Mahmoud takes the narrator to the kiosk, has her sit on his lap, and touches her chest and shoulders. The narrator kisses his face, and then he tells her they should go to meet Dalal.

Dalal and Mahmoud fight in the car, and he loses control and crashes them into a hedge. Dalal has blood on her face and passes out, and Mahmoud drives the girls home. Their mother and sisters help them in, asking them what happened and concerned about the fact that they were with a strange boy. The narrator keeps quiet, and as she falls asleep, Dalal smiles at her. The narrator knows that Dalal won't hit her or yell at her again, since she protected Dalal's secret.

"MANSOURA"

Sheikh Zeidan leads a crew of men who lay pipe. At the campsite, he tells a newcomer the story of Mansoura. She was a beautiful woman with great powers, whom every man loved. She married a strong, good man named Sayyid, and they were initially very happy. Then Sayyid took a job guarding the bean crop of a man named Hindawi. Hindawi would go to Mansoura at night when Sayyid was away. It is not certain whether he would rape her or whether she submitted to his advances out of loneliness. The villagers began singing lewd songs about Mansoura's honor, but Sayyid did not realize that they were about his wife.

At Mansoura's urging, Sayyid quits guarding Hindawi's farm. Hindawi obsesses about Mansoura and meets her at the canal to convince her to leave Sayyid for him. She refuses, and while arguing, she slips into the canal and drowns. Hindawi tells no one of his meeting with Mansoura, and Sayyid is put in prison for murder when Mansoura's body is found.

Hindawi flees the area and works with the men laying pipe. One day, Hindawi looks up at the bulldozer as it is lowering pipe, and he grows terrified. The pipe falls from the arm of the bulldozer and crushes him. Just before dying, he says, "Mansoura, you cruel one." Because of this legend, the men chant Mansoura's name as they lay pipe, to ask for her help to make their work easier.

"THE LONG NIGHT OF WINTER"

Zennouba awakes to find that her husband is not in bed. She starts to think back on her life, especially her loss of freedom since puberty. In order to keep their land in the family, she was married to her cousin Hagg. Sex with Hagg was unpleasant, but eventually he began sleeping with the servant girls. When she asked him for a divorce, Hagg revealed that Zennouba's own father did the same, so why should he grant her a divorce? Zennouba's adoration and reverence toward her father are wounded. She wonders if all women are doomed to the same fate.

Hagg returns to bed and Zennouba notices it's almost dawn. She wakes the servant girl and asks her to fetch hot water for a bath. Zennouba thinks that she, like the servant girl, was once beautiful. She has the girl scrub her back so hard with a loofah that it is actually painful.

"MY WORLD OF THE UNKNOWN"

The narrator's husband has been transferred to a country town. She journeys there to find a suitable house. A house on the canal resembles an image from her dreams, and she wishes to occupy it. A young woman named Aneesa has been squatting there with her child, and Aneesa tries to prevent the narrator from entering. Kamil, one of her husband's employees, tells the narrator that the local people believe that spirits inhabit the house, but the narrator is determined to live there.

A short time later, the narrator returns to begin moving in. Once again, Aneesa confronts the narrator, telling her to leave. Eventually the authorities come to take Aneesa and her child away, and Aneesa points under the house and tells the narrator, "I'll leave her to you."

One day, the narrator sees a huge, beautiful snake. She feels intoxicated and elated at the sight, but when she tells her husband, he boards up the crack where the snake has disappeared. A sheikh from the town is summoned. He tells the narrator that the snake is a female spirit, one of the monarchs of the earth, and should be considered a blessing. The narrator is skeptical, but later she begins to fantasize about seeing the snake again. Though she fulfills her duties as the woman of the house, she becomes more isolated and sits around lazily. Her fantasies become sexual and she is consumed by a painful yearning for the snake.

The snake reappears and her sexual desires are fulfilled. However, the narrator again tells her husband that she has seen a snake, and he boards up a hole in their bedroom wall. The snake later tells the narrator that there is no sin in their actions, as they are now married and the narrator will have "abiding youth and the delights of love." They carry on their love affair. The narrator's vitality increases and she is taken through worlds of unimaginable beauty. Their affair lasts many months.

Then the narrator's husband kills a snake, breaking the pact of peace between snakes and man. The snake comes once more to bid the narrator goodbye, in a passionate embrace, and tells her they must leave. The narrator still yearns for her snake lover and hopes that one day she will reappear.

"AT THE TIME OF THE JASMINE"

Hassan is traveling by train to his hometown because his father has recently died. Hassan thinks back to images of his father making ablutions before daily prayer and of his father's pride in young Hassan. Then, Hassan spent his adolescence with foreign tutors and his love for his father became frozen. Hassan abandoned emotions and instead began to rule his life with reason and rational standards. He eventually opened an accounting office in Cairo and hardly ever returned home. When his daughter was born, Hassan's father sent him a telegram saying to name her Jasmine. Hassan's wife later left him and took their daughter back to Turkey, her homeland.

The men of the town greet Hassan when he arrives for his father's funeral. The jasmine in the air causes him to cough badly. The burial rites begin, and tears come to Hassan's eyes when he sees his father's body. The body is washed and carried to the grave. It is Hassan's duty to cut the burial shroud away before his father is buried. As the men remember his father, Hassan thinks to himself that they knew his father better than he did. Hassan generously offers to pay for a feast for all of the men.

That night, Hassan finds that his father mentioned Jasmine in his will. He regrets that he never brought Jasmine to meet his father. Hassan also regrets that he did not go on a pilgrimage with his father, something that his father mentioned once. He wakes during the night and thinks, "Father, you gave me a real beating tonight," referring to his own emotional suffering as a result of death and regrets.

"THE FLAT IN NAKSHABANDI STREET"

Aziza is a seventy-year-old spinster who lives with her nephew, Mahmoud, and their servant, Waheeba. Aziza had lived with her brother, Saleh, until Saleh and Mahmoud's parents died. She then moved in with Mahmoud and now lives off of their family savings. Whenever she hears of a death, she attends the funeral, regardless of whether she knew the person well, and leads the women in mourning. This is the only time she leaves the house. She spends most of her time yelling at Waheeba or looking out the window, often scolding boys in the street.

Mahmoud talks to Aziza about his desire to privately tutor some of his students at home, but Aziza rejects the idea. Mahmoud, who is outwardly very agreeable to Aziza, leaves to smoke in his room and think about his desire to tutor a young girl in hopes of meeting one of their older sisters and possibly finding a wife. He secretly has sex with Waheeba at night and wonders if his aunt knows this is going on. He puts on some cologne, studies his face in the mirror, and goes out.

D

The call to prayer comes. Aziza no longer prays, thinking that she has done much praying in her life, and besides, she has not committed the sins of other women and has acquired much grace by attending so many funerals.

Waheeba leaves to buy vegetables. This is her time of freedom, when she can meet up with friends at the market, often retelling stories of the household in such a way as to make it seem that she has the upper hand. Meanwhile, Aziza wonders what Waheeba during her time away from the apartment. Aziza also relishes the thought of how much money she has saved up for Mahmoud's inheritance—over 54,000 pounds. She is very proud and grows happy at the thought of surprising him someday. Aziza also ponders Mahmoud's relations with Waheeba, which she is well aware of. She decides it is best to hide both the amount of money in the bank and her knowledge of this affair. Aziza hopes to maintain the current routine as long as possible. Suddenly, though, she suffers a heart attack, and sits clenched with terror, waiting for Mahmoud or Waheeba to return.

"DEGREES OF DEATH"

The narrator is a young girl. Her grandmother buys her some rabbits. She spends her time lying in the enclosure built for the rabbits, watching their leisurely existence, and eventually they have babies. Of all the animals on their farm, these are the only ones with which she has bonded. Then one day she sees Nanny Zareefa, the servant, cut the throat of one of the baby rabbits. The narrator runs home, upset at the sight of the slaughter and the loss of its life. She realizes that for adults, there are degrees of death, varying in importance between man and animals, and even between certain men and others.

"THE KITE"

Widad lives alone. Her children have grown up and moved away, and her husband Ahmed has died, so she lives a strict, unchanging routine, caring for her chickens and the property. She knows each chicken and its particular characteristics. Widad regrets that she never learned the verses used in the daily prayers and is too shy to ask the neighbors if she could join them in their prayers, but in her simple way she still thanks and praises Allah. Her only interaction with others is when she sits on her bench outside and watches people pass by.

Mitwalli, her childhood sweetheart, has come to ask her to marry him. She loved him when she was younger, but her father arranged for her to marry Ahmed, and she did not object. Widad tells Mitwalli that he should have come thirty years ago, and they are both old now so it is too late. Mitwalli says that the past is over, and they both have the right to live out the rest of their lives happily. He tells her he will come back tomorrow for her answer.

Widad thinks that she should live the rest of her life alone. But suddenly she notices a kite swoop down and grab one of the chicks from the courtyard. She is upset, and her only thoughts are about how to prevent this from happening again. That night she has a vision of Mitwalli standing over the chickens to protect them. She also dreams of standing behind him during his daily prayers, as she once did with Ahmed, and she is filled with contentment.

"JUST ANOTHER DAY"

The narrator is an old woman who feels like a useless burden since her children have grown up. Today she decides to stay in bed, thinking that it makes no difference if she doesn't get up. Every day she had the same routine, going to the market for food and meeting the same people. Once a month she went to the center of the city and bought a scarf or slippers, which she probably wouldn't wear. She simply used the act of shopping to pass the time and actually spends more and more of her time living in past memories.

She thinks of the gardener in her father's country house, spraying water on the lime trees. The vision is interrupted by her daughter coming into the room to ask if she has had a nice rest. Her son, too, approaches, and then her children leave and close the door to the room. Later she hears the voice of her brother, who has not visited her in years. She also hears the voice of his wife, with whom she doesn't get along. Finally a woman comes in and begins undressing her, and a reciter is reading the funeral verses from the Qur'an. A feeling of peace flows over her and she abandons herself to the funeral ritual.

CHARACTER LIST

D

"DISTANT VIEW OF A MINARET"

The Wife The protagonist of the story who is sexually dissatisfied with her marriage but has given up any attempt to change the situation. The wife is indifferent to the fact that her husband may be having affairs with other women. She wishes she had a house with a garden, but they live in the city because of her husband's job.

The Husband A man who cares only for his own sexual fulfillment. The husband gives no consideration to his wife's desires and flippantly refers to relationships he's had with other women.

"BAHIYYA'S EYES"

Bahiyya An older women who is going blind. Bahiyya tends to ramble, and she proposes that her eyes are going blind from all the tears she's cried. She laments being born a woman in her society, in which others have control over her life.

"TELEPHONE CALL"

The Widow The narrator, who has just lost her husband. The widow hopes for a sign from beyond the grave and places all of her faith in the idea that a late-night phone call is her dead husband communicating with her.

"THURSDAY LUNCH"

The Wife A fifty-year-old woman who wishes she could talk to someone about her failing marriage. The wife was close to her sister, who recently died. She has always been somewhat afraid to open up to her own mother, but she blames her mother's closed-in personality.

The Mother A well-groomed Turkish woman living in an expensively decorated apartment with a servant. The mother was truly in love with her husband, who died twenty-four years ago, and, despite her reserved nature, she makes an attempt to connect with her daughter.

"AN INCIDENT IN THE GHOBASHI HOUSEHOLD"

Zeinat The mother of the Ghobashi family. Zeinat is strong and practical, in charge of the household since her husband left to work in Libya. She is not afraid to lie in order to protect her child, Ni'ma, and to save the honor of the family.

Ni'ma The oldest daughter of the Ghobashi family. Ni'ma has gotten illegitimately pregnant. Instead of facing her predicament, Ni'ma suggests she commit suicide.

Ghobashi The father and head of the household. Ghobashi does his best to care for his family.

"BADRIYYA AND HER HUSBAND"

Badriyya A naïve, romantic young woman who marries Omar, a good-for-nothing womanizer. Badriyya is so adamant about holding on to her fantasies about Omar saving her from the boring routine of her life that she refuses to acknowledge his behavior.

Omar Badriyya's husband, who was just released from prison for stealing tires. Omar talks of grand plans for his life but spends all of his time drinking, doing drugs, and sleeping with other women.

Badriyya's Mother A woman who lives with Badriyya and Omar. Badriyya's mother initially disapproves of Omar, but after he gives her some attention, she changes her opinion of him.

Badriyya's Uncle A man who lives in a nearby town and tries to convince Badriyya not to marry Omar. Badriyya's uncle recognizes Omar's character flaws but ultimately allows Badriyya to make her own decisions.

"ME AND MY SISTER"

Youngest Sister The innocent narrator of the story who is abused by her sister Dalal. The narrator's only friend is her older sister, Nagwa. She is too young to understand adult behavior and provides innocent description and perspective. She desires approval from both Dalal and their father.

Dalal The narrator's older sister, who lies to their mother in order to meet with her boyfriend, Mahmoud. Dalal brings the narrator along so as to not arouse suspicion. She wants to marry Mahmoud, but her father is arranging a marriage for her with someone else.

Mahmoud Dalal's boyfriend. Mahmoud buys the narrator chocolates, but his character is questionable since he fondles her in Dalal's absence. He likes Dalal but is not interested in marriage.

"MANSOURA"

Mansoura A woman of great beauty and mysterious powers. Mansoura loves Sayyid and seems righteous and honorable. It is unclear whether she willingly cheats on Sayyid or is raped by Hindawi. She tragically drowns but avenges her death from beyond the grave.

Sayyid Mansoura's husband, who goes to work for Sayyid. Sayyid is strong and good-hearted but naïve, unable to realize that the folk songs he sings are about his unfaithful wife.

Hindawi The antagonist who employs Sayyid so that he can sneak off to seduce Mansoura while Sayyid works. Hindawi is cowardly, dishonorable, and obsessed with Mansoura. He flees after Mansoura's death so that Sayyid will not find and kill him.

Sheikh Zeidan An older man who oversees the crew of men laying sewage pipe in the Mansoura canal. Sheikh Zeidan narrates the legendary tale of Mansoura to explain why the men chant her name as they lay pipe.

"THE LONG NIGHT OF WINTER"

Zennouba The protagonist whose husband cheats on her with the servant girls. Zennouba is devastated to hear that her venerable father also cheated on his wife. She was initially angry at her husband's behavior but is now indifferent and frustrated because they have to continually find new servants.

Hagg Zennouba's husband, who sleeps with the servant girls. Hagg is rough and uncaring.

Nargis The new servant girl in the house. Nargis is submissive and obedient.

"MY WORLD OF THE UNKNOWN"

The Wife A wise, strong woman who is seduced by a snake who is a monarch of the spirit world. The wife yearns for the snake and develops an unhealthy obsession, during which she becomes lazy and indifferent. However, she does act graciously toward Aneesa, the vagrant woman who claims the house as her own, and she is independent enough to travel alone and choose a house for the family.

The Snake A powerful spirit who has taken the form of a snake. The snake is wise and benevolent; she loves the narrator and bestows the gifts of youth, vitality, and sexual satisfaction upon her.

Aneesa The mad woman with a child who tries to stop the narrator from inhabiting the house. Aneesa eventually recovers her mental facilities after the authorities take her away.

The Husband A government worker whose transfer brings the family to the town where the spirit-inhabited house is. The husband unknowingly breaks the pact with the spirit world by killing a snake.

"AT THE TIME OF THE JASMINE"

Hassan The protagonist, who has traveled home for the burial of his father. Hassan has neglected his emotions for most of his life, preferring to live by reason and rational conventions. His inaction led to poor relations with his father, his wife, and his daughter. At his father's funeral, he feels sadness and regret.

D

Hagg Aballah Shalabi The protagonist's father, who has just died. Hagg Aballah was proud of his young son and hoped to one day go on a pilgrimage with him. The villagers knew him as a great horseman and said he could tell who was approaching and when by putting his ear to the ground and listening.

"THE FLAT IN NAKSHABANDI STREET"

Aziza An old spinster who lives with her nephew and their servant. Aziza is a somewhat hostile woman who spends her time criticizing the servant and yelling at children. She leaves the house only to attend funerals, where she leads the women in mourning. She is fond of her nephew and takes pleasure in thinking of the large inheritance she will leave him.

Mahmoud A bachelor and teacher who lives with his aunt, Aziza. Mahmoud secretly sleeps with the servant, Waheeba, and wishes to meet a woman to marry. Though he is agreeable with Aziza, he wishes he had more control, for he has to hide his smoking from her and submit to her opinions.

Waheeba A servant for Mahmoud and Aziza. Waheeba is a divorcee and secretly sleeps with Mahmoud. She enjoys her time out of the house, when she meets with friends and tells stories about the household, usually altering the stories to make herself appear to have the upper hand.

"DEGREES OF DEATH"

The Little Girl A small child who lives on a farm and receives two rabbits from her grandmother. The narrator becomes very attached to the animals. She feels guilty and responsible when Nanny Zareefa kills one of the baby rabbits, and she gains a realization that death comes in varying degrees of significance.

Nanny Zareefa A servant who kills one of the baby rabbits. Nanny Zareefa doesn't realize that the narrator sees the killing.

"THE KITE"

Widad A widow who lives alone and cares for chickens. Widad doesn't believe in second chances and thinks that now is the time to live out the rest of her life, alone, in her unchanging routine. She is devastated when a kite swoops down and snatches one of her chicks; this leads her to rethink her recent marriage proposal.

Mitwalli Widad's childhood sweetheart, recently widowed. Mitwalli comes to propose to Widad in hopes that they can live the rest of their lives together.

"JUST ANOTHER DAY"

The Old Woman An aged woman who feels useless and no longer finds the strength to live her boring routine. The old woman does not realize she has died until she hears a man reading the funeral prayers from the Qur'an.

ANALYSIS OF MAJOR CHARACTERS

BADRIYYA, "BADRIYYA AND HER HUSBAND" Badriyya is idealistic and naïve, and her hope that her marriage to Omar will resemble a fairy tale is her downfall. She ignores Omar's shortcomings because she still believes Omar will rescue her from the "long, dark tunnel" of her life. When he talks about his big plans for starting his own café, she thinks of him as "ambitious," even though her uncle tells her Omar is all talk. When Omar stays out late at night and comes home drunk, Badriyya believes his explanation that he was scouting out possible sites for the café. Badriyya wants so badly for Omar to be her knight in shining armor that she refuses to question anything he says. The alternative to life with Omar is a life alone: if she divorces him, she'll once again feel as though life is hopeless and dark.

Like many of Rifaat's female characters, Badriyya is sexually unfulfilled—though married, she is still a virgin. She hints at sex, but Omar tells her that he must concentrate on starting his café. Badriyya is completely powerless in this marriage. However, she is eventually jolted from her idealistic dream when a shopkeeper tells Badriyya that Omar is sleeping around. Though she's unsure whether she'll have the strength to turn Omar away when he tries to come home, she hopes she does. Her fear isn't rooted only in the end of the relationship; the harder part is giving up her dream of being saved.

D

THE WIFE, "MY WORLD OF THE UNKNOWN" The narrator, the wife of a government official, never explicitly indicates that her marriage to her husband is unsatisfying, but because she is so easily seduced by the snake-spirit that inhabits their home, she reveals the extent of her unhappiness and dissatisfaction. The snake provides fulfillment in every capacity. She satisfies the narrator sexually, lavishes her with youth and vitality, and takes her to hidden spirit worlds. The adventure of the relationship completely eclipses her domestic life. However, the narrator is initially ambivalent about the snake. She is attracted to the snake, then she tells her husband to board up the house's cracks so the snake can't enter, then she yearns for the snake. Her request to her husband is significant. Though the snake is female, it has a phallic form, and it eventually replaces the husband in the role of sexual partner. When the wife asks her husband to help keep the snake out, she is making a final attempt to impel him to take action before she seeks sexual fulfillment in other ways. Later, when the wife stops up the cracks in the wall, it is in a playful, teasing way, which illustrates how she has changed from being fearful of her sexuality to embracing it.

In the narrator's fantasy world of passionate sexual fulfillment, adventurous romping through other worlds, and love with a companion who is considerate and giving, we find the model of an ideal relationship—the only clear representation of an ideal relationship in all of Rifaat's stories. Though the events are likely only products of the narrator's imagination, it shows a true understanding of what characterizes fulfillment in marriage.

HASSAN, "AT THE TIME OF THE JASMINE" Hassan, an emotionless, rational accountant, left the small town where he grew up and hardly ever returns to see his family. He is consistently guilty of inaction, and he neglects his own emotional life. When he returns home for his father's funeral, he can no longer ignore his feelings. Hassan's flashbacks reveal his inaction, which he now regrets. He never brought his daughter, Jasmine, to his hometown to meet his father, and now it is too late. Hassan is as baffled as he is sad: he has suppressed his emotions for so long that their reappearance is confusing.

After the funeral ceremony, Hassan offers to pay for a feast for the men in the village. The men are grateful for his unexpected generosity, but it seems as though Hassan is trying to compensate for the guilt he feels because these men know his father better than he does. He again feels guilty when he discovers that his father has left Jasmine some of his inheritance. Even though Hassan was never considerate enough to bring Jasmine to the town, his father remembered her and probably longed to meet her. When Hassan goes to sleep that night, he feels truly exhausted and emotionally beaten down. The weight of what has happened begins to sink in, but whether or not Hassan will be permanently changed because of it is unclear.

THEMES, MOTIFS, AND SYMBOLS

THEMES

THE IMPORTANCE OF LOVE IN MARRIAGE Most of the marriages in Alifa Rifaat's stories are unhappy. Many of the husbands cheat, and the wives are dissatisfied both sexually and emotionally. This is not too surprising, since most of the marriages in the stories—and in Islamic communities—are arranged marriages, so the husband and wife are not in love before marrying. Often, the marriage is arranged so that land or wealth can be kept in the family, as in the case of Zennouba in "The Long Night of Winter." Clearly, Rifaat believes two main things about marriage in the Islamic world: marriages should not be arranged, and husbands should meet the emotional and sexual needs of their wives. Arranged marriages completely ignore the desires of the women.

In her stories, Rifaat makes clear that sexual intercourse should be enjoyable for both husband and wife. "Enjoyment" does not refer only to physicality; the act of sex should be one of consideration, leading to a stronger bond. For example, in "Distant View of a Minaret," the husband and wife do not connect on a sexual level at all. The husband is concerned only with his own sexual urges, and he prevents his wife from experiencing sexual pleasure. He is even cruel to her, telling her that he has had sexual experiences with other women. The wife resembles a slave or a concubine, rather than a life partner.

THE TYRANNY OF HUSBANDS Rifaat's depictions of husbands are not favorable. In "Distant View of a Minaret" and "The Long Night of Winter," both husbands are disgusting and animal-like while having sex. In "Distant View of a Minaret," Rifaat describes the husband's face in "ugly contortions," and in "The Long Night of Winter," the husband has "evil-smelling breath" and repugnant, "rough hands." The men are selfish and often have affairs. In "The Long Night of Winter," the wife Zennouba asks her mother if it is true that her father also had affairs. Her mother tells her that, "All men are like that." In "Badriyya and Her Husband," Badriyya's husband Omar is a worthless womanizer who lies to Badriyya and never even sleeps with her.

THE IMPACT OF DEATH ON THE LIVING Death permeates the stories in *Distant View of a Minaret*, and with it are those who are still alive but who are left stunned, sad, and bewildered, never to be the same. In "Telephone Call," the widowed narrator believes a late-night phone call could be a message from her dead husband. Her life begins to resemble death: she sleeps during the day, when the rest of the world lives and carries on their day-to-day life, and she stays up through the dark and lonely night, thinking of her dead husband. She wants to know that there is life after death, so that she can be comforted by the fact that she and her husband will someday be reunited. In "Thursday Lunch," the narrator's mother confesses that she has thought of her dead husband every day since his death twenty-four years ago. Death may separate lovers, but the love remains.

The changes death brings are not always unwelcome. In "Just Another Day," the narrator is an old woman who endures a tiresome, unchanging routine. She feels she is a useless burden to her children, and she struggles to find activities that will eat away at time. But death releases the narrator from routine. When she finally realizes she has died, she willingly and happily gives in to death. Widad in "The Kite" has a similar attitude of relief. She, too, is in a routine, and though she doesn't dislike it, she has come to terms with the fact that she is in the last phase of life and will soon die. By facing death and realizing its inevitability, she alleviates her own fear of death and the change it brings.

THE COST OF FREEDOM FOR WOMEN In *Distant View of a Minaret*, women endure many restrictions, and a woman's freedom and power come only at the sacrifice of her life, marriage, or honesty. In "The Incident in the Ghobashi Household," Zeinat must lie to protect her pregnant, unmarried daughter and the family honor, and the money she gave her daughter was money she'd kept secret from her husband. For an Islamic woman, financial power sometimes comes only as a result of dishonest behavior. In "The Flat in Nakshabandi Street," Aziza controls the household and its finances, but she's never had a husband, and she'd never really explored her freedom: she leaves her apartment only for funerals. In "Mansoura," the only time Mansoura successfully fends off Hindawi's sexual advances is when she falls into a canal and drowns. After her death, Mansoura attains a supernatural power, and she crushes Hindawi beneath the arm of the bulldozer. Mansoura avenges Hindawi's wrongdoings, but only at the cost of her own life.

MOTIFS

DAILY PRAYERS In six of the stories in *Distant View of a Minaret*, characters stop what they're doing for prayers, which Muslims do five times a day. In "Distant View of a Minaret," the call comes just as the husband and wife are having sex, and, in a way, it liberates the wife so that she may pray, make coffee, and carry on with the rest of her day. In "Telephone Call," the narrator expects the morning call to prayer to come soon, to end another night of staying up and longing for her dead husband. In "An Incident in the Ghobashi Household," Zeinat has woken up to find that her daughter is showing signs of pregnancy, but before she attends to this dilemma, she makes her ablutions and performs the daily prayer. The men working on the canal in "Mansoura" finish their day and say the last of the daily prayers before gathering around the fire to hear the legend of Mansoura. And in "The Kite," though Widad does not know any verses of the Qur'an and cannot perform the daily prayers, she makes gestures of gratitude and thinks back to when her husband was alive and she could stand behind him as he prayed.

Only one character hears the call to prayer and does not pray: Aziza in "The Flat in Nakshabandi Street." As others begin to pray in the street, Aziza thinks to herself that she no longer has to pray. This, she feels, is because she has prayed enough during her lifetime, she has not committed the sins of married women, and she leads the women in funeral dirges during every funeral she attends. Her self-righteousness is striking when compared to the humble obedience of the characters in other stories.

RELIGION IN DAILY LANGUAGE Muslims' daily language includes praise and thanks to Allah. In "Bahiyya's Eyes," Bahiyya's language makes her faith in Allah clear. The story opens with the sentence, "We praise Him and thank Him for His favour for whatever He decides." Bahiyya praises Allah despite the fact that she has not been allowed to live fully because of the restrictions placed on women in her society. She constantly references "Allah's hands," a phrase that demonstrates her faith that whatever happens, regardless of how tragic, is Allah's will. Bahiyya also uses phrases such as "Allah have mercy on her," "Allah bless you," or "Allah forgive me," which are simply habits of speech rather than true prayers. Other stories contain similar language. In "Thursday Lunch," the narrator converses with her mother's servant, making small talk that is punctuated with the phrase "Thanks be to God." In "An Incident in the Ghobashi Household," the phrase "May Allah keep him (or her) safe" is used twice, when the characters refer to travel. These phrases are simply part of everyday language in an Islamic society. By using them in the stories, Rifaat sets her collection firmly in an Islamic setting.

WIDOWS Most of the characters in *Distant View of a Minaret* are widows, and the state of widowhood takes different shapes with each woman. In "Distant View of a Minaret," the wife is not emotionally connected to her husband, and she feels calm when he dies. When Bahiyya's husband dies in "Bahiyya's Eyes," Bahiyya feels like a stranger in her own village: other women avoid her for fear that she'll steal their husbands. In "Thursday Lunch," the narrator's widowed mother confesses that she has constantly thought of her dead husband for the past twenty-four years. The widow in "Telephone Call" loved her husband enough to seek signs of him from beyond the grave. The women in "The Kite" and "Just Another Day" are widows as well.

Some of the women who are not actually widows lead lonely lives that resemble those of widows. In "Badriyya and Her Husband," Badriyya is married to a selfish womanizer and has not even had sex with him. In "The Long Night of Winter," Zennouba must constantly deal with her husband's affairs with the servant girls. In "At the Time of the Jasmine," Hassan's wife has left him and now lives in her homeland of Turkey, and she basically leads a widow's life. Each of these wives must find the strength to endure a lonely life.

SYMBOLS

THE SNAKE In "My World of the Unknown," the narrator/wife falls in love with a snake, which is also a monarch from the spirit world. Traditionally, the serpent is known as the creature that tempted Eve in the Garden of Eden. When the snake deceives Eve into eating from the fruit of the forbidden tree of wisdom, Eve seduces Adam into partaking as well, and they are both exiled from the Garden of Eden by God. The snake in this short story is also a seducer, but she does not seem evil or demonic. In fact, she tells the wife that their affair is not shameful, because in the eyes of Allah they are now married. The narrator presents the snake as a creature that brings only good to her life and overturns the equating of sex and sin. The snake represents what seems to be lacking in her marriage with her husband. The snake's shape also renders it a phallic symbol, and it indeed brings the narrator sexual pleasure. The narrator seems to be willing to give up her husband in his entirety in exchange for this single representation of a sexual organ, which she immediately finds beautiful and begins to yearn for. However, in the context of Rifaat's other stories, the narrator's desire is natural: an important part of a successful relationship is the sexual connection.

THE CANAL In Egyptian culture, water is viewed as a source of life. The Nile River and the irrigation systems it feeds have been vital to the success of Egyptian civilization since the time of the pharaohs. Strangely, Rifaat depicts the canal in "Mansoura" as a representation of death and tragedy. Mansoura dies when she slips into the canal during a confrontation with Hindawi, a man who is obsessed with her. At the end of the story, the canal is a setting for another death. Hindawi flees town to avoid being killed by Sayyid, and he takes a job laying pipe in the canal. The ghost of Mansoura avenges her death by causing a piece of pipe to fall and crush Hindawi. The canal is far from life-giving; Rifaat has turned a traditional symbol on its head.

IMPORTANT QUOTATIONS EXPLAINED

---

1. *She returned to the living room and poured out the coffee for herself. She was surprised at how calm she was.*

This phrase is from the last line of "Distant View of a Minaret." The husband has just died, and the wife is not terribly upset about his passing. Sex for her was simply another one of her daily chores, and because of his inconsideration during intercourse and in talking about other women, his death does not elicit any grieving. After she finds him dead in their bed, the wife continues her normal routine: after sending her son out for the doctor, she sits down for her afternoon coffee. Outside the context of the story, the wife may seem cold, but the husband's inconsideration and selfishness make the wife's reaction understandable. Rifaat suggests that within a marriage, a husband and wife have a duty to fulfill each other, both emotionally and sexually. Because the husband completely fails in this regard, there is no love in the relationship, and no reason for the wife to grieve.

---

2. *"Isn't it better, when he returns, for your father to find himself with a legitimate son [rather] than an illegitimate grandson?"*

This quote is the last line of "An Incident in the Ghobashi Household." Zeinat's unmarried daughter, Ni'ma, has gotten pregnant. Zeinat's husband is away for many months for work, so Zeinat will pretend that the baby is hers, rather than Ni'ma's. She sends Ni'ma away to have the baby in secret and tells her to return in the night. When Ni'ma questions this plan, Zeinat explains that it is best to lie to Ghobashi because of the dishonor he would experience from knowing Ni'ma had an illegitimate child. Though Zeinat is willing to deceive her husband, her decision is rooted in good intentions. However, she must explain herself to Ni'ma, who doesn't seem to understand the significance of what has happened. Zeinat must convince Ni'ma that her plan is the best solution to this predicament.

---

3. *"Daughter, I'm not crying now because I'm fed up or regret that the Lord created me a woman. No, it's not that. It's just that I'm sad about my life and my youth that have come and gone without my knowing how to live them really and truly as a woman."*

This quote is the last line of "Bahiyya's Eyes." Bahiyya has faith in Allah, and when she says that she does not regret that the Lord created her a woman, she demonstrates her belief that all that happens in life is in accordance with Allah's will. However, she laments some of the events that have befallen her: she was abused by her brother, castrated by the village women, forced into an arranged marriage when she was in love with someone else, and obliged to live in solitude after being widowed at an early age.

Rifaat's message in this story seems to be that Bahiyya's feeling of hopelessness could have been avoided or overcome if her society granted more freedom to women. Bahiyya was told to endure her brother's pinching, hitting, and demands because he would be the man of the family someday, and Bahiyya would be forced to obey him then. If women in her society were allowed to choose their own husbands, she certainly would have married her childhood sweetheart instead of the man her father chose. These two examples illustrate the fact that Bahiyya's life was ruled by men, so she was unable to live fully. Now, in her old age, she feels sad about her wasted youth and life.

---

4. *"Only blood," he said, "washes dishonor clean."*

These words were spoken by Sayyid in "Mansoura" after his wife, Mansoura, is found dead after falling into a canal to escape Hindawi, Sayyid's employer, who was trying to convince Mansoura to resume her affair with him. Prior to her death, Hindawi had cunningly employed Sayyid all day and night, and he would sneak into Mansoura's house while Sayyid was away. Mansoura convinced Sayyid to quit his employment with Hindawi, but Hindawi could not live without her, so he approached Mansoura at the canal. When Mansoura's body washes up, Sayyid is accused of murdering her in a jealous rage. In the quote above, he is confessing to the crime. The narrator of the story explains that Sayyid confesses out of pride, so that he can serve a short sentence and then find and kill the real murderer.

Even though Sayyid seems to be talking about Mansoura's blood in this quote, it is Hindawi's blood that is finally spilled in order to erase the dishonor that has been done against Mansoura and Sayyid. At the close of this legend about the Mansoura Canal, the narrator explains that Hindawi fled the town for fear that Sayyid would kill him. Hindawi joined the narrator, Sheikh Zeidan, as a worker laying pipe in the canal. While Hindawi is working, he sees a vision of Mansoura above a crane that suddenly drops a pipe on him and kills him. Mansoura avenges her death, and Hindawi pays for his dishonor with his blood.

---

5. *"Father, you gave me a real beating tonight."*

Hassan speaks these words at the end of "At the Time of the Jasmine." Hassan has spent the day at the burial ceremony of his father, Hagg. Just before sleeping, Hassan thinks back on his relationship with his father and regrets not having spent more time developing it. Hagg never even got to meet Hassan's daughter, Jasmine, nor did he fulfill his wish of making a pilgrimage with Hassan. While reflecting on these things and experiencing anger and grief, Hassan feels as if he has been beaten with his father's staff. Hagg never actually beat Hassan with his staff—he would simply wave it at Hassan when he was a boy and threaten to beat Hassan if he was insubordinate. Tonight, Hassan is so emotionally devastated that he feels as if he has received a real beating.

Hassan had ignored his emotional life for so long that when he experiences loss and regret over his father's death, he is completely unprepared. When Hassan says that he has been given a "real" beating, he feels as though he is being punished for his inaction. As a child, if he misbehaved, he would be threatened by Hagg and then be given the opportunity to change his behavior. This situation is different: Hassan does not have the opportunity to alter the past. His father is dead, so it is too late for Hassan to change the fact that he has ignored his father and failed to foster a relationship with him.

Emma

Jane Austen (1775–1817)

E

CONTEXT

Jane Austen, whom some critics consider England's best novelist, was born in 1775 in Steventon, England. The seventh of eight children, Austen lived with her parents for her entire life, first in Steventon and later in Bath, Southampton, and Chawton. Her father was the parish rector in Steventon, and, though not wealthy, her family was well connected and well educated. Austen briefly attended boarding school in Reading but received the majority of her education at home. According to rumor, she had a brief love affair when she was twenty-five, but it did not lead to a marriage proposal. Two years later, she accepted and then quickly rejected a proposal. She remained unmarried for the rest of her life. Austen died in 1817, at age forty-one, of Addison's disease.

Austen began writing stories at a very young age and completed her first novel in her early twenties. However, she did not publish until 1811, when *Sense and Sensibility* appeared anonymously, followed by *Pride and Prejudice* (1813) and *Mansfield Park* (1814). *Emma*, which appeared in 1816, was the last novel published during Austen's lifetime. (*Northanger Abbey* and *Persuasion* appeared posthumously.)

Austen's novels received little critical or popular recognition during her lifetime, and her identity as a novelist was not revealed until after her death. As admired as Austen's novels later became, critics have had a difficult time placing them within literary history. She is known for her gently satirical portraits of village life and of the rituals of courtship and marriage, but she wrote during the Romantic period, when most major writers were concerned with a very different set of interests and values. Romantic poets confronted the hopes and failures of the French Revolution and formulated new literary values centered on individual freedom, passion, and intensity. In comparison, Austen's detailed examination of the rules of decorum that govern social relationships, and her insistence that reason and moderation are necessary checks on feeling, make her seem out of step with the literary times. One way to understand Austen's place in literary history is to think of her as part of the earlier eighteenth century, the Age of Reason, when literature was associated with wit, poise, and propriety. Her novels certainly belong to an eighteenth-century genre, the comedy of manners, which examines the behavior of men and women of a single social class.

Rather than dismiss Austen as a writer who shuns the artistic and political movements of her time, it is perhaps more useful to think of her as an early feminist. Critics have pointed out that the Romantics, who were almost exclusively male, offered a poor model of literary fulfillment for the ambitious woman of the time. While male writers such as Percy Bysshe Shelley and Lord Byron possessed the freedom to promote their own individuality through wide travel and sexual and military adventurism, women were largely denied these freedoms. For women, the penalty for sexual freedom was social ostracism, poverty, and worse. In *Sense and Sensibility*, Austen describes explicitly the danger that cultivating emotion posed for women of her time.

In this social context, Austen's commitment to reason and moderation can be seen as feminist and progressive rather than conservative. The intelligence and resourcefulness of her heroines stand in constant contrast to the limits of the constricted world of courtship and marriage defining their sphere of action. While reading *Emma*, it is interesting to consider to what extent Austen accepts or questions the idea that marriage represents a woman's maturity and fulfillment.

Some consider *Emma* Austen's best and most representative novel. It is also her longest novel and, by many accounts, her most difficult. Long praised for its rich domestic realism, *Emma* also presents puzzling questions: how can a character as intelligent as Emma be wrong so often? When does Austen expect us to sympathize with Emma, and when does she expect us to criticize her? Is the ending as genuinely happy as it is presented to be, or does Austen subtly inject a note of subversive irony into it? That these questions are on some level unanswerable ensures that *Emma* will be read again and again.

PLOT OVERVIEW

Although convinced that she herself will never marry, Emma Woodhouse, a precocious twenty-year-old resident of the village of Highbury, imagines herself to be naturally gifted in conjuring love matches. After self-declared success at matchmaking between her governess and Mr. Weston, a village widower, Emma takes it upon herself to find an eligible match for her new friend, Harriet Smith. Though Harriet's parentage is unknown, Emma is convinced that Harriet deserves to be a gentleman's wife and sets her friend's sights on Mr. Elton, the village vicar. Meanwhile, Emma persuades Harriet to reject the proposal of Robert Martin, a well-to-do farmer for whom Harriet clearly has feelings.

Harriet becomes infatuated with Mr. Elton under Emma's encouragement, but Emma's plans go awry when Elton makes it clear that his affection is for Emma, not Harriet.

Emma realizes that her obsession with making a match for Harriet has blinded her to the true nature of the situation. Mr. Knightley, Emma's brother-in-law and treasured friend, watches Emma's matchmaking efforts with a critical eye. He believes that Mr. Martin is a worthy young man whom Harriet would be lucky to marry. He and Emma quarrel over Emma's meddling, and, as usual, Mr. Knightley proves to be the wiser of the pair. Elton, spurned by Emma and offended by her insinuation that Harriet is his equal, leaves for the town of Bath and marries a girl there almost immediately.

Emma is left to comfort Harriet and to wonder about the character of a new visitor expected in Highbury—Mr. Weston's son, Frank Churchill. Frank is set to visit his father in Highbury after having been raised in London by his aunt and uncle, who have taken him as their heir. Emma knows nothing about Frank, who has long been deterred from visiting his father by his aunt's illnesses and complaints. Mr. Knightley is immediately suspicious of the young man, especially after Frank rushes back to London merely to have his hair cut. Emma, however, finds Frank delightful and notices that his charms are directed mainly toward her. Though she plans to discourage these charms, she finds herself flattered and engaged in flirtation with the young man. Emma greets Jane Fairfax, another addition to the Highbury set, with less enthusiasm. Jane is beautiful and accomplished, but Emma dislikes her because of her reserve and, the narrator insinuates, because she is jealous of Jane.

Suspicion, intrigue, and misunderstandings ensue. Mr. Knightley defends Jane, saying that she deserves compassion because, unlike Emma, she has no independent fortune and must soon leave home to work as a governess. Mrs. Weston suspects that the warmth of Mr. Knightley's defense comes from romantic feelings, an implication Emma resists.

Everyone assumes that Frank and Emma are forming an attachment, though Emma soon dismisses Frank as a potential suitor and imagines him as a match for Harriet. At a village ball, Knightley earns Emma's approval by offering to dance with Harriet, who has just been humiliated by Mr. Elton and his new wife. The next day, Frank saves Harriet from gypsy beggars. When Harriet tells Emma that she has fallen in love with a man above her social station, Emma believes that she means Frank. Knightley begins to suspect that Frank and Jane have a secret understanding, and he attempts to warn Emma. Emma laughs at Knightley's suggestion and loses Knightley's approval when she flirts with Frank and insults Miss Bates, a kindhearted spinster and Jane's aunt, at a picnic. When Knightley reprimands Emma, she weeps.

News comes that Frank's aunt has died, and this event paves the way for an unexpected revelation that slowly solves the mysteries. Frank and Jane have been secretly engaged; his attentions to Emma have been a screen to hide his true preference. With his aunt's death and his uncle's approval, Frank can now marry Jane, the woman he loves. Emma worries that Harriet will be crushed, but she soon discovers that it is Knightley, not Frank, who is the object of Harriet's affection. Harriet believes that Knightley shares her feelings. Emma finds herself upset by Harriet's revelation, and her distress forces her to realize that she is in love with Knightley. Emma expects Knightley to tell her he loves Harriet, but, to her delight, Knightley declares his love for Emma. Harriet is soon comforted by a second proposal from Robert Martin, which she accepts. The novel ends with the marriage of Harriet and Mr. Martin and that of Emma and Mr. Knightley, resolving the question of who loves whom after all.

CHARACTER LIST

Emma Woodhouse The protagonist of the novel. In the well-known first sentence of the novel, the narrator describes Emma as "handsome, clever, and rich, with a comfortable home and happy disposition." In some ways, twenty-year-old Emma is mature for her age. Because her mother is dead and her older sister is married, she is already the head of her father's household. She cares for her father and oversees the social goings-on in the village of Highbury. Emma's misplaced confidence in her abilities as a matchmaker and her prudish fear of love constitute the central focus of the novel, which traces Emma's mistakes and growing self-understanding.

Mr. George Knightley Emma's brother-in-law and the Woodhouses' trusted friend and advisor. Knightley is a respected landowner in his late thirties. He lives at Donwell Abbey and leases property to the Martins, a family of wealthy farmers whom he likes and counsels. Knightley is the only character who is openly critical of Emma, pointing out her flaws and foibles with frankness, out of genuine concern and care for her. In this respect, he acts as a stand-in for Austen's and the reader's judgments of Emma.

Mr. Woodhouse Emma's father and the patriarch of Hartfield, the Woodhouse estate. Though Mr. Woodhouse is nervous, frail, and prone to hypochondria, he is also known for his friendliness and his attachment to his daughter. He is very resistant to change, to the point that he is unhappy to see his daughters or Emma's governess marry. In this sense, he impedes Emma's growth and acceptance of her adult destiny. He is often foolish and clearly not Emma's intellectual equal, but she comforts and entertains him with insight and affection.

Harriet Smith A pretty but unremarkable seventeen-year-old woman of uncertain parentage, who lives at the local boarding school. Harriet becomes Emma's protégé and the object of her matchmaking schemes.

Frank Churchill Mr. Weston's son and Mrs. Weston's stepson. Frank Churchill lives at Enscombe with his aunt and uncle, Mr. and Mrs. Churchill. He is considered a potential suitor for Emma, but she learns that though Frank is attractive, charming, and clever, he is also irresponsible, deceitful, rash, and ultimately unsuited to her.

E

Jane Fairfax Miss Bates's niece, whose arrival in Highbury irritates Emma. Jane rivals Emma in accomplishment and beauty; she possesses a kind heart and a reserved temperament. Because Jane lacks Emma's fortune, she must consider employment as a governess, but her marriage to Frank Churchill saves her from that fate.

Mrs. Weston Formerly Miss Taylor, Emma's beloved governess and companion. Known for her kind temperament and her devotion to Emma, Mrs. Weston lives at Randalls with her husband, Frank Churchill's father.

Mr. Weston The widower and proprietor of Randalls, who has just married Miss Taylor when the novel begins. Mr. Weston has a son, Frank, from his first marriage to Miss Churchill (Frank was raised by Miss Churchill's sister and brother-in-law). Mr. Weston is warm, sociable, and perpetually optimistic.

Mr. Elton The village vicar, a handsome and agreeable man considered a welcome addition to any social gathering. When Mr. Elton reveals his indifference to Harriet and his desire to marry Emma, only to take a bride at Bath shortly thereafter, he comes to seem proud, conceited, and superficial.

Mr. Robert Martin A twenty-four-year-old farmer. Mr. Martin is industrious and good-hearted, though he lacks the refinements of a gentleman. He lives at Abbey-Mill Farm, a property owned by Knightley, with his mother and sisters.

Miss Bates A friend of Mr. Woodhouse and aunt of Jane Fairfax. Miss Bates is a middle-aged spinster without beauty or cleverness but with universal goodwill and a gentle temperament. Emma's impatient treatment of her reveals the less attractive parts of Emma's character.

Isabella Knightley Emma's older sister, who lives in London with her husband, Mr. John Knightley, and their five children. Isabella is pretty, amiable, and completely devoted to her family, but slow and diffident compared to Emma. Her domesticity provides a contrast to the independent celibacy Emma imagines for herself.

Mr. John Knightley Emma's brother-in-law, and Mr. George Knightley's brother. As a lawyer, John Knightley is clear-minded but somewhat sharp in temper, and Emma and her father are sometimes displeased with his severity.

Mrs. Elton Formerly Augusta Hawkins. Mrs. Elton hails from Bristol and meets Mr. Elton in Bath. She is somewhat attractive and accomplished; she has some fortune and a well-married sister, but her vanity, superficiality, and vulgar overfamiliarity offset her admirable qualities.

Mrs. Churchill Mr. Weston's ailing former sister-in-law and Frank Churchill's aunt and guardian. Mrs. Churchill is known to be capricious, ill-tempered, and extremely possessive of Frank. Frank is able to marry Jane Fairfax, as he desires, only after Mrs. Churchill's death.

Colonel Campbell A friend of Jane Fairfax's father who lives in London and who takes charge of orphaned Jane when she is eight years old. Colonel Campbell feels great affection for Jane but is unable to provide her with an inheritance.

Mrs. Dixon The Campbells' daughter and Jane's friend. Mrs. Dixon lacks beauty and lives with her husband in Ireland.

Mr. Dixon Husband to the Campbells' daughter. Emma suspects that Mr. Dixon had a romance with Jane Fairfax before his marriage.

Mrs. Goddard Mistress of the local boarding school. Mrs. Goddard introduces Harriet Smith to the Woodhouses.

Mrs. Bates The mother of Miss Bates and friend of Mr. Woodhouse. An elderly woman, Mrs. Bates is quiet, amiable, and somewhat deaf.

Mr. Perry An apothecary and associate of Emma's father. Mr. Perry is highly esteemed by Mr. Woodhouse for his medical advice even though he is not a proper physician, and Mr. Woodhouse argues with his daughter Isabella over Perry's recommendations.

Elizabeth Martin Mr. Martin's kind sister, with whom Harriet was good friends before meeting Emma and turning down Mr. Martin's marriage proposal. Harriet's feelings of guilt and her desire to rekindle her relationship with Elizabeth pose a dilemma for Emma, who finds the Martins pleasant, worthy people, but worries that Harriet may be tempted to accept Mr. Martin's offer if she again grows close with the family.

Mr. and Mrs. Cole Tradespeople and longtime residents of Highbury whose good fortune of the past several years has led them to adopt a luxurious lifestyle that is only a notch below that of the Woodhouses. Offended by their attempt to transcend their "only moderately genteel" social status, Emma has long been preparing to turn down any dinner invitation from the Coles in order to teach them their folly in thinking they can interact socially with the likes of her family. Like the Martins, the Coles are the means through which Emma demonstrates her class-consciousness.

ANALYSIS OF MAJOR CHARACTERS

EMMA WOODHOUSE The narrator introduces Emma to us by emphasizing her good fortune: "handsome, clever, and rich, with a comfortable home and happy disposition," Emma "had lived nearly twenty-one years in the world with very little to distress or vex her." But, the narrator warns us, Emma possesses "the power of having rather too much her own way, and a disposition to think a little too well of herself." Emma's stubbornness and vanity produce many of the novel's conflicts, as Emma struggles to develop emotionally.

Emma makes three major mistakes. First, she attempts to make Harriet into the wife of a gentleman, when Harriet's social position dictates that she would be better suited to the farmer who loves her. Then, she flirts with Frank Churchill even though she does not care for him, making unfair comments about Jane Fairfax along the way. Most important, she does not realize that, rather than being committed to staying single (as she always claims), she is in love with and wants to marry Mr. Knightley. Though these mistakes seriously threaten Harriet's happiness, cause Emma embarrassment, and create obstacles to Emma's own achievement of true love, none of them has lasting consequences. Throughout the novel, Knightley corrects and guides Emma; in marrying Knightley, Emma signals that her judgment has aligned with his.

Austen predicted that Emma would be "a character whom no one but me will much like." Though most of Austen's readers have proven her wrong, her narration creates many ambiguities. The novel is narrated using free indirect discourse, which means that, although the all-knowing narrator speaks in the third person, she often relates things from Emma's point of view and describes things in language we might imagine Emma using. This style of narration creates a complex mixture of sympathy with Emma and ironic judgment on her behavior. It is not always clear when we are to share Emma's perceptions and when we are to see through them. Nor do we know how harshly Austen expects us to judge Emma's behavior. Though this narrative strategy creates problems of interpretation for the reader, it makes Emma a richly multidimensional character.

Emma does not have one specific foil, but the implicit distinctions made between her and the other women in the novel offer us a context within which to evaluate her character. Jane is similar to Emma in most ways, but she does not have Emma's financial independence, so her difficulties underscore Emma's privileged nature. Mrs. Elton, like Emma, is independent and imposes her will upon her friends, but her crudeness and vanity reinforce our sense of Emma's refinement and fundamentally good heart. Emma's sister, Isabella, is stereotypically feminine—soft-hearted, completely devoted to her family, dependent, and not terribly bright. The novel implicitly prefers Emma's independence and cleverness to her sister's more traditional deportment, although we are still faced with the paradox that though Emma is clever, she is almost always mistaken.

MR. KNIGHTLEY Mr. Knightley serves as the novel's model of good sense. From his very first conversation with Emma and her father in Chapter 1, his purpose—to correct the excesses and missteps of those around him—is clear. He is unfailingly honest but tempers his honesty with tact and kindheartedness. Almost always, we can depend upon him to provide the correct evaluation of the other characters' behavior and personal worth. He intuitively understands and kindly makes allowances for Mr. Woodhouse's whims; he is sympathetic and protective of the women in the community, including Jane, Harriet, and Miss Bates; and, most of all, even though he frequently disapproves of her behavior, he dotes on Emma.

Knightley's love for Emma—the one emotion he cannot govern fully—leads to his only lapses of judgment and self-control. Before even meeting Frank, Knightley decides that he does not like him. It gradually becomes clear that Knightley feels jealous—he does not welcome a rival. When Knightley believes Emma has become too attached to Frank, he acts with uncharacteristic impulsiveness in running away to London. His declaration of love on his return bursts out uncontrollably, unlike most of his prudent, well-planned actions. Yet Knightley's loss of control humanizes him rather than making him seem like a failure.

Like Emma, Knightley stands out in comparison to his peers. His brother, Mr. John Knightley, shares his clear-sightedness but lacks his unfailing kindness and tact. Both Frank and Knightley are perceptive, warm-hearted, and dynamic; but whereas Frank uses his intelligence to conceal his real feelings and invent clever compliments to please those around him, Knightley uses his intelligence to discern right moral conduct. Knightley has little use for cleverness for its own sake; he rates propriety and concern for others more highly.

FRANK CHURCHILL Frank epitomizes attractiveness in speech, manner, and appearance. He goes out of his way to please everyone, and, while the more perceptive characters question his seriousness, everyone except Knightley is charmed enough to be willing to indulge him. Frank is the character who most resembles Emma, a connection she points out at the novel's close when she states that "destiny . . . connect[s] us with two characters so much superior to our own." Like Emma, Frank develops over the course of the novel by trading a somewhat vain and superficial perspective on the world for the seriousness brought on by the experience of genuine suffering and love. He is a complex character because though we know we should judge him harshly in moral terms, we cannot help but like him more than he deserves to be liked.

JANE FAIRFAX Jane's beauty and accomplishment immediately make her stand out, but we are likely to follow Emma's lead at first and judge Jane uninteresting on account of her reserve. As Jane gradually betrays more personality and emotion, she indicates that she harbors some secret sorrow. Eventually, she and Emma push the cloudy confusion behind and become friends. The contrast between Jane's delicate sense of propriety and morality and the passionate nature of her feelings is much more dramatic than any of the conflicts that Emma experiences. Jane's situation too is much more dire than Emma's: if Jane does not wed, she must become a governess, because she lacks any money of her own. The revelation of Jane's secret engagement to Frank makes Jane seem more human, just as Knightley's humanity is brought out by his love for Emma.

THEMES, MOTIFS, AND SYMBOLS

THEMES

THE RELATIONSHIP BETWEEN MARRIAGE AND SOCIAL STATUS *Emma* is structured around a number of marriages recently consummated or anticipated, and, in each case, the match solidifies the participant's social status. In Austen's time, social status was determined by a combination of family background, reputation, and wealth—marriage was one of the main ways in which one could raise one's social status. This method of social advancement was especially crucial to women, who were denied the possibility of improving their status through hard work or personal achievement.

Yet, the novel suggests, marrying too far above oneself leads to strife. Mr. Weston's first marriage to Miss Churchill had ostensibly been a good move for him, because she came from a wealthy and well-connected family (Mr. Weston is a tradesman), but the inequality of the relationship caused hardship for both. He marries Mrs. Weston just prior to the novel's opening, and this second marriage is happier because their social statuses are more equal—Mrs. Weston is a governess and thus very fortunate to be rescued from her need to work by her marriage. Emma's attempt to match Harriet with Mr. Elton is also shunned by the other characters as inappropriate. Since Harriet's parentage is unknown, Emma believes that Harriet may have noble blood and encourages her to reject what turns out to be a more appropriate match with Robert Martin. By the time it is revealed that Harriet is the daughter of a tradesman, Emma admits that Mr. Martin is more suitable for her friend.

The relationship between marriage and social status creates hardship for other characters. Frank Churchill must keep his engagement to the orphan Jane Fairfax secret because his wealthy aunt would disapprove. Jane, in the absence of a good match, is forced to consider taking the position of a governess. The unmarried Miss Bates is threatened with increasing poverty without a husband to take care of her and her mother. Finally, the match between Emma and Mr. Knightley is considered a good one not only because they are well matched in temperament but also because they are well matched in social class.

E

THE CONFINED NATURE OF WOMEN'S EXISTENCE The novel's limited, almost claustrophobic scope of action gives us a strong sense of the confined nature of a woman's existence in early-nineteenth-century rural England. Emma possesses a great deal of intelligence and energy, but the best use she can make of these is to attempt to guide the marital destinies of her friends, a project that gets her into trouble. The alternative pastimes depicted in the book—social visits, charity visits, music, artistic endeavors—seem relatively trivial, at times even monotonous. Isabella is the only mother focused on in the story, and her portrayal suggests that a mother's life offers a woman little use of her intellect. Yet, when Jane compares the governess profession to the slave trade, she makes it clear that the life of a working woman is in no way preferable to the idleness of a woman of fortune. The novel focuses on marriage because marriage offers women a chance to exert their power, if only for a brief time, and to affect their own destinies without adopting the labors or efforts of the working class. Participating in the rituals of courtship and accepting or rejecting proposals is perhaps the most active role that women are permitted to play in Emma's world.

THE BLINDING POWER OF IMAGINATION *Emma* offers sharply critical illustrations of the ways in which personal biases or desires blind objective judgment. Emma cannot understand the motives that guide Mr. Elton's behavior because she imagines that he is in love with Harriet. She later admits to herself that "[s]he had taken up the idea, she supposed, and made everything bend to it." Meanwhile, Mr. Elton's feelings for Emma cause him to mistake her behavior for encouragement. The generally infallible Mr. Knightley cannot form an unbiased opinion about Frank Churchill because he is jealous of Frank's claim on Emma, and Emma speaks cruelly of Jane because her vanity makes her jealous of Jane's accomplishments. Emma's biases cause her to invent an attachment between Harriet and Frank and blind her to the fact that Harriet actually has feelings for Knightley. At the same time, Frank's desire to use Emma as a screen for his real preference causes him to mistakenly believe that she is aware of the situation between him and Jane. The admirable, frequently ironic detachment of the narrator allows us to see many of these misunderstandings before the characters do, along with the humorous aspects of their behavior. And the plot is powered by a series of realizations that permit each character to make fuller, more objective judgments.

THE OBSTACLES TO OPEN EXPRESSION The misunderstandings that permeate *Emma* are created, in part, by the conventions of social propriety. To differing degrees, characters are unable to express their feelings directly and openly, and their feelings are therefore mistaken. While the novel by no means suggests that the manners and rituals of social interaction should be eliminated, Austen implies that the overly clever, complex speech of Mr. Elton, Frank Churchill, and Emma deserves censure. She presents Mr. Martin's natural, warm, and direct manner of expressing himself as preferable to Mr. Elton's ostentatious and insincere style of complimenting people. Frank, too, possesses a talent for telling people exactly what they want to hear, and Knightley's suspicions of Frank's integrity are proven valid when it turns out that Frank has been misleading Highbury and hiding his true feelings for Jane. The cleverness of Frank's and Emma's banter gets them both into trouble by upsetting Jane, about whom Emma says indiscreet and unfair things. Emma and Frank's flirting at the Box Hill party hurts both Knightley and Jane. Moreover, Emma forgets herself to the extent that she cruelly insults Miss Bates. Austen seems to prefer Knightley and Martin's tactful tacitness to the sometimes overly gregarious commentary of Emma, Mr. Elton, and Frank, and, as a result, the author gives the latter characters' contrived speech a misleading influence on the story as a whole.

MOTIFS

VISITS The main events of the novel take place during visits that the characters pay to each other. The frequency and length of visits between characters indicates the level of intimacy and attachment between them. Frank's frequent visits to Hartfield show his relationship with Emma to be close, though in hindsight we recognize that Frank also continually finds excuses to visit Jane. Mr. Knightley's constant presence at Hartfield indicates his affection and regard for Emma. Emma encourages Harriet to limit a visit with the Martin family to fifteen minutes, because such a short visit clearly indicates that any former interest has been lost. Emma is chastised for her failure to visit Miss Bates and Jane more often; when she takes steps to rectify this situation, she indicates a new concern for Miss Bates and a new regard for Jane.

PARTIES More formal than visits, parties are organized around social conventions more than around individual attachments—Emma's hosting a dinner party for Mrs. Elton, a woman she dislikes, exemplifies this characteristic. There are six important parties in the novel: the Christmas Eve party at Randalls, the dinner party at the Coles', the dinner party given for Mrs. Elton, the dance at the Crown Inn, the morning party at Donwell Abbey, and the picnic at Box Hill. Each occasion provides the opportunity for social intrigue and misunderstandings, and for vanities to be satisfied and connections formed. Parties also give characters the chance to observe other people's interactions. Knightley observes Emma's behavior toward Frank and Frank's behavior toward Jane. Parties are microcosms of the social interactions that make up the novel as a whole.

CONVERSATIONAL SUBTEXTS Much of the dialogue in *Emma* has double or even triple meanings, with different characters interpreting a single comment in different ways. Sometimes these double meanings are apparent to individual characters, and sometimes they are apparent only to the alert reader. For example, when Mr. Elton says of Emma's portrait of Harriet, "I cannot keep my eyes from it," he means to compliment Emma, but she thinks he is complimenting Harriet. When, during the scene in which Mr. Knightley proposes to Emma, Emma says, "I seem to have been doomed to blindness," Knightley believes she is speaking of her blindness to Frank's love of Jane, but she is actually referring to her blindness about her own feelings. One of our main tasks in reading the novel is to decode all of the subtexts underlying seemingly casual interactions, just as the main characters must. The novel concludes by unraveling the mystery behind who loves whom, which allows us to understand Austen's subtext more fully.

SYMBOLS

THE RIDDLE Also known as charades, riddles in the novel take the form of elaborate wordplay. They symbolize the pervasive subtexts that wait to be decoded in characters' larger social interactions. In Chapter 9, Mr. Elton presents a riddle to Emma and Harriet. Emma decodes it immediately as "courtship," but she decodes it wrong in the sense that she believes it is meant for Harriet rather than herself. This wordplay also makes an appearance during the Box Hill party, when Mr. Weston makes an acrostic for Emma.

THE WORD GAME Similar to the riddle, a word game is played in Chapter 41 between Emma, Frank, and Jane. It functions as a metaphor for the partial understandings and misunderstandings that exist among Emma, Frank, Jane, and Mr. Knightley. As Mr. Knightley looks on, Frank uses child's blocks to create words for the ladies to decode, though these words mean different things to each of them. Frank makes the word "blunder," which Jane understands as referring to a mistake he has just made, but whose meaning is opaque to Emma and Knightley. He then makes the word "Dixon," which Emma understands as a joke on Jane, and which baffles Knightley. In truth, everyone "blunders" in different ways that evening, because no one possesses complete enough information to correctly interpret everything that is going on.

TOKENS OF AFFECTION A number of objects in the novel take on symbolic significance as tokens of affection. Mr. Elton frames Emma's portrait of Harriet as a symbol of affection for her, though Emma misunderstands it as a symbol of affection for Harriet. Harriet keeps court plaster and a pencil stub as souvenirs of Mr. Elton. When the engagement between Jane and Frank is briefly called off, she returns his letters to symbolize her relinquishment of his affection.

IMPORTANT QUOTATIONS EXPLAINED

---

1. *The real evils, indeed, of Emma's situation were the power of having rather too much her own way, and a disposition to think a little too well of herself: these were the disadvantages which threatened alloy to her many enjoyments. The danger, however, was at present so unperceived, that they did not by any means rank as misfortunes with her.*

E

This passage, which appears early in the first chapter, foreshadows the novel's structure as a whole. What Emma fails to perceive—that it is possible to have too much of one's own way or to be too satisfied with oneself—is exactly what she learns over the course of the novel. She is permitted too much influence over Harriet and comes to understand that this power threatens not only Harriet's happiness but also her own. Her flirtations with Frank Churchill satisfy her vanity, but they also expose her to embarrassment and hurt and mislead Mr. Knightley. This quotation also displays Austen's gift for understatement. The narrator's commentary on Emma seems merely part of a standard character introduction. Like so many of the statements in the book, we can only feel the full force of the narrator's observation upon a second reading.

---

2. *The first error, and the worst, lay at her door. It was foolish, it was wrong, to take so active a part in bringing any two people together. It was adventuring too far, assuming too much, making light of what ought to be serious—a trick of what ought to be simple. She was quite concerned and ashamed, and resolved to do such things no more.*

These are Emma's reflections after Mr. Elton proposes in Chapter 16, revealing to her that she was wrong in thinking him attached to Harriet. Though Emma is never totally cured of her impulse to make matches for others, here she rightly diagnoses what is wrong with her matchmaking. Courtship should be serious and simple; it should flow naturally from spontaneous affinities and affection between two people. In the novel, courtship rarely follows these guidelines. Mr. Elton's courtship of Emma is marked by the artificiality and ostentation of his compliments, which reveal his underlying lack of real feeling for her. Frank and Emma's flirtation is light and elaborate in its wit, again signaling us that they are not truly meant for each other. At the end of the novel, Mr. Knightley's direct and simple proposal embodies the ideal proposed here.

---

3. *She was vexed beyond what could have been expressed—almost beyond what she could conceal. Never had she felt so agitated, so mortified, grieved, at any circumstance in her life. She was most forcibly struck. The truth of his representation there was no denying. She felt it at her heart. How could she have been so brutal, so cruel to Miss Bates! How could she have exposed herself to such ill opinion in any one she valued! And how suffer him to leave her without saying one word of gratitude, of concurrence, of common kindness!*

This phrase comes at the end of Chapter 43. After being reprimanded by Mr. Knightley for insulting Miss Bates at the Box Hill picnic, a deluge of remorse comes over Emma as she realizes the cruelty of her behavior. This quotation marks the point at which Emma's growing self-understanding, which helps her feel how wrongly she has treated Miss Bates, coincides with her growing attachment to Knightley. Her increasing self-knowledge is thus weighted, because it will bring her to or separate her from true love. This moment is also Emma's most emotional in the novel, and it is narrated directly, unlike Mr. Elton's proposal and Emma's response to Mr. Knightley's proposal. That the narrative so directly accesses Emma's remorse underscores its seriousness—it is as if her thoughts have overpowered the narrator's ability to relate them.

E

4. *Emma's eyes were instantly withdrawn; and she sat silently meditating, in a fixed attitude, for a few minutes. A few minutes were sufficient for making her acquainted with her own heart. A mind like hers, once opening to suspicion, made rapid progress; she touched, she admitted, she acknowledged the whole truth. Why was it so much worse that Harriet should be in love with Mr. Knightley than with Frank Churchill? Why was the evil so dreadfully increased by Harriet's having some hope of a return? It darted through her with the speed of an arrow that Mr. Knightley must marry no one but herself!*

This passage, from Chapter 47, comes in the midst of Emma's conversation with Harriet in which Harriet confesses her feelings for Mr. Knightley. For the majority of the novel, Emma's suspicions and her attention have been misdirected, focusing on Harriet's possible matches and on her speculations about Jane. Once her perceptiveness and ability to see beyond appearances are finally directed appropriately (after her realization that Frank and Jane are engaged), she makes a swift leap forward in her own self-understanding. However, Emma does not come to the realization that she loves Knightley on her own; only her jealousy of Harriet brings her there. The relationship between Emma and Knightley, though based on their private history together, takes shape only in the context of the surrounding web of social relationships.

---

5. *Seldom, very seldom does complete truth belong to any human disclosure; seldom can it happen that something is not a little disguised, or a little mistaken; but where, as in this case, though the conduct is mistaken, the feelings are not, it may not be very material.*

This observation, which follows Emma and Mr. Knightley's betrothal in Chapter 49, could serve as the novel's motto. It says that although almost all human speech holds something back, or doesn't tell the entire truth, as long as the speech is loyal to the speaker's feelings, the fact that we talk without complete truth is not a big deal. The novel is filled with disguises and mistakes. Some are more reprehensible than others, and some are more avoidable than others. Though Elton's insincerity and Frank's conscious deception are critically portrayed—and Emma's mistakes gently corrected—we are left with the sense that, to some degree, misunderstandings are made inevitable by the social conventions that govern human intercourse, and by the imperfections of human communication itself. The remedy for such imperfect communication, according to this quotation, is the genuine emotion of the human heart.

Frankenstein

Mary Wollstonecraft Shelley (1797–1851)

NOTE: In 1831, Shelley completed a revision of Frankenstein in which she changed several minor, but not insignificant, facts. Most importantly, in the 1831 revision, Elizabeth Lavenza is an orphan adopted from a poor Italian family; she is not Victor Frankenstein's cousin. Where appropriate, differences between the two versions are noted in the text. Chapter numbers are taken from the 1831 edition.

CONTEXT

In the summer of 1816, a young, well-educated woman from England traveled with her lover to the Swiss Alps. Unseasonable rain kept them trapped inside their lodgings, where they entertained themselves by reading ghost stories. At the urging of renowned poet Lord Byron, a friend and neighbor, they set their own pens to paper, competing to see who could write the best ghost story. The young woman, Mary Wollstonecraft Godwin, took the prize, having composed a story creepy enough not only to take its place alongside the old German tales that she and her Alpine companions had been reading, but also to become a bestseller in her time and a Gothic classic that still resonates with readers almost two centuries later.

Mary Wollstonecraft Shelley was born Mary Wollstonecraft Godwin on August 30, 1797, in London, of prime literary stock. Her mother, Mary Wollstonecraft, was the author of *A Vindication of the Rights of Woman*, a feminist tract encouraging women to think and act for themselves. Wollstonecraft died giving birth to Shelley, leaving her daughter in the care of her husband, William Godwin, a member of a circle of radical thinkers in England that included Thomas Paine and William Blake among its ranks. Shelley's upbringing in this rarefied atmosphere exposed her at an early age to cutting-edge ideas, and it forged useful connections for her to such notables as Lord Byron.

Another of the literary types that Shelley met as a teenager was Percy Bysshe Shelley, a dashing young poet. Sparks flew, and, in 1814, they ran away together for a tour of France, Switzerland, and Germany—Shelley escaping her family and Percy his wife. At first blissful, their affair soon came under strain. Percy's relationship with Shelley waxed and waned with the demands of his wife, Harriet; meanwhile, Shelley busied herself with another man. Despite these distractions, the relationship endured and was eventually formalized under tragic circumstances: Harriet, pregnant with Percy's child, drowned herself in London in November of 1816; Shelley and Percy were married weeks later.

The union between Shelley and Percy was not only romantic but also literary. Percy edited Shelley's manuscript for *Frankenstein* and is commonly supposed to have written the preface under her name. *Frankenstein* was published on January 1, 1818, and became an immediate bestseller. Unfortunately for Shelley, this success was a single bright spot amid a series of tragedies. From 1815 to 1819, three of her four children died in infancy; in 1822, Percy drowned off the shore of Tuscany, leaving Shelley a widow and single mother. Shelley turned to her husband's poetry and prose, editing and publishing his *Posthumous Poems* in 1824 and his *Poetical Works and Letters* in 1839. She spent the rest of her time on her own writing, publishing *Valperga* in 1823, *The Last Man* in 1826, *The Fortunes of Perkin Warbeck* in 1830, *Lodore* in 1835, and *Falkner* in 1837. Serious illness plagued Shelley, and she died in London in February 1851.

PLOT OVERVIEW

In a series of letters, Robert Walton, the captain of a ship bound for the North Pole, recounts to his sister back in England the progress of his dangerous mission. Successful early on, the mission is soon interrupted by seas full of impassable ice. Trapped, Walton encounters Victor Frankenstein, who has been traveling by dog-drawn sledge across the ice and is weakened by the cold. Walton takes him aboard the ship, helps nurse him back to health, and hears the fantastic tale of the monster that Frankenstein created.

Victor first describes his early life in Geneva. At the end of a blissful childhood spent in the company of Elizabeth Lavenza (his cousin in the 1818 edition, his adopted sister in the 1831 edition) and friend

Henry Clerval, Victor enters the university of Ingolstadt to study natural philosophy and chemistry. There, he is consumed by the desire to discover the secret of life and, after several years of research, becomes convinced that he has found it.

Armed with the knowledge he has long been seeking, Victor spends months feverishly fashioning a creature out of old body parts. One climactic night, in the secrecy of his apartment, he brings his creation to life. When he looks at the monstrosity that he has created, however, the sight horrifies him. After a fitful night of sleep, interrupted by the specter of the monster looming over him, he runs into the streets, eventually wandering in remorse. Victor runs into Henry, who has come to study at the university, and he takes his friend back to his apartment. Though the monster is gone, Victor falls into a feverish illness.

Sickened by his horrific deed, Victor prepares to return to Geneva, to his family, and to health. Just before departing Ingolstadt, however, he receives a letter from his father informing him that his youngest brother, William, has been murdered. Grief-stricken, Victor hurries home. While passing through the woods where William was strangled, he catches sight of the monster and becomes convinced that the monster is his brother's murderer. Arriving in Geneva, Victor finds that Justine Moritz, a kind, gentle girl who had been adopted by the Frankenstein household, has been accused. She is tried, condemned, and executed, despite her assertions of innocence. Victor grows despondent, guilty with the knowledge that the monster he has created bears responsibility for the deaths of two innocent loved ones.

Hoping to ease his grief, Victor takes a vacation to the mountains. While he is alone one day, crossing an enormous glacier, the monster approaches him. The monster admits to the murder of William but begs for understanding. Lonely, shunned, and forlorn, he says that he struck out at William in a desperate attempt to injure Victor, his cruel creator. The monster begs Victor to create a mate for him, a monster equally grotesque to serve as his sole companion.

Victor refuses at first, horrified by the prospect of creating a second monster. The monster is eloquent and persuasive, however, and he eventually convinces Victor. After returning to Geneva, Victor heads for England, accompanied by Henry, to gather information for the creation of a female monster. Leaving Henry in Scotland, he secludes himself on a desolate island in the Orkneys and works reluctantly at repeating his first success. One night, struck by doubts about the morality of his actions, Victor glances out the window to see the monster glaring in at him with a frightening grin. Horrified by the possible consequences of his work, Victor destroys his new creation. The monster, enraged, vows revenge, swearing that he will be with Victor on Victor's wedding night.

Later that night, Victor takes a boat out onto a lake and dumps the remains of the second creature in the water. The wind picks up and prevents him from returning to the island. In the morning, he finds himself ashore near an unknown town. Upon landing, he is arrested and informed that he will be tried for a murder discovered the previous night. Victor denies any knowledge of the murder, but when shown the body, he is shocked to behold his friend Henry Clerval, with the mark of the monster's fingers on his neck. Victor falls ill, raving and feverish, and is kept in prison until his recovery, after which he is acquitted of the crime.

Shortly after returning to Geneva with his father, Victor marries Elizabeth. He fears the monster's warning and suspects that he will be murdered on his wedding night. To be cautious, he sends Elizabeth away to wait for him. While he awaits the monster, he hears Elizabeth scream and realizes that the monster had been hinting at killing his new bride, not himself. Victor returns home to his father, who dies of grief a short time later. Victor vows to devote the rest of his life to finding the monster and exacting his revenge, and he soon departs to begin his quest.

Victor tracks the monster ever-northward into the ice. In a dogsled chase, Victor almost catches up with the monster, but the sea beneath them swells and the ice breaks, leaving an unbridgeable gap between them. At this point, Walton encounters Victor, and the narrative catches up to the time of Walton's fourth letter to his sister.

Walton tells the remainder of the story in another series of letters to his sister. Victor, already ill when the two men met, worsens and dies shortly thereafter. When Walton returns, several days later, to the room in which the body lies, he is startled to see the monster weeping over Victor. The monster tells Walton of his immense solitude, suffering, hatred, and remorse. He asserts that now that his creator has died, he too can end his suffering. The monster then departs for the northernmost ice to die.

CHARACTER LIST

Victor Frankenstein The doomed protagonist and narrator of the main portion of the story. Studying in Ingolstadt, Victor discovers the secret of life and creates an intelligent but grotesque monster, from whom he recoils in horror. Victor keeps his creation of the monster a secret, feeling increasingly guilty and ashamed as he realizes how helpless he is to prevent the monster from ruining his life and the lives of others.

The monster The eight-foot-tall, hideously ugly creation of Victor Frankenstein. Intelligent and sensitive, the monster attempts to integrate himself into human social patterns, but all who see him shun him. His feeling of abandonment compels him to seek revenge against his creator.

Robert Walton The Arctic seafarer whose letters open and close *Frankenstein*. Walton picks the bedraggled Victor Frankenstein up off the ice, helps nurse him back to health, and hears Victor's story. He records the incredible tale in a series of letters addressed to his sister, Margaret Saville, in England.

Alphonse Frankenstein Victor's father, very sympathetic toward his son. Alphonse consoles Victor in moments of pain and encourages him to remember the importance of family.

Elizabeth Lavenza An orphan, four to five years younger than Victor, whom the Frankensteins adopt. In the 1818 edition of the novel, Elizabeth is Victor's cousin, the child of Alphonse Frankenstein's sister. In the 1831 edition, Victor's mother rescues Elizabeth from a destitute peasant cottage in Italy. Elizabeth embodies the novel's motif of passive women, as she waits patiently for Victor's attention.

Henry Clerval Victor's boyhood friend, who nurses Victor back to health in Ingolstadt. After working unhappily for his father, Henry begins to follow in Victor's footsteps as a scientist. His cheerfulness counters Victor's moroseness.

William Frankenstein Victor's youngest brother and the darling of the Frankenstein family. The monster strangles William in the woods outside Geneva in order to hurt Victor for abandoning him. William's death deeply saddens Victor and burdens him with tremendous guilt about having created the monster.

Justine Moritz A young girl adopted into the Frankenstein household while Victor is growing up. Justine is blamed and executed for William's murder, which is actually committed by the monster.

Caroline Beaufort The daughter of Beaufort. After her father's death, Caroline is taken in by, and later marries, Alphonse Frankenstein. She dies of scarlet fever, which she contracts from Elizabeth, just before Victor leaves for Ingolstadt at age seventeen.

Beaufort A merchant and friend of Victor's father, and the father of Caroline Beaufort.

Peasants A family of peasants, including a blind old man, De Lacey; his son and daughter, Felix and Agatha; and a foreign woman named Safie. The monster learns how to speak and interact by observing them. When he reveals himself to them, hoping for friendship, they beat him and chase him away.

M. Waldman The professor of chemistry who sparks Victor's interest in science. He dismisses the alchemists' conclusions as unfounded but sympathizes with Victor's interest in a science that can explain the "big questions," such as the origin of life.

M. Krempe A professor of natural philosophy at Ingolstadt. He dismisses Victor's study of the alchemists as wasted time and encourages him to begin his studies anew.

Mr. Kirwin The Scottish magistrate who accuses Victor of Henry's murder.

ANALYSIS OF MAJOR CHARACTERS

VICTOR FRANKENSTEIN Victor Frankenstein's life story is at the heart of *Frankenstein*. A young Swiss boy, he grows up in Geneva reading the works of the ancient and outdated alchemists, a background that serves him ill when he attends university at Ingolstadt. There he learns about modern science and, within a few years, masters all that his professors have to teach him. He becomes fascinated with the "secret of life," discovers it, and brings a hideous monster to life. The monster proceeds to kill Victor's youngest brother, best friend, and wife; he also indirectly causes the deaths of two other innocents, including Victor's father. Though torn by remorse, shame, and guilt, Victor refuses to admit to anyone the horror of what he has created, even as he sees the ramifications of his creative act spiraling out of control.

Victor changes over the course of the novel from an innocent youth fascinated by the prospects of science into a disillusioned, guilt-ridden man determined to destroy the fruits of his arrogant scientific endeavor. Whether as a result of his desire to attain the godlike power of creating new life or his avoidance of the public arenas in which science is usually conducted, Victor is doomed by a lack of humanness. He cuts himself off from the world and eventually commits himself entirely to an animalistic obsession with revenging himself upon the monster. At the end of the novel, having chased his creation ever northward, Victor relates his story to Robert Walton and then dies. With its multiple narrators and, hence, multiple perspectives, the novel leaves the reader with contrasting interpretations of Victor: classic mad scientist, transgressing all boundaries without concern, or brave adventurer into unknown scientific lands, not to be held responsible for the consequences of his explorations.

THE MONSTER The monster is Victor Frankenstein's creation, assembled from old body parts and strange chemicals, animated by a mysterious spark. He enters life eight feet tall and enormously strong but with the mind of a newborn. Abandoned by his creator and confused, he tries to integrate himself into society, only to be shunned universally. Looking in the mirror, he realizes his physical grotesqueness, an aspect of his persona that blinds society to his initially gentle, kind nature. Seeking revenge on his creator, he kills Victor's younger brother. After Victor destroys his work on the female monster meant to ease the monster's solitude, the monster murders Victor's best friend and then his new wife.

While Victor feels unmitigated hatred for his creation, the monster shows that he is not a purely evil being. The monster's eloquent narration of events (as provided by Victor) reveals his remarkable sensitivity and benevolence. He assists a group of poor peasants and saves a girl from drowning, but because of his outward appearance, he is rewarded only with beatings and disgust. Torn between vengefulness and compassion, the monster ends up lonely and tormented by remorse. Even the death of his creator-turned-would-be-destroyer offers only bittersweet relief: joy because Victor has caused him so much suffering, sadness because Victor is the only person with whom he has had any sort of relationship.

ROBERT WALTON Walton's letters to his sister form a frame around the main narrative, Victor Frankenstein's tragic story. Walton captains a North Pole–bound ship that gets trapped between sheets of ice. While waiting for the ice to thaw, he and his crew pick up Victor, weak and emaciated from his long chase after the monster. Victor recovers somewhat, tells Walton the story of his life, and then dies. Walton laments the death of a man with whom he felt a strong, meaningful friendship beginning to form.

Walton functions as the conduit through which the reader hears the story of Victor and his monster. However, he also plays a role that parallels Victor's in many ways. Like Victor, Walton is an explorer, chasing after that "country of eternal light"—unpossessed knowledge. Victor's influence on him is paradoxical: one moment he exhorts Walton's almost-mutinous men to stay the path courageously, regardless of danger; the next, he serves as an abject example of the dangers of heedless scientific ambition. In his ultimate decision to terminate his treacherous pursuit, Walton serves as a foil (someone whose traits or actions contrast with, and thereby highlight, those of another character) to Victor, either not obsessive enough to risk almost-certain death or not courageous enough to allow his passion to drive him.

THEMES, MOTIFS, AND SYMBOLS

THEMES

THE DANGER OF KNOWLEDGE The pursuit of knowledge is at the heart of *Frankenstein*, as Victor attempts to surge beyond accepted human limits and access the secret of life. Likewise, Robert Walton attempts to surpass previous human explorations by endeavoring to reach the North Pole. This ruthless pursuit of knowledge proves dangerous, as Victor's act of creation eventually results in the destruction of everyone dear to him, and Walton finds himself perilously trapped between sheets of ice. Whereas Victor's obsessive hatred of the monster drives him to his death, Walton ultimately pulls back from his treacherous mission, having learned from Victor's example how destructive the thirst for knowledge can be.

THE SUBLIMITY OF NATURE The sublime natural world, embraced by Romanticism (late-eighteenth century to mid-nineteenth century) as a source of unrestrained emotional experience for the individual, initially offers characters the possibility of spiritual renewal. Mired in depression and remorse after the deaths of William and Justine, for which he feels responsible, Victor heads to the mountains to lift his spirits. Likewise, after a hellish winter of cold and abandonment, the monster feels his heart lighten as spring arrives. The influence of nature on mood is evident throughout the novel, but for Victor, the natural world's power to console him wanes when he realizes that the monster will haunt him no matter where he goes. By the end, as Victor chases the monster obsessively, nature, in the form of the Arctic desert, functions simply as the symbolic backdrop for his primal struggle against the monster.

THE MISERY OF SECRECY Victor conceives of science as a mystery to be probed; its secrets, once discovered, must be jealously guarded. He considers M. Krempe, the natural philosopher he meets at Ingolstadt, a model scientist: "an uncouth man, but deeply imbued in the secrets of his science." Victor's entire obsession with creating life is shrouded in secrecy, and his obsession with destroying the monster remains equally secret until Walton hears his tale.

Whereas Victor continues in his secrecy out of shame and guilt, the monster is forced into seclusion by his grotesque appearance. Walton serves as the final confessor for both, and their tragic relationship becomes immortalized in Walton's letters. In confessing all just before he dies, Victor escapes the stifling secrecy that has ruined his life; likewise, the monster takes advantage of Walton's presence to forge a human connection, hoping desperately that at last someone will understand, and empathize with, his miserable existence.

F

MOTIFS

MONSTROSITY The monster lies at the center of the action in *Frankenstein*. Eight feet tall and hideously ugly, the monster is rejected by society. However, his monstrosity results not only from his grotesque appearance but also from the unnatural manner of his creation, which involves the secretive animation of a mix of stolen body parts and strange chemicals. He is a product not of collaborative scientific effort but of dark, supernatural workings.

The monster is only the most literal of a number of monstrous entities in the novel, including the knowledge that Victor used to create the monster (see "Dangerous Knowledge"). One can argue that Victor himself is a kind of monster, as his ambition, secrecy, and selfishness alienate him from human society. Ordinary on the outside, he may be the true "monster" inside, as he is eventually consumed by an obsessive hatred of his creation. Finally, many critics have described the novel itself as monstrous, a stitched-together combination of different voices, texts, and tenses.

TEXTS AND LANGUAGE Frankenstein is overflowing with texts: letters, notes, journals, inscriptions, and books fill the novel, sometimes nestled inside each other, other times simply alluded to or quoted. Walton's letters envelop the entire tale; Victor's story fits inside Walton's letters; the monster's story fits inside Victor's; and the love story of Felix and Safie and references to Paradise Lost fit inside the monster's story. This profusion of texts is an important aspect of the narrative structure, as the various writings serve as concrete manifestations of characters' attitudes and emotions.

Language plays an enormous role in the monster's development. By hearing and watching the peasants, the monster learns to speak and read, which enables him to understand the manner of his creation, as described in Victor's journal. He later leaves notes for Victor along the chase into the northern ice, inscribing words in trees and on rocks, turning nature itself into a writing surface.

PASSIVE WOMEN For a novel written by the daughter of an important feminist, *Frankenstein* is strikingly devoid of strong female characters. The novel is littered with passive women who suffer calmly and then expire: Caroline Beaufort is a self-sacrificing mother who dies taking care of her adopted daughter; Justine is executed for murder, despite her innocence; the creation of the female monster is aborted by Victor because he fears being unable to control her actions once she is animated; Elizabeth waits, impatient but helpless, for Victor to return to her, and she is eventually murdered by the monster. One can argue that Shelley renders her female characters so passive and subjects them to such ill treatment in order to call attention to the obsessive and destructive behavior that Victor and the monster exhibit.

ABORTION The motif of abortion recurs as both Victor and the monster express their sense of the monster's hideousness. About first seeing his creation, Victor says: "When I thought of him, I gnashed my teeth, my eyes became inflamed, and I ardently wished to extinguish that life which I had so thoughtlessly made." The monster feels a similar disgust for himself: "I, the miserable and the abandoned, am an abortion, to be spurned at, and kicked, and trampled on." Both lament the monster's existence and wish that Victor had never engaged in his act of creation.

The motif appears also in regard to Victor's other pursuits. When Victor destroys his work on a female monster, he literally aborts his act of creation, preventing the female monster from coming alive. Figurative abortion materializes in Victor's description of natural philosophy: "I at once gave up my former occupations; set down natural history and all its progeny as a deformed and abortive creation; and entertained the greatest disdain for a would-be science, which could never even step within the threshold of real knowledge." As with the monster, Victor becomes dissatisfied with natural philosophy and shuns it not only as unhelpful but also as intellectually grotesque.

SYMBOLS

LIGHT AND FIRE "What could not be expected in the country of eternal light?" asks Walton, displaying a faith in, and optimism about, science. In *Frankenstein*, light symbolizes knowledge, discovery, and enlightenment. The natural world is a place of dark secrets, hidden passages, and unknown mechanisms; the goal of the scientist is then to reach light. The dangerous and more powerful cousin of light is fire. The monster's first experience with a still-smoldering flame reveals the dual nature of fire: he discovers excitedly that it creates light in the darkness of the night, but also that it harms him when he touches it.

The presence of fire in the text also brings to mind the full title of Shelley's novel, Frankenstein: or, The Modern Prometheus. The Greek god Prometheus gave the knowledge of fire to humanity and was then severely punished for it. Victor, attempting to become a modern Prometheus, is certainly punished, but unlike fire, his "gift" to humanity—knowledge of the secret of life—remains a secret.

IMPORTANT QUOTATIONS EXPLAINED

---

1. *I saw—with shut eyes, but acute mental vision—I saw the pale student of unhallowed arts kneeling beside the thing he had put together. I saw the hideous phantasm of a man stretched out, and then, on the working of some powerful engine, show signs of life and stir with an uneasy, half-vital motion. Frightful must it be, for supremely frightful would be the effect of any human endeavor to mock the stupendous mechanism of the Creator of the world.*

Taken from Mary Shelley's Author's Introduction to the 1831 edition of *Frankenstein*, this passage describes the vision that inspired the novel and the prototypes for Victor and the monster. Shelley's image evokes some of the key aspects of the novel, such as the utter unnaturalness of the monster ("an uneasy, half-vital motion"), the relationship between creator and created ("kneeling beside the thing he had put together"), and the dangerous consequences of misused knowledge ("supremely frightful would be the effect of . . . mock[ing] . . . the Creator").

---

2. *Did I request thee, Maker, from my clay To mould me Man, did I solicit thee From darkness to promote me?*

This line appears on the title page of the novel and come from John Milton's *Paradise Lost*, when Adam bemoans his fallen condition (Book X, 743–745). The monster conceives of himself as a tragic figure, comparing himself to both Adam and Satan. Like Adam, he is shunned by his creator, though he strives to be good. These rhetorical questions epitomize the monster's ill will toward Victor for abandoning him in a world relentlessly hostile to him and foist responsibility for his ugliness and eventual evil upon Victor.

3. *What may not be expected in a country of eternal light?*

This phrase comes from Walton's first letter to his sister in England. It encapsulates one of the main elements of *Frankenstein*—that of light as a symbol of knowledge and discovery. Walton's quest to reach the northernmost part of the earth is similar in spirit to Victor's quest for the secret of life: both seek ultimate knowledge, and both sacrifice the comfort of the realm of known knowledge in their respective pursuits. Additionally, the beauty and simplicity of the phrasing epitomize the eighteenth-century scientific rationalists' optimism about, and trust in, knowledge as a pure good.

4. *So much has been done, exclaimed the soul of Frankenstein—more, far more, will I achieve; treading in the steps already marked, I will pioneer a new way, explore unknown powers, and unfold to the world the deepest mysteries of creation.*

Victor utters these words in Chapter 3 as he relates to Walton how his chemistry professor, M. Waldman, ignited in him an irrepressible desire to gain knowledge of the secret of life. Victor's reference to himself in the third person illustrates his sense of fatalism—he is driven by his passion, unable to control it. Further, the glorious, assertive quality of his statement foreshadows the fact that Victor's passion will not be tempered by any consideration of the possible horrific consequences of his search for knowledge. Additionally, this declaration furthers the parallel between Walton's spatial explorations and Frankenstein's forays into unknown knowledge, as both men seek to "pioneer a new way," to make progress beyond established limits.

5. *I, the miserable and the abandoned, am an abortion, to be spurned at, and kicked, and trampled on.*

In Walton's final letter to his sister, he recounts the words that the monster speaks to him over Victor's dead body. This eruption of angry self-pity as the monster questions the injustice of how he has been treated compellingly captures his inner life, giving Walton and the reader a glimpse into the suffering that has motivated his crimes. This line also evokes the motif of abortion: the monster is an unwanted life, a creation abandoned and shunned by his creator.

In *Frankenstein*, how does the relationship between Victor and the creature relate to the relationship among the Biblical figures of God, Adam, and Satan?

In *Frankenstein*, Mary Shelley complicates the Biblical creation story of God and Adam. Here, Victor Frankenstein and his creature both contain elements of God, Adam, and even Satan.

At first glance, Victor is God to Frankenstein's Adam. Victor has formed the creature through his work and created him in his image. The creature is like Adam in that he develops his own thoughts and feelings and turns to Victor for help. Frankenstein and Adam both become frustrated by the limitations placed on them by their creators: Victor will not create a female for the creature to live with, and God forbids Adam to eat of the Tree of Knowledge. Both Frankenstein and Adam attempt to gain power in relation to their respective creators through their crimes: Adam steals knowledge, and Frankenstein uses intimidation and coercion. In the process, each ends up losing whatever happiness he once had.

A major problem with comparing Frankenstein and Adam is that it leaves Victor to play God, when in fact Victor is more closely aligned with Satan. Much like Satan, Victor aspires to greatness, and in doing so, he transgresses moral boundaries. Satan is one of the highest ranked angels in the heavenly system—an archangel, sitting at the foot of God—but wants greater power. He attempts to overthrow God and he is consequently banished to Hell. Similar to Satan's fall, Victor's creation brings him unhappiness, the loss of loved ones, and perpetual torture. Victor even references Satan in describing himself: "All my speculations and hopes are as nothing; and, like the archangel who aspired to omnipotence, I am chained in an eternal hell" (Chapter XXIV).

While Victor's offense links him to Satan, his punishment connects him to Adam. Adam's punishment is to be cast out from the Garden of Eden and forced into a life of hardship. Victor's life, too, changes from a happy and social one to a solitary, miserable existence. In Victor's punishment, the creature becomes the punishing

God, destroying both his Eve and Eden. Adam is forced to leave his Paradise, but he is allowed to keep his companion Eve with him. Victor's Paradise—his home life in Geneva—is destroyed piece by piece. His youngest brother is killed, a close family friend is wrongfully hanged as his murderer, his father is overcome with grief, and, finally, the two people most important to him, Clerval and Elizabeth, meet a horrible end at the hands of Frankenstein.

Shelley solidifies the torturous existence of both Victor and the creature by using repeated images of hellfire, which links both of them with Satan. Attempting to deal with Justine's wrongful arrest, Victor writes, "I bore a hell within me, which nothing could extinguish" (Chapter VIII). The creature also makes reference to his miserable existence after failing to join human society, moaning, "I, like the arch-fiend, bore a hell within me" (Chapter XXIV).

The figures of Adam, God, and Satan are inextricably woven throughout Shelley's *Frankenstein.* Frankenstein is a rejected Adam, a vengeful Satan, and a punishing God for Victor. Victor also seems to fit into all three characters—a creating God, a striving Satan, and a punished Adam. Both Victor and the creature contain different elements of each character, which deepen the reader's understanding of Shelley's masterful tale.

The Handmaid's Tale

Margaret Atwood
(1939–)

CONTEXT

Margaret Atwood was born in Ottawa, Ontario, on November 18, 1939. She published her first book of poetry in 1961 while attending the University of Toronto. She later received degrees from both Radcliffe College and Harvard University and pursued a career in teaching at the university level. Her first novel, *The Edible Woman*, was published in 1969 to wide acclaim. Atwood continued teaching as her literary career blossomed. She has lectured widely and has served as a writer-in-residence at colleges ranging from the University of Toronto to Macquarie University in Australia.

Atwood wrote *The Handmaid's Tale* in West Berlin and Alabama in the mid-1980s. The novel, published in 1986, quickly became a best-seller. *The Handmaid's Tale* falls squarely within the twentieth-century tradition of anti-utopian, or "dystopian," novels, exemplified by classics such as Aldous Huxley's *Brave New World* and George Orwell's *1984*. Novels in this genre present imagined worlds and societies that are not ideals but instead are terrifying or restrictive. Atwood's novel offers a strongly feminist vision of dystopia. She wrote it shortly after the elections of Ronald Reagan in the United States and Margaret Thatcher in Great Britain, during a period of conservative revival in the West partly fueled by a strong, well-organized movement of religious conservatives who criticized what they perceived as the excesses of the "sexual revolution" of the 1960s and 1970s. The growing power of this "religious right" heightened feminist fears that the gains women had made in previous decades would be reversed.

In *The Handmaid's Tale*, Atwood explores the consequences of a reversal of women's rights. In the novel's nightmare world of Gilead, a group of conservative religious extremists has taken power and turned the sexual revolution on its head. Feminists argued for liberation from traditional gender roles, but Gilead is a society founded on a "return to traditional values" and gender roles, and on the subjugation of women by men. What feminists considered the great triumphs of the 1970s—namely, widespread access to contraception, the legalization of abortion, and the increasing political influence of female voters—have all been undone. Women in Gilead are not only forbidden to vote, they are forbidden to read or write. Atwood's novel also paints a picture of a world undone by pollution and infertility, reflecting 1980s fears about declining birthrates, the dangers of nuclear power, and environmental degradation.

Some of the novel's concerns seem dated today, and its implicit condemnation of the political goals of America's religious conservatives has been criticized as unfair and overly paranoid. Nonetheless, *The Handmaid's Tale* remains one of the most powerful recent portrayals of a totalitarian society and one of the few dystopian novels to examine in detail the intersection of politics and sexuality. The novel's exploration of the controversial politics of reproduction seems likely to guarantee Atwood's novel a readership well into the twenty-first century.

Atwood lives in Toronto with novelist Graeme Gibson and their daughter, Jess. Her novel, *The Blind Assassin*, won Great Britain's Booker Prize for literature in 2000.

PLOT OVERVIEW

Offred is a Handmaid in the Republic of Gilead, a totalitarian and theocratic state that has replaced the United States of America. Because of dangerously low reproduction rates, Handmaids are assigned to bear children for elite couples that have trouble conceiving. Offred serves the Commander and his wife, Serena Joy, a former gospel singer and advocate for "traditional values." Offred is not the narrator's real name—Handmaid names consist of the word "of" followed by the name of the Handmaid's Commander. Every month, when Offred is at the right point in her menstrual cycle, she must have impersonal, wordless sex with the Commander while Serena sits behind her, holding her hands. Offred's freedom, like the freedom of all women, is completely restricted. She can leave the house only on shopping trips, the door to her room cannot be completely shut, and the Eyes, Gilead's secret police force, watch her every public move.

As Offred tells the story of her daily life, she frequently slips into flashbacks, from which the reader can reconstruct the events leading up to the beginning of the novel. In the old world, before Gilead, Offred had an affair with Luke, a married man. He divorced his wife and married Offred, and they had a child together. Offred's mother was a single mother and feminist activist. Offred's best friend, Moira, was fiercely independent. The architects of Gilead began their rise to power in an age of readily available pornography, prostitution, and violence against women—when pollution and chemical spills led to declining fertility rates. Using the military, they assassinated the president and members of Congress and launched a coup, claiming that they were taking power temporarily. They cracked down on women's rights, forbidding women to hold property or jobs. Offred and Luke took their daughter and attempted to flee across the border into Canada, but they were caught and separated from one another, and Offred has seen neither her husband nor her daughter since.

After her capture, Offred's marriage was voided (because Luke had been divorced), and she was sent to the Rachel and Leah Re-education Center, called the Red Center by its inhabitants. At the center, women were indoctrinated into Gilead's ideology in preparation for becoming Handmaids. Aunt Lydia supervised the women, giving speeches extolling Gilead's beliefs that women should be subservient to men and solely concerned with bearing children. Aunt Lydia also argued that such a social order ultimately offers women more respect and safety than the old, pre-Gilead society offered them. Moira is brought to the Red Center, but she escapes, and Offred does not know what becomes of her.

Once assigned to the Commander's house, Offred's life settles into a restrictive routine. She takes shopping trips with Ofglen, another Handmaid, and they visit the Wall outside what used to be Harvard University, where the bodies of rebels hang. She must visit the doctor frequently to be checked for disease and other complications, and she must endure the "Ceremony," in which the Commander reads to the household from the Bible, then goes to the bedroom, where his Wife and Offred wait for him, and has sex with Offred. The first break from her routine occurs when she visits the doctor and he offers to have sex with her to get her pregnant, suggesting that her Commander is probably infertile. She refuses. The doctor makes her uneasy, but his proposition is too risky—she could be sent away if caught. After a Ceremony, the Commander sends his gardener and chauffeur, Nick, to ask Offred to come see him in his study the following night. She begins visiting him regularly. They play Scrabble (which is forbidden, since women are not allowed to read), and he lets her look at old magazines like *Vogue*. At the end of these secret meetings, he asks her to kiss him.

During one of their shopping trips, Ofglen reveals to Offred that she is a member of "Mayday," an underground organization dedicated to overthrowing Gilead. Meanwhile, Offred begins to find that the Ceremony feels different and less impersonal now that she knows the Commander. Their nighttime conversations begin to touch on the new order that the Commander and his fellow leaders have created in Gilead. When Offred admits how unhappy she is, the Commander remarks, "[Y]ou can't make an omelette without breaking eggs."

After some time has gone by without Offred becoming pregnant, Serena suggests that Offred have sex with Nick secretly and pass the child off as the Commander's. Serena promises to bring Offred a picture of her daughter if she sleeps with Nick, and Offred realizes that Serena has always known the whereabouts of Offred's daughter. The same night that Offred is to sleep with Nick, the Commander secretly takes her out to a club called Jezebel's, where the Commanders mingle with prostitutes. Offred sees Moira working there. The two women meet in a bathroom, and Offred learns that Moira was captured just before she crossed the border. She chose life in Jezebel's over being sent to the Colonies, where most political prisoners and dangerous people are sent. After that night at Jezebel's, Offred says, she never sees Moira again. The Commander takes Offred upstairs after a few hours, and they have sex in what used to be a hotel room. She tries to feign passion.

Soon after Offred returns from Jezebel's, late at night, Serena arrives and tells Offred to go to Nick's room. Offred and Nick have sex. Soon they begin to sleep together frequently, without anyone's knowledge. Offred becomes caught up in the affair and ignores Ofglen's requests that she gather information from the Commander for Mayday. One day, all of the Handmaids take part in a group execution of a supposed rapist, supervised by Aunt Lydia. Ofglen strikes the first blow. Later, she tells Offred that the so-called rapist was a member of Mayday and that she hit him to put him out of his misery.

Shortly thereafter, Offred goes out shopping, and a new Ofglen meets her. This new woman is not part of Mayday, and she tells Offred that the old Ofglen hanged herself when she saw the secret police coming for her. At home, Serena has found out about Offred's trip to Jezebel's, and she sends her to her room, promising punishment. Offred waits there, and she sees a black van from the Eyes approach. Then

Nick comes in and tells her that the Eyes are really Mayday members who have come to save her. Offred leaves with them, over the Commander's futile objections, on her way either to prison or to freedom—she does not know which.

The novel closes with an epilogue from 2195, after Gilead has fallen, written in the form of a lecture given by Professor Pieixoto. He explains the formation and customs of Gilead in objective, analytical language. He discusses the significance of Offred's story, which has turned up on cassette tapes in Bangor, Maine. He suggests that Nick arranged Offred's escape but that her fate after that is unknown. She could have escaped to Canada or England, or she could have been recaptured.

CHARACTER LIST

Offred The narrator and protagonist. Offred belongs to the class of Handmaids, fertile women forced to bear children for elite, barren couples. Handmaids show which Commander owns them by adopting their Commanders' names, such as Fred, and preceding them with "Of." Offred remembers her real name but never reveals it. She no longer has family or friends, though she has flashbacks to a time in which she had a daughter and a husband named Luke. The cruel physical and psychological burdens of her daily life in Gilead torment her and pervade her narrative.

The Commander The head of the household where Offred works as a Handmaid. The Commander initiates an unorthodox relationship with Offred, secretly playing Scrabble with her in his study at night. He often seems a decent, well-meaning man, and Offred sometimes finds that she likes him in spite of herself. He almost seems a victim of Gilead, making the best of a society he opposes. However, we learn from various clues and from the epilogue that the Commander was actually involved in designing and establishing Gilead.

H

Serena Joy The Commander's Wife. Serena worked in pre-Gilead days as a gospel singer, then as an anti-feminist activist and crusader for "traditional values." In Gilead, she sits at the top of the female social ladder, yet she is desperately unhappy. Serena's unhappiness shows that her restrictive, male-dominated society cannot bring happiness even to its most pampered and powerful women. Serena jealously guards her claims to status and behaves cruelly toward the Handmaids in her household.

Moira Offred's best friend from college. Moira is a lesbian and a staunch feminist; she embodies female resourcefulness and independence. Her defiant nature contrasts starkly with the behavior of the other women in the novel. Rather than passively accept her fate as a Handmaid, she makes several escape attempts and finally manages to get away from the Red Center. However, she is caught before she can get out of Gilead. Later, Offred encounters Moira working as a prostitute in a club for the Commanders. At the club, Moira seems resigned to her fate, which suggests that a totalitarian society can grind down and crush even the most resourceful and independent people.

Aunt Lydia The Aunts are the class of women assigned to indoctrinate the Handmaids with the beliefs of the new society and make them accept their fates. Aunt Lydia works at the "Red Center," the reeducation center where Offred and other women go for instruction before becoming Handmaids. Although she appears only in Offred's flashbacks, Aunt Lydia and her instructions haunt Offred in her daily life. Aunt Lydia's slogans and maxims drum the ideology of the new society into heads of the women, until even those like Offred, women who do not truly believe in the ideology, hear Gilead's words echoing in their heads.

Nick A Guardian (a low-level officer of Gilead assigned to the Commander's home) who works as a gardener and chauffeur. Nick and Offred have a sexual chemistry that they get to satisfy when Serena Joy orchestrates an encounter between them in an effort to get Offred pregnant. After sleeping together once, they begin a covert sexual affair. Nick is not just a Guardian; he may work either as a member of the Eyes, Gilead's secret police, or as a member of the underground Mayday resistance, or both. At the end of the novel, Nick orchestrates Offred's escape from the Commander's home, but we do not know whether he puts her into the hands of the Eyes or the resistance.

Ofglen Another Handmaid who is Offred's shopping partner and a member of the subversive "Mayday" underground. At the end of the novel, Ofglen is found out, and she hangs herself rather than face torture and reveal the names of her co-conspirators.

Cora A servant in the Commander's household. Cora belongs to the class of Marthas, infertile women who do not qualify for the high status of Wives and so work in domestic roles. Cora seems more content with her role than her fellow Martha, Rita. She hopes that Offred will be able to conceive, because then she will have a hand in raising a child.

Janine An acquaintance of Offred's from the Red Center. After Janine becomes a Handmaid, she takes the name Ofwarren. She has a baby, which makes her the envy of all the other Handmaids in the area, but the baby later turns out to be deformed—an "Unbaby"—and there are rumors that her doctor fathered the child. Janine is a conformist, always ready to go along with what Gilead demands of her, and so she endears herself to the Aunts and to all authority figures. Offred holds Janine in contempt for taking the easy way out.

Luke A man who, in the days before Gilead, had an affair with Offred while he was married to another woman, then got a divorce and became Offred's husband. When Gilead comes to power, Luke attempts to escape to Canada with Offred and their daughter, but they are captured. He is separated from Offred, and the couple never see one another again. The kind of love they shared is prohibited in Gilead, and Offred's memories of Luke contrast with the regimented, passionless state of male-female relations in the new society.

Offred's Mother A single parent and a feminist activist, whom Offred remembers in flashbacks to her pre-Gilead world. One day during her education at the Red Center, Offred sees a video of her mother as a young woman, yelling and carrying a banner in an antirape march called Take Back the Night. She embodies everything the architects of Gilead want to stamp out.

Aunt Elizabeth One of the Aunts at the Red Center. Moira attacks her and steals her Aunt's uniform during her escape from the Red Center.

Rita A Martha, or domestic servant, in the Commander's household. Rita seems less content with her lot than Cora, the other Martha working there.

Professor Pieixoto The guest speaker at the symposium that takes place in the epilogue to *The Handmaid's Tale*. Professor Pieixoto and another academic, working at a university in the year 2195, transcribed Offred's recorded narrative; his lecture details the historical significance of the story that we have just read.

ANALYSIS OF MAJOR CHARACTERS

OFFRED Offred is the narrator and the protagonist of the novel, and we are told the entire story from her point of view, experiencing events and memories as vividly as she does. She tells the story as it happens and shows us the travels of her mind through asides, flashbacks, and digressions. Offred is intelligent, perceptive, and kind. She possesses enough faults to make her human, but not so many that she becomes an unsympathetic figure. She also possesses a dark sense of humor—a graveyard wit that makes her descriptions of the bleak horrors of Gilead bearable, even enjoyable. Like most of the women in Gilead, she is an ordinary woman placed in an extraordinary situation.

Offred is not a hero. Although she resists Gilead inwardly, once her attempt at escape fails, she submits outwardly. She is hardly a feminist champion; she had always felt uncomfortable with her mother's activism, and her pre-Gilead relationship with Luke began when she became his mistress, meeting him in cheap hotels for sex. Although friends with Ofglen, a member of the resistance, she is never bold enough to join up herself. Indeed, after she begins her affair with Nick, she seems to lose sight of escape entirely and suddenly feels that life in Gilead is almost bearable. If she does finally escape, it is because of Nick, not because of anything she does herself. Offred is a mostly passive character, good-hearted but complacent. Like her peers, she took for granted the freedoms feminism won and now pays the price.

THE COMMANDER The Commander poses an ethical problem for Offred, and consequently for us. First, he is Offred's Commander and the immediate agent of her oppression. As a founder of Gilead, he also bears responsibility for the entire totalitarian society. In person, he is far more sympathetic and friendly toward Offred than most other people, and Offred's evenings with the Commander in his study offer her a small respite from the wasteland of her life. At times, his unhappiness and need for companionship make him seem as much a prisoner of Gilead's strictures as anyone else. Offred finds herself feeling sympathy for this man.

Ultimately, Offred and the reader recognize that if the Commander is a prisoner, the prison is one that he himself helped construct and that his prison is heaven compared to the prison he created for women. As the novel progresses, we come to realize that his visits with Offred are selfish rather than charitable. They satisfy his need for companionship, but he doesn't seem to care that they put Offred at terrible risk, a fact of which he must be aware, given that the previous Handmaid hanged herself when her visits to the Commander were discovered. The Commander's moral blindness, apparent in his attempts to explain the virtues of Gilead, is highlighted by his and Offred's visit to Jezebel's. The club, a place where the elite men of the society can engage in recreational extramarital sex, reveals the rank hypocrisy that runs through Gileadean society.

Offred's relationship with the Commander is best represented by a situation she remembers from a documentary on the Holocaust. In the film, the mistress of a brutal death camp guard defended the man she loved, claiming that he was not a monster. "How easy it is to invent a humanity," Offred thinks. In other words, anyone can seem human, and even likable, given the right set of circumstances. But even if the Commander is likable and can be kind or considerate, his responsibility for the creation of Gilead and his callousness to the hell he created for women means that he, like the Nazi guard, is a monster.

SERENA JOY Though Serena had been an advocate for traditional values and the establishment of the Gileadean state, her bitterness at the outcome—being confined to the home and having to see her husband copulating with a Handmaid—suggests that spokeswomen for antifeminist causes might not enjoy getting their way as much as they believe they would. Serena's obvious unhappiness means that she teeters on the edge of inspiring our sympathy, but she forfeits that sympathy by taking out her frustration on Offred. She seems to possess no compassion for Offred. She can see the difficulty of her own life, but not that of another woman.

H

The climactic moment in Serena's interaction with Offred comes when she arranges for Offred to sleep with Nick. It seems that Serena makes these plans out of a desire to help Offred get pregnant, but Serena gets an equal reward from Offred's pregnancy: she gets to raise the baby. Furthermore, Serena's offer to show Offred a picture of her lost daughter if she sleeps with Nick reveals that Serena has always known of Offred's daughter's whereabouts. Not only has she cruelly concealed this knowledge, but she is willing to exploit Offred's loss of a child in order to get an infant of her own. Serena's lack of sympathy makes her the perfect tool for Gilead's social order, which relies on the willingness of women to oppress other women. She is a cruel, selfish woman, and Atwood implies that such women are the glue that binds Gilead.

MOIRA Moira's relationship with Offred epitomizes female friendship. Gilead claims to promote solidarity between women, but, in fact, it only produces suspicion, hostility, and petty tyranny. The kind of relationship that Moira and Offred maintain from college onward does not exist in Gilead. In Offred's flashbacks, Moira also embodies female resistance to Gilead. She is a lesbian, which means that she rejects male-female sexual interactions, the only kind that Gilead values. More than that, she is the only character who stands up to authority directly by making two escape attempts, one successful, from the Red Center. The manner in which she escapes—taking off her clothes and putting on the uniform of an Aunt—symbolizes her rejection of Gilead's attempt to define her identity. From then on, until Offred meets up with her again, Moira represents an alternative to the meek subservience and acceptance of one's fate that most of the Handmaids adopt. When Offred runs into Moira, Moira has been recaptured and is working as a prostitute at Jezebel's, servicing the Commanders. Her fighting spirit seems broken, and she has become resigned to her fate. After embodying resistance for most of the novel, Moira comes to exemplify the way a totalitarian state can crush even the most independent spirit.

THEMES, MOTIFS, AND SYMBOLS

THEMES

WOMEN'S BODIES AS POLITICAL INSTRUMENTS Because Gilead was formed in response to the crisis caused by dramatically decreased birthrates, the state's entire structure, with its religious trappings and rigid political hierarchy, is built around a single goal: control of reproduction. The state tackles the problem head-on by assuming complete control of women's bodies through their political subjugation. Women cannot vote, hold property or jobs, read, or do anything else that might allow them to become subversive or independent and thereby undermine their husbands or the state. Despite all of Gilead's pro-women rhetoric, such subjugation creates a society in which women are treated as subhuman. They are reduced to their fertility, treated as nothing more than a set of ovaries and a womb. In one of the novel's key scenes, Offred lies in the bath and reflects that, before Gilead, she considered her body an instrument of her desires; now, she is just a mound of flesh surrounding a womb that must be filled in order to make her useful. Gilead seeks to deprive women of their individuality in order to make them docile carriers of the next generation.

LANGUAGE AS A TOOL OF POWER Gilead creates an official vocabulary that ignores and warps reality in order to serve the needs of the new society's elite. Having made it illegal for women to hold jobs, Gilead creates a system of titles. Whereas men are defined by their military rank, women are defined solely by their gender roles as Wives, Handmaids, or Marthas. Stripping them of permanent individual names strips them of their individuality, or tries to. Feminists and deformed babies are treated as subhuman, denoted by the terms "Unwomen" and "Unbabies." Blacks and Jews are defined by biblical terms ("Children of Ham" and "Sons of Jacob," respectively) that set them apart from the rest of society, making their persecution easier. There are prescribed greetings for personal encounters, and to fail to offer the correct greetings is to fall under suspicion of disloyalty. Specially created terms define the rituals of Gilead, such as "Prayvaganzas," "Salvagings," and "Particicutions." Dystopian novels about the dangers of totalitarian society frequently explore the connection between a state's repression of its subjects and its perversion of language ("Newspeak" in George Orwell's *1984* is the most famous example), and *The Handmaid's Tale* carries on this tradition. Gilead maintains its control over women's bodies by maintaining control over names.

H

THE CAUSES OF COMPLACENCY In a totalitarian state, Atwood suggests, people will endure oppression willingly as long as they receive some slight amount of power or freedom. Offred remembers her mother saying that it is "truly amazing, what people can get used to, as long as there are a few compensations." Offred's complacency after she begins her relationship with Nick shows the truth of this insight. Her situation restricts her horribly compared to the freedom her former life allowed, but her relationship with Nick allows her to reclaim the tiniest fragment of her former existence. The physical affection and companionship become compensation that make the restrictions almost bearable. Offred seems suddenly so content that she does not say yes when Ofglen asks her to gather information about the Commander.

Women in general support Gilead's existence by willingly participating in it, serving as agents of the totalitarian state. While a woman like Serena Joy has no power in the world of men, she exercises authority within her own household and seems to delight in her tyranny over Offred. She jealously guards what little power she has and wields it eagerly. In a similar way, the women known as Aunts, especially Aunt Lydia, act as willing agents of the Gileadean state. They indoctrinate other women into the ruling ideology, keep a close eye out for rebellion, and generally serve the same function for Gilead that the Jewish police did under Nazi rule.

Atwood's message is bleak. At the same time that she condemns Offred, Serena Joy, the Aunts, and even Moira for their complacency, she suggests that even if those women mustered strength and stopped complying, they would likely fail to make a difference. In Gilead the tiny rebellions of resistances do not necessarily matter. In the end, Offred escapes because of luck rather than resistance.

MOTIFS

SEXUAL VIOLENCE Sexual violence, particularly against women, pervades *The Handmaid's Tale*. The prevalence of rape and pornography in the pre-Gilead world justified to the founders their establishment of the new order. The Commander and the Aunts claim that women are better-protected in Gilead, that they are treated with respect and kept safe from violence. Certainly, the official penalty for rape is terrible: in one scene, the Handmaids tear apart with their bare hands a supposed rapist (actually a member of the resistance). Yet, while Gilead claims to suppress sexual violence, it actually institutionalizes it, as we see at Jezebel's, the club that provides the Commanders with a ready stable of prostitutes to service the male elite. Most important, sexual violence is apparent in the central institution of the novel, the Ceremony, which compels Handmaids to have sex with their Commanders.

RELIGIOUS TERMS USED FOR POLITICAL PURPOSES Gilead is a theocracy—a government in which there is no separation between state and religion—and its official vocabulary incorporates religious terminology and biblical references. Domestic servants are called "Marthas" in reference to a domestic character in the New Testament; the local police are "Guardians of the Faith"; soldiers are "Angels"; and the Commanders are officially "Commanders of the Faithful." All the stores have biblical names: Loaves and Fishes, All Flesh, Milk and Honey. Even the automobiles have biblical names like Behemoth, Whirlwind, and Chariot. Using religious terminology to describe people, ranks, and businesses whitewashes political skullduggery in pious language. It provides an ever-present reminder that the founders of Gilead insist they act on the authority of the Bible itself. Politics and religion sleep in the same bed in Gilead, where the slogan "God is a National Resource" predominates.

SIMILARITIES BETWEEN REACTIONARY AND FEMINIST IDEOLOGIES Although *The Handmaid's Tale* offers a specifically feminist critique of the reactionary attitudes toward women that hold sway in Gilead, Atwood occasionally draws similarities between the architects of Gilead and radical feminists such as Offred's mother. Both groups claim to protect women from sexual violence, and both show themselves willing to restrict free speech in order to accomplish this goal. Offred recalls a scene in which her mother and other feminists burn porn magazines. Like the founders of Gilead, these feminists ban some expressions of sexuality. Gilead also uses the feminist rhetoric of female solidarity and "sisterhood" to its own advantage. These points of similarity imply the existence of a dark side of feminist rhetoric. Despite Atwood's gentle criticism of the feminist left, her real target is the religious right.

SYMBOLS

CAMBRIDGE, MASSACHUSETTS The center of Gilead's power, where Offred lives, is never explicitly identified, but a number of clues mark it as the town of Cambridge. Cambridge, its neighboring city of Boston, and Massachusetts as a whole were centers for America's first religious and intolerant society—the Puritan New England of the seventeenth century. Atwood reminds us of this history with the ancient Puritan church that Offred and Ofglen visit early in the novel, which Gilead has turned into a museum. The choice of Cambridge as a setting symbolizes the direct link between the Puritans and their spiritual heirs in Gilead. Both groups dealt harshly with religious, sexual, or political deviation.

HARVARD UNIVERSITY Gilead has transformed Harvard's buildings into a detention center run by the Eyes, Gilead's secret police. Bodies of executed dissidents hang from the Wall that runs around the college, and Salvagings (mass executions) take place in Harvard Yard, on the steps of the library. Harvard becomes a symbol of the inverted world that Gilead has created: a place that was founded to pursue knowledge and truth becomes a seat of oppression, torture, and the denial of every principle for which a university is supposed to stand.

THE HANDMAIDS' RED HABITS The red color of the costumes worn by the Handmaids symbolizes fertility, which is the caste's primary function. Red suggests the blood of the menstrual cycle and of childbirth. At the same time, however, red is also a traditional marker of sexual sin, hearkening back to the scarlet letter worn by the adulterous Hester Prynne in *The Scarlet Letter*, Nathaniel Hawthorne's tale of Puritan ideology. While the Handmaids' reproductive role supposedly finds its justification in the Bible, in some sense they commit adultery by having sex with their Commanders, who are married men. The wives, who often call the Handmaids sluts, feel the pain of this sanctioned adultery. The Handmaids' red garments, then, also symbolize the ambiguous sinfulness of the Handmaids' position in Gilead.

A PALIMPSEST A palimpsest is a document on which old writing has been scratched out, often leaving traces, and new writing put in its place; it can also be a document consisting of many layers of writing simply piled one on top of another. Offred describes the Red Center as a palimpsest, but the word actually symbolizes all of Gilead. The old world has been erased and replaced, but only partially, by a new order. Remnants of the pre-Gilead days continue to infuse the new world.

THE EYES The Eyes of God are Gilead's secret police. Both their name and their insignia, a winged eye, symbolize the eternal watchfulness of God and the totalitarian state. In Gilead's theocracy, the eye of God and of the state are assumed to be one and the same.

IMPORTANT QUOTATIONS EXPLAINED

---

1. *Ordinary, said Aunt Lydia, is what you are used to. This may not seem ordinary to you now, but after a time it will. It will become ordinary.*

This comment is from the end of Chapter 6. Offred and Ofglen are standing by the Wall, looking at the bodies of people who have been hanged by Gilead. The sight horrifies Offred, but she strains to push aside her repugnance and substitute an emotional "blankness." As she represses her natural revulsion, she remembers Aunt Lydia's words about how life in Gilead will "become ordinary." Aunt Lydia's statement reflects the power of a totalitarian state like Gilead to transform a natural human response such as revulsion at an execution into "blankness," to transform horror into normalcy. Aunt Lydia's words suggest that Gilead succeeds not by making people believe that its ways are right, but by making people forget what a different world could be like. Torture and tyranny become accepted because they are "what you are used to."

---

2. *I would like to believe this is a story I'm telling. I need to believe it. I must believe it. Those who can believe that such stories are only stories have a better chance. If it's a story I'm telling, then I have control over the ending. Then there will be an ending, to the story, and real life will come after it. I can pick up where I left off.*

These lines from the end of Chapter 7, reflect the connection between Offred's story, her readers, her lost family, and her inner state. These words suggest that Offred is not recounting events from afar, looking back on an earlier period in her life. Rather, she is describing the horror of Gilead as she experiences it from day to day. For Offred, the act of telling her story becomes a rebellion against her society. Gilead seeks to silence women, but Offred speaks out, even if it is only to an imaginary reader, to Luke, or to God. Gilead denies women control over their own lives, but Offred's creation of a story gives her, as she puts it, "control over the ending." Most important, Offred's creation of a narrative gives her hope for the future, a sense that "there will be an ending . . . and real life will come after it." She can hope that someone will hear her story, or that she will tell it to Luke someday. Offred has found the only avenue of rebellion available in her totalitarian society: she denies Gilead control over her inner life.

---

3. *I used to think of my body as an instrument, of pleasure, or a means of transportation, or an implement for the accomplishment of my will . . . Now the flesh arranges itself differently. I'm a cloud, congealed around a central object, the shape of a pear, which is hard and more real than I am and glows red within its translucent wrapping.*

This passage is from Chapter 13, when Offred sits in the bath and contrasts the way she used to think about her body to the way she thinks about it now. Before, her body was an instrument, an extension of herself; now, her self no longer matters, and her body is only important because of its "central object," her womb, which can bear a child. Offred's musings show that she has internalized Gilead's attitude toward women, whereby women are treated not as individuals but as objects important only for the children they can bear. Women's wombs are a "national resource," the state insists, using language that dehumanizes women and reduces them to, as Offred puts it, "a cloud, congealed around a central object, which is hard and more real than I am."

4. *He was not a monster, to her. Probably he had some endearing trait: he whistled, offkey, in the shower, he had a yen for truffles, he called his dog Liebchen and made it sit up for little pieces of raw steak. How easy it is to invent a humanity, for anyone at all. What an available temptation.*

In this quotation, from Chapter 24, Offred remembers a documentary that she watched about a woman who was the mistress of a Nazi death camp guard. She recalls how the woman insisted that her lover was not a "monster," and she compares that woman's situation to her own, as she spends her evenings with the Commander and comes to almost like him. The Commander seems like a good person: he is kind, friendly, genial, and even courtly to Offred. Yet he is also the agent of her oppression—both directly, as her Commander, and indirectly, through his role in constructing the oppressive edifice of Gileadean society. Like the concentration camp guard, he is "not a monster, to her"; yet he is still a monster. Offred suggests that it is "easy," when you know an evil person on a personal level, to "invent a humanity" for them. It is a "temptation," she says, meaning that no one wants to believe that someone they know is a monster. But in the case of the Commander, that temptation must be resisted. He may be kind and gentle, but he still bears responsibility for the evil of Gilead.

5. *The problem wasn't only with the women, he says. The main problem was with the men. There was nothing for them anymore . . . I'm not talking about sex, he says. That was part of it, the sex was too easy . . . You know what they were complaining about the most? Inability to feel. Men were turning off on sex, even. They were turning off on marriage. Do they feel now? I say. Yes, he says, looking at me. They do.*

This passage, from the end of Chapter 32, recounts the Commander's attempt to explain to Offred the reasons behind the foundation of Gilead. His comments are ambiguous, perhaps deliberately so, but they are the closest thing to a justification for the horror of Gilead that any character offers. He suggests that feminism and the sexual revolution left men without a purpose in life. With their former roles as women's protectors taken away, and with women suddenly behaving as equals, men were set adrift. At the same time, changing sexual mores meant that sex became so easy to obtain that it lost meaning, creating what the Commander calls an "inability to feel." By making themselves soldiers, providers, and caretakers of society again, men have meaning restored to their lives. This sounds almost noble, except that in order to give meaning to men's lives, both men and women have lost all freedom. The benefits of the new world are not worth the cost in human misery.

Herland

Charlotte Perkins Gilman (1860–1935)

CONTEXT

At the time of her death in 1935, Charlotte Perkins Gilman was as famous for her political and journalistic writing as she was notorious for her unconventional personal life. In her time, Gilman was known as a crusading journalist and feminist intellectual, a follower of such pioneering women's rights advocates as Susan B. Anthony, Elizabeth Cady Stanton, and Harriet Beecher Stowe, Gilman's great-aunt. Gilman was concerned with political inequality and social justice in general, but the primary focus of her writing was the unequal status of women within the institution of marriage. In such works as *Concerning Children* (1900), *The Home* (1904), and *Human Work* (1904), Gilman argued that women's confinement to the domestic sphere robbed them of the expression of their full powers of creativity and intelligence, while simultaneously robbing society of women whose abilities suited them for professional and public life. An essential part of her analysis was that the traditional power structure of the family made *no one* happy—not the woman who was made into an unpaid servant, not the husband who was made into a master, and not the children who were subject to both. Her most ambitious work, *Women and Economics* (1898), analyzed the hidden value of women's labor within the capitalist economy. She argued, as she would throughout her work, that financial independence for women could only benefit society as a whole.

Gilman's analysis of women's status in society was deeply rooted in her own situation. In 1886, early in her first marriage and not long after the birth of her daughter, Charlotte Perkins Stetson (as she was then known) was stricken with a severe case of depression. In her 1935 autobiography, *The Living of Charlotte Perkins Gilman*, she describes her "utter prostration" by "unbearable inner misery" and "ceaseless tears," a condition only made worse by the presence of her husband and her baby. She was referred to Dr. S. Weir Mitchell, then the country's leading specialist in nervous disorders, who believed that such postpartum depression was brought by too much mental activity and not enough attention to domestic affairs. Mitchell's treatment in such cases was a "rest cure" of forced inactivity. For Gilman, this treatment was a disaster. Prevented from working, writing, and even reading, she sank deeper into depression, and she soon had a nervous breakdown. At her worst, she crawled into closets and under beds, clutching a rag doll. Eventually, Gilman realized that the powerlessness she felt as a wife, mother, and subject of a male-dominated medical regime was an extreme instance of the powerlessness all women were made to feel in a culture that refused to take their thoughts and desires seriously.

Once she abandoned Mitchell's rest cure, Gilman's condition improved, though she claimed to feel the effects of the ordeal for the rest of her life. She based her best-known work of fiction, the classic short story "The Yellow Wallpaper," on the experience. Leaving behind her husband and child, a decision that made her a figure of scandal, Charlotte Perkins Stetson (she took the name Gilman after a second marriage, to her cousin) embarked on her famous career as a journalist, lecturer, and publisher. She published a monthly magazine, *The Forerunner*, writing the contents of each issue herself, down to the advertising copy. *The Forerunner* reflected Gilman's wide-ranging interests in feminism, politics, socialist economics, and history, and Gilman serialized several works of fiction in its pages. *Herland*, a utopian novel in which a trio of modern men discovers a lost country populated entirely by women, appeared in the magazine in 1915.

Herland is part of a long tradition of utopian fiction, a tradition stretching all the way back to Plato's *Republic*. In a utopian work, an imaginary country, usually one discovered or described by the narrator, serves as an example of an "ideal" political and social state and is contrasted with an actual earthly society. The genre takes its name from Thomas More's classic *Utopia* (1516), the title of which means "nowhere" in Greek. Many later fictional utopias are satirical, using the imaginary land to represent the worst aspects of society. Jonathan Swift's *Gulliver's Travels* (1726) is perhaps the best example of such a satirical utopia.

In the twentieth century, an extreme form of the negative utopia appeared, called the "dystopia," in which a nightmarish future version of society is shown to result from certain trends in contemporary culture. The most famous dystopian fictions are Aldous Huxley's *Brave New World* (1932) and George Orwell's *1984* (1948). Toward the end of the nineteenth century, a great deal of straightforwardly utopian writing appeared, often inspired by socialist politics. William Morris's *News from Nowhere* (1890) is one such leftist utopia, as is Edward Bellamy's *Looking Backward* (1896). The science-fiction pioneer H. G. Wells wrote several similar works.

Herland is one of the most notable examples of this revival of utopian literature, though it slipped from view after its first publication and was only rediscovered in the late 1970s. Since then, Gilman's skillful use of the utopian genre, as well as its humor and sharp feminist analysis, has helped to solidify her reputation as a major writer. Gilman's work continues to be an influence on such authors as Ursula K. LeGuin, Marge Piercy, and Margaret Atwood, each of whom has written fiction in which the conventions of science fiction and utopian writing are adapted to a feminist critique of society—much as Gilman does so brilliantly in *Herland*.

PLOT OVERVIEW

Three adventurous friends—Vandyck Jennings (the narrator, also called Van), Terry Nicholson, and Jeff Margrave—join a scientific expedition to one of the few remaining uncharted areas of the world, although Van leaves the exact region ambiguous as he tells the story. As they travel, the friends hear persistent rumors of a strange land, hidden high in the mountains, that is populated only by women. Intrigued, the men investigate the rumors and do, in fact, find evidence of an advanced, isolated culture in the mountains, cut off from the rest of the world. Doubtful about the existence of an all-female country, the men are nevertheless excited by the chance to explore an unknown land, and they resolve to return on their own to find it. The three are driven by a genuine desire for knowledge, a love of adventure, and, although Van is ashamed to admit it, by fantasies stoked by the tales they have heard of a land full of women without men.

The friends equip an expedition back to the hidden plateau and begin to survey the area using Terry's airplane. From the air, they see signs of an advanced civilization and decide to land. As they explore the hidden country, the men notice the obvious cultivation of the forests and the great skill with which the roads have been laid. Terry takes these signs of agricultural and technological skill as evidence that there must be men around after all.

At first, the men are unable to discover any of the inhabitants, but soon they notice three young women watching them from the trees. The men make several attempts to entice them to come closer but have little luck, although the women obviously find the men interesting. Terry uses a necklace to draw one of the women closer, then makes a grab for her. The women flee, showing amazing athleticism. The men give chase but are soon left behind. The men follow them into the nearest settlement, where they are greeted by a large gathering of women. The women are unlike any the men have ever encountered: strong, self-confident, clearly intelligent, and obviously unafraid of men. The women indicate that they want the men to follow them, but the three friends are unwilling to be taken into custody. The men decide to make a break for it, but they are soon overcome by the women, who drug them into unconsciousness.

The men awake to find themselves unharmed but captive. The women treat the men well and begin to teach them their language, although the men are still not allowed to roam freely. After a while, the men, especially Terry, become impatient and decide to attempt an escape. They fashion a crude rope and lower themselves to the ground outside their window. From there, the men sneak back toward their airplane, hiding themselves carefully during the day. When they find the airplane, the men also encounter the three young women they met upon their arrival: Celis, Alima, and Ellador. The men begin talking to the women and become so distracted that they are soon recaptured. Back in custody, the men learn that their escape attempt had been anticipated and that they had, in fact, been observed the whole time.

Now resigned to their gentle captivity, the men begin to question their tutors about the history and organization of what they have come to call "Herland." They are told that Herland has been without men for 2,000 years, ever since a sequence of wars, natural disasters, and internal strife combined to leave a small population of women alone atop their hidden plateau. Forced to fend for themselves under extreme circumstances, the women organized their society along the most rational lines possible, realizing that they would never survive without cooperation. After a time, a young girl miraculously became pregnant, and her descendants (each of whom was female, and each of whom inherited the gift of solo reproduction) are the present inhabitants of Herland. Over time, the women of Herland developed a peaceful, orderly, highly efficient society in which competition, crime, and antisocial behavior are unknown. As befits a society of mothers, childbearing is the greatest honor of the women's lives, as well as their highest duty. In fact, Herland is essentially a giant family, an organic community pursuing the common good. As such, property is held in common, there is a loose system of authority based on experience and wisdom, and the wellbeing and education of children are the highest priorities.

As the men, especially Van and Jeff, come to learn about and appreciate the social structure of Herland, the women begin to learn, through the men, about the outside world. All three men begin with the assumption that any comparison of Herland and the "civilized" world of Europe and the United States will be to the advantage of the latter. Van and Jeff, however, soon realize that, in comparison to the society they have left behind, Herland is a veritable paradise. The women of Herland are shocked to hear of the poverty, disease, exploitation, and violence of the modern world, so much so that the men find themselves dissembling out of shame and often hiding the full truth. The women are able to perceive the true nature of the society the men describe, despite their reticence: women are particularly exploited in the competitive, money-driven modern world, as their maternal function is used to keep them in a subordinate position. The women are horrified to learn of the practice of abortion, for example, seeing it as violence against motherhood itself. The more Van and Jeff see of Herland, the more they are convinced of its goodness and of the fundamental sickness of their own society. Terry, however, refuses to see anything good in Herland apart from the beauty of its inhabitants. Terry is convinced that women are naturally subordinate to men and that women, in fact, desire to be "mastered" by men. The very existence of Herland is an affront to Terry's sensibilities, and the more he learns of it, the more he resents the "unnatural" state of affairs.

The women of Herland are themselves concerned about their lack of men, feeling that their society would benefit from a masculine perspective and contribution. Accordingly, Celis, Alima, and Ellador are encouraged to continue the courtship the men had so crudely begun upon their first arrival. The primary obstacle the lovers have to overcome is the assumption, by the men, that theirs is the active, dominant role in the relationship. The young women see themselves as equal partners with the men and cannot understand why the men would want it any other way. Jeff is a romantic, full of chivalry and southern notions of gallantry, and his tendency to put women on a pedestal sometimes becomes condescending and hampers his relationship with Celis. Jeff is, however, the most ardent convert to the ways of Herland. Terry, in contrast, woos Alima in a brusque, aggressive way, convinced that she desires a "masterful" man and that all men should have a submissive mate. Alima is fascinated by Terry, but wary; the two quarrel and make up often. Van and Ellador have the best, most equal relationship, soon becoming best friends and true lovers. The entire society of Herland watches the three couples with great interest, seeing that the outcome of the experiment could determine the future of Herland and mark their return to a "bisexual" state.

At the insistence of the men, a marriage ceremony is arranged for the three couples. After the wedding, the women are uncomfortable with the idea of "private life," preferring to remain part of the larger community. They are also confused by the notion of nonprocreative sexual activity. The men respond to this new challenge in different ways. Jeff is a thorough believer in the superiority of Herland. Van wants to find some way to combine the best aspects of companionate marriage as he understands it, including romantic and sexual intimacy, with the socially minded attitude of Herland, in which the needs of the larger group always prevail. Ellador shares this desire, feeling romantic love for Van along with her familial desire to procreate for the community. Terry is outraged by Alima's continued insistence on her own autonomy, feeling that he now "owns" Alima by marriage.

Terry's sexual advances become more aggressive and even brutal, and Alima is forced to defend herself physically. The leaders of Herland are shocked by Terry's attempted rape of Alima and decide to exile the men. Celis is now pregnant, much to the joy of the Herlanders, and so Jeff decides to stay behind with her forever. Terry is more than pleased to leave Herland behind. Though he threatens at first to return in force, he eventually promises to keep the location of the plateau a secret. Ellador decides to accompany Van in order to see the outer world in his company and to report back on what she observes to Herland. Taking the airplane on which the men first arrived, Terry, Van, and Ellador return to the troubled world below.

CHARACTER LIST

Alima One of the three young women the men meet when they first arrive in Herland. Alima is attracted to Terry and eventually marries him. Terry and Alima have a stormy relationship, which ends badly when Terry tries (unsuccessfully) to force himself on Alima soon after their wedding. Like all the women of Herland, Alima is strong and self-confident and would never consent to an unequal relationship with a man.

Celis One of the three young women the men meet when they first arrive in Herland. Celis and Jeff are drawn to one another and later marry. Celis is mild-mannered and kind, but she is puzzled by Jeff's courtly insistence on treating her as if she were weaker than she actually is. In general, however, they are happy, and Celis becomes the mother of the first "fathered" child in Herland's 2,000-year history.

Ellador One of the three young women the men meet when they first arrive in Herland. Ellador is the most intellectually curious of the group. The relationship between Ellador and Van is the most successful of the three couples, as it is based on a close friendship and mutual respect. Ellador takes a great interest in the world beyond Herland, convinced that there must be good in the world of men, despite the testimony of Van and Jeff. When Van and Terry are forced to return home, Ellador agrees to accompany them, motivated by love of Van, curiosity about the world, and a desire to act as Herland's representative.

Vandyck Jennings One of the three explorers who discover Herland, and the novel's narrator. A sociologist by training, Van is the "philosopher" of the group—the one who understands Herland most fully and critically—and the one who is most convinced that Herland has much to teach the outside world. Van has some difficulty adjusting to a society in which women are simply "people" and not a protected and constrained "weaker sex," but once he makes the shift, Van sees the revolutionary implications of such a change more deeply than do his friends.

Jeff Margrave One of the three explorers who discovers Herland. A doctor and a botanist, Jeff is also a southern gentleman, with refined, romantic notions of idealized femininity, notions that are strongly challenged by the athletic, independent women of Herland. Jeff falls in love with Celis and puzzles her with his insistence that he take care of her, rather than simply treat her as an equal partner. Jeff soon comes to prefer Herland to any country on Earth, though his appreciation of Herlandian culture is tinged with his generally unrealistic, idealized vision of womanhood.

Terry Nicholson One of the three explorers who discovers Herland. Terry is the driving force behind the expedition to Herland and the most forceful of the three friends. A classic male chauvinist, Terry fancies himself quite the ladies' man and prides himself on his knowledge of and control over the female mind. Convinced that women like to be "mastered" both emotionally and physically by men, Terry is completely flummoxed by the women of Herland, who don't need men at all. Terry is unable to relate to women as equals, and this inability dooms his relationship with Alima.

Moadine One of the older women who tutors the three men in the ways of Herland. Moadine is charged with guiding Terry, a difficult task she approaches with a great deal of patience. Terry is convinced that he has Moadine outsmarted, but Van sees that Moadine is humoring Terry as she would a small child, concealing her amusement at his conceited ways.

Somel One of the older women who tutors the three men in the ways of Herland. Somel is a wise and knowledgeable guide to the history and customs of Herland. As she teaches Van, Somel is also gathering information from him regarding his own society. Though Van often sugarcoats or omits the truth, Somel is able to cut through his obfuscation and build an accurate—and ugly—picture of the modern world.

Zava One of the older women who tutors the three men in the ways of Herland. Zava deals with Jeff in particular, and she reminds him of one of his aunts.

ANALYSIS OF MAJOR CHARACTERS

ELLADOR In many ways, Ellador is Gilman's ideal woman. Beautiful and athletic, an unusual combination in the literature of Gilman's time, Ellador defies the frail, delicate Victorian feminine ideal without seeming in any way masculinized or unwomanly. She is intelligent, courageous, and curious about the larger world. She is also a career woman: her work as a forester is inspired by the praise she received as a child for helping destroy an insect pest that threatened Herland's trees. All of these aspects combine to make Ellador a walking rebuke to the stereotype of the modern, "liberated" woman as a waspish, unfulfilled man-hater. Gilman means for Ellador to exemplify woman's *human* potential—that is, woman's potential for wholeness, beyond the conventional boundaries of traditional femininity. Given the chance, Gilman is saying, women can be like Ellador: equal to a man spiritually, intellectually, and even physically.

Ellador's mission to the outside world is part of her quest for an understanding of human nature in its wholeness. Ellador senses that, despite the amazing progress made in Herland, their society remains incomplete as long as there is no contribution from the masculine half of humanity. Ellador is driven to understand the masculine "other" both through her romantic relationship with Van and, at the end of the novel, by exploring the outside world in his company. There is still a tentative, unsettled quality to Ellador's relationship with Van at the conclusion of the novel, as though both the characters and the author were still trying to figure out what a truly equal sexual relationship would look like. In a typically clever reversal of traditional characterization, Gilman has Ellador in the role of cool rationalist, not seeing the point of nonprocreative sexuality—while Van argues for the emotional, passionate, romantic (and traditionally "feminine") side of sexuality. If the women of the future are anything like Ellador, Gilman seems to say, many of our traditional expectations will have to be radically revised.

JEFF Jeff and Terry are a matched pair—opposite sides of the same sexist coin. Where Terry represents the macho, domineering aspects of patriarchal society, Jeff represents the genteel, idealistic attitudes that often accompany and help to justify a system of sexual inequality. Gilman's point is that Terry's brutality and Jeff's gentility are both predicated on a shared belief in the natural inferiority of women. In Jeff's case, the assumption is that women are naturally delicate, sweet, placid creatures who need looking after. Jeff fancies himself as part of the tradition of the southern gentleman, which, in turn, was based on the tradition of knightly chivalry and courtly love. Gilman wants her readers to see that the object of a gentleman's chivalry is just that: an object, an idol created in order to be worshipped, and not a living, feeling woman with independent thoughts and autonomous desires. According to Jeff's beliefs, women are just as controlled and powerless as under Terry's beliefs, although Jeff's way is certainly a much nicer, more sensitive means of control.

H

The more Jeff learns about Herland, the more enamored of its social system he becomes. As Van points out, Jeff's natural inclination to "worship" and idealize women leads him to embrace Herland's ways like a religious convert and to reject the male-dominated outside world entirely. Jeff's embrace of Herland, however, is based more on emotion than anything else, and he seems to think that a woman-dominated society would be preferable in every way to a male-dominated one, mostly because women are simply better, kinder, more moral people than are men. But here Jeff misses the point. Herland is better not because it is dominated by women but because there is no domination of anyone, by anyone, at all. By the end of the novel, Jeff is still struggling to see women as *equals*, not angelic superiors. Gilman seems to reward Jeff at the end of the novel, both by allowing him to remain in Herland and by having him be the father of Herland's first naturally conceived child in 2,000 years.

TERRY On the surface, Terry seems to undergo the most drastic transformation of any character in the novel. At first, Terry seems confident, funny, courageous, a natural leader of men, and, we are told, a charmer of ladies. Later, however, he is shown to be a bully, an abuser, and a fool. Terry hasn't changed; rather, his true character has been revealed, and Van, the narrator, has come to see him in a new light. Terry arrives in Herland with a theory that men are naturally superior to women and that, consequently, every woman naturally enjoys being "mastered" by her man. This notion is part of the bedrock of Terry's identity and the source of his self-image. In Gilman's time, men of Terry's type were referred to as "blackguards" (as opposed to "gentlemen" like Jeff), and Gilman is saying that one sign of the unhealthy state of our male-dominated culture is the way blackguards such as Terry are viewed as lovable rogues and not seen for the domineering, often violent sexists that they are. The task of a decent society, Gilman suggests, is to turn the laudable energy and drive of men such as Terry in a less anti-social, anti-woman direction.

Though Terry imagines himself a rugged individualist, he is actually just as dependent on women as he imagines women are on men. Without a woman to admire him, flirt with him, and be impressed by his bluster, Terry's sense of himself as a man is challenged, and he becomes deeply insecure. Faced with a woman such as Alima, who is a match for him physically and intellectually and who has no desire to be subservient to a man, Terry doesn't know what to do. Unlike Jeff, who is thoroughly converted to Herland's ways, and unlike Van, who, though cautious, hopes to understand and learn from them, Terry's response is to reject Herland and to insist ever more stridently on his male prerogatives. Once his fantasies are exploded, he cannot even see the beauty of Herland's inhabitants, whom Terry sees as unwomanly because of their self-confidence, a society not of women, but of "neuters." The more strident Terry becomes, however, the more foolish he looks, and the more estranged he becomes from his lover and even his friends.

VAN At the beginning of the novel, Van makes clear that he is proud of his training as a sociologist, which requires him to be versed in just about every other science. Sociology concerns the organization of human life in general, and in Herland he finds the perfect test case of a social structure unlike any other on Earth. He is fascinated, but his interest is much more intellectual, and much less personal, than that of Jeff or Terry. Van is more critical in his approach to Herland than either Jeff or Terry, and he makes a genuine effort to understand the principles on which the country is built in order to understand whether or not the place *works*. Van soon finds that Herland has the "advanced" civilizations of Europe and the United States beat in almost every way. Van's eventual endorsement of Herland is more impressive than Jeff's, since he is the most reasonable, objective, and well rounded of the three men.

Whenever Van is confronted by an aspect of Herlandian society that shocks his traditional sensibilities (for example, when he learns that children are raised by specialists, not by their own mothers), his study of different cultures helps him to see the advantages of a new and different social arrangement. Van's preference is to judge a situation based on the evidence he has before him, not to prejudge it according to a theory. He finds that the sexist assumptions he acquired simply by living in his society are quickly overturned by his experiences and observations in Herland. Thanks to his discussions with Ellador and Somel, Van comes to see that much of what seems "natural" in our society is in fact quite arbitrary, and that things could be, and in many cases ought to be, arranged differently. Van's rational approach helps him in his relationship with Ellador, since he is able to adjust more quickly than the other men to a romantic relationship that upends his prior notions of romance.

THEMES, MOTIFS, AND SYMBOLS

THEMES

THE SUBDUING OF WOMEN'S HUMANITY In *Herland* and other writings, Gilman shows that her society is unjust to women and does not allow them to achieve their full human potential. Women's lives, she reveals, are too consumed by difficult, unremunerated "women's work," such as childbearing, child rearing, and domestic labor. Because women are limited to this domestic world, they are made out to be less "fully human" than men in their potential for development. Given the chance, Gilman says, women can embrace the whole of life just as much men, and the women of Herland—strong, intelligent, and self-reliant—are the fictional embodiment of this point. All three of the male characters in *Herland* start out with the assumption of female inferiority, and all three must eventually alter their world views in their dealings with the Herlandian women, to varying degrees of success.

The men's relationships with Ellador, Celis, and Alima show the difficulties that arise when women demand to be treated as equals in love as well as in society. Terry and Alima end in open conflict, while Jeff and Celis simply fail to understand one another at all. Van eventually relates to Ellador as a full human being, not merely a woman, and Gilman portrays their relationship as the most successful. Gilman suggests that once equality between men and women has been established, romantic partners will achieve a sense of privacy and pleasure in sexual difference. As Van and Ellador begin their journey at the end of the novel, part of their mission is to completely re-imagine the sexual and romantic bond between men and women, with the full humanity of women as part of the equation.

THE RATIONALISM OF HERLAND'S SOCIETY Herland is organized along socialist lines and represents an idealized form of how society should behave. In a socialist economy, the government manages business, industry, and economic activity on behalf of the people. This is the opposite of a "free enterprise" system, in which the central authority may regulate industrial and commercial activity, but not control or direct it. One of socialism's attractions is that it proposes to replace a social structure based on competition and individualism with one based on community and cooperation. Thanks to Herland's isolated location and the extreme interdependence of its inhabitants, its members must put the community's needs before their own. Herland is organized more as a family than as a state, and each member is happy to sacrifice for the greater good. From the communal farming of the forests to the common education of the young, Herland is organized around the principle that work and reward are to be shared by all, to the maximum benefit of the greatest number. Herlandian society is therefore highly rationalized. The entire community deals with internal problems, without favoritism, individual ambition, or family feeling to interfere with reaching the most rational solution.

Perhaps the most striking example of Herland's rational society is the way the women calmly embrace the population controls required to sustain the population on their isolated plateau. Although many of the women would prefer to have multiple children, they are limited to just one, and some are forbidden to reproduce at all so that bad qualities may be "bred out" of the population. Van is struck by the simplicity of this solution and by the shared sacrifice required of all of the women to make it work. Van comes to see his own society as simply an aggregation of individuals, each in competition with the other, and predicated on the oppression of the female half of the population. Gilman argues that disease, crime, war, pollution, and poverty, all unknown in Herland, would be conquered if they were viewed as issues for the whole society to tackle and if society had the power to remake itself along the most rational lines.

THE REJECTION OF TRADITION The extreme rationalization of Herlandian society is possible in part because of Herland's complete rejection of tradition. For example, when Jeff mentions that the men's society is based on traditions thousands of years old, Moadine responds that Herland has no laws over one hundred years old and very few over twenty. Having been created essentially from scratch, the laws and customs of Herland are subject to constant scrutiny and revision. The women see their society and culture as human creations, meant to serve human needs in the present, so neither the institutions nor the practices of the past are sacred. Even the games the children play are new inventions, created for their educational value. Religious tradition is no exception, and the religion of Herland is a rather simple worship of motherhood and nature, in which there is no vested authority or sacred canon and from which all negative or unpleasant aspects have been purged.

Though Van initially views the women's attitude toward the past as irreverent and disrespectful, Ellador explains that, from the Herlandian perspective, it makes no sense to give the same weight to the opinions of ancestors as to those of the present generation. Knowledge and understanding have increased over the years, and the best way to honor the departed women of Herland is to continue their example of conscious improvement of the land and of themselves. Gilman understands that her project of advancing feminism and moving the United States toward a socialist economy places her in direct opposition to many firmly rooted traditions, especially those regarding the family. Gilman saw traditional Christianity as opposed to many of the changes she was proposing. By subjecting tradition in general, and Christianity in particular, to the reasonable but quite sharp questions of the women of Herland, Gilman hopes to displace tradition from its privileged seat and thereby prepare the way for serious political changes.

THE SANCTITY OF MOTHERHOOD The women of Herland have a nearly religious attitude toward motherhood. The rationality and the constant drive for self-improvement that mark Herland's culture are meant to be in service to the overarching ideal of motherhood. The miraculous ability of the women of Herland to conceive children on their own leads them to see motherhood as the central aspect of their beings—their greatest duty and their greatest honor. They think of God as a sacred mother, a personification of the love that pervades the whole universe. One of the sharpest contrasts Gilman draws is between the judgmental, patriarchal male God of Western monotheism and the nurturing, mothering, female spirit of Herland's religion.

In addition to being a religious imperative, motherhood in Herland is the dominant principle of social organization. Each woman in Herland is allowed, with rare exception, to give birth only once, and she does not raise her child herself. Instead, children are raised by specialists, as their education and nurturing are simply too important to society as a whole to be left in private hands. Each child has a whole country of mothers, and each woman has millions of objects for her boundless love. In a society that truly values mothers and children, Gilman suggests, children are not possessions, and motherhood is not merely incidental to a woman's sexual being. One of the major problems for Van and Ellador's marriage is Ellador's inability to grasp the idea that sex has a romantic, pleasurable aspect as well as a procreative function. Any social arrangement in which children are not the highest priority seems immoral to the women of Herland, and this perspective that makes the men unwilling to admit how often children are neglected in the "civilized" world. The women are horrified when Van mentions abortion. For Gilman, Somel's extreme, disbelieving reaction to the reality of abortion is one more piece of evidence that our society, not Herland's, is the truly strange one.

MOTIFS

EMBARRASSING CONTRASTS In *Herland*, Gilman contrasts the way things are done in Herland and the way "we" do things. At first, these contrasts seem neutral, the incidental differences any two cultures would have. As the men become more familiar with Herland, however, a pattern emerges. In any realm in which there is a contrast between the customs of Herland and those of the outer world, the policies of Herland inevitably appear to be more rational and more effective. One example is the contrast drawn in the matter of the domestication of animals. Herland's cats are model citizens, intelligent, healthy, and beautiful. They have been systematically bred for good behavior, chasing rodents only and leaving birds alone. Somel and Zava are shocked and disgusted to hear about the dirt, danger, and disease associated with dogs in the outer world and marvel that such a situation is tolerated. Eventually, after increasingly embarrassing comparisons, Van and his friends are forced to wonder why their society *does* tolerate such things. At every stage of the novel, Gilman contrasts a society built on reason, equality, and cooperation—all standards we claim to value—with one organized along the lines we have in fact chosen: tradition, inequality, and competition.

FEMALE PHYSICAL PROWESS When Van, Terry, and Jeff first encounter their future brides, the extreme physical prowess of Herland's women is strikingly clear. This encounter is only the first in a series of scenes in which Gilman shows our conventional notions of male physical superiority to be completely inaccurate, at least in the case of the Herlandians. Gilman uses the women's amazing athleticism to illustrate one of her recurring points: that the inferiority and supposed weakness of women is entirely a product of culture. For instance, during their confinement and education into the customs of Herland, the men are allowed to exercise—and are humiliated by the ease with which the older women match and beat them. Later, the men play a stone-tossing game with the three girls, who easily beat them. Van comments on the naturalness of the girls' physicality—vastly different from the women back home. Gilman wants to show that women would soon cease to be the "weaker sex" if they were not treated as such. The assumption of female frailty becomes a self-fulfilling prophecy, in which women are sheltered because they are weak and weak because they are sheltered. The unique history of Herland explodes the myth of female weakness.

SYMBOLS

THE WELL-TENDED FORESTS One of the first observations the men make about Herland is how carefully the forestland around the city is maintained, and Jeff confirms that every tree in the forest is fruit- or nut-bearing, or in some way useful. The entire forest is not so much a wilderness as an immense garden. The forests exemplify the Herlandian way, especially with regard to nature. First, the forests are completely under human control. Every aspect of the ecosystem has been rationalized and made to serve the women in the most efficient way possible, but without the waste and ugliness associated with industrial exploitation. The useful, pleasant aspects of nature have been encouraged to flourish, and the aggressive, wasteful elements have been bred out. The women have gently forced nature to cooperate.

Though men such as Terry associate nature with ferocity and physical challenge, the Herlandian forests represent a different kind of relationship between humans and their environment. Natural life is humanized; it cooperates with and supports humanity rather than reduces human behavior to so-called "natural laws" that tend to favor competition and the domination of the strong over the weak. The women are disgusted to learn the barest details of the modern meat industry, which stands in sharp contrast to the Herlandian women's relationship to their well-tended forests.

HERLANDIAN CLOTHES Contrary to the men's expectations, the Herlandian women's clothes are not frivolous, but rather, practical and stylish: the women wear a one-piece undergarment, hose, and either a tunic or a long robe, which is attractively stitched and has many useful pockets. In our society, women are often assumed to be vain and frivolous because of their clothing, and thus, Gilman uses the Herlandians' clothing to confound the shortsighted expectations of the men, who are forced to admit that the women are no less attractive for having shorter hair and practical clothes. In time, Jeff and Van even come to prefer the Herlandian style. The men, too, must adopt Herlandian dress, and they find the clothes comfortable and becoming, which suggests that Herland's style is fitting for both men and women alike. When Van eventually leaves Herland, he misses the clothing, and, by extension, the eminently reasonable, attractive, and comfortable lifestyle that those clothes represent.

IMPORTANT QUOTATIONS EXPLAINED

---

1. *They were not young. They were not old. They were not, in the girl sense, beautiful. They were not in the least ferocious. . . . I had the funniest feeling . . . of being hopelessly in the wrong that I had so often felt in early youth when my short legs' utmost effort failed to overcome the fact that I was late to school.*

In Chapter 2, the men have their first encounter with the women of Herland, and things do not at all go as they had planned. In this passage, Van begins to sense that these women are unlike any he has ever encountered, and that perhaps he has misjudged what women *could* be. These women are not afraid of the three explorers, and they do not seem like "savages" or belligerent "amazons" at all. Van cannot determine how old the women are, but in their presence he begins to feel young and timid. Van's feeling that he is perpetually in the wrong stays with him throughout his time in Herland.

In Herland, the men do, in effect, become like little boys again. Compared to the full humanity represented by the women of Herland, the kind of masculinity represented by all three men, particularly by Terry, is a kind of childishness, the mark of an incomplete personality. Van's early sensitivity to his position with regard to the women shows that he is willing to learn from the situation in which he finds himself. Terry, on the other hand, cannot really see the women. Since they are not beautiful "in the girl sense," he cannot even recognize them as women. If Van feels like a child at first, he soon grows into a new kind of man, while Terry retreats into his childish version of what it means to be a man.

H

---

2. *[Terry] squared his broad shoulders and lifted his chest. "We do not allow our women to work. Women are loved—idolized—honored—kept in the home to care for the children."*
   "What is 'the home'?" asked Somel a little wistfully.
   But Zava begged: "Tell me first, do no women work, really?"
   "Why, yes," Terry admitted. "Some have to, of the poorer sort."
   "About how many—in your country?"
   "About seven or eight million," said Jeff, as mischievous as ever.

This exchange, from the end of Chapter 5, is one of several conversations in which the pretenses and false ideals of modern society are exposed to the gentle, ironic questioning of the women of Herland. Gilman achieves her effect in part by having the men explain their society's gender relations to a group of women wholly unfamiliar with what is considered to be "normal" behavior between men and women. In this situation, the men find themselves straining to find the logic behind such institutions as marriage and the family, and in the process, they often reveal more than they intend. For example, Terry is thoroughly in character here, flexing his muscles as he flexes his ideas. He is unaware of how strange it must sound to the Herlandians to hear him speak of men "allowing" women to work, or of "honoring" them by "keeping" them in the home.

Jeff, on the other hand, is more than halfway converted to the Herlandian way of thinking, and he is happy to point out that the supposedly normal, preferred domestic situation Terry describes is actually far from typical, thanks to the economic inequalities of modern society. Even more important for Gilman's purposes, the reader is learning to see traditional arrangements in a new way, just as the men are. For the reader as well, the chain of linked verbs that Terry uses ("women are loved—idolized—honored—kept") begins to take on new and more ominous levels of meaning.

3. *We soon grew to see that mother-love has more than one channel of expression. I think the reason our children are so—so fully loved, by all of us, is that we never—any of us—have enough of our own.*

Somel says these words to Van toward the end of Chapter 6, during one of their long discussions about the idea of motherhood in Herland. Gilman wants to show that even though the women have lived without men for so long, they are not less feminine than other women and not unnatural in their feelings. These women experience a desire for motherhood as great as any woman's, but it is a desire likely bound to go unfulfilled to some extent. The vast majority of the women of Herland are allowed only one child, even though they might personally want to bear more. This great sacrifice is one of the elements that allows Herland to function as well as it does, and it represents the highest expression of their communal, socialist system.

Trapped on their plateau, uncontrolled reproduction by the women would soon lead to overpopulation, which would be fatal to the whole group. Although each woman sacrifices a bit of her personal motherhood, she does so knowing that the larger motherhood of the community can grow thanks to her sacrifice. Every duty, every responsibility undertaken by an individual in Herland, every creative or constructive act, is a contribution to the mothering function of society as a whole. The sacred nature of motherly love is the one unquestioned value of Herland's women and the foundation of all of their other values. Everything from their religious notions to their agriculture is determined by a desire to place the raising and cherishing of children at the center of life. However, Somel's admission that none of the women ever have "enough" children is an acknowledgement that life in Herland, as ideal as it seems, is not perfect.

4. *I found that much, very much, of what I had honestly supposed to be a physiological necessity was a psychological necessity—or so believed. I found, after my ideas of what was essential had changed, that my feelings changed also.*

In Chapter 11, Van reflects on his own psychology as he struggles to understand Ellador's continuing independence after the two have been wed. Ellador and the other women do not understand the notion the men have brought with them of married privacy. Indeed, the idea of "private families" is completely alien to Herland, where the larger group always overrides any such smaller connections between individuals. The real frustration for Van is in the matter of romantic or recreational sexuality. Ellador simply has no interest in sex, aside from its procreative purposes, and to her the idea that sexual pleasure could be an end in itself seems odd, even unnatural. Van does his best to entice her, but Ellador is a skilled psychologist, and she is able to steer the relationship away from sexuality and back toward simple friendship. Van is smart enough to see what Ellador is doing, and over time he begins to experience the changes he details above.

Van eventually puts his sexual drive at the service of his rational will, just as the women of Herland have done, thus overturning the common assumption that the sex drive is essentially unstoppable, especially in men. Gilman is aware that such beliefs about the male physiological "need" for sex are behind many of the excuses made for male sexual misconduct, from adultery to promiscuity and even to rape. However, Van finds he has much more self-control than he ever thought possible. Later, Van continues to make the case that sexuality can be expressive of true love, even when reproduction is not the object, but he does so in terms of spiritual union, not simple physical desire. Ellador is much more open to this argument, and it is clear that their discussion of sex does not end when the novel does.

5. *When we say* men, man, manly, manhood, *and all the other masculine-derivatives, we have in the background of our minds a huge vague crowded picture of the world and all its activities. . . . And when we say* women, *we think* female—*the sex.*

But to these women . . . the word woman *called up all that big background, so far as they had gone in social development; and the word* man *meant to them only* male—*the sex.*

Toward the end of the novel, in Chapter 12, the men are faced with expulsion from Herland, thanks to Terry's attack on Alima. Ellador, eager to join Van in exile and to see the outside world, imagines that

Van must be homesick. Van tries to explain how different his feelings about men and women are after a year in Herland, and he realizes that his thinking has changed in a fundamental way. Now, when he thinks of humanity or "mankind," he includes women and womanliness as fully part of the equation, not merely as a subset of a larger entity. Before his experiences in Herland, Van unconsciously thought of women as a kind of man—attractive, but weaker and not representative of the group as a whole. Previously, whenever Van thought of history and the progress of human achievement, he'd really been thinking of men and things men had done.

Van can now see that he'd excluded half of humanity from full membership in the group. The same situation applies in reverse for the women of Herland. In the absence of men, these women have come to think of men as a kind of woman, and to assume that the men of the outside world must be as devoted to reason, cooperation, and children as they are. This assumption, says Van, is partly why Terry's attempted rape comes as such a shock to the women. Terry's act was a particularly male kind of violence, directed at another person, not as a person, but as a woman. As they come to understand the outside world, the women of Herland must expand their definition of humanity, just as the men have had to. The difference is that the information they will have to assimilate is not entirely benign.

The House of Mirth

Edith Wharton (1862–1937)

CONTEXT

Edith Wharton was born into a wealthy New York family on January 24, 1862, as Edith Newbold Jones. In 1885, she married Edward Wharton, a Boston banker, who was twelve years her senior. They divorced in 1913 after thirty unhappy years of marriage as a result of Edward's many public infidelities and his declining mental state. For several years toward the end of her marriage, she had an affair with American bisexual journalist William Morton Fullerton. In 1907, Wharton moved to France, where, during World War I, she worked for the Red Cross and wrote many articles about her experiences on the front lines. She was a close friend of Theodore Roosevelt, F. Scott Fitzgerald, and Ernest Hemingway, among other prominent intellectuals of her time. Famous not only for her writing, Wharton is well known for her skills as a landscape architect. The Mount, her self-designed estate in Lennox, Massachusetts, exemplifies this skill.

H

Wharton began her writing career in 1897 with the publication of *Decoration of Houses*. During the 1890s, she also submitted many short stories to *Scribner's Magazine*. Wharton's first literary success, and the first of her best-sellers, was *The House of Mirth* (1905). The tragic tone of the novel, combined with Wharton's sharp wit, provides a telling picture of the rungs of society at the turn of the century. In 1920, she wrote *The Age of Innocence*, one of her most famous novels, for which she won the Pulitzer Prize. Wharton wrote over forty books in forty years, including novels, poems, essays, travel books, and her autobiography, *A Backward Glance* (1934). Wharton was raised in the aristocracy of Old New York, and her works offer profound insight into the society of the privileged class, and her themes center around topics such as the conflict between social and individual fulfillment, repressed sexuality, and the manners of old families and the *nouveau riche*, who had made their fortunes in more recent years. Wharton was the first woman to be awarded the Pulitzer Prize for Fiction, an honorary Doctorate of Letters from Yale University, and full membership to the American Academy of Arts and Letters. Although Wharton died in 1937, her editor published her unfinished novel, *The Buccanneers*, in 1938.

In America's Gilded Age (between 1876 and 1901, approximately), the rich got much richer, and the poor got much poorer. It was a time of great industrial expansion in the United States and a time when the stock market was doing very well. Great cities such as New York became worlds of extremes, where on one block lived millionaires in mansions and on another block lived immigrant families in tenements. It is in this environment that Edith Wharton chose to set her first major novel.

Because of her family's social position, Wharton knew the upper-crust New York society well, and she knew how cruel it could be. Her intention for *The House of Mirth* was not only to satirize this society but also to show the profoundly tragic suffering that goes on inside it. To be sure, *The House of Mirth* condemns the elitist world of women such as Bertha Dorset; it does so by promoting the age-old ideal that you can't buy happiness. The most content person in the novel may be Lawrence Selden, who is comfortable with his modest wealth and remains a detached observer of the upper-crust. Lily Bart, the protagonist, is trapped by her obsession with money, which prevents her from marrying the man she really loves because he is not wealthy enough.

The House of Mirth is about the personal struggle to fit into society and, ultimately, to get married. This places the book in a long-standing literary tradition known as the novel of manners, a form developed most notably by Sir Walter Scott and Jane Austen. Austen's *Pride and Prejudice* (1813) and *Sense and Sensibility* (1811) are pioneer works of this literary genre. The tradition developed in England throughout the nineteenth century, as authors such as George Eliot and Henry James explored the place of women in society and the social effect of marriage, showing in particular the problems that come with marriage and conforming to society. A novel of manners generally follows four conventions: the protagonist is usually a single woman looking to get married; socioeconomic class must be a factor in determining whom she will marry; there must be many scenes that portray the proper and improper way to act within high society and that outline relations between classes; and it usually ends with either the marriage or the death of the protagonist.

During the late nineteenth century, the novel of manners was one of the most popular novel genres, but it was also a predominantly British form. Many people questioned whether such a genre could exist in America, where there are no official social classes. Wharton adapted the form in her own way to better suit New York society. Instead of a legitimized aristocracy, Wharton creates a social circle comprised of elegant New York snobs. Class mobility, not present in most British manners novels, is a large factor in *The House of Mirth*, which shows the attempts of Lily to assimilate herself into the elite group, only to slide down the social scale into the working class before her death. In fact, Lily's primary goal is not to marry for happiness, as is seen in many Austen characters, for example, but rather, for social security. A marriage to Percy Gryce, Lily decides at the beginning of the novel, would be the best way to assure herself of good social standing and a steady income.

The House of Mirth also examines the long physical and mental decline of a young woman who, because of her own cowardice and indecision, slips out of social prominence into poverty and dinginess. The novel presents a very harsh dose of reality and ends rather pathetically. Instead of marrying and living happily ever after, or tragically dying during childbirth (the two most common endings in the genre), Lily fades away slowly and commits suicide, perhaps unintentionally, as a means of escaping from a lower-class world in which her upper-class sensibilities cannot survive.

Wharton's manipulation of the genre makes the novel a good example of the American realism movement, which began roughly after Reconstruction (the late 1870s) and lasted until just after World War I (the early 1920s). The English novel of manners was developed during the Romanticism movement, which placed a literary emphasis on emotion rather than reason, and the ideal rather than reality. Realism, to which Wharton subscribed, grew out of Darwinist ideas of natural selection and survival of the fittest. To Wharton, the existing novel of manners had not adequately dealt with the fall from society that many people in New York experienced if they ran out of money or did not marry well. *The House of Mirth*, then, can perhaps best be viewed as an attempt to add a very dark truth to an otherwise optimistic genre, an attempt consistent with the literary spirit of the time in which Wharton was writing.

PLOT OVERVIEW

Lily Bart is an attractive woman with some important social and family ties, but at the age of twenty-nine, she is still unmarried. Since the death of her mother, who had an intense hatred for "dinginess," Lily has lived with her aunt, Mrs. Peniston. However, Lily spends much of her time staying at the Bellomont, the out-of-town estate of the wealthy and well-established Gus and Judy Trenor. At the Bellomont, Judy regularly throws extravagant parties that are attended by most of the New York upper-crust. They play bridge for money, which is problematic for Lily because she has a gambling addiction that ruins her financially.

Lily has two main goals: marriage and wealth. She hopes to marry a rich man, thereby securing her place in society, but due to her own indecision, she passes up numerous chances, always thinking she can do better. Unfortunately, Lily's true love, Lawrence Selden, does not have enough money for Lily to consider him a viable partner.

Lily hears about the stock market at the Bellomont and decides that she would like to get involved in investment. She asks Gus Trenor to invest her small sum of money for her, and he readily assents because he is secretly attracted to Lily and wants her to spend time with him. The investments pay off, and as Lily begins to make money from Wall Street, she begins to spend lavishly. Later, to her horror, Trenor tries to proposition her, and she learns that he has not been investing her money—of which there is none—but rather his own; he has been giving her his profits. He says that she may pay him back by spending time with him, but Lily withdraws quickly from his presence and resolves that she will somehow pay him back, although she does not know how.

Lily takes a sudden vacation to the Mediterranean with George and Bertha Dorset and the young Ned Silverton, but she soon learns that she is being brought along to distract George while Bertha has an affair with Ned. When Lily begins to associate with European royalty, Bertha becomes jealous and kicks her off the yacht, starting a nasty rumor that Lily and George are having an affair, which leads to Lily's expulsion from society.

Lily returns to America to learn that her aunt has died, leaving her with only $10,000, which is just enough to pay off her debt to Trenor, although Lily cannot have the money until one year has elapsed. In the meantime, Lily tries desperately to rebuild her reputation in society, but fails and moves in with Gerty Farish, Selden's cousin. She takes up jobs as a secretary and milliner (hat maker) before finally moving into a boarding house and leading a meaningless life. She begins to take sleeping pills to help her get over her fear and loneliness until the day when her check from her aunt's estate finally arrives. She pays off all of her debts with the money, then overdoses (perhaps intentionally) on sleeping pills. The next day, Selden shows up at her apartment with the intention of proposing marriage to her, only to find her dead, with all of her debts paid off.

CHARACTER LIST

Lily Bart The protaganist of the novel and an unmarried twenty-nine-year-old woman who desires to be a social success. Lily's mission is to marry a relatively wealthy man, thereby ensuring her financial stability and a place in the higher levels of New York society. Unfortunately, her desire to marry someone wealthy clashes with her feelings for Lawrence Selden, a man of modest means whom she truly loves. She also suffers from an inability to make decisions, which causes her to pass up several good marriage opportunities in hopes that she can do better. Book Two chronicles Lily's gradual expulsion from society after a false rumor spreads that she has had an extramarital affair. She eventually joins the working classes before dying at the end of the novel from a sleeping pill overdose.

Lawrence Selden A detached observer of the New York society that Lily aspires to join. Selden is a lawyer by profession, but he is not particularly wealthy, which prevents Lily from marrying him even though they love each other. Throughout the novel, Selden struggles between his desire to remain detached from society and his wish to court Lily and convince her to marry him. At the end of the novel, he finally resolves to propose marriage to Lily, but his decision comes too late—he finds her dead in her apartment.

H

Bertha Dorset The wife of George Dorset and the novel's antagonist. Most of the characters (perhaps including her husband) know that Bertha has a history of extramarital affairs, one of which may have been with Lawrence Selden. She is described as a nasty woman who enjoys making other people miserable, especially her own husband. She invites Lily on a cruise with her, her husband, and Ned Silverton around the Mediterranean, but only so Lily will distract George while Bertha has an affair with Ned. Bertha spreads the rumor that Lily and George are having an affair, then uses her money and influence to keep Lily out of the society forever.

Gerty Farish Selden's cousin. Gerty is a kind, generous woman who does a lot of charity work. In Book Two, she becomes one of Lily's only friends, giving her a place to stay and taking care of her when everyone else abandons her.

Simon Rosedale A dedicated social climber who owns many stocks and lots of property. At the end of the novel, Rosedale asks Lily to marry him, an opportunity that she initially passes up. Later on, he becomes her friend and visits her after she becomes very poor and very sick.

Gus Trenor Husband of Judy. Trenor is a lonely, moody man who has a particular liking for Lily even though he is married. In Book One, Lily asks him to invest her money for her in the stock market. Instead, Trenor invests his own money and gives Lily the profits. When Lily finds out that the money is not truly hers, she resolves to pay Trenor back rather than agree to spend time with him.

Percy Gryce A young, rich, eligible bachelor on whom Lily sets her sights early in the novel. Unfortunately, just as Lily decides she must marry him, Gryce announces his engagement to Evie Van Osburgh. He is another missed opportunity for Lily.

Judy Trenor A close friend of Lily's. Judy is the social overseer of the events at the Bellomont, her out-of-town estate. She regularly hosts large bridge parties and gives Lily a place to stay for up to weeks at a time. She all but disappears in Book Two.

Carry Fisher A woman known for bringing newcomers, such as the Brys, into society. After Lily has been expelled from the upper class by Bertha, Carry is one of the few people who still shows compassion toward her, offering Lily support and money.

George Dorset The husband of Bertha. George does not factor into the novel regularly until Book Two, when he begins to realize that his wife is cheating on him with Ned Silverton. To complicate the matter, George seems to fancy Lily, although she will not ever see him again after people spread rumors that the two of them had an affair.

Ned Silverton A young man who accompanies Lily and the Dorsets on their Mediterranean cruise. A rich man, Silverton has an affair with Bertha but manages to keep it concealed from most of society.

Mrs. Peniston Lily's wealthy aunt who lives on Fifth Avenue. Mrs. Peniston became Lily's guardian after Lily's mother died. When Mrs. Peniston hears rumors that Lily had an affair and learns that Lily gambles on Sundays, she disinherits her before her death at the beginning of Book Two, and leaves most of her estate to other relatives.

Jack Stepney and Gwen Stepney Lily's cousin and his wife. Jack married Gwen Van Osburgh in Book One and is a regular member of society. In Book Two, he agrees to shelter Lily for the night after she is kicked off the yacht by Bertha. Jack and Gwen are very wealthy.

Grace Stepney Lily's competetive cousin. When Lily asks Grace for financial assistance, Grace flatly refuses.

ANALYSIS OF MAJOR CHARACTERS

LILY BART The protagonist of the novel, Lily Bart, is a beautiful young woman searching for the right husband who will give her the money and status to remain in upper-class New York social circles. While she has a streak of the romantic in her, her primary focus is on the wealth and social status of potential suitors, and she casts aside many options, believing she can do better. The novel follows a two-year period in Lily's life as she moves from party to party, struggling to stay within the favor of the wealthy while mounting larger and larger debts. Unfortunately, her precarious financial situation forces her to try some risky investing with the help of a married man, which ends up backfiring and resulting in her being cast out of the circles she so desperately wishes to join. When her family rejects her for the same untrue rumors, Lily is forced to join the middle class, working as a hat maker. Her slide into poverty and depression continues, and eventually, Lily takes too large a dose of sleeping medication—perhaps accidentally—and dies in her sleep. Her focus on financial success never allows her to truly consider a marriage to Selden, her truest friend and most ideal match.

LAWRENCE SELDEN Lawrence Selden, a young lawyer, is the only person in the novel who is able to move within the elite social circles and yet view them with the detached scrutiny of an outsider. Not wealthy himself, Selden has a distant relationship to money, believing love and happiness to be found instead of purchased. He is one of Lily's few consistent friends, always providing lively banter, a shoulder to cry on, and honest advice. Selden's rational thinking often overpowers his romantic side, and it eventually causes him to realize how much he is in love with Lily—a few hours too late.

GEORGE AND BERTHA DORSET George and Bertha Dorset are an extremely wealthy couple trapped in a loveless marriage. Bertha is an obnoxious, manipulative socialite who uses gossip and wealth to get what she wants, including the attention of other men. Initially, Bertha pursues Selden, and later she uses Lily as a distraction for George so she can have an affair with another young bachelor. Bertha then becomes jealous of George's affection for Lily and spreads rumors that result in Lily's expulsion from society. In the meantime, George is dragged along through his wife's escapades, eventually looking for divorce and Lily's hand in marriage.

GUS AND JUDY TRENOR The Trenors are another socialite couple who often host large events at their home, Bellomont. Mrs. Trenor is a gossip and spends much of her day fretting over the minutiae of entertaining—which guests are the most desirable to invite, which have been "stolen" by another conflicting event, and which unmarried men and women should be set up together. Gus Trenor looks to other women for the attention his wife doesn't give him. A notorious flirt, Gus is drawn to Lily, and he uses his financial investment skills and a large sum of his own money in a risky investment for Lily. This money becomes the focal point of the second half of the novel, as Lily commits herself to repaying her debt.

H

SIMON ROSEDALE Mr. Rosedale aspires to the social circles of the wealthy. Building his fortune in real estate, Rosedale initially appears as the owner of Selden's apartment building who catches Lily leaving what appears to be a lover's meeting with Selden. The path of Rosedale's rise to financial success and place in society sits in opposition to Lily's decline and death; while she starts as a member of the inner circles and falls from their graces, he works his way up to a point where he no longer is interested in marrying her. Despite the differences in their social standing by the end of the book, Rosedale is still kind to Lily, and he offers her money when he runs into her after she has lost her hat-making job.

THEMES, MOTIFS, AND SYMBOLS

THEMES

THE SAFETY OF LOVE AND DEATH In *The House of Mirth*, Wharton presents love and death as the only two safe places for a woman to be. Lily especially subscribes to this theory, feeling hounded by her debts and financial woes and surrounded by loveless marriages. Love or death seem to be the only possibilities for salvation. In Book Two, Lily finds herself at a crossroads—either she can choose love, marry Selden, and find happiness without wealth; or she will find rest in the finality of death. Lily's obsession with wealth and luxury continually prevents her from acknowledging and accepting Selden's love, and so the safety love can offer is not a viable choice for her. She is left with death as her only option.

THE UNCIVILIZATION OF MANNERS The social expectation of politeness, good manners, and the acting required to maintain a constant façade of enjoying one another's company dominate all of the parties and interactions between the members of the elite circles in *The House of Mirth*. Lily recognizes the difference between a conversation she has with Selden, where they are both real and sometimes less-than-flattering in the honesty of their responses, and the acting she does with Mrs. Trenor and the other socialites, where they focus solely on gossip and pretense and are constantly calculating in order to manipulate one another. The artificiality of the good manners of the "most civilized" characters in the novel demonstrates just how bad their manners actually are. Lying, cheating, stealing, adultery, spreading rumors, and generally being hurtful and mean are common occurrences within this circle. Lily recognizes this, and at times she longs for the honesty and realness of her relationship with Selden. However, she isn't able to detach herself from her desire for wealth, which demands that she continue to play the same manipulative game as the other socialites in order to get what she wants.

FREEDOM VS. SLAVERY Lily's relationship with money is obviously fraught with tension and drama, and she often describes the relationship in terms of freedom and slavery. When she has money and is able to pay her debts, she feels a sense of unparalleled freedom. But when the money is gone and her debts overwhelm her, she likens her situation to that of slavery—she is a slave to the whims and desires of others, a slave to the social demands of the upper-class circles, and a slave to her own inability to be happy without money. The idea of freedom and slavery also fits the different roles of the sexes. Percy Gryce, a wealthy, eccentric young bachelor, has large amounts of freedom, simply by virtue of his being a man. As a young woman, especially one without great wealth, Lily can never live the life of Selden or Gryce, and instead she must find a match that will ensure her protection and security. She will never have the freedom that the men have.

MOTIFS

GAMBLING AND LUCK Gambling and luck appear throughout *The House of Mirth*. Lily gambles at the socialite parties and loses her spending money. She gambles again on the stock market with the help of Gus Trenor. Throughout the novel, she gambles with love, continually staying in the game instead of taking various suitors' marriage proposals, always believing she can win a bigger and better "hand." Unfortunately, Lily's luck takes a definite turn for the worse. She loses her large sum in the stock market, then inadvertently makes an enemy of Bertha Dorset, who spreads rumors that hurt Lily even more. Even Lily's death can be seen as unlucky—Wharton doesn't make clear whether Lily intends to overdose on sleeping medication or whether her decision to take a little extra really is because she wants to sleep longer. Regardless, the reader is left with a sense that Lily's whole life could have been changed drastically were she to have had a little better luck.

SYMBOLS

MONEY *The House of Mirth* deals with American class hierarchies, which are dictated by money, unlike European classes, where nobility is predetermined and not totally dependent upon wealth. Thus money is the only way in—and out—of the upper class circles that Lily frequents. More than access, money also ranks individuals within the circle. Percy Gryce is the most desired bachelor for a time because of his extraordinary wealth, and the Trenors are continually hosting events because of their financial resources. Money is also linked with power: Bertha Dorset's version of Lily and George's relationship is believed over Lily's simply because Bertha is richer. Money defines characters as well. Selden is partially defined by his lack of desire for wealth, in contrast with the rest of the characters. Most important for this novel, money drives the plot of Lily's fall from upper-class eligible socialite to outcast working-class spinster.

IMPORTANT QUOTATIONS EXPLAINED

---

1. *Society is a revolving body which is apt to be judged according to its place in each man's heaven; and at present it was turning its illuminated face to Lily.*

This observation, from Book One, Chapter Four, shows Lily at the height of her confidence in searching for a husband. She has just finished laying what she believes will be the groundwork for making Percy Gryce, an extremely wealthy but socially awkward bachelor, want to marry her. Lily is indeed basking in the glow of social success, feeling the attention of others and the much-desired success in finding a potential husband whose wealth would give her security and stability. She has pushed her romantic ideas about love and her relationship with Selden from her mind and has made the logical, calculated decision to pursue Gryce. This decision makes her feel as though she is in control and winning the game of manipulation and artifice that is upper class socializing. Unfortunately, just as society is at this moment turning "its illuminated face" to her, it will also continue to revolve, taking its glorious light elsewhere and leaving Lily in the dark. This passage and others contribute to the idea that perhaps Lily has little control over her existence, and that larger forces—such as fate or luck—might be more influential in determining the outcome of the story.

---

2. *I wasn't meant to be good.*

This comment appears late in Book Two, after Lily has been sinking lower and lower into poverty and despair. She sits at Gerty's table, talking about two other women who have found themselves penniless, and begins to see the parallels to her own situation. Lily is starting to acknowledge that despite her best efforts, luck has been against her, and she may never be rich and esteemed. Here, "good" refers to being wealthy, a member of the upper-class elite social circles, and having a secure marriage. This definition reflects how deeply rooted this desire for money and status is in Lily. She cannot confine herself to the artificial behavior of the upper-class women, she cannot settle on a marriage that isn't the best, and she cannot decide between the happiness of true love and the happiness of wealth.

---

3. *That was all he knew—all he could hope to unravel of the story. The mute lips on the pillow refused him more than this—unless indeed they had told him the rest in the kiss they had left upon his forehead. Yes, he could now read into that farewell all that his heart craved to find there; he could even draw from it courage not to accuse himself for having failed to reach the height of his opportunity.*

The passage appears at the end of the novel, when Selden finds Lily's cold body after she has killed herself by overdosing on sleeping medication. He has also found Lily's check to Trenor and is unsure of what to make of it. In his grief, Selden reflects back to the last time he saw Lily, when she kissed him on the forehead and said goodbye, presumably for a short while, and finds in that moment that she had loved him too. He also finds the courage to not blame himself for being too late in discovering his own feelings for her. This bedside moment returns the reader's focus to romantic love. It also somewhat redeems Lily's character by both allowing for the possibility of her death being an accident and bringing

H

her love for Selden up again at the very end of the novel. The reappearance of true love gives Lily's tragic end a fated, pitiable spin, instead of a desperate, money-hungry tone. Also, it is appropriate that Selden, who opened the novel by observing Lily from across the train station, finish the novel observing her even more intimately, but with just as many questions in his mind.

The House of the Spirits

Isabel Allende (1942–)

CONTEXT

Isabel Allende, one of the most successful contemporary Latin American woman novelists, was born in 1942. Although she was born in Lima, Peru, Allende is Chilean. As a child, she traveled throughout Latin America and beyond, thanks to her father and stepfather's diplomatic careers. In 1962, Allende married Manuel Frias. She soon gave birth to their daughter, Paula, and their son, Nicolas. Beginning in 1967, Allende worked as a journalist for a number of magazines and newspapers in Chile. In 1970, her uncle, Salvador Allende, became the first socialist to be elected president of Chile. In 1973, he was assassinated in a military coup led by General Augusta Pinochet. Due to increasing political tensions in Chile, Allende and her family fled to Venezuela in 1975. She lived there for thirteen years, continuing to work as a journalist and beginning to write novels. In 1987, Allende and Frias were divorced. A year later, Allende married Willie Gordon in San Francisco and settled down in nearby San Rafael, California. In 1992, her daughter Paula died of porphyria.

H

Written and first published in Spanish in 1982, *The House of the Spirits* was Allende's first book. It received enormous critical and popular acclaim and, in 1985, was translated into English. In 1993, it was released as a film with a star-studded cast. Allende has written numerous other novels, including *The Stories of Eva Luna* (1991), *The Infinite Plan* (1994), and a biography of her daughter, *Paula* (1996).

Many elements in *The House of the Spirits* are based on Allende's own life. The political events in the unnamed country in the novel are quite similar to those that occurred in Chile. As Allende later explained in *Paula*, many of the characters in *The House of the Spirits* are based on members of her own family. In fact, *The House of the Spirits* began as a letter Allende wrote to a dying uncle. However, *The House of the Spirits* is a novel, and there is no exact correlation between it and any real events or characters.

The House of the Spirits is a prime example of magical realism, along with Gabriel Garcia Marquez's *One Hundred Years of Solitude*. Primarily a Latin American tradition, magical realism is characterized by the simple, straightforward presentation of strange, magical events. For example, characteristics such as Clara's clairvoyance are compared to her brother's lameness. The characters in magical realist fiction experience and accept the unbelievable with calm rationality. When Clara dreams that her mother's severed head is missing, for example, she borrows a car and goes to find it, and then she puts it in a hatbox and forgets about it. Magical realist novels are often long family sagas, told with little respect for clear temporal succession. They often employ strategies of foreshadowing and repetition, both of which are prevalent in *The House of the Spirits*, especially in Clara's predictions of future events and in the recurrence of the names Pedro and Esteban.

PLOT OVERVIEW

On the day that the priest accused her of being possessed by the devil and that her Uncle Marcos's body was delivered to her house accompanied by a puppy, Barrabás, Clara del Valle began keeping a journal. Fifty years later, her husband Esteban and her granddaughter Alba refer to these journals as they piece together the story of their family.

Clara is a young girl when Barrabás arrives at the del Valle house. Her favorite sister, Rosa the Beautiful, is engaged to Esteban Trueba. Clara is clairvoyant and is able to predict almost every event in her life. She is not able to change the future, only to see it. While Esteban is off in the mines trying to make his fortune, Rosa is accidentally poisoned in place of her father, Severo del Valle. Rosa dies. Clara is so shocked by the events that she stops talking. Nine years later, Esteban has made a fortune with his family property, Tres Marias, thanks to his hard work and to his exploitation of the local peasants. On top of exploiting their labor, Esteban exploits all of the young girls of the peasant families, notably Pancha, for his sexual satisfaction. In addition to the peasant girls, Esteban also has sexual relations with prostitutes, including Transito Soto. Transito and Esteban become friends, and he lends her money to move to the city. Esteban's mother is about to die, and he returns to the city, where he pays a visit to the del Valle home. Esteban and Clara become engaged and marry. They move into the big house on the corner that Esteban built for them. Esteban's sister Ferula moves in with them.

About a year after they are married, Clara and Esteban's first child, Blanca, is born. When the family travels to Tres Marias for the summer a few years later, Blanca meets Pedro Tercero and they fall in love. Pedro Tercero is the son of Pedro Segundo, the peasant foreman of Tres Marias. Toward the end of the summer, Clara becomes pregnant again, this time with twins who, she announces, will be named Jaime and Nicolas. Days before the twins are due, Clara's parents are killed in a car accident. Rescuers are unable to find Nivea's head. No one wants to tell Clara that Nivea is buried headless, because they do not want to upset her just before the birth. Clara, however, realizes that her mother's head has not been found and makes Ferula go with her to find it. As soon as she recovers her mother's head, Clara goes into labor. Over the years, Ferula and Clara have developed a deep friendship. Ferula's feelings for Clara border on passionate love, and she and Esteban develop a rivalry over Clara's affections. One morning, Esteban comes home unexpectedly and finds Ferula in Clara's bed. Esteban kicks Ferula out of the house. As she leaves, Ferula curses Esteban to eternal loneliness.

Blanca and Pedro Tercero's love grows as they mature, and they soon realize that Esteban would disapprove if he knew. In addition to being of different classes, Pedro Tercero is a revolutionary, while Esteban is a conservative. Blanca and Pedro Tercero continue their romance in secret. Several years later, they are exposed to Esteban by Jean de Satigny, who is trying to ingratiate himself with Esteban so he can become either his business partner or his son-in-law. Esteban makes Blanca leave Tres Marias and tries to kill Pedro Tercero. In his anger, Esteban hits Clara. She never talks to him again. For several years, although they live in the same house, they almost never see each other. Jaime and Nicolas finish boarding school and return home. Jaime studies medicine, and Nicolas dabbles in spirituality and inventing. Esteban becomes very involved in the Conservative party, runs for Senate, and is elected. Esteban and Clara eventually return to a civil, if silent, relationship.

A few years later, Blanca gets pregnant. Esteban tells her that he has killed Pedro Tercero and forces her to marry Jean de Satigny. About six months after they are married, Blanca discovers Jean de Satigny's unusual sexual practices and leaves him. She gives birth to her daughter Alba as soon as she arrives home at the big house on the corner. Miguel, the younger brother of a friend and lover of Nicolas and Jaime, watches Alba's birth from a closet.

According to Clara, Alba is born lucky. She is raised by her entire family, inspiring great love in all. She is the only member of the family to develop a close and loving relationship with Esteban. Although she thinks that Jean de Satigny is her father and that he is dead, Alba meets Pedro Tercero and establishes a friendship with him. To the great sadness of everyone but herself, Clara dies. When she is eighteen, Alba enters the university where she meets Miguel, and they fall in love. Miguel is a revolutionary. They participate in some of the growing number of anticonservative protests that are springing up around the country.

To everyone's surprise, the socialists win the elections. Pedro Tercero joins the government. The peasants take over Tres Marias. Esteban tries to stop them and is taken hostage. At Blanca's request, Pedro Tercero intervenes and saves Esteban. Esteban and the conservatives do all they can to discredit the socialists, including preparing a military coup. A few months later, there is a military coup. Jaime, who is friends with the Socialist president, is killed. Miguel joins the guerrillas, and Pedro Tercero goes into hiding in the big house on the corner. Esteban is at first pleased with the coup but soon realizes that it results not in the conservatives' return to power but in the establishment of a military dictatorship. He is powerless to do much other than to help Blanca and Pedro Tercero escape to Canada.

The colonel at the head of the dictatorship abducts Alba. He turns out to be Esteban Garcia, Pancha and Esteban Trueba's grandson. Before she died, Pancha told Esteban the story of his ancestry. Esteban slowly made his way up the ranks of the military, and in the process he acquainted himself with Esteban Trueba and his family, especially Alba. Under the guise of finding out where Miguel is, Esteban Garcia exacts revenge on Alba for his grandmother's mistreatment. Desperate to find Alba, Esteban turns to Transito Soto, who runs the Christopher Columbus, a brothel-turned-hotel. Thanks to the connections she has established through her sex work, Transito is able to repay the favor Esteban did for her years before, and she assures that Alba is returned home. Alba and Esteban have just begun to write the story of their family when Esteban dies. Alba carries forth the project, pregnant with a child whose father is either Miguel or one of the men who raped her while she was in detention.

CHARACTER LIST

Clara Severo and Nivea del Valle's daughter, Esteban's wife, and Blanca, Jaime, and Nicolas's mother. The key female figure in the novel, Clara is the connection between the Trueba and del Valle families. She is clairvoyant and only sporadically attentive to domestic chores, but she holds her family together through her love and predictions. She is always surrounded by animals and flowers. Clara marries Esteban because she understands that it is her fate. After he hits her, she never talks to him again, but she maintains a civil relationship with him until her death.

Esteban Trueba The patriarch of the Trueba family. Esteban narrates sections of the novel in the first person. He builds a vast fortune through hard work, a violent temper, and Conservative politics. He marries Clara and becomes a senator. Esteban's penchant for turning his violence on his workers and his family creates deep tensions in the family, which are finally resolved through his love and respect for his granddaughter, Alba.

Alba Blanca and Pedro Tercero's daughter, and Clara and Esteban's granddaughter. Alba reunites the family after her grandparents' estrangement, through her love for them and their love for her. She devotes her life to her family and to her love for Miguel. Alba becomes the object of all of Esteban Garcia's hatred. In the epilogue, Alba emerges as the voice behind the third-person narration of the story.

Blanca Clara and Esteban's first born. Blanca falls in love with Pedro Tercero at a young age and throughout her life defies her father to meet with him as often as possible. Blanca is caught with Pedro Tercero, and they are forced to separate for a time, during which Blanca is forced to marry Jean de Satigny. Blanca leaves Jean just before giving birth to Alba, her daughter by Pedro Tercero. Blanca raises Alba in her parents' house and continues meeting Pedro Tercero but refuses to run away with him until after the military coup, when they flee together to Canada.

H

Pedro Tercero Pedro Segundo's son. As a young boy, Pedro Tercero falls deeply in love with Blanca and continues to love her throughout his life. As he reaches adolescence, Pedro Tercero becomes a revolutionary and a songwriter. He is greatly respected by the peasants, and his music is very popular with revolutionary students. First for his revolutionary activities and then for his relations with Blanca, Pedro Tercero is banned from Tres Marias, but he continues to meet Blanca in secret. He eventually pays for these meetings with three of his fingers, but he still does not give up Blanca. When the Socialists come to power, Pedro Tercero joins the government. At Blanca's request, he saves Esteban's life. After the military coup, Esteban saves his life and helps him to escape to Canada with Blanca.

Pedro Segundo Pedro Garcia's son. Pedro Segundo is the foreman and caretaker of Tres Marias. Although he works closely with Esteban for much of his life, he never becomes friends with him, but he does develop a close friendship with Clara. Pedro Segundo never joins the revolutionaries, nor does he denounce them. He leaves Tres Marias after Esteban discovers that his son, Pedro Tercero, is Blanca's lover.

Esteban Garcia Pancha and Esteban Trueba's grandson. Esteban Garcia despises Esteban Trueba for not allowing him to be acknowledged. As a boy, he turns Pedro Tercero in to Esteban. Later, he requests Esteban's help to enter the police force and eventually rises to become the leader of the military coup, in the process venting much of his anger on Alba.

Pedro Garcia The father of Pedro Segundo. Pedro Garcia is one of the oldest residents of Tres Marias. Wise in the ways of nature, Pedro Garcia rids the property of the ant plague and sets all of Esteban's bones when they are broken in an earthquake.

Ferula Esteban Trueba's older sister. Ferula is jealous of Esteban. After Dona Ester's death, she moves in with Esteban and Clara. Ferula and Clara become great friends, and Ferula secretly desires Clara. When Esteban discovers Ferula in bed with Clara, he throws Ferula out of the house forever. As she leaves, Ferula curses Esteban. Many years later, Ferula dies in one of the city's poor neighborhoods. Clara washes Ferula's body herself.

Rosa the Beautiful The oldest del Valle daughter. Rosa is exceptionally beautiful, with transparent skin, yellow eyes, and green hair. She is engaged to Esteban Trueba but dies before they can marry, accidentally poisoned by brandy intended for Severo.

Miguel Amanda's younger brother. Miguel first sees Alba at her birth, and when he meets her again eighteen years later, he falls in love with her. Their relationship lasts through the end of the book. Miguel is also a revolutionary who joins the guerrillas after the military coup.

Jaime One of Esteban and Clara's twin boys. Jaime studies medicine and devotes his life to helping the poor.

Nicolas Jaime's twin brother. Nicolas inherits Uncle Marcos's penchant for travel and invention. He pursues spiritual enlightenment, embarrassing Esteban, and is sent out of the country.

Nana The housekeeper and nurse of the del Valle family. Nana is especially close to Clara. After Severo and Nivea's deaths, Nana moves to the Trueba household as their housekeeper.

Pancha A peasant girl at Tres Marias. Pancha is raped by Esteban Trueba, taken into his house as a housekeeper, and then thrown out when she becomes pregnant. She is the mother of an illegitimate son of Esteban Trueba's, who is the child's namesake. Pancha passes on to her son Esteban Garcia and then her grandson Esteban Garcia her resentment toward Esteban Trueba.

Jean de Satigny Blanca's husband. Jean de Satigny is a French immigrant who wants to join de Trueba family through business or marriage. He is able to marry Blanca thanks to his revelation of her affair and her subsequent pregnancy. When Blanca discovers his sexual eccentricities, she leaves him.

H

Nivea del Valle The mother of Clara, Rosa, and thirteen other children. Nivea is a suffragette. She dies after being decapitated in a car accident.

Severo del Valle Clara's father. Severo is a businessman who becomes a politician with the Liberal party.

Uncle Marcos Nivea's favorite brother, and Clara's favorite uncle. Uncle Marcos is an explorer and inventor who stays with the del Valle family between trips. Although Uncle Marcos dies early on, he leaves his books and stories, which pass on to every del Valle-Trueba child.

Dona Ester Trueba A direct descendant of one of Peru's oldest families. In her youth, Ester fell in love with and married the lower class immigrant Trueba. The money she brought to the marriage quickly ran out, her husband died, and she is afflicted by severe arthritis, which confines her to a wheelchair. She dies shortly after Esteban has finished restoring Tres Marias.

Transito Soto A prostitute that Esteban Trueba first encounters while restoring Tres Marias. Transito borrows money from Esteban to move to the city and establish a brothel there. In good faith, Transito returns the favor to Esteban many years later by helping him secure Alba after she is captured.

Amanda A lower-class woman, active in university counter-culture. Amanda has a relationship with Nicolas and gets pregnant. Jaime, who is in love with her, performs the abortion. Shortly after the abortion, Amanda disappears from the story. She reappears twenty years later when Jaime helps to save her from illness due to drug addiction.

Ana Diaz A student revolutionary who first meets Alba during the occupation of the university. Later, Ana helps Alba survive in the military dictator's detention centers.

Father Jose Dulce Maria A revolutionary priest from Tres Marias. Father Jose teaches and repeatedly helps Pedro Tercero.

The Candidate An unnamed character who runs for president for the Socialist Party every single year, never expecting to win. Over these years he and Jaime become friends. He is as surprised as the Conservatives are when he wins the election. He does his best as president, but he has great difficulties running the country in the face of the Conservatives' attempts to undermine his government. He is one of the first people killed during the Military Coup.

Rumanian Rostipov An itinerant doctor who diagnoses Clara's mutism. Rumanian realizes that Clara has stopped speaking because she does not want to speak.

Professor Sebastian Gomez A professor at the university that Alba and Miguel attend. Sebastian Gomez helps them to organize the occupation of the school.

The Poet An unnamed character who is friends with Clara and a frequent visitor at the big house on the corner.

The King of the Pressure Cookers One of Blanca's many suitors. Esteban does not like him because he appears to be Jewish.

Barrabas The del Valle's dog.

ANALYSIS OF MAJOR CHARACTERS

CLARA Clara is barely aware of the material world. She is most interested in communicating with spirits and pays attention to mundane details such as domestic chores only in times of extreme necessity. Clara is often described as floating through the world. At times, this refers to her literally levitating; at other times, it shows the way she is able to ignore much of what she does not want to deal with. Clara's temper is extremely calm. She inspires great respect and devotion in all those who meet her, from Esteban to his sister Ferula to his foreman Pedro Segundo. Although she can see it in advance, Clara never fights her destiny. She is not, however, passive. When she faces a situation that she does not like, she proceeds to change it in quiet, subtle ways, such as adding little rooms to the big house on the corner bit by bit until, although it looks the same on the outside, it is completely transformed. Clara's character changes very little as she grows from a young girl into an old woman.

H

BLANCA Blanca is very close to her mother and very distant from her father. She is raised by Clara and Ferula together and quickly devises illnesses that get her returned home when she is sent away to school. Unlike her mother, Blanca is quite practical. After her divorce from Jean de Satigny, and even moreso after Clara's death, Blanca runs the big house on the corner. Like both of her parents, Blanca is incredibly stubborn. Even while she runs his house, she never asks for a cent from her father, instead supporting herself through her ceramics.

Blanca is defined primarily by her love for Pedro Tercero. However, she is not simply attached to him. In fact, for most of the novel she is separated from Pedro Tercero as much by her own choice as by outside circumstance. It is precisely the idea of her love for Pedro Tercero that defines Blanca more than any actual relationship the two may have.

ALBA Alba is defined primarily through the effects she has on those around her and through her reactions to their actions. It is in fact in reaction to her detention, torture, and rape at the hands of Esteban Garcia that she convinces her grandfather to help her write the story of their family in order to, as she puts it, "reclaim the past and overcome terrors of my own."

ESTEBAN TRUEBA Esteban is obsessive, violent, and materialistic. He devotes his life to his business and political careers, determined first to become rich and then to become powerful. He owes much of his success to the labor of the peasants at Tres Marias, but he never treats them with respect or equality. From the time he becomes engaged to Clara through the end of his life, Esteban is passionately in love with her. His love for her is so strong it is like an obsession. It is not, however, enough to curb his temper, even toward her. Esteban achieves his material goals but is not able to be close to anyone except his granddaughter Alba. As he ages, Esteban begins to see the negative outcomes of his violent, selfish actions and becomes increasingly aware of how lonely he is.

THEMES, MOTIFS, AND SYMBOLS

THEMES

THE STRUGGLE BETWEEN CLASSES The major characters in *The House of the Spirits* come from two opposing classes: the landed aristocracy and the peasants. Most of the population of Latin America, as well as all of the characters in the novel, belong to one of these two classes. Essentially the only other class distinction that might be drawn is that occupied by those in civil service. Peasants can join the police force or the army and gain access to education and a higher class status, which is the case of Esteban Garcia. The del Valle and Trueba families represent the land-owning upper-class criollos (a criollo is a person who is born and raised in South America but is a direct descendant of Spaniards), while the Garcias represent the peasants. The two classes come into conflict because one (upper) owns the land that the other (lower) works on. Especially in rural areas such as Tres Marias, the upper classes control all of the infrastructure, such as schools, transportation, banks, and hospitals, as well as all of the capital. As the upper classes prosper, conflict mounts when that prosperity is not equally distributed.

Several different attitudes are presented toward this inequality in *The House of the Spirits*. Esteban Trueba represents the conservative view—that the status quo should be maintained and that there is no reason for the peasants to share in the upper class's wealth or to change their situation. Pedro Tercero Garcia represents the revolutionary peasants who will work to make that change happen. The Trueba women, as well as Jaime, support the peasants. This sets up an important alliance between all of those who are subjugated by the patriarchal system.

Simply by making class struggle a major theme of the novel, *The House of the Spirits* supports the view of the peasants: the conservatives would not see class struggle as a problem, let alone a topic around which to organize a novel. The third person narration of the story is in fact given in the perspective of Alba, a staunch supporter of the socialist revolution. Alba's views also prevail in the retrospective commentary of Esteban Trueba, who slowly comes to accept his granddaughter's position.

THE POWER OF WOMEN The protagonists of the novel are all women who work in different and subtle ways to assert their rights. *The House of the Spirits* can be seen as a woman-centered response to the paradigmatic text of magical realism: Gabriel Garcia Marquez's *One Hundred Years of Solitude*. Where *One Hundred Years of Solitude* centers around three generations of men, with the women whom they love as important but secondary characters, *The House of the Spirits* does the opposite. Clara, Blanca, and Alba remain the focus of the story, while Esteban, Pedro Tercero, and Miguel enter the story because they are the men those women love or marry. Experiences particularly central to the lives of women dominate the minor as well as the major events in the story, such as the detailed descriptions of each childbirth and the abortion, as well as the presentation of physical and sexual violence against women.

Aside from Nivea's commitment to female suffrage, the women rarely explicitly condemn gender inequality. Each woman's life is, however, marked by it. All of the women in *The House of the Spirits* are strong women who do not bow to mistreatment. They choose subtle responses the situations, though, instead of outright revolt. This very method of resistance can be seen as particularly feminine. If violence and activity are male traits, while gentleness and passivity are female ones, *The House of the Spirits* shows that this does not mean that men accomplish things and change things while women do not. On the contrary, the women in *The House of the Spirits* effect more long-lasting and drastic changes than do any of the men. While the men lead revolutions that topple governments, those revolutions are themselves quickly toppled. The women's subtler methods of teaching literacy and basic healthcare, setting curses, and refusing to speak are far more effective in exacting permanent change.

THE IMPORTANCE OF GENEALOGY Although genealogy is a subtle theme in the novel, it is ultimately the source of the denouement. Almost all of the characters in the story belong to either the del Valle-Trueba family, or else to the Garcia family. The family name or genealogy to which each character belongs determines her or his class position. Genealogy does not, however, follow simply from biological parenting. In fact, the bloodlines of the Trueba and Garcia families cross repeatedly, but Esteban Trueba works hard to assure that their family names and their genealogies do not. In the novel, it is less whose genes you share and more the last name you carry that determines genealogy. At the birth of each child, the question of last name is raised. In addition, at each point that a character wishes to mark a drastic shift in alliances away from their father or family, they change their last name. Despite Esteban's efforts to make genealogy by name the only type of genealogy that matters, his refusal to acknowledge some of his biological children ultimately comes back to haunt him.

CIVILIZATION VS. BARBARITY The unnamed country in *The House of the Spirits*, like Allende's native Chile, is divided between modern city and largely undeveloped countryside, and between an aristocratic and a peasant class, with little in between. One of the oldest tropes or models for understanding the great divergences in Latin American culture is that of culture versus nature or civilization versus barbarity.

The traditional view of civilization and barbarity holds that while nature is bountiful and has restorative powers, it is barbaric and needs the influence of civilization in order to be productive. This same view considers civilization the realm of the upper classes and the cities; it is rational and well ordered. While several of the characters in *The House of the Spirits* subscribe to these traditional views, the novel works to break down any neat divisions between civilization and barbarity. The beliefs and practices of those who believe themselves to be civilized are shown to often be inhumane, irrational, ineffective, and backward. At the same time, the "barbaric" peasants demonstrate the most levelheaded, successful responses to everything from natural disasters to politics.

MOTIFS

WRITING *The House of the Spirits* begins and ends with the narrators referring explicitly to her use of Clara's journals in order to write the story at hand. Of course, the words of this narrator were written by Isabel Allende. Allusions to Clara's writing pervade the novel. Special attention is given to the ways in which each woman learns to write, and the moments when writing acquires meaning in her life. Both Clara and Alba first learn how to write and then learn how to use writing. Writing serves as testimony both on a personal and on a political level, bearing witness to events for the purpose of broadcasting them to a wider audience that may be able to learn from or even remedy the events testified to. On the personal level, Alba and other family members are able to piece together their "true" family history based on Clara's writings; on the political level, Alba is able to testify to the abuses of power of the military regime through her writing. Alba's writing is also a metaphor for Isabel Allende's writing of *The House of the Spirits* as a testimony to events that took place in her native Chile during her lifetime.

FATE Chance or strange twists of fate recur repeatedly in *The House of the Spirits*. These are thematized in Clara's clairvoyance, which allows her to understand people's fates and to predict the future. They also structure the plot, which revolves around the encounters and reencounters of members of the del Valle-Trueba family and the Garcia family with each other and with their natural and political environment. Each of the romantic couples in the novel meets seemingly by chance at a young age and years later realizes that things were meant to be. Just as loves return and persist through a strange combination of chance and design, so do other connections, such as friendships and debts. Although Clara must come to realize that she can predict but not change the future, fate is not an entirely arbitrary experience in *The House of the Spirits*. Rather, each character's fate is the result of all of their actions, great and small, just as the country's fate is determined by the particular combination of political influences that those characters exert.

SYMBOLS

THE BIG HOUSE ON THE CORNER Esteban builds a big house on the corner that on the surface is straightforward, if somewhat ostentatious. Similarly, *The House of the Spirits* can be read as a traditional romance novel, following a single family over several generations. However, Esteban's house ends up full of complicated and impractical additions. Despite its apparently traditional structure, *The House of the Spirits* contains an enormous number of complicated twists of plot. The title of the novel underlines the association: *The House of the Spirits* refers both to the book as a whole, and also to the big house on the corner, which, thanks to Clara, is always full of ghosts and spirits.

IMPORTANT QUOTATIONS EXPLAINED

---

1. *Barrabas came to us by sea, the child Clara wrote in her delicate calligraphy. She was already in the habit of writing down important matters, and afterward, when she was mute, she also recorded trivialities, never suspecting that fifty years later I would use her notebooks to reclaim the past and overcome terrors of my own.*

These are the first words of the novel, and they are repeated, almost exactly but in reverse order, as the last words of the novel. The "I" in this quote is Alba, speaking about her grandmother. Although Alba is one of the principal narrators of the story, she almost always uses the third person. This sentence and the epilogue are the only two places she expresses herself in the first person. Clara is Alba's grandmother.

Writing is thematized in *The House of the Spirits*. This is a metatextual gesture: by having her characters openly discuss writing, Allende refers to her own process of creating *The House of the Spirits*. We do not learn until the epilogue that the "I" from these opening lines is Alba. It is easy to assume that the "I" here refers to Allende herself, since it talks about the process of writing the text we are reading. While Alba is in many ways based on Allende, it is important to distinguish the two. Allende purposefully created Alba as a character who is both the subject of the novel and one of its narrators.

---

2. *At birth Rosa was white and smooth, without a wrinkle, like a porcelain doll, with green hair and yellow eyes—the most beautiful creature to be born on earth since the days of original sin, as the midwife put it, making the sign of the cross.*

Rosa is Clara's older sister. She is Esteban's first fiancé but dies before they can be married. This passage is a perfect example of the way magic realism works in the novel. It is not realistic for anyone to have pure white skin, green hair, and yellow eyes, but in the novel, Rosa is a very real character. Although her beauty is otherworldly, she has to deal with it in very real and realistic ways. She has to tan very carefully because her skin is so pale, and she must wash her hair with special herbs to make it a more natural color.

The midwife's reference to original sin and her making the sign of the cross emphasize that the setting for the novel is a Catholic country. Within that context, if Rosa is to remain untouched by original sin, she must be a saint or die young. Her mother realizes that Rosa is too beautiful to last and is not surprised when she dies before marrying Esteban.

---

3. *He could hardly guess that the solemn, cubic, dense, pompous house, which sat like a hat amidst its green and geometric surroundings, would end up full of protuberances and incrustations, of twisted staircases that led to empty spaces, of turrets, or small windows and could not be opened, doors hanging in midair, crooked hallways, and portholes that linked the living quarters so that people could communicate during the siesta, all of which were Clara's inspiration.*

Esteban builds the big house on the corner, described here, during his courtship with Clara. This description of the house is given as Esteban is building it but foreshadows what will happen to the house throughout the course of the novel. The elements that Esteban and Clara contribute to the house reflect their respective characters. Esteban is practical and serious, while Clara is imaginative and creative.

The big house on the corner is a metaphor for the novel itself: it is straightforward and clear on the surface but contains many complications and intricacies within. *The House of the Spirits* may seem like a traditional romance novel, following a single family over several generations, but it is full of plot twists and intrigue. The title *The House of the Spirits* refers both to the book as a whole and also to the big house on the corner, which, thanks to Clara, is always full of ghosts and spirits.

---

4. *"I set my curse on you, Esteban!" Ferula shouted back. "You will always be alone! Your body and soul will shrivel up and you'll die like a dog!"*

After discovering her in bed with Clara, Esteban throws Ferula out of his house and tells her that if he ever sees her near his family again, he will kill her. Ferula goes, leaving this curse on her brother. Every action in *The House of the Spirits* eventually comes back to haunt or help the characters. It is not necessary, therefore, for Ferula to curse Esteban in order for his cruelty to her to affect him later on in life. The curse here works as a foreshadowing. Ferula predicts as much as she causes what will happen to Esteban. Fitting the tradition of magical realism, however, this curse also works quite literally. Not only is Esteban increasingly estranged from his family, but his body actually begins to shrink enough for Esteban to notice it and to travel to the United States to consult doctors there.

5. *Alba did not see Esteban Garcia again until he was standing next to her in the university parking lot, but she could never forget him. She told no one of that repulsive kiss or of the dreams that she had afterward, in which Garcia appeared as a green beast that tried to strangle her with his paws and asphyxiate her by shoving a slimy tentacle down her throat.*

Esteban Garcia is Esteban Trueba's illegitimate grandson; Alba is Esteban Trueba's legitimate granddaughter. Alba does not know who Esteban Garcia is, but he haunts her. They meet, seemingly by accident, three different times. The scene in the university parking lot, which is the source for these reflections, is the third. They will meet one more time, when he will torture her.

The two sides of Esteban Trueba's character are represented and played out in his two grandchildren. Esteban Trueba's two most notable traits are his love for Clara and his mistreatment of the peasants. The first produces Alba; the second produces Esteban Garcia. Just as everything in the novel comes back around, although not always in the most fair of manners, Alba and Esteban Garcia's relationship works as the revenge of the peasants for Esteban Trueba's actions. The blurry lines between dreams and reality are demonstrated here as well. The strange creature who haunts Alba's dreams turns out to be a very real person who has literally lurked around her house and her life, waiting for a chance to avenge himself on her. All of the different times of the novel also come to play here in this passage: the moment when Alba meets Esteban Garcia in the parking lot, all of the other times she has met and will meet him, the time before either of them was born when the nightmare was unleashed, and the time after their last meeting when Alba will try to make sense of it all.

The House on Mango Street

Sandra Cisneros (1954–)

CONTEXT

Sandra Cisneros was born in 1954 in Chicago to a Spanish-speaking Mexican father and an English-speaking mother of Mexican descent. She was the third child and only daughter in a family of seven children. While she spent most of her childhood in one of Chicago's Puerto Rican neighborhoods, she also traveled back and forth to Mexico with her family. Cisneros has published two books of poetry, *My Wicked Wicked Ways* (1992) and *Loose Woman* (1995); a children's book titled *Hair/Pelitos* (1997); a collection of stories titled *Woman Hollering Creek and Other Stories* (1992); and, most recently, a second novel, *Caramelo* (2003).

H

Cisneros is part of a group of Chicana and Latina writers who became prominent in the 1980s and 1990s, among them Gloria Anzaldua, Laura Esquivel, and Julia Alvarez. *Chicana* refers to a woman of Mexican descent who lives in the United States. *Latina* is a more encompassing word, referring to women from all Latin-American countries. These women were part of a larger group of American minority women, such as Amy Tan and Toni Morrison, who found success as writers at the end of the twentieth century. While many of them had been writing for some time, renewed interest in the issues of race and gender in the 1980s provided a milieu in which their work became a vital part of the dialogue taking place.

The House on Mango Street received mostly positive reviews when it was published in 1984, and it has sold more than two million copies worldwide. However, some male Mexican-American critics have attacked the novel, arguing that by writing about a character whose goal is to leave the barrio (a neighborhood or community where most of the residents are of Spanish-speaking origin), Cisneros has betrayed the barrio, which they see as an important part of Mexican tradition. Others have criticized the novel as encouraging assimilation, labeling Cisneros a *vendida*, or sellout. Such critics have condemned Cisneros for perpetuating what they see as negative stereotypes of Mexican-American men (the wife-beaters, the overbearing husbands), while at the same time contending that the feminism Cisneros embraces was created by white women. Cisneros's defenders claim that a Mexican-American woman's experiences are very different from the experiences of a Mexican-American man, and that it's therefore unfair to expect Cisneros, a woman, to present a unified front with male Mexican-American writers. In *The House on Mango Street*, Cisneros focuses on the problems of being a woman in a largely patriarchal Hispanic society.

The House on Mango Street consists of what Cisneros calls "lazy poems," vignettes that are not quite poems and not quite full stories. The vignettes are sometimes only two or three paragraphs long, and they often contain internal rhymes, as a poem might. This form also reflects a young girl's short attention span, flitting from one topic to another, never placing too much importance on any one event. Within these very short pieces, Cisneros introduces dozens of characters, some only once or twice, and in this way, the structure of the novel imitates the geography of the barrio. No one person has very much space, either in the barrio or on the page, and the neighborhood is small enough that even a young girl can know everyone in it by name. The conflicts and problems in these little stories are never fully resolved, just as the fates of men, women, and children in the barrio are often uncertain. Finally, the novel's structure suggests the variable fate of Chicana women, whose life stories often depend on men. Without a dominant, omniscient, masculine voice to tell the women's stories, their narratives are left waiting and unresolved.

Critics have compared *The House on Mango Street* to Virginia Woolf's *A Room of One's Own*, a long essay in which Woolf asserts that women need a place and financial resources of their own in order to write successfully. The protagonist in *The House on Mango Street*, Esperanza, does long for a place of her own, but writing is a way for her to get that place, not the other way around. In this way, *The House on Mango Street* is more similar to *A House for Mr. Biswas*, by British colonial novelist V. S. Naipaul, in which an Indian in Trinidad struggles to balance his interactions with his wife's extended family with his dream of possessing his own private space. In many ways, *The House on Mango Street* is a traditional bildungsroman—that is, a coming-of-age story. Only one year passes over the course of the novel, but Esperanza matures tremendously during this period. The novel resembles other artists' coming-of-age stories, including James Joyce's *A Portrait of the Artist as a Young Man*. Like the hero of that novel, Stephen Dedalus, Esperanza has a keen eye for observation and is gifted in her use of language.

Though Esperanza experiences two sexual assaults, this work should not be considered a sexual-abuse novel. For the young girls in *The House on Mango Street*, assault is only one aspect, and not a particularly shocking one, of growing up. The assault may change Esperanza's view of sex and men, but it does not make her want to leave the barrio—that desire begins to grow well before the assaults happen. Some feminist critics blame Cisneros for not criticizing men more strongly in the novel. After Esperanza is raped, she does not blame the boys who did it, only the girl who was not there when Esperanza needed her and the women who have not debunked romantic myths about sex. In Esperanza's world, male violence is so ordinary that blaming them for the rape would be unusual. The boys, as she says in an early section, live in their own worlds. By completely separating the men's world from the women's, Cisneros indicts both men and her culture. Her criticism is even more powerful because she veils her anger instead of making it explicit. In *The House on Mango Street*, Cisneros demonstrates her ability to critique her culture without openly or unfairly condemning it.

PLOT OVERVIEW

In a series of vignettes, *The House on Mango Street* covers a year in the life of Esperanza, a Chicana (Mexican-American girl), who is about twelve years old when the novel begins. During the year, she moves with her family into a house on Mango Street. The house is a huge improvement from the family's previous apartment, and it is the first home her parents actually own. However, the house is not what Esperanza has dreamed of, because it is run-down and small. The house is in the center of a crowded Latino neighborhood in Chicago, a city where many of the poor areas are racially segregated. Esperanza does not have any privacy, and she resolves that she will someday leave Mango Street and have a house all her own.

Esperanza matures significantly during the year, both sexually and emotionally. The novel charts her life as she makes friends, grows hips, develops her first crush, endures a sexual assault, and begins to write as a way of expressing herself and as a way to escape the neighborhood. The novel also includes the stories of many of Esperanza's neighbors, giving a full picture of the neighborhood and showing the many possible paths Esperanza may follow in the future.

After moving to the house, Esperanza quickly befriends Lucy and Rachel, two Chicana girls who live across the street. Lucy, Rachel, Esperanza, and Esperanza's little sister, Nenny, have many adventures in the small space of their neighborhood. They buy a bike, learn exciting stories about boys from a young woman named Marin, explore a junk shop, and have intimate conversations while playing Double Dutch (jumping rope). The girls are on the brink of puberty and sometimes find themselves sexually vulnerable, such as when they walk around their neighborhood in high-heeled shoes or when Esperanza is kissed by an older man at her first job. During the first half of the year, the girls are content to live and play in their child's world. At school, Esperanza feels ashamed about her family's poverty and her difficult-to-pronounce name. She secretly writes poems that she shares only with older women she trusts.

Over the summer, Esperanza slips into puberty. She suddenly likes it when boys watch her dance, and she enjoys dreaming about them. Esperanza's newfound sexual maturity, combined with the death of two of her family members, her grandfather and her Aunt Lupe, bring her closer to the world of adults. She begins to closely watch the women in her neighborhood. This second half of *The House on Mango Street* presents a string of stories about older women in the neighborhood, all of whom are even more stuck in their situations and, quite literally, in their houses, than Esperanza is. Meanwhile, during the beginning of the following school year, Esperanza befriends Sally, a girl her age who is more sexually mature than Lucy or Rachel. Sally, meanwhile, has her own agenda. She uses boys and men as an escape route from her abusive father. Esperanza is not completely comfortable with Sally's sexual experience, and their friendship results in a crisis when Sally leaves Esperanza alone, and a group of boys sexually assaults Esperanza in her absence.

Esperanza's traumatic experiences as Sally's friend, in conjunction with her detailed observations of the older women in her neighborhood, cement her desire to escape Mango Street and to have her own house. When Esperanza finds herself emotionally ready to leave her neighborhood, however, she discovers that she will never fully be able to leave Mango Street behind, and that after she leaves she'll have to return to help the women she has left. At the end of the year, Esperanza remains on Mango Street, but she has matured extensively. She has a stronger desire to leave and understands that writing will help her put distance between herself and her situation. Though for now writing helps her escape only emotionally, in the future it may help her to escape physically as well.

CHARACTER LIST

MAJOR CHARACTERS

Esperanza The novel's heroine and narrator, an approximately twelve-year-old Chicana (Mexican-American girl). Esperanza is a budding writer who wishes for a home of her own. *The House on Mango Street* chronicles a year in her life as she matures emotionally and sexually. The name Esperanza means "hope" in Spanish.

Rachel and Lucy Esperanza's best friends. Rachel and Lucy are Mexican-American sisters who live across the street from Esperanza. Lucy, the older sister, was born in Texas, while Rachel, the younger, was born in Chicago. Esperanza eventually chooses a more sexually mature friend, Sally.

Sally A young girl whom Esperanza befriends the same year she moves to Mango Street. Sally is the same age as Esperanza but is sexually bold and seems quite glamorous to Esperanza. She is not a good friend to Esperanza, abandoning her time and again to go off with boys. She has a physically abusive father and runs off before eighth grade to marry a man who won't let her see her friends or leave the house. Esperanza feels protective of Sally.

Nenny Esperanza's little sister. Nenny, whose real name is Magdalena, is a pretty, dreamy little girl for whom Esperanza is often responsible. Since Nenny is immature, she is often a source of embarrassment for Esperanza when the two of them play with Rachel and Lucy.

Marin A young woman from Puerto Rico who lives with her cousin's family. Marin spends most of her time baby-sitting and so cannot leave the house. She sells makeup for Avon and teaches Esperanza and her friends about the world of boys. Although she has a fiancé back in Puerto Rico, she also dreams about American men taking her away from Mango Street to the suburbs. At the end of the year, her cousins send her back to Puerto Rico.

Papa Esperanza's father. Originally from Mexico, Papa is less domineering than the other father figures in the neighborhood. He works most of the time and is rarely home.

Mama Esperanza's mother. Mama grew up in the United States. She is one of the strongest-willed and smartest women in the novel, yet she seems to influence Esperanza very little. She is sometimes a source of comfort for Esperanza. All of her admirable attributes are lost on Esperanza because Mama has not escaped Mango Street to live somewhere nicer.

Alicia Esperanza's friend who attends a local university. Since Alicia's mother died, her father forces her to take over the family's domestic chores. Alicia is a rare example of a neighborhood girl who has not tried to escape the neighborhood through marriage, but instead works hard and hopes to change her life from within.

Cathy Esperanza's first friend in the neighborhood. Cathy's family moves out the week after Esperanza's family moves in. She discourages Esperanza from becoming friends with Rachel and Lucy. She is one of the few characters who is not from Mexico or Latin America.

MINOR CHARACTERS IN ORDER OF APPEARANCE

Carlos and Kiki Esperanza's younger brothers. Carlos and Kiki appear infrequently, and Esperanza explains that they live in a different, male world.

Meme Ortiz The new resident of Cathy's house. Meme's real name is Juan, and he has a dog with two names.

Louie The eldest sibling in a Puerto Rican family that lives in the basement of the Ortiz house. Louie is friends with Esperanza's brothers, while Esperanza is friends with Louie's cousin Marin. Louie's other cousin appears once with a stolen car, only to get arrested later that afternoon.

The Vargas Kids An unspecified number of poorly raised, vagrant siblings whose father has abandoned them. One of the Vargas kids, Angel Vargas, dies after falling from a great height.

Uncle Nacho Esperanza's friendly uncle, who gets her to dance at her cousin's baptism in "Chanclas."

Aunt Lupe Esperanza's aunt. In her youth, Lupe was a vibrant, beautiful swimmer, but now she is old, blind, and bedridden. She listens to Esperanza's poems and encourages her to keep writing, but Esperanza and her friends mock Lupe behind her back.

Elenita A witch woman Esperanza visits to have her fortune told. Elenita reads Tarot cards and tells Esperanza that she will have "a home in the heart."

Ruthie A childish grown-up neighbor who enjoys playing with Esperanza and her friends. Ruthie's mother, Edna, is a landlady for the large building next door and ignores Ruthie.

Geraldo A Mexican man Marin meets at a dance. Geraldo dies in a car accident the evening she meets him. Nobody, including Marin, knows anything about him, including his last name.

Mamacita The overweight Mexican wife of another neighbor. Mamacita comes to America at great expense to her husband, but she is wildly unhappy. She never learns English and never leaves her third-floor apartment.

Rafaela A neighborhood woman whose husband locks her in their apartment because he is afraid she'll run off. Rafaela sends money down on a clothesline to Esperanza and her friends so they can buy her sweet juices from the convenience store.

Minerva The married woman in the neighborhood who is most similar to Esperanza. Minerva and Esperanza share their poems with each other. She is only two years older than Esperanza but already has a husband and two children. Her husband leaves for long periods, only to return in a violent rage.

Tito A neighborhood boy who relates to girls in violent and sexual ways. Tito flirts with Esperanza by pushing her in front of an open fire hydrant, and later he steals Sally's keys in order to get her to kiss him and his friends.

Sire Esperanza's first crush. Sire sometimes stares at Esperanza, and though she is afraid, she tries sometimes to look back at him. Sire and his girlfriend Lois hang around outside late at night. Esperanza's father tells her Sire is a punk, and Esperanza's mother tells her Lois is the kind of girl who will go with a boy into an alley.

Earl A neighbor who works nights and tries to sleep during the day. Earl sometimes brings women home with him for short periods. The neighbors see these women at different times, and each thinks a different woman is his wife, but the women are probably prostitutes.

The Three Sisters Old ladies whom Esperanza meets at Lucy and Rachel's baby sister's wake. The three sisters are mysterious and guess Esperanza's hopes and dreams. They advise Esperanza always to return to Mango Street after she leaves it.

ANALYSIS OF MAJOR CHARACTERS

ESPERANZA As Esperanza matures during the year that makes up *The House on Mango Street*, she experiences a series of awakenings, the most important being a sexual awakening. At the beginning of the novel, Esperanza is not quite ready to emerge from the asexuality of childhood. She is completely ignorant about sex and says that boys and girls live in completely different worlds. She is so much a child that she cannot even speak to her brothers outside of the house. When she becomes an adolescent, she begins to experiment with the power she, as a young woman, has over men. Marin teaches her fundamental facts about boys, but the first major step in Esperanza's awareness of her sexuality is when she and her friends explore the neighborhood in high-heeled shoes. She relishes the power the shoes seem to give her, and she plays with the idea that physical beauty could help her escape the squalor of her surroundings. Esperanza quickly learns, however, that the patriarchal society in which she lives denies the power of female sexuality. The bum who attempts to kiss Rachel is the first in a series of men who will use force to take what girls don't want to give freely. After being sexually assaulted, Esperanza decides to try to forget some of what she has learned about sex in the past year in order to focus on writing. By the end of the novel, Esperanza's views on sex have evolved, and she rejects sex as a means of escape.

Esperanza's moral sense develops from an intense individualism to a feeling of responsibility toward the people in her community. As a child, Esperanza wants only to escape Mango Street. Her dreams of self-definition don't include the fact that she has any responsibility to her family or to the people around her, and she wishes to leave them all behind. Once Esperanza has become familiar with the people in her neighborhood, however, she begins to feel affection and, ultimately, responsibility for them. She no longer sees herself as an individual striving for self-determination. Instead, she recognizes herself as a member of a social network who must give back to her community in order to break the cycle of poverty that plagues the neighborhood. Esperanza also develops feelings of moral responsibility toward her community of women. Her negative experiences as Sally's friend show that she has the courage to try to help her friends, even if they do not always understand that they need to help her as well. Not until she talks with the three sisters and Alicia, however, does Esperanza understand that helping the neighborhood women will be a lifelong effort.

Esperanza's final and most important awakening is her realization of her writing ability, which gives her the means to escape from Mango Street. Because Esperanza is a writer, she is a keen observer, and we see her powers of observation mature. She is present in all of the early stories she narrates, but by the middle of the novel she is able to narrate stories based wholly on observation of the people around her. This change shows that she is becoming an artist, and also that she is becoming more detached from her neighborhood, since she does not always see herself in the stories she tells. By the end of *The House on Mango Street*, she knows she has become more detached from her home through her writing. Although she has not yet found a home of her own, her writing has helped her to find privacy within herself.

SALLY When Esperanza begins desiring boys, she seeks out a friend in Sally, whom boys find desirable. Sally seems to be beautiful and cruel, like the women Esperanza admires in movies. She leans against the fence at school and doesn't talk to anyone. Rumors about Sally's promiscuity circulate, but Esperanza doesn't believe them. Instead, she thinks of Sally as a kindred spirit, someone who also spends her time dreaming of escaping the neighborhood. Sally, however, is not interested only in driving boys crazy and then laughing them away, as the women in the movies do. Instead, she finds safety and comfort in sex, feelings she does not find at home with her abusive father. Sally's sexual exploits make Esperanza uncomfortable, since at this point Esperanza is interested in sex only abstractly. Eventually, this discomfort becomes extreme, and Sally ends up putting Esperanza in physical danger. Sally herself changes little, but Esperanza's understanding of her changes dramatically. Esperanza's experiences as Sally's friend make Esperanza realize she has tried to mature too quickly. In the end, Sally is a pitiable, not enviable, figure in Esperanza's life.

NENNY As the younger sister, Nenny is often Esperanza's responsibility, and though her innocence is a major source of annoyance for Esperanza, it also signals Nenny's independence. In many ways, Nenny is a pesky little sister. Esperanza must introduce Nenny to her new friends and keep her away from bad influences, such as the Vargas kids. Nenny also has qualities that Esperanza covets, including two names ("Nenny" is short for "Magdalena"), pretty eyes, and shiny, straight hair. Though Nenny can be a nuisance and a tag-along, and her actions often embarrass and annoy Esperanza, she frequently demonstrates her independence. When Esperanza, Rachel, and Lucy make up chants about hips, Nenny recites old chants that everyone already knows. Similarly, when Rachel and Lucy describe clouds with creative metaphors, Nenny gives the clouds everyday names such as Jose and Alicia. Nenny's apparent refusal to be creative embarrasses Esperanza, but her choices suggest she has her own way of surviving on Mango Street.

Nenny and Esperanza don't seem very much alike, but their differences in age and sociability mask their fundamental similarities. Nenny and Esperanza laugh at the same things, even those things others don't understand are funny. More important, Nenny and Esperanza are both dreamers. While Esperanza imagines a world outside the barrio, Nenny turns the outside world into the barrio by giving the clouds the same names as her neighbors. By doing so, she enlarges her world and makes it bearable. She turns Mango Street into the center of the universe, a place where she can be happy. Nenny and Esperanza are also very steadfast in their ideas, though Nenny is less likely to go along with the other girls if her views differ. While Esperanza, Lucy, and Rachel bounce ideas off each other, Nenny pursues her own idea. She is not distracted from her dreams, even when the other girls give her dirty looks. Despite Nenny's similarities to Esperanza, Nenny does not have as much a part in Esperanza's narrative as other women. Esperanza observes most of the women in her life closely and gives each of them a chapter—except for Nenny. Nenny ultimately recedes from view as Esperanza pursues life beyond Mango Street.

THEMES, MOTIFS, AND SYMBOLS

THEMES

THE POWER OF LANGUAGE Throughout *The House on Mango Street*, particularly in "No Speak English," those who are not able to communicate effectively (or at all) are relegated to the bottom levels of society. Mamacita moves to the country to be with her husband, and she becomes a prisoner of her apartment because she does not speak English. She misses home and listens to the Spanish radio station, and she is distraught when her baby begins learning English words. His new language excludes her. Similarly, Esperanza's father could not even choose what he ate when he first moved to the country, because he did not know the words for any of the foods but ham and eggs. Esperanza's mother may be a native English speaker, but her letter to the nuns at Esperanza's school is unconvincing to them in part because it is poorly written.

Esperanza observes the people around her and realizes that if not knowing or not mastering the language creates powerlessness, then having the ability to manipulate language will give her power. She wants to change her name so that she can have power over her own destiny. Her Aunt Lupe tells her to keep writing because it will keep her free, and Esperanza eventually understands what her aunt means. Writing keeps Esperanza spiritually free, because putting her experiences into words gives her power over them. If she can use beautiful language to write about a terrible experience, then the experience seems less awful. Esperanza's spiritual freedom may eventually give her the power to be literally free as well.

H

THE STRUGGLE FOR SELF-DEFINITION The struggle for self-definition is a common theme in a coming-of-age novel, or bildungsroman, and in *The House on Mango Street*, Esperanza's struggle to define herself underscores her every action and encounter. Esperanza must define herself both as a woman and as an artist, and her perception of her identity changes over the course of the novel. In the beginning of the novel, Esperanza wants to change her name so that she can define herself on her own terms instead of accepting a name that expresses her family heritage. She wants to separate herself from her parents and her younger sister in order to create her own life, and changing her name seems to her an important step in that direction. Later, after she becomes more sexually aware, Esperanza would like to be "beautiful and cruel" so men will like her but not hurt her, and she pursues that goal by becoming friends with Sally. After she is assaulted, she doesn't want to define herself as "beautiful and cruel" anymore, and she is, once again, unsure of who she is.

Eventually, Esperanza decides she does not need to set herself apart from the others in her neighborhood or her family heritage by changing her name, and she stops forcing herself to develop sexually, which she isn't fully ready for. She accepts her place in her community and decides that the most important way she can define herself is as a writer. As a writer, she observes and interacts with the world in a way that sets her apart from non-writers, giving her the legitimate new identity she's been searching for. Writing promises to help her leave Mango Street emotionally, and possibly physically as well.

SEXUALITY VS. AUTONOMY In *The House on Mango Street*, Esperanza's goals are clear: she wants to escape her neighborhood and live in a house of her own. These ambitions are always in her mind, but as she begins to mature, the desire for men appears in her thoughts as well. At first, the desire to escape and the desire for men don't seem mutually exclusive, but as Esperanza observes other women in the neighborhood and the marriages that bind them, she begins to doubt that she can pursue both. Most of the women Esperanza meets are either trapped in marriages that keep them on Mango Street or tied down by their children. Esperanza decides she does not want to be like these women, but her dire observations of married life do not erase her sexual yearnings for neighborhood boys.

Esperanza decides she'll combine sexuality with autonomy by being "beautiful and cruel" like Sally and the women in movies. However, Esperanza finds out that being "beautiful and cruel" is impossible in her male-dominated society when she experiences sexual assault. In her dreams about being with Sire, Esperanza is always in control, but in her encounter with the boys who assault her, she has no power whatsoever. The assault makes Esperanza realize that achieving true independence won't be possible if she pursues relationships with the men in her neighborhood. She puts aside her newfound sexual awareness, rejoins Lucy and Rachel, her less sexually mature friends, and spends her time concentrating on writing instead of on boys. She chooses, for the present, autonomy over sexuality, which gives her the best chance of escape.

WOMEN'S UNFULFILLED RESPONSIBILITIES TO EACH OTHER Early in the novel, Esperanza says that boys and girls live in different worlds, and this observation proves true of men and women in every stage of life. Since the women's world is often isolating and grants women so little power, Esperanza feels that women have a responsibility to protect and make life easier for each other. However, on Mango Street, this responsibility goes unfulfilled. The boys and men in *The House on Mango Street* are consistently violent, exploitative, or absent, but their world is so foreign to the women that no woman rebels against the men or calls for them to change. Esperanza may call out for women to help each other in the face of the unchanging male world, but no one answers.

Esperanza accepts more responsibility for women as she matures, and as she does, she confronts other women's indifference more directly. At first Esperanza is responsible only for her younger sister, Nenny, but her responsibilities grow when she befriends Sally. Esperanza tries to save Sally from having to kiss a group of boys in "The Monkey Garden." However, when Esperanza tries to enlist one of the boys' mothers to help her, the mother refuses. Later, Sally abandons Esperanza and leaves her vulnerable to male attackers in "Red Clowns." Esperanza expects female friends to protect each other, and Sally does not fulfill this responsibility. Ultimately, Esperanza understands that even if and when she leaves Mango Street, she will continue to take responsibility for the women in her neighborhood. She feels the responsibility deeply and will not forget it.

MOTIFS

NAMES Esperanza is one of the only characters in *The House on Mango Street* with just one name—most characters have two. Some have a real name and a nickname, such as Nenny, whose real name is Magdalena, and Aunt Lupe, whose real name is Guadeloupe. Others have an English name and a Spanish name, such as Meme Ortiz, whose Spanish name is Juan, and Meme's dog, which has unspecified names in both languages. These dual or multiple names emphasize the mix of cultures and languages that make up Esperanza's neighborhood and the difficulties her neighbors have in figuring out who they are, in their families, their neighborhood, even their country.

The power of names to transform and empower fascinates Esperanza, who struggles with how to define herself. She mentions the transforming power of names in "My Name," where she picks Zeze the X as a new name for herself. She also gives her current name, Esperanza, several definitions in order to make it more powerful. In "And Some More," Esperanza discusses the fact that the Eskimos have thirty names for snow. She speculates that the Eskimos have so many names for snow because snow is so important to them, which suggests that the more names a person has, the more important he or she is. Rachel rejoins by saying that her cousin has three last names and two first names, indicating that she, too, shares the theory that the more names one has, the better. Eventually, Esperanza places more importance on language and description than on naming alone, but her obsession with naming shows an early understanding of the importance of language.

FALLING Throughout *The House on Mango Street*, people fear falling and sometimes actually fall, which suggests the constant threat of failure or injury. Images of falling appear frequently. Angel Vargas and Meme both fall from significant heights, both with disastrous results. Marin waits for a star to fall to change her life. Esperanza even describes herself as floating in an early vignette, as a red balloon on a tether. When she finally abandons her tether, she hopes she'll fly away and not fall to the ground as

Angel and Meme did. Esperanza faces the same fear of falling that her neighbors do, and she hopes for a different fate.

WOMEN BY WINDOWS Mango Street is full of women who are trapped by their husbands, fathers, children, or their own feelings of inadequacy. Esperanza's long-dead great-grandmother married unwillingly and spent her whole life sitting sadly by her window. Four women in Esperanza's neighborhood are trapped in their apartments—Mamacita, Rafaela, Minerva, and Sally. They sit by their windows all day and look down onto the street. The group makes up a kind of community, but these women cannot communicate, and each keeps to her place without much complaint. Esperanza is determined not to become a woman sitting by a window, and she understands there is something amiss among the women in her world. Eventually, she tries to help by supporting women when she can. For now, however, the women represent a disturbing failure: that of the more liberated women to help their confined and unhappy neighbors.

SYMBOLS

SHOES Shoes in *The House on Mango Street* frequently evoke images of sex and adult femininity, and for Esperanza they illustrate the conflict she feels between her emerging sexual attractiveness and her desire for independence. Esperanza makes the connection between shoes and sex for the first time when she, Lucy, and Rachel try on high- heeled shoes a neighbor gives them. The shoes transform their scarred, childish feet and legs into long, slim women's legs, and what began as a childhood game of dress-up becomes something more dangerous, as male neighbors ogle them hungrily. That afternoon, they are happy to abandon the shoes, claiming they are bored with them. For the moment, Esperanza can smoothly shed her new sexual attractiveness and become a child again.

When shoes appear again, Esperanza can't discard them so easily. When Esperanza attends a dance and wears brown saddle shoes with her pretty new dress, she is almost paralyzed with embarrassment and self-consciousness. Men ask her to dance, and she wants to dance, but she wants more to hide her worn-out little-girl shoes. Though she eventually dances with her uncle and relishes the stares of a boy, she is aware of her clunky shoes the entire time. When Esperanza wants to befriend Sally, who is sexually mature, she describes Sally's black suede shoes and wonders if she can convince her mother to buy her a similar pair. When Sally abandons Esperanza in the monkey garden in order to fool around with boys, Esperanza thinks her own feet look foreign. Finally, in Esperanza's vision of her dream house, her shoes are beside the bed, suggesting that she does have or will have some measure of control over her own sexuality, if only in her imagination.

TREES Esperanza expresses respect and admiration for trees throughout *The House on Mango Street*, and her affection stems from her identification with their appearance, resilience, and independence. In "Four Skinny Trees," Esperanza personifies the trees in her front yard, saying she and they understand each other, even that they teach her things. She relates to the trees because they don't seem to belong in the neighborhood and because they persevere despite the concrete that tries to keep them in the ground. Esperanza herself does not seem to belong, and she plans to persevere despite the obstacles posed by her poor neighborhood. Esperanza views the trees almost as a reflection of herself, comparing her own skinny neck and pointy elbows to the tree's spindly branches.

The tree in Meme Ortiz's backyard has particular resonance for Esperanza. Even though the tree eventually turns out to be dangerous, since Meme jumps out of it and breaks both of his arms, Esperanza claims it is the most memorable part of Meme's backyard. She points out that the tree is full of squirrels and that it dwarfs her neighborhood in age and size. This tree has flourished even more than the trees in her front yard have, again without anybody doing much to help it. Meme's hardy tree was probably once like the elms in Esperanza's yard, which suggests that Esperanza will perhaps be able to grow into a strong and independent woman despite the setbacks in her first year on Mango Street.

POETRY *The House on Mango Street* contains many small poems and references to poems, which emphasize the importance of language to Esperanza and her neighbors. These references and poems include a poem Esperanza writes, jump-roping chants, and simple, internal rhymes within paragraphs of the text. We never hear some of the poems, such as those Esperanza recites to Ruthie, or those Minerva writes. The abundance of poetry suggests that the women and girls on Mango Street try to make their lives better by describing the world with beautiful language. The novel itself, with its many internal rhymes, is in some ways Esperanza's long poem, her attempt to make some of the unpoetic aspects of her life less hard and more ordered through poetry.

IMPORTANT QUOTATIONS EXPLAINED

---

1. *In English my name means hope. In Spanish it means too many letters. It means sadness, it means waiting.*

This remark, from the section "My Name," occurs before Esperanza says her name for the first time. Esperanza's characterization of her name shows how she channels her dissatisfaction with her given name into creativity and word play. What Esperanza says here about the word *esperanza* is neither intuitive nor true. In Spanish, *esperanza* means "hope." The word does not have a dictionary definition in English. When Esperanza says her name means "waiting," she has taken the Spanish verb *esperar*, which means "to wait or expect," and superimposed it on the noun *hope*. Similarly, sadness may come from the opposite of *esperanza*, *desesperarse*, or "despair." Later in the chapter Esperanza says she would like to give herself a new name, but she has already given her old name new meaning, using a similar-looking word with a different definition. By refusing to accept the word's conventional definitions, Esperanza shows that she possesses a writer's gift for interpretation and storytelling.

On a more literal level, the words Esperanza has chosen to associate with the Spanish meaning of her name are very negative. She has taken a positive word, *hope*, and given it three negative descriptions. The first, "too many letters," is a description of the word as it is written. As an American schoolgirl, Esperanza is frustrated by the physical difficulty of her name, which sets her apart from others. Even her siblings, Nenny, Carlos, and Kiki, have simpler, less foreign-sounding names. The next two negative descriptions are associations she has with herself. As her current self with her current name, Esperanza's life is full of sadness and waiting. Esperanza says her inner self is described by the name "Zeze the X." Zeze the X is the version of Esperanza who does not belong in the barrio.

---

2. *Until then I am a red balloon, a balloon tied to an anchor.*

Esperanza describes herself as a red balloon in "Boys and Girls" before she has made any friends in her new neighborhood. Until she has a best friend with whom she can share her secrets and who will understand her jokes, she believes she will be this red balloon. The image of the balloon suggests that she feels she is floating in anticipation of something and that she feels isolated. The color red suggests that she stands out in the neighborhood. Esperanza finds friends, Lucy and Rachel, soon after this section, but the feeling of being a balloon persists. She is still floating because she feels she does not fit in on Mango Street, and she is still isolated because she does not share her deepest secrets with her friends. In "Laughter" we learn that Esperanza's sister Nenny, not her new friends, laughs at her jokes without her having to explain them.

Esperanza has chosen to think of herself as something floating, and in this way she is similar to some of the other children on Mango Street. Both Meme Ortiz and Angel Vargas fall from great heights in early vignettes. Meme breaks both of his arms, while Angel dies. Both children are trying to fly in order to escape their lives on Mango Street. In this quote Esperanza describes herself as floating, but also as tethered to the earth. When she finally abandons her tether, she would like to fly away instead of falling, as the others have. She will either have to find a way to return to the ground without hurting herself, or to fly away without falling. By the end of *The House on Mango Street*, Esperanza discovers she is not unique in her neighborhood, but does, in fact, belong there. Only at that point can Esperanza let go of this particular metaphor and realize that she cannot float away from her community for good. She must leave it gradually and eventually return.

3. *She looked out the window her whole life, the way so many women sit their sadness on an elbow. I wonder if she made the best with what she got or was she sorry because she couldn't be all the things she wanted to be. Esperanza. I have inherited her name, but I don't want to inherit her place by the window.*

Esperanza says this of her great-grandmother and namesake, Esperanza. Her great-grandmother is the first of many women in *The House on Mango Street* who spend their lives looking out the window and longing for escape. Esperanza resolves not to end up like her great-grandmother even before she meets the other trapped women on Mango Street. These modern women, including Mamacita, Rafaela, Minerva (whose window is broken), and Sally (who has to look at the floor instead of out the window) give Esperanza an even more vivid picture of what it is like to be trapped, hardening her resolve not to be like the first Esperanza.

By repeatedly connecting the window image to the trapped women on Mango Street, Cisneros depicts a row of third-floor apartments as jail cells. Some of the women are stuck in these cells because of their husbands, but Esperanza implies that some of them could do more to change their situations. Esperanza wonders if her great-grandmother made the best of her situation, or if instead she turned her anger at her husband inward, and therefore hurt herself more than her husband could have. Esperanza asks this question only once, and she does not apply it to any of the other women she meets. Her capacity for both empathy and pity grows as she understands their particular stories better than the story of her great-grandmother, whom she never met.

4. *Sally, you lied, you lied. He wouldn't let me go. He said I love you, I love you, Spanish girl.*

H

Esperanza says this in "Red Clowns," after a group of boys has sexually assaulted her at a carnival. She repeats the accusation that her friend lied, blaming Sally for the assault instead of the boys who have hurt and traumatized her. Esperanza blames Sally for not returning after she goes off with an older boy, but the accusation goes deeper than that. Esperanza is angry that girls perpetuate the myth that sex goes hand in hand with love. "I love you, Spanish girl" is a taunting, violent refrain that has no place in the picture of sex that popular culture presents to young girls. Esperanza understands that popular media may never change, but at the very least the women who have more experience, like Sally, should debunk the myth so reality would not be such a surprise to girls like Esperanza.

Esperanza's accusation here is the culmination of a theme that is implicit in much of *The House on Mango Street*: men will not change, so women need to help each other. In "The Monkey Garden," the section before "Red Clowns," Esperanza sees Tito's mother as complicit in Sally's exploitation, since she refuses to see that her son is doing something wrong. Esperanza reacts by crying alone in a corner of the Monkey Garden. In "Red Clowns," Esperanza's pain is more acute. She screams out her accusation. Her experience with the disloyal Sally leads to Esperanza's resolution to come back to help the other women on Mango Street once she leaves. She does not want to leave the women behind in a dangerous place the way Sally left her.

5. *No, this isn't my house I say and shake my head as if shaking could undo the year I've lived here. I don't belong. I don't ever want to come from here.*

This is Esperanza's reply to Alicia in "Alicia & I Talking on Edna's Steps" after Alicia insists that Esperanza does have a house, and that it is right there on Mango Street. This exchange occurs near the end of the novel, when Esperanza is realizing she does indeed belong on Mango Street. Instead of insisting that she does not belong, here she says she doesn't *want* to belong, which suggests that Esperanza understands that she actually does. She has realized that she is not intrinsically different from the other women in her neighborhood. She has met other women in the neighborhood who write, women who share her desire to escape, women who are interested in boys, and women, like Alicia, who desire education. Her previous feelings of superiority and difference were only childish ways of obscuring the truth: Mango Street is part of Esperanza. No matter how far she goes, she will never truly escape it.

How the Garcia Girls Lost Their Accents

Julia Alvarez (1950–)

CONTEXT

How the Garcia Girls Lost Their Accents is a family epic that follows several generations of the Garcia and de la Torre families as they struggle to hold together a sense of family solidarity in the midst of migration, divorces, family disputes, and cultural change. Like the Garcia sisters of the novel, Julia Alvarez was born in the Dominican Republic and immigrated to the United States in 1960. She published *How the Garcia Girls . . .* in 1991, and this was followed by several others that also dealt with Dominican women immigrants. Alvarez wrote the novel during a period of increased immigration from the Dominican Republic, when the community of Dominicans living in the United States expanded. Along with other writers and artists, Alvarez contributed to the articulation of a new Dominican-American identity. In addition, this novel shares a space along with other works written by Caribbean immigrants who wanted to explore the experience of Spanish speakers and their descendants in the United States. The geographic proximity of the United States, as well as its historical and continuing political influence in this region, distinguishes the experiences of these communities from other immigrant groups.

Alvarez's protagonists share some things in common with the typical Dominican immigrant experience, such as the painful dislocation of family ties and difficult cultural readjustments. It is important to keep in mind, however, that most Dominicans living in the United States did not come from the privileged background that the Garcia family enjoyed. Though the girls dwell on the financial hardship they faced during the first year of life in the United States, the family drew on tremendous financial and political resources that many Dominicans did not enjoy. They perceive hardship only in comparison to the lavish and luxurious lifestyle they were used to in the Dominican Republic, where different economic conditions meant that the family could afford numerous servants and expansive estates. Even in the United States, the girls were given expensive private education and numerous opportunities to travel. In this sense, the novel does not represent the typical Dominican immigrant experience. However, it contributed to mainstream awareness of the differences between American and Dominican culture, as well as the psychological difficulties facing children who are forced to suddenly move from one cultural context to another.

For Hispanic communities in the United States, the question of whether the Garcia girls have truly lost their accents is critical. Hispanic communities have not integrated into the mainstream in the same ways that previous immigrant communities have, indicating the differences between previous patterns of migration and the current pressures that Hispanics face. Alvarez's novel illustrates a desire to retain access to the language and culture of the home nation while also incorporating oneself into the new country's culture, economy, and political system.

PLOT OVERVIEW

The four Garcia sisters, Carla, Sandra, Yolanda, and Sofia, enjoy a fairly sheltered and luxurious childhood in the Dominican Republic. They often receive exciting presents from FAO Schwarz in the United States. Carla remembers an iron bank representing Mary ascending to heaven, which she gave to one of the family's maids, who was later dismissed for stealing the bank. Yolanda plays with her boy cousin and shows him her genitals in exchange for a Human Body doll and modeling clay. She also steals a newborn kitten from its mother and puts it inside a drum that she plays until she grows bored and throws the kitten outside, where it hobbles away. The mother cat appears to her in nightmares. Sandra wants to be an artist, but her irrepressible spirit gets her in trouble, and she is thrown out of art class. She later comes upon a naked, chained, insane sculptor who scares her, and she falls and breaks her arm. She loses her artistic vision and settles for being the sculptor's muse when she realizes he had used her face in a representation of the Virgin Mary.

When their father, Carlos, gets in trouble with the secret police for agitating against the military dictatorship, the family enlists the help of a CIA operative, Vic, to get them out of the country. They flee to New York City, where they have trouble adjusting culturally and materially. Laura, the sisters' mother, comes from a wealthy and influential family in the Dominican Republic and does not like having to become a middle-class nobody in the United States. She finds comfort in supporting her daughters' endeavors, such as Yolanda's poetry and Sofia's defiance of her father's overprotective nature.

Dr. Fanning, a friend of the family, helps Carlos get a medical fellowship and offers to take the family out for a celebratory dinner once they get settled in the United States. Laura wants to make a good impression and pressures the girls to behave themselves and not ask for any special treats. After Sandra sees Mrs. Fanning kiss her father in the restroom, she insists that Dr. Fanning buy her a flamenco doll. Carla has trouble fitting into American school settings and is harassed by abusive and prejudiced schoolboys. She also is nearly molested by a perverted exhibitionist in a car. Yolanda begins to write in English and finds a way to express her own voice, though she starts off by imitating Walt Whitman. Her father criticizes her insubordination, which Yolanda perceives to be intellectual independence. Sofia is sent to the Dominican Republic as punishment for using marijuana, though she ends up getting into more trouble by spending time without a chaperone with her illegitimate cousin, Manuel.

In college, Yolanda has trouble relating to men, since she is turned off by the vocabulary men use to describe sex. Though she is attracted to a boy named Rudy, she will not sleep with him, and he accuses her of being frigid. She is hurt by this but later realizes that he was just a jerk. She later marries a man she thinks she loves, John, though at a certain point they have problems communicating. Like Rudy, he does not understand her Dominican cultural heritage and cannot appreciate the Spanish language. When Yolanda stops trusting and loving John, she cannot understand the words he uses and hears only "babble, babble." She has a mental breakdown at her parents' house, during which she can only quote and misquote bits of things she has read and heard throughout her life. She spends time in a mental hospital until she recovers. Her sister Sandra also has a mental breakdown, during which she thinks she is regressing through evolution and will eventually cease to be human.

After Sandra is released from the hospital, Sofia plans to reconcile with her father during a birthday party. She breaks tradition, in that the daughters usually come home for their father's birthday, but she hosts the party at her house to show off her German husband and two blond children. She and her father had fought when he accused her of sleeping around during a trip to Colombia, where she met her husband, Otto. She ran away from home to assert her independence and later married Otto. Though the party is going well, Sofia is hurt that her father does not express more affection toward her. She humiliates him with a seductive kiss in the ear as part of a party game.

Yolanda returns to the Dominican Republic, possibly for good, to embrace her extended family and cultural roots. Her family thinks she's crazy for driving into the countryside by herself, but she ignores them. She gets lost looking for fresh guavas and then gets a flat tire. When approached by two men, she panics and pretends not to speak any Spanish. Yolanda feels more comfortable in her English-speaking American identity than with the Dominican side of her personality.

CHARACTER LIST

Carlos The overprotective father of the four Garcia sisters. Carlos resists the military dictatorship in the Dominican Republic and, as a result of his political activities, the family must flee to the United States.

Laura The mother of the four sisters. Laura must adjust to cultural and material differences in the United States, where her family name and privilege mean much less than it had in the Dominican Republic. She is proud and supportive of her daughters.

Carla The oldest of the Garcia sisters. Carla has the most difficulty adjusting to school and the English language after the move to the United States. She eventually becomes a psychologist.

Sandra The second-oldest daughter. Sandi feels stifled and frustrated as a child, and she loses her artistic vision after she suffers a broken arm. She has a mental breakdown as an adult.

Yolanda The rebellious tomboy of the family in the Dominican Republic. Once in the United States, Yolanda becomes a poet. Her difficulties with men and a painful divorce bring about a mental breakdown.

Sofia The youngest daughter of the Garcia family. Sofia's wild and rebellious streak comes out during her adolescence, when she challenges her father's authority and runs away to Germany to marry Otto.

Mundin Yolanda's favorite cousin, who asks her to prove she is a girl in exchange for pink modeling clay when they are children. Mundin later protects Sofia and Manuel from getting into trouble for having sex.

Manuel Sofia's boyfriend while she lived on the Island and her illegitimate cousin on her father's side of the family.

Victor Hubbard An American CIA operative who arranges for Carlos and his family to escape to the United States. Victor responds to the code phrase "come get your tennis shoes" and likes to intimidate the local police and sleep with young girls.

Otto A man whom Sofia meets while traveling in Colombia. Otto and Sofia fall in love, he writes her love letters, and she runs away from home to be with him in Germany.

Chucha The Garcia family's Haitian maid in the Dominican Republic. Chucha practices voodoo and sleeps in a coffin.

Gladys The family's Dominican maid. Gladys is fired for accepting a toy bank from Carla as a present.

Dr. Fanning A friend of the Garcia family who arranges for Carlos's medical fellowship and helps the family when they first arrive in the United States.

Mrs. Fanning A woman who kisses Carlos in the restroom of a Spanish restaurant during a celebratory dinner and ruins Sandra's enjoyment of a flamenco act.

John Yolanda's husband. John ceases to make sense to her and speaks only in a babbling gibberish once she realizes she doesn't love him anymore.

Rudy Yolanda's first boyfriend, who becomes frustrated because she doesn't want to have sex. Yolanda feels very insecure because of her experience with Rudy until she realizes that he had been a jerk all along.

Dona Charito Sandra's childhood art teacher, who disciplined her for disobedience instead of encouraging her talent and enthusiasm for art.

Don Jose Dona Charito's insane sculptor husband, who terrified Sandra and made her fall and break her arm. Don Jose later puts Sandra's face on a statue of the Virgin Mary.

Trujillo A real-life Dominican dictator who lives next door to the de la Torre compound in the novel and takes walks with his grandson through the adjoining grounds. His secret police threaten Carlos's and others' lives.

ANALYSIS OF MAJOR CHARACTERS

CARLOS Though the novel focuses primarily on the Garcia girls, the girls' father, Carlos, has his own set of struggles to face. Carlos agitates against Trujillo's military dictatorship, which leads to his family's flight from the Dominican Republic to the United States. As a doctor, he must face the humiliation of having to re-establish his professional reputation and credentials and not being able to provide for his family in the manner they were used to back home on the Island. He also has difficulty accepting that his daughters will mature and assimilate into American culture. He fights with his daughters when they show a spark of independence or individuality, and he insists that they must behave as Dominican women would, even though this is an unrealistic expectation. Because he left the Dominican Republic as a mature man and his daughters left when they were young children, he is in many ways culturally distinct from them. They have trouble tolerating his Dominican values when they clash with the American attitudes they have adopted regarding sexuality and gender relations.

LAURA Laura comes from a very wealthy, privileged, and influential family in the Dominican Republic. As a daughter of the de la Torre clan and a doctor's wife, she considers herself entitled to a degree of social respect and material privilege that is unrealistic to expect as a recent immigrant. Her frustration with the challenges of immigration is reflected in her snobbery, yet she attempts to make a new identity for herself as an American wife, mother, and inventor of household gadgets. She defends her daughters' individuality and creativity and supports them through their mental breakdowns. She is intensely proud of her family name, her children, and her grandchildren.

CARLA As the oldest daughter, Carla feels most out of place in the United States and has the most trouble fitting into her new social and cultural environment. She is harassed at school by malicious and prejudiced boys, and she feels isolated by her limited English language abilities. Her discomfort with puberty is exacerbated by an encounter with a perverted American exhibitionist in a car. She deals with these issues later in life by becoming a psychologist and analyzing her family's myriad mental problems.

SANDRA When Sandra is a child, her artistic abilities are frustrated by poor art instruction and a terrible fall that breaks her arm. She feels stifled as a child by her parents' desires to fit into American culture and is criticized for expressing her own hopes and needs. She grows disillusioned with American virtue after watching a drunk woman kiss her father. Her inability to express herself artistically or personally leads to an eventual mental breakdown, characterized by her belief that she is moving backward through evolution and is losing her humanity. This loss of humanity symbolizes her loss of artistic inspiration and a sense of her own unique identity.

YOLANDA Yolanda is the tomboy of the family and is a troublemaker as a child. She is haunted by the memory of a kitten that she kidnapped from its mother, as well as the fear she felt as the family struggled to leave the Dominican Republic. Once in the United States, she has difficulty interacting with men in sexual and romantic situations and eventually divorces her husband, John. This heartbreak leads to a mental breakdown and the inability to use language in a meaningful way. This is a particularly traumatic experience for Yolanda, since she is a poet and therefore places particular importance on language. She returns to the Dominican Republic after her divorce in order to reconnect to her cultural roots, though she finds she has forgotten her Spanish and stands out culturally. When faced with a challenging situation, such as car trouble at night in the middle of nowhere, she feels most comfortable in her identity as an English-speaking American woman, rather than a Dominican immigrant. She is the sister who most enjoys taking on the role of storyteller, and she hopes to untangle the past to better understand the trauma that underlies the various struggles of the entire family.

SOFIA Sofia, the youngest daughter, does not have many clear memories of life in the Dominican Republic, but she does remember the Haitian maid, Chucha, who performed voodoo spells. When she gets older, she has "non-stop boyfriends," runs off with Otto from Germany, and develops a tense and often openly hostile relationship with her father. After a failed relationship with a Dominican boyfriend, she embraces American attitudes toward sexual relationships. She challenges sexual double standards that she finds to be more pronounced in traditional Dominican culture and claims her sexual independence. She and her father begin to reconcile when she has children, but at his birthday party she continues to flaunt her sexuality and his powerlessness to control it by kissing his ear in a particularly seductive way.

THEMES, MOTIFS, AND SYMBOLS

THEMES

THE ROOTS OF FAMILY CONFLICT The interpersonal conflict within the Garcia family takes root during the point of political and cultural rupture, when the family had to leave the Dominican Republic. The fragmentation of the extended family in 1960 due to immigration leads to a spiraling dissolution of the Garcia nuclear family. As the girls mature, they grow increasingly distant from one another, their parents, and their relatives on the Island. Their integration into American culture tears them further apart from their family roots and leaves them badly prepared to deal with their parents' more traditional perspectives. During Sofia's rebellious phase, she leaves home and prompts a serious rift in the family. Carla's clinical indifference toward the family also reveals interpersonal distance. The fact that the Garcia parents commit their daughters to mental hospitals so quickly indicates that they cannot reach out to their daughters during emotionally challenging times. Though the origins of the family conflict are in the past, the effects continue to reverberate even when the girls begin families of their own.

THE PROBLEMS POSED BY SEXUALITY Sexuality poses problems for nearly every character in the novel. Yolanda's problems begin with her cousin, who promised her a Human Body doll if she'd drop her pants. She has continuing problems with a boyfriend, Rudy, who calls her frigid, and her husband, John, whom she eventually divorces. Sofia uses sexuality as a tool to rebel against her father and assert her independence. Carla sees sexuality as an embarrassing and possibly threatening aspect of human psychology, a perspective that stems from her exposure to a perverted exhibitionist in a green car. Sandra's perception of sexuality is not explicitly discussed, but it must have been influenced by her experience watching a drunk woman, Mrs. Fanning, kissing her father in the restroom while out to dinner with the entire family. All four sisters feel caught between Dominican sexual and gender norms, framed within a traditional Catholic ideology, and more liberal American and even feminist standards of behavior.

THE MEANING OF LANGUAGE Language has different cultural and literary meanings for each of the members of the Garcia family. Laura uses adopted idioms carelessly, yet always effectively communicates her meaning even if she mixes up the particular images. Yolanda would never be so careless, since she considers herself a poet with a highly discerning literary perspective. Her husband John's monolingual limitations frustrate her and lead to the end of their relationship, when they lose the ability to communicate effectively. The deterioration of her ability to make sense of language also signals her imminent mental breakdown. Sandra's breakdown is also preceded by her fear that she'll lose the ability to read and reason with language, indicating that humanity for her is symbolized by language itself. Carla's difficulties fitting into American society and communicating with the authorities, such as teachers and the police, stem from her limited English ability. For her, language has the power to exclude and isolate, in addition to the power to connect and facilitate interactions.

MOTIFS

NICKNAMES Throughout the novel, nicknames are used to convey a sense of intimacy. This intimacy can be positive, such as when the Garcia daughters refer to their mother as Mami to express affection. On the other hand, nicknames can convey a negative sense of being overly familiar, such as when John refers to Yolanda as Josephine, anglicizing her name and distorting her identity in the process.

SYMBOLS

THE MOTHER CAT The mother cat that haunts Yolanda's dreams symbolizes her home, the Dominican Republic, which reproaches her for leaving. The violation the cat suffers in losing its kitten represents the pain of a country that has lost its children, who cannot find their way home again. Yolanda is unable to find her roots when she returns home in the first chapter, representing the culmination of her search to reclaim what was lost when her family left the Dominican Republic.

THE BLACK BIRD The black bird that emerges from Yolanda's throat and attacks Dr. Payne symbolizes her fears that language, specifically her own words, could hurt the people she cares about. Her affection for and attraction to Dr. Payne is threatened by the aggressive and ugly words that could come out of her mouth. The bird freely moves from the room through the window screen, just as Yolanda might be able to freely speak her own mind if she were able to stop misquoting others and truly express her love and desires.

GUAVAS The guavas Yolanda craves when she arrives on the Island symbolize her desires to reconnect to the best memories of her childhood. She hopes the taste of the guavas will take her back to a vivid experience from the past. Instead, the outing highlights how culturally unprepared she is to pass as a Dominican woman, and how culturally American she has become as an adult.

SNOW Snow symbolizes hope for the future and the positive aspects of the American dream, as well as the terrifying potential of the unknown. Yolanda's first experience of snow makes her think of atomic fallout, and she terrifies her class with a warning of imminent doom. Once she realizes her mistake, the snow comes to symbolize the culmination of her long-held hope to experience a mysterious and wondrous occurrence she has only heard about. The unique nature of each snowflake also symbolizes the possibilities that America offers Yolanda to explore her identity and express a new voice.

IMPORTANT QUOTATIONS EXPLAINED

1. *She has been too frightened to carry out any strategy, but now a road is opening up before her. She clasps her hands on her chest—she can feel her pounding heart—and nods. Then, as if the admission itself loosens her tongue, she begins to speak, English, a few words, of apology at first, then a great flood of explanation . . .*

In Chapter 1, Yolanda gets lost while gathering fresh guavas in the countryside and gets a flat tire. While stranded, two men approach and ask if she needs help. She is frozen with terror until they ask if she is an American. At this point, she begins speaking English, which the men do not understand, and assents that she is indeed American. This is ironic, because the purpose for her trip to the Dominican Republic was to assert her Dominican identity and reconnect to her cultural and family roots. Yet she fears interacting with Dominicans outside the safety of the family compound. During this moment of panic, she feels most comfortable pretending not to understand a word of Spanish. Her behavior is considered strange by Dominican standards, since a woman would not be out alone after dark looking for fruit. She can explain herself only by remaining tightly enclosed within her American identity and sticking to the English language.

2. *His face darkened with shame at having his pleasure aroused in public by one of his daughters. He looked from one to the other. His gaze faltered. On the face of his youngest was the brilliant, impassive look he remembered from when she had snatched her love letters out of his hands.*

In Chapter 2, Carlos and Sofia attempt to reconcile their differences during his birthday party. Yet Sofia feels slighted by how her father treats her other sisters, and she decides to humiliate him during a party game. A seductive kiss in the ear leads to his shame and anger. The moment when she snatched back her love letters was the moment that led to the family rift, so the fact that Sofia continues to wear her brilliant and impassive look indicates that there has been no reconciliation. This look shows her pride in displaying her sexual independence from her father, and her unwillingness to feel the shame he insists is appropriate.

3. *The words tumble out, making a sound like the rumble of distant thunder, taking shape, depth, and substance. Yo continues: "Doc, rock, smock, luck," so many words. There is no end to what can be said about the world.*

After Yolanda's stay in the mental hospital in Chapter 3, she begins to reclaim language and its meanings. Following the period when she could only quote or misquote things she had read or heard, she is able to label objects and play word games. By rhyming and naming, Yolanda regains the ability to use language and convey meaning. This moment signals a recovery from her mental breakdown. Her realization that there are limitless things to be said about the world indicates that an artistic as well as emotional healing has taken place. She is prepared to write to a broader audience, as well as communicate with the people she loves and cares about.

4. *So, Laura thinks. So the papers have cleared and we are leaving. Now everything she sees sharpens as if through the lens of loss—the orchids in their hanging straw baskets, the row of apothecary jars Carlos has found for her in old druggists' throughout the countryside, the rich light shafts swarming with a golden pollen. She will miss this glorious light warming the inside of her skin and jewelling the trees, the grass, the lily pond beyond the hedge.*

The moment when Laura realizes that she and her family will leave the Dominican Republic for an indefinite period of time signals a dramatic and traumatic transition. The proximity of this turning point leads her to view her surroundings in different ways. The details of her home that previously hid in the background of her perceptions come forward to occupy her attention. The light and plants, which will be different in the United States, come to have a significance that fixes itself permanently into her consciousness. During the moment when she prepares for change, Laura focuses on the essence of what she loves most about the Dominican Republic, the light that contributes to a distinctive sense of place.

---

5. *There are still times I wake up at three o'clock in the morning and peer into the darkness. At that hour and in that loneliness, I hear her, a black furred thing lurking in the corners of my life, her magenta mouth opening, wailing over some violation that lies at the center of my art.*

The cat that continues to appear in Yolanda's dreams represents her home, the Dominican Republic, which reproaches her for leaving. This psychological distress unfolds into further traumas, which can be traced back to her being uprooted from the Dominican Republic, her culture, and her extended family at a very young age. This passage concludes the novel, indicating that this haunting is the root and simultaneous conclusion of her sense of violation. This violation stems from her experience as a child immigrant, and becomes the focus of her creative endeavors and her mature understanding of her cultural and personal identity. Her writing and poetry will center on the haunting that begins with the black cat and continues throughout her adult life as she struggles to incorporate the past into her plans for the future.

I Know Why the Caged Bird Sings

Maya Angelou (1928–)

CONTEXT

Maya Angelou was born Marguerite Anne Johnson on April 4, 1928, in St. Louis, Missouri. Her older brother, Bailey Johnson, Jr., could not pronounce her name when he was little, so he called her Mya Sister, then My, which eventually became Maya. When Angelou was three years old, her parents divorced and sent their children to live in the rural, segregated town of Stamps, Arkansas, with their paternal grandmother, Annie Henderson. During their teens, they lived with their mother, Vivian Baxter, in California. At the age of fifteen, Angelou began her career as a civil-rights activist of sorts. She battled racism with dogged persistence and succeeded in becoming the first African American hired to the position of streetcar conductor in San Francisco.

Angelou has remained a civil-rights activist throughout her life. At the request of Dr. Martin Luther King, Angelou became the northern coordinator for the Southern Christian Leadership Conference in the 1960s. Presidents Gerald Ford and Jimmy Carter also respected her leadership qualities. Ford appointed her to the American Revolutionary Bicentennial Advisory Commission, and Carter appointed her to the National Commission on the Observance of the International Woman's Year. At President Bill Clinton's request, she wrote and delivered a poem, "On the Pulse of Morning," for his 1993 presidential inauguration, becoming only the second poet in American history to receive such an honor.

Angelou's work in the arts includes writing, film, and theater. She moved to New York and earned a role in the Gershwin opera *Porgy and Bess*. Along with the rest of the cast, she toured nearly two-dozen countries in Europe and Africa from 1954 to 1955. After marrying a South-African freedom fighter, Angelou lived in Cairo, Egypt, for several years, where she edited an English- language newspaper. Later, she taught at the University of Ghana and edited the *African Review*.

Angelou often shared stories about her unusual, intense, and poignant childhood, and her friends and associates encouraged her to write an autobiography. In 1969, Angelou published *I Know Why the Caged Bird Sings*, the first in a series of autobiographical works. It quickly became a best-seller and was nominated for the National Book Award. Angelou's *Georgia, Georgia* (1971) became the first original screenplay by a black woman to be produced and filmed. *Just Give Me a Cool Drink of Water 'fore I Die* (1971), a collection of poetry, was nominated for the Pulitzer Prize. Angelou was also nominated for an Emmy award for her performance in the film adaptation of Alex Haley's *Roots*. By 1995, she had spent two years on *The New York Times* Paperback Nonfiction Bestseller list, becoming the first African-American author to achieve such success.

Out of her five autobiographies, *I Know Why the Caged Bird Sings* is probably Angelou's most popular and critically acclaimed volume. The book is now frequently read as a complement to fictional works that delve into the subject of racism, such as Harper Lee's *To Kill a Mockingbird* (1960) and Ralph Ellison's *Invisible Man* (1952). It has often been cut from reading lists because it involves honest depictions of Angelou's sexuality and her experience of being raped as a child. She wrote *I Know Why the Caged Bird Sings* at a time when autobiographies of women, and particularly black women, had begun to proclaim women's significance in the mainstream as thinkers and activists. Angelou's book conveys the difficulties associated with the mixture of racial and gender discrimination endured by a southern black girl. At the same time, she speaks to many other issues, such as the relationships between parents and children, child abuse, and the search for one's own path in life.

PLOT OVERVIEW

In *I Know Why the Caged Bird Sings*, Maya Angelou describes her coming of age as a precocious but insecure black girl in the American South during the 1930s and subsequently in California during the 1940s. Maya's parents divorce when she is only three years old and ship Maya and her older brother, Bailey, to live with their paternal grandmother, Annie Henderson, in rural Stamps, Arkansas. Annie, whom they call Momma, runs the only store in the black section of Stamps and becomes the central moral figure in Maya's childhood.

As young children, Maya and Bailey struggle with the pain of having been rejected and abandoned by their parents. Maya also finds herself tormented by the belief that she is an ugly child who will never measure up to genteel white girls. She does not feel equal to other black children. One Easter Sunday, Maya is unable to finish reciting a poem in church, and feeling ridiculed and a failure, Maya races from the church crying, laughing, and wetting herself. Bailey sticks up for Maya when people actually make fun of her to her face, wielding his charisma to put others in their place.

Growing up in Stamps, Maya faces a deep-seated southern racism manifested in wearying daily indignities and terrifying lynch mobs. She spends time at Momma's store, observing the cotton-pickers as they journey to and from work in the fields. When Maya is eight, her father, of whom she has no memory, arrives in Stamps unexpectedly and takes her and Bailey to live with their mother, Vivian, in St. Louis, Missouri. Beautiful and alluring, Vivian lives a wild life working in gambling parlors. One morning Vivian's live-in boyfriend, Mr. Freeman, sexually molests Maya, and he later rapes her. They go to court, and afterward, Mr. Freeman is violently murdered, probably by some the underground criminal associates of Maya's family.

In the aftermath of these events, Maya endures the guilt and shame of having been sexually abused. She also believes that she bears responsibility for Mr. Freeman's death because she denied in court that he had molested her prior to the rape. Believing that she has become a mouthpiece for the devil, Maya stops speaking to everyone except Bailey. Her mother's family accepts her silence at first as temporary post-rape trauma, but they later become frustrated and angry at what they perceive to be disrespectful behavior.

To Maya's relief, but Bailey's regret, Maya and Bailey return to Stamps to live with Momma. Momma manages to break through Maya's silence by introducing her to Mrs. Bertha Flowers, a kind, educated woman who tells Maya to read works of literature out loud, giving her books of poetry that help her to regain her voice.

During these years in Stamps, Maya becomes aware of both the fragility and the strength of her community. She attends a church revival during which a priest preaches implicitly against white hypocrisy through his sermon on charity. The spiritual strength gained during the sermon soon dissipates as the revival crowd walks home past the honky-tonk party. Maya also observes the entire community listening to the Joe Louis heavyweight championship boxing match, desperately longing for him to defend his title against his white opponent.

Maya endures several appalling incidents that teach her about the insidious nature of racism. At age ten, Maya takes a job for a white woman who calls Maya "Mary" for her own convenience. Maya becomes enraged and retaliates by breaking the woman's fine china. At Maya's eighth-grade graduation, a white speaker devastates the proud community by explaining that black students are expected to become only athletes or servants. When Maya gets a rotten tooth, Momma takes her to the only dentist in Stamps, a white man who insults her, saying he'd rather place his hand in a dog's mouth than in hers. The last straw comes when Bailey encounters a dead, rotting black man and witnesses a white man's satisfaction at seeing the body. Momma begins to fear for the children's well-being and saves money to bring them to Vivian, who now lives in California.

When Maya is thirteen, the family moves to live with Vivian in Los Angeles and then in Oakland, California. When Vivian marries Daddy Clidell, a positive father figure, they move with him to San Francisco, the first city where Maya feels at home. She spends one summer with her father, Big Bailey, in Los Angeles and has to put up with his cruel indifference and his hostile girlfriend, Dolores. After Dolores cuts her in a fight, Maya runs away and lives for a month with a group of homeless teenagers in a junkyard. She returns to San Francisco strong and self-assured. She defies racist hiring policies in wartime San Francisco to become the first black streetcar conductor at age fifteen. At sixteen, she hides her pregnancy from her mother and stepfather for eight months and graduates from high school. The account ends as Maya begins to feel confident as a mother to her newborn son.

CHARACTER LIST

Maya Angelou (born Marguerite Ann Johnson) The protagonist of the work. Angelou writes about her experiences growing up as a black girl in the rural South and in the cities of St. Louis, Los Angeles, and San Francisco. She has an unusual degree of curiosity and perceptiveness. Haunted by her displacement from her biological parents and her sense that she is ugly, she often isolates herself, escaping into her reading. This autobiography traces the start of her development into an independent, wise, and compassionate woman.

Bailey Johnson, Jr. Maya's older brother. Like Maya, he is intelligent and mature beyond his age. Though Bailey enjoys sports and fares well in social situations, he also shows deep compassion for his isolated sister. Bailey senses the negative influences of racism, but to protect himself from despair, he chooses to anesthetize himself and subdue his soul until the negative moment passes.

Annie Henderson (Momma) Maya and Bailey's paternal grandmother. Momma raises them for most of their childhood. She owns the only store in the black section of Stamps, Arkansas, and it serves as the central gathering place for the black community. She raises the children according to stern Christian values and strict rules. Though she never reacts with emotion, both children feel her love anyway.

Vivian Baxter Bailey and Maya's mother. Although Vivian has a nursing degree, she earns most of her money working in gambling parlors or by gambling herself. Though Vivian and Momma have very different values, they are both strong, supportive women. A somewhat inattentive mother, Vivian nevertheless treats her children with love and respect.

Big Bailey Johnson Maya and Bailey's father. Despite his lively personality, Big Bailey is handsome, vain, and selfish. He stands out among the other rural blacks because of his proper English and flashy possessions. Maya implies that Big Bailey's pretensions result from his disenfranchisement as a black man in the United States. Big Bailey does not respect, care for, or connect with Maya.

Willy Johnson Momma's son, who is in his thirties. Crippled in a childhood accident, Uncle Willy lives his entire life with Momma. He suffers insults and jokes because of his disability. Like Momma, he is a devout Christian, and he acts as the children's disciplinarian and protector.

Daddy Clidell Vivian's second husband, whom she marries after her children join her in California. Although Maya initially tries to dismiss him, Daddy Clidell becomes the only real father Maya knows. He combines the virtues of strength and tenderness and enjoys thinking of himself as Maya's father. He introduces her to his con-men friends and teaches her how to play poker. A successful businessman despite his lack of education, he remains modest and confident.

Mr. Freeman Vivian's live-in boyfriend in St. Louis. When Maya and Bailey move to St. Louis, Mr. Freeman sexually molests and rapes Maya, taking advantage of her need for physical affection and her innocent, self-conscious nature. In retrospect, Maya feels partly responsible for Mr. Freeman's fate, and her guilt over his murder haunts her throughout her childhood.

Mrs. Bertha Flowers A black aristocrat living in Stamps, Arkansas. One of Maya's idols, Mrs. Flowers becomes the first person to prod Maya out of her silence after Maya's rape, taking an interest in Maya and making her feel special. Maya respects Mrs. Flowers mainly for encouraging her love of literature.

Mrs. Viola Cullinan A southern white woman in Stamps and Maya's first employer. Perhaps unwittingly, Mrs. Cullinan hides her racism under a self-deceptive veneer of gentility. Her disrespect for Maya's wish to be called by her given name leads to Maya's subtly rebellious smashing of the Cullinans' china.

Glory (formerly Hallelujah) Mrs. Cullinan's cook. A descendent of the slaves once owned by the Cullinan family, Glory's acceptance of Mrs. Cullinan's condescending and racist renaming practices contrasts with Maya's resistance.

Mr. Edward Donleavy A white speaker at Maya's eighth-grade graduation ceremony. Mr. Donleavy insults the black community by talking condescendingly, but not explicitly, of their limited potential in a racist society. His racist tone casts a pall over the graduation and infuriates Maya.

Henry Reed The valedictorian of Maya's eighth-grade graduating class. Henry leads the class in "Lift Ev'ry Voice and Sing," popularly known as the Black National Anthem, and renews his community's pride following Mr. Donleavy's speech. This moment catalyzes Maya's great pride in her heritage and also inspires her passion for black poets and orators.

Dolores Stockland Big Bailey's prim-and-proper live-in girlfriend in Los Angeles. Maya spends the summer with them when she is fifteen and drives Dolores into a jealous rage. Maya's decision to show compassion toward her shows Maya's capacity for mercy, despite her self-aware and proud nature.

Louise Kendricks Maya's first friend outside her family. When she is with Louise, Maya is able to escape her troubles and play like a child should.

Tommy Valdon An eighth-grader who writes Maya a valentine. Maya reacts with hostility at first, distrusting any man's advances after the rape. She softens when Tommy writes her another letter showing that his interest in her is sincere.

Joyce Bailey's first love, with whom he loses his virginity. Joyce's relationship with Bailey foreshadows the troubles associated with adolescent sexuality that Maya will experience in San Francisco. Four years older than Bailey, Joyce turns his innocent displays of sexual curiosity playing "Momma and Papa" into sexual intercourse and eventually runs away with a railroad porter whom she meets at the store, leaving Bailey heartbroken and morose.

Dr. Lincoln A white dentist in Stamps to whom Momma lent money during the Great Depression. Momma's staunch effort to appeal to Dr. Lincoln's sense of ethics to support her in treating Maya's tooth shows both her resolve and her ability to act somewhat unethically out of necessity. The scene also reinforces Maya's impression of Momma as a superhero.

Stonewall Jimmy, Spots, Just Black, Cool Clyde, Tight Coat, and Red Leg Daddy Clidell's con-men friends, who teach Maya that it is possible to use white prejudice to gain advantage over whites. They represent creativity and the ethics that result from necessity and desperation.

Mrs. Florida Taylor Mr. Taylor's wife of forty years. Maya attends Florida's funeral and confronts her own mortality for the first time.

Miss Kirwin Maya's teacher in San Francisco. Miss Kirwin treats Maya like an equal human being, regardless of her color.

ANALYSIS OF MAJOR CHARACTERS

MARGUERITE ANN JOHNSON (MAYA) At the beginning of *I Know Why the Caged Bird Sings*, Maya is a precocious young girl suffering not just from the typical traumas associated with being black and female in America but also from the trauma of displacement. Smart and imaginative, Maya nevertheless feels that people judge her unfairly due to her ungainly appearance. Feeling misunderstood, she fantasizes that she is a blond-haired, blue-eyed girl trapped in a "black ugly dream" and will soon wake up and reveal her true self. Maya describes her social and familial displacement as "unnecessary insults" on top of the general difficulties associated with growing up as a black girl in the segregated American South. The South presents Maya with three tremendous impediments: white prejudice, black powerlessness, and female subjugation.

In addition to these broad societal obstacles, Maya endures many personal traumas in her lifetime. Her parents abandon her and Bailey when Maya is three, and her sense of abandonment and her need for physical affection lead to further struggles. Five years later, she must leave the only home she has known and live in an unknown city where she seeks comfort in Mr. Freeman, who molests and rapes her. At age ten, having already witnessed callous whites mistreating the people she loves most, such as Momma, Maya begins to experience racism directly. Mrs. Cullinan tries to rename and demean her, and Dr. Lincoln, the racist white dentist, says he would rather stick his hand in a dog's mouth than treat Maya's problem. In San Francisco, Maya's confusion about sexuality is compounded when she becomes pregnant at age sixteen.

Angelou's autobiography documents her victories and successes as well. With Bailey's and Momma's unwavering love and later encouragement from Vivian, Daddy Clidell, and numerous role models and friends, Maya gains the strength to overcome difficulties and realize her full potential. She learns to confront racism actively and eventually secures a position as the first black conductor aboard a San Francisco streetcar, which is perhaps her crowning achievement in the book. She also learns to confront her own failings with dignity and honor, never forgetting her guilt about lying in court and, in the Los Angeles junkyard, realizing the need to think not just in terms of black and white but in terms of humanity in all its diversity. She shows the power of forgiveness as she tries to find positive qualities in Big Bailey and to show compassion toward Dolores. She remains insecure, especially about her sexuality and appearance, but eventually she learns to trust her own abilities, as we see in the final scene, when she realizes that she will be able to care for her newborn son.

BAILEY JOHNSON, JR. Maya's older brother by one year, Bailey is the most important person in Maya's life throughout her childhood. When moved around from place to place, Bailey and Maya depend on each other to achieve some semblance of stability and continuity in their lives. Unlike Maya, Bailey is graceful, attractive, outgoing, and charming, and many consider him the jewel of his family. Bailey uses his skills and status to protect Maya. With his charms, he defends her against criticism and insults. Bailey and Maya share not just tragedies but also private jokes and a love of language and poetry.

One of the most striking differences between Maya and Bailey is their ability to confront racism. Bailey explains to Maya early on that when he senses the negative effects of racism, he essentially puts his soul to sleep so that he can forget the incident. Maya, however, learns to resist racism actively. Bailey and Maya grow further apart as they go through adolescence, and Bailey continues to withdraw deeper into himself. Even so, Maya continues to confide in him, asking for advice about her pregnancy. He continues to show his love for her as well, replying quickly to his sister and giving caring advice.

The return to Stamps from St. Louis traumatizes Bailey, and though he never blames his sister, he remains tormented by his longing for his mother. He expresses his longing through moodiness, sarcasm, and a bold assertion of his independence. In Stamps, he finds outlets for his longing for maternal affection by watching the white movie star who looks like Vivian and by playing "Momma and Papa" with Joyce, his buxom girlfriend who is four years his senior. In San Francisco, Bailey tries to win his mother's approval by imitating the people she befriends—he becomes the pimp-like boyfriend of a white prostitute. Bailey moves out at age sixteen and gets a job on the Southern Pacific Railroad, explaining that he and Vivian have come to an understanding with each other and that he has grown wise beyond his years.

ANNIE HENDERSON (MOMMA) Maya and Bailey's paternal grandmother, Momma, raises them for most of their childhood. She owns the only store in the black section of Stamps, Arkansas, and it serves as the central gathering place for the black community. She has owned the store for about twenty-five years, starting it as a mobile lunch counter and eventually building the store in the heart of the black community. Not knowing that Momma was black, a judge once subpoenaed her as "Mrs. Henderson," which cemented her elevated status in the mind of the black community. Momma is also the moral center of the family and especially of Maya's life. Momma raises the children according to stern Christian values and strict rules. She is defined by an unshakable faith in God, her loyalty to her community, and a deep love for everything she touches. Despite the affection she feels for her grandchildren, she cares more about their well-being than her own needs, extracting them from the Stamps community when the racist pressures begin to affect Bailey negatively.

While in Stamps, Momma teaches Maya how to conduct herself around white people. She chooses her words, emotions, and battles carefully, especially when race plays a role. Momma considers herself a realist regarding race relations. She stands up for herself but believes that white people cannot be spoken to without risking one's life. When three nasty poor white children mock Momma from the yard one afternoon, Maya watches furiously, but Momma maintains her dignity by not even acknowledging their taunts. Though stern and not given to emotional or affectionate displays, Momma conveys the depth of her love for Maya and Bailey throughout the book.

VIVIAN BAXTER Although she has a nursing degree, Maya and Bailey's mother earns her money working in gambling parlors. Vivian's parents and brothers are tough city dwellers who thrive in St. Louis amid the chaos of Prohibition, and Vivian seems to have inherited the family's wild streak. Though her lifestyle differs greatly from that of Momma, Vivian is also strong, proud, practical, and financially independent. She is also devastatingly beautiful—it is fitting that Maya and Bailey discover a white actress with a striking likeness to their mother because to them Vivian appears as a goddess performer who exists in her own personal spotlight. Maya is dumbstruck by Vivian's magnetic beauty, and Bailey falls in love with her at first sight. Maya believes Vivian initially sent them away because Vivian was, in Maya's opinion, too gorgeous to have children.

Vivian always treats Maya and Bailey well, and it is hard to imagine that she would have sent them so far away as young children. At the same time, however, even when they live together, the children remain peripheral to Vivian's life. Even after living together for some time and growing closer, Maya notes that Vivian notices Maya not out of the corner of her eye but "out of the corner of her existence." Showing her practical nature, Vivian sees no need to focus attention on Maya as long as Maya is healthy, well-clothed, and at least outwardly happy.

Throughout the book, Vivian oscillates between her gifts and limitations as a parent. In St. Louis, Vivian does not realize the danger of leaving her young daughter at home with a man who spends all day pining and waiting for her to come home. She does, however, demonstrate a high degree of maternal intuition when her live-in boyfriend, Mr. Freeman, sexually molests and rapes Maya. Without even knowing what has happened, Vivian kicks him out of the house immediately. Later, however, she proves unable to deal with Maya's post-rape trauma, and Maya and Bailey go back to Stamps. Similarly, in San Francisco, Vivian's lifestyle prevents her from actively engaging her daughter about her sexuality, leading indirectly to Maya's pregnancy. Even so, when Maya becomes pregnant, Vivian supports and encourages her without condemnation, and it is Vivian who gives Maya her first and most important lesson about trusting her maternal instincts. Maya admires Vivian's unflinching honesty, strength, and caring nature, despite her frequent fumbling as a parent.

BIG BAILEY JOHNSON Maya and Bailey's father exemplifies ignorant, parental neglect. He is handsome and vain, and he speaks with proper English, almost to the point of caricaturing a stereotypical upper-class white man of the time. Big Bailey ruins his own attempts to reconnect with his children, particularly with Maya. Absent from the children's lives for years, he arrives in Stamps out of the blue one year, impressing the children and everyone else in town with his congenial nature and his fancy car and clothing, but Maya feels neither glad nor sad to see him go when they reach St. Louis. She regards him as a stranger, for he shows little genuine effort to care for her. Though he resurfaces at the end of the book when Maya is fifteen and living in California, Big Bailey has not changed. Maya learns more about him—that he lives in a trailer park and suffers from many of the same troubles that afflict other black men trying to advance in the world—but he fails to try to learn anything about Maya. Even though Maya enjoys seeing her father's jubilant spirit in Mexico, the harsh reality of his selfishness continually undermines his appeal.

When Big Bailey first appears in the book, Maya questions whether he obtains his possessions legally as a railroad porter or whether he advances through illegal means. At that point, he exemplifies the ethics of necessity seen elsewhere in the book, in which blacks compromise ethical behavior to break through the walls of racial injustice. Later, regardless of his methods, he exemplifies the tragedy of the American black man trying to advance in a white society obsessed with class, paying more attention to his image than to his family.

THEMES, MOTIFS, AND SYMBOLS

THEMES

THE EFFECTS OF RACISM AND SEGREGATION Maya confronts the insidious effects of racism and segregation in America at a very young age. She internalizes the idea that blond hair is beautiful and that she is a fat black girl trapped in a nightmare. Stamps, Arkansas, is so thoroughly segregated that as a child Maya does not quite believe that white people exist. As Maya gets older, she is confronted by more overt and personal incidents of racism, such as a white speaker's condescending address at her eighth-grade graduation, her white boss's insistence on calling her Mary, and a white dentist's refusal to treat her. The importance of Joe Louis's world championship boxing match to the black community reveals the dearth of publicly recognized African American heroes. It also demonstrates the desperate nature of the black community's hope for vindication through the athletic triumph of one man. These unjust social realities confine and demean Maya and her relatives. She comes to learn how the pressures of living in a thoroughly racist society have profoundly shaped the character of her family members, and she strives to surmount them.

THE DEBILITATING EFFECTS OF DISPLACEMENT Maya is shuttled around to seven different homes between the ages of three and sixteen: from California to Stamps to St. Louis to Stamps to Los Angeles to Oakland to San Francisco to Los Angeles to San Francisco. As expressed in the poem she tries to recite on Easter, the statement "I didn't come to stay" becomes her shield against the cold reality of her rootlessness. Besieged by the "tripartite crossfire" of racism, sexism, and power, young Maya is belittled and degraded at every turn, making her unable to put down her shield and feel comfortable staying in one place. When she is thirteen and moves to San Francisco with her mother, Bailey, and Daddy Clidell, she feels that she belongs somewhere for the first time. Maya identifies with the city as a town full of displaced people.

Maya's personal displacement echoes the larger societal forces that displaced blacks all across the country. She realizes that thousands of other terrified black children made the same journey as she and Bailey, traveling on their own to newly affluent parents in northern cities, or back to southern towns when the North failed to supply the economic prosperity it had promised. African Americans descended from slaves who were displaced from their homes and homelands in Africa, and following the Emancipation Proclamation in 1862, blacks continued to struggle to find their place in a country still hostile to their heritage.

RESISTANCE TO RACISM Black people's resistance to racism takes many forms in *I Know Why the Caged Bird Sings*. Momma maintains her dignity by seeing things realistically and keeping to herself. Big Bailey buys flashy clothes and drives a fancy car to proclaim his worth and runs around with women to assert his masculinity in the face of dehumanizing and emasculating racism. Daddy Clidell's friends learn to use white peoples' prejudice against them in elaborate and lucrative cons. Vivian's family cultivates toughness and establishes connections to underground forces that deter any harassment. Maya first experiments with resistance when she breaks her white employer's heirloom china. Her bravest act of defiance happens when she becomes the first black streetcar conductor in San Francisco. Blacks also used the church as a venue of subversive resistance. At the revival, the preacher gives a thinly veiled sermon criticizing whites' charity, and the community revels in the idea of white people burning in hell for their actions.

MOTIFS

STRONG BLACK WOMEN Though Maya struggles with insecurity and displacement throughout her childhood, she has a remarkable number of strong female role models in her family and community. Momma, Vivian, Grandmother Baxter, and Bertha Flowers have very different personalities and views on life, but they all chart their own paths and manage to maintain their dignity and self-respect. None of them ever capitulates to racist indignities.

Maya also charts her own path, fighting to become the first black streetcar conductor in San Francisco, and she does so with the support and encouragement of her female predecessors. Maya notes at the end of Chapter 34 that the towering character of the black American woman should be seen as the predictable outcome of a hard-fought struggle. Many black women fall along the way. The ones who can weather the storm of sexism and racism obviously will shine with greatness. They have survived, and therefore, by definition, they are survivors.

LITERATURE Maya's first love is William Shakespeare. Throughout her life, literature plays a significant role in bolstering her confidence and providing a world of fantasy and escape. When feeling isolated in St. Louis, she takes refuge in the library. She describes Mrs. Bertha Flowers as being like women in English novels. Mrs. Flowers helps Maya rediscover her voice after her rape by encouraging her to use the words of other writers and poets. Maya continually quotes and refers to the literature she read throughout her childhood. For instance, at one point she simply gives San Francisco the title "Pride and Prejudice" without referring specifically to Jane Austen's novel of the same name. Bailey appreciates Maya's love of literature. He often presents her with gifts, such as the book of Edgar Allen Poe's work that he and Maya read aloud while walking in their backyard in Stamps.

NAMING Maya's real name is Marguerite, and most of her family members call her Ritie. The fact that she chooses to go by Maya as an adult, a name given to her by her brother, Bailey, indicates the depth of love and admiration she holds for him. When Maya reunites with her mother and her mother's family in

St. Louis at age eight, one of her uncles tells her the story of how she got this name. Thus, finding her family is connected with finding her name and her identity. Indeed, for African Americans in general, Maya notes, naming is a sensitive issue because it provides a sense of identity in a hostile world that aims to stereotype blacks and erase their individuality and identity. Consequently, given the predominance of pejoratives like *nigger* so often used to cut down blacks, Maya notes the danger associated with calling a black person anything that could be loosely interpreted as insulting. Besides the obvious fact that Mrs. Cullinan does not take the time to get Maya's name right in the first place, Mrs. Cullinan wishes to manipulate Maya's name for her own convenience, shortening it to Mary, illustrating that she cares very little about Maya's wishes or identity. Maya becomes enraged, and the incident inspires her to commit her first act of resistance.

SYMBOLS

THE STORE Momma's store symbolizes the rewards of hard work and loyalty and the importance of a strong and devout community. It is a central gathering place in Stamps and the center of Maya's childhood. There she witnesses the cycles of nature and labor, tending to workers in the cotton-picking season and canners during the killing season. Maya notes that until she left Arkansas for good at age thirteen, the Store was her favorite place to be.

MAYA'S EASTER DRESS The lavender taffeta dress that Momma alters for Maya on Easter symbolizes Maya's lack of love for herself and her wish for acceptance through transformation. She believes that beauty means *white* beauty. Hanging by the sewing machine, the dress looks magical. Maya imagines that the dress will reveal her true self to people who will then be shocked by her beauty. Harsh reality strikes on Easter morning, however, when she realizes that the dress is only a white woman's throwaway that cannot wake her from her black nightmare. Maya learns that her transformation will have to take place from within.

IMPORTANT QUOTATIONS EXPLAINED

---

1. *If growing up is painful for the Southern Black girl, being aware of her displacement is the rust on the razor that threatens the throat. It is an unnecessary insult.*

This vivid assertion ends the opening section of *I Know Why the Caged Bird Sings*. Although this section, which acts as a prologue, mostly emphasizes the point of view of Maya at five or six years old, this statement clearly comes from Angelou's adult voice. Looking back on her childhood experiences, Maya notes that she not only fell victim to a hostile, racist, and sexist society, but to other social forces as well, including the displacement she felt from her family and her peers. Maya feels displaced primarily because when she was three years old, her parents sent her away to live with her grandmother. This early separation, as well as subsequent ones, leaves her feeling rootless for most of her childhood. Angelou's autobiography likens the experience of growing up as a black girl in the segregated American South to having a razor at one's throat. Her constant awareness of her own displacement—the fact that she differed from other children in appearance and that she did not have a sense of belonging associated with anyone or anyplace—becomes the "unnecessary insult" that she must deal with at such a young age. Over the course of the work, Maya details numerous negative effects of such displacement, including her susceptibility to Mr. Freeman's sexual molestation.

---

2. *A light shade had been pulled down between the Black community and all things white, but one could see through it enough to develop a fear-admiration-contempt for the white "things"—white folks' cars and white glistening houses and their children and their women. But above all, their wealth that allowed them to waste was the most enviable.*

In this passage in Chapter 8, Angelou captures Maya's childlike observations about what makes white people different. Her fixation on clothing as a sign of difference also refers back to the incident in church when she suddenly realizes that her fairy-tale taffeta dress is really an old, faded white woman's hand-me-down. Stamps, Arkansas, suffers so thoroughly from segregation, and Maya's world is so completely enmeshed in the black community, that she often finds it hard to imagine what white people look like. They appear to her more like spectral ghosts with mysterious powers—and wonderful possessions—than as fellow human beings. At the same time, from a young age Maya knows that white people bear responsibility for the suffering of the cotton-pickers. She also learns from Momma that it is best not to address any white people directly, as it might lead to mortal danger. Momma goes so far as never to even speak about white people without using the title "they."

---

3. *My race groaned. It was our people falling. It was another lynching, yet another Black man hanging on a tree. One more woman ambushed and raped. . . . This might be the end of the world. If Joe lost we were back in slavery and beyond help. It would all be true, the accusations that we were lower types of human beings. Only a little higher than the apes.*

In this scene in Chapter 19, Maya crowds around the Store's radio with the rest of the community to listen to Joe Louis defend his world heavyweight boxing title. As Maya conveys in this passage, the entire black community has its hopes and psychological salvation bound up in the fists of Louis, "the Brown Bomber." This passage describes the precarious nature of black pride in the face of hostile oppression, highlighting the staggering and wrenching significance this boxing match held for the community as the community teeters between salvation and despair. The rarity of black people achieving public acclaim in both the black and white communities meant that the few who managed to do so had to bear the expectations of the black community.

The match becomes an explicit staging of black against white. Louis's loss would mean the "fall" of the race and a return to the idea that whites had a right to denigrate black people. Cynics might say that Louis's win does little more than stave off the black community's psychological despair. It does not turn the tables on whites because there is no denying that whites still hold all of the power. His public victory, however, proves to blacks in the Store that they are the most powerful people in the world and enables them to live another day with strength and vigor in the face of oppression. Racism plays many psychological games with blacks and whites, and perhaps Louis's public recognition helps to teach both whites and blacks to accept African Americans as equals.

I

---

4. *Bailey was talking so fast he forgot to stutter, he forgot to scratch his head and clean his fingernails with his teeth. He was away in a mystery, locked in the enigma that young Southern Black boys start to unravel, start to try to unravel, from seven years old to death. The humorless puzzle of inequality and hate.*

In this passage in Chapter 25, Bailey reels from having encountered a dead, rotting black man and having witnessed a white man's lighthearted satisfaction at seeing the body. Maya emphasizes that the traumatic experience forces him to *try* to confront a degree of hatred that he cannot comprehend. Maya does not say that he succeeds in comprehending the reasoning behind white hatred. Bailey asks Uncle Willy to explain how colored people had offended whites originally, but both Uncle Willy and Momma try to hide the sickening, debilitating truth from Bailey. This section draws attention to the idea that Bailey's life depended upon him not understanding or attempting to understand how racism operates against black men. Bailey's experience here precipitates Momma's decision to remove the children from both the physical and psychological dangers associated with growing up in the South. This quote also illustrates the fact that while Angelou writes mostly about the experiences of black girls and women living in the segregated South, she also empathizes with the experiences of her male relatives.

5. *The Black female is assaulted in her tender years by all those common forces of nature at the same time that she is caught in the tripartite crossfire of masculine prejudice, white illogical hate and Black lack of power. The fact that the adult American Negro female emerges a formidable character is often met with amazement, distaste and even belligerence.*

This passage in Chapter 34 addresses why black women have strength of character. Maya says that most of the strong black women in her novel are "survivors." They have strong characters quite simply because they have survived against impossible odds. Therefore, they obviously show heroism, courage, and strength. Moreover, Maya states that the odds pitted against black women include not only the triple threat of sexism, racism, and black powerlessness, but also the simultaneous presence of "common forces of nature" that assault and confuse all children. Maya has had to grow up more quickly than the children around her. Her experiences—driving the car in Mexico, living in the junkyard, returning to witness Bailey move out of the house, and then successfully fighting to get a job as the first black conductor on the San Francisco streetcars, rather than go back to a school where she would not belong—have made her feel displaced and older than her years. Maya is already on her way toward becoming "a formidable character" as a result of the many assaults she deals with in "her tender years," but this does not mean that Maya is an adult. Maya's discussion of the "common forces of nature" foreshadows how her journey of survival has yet to meet the obstacles of adolescence, sexuality, and teenage pregnancy. These obstacles face all children, but for black females, they exacerbate an already difficult situation.

I, Rigoberta Menchu

Rigoberta Menchu
(1959–)

CONTEXT

When *I, Rigoberta Menchu* hit bookstores as *Me Llamo Rigoberta Menchu Y Asi Me Nacio La Conciencia* in 1983, only a handful of intellectuals and political activists around the world knew how difficult life had become for thousands of Indian people living in Guatemala under an abusive military dictatorship. Rigoberta Menchu was twenty-four years old and living in exile in Mexico City, and around the world, people responded to her vivid, often shocking words and images.

I, Rigoberta Menchu rose from a weeklong marathon of interviews with Menchu, conducted by the Venezuelan anthropologist Elisabeth Burgos-Debray, the book's editor, in Paris in 1982. The book was eventually translated into twelve languages, including English in 1984, and introduced into the curriculum at several prominent universities, spawning a flurry of dissertations. In human rights circles, Menchu's name gradually became familiar. In 1992, Menchu won the Nobel Peace Prize, and the general public became aware of her and her cause. After she won the Nobel Prize, Menchu became a UNESCO Goodwill Ambassador and launched a human rights foundation.

Born on January 9, 1959 in Chimel, a settlement in the rugged northwestern region of Guatemala, Menchu was the sixth of nine children. Her mother, Juana Tum, was a healer and a midwife. Menchu's father, Vicente, was a laborer, preacher, and widely acknowledged leader in the village that Menchu and her family called home. A member of the Quiche (pronounced Kee-chay) Indians, one of twenty-two groups descended from the Mayans, Menchu was raised in a community that interwove traditional, ancient Mayan beliefs with those introduced by the Roman Catholic Church. Political action became another important thread in Menchu's childhood tapestry, because she was frequently exposed to the effects of a Guatemalan civil war that broiled throughout her youth and continued, with increased fervor, through the 1980s and into the 1990s. It came to an end in 1996, largely because of Menchu's efforts. After she went into exile in 1981 and even more after she won the Nobel Prize in 1992, Menchu frequented the headquarters of the United Nations in her traditional Mayan attire and, often, bare feet.

During Menchu's early years, *ladinos*, or Spanish descendents, made up the dominant class in Guatemala and ruled in society, business, and the government, creating a vast separation between the wealthy minority and the poverty-stricken peasant majority in Guatemala. Menchu's Quiche people lived off of the maize, potatoes, and beans they grew in the cool, humid slopes of the Altiplano. Their homes were simple hovels that lacked electricity, running water, and sewage. To make ends meet, Menchu's family, like many Indian families, were forced to work at the coffee and cotton plantations, or *fincas*, that dotted the Guatemalan landscape.

When Menchu and her family went to work at the plantations, their lives essentially belonged to the wealthy plantation owners. These owners pressured them to run up debts at plantation stores and cantinas, and when they returned to the mountains, they often had just a trace more money than when they started. This experience was common for Indian laborers in Guatemala, many of whom lost children to starvation, disease, or harsh pesticides that rained down on Indian families while they worked in the fields.

As Guatemalan rebels began to take up arms against those in power, their guerilla armies frequently hid out in Guatemala's high country, near Menchu's village. Caught in the crossfire between the ladino-controlled Guatemalan government and the guerillas, many Indians, including members of the Menchu family, became sympathetic to the guerillas and embraced their cause. Even Indians who didn't have guerilla sympathies were frequently targeted by the government as suspected communists. Frustrated by the abuses of his people at the hands of the Guatemalan government and the wealthy landowners who repeatedly attempted to wrench his fertile land away from him, Vicente Menchu joined with other peasant leaders to form the Peasant Unity Committee (the CUC) in 1978. Before he died in 1980, Vicente Menchu asked his daughter to continue his fight. Words became Menchu's chief weapon.

During the 1990s, *I, Rigoberta Menchu* was the subject of increasing controversy and debate, which came to a head when David Stoll, an American anthropologist, traveled to Guatemala and, through interviews with Menchu's family and neighbors, picked apart the accounts that Menchu communicated with such vivid detail in the book. In his 1999 book, *Rigoberta Menchu and the Story of All Poor Guatemalans*, Stoll claimed that Menchu made up or overstated many of her reports, including a searing account of what it was like to watch as her younger brother was burned to death in public by the Guatemalan military. Though billed as an autobiography, Menchu's book falls in line with the Latin-American storytelling and literary tradition known as *testimonio*, or testimony, in which one speaker presents the story of an entire community or group as though it were his or her own. Menchu's defenders believe that *I, Rigoberta Menchu* doesn't have to stand up to scrutiny regarding its truth. In its portrayal of the troubles that the entire Indian population faced in Guatemala, they say, the book is accurate.

Attackers argue that Menchu ought to be held responsible for the holes in her story, and many accuse her of taking advantage of the violent situation in her country to further her left-leaning political beliefs. Others claim she was involved with Guatemalan guerilla groups. Still others question the authorship of *I, Rigoberta Menchu*, suggesting that Elisabeth Burgos-Debray influenced the finished product more than she should have. Though some groups claimed Menchu ought to be stripped of her Nobel Prize, the Nobel committee refused, stating that Menchu's record as a human rights activist stands alone, regardless of the controversy surrounding her autobiography. In 1998, Menchu published her own memoir, *Crossing Borders*, which picks up where *I, Rigoberta Menchu* left off.

PLOT OVERVIEW

During a visit to Paris as part of the Guatemalan political organization known as "the 31 January Popular Front," Rigoberta Menchu meets Venezuelan anthropologist Elisabeth Burgos-Debray and agrees to tell her life story so that it can be transformed into a book. The two work feverishly for several days, Burgos-Debray questioning Rigoberta, who tells her story in Spanish, her second language. The result is several hours' worth of recorded interviews that Burgos-Debray transcribes and arranges as *I, Rigoberta Menchu*.

As far back as Rigoberta, a Quiche Indian, can recall, her life has been split between the highlands of Guatemala, known as the Altiplano, and low country plantations, or fincas. Each year, she and her family spend about eight months at the fincas working for ladinos, Guatemalans of Spanish descent. Starvation and malnutrition are constants at the finca, and the Indians are routinely sprayed with pesticides. Rigoberta and her people find respite in the months they spend in their small village in the Altiplano that they call home. In the deeply wooded Altiplano, Rigoberta's life centers around the ceremonies and traditions of her community, many of which celebrate the natural world. At the fincas, she and her people struggle to survive in cramped, miserable conditions at the mercy of wealthy landowners and their overseers. They move between the two worlds each year in a truck covered with a tarp, and by the time she is eight years old, Rigoberta is already a hard worker, capable of picking several pounds of coffee each day.

Though she lives in a traditional Indian society, Rigoberta's awareness of a world beyond the finca and the Altiplano begins to dawn when she is still quite young. When her younger brother, Nicolas, dies of malnutrition while at the finca, Rigoberta begins to feel both angry and afraid of what the future will hold for her. Visiting Guatemala City, the capital of Guatemala, with her father, whom she idolizes, Rigoberta is at once terrified and compelled. As she grows older and begins to develop a conscience, Rigoberta starts to yearn for change, both for herself and for her community. She craves education and wishes above all to learn to speak Spanish so that she can explore the world outside of the Altiplano and the finca. Though she begins to follow in her father's footsteps and take on leadership duties in her community, she also yearns to learn about the world and its people.

When she's offered a job as a maid at the home of a wealthy landowner in Guatemala City, Rigoberta leaps at the opportunity, hoping she'll get a chance to master Spanish. Immediately upon arriving in Guatemala City, however, she understands the discrimination that exists for people of her heritage. At the landowner's home, even the dog is treated better than she. The most influential force in Rigoberta's life as she figures out the various household tasks is Candelaria. Like Rigoberta, Candelaria is an Indian, yet she has learned to speak Spanish and dresses as a ladino. She has also figured out how to get under the mistress's skin and routinely sabotages her by neglecting certain chores and talking back. When Rigoberta's father comes to the mistress's house and asks for money, Candelaria convinces the mistress to contribute. Rigoberta doesn't follow in Candelaria's footsteps right away, but Candelaria's rebellious spirit has an impact on her that continues even after Candelaria is booted out of the house.

Upon returning from her work in the capital, Rigoberta finds out that her father has been jailed because he refused to cooperate with ladino landowners who attempt to claim the land in the Altiplano where Rigoberta's community lives. This is the first of several times that Rigoberta's father is jailed, and Rigoberta and her siblings work constantly to free him for good. After the landowners and the government repeatedly hoodwink the Indians, the Indians decide to defend their lands and rebel against the Guatemalan powers. Led in part by Rigoberta's father, they form the Peasant Unity Committee, or CUC, to pool their resources against the powerful ladino government and business owners. By this time, Rigoberta has taken a leadership role in her community, and she and the rest of her family play a major part in helping the Indians develop strategies to defend their lands against the Guatemalan army. The Indians rely on simple weapons such as traps and knives to fight back, and they are inspired in their cause by the Bible's stories of disenfranchised populations and people.

After securing her own people's holdings, Rigoberta goes on the road as a representative of the CUC, helping Indian communities secure their lands and outsmart the Guatemalan army. As the CUC becomes increasingly influential, Rigoberta and her family find themselves more at risk. First, Rigoberta's brother, Petrocinio, is kidnapped and burned alive while Rigoberta's entire family and village are forced to watch. Then Rigoberta's father leads an offensive on Guatemala City and is killed along with a group of protesters while storming the Spanish Embassy. Finally, Rigoberta's mother is kidnapped, raped, tortured, and murdered. Rigoberta responds by renouncing marriage and motherhood and becoming more involved in the peasant cause, leading strikes and other rebellious actions until she finds herself in danger and is forced into exile. Though Rigoberta's sisters join the guerilla army to fight for the rights of Guatemala's Indian peasants, Rigoberta decides to take a diplomatic route, telling stories of her people and putting legislation into place as a way of furthering the rights of Indians.

CHARACTER LIST

Rigoberta Menchu The narrator and protagonist of *I, Rigoberta Menchu*. Proud, hardworking, and idealistic, Rigoberta is a Quiche Indian who finds herself poised for leadership when her people are persecuted and exploited by the powerful Guatemalan dictatorship. Rigoberta oscillates between despair and anger as she gains the skills and confidence that enable her to make a difference in her community and in the world. Fiercely traditional, Rigoberta defends her family and fellow Indians, celebrating the folkways and stories that have been passed down for generations. Rigoberta repeatedly pursues activities that aren't typical among the women in her culture. Eventually, Rigoberta becomes a radical political activist who travels throughout the world, telling her story and furthering the Guatemalan peasant cause.

Elisabeth Burgos-Debray The editor of *I, Rigoberta Menchu*. Burgos-Debray interviewed, recorded, transcribed, and arranged Rigoberta's autobiography. Though Burgos-Debray's presence is only implied in the action of *I, Rigoberta Menchu*, she shapes the story. An educated, left-leaning anthropologist, Burgos-Debray sympathizes with Rigoberta and holds a romantic view of her and her fellow Indian peasants. Cooking the traditional dishes that are staples in both women's homelands, for instance, Burgos-Debray feels a deep connection with Rigoberta, but Rigoberta doesn't return the connection because she mistrusts ladinos and other outsiders.

Vicente Menchu Rigoberta's father. A leader in his community, the Roman Catholic Church, and the CUC, Vicente is Rigoberta's chief role model. From early in Rigoberta's life, Vicente presses on her his hope that she'll continue his cause. Vicente was an orphan who entered the Guatemalan army at a young age before he met and married Juana Tum, and he is committed to his family and the Indian community. Despite his apparent strength, he can also be thin-skinned, sometimes escaping his problems by drinking alcohol.

Juana Tum Rigoberta's mother. A traditional Indian healer, Juana believes strongly in upholding the values and practices of the elders and the ancestors. However, she wholeheartedly embraces the cause of the Guatemalan peasants and is able to unite people in simple but powerful ways. After seeing three of her sons die at the hands of the Guatemalan landowners and government, Juana becomes more militant and even sympathizes with guerillas who live in the mountains near her village.

Petrocinio Rigoberta's older brother. Petrocinio is singled out by the Guatemalan military for his work as a catechist and as a community leader among the Guatemalan peasants. Rigoberta, her family, and their community must watch as he is burned alive by the Guatemalan military, which galvanizes their commitment to fight for Indian rights.

Candelaria Another maid in the landowner's house, where Rigoberta works in Guatemala City. Candelaria is a "ladinized" Indian, which means she speaks Spanish and wears ladino clothing, not the traditional Indian dress. Confident and street-smart, Candelaria shows Rigoberta how to perform household duties at the landowner's house, but she also teaches her how to sabotage wealthy landowners and what it takes to stand up to authority. She is a survivor who holds onto her dignity, even though she is eventually thrown out of the landowner's house.

Nicolas Rigoberta's little brother. Two-year-old Nicolas succumbs to illness at the finca. His death spurs Rigoberta's dawning realization of her people's exploitation and her understanding of what life means for Indians living in Guatemala. Upon Nicholas's death, Rigoberta feels angry and wishes to make changes in her own life and the lives of her people.

The Mistress The wife of the wealthy landowner who hires Rigoberta to work as a maid in Guatemala City. The mistress hates Indians but also relies on their strong work ethic to keep her household running. She sees Rigoberta and Candelaria as an extension of her household and expects them to behave and dress appropriately. Yet she also mistreats them, feeding her dog better food than she sets aside for the Indians.

Rigoberta's Younger Sister A member of the Guerilla army. Rigoberta's twelve-year-old sister visits Rigoberta while Rigoberta is in hiding in Guatemala and reminds her that being a revolutionary isn't born of something good but of "wretchedness and bitterness."

Rigoberta's Youngest Sister A member of the guerilla army. Rigoberta's youngest sister says she can honor her mother only by taking up arms.

Maria Rigoberta's friend at the finca. Maria exists only in Rigoberta's memory, but her death sets off a rage within Rigoberta that energizes her commitment to become a leader among her people and to do whatever it takes to transform the dismal lot most Indians face.

The Old Woman A resident in one of the communities where Rigoberta organizes the Guatemalan peasant movement. A widow who has lost her entire family, the Old Woman is tired of fighting the Guatemalan government. However, she is also willing to take more risks than her neighbors in rebelling against them and ends up killing a member of the Guatemalan army. Because she has traits that appear in legends and myths cross-culturally, the Old Woman is an archetypal figure.

Dona Petrona Chona A friend of Rigoberta's from the finca. Dona Petrona Chona, the mother of two small children, is murdered after she refuses advances from the landowner's son. Her role in *I, Rigoberta Menchu* is highly symbolic and suggests the fractured identity of Rigoberta and all of the Indian people. Like the Old Woman, Dona Petrona Chona is also an archetypal mother figure.

Kjell Laugerud Garcia The president of Guatemala from 1974–1978. Rigoberta refers to him as Kjell Laugerud, and he tells the Indians he sympathizes with them. However, he then betrays them and sides with the Guatemalan landowners.

Lucas Garcia The president of Guatemala from 1978–1982. Lucas Garcia is more aggressive toward the Indians than was Kjell Laugerud. He sets up military bases in the Altiplano, where his soldiers routinely rape, torture, and kidnap Indians.

ANALYSIS OF MAJOR CHARACTERS

RIGOBERTA MENCHU Rigoberta Menchu, a Quiche Indian, pushes herself and others past victimhood to empowerment. A survivor to the core, Rigoberta begins as a meek and obedient daughter, but she gradually gains a strong, militant sense of her individual rights and the rights of her people. Though Rigoberta's alliance to elders and to her father in particular is fierce and unyielding, she nonetheless yearns to change the future for herself and others like her. Though she is repeatedly reminded during tribal ceremonies that all Indians must succumb to a life of hard work, misery, and suffering, she refuses to accept her lot. When her brother Nicholas dies of malnutrition at the finca, Rigoberta grows angry, not despondent. Over time, this anger motivates her. Later, as many other members of her family, including her mother and father, are murdered, Rigoberta grows increasingly militant. She sees the merits of violence as a means to an end, yet she stops short of joining the Guatemalan guerillas.

As a young girl working on Guatemalan plantations, Rigoberta works hard and recognizes the virtue of continuing to labor at certain tasks, even when it appears there is no end to what must be done. Later, Rigoberta applies her work ethic to political change, realizing that patience is a key component to any worthwhile effort. Though early attempts to learn Spanish are thwarted, for example, she doesn't give up on her dream and eventually succeeds in learning the language. Highly adaptable, Rigoberta is able to blend teachings from Roman Catholic missionaries with Indian beliefs and rituals that have been passed down for ages. As she forges her political ideologies, which center on peasant rights and the inherent value of the poor, Rigoberta molds her Catholic beliefs to support her ideology, rejecting the Roman-Catholic hierarchy while embracing certain stories from the Bible and the figure of Christ as leader of the poor. Rigoberta is at once extremely traditional and radically modern. While she carefully preserves the ancient ways of her people by chronicling birth and death ceremonies in painstaking detail, for example, she also renounces motherhood and marriage so she can follow in her father's footsteps, a radical move for a woman in any society but especially in one as traditional and old-fashioned as that of the Quiche Indians.

VICENTE MENCHU, RIGOBERTA'S FATHER Vicente Menchu is perhaps the most influential person in Rigoberta's life. Despite a checkered past that includes orphanhood, a stint in the Guatemalan military, and occasional bouts of alcoholism, Rigoberta's father is a leader in his village. To Rigoberta and, indeed, many Indians, he is larger than life, an embodiment of strength, solidarity, and courage. Early in Rigoberta's life, he takes her to Guatemala City and leads her through the streets of the capital, giving her a first glimpse of the Guatemalan government in action at the INTA (the Guatemalan National Institute for Agrarian Transformation). Though frequently absent from the Altiplano, Rigoberta's father stays tied to his roots, routinely reminding Rigoberta not to forget about her ancestors. He also underscores the necessity for resistance as a form of preserving cultural identity.

JUANA MENCHU TUM, RIGOBERTA'S MOTHER Rigoberta's mother is a keeper of traditions and the old ways of doing things. A traditional Indian healer, she has an intimate relationship with nature, knowing, for example, when it's about to rain or the best time to sow crops. Although not articulate in political affairs, she is able to weave protest into simple acts, such as tending to guerilla soldiers when they are ill or cooking for protesters. Her influence on Rigoberta is subtle. Though Rigoberta considers her father to have far more impact on her evolution, she continues to obey her mother in certain powerful ways, such as continuing to dress in traditional Indian apparel, which profoundly affects her interactions with others.

Throughout *I, Rigoberta Menchu*, Rigoberta's mother exhibits a high level of endurance, gracefully bearing difficult trials, such as watching her children die, one by one, in sometimes violent ways. She is able to absorb difficult experiences, whereas Rigoberta's father sometimes runs away or drinks to deal with trauma. Even as she approaches death, Rigoberta's mother exhibits strength and courage that last, and this point is driven home by the way the earth slowly absorbs her body after she dies—she doesn't disappear immediately.

CANDELARIA Though she is just a maid working in the home of a wealthy Guatemala City landowner, Candelaria manages to resist and rebel against those who assume power over her. She has an enormous impact on Rigoberta, proving to her that something as simple as cleaning can be infused with revolution. Though she has assumed a ladino identity, Candelaria retains her sense of self. She protects Rigoberta from the conniving mistress for whom they work, and when Rigoberta's father comes to ask for money, Candelaria talks the mistress into contributing. Candelaria appears in *I, Rigoberta Menchu* just before Rigoberta must tap into her own rebellious nature. In many ways, Rigoberta inherits some of Candelaria's traits as she presses forth as an activist in the CUC.

THEMES, MOTIFS, AND SYMBOLS

THEMES

THE POWER OF LANGUAGE While several of Rigoberta's siblings choose to fight the peasant cause by joining a guerilla group, Rigoberta understands that she can fight using words and stories. *I, Rigoberta Menchu* comes directly from this impulse. Working with Burgos-Debray, Menchu clearly realized that her autobiography would be a powerful tool in bringing about change for the Guatemalan people. By her own admission in the closing lines of the book, Rigoberta selectively chooses exactly what she will reveal about herself and her people. A master of rhetoric who learned how to preach about the Bible early in her life, she appears keenly aware of the emotion she wants to stir among her listeners and readers. As a girl, when Rigoberta realizes she wants to bring about change, her mind turns immediately to mastering the Spanish language and learning how to read. Despite the fact that this idea threatens Rigoberta's father, she nonetheless pursues the language doggedly, knowing that these skills will help her succeed in the larger world.

THE COST OF PROGRESS Progress isn't necessarily a positive element for Rigoberta and her people, who often find themselves bearing the burden of advancements initiated by the white man. The Indians in Rigoberta's village react by resisting progress and clinging to their way of life in the Altiplano. Elders and ancestors, emblems of the past, are celebrated in tribal ceremonies, whereas modern trappings such as Coca-Cola are condemned for their role in diluting Indian identity. When ladino landowners come to seize the land of Rigoberta's people in the name of progress, Rigoberta and her fellow villagers take up machetes, build traps, and unite in militaristic fashion. In their efforts to preserve the old ways, the Indians must resort to violent activities that distance them from their ancestors. In effect, even those who would rather not move forward are, by their proximity to change and advancement, forced to comply. Through progress, Rigoberta wins the freedom to pursue education and life outside of the Altiplano and to make her own choices, such as renouncing marriage and motherhood. Progress also enables her to approach the United Nations, appealing to the basic humanity that links people of all races and creeds.

THE VIRTUE OF HARD WORK Whether they are at home in the Altiplano or on the job at the fincas, Rigoberta and her people embrace manual labor wholeheartedly. By the time she is eight years old, Rigoberta has already developed fingers dexterous enough to pluck coffee beans from bushes without breaking a twig, and a back strong enough to haul pounds of coffee. She feels significant pride in these accomplishments, despite the pain she's endured. It isn't necessarily difficult labor that causes Rigoberta and her people to resent ladinos but rather the ladinos' lack of respect for the Indians' basic needs and their way of life. When she becomes a maid in the capital, Rigoberta dutifully performs the tasks that are expected of her, even those as foreign and seemingly pointless as ironing. Meanwhile, Rigoberta regards the mistress with disdain, noting in particular that she spends her days doing nothing. As Rigoberta moves away from manual labor and into working for the CUC and other peasant groups, she maintains a high level of activity, passing out flyers and discussing her cause with any who are interested. Clearly, the drive to work is important to Rigoberta, and it is indeed her and her people's persistence that makes the CUC cause take hold.

MOTIFS

TRADITION *I, Rigoberta Menchu* opens with a thorough, textured account of the traditions that surround the process of giving birth in Rigoberta's culture. Throughout the book, Rigoberta repeatedly returns to explanations and descriptions of traditions surrounding other aspects of Quiche Indian life, including marriage, death, and the harvesting of the maize. Both Rigoberta and Burgos-Debray assert that keeping traditions alive is a way of preserving the Indian community and fighting against the Guatemalan dictatorship that threatens it. Modern elements that pull people away from tradition contrast with the traditions that make the work compelling. This contrast creates a tension that mirrors the tension Rigoberta feels as she steps outside the standard role of an Indian woman. The impact of Candelaria choosing to dress as a ladino, for example, or Rigoberta deciding not to have children are heightened because such occurrences are placed against Rigoberta's emphasis on the way things have always been done.

COMMUNITY Early in Rigoberta's story, her definition of community includes only those with whom she lives in the Altiplano. As her community is persecuted along with other Indian groups, Rigoberta's sense of community broadens to include all of the Guatemalan Indians. Later, as her community is virtually destroyed and she goes into exile, she must again redefine community to stand for all those with whom she works to liberate her people. In Rigoberta's imagination and through storytelling, however, she keeps the idea of her community on the Altiplano alive.

STORYTELLING The text of *I, Rigoberta Menchu* originated from an extended storytelling session in which Rigoberta told her experiences to Burgos-Debray, and Rigoberta continuously breaks the action to insert more stories of her past. Storytelling informs the very structure of the book, but it also is an important part of how characters in the work interact with one another. When the Old Woman meets Rigoberta and the community after killing the soldier, she joyously tells a story about it. During marriage ceremonies, Indian elders tell stories of their past. Stories distill the many chaotic elements of the strife between Guatemalans and Indians, allowing Rigoberta to draw readers in and make them care about what she has been through.

SYMBOLS

THE LORRY The lorry, with its closed sides, represents the darkness Rigoberta and other Indians exist within before they reach the point when they can no longer ignore the exploitation the ladinos have brought to them. People become sick in the lorry, but they also become sick of the oppressive conditions under which the Guatemalan government and landowners force them to live. After Rigoberta watches her brother die and grows angry for the first time, she sees her surroundings more clearly while returning to the Altiplano by bus. No longer kept in the dark, she has important insight that powers her efforts to reclaim her people's rights. As *I, Rigoberta Menchu* unfolds, Rigoberta is usually the one who can see things clearly, and she must tell others how to defend themselves.

RIGOBERTA'S CORTE Rigoberta rips the *corte*, or skirt, that the mistress gives her in half, which signifies her ripping away from tradition and the obedient identity she has always known within her community. Until this point, Rigoberta's stance has been to cover her growing anger with sweetness and submission. Her experience working as a maid in a ladino household and the example of Candelaria reveal to her that in order to claim her rights and the rights of her people, she must become more assertive, even aggressive. In remaining chapters, Rigoberta becomes more and more militant and less and less the timid, obedient servant she is when she arrives in the capital. Rigoberta's mother continuously reminds her to continue wearing her *corte* and *huipil*, important parts of traditional Indian dress, a request that Rigoberta respects and follows. Still, to fight the Guatemalan government and landowners, Rigoberta must, in effect, rip away from the traditional fabric of her life.

THE OLD WOMAN In *I, Rigoberta Menchu*, the Old Woman is an archetypal figure, which is an element that occurs cross-culturally in literature. She symbolizes the ancestors that Rigoberta and her people look up to, but she is also the first Indian in the work who commits murder. The Old Woman's willingness to kill in the name of justice and liberty gives other Indians permission, from the ancestors and elders, to take life. The Old Woman is also a fierce defender of her culture and its people, and will stop at nothing to protect the younger generation, even though her own family has been killed. Able to summon enough strength to take down a soldier, the Old Woman also signifies the idea that those who appear meek or feeble might, in actuality, be capable of strong, powerful acts.

IMPORTANT QUOTATIONS EXPLAINED

---

1. *My Name is Rigoberta Menchu. I am 23 years old. This is my testimony. I didn't learn it from a book and I didn't learn it alone. I'd like to stress that it's not only* my *life, it's also the testimony of my people. . . . My story is the story of all poor Guatemalans. My personal experience is the reality of a whole people.*

These passages open *I, Rigoberta Menchu* and are the first words we hear from Rigoberta as she begins her story. Rigoberta makes it clear from the outset that she is a representative of her community, speaking not only for herself but also for her people. This attitude reflects the Latin American tradition of *testimonio*, in which events that have happened to a person's community can be adopted and retold as though they have happened to an individual. This device allows Rigoberta to communicate both events that happened to her and experiences of other Guatemalans in a way that is cohesive and compelling. By using such a technique, however, Rigoberta opened herself to criticism regarding the accuracy of her account, particularly by the anthropologist David Stoll, who spent a number of years working to discredit Rigoberta, based on the notion that what she presented in her book was fact. Though *I, Rigoberta Menchu* has been widely referred to as an autobiography, this label is somewhat misleading. In actuality, as Rigoberta says here, the work is a testimony, defined as a story that serves as evidence of some wrong that has been committed.

By stating that she "learned" her testimony, Rigoberta reminds readers that its telling has been influenced by others and that the experience she presents in the following pages has been minted consciously, not only by her but by the collective entity of her people. Rigoberta illustrates the closely knit quality of her community here, and throughout the work she develops her own attitudes about the world as she reflects on the values passed down to her from ancestors and elders. For Rigoberta, there is no such thing as an identity completely separate from the Indian community. This stance informs her approach to telling the story and allows her to plug images and details into events she did not actually witness but only heard about from other community members. Aside from enriching the work, such descriptive elements help Rigoberta build her case because she was, indeed, working to gain support for her human rights efforts at the United Nations when *I, Rigoberta Menchu* was published.

---

2. *From then on, I was very depressed about life because I thought, what would life be like when I grew up? I thought about my childhood and all the time that had passed. I'd often seen my mother crying. . . . I was afraid of life and I'd ask myself: "What will it be like when I'm older?"*

This passage appears in Chapter XIII, just after Rigoberta's friend, Maria, is poisoned on the finca. Seeing both her brother and a friend die at the fincas makes Rigoberta depressed, then angry. She questions here what the future will hold for her and responds by feeling afraid. Throughout the remainder of the work, Rigoberta replaces fear with action and independence. Her impulse to respond and engage with her world is present in these passages, as she chooses to be an active player in the events that surround her. Looking at her weeping mother, whose spirit appears to be defeated in this quotation by the ills that have been thrust upon her, Rigoberta responds not by crying but by asking a powerful, somewhat political question. Though Rigoberta is only fourteen years old when this passage takes place, she interprets the events that have happened to her people not as sentences that are unstoppable and must be endured but as conditions that can be improved and changed.

Rigoberta will not rest until she is given a satisfactory answer to the question of what the future holds for her and for all poor Guatemalans. By asking this question of herself, she is motivated to incite change in her own life. This passage is somewhat a turning point in Rigoberta's development as a woman, as she comes to the understanding that advancement must begin with her. This dissatisfaction with the present conditions and hope for a changed future compel Rigoberta to leave the relative safety of the Altiplano in search of knowledge, first as a maid in the capital and later as a human rights worker and political organizer. Rigoberta takes such a step despite being afraid of life, a bravery she exhibits throughout the work and one that is repeated in actions taken by other members of her family and by Guatemalan peasants throughout her country.

3. *We were going to ask for two days holiday and if they didn't give it to us we'd go and spend Christmas somewhere else. But I was anxious. I couldn't do it then, perhaps because of the way my parents had brought me up. I was incapable of disobedience. And those employers exploited my obedience. They took advantage of my innocence.*

This passage appears near the end of Chapter XIV, just before Candelaria is fired. It demonstrates the conflict Rigoberta feels upon realizing that, to force change, she will have to become less compliant and obedient. The "we" Rigoberta refers to here is Candelaria and Rigoberta. As maids at the landowner's home, Rigoberta and Candelaria often must work together, but Candelaria spearheads rebellious acts, including killing and plucking chickens for the Christmas feast but then refusing to dress them. Candelaria is at once a foil for Rigoberta and a role model: through her, Rigoberta begins to understand that one of the few options Indians have for communicating their dissatisfaction with the ladinos who exploit them is to rebel by not catering to the ladinos. Though Rigoberta claims here that she was incapable of disobedience, she quickly learns to become comfortable with going against those in power.

In her autobiography, Rigoberta refers to the ladino opinion that the Mayan Indians were weak and submissive, which contributed to the downfall of the Mayan culture. She rejects this notion, yet in this passage, she stresses the fact that her parents raised her to be submissive. The price of progress is an important theme in *I, Rigoberta Menchu*, because, as Rigoberta points out in this passage, bringing about change sometimes involves changing identity and going against the manners that have been passed down from previous generations. The fact that Candelaria and Rigoberta choose Christmas, a season of tradition for the ladinos, as the time in which they will begin to sabotage their employer works to heighten the tension Rigoberta experiences as she pulls away from the expectations of her elders and ancestors in an attempt to protect the values they have passed on to her.

I

4. *"A revolutionary isn't born out of something good," said my sister. "He is born out of wretchedness and bitterness. This just gives us one more reason. We have to fight without measuring our suffering, or what we experience, or thinking about the monstrous things we must bear in life."*

This passage occurs in Chapter XXXIII, when Rigoberta has gone into hiding in Guatemala. It is one of the few times we hear from Rigoberta's sister, age twelve, who remains nameless. In the following chapter, Rigoberta tells her little sister's story, and we learn that this sister joined the guerillas many years earlier, at the age of eight. This is contrary to Rigoberta's response, which is to take a diplomatic approach to fighting for the rights of her people. These two young women embody the dilemma of whether to fight with weapons or take on the peaceful protests of such activists as Gandhi or Martin Luther King, Jr. Though she is a few years younger than Rigoberta, Rigoberta's sister embraces the dark underbelly of the movement in which she and her other sister are involved. She bluntly reminds Rigoberta that there isn't anything romantic to the lot they have been given in life.

Rigoberta holds on to her idealism despite these dire sentiments. She maintains the belief that her efforts and the efforts of the other *companeros* will ultimately end in something positive. Rigoberta's sister, on the other hand, views life as "monstrous" and revolutionaries as coming into the world out of wretchedness and bitterness. This view contrasts sharply with the idea of birth as Rigoberta illustrates it in the opening chapter of *I, Rigoberta Menchu*, where children are born into lives of hard work but are celebrated by the community. Rigoberta's sister's words are a harsh reminder of the loss of community infrastructure the Indian people have endured. For her, an identity of revolutionary has replaced that of Quiche Indian. Rigoberta resists this jadedness as she continues to identify with the way things used to be in her community and to hope for a reconstruction of traditional Indian identity.

5. *I'm still keeping my Indian identity a secret. I'm still keeping secret what I think no one should know. Not even anthropologists or intellectuals, no matter how many books they have, can find out all our secrets.*

These words close *I, Rigoberta Menchu,* and they are the last we hear from Rigoberta. Her reference to anthropologists is a reminder of the constant presence of Burgos-Debray in the preparation of the work. Throughout the autobiography, Rigoberta tells her story with remarkable candidness. Here, however, she reveals that she has selectively divulged information about her identity, which gives her the final authority and raises the question of what she held back in her story. The exact nature of her relationship with Burgos-Debray is also unclear. In the introduction to *I, Rigoberta Menchu,* Burgos-Debray conveyed her relationship with Rigoberta as being extremely collegial, even familial, because the two shared a Latin heritage. Yet Rigoberta's closing words contradict the sense that she bonded with Burgos-Debray and instead casts the impression that perhaps Rigoberta didn't trust Burgos-Debray to the extent that Burgos-Debray claimed in her introduction. This serves as a reminder that Indians might perceive their relationship with those who are outside of their community, whether they are ladinos, Europeans, or Americans, differently than do those outsiders.

Incidents in the Life of a Slave Girl

Harriet Jacobs (1813–1897)

CONTEXT

Harriet Jacobs was born into slavery in 1813 near Edenton, North Carolina. She enjoyed a relatively happy family life until she was six years old, when her mother died. Jacobs's mistress, Margaret Horniblow, took her in and cared for her, teaching her to read, write, and sew. When Horniblow died, she willed the twelve-year-old Jacobs to her niece, and Jacobs's life soon took a dramatic turn for the worse. Her new mistress's father, Dr. James Norcom ("Dr. Flint" in *Incidents*), subjected Jacobs to aggressive and unrelenting sexual harassment. At age sixteen, afraid that Norcom would eventually rape her, Jacobs began a relationship with a white neighbor, Samuel Tredwell Sawyer ("Mr. Sands" in *Incidents*), and with him she had two children while still in her teens. Instead of discouraging Norcom, Jacobs's affair only enraged him. In 1835, he sent her away to a life of hard labor on a plantation he owned, also threatening to break in her young children as field hands.

Jacobs soon ran away from the plantation and spent almost seven years hiding in a tiny attic crawl space in her grandmother's house. She was unable to sit or stand, and she eventually became permanently physically disabled. In 1842, Jacobs escaped to New York and found work as a nanny in the household of a prominent abolitionist writer, Nathaniel Parker Willis. She was eventually reunited with her children and later joined the antislavery movement. In 1861, the year the Civil War began, Jacobs published *Incidents in the Life of a Slave Girl, Written by Herself*, under the pseudonym Linda Brent.

During the 1850s, when Jacobs was writing her book, slavery was a highly explosive issue in the rapidly expanding United States. Americans argued bitterly over whether or not slavery should be allowed in new territories like California, Kansas, and Nebraska. The Compromise of 1850 sought to hold the Union together by designating California a free state, but it also enacted the Fugitive Slave Act, which facilitated the recapture of runaway slaves. The solution was only temporary, and the divisions that led to the Civil War continued to deepen. In 1854, the Kansas-Nebraska Act led to bloody confrontations between pro- and anti-slavery settlers in those territories. In response to these conflicts, the Underground Railroad became more active and abolitionists increased their propaganda efforts, in which slave narratives such as *Incidents* played a crucial part.

Slave narratives were the dominant literary mode in early African-American literature. Thousands of accounts, some legitimate and some the fictional creations of white abolitionists, were published in the years between 1820 and the Civil War. These were political as well as literary documents, used to promote the antislavery cause and to answer pro-slavery claims that slaves were happy and well-treated. Most slave narratives feature graphic descriptions of the violent whippings and severe deprivation inflicted on slaves, attempting to appeal to the emotions and conscience of white readers. Some of the most famous narratives, such as Frederick Douglass's *Narrative of the Life of Frederick Douglass*, also tell the inspiring story of a brutalized slave's journey toward self-definition and self-assertion. Like other slave narratives, *Incidents in the Life of a Slave Girl* chronicles the abuses of slavery, the slave's struggle for self-definition and self-respect, and the harrowing details of a dangerous escape. However, Jacobs's story also emphasizes the special problems faced by female slaves, particularly sexual abuse and the anguish of slave mothers who are separated from their children. Because of its unique point of view, and because of the skilled, novelistic way Jacobs tells her tale, the book has become one of the most celebrated slave narratives of all time.

Critics have compared the style and structure of *Incidents* to the hugely popular "sentimental novels" of the nineteenth century, many of which tell the story of a young girl fighting to protect her virtue from a sexually aggressive man. Jacobs knew that her contemporaries would see her not as a virtuous woman but as a fallen one and would be shocked by her relationship with Sawyer and the illegitimate children it produced. In spite of her embarrassment, Jacobs insisted on telling her story honestly and completely, determined to make white Americans aware of the sexual victimization that slave women commonly faced and to dramatize the fact that they often had no choice but to surrender their "virtue."

When it was published, *Incidents in the Life of a Slave Girl* was well-received and accepted as a legitimate documentation of the horrors of slavery. For most of the twentieth century, however, scholars believed the book to be a fictional tale written to further the abolitionist cause, and that "Linda Brent," its protagonist, had never really existed. They speculated that Lydia Maria Child, who was a successful novelist as well as an activist, must have been the memoir's real author. Not until the 1980s, when the critic Jean Fagan Yellin discovered a cache of letters from Harriet Jacobs to Lydia Maria Child, did Jacobs again receive credit for her work. Yellin went on to research Jacobs's life and verify that the events of *Incidents* are true and accurate.

After writing her book, Jacobs continued to work to help those she had left behind in slavery. During and after the Civil War, she aided black refugees behind Union lines and nursed African-American soldiers. After the war, she returned to the South and worked for many years to help freed slaves, founding two free schools for blacks and traveling to England to raise money for the freedmen. Jacobs died in Washington, D.C., in 1897.

PLOT OVERVIEW

Incidents in the Life of a Slave Girl opens with an introduction in which the author, Harriet Jacobs, states her reasons for writing an autobiography. Her story is painful, and she would rather have kept it private, but she feels that making it public may help the antislavery movement. A preface by abolitionist Lydia Maria Child makes a similar case for the book and states that the events it records are true.

I

Jacobs uses the pseudonym Linda Brent to narrate her first-person account. Born into slavery, Linda spends her early years in a happy home with her mother and father, who are relatively well-off slaves. When her mother dies, six-year-old Linda is sent to live with her mother's mistress, who treats her well and teaches her to read. After a few years, this mistress dies and bequeaths Linda to a relative. Her new masters are cruel and neglectful, and Dr. Flint, the father, soon begins pressuring Linda to have a sexual relationship with him. Linda struggles against Flint's overtures for several years. He pressures and threatens her, and she defies and outwits him. Knowing that Flint will eventually get his way, Linda consents to a love affair with a white neighbor, Mr. Sands, saying that she is ashamed of this illicit relationship but finds it preferable to being raped by the loathsome Dr. Flint. With Mr. Sands, she has two children, Benny and Ellen. Linda argues that a powerless slave girl cannot be held to the same standards of morality as a free woman. She also has practical reasons for agreeing to the affair: she hopes that when Flint finds out about it, he will sell her to Sands in disgust. Instead, the vengeful Flint sends Linda to his plantation to be broken in as a field hand.

When she discovers that Benny and Ellen are to receive similar treatment, Linda hatches a desperate plan. Escaping to the North with two small children would be impossible. Unwilling to submit to Dr. Flint's abuse, but equally unwilling to abandon her family, she hides in the attic crawl space in the house of her grandmother, Aunt Martha. She hopes that Dr. Flint, under the false impression that she has gone North, will sell her children rather than risk having them disappear as well. Linda is overjoyed when Dr. Flint sells Benny and Ellen to a slave trader who is secretly representing Mr. Sands. Mr. Sands promises to free the children one day and sends them to live with Aunt Martha. But Linda's triumph comes at a high price. The longer she stays in her tiny garret, where she can neither sit nor stand, the more physically debilitated she becomes. Her only pleasure is to watch her children through a tiny peephole, as she cannot risk letting them know where she is. Mr. Sands marries and becomes a congressman. He brings Ellen to Washington, D.C., to look after his newborn daughter, and Linda realizes that Mr. Sands may never free her children. Worried that he will eventually sell them to slave traders, she determines that she must somehow flee with them to the North. However, Dr. Flint continues to hunt for her, and escape remains too risky.

After seven years in the attic, Linda finally escapes to the North by boat. Benny remains with Aunt Martha, and Linda is reunited with Ellen, who is now nine years old and living in Brooklyn, New York. Linda is dismayed to find that her daughter is still held in virtual slavery by Mr. Sands's cousin, Mrs. Hobbs. She fears that Mrs. Hobbs will take Ellen back to the South, putting her beyond Linda's reach forever. She finds work as a nursemaid for a New York City family, the Bruces, who treat her very kindly. Dr. Flint continues to pursue Linda, and she flees to Boston. There, she is reunited with Benny. Dr. Flint now claims that the sale of Benny and Ellen was illegitimate, and Linda is terrified that he will re-enslave all of them. After a few years, Mrs. Bruce dies, and Linda spends some time living with her children in Boston. She spends a year in England caring for Mr. Bruce's daughter, and for the first time in her life she enjoys freedom from racial prejudice. When Linda returns to Boston, Ellen goes to boarding school and Benny moves to California with Linda's brother William. Mr. Bruce remarries, and Linda takes a position caring for their new baby. Dr. Flint dies, but his daughter, Emily, writes to Linda to claim ownership of her. The Fugitive Slave Act is passed by Congress, making Linda extremely vulnerable to kidnapping and re-enslavement.

Emily Flint and her husband, Mr. Dodge, arrive in New York to capture Linda. Linda goes into hiding, and the new Mrs. Bruce offers to purchase her freedom. Linda refuses, unwilling to be bought and sold yet again, and makes plans to follow Benny to California. Mrs. Bruce buys Linda anyway. Linda is devastated at being sold and furious with Emily Flint and the whole slave system. However, she says she remains grateful to Mrs. Bruce, who is still her employer when she writes the book. She notes that she still has not yet realized her dream of making a home for herself and her children to share. The book closes with two testimonials to its accuracy, one from Amy Post, a white abolitionist, and the other from George W. Lowther, a black antislavery writer.

CHARACTER LIST

Linda Brent The book's protagonist and a pseudonym for the author. Linda begins life innocently, unaware of her enslaved state. In the face of betrayal and harassment at the hands of her white masters, she soon develops the knowledge, skills, and determination that she needs to defend herself. Linda is torn between a desire for personal freedom and a feeling of responsibility to her family, particularly her children.

Dr. Flint Linda's master, enemy, and would-be lover. Although Dr. Flint has the legal right to "use" Linda in any way he chooses, he seeks to seduce her by means of threats and trickery rather than outright force. Linda's rebelliousness enrages him, and he becomes obsessed with the idea of breaking her will. Throughout the long battle over Linda's right to own herself, Dr. Flint never shows any sign of remorse or understanding that she is a person with rights and feelings.

Aunt Martha Linda's maternal grandmother and chief ally. Aunt Martha is pious and patient, suffering silently as she watches her children and grandchildren sold off and abused by their masters. Aunt Martha also represents a kind of maternal selfishness, grieving when her loved ones escape to freedom because she will never see them again. For her, family ties must be preserved at all costs, even if it means a life spent in slavery.

Mrs. Flint Linda's mistress and Dr. Flint's jealous wife. Mrs. Flint is characterized mainly by her hypocrisy. She is a church woman who supposedly suffers from weak nerves, but she treats her slaves with callousness and brutality. Mrs. Flint demonstrates how the slave system has distorted the character of southern women.

Mr. Sands Linda's white lover and the father of her children. Mr. Sands has a kindlier nature than Dr. Flint, but he feels no real love or responsibility for his mixed-race children. He repeatedly breaks his promises to Linda that he will free them.

Uncle Benjamin Linda's beloved uncle, a slave who defies and beats his master and then runs away. Uncle Benjamin's successful escape inspires Linda, but also shows her that to run away means to give up all family and community ties.

Benny and Ellen Linda's children with Mr. Sands. Linda loves Benny and Ellen passionately, and her feelings about them drive the book's action. Benny and Ellen are dutiful children but otherwise are not characterized in great detail.

Uncle Phillip Linda's other uncle, instrumental in her escape. Uncle Phillip is reliable and moderate, remaining in the South with his family long after his mother, Aunt Martha, buys his freedom.

William Linda's brother, to whom she is close. William's escape from Mr. Sands, his relatively "kind" master, shows that even a privileged slave desires freedom above all else.

Aunt Nancy Linda's maternal aunt and Mrs. Flint's slave. A martyr figure, Aunt Nancy is slowly killed by Mrs. Flint's abuse.

Peter A family friend who helps Linda escape. Peter urges Linda to risk the escape he has planned rather than to remain in her attic hideaway.

The "white benefactress" An upper-class white friend of Aunt Martha's who hides Linda for a while. She is not named even with a pseudonym and is one of the few genuinely sympathetic slave owners in the book.

Betty A slave in the household of the white benefactress. Betty is uneducated but an intelligent, loyal, and resourceful slave who provides material assistance and encouragement to Linda.

Sally A family friend who lives with Aunt Martha and helps Linda escape into hiding.

Aggie An old slave woman who tells Aunt Martha to rejoice that William has run away. Aggie provides a counterpoint to Aunt Martha's reluctance to see her loved ones escape to the North.

Emily Flint Dr. Flint's daughter and Linda's legal "owner." Emily Flint serves mainly as Dr. Flint's puppet, sometimes writing Linda letters in her name, trying to trick her into returning to Dr. Flint.

Mr. Dodge Emily Flint's husband, who seeks to recapture Linda after Dr. Flint dies. Although Mr. Dodge is northern by birth, entering southern society has made him feel as floundering and desensitized as any native-born slave holder.

Nicholas Flint Dr. Flint's son. Nicholas is essentially a carbon copy of his father, with the same lecherous tendencies toward his female slaves that Dr. Flint has.

Young Mrs. Flint Nicholas's bride. Seemingly kind at first, young Mrs. Flint provides further evidence of the cruelty of slaveholding women when she orders an elderly slave to eat grass.

Mrs. Hobbs Mr. Sands's New York cousin, to whom he "gives" Ellen. Mrs. Hobbs is a little slice of the Old South in Brooklyn, selfishly treating Ellen as property and highlighting the continued danger for escaped slaves even after they reach the Free States.

Mr. Thorne A southerner visiting Brooklyn who betrays Linda's whereabouts to Dr. Flint. Like Mrs. Hobbs, Mr. Thorne signals that a fugitive slave can never feel safe again.

Mrs. Bruce (#1) Linda's first employer in New York City. Mrs. Bruce is a kindly Englishwoman who helps Linda hide from the Flints. She dies and is replaced by Mrs. Bruce #2.

Mr. Bruce Mrs. Bruce's husband, who takes Linda on a trip to England.

Mrs. Bruce (#2) Mr. Bruce's second wife. The second Mrs. Bruce is an abolitionist American who protects Linda at great risk to herself and ultimately buys her freedom from Mr. Dodge. Linda claims to be very grateful to Mrs. Bruce but is also very upset at being purchased by her.

Amy and Isaac Post Abolitionist antislavery friends of Linda's in Rochester. The Posts appear in the book under their real names. They show Linda that it is possible for white people to treat her as an equal.

Reverend and Mrs. Durham Free blacks, and the first people Linda meets in Philadelphia. The Durhams, with their legitimate marriage and morally upstanding lives, remind Linda that slavery has robbed her of the chance to have a normal existence.

Fanny A slave friend of Linda's with whom she escapes by boat to the North. Fanny had the devastating experience of watching all of her children be sold to slave traders.

Miss Fanny An elderly woman and the sister of Aunt Martha's mistress. Miss Fanny buys and frees Aunt Martha when Dr. Sands puts her on the auction block.

Luke An acquaintance of Linda's from home whom she meets on the street in New York. Luke has escaped by stealing money from his dead master, and Linda uses him as an example of how slaves cannot be judged by the same moral standards as free citizens.

ANALYSIS OF MAJOR CHARACTERS

LINDA BRENT An innocent young slave girl, Linda must grow up fast when she finds herself in the clutches of a morally corrupt master. She begins life with a secure attachment to her parents, who take excellent care of her for her first six years. They don't tell her she is a slave, which enables her to develop a strong sense of self-worth that later allows her to overcome major obstacles. Linda is confident and spirited, and she never really accepts the fact that she is the property of another person. Although she is exposed to the most degrading treatment at the hands of Dr. Flint, she never loses her self-respect or her desire to have a normal home and family. She is devoted to her children and willing to endure great suffering for their sake.

Just as she refuses to acknowledge the legitimacy of the slave system, Linda totally rejects her master's claim that she is his property, body and soul. She is an independent spirit, and Dr. Flint's sexual harassment only intensifies her desire to control her own life. Linda is clever, rebellious, and strong-willed, and from the start, she lets Dr. Flint know that she will never submit to his advances. She enters into a battle of wills with him and at times even expresses a perverse satisfaction at tricking him or making him angry. Her independence also leads her to have an affair with Mr. Sands, largely to spite Flint and retain some control over her sexuality. Although she doesn't love Mr. Sands and believes that it is wrong to have sex with him, she takes satisfaction in her ability to choose whom to sleep with. Similarly, when she hides in an attic crawl space for seven years, substituting a life of physical suffering over the relatively "easy" existence she would have had as Dr. Flint's concubine, Linda once again expresses her strong desire to be psychologically and spiritually independent.

As Linda grows up, and particularly after she becomes a mother, her rebellious and independent nature is somewhat modulated. As a young girl, Linda dreams only of escaping slavery for a better life in the North. After becoming a mother, she still wants freedom, but she also feels deeply attached to her children, who are also Dr. Flint's property. She is unwilling to leave them and worries about what will become of them if she runs away. Unlike some of the male characters in the book, she cannot simply sever all of her emotional ties and start over in the North. Most of Linda's actions are directed by this essential emotional and moral conflict. She is torn between her independent nature and her maternal feelings, which urge her to sacrifice her own opportunity for freedom to save her children. In the end, motherhood wins out, although Linda's bold spirit is never extinguished.

DR. FLINT Although he is based on Harriet Jacobs's real-life master, Dr. Flint often seems more like a melodramatic villain than a real man. He is morally bankrupt and lacks any redeeming qualities. He is thoroughly one-dimensional, totally corrupted by the power that the slave system grants him. He sees no reason not to use and abuse his slaves in any way he chooses, and he never shows any signs of sympathy for them or remorse for his crimes. If Dr. Flint expresses kindness, it is invariably a ruse to try to get Linda to sleep with him. Dr. Flint represents the cruelty, callousness, and treachery of the entire slave system.

Dr. Flint loves power above all else, and it often seems that forcing Linda to submit to him is more important to him than simply sleeping with her. He is galled and infuriated by her defiance, and he becomes obsessed with the idea of breaking her will. Rather than simply raping her, he persists in his efforts make her acknowledge his mastery. When Linda escapes, he pursues her relentlessly, putting himself hundreds of dollars in debt to chase her to New York. After his death, his venom and determination seem to be reincarnated in the form of his son-in-law, Mr. Dodge. Dr. Flint neither changes nor grows over the course of the narrative. His malice, representing all of the evils of slavery, appears to affect Linda even from beyond the grave.

AUNT MARTHA Aunt Martha is one of the narrative's most complex characters, embodying Jacobs's ambivalence about motherhood and maternal love. She is a second mother to Linda, a positive force in her life, and a paragon of honesty and decency. She is loving and family-oriented, representing an ideal of domestic life and maternal love. She works tirelessly to buy her children's and grandchildren's freedom. Her unwavering piety leads her to attribute her enslavement to God's will and to patiently bear the loss of her children to slave traders. Beneath her gentle veneer, Aunt Martha is a powerful figure with considerable standing in her community. She is the only black woman in the narrative with her own home. On more than one occasion, she rebukes slave holders who harm her relatives, even telling Dr. Flint to his face that he is going to hell for his treatment of Linda.

Although she is generally a positive character, there is a dark side to Aunt Martha's domesticity. She prizes home and family first and foremost, loving her children and grandchildren so possessively that she cannot bear the thought of being separated from them. She is essential to Linda's survival, but at times her maternal power threatens to suffocate her loved ones. She would rather see them in slavery than have them run away from her to freedom. She mourns the successful escape of her son, Benjamin, who has been dreadfully abused by his master. She repeatedly urges Linda not to run away. When Linda hides in Aunt Martha's attic crawl space, it is as if she has been locked away in a prison of Martha's creation. In the end, Aunt Martha manages to let Linda go, but only when it is clear that to stay would spell total disaster.

THEMES, MOTIFS, AND SYMBOLS

THEMES

THE CORRUPTING POWER OF SLAVERY Jacobs takes great pains to prove that there can be no "good" slave masters. She argues that slavery destroys the morality of slave holders, almost without exception. Slave holders such as Dr. Flint become inhumane monsters. With no legal checks on their behavior, they inflict every conceivable kind of torture on their servants. Most slave masters view slaves as little more than animals or objects, never acknowledging their humanity. But even "kindly" slave holders, such as Mr. Sands, show themselves capable of betraying their slaves when it is convenient or profitable. Mr. Sands promises to free his slave children and may even intend to do so at first. However, in the slave system, such good intentions are easily forgotten. If a slave owner such as Mr. Sands encounters financial problems, he will likely be tempted to sell his own children to get himself out of trouble. Thus, slavery distorts even the most basic emotional instinct: the love of a parent for a child.

Slaves also suffer from the influence of the slave system on their moral development. Linda does not condemn slaves for illegal or immoral acts such as theft or adultery, saying that they usually have no choice but to behave this way. However, she also points out that slaves have no reason to develop a strong ethical sense, as they are given no ownership of themselves or final control over their actions. This is not their fault, but the fault of the system that dehumanizes them. Slaves are not evil like their masters, but important parts of their personalities are left undeveloped.

DOMESTICITY AS PARADISE AND PRISON At the end of *Incidents*, Linda states that she is still waiting to have her greatest dream fulfilled—that of creating a real home for herself and her children. The desire for a comfortable and safe home runs throughout this book, reflecting the cult of domesticity that would have been familiar to Jacobs's mostly white female readers in the nineteenth century. During Jacobs's time, women were relegated to the domestic sphere and expected to find all of their fulfillment in caring for their homes and children. Women were considered to be housewives by their very natures, unfit for any other kind of life. As a black woman excluded from this value system, unable even to live with her children, Linda's longing for a home is understandable.

Jacobs does not always present the domestic sphere as an uncomplicated good. Aunt Martha, the book's representative of domesticity and the only black woman Linda knows who has a real home, is both a positive and a negative character. She is caring and stable, the backbone of her family and a paragon of domestic virtue. Her tidy home is a refuge and a lifeline for Linda from the time her own mother dies. But at times in which Linda needs encouragement in her quest for freedom and independence, Aunt Martha and her house become a discouraging, even confining force. Placing her children's needs above her own, Linda remains a virtual captive in Aunt Martha's home until she is permanently crippled. Hence, home and family are valuable, but they must be balanced with personal freedom. Otherwise, they may overwhelm a woman's individuality.

THE PSYCHOLOGICAL ABUSES OF SLAVERY Most slave narratives emphasize the physical brutality and deprivation that slaves were forced to endure, presenting gory descriptions of beatings and lynchings to shock the reader. Jacobs does not ignore such issues, but her focus on slaves' mental and spiritual anguish makes an important contribution to the genre. As a slave with a relatively "easy" life, Linda does not have to endure constant beatings and hard physical labor. However, she and many of the other slaves around her suffer greatly from being denied basic human rights and legal protection. Men and women are not permitted to marry whomever they choose—they often are not allowed to marry at all. Women are frequently forced to sleep with the masters they despise. Worst of all, families are torn apart, with children sold to a place far away from their parents. Thus, even slaves who are not beaten or starved are stripped of their humanity. When Linda states that she would rather be a desperately poor English farm laborer than a "pampered" slave, she underscores the point that slavery's mental cruelty is every bit as devastating as its physical abuses.

MOTIFS

FRACTURED FAMILY TIES There is only one intact black family in this book, and it does not live in the South. The happy Durham family, whom Linda meets in Philadelphia, contrasts starkly with the situation of black families living under slavery. Aunt Martha struggles to keep her family together, but sees nearly all of her children sold. Linda is taken away from her father at age six to live with her mistress. Her mistress acts as a sort of mother to Linda, but she shows how little this relationship means to her when she treats Linda as property in her will. Linda is also denied the right to raise her own children and meets many women who will never see their children again. Slaves are often not allowed to marry, and if they are, husband and wife cannot always live together. White men father children with black women but feel no parental obligation to them, and they abuse them or sell them as if they were unrelated. If a white woman and a black man have a child together, the woman's family will frequently have the infant killed. Even privileged white families do not care for their own children, fostering them out to slave wet nurses. Finally, pseudofamilial ties that develop between white and black half-siblings and foster siblings are broken as soon as the whites deem it appropriate. Normal human relationships simply cannot survive the disruptions of the slave system.

CONFINEMENT Linda's seven-year imprisonment in Aunt Martha's attic may be the narrative's most spectacular example of confinement, but it is not the only one. Dr. Flint seeks to lock Linda up in an isolated cottage in the woods so he can sleep with her freely. Linda's Uncle Benjamin is jailed for six months before he finally escapes. Dr. Flint imprisons Linda's brother and small children when he finds that she has run away. Linda herself is confined in several places, including under the floorboards of her the house of her "white benefactress." She continues to feel circumscribed by slavery even after she reaches New York. After the passage of the Fugitive Slave Act, she becomes a virtual prisoner in her employers' home. The greatest confinements of all, though, may be mental. Masters keep slaves trapped by ignorance: unable to read, they cannot question the pro-slavery claims that the Bible dictates their condition. They know nothing of life beyond their immediate surroundings, and many believe that free blacks in the North are starving in the streets and begging to return to slavery.

GRAPHIC VIOLENCE Violence is a motif common to all slave narratives, and *Incidents* is no exception. One of Linda's earliest memories is hearing Dr. Flint brutally whip one of his plantation slaves. She recalls seeing the blood and gore on the walls the next morning. Mrs. Flint, a supposed Christian, orders slaves whipped until they bleed and spits in their food so they will have to go hungry. She forces Aunt Nancy to sleep on the floor outside her room, continuing this practice even when Nancy is pregnant, causing her to give birth to many stillborn babies. Mrs. Flint's treatment of Aunt Nancy, as Linda points out, amounts to murder committed very slowly. Slaves are burned, frozen, and whipped to death. Their wounds are washed with brine for further agonizing torture. Jacobs includes such accounts throughout the book, narrating them in detail to shock the reader into sympathy for slaves and to goad him or her into joining the abolitionist movement. Such stories of violence also counteract the common proslavery claim that most slaves were well cared for and led happy, peaceful lives.

SYMBOLS

DR. FLINT Dr. Flint is based on Harriet Jacobs's real-life master, and there is no reason to think that she exaggerated his vicious nature. Through historical research, scholars have confirmed that her depiction of him is accurate. However, in addition to his role in the true events of Jacobs's life story, Dr. Flint also functions as the book's main symbol of the slave system. He is monstrously cruel, hypocritical, and conniving, and he never experiences a moment of guilt, self-doubt, or sympathy for his victims. Given absolute power by the slave system, Flint never questions his right to do whatever he pleases to his slaves. He will accept nothing less than total submission from them. Dr. Flint aptly symbolizes the defining qualities of slavery: lust for power, moral corruption, and brutality. When Linda defies him, she threatens the legitimacy of slavery itself—hence his insistence on "mastering" her.

AUNT MARTHA Aunt Martha, religious, domestic, and patient, represents ideals of womanhood and femininity that were important in Jacobs's time. She lives for her home and her children and wants only to keep her family intact. She is so humble and pious that she believes that God has ordained her a slave for her own good. All of this is in keeping with a set of sexual stereotypes called the Cult of Domesticity (sometimes called "True Womanhood"), which dictated that women were essentially pure, submissive, pious, and oriented toward the private realm of home and family. Jacobs presents Aunt Martha as a sympathetic, virtuous figure, but also uses her to question some of the "feminine" values she represents, particularly as they apply to black women. Her virtue, patience, and piety go unrewarded, as she sees most of her children and grandchildren sold away or escaped to the North. Her last child, Aunt Nancy, is slowly killed by slavery. Aunt Martha's story suggests that if slave women try to adhere to white middle-class ideas of how women should behave, they will be rewarded only with greater suffering.

THE LOOPHOLE OF RETREAT Linda's attic hideout, a place where she is so restricted that she cannot sit or stand, represents all of the forces that keep her from being free. Conversely, it also represents the space of freedom she creates for herself in her own mind. Like slavery, the attic confines Linda's body in terrible ways. She suffers physically and psychologically, losing her ability to speak and walk and becoming despairing and depressed. Her time in the attic almost kills her, which causes the reader to recall how Dr. Flint had claimed his right, under the laws of slavery, to do so himself. However, the attic is also a prison of Linda's own choosing, and in this regard it differs from the imposed confinement of slavery. By going into hiding, she rejects Dr. Flint's claim to own her soul as well as her body. Just as she decides to have consensual sex with Mr. Sands to avoid forced sex with Dr. Flint, she chooses the tortures of the attic over Flint's luxurious cottage in the woods. She may have replaced one set of physical and emotional hardships with another, but she has claimed her mind and spirit as her own. The "loophole," a peephole through which she can watch the outside world, symbolizes the spiritual freedom Linda finds even in seemingly restricted circumstances.

IMPORTANT QUOTATIONS EXPLAINED

---

1. *READER, be assured this narrative is no fiction. I am aware that some of my adventures may seem incredible; but they are, nevertheless, strictly true. I have not exaggerated the wrongs inflicted by Slavery; on the contrary, my descriptions fall far short of the facts.*

Jacobs opens her autobiography with these boldly stated instructions to her mostly white readers. This passage seeks to preempt a common criticism aimed at slave narratives by proslavery forces: that they were fabricated or inaccurate. Jacobs knows that many white northerners will be unwilling to accept her story, so she must assert her authority over her narrative from the start. She literally orders her readers to "be assured," establishing an active, confident narrative voice. Also, Jacobs is about to make her sexual transgressions public, and she cannot trust genteel readers to be sympathetic. Therefore, she lets her audience know that whatever their interpretation of her story, she will remain firmly in control of it. Even as she asserts power over her readers, Jacobs also creates a feeling of intimacy with them by addressing them directly. This is an important strategy, given the sexually frank and politically controversial nature of her text. By making her narrator seem like a real person with whom readers can identify, she makes them less likely to automatically reject her story as unbelievable or immoral.

2. *Slavery is terrible for men; but it is far more terrible for women. Superadded to the burden common to all, they have wrongs, and sufferings, and mortifications peculiarly their own.*

This passage from Chapter XIV embodies Jacobs's most important contribution to the literature of slavery—her depiction of the emotional anguish of slave women. Most slave narratives were written by men, and followed a standard formula that placed great emphasis on bodily pain and physical endurance. They included graphic descriptions of whippings and other physical abuses that stripped the slave of his masculinity. In order to reclaim his manhood, the slave had to assert bodily control over his master by fighting him. The male slave then endured more physical suffering during his dangerous and solitary escape to the North. As a female slave with a very different story to tell, Jacobs creates a new type of slave narrative. She emphasizes that whether or not they are beaten, starved, or made to work in the fields, all female slaves suffer horrible mental tortures such as sexual harassment and the loss of their children. In repeated anecdotes, she portrays the emotional agony of mothers whose children are taken from them, as well as the shame of slave girls who are sexually victimized by white men. For these women, such experiences were just as difficult as any physical punishment, if not more so.

3. *When he told me that I was made for his use, made to obey his command in* every *thing; that I was nothing but a slave, whose will must and should surrender to his, never before had my puny arm felt half so strong.*

In this passage, Linda realizes that although Dr. Flint has complete legal authority over her, she nonetheless has the power to resist him. His goading causes her to erupt into the rebelliousness that will come to define her character and will direct the course of her future. The statement appears in Chapter IV, after Linda relates that Aunt Martha believes slavery to be God's will. Linda and William, taught by their parents to view themselves as self-respecting human beings, do not agree with their grandmother's submissive, fatalistic attitude. They both long to take control of their own destinies. Soon after her encounter with Dr. Flint, Linda advises William to be patient and forgiving in the face of Nicholas Flint's abusiveness. However, as soon as she recommends this course of action, it occurs to her that she herself has no intention of submitting to Dr. Flint's control. Linda realizes that she will never be able to bear slavery passively, and notes that the "war of [her] life had begun." This is an important moment of awakening for her, in which she finds that although Flint owns her body, she can remain spiritually free.

4. *Pity me, and pardon me, O virtuous reader! You never knew what it is to be a slave; to be entirely unprotected by law or custom; to have the laws reduce you to the condition of a chattel, entirely subject to the will of another.*

In this remark from Chapter X, Jacobs makes one of her narrative's most powerful and radical claims: that other women have no right to condemn her for her shocking revelations about her sexual history unless they have been similarly victimized. As in the Preface, she uses a direct tone, taking charge of the reader at a controversial moment and asserting her right to interpret her own life story. If you have never been powerless in the face of sexual harassment and abuse, Jacobs argues, you cannot possibly understand what she has been through. The implication is that slaves should not be judged according to the moral and legal standards of the free world at all. Since slaves have no control over their bodies and destinies, they cannot reasonably be convicted of unethical or illegal actions. Elsewhere in the book, Jacobs makes similar arguments about slaves' relationships to crime and the law, even defending the right of a slave to steal from his master on the grounds that all slaves are owed a lifetime of unpaid wages.

5. *Reader, my story ends with freedom; not in the usual way, with marriage. I and my children are now free! We are as free from the power of slave holders as are the white people of the north; and though that, according to my ideas, is not saying a great deal, it is a vast improvement in my condition.*

In this passage from Chapter XVI, Jacobs explicitly refers to the novelistic conventions she has used to shape her autobiography. *Incidents* borrows much from melodramatic novels, known as "sentimental fiction," which also featured lovely virgins trying to preserve their virtue, lecherous villains, desperate mothers, and enterprising young men. Although Jacobs tells a true story, she uses the popular literature with which her readers were familiar to help them accept and understand her unconventional, even radical, tale. However, *Incidents* also departs from sentimental fiction in important ways, as this quote reminds us. The heroine does not preserve her virtue. She has no valiant male protector, and the villain dies peacefully at home rather than receiving his just desserts. And, as Jacobs notes, the story does not end with the inevitable wedding. Not only is Jacobs still unmarried, but she still does not even have a home of her own, as she points out shortly after this passage. Thus, even as her writing strategy allows her readers to identify with her story, it also challenges the literary conventions of the time. Jacobs makes the point elsewhere in the narrative that slaves cannot be judged according to the laws and morals of the free world. Similarly, she implies here, the "life of a slave girl" cannot be written according to the usual plot lines.

Iola Leroy

Frances Harper
(1825–1911)

CONTEXT

Frances Ellen Watkins Harper, born in 1825, enjoyed a prolific career in the public spotlight until her death in 1911. Harper's *Iola Leroy; or, Shadows Uplifted*, published in 1892, is arguably the first novel written by an African-American woman. There is some speculation among literary critics that perhaps Amelia Johnson's *In God's Way* or Emma Dunham Kelly's *Megda* may have been published in 1891. However, it is fairly undisputed that Harper was the first African-American woman to publish a short story, "The Two Offers," written in 1859. Also well known as a poet, Harper published nine volumes of poetry, mostly organized around the theme of equal rights for blacks.

Harper's career was not limited to writing essays and literature. An influential orator, Harper was particularly active in reform movements that advocated for women's rights, suffrage, temperance, and the abolition of slavery, and her lectures sometime seeped into her literature. For instance, among other commitments to social causes, Harper was active in establishing Sunday school for black children, helping to launch the National Association for Colored Women, and promoting voting rights for blacks and women with Elizabeth Cady Stanton, Susan B. Anthony, and Frederick Douglas. Harper's vision for social reform likely began when she was a child, as she was raised by her uncle, the prominent abolitionist William J. Watkins, and his wife. Before becoming active in the Underground Railroad and other abolitionist movements, Harper taught at the Union Seminary for freed blacks in Ohio as its first female instructor. Accompanied by her daughter, Harper lectured in the South for several years following a short marriage that ended upon the death of her husband, Fenton Harper. In her speeches, she focused on the issue of reshaping the nation via social reform and civil rights for blacks and elaborated on the condition of black women laborers. Harper emphasized religious and family values that countered the ideological impulses of the Gilded Age during which she published—a period of intense political, economic, and industrial upheaval. Harper later resided in Philadelphia, where she published *Iola Leroy*.

Harper wrote *Iola Leroy* during "the women's era," a period from 1890–1910 in which women writers produced volumes of work. In the late eighteenth and early nineteenth centuries, the ideology of the Cult of True Womanhood pervaded American culture and enforced the idea that a virtuous woman's civic duty was to nurture her husband and children and to remain within the confines of the home. *Iola Leroy* challenges this social and cultural norm, often the topic of previous literary works. The protagonist, Iola, works as a nurse, an accountant, and a teacher, and she is an outspoken intellectual. *Iola Leroy* also counters the idea that women should be meek and docile, as dictated by a male-dominated society. Several critics also note that *Iola Leroy* resists the literary convention of the tragic mulatta character that was popular in writings of the 1850s and 1860s. These texts often portrayed miscegenation, or racial mixing, as a catalyst to a female character's demise.

Iola Leroy explores the nineteenth-century ideology that the degree of blackness of one's skin determined one's social class and civil rights. The emphasis on biology, or genetic composition, fixed one's place in society and determined one's worth. This ideology stemmed from scientific principles of the eighteenth century, the Age of Enlightenment, which valued the importance of keeping the white race pure and therefore condemned racial mixing. Western science promoted the idea that life forms were arranged according to a hierarchy. Plants and animals were at the bottom of this "great chain of being," and angels, saints, and God ranked at the top. Whites fell between animals and deities. Blacks' status fell between animals and whites, thus rendering them subhuman. This ideology fueled misperceptions of blacks and rendered miscegenation unacceptable. *Iola Leroy* responds to this ideology and emphasizes the need to elevate the black race by demonstrating its equality with the white race.

The novel is set during Civil War, 1861–1865, and Reconstruction, 1865–1877. Although slavery ended with the Thirteenth Amendment in 1865, racist sentiment against blacks persisted. Harper wrote the novel just after the Supreme Court condoned the Jim Crow laws, which segregated blacks and whites. This continued racial strife influenced the text's genre as a novel of protest, particularly notable in its characterization, plot, and theme. The author's "Note" explains that the novel seeks to inspire blacks to empower or uplift themselves and to move whites to amend the oppression of blacks. For Harper, Christianity provides the means for attaining these goals. Other prominent authors of the period also echoed the importance of religion in ameliorating the racially divided nation, particularly Harriet Beecher Stowe in her widely read novel, *Uncle Tom's Cabin*. *Iola Leroy* was a form of popular literature that therefore had a mass readership, but critics disagree over Harper's intended audience. Some critics contend that Harper wrote for a white Christian audience, while others recognize that her audience was the black Christian population. *Iola Leroy* was largely overlooked as part of the African-American literary canon until the 1970s and 1980s, probably due to dawning of the black feminist literary movement.

PLOT OVERVIEW

The novel's opening chapters establish the Civil War setting, delve into the sociopolitical debates surrounding the war, and illustrate the lives of slaves, particularly Uncle Daniel, Aunt Linda, Robert Johnson, and Tom Anderson. In the North Carolina marketplace, Tom and Robert meet to secretly discuss the Union army's progress against the South. Soon after, the slaves desert their owners and join the Union army. Uncle Daniel leads a clandestine prayer meeting in the woods, the only safe location for slaves to congregate and worship.

Iola Leroy, a slave with a white complexion and blue eyes, is held captive by the abusive Master Tom. Tom Anderson arranges for the Union army to rescue Iola. Exiled from family and home, Iola becomes a nurse in the army. Tom is wounded in a skirmish with Confederate forces, and Iola's attempts to restore his health are in vain. Dr. Gresham, a white Union hospital physician, develops affection for Iola but is disturbed by her tender care of Tom, a black man. Dr. Gresham despises miscegenation, or racial mixing, and checks his feelings for Iola when he learns that she is a mulatta, a woman who is both black and white. Nevertheless, Dr. Gresham cannot suppress his feelings and proposes to Iola.

To explain Iola's condition as a slave, the novel flashes back to her parents' courtship and marriage. The time sequence is out of order to develop conflict and suspense. Iola's father, Eugene Leroy, is a wealthy southern slave owner. When he becomes ill, Leroy's friends abandon him. A compassionate slave, Marie, who is one-quarter black, tends to Leroy. Grateful for Marie's care, the love-struck Leroy sends Marie to a northern school, frees her from slavery, and, despite protests from his cousin Alfred Lorraine, proposes to her. The couple marry, and Marie bears three children who are one-eighth black, but they decide to raise Harry, Iola, and Gracie as white. To protect them from prejudice and slavery, the Leroys lead a solitary life and later send their children to northern schools. Marie predicts that Lorraine, who shuns her and her children because they are mulatto, will sell them into slavery upon Leroy's death.

The novel skips ahead several years to Iola's childhood in a northern school. Ironically, Iola professes a pro-slavery stance. In a letter to her parents, she details a controversial incident at school—a black girl's enrollment. The novel's nonlinear structure creates irony and foreshadows conflict, for the reader already knows that Iola is an enslaved mulatta. Upon Leroy's death from yellow fever, Lorraine orchestrates the family's demise, finagling legal loopholes to overtake Leroy's property, to void Leroy and Marie's marriage, and to nullify Marie's freedom. Then, he nefariously sells Marie and her children as slaves. Marie discloses Iola's true identity as a mulatta. Marie and Gracie also catch yellow fever, and Gracie dies.

The plot shifts back to the present. Iola rebuffs Dr. Gresham's proposal because she refuses to marry a man whose race has oppressed her family and the black community via slavery. Iola begins to accept her identity as black, and she resolves to locate her mother before committing to any marriage. Meanwhile, Harry remains at school in Maine, unaware of his family's tragedy until he receives a letter from Iola. When he learns of his real identity and his family's separation, he becomes ill. Later, Harry joins the Union army's black regime. While he hesitates to associate himself with a race ostracized as lower class and inferior, Harry chooses to pass as black. Iola later nurses Robert, hurt in battle. She sings to soothe him, and he recognizes the song as his mother's. Coincidentally, the two discover that they are relatives. Robert is Marie's sister and Iola's uncle. As the Civil War ends, the Union hospital closes. Iola briefly teaches at a school for freed slaves. Robert revisits the Johnson plantation, where he was enslaved, and discovers a thriving settlement of freed blacks, including Uncle Daniel and Aunt Linda. Harry awakens from a war injury with his mother unexplainably at his bedside. Within the context of religious events, the slaves' families reunite. At a prayer meeting, Robert reclaims his long-lost mother, Harriet. Harry and Iola reconnect at a Methodist Conference.

While Marie and her children move to Georgia and relish their time together, Harriet and Robert travel to the North. Eventually, Iola and Marie reunite with Harriet. Robert and Iola confront discrimination in the northern housing market, and as a black woman, Iola struggles to find employment. The Leroy family associates with progressive northern thinkers, including Dr. Latimer, Dr. Gresham, and Miss Delany, who gather at a *conversazione* to discuss the post-war sociopolitical conditions facing the black race. The group aims to sway public opinion about blacks' achievements, and the astute Dr. Latimer, a mulatto, proves his scholarly ability before Dr. Latrobe, a white southerner skeptical of blacks' intellectual equality. Lorraine becomes a Confederate soldier and dies in the war.

The convoluted plot revolves around and questions the social implications of miscegenation. Iola rejects Dr. Gresham's second proposal as she now fully perceives herself as a black woman who intends to marry a black man. Dr. Latimer decides to pass as black, sacrificing family fortune and the upward mobility granted to whites. Both fervent proponents for blacks' rights, Dr. Latimer and Iola fall in love and marry. Harry is engaged to Miss Delany, a college-educated black woman and teacher. The plight of slave owner and slave has reversed. The slave owners have deteriorated. Master Gundover, Aunt Katie's slave owner, died, and Mrs. Johnson, now poor, depends on Robert's financial support. However, the former slaves prosper and return to North Carolina to elevate the black community. Dr. Latimer and Iola succeed in their respective careers as physician and teacher. Harry and Miss Delany operate a school. Robert purchases land, which he resells to the needy. While Uncle Daniel and Harriet retire, Marie volunteers in the community. The reunited Leroy family toils as advocates for racial empowerment and civil rights.

CHARACTER LIST

Iola Leroy A mulatta woman, former slave, and the novel's protagonist. Iola's parents raised her as white, but she eventually embraces her black heritage and later marries a mulatto man, Dr. Latimer. Even as a slave, Iola exhibits inner strength and optimism. She exudes feminist qualities in her independent spirit and her desire to work outside the home as a teacher, accountant, nurse, and staunch advocate for racial equality.

Dr. Gresham A physician in the Union hospital and Iola's suitor. Dr. Gresham embodies one of the novel's main conflicts, that between professing beliefs and living them through action. While he castigates slavery, advocates for blacks' equal rights, and even vocally supports Dr. Latimer's choice to publicly proclaim himself black, Dr. Gresham, a white man, will marry Iola only if she hides her identity as a mulatta woman and opts to pass as white.

Dr. Latimer A physician, firm proponent of equal rights, and Iola's husband. Dr. Latimer's scholarly accomplishments challenge Dr. Latrobe's beliefs that blacks are intellectually inferior to whites. In dispelling Dr. Latrobe's misperceptions of blacks, the mulatto Dr. Latimer resists the racial stereotypes rampant in the nineteenth century. Dr. Latimer is principled and committed to uplifting the black race, and he encourages Iola to enlist her talents for the same social cause.

Robert Johnson Lieutenant in a black unit of the Union army, former slave, and Iola's long-lost uncle. Robert is literate, articulate, hard working, and courageous. He rallies the slaves in their efforts to abandon the plantations, owns a successful business, and quickly rises in the army's ranks. Generous and forgiving, Robert offers financial support to his former slave mistress after the Civil War dismantles the slave system and her plantation, leaving her destitute. Robert is also a mulatto who could pass as white.

Harry Leroy Iola's brother, Miss Delany's fiancé, and a soldier in the Union army's black regimen. Harry initially wavers about his decision to pass as black, unwilling to accept the decline in social status that accompanies such a choice. At times portrayed as lacking confidence and appearing physically weak, Harry's resolve strengthens throughout the novel, and he becomes more assertive and proud of identifying himself as black.

Marie Leroy Iola and Harry's mother, Eugene Leroy's wife, and a former slave. As a mulatta herself, Marie is conflicted over her husband's refusal to inform their children of their black heritage. The merciful and compassionate Marie cares for her slave master during his illness and his spiritual decline. Overtly maternal, Marie is dedicated to her children. She is also industrious and employs her skills in the domestic arts to sustain herself financially.

Eugene Leroy Iola's white father and a wealthy Southern plantation and slave owner. Leroy leads a morally depraved and spiritually empty lifestyle fraught with carousing and carelessness until he falls ill. Progressive in thought and bold in his actions, Leroy marries a slave, Marie, at a time when southern culture deemed him a social pariah for doing so. However, the cautious father overprotects his children and hides their true identities from them.

Alfred Lorraine A Confederate supporter, cousin to Eugene Leroy, and the novel's antagonist to Iola and her family. Alfred, corrupt and wicked, destroys the Leroy family for a financial payoff. Lorraine objectifies women and commodifies blacks. That is, he dehumanizes the race as mere property to be sold for monetary gain.

Aunt Linda A slave on the Johnson plantation. Aunt Linda's clairvoyant visions reveal her strong faith, as she predicts the slaves' freedom and ultimate salvation. She also acts as a preacher of sorts who converses regularly with other characters about leading a moral life, and she endorses pro-suffrage and antislavery sentiment. Intelligent and worldly, the feminist Aunt Linda establishes her own business and contributes her earnings toward purchasing a home for herself and her husband.

Miss Delany Harry's fiancée and a teacher and community leader. Miss Delany is a college-educated black woman who represents a model for the race, as she devotes her time to intellectual pursuits and teaching women. Strong-willed and opinionated, yet fraught with feminine decorum, Miss Delany freely expresses her views about racial uplift even among a group of men. Harper emphasizes that Miss Delany is not a mulatta and praises Harry's marriage to this successful black woman.

Tom Anderson A resourceful, high-spirited, intelligent slave. Tom joins the Union army with Robert Johnson. Remarkably selfless, Tom functions as a Christ figure who orchestrates Iola's rescue from an abusive slave owner and sacrifices his life to save his fellow soldiers. Tom's character attests to slaves' innate intelligence despite their masters' rejection of a formal education for them.

Uncle Daniel Aunt Katie's husband, loyal slave to his master, and storyteller. Uncle Daniel leads prayer meetings and shares stories with the slaves, particularly his personal slave narrative. His character is a vehicle for the oral tradition.

Dr. Latrobe A southern colleague of Dr. Latimer and Dr. Gresham with racist attitudes about blacks.

Aunt Katie Uncle Daniel's wife and a slave on the Gundover plantation. The benevolent Aunt Katie represents Christian forgiveness, as she does not seek retribution against her former owners who sequestered her from her husband and who physically assaulted her.

Master Gundover Aunt Katie's slave owner. Master Gundover embodies the hypocrisy of Christian believers who own, and therefore dehumanize, slaves.

Master Thurston Uncle Daniel's slave owner. Master Thurston entrusts Uncle Daniel with guarding his money while he fights in the Confederate army, and he exemplifies the slave owner who, though kind, still suppresses and brutalizes blacks because he embraces the institution of slavery.

Mrs. Johnson Robert Johnson's slave owner. While Mrs. Johnson teaches Robert to read and treats him fairly kindly, she does believe that Robert is unequal to whites.

Harriet A former slave and Robert and Marie's mother. Harriet reunites with her son and daughter after nearly thirty years of separation.

Louis Bastine An attorney hired by Alfred Lorraine. Despite his scruples about the institution of slavery, Louis nonetheless deceitfully kidnaps Iola and delivers her into the hands of Lorraine, ostensibly setting in motion her inevitable sale at the slave auction block.

Captain Sybil A Union army leader and friend to Robert. Captain Sybil frequently engages Robert in heavy discussions about slavery and its political, social, and religious ramifications.

ANALYSIS OF MAJOR CHARACTERS

IOLA LEROY Because of her complex racial background, Iola has a complicated relationship with race and biology. To protect their mulatto children from discrimination, Iola's mother, a mulatta, and her father, a white slave owner, raise Iola as white and sequester themselves from southern society. Unaware that she is a mulatta, Iola ironically adopts a pro-slavery attitude, for she believes her father treats his slaves kindly. However, after Iola endures family tragedy and coercion into slavery, her perspective changes and she begins to gain more awareness about her identity and more confidence in her convictions. For example, she shuns Dr. Gresham's marriage proposal because he is white, and his race has been responsible for slavery. However, she hesitates to admit to prospective employers that she is a mulatto and doesn't disclose her true identity until she experiences prejudice at work. Ultimately, she not only accepts but embraces her black heritage. She marries Dr. Latimer, a mulatto man. She publicly asserts herself as black and devotes her life to empowering blacks through education and securing civil rights.

As she develops her racial identity, Iola fosters feminist qualities as well, and in a way, Harper uses her as a vehicle to present her social agenda, which upholds feminist tenets. For example, Iola refuses to marry Dr. Gresham, even though doing so would grant her financial security and upper-class social standing. Instead, Iola chooses to remain independent and prioritizes reuniting her family. Iola's refusal of Dr. Gresham and her efforts to find her family are intertwined with her acknowledgment of her identity as a black woman. Even though Iola becomes financially well-off with Robert providing for her, she nonetheless determines that women should support themselves by learning a marketable skill. Iola labors in the public sphere at a time when few women of her social class worked outside the home, and she ultimately maintains a career as a teacher. Further, Iola openly expresses her opinions at the *conversazione*, and her confidence and self-assertion reflect her belief that she is equal to the male intellectuals at the event. Iola also transcends her victimization as a slave. Her strength and self-determination overturn the popular nineteenth-century literary motif of the tragic mulatta whose fate is doomed.

DR. GRESHAM Dr. Gresham, a white physician, never succeeds in making his views on race consistent. As the son of a northern abolitionist, he publicly and avidly supports blacks and their quest for equal rights. However, he romanticizes blacks by pitying them and seeking to rescue them from their suffering, and though he loves Iola, he can't allow himself to marry a woman who acknowledges her black heritage. He wholeheartedly supports Dr. Latimer's right to assert his mulatto identity and to support black rights. However, while Dr. Gresham does encourage Iola to advocate on behalf of the black race, he explicitly expresses his desire for her to pass as white, especially in his family's presence. Such hypocrisy represents the conflict that lies at the center of the novel and which Harper addresses on multiple levels of religious and moral issues—incongruence between beliefs and actions.

Dr. Gresham reveals the prevalence of discrimination not only against blacks but also against women. For example, he wants Iola to completely erase her black heritage and essentially repudiate her mother's existence. He fully recognizes and backs Dr. Latimer's career and his advocacy for blacks, but he discounts Iola's career goals, telling her she is destined to fail in her objective to uplift the black race in the South through community action. Through Dr. Gresham, Harper also addresses class issues associated with race and gender. Dr. Gresham warns Iola that marrying outside of the white race will lower her social class, revealing his preoccupation with upward mobility, surface appearances, and how society judges him.

DR. LATIMER Throughout *Iola Leroy*, Dr. Latimer remains passionately committed to the social cause of empowering blacks, and unlike Dr. Gresham, he lives his beliefs. Though he is a mulatto who appears white, he decides to pass as black and to relinquish his white grandmother's inheritance. He sacrifices his lucrative medical practice in the North to serve the needy in the South. Passing as white would have given Dr. Latimer a comfortable upper-class existence, but he freely chooses a life fraught with toil. The fact that Dr. Latimer is a learned scholar and a doctor who presents his research at conferences demonstrates blacks' intelligence, and his nobility and purity overturn the nineteenth-century misconception that blacks were inferior to whites. Through Dr. Latimer, Harper attempts to reverse ingrained cultural and social assumptions about blacks' status as unequal.

Dr. Latimer also helps emphasize and promote black authorship and scholarly contributions. He urges Iola to write a book for a black audience and encourages her to be a voice for her race and a model for what it can attain. Dr. Latimer attests to the idea that blacks must create their own literature and scholarship to shape a legacy of intellectual achievement. In addition, according to Dr. Latimer, white authors cannot satisfactorily write about blacks' history and life experience. He attempts to inspire Iola to accomplish what Harper herself realized through her career as a poet, novelist, essayist, and orator. Indeed, Dr. Latimer's deep respect for Iola, her pursuit of knowledge, and her socially conscious contributions to society eventually becomes love. Theirs is an intellectualized romance, and Harper deliberately fashions the relationship as such to reinforce to her audience blacks' intelligence and purity.

THEMES, MOTIFS, AND SYMBOLS

THEMES

THE DOUBLE OPPRESSION OF RACE AND GENDER Race and gender prove to be two daunting obstacles for the women in *Iola Leroy*, and success depends on the women's ability to keep a strong black feminist stance. Prescribed female roles and racial prejudice hinder Aunt Linda and Iola in their ambitions and endeavors, but they resist the expectation that women's work is nurturing children and husbands. Both characters transcend the confines of the home, and Iola believes that working in public is key to marital success. She repeatedly encounters racism while pursuing her career, and only through the white Mr. Cloten does she secure an accountancy position. To finance a home, Aunt Linda, an entrepreneur, sells pies while her husband is at war. She exerts power over her husband, who disagrees about the purchase; however, due to slavery, she remains illiterate and thus subjugated.

BIOLOGICAL VS. SOCIAL CONDITIONS OF RACE In *Iola Leroy*, Harper explores the biological and social bases of race and raises the question of which plays a larger role in forming identity. Iola, Harry, and Dr. Latimer, born of slave mothers, struggle with whether or not to pass as white and hide their genetic composition as black. During the nineteenth century, when *Iola Leroy* takes place, physical appearance signified intelligence, morality, and power, and these characters' choices of whether to live as white or black have serious consequences. Dr. Latimer, a mulatto who appears white, chooses to live as black, and his intellectual successes contrast Dr. Latrobe's racist belief that blacks are inferior to whites. Iola and Harry, who were raised as white and appear white, later choose to pass as black. Iola labels herself "the Iola of now," a black activist who marries a mulatto and repudiates Dr. Gresham because his whiteness links him to slavery. Fearing social and familial disapproval of his love for a black woman, Dr. Gresham begs Iola to pass as white, but she refuses, bringing much hardship to her life. For these characters, "blackness" and "whiteness" mean much more than biology and dictate an entire world view.

MOTIFS

THE CONTRAST OF DARKNESS AND LIGHT Images of darkness and light pervade Harper's novel and serve several purposes. Shadows suggest blacks' exile from Africa and coercion into slavery. The "uplifted shadows" of the title of the novel itself, *Iola Leroy; or, Shadows Uplifted*, suggest freedom both from bondage and racial empowerment. The image also holds religious meaning. Harper's note at the beginning of the novel mentions "light beyond the darkness" and "hope in God's great justice," linking light with salvation. Dr. Gresham believes that Iola should hide her status as a mulatta, especially from his upper-class, white family, which Iola considers a "veil of concealment." Dr. Latimer likewise lifts this "veil" in asserting his black heritage. The blond-haired, blue-eyed doctor refused to stifle his identity and "stood in his own light," when he could have passed for a white man and profited from his grandmother's inheritance. Light emanates from Iola's "luminous" and "lustrous" eyes as she sings to Tom and admits her love for Dr. Latimer. Harper associates blacks with light images, suggesting truth, goodness, and intelligence, which is a marked difference from the prevalent idea of the time that blacks were inferior in intellect, moral judgment, and appearance.

THE CHRISTIAN RELIGION Harper believes that Christianity will unify the North and South, and she uses a sentimental style to arouse empathy in her Christian audience for blacks' condition. Dialogue between characters speaks indirectly to readers, emphasizing that religion must be lived in actions. Harper criticizes characters who hypocritically attest to upholding Christian beliefs. For example, Master Gundover attempts to force a slave to publicly confess sins before a preacher, but the preacher condones the slave's actions and admonishes Gundover's contradictory testament to Christianity and ownership of slaves. Characters of both races exemplify Harper's religious ideal. Dr. Latimer relinquishes his prosperous career to serve freed slaves in the South, and Harper compares him to Moses and Nehemiah, Biblical figures who led oppressed peoples to freedom. Further, Mr. Cloten supports Iola's right to work as an accountant in his store. At the *conversazione*, Iola compares blacks to Jesus, a figure who had been oppressed but later exalted. Iola declares that the afflicted, like Jesus, will be uplifted and that the Christian religion will lead the country to glory.

LITERACY AND AUTHORSHIP Harper saturates *Iola Leroy* with the concept of literacy as a means of empowerment and incorporates various genres, including sentimentalism, historical fiction, social protest, and slave narrative, into the novel to exhibit her intellectual, artistic accomplishments, and to idealize her characters. Eclectic modes of writing also advance the plot and the theme. Prior to realizing her true identity, Iola writes to her parents about a black student's enrollment in school, which she considers atypical. Iola's letter to Harry, revealing his heritage and warning him to remain distant, propels the plot, guaranteeing Harry's safety. The *conversazione*'s academic papers and poetry evoke the theme of racial uplift and demonstrate blacks' intellectual achievements. The slaves' code language is a form of verbal literacy. Harper depicts slaves as innately intelligent because they create their own system of language. African American literature frequently includes the motif of writing to elicit the power of literacy in delivering slaves to freedom and to prove blacks' intellectual abilities.

SYMBOLS

BIRTHMARKS Robert and Marie both have birthmarks, which represent the freed slaves' hopes for family reunification. Since slavery has dislocated their family for nearly a generation, the only knowledge that Iola and Robert have of their more distant relatives is their physical descriptions. Their grandmother's slave song is the sole memory that Iola and Robert share. Robert recalls the mole on Marie's cheek, and Iola's photo of her mother convinces Robert that Marie is his sister. Robert displays "a red spot on his temple" that identifies him as Iola's uncle. Family is of the utmost importance—Iola even refuses to marry Dr. Gresham because she prioritizes finding her long-lost mother. Birthmarks identify individuality and family legacy and offer hope that families will one day be reunited.

NATURAL IMAGERY Harper rarely describes setting, but the descriptions of natural imagery that she does include work symbolically to offer unique perspectives on the events taking place. Prior to the Civil War, slaves held their secret prayer meetings in the dismal woods. Harper's transformation of the post-war North Carolina countryside to a fertile, blossoming setting symbolizes rebirth and optimism—a passage from slavery to freedom. When Dr. Latimer and Iola arrive in North Carolina, their home is shrouded in flowers, which suggests both the South's renewal and the couple's crossing of a threshold into married life. Harper also details the natural imagery surrounding two marriage proposal scenes. Dr. Latimer's proposal to Iola occurs amidst the end of summer on a beautiful day, and the lovely scenery Harper describes suggests contentment and the rightness of the decision to get married, particularly for strong young women such as Iola. Harry proposes to Miss Delany on a carriage ride through a forest, and Miss Delany comments on the "stately pines that remind [her] of a procession of hooded monks." This metaphor refers to the sanctity and purity of marriage.

AUNT LINDA The character of Aunt Linda serves as a symbol of optimism, and her visionary capability develops the novel's theme of vanquishing slavery and foreshadows the novel's plot. Aunt Linda has premonitions of liberation and transcendence for blacks, and she predicts the North's victory in the war and the subsequent abolition of slaves. She seems certain of her visions of glory and freedom from captivity and thus exudes positive energy and enthusiasm. From one of her visions, Aunt Linda predicts Iola's arrival in the South and her success in ameliorating conditions for black women. Aunt Linda sees blacks as uplifted, and, because of her visions, she herself is elevated to a role akin to a Biblical figure or an oracle who predicts the future.

IMPORTANT QUOTATIONS EXPLAINED

---

1. *I ain't got nothing 'gainst my ole Miss, except she sold my mother from me. And a boy ain't nothin' without his mother. I forgive her, but I never forget her, and never expect to. But if she were the best woman on earth I would rather have my freedom than belong to her.*

Robert makes this remark in Chapter II as the slaves discuss abandoning their masters' plantations to join the Union army and seek their freedom. Robert responds to Uncle Daniel's criticism of his plan to desert Mrs. Johnson, Robert's slave mistress who taught him to read and who treats him rather kindly. Unlike Uncle Daniel, Robert rejects the institution of slavery, no matter how benevolently his owner treats him. The slave system bears responsibility for slave families' dislocation, exile from their homeland, and breakdown of individuals' self-possession. Harper constructs *Iola Leroy* around such issues of identity—self-perception and family unity. One of the novel's main themes elaborates on how slavery fractures the family unit and slaves' subsequent attempts to reconstruct surrogate families via the slave community on the plantations, as well as freed or fugitive slaves' efforts to reunite with their biological families who had been sold or separated from them. The novel's structure and plot lines trace the Leroy family's fracture and reunification.

Through this quotation, Harper also explores gender roles and critiques political events. Robert's comment reveals a provocative gender role reversal. A woman, Mrs. Johnson, holds a position of power over a subordinate man, Robert. Robert is forced to take Mrs. Johnson's last name, which strips him of his identity and family ties and elucidates his lowly social status as a slave. Though he flouts Mrs. Johnson's authority over him, Robert does esteem his mother, and here Harper likely draws from the tradition of sentimental novels, which tend to elevate mother figures. In ungluing Robert's domestic center, his family, Harper not only depicts the reality of slave life but also evokes the reader's sympathy. Robert's comment also enables Harper to address the national political milieu. Harper responds to United States legislation, such as the reversal of the Fugitive Slave Act—a small step toward freedom for blacks. Nevertheless, Harper wrote the novel during a time of increasing racial strife, in the 1890s, when the Jim Crow laws that cemented separation between blacks and whites were condoned by the Supreme Court.

---

2. *Uncle Robert, [. . .] I have a theory that every woman ought to know how to earn her own living. [A] great amount of sin and misery springs from the weakness and inefficiency of women. [E]very woman should have some skill or art which would insure her at least a comfortable support. I believe that there would be less unhappy marriages if labor were more honored among women.*

Iola proclaims these feminist opinions in Chapter XXIV after enduring and escaping her fall into slavery and reuniting with her mother and while living in the North with her uncle, Robert. Iola firmly believes that women should pursue their own interests and develop unique, marketable skills. She calls for individualism, a fundamental principle in the United States, and she likewise endorses feminism to a degree. In the early days of the country's development, marriage was considered more of an economic transaction than a romantic union. Women's dowries were essential to a marriage, and a husband and wife's relationship was deemed somewhat of a commodity in which men possessed, or owned, women. In this sense, women were subjugated. Women at the time were expected to remain in the home and to reign over only the designated domestic responsibilities. This social custom stemmed from the Cult of True Womanhood, earlier ideological beliefs that restricted women's roles to the domestic circle.

In questioning women's presence in the workplace, Harper seems to invert the idea of true womanhood. That is, she challenges the prescribed gender role allotted to women that essentially and narrowly defined their work as solely housework. Harper reconsiders women's ability to contribute financially to married and family life. Iola contends that women should attain their own goals outside of the home and that such self-affirmation will enhance and strengthen the bonds of marriage. Iola goes so far as to ascertain that women's inability to work beyond the domestic unit does not merely enervate or weaken marriage but is also equivalent to committing a "sin." Therefore, Iola equates keeping women inside the home to complete specific domestic tasks with moral corruption.

3. *[. . .] Lindy warn't satisfied wid rentin' so I buyed a piece ob lan', an' I'se glad now I'se got it. Lindy's got a lot ob gumption; knows most as much as a man. She ain't got dat long head fer nuffin. She's got lots ob sense, but I don't like to tell her so.*

Aunt Linda's husband, Salters, explains his perceptions of Aunt Linda's authority to Iola, Robert, and Uncle Daniel in Chapter XIX. Salters makes this comment during Robert and Iola's visit to the former Johnson plantation following the Civil War and the slaves' emancipation. Through her monetary contributions to purchasing their home, Aunt Linda makes financial decisions and controls money—tasks clearly designated to men at that time. While Salters admits his affection and respect for his wife, his reveals in these words that he desires to keep her in her place—subordinate to him. He fears she will exert too much influence over him and usurp the decision-making power assigned to men. In short, Aunt Linda is a threat to Salters's masculinity. According to Salters, Aunt Linda is *almost* as intelligent as a man. His carefully chosen words reveal a layer of sexism buried beneath his admiration for his wife's practicality and intellectual curiosity.

Harper incites black feminism in the novel, and she explores the notion that black women are doubly oppressed—subjugated because they are black and because they are female. Aunt Linda suffers through the physical and emotional abuse of slavery and remains illiterate because her former owner forbade her to become educated. A former slave, Aunt Linda also exists under the reign of her husband, who secretly respects and admires her but remains silent and aloof about his appreciation for her persistence in urging him to purchase their own home. Resilient and faithful, Aunt Linda surmounts her trials and continues to blatantly declare her opinions and desires. She even becomes a businesswoman who successfully sells her pies to survive while her husband is at war. Harper presents other strong female characters as well, such as Miss Delany and Iola, who are educated and career-oriented. Aunt Linda is an entrepreneur, an assertive wife, and an active community member, and she and the other strong women celebrate black women's determination and perseverance in the face of multiple obstacles in their private lives and in the broader realm of society.

4. *"But, Mr. Bascom," Harry said, "I do not understand this. It says my mother and father were legally married. How could her marriage be set aside and her children robbed of their inheritance? This is not a heathen country. I hardly think barbarians would have done any worse; yet this is called a Christian country."*
   "Christian in name," answered the principal.

In Chapter XIV, a distraught and stupefied Harry attempts to comprehend the legality of his sudden change in race, social status, and family situation upon his father's death and Lorraine's subsequent manipulation. At his boarding school in Maine, Harry is perplexed by the letter from Iola explicating the dissolution of his parents' marriage, his mother's real background as a mulatta, and the family's plunge into slavery. Harry and Mr. Bascom wrestle with the moral contradiction of the legal existence of the slave trade in a purportedly Christian nation. Harper's purpose in penning the novel emerges in its overarching theme—advocacy for a renewal of Christian values as the method for mending the country's disunity, the North's and South's impasse on political and social issues, namely slavery. Harper exposes the false nature of a Christian government that enabled the slave trade to flourish, dehumanized an entire race, and harbored slave owners.

Harper also uses characters to generate a theme and to transcribe her own views as a champion of both a pro-abolition platform and pro-equal rights policies for blacks and women. *Iola Leroy* is rich in dialogue, and this interaction among characters serves as a means of delivering Harper's political and social agendas. The characters directly translate Harper's beliefs to the audience. For example, Mr. Bascom is a northerner and an active abolitionist whom Eugene Leroy entrusts to care for Harry and who acts as a mentor to the young boy. The principal's concise, pointed statement is a loaded accusation that exposes the hypocrisy and sanctimoniousness, or false piety, of slave owners who profess themselves to be Christian. Mr. Bascom's simple reply to Harry also unleashes a broader charge against the nation as a whole, particularly its legal and government institutions. Harper makes a purposeful political statement via literary elements—characters and dialogue.

5. *Doctor, were I your wife, are there not people who would caress me as a white woman who would shrink from me in scorn if they knew I had one drop of Negro blood in my veins? [. . .] No, Doctor, I am not willing to live under a shadow of concealment which I thoroughly hate as if the blood in my veins were an undetected crime of my soul.*

This quotation appears in Chapter XXVII when Dr. Gresham proposes to Iola for the second time. Iola again rejects Dr. Gresham's offer, adamantly citing his hypocritical desire for her to silence any acknowledgment of her black heritage and warning that society's scathing view of blacks would inevitably affect her, marring her marriage to the white Dr. Gresham. Further, Iola speculates that Dr. Gresham's circle of friends and family would belittle her and defame her character if they discovered her true biological make-up. While she appears to be of the white race, Iola consciously opts to identify herself as black. Dr. Gresham's protests of Iola's pride in her black roots indicate his discomfort with miscegenation. In Harper's time, a person's civil rights and social status were defined according to his or her position on the Great Chain of Being, a racist, flawed scientific scale that measured a person's worth according to skin tone, ranking whites ahead of blacks on the spectrum.

Harper uses figurative language to reinforce Iola's insistence in her affirmation of her racial identification as black. The "shadows of concealment" refer to the novel's title and bear particular significance. Through this metaphor that compares passing as white to hiding her true identity, Iola rebuffs Dr. Gresham's recommendation that she align herself with the white race. The "shadow" refers to darkness, a motif that runs throughout the novel. In this instance, the shadow represents a falseness, a veil of sorts, that posing as white would bring upon Iola. Also, Iola refers to "an undetected crime of [her] soul," a simile that likens being black to unconsciously committing a criminal act. This comparison alludes to the political and legal fallout associated with a person's biology. For Iola, being born black carries the burden of unwarranted prejudice.

Jane Eyre

Charlotte Brontë (1816–1855)

CONTEXT

Charlotte Brontë was born in Yorkshire, England, on April 21, 1816, to Maria Branwell and Patrick Brontë. Because Brontë's mother died when Brontë was five years old, Brontë's aunt, a devout Methodist, helped her brother-in-law raise his children. In 1824, Brontë and three of her sisters—Maria, Elizabeth, and Emily—were sent to Cowan Bridge, a school for clergymen's daughters. When an outbreak of tuberculosis killed Maria and Elizabeth, Charlotte and Emily were brought home. Several years later, Brontë returned to school, this time in Roe Head, England. She became a teacher at the school in 1835 but decided after several years to become a private governess instead. She was hired to live with and tutor the children of the wealthy Sidgewick family in 1839, but the job was a misery to her and she soon left it. Once Brontë recognized that her dream of starting her own school was not immediately realizable, she returned to working as a governess, this time for a different family. Finding herself equally disappointed with governess work the second time around, Brontë recruited her sisters to join her in more serious preparation for the establishment of a school.

Although the Brontës' school was unsuccessful, their literary projects flourished. At a young age, the children created a fictional world they named Angria, and their many stories, poems, and plays were early predictors of shared writing talent that eventually led Emily, Anne, and Charlotte to careers as novelists. As adults, Charlotte suggested that she, Anne, and Emily collaborate on a book of poems. The three sisters published under male pseudonyms: Charlotte's was Currer Bell, while Emily and Anne wrote as Ellis and Acton Bell, respectively. When the poetry volume received little public notice, the sisters decided to work on separate novels but retain the same pseudonyms. Anne and Emily produced their masterpieces in 1847, but Charlotte's first book, *The Professor*, never found a willing publisher during her lifetime. Charlotte wrote *Jane Eyre* later that year. The book, a critique of Victorian assumptions about gender and social class, became one of the most successful novels of its era, both critically and commercially.

Autobiographical elements are recognizable throughout *Jane Eyre*. Jane's experience at Lowood School, where her dearest friend dies of tuberculosis, recalls the death of Brontë's sisters at Cowan Bridge. The hypocritical religious fervor of the headmaster, Mr. Brocklehurst, is based in part on that of the Reverend Carus Wilson, the Evangelical minister who ran Cowan Bridge. Brontë took revenge upon the school that treated her so poorly by using it as the basis for the fictional Lowood. Jane's friend Helen Burns's tragic death from tuberculosis recalls the deaths of two of Brontë's sisters, Maria and Elizabeth, who succumbed to the same disease during their time at Cowan Bridge. Additionally, John Reed's decline into alcoholism and dissolution is most likely modeled upon the life of Brontë's brother Branwell, who slid into opium and alcohol addictions in the years preceding his death. Finally, like Brontë, Jane becomes a governess—a comparatively neutral vantage point from which to observe and describe the oppressive social ideas and practices of nineteenth-century Victorian society.

The plot of *Jane Eyre* follows the form of a bildungsroman, which is a novel that tells the story of a child's maturation and focuses on the emotions and experiences that accompany and incite his or her growth to adulthood. In *Jane Eyre*, there are five distinct stages of development, each linked to a particular place: Jane's childhood at Gateshead, her education at the Lowood School, her time as Adele's governess at Thornfield, her time with the Rivers family at Morton and at Marsh End (also called Moor House), and her reunion with and marriage to Rochester at Ferndean. From these various experiences, Jane becomes the mature and steady-handed woman who narrates the novel retrospectively.

But the bildungsroman plot of *Jane Eyre*, and the book's element of social criticism, are filtered through a third literary tradition— that of the Gothic horror story. Like the bildungsroman, the Gothic genre originated in Germany. It became popular in England in the late eighteenth century, and it generally describes supernatural experiences, remote landscapes, and mysterious occurrences, all of which are intended to create an atmosphere of suspense and fear. Jane's encounters with ghosts, dark secrets, and sinister plots add a potent and lingering sense of fantasy and mystery to the novel.

After the success of *Jane Eyre*, Brontë revealed her identity to her publisher and went on to write several other novels, most notably Shirley in 1849. In the years that followed, she became a respected member of London's literary set. But the deaths of siblings Emily and Branwell in 1848, and of Anne in 1849, left her feeling dejected and emotionally isolated. In 1854, she wed the Reverend Arthur Nicholls, despite the fact that she did not love him. She died of pneumonia, while pregnant, the following year.

PLOT OVERVIEW

Jane Eyre is a young orphan being raised by Mrs. Reed, her cruel, wealthy aunt. A servant named Bessie provides Jane with some of the little kindness she receives, telling her stories and singing songs to her. One day, as punishment for fighting with her bullying cousin John Reed, Jane's aunt imprisons Jane in the red-room, the room in which Jane's Uncle Reed died. While locked in, Jane, believing that she sees her uncle's ghost, screams and faints. She wakes to find herself in the care of Bessie and the kindly apothecary Mr. Lloyd, who suggests to Mrs. Reed that Jane be sent away to school. To Jane's delight, Mrs. Reed concurs.

Once at the Lowood School, Jane finds that her life is far from idyllic. The school's headmaster is Mr. Brocklehurst, a cruel, hypocritical, and abusive man. Brocklehurst preaches a doctrine of poverty and privation to his students while using the school's funds to provide a wealthy and opulent lifestyle for his own family. At Lowood, Jane befriends a young girl named Helen Burns, whose strong, martyrlike attitude toward the school's miseries is both helpful and displeasing to Jane. A massive typhus epidemic sweeps Lowood, and Helen dies of consumption. The epidemic also results in the departure of Mr. Brocklehurst by attracting attention to the insalubrious conditions at Lowood. After a group of more sympathetic gentlemen takes Brocklehurst's place, Jane's life improves dramatically. She spends eight more years at Lowood, six as a student and two as a teacher.

J

After teaching for two years, Jane yearns for new experiences. She accepts a governess position at a manor called Thornfield, where she teaches a lively French girl named Adèle. The distinguished housekeeper Mrs. Fairfax presides over the estate. Jane's employer at Thornfield is a dark, impassioned man named Rochester, with whom Jane finds herself falling secretly in love. She saves Rochester from a fire one night, which he claims was started by a drunken servant named Grace Poole. But because Grace Poole continues to work at Thornfield, Jane concludes that she has not been told the entire story. Jane sinks into despondency when Rochester brings home a beautiful but vicious woman named Blanche Ingram. Jane expects Rochester to propose to Blanche. But Rochester instead proposes to Jane, who accepts almost disbelievingly.

The wedding day arrives, and as Jane and Mr. Rochester prepare to exchange their vows, the voice of Mr. Mason cries out that Rochester already has a wife. Mason introduces himself as the brother of that wife—a woman named Bertha. Mr. Mason testifies that Bertha, whom Rochester married when he was a young man in Jamaica, is still alive. Rochester does not deny Mason's claims, but he explains that Bertha has gone mad. He takes the wedding party back to Thornfield, where they witness the insane Bertha Mason scurrying around on all fours and growling like an animal. Rochester keeps Bertha hidden on the third story of Thornfield and pays Grace Poole to keep his wife under control. Bertha was the real cause of the mysterious fire earlier in the story. Knowing that it is impossible for her to be with Rochester, Jane flees Thornfield.

Penniless and hungry, Jane is forced to sleep outdoors and beg for food. At last, three siblings who live in a manor alternatively called Marsh End and Moor House take her in. Their names are Mary, Diana, and St. John (pronounced "Sinjin") Rivers, and Jane quickly becomes friends with them. St. John is a clergyman, and he finds Jane a job teaching at a charity school in Morton. He surprises her one day by declaring that her uncle, John Eyre, has died and left her a large fortune: 20,000 pounds. When Jane asks how he received this news, he shocks her further by declaring that her uncle was also his uncle: Jane and the Riverses are cousins. Jane immediately decides to share her inheritance equally with her three new-found relatives.

St. John decides to travel to India as a missionary, and he urges Jane to accompany him—as his wife. Jane agrees to go to India but refuses to marry her cousin because she does not love him. St. John pressures her to reconsider, and she nearly gives in. However, she realizes that she cannot abandon forever the man she truly loves when one night she hears Rochester's voice calling her name over the moors. Jane immediately hurries back to Thornfield and finds that it has been burned to the ground by Bertha

Mason, who lost her life in the fire. Rochester saved the servants but lost his eyesight and one of his hands. Jane travels on to Rochester's new residence, Ferndean, where he lives with two servants named John and Mary.

At Ferndean, Rochester and Jane rebuild their relationship and soon marry. At the end of her story, Jane writes that she has been married for ten blissful years and that she and Rochester enjoy perfect equality in their life together. She says that after two years of blindness, Rochester regained sight in one eye and was able to behold their first son at his birth.

CHARACTER LIST

Jane Eyre The protagonist and narrator of the novel. Jane is an intelligent, honest, plain-featured young girl forced to contend with oppression, inequality, and hardship. Although she meets with a series of individuals who threaten her autonomy, Jane repeatedly succeeds at asserting herself and maintaining her principles of justice, human dignity, and morality. She also values intellectual and emotional fulfillment. Her strong belief in gender and social equality challenges the Victorian prejudices against women and the poor.

Edward Rochester Jane's employer and the master of Thornfield. Rochester is a wealthy, passionate man with a dark secret that provides much of the novel's suspense. Rochester is unconventional, ready to set aside polite manners, propriety, and consideration of social class in order to interact with Jane frankly and directly. He is rash and impetuous and has spent much of his adult life roaming about Europe in an attempt to avoid the consequences of his youthful indiscretions. His problems are partly the result of his own recklessness, but he is a sympathetic figure because he has suffered for so long as a result of his early marriage to Bertha.

St. John Rivers Jane's benefactor after she runs away from Thornfield. St. John (pronounced "Sinjin"), along with his sisters, Mary and Diana, gives Jane food and shelter. The minister at Morton, St. John is cold, reserved, and often controlling in his interactions with others. Because he is entirely alienated from his feelings and devoted solely to an austere ambition, St. John serves as a foil for Edward Rochester.

Mrs. Reed Jane's cruel aunt, who raises her at Gateshead Hall until Jane is sent away to school at age ten. Later in her life, Jane attempts reconciliation with Mrs. Reed, but the old woman continues to resent her because her husband had always loved Jane more than his own children.

Bessie Lee The maid at Gateshead. Bessie is the only figure in Jane's childhood who regularly treats her kindly, telling her stories and singing her songs. Bessie later marries Robert Leaven, the Reeds' coachman.

Mr. Lloyd The Reeds' apothecary, who suggests that Jane be sent away to school. Always kind to Jane, Mr. Lloyd writes a letter to Miss Temple, confirming Jane's story about her childhood and clearing Jane of Mrs. Reed's charge that she is a liar.

Georgiana Reed Jane's cousin and one of Mrs. Reed's two daughters. The beautiful Georgiana treats Jane cruelly when they are children, but later in their lives she befriends her cousin and confides in her. Georgiana attempts to elope with a man named Lord Edwin Vere, but her sister, Eliza, alerts Mrs. Reed of the arrangement and sabotages the plan. After Mrs. Reed dies, Georgiana marries a wealthy man.

Eliza Reed Jane's cousin and one of Mrs. Reed's two daughters (along with her sister, Georgiana). Not as beautiful as her sister, Eliza devotes herself somewhat self-righteously to the church and eventually goes to a convent in France where she becomes the Mother Superior.

John Reed Jane's cousin, Mrs. Reed's son, and brother to Eliza and Georgiana. John treats Jane with appalling cruelty during their childhood and later falls into a life of drinking and gambling. John commits suicide midway through the novel when his mother ceases to pay his debts for him.

Helen Burns Jane's close friend at the Lowood School. Helen endures her miserable life there with a passive dignity that Jane cannot understand. Helen dies of consumption in Jane's arms.

Mr. Brocklehurst The cruel, hypocritical master of the Lowood School. Mr. Brocklehurst preaches a doctrine of privation while stealing from the school to support his luxurious lifestyle. After a typhus epidemic sweeps Lowood, Brocklehurst's shifty and dishonest practices are brought to light and he is publicly discredited.

Maria Temple A kind teacher at Lowood who treats Jane and Helen with respect and compassion. Along with Bessie Lee, Maria serves as one of Jane's first positive female role models. Miss Temple helps clear Jane of Mrs. Reed's accusations against her.

Miss Scatcherd Jane's sour and vicious teacher at Lowood, Miss Scatcherd behaves with particular cruelty toward Helen.

Alice Fairfax The housekeeper at Thornfield Hall. Alice is the first to tell Jane that the mysterious laughter often heard echoing through the halls is, in fact, the laughter of Grace Poole—a lie that Rochester himself often repeats.

Bertha Mason Rochester's clandestine wife. Bertha is a formerly beautiful and wealthy Creole woman who has become insane, violent, and bestial. She lives locked in a secret room on the third story of Thornfield and is guarded by Grace Poole, whose occasional bouts of inebriation sometimes enable Bertha to escape. Bertha eventually burns down Thornfield, plunging to her death in the flames.

Grace Poole Bertha Mason's keeper at Thornfield, whose drunken carelessness frequently allows Bertha to escape. When Jane first arrives at Thornfield, Mrs. Fairfax attributes to Grace all evidence of Bertha's misdeeds.

Adèle Varens Jane's pupil at Thornfield. Adèle is a lively though somewhat spoiled child from France. Rochester brought her to Thornfield after her mother, Celine, abandoned her. Although Celine was once Rochester's mistress, he does not believe himself to be Adèle's father.

Celine Varens A French opera dancer with whom Rochester once had an affair. Although Rochester does not believe Celine's claims that he fathered her daughter Adèle, he nonetheless brought the girl to England when Celine abandoned her. Rochester had broken off his relationship with Celine after learning that Celine was unfaithful to him and interested only in his money.

Sophie Adèle's French nurse at Thornfield.

Richard Mason Bertha's brother. During a visit to Thornfield, Richard is injured by his mad sister. After learning of Rochester's intent to marry Jane, Mason arrives with the solicitor Briggs in order to thwart the wedding and reveal the truth of Rochester's prior marriage.

Mr. Briggs John Eyre's attorney, Mr. Briggs helps Richard Mason prevent Jane's wedding to Rochester when he learns of the existence of Bertha Mason, Rochester's wife. After John Eyre's death, Briggs searches for Jane in order to give her her inheritance.

Blanche Ingram Blanche Ingram is a beautiful socialite who despises Jane and hopes to marry Rochester for his money.

Diana Rivers Jane's cousin and the sister of St. John and Mary. Diana is a kind and intelligent person, and she urges Jane not to go to India with St. John. She serves as a model for Jane of an intellectually gifted and independent woman.

Mary Rivers Jane's cousin, the sister of St. John and Diana. Mary is a kind and intelligent young woman who is forced to work as a governess after her father loses his fortune. Like her sister, she serves as a model for Jane of an independent woman who is also able to maintain close relationships with others and a sense of meaning in her life.

Rosamond Oliver The beautiful daughter of Mr. Oliver, Morton's wealthiest inhabitant. Rosamond gives money to the school in Morton where Jane works. Although she is in love with St. John, she becomes engaged to the wealthy Mr. Granby.

John Eyre Jane's uncle, who leaves her his vast fortune of 20,000 pounds.

Uncle Reed Mrs. Reed's late husband. In her childhood, Jane believes that she feels the presence of Uncle Reed's ghost. Because he was always fond of Jane and her mother (his sister), Uncle Reed made his wife promise that she would raise Jane as her own child. It is a promise that Mrs. Reed does not keep.

ANALYSIS OF MAJOR CHARACTERS

JANE EYRE From the beginning of the novel, Jane possesses a sense of self-worth and dignity, a commitment to justice and principle, a trust in God, and a passionate disposition. Her integrity is continually tested over the course of the novel, and Jane must learn to balance the frequently conflicting aspects of herself so as to find contentment. An orphan since early childhood, Jane initially feels exiled and ostracized, and the cruel treatment she receives from her Aunt Reed and her cousins only exacerbates her feeling of alienation. Afraid that she will never find a true sense of home or community, Jane feels the need to belong somewhere—to find "kin," or at least "kindred spirits." This desire tempers her equally intense need for autonomy and freedom.

In her search for freedom, Jane struggles with the question of what type of freedom she wants. While Rochester initially offers Jane a chance to liberate her passions, Jane comes to realize that such freedom could also mean enslavement—by living as Rochester's mistress, she would be sacrificing her dignity and integrity for the sake of her feelings. St. John Rivers offers Jane another kind of freedom: the freedom to act unreservedly on her principles. He opens to Jane the possibility of exercising her talents fully by working and living with him in India. Jane eventually realizes, though, that this freedom would also constitute a form of imprisonment, because she would be forced to constantly keep her true feelings and her true passions in check.

Charlotte Brontë may have created the character of Jane Eyre as a means of coming to terms with elements of her own life. Much evidence suggests that Brontë, too, struggled to find a balance between love and freedom and to find others who understood her. At many points in the book, Jane voices the author's then-radical opinions on religion, social class, and gender.

EDWARD ROCHESTER Despite his stern manner and not particularly handsome appearance, Edward Rochester wins Jane's heart. She feels they are kindred spirits, and he is the first person in the novel to offer Jane lasting love and a real home. Although Rochester is Jane's social and economic superior, and although men were widely considered to be naturally superior to women in the Victorian period, Jane is Rochester's intellectual equal. Moreover, after their marriage is interrupted by the disclosure that Rochester is already married to Bertha Mason, Jane is proven to be Rochester's moral superior.

Rochester regrets his former libertinism and lustfulness; nevertheless, he has proven himself to be weaker in many ways when compared to Jane. Jane feels that living with Rochester as his mistress would mean the loss of her dignity. Ultimately, she would become degraded and dependent upon Rochester for love, while unprotected by any true marriage bond. Jane will only enter into marriage with Rochester after she has gained a fortune and a family, and after she has been on the verge of abandoning passion altogether. She waits until she is not unduly influenced by her own poverty, loneliness, psychological vulnerability, or passion. Additionally, because Rochester has been blinded by the fire and has lost his manor house at the end of the novel, he has become weaker while Jane has grown in strength—Jane claims that they are equals, but the marriage dynamic has actually tipped in her favor.

ST. JOHN RIVERS St. John Rivers is a foil for Edward Rochester. Whereas Rochester is passionate, St. John is austere and ambitious. Jane often describes Rochester's eyes as flashing and flaming, whereas she constantly associates St. John with rock, ice, and snow. Marriage with Rochester represents the abandonment of principle for the consummation of passion, but marriage to St. John would mean sacrificing passion for principle. When he invites her to come to India with him as a missionary, St. John offers Jane the chance to make a more meaningful contribution to society than she would as a housewife. At the same time, life with St. John would mean life without true love, in which Jane's need for spiritual solace would be filled only by retreat into the recesses of her own soul. Independence would be accompanied by loneliness, and joining St. John would require Jane to neglect her own legitimate needs for love and emotional support. Her consideration of St. John's proposal leads Jane to understand that, paradoxically, a large part of one's personal freedom is found in a relationship of mutual emotional dependence.

HELEN BURNS Helen Burns, Jane's friend at Lowood School, serves as a foil for Mr. Brocklehurst as well as for Jane. While Mr. Brocklehurst embodies an evangelical form of religion that seeks to strip others of their excessive pride or of their ability to take pleasure in worldly things, Helen represents a mode of Christianity that stresses tolerance and acceptance. Brocklehurst uses religion to gain power and to control others; Helen ascetically trusts her own faith and turns the other cheek to Lowood's harsh policies.

Although Helen manifests a certain strength and intellectual maturity, her efforts involve self-negation rather than self-assertion, and Helen's submissive and ascetic nature highlights Jane's more headstrong character. Like Jane, Helen is an orphan who longs for a home, but Helen believes that she will find this home in Heaven rather than Northern England. And while Helen is not oblivious to the injustices the girls suffer at Lowood, she believes that justice will be found in God's ultimate judgment—God will reward the good and punish the evil. Jane, on the other hand, is unable to have such blind faith. Her quest is for love and happiness in this world. Nevertheless, she counts on God for support and guidance in her search.

THEMES, MOTIFS, AND SYMBOLS

THEMES

LOVE VS. AUTONOMY *Jane Eyre* is very much the story of a quest to be loved. Jane searches not just for romantic love but also for a sense of being valued—of belonging. Yet Jane must learn how to gain love without sacrificing and harming herself in the process. Her fear of losing her autonomy motivates her refusal of Rochester's marriage proposal. Jane believes that "marrying" Rochester while he remains legally tied to Bertha would mean rendering herself a mistress and sacrificing her own integrity for the sake of emotional gratification. On the other hand, her life at Moor House tests her in the opposite manner. There, she enjoys economic independence and engages in worthwhile and useful work, teaching the poor; yet she lacks emotional sustenance. Although St. John proposes marriage, offering her a partnership built around a common purpose, Jane knows their marriage would remain loveless. However, the events of Jane's stay at Moor House are necessary tests of Jane's autonomy. Only after proving her self-sufficiency to herself can she marry Rochester and not be asymmetrically dependent upon him as her "master." The marriage can be one between equals.

THE BALANCE BETWEEN BODY AND SPIRIT Throughout the novel, Jane struggles to find the right balance between moral duty and earthly pleasure, between obligation to her spirit and attention to her body. She encounters three main religious figures: Mr. Brocklehurst, Helen Burns, and St. John Rivers. Each represents a model of religion that Jane ultimately rejects as she forms her own ideas about faith and principle and their practical consequences.

Mr. Brocklehurst illustrates the dangers and hypocrisies that Brontë perceived in the nineteenth-century Evangelical movement. Mr. Brocklehurst adopts the rhetoric of Evangelicalism when he claims to be purging his students of pride, but his method of subjecting them to various privations and humiliations, such as when he orders that the naturally curly hair of one of Jane's classmates be cut so as to lie straight, is entirely un-Christian. Of course, Brocklehurst's proscriptions are difficult to follow, and his hypocritical support of his own luxuriously wealthy family at the expense of the Lowood students shows Brontë's wariness of the Evangelical movement. Helen Burns's meek and forbearing mode of Christianity, on the other hand, is too passive for Jane to adopt as her own, although she loves and admires Helen for it. St. John Rivers provides another model of Christian behavior. His is a Christianity of ambition, glory, and extreme self-importance. St. John urges Jane to sacrifice her emotional deeds for the fulfillment of her moral duty, offering her a way of life that would require her to be disloyal to her own self.

Although Jane ends up rejecting all three models of religion, she does not abandon morality, spiritualism, or a belief in a Christian God. When her wedding is interrupted, she prays to God for solace. As she wanders the heath, poor and starving, she puts her survival in the hands of God. She strongly objects to Rochester's lustful immorality, and she refuses to consider living with him while church and state still deem him married to another woman. Even so, Jane can barely bring herself to leave the only love she has ever known. She credits God with helping her to escape what she knows would have been an immoral life. Jane ultimately finds a comfortable middle ground. Her spiritual understanding is not hateful and oppressive like Brocklehurst's, nor does it require retreat from the everyday world as Helen's and St. John's religions do. For Jane, religion helps curb immoderate passions, and it spurs one on to worldly efforts and achievements. These achievements include full self-knowledge and complete faith in God.

THE PROBLEMS OF SOCIAL CLASS Jane Eyre is critical of Victorian England's strict social hierarchy. Brontë's exploration of the complicated social position of governesses is perhaps the novel's most important treatment of this theme. Like Heathcliff in *Wuthering Heights*, Jane is a figure of ambiguous class standing and, consequently, a source of extreme tension for the characters around her. Jane's manners, sophistication, and education are those of an aristocrat, because Victorian governesses, who tutored children in etiquette as well as academics, were expected to possess the "culture" of the aristocracy. Yet, as paid employees, they were more or less treated as servants; thus, Jane remains penniless and powerless while at Thornfield. Jane's understanding of the double standard crystallizes when she becomes aware of her feelings for Rochester; she is his intellectual, but not his social, equal. Even before the crisis surrounding Bertha Mason, Jane is hesitant to marry Rochester because she senses that she would feel indebted to him for "condescending" to marry her. Jane's distress, which appears most strongly in Chapter 17, seems to be Brontë's critique of Victorian class attitudes.

Jane herself speaks out against class prejudice at certain moments, but nowhere in *Jane Eyre* are society's boundaries bent. Ultimately, Jane is able to marry Rochester as his equal only because she has almost magically come into her own inheritance from her uncle.

THE OPPRESSION OF WOMEN Jane struggles continually to achieve equality and overcome oppression. In addition to class hierarchy, she must fight against patriarchal domination—against those who believe women to be inferior to men and try to treat them as such. Three central male figures threaten her desire for equality and dignity: Mr. Brocklehurst, Edward Rochester, and St. John Rivers. All three are misogynistic on some level. Each tries to keep Jane in a submissive position, where she is unable to express her own thoughts and feelings. In her quest for independence and self-knowledge, Jane must escape Brocklehurst, reject St. John, and come to Rochester only after ensuring that they may marry as equals. This last condition is met once Jane proves herself able to function, through the time she spends at Moor House, in a community and in a family. She will not depend solely on Rochester for love, and she can be financially independent. Furthermore, Rochester is blind at the novel's end and thus dependent upon Jane to be his "prop and guide." In Chapter 12, Jane articulates what was for her time a radically feminist philosophy:

> *Women are supposed to be very calm generally: but women feel just as men feel; they need exercise for their faculties, and a field for their efforts as much as their brothers do; they suffer from too rigid a restraint, too absolute a stagnation, precisely as men would suffer; and it is narrow-minded in their more privileged fellow-creatures to say that they ought to confine themselves to making puddings and knitting stockings, to playing on the piano and embroidering bags. It is thoughtless to condemn them, or laugh at them, if they seek to do more or learn more than custom has pronounced necessary for their sex.*

J

MOTIFS

FIRE AND ICE Fire and ice appear throughout *Jane Eyre*. The former represents Jane's passions, anger, and spirit, while the latter symbolizes the oppressive forces trying to extinguish Jane's vitality. Fire is also a metaphor for Jane, as the narrative repeatedly associates her with images of fire, brightness, and warmth. In Chapter 4, she likens her mind to "a ridge of lighted heath, alive, glancing, devouring." We can recognize Jane's kindred spirits by their similar links to fire; thus we read of Rochester's "flaming and flashing" eyes. After he has been blinded, his face is compared to "a lamp quenched, waiting to be relit."

Images of ice and cold, often appearing in association with barren landscapes or seascapes, symbolize emotional desolation, loneliness, or even death. The "death-white realms" of the arctic that Bewick describes in his History of British Birds parallel Jane's physical and spiritual isolation at Gateshead. Lowood's freezing temperatures—for example, the frozen pitchers of water that greet the girls each morning—mirror Jane's sense of psychological exile. Finally, at Moor House, St. John's frigidity and stiffness are established through comparisons with ice and cold rock.

SUBSTITUTE MOTHERS Poet and critic Adrienne Rich has noted that Jane encounters a series of nurturing and strong women on whom she can model herself, or to whom she can look for comfort and guidance: these women serve as mother-figures to the orphaned Jane. The first such figure that Jane encounters is the servant Bessie, who soothes Jane after her trauma in the red-room and teaches her to find comfort in stories and songs. At Lowood, Jane meets Miss Temple, who has no power in the world at large, but possesses great spiritual strength and charm. Not only does she shelter Jane from pain, she also encourages her intellectual development. Jane also finds a comforting model in Helen Burns, whose lessons in stamina teach Jane about self-worth and the power of faith.

After Jane and Rochester's wedding is cancelled, Jane finds comfort in the moon, which appears to her in a dream as a symbol of the matriarchal spirit. Jane sees the moon as "a white human form" shining in the sky, "inclining a glorious brow earthward." She tells us: "It spoke to my spirit: immeasurably distant was the tone, yet so near, it whispered in my heart—"My daughter, flee temptation." Jane answers, "Mother, I will." Waking from the dream, Jane leaves Thornfield. Jane finds two additional mother-figures in the characters of Diana and Mary Rivers. Rich points out that the sisters bear the names of the pagan and Christian versions of "the Great Goddess": Diana, the Virgin huntress, and Mary, the Virgin Mother. Unmarried and independent, the Rivers sisters love learning and reciting poetry and live as intellectual equals with their brother St. John.

SYMBOLS

BERTHA MASON Bertha Mason is a complex presence in *Jane Eyre*. She impedes Jane's happiness, but she also catalyses the growth of Jane's self-understanding. The mystery surrounding Bertha establishes suspense and terror to the plot and the atmosphere. Further, Bertha serves as a remnant and reminder of Rochester's youthful libertinism. Yet Bertha can also be interpreted as a symbol. Some critics have read her as a statement about the way Britain feared and psychologically "locked away" the other cultures it encountered at the height of its imperialism. Others have seen her as a symbolic representation of the "trapped" Victorian wife, who is expected never to travel or work outside the house and becomes ever more frenzied as she finds no outlet for her frustration and anxiety. Within the story, then, Bertha's insanity could serve as a warning to Jane of what complete surrender to Rochester could bring about.

One could also see Bertha as a manifestation of Jane's subconscious feelings—specifically, of her rage against oppressive social and gender norms. Jane declares her love for Rochester, but she also secretly fears marriage to him and feels the need to rage against the imprisonment it could become for her. Jane never manifests this fear or anger, but Bertha does. Thus, Bertha tears up the bridal veil, and it is Bertha's existence that indeed stops the wedding from going forth. And when Thornfield comes to represent a state of servitude and submission for Jane, Bertha burns it to the ground. Throughout the novel, Jane describes her inner spirit as fiery. Bertha seems to be the outward manifestation of Jane's interior fire. Bertha expresses the feelings that Jane must keep in check.

J

THE RED-ROOM The red-room symbolizes what Jane must overcome in her struggles to find freedom, happiness, and a sense of belonging. In the red-room, Jane's position of exile and imprisonment first becomes clear. Although Jane is eventually freed from the room, she continues to be socially ostracized, financially trapped, and excluded from love; her sense of independence and her freedom of self-expression are constantly threatened. The red-room's importance as a symbol continues throughout the novel. It reappears as a memory whenever Jane makes a connection between her current situation and that first feeling of being ridiculed. Thus she recalls the room when she is humiliated at Lowood. She also thinks of the room on the night that she decides to leave Thornfield after Rochester has tried to convince her to become an undignified mistress. Her destitute condition upon her departure from Thornfield also threatens emotional and intellectual imprisonment, as does St. John's marriage proposal. Only after Jane has asserted herself, gained financial independence, and found a spiritual family—which turns out to be her real family—can she wed Rochester and find freedom in and through marriage.

IMPORTANT QUOTATIONS EXPLAINED

---

1. *I am glad you are no relation of mine. I will never call you aunt again as long as I live. . . . You think I have no feelings, and that I can do without one bit of love or kindness; but I cannot live so: and you have no pity. I shall remember how you thrust me back . . . into the red-room . . . I will tell anybody who asks me questions this exact tale. 'Ere I had finished this reply, my soul began to expand, to exult, with the strangest sense of freedom. . . .*

This passage, part of Jane's outburst to her aunt just prior to her departure from Gateshead for Lowood School, appears in Chapter 4. In the passage, Jane solidifies her own orphanhood, severing her ties to the little semblance of family that remained to her ("I will never call you aunt again as long as I live," she tells Mrs. Reed). Jane asserts her fiery spirit in her tirade, and she displays a keen sense of justice and a recognition of her need for love. Along with familial liberation, the passage marks Jane's emotional liberation. Jane's imprisonment in the red-room has its psychological counterpart in her emotional suppression, and it is not until she speaks these words to Mrs. Reed that she feels her "soul begin to expand." Lastly, the passage highlights the importance of storytelling as revenge and also as a means of empowerment. Jane declares that she will "tell anybody who asks me questions this exact tale"—via authorship, Jane asserts her authority over her tyrannical aunt.

---

2. *"[T]ell him you love him and will be his. Who in the world cares for you? . . . " Still indomitable was the reply: "I care for myself. The more solitary, the more friendless, the more unsustained I am, the more I will respect myself. I will keep the law given by God; sanctioned by man. . . . Laws and principles are not for the times when there is no temptation . . . They have a worth—so I have always believed; and if I cannot believe it now, it is because I am insane—quite insane: with my veins running fire . . .*

In this quotation, near the end of Chapter 27, Jane asserts her strong sense of moral integrity over and against her intense immediate feelings. Rochester has been trying to convince her to stay with him despite the fact that he is still legally married to Bertha Mason. His argument almost persuades Jane: Rochester is the first person who has ever truly loved her. Yet she knows that staying with him would mean compromising herself, because she would be Rochester's mistress rather than his wife. Not only would she lose her self-respect, but she would probably lose Rochester's, too, in the end. Thus, Jane asserts her worth and her ability to love herself regardless of how others treat her.

The passage also sheds light upon Jane's understanding of religion. She sees God as the giver of the laws by which she must live. When she can no longer trust herself to exercise good judgment, she looks to these principles as an objective point of reference.

Jane's allusions to her "madness" and "insanity" bring out an interesting parallel between Jane and Bertha Mason. It is possible to see Bertha as a double for Jane, who embodies what Jane feels within—especially since the externalization of interior sentiment is a trait common to the Gothic novel. Finally, the description of Jane's blood running like "fire" constitutes one of many points in the book in which Jane is associated with flames.

---

3. *As his curate, his comrade, all would be right: I would cross oceans with him . . . ; toil under Eastern suns, in Asian deserts with him . . . ; admire and emulate his courage and devotion and vigour: accommodate quietly to his masterhood; smile undisturbed at his ineradicable ambition. . . . I should suffer often, no doubt, attached to him only in this capacity: my body would be under a rather stringent yoke, but my heart and mind would be free. . . . There would be recesses in my mind which would be only mine, to which he never came; and sentiments growing there, fresh and sheltered, which his austerity could never blight, nor his measured warrior-march trample down: but as his wife—at his side always, and always restrained, and always checked—forced to keep the fire of my nature continually low, to compel it to burn inwardly and never utter a cry, though the imprisoned flame consumed vital after vital—this would be unendurable.*

This passage appears in Chapter 34. St. John Rivers has just asked Jane to join him as his wife on his missionary trip to India. Jane dramatizes the interior conflict involved in making her decision. In many ways, the proposal tempts her. It is an opportunity to perform good works and to be more than a governess, schoolteacher, or housewife—the roles traditionally open to women. Jane's teaching jobs at Lowood, Thornfield, and Morton have all made her feel trapped, and she would not mind enduring hardships for a cause in which she truly believes. Yet, St. John's principles—"ambition," "austerity," and arrogance—are not those that Jane upholds.

Misguided religion threatens to oppress Jane throughout the book, and St. John merely embodies one form of it. He also embodies masculine dominance, another force that threatens Jane like a "stringent yoke" over the course of the novel. Thus she describes St. John's "warrior-march" and notes his assertion of his "masterhood." Jane must escape such control in order to remain true to herself, for she realizes that her conventional manner of dealing with oppression—by retreating into herself, into the recesses of her imagination, into conversation with herself—cannot constitute a way of life. In her rejection of Rochester, Jane privileged principle over feeling; she is now aware of the negative effects that such emotional repression can have. Feeling, too, must play a role in one's life: a balance must be struck.

---

4. *[T]he restlessness was in my nature . . . Then my sole relief was to walk along the corridor of the third story, backwards and forwards . . . and, best of all, to open my inward ear to . . . a tale my imagination created, and narrated continuously; quickened with all of incident, life, fire, feeling, that I desired and had not in my actual existence. . . . Millions are condemned to a stiller doom than mine, and millions are in silent revolt against their lot. . . . Women are supposed to be very calm generally: but women feel just as men feel . . . [I]t is narrow-minded . . . to say that they ought to confine themselves to making puddings and knitting stockings, to playing on the piano and embroidering bags.*

This passage appears in Chapter 12, in the midst of Jane's description of her first few weeks at Thornfield. The diction highlights Jane's feelings of imprisonment (she paces the corridors like a caged creature), and her longings for freedom and equality. Jane's words are also relevant to Brontë's own experience as a writer, and to the general condition of Victorian women. The images of restlessness and pacing, of feeling "stagnation" and "too rigid a restraint," are examples of the book's central idea of imprisonment. In addition to instances of physical imprisonment, Jane must also escape the fetters of misguided religion (represented by Brocklehurst), of passion without principle (represented at first by Rochester), and of principle without passion (represented by St. John Rivers)—not to mention those of society.

Brocklehurst, Rochester, and St. John may also threaten Jane with the fetters of patriarchy, which is the specific force that Jane resists in this passage. Jane extends her feeling of entrapment to her fellow women, and these sentences constitute Brontë's feminist manifesto. As she describes the "doom" to which "millions in silent revolt against their lot" are condemned, Brontë criticizes what she believed to be stifling Victorian conceptions of proper gender roles. The passage explicitly states that the Victorian wife suffers from being metaphorically "locked up." Bertha Mason, who is eventually rendered nearly inhuman when her neglected, suppressed feelings turn to madness and fury, may be viewed as a symbol of the imprisoned female's condition. The passage suggests that Brontë's writing may have been her means of coping with such rage. Jane describes her retreat into her own mind, to find freedom in her imagination. While Brontë's greatest triumphs were the result of such self-retreat, her heroine's achievement is the balance she strikes between her need for autonomy and her desire to be an active member of society.

---

5. *I have now been married ten years. I know what it is to live entirely for and with what I love best on earth. I hold myself supremely blest—blest beyond what language can express; because I am my husband's life as fully as he is mine. No woman was ever nearer to her mate than I am: ever more absolutely bone of his bone, and flesh of his flesh . . . To be together is for us to be at once as free as in solitude, as gay as in company. . . . [T]o talk to each other is but a more animated and an audible thinking. All my confidence is bestowed on him, all his confidence is devoted to me; we are precisely suited in character—perfect concord is the result.*

This, one of the final passages of *Jane Eyre*, summarizes the novel's "happy ending." Its implications have generated much debate over the way Brontë chose to conclude her book. Some critics view Jane as having sacrificed her autonomy—no longer her own person, she and Rochester have merged, sharing one heart, each possessing the "bone" and "flesh" of the other. One might also argue that Jane relinquishes her powers of thought and expression—two characteristics that have defined her for most of the novel. Suddenly, the otherwise imaginative Jane equates her "thinking" to her conversations with Rochester—she even finds the conversations "more animated." Similarly, although ten years have elapsed since the wedding, the otherwise eloquent Jane suddenly claims that she is unable to find any "language" to "express" her experiences during this period.

This passage can also be read as Jane's affirmation of the equality between her and Rochester, as testimony that she has not "given up" anything. The passage is followed in the novel by a report on St. John Rivers. Emphasizing St. John's desires for "mastery" and his "warrior" characteristics, Jane describes a controlling patriarch. While Rochester may have been such a figure at the beginning of the novel, his character has changed by its conclusion. He has lost his house, his hand, and his eyesight to a fire, and the revelation of his youthful debaucheries has shown him to be Jane's moral inferior. Rochester can no longer presume to be Jane's "master." Moreover, Jane has come to Rochester this second time in economic independence and by free choice; at Moor House she found a network of love and support, and she does not depend solely on Rochester for emotional nurturance. We may see Jane's description of St. John as her reminder that the marriage she rejected would have offered her a much more stifling life. By entering into marriage, Jane does enter into a sort of "bond"; yet in many ways this "bond" is the "escape" that she has sought all along. Perhaps Brontë intended for Jane's closing words to celebrate her attainment of freedom; it is also possible that Brontë meant for us to bemoan the tragic paradox of Jane's situation.

What role does colonialism play in the relationship between Rochester and Bertha in *Jane Eyre*?

In Charlotte Brontë's *Jane Eyre*, we can understand the relationship between Rochester and Bertha by understanding how it is similar to eighteenth-century colonialism (the control of a powerful country over part or all of a less powerful one). Brontë's Rochester both embodies and rejects colonialism in his relationship with his wife Bertha, moving from being her captive to her captor. Neither character is ever free of their colonial bonds.

Rochester's relationship with Bertha begins as a business deal. As the second son under primogeniture (the right of an oldest son to inherit a family's wealth), Rochester will not inherit his father's fortune. Therefore, his family arranges his marriage into a wealthy Creole family of Spanish Town, Jamaica. This family wants to marry their daughter Bertha into Rochester's upper-class English lineage. Rochester travels to Jamaica to meet his fiancée and is quickly cast under the spell of this tall, mysterious, exotic beauty and the charms of her Creole society.

Rochester soon awakens from this spell to discover that he has been tricked; his seemingly perfect wife has a family history of insanity, a "violent and unreasonable temper," and is totally incompatible with him socially and intellectually (Chapter XXVII). Rochester becomes the victim of Bertha's violent, tyrannical attacks because he refuses to restrain her by force. As Bertha's mental instability grows, the shackles on Rochester tighten: her outbursts grow worse daily, forcing them to retreat from society, and he discovers he cannot legally divorce her because of her diagnosed insanity.

This situation escalates until, one night, a sleepless Rochester is driven to the brink of suicide by Bertha's ranting and raving. Gun in hand, he is about to end his misery when "a wind fresh from Europe blew over the ocean and rushed through the open casement" (Chapter XXVII). The storm breaks, and Rochester sees a way out of his hell. Taking Bertha with him, he returns to Europe, where he again enjoys the social and intellectual benefits of upper-class English society. Ironically, while “the Atlantic . . . thunder[s] in glorious liberty” for Rochester, the passage to England marks the beginning of Bertha’s captivity (Chapter XXVII).

Rochester’s decision to leave Jamaica both echoes and rejects the actions of Europeans in the New World. Having taken the prizes and wealth of his colony, Rochester returns to civilized England, treasure in tow. Thus he exemplifies the greedy merchant using native heathens of foreign lands to reap maximum profit. Yet by turning his back on the West Indies and returning to England, Rochester also rejects colonialism. Once “piqued” and “allured” by the exotic beauty and treasure of this faraway land, he now wants only to escape Jamaica, and “let her connection with [him] be buried in oblivion” (Chapter XXVII). In England Rochester is free again, but his liberty costs Bertha *her* freedom and begins her colonial nightmare.

Bertha’s oppression echoes that of slaves taken from Africa to work on American plantations. Taken from her homeland against her will, she is stowed away in the bottom of the ship, hidden from other passengers, just as slaves were transported during the slave trade. Upon arrival in England, Rochester imprisons her in the attic of his home, her existence known only to himself and her jailkeeper. In her new home, her condition worsens and she becomes more like the plantation slave and less like the exotic beauty she once was.

Despite her diminishing mental faculties, Bertha engineers several escapes from her holding cell, during which she attacks Rochester and various visitors to Thornfield Hall using makeshift weapons, unguarded candles, and even her teeth. One escape brings her face to face with Jane, who describes her as “tall and large, . . . with a savage face, red eyes, and black eye-brows widely raised over blood-shot eyes” (Chapter XXV). Bertha no longer resembles the exotically elegant Creole beauty of Spanish Town. Instead, she reminds Jane of “the foul German spectre—the

Vampyre" (Chapter XXV). Rochester also refers to his wife in bestial terms, calling her a "monster" and a "thing" with a "black and scarlet visage," "pygmy intellect," "gross, impure, depraved" nature, and a room like "a wild beast's den—a goblin's cell" (Chapter XXVII). These descriptions echo the racist colonial associations between dark skin and monstrosity, bestiality, and evil. Bertha is now indistinguishable from the colonial slave.

The mutual oppression of Bertha and Rochester haunts the novel. Rochester will never be rid of Bertha. Only through her death can he take Jane as his bride, though he cannot hide the physical scars of Bertha's final moments. Bertha never escapes her marriage to Rochester. Her mental instability escalates as her situation worsens, and her tragic death becomes a humane end to her suffering. Neither Rochester nor Bertha set out to intentionally destroy the other; both were looking to profit from the colonial system. In these characters, Brontë demonstrates how everyone suffers under colonial imperialism.

Journey into the Whirlwind

Eugenia Ginzburg (1904–1977)

CONTEXT

An understanding of Eugenia Ginzburg's memoir, *Journey into the Whirlwind,* begins with an understanding of the fallout from the Russian Revolution of 1917. After the revolution, the Bolshevik leader Vladimir Lenin spoke up about the presence of "enemies of the people" within the government. These class enemies, he said, were no better than criminals and therefore must be imprisoned. Thousands of state officials were accused of corruption, and both political dissidents and innocent people were carted off to labor camps and prisons. By 1930, this system of labor camps was known as the Gulag, a name that has since sent chills up and down the spines of millions of people in Russia and beyond. The Gulag was both the government's answer to the question of how to punish its political criminals and a solution to the nation's growing need for cheap labor. Prisoners of the Gulag were sent into exile in Siberia and put to work, toiling in backbreaking and often fatal conditions. Meanwhile, the rest of the population lived in a state of terror, afraid to make the slightest criticism of a government that was perpetuating such atrocities.

The Gulag peaked in intensity during the late 1930s, when *Journey into the Whirlwind* is set. During this time, the Soviet Union, under the rule of the Communist leader Joseph Stalin, underwent a period of intense repression, mass imprisonment, and penal executions known as the Great Purge. By 1938, after the Great Purge was over, almost two million people had been incarcerated. The Communist Party leadership visited horrifying punishment on these individuals in order to prevent government opposition from rising. Anyone who was seen as a potential threat to the party, even if the charges could not be proved, was arrested, thrown in prison, sent off to remote areas to work in a labor camp, or executed.

Journey into the Whirlwind, published in 1967, is the first of Ginzburg's two books detailing her eighteen years in the prison system following her arrest during the Great Purge. It begins with a few ominous pages describing the air of fear in late 1934, then recounts her arrest, interrogation, trial, incarceration, and subsequent movement from prison to prison, ending with her time in the Kolyma camps at the easternmost edge of Siberia. There, the guards subjected Ginzburg and her fellow prisoners to barbaric tortures, forcing them to fell trees in frigid temperatures and on empty stomachs and to live in the most primitive and unsanitary of conditions. Historians believe approximately five million people were forced to work in Kolyma during the height of the Gulag's existence, most of them "political criminals" like Ginzburg. Only an incredibly small number of them, perhaps as low as 2 or 3 percent, survived the experience. In the second installment of her memoir, *Within the Whirlwind,* Ginzburg picks up where she leaves off in the first book, when she becomes a medical attendant at a prison facility. This reassignment is a "lucky break," saving her from the hell of Kolyma and imminent death.

Ginzburg narrates her story with heartbreaking emotion as well as the perfectly framed observations of a seasoned writer and intellectual. Prior to her arrest, Ginzburg was a professor specializing in Communism at a top Soviet university, as well as a published author with connections to the local party paper, *Red Tartary*. Her considerable mental power and strength of character are evident everywhere in the book, from her poetry recitations to her sly plots to trick the guards to her unshakable moral compass. Ginzburg herself is an inspiring character, a longtime Communist with devout party loyalties who refuses to give in to the interrogators' soul-shaking tortures. Having been unfairly accused, she clings to her innocence and does not let even the terror of the prison system diminish her joy at being called "comrade." But Ginzburg's own inspirational narrative is set against the backdrop of the stories of less scrupulous characters, including fellow purge victims-turned-informants and "real" (not political) criminals. The real villains of the book, of course, are the interrogators and vicious guards, many of whom later fall prey to the purge themselves. Ginzburg's memoir is astonishing for its clear-eyed vision of the cruelties man is capable of visiting upon his fellow man.

Journey into the Whirlwind is also striking in its conclusion that, while man can sink to incredible moral lows, he can also become transcendent in the medium of art. During her eighteen years in the worst of prisons, Ginzburg revels in the fast friendships she is able to cultivate even in the darkest circumstances, and poetry is a tie that binds her strongly to her fellow inmates. Ginzburg is a fierce lover of poetry, and words and poems are her prison saviors. Russian culture is famous for prizing its poets and artists, who have for centuries sung beautifully about the horrors of war, hate, death, and other grim realities. Ginzburg's own memoir falls in neatly with that tradition, even referencing several famous Russian poets. Though its subject is a truth so appalling it can sometimes seem unbelievable, the prose in which that truth is rendered makes for a uniquely compelling read.

The ability to communicate is the last and most valuable quality one can possess, a truth made even more poignant by the fact that Ginzburg, who died in Moscow in 1977, did not live to see her memoirs published in her native country. However, her words have lived on. In *Journey into the Whirlwind*, Ginzburg insists that the lives of the millions killed by Stalin and his henchmen must not be forgotten but instead should be retold and remembered. By telling her own story, she effectively enters those millions of other stories into the annals of history. Her book is a document testifying to the incredible tenacity of the human spirit. It evidences the sheer force of the human will to survive even the most degrading and abysmal conditions—and to emerge all the stronger for it.

PLOT OVERVIEW

Journey into the Whirlwind, Eugenia Ginzburg's memoir of her imprisonment during the era of Stalin's purges, is divided into two parts. Part One details her arrest, trial, and two years of solitary confinement. Part Two deals with her reassignment to Kolyma, a group of Gulag prison camps deep in Siberia, at the easternmost edge of the country.

Part One begins with a phone call. It is December 1, 1934, and the voice on the phone tells Ginzburg that someone has assassinated Kirov, the secretary of the Communist Party's General Committee. His murder generates paranoia about the dissident political elements within the party, and the government tightens its grip on society. Ginzburg is personally drawn into the fray when her old friend, Professor Elvov, is arrested in 1935, for having written a chapter of a history book with so-called Trotskyist undertones. Her association with Elvov places her under intense suspicion. The party officials in Kazan, her hometown, are quick to accuse her of failing to condemn Elvov's disloyalty to the party. Ginzburg refuses to admit her guilt and is called in for questioning by Comrade Beylin. Beylin and his colleague Malyuta initially let Ginzburg off with a lesser charge of "insufficient vigilance," but soon Ginzburg finds herself facing a number of increasingly cruel interrogators.

In 1936, Ginzburg, a fiercely devoted Communist, sees Stalin, the Communist leader, for the first and only time in her life. Instead of idolizing Stalin, however, she sees him as "ugly" and has a vision of his evil. Ginzburg then travels to Moscow to appeal her case to the court at Ilyinka Street, where many other accused people are waiting in line. Sidorov, a political commissar, is sympathetic to Ginzburg's plight, but in the end Ginzburg must turn in her party card, and, eight days later, she is arrested by the sadistic Captain Vevers.

Ginzburg is incarcerated in the prison cellars at Black Lake Street, along with a pretty young woman named Lyama. Ginzburg cannot stomach the foul-smelling fish that is served as prison food, so Lyama eats both of their portions. Lyama explains that it is important to find ways of communicating with the other prisoners. The interrogators call Ginzburg in for continued questioning, using techniques ranging from sleep deprivation to starvation, but Ginzburg continues to refuse to admit guilt or to turn others in.

Ginzburg hears other prisoners knocking on the walls, and she remembers a page from a book that explains the prison alphabet, a series of tapping noises. By tapping and translating others' taps, Ginzburg learns about the prison and its inmates. She and Lyama get a new cellmate, Ira.

As part of the ongoing interrogation, Ginzburg's former colleagues from the magazine *Red Tartary* are called in to confront her. Ginzburg is dismayed to learn that both Volodya Dyakonov and Nalya Kozlova have agreed to sign the interrogators' documents. Soon after, Ginzburg is taken to another prison, which is dirtier but less strict. Ginzburg meets her new cellmates and a new system of communication—spreading news throughout the prison by setting it to opera melodies and singing. Before long, Ginzburg moves again, this time to Moscow. She and her fellow inmates travel in coaches, like "human freight." At the new prison, Butkryki, Ginzburg hears the screams of prisoners being tortured.

Ginzburg appears before the military tribunal, fully expecting to receive the death sentence. Instead, she is given ten years' imprisonment. She is momentarily elated.

After a brief stay at the Pugachev Tower, a facility for prisoners about to be deported, Ginzburg is taken by train to Yaroslavl. There she serves two years, along with her cellmate, Julia. At the end of the two years, Ginzburg's prison sentence is revised and she is reassigned, along with the other inmates, to a corrective labor camp.

Part Two begins with a group of seventy-six female prisoners boarding Car Number 7, a train compartment labeled "special equipment." After a harrowing monthlong journey in what is essentially a cattle car, the prisoners arrive at a transit camp near Vladivostok. Here the women mingle, through barbed wire, with male prisoners, gorging themselves on romantic emotion and searching for familiar faces. Ginzburg spends a month at this camp before being taken by ship to Kolyma, deep in the northeast region of Siberia.

Life aboard the SS *Dzhurma* is even more wretched than life in Car 7 and Yaroslavl. Ginzburg falls deathly ill and is taken to the sick ward, where ailing men and women are grouped together in very tight quarters. She goes in and out of consciousness during the trip and comes to on land, in a warm pine bath prescribed by a doctor. She is in the infirmary at Magadan camp and under the care of a nurse who helps Ginzburg regain her health. When Ginzburg is well again, she rejoins the other prisoners and is put to work.

Ginzburg bribes the team leader, who assigns the prisoners to various work locations, and lands in the cozy environment of a guesthouse, where she does housework. Later she works in the kitchen of the men's quarters. Soon, her luck runs out, however, and she is sent off with the convoy to the camp at Elgen, where she must fell trees in frigid temperatures. During this time, death keeps knocking. But she has another lucky break when a doctor performing a routine medical inspection on Ginzburg recognizes her and says he knows her son. The doctor gets Ginzburg reassigned as a medical attendant in a children's home, rescuing her from the often-fatal conditions of the camp at Elgen.

In a brief epilogue, Ginzburg writes that hers is merely "the story of an ordinary Communist woman." However, she also notes that during her imprisonment she tried her best to observe and commit her observations to memory so that she could one day tell of "the things that have been and shall be no more."

CHARACTER LIST

Eugenia Semyonovna Ginzburg The author and narrator. Ginzburg is a loyal Communist Party member, historian, writer, mother, and wife with a passion for poetry and a writer's gift for observation and memorization. Her clearheaded perception of the atrocities of prison life is fuel for her strong moral imperative to survive the injustices she is forced to suffer.

Pavel Vasilyevich Aksyonov Ginzburg's husband and a leading member of the Tartar Province Committee. Aksyonov stands by his wife throughout the time leading to her arrest. Later, he, too, is arrested, as Ginzburg learns in prison.

Alyosha Ginzburg's elder son and one of the couple's two children. Alyosha is nine years old in 1935, when the story begins. Ginzburg never sees him again after being taken to jail.

Vaska Ginzburg's younger son. When the book begins in 1935, Vaska is two.

Professor Elvov A friend and colleague of Ginzburg and a member of the party's municipal committee. Before the start of Ginzburg's memoir, Elvov writes a chapter of a book on the history of the Bolsheviks that Stalin later denounces as containing "Trotskyist ideas." After Kirov's death, Elvov is arrested on suspicion of being a Trotskyist. Ginzburg's association with Elvov results in her arrest and trial.

Alexandra Alexandrovna The office typist at *Red Tartary*. Alexandrovna advises Ginzburg to admit her guilt, but Ginzburg does not listen.

Comrade Beylin Ginzburg's first interrogator. Redheaded Comrade Beylin meets Ginzburg for the first time at Livadia, the regional committee's country villa.

Malyuta Another of Ginzburg's interrogators. Malyuta works alongside Beylin, playing "bad cop" to Beylin's "good cop."

Avdotya Vasilyevna Aksyonova Ginzburg's mother-in-law. Aksyonova is a simple peasant woman, but she seems to understand better than Ginzburg the dangers lying in wait. Ginzburg refers to her as "Grandmother."

Yaroslavsky The editor of the *History of the All-Union Communist Party*, to which Elvov contributed his ill-fated article on the Bolsheviks. Yaroslavsky somehow escapes persecution himself and becomes one of Ginzburg's tormentors.

Makarova Ginzburg's companion on the train back to Moscow after her summons by Beylin. Makarova prevents Ginzburg from committing suicide by restraining Ginzburg when she is about to jump off the train.

Biktashev A former student of Ginzburg's. Biktashev serves as secretary of the Kazan committee, which expels his onetime teacher from the party.

Vevers The NKVD official who calls Ginzburg in after her expulsion from the party and pronounces her under arrest. Vevers has a chilling grimace, which, as Ginzburg later learns, all interrogators are forced to practice in the mirror.

Lyama Shepel Ginzburg's cellmate in the cellars at Black Lake. Lyama, whose real name is Lydia, had worked for the Chinese–Far Eastern Railway, but, upon her return, she was arrested as a spy, like so many other CFER workers.

Interrogator Livanov Ginzburg's interrogator in the cellars at Black Lake. Livanov cheers Ginzburg briefly with his seemingly placid demeanor, his Kazan accent, and his old-fashioned speech patterns, but Ginzburg soon realizes how devoted Livanov is to his work.

Tsarevsky The State Security Lieutenant. Like many other officials at Black Lake, Tsarevsky is maniacal and sadistic.

J

Major Yelshin The deceptively kind-looking interrogator who asks Ginzburg to write out her confession. Later, Yelshin passes through Kolyma as a prisoner while Ginzburg is working in the kitchen.

Garey Sagidullin A fellow prisoner at Black Lake. Sagidullin is a Leninist who was arrested in 1933 and occupies the cell next to Ginzburg's, often tapping on their shared wall.

Ira Yegereva The third prisoner in Ginzburg's jail cell, along with Lyama. Ira is a postgraduate student whom Ginzburg saw once or twice at the university.

Lieutenant Bikchentayev Another interrogator at Black Lake.

Volodya Dyakonov A former writer on Ginzburg's staff at *Red Tartary*. Dyakonov is brought in as a witness against Ginzburg while she is being held at Black Lake.

Nalya Kozlova Another staff member of *Red Tartary*. Kozlova is also brought in as a witness against Ginzburg and calmly signs her statement.

Yefrem Medvedyev A fellow prisoner whom Ginzburg speaks to on the Black Maria. Yefrem and Ginzburg first knew each other when he was a postgraduate student at the Marxist Institute.

Big Anna A fellow inmate at the Krasin Street prison. Big Anna is in jail for telling political jokes.

Lydia Another inmate at the Krasin Street prison. Lydia is a seasoned prisoner, having been incarcerated many times.

Little Anna A party activist and another inmate at Krasin Street.

Nina Yet another inmate at Krasin Street. Nina is an honest working girl who is in jail for failing to report overhearing a joke about Stalin.

Nadezhda Derkovskaya Another Krasin Street inmate, who was arrested along with her son.

Zinaida Abramova The wife of the head of the Council of the People's Commissars of the Tartar Republic. Zina, as she is known, seems bewildered by her first experience in prison and is convinced she is going to be released. Instead, the interrogators beat her.

Julia Karepova A biologist and orthodox party member who shares the Black Maria with Ginzburg. In a twist of fate, Julia later becomes Ginzburg's cellmate at Yaroslavl.

Rimma Faridova Another passenger in the Black Maria. Rimma caves and signs whatever the interrogators put before her.

Anna Zhilinskaya Ginzburg's roommate in the Pugachev Tower and a fellow historian. Anna has already spent time in the Lubyanka prison, and her outlook on her future is very grim.

Tanya Andreyeva A cheerful cellmate in the Pugachev Tower.

The Nabob Ginzburg's name for the sadistic senior warder in Yaroslavl prison.

Yaroslavsky A prison guard at Yaroslavl. Yaroslavsky brings Ginzburg and Julia their requested books and has a kindly, youthful appearance.

Vulturidze The new prison governor of Yaroslavl, whose real name Ginzburg never learns. Instead, she gives him the nickname "Vulturidze" after a vulturelike character in a film who kills the "dovelike" heroine.

Fisa Korkodinova A strong, articulate woman who is elected the *starosta*, or spokesperson, of Car 7.

Tanya Stankovskaya One of the passengers in Car 7. Tanya suffers from pellagra, and the other women fear she will die before they reach Kolyma. Tanya resolves to make it to the destination alive, and she succeeds.

Tamara Varazashvili Another inmate of Car 7. Tamara demands increased water rations from the guards but in vain. She is later racked by guilt when two other inmates are punished as a result of her demands.

The Brigand The officer in charge of the women in Car 7.

Lena Solovyova One of the Car 7 inmates from Suzdal prison, another solitary confinement facility for women. Lena recognizes Ginzburg as an old acquaintance from Moscow.

J

Vasek A prison trusty in the transit camp. Vasek alerts Ginzburg when she is about to be taken to Kolyma.

Dr. Angelina Klimenko Ginzburg's doctor in the Magadan camp infirmary. Dr. Klimenko is married to an NKVD investigator and has a very kindly disposition. She takes it upon herself to nurse Ginzburg back to health after a near-fatal bout with illness.

Verka The team leader at Kolyma who is responsible for assigning the prisoners to work. Verka takes Ginzburg's colorful jacket and, in return, assigns her to do comfortable, easy work in the guesthouse. Later, in response to a monetary bribe, she assigns Ginzburg to the kitchen in the male compound.

Rudolf One of the men awaiting deportation from Kolyma in the guesthouse where Ginzburg works. Rudolf takes a liking to Ginzburg and, along with his friends, gives her money to bribe the prison guard into giving her light work.

Helmut A deaf Volga German man who works alongside Ginzburg in the prison kitchen. Helmut grows fond and protective of Ginzburg after she makes an effort to communicate with him by writing things down.

Dr. Petukhov A doctor who performs medical inspections at Elgen. Dr. Petukhov recognizes Ginzburg as the relative of one of his good friends and arranges for her to become a medical attendant in the children's home, despite her lack of medical training.

ANALYSIS OF MAJOR CHARACTER

EUGENIA SEMYONOVNA GINZBURG Eugenia Semyonovna Ginzburg, born in 1896, is not quite thirty when her narrative begins in December 1934. She is the wife of a high-ranking member of the Communist Party's Tartar Province Committee, as well as a mother to two young sons. She has a teaching position at a Communist university in Kazan and works for the local Communist newspaper, *Red Tartary*. She is, by all accounts, an extremely loyal party member, and she admits she would have been willing "to die for the Party" before she was expelled from it. Even after her eighteen-year imprisonment, she says she remains an ordinary Communist woman at heart, and she still takes pride at being called a comrade. Her unjust incarceration poisons her only against the sadistic prison warden and the barbarians who serve as interrogators. From the first page of the memoir, however, Ginzburg reveals her secret dislike of Stalin, calling it a "vague disquiet." Publicizing such an opinion would have been impossible for Ginzburg in those dangerous years leading up the Great Purge of 1937, and we must wonder whether it is Ginzburg the reflective narrator or Ginzburg the woman of not yet thirty who senses in Stalin something less than the hero he was to become in Russia.

In stark contrast to the questionable ethics of those around her, Ginzburg's own moral core seems unassailable. Her reasons for not confessing to a crime she did not commit are poignant, and they seem even more remarkable as so many people around her weaken and confess. She carefully withholds judgment for those who, under torture, can no longer hold out. Ginzburg is also honest in admitting she was fortunate to miss the worst of Stalin's terrors. She escaped many of the painful physical tortures the interrogators later devised for prisoners, suffering "only" a rash of psychological tortures. Still, even the most standard and commonplace torments of a Soviet-era prison were soul shaking, and Ginzburg's steadfastness in the face of constant pressure is inspiring. Ginzburg constantly exudes a solidity of presence and a grounded nature that emphasizes the unscrupulousness of her captors.

Ginzburg possesses not just the moral imperative to tell her story but also a passion for language, a writer's gift for observation, and an astonishing memory. She turns her clearheaded perceptions of the atrocities of prison life into riveting and vivid imagery. Despite her gift for painfully beautiful phrasing and the occasional rhetorical flourish, she is never so sentimental or subjective as to seem dishonest, and the narrative is generally very straightforward. Ginzburg tells her story with a rawness that is not at all dated. She employs her warm sense of humor, investing even the dreariest and most inhumane scenarios with a lighthearted human touch, such as when she laughs over her cellmate's paranoia that a crevice in the wall is really a secret spy hole. Ginzburg's genial and evenhanded prose suggests that her survival secret was not just to preserve her body but also to safeguard the kernel of humanity implicit in humor, puns, artistic allusions, and compassion even for one's enemies.

Though she is a real historical figure, Ginzburg has all the trappings of a classic literary heroine, and her narration is as rich and engaging as any classic work of fiction. Ginzburg is communicative, compassionate, and genuinely concerned for those around her. She is also intelligent, well read, and loyal to those who are loyal to her. It's easy to see why Ginzburg, fluent in several languages, was able to make so many friends in such a short time, and how she was able to parlay those associations into so many turns of good fortune. Like any good literary heroine, Ginzburg is no self-contained protagonist but rather exists to reflect upon the lives of those around her. Her awareness of everything around her is one aspect of Ginzburg's personality that makes her memoir so compelling as well as such a damning account of Stalin's prison era. Ginzburg is constantly looking around, observing her surroundings, even feeling the walls and floors in the dark when she is thrown into a pitch-black punishment cell. She strives deliberately to commit verses and lines of dialogue to memory so that she can later draw upon a mental reservoir of facts. Ginzburg is, as she presents herself in this memoir, the perfect narrator for an account of a prison system that, because so many of its victims disappeared, needed one witness who was able to speak eloquently and knowledgably on behalf of so many.

THEMES, MOTIFS, AND SYMBOLS

THEMES

THE WILL TO SURVIVE In *Journey into the Whirlwind*, the will to survive perseveres despite all odds, even when those odds reduce the chance of survival nearly to zero. Many characters who seem close to death are able to battle, by sheer will, either to regain their strength or to hang on to life longer than anyone might have reasonably thought possible. Tanya, for example, seems about to expire at any moment during the train journey eastward, but she tells Ginzburg she'll make it to the end of the journey—and she does. By actually giving voice to her determination, Tanya is able to make it a reality. Ginzburg, too, comes close to death several times, and each time there is an implicit echo of an early declaration: "I intended to survive. Just to spite them." Having been spared the death sentence, Ginzburg makes it her goal simply to stay alive, and this fortitude drives her story forward.

THE DESIRE FOR COMPANIONSHIP Though at first it might seem ironic for a memoir that details the life of a woman in solitary confinement to be concerned with companionship, Ginzburg's narrative testifies to the deep longing for connection between human beings. At the most fundamental level, Ginzburg's memoir is about being thrown in prison, cut off from family, and separated in almost every way from society. As deprivation induces a desire to fill the void, a prisoner such as Ginzburg, particularly a prisoner in solitary confinement, naturally desires companionship. Such is the case whenever Ginzburg finds herself in a cell with another prisoner, both of them inevitably talking each other hoarse. Ginzburg also finds a great deal of comfort in reciting and reading poetry, which gives her the sense of communing with the outside world. Moreover, the crux of the Communist system, to which Ginzburg adheres even after her arrest, is communality. A real sense of companionship exists among the party members toward the beginning of the memoir, and real emotion fills Ginzburg's tone whenever she writes the word *comrade*.

THE NEED FOR COMMUNICATION The fact that Ginzburg relates her experience to others in the form of a written narrative speaks to the intrinsic human desire to share significant experiences. Storytelling is a fundamental form of communication, and a published book is communication in a print medium, not so different from the tapping on the prison walls or singing news set to opera melodies, as Ginzburg does in prison. No matter how fierce the oppressors in any of the Soviet prisons, the prisoners still manage to find a way to communicate. Just as the poetry of great Russian writers inspires Ginzburg throughout her ordeal because they show her she is not alone, so is Ginzburg's own memoir both a testimony to her experience and a sort of message in a bottle to future generations. On the levels of political ideology, storytelling, characterization, and historical reportage, communication between writer and sympathetic listener is at the heart of the memoir.

MOTIFS

POETRY Russian poetry occupies a special place in *Journey into the Whirlwind*. Lines from a single poem recur throughout the text ("penal servitude—what bliss!"), and authors are cited or quoted from at length. Both Ginzburg and her fellow prisoners, from Garey in the cellars at Black Lake to the women on the train car, engage in the recitations. Russian culture is known for its brilliant literature, particularly when the subject is bleakness or gloominess, and it is fitting that Ginzburg should find at her mental disposal such a wealth of appropriate poems and texts. The countless poetic allusions show art to be an effective antidote to the depressing monotony of prison life. These allusions appeal to the private inner core, shielded from all else and unreachable even by the government's long arm.

MOTION AND STASIS Prison itself implies a literal stillness, an inability to move freely, and for much of the narrative, the concept of stasis is at the forefront. Even when Ginzburg is under suspicion of arrest but has not yet been arrested, she is confined to her house in Kazan or takes brief walks in circles around her neighborhood. This inability to move freely—or, more accurately, the mundane repetition of daily activities—contrasts the eastward, almost linear movement of the train carrying its special cargo. The competing concepts of movement and immobility characterize the life of a prisoner in Stalin's Gulag. Prisoners must wait and wait in the prison cell until it is time to move, and they then move either to another cell, to trial, or to await an even worse fate.

FOOD Throughout *Journey into the Whirlwind*, Ginzburg uses food to emphasize narrative points and highlight moral themes. Ginzburg refuses the food her interrogators offer her under duress and refuses bread when she is locked in the punishment cell, demonstrating to her captors that the loss of her freedom does not mean she is without self-control. Elsewhere, Ginzburg uses gifts of food to depict generosity, such as when the merchants outside the train car thrust water, spring onions, and other foods into the prisoners' hands. Perhaps the most notable appearance of food is near the book's conclusion, when Ginzburg, having been subjected to bouts of forced as well as self-imposed starvation, finds herself working in the kitchen of the men's camp at Kolyma. Now that she has a hand in food distribution, she is able to demonstrate her considerable compassion by sending a piece of bread out to the prisoner Yelshin, who, as her interrogator much earlier in the narrative, had taunted Ginzburg by offering a plate of ham and cheese sandwiches in exchange for her signed confession.

SYMBOLS

PHONE CALLS Throughout *Journey into the Whirlwind*, phones and phone calls are emblematic of authority, the intrusion of the public into the private sphere, and the connectedness of the domestic and the official. *Journey* begins with a phone call that informs Ginzburg of Kirov's death. Shortly thereafter, Ginzburg and her family wait anxiously for the phone call that will signal her imminent arrest. The shrill sound of the phone is also a perfect representation of the nervousness generated by the calls, combined with a sense of strident, piercing authority.

WATCHES Two notable watches appear in *Journey into the Whirlwind*, and both suggest in some way that familiar time has come to an end. The first watch is a gift from Aksyonov to Ginzburg, and it falls into a snowbank as the husband and wife are taking a walk near their home. This occurs shortly before Ginzburg's arrest and foreshadows the cessation of her life as she knows it. The loss of the watch augurs the period of Ginzburg's life in which time passes not in minutes or hours but in the interminability of the prison cell. The second watch is confiscated from Ginzburg upon her arrival at the cellars at Black Lake, just after her arrest. When she receives the watch back later, before being transferred to the Krasin Street prison, she notices that it stopped the day of her arrest. The symbolic implication is, of course, that time stopped that day.

IMPORTANT QUOTATIONS EXPLAINED

---

1. *Don't you know he's been arrested? Can you imagine anyone's being arrested unless there's something definite against him?*

These words, from Part One, Section 3, are spoken by a nameless speaker at a party meeting at the *Red Tartary* office just after Elvov's arrest. When Ginzburg finds herself accused of not doing enough to condemn Elvov in the first place, her protests are met with indignation and anger. Again and again, the other party members ask her why she did nothing to indicate that Elvov was not to be trusted. When Ginzburg tries to use common sense, explaining that no one else had criticized Elvov prior to his arrest and that he was even an elected municipal leader, the party officials refuse to listen to reason. Finally, Ginzburg asks them how they even know, for certain, that Elvov is guilty. That's when they explode, asking, "Can you imagine anyone's being arrested unless there's something definite against him?" This question epitomizes the atmosphere at the time, in which anyone accused was considered guilty beyond question. A trial was a mere formality, as in Ginzburg's own case. The accusers would not listen to reason and would not even consider the possibility of innocence. Once someone was accused, he or she was tainted, and the stain of that person's possible offense could never be washed off.

This quote is part of a series of questions and answers. Ginzburg presents much of her confrontation with the party leaders in detail, providing a sort of transcript of the meeting. One of the effects of doing so is to elicit a feeling of outrage. The party's answers are so clearly inane that no reasonable person today could find them adequate. No one could find their reasoning sufficient justification for imprisoning a person, let alone sentencing him or her to prison for years or possibly executing him. Ginzburg's method of quoting the party leader's responses is an effective rhetorical device as well as a clever means of letting the facts speak for themselves.

---

2. *There are no more fervent friendships than those made in prison.*

This statement from Part One, Section 19, comes just after Ginzburg is taken to interrogation and separated from Lyama and Garey and underscores one of the book's central themes: it is human nature to reach out for companionship and communication. Again and again, Ginzburg pays homage to those with whom she endured the horrors of prison and with whom, as a result, she became friends. She writes effusively, almost sentimentally, about the people who affected her during her incarceration. We get to know characters such as Lyama and Julia very well, and their personalities and experiences reflect Ginzburg's own. Prison cells have no mirrors, but cellmates can function as both friend and reflection. Julia and Ginzburg often remark on each other's wasted appearance, and Ginzburg's frequent descriptions of other women's dirty hair, misaligned teeth, peeling skin, and emaciated bodies reveals her own probable physical condition. Ginzburg also reserves a tone of awe for the women who, despite their imprisonment, manage to retain their outward femininity, letting their hair grow long or flashing their eyes "like diamonds."

Given this intensive scrutiny of cellmates, intense relationships are inevitable. Ginzburg grows to call Lyama her "sister," and there is an overwhelming sense that many of the other female inmates become like a family to Ginzburg, standing in for the real family she has lost. When the male prisoners arrive at the transit camp, the women inevitably fall passionately in love with many of them, seeing in them traces of their absent lovers, fathers, and sons. Ginzburg herself admits that she sees her husband in many of their faces. It is human nature to desire connections with others, and nowhere is that desire more insistent than in prison, where it is so often thwarted.

---

3. *As I lay awake on my plank bed, the most unorthodox thoughts passed through my mind—about how thin the line is between high principles and blinkered intolerance, and also how relative are all human systems and ideologies and how absolute the tortures which human beings inflict on one another.*

This passage comes in Part One, Section 20, as Ginzburg lies on her plank bed at the Krasin Street prison. She has recently been transported from the hellish cellars at Black Lake and has just received a box of cigarettes in a package from her mother. Because she does not smoke, she offers them to a fellow inmate who is a Social Revolutionary. The woman thanks Ginzburg but then asks a fellow Social Revolutionary if she should accept cigarettes from a Communist. The answer she receives is "No," and so she refuses Ginzburg's offer. Later, as Ginzburg drifts off to sleep, she considers the steadfastness, even the stupidity, with which some people hold to their ideals. Her cellmate, a desperate cigarette smoker, will suffer through her withdrawal in order to avoid something as benign as taking cigarettes from an enemy. Ginzburg, however, has no qualms about offering a source of comfort to a fellow prisoner, even one whose political views she disagrees with. She sees no reason for the prisoners to erect artificial walls of prejudice when so many real walls already exist around them. Her cellmate's "blinkered intolerance" is little more than bias, an unwillingness to separate a person's compassion from his or her political ideologies.

When Ginzburg speaks of "the tortures which human beings inflict on one another," she is speaking not just of the physical tortures visited upon the inmates by the interrogators or the prison guards. She is also speaking of the hurts and discriminations prisoners visit on fellow prisoners. People of varying cultures, backgrounds, ideologies, and religions fill the prisons, and Ginzburg accurately describes the multiplicity and relativity of belief systems. She makes clear that in addition to the diversity of ethnic backgrounds and languages being spoken, there is the attendant diversity of political ideologies. People do not separate themselves solely on the basis of cultural affiliations, religion, or ancestry but also on the basis of moral doctrines and ideologies. Yet as Ginzburg points out, at least one universal constant exists: the willingness of men and women from all walks of life to use those differences as justification for bullying others.

J

---

4. *I intended to survive. Just to spite them.*

This remark appears in Part One, Section 30, just after Ginzburg receives her ten-year prison sentence. The judges' decision turns out to be, contrary to all expectations, a reprieve from the death sentence Ginzburg has been dreading. She is, at least for the moment, overjoyed, and she wants to do everything in her power to outlive the judges who have put her in prison. Ginzburg believes there is no way there can be ten more years of the same repression. She is certain some of the party leadership will come together and rise up against the injustices being committed on so many of the party's members. Now that she has avoided death, she wants to endure prison long enough to see the day when she and other innocent victims are liberated.

This quote reveals Ginzburg's fierce determination to endure the torments of prison life as well as her sense of humor even in the darkest moments. There is an impertinent, almost mischievous tone to the statement, "Just to spite them," and Ginzburg describes herself earlier in this passage as being "cheerful," much to the amazement of the wardens and the wardress setting out Ginzburg's dinner. Ginzburg is deeply serious about her conviction, but she also has the strength, creativity, and wit necessary to endure her hellish circumstances. The idea of survival is at the heart of *Journey into the Whirlwind*. Throughout the memoir are many examples of prisoners who succumb to the horrors of confinement and die, but there are also many brave inmates who, despite being ferociously ill, survive by sheer force of will. Tanya, for instance, survives the long train journey into eastern Russia despite appearing to be close to death.

Although everyone else in Car 7 believes she'll die, Tanya assures them she'll make it to the end of the line—and she does. Intoning a statement such as "I intended to survive" seems to be almost enough to make it true.

---

5. *It's penal servitude—what bliss!*

This exclamation appears in Part One, Section 30, and is one of the most important phrases in the book. Ginzburg borrows the line from a poem by Boris Pasternak called "Lieutenant Schmidt." The entire passage, which Ginzburg includes, reads: "The indictment stretched, mile on mile, / Pit-shafts mark our weary way. / We greet out sentence with a smile— / It's penal servitude! What bliss!"

Pasternak's poem is understandably appealing to Ginzburg after her own experience before the military tribunal and her ten-year prison sentence. Because she was anticipating a death sentence, she does indeed feel that a term of penal servitude is "bliss" in comparison. Ginzburg, like Pasternak, smiles when she hears her sentence. Moreover, her own text, in the wake of her sentence, is punctuated with exclamation points. Ginzburg even takes Pasternak's line as the title of a subsection because she feels so closely allied to him and his own experience of sentencing.

After the initial appearance of the quotation, Ginzburg takes up Pasternak's quotation as a refrain. She uses it again most notably at the start of her train journey to Kolyma. Her reassignment to the labor camp is, at least while it is still in the future, an antidote to the stifling inactivity of solitary confinement. One of the horrors of the prison enclosure at Yaroslavl is that is restricts the inmates' access to fresh air and sunlight, so much so that Ginzburg starts to fantasize about being outside in the open air. Thus there is at least some earnestness to her quotation, "Penal servitude—what bliss!" Of course, through the lens of history, and through Ginzburg's own knowledge of what actually happened, the quotation is also dripping with irony. There is certainly nothing blissful about the work Ginzburg does in the prison camps. In fact, while serving out the rest of her sentence, Ginzburg thinks back to her days in solitary confinement with "affection." In that respect, Pasternak's quote, as used by Ginzburg, symbolizes the ignorance that is bliss to the prisoner who does not know what is coming.

The Joy Luck Club

Amy Tan
(1952–)

CONTEXT

Amy Tan was born in Oakland, California, in 1952. Her parents, both Chinese immigrants, lived in various towns in California before eventually settling in Santa Clara. When Tan was in her early teens, her father and one of her brothers each died of a brain tumor within months of each other. During this period, Tan learned that her mother had been married before, in China. Tan's mother had divorced her first husband, who had been abusive, and had fled China just before the Communist takeover in 1949. She left behind three daughters, whom she would not see again for nearly forty years.

After losing her husband and son, Tan's mother moved her family to Switzerland, where Tan finished high school. During these years, mother and daughter argued about Tan's college and career plans. Tan eventually followed her boyfriend to San Jose City College, where she earned a bachelor's and a master's degree in English and linguistics, despite her mother's wish that she study medicine.

After Tan married her boyfriend, Louis DeMattei, she began to pursue a Ph.D. in linguistics. She later abandoned the program in order to work with developmentally disabled children. Then she became a freelance business writer. Although she was successful, she found writing for corporate executives unfulfilling. She began to write fiction as a creative release.

Meanwhile, Tan's mother was suffering from a serious illness, and Tan resolved to take a trip to China with her mother if she recovered. In 1987, after her mother returned to health, they traveled to China, where Tan's mother was reunited with her daughters and Tan met her half-sisters. The trip provided Tan with a fresh perspective on her mother, and it served as the key inspiration for her first book, *The Joy Luck Club*. Soon after its publication in 1989, *The Joy Luck Club* garnered enthusiastic reviews, remaining on the *New York Times* bestseller list for many months. It won both the National Book Award and the *L.A. Times* Book Award in 1989.

Tan continues to publish popular works. In response to the widely held opinion that she writes with a social aim—to portray the Chinese-American experience—Tan often emphasizes that she writes first and foremost as an artist. She argues that her bicultural upbringing is her work's source of inspiration but not its primary subject. Through her writing, Tan approaches issues that are universally applicable to all groups of people. She explores themes of family and memory, as well as the conflicts of culture that arise in so many American communities.

PLOT OVERVIEW

The Joy Luck Club contains sixteen interwoven stories about conflicts between Chinese immigrant mothers and their American-raised daughters. The book hinges on Jing-mei's trip to China to meet her half-sisters, twins Chwun Yu and Chwun Hwa. The half-sisters remained in China because Jing-mei's mother, Suyuan, was forced to leave them on the roadside during her desperate flight from Japan's invasion of Kweilin during World War II. Jing-mei was born to a different father years later, in America. Suyuan intended to return to China for her other daughters, but she failed to find them before her death.

Jing-mei has taken her mother's place playing mahjong in a weekly gathering her mother had organized in China and revived in San Francisco: the Joy Luck Club. The club's other members—Lindo, Ying-ying, and An-mei—are three of her mother's oldest friends and fellow immigrants. They tell Jing-mei that just before Suyuan died, she had finally succeeded in locating the address of her lost daughters. The three women repeatedly urge Jing-mei to travel to China and tell her sisters about their mother's life. But Jing-mei wonders whether she is capable of telling her mother's story, and the three older women fear that Jing-mei's doubts may be justified. They fear that their own daughters, like Jing-mei, may not know or appreciate the stories of their mothers' lives.

The novel is composed of four sections, each of which contains four separate narratives. In the first four stories of the book, the mothers, speaking in turn, recall with astonishing clarity their relationships with their own mothers, and they worry that their daughters' recollections of them will never possess the same intensity. In the second section, these daughters—Waverly, Jing-mei, Lena, and Rose—relate their recollections of their childhood relationships with their mothers; the great lucidity and force with which they tell their stories prove their mothers' fears at least partially unfounded. In the third group of stories, the four daughters narrate their adult dilemmas—troubles in marriage and with their careers. Although they believe that their mothers' antiquated ideas do not pertain to their own very American lifestyles, their search for solutions inevitably brings them back to their relationships with the older generation. In the final group of stories, the mothers struggle to offer solutions and support to their daughters, in the process learning more about themselves. Lindo recognizes through her daughter Waverly that she has been irrevocably changed by American culture. Ying-ying realizes that Lena has unwittingly followed her passive example in her marriage to Harold Livotny. An-mei realizes that Rose has not completely understood the lessons she intended to teach her about faith and hope.

Although Jing-mei fears that she cannot adequately portray her mother's life, Suyuan's story permeates the novel via Jing-mei's voice: she speaks for Suyuan in the first and fourth sections, the two "mothers' sections," of the novel. Suyuan's story is representative of the struggle to maintain the mother-daughter bond across cultural and generational gaps; by telling this story as her mother's daughter, Jing-mei enacts and cements the very bond that is the subject of Suyuan's story. When Jing-mei finally travels to China and helps her half-sisters to know a mother they cannot remember, she forges two other mother-daughter bonds as well. Her journey represents a reconciliation between Suyuan's two lives, between two cultures, and between mother and daughter. This enables Jing-mei to bring closure and resolution to her mother's story, but also to her own. In addition, the journey brings hope to the other members of the Joy Luck Club that they too can reconcile the oppositions in their lives between past and present, between cultures, and between generations.

CHARACTER LIST

The character list is divided into four sections, according to the mother-daughter pairs who narrate *The Joy Luck Club*'s sixteen stories. Each family's list includes family members along with other characters associated with the family or who appear exclusively in the family's stories.

WOO FAMILY

Jing-mei (June) Woo The newest member of the Joy Luck Club, having taken her mother Suyuan's place after her death. The other members of the Joy Luck Club give Jing-mei money to travel to China so that she can find her mother's long-lost twin daughters, Chwun Yu and Chwun Hwa, and tell them Suyuan's story, but Jing-mei fears that she is not up to the task.

Suyuan Woo Jing-mei's mother and the founder of the Joy Luck Club, a group of women who come together once weekly to play mahjong. Suyuan started the club in China, in the early days of her first marriage. During her flight from a war-torn area of China, Suyuan lost her twin daughters, Chwun Yu and Chwun Hwa. In San Francisco, Suyuan revived the Joy Luck Club with Lindo, An-mei, and Ying-ying.

Canning Woo Suyuan's second husband and the father of her daughter Jing-mei. Canning met Suyuan in the hospital in Chungking, where she recovered from her flight from Kweilin. After Suyuan's death, he travels to China with Jing-mei to meet her children.

Wang Chwun Yu and Wang Chwun Hwa Suyuan's twin daughters by her first husband, Wang Fuchi, and the half-sisters of Jing-mei. When an officer warned Suyuan to go to Chungking with her daughters to be with Wang Fuchi, Suyuan knew the Japanese were going to invade Kweilin. After many hardships and the onset of dysentery, Suyuan was forced to leave the twins by the side of the road, but Jing-mei and Canning are reunited with them at the end of the novel and tell them their mother's story.

JONG FAMILY

Lindo Jong A member of the Joy Luck Club. Lindo teaches the power of invisible strength to her daughter Waverly, instilling in her the skills that contribute to Waverly's talent in chess. She fears that in trying to give Waverly American opportunities, she may have undermined her daughter's Chinese identity; Lindo also fears that she herself may have become too assimilated.

Waverly Jong The youngest of Lindo and Tin Jong's children. Waverly has always been a model of success, winning chess tournaments as a child and eventually building a lucrative career as an attorney. Jing-mei has always felt a rivalry with her, somewhat imposed by their competitive mothers. Much of Waverly's talent in chess stemmed from her ability to hide her thoughts and channel invisible powers. Waverly fears what her mother will say about her white fiancé, Rich.

Tin Jong Lindo's second husband. Tin is the father of her three children: Vincent, Waverly, and Winston.

Vincent Jong Lindo and Tin Jong's second child. When Vincent received a secondhand chess set at a church-sponsored Christmas party, his sister Waverly discovered her interest and talent in chess.

Winston Jong Lindo and Tin Jong first child. Winston was killed in a car accident at the age of sixteen.

Huang Tyan-yu Lindo Jong's first husband, in China. Tyan-yu's mother was Huang Taitai. When Tyan-yu and Lindo were one and two, respectively, a matchmaker arranged for their marriage. Pampered and self-centered, Tyan-yu makes Lindo's life extremely unpleasant when she comes to live with his family at the age of twelve. When Lindo is sixteen, they get married, but Tyan-yu remains very much a boy. He has no desire for Lindo, but he is too afraid to admit it.

Huang Taitai Tyan-yu's mother. When Lindo came to live in her household at the age of twelve, Taitai trained her to be the epitome of the obedient wife. Domineering and tyrannical, Taitai made Lindo's life miserable and ignorantly blamed her for the fact that Lindo and Tyan-yu had no children.

Marvin Chen Waverly's first husband and the father of her daughter, Shoshana. Waverly's mother Lindo was very critical of Marvin, always pointing out his faults. Soon, Waverly could see nothing but his shortcomings and consequently divorced him. Waverly fears that the same thing will happen when she marries Rich.

Shoshana Chen Waverly's four-year-old daughter. Waverly's unconditional love for Shoshana teaches her about maternal devotion.

Lindo's Mother After Lindo was engaged at the age of two, Lindo's mother began to talk about Lindo as if she were already her mother-in-law Huang Taitai's daughter. Lindo knows that her mother did so only because she wanted to keep herself from feeling too attached to the daughter she loved so dearly but had already given away.

Rich Schields Waverly's white fiancé. Waverly wants to tell her mother, Lindo, about their engagement, but she is afraid that Lindo will criticize Rich to the point that she will be unable to see anything but his faults. Rich loves Waverly unconditionally, but Waverly fears that a bad first impression will unleash a flood of criticism from Lindo.

HSU FAMILY

An-mei Hsu One of the members of the Joy Luck Club. An-mei has learned important lessons about the dangers of passivity and the necessity of speaking up for herself, but, she notes with pain, she has not passed on these lessons to her daughter Rose. Although she has lost most of her faith in God, An-mei maintains a certain faith in the human power of will and effort.

Rose Hsu The youngest of An-mei and George Hsu's three daughters. Rose married Ted Jordan, despite protests from both An-mei and Mrs. Jordan. She has always allowed Ted to make all of the decisions, but when Ted asks her to take on some of the responsibility, Rose's relationship with Ted disintegrates. An-mei helps Rose understand that she needs to assert herself.

Bing Hsu The youngest of An-mei's and George Hsu's seven children. When Bing was four years old, the entire Hsu family took a trip to the beach, and Bing drowned. Rose, rather irrationally, blames herself for the death. An-mei had faith that God and her *nengkan*, or her belief in her power to control her fate, would help her find Bing, but the boy never turned up.

George Hsu An-mei's husband and Rose's father.

J

An-mei's Mother A strong but sorrowful woman who, after being widowed while still young, was tricked into becoming the fourth wife of Wu Tsing. She went to live in his household in the city of Tientsin. When An-mei's grandmother, Popo, dies, An-mei goes to live with her mother in the city. Eventually, An-mei's mother commits suicide so that An-mei will not live a life of shame and unhappiness. An-mei's mother teaches her daughter to sacrifice herself for her family, to swallow her tears, to mask her pain, and to beware of people who seem too kind or generous.

Popo An-mei's maternal grandmother. When An-mei's mother married Wu Tsing, Popo disowned her. According to traditional Chinese values, it was a disgrace that her widowed daughter had not only remarried but had remarried as a third concubine. Five years after leaving, An-mei's mother returned because Popo had fallen terminally ill and, according to superstitious healing methods, sliced off a piece of her flesh to put in a broth for Popo.

Wu Tsing A wealthy Chinese merchant who took An-mei's mother as his third concubine, or "Fourth Wife." Wu Tsing was easily manipulated by Second Wife and was, at root, a coward. When An-mei's mother commits suicide, he fears the vengeance of her ghost and thus promises to raise An-mei in wealth and status.

Second Wife Wu Tsing's first concubine. Second Wife entirely dominates the household in Tientsin, providing an example of extreme female power in a patriarchal society. Yet hers is a cruel power: she is deceptive and manipulative. She banks on her husband's fear of ghosts by faking suicides so that he will give her what she wants, and she trapped An-mei's mother into marrying Wu Tsing so as to fulfill his wish for heirs without losing her authority. At first, Second Wife manipulates An-mei into liking her by giving her a pearl necklace, but An-mei's mother shows An-mei the deceptiveness of appearances by shattering one of the "pearls" with her foot in order to prove that it is actually glass. An-mei repeats this action after her mother's suicide, and Second Wife is the first figure against whom An-mei learns to assert her own strength.

J

Syaudi The son of An-mei's mother and her second husband, Wu-Tsing, but taken by Second Wife as her own. An-mei learned that Syaudi was her brother through Yan Chang, her mother's servant.

Ted Jordan Rose's estranged husband. When they were dating, Ted made all the decisions. Later, he asks for a divorce and is surprised when Rose stands up for herself.

ST. CLAIR FAMILY

Ying-ying St. Clair A member of the Joy Luck Club. As a child, Ying-ying was headstrong and independent. Yet she slowly develops a fatalism and passivity; rarely speaking her mind, she allows her American husband, Clifford St. Clair, to translate incorrectly her feelings and thoughts. Once she realizes that her daughter Lena exhibits the same qualities in her own marriage, Ying-ying recognizes her weakness and resolves to tell Lena her story.

Lena St. Clair The only child of Ying-ying and Clifford St. Clair. When Lena married Harold Livotny, she unwittingly began to follow Ying-ying's passive example, believing herself incapable of control in her marriage and her career.

Clifford St. Clair Ying-ying's second husband. Clifford never learned to speak Chinese fluently, and Ying-ying never learned to speak English fluently. Clifford often puts words into his wife's mouth.

Ying-ying's Amah Ying-ying's childhood nursemaid. She loved Ying-ying as if she were her own child and tried to instill traditional Chinese feminine values in her—values that Ying-ying will later regret having adopted.

Harold Livotny Lena St. Clair's husband. Since the beginning of their relationship, Harold has insisted that they split the cost of everything they share. He says that keeping their finances separate makes their love purer. However, what he believes will keep them independent and equal in fact renders Lena rather powerless.

ANALYSIS OF MAJOR CHARACTERS

JING-MEI (JUNE) WOO In a way, Jing-mei Woo is the main character of *The Joy Luck Club*. Structurally, her narratives serve as bridges between the two generations of storytellers, as Jing-mei speaks both for herself and for her recently deceased mother, Suyuan. Jing-mei also bridges America and China. When she travels to China, she discovers the Chinese essence within herself, thus realizing a deep connection to her mother that she had always ignored. She also brings Suyuan's story to her long-lost twin daughters, and, once reunited with her half-sisters, gains an even more profound understanding of who her mother was. For the most part, Jing-mei's fears echo those of her peers, the other daughters of the Joy Luck Club members. They have always identified with Americans (Jing-mei also goes by the English name "June") but are beginning to regret having neglected their Chinese heritage. Her fears also speak to a reciprocal fear shared by the mothers, who wonder whether, by giving their daughters American opportunities and self-sufficiency, they have alienated them from their Chinese heritage.

Jing-mei is representative in other ways as well. She believes that her mother's constant criticism bespeaks a lack of affection, when in fact her mother's severity and high expectations are expressions of love and faith in her daughter. All of the other mother-daughter pairs experience the same misunderstanding, which in some ways may be seen to stem from cultural differences. What Tan portrays as the traditional Chinese values of filial obedience, criticism-enveloped expressions of love, and the concealment of excessive emotions all clash with the daughters' "American" ideas about autonomy, free and open speech, and self-esteem. However, by eventually creating a bridge between China and America, between mothers and daughters, Jing-mei ultimately reconciles some of these cultural and generational differences, providing hope for the other mother-daughter pairs.

SUYUAN WOO Suyuan Woo is a strong and willful woman who refuses to focus on her hardships. Instead, she struggles to create happiness and success where she finds it lacking. It is with this mentality that she founds the original Joy Luck Club while awaiting the Japanese invasion of China in Kweilin. Her sense of the power of will can at times cause problems, such as when Suyuan believes that her daughter Jing-mei can be a child prodigy if only the Woos can locate her talent and nurture it well enough. This leads to a deep resentment in Jing-mei. Yet it is also by virtue of Suyuan's will that she eventually locates her long-lost twin daughters in China. Only her death prevents her from returning to them.

J

Suyuan shares many characteristics with her fellow mothers in the Joy Luck Club: fierce love for her daughter, often expressed as criticism; a distress at her daughter's desire to shake off her Chinese identity in favor of an American one; and a fear that she may be alienated from her daughter either because of her own actions or because of their divergent ages and cultural upbringings.

AN-MEI HSU At an early age, An-mei Hsu learns lessons in stoic and severe love from her grandmother, Popo, and from her mother. Her mother also teaches her to swallow her tears, to conceal her pain, and to distrust others. Although An-mei later learns to speak up and assert herself, she fears that she has handed down a certain passivity to her daughter Rose.

An-mei sees "fate" as what one is "destined" to struggle toward achieving. When her youngest child Bing dies, An-mei ceases to express any outward faith in God, but retains her belief in the force of will. Rose initially believed that the death had caused her mother to lose faith altogether, but she eventually realizes that she may have misinterpreted her mother's behaviors.

ROSE HSU JORDAN Rose Hsu Jordan finds herself unable to assert her opinion, to stand up for herself, or to make decisions. Although she once displayed a certain strength, illustrated by her insistence on marrying her husband, Ted, despite her mother's objections and her mother-in-law's poorly concealed racism, she has allowed herself to become the "victim" to Ted's "hero," letting him make all of the decisions in their life together. She finally needs her mother's intervention in order to realize that to refuse to make decisions is in fact itself a decision: a decision to continue in a state of subservience, inferiority, and ultimate unhappiness.

Rose's youngest brother, Bing, died when he was four years old. Because Bing drowned at the beach while Rose was supposed to be watching him, Rose feels responsible for his death, despite the fact that the rest of the family does not hold Rose accountable. Her refusal to take on future responsibilities may stem from her fear of future blame should misfortunes occur.

LINDO JONG Lindo Jong learns from an early age the powers of "invisible strength"—of hiding one's thoughts until the time is ripe to reveal them and of believing in one's inner force even when one finds oneself at a disadvantage. She discovers these values while in China, caught in a loveless marriage and oppressed by the tyranny of her mother-in-law. By playing upon her mother-in-law's superstition and fear, Lindo eventually extricates herself from the marriage with her dignity intact, and without dishonoring her parents' promise to her husband's family. Lindo later teaches these skills of invisible strength—for which she uses the wind as a metaphor—to her daughter Waverly. Her lessons nurture Waverly's skill at chess, but Waverly comes to resent her mother's control and seeming claims of ownership over her successes. Eventually, Waverly seems to become ashamed of Lindo and misunderstands her as a critical, controlling, and narrow-minded old woman.

Lindo perhaps experiences the largest crisis of cultural identity of any of the characters. She regrets having wanted to give Waverly both American circumstances and a Chinese character, stating that the two can never successfully combine. She thinks that from the moment she gave Waverly an American name—she named her after the street where the family lived—she has allowed her daughter to become too American, and consequently contributed to the barrier that separates them. At the same time, however, she recognizes her own American characteristics and knows that she is no longer "fully Chinese": during her recent visit to China, people recognized her as a tourist. Distressed by this, Lindo wonders what she has lost by the alteration. Her strategies of concealing inner powers and knowledge may be related to her ability to maintain what Waverly characterizes as a type of "two-facedness"—an ability to switch between a "Chinese" and an "American" face, depending on whom she is with.

WAVERLY JONG From her mother, Waverly inherits her "invisible strength"—her ability to conceal her thoughts and strategize. Although she applies these to chess as a child, she later turns them on her mother, Lindo, as well, imagining her struggles with her mother as a tournament. Waverly's focus on invisible strength also contributes to a sense of competitiveness: she feels a rivalry with Jing-mei and humiliates her in front of the others at Suyuan's New Year's dinner. Yet Waverly is not entirely self-centered: she loves her daughter, Shoshana, unconditionally. Nor is she without insecurities: she fears her mother's criticism of her fiancé, Rich. In fact, it seems that Waverly tends to project her fears and dislikes onto her mother. As she sits through dinner with her parents and Rich, she becomes distraught as she imagines her mother's growing hatred of her fiancé. Yet, later on, she realizes that her mother in fact likes Rich—Waverly was the one with the misgivings, perhaps a sort of cultural guilt: Rich is white, and Waverly does not like to think that she has lost her ties to her Chinese heritage.

YING-YING ST. CLAIR Ying-ying was born in the year of the Tiger, a creature of force and stealth. However, when her nursemaid tells her that girls should be meek and passive, Ying-ying begins to lose her sense of autonomous will. Furthermore, at an early age Ying-ying's profound belief in fate and her personal destiny led to a policy of passivity and even listlessness. Always listening to omens and signs, she never paid attention to her inner feelings. Because she believed that she was "destined" to marry a vulgar family friend, she did nothing to seriously prevent the marriage, and even came to love her husband, as if against her will. When he died, she allowed the American Clifford St. Clair to marry her because she sensed that he was her destiny as well. For years she let Clifford mistranslate her clipped sentences, her gestures, and her silences.

Only after Ying-ying realizes that she has passed on her passivity and fatalism to her daughter Lena does she take any initiative to change. Seeing her daughter in an unhappy marriage, she urges her to take control. She tells Lena her story for the first time, hoping that she might learn from her mother's own failure to take initiative and instead come to express her thoughts and feelings. Lena, too, was born in the year of the Tiger, and Ying-ying hopes that her daughter can live up to their common horoscope in a way that she herself failed to do. Moreover, in this belief in astrology Ying-ying finds a sort of positive counterpart to her earlier, debilitating superstitions and fatalism, for it is a belief not in the inevitability of external events but in the power of an internal quality.

LENA ST. CLAIR Lena St. Clair is caught in an unhappy marriage to Harold Livotny. Harold insists that the couple keep separate bank accounts and use a balance sheet to detail their monetary debts to one another. Although he believes that this policy will keep money out of the relationship, it in fact accomplishes the opposite, making money and obligation central to Lena and Harold's conjugal life. Lena has inherited her mother Ying-ying's belief in superstition and deems herself incapable of reversing what is "fated" to happen. She fails to take initiative to change her relationship, despite her recognition of its dysfunctional elements.

While still a child, Lena learns an important lesson from her neighbors. She constantly hears the mother and daughter in the adjacent apartment yelling, fighting, and even throwing things. She is shocked by the difference between these noisy confrontations and her own relationship with her mother, which is marked by silences and avoidance of conflict. Yet, when she realizes that the shouting and weeping she hears through the wall in fact express a kind of deep love between mother and daughter, she realizes the importance of expressing one's feelings, even at the cost of peace and harmony. Although the neighboring family lives a life of conflict and sometimes even chaos, they possess a certainty of their love for each other that Lena feels to be lacking in her own home. Reflecting back on this episode of her life, Lena begins to realize how she might apply the lesson she learned then to her married life with Harold.

THEMES, MOTIFS, AND SYMBOLS

THEMES

THE CHALLENGES OF CULTURAL TRANSLATION Throughout *The Joy Luck Club*, the various narrators meditate on their inability to translate concepts and sentiments from one culture to another. The incomplete cultural understanding of both the mothers and the daughters owes to their incomplete knowledge of language. Additionally, the barriers that exist *between* the mothers and the daughters are often due to their inability to communicate with one another. Although the daughters know some Chinese words and the mothers speak some English, communication often becomes a matter of translation, of words whose intended meaning and accepted meaning are in fact quite separate, leading to subtle misunderstandings.

The first mention of this difficulty with translation occurs when Jing-mei relates the story of her mother's founding of the Joy Luck Club. After attempting to explain the significance of the club's name, Jing-mei recognizes that the concept is not something that can be translated. She points out that the daughters think their mothers are stupid because of their fractured English, while the mothers are impatient with their daughters who don't understand the cultural nuances of their language and who do not intend to pass along their Chinese heritage to their own children. Throughout the book, characters bring up one Chinese concept after another, only to accept the frustrating fact that an understanding of Chinese culture is a prerequisite to understanding its meaning.

J

THE POWER OF STORYTELLING Because the barriers between the Chinese and the American cultures are exacerbated by imperfect translation of language, the mothers use storytelling to circumvent these barriers and communicate with their daughters. The stories they tell are often educational, warning against certain mistakes or giving advice based on past successes. For instance, Ying-ying's decision to tell Lena about her past is motivated by her desire to warn Lena against the passivity and fatalism that Ying-ying suffered. Storytelling is also employed to communicate messages of love and pride, and to illumine one's inner self for others.

Another use of storytelling concerns historical legacy. By telling their daughters about their family histories, the mothers ensure that their lives are remembered and understood by subsequent generations, so that the characters who acted in the story never die away completely. In telling their stories to their daughters, the mothers try to instill them with respect for their Chinese ancestors and their Chinese pasts. Suyuan hopes that by finding her long-lost daughters and telling them her story, she can assure them of her love, despite her apparent abandonment of them. When Jing-mei sets out to tell her half-sisters Suyuan's story, she also has this goal in mind, as well as her own goal of letting the twins know who their mother was and what she was like.

Storytelling is also used as a way of controlling one's own fate. In many ways, the original purpose of the Joy Luck Club was to create a place to exchange stories. Faced with pain and hardship, Suyuan decided to take control of the direction of her life. The Joy Luck Club did not simply serve as a distraction; it also enabled transformation—of community, of love and support, of circumstance. Stories work to encourage a certain sense of independence. They are a way of forging one's own identity and gaining autonomy. Waverly understands this: while Lindo believes that her daughter's crooked nose means that she is ill-fated, Waverly dismisses this passive interpretation and changes her identity and her fate by reinventing the story that is told about a crooked nose.

THE PROBLEM OF IMMIGRANT IDENTITY At some point in the novel, each of the major characters expresses anxiety over her inability to reconcile her Chinese heritage with her American surroundings. Indeed, this reconciliation is the very aim of Jing-mei's journey to China. While the daughters in the novel are genetically Chinese (except for Lena, who is half Chinese) and have been raised in mostly Chinese households, they also identify with and feel at home in modern American culture. Waverly, Rose, and Lena all have white boyfriends or husbands, and they regard many of their mothers' customs and tastes as old-fashioned or even ridiculous. Most of them have spent their childhoods trying to escape their Chinese identities: Lena would walk around the house with her eyes opened as far as possible so as to make them look European. Jing-mei denied during adolescence that she had any internal Chinese aspects, insisting that her Chinese identity was limited only to her external features. Lindo meditates that Waverly would have clapped her hands for joy during her teen years if her mother had told her that she did not look Chinese.

As they mature, the daughters begin to sense that their identities are incomplete and become interested in their Chinese heritage. Waverly speaks wishfully about blending in too well in China and becomes angry when Lindo notes that she will be recognized instantly as a tourist. One of Jing-mei's greatest fears about her trip to China is not that others will recognize her as American, but that she herself will fail to recognize any Chinese elements within herself.

Of the four mothers, Lindo expresses the most anxiety over her cultural identity. Having been spotted as a tourist during her recent trip to China, she wonders how America has changed her. She has always believed in her ability to shift between her true self and her public self, but she begins to wonder whether her "true" self is not, in fact, her American one. Even while a young girl in China, Lindo showed that she did not completely agree with Chinese custom. She agonized over how to extricate herself from a miserable marriage without dishonoring her parents' promise to her husband's family. While her concern for her parents shows that Lindo did not wish to openly rebel against her tradition, Lindo made a secret promise to herself to remain true to her own desires. This promise shows the value she places on autonomy and personal happiness—two qualities that Lindo associates with American culture.

J

Jing-mei's experience in China at the end of the book certainly seems to support the possibility of a richly mixed identity rather than an identity of warring opposites. She comes to see that China itself contains American aspects, just as the part of America she grew up in—San Francisco's Chinatown—contained Chinese elements. Thus, her first meal in China consists of hamburgers and apple pie, per the request of her fully "Chinese" relatives. Perhaps, then, there is no such thing as a pure state of being Chinese, a pure state of being American; all individuals are amalgams of their unique tastes, habits, hopes, and memories. For immigrants and their families, the contrasts within this amalgam can bring particular pain as well as particular richness.

MOTIFS

CONTROL OVER ONE'S DESTINY *The Joy Luck Club* contains an ongoing discussion about the extent to which characters have power over their own destinies. Elements from the Chinese belief system—the twelve animals of the zodiac, the five elements—reappear in the characters' explanations of their personalities. For example, Ying-ying St. Clair speaks about how she and her daughter, Lena, are both Tigers, according to the years in which they were born. The "black" side of her Tiger personality is that she waits, like a predator, for the right moment for the "gold" side to act—the right moment to snatch what she wants. Yet Ying- ying's behavior contradicts this symbolic explanation of her character. Ironically, her belief in "fate" ends up negating her understanding of her "fated" nature. She believes she is destined to marry a certain vulgar older man in China, does so, and then ends up feeling bereft after she learns of his infidelity. She shows she can take matters into her own hands when she aborts the fetus of the unborn child from her first marriage, but then falls back into the same trap when she "allows" Lena's father, Clifford, to marry her because she thinks it is her destiny. She lives in constant anxiety and fear from tragedies that she believes she is powerless to prevent.

Jing-mei and her mother also clash because of their opposing concepts of destiny. Suyuan believes that Jing-mei will manifest an inner prodigy if only she and her daughter work hard enough to discover and cultivate Jing-mei's talent. Jing-mei, on the other hand, believes that there are ultimately things about her that cannot be forced; she is who she is.

An-mei Hsu seems to possess a notion of a balance between fate and will. She believes strongly in the will, and yet she also sees this will as somehow "fated." While her faith in her ability to will her own desires becomes less explicitly religious after the loss of her son Bing, An-mei never resigned herself, as Ying-ying does, to thinking that human beings have no control over what happens to them. Thus, when Rose asks why she should try to save her marriage, saying there is no hope, no reason to try, An-mei responds that she should try simply because she "must." "This is your fate," she says, "what you must do." Rose comes to realize that for her mother, the powers of "fate" and "faith" are co-dependent rather than mutually exclusive.

SEXISM Sexism is a problem common to both Chinese and American cultures, and as such they are encountered by most of the characters in the novel. In China, for example, Lindo is forced to live almost as a servant to her mother-in-law and husband, conforming to idealized roles of feminine submission and duty. Because An-mei's mother is raped by her future husband, she must marry him to preserve her honor whereas he, as a man, may marry any number of concubines without being judged harshly. Indeed, it is considered shameful for An-mei's mother to marry at all after her first husband's death, to say nothing of her becoming a concubine, and An-mei's mother is disowned by her mother (Popo) because of the rigid notions of purity and virtue held by the patriarchal Chinese society. Ying- ying's nursemaid tells her that girls should never ask but only listen, thus conveying her society's sexist standards for women and instilling in Ying-ying a tragic passivity.

In America, the daughters also encounter sexism as they grow up. Waverly experiences resistance when she asks to play chess with the older men in the park in Chinatown: they tell her they do not want to play with dolls and express surprise at her skill in a game at which men excel. Rose's passivity with Ted is based on the stereotypical gender roles of a proactive, heroic male and a submissive, victimized female. Lena's agreement to serve as a mere associate in the architecture firm that she helped her husband to found, as well as her agreement to make a fraction of his salary, may also be based on sexist assumptions that she has absorbed. Tan seems to make the distinction between a respect for tradition and a disrespect for oneself as an individual. Submission to sexist modes of thought and behavior, regardless of cultural tradition, seems to be unacceptable as it encompasses a passive destruction of one's autonomy.

SACRIFICES FOR LOVE Many of the characters make great sacrifices for the love of their children or parents. The selflessness of their devotion speaks to the force of the bond between parent and child. An-mei's mother slices off a piece of her own flesh to put in her mother's soup, hoping superstitiously to cure her. An-mei's mother's later suicide could also be seen not as an act of selfish desperation but as one of selfless sacrifice to her daughter's future happiness: because Wu-Tsing is afraid of ghosts, An-mei's mother knows that in death she can ensure her daughter's continued status and comfort in the household with more certainty than she could in life. Later, An-mei throws her one memento of her mother, her sapphire ring, into the waves in hopes of placating the evil spirits that have taken her son Bing. So, too, does Suyuan take an extra job cleaning the house of a family with a piano, in order to earn Jing-mei the opportunity to practice the instrument. These acts of sacrifice speak to the power of the mother-daughter bond. Despite being repeatedly weakened—or at least tested—by cultural, linguistic, and generational gulfs, the sacrifices the characters make prove that this bond is not in danger of being destroyed.

SYMBOLS

SUYUAN'S PENDANT In Jing-mei's story "Best Quality," she discusses the jade pendant her mother, Suyuan, gave her, which she called her "life's importance." Over the course of the story, the symbolic meaning of the pendant changes. At first, Jing-mei found the pendant garish and unstylish; to her it represented the cultural differences between herself and her mother. After Suyuan's death, however, Jing-mei comes to see it as a symbol of her mother's love and concern. It is particularly interesting to note that, in its very ability to change meanings, the pendant gains an additional symbolism: it symbolizes the human power to assign new meanings to the phenomena around us. The development that Jing-mei undergoes in understanding the gift of the pendant symbolizes her development in understanding her mother's gestures in general. While Jing-mei used to interpret many of her mother's words as expressions of superstition or criticism, she now sees them as manifesting a deep maternal wisdom and love.

LENA'S VASE In the story "Rice Husband," a vase in Lena's home comes to symbolize her marriage. Lena had placed the vase upon a wobbly table; she knew the placement of the vase there was dangerous, but she did nothing to protect the vase from breaking. Like the vase, Lena's marriage is in danger of falling and shattering. According to the text, it was Lena's husband, Harold, who built the wobbly table when he was first studying architecture and design. If one takes this information as similarly symbolic, one might say that the precariousness of the marriage may result from Harold's failure to be "supportive" enough, "solid" enough in his commitment. In any case, Lena, too, is to blame: as with the vase, Lena realizes that her marriage is in danger of shattering, but she refuses to take action. When Ying-ying "accidentally" causes the vase to break on the floor, she lets Lena know that she should prevent disasters before they happen, rather than stand by passively as Ying-ying herself has done throughout her life.

LINDO'S RED CANDLE When Lindo Jong is married, she and her husband light a red candle with a wick at each end. The name of the bride is marked at one end of the candle, and the name of the groom at the other. If the candle burns all night without either end extinguishing prematurely, custom says that the marriage will be successful and happy. The candle has a symbolic meaning—the success of the marriage—within the Chinese culture, but within the story it also functions as a symbol of traditional Chinese culture itself: it embodies the ancient beliefs and customs surrounding marriage.

Lindo feels conflicted about her marriage: she desperately does not want to enter into the subservience she knows the wedding will bring, yet she cannot go against the promises her parents made to her husband's family. In order to free herself from the dilemma, she secretly blows out her husband's side of the candle. A servant relights it, but Lindo later reveals to her mother-in-law that the flame went out, implying that it did so without human intervention. By blowing out the flame, Lindo takes control of her own fate, eventually extricating herself from an unhappy marriage. Thus, the candle also symbolizes her self-assertion and control over her own life.

It is important to consider the candle's original symbolism as a sign of tradition and culture, for it is by playing upon the traditional beliefs and superstitions that Lindo convinces her mother-in-law to annul the marriage. Her act of blowing out the candle would have been meaningless without an underlying, preestablished network of belief. Thus the candle, first a symbol of tradition, then of self-assertion, ultimately comes to symbolize the use of tradition in claiming one's own identity and power.

IMPORTANT QUOTATIONS EXPLAINED

---

1. *"What will I say? What can I tell them about my mother? I don't know anything. . . ." The aunties are looking at me as if I had become crazy right before their eyes. . . . And then it occurs to me. They are frightened. In me, they see their own daughters, just as ignorant. . . . They see daughters who grow impatient when their mothers talk in Chinese . . . who will bear grandchildren born without any connecting hope passed from generation to generation.*

This quotation, which is found at the end of the first story, "The Joy Luck Club," establishes some of the central themes of the novel. The passage establishes Jing-mei Woo as a representative of the book's younger generation, the American-born daughters who feel largely out of touch with their Chinese identities and with their Chinese mothers. As Jing-mei acknowledges this, she also shows a deep sympathy with the older generation. She understands their fears about their daughters, their distress at the idea that their hopes and dreams may not survive them in these modern American women for whom so many of the old values no longer have meaning.

However, even while Jing-mei perceives the mother-daughter gap from both sides, this double perception ultimately serves not to accentuate the gap, but to bridge it. Throughout the novel, Jing-mei provides the connecting voice between the generations. She tells both the story of an American-born daughter longing for independence and the story of her mother, who fought hard to give her daughters the freedoms that she never had. Thus, by the last chapter of the book, Jing-mei will come to represent a figure of hope for both generations, that they might understand each other better than they had thought, that they might share in a dialogue of love that often transcends linguistic and cultural barriers.

2. *I . . . looked in the mirror. . . . I was strong. I was pure. I had genuine thoughts inside that no one could see, that no one could ever take away from me. I was like the wind. . . . And then I draped the large embroidered red scarf over my face and covered these thoughts up. But underneath the scarf I still knew who I was. I made a promise to myself: I would always remember my parents' wishes, but I would never forget myself.*

In this quotation, which is from Lindo Jong's narrative "The Red Candle," Lindo introduces what will become an important link between herself and her daughter Waverly. Here she narrates how she first came to recognize her inner invisible strength, a strength that her daughter will inherit and come to use in her chess matches. This strength gives Lindo the power to endure the hardships that a restrictive and patriarchal society forces upon her. She stares into the mirror as she prepares for her arranged marriage to a man she does not love, knowing that to flee the marriage would be to go back on her parents' promise to her husband's family. Yet she also makes a promise to herself, which she is determined to honor with equal devotion. Lindo's lesson in balancing duty to one's parents and duty to oneself also links her to her own daughter, and to all of the daughters in the book, who must learn to revere their heritage and their elders without becoming passive or giving up their own desires and aspirations. While the struggle for this balance often alienates mothers and daughters, it also brings them closer together, for all of them have faced this challenge at some point in their lives, whether or not the mothers choose to recollect it.

The central event in this passage—Lindo's recognition of her value and her subsequent covering of it with her scarf—symbolizes another lesson in balance. She learns to listen to her own heart and maintain her strength even as she hides these away beneath the scarf. She knows that sometimes the strongest force is a hidden one. Although this gesture of concealment can also easily become a gesture of passivity, Lindo escapes the passivity that characterizes so many of the other female characters in *The Joy Luck Club* because she knows when to expose what she hides.

3. *"A mother is best. A mother knows what is inside you," she said. . . . "A psyche-atricks will only make you hulihudu, make you see heimongmong."*

   Back home, I thought about what she said. . . . [These] were words I had never thought about in English terms. I suppose the closest in meaning would be "confused" and "dark fog." But really, the words mean much more than that. Maybe they can't be easily translated because they refer to a sensation that only Chinese people have. . . .

This quotation is from Rose Hsu Jordan's story "Without Wood." Rose and her mother An-mei sit in church and speak about Rose's visits to the psychiatrist. Challenging her daughter's adherence to what she feels is an odd Western convention, An-mei asks Rose why she feels she must tell a psychiatrist—a complete stranger—about her marital woes, when she refuses to confide in her mother about them.

Linguistic barriers between Chinese and American cultures are especially prominent in this section of the novel, "American Translation." The passage highlights linguistic discrepancy twice. In the first instance, An-mei appears unable to pronounce "psychiatrist." Yet her mispronunciation may also be deliberate: by calling the doctor a "psyche-atricks," she may be deviously disparaging him as someone who plays tricks on the psyche—a quack not to be trusted. The second illustration of language barriers arises in Rose's own meditations on the Chinese words her mother has used. She struggles to explain them and then wonders whether they can be "translated" into English at all.

While one might find substitutes for them in English, she doubts whether the true feeling they connote can be felt by a non-Chinese person. The question then becomes whether these problems of translation inevitably alienate immigrant mothers from their American-born daughters, leading to the situation that An-mei complains of: a situation in which mother and daughter are unable to confide in each other or discuss their inner experiences with one another—in which they must go to strangers for help and support.

4. *Her wisdom is like a bottomless pond. You throw stones in and they sink into the darkness and dissolve. Her eyes looking back do not reflect anything.*

 I think this to myself even though I love my daughter. She and I have shared the same body. . . . But when she was born, she sprang from me like a slippery fish, and has been swimming away ever since. All her life, I have watched her as though from another shore. And now I must tell her everything about my past. It is the only way to . . . pull her to where she can be saved.

This passage comes from the beginning of Ying-ying St. Clair's second narrative, "Waiting Between the Trees." Seeing her daughter Lena in a painful marriage, Ying-ying resents her daughter's stubborn refusal to learn from her the Chinese ways of thinking, which Ying-ying regards as wiser than the American ways. Yet she also acknowledges the extent to which her own passivity has led to her daughter's failure to stand up for herself in a dysfunctional marriage. Thus, she knows that the only way to save her daughter is to tell her story, the story of how her submission to fate and other people's wills led to discontent and even agony.

The imagery here creates an especially potent effect and resonates throughout the novel. Although Ying-ying thinks of herself and her daughter as having shared the same body, as being of the same flesh, she also sees Lena as having sprung away like a slippery fish that now exists on a distant shore. Significantly, while many of the mother-daughter pairs view themselves as reflections of one another, Ying-ying looks into Lena's eyes and sees not her reflection but a "bottomless pond." What joins the women—their mutual passivity—is also what divides them.

Ying-ying's notion that the telling of a story can "save" her daughter is not unique in *The Joy Luck Club*. Throughout the book, the mothers insist on the importance of stories not only in guiding their daughters and protecting them from pain, but also in preserving their own memories and hopes, keeping their culture alive.

J

5. *. . . I wanted my children to have the best combination: American circumstances and Chinese character. How could I know these two things do not mix? I taught [my daughter] how American circumstances work. If you are born poor here, it's no lasting shame. . . . In America, nobody says you have to keep the circumstances somebody else gives you. She learned these things, but I couldn't teach her about Chinese character . . . How not to show your own thoughts, to put your feelings behind your face so you can take advantage of hidden opportunities. . . . Why Chinese thinking is best.*

In this passage from "Double Face," Lindo Jong questions the feasibility of the mixed cultural identity she once wished for her daughter. She fears that Chinese identity has come to constitute merely Waverly's exterior, while American identity dominates her interior self. Lindo blames herself for Waverly's lopsided duality. Yet, from Waverly's own narrative, we know that Lindo's fears are not entirely justified: Waverly exhibits a deep respect and concern for her Chinese identity. Waverly attributes much of her early talent in chess to her mother's lessons in how "not to show [her] thoughts," and she seems to have brought this skill to her adulthood.

Just as Lindo's fears are exaggerated, her descriptions of the American and Chinese ways of life also appear idealized: she seems to believe somewhat naïvely in the "American Dream," the notion of equal opportunity for all. At the same time, she describes Chinese thinking as "best" and speaks of the Chinese values of obedience and modesty as if they were universally ascribed to in China. Thus, when Lindo fears that the American and Chinese cultures cannot mix, she is contemplating the combination of two extremes. In reality, each identity is itself mixed: just as the American culture is not wholly about autonomy and liberty, the Chinese culture is not wholly about passivity, obedience, and self-restraint. Nonetheless, the challenge of finding a way to combine aspects of both into one's own unique personality is a challenge faced not only by Waverly, but all of the novel's daughter characters—even, to some extent, by the mother characters, as they become increasingly accustomed to their lives in the United States.

The Joys of Motherhood

Buchi Emecheta (1944–)

CONTEXT

Buchi Emecheta is one of a growing number of African women writers who have set their authorial eyes on the conditions of women living both on their home continent and abroad. She takes her place among Tsitsi Dangarembga, Miriama Ba, Bessie Head, Ama Ata Aidoo, Lauretta Ngcobo, and Lindsey Collen, to name a few, as writers who have formed an intense new voice of African womanhood. Emecheta has published more than twenty works, including the novels *Double Yoke, The Bride Price, Head above Water, Destination Biafra,* and *Kehinde.* Each is an exploration of what it means to be a woman and a mother in rapidly evolving societies where traditions and mores are in a constant state of flux. While some of her novels mirror her own experience as an expatriate living in London, her work mostly focuses on her native country of Nigeria. *The Joys of Motherhood* is among her most pivotal works, as it offers critical commentary on colonialism, tradition, capitalism, and women's roles as they come to affect one woman, Nnu Ego, and her family.

Emecheta's work is not strictly *feminist* in the western sense of the term, and she does not fully identify with Western feminist ideals. Many African women have not typically viewed themselves as domestic drudges, confined to the endless domestic cycles of childbearing and child rearing. Instead, Emecheta and others have pointed out that African women have a different cultural understanding of the role and function of work, identifying themselves as powerful economic forces who have always been a significant source of the family's income.

Still, Emecheta does not back down when it comes to critiquing the often repressive attitudes commonly held by many Ibo men of her generation. The Ibo, sometimes referred to as the Igbo, are a group of people who originally settled in southeastern Nigeria. Traditional Ibo culture called for strict regulation of women's roles and a proscribed subservience to men. In her novels, Emecheta is often critical of authoritarian Ibos who take advantage of male privilege, citing it as a justification for the oppression of their wives and daughters. Emecheta has always defended polygamy, or multiple marriage, seeing the system as a necessary community that aids in the rearing of children. However, she argues that it is not a presumed right that every man holds, especially when the husband is unable to afford and support additional family members. She sees the unquestioning application of repressive attitudes and behaviors as systematically silencing women and barring them from realizing their full potential.

Another source of conflict and change in Emecheta's work is the colonial influence. Emecheta turns her critical eye to the mostly white Europeans whose governments seize control of various African nations, fundamentally annexing them. European powers turn to developing parts of Africa as a rich source of raw materials, products, and labor. This foreign presence not only brings a new economic order to the colonized nation but influences and alters the values, community standards, and ways of life of the native residents. In *The Joys of Motherhood,* the family is affected most profoundly. The young are lured by the promise of higher education and the temptations of wealth, individual advancement, and personal gain. The colonial influence challenges and effectively erodes the communal and clan value systems that once defined and unified the Ibo.

These concerns are simply backdrops to the human drama Emecheta anchors firmly at the heart of her novel. Emecheta's art lies in her exploration of individual lives buffeted and shaped by larger social, economic, and national concerns. Nnu Ego stands as both a test case and a warning to a society that traditionally values motherhood at the expense of all other roles women could assume. Nnu Ego is caught between worlds and between diverse, often warring traditions. Change and resolution come only at the expense of her happiness and her illusions.

PLOT OVERVIEW

Nnu Ego, the protagonist, stumbles across the Yaba compound, almost delusional with grief. She makes her way to the waterfront, heading to Carter Bridge, intent on throwing herself off.

The action shifts to twenty-five years previous to this moment, in the village of Ogboli in the Ibuza homeland. Agbadi, the esteemed local chief, is enamored by the one woman he cannot possess, the beautiful and strong-willed Ona. During a hunting trip, Agbadi is gored by an injured elephant and not expected to live long. Ona slowly nurses him back to health. As he heals, he humiliates her in the compound by loudly forcing his sexual attentions on her. She becomes pregnant as the result of this union. If it is a boy, the child will belong to Ona's father, but if it is a girl, Agbadi will accept responsibility. When Nnu Ego is born, a medicine man concludes that her *chi*, or guiding spirit, is the slave girl who was forcibly killed and buried with one of Agbadi's wives. Within the year, Ona dies during childbirth.

Sixteen years later, Nnu Ego is of marrying age. She is first betrothed to Amatokwu. When she does not become pregnant, relations cool between her and Amatokwu, and she is soon moved to another hut to make room for a new wife. Nnu Ego is relegated to working in the fields and taking care of the new wife's infant son. When Amatokwu catches Nnu Ego breast-feeding the hungry child, he beats her. Nnu Ego returns to her father to rest and recover, and the marriage ties are severed. Dedicated to finding his daughter a better match, Agbadi arranges a marriage between Nnu Ego and Nnaife, who lives in faraway Lagos. Nnaife's older brother escorts Nnu Ego to the city and her new life with Nnaife.

Nnaife and Nnu Ego live in the Yaba compound, where Nnaife does laundry for the Meers, a British couple. Happy in her marriage, Nnu Ego becomes pregnant and gives birth to a son, Ngozi. She also starts her own business selling cigarettes and matches beside the road. One morning, she discovers Ngozi dead in their one-room home. Distraught and devoid of hope, she rushes to the waterfront to throw herself off Carter Bridge. Nwakusor, an Ibo man coming off his shift at work, prevents her with the help of the crowd that has gathered.

J

Recovering from Ngozi's death is a slow and painful process. Eventually, Nnu Ego becomes pregnant again and gives birth to Oshia. She decides to focus solely on raising the child instead of making extra income at her market stall. But economic pressures set in when the Meers return to England and Nnaife is suddenly out of a job. Nnu Ego resumes her local trade in cigarettes. Nnaife eventually secures a position that takes him far from home, working for a group of Englishmen. While he is away, British soldiers enter the abandoned compound and tell Nnu Ego that she and Oshia must vacate the premises. Nnu Ego takes a rented room in another part of town, where she gives birth to another son, Adim. Left on their own, the family slowly succumbs to malnutrition. Neighbors step in to help. Nnu Ego returns from her search for more contraband cigarettes to find that her husband has returned, flush with money. Nnu Ego secures a permanent stall in the marketplace and pressures Nnaife to find his next job.

One evening, Nnaife's friends arrive with the news that his brother has died in Ibuza. Nnaife has inherited all of his brother's wives, but only one will come to live with them in Lagos. Adaku arrives with her daughter, setting off tensions and rivalry between the two women. As Nnu Ego tries to sleep nearby, Nnaife invokes his rights as a husband and has sexual relations with Adaku. Nnaife starts a new job cutting grass for the railroad. With less space and more mouths to feed, Nnu Ego and Adaku become pregnant around the same time. Nnu Ego gives birth to twin girls, while Adaku's son dies shortly after he is born. Feeling they are not being given enough money to support the household, the women go on strike. Nnu Ego's firm resolve eventually wavers, and she cooks a large conciliatory meal. But Nnaife does not come home to enjoy it. He has been forced to join the army and is shipped off to India and then Burma to fight in World War II.

With Nnaife away and his pay partially secure in a savings account, Nnu Ego, again pregnant, takes her family to Ibuza and to the deathbed of her father. After his two funerals, Nnu Ego is unwilling to return to Lagos. However, Adankwo, the eldest wife of Nnaife's older brother, urges her to return to the city to keep an eye on Adako. Nnu Ego returns to find that Nnaife had been home for a brief visit and had left some money for her that she failed to receive. Relations between Nnu Ego and Adako grow increasingly strained, culminating in Nnu Ego's rude and brusque treatment of one of Adako's visiting cousins. When Nnaife's friends step in to resolve the conflict, Adako decides that she and her daughters will move out on their own. Impoverished once again, Nnu Ego spends the last of her savings before learning she had not been receiving her husband's yearly stipends due to an institutional error. Nnaife returns and spends most of this windfall. Though Nnu Ego is pregnant again, Nnaife decides to return to Ibuza, where he impregnates Adankwo and returns with a teenage bride, Okpo. Nnu Ego gives birth to twin girls.

The family moves to a mud house in another part of town. First Oshia and then Adim announce their intentions of furthering their educations. When Oshia tells Nnaife he has won a scholarship to study in the United States, Nnaife denounces him for his dereliction of his filial duty. Taiwo's marriage is arranged to an Ibo clerk, but Kehinde runs away to marry a Yoruba. Hearing the news, Nnaife flies into a rage and attempts to murder Kehinde's father-in-law with his cutlass. Nnaife is put in jail, tried, and sentenced to five years, a stint that is reduced provided he return to Ibuza after his release. Nnu Ego has also returned to her homeland, where she dies several years later, alone by the roadside. Oshia returns to honor Nnu Ego with a costly funeral, befitting her sacrifices as a mother.

CHARACTER LIST

Nnu Ego The novel's protagonist. At the beginning of the novel, slim, long-necked Nnu Ego is known for her youthful beauty and is often compared to her mother, the high-spirited Ona. Although she has her mother's strength and singleness of purpose, she is more polite and compliant and less aggressive and outspoken than Ona. She leaves her husband after she cannot get pregnant, and she later attempts suicide when her firstborn is found dead. Eventually, she settles into a bittersweet life of challenge and sacrifice with Nnaife and her children in Lagos.

Amatokwu Nnu Ego's first husband. When Amatokwu fails to impregnate Nnu Ego, he eventually asks her to move to an outer hut to make room for his second wife. He forces Nnu Ego to work in the fields if she cannot be productive bearing children. When he discovers Nnu Ego breast feeding his second wife's son, he savagely beats her, prompting their eventual divorce. Despite the abuse, Nnu Ego still holds him up as the standard of Ibo manhood.

Nnaife Nnu Ego's second husband. Nnaife is short, with a large paunch, pale skin, puffy cheeks, and untraditionally long hair. He is both sensitive and tender with his wife as well as nasty and unsympathetic about the demands made of her as a woman. After he loses his job washing for the Meers, he becomes an assistant to a group of Englishmen and is then employed cutting grass for the railroad, where he is forced to join the army. He is sent to India and Burma to fight in World War II. Eventually disillusioned with his life and family, he attempts to murder Kehinde's Yoruba father-in-law and is sentenced to five years in prison. When he is released early, he returns to Ibuza a broken man.

Ngozi Nnu Ego and Nnaife's first child. Ngozi dies in infancy, and his death marks a turning point in the novel, prompting Nnu Ego's suicide attempt. He is a source of guilt and regret, a specter that haunts Nnu Ego for years.

Adaku Nnaife's brother's wife whom Nnaife inherits when his brother dies. Young, attractive, peaceful, and self-satisfied, Adaku joins the family in Lagos and soon starts a thriving and lucrative business selling in the marketplace. Her wealth and success go unrecognized because she bears no sons, only two daughters. Tired of her role of inferiority, she moves out of the household and threatens to become a prostitute. The name *Adaku* means "daughter of wealth."

Adankwo The eldest wife of Nnaife's older brother. Tough, strong, wiry, and dependable, Adankwo is in her early forties and a voice of wisdom and reason among the Ibuza women. She advises Nnu Ego to return home to Lagos in order to keep an eye on Adaku. When Nnaife impregnates her with her last child, she refuses to return to Lagos with him and arranges to have Okpo sent instead.

Adimabua The second living son of Nnu Ego and Nnaife, known as Adim. Observant and intelligent, Adim grows up in the shadow of his older brother. He quickly figures out the entitlement due him as a male and realizes the opportunities denied him as the second oldest. Quick to act, he prevents his father from murdering the Yoruba butcher. Like Oshia, Adim aspires to better things and later leaves Nigeria to pursue his education in Canada. His name means "now I am two" and shows his place in the male hierarchy of the family.

Agbadi Nnu Ego's father. Agbadi is a highly respected local chief known for both his skill at oratory and for his physical prowess. Cold, disrespectful, and cruel to his wives, he is loving and indulgent to his daughter, whom he treats as the embodiment of and last link to his beloved mistress, Ona. He is a constant source of support and a voice of reason in Nnu Ego's life.

Cordelia Ubani's wife. Cordelia is kindhearted and a good friend to Nnu Ego when she makes the initially tough transition to life in Lagos. She is also a source of jealousy and conflict. Nnu Ego resents the easier, more stable life Cordelia seems to have, an attitude that sparks squabbles and petty disagreements between the women. Her name reveals the colonial influence on the region.

Mama Abby A prosperous Ibo woman and confidant of Nnu Ego's. Mama Abby earns respectability through the advancement of her son, the intelligent, upwardly mobile Abby. Her husband was a European who had worked in the Nigerian colonial service. He eventually returned to Europe, leaving his family well provided for. She, too, is of a mixed racial background. Slim, ladylike, and an eventual mother figure to Nnu Ego, Mama Abby is considered upper class but likes to live modestly with other Ibos. Many of the men view her as a negative influence and do not want their wives associating with her.

Dr. Meers Nnaife and Ubani's employer. Dr. Meers is the chief occupant of the Yaba compound and works at the Forensic Science Laboratory in Taba. The doctor makes little attempt to hide his racist attitudes concerning his African employees, overtly calling Nnaife a "baboon."

Mrs. Meers Dr. Meers's wife. Mrs. Meers, the only white female character in the novel, has gray, sunken eyes, and appears to have been prematurely aged by the climate and her life in West Africa. She believes she is kind to her African staff, chiding her husband for his racist remarks, but at the same time she maintains a haughty and aloof demeanor of social superiority in their presence.

Obi Umunna Ona's father. A great chief and doting father, Obi Umunna is particularly protective of his daughter's honor and freedom. He allows her to have lovers but does not force her to commit to a marriage. He prizes only an elusive male heir, which his daughter never produces. He is ridiculed for not finding a suitable match for his daughter and viewed by some as an ineffective father because of it.

Okpo Nnaife's sixteen-year-old bride. Okpo is sent to Lagos to live with the family when Adankwo refuses to leave Ibuza. Though she is Nnaife's wife, Okpo has childlike qualities herself. She understands her traditional role as a wife and praises and flatters Nnu Ego for raising such clever and accomplished children.

Ona Nnu Ego's mother. Ona is known for her catlike grace and youthful exuberance as she runs about the village with her breasts exposed. She wears expensive waist beads and is later held to be conservative, haughty, cold, and remote when she wins the role of Agbadi's favorite mistress. She is often reminded of her place as an Ibuzan women when she openly challenges and taunts her lover.

Oshiaju Nnu Ego's oldest surviving son, known as Oshia. Medicine men predict Oshiaju will be an intelligent man of infinite resources whose success will provoke jealousy in others. Tender and firm, Oshia physically resembles his father. He aggressively pursues higher education, working in a laboratory in Lagos and eventually winning a scholarship to a university in America. His name means "the bush has refused this," referencing his health and the long life predicted for him.

Taiwo and Kehinde Nnu Ego and Nnaife's oldest twin girls. Kehinde is quieter and more introspective than Taiwo. She radically breaks with tradition by marrying a Yoruba man. Taiwo is the more fun-loving and adaptable twin. She aspires for a dependable husband and stable home life, both of which she finds with the clerk Magnus. He finds his ideal match in an uneducated wife content with the more traditional role of bearing and raising children.

Ubani Friend of the Owulums. At first, Ubani is a cook in the Meers's compound. A good provider, he later gets Nnaife a job cutting grass for the railroad. He is a stable presence in the lives of those around him. He is the one who calmly informs Nnaife that his son, Ngozi, has died.

ANALYSIS OF MAJOR CHARACTERS

NNU EGO Nnu Ego starts out as an innocent, somewhat naïve girl filled with hope and anticipation of the joys and rewards motherhood will bring her. Unlike her mother, Ona, Nnu Ego is not a radical or antagonistic presence, and she dutifully accepts and fulfills her role as a woman in Ibo society. Her initial quest is for justification and validation. When she cannot conceive with her first husband, Amatokwu, the marriage is dissolved and she is filled with apprehension and shame. When her second marriage, to Nnaife, produces a highly prized son, she realizes the happiness denied her, only to have her joy shattered when Ngozi dies in infancy. The death of the child becomes, by extension, the death of Nnu Ego. She sees no reason to live if she cannot succeed in the single role of bearing and rearing children. Slowly, she comes to new realizations about what is truly important to her, and these epiphanies force her to re-examine her role and function as a woman in Ibo society.

Though she is distraught over the death of Ngozi, Nnu Ego feels guilty relief when, later, a daughter arrives stillborn. She begins to examine her essential worth as a woman. Although she becomes a vital economic force in the community, essentially setting up her own business to help her family survive, she is seen as merely an economic unit, a machine for producing and rearing male heirs. Nnu Ego comes to believe that aspirations of being solely a mother and provider are too limiting and dispiriting. Rather than looking forward to a quiet life where she will be well provided for by her sons and daughters, she is a victim of her times, caught at a critical turning point in West-African social history. Rather than serving the collective unit of the family, her children pursue their own courses and seek to place their own self-fulfillment and individual destinies before their family responsibilities. Nnu Ego's hope and joy become disillusionment as she dies, alone, at the side of the road, an ambivalent figure with little to show for her years of selflessness and sacrifice.

NNAIFE Nnaife, Nnu Ego's husband, is the chief male presence in *The Joys of Motherhood*, the counterpart and mirror reflection of his wife. The two stand on opposite sides of a similar conflict. While Nnu Ego must reconcile her own disillusionment with motherhood, Nnaife faces his own struggles in the wake of evolving tradition and the slow dissolve of their family structure. Nnu Ego calls Nnaife's masculinity into question from the early days of their marriage. Nnaife is filled with pride at the responsibilities he has as a launderer in the Meers household, a role no Ibo man would have filled in previous generations. Nnaife is forced to compromise in a world where capitalism reigns and where power is in the hands of white colonialists. Still, despite changing with the times, Nnaife retains his traditional notions of his role as father, husband, and man. But in his modern urban context, he is viewed more as a functionary, a mere figurehead of a family that is mostly supported and held together by the efforts of Nnu Ego.

Nnaife is a passive, ineffective figure whose lack of ambition or connections does little to further the livelihood of his family. He allows others to control or intercede for him, all the while believing he is a figure of power, strength, and action. As traditions and times change, they render Nnaife increasingly ineffective in his role as a male authority figure. In the end, he simply playacts at the part of the blustering patriarch rather than truly embodying or living up to the duties he is expected to fulfill. He emerges as an emasculated figure and is unmasked as a poor provider and a drunk, the equivalent of a deadbeat dad. As Nnaife's traditional male identity grows weaker and more threatened, he descends deeper into alcoholism and an aloof, willful detachment, both of which serve as safeguards and antidotes to reality. In a final act of desperation, he threatens to kill his own daughter and her new father-in-law. In his skewed vision of the world, individual lives and the happiness of his daughter are secondary to more abstract notions of family reputation, honor, and tradition. His subsequent imprisonment serves as symbolic punishment for a man who has grown so out of step with the world around him.

OSHIA Oshia, Nnu Ego's oldest surviving son, is an emblem of the new order, the next generation that would alter the nature of modern Nigerian society. However, he is not a radical figure, out to break entirely with traditional modes or to topple the institution of the family. Through most of his formative years, he is the ideal and dutiful son, fulfilling the high hopes Nnu Ego cherishes of the honor and comfort he will eventually bestow on her. Although he and his brother, Adim, obediently tend the family stall in the marketplace, they later lament the time they were forced to sacrifice from pursuing their studies. Caught between two worlds, Oshia must live up to the expectations his parents place on him while satisfying his own desire to better himself through education.

Oshia's ambition and intelligence eventually overpower his obligations to the traditional order. He represents a general shift in Nigerian society as new influences and new options became available to Ibos such as Nnaife. Oshia chooses his own individual destiny over his responsibilities to the collective, which makes him a failure and a disappointment to his parents. Ironically, while Oshia works as a research scientist and wins a scholarship to study in the United States, his academic achievements do not make up for his failure to remain in Lagos to support his family. Still, Oshia never completely turns his back on his origins. He honors his culture and pays homage to the sacrifices his mother made by funding an elaborate funeral service for her.

THEMES, MOTIFS, AND SYMBOLS

THEMES

THE INFLUENCES OF COLONIALISM The Owulum family and their experiences are dramatically influenced by the forces of the colonialist world in which they live. Emecheta portrays colonialism ambiguously in *The Joys of Motherhood*. It forces native populations to adopt and adhere to systems and beliefs foreign to their own. Capitalism, Christianity, and European notions of education and conduct all effectively alter and threaten traditional Nigerian culture. The effects eventually touch all levels of society, eroding tradition and trickling down to harm both families and individuals. Without the changes colonialism and its practitioners ushered in, Nnu Ego's joy as a mother and the cohesive and interdependent family she long desired could have remained intact and uncompromised. The tragedy of Nnu Ego's story is that she cannot recognize and embrace change—and that these changes themselves, embraced or not, are not entirely positive forces.

THE INDIVIDUAL VS. THE COLLECTIVE In Nnu Ego's traditional vision of the family, individual concerns are secondary to the livelihood of the group. Several times in the novel, Emecheta portrays the family as a small corporation, each member contributing to the success and well-being of the "company" as a whole. The younger generation, however, views the family arrangement quite differently. Oshia's love of learning and desire for an education take him the farthest from the family fold. He makes a severe break with tradition when he accepts a scholarship to study in the United States, where he eventually marries a white woman. Adim, in his own right, retaliates against the strict hierarchies implicit in the family structure. Traditionally, as the second son, his own interests and desires are squelched so that the eldest and the family as a whole can be supported and lifted up. Adim similarly throws off the mantle of tradition and pursues a path much like Oshia's. The change appears just as dramatically in one of Nnu Ego's daughters, Kehinde, who desires to break with traditional and societal taboos. Rather than accepting the course that would be best for her family, she asserts her right to happiness and her right to select a mate of her own choosing.

J

THE DANGER OF RESISTING CHANGE In the rapidly changing world of Lagos, traditional Ibo culture struggles to continue, and Nnu Ego must find a new and different form of pleasure in her honored status as a mother. Her children's education and achievements are now becoming the benchmarks of good parenting rather than threats to the repressive traditions that required the next generation to forgo their own goals in service to and respect for the family. The traditions and rituals of the past provide balance, order, and security in a changing world, but those unwilling or unable to compromise or to accept change end up broken and alone. Nnaife is literally punished, with imprisonment, when he cannot accept his daughter marrying into a Yoruba family. Nnu Ego's punishment is more psychological and emotional, culminating with her dying alone at the side of a road.

THE AMBIGUOUS REWARDS OF MOTHERHOOD In *The Joys of Motherhood*, motherhood is the source of not only Nnu Ego's greatest joys but also her greatest defeats. As a girl, she is taught that her sole functions are to bear and raise children. Her initial struggle to conceive and her utter self-defeat when she is unable to exemplify how strongly she believes in this uniquely female destiny that her culture has prescribed. The idea of motherhood informs her fantasies and her dreams. Yet when Nnu Ego actually becomes a mother and struggles to raise her growing family, her idealism begins to change. Nnu Ego ultimately regrets having so many children and investing so much of her life in them since they seem to have little concern for her well-being. She forces herself to accept a vision of motherhood that has been radically modified from the ideas she once cherished. Instead of an honored and revered figure, Nnu Ego becomes a sacrificial lamb, one who gave to her family selflessly while receiving little, if not nothing, in return.

MOTIFS

BLURRED GENDER ROLES Nnu Ego and Nnaife, who embody the stereotypical roles of Ibo men and women, represent the traditional thinking of their society and their generation. Yet their world is in flux. The old, formerly unquestioned attitudes have begun to change. Boys do not necessarily serve as their family's main support. Girls gain respect and power for their skills and education, not just an increased bride price. For the older generation, these changes in perception are often startling and unsettling, as once-solid gender definitions become more fluid. Nnu Ego reacts unfavorably to the fact that her husband is employed washing the personal garments of a woman. She feels such subservience "[robs] him of his manhood." At the same time, Nnu Ego herself is not untouched by the transformation and blurring of gender roles. While her identity is almost entirely dependent on her status as a mother, she occasionally assumes the traditionally male role of provider and breadwinner to support her family.

LANGUAGE BARRIERS Characters in *The Joys of Motherhood* often have difficulty understanding one another. These communication barriers suggest a world of division and separation, where English, Hausa, Yoruba, Ibo, and the various other native dialects of Nigeria intersect. Mrs. Meers and Nnaife are deeply connected in their relationship as employer and employee, yet language separates them as much as race and class do—they cannot even pronounce each other's names correctly. When soldiers enter the Yaba compound to evict Nnu Ego and Oshia, the sharp, foreign words they shout at her are as frightening and daunting as the yelps of the snarling dogs. Language divides and alienates individuals as well as families, communities, and the nation as a whole. In the novel, language barriers and lapses in communication suggest a deeper problem infecting Nigerian society: they indicate an inability to connect to and understand the outside world. Even when characters speak the same language, they still fail to fully comprehend one another's actions and intentions. For example, Nnu Ego has no idea that Oshia does not plan to stop his schooling so he can return to the family and support them.

VISION Nnu Ego's vision of the world, as well as her literal vision, frequently falter as she loses her illusions in the face of new realities. References to imperfect or unreliable sight abound, particularly in the first half of the novel, when Nnu Ego is most mired in her illusions. When Nnu Ego gets married, her vision of the world is distorted by her unrealistic ideas about motherhood and her duty as a woman. During Nnu Ego's desperate suicide attempt, Emecheta calls attention to her distorted vision. When Nnu Ego first appears, she is stumbling about, blind with grief, "her eyes unfocused and glazed, looking into vacancy." Later, Emecheta equates Nnu Ego with the blind Hausa beggar whom she nearly knocks over in her hasty retreat from the site of Ngozi's death. She runs straight into the man "as if she too was without the use of her eyes." Nnu Ego's impaired vision suggests her lack of insight. By the end of the novel, realization settles on her, and, for better or worse, Nnu Ego is finally able to see her life for what it is.

SYMBOLS

THE CHILD The pervasive image of the child in *The Joys of Motherhood* represents the destiny and supposed common goal of Ibo women. Children represent a complement to a woman's identity, and her life is viewed as incomplete or unjustified unless she has had children. The child is consistently and idealistically portrayed as an image of completion and female self-fulfillment. These abstract notions of motherhood and its attendant joys inform Nnu Ego's early years. Her dreams are haunted by visions, including images of babies in peril or children being taken away by her *chi*. Nnu Ego conjures fantasies of kidnapping Amatokwu's son and running off to raise the child alone in bliss. As the novel progresses, however, the iconic significance of the child changes. Children are still viewed as a delight, but they are also a source of agony and deep emotional pain. When Nnu Ego slowly strips away her illusions about motherhood and her unrealized expectations, she is left with the unadorned reality of her life as it is, not as she wants it to be.

PALM WINE Palm wine suggests Nnaife's refusal to confront reality and his failure to be an active force in shaping and guiding his family. On one level, palm wine represents the negative influences and social ills of life in the city. It also stands for a shirking of male responsibility, and drunkenness becomes emblematic of Nnaife's detachment as a father. He prefers intoxication to the living reality of what his family has become. At one point, about to drink a glass of palm wine, Nnaife states that the wine in the glass is the only truth he knows. His drinking only masks other problems, and his alcohol abuse plays a key role in sealing his fate during his trial for attempted murder.

CARTER BRIDGE In addition to the account of Nnu Ego's actual suicide attempt, references to Carter Bridge appear in the novel both explicitly and teasingly in Nnu Ego's random thoughts and memories of the past. The bridge serves as an ambiguous or double symbol, standing for various impressions and emotional states at the same time. On the one hand, Nnu Ego sees it as salvation, a gateway to freedom. Suicide is the only way she can address the pain of losing her child, but it is also her frantic response to the claustrophobic and predetermined role she finds herself cast in as an Ibo woman. At the same time, the bridge stands as an emblem of shame. Shame lurks in Nnu Ego's irrational response to the death of Ngozi and in her desire to seek death as a means of accepting her "failure" as a mother. Shame also lies in her desire to sidestep the expectation that she would bear male heirs. For Nnu Ego, the edge of the bridge represents the precarious intersection of failure and freedom, life and death.

IMPORTANT QUOTATIONS EXPLAINED

---

1. *Her love and duty for her children were like her chain of slavery.*

This comment, appearing in Chapter 10, summarizes one of the novel's main themes: that motherhood brings ambiguous joys. While the title of the novel promises a warm portrait of the joys and rewards of motherhood, the novel itself charts a much different course for Nnu Ego and many of the other women who make up her Ibo community. Rather than a self-fulfilling and life-giving role, motherhood and the responsibilities it creates become a form of enslavement. For Nnu Ego, her life, hope, and identity depend on her ability to bear children. In the eyes of society, she has no other primary function and no other means of achieving rank and respect.

Nnu Ego's struggle is twofold. First, she fears she will face the fate of a barren, cast-off woman when she does not become pregnant after her marriage to her first husband, Amatokwu. Later, when she is blessed with several offspring, she is ill-equipped to feed and clothe them, and the family slides deeper into poverty. Finally, when Oshia, Adim, and Kehinde turn their backs on their familial responsibilities and pursue lives of their own, Nnu Ego questions the point of all the sacrifices and self-denial she has endured, for her children's sake, through the years.

---

2. *Men here are too busy being white men's servants to be men. We women mind the home. Not our husbands. Their manhood has been taken away from them. The shame is that they don't know it.*

Cordelia, Ubani's wife, speaks these words in Chapter 4, and they underscore the blurring of gender roles that many Ibo families face in Lagos. Colonialism and the modern world, with its capitalist-based labor systems, leave their mark on the novel's male characters and help erode the traditional role of men in twentieth-century West-African society. While the men still see themselves as the heads of their households, the women view their husbands' evolving economic roles differently. The need to work, specifically in the service of white colonialists, has compromised the men as figures of authority and drained them of their once-unquestioned power as the dominant member of the family. Ubani and Nnaife are diminished in their wives' eyes by their service to the Meers family, which casts them in a subservient role. In making this statement, Cordelia indicates that she agrees with Nnu Ego, who has little respect for her husband and the pride and delight he takes in laundering Mrs. Meers's linens and underclothes. Nnu Ego compares the early days of her marriage to Nnaife to being with a middle-aged woman instead of a man. These sentiments echo the novel's pervading sense that Lagos perverts and permanently alters tradition, robbing the individual of identity or, in this case, manhood.

---

3. *She had been trying to be traditional in a modern urban setting. It was because she wanted to be a woman of Ibuza in a town like Lagos that she lost her child. This time she was going to play according to the new rules.*

In Chapter 7, soon after Oshia is born, Nnu Ego reflects on her conduct and actions during Ngozi's infancy and early death. The pressure of tending to her new child and maintaining her market stall proved to be too much. Nnu Ego feels that the all-encompassing dual roles of mother and provider directly led to her baby's death, even though these roles were expected of her. Traditionally, Ibuza women were the providers, but in the new world and economic order of Lagos, men have become the family's sole economic source. Nnu Ego concludes that they are living now in a "white man's world," where supporting the family is the man's duty. With the breakdown of the traditional family order, without an extended clan of parents and grandparents to assist with child rearing, the full burden of child care falls to the mother. Nnu Ego concludes that in order to ensure the health and livelihood of her son, she must embrace the changes her new life in Lagos have forced on her. She forgoes the extra income her selling and trading would bring in to dutifully fulfill what she believes is her greater and more valuable role as mother and nurturer.

---

4. *On her way back to their room, it occurred to Nnu Ego that she was a prisoner, imprisoned by her love for her children, imprisoned in her role as the senior wife.*

This description appears in Chapter 11. As an Ibo woman, Nnu Ego can pursue only one life path: she must produce children, preferably boys. As Nnu Ego gets older and becomes more deeply involved in her role as a mother, she sees more clearly the restrictions and limitations of this set course. She also feels she is society's scapegoat. When the children bring honor or fulfill their duty to their family, they are a reflection on their father. When they tarnish or shame the family name or fail to live up to their responsibility to their parents, the failing is placed squarely on the mother's shoulders. This double standard saddens Nnu Ego. She is trapped in this role, and her destiny and reputation are commingled with those of her children—no matter what the outcome. This restrictive arrangement extends to the hierarchy of multiple wives, or plural marriage, which is common in West-African society. As the senior wife, Nnu Ego is expected to endure the humiliation when Adaku, Nnaife's crafty and attractive second wife, arrives in Lagos and becomes part of the Owulum family. Rather than being an object of respect and veneration, Nnu Ego is expected to calmly accept the slights and insults her husband and family visit on her. She is even subjected to the sounds of Nnaife and Adaku having sexual relations in the same room in which she herself sleeps.

J

---

5. *God, when will you create a woman who will be fulfilled in herself, a full human being, not anybody's appendage? she prayed desperately.*

Nnu Ego poses this question in her prayer in Chapter 15. As an Ibo mother, Nnu Ego is expected to arm her sons for the future, at the expense of her daughters. Society views the girls as having little worth, valuable only for the bride price they will one day fetch when their marriage is arranged. Without the context of marriage and the family, an Ibo woman has neither an identity nor an inherent worth beyond the production of the next generation. However, in the new economic and social order of Lagos, both men's and women's roles change. Nnu Ego anticipates the day when individual women will be of prime importance, rather than simply being vehicles that serve and aid the collective at the expense of the self. Nnu Ego views the traditional role of Ibo women as amounting to a qualified or partial life. Rather than lives of sacrifice, Nnu Ego hopes women can achieve lives of satisfaction and self-fulfillment. In Nnu Ego's world, women are seen as tools, or as appendages that simply extend men's will. The traditional Ibo family construct demands that women deny or downplay personal fulfillment and self-realization in service to the group-oriented duties they are expected to perform.

Krik? Krak!

Edwidge Danticat
(1969–)

CONTEXT

Edwidge Danticat was born in Haiti in 1969 and grew up during a tumultuous period in the country's history. By the time Danticat was four years old, both of her parents had left Haiti for the United States, but Danticat stayed with her aunt and uncle in Port-au-Prince, the capital. While there, she learned Haitian storytelling traditions, which is where *Krik? Krak!* gets its title. In Haiti, *krik?* is a request to tell a story, and obliging listeners answer *krak*. Danticat began writing stories as a child, and in 1981, when she was twelve, she joined her parents in Brooklyn, where she began speaking English instead of her native Creole (a blend of African dialects and French). After attending Barnard College, she went to Brown University to earn an MFA in creative writing. All of Danticat's books deal with the Haiti that Danticat knew as a child, its tortured history, and the complicated politics that caused her to leave the country.

Danticat's first novel, *Breath, Eyes, Memory* (1994), is narrated by Sophie, a Haitian girl with a history that is superficially similar to Danticat's own. Sophie is raised by her aunt in Haiti until she joins her mother in New York at age twelve. When Sophie finds out she was conceived when her mother was raped, their relationship, already difficult because of their long separation, becomes strained by issues of sexuality. *Krik? Krak!* (1995) was published next and nominated for a National Book Award. Danticat's next novel, *The Farming of the Bones* (1998), concerns the 1937 massacre of Haitians who were trying to leave the Dominican Republic, an action ordered by its dictator, Rafael Trujillo Molinas. The massacre is also the subject of the short story "Nineteen Thirty-Seven" in *Krik? Krak!*. Recently, Danticat published *The Dew Breaker* (2004) about a man who used to be a torturer for the Haitian government and the many lives he affected. Danticat has also been involved with several anthologies of writings by diverse Haitian and Haitian-American authors. She often says that her voice is only one of many representing the Haitian people and refuses to be a spokesperson for the whole nation.

Haiti is on the island of Hispaniola, which it shares with the Dominican Republic. Columbus landed on Hispaniola in 1492 and claimed it for the Spanish, who imported African slaves to work on plantations. However, the Spanish population was concentrated on the eastern half of the island, and French pirates began conquering the western half. In 1697, a treaty gave the French possession of what is now Haiti. Producing abundant amounts of sugar, indigo, cotton, tobacco, and rum, among other things, Haiti quickly became one of the most economically successful settlements in the Caribbean. However, the profitable exploitation of slaves came to an end as repressed mulattoes and then black slaves began to revolt. In 1791, a slave named Boukman used voodoo priests and rituals to lead the first significant slave revolt. This set off a number of smaller revolts, leading to the revolution of the slave and General Toussaint L'Ouverture, who took control of all of Hispaniola, oversaw the end of slavery on the island, and established Haiti's independence in 1804. Toussaint was killed by Napoleon, but Haiti remained independent. Its first ruler, Dessalines, made it a military force and executed the majority of the country's white population.

Haiti's former wealth all but disappeared, replaced by an extreme poverty and illiteracy that only worsened over the next few centuries. Early twentieth-century attempts by the United States to establish security in the country, including an American occupation of Haiti from 1915 to 1934, failed. In 1957, a fraudulent election made a doctor named François "Papa Doc" Duvalier Haiti's president. Duvalier became a despotic ruler and declared himself "president for life." His *tonton macoutes*, a ruthless secret police named after a mythical Haitian monster, terrorized the nation, arresting or killing the government's critics. Duvalier compared himself to both Haitian voodoo spirits and Jesus Christ, exploiting the country's religious influences. He avoided deposition by the United States by opposing communism and allied himself with the Dominican Republic's dictator, Trujillo (who in 1937 had massacred Haitians at the Dominican border). But while Duvalier's political power and wealth increased, Haiti became the poorest country in the Americas. Duvalier stole as much money and land from his people as possible, using foreign aid money for his personal gain. The small percentage of educated Haitians fled the country for economic or political reasons.

When Duvalier died in 1971, his son, Jean-Claude "Baby Doc" Duvalier, continued his legacy of political tyranny and economic exploitation while making superficial reforms to improve Haiti's international reputation. "Baby Doc" was deposed in 1986 because of opposition from both the Haitian people and the United States government. He left behind a power vacuum that resulted in military control, despite many attempts at democratic elections. In 1991, democracy seemed to be established with the election of Jean Bertrand Aristide. However, Aristide was overthrown months later by a military coup. In 1994, the United States government, under pressure from its Haitian citizens, restored Aristide to the presidency with threats of military invasion. Several democratic elections followed, but Haiti's political status remains unstable, and its economic conditions are still the worst in the western hemisphere. Communities of Haitian immigrants and their Haitian-American descendants, including Danticat, remain in the United States.

PLOT OVERVIEW

Krik? Krak! contains nine stories and an epilogue. Although the stories take place in Port-au-Prince or Ville Rose, Haiti, or New York, they do not overlap. The only exception is "Between the Pool and the Gardenias," which mentions women from earlier stories. All the stories are all about Haitian women trying to understand their relationships to their families and to Haiti. The epilogue, "Women Like Us," suggests that these women are related. The epilogue's unnamed narrator, possibly Danticat herself, notices her similarity to her mother and female ancestors. These women cook to express sorrow, but the narrator chooses to write. Her mother doesn't approve because Haitian writers are often killed. However, the narrator's female ancestors are united in death, and she uses stories to keep their history alive.

"CHILDREN OF THE SEA"

Two nameless narrators are in love and write each other letters they will never read. The female narrator is angry that her father opposes their love, but she finds out he gave up all his possessions to protect her from the *macoutes*. The female narrator's family hears the *macoutes* kill her neighbor, whose son was in the Youth Federation. The male narrator, also a member, has fled Haiti. In his boat is a pregnant teenager, Célianne, who was raped by a *macoute*. Days after her baby dies, she throws it and herself overboard. The female narrator sees a black butterfly and knows the male narrator has died too.

"NINETEEN THIRTY-SEVEN"

"Nineteen Thirty-Seven" is narrated by Josephine, whose mother is imprisoned as a witch. Hours before Josephine's birth, her mother swam across a blood-filled river to Haiti from the Dominican Republic, where Haitians were slaughtered, including Josephine's grandmother. Every year, Josephine and her mother performed rituals at the Massacre River. When Josephine visits her increasingly frail mother, she never says anything, but she brings a Virgin Mary statue that her mother makes cry using wax and oil. When Josephine's mother dies, Jacqueline, another ritual performer, takes Josephine to see her body burned.

"A WALL OF FIRE RISING"

Guy, Lili, and their son, Little Guy, live in a one-room shack. They get excited when Little Guy gets to play a revolutionary at school, and Guy gets extra work cleaning bathrooms at a plantation. Little Guy spends all his time learning lines while Guy dreams of stealing the plantation's hot air balloon. Lili doesn't approve, but one day she sees Guy flying the balloon. Guy captures the neighborhood's attention and jumps out. Little Guy recites the lines from his play over Guy's dead body.

"NIGHT WOMEN"

"Night Women" concerns a prostitute who practices her profession next to her young, sleeping son's bed. She tells him she gets made up before bedtime because she's waiting for an angel to come. She worries he'll someday find out the truth, especially as she sees him becoming older and more sexually aware. If he ever wakes to find her with one of her regular married men, she will tell him it's his father, visiting for one night. When he asks about the angels, she tells him they haven't come yet.

"BETWEEN THE POOL AND THE GARDENIAS"

Marie finds a dead baby in the street. She names it Rose and tells it about her miscarriages, her cheating husband, and the Dominican pool-cleaner who slept with her once. Marie pretends the household where she works belongs to her and imagines her female ancestors visiting her. When the baby rots, she covers it with perfume, but she finally decides the flies are trapping Rose's spirit and buries Rose by the gardenias. The Dominican calls the police, claiming Marie killed the baby for evil purposes.

"THE MISSING PEACE,"

Emilie Gallant, Lamort's grandmother's boarder, asks Lamort to take her secretly to a mass grave where Emilie's mother, a supporter of the old government, may have been dumped. A soldier tries to stop Emilie, who defies him. Lamort says "peace," a password given to her by a flirtatious soldier, but he appears and says the password has changed. Emilie tells Lamort she doesn't have to please her grandmother. Lamort's name means "death" because her mother died when she was born, but when she goes home she demands to be called Marie Magdalènene, her mother's name.

"SEEING THINGS SIMPLY"

Princesse passes a flirtatious drunk watching cockfights on her way to visit Catherine, a foreign painter. Princesse poses nude while Catherine paints and talks about art. Princesse feels uncomfortable at first, but as long as no one else can see her, she relaxes. Sometimes Catherine paints her outdoors, wearing clothes. When Catherine's mentor dies, Catherine goes to Paris without telling Princesse. When she returns, she gives Princesses a nude painting of her by the ocean. Princesse is inspired to create art herself and sketches the cockfight-watching drunk in the sand.

"NEW YORK DAY WOMEN"

"New York Day Women" takes place in New York rather than Haiti. Suzette spots her mother, who never leaves Brooklyn, in Midtown. As Suzette follows her mother, undetected, she thinks about the critical things her mother says about family or Haiti or Suzette. In a playground, a woman wearing workout clothes leaves her young son with Suzette's mother for an hour. Suzette's mother and the son seem quite fond of each other. Suzette wonders whether her mother would have said hello, had she seen her.

K

"CAROLINE'S WEDDING"

Grace's mother (Ma) is upset that Grace's sister, Caroline, is marrying Eric, who isn't Haitian. Ma makes bone soup every day, which she believes will end Caroline's engagement. Grace begins dreaming about her father, as she did when he died of cancer. In order to get a visa, Grace's father married a widow, then divorced her to bring his real family to the United States. Ma worries that Caroline thinks no one but Eric will love her. Before the ceremony, Caroline becomes very nervous, but Ma reassures her. There is a heavy sadness over the family because they know Caroline will never again be as close to them as she has been all her life. Ma asks Grace to burn her belongings when she dies so no one will feel sorry for her. Grace refuses. She visits her father's grave to tell him about the wedding and her new U.S. citizenship, and when she returns home, she helps her mother make bone soup.

CHARACTER LIST

"CHILDREN OF THE SEA"

Male narrator An educated young man who opposes the Haitian government. The male narrator has no hope for the future and worries he will never again see the female narrator, whom he loves. He's upset by the suffering he sees around him, but he's so used to it that he no longer expresses pain. In the end, he gives in to death.

Female narrator A young woman very much in love. The female narrator clings to the hope that the male narrator is alive and they will somehow be reunited. She does not openly defy her father, though she hates him for disapproving of her lover. She's angry at the world for preventing her love, but she's powerless to do anything about it.

Papa The female narrator's father. Papa is controlling but only because he wants what is best for his family, and he feels guilty when he makes them unhappy. He refuses to endanger his family for the sake of others in need.

Célianne The pregnant teenager in the male narrator's boat. Célianne is in shock from the experiences she had with the *macoutes*, who forced her brother to rape their mother and then raped her. When her baby dies, she finally gives in to her despair.

Manman The female narrator's mother. Manman has high ideals about love and responsibility and is horrified when she must listen helplessly to her neighbor's murder.

"NINETEEN THIRTY-SEVEN"

Josephine A young woman whose mother is in prison. Josephine is sad and confused about the rumors about her mother. She doesn't know how to express her love for her mother and can never talk when she visits her, though she feels like crying. When her mother dies, she finally understands why she paid tribute to her grandmother in such strange ways and embraces the tradition herself.

Manman Josephine's mother, imprisoned for being a witch. Manman was traumatized when she saw her own mother murdered, but she had the strength to save Josephine by fleeing Dominica. Manman tries to explain her behavior but always cryptically. She suffers in prison and takes comfort in Josephine's visits, but she resents Josephine's silence.

Jacqueline A woman who lost her mother. Jacqueline participates in the same rituals Manman did, which makes Josephine feel close to her. Jacqueline's actions encourage Josephine to embrace her mother's traditions.

"A WALL OF FIRE RISING"

K

Guy A poor man working to feed his family. Guy is frustrated with his inability to give his family security and ashamed of the menial work he does. He dreams of starting over. Guy loves Lili and is proud of Little Guy, but they remind him of his failure. He reveals the depth of his despair when he kills himself.

Lili A wife who must frequently make ends meet. Lili is strong and resourceful and tries to keep her family happy. She derives genuine happiness from their success and manages to be content with what she has. She's afraid of Guy's ambitions, but she's cautiously hopeful for Little Guy's future.

Little Guy A young boy chosen to play the revolutionary Boukman at school. Little Guy is proud to share this achievement with his parents, whom he admires. He's extremely dedicated and gets painfully nervous about making a mistake. Little Guy reveals his independence when he mourns Guy with a tearful recitation of the lines Guy was so proud of.

"NIGHT WOMEN"

Narrator A young single mother and prostitute. The narrator hates her job but needs it to support her son. She makes up lies about angels to protect him and wants to believe them herself. She is totally enamored of her son, in an almost sexual way. She convinces herself that women who work during the day lack her independence.

"BETWEEN THE POOL AND THE GARDENIAS"

Marie The daughter of Josephine from "Nineteen Thirty-Seven" and a maid. Marie has suffered many miscarriages and left a cheating husband. She is so desperate for love that she imagines a dead baby to be alive and tells it all her disappointments. She imagines her female ancestors watching over her, silently pressuring her to continue the family line.

"THE MISSING PEACE"

Lamort A teenage girl who defies her grandmother by sneaking out to take foreigners, usually journalists, to the cemetery. Lamort is virtuous when avoiding Raymond's advances, but she resents her grandmother for holding her mother's death against her. She is independent and feels important when she can help people like Emilie.

Emilie Gallant An American journalist who is searching for her mother and who supported the old government. Emilie is kind to Lamort but angry at the government that killed her mother, and she is unable to hide her hatred. Emilie embodies the independent woman for Lamort and gives her the courage to assert herself.

Lamort's grandmother Lamort's grandmother, who dictates how she should act. Lamort's grandmother says people are judged by their actions and constantly reminds Lamort to be careful. She disapproves of Emilie's independence and blames Lamort for her mother's death.

Raymond A young soldier who switched alliances when the new government came to power. Raymond brags about his adventures as a soldier to impress Lamort. He protects Lamort when he has to, but he doesn't really care for her.

"SEEING THINGS SIMPLY"

Princesse A young student who poses nude for a foreign artist. Princesse wants to keep her actions secret from the town, but she's comfortable in her own skin. She is fascinated by Catherine's views on art, and she's sensitive to the beauty around her. She hopes to create beauty herself someday.

Catherine A painter who teaches Princesse about art and life. Catherine cares about Princesse, but she also imposes her strong ideas about the world on her. Catherine is stubborn, and her drinking suggests that she doesn't care about social norms.

"NEW YORK DAY WOMEN"

Suzette A young Haitian woman who works in New York's Midtown. Suzette thinks of her mother as a bit of a nag and is shocked to find that there are things she doesn't know about her. However, Suzette does love her mother, and she wants her approval even though she ignores her criticisms.

Suzette's mother A Haitian immigrant who is very set in her ways. Suzette's mother wants Suzette to be like her and frequently criticizes her. She dreams about winning the lottery but doesn't play it, and she talks about Haiti but cannot face its suffering by visiting. Suzette's mother is ashamed of her menial job.

"CAROLINE'S WEDDING"

Grace A Haitian immigrant in her mid-twenties who just became an American citizen. Grace, whose real name is Gracina, doesn't feel fully part of either Haitian or American culture. She is very close to both her sister and her mother and tries to defend each against the other's frustrations. Family is all she really has, so although she wants Caroline to be happy, she cannot help but be sad that Caroline is leaving.

Ma Grace and Caroline's mother. Ma maintains her Haitian traditions and beliefs twenty-five years after leaving. Ma is sad to see Caroline with a non-Haitian because the marriage represents the end of Haitian culture in their family. She's ashamed that her husband stopped loving her and that she has nothing but her daughters, who will leave her.

Caroline A young Haitian-American woman about to get married. Caroline is loving but independent and embraces the freedoms of America while rejecting her mother's traditional Haitian expectations. Caroline acts confident but feels a hidden insecurity, especially about her missing forearm.

Eric A Bahamian janitor engaged to Caroline. Eric is a bit slow but very kind, and he truly cares about Caroline. He even tries to please her impossible mother.

ANALYSIS OF MAJOR CHARACTERS

GRACE, "CAROLINE'S WEDDING" Grace is the backbone of her family. Both her mother and her sister, Caroline, depend on and confide in her, and she negotiates between the traditional Haitian values of her mother and Caroline's American independence. Grace wants to take care of her family and make them proud. She sees the best in people and trusts them to make their own decisions, so she's supportive of both Caroline's engagement and her mother's inability to break her ties to Haiti. Yet Grace's competent negotiations reveal her own personal difficulty: she feels neither completely Haitian nor completely American. She still feels a strong connection to Haiti, but she feels guilty for being the reason her parents had to leave. She feels oppressed by the culture she has inherited, which makes her rebel against her mother's superstition. Grace is still searching for her place in the world. Although she doesn't realize it, she's jealous of Caroline for making a new place for herself in her own family. Grace feels betrayed when Caroline leaves home for good. She is terrified of change and loss and doesn't want to forget her past. Eventually, her new passport gives her a sense of belonging. As a true American, she feels secure enough to embrace the Haitian traditions she once resisted by helping her mother make bone soup.

JOSEPHINE, "NINETEEN THIRTY-SEVEN" Josephine knows well the painful legacy she has inherited. Her mother had to choose whether to save Josephine's life or try to save her grandmother's, so Josephine's birth depended on her grandmother's death. She feels a bond with her grandmother and her mother as a result of the rituals her mother made her take part in at Massacre River, even though she has never understood them. Josephine is awed by her mother's rituals and stories, and she has absorbed them more than she realizes. When Jacqueline visits her, Josephine asks questions that only a fellow performer of the rituals would understand. Despite the strength this tradition gives her, Josephine feels overwhelmed by the depressing world around her and helpless to change it. She doesn't know how to connect with her mother, perhaps because she is ashamed of her inability to help her. She attempts to be strong by hiding her profound sorrow. Though she cannot express it, Josephine highly values her relationship with her mother and the tradition of which she is part.

LAMORT, "THE MISSING PEACE" Lamort, naïve and uneducated, doesn't worry too much about her own well-being because she has a low sense of self-worth. Her grandmother blames her for her mother's death and is never satisfied with her behavior. Lamort never had a mother, and she is desperate for approval—from her grandmother, Raymond, Emilie, or anyone else. She tries to please her grandmother by living up to her standards of propriety and wishes she could be more experienced and intelligent. She looks up to independent women like Emilie and feels important when she can help them, so she does so eagerly, even when serious risk is involved. Lamort accepts the violent, dangerous state of her world, so courage comes easily to her. She thinks nothing of bravely coming up with excuses to protect Emilie from Toto, the soldier who stops them when they try to go to the churchyard. Emilie's compliments and dependence on Lamort encourage Lamort to be brave in her personal life as well, and their adventure together empowers her to stand up to her grandmother.

PRINCESSE, "SEEING THINGS SIMPLY" Princesse is modest, but she has a strong sense of self-confidence. She is unfazed by the advances of the drunk watching the cockfights and even humors him when he flirts with her. She thinks Catherine paints her because she's willing to be naked and not because she's particularly beautiful, but this doesn't bother her. Princesse admires Catherine and her sophistication, but she can also be childlike and playful. She fears negative attention and won't drink the rum Catherine offers her, but she doesn't believe in society's standards of propriety. Eventually, however, she feels daring enough to drink a little rum. Princesse is fascinated by the world and excited to learn about it. Though Princesse's standard of living is probably not much better than that of the protagonists in the other stories, she notices the beauty around her and wants to capture it. She is willing to dedicate herself entirely to art, as she shows when she "draws" on her undershirt with her own blood. Princesse is ambitious and inspired, and Catherine's painting of her makes her feel special for her part in its creation.

MARIE, "BETWEEN THE POOL AND THE GARDENIAS" Marie has a childlike ignorance that, paired with her great disappointment with life, encourages her to exist in a fantasy world, out of touch with reality. When she couldn't take her miscarriages and her husband's cheating any longer, she escaped her village life for the city. When her life as a maid fails to satisfy her, she escapes into a world where the dead baby she finds is her living daughter and the household where she works is her own home. Nothing in the world matters to her, and the only people she feels close to are the imagined ghosts of her dead mother and ancestors. She wants to die so she can join them. Marie sees the real world as a cruel place and feels worthless because of her inability to have a child and continue her ancestral line. Marie is religious and superstitious. She bitterly resents her employers for their comfortable lifestyle and their dismissal of her as an ignorant peasant. She feels anonymous and knows that no one loves her, which gives her an overwhelming sense of despair.

THEMES, MOTIFS, AND SYMBOLS

THEMES

THE DIVERSITY OF SUFFERING The stories in *Krik? Krak!* demonstrate that everyone experiences suffering in his or her own unique way. The characters in the collection come from diverse backgrounds and have very different experiences, but to a certain extent, they all share the same pain. The despair of Célianne in "Children of the Sea" as she throws herself into the ocean is felt by the male narrator of the same story when he embraces death and by Grace's mother in "Caroline's Wedding" when she goes to a mass for refugees who, like Célianne, died at sea. But while these and other characters all see the same horrible things happening to the people and the nation they love, they all have their own reactions. Guy, in "A Wall of Fire Rising," tries to defy his hopelessness by stealing a brief moment of glory, even though he knows it must end in death. The mother in "New York Day Women" makes a new life for herself in the United States, but she still can't face the suffering she left behind. As Danticat often explains, there is no universal Haitian experience because the people who suffer remain individuals.

FAMILY AS A SOURCE OF POSTERITY In a country with a violent, complicated past, stories are passed on from mothers to daughters to preserve a sense of history and create a record for the future. In "The Missing Peace," Emilie tells Lamort they should write down what has happened for posterity, but Lamort answers that she has posterity in the form of her family. She means that she has inherited her mother's and her grandmother's experiences, and when she is old, her own daughters will inherit her experiences. Similarly, Josephine's mother tells her in "Nineteen Thirty-Seven" that her birth made up for her grandmother's death. Death broke one link in the family chain, but a new one was formed. Many of the characters in *Krik? Krak!* sense the presence of their dead ancestors and feel connected to their pain. They understand their place in the world in terms of their mothers' and ancestors' experiences, and they pass these experiences on to their children in order to keep the family history alive. In the epilogue, "Women Like Us," the narrator explains that these past experiences are what fuel her writing, giving her oppressed ancestors a voice.

THE DANGEROUS POWER OF HOPE Hope has the power to give people strength in times of suffering, but it also threatens to blind them to reality. Most of the characters in *Krik? Krak!* hold on to hope in order to keep themselves alive. In "Night Women," the narrator makes up stories about an angel coming to rescue her and her son in order to hide the truth from him, but she also uses these stories to escape the harsh reality of her life. Similarly, in "Seeing Things Simple," Princesse avoids the world around her by dreaming of becoming an artist and immersing herself in the reality of a foreign painter. These characters survive by denial and wait for the day when such denial will no longer be necessary. However, this coping strategy can be dangerous. In "Between the Pool and the Gardenias," Marie's hope becomes a delusion when she pretends to find the daughter she always wanted. This fantasy leads her to hold on to the baby even as it begins to rot, and she is finally arrested when the pool-cleaner, whom Marie had convinced herself cared about her, accuses her of witchcraft. Several other characters find out that too much hope can result in crippling despair when reality sets in.

MOTIFS

IMAGINED DIALOGUE Imagined conversations often structure characters' relationships in *Krik? Krak!*. "Children of the Sea" consists of letters that are never exchanged. Their letters are, in effect, more like journal entries than letters: they reveal more about how the characters feel about each other and how they feel in general than real letters would. In a different way, Suzette's narration of "New York Day

Women" is peppered with quotations she imagines her mother saying. Suzette's consciousness of these quotations as she follows her mother around New York reveals the sensibility she has inherited from her mother, even though she distances herself from her mother's beliefs. This narrative technique shows the impact people have on each other and on their understanding of the world, especially when making sense of the world is difficult to do independently.

RELIGIOUS ICONOGRAPHY Religious iconography shows the often-conflicted interaction between Haiti's native voodoo religion and the Christianity imposed on the Haitian people by Europeans. Though Christianity represents oppression, many of the characters in these stories have embraced Christian beliefs as their own, even while clinging to voodoo rituals. In "Caroline's Wedding," Grace's mother goes to mass regularly, but she also believes in superstitions, such as the magical powers of bone soup. Similarly, in "Nineteen Thirty-Seven," Josephine's mother practically worships a statuette of the Virgin Mary, but she believes it has mystical qualities that don't belong to the Christian tradition. She incorporates these qualities into voodoo rituals to honor her ancestors. Any postcolonial nation has difficulties reconciling native traditions with colonial ones, but religion, a particularly significant area, proves to be an anomaly: in Haiti, beliefs that should be in conflict with each other are all embraced without question. The hybrid religion that results shows how Haiti's national identity is influenced by both its native roots and its colonial history.

WATER The constant references to water in *Krik? Krak!* suggest the limitations of the characters' worlds. As half of an island, Haiti is surrounded by water, which symbolically serves to contain the country's troubles. Refugees leave Haiti by boat, overcoming the limits the sea imposes on them and thus the limits of Haitian politics and poverty. But this obstacle is not so easy to overcome. "Children of the Sea" shows how the ocean holds the dead bodies of many Haitians who have tried to flee their desperate lives. The water that defines their world continues to overwhelm them even as they escape it, and it often claims them for its own. In "Nineteen Thirty-Seven," water separates Haiti from the Dominican Republic as the Massacre River, and almost everyone who tries to cross it is killed. In "Seeing Things Simply," however, Princesse sees beauty in the ocean. She sees not limits but possibilities in its vast, watery world, and she sees hope in the horizon, where the sea meets the sky. The characters who do escape Haiti, in "New York Day Women" and "Caroline's Wedding," live in New York, a city of islands, where water surrounds them and connects them to the lives they left behind.

SYMBOLS

CRYING Crying represents life, which in Haiti is always marked by pain. Crying expresses suffering, and as long as Haitians live, they suffer and therefore cry. Danticat indicates that both Célianne's baby in "Children of the Sea" and the dead baby in "Between the Pool and the Gardenias" are dead by noting that they do not cry. For Marie, the absence of crying is positive in a way. She wishes no babies cried, because a dead baby cannot feel pain. In "Nineteen Thirty-Seven," Josephine tries not to cry in order to suppress her suffering, as well as her mother's. But Josephine's mother makes the Madonna statuette cry because her suffering has not died, and she needs to express it somehow. Similarly, in "Women Like Us," the narrator's mother compares the sound of her writing to the sound of crying, and the narrator agrees that writing is a form of crying. She writes to express her suffering and the suffering of her ancestors and to keep their painful stories alive. In a way, the whole story collection is one deep cry, expressing the emotional pain of its characters.

BUTTERFLIES In *Krik? Krak!*, butterflies suggest the understanding of harsh realities. In "Children of the Sea," the female narrator explains that different butterflies can deliver different messages, but in a troubled country such as Haiti, nearly all the messages are bad ones. When the black butterfly at the end of "Children of the Sea" lands on the female narrator, she knows the male narrator has died. At the end of "The Missing Peace," Lamort describes Raymond as a soldier who likes butterfly-shaped leaves because she realizes he has embraced the reality of political conflict and violence. The narrator of "Night Women" imagines her son as a butterfly in the middle of a stream because she knows he is too distant for her to protect him. Butterflies are elusive, hard to catch or to control, much like the suffering of the characters. They represent change, the blossoming of a lowly caterpillar into a bigger, greater creature, just as the characters' daily pain blossoms into greater, unavoidable tragedy.

BRAIDING Braiding suggests the combination of unique strands into a coherent, more beautiful whole, an apt description of what *Krik? Krak!* does with the characters' unique stories. Although this symbol appears only in the epilogue, it represents the book as a whole. In the epilogue, the narrator explains that writing is like braiding because it forces separate elements to build a single, unified meaning. It can be challenging, and if the hair doesn't cooperate, the result isn't always pretty. But there is something soothing about the process, the rhythmic performance of a skill that is both challenging and routine. To the narrator, it comes naturally. It is also a tradition she has inherited from her mother and her ancestors, who used to braid her hair when she was a child. Although the narrator's mother doesn't write or even approve of her writing, the storytelling traditions she has handed down to the narrator are the foundations of her writing. Although the narrator tells stories, or braids, in her own way, she maintains her Haitian inheritance by doing so.

IMPORTANT QUOTATIONS EXPLAINED

---

1. *I also know there are timeless waters, endless seas, and lots of people in this world whose names don't matter to anyone but themselves.*

The male narrator writes these words at the beginning of "Children of the Sea," soon after he sets out for the United States in a tiny boat. His words emphasize how common and almost meaningless suffering is in Haiti. Every Haitian, not just the ones on the male narrator's boat, has a reason to flee the country, whether for political, economic, or personal reasons. Their stories are painful and touching, but so many stories exist that listening to or caring about them all is impossible. Each person must focus on his or her own difficult past and unsure future. The suffering they share makes them anonymous. The entirety of the Haitian problem is so great that no individual matters too much. The male narrator also understands that, like the "timeless waters," this suffering is nothing new. Haiti and many other places have been consumed by suffering for centuries, and people in these places will likely continue to suffer. This realization makes the male narrator's despair both inevitable and understandable. Danticat points out that maintaining hope is almost impossible when everyone is so familiar with pain and no relief is in sight. Somewhere between Haiti and the United States, the male narrator sees that suffering is as great as the ocean, and all he can do is navigate it in the foolish hope of one day reaching safety.

---

2. *[P]eople are just too hopeful, and sometimes hope is the biggest weapon of all to use against us. [P]eople will believe anything.*

This statement, which the female narrator's mother, Manman, makes when she hears rumors that the old president might be returning to Port-au-Prince in "Children of the Sea," shows how desperate the Haitian people are for something good to happen. Even a highly unlikely rumor has the power to revitalize the hope of a community worn out by the horror of daily life. The Haitians have been scared and angry for such a long time that they need something to be happy about, so they cling to whatever they can. This is true for many of the characters in *Krik? Krak!*, including Guy in "A Wall of Fire Rising," the narrator of "Night Women," and even Princesse, who dreams of becoming an artist in "Seeing Things Simply." They want to believe good exists in the world and that their lives will get better, but their rare moments of optimism are constantly proven to be ill-founded. Hope is all they have, but every disappointment suggests they can't keep even that.

This remark emphasizes the reality, and even the necessity, of Haitian despair. Even hope is a bad thing in the Haitians' world because it is more likely to be a trap than a true sign of good things to come. In "Children of the Sea," the people who let hope get the best of them and believe the rumor go to the airport to greet the returning president, where they are arrested or killed by the *macoutes*. Only the realist, who accepts the horrific state of Haiti, can survive. Haitians are better off embracing their hopelessness because that way they won't be disappointed or even killed. Hope may be the best thing in a Haitian's life, but despair—a total abandonment of hope—is the only real option. Of course, despair is not much better, as Celianne shows when she kills herself and the male narrator shows when he gives in to death. The horrors of Haitian life lead only to death, whether one embraces despair or foolishly clings to hope.

3. *It's so easy to love somebody, I tell you, when there's nothing else around.*

This comment appears in "Between the Pool and the Gardenias" when Marie tells Rose about her life. It shows the loneliness of a Haitian woman who has lost everything. In Marie's case, her numerous miscarriages and her unfaithful husband made her so unhappy that she had to leave Ville Rose. She has no family because her grandmother, from "Nineteen Thirty-Seven," was killed for being a witch, and her godmother, Lili, from "A Wall of Fire Rising," killed herself when she lost her husband to despair. Nothing good has happened to Marie, so she looks for any good she can find or invent. Marie goes so far as to convince herself that the dead baby she finds on the street is alive and even her own. She is so desperately lonely that she needs something to love.

Love is vital to survival in the cruel poverty of Haiti. Marie has lost every other person she has loved and who has loved her, so she tries to create love in unlikely places. She sleeps with the Dominican pool-cleaner even though she doesn't know his name, and she is saddened when he ignores her. She pretends the dead baby is alive so she can pretend it loves her back. This need for love is an important motivator in many of the stories. In "Nineteen Thirty-Seven," Josephine's mother looks forward to Josephine's visits because they represent a daughter's love and sustain her even as she slowly starves to death. Lamort in "The Missing Peace" needs to win her grandmother's love by living up to her standards, and she risks her life to win the affection of her grandmother's foreign boarders. In "Caroline's Wedding," Grace's mother clings to the past because her husband still loved her then. The suffering of loss and hopelessness seem bearable when a woman has love to support her.

4. *These were our bedtime stories. Tales that haunted our parents and made them laugh at the same time. We never understood them until we were fully grown and they became our sole inheritance.*

These words appear in "Caroline's Wedding," when Grace remembers her father's favorite jokes, and they emphasize the importance of storytelling in passing on Haitian traditions. The jokes Grace remembers aren't technically stories, but they capture the hopes and fears of the Haitian people as well as any stories would. The jokes are both lighthearted and serious: their subject matter is so grave that it must be delivered with a dose of humor. Talking about such things would be too difficult otherwise. The specific joke Grace remembers is about God fearing Papa Doc Duvalier, who would steal God's throne if given a chance. Though the joke is meant to be funny, it is a poignant reminder of the ruthlessness of Haitian politics and the hatred the Haitian people have for their corrupt leaders. It is both funny and depressing because, in a way, the sentiment is true. Grace's father could show his young daughters his great sorrow about his country without frightening them because he treated it as a joke. In a country where violence and poverty threaten to destroy everyone who doesn't leave, such storytelling and passing on of tradition, even outside of the country, is necessary to keep its culture alive.

Though Grace didn't understand her father's jokes as a child, they subtly shaped her understanding of her own Haitian culture. She grew up in a household where her parents told stories about Haiti all the time, so she accepted the country's importance without thinking about it. Her knowledge of Haitian politics originated in these stories, and as she grew older she understood more and more. As a young immigrant growing up in America, Grace might easily have lost all sense of connection to Haiti, but her parents' stories kept that connection alive.

5. *The women in your family have never lost touch with one another. Death is a path we take to meet on the other side.*

This passage, spoken by the narrator of the epilogue, "Women Like Us," reveals the strong bond Haitian women feel with their female relatives. The women in these stories feel very close even to the relatives who have died because they all have suffered many of the same things. In Haiti, poverty and political oppression have been constants for centuries, so generation after generation of Haitian women have had to deal with similar problems. In "Nineteen Thirty-Seven," Josephine and her mother perform rituals to honor her grandmother, who was slaughtered by a cruel government, until Josephine's mother is also imprisoned and essentially killed by the police. The chain of suffering continues with Josephine's daughter, Marie, in "Between the Pool and the Gardenias," when her insanity, caused by her despair, results in her arrest and probable death in prison. Marie, like Josephine and many of the women in the collection, turns to the ghosts of her female ancestors for comfort. The female bond in families also helps to perpetuate Haitian tradition, as Grace learns in "Caroline's Wedding."

The Haitian belief that women are tied to their dead female ancestors also provides a way of coping with death. In a world where death is easier than life, whether because of imprisonment, hunger, or despair, as in the case of Lili from "A Wall of Fire Rising," viewing death as a source of happiness brings comfort. When the Haitian women in Danticat's stories die, they expect to be reunited with their female ancestors, and they often sense the ghosts of those ancestors communicating with them. The narrator of the epilogue hopes to channel these communications into her stories, thus providing an outlet for the suffering she has inherited from her female ancestors. The suffering they share is so strong that it deserves to be expressed, and she hopes to do this through her writing. Because her female ancestors can speak from beyond the grave, death is not an end of life but rather a source of relief from earthly pain.

Lieutenant Nun

Catalina de Erauso (1585–1635)

CONTEXT

Lieutenant Nun: Memoir of a Basque Transvestite in the New World is Catalina de Erauso's memoir about her experiences during the early 1600s in Spain and South America. Catalina was born in 1585 into a wealthy Basque family. Her parents, María Pérez de Galarraga y Arce and Captain don Miguel de Erauso, were native-born residents of San Sebastian, Spain, a city located in the Spanish Basque province of Guipúzcoa. Though the Basque people are technically Spanish citizens, they are thought to be the oldest ethnic group in Europe and have their own distinct language. Solidarity among the Basque people runs high, although they are still loyal to the Spanish crown.

In 1492, Christopher Columbus discovered the Americas on a voyage sponsored by the Spanish crown, opening the door to colonization in the area. During the sixteenth century, Spain dedicated enormous amounts of money and manpower to exploration and colonization. The heart of the Spanish-American empire was called New Spain and was located in present-day Mexico. However, the Spanish also laid claim to much of South America, conquering the indigenous peoples and killing any who resisted Spanish rule.

In approximately 1589, when de Erauso was four years old, her parents placed her in a Dominican convent. We know from other historical accounts that they did the same with three of her sisters and that consigning female children to become future nuns was a not uncommon way of displaying loyalty to the Catholic Church. In 1600, de Erauso, at the age of fifteen, ran away from the convent, disguised herself as a man, and took a number of jobs as a page before she left for South America. During her time in the New World, de Erauso, still disguised as a man, served as a soldier in Peru and Chile, fighting for the Spanish cause.

De Erauso came of age during Spain's golden age and the Catholic Counter-Reformation. During this time, the role of women was extremely limited. Spanish society was heavily male-dominated and intensely religious, which meant that freedoms for women, both civil and religious, were rare. Even men themselves faced a great deal of constraint, and they had very few opportunities to break out of their rigid society's confines. One of the few means of escape for men was leaving for the New World, either to assist in the military conquest of the indigenous peoples or to become a missionary and help convert them to Catholicism. Leaving for the New World allowed men to escape their pasts and gave them vastly expanded chances to shape their futures in ways that were unavailable to them in Spain. By dressing as a man, de Erauso allowed herself the same opportunities, which must have appeared considerably more attractive than spending the rest of her life in the convent where she had resided since age four—the fate of her three sisters.

Once de Erauso returned to Europe, she revealed herself as a woman and became a celebrity due to the reputation she created for herself in South America. In 1625, she presented herself to the king and was granted a military pension in honor of her service to Spain. She later met with the Pope in Rome, who granted her permission to continue dressing as a man, which was especially significant considering Spain's history of outlawing female cross-dressing.

De Erauso wrote her autobiography sometime between 1626, the year the memoir ends, and 1630. She was likely influenced by the Spanish literary convention that would later become known as the *picaresque novel*, which was introduced in Spain in the sixteenth century but became more popular in the early 1600s—the time that Catalina was writing her memoir. A picaresque novel is a work of fiction that details the exploits of an adventurous or troublemaking protagonist. Although her work is nonfiction and features a female protagonist, it is still firmly planted in the picaresque tradition.

Little is conclusively known about de Erauso's life after the close of her memoir. Some critics have suggested that she herself did not write her memoir and that it may have been penned by someone who was acquainted with her fame and deeds, someone who may have been working under de Erauso's own supervision. In 1629, de Erauso signed over her portion of the family estate to her sister Mariana. The next year, she left again for the New World, where she remained for the rest of her life, under the name Antonio de Erauso. In the centuries since then, many books, plays, and films have been made based on de Erauso's exploits and her astonishing secret.

PLOT OVERVIEW

At the age of four, Catalina de Erauso, born in the Basque area of Spain in 1585, is placed in a Dominican convent, where she trains until the age of fifteen to become a nun. On March 18, 1600, Catalina runs away from the convent and fashions herself a suit of male clothes out of her convent garments. Thus she begins her life as a man.

She obtains a number of jobs, including one as a page for the king's secretary. While in his employ, she encounters her father, who is petitioning for help in finding his missing daughter. Her father does not recognize her. She again tempts fate and returns to her old convent for mass, where her mother is in attendance. Catalina's mother also does not recognize her.

Catalina's journeys through the New World begin when she meets her uncle, a sea captain who, not recognizing her, signs her on as a ship's boy. Eventually Catalina flees the ship, stealing money from her uncle as she leaves for Panama, and embarks on a series of jobs and adventures. A number of violent episodes ensue, which often lead Catalina to flee into a local church for safety. At that time, police were barred from invading the sanctity of a church, thus granting criminals inside sanctuary. Catalina's tendency to get into violent and criminal scrapes leads her to take frequent advantage of this legal loophole.

Catalina also has a number of problematic encounters with young ladies. Some want to marry her, forcing her to ward off their advances. But in one situation, Catalina is dismissed from her position for inappropriate behavior with the sister-in-law of her master. She signs up for the army and soon travels to Chile, where she becomes a soldier for her brother, who does not recognize her. Although they generally get along well, after three years they fight over a woman, and Catalina is banished to another town. She manages to distinguish herself in battle, both for her bravery and for her propensity for violence. She kills many people, both on and off the battlefield, and is constantly running from the law.

When a friend asks her to be his second in a duel, she agrees. During the course of the duel, she kills the other man's second, who turns out to be her own brother. She retreats to the church to avoid arrest, and from there, wracked with sorrow, she watches her brother's funeral. After months of hiding out in the church, Catalina leaves town and joins up with two other army deserters, who eventually die of starvation during their journey. Catalina is rescued by a half-Indian woman who wants Catalina to marry her daughter. At the same time, a local vicar tries to persuade her to marry his niece. Although she accepts their gifts, she eventually abandons them both.

Catalina assists in suppressing the Alonso Ibáñezi uprising and is part of a bloody battle where thousands of Indians are butchered. She is accused of committing a crime that she is innocent of, and although she is tortured, she refuses to admit to it. Soon after, she is accused of a murder that she actually has committed, but she refuses to admit to this crime either. She is nearly put to death until a fellow Basque halts the execution.

In Bolivia, the daughter of a nun begs Catalina to help her escape her husband, who is about to kill her for infidelity. The husband then tries to kill them both, but Catalina gets the woman to the safety of her mother's convent. Catalina then goes to Peru to investigate crimes in the area. Soon after, she kills a man for insulting her and is sentenced to death. Due to a technicality in the church doctrine, she gains her freedom by taking communion and spitting it into her hand, holding onto the host until she is taken into a church, where she is granted sanctuary.

In Lima, she joins Spanish troops who are being attacked by the Dutch and then returns to the city of Cuzco, where she gets into a bloody fight over a game of cards. She kills her opponent, "the Cid," who inflicts mortal wounds on her as well. Thinking she is going to die, she makes a full confession to a priest.

Although she survives, she is wanted by the law. Her brushes with the constables grow more and more dangerous, and she is eventually surrounded by officers who have been given orders to kill her. A bishop intervenes and takes Catalina into the safety of his house. Catalina finally admits to the bishop that she is a woman, and when he expresses doubts, she gamely offers to submit to a medical examination. During the examination, she is proven to be not only a woman but a virgin, and the bishop vows to help her.

She is sent to a nunnery while the church investigates her past to find out if she ever took vows to become a nun. Her story spreads far and wide, and by 1620 she is well known throughout Spain. When, two years later, it is confirmed that she never took her vows, she is allowed to leave the convent and begin her life as a Spanish celebrity. She goes to Madrid and presents herself to the king, who, in 1625, grants her a pension for her service to Spain.

Catalina travels to Rome, where she meets Pope Urban the Eighth and tells him about her life and travels. She tells him that she is a woman and a virgin, and he gives her permission to continue to dress in men's clothing.

Catalina ends her memoir with a short tale about being confronted by two prostitutes, whom she insults because they address her as a woman.

CHARACTER LIST

Catalina The narrator of the memoir that covers twenty-six years of her life. Catalina escapes a convent at the age of fifteen and lives her life as a man, joining the army and inciting violence both on and off the battlefield. Although Catalina does not exhibit significant emotional growth during this time, she is weighed down by the secret that she keeps—that of her biological gender—and much of the focus of her memoir is the price she pays to keep this secret. Catalina also explores her conflicting feelings about the church and God, as well as her intense patriotism toward her native country, Spain.

Captain don Miguel de Erauso Catalina's father, a native-born resident of San Sebastian, Spain. Captain de Erauso is genuinely anguished by Catalina's flight from the convent and resolutely searches for her, even going to the king's secretary for assistance. He does not recognize Catalina when he sees her dressed as a page, but expresses great concern for her.

María Pérez de Galarraga y Arce Catalina's mother, sister to the prioress of the convent that Catalina is placed in at the age of four. María does not recognize Catalina when she sees her, now age fifteen and dressed as a man, at mass.

Captain Miguel de Erauso Catalina's brother, the secretary to Governor Alonso de Ribera. Miguel cares about his family deeply, although he does not recognize Catalina when she joins his company. He is a loyal Basque, expressing great concern for Catalina merely because of her Basque hometown, and exhibits great enthusiasm and depth of feeling during his short appearance in Catalina's memoir. Eventually, Catalina unknowingly kills him during a duel. Catalina's relationship with him is the closest relationship in her life.

L

Agustín de Carvajal ("The Bishop") The Augustine friar who served as bishop of Guamanga from 1612 until his death in 1620. The bishop risks his life to help Catalina escape the constables in Guamanga, and he is one of the only people to get through Catalina's tough exterior. She is deeply touched by his spirituality and refers to him as a "saintly man." He is the first person to whom she confesses the truth of her biological gender. Bearing out her faith in his caring and belief in honor, he protects Catalina after she makes her confession.

Brother Luis Ferrer de Valencia The priest who arrives to take Catalina's confession after her near-death battle with the Cid. Catalina implies that she tells Brother Luis that she is a woman. The priest is kind and encouraging to Catalina, who describes him as being a "great man."

The Half-Indian Woman The daughter of a Spaniard and an Indian woman, and a widow. The half-Indian woman treats Catalina well and feels pity for Catalina's destitution. She is wealthy and hopes to marry her daughter to Catalina.

The Half-Indian Woman's Daughter A girl Catalina refuses to marry, describing her as being "as black and ugly as the devil himself."

Captain Esteban Eguiño Catalina's uncle, also the first cousin of Catalina's mother. Esteban hires her on as ship's boy on his vessel, and although he does not recognize her as his niece, as a loyal Basque he allows Catalina to curry favor with him simply due to the fact that her background is also Basque.

The Cid A dark, hairy giant known as "the Cid." The Cid attempts to steal from Catalina during a card game. He is quite brazen in his behavior and doesn't hesitate to defend himself when Catalina reacts with violence. Although he wounds Catalina badly, he dies almost at once.

Reyes An arrogant young man who starts an argument with Catalina. When confronted by Catalina, Reyes does not back down and instead responds with threats of violence. He is a proud young man with loyal friends, and he is willing to go to great lengths to defend his honor.

María Dávalos The daughter of the late Captain Juan Dávalos and Dõna María de Ulloa, who is a nun and founded a convent. María is brave and adventurous, urging Catalina to cross a river that frightens even Catalina. María has been unfaithful to her husband with the bishop's nephew and enlists Catalina's help in escaping her vengeful husband.

Pope Urban the Eighth The Pope of the Catholic Church, residing in Rome. The Pope is willing to allow Catalina to rebel against propriety and continue dressing as a man, while urging her to lead an honest existence. A gracious ruler, he believes Catalina's virginity is much more significant than her cross-dressing in defining her character.

ANALYSIS OF MAJOR CHARACTERS

CATALINA At the beginning of her memoir, Catalina is a young woman living in a convent, on the verge of taking her vows to become a nun. She eventually transforms herself into a soldier with a male persona, adept at killing both on and off the battlefield. In positioning herself as a man, she exhibits many stereotypically male traits, including bravado, competitiveness, and aggressiveness. She possesses a quick temper and responds to insults with her sword. She writes very little about her feelings—her memoir is almost entirely devoid of introspection. She appears to have no compunction about killing men for reasons as trivial as offending her over a game of cards. Despite the fact that she generally depends on violence to solve problems in her day-to-day life, she is very intelligent, and many times she survives by using only her wits. She moves from place to place regularly, never settling down or developing close relationships with others, perhaps for fear that they will discover her greatest secret—that she is a woman.

Although *Lieutenant Nun* covers more than twenty-six years, Catalina shows very little personal or emotional growth. The Catalina at the end of the memoir is nearly identical to the Catalina from the beginning; the passage of time is apparent only when Catalina writes that it has. Her development is primarily in terms of the violence she commits. She becomes a better soldier over the years, and she also becomes more readily able to kill at the smallest provocation. Despite her abilities as a soldier, or perhaps because of them, she rarely expresses emotion. One of the few times she describes how she feels is when she expresses joy about meeting her brother. Another is when she is plunged into despair after killing him. Catalina's life, and her secret identity as a woman, doesn't allow for many intimate relationships. Her relationship with her brother is the most important relationship in her life, but she devotes only a few words to it. Catalina clearly values her skill and prowess as a soldier and as a man far more than she does her emotional development, which she likely associates with her biologically designated gender—one she has worked so hard to hide.

THEMES, MOTIFS, AND SYMBOLS

THEMES

THE CREATION OF MASCULINITY Catalina's ability to transform herself into a man and live undetected for more than two decades suggests that gender is constructed, not innate, and that masculinity can be created. Throughout her memoir, from her teen years until her forties, Catalina builds up her masculine façade. She emphasizes only the qualities in herself that would be identified as traditionally masculine, and she omits any characteristics that would be deemed female. Catalina is no longer the victim of violence, as she was as a child and teenager; now she is combative and violent and kills many men. She is boastful and aggressive in a conventionally masculine manner, and her life as a soldier only reinforces these masculine traits. Her training as a warrior also helps her make decisions quickly, without weighing the consequences of her actions.

Her machismo is never more apparent than when she kills one of her fellow lieutenants for calling her a "cuckold," that is, a man whose wife is sexually unfaithful. This is an insult that is designed specifically to be leveled at a man—and Catalina has embraced her masculine alter-ego so thoroughly that she is willing to kill to defend her male honor. In deciding to dress as a man, Catalina learns how much of traditional masculinity and violent behavior is a construct, for she makes herself into a bold and violent killer by the force of her own determination. After living as a man for more than two decades, there are almost no traditionally feminine characteristics apparent in Catalina's personality.

THE IMPORTANCE OF A RELATIONSHIP WITH GOD Although Catalina's relationship with God fluctuates throughout her life, she always sees religion and God as avenues to forgiveness, redemption, and, sometimes most important, rescue. Although Catalina does not appear to be particularly devout, religion infuses her character, and she often credits God for helping her out of tight situations. Yet Catalina turns to God only out of sheer desperation. She visits a church only when trying to escape arrest and imprisonment, and she gives thanks to God only in moments where her life is at risk. Her vision of God seems to be of a benevolent being who allows her to escape punishment for her crimes, which is why she often flees to a church or cathedral immediately after committing a crime, in order to escape retribution. Despite her unwillingness to write about her relationship with God except in crisis, Catalina's religious beliefs are clearly integral to her character. Her belief that God is responsible for allowing her to escape punishment for her crimes relieves her of guilt and frees her to continue her criminal lifestyle.

THE POWER OF DISGUISE Throughout *Lieutenant Nun*, disguise gives Catalina power. When she leaves the convent, clothing is her disguise and means of changing her gender identity. This disguise and the bravery that donning it requires are the most important factors in her escape, as well as in assuring her safety. Not only does her disguise allow her to camouflage herself as a man, but it also allows her to feel masculine enough to develop a male persona. As a teenager, Catalina explores whether her disguise will fool others. When neither her aunt nor her father recognize her, Catalina risks going back to the convent, where she eludes detection by her mother and, presumably, the nuns and novices with whom she had spent eleven years. Catalina clearly intends this return as a test to bolster her confidence, and she passes easily. Her attitude is as vital to her disguise as her clothing is. Catalina also uses a disguise to change more than just her sex. She changes identities when it suits her and gives false identification many times when being pursued by the law. Catalina views her external identity as fluid, and she uses this fluidity to her advantage.

MOTIFS

PICARESQUE-STYLE MEMOIR Catalina's memoir follows the form of a traditional picaresque novel, a Spanish literary convention that was popular during her lifetime. Traditionally, the Spanish picaresque novel is about a loveable Spanish rogue's adventures and is often episodic in nature. The rogue often has to live by his wits, has experiences with different social classes, and is usually traveling during the course of the story. Catalina's memoir differs from the classic Spanish picaresque in two very dramatic ways—she is female, and her memoir is nonfiction (although some critics have questioned the latter). It is possible that Catalina herself was influenced by some of these works, which may explain why her memoir is told in a series of episodes rather than in standard chronological narrative form. As in many picaresque novels, Catalina's recounting of her trials is often humorous, and although she uses violence to survive, she just as often has to rely on her intelligence.

IMPERMANENCE One of the defining characteristics of Catalina's story is the fleeting nature of the relationships and events in her life. The people closest to Catalina are often introduced in a few sentences and then never mentioned again. She travels from town to town and country to country, only rarely mentioning the differences between places. Even her social station changes rapidly—she goes from a page to the king's secretary to a violent street thug, from a soldier to a deserter, and from a worker for the sheriff to a brutal killer. The impermanent nature of the events in Catalina's life propels her story forward. Her memoir is based on action, not emotion, and what moves the reader from one chapter to the next is the rapid pace of events in Catalina's life. Catalina's lack of stability also helps her keep her biological gender a secret.

VIOLENCE As Catalina grows older, her violent behavior becomes more and more pronounced as a means of protecting her honor, and these violent episodes trigger most of the action in the memoir. Catalina's story begins when she runs away from the convent, an event precipitated by a savage beating she receives from one of the nuns. Once Catalina starts disguising herself as a man, the violence escalates:

she stabs Reyes and must leave town, and many times she kills men over cards and flees into churches until the furor dies down. Many of the transitional events in Catalina's story are precipitated by violence, and Catalina clearly feels that in order to maintain her honor she must commit these acts. Honor is extremely important in a society where the representation of public self is far more important than one's private inner life, and for Catalina, violence and honor are inextricably intertwined.

SYMBOLS

CHURCHES Though Catalina's relationship with religion is often tenuous, she regularly turns to churches in times of need. Laws at the time prevented police and other officers from invading the sanctuary of a church, thus allowing criminals a safe haven from arrest as long as they stayed inside the church walls. Though this may well be the only reason that Catalina seeks refuge in churches when she is in desperate situations, her reasoning for seeking sanctuary in a church seems more complex than that. Catalina was raised in a convent, and the priests and nuns were the only family and authority figures she likely encountered on a regular basis. Therefore, it is not surprising that she turns to the church in times of distress. Although she never explicitly mentions her views on specific religious doctrine, Catalina clearly finds some emotional support in the church and what it stands for. To her, the church represents a surrogate family, and she finds relief, both legally and emotionally, within its walls.

CLOTHING Clothing is Catalina's representation of self, and her ability to change it allows her to change her very identity. Catalina's original deception depended solely on the boy's clothes she created for herself, and though two decades of cultivating her male persona have pushed that disguise deeper than skin-level, clothing still represents disguise and the ability to transform. Although Catalina often covers years in single sentences, she nonetheless makes mention of each new set of clothing she receives during her first decade living with a male identity. Her frequent mentions of clothes in these chapters underscore clothes' importance in this time in her life. Each additional gift of clothing, such as from the half-Indian woman and the vicar, reaffirms Catalina's male identity and allows her to continue under the pretense. Clothing enables the fluidity of her identity and also publicly reinforces the identity she has chosen for herself.

IMPORTANT QUOTATIONS EXPLAINED

---

1. *And a couple of days later, she let me know it would be fine by her if I married her daughter—a girl as black and ugly as the devil himself, quite the opposite of my taste, which has always run to pretty faces.*

Many critics believe that this passage, from Chapter 7, offers evidence of Catalina's sexual preference for women. However, the phrase *pretty faces* does not necessarily refer to women, and all the line really proves is that Catalina has a predilection for attractive faces, whether they be men or women. Better evidence of Catalina's possible preference for women lies in the tone she uses to talk about her relationships with women, which are much more playful and flirtatious than her relationships with men. Otherwise, Catalina is deliberately coy about her sexuality and erotic life. This reticence is not surprising, given the time and place that her memoir was written, and the line about *pretty faces* stands out because such an idea was taboo. At the very least, this line is Catalina's way of admitting that despite how she portrays herself, she is not unaffected by desire.

This passage also reveals Catalina's racism, but this, too, must be understood within the context of her era. She describes the half-Indian woman's daughter as being "as black and ugly as the devil himself," which suggests that her skin color is as much an impediment to their marriage as Catalina's sex. Catalina's descriptions of the Indians are no different from her descriptions of her horses. She describes them in terms of whether they serve her purposes or impede them, but she does not name them or give them any human characteristics. Such attitudes were not unusually in seventeenth-century Spain. The Spaniards who helped colonize South America used a system of land distribution called *encomiendas* that rendered the local Indians virtual slaves. In this context, Catalina's view of the Indians as little more than animals is not surprising.

2. *It just goes to show that persistence and hard work can perform miracles, and it happens regularly—especially in the Indies!*

This line closes Chapter 10 and summarizes Catalina's feelings after she is released from the prison where she had been incarcerated for a crime she did not commit and sentenced to ten years of hard labor without pay. Catalina is jailed and released for numerous crimes throughout her memoir, but few seem as miraculous to her as this one, perhaps because in this case she is genuinely innocent. Catalina makes clear that she believes miracles are more likely to occur in the New World than anywhere else. The thrust for colonization was based on the belief that a man, even one with a murky past, could conquer new lands and become incredibly rich, something that would be considered nothing short of a miracle in Spain. Catalina recognizes that the New World has allowed her to live freely as a man and keep her biological gender secret—a feat that would have been unlikely in Spain. Catalina's ability to conceal her biological gender and evade detection is the result of her persistence and hard work, but underneath Catalina's bravado, she recognizes how miraculous it is that a fifteen-year-old girl could accomplish such a feat.

This quote also reflects Catalina's deep religious beliefs. Her beliefs remain deeply ingrained even after she leaves the convent, which isn't surprising, since she was raised by the nuns since the age of four. She often makes light of her religious feelings, but she reveals her faith in the most emotional lines of her memoir, though it is unclear how much credit she attributes directly to God. These sincerely held, although not openly apparent, religious convictions are the basis for Catalina's belief in the possibilities of miracles. However, she eventually displays a shift in her attitude toward religion, and as an adult she is more likely to attribute the miracles she sees to persistence and hard work rather than to God, even if she can't fully discount his influence.

3. *And seeing that he was such a saintly man, and feeling as if I might already be in the presence of God, I revealed myself to the bishop and told him, "Senõr, all of this that I have told you . . . in truth, it is not so. The truth is this: that I am a woman. . . ."*

L

In Chapter 20, after Catalina has been relentlessly pursued by the law, she is rescued by a bishop who both keeps her out of prison and saves her life. For the first time in her many decades of living as a man, Catalina confesses the truth of her biological gender. Her choice of confidant is especially significant. Despite Catalina's official rejection of the church, she still gravitates toward the church in times of trouble. This is partially due to the church's ability to protect her, but it also indicates her desire to seek absolution from the church for her sins. At the moment when she thinks she is near either death or arrest, she confesses her sins to a bishop and tells him the truth about her sex. Catalina was raised in the church, and her relationship with it is much like that of a child to a parent. Catalina rebels against many of the church's rules and laws, but when she reaches a point of desperation, she seeks acknowledgement of and forgiveness for her greatest secret.

4. *Brother Luis Ferrer de Valencia, who is a great man, arrived and took my confession—and seeing as how I was about to die, I told him the truth about myself.*

Although Catalina is ambiguous about whether or not she has told anyone before the bishop about her biological gender, she strongly implies in Chapter 18 that she reveals it to another priest as well. The clear implication of this statement—coupled with the astonishment the priest expresses at her words—is that she has told him she is actually a woman. Her downplaying of this possible first confession may stem from the priest's failure to react expansively enough to her news. When she tells the bishop, she revels in his intense astonishment and offers to submit to a medical examination. She may very well have been disappointed when the first priest did not react this way—and so minimized the importance of the incident in her memoir, finding it lacking in drama and effect.

5. *At one point during the afternoon, I found myself chatting with three cardinals, one of whom, Cardinal Magalón, told me that my only fault was that I was a Spaniard. To this I replied, "With all due respect, your Holiness, that is my only virtue."*

This is the last line of Chapter 25, and it appears after Catalina receives permission from the Pope to dress in men's clothing. Although the memoir has one more short chapter, this line serves as an appropriate ending. Catalina has renounced her conventional Christian and female identities, but she has not made any attempt to rid herself of her heritage, namely her identity as a Spaniard and a Basquero. Catalina attempts to deny her past at all possible turns, yet when asked where she comes from, she readily says she is Basque, although she falsifies the names of her parents. Each time she admits her Basque heritage, she is rewarded with favors and camaraderie from other Basqueros. Catalina makes clear that her Basque and Spanish heritage trumps all other affiliations, including gender identification or the sworn duty to uphold the law. As Catalina readily abandons her identity and her past, what she holds onto—her heritage—becomes increasingly important.

In this quotation, Catalina minimizes the importance of her Basque identity to her. The Basques are technically Spaniards, so Catalina is including her Basque self when she talks about her national identity as being her only virtue. However, to the Basque people, self-identification as a Basquero is of the utmost importance and supersedes all other loyalties—Basques identify as Basques first and as Spaniards second. Growing up as a Spanish Basque, Catalina had ample opportunity to feel marginalized and oppressed, as she also felt as a woman. However, her connection with her cultural identity proves to be much stronger than that with her sex, for she is willing to abandon her identity as a woman but not as a Basque. Catalina's Basque and Spanish identity both defines her as a person and is responsible for saving her life on many occasions. Strangers who know nothing about Catalina except her cultural background believe her Basque identity trumps any crimes she may have committed, thus encouraging her to believe that perhaps her only virtue is her heritage.

Little Women

Louisa May Alcott (1832–1888)

CONTEXT

Louisa May Alcott was born on November 29, 1832, the second daughter of Amos Bronson and Abigail "Abba" May Alcott. She was raised in Concord, Massachusetts, a small town to the north of Boston that was home to many great writers of the day. Ralph Waldo Emerson, Nathaniel Hawthorne, and Henry David Thoreau were neighbors to the Alcotts. All of these writers were part of the transcendentalist movement during the New England Renaissance. Transcendentalists believed that one could find spirituality through nature and reason. They were an optimistic group who believed humans were capable of great thoughts, and they advocated nonconformity and being true to one's inner self.

Amos Bronson Alcott was not a particularly responsible father or husband, although he was an enthusiastic transcendentalist philosopher, abolitionist, and teacher. He failed to provide enough money to support his family, and their poverty was so dire that in twenty years, they moved twenty times. Louisa's mother acted as head of the household, and when Louisa grew older, she also took on much of the burden.

Alcott had an older sister, Anna, and two younger sisters, Lizzie and Abba May. These names are noticeably similar to the names Alcott gives her characters in *Little Women* (1868) (Meg, Beth, and Amy). Her sister Lizzie died at age twenty-two after a bout of scarlet fever. Alcott also had a brother, Dapper, who died in infancy.

Alcott was educated at home by her father. She loved to read and write and enjoyed borrowing books from Emerson's large library. As a child, Alcott struggled with the ladylike behavior that was expected of girls in the nineteenth century. Though she was required to be calm and stay at home, Alcott was a tomboy whose favorite childhood activity was running wild through the fields of Concord. She had an unladylike temper that she struggled to control.

Like Jo March in *Little Women*, Alcott could not get over her disappointment in not being a boy, since opportunities for women were limited. When the Civil War broke out in 1861, Alcott had an urge to go and fight in it. Like most transcendentalists, she supported the Northern side of the conflict because she was against slavery. But since she was female and thus could not join the military, she signed up to be a Union nurse and was stationed in Washington, D.C. Later in life, Alcott became active in the women's suffrage movement in the United States, whose supporters sought to extend the right to vote to women. Alcott's feminist sympathies are expressed through the character of Jo March in *Little Women*.

Though she never married or had a family of her own, Alcott was devoted to her parents and her sisters. She understood that for women, having a family meant professional loss, and having a profession meant personal loss. *Little Women* dramatizes this struggle between the desire to help one's family and the desire to help oneself. Alcott caught pneumonia while working as a nurse in the Civil War. She was treated with calomel, a mercury compound, and this treatment gave her mercury poisoning. For twenty years, Alcott was weak, suffered intense pain, and was plagued by hallucinations that could only be controlled with opium. Her right hand hurt her so badly that she had to learn how to write with her left hand. She also lost her hair because of the illness. Alcott died on March 6, 1888, and was buried in Sleepy Hollow Cemetery in Concord, Massachusetts, alongside her father, Emerson, Hawthorne, and Thoreau.

Alcott is most famous for her domestic tales for children, which brought her fame and fortune during her lifetime. Alcott also wrote sensationalist gothic novels, such as *A Long Fatal Love Chase* (1866), and serious adult novels, such as *Moods* (1864) and *Work: A Story of Experience* (1872), which received middling reviews. *Little Women* and Alcott's other domestic novels have enjoyed more popularity than her novels of other genres. Alcott did not particularly like *Little Women*; she wrote it at the request of her publisher, and upon its great success, worried that she was doing nothing more than writing "moral pap" fit for children.

Little Women possesses many qualities of the didactic genre, a class of works that have a moral lesson. *Little Women* does not preach directly to the reader, however, as did much didactic fiction of its time.

The narrator refrains from too much explicit moralizing, allowing us to draw our own lessons from the outcome of the story.

Because Jo learns to behave and becomes a lady at the end of the novel, it is possible to assume that Alcott wants to teach her readers that conformity is good. Interestingly, however, *Little Women* has been championed by feminists for more than a century because untamed Jo is so compellingly portrayed. Also, in the novel's characterization of the March sisters, rebellion is often valued over conformity. So while *Little Women* can be called a didactic novel, the question of what it teaches remains open.

PLOT OVERVIEW

Alcott prefaces *Little Women* with an excerpt from John Bunyan's seventeenth-century work *The Pilgrim's Progress*, an allegorical novel about leading a Christian life. Alcott's story begins with the four March girls—Meg, Jo, Beth, and Amy—sitting in their living room, lamenting their poverty. The girls decide that they will each buy themselves a present in order to brighten their Christmas. Soon, however, they change their minds and decide that instead of buying presents for themselves, they will buy presents for their mother, Marmee. Marmee comes home with a letter from Mr. March, the girls' father, who is serving as a Union chaplain in the Civil War. The letter inspires the girls to bear their burdens more cheerfully and not to complain about their poverty.

On Christmas morning, the girls wake up to find books, probably copies of *The Pilgrim's Progress*, under their pillows. Later that day, Marmee encourages them to give away their breakfast to a poor family, the Hummels. Their elderly neighbor, Mr. Laurence, whom the girls have never met, rewards their charitable activities by sending over a feast. Soon, Meg and Jo are invited to attend a New Year's Party at the home of Meg's wealthy friend, Sally Gardiner. At the party, Jo retreats to an alcove, and there meets Laurie, the boy who lives with Mr. Laurence. While dancing, Meg sprains her ankle. Laurie escorts the sisters home. The Marches regret having to return to their daily routine after the holiday festivities.

Jo visits Laurie when he is sick and meets his grandfather, Mr. Laurence. She inadvertently insults a painting of Mr. Laurence in front of the man himself. Luckily, Laurie's grandfather admires Jo's spunk, and they become friends. Soon, Mr. Laurence meets all of the sisters, and Beth becomes his special favorite. Mr. Laurence gives her his deceased granddaughter's piano.

The girls have various adventures. Amy is caught trading limes at school, and the teacher hits her as punishment. As a result, Mrs. March withdraws her daughter from school. Jo refuses to let Amy go with her to the theater. In retaliation, Amy burns Jo's manuscript, and Jo, in her anger, nearly lets Amy drown while ice-skating. Pretty Meg attends her friend Annie Moffat's party and, after allowing the other girls to dress her up in high style, learns that appearances are not everything. While at the party, she hears that people think she intends to marry Laurie for his money.

That year, the Marches form the Pickwick Club, in which they write a family newspaper. In the spring, Jo smuggles Laurie into one of the club meetings, and he becomes a member, presenting his new circle with a postbox. At the beginning of June, the Marches decide to neglect their housework. At the end of a lazy week, Marmee takes a day off too. The girls spoil a dinner, but everyone ends up laughing over it. One day, Laurie has English friends over, and the Marches go on a picnic with them. Later, Jo gets a story published for the first time.

One dark day, the family receives a telegram saying that Mr. March is sick in the hospital in Washington, D.C. Marmee goes to tend to him, and Jo sells her hair to help finance the trip. Chaos ensues in Marmee's wake, for the girls neglect their chores again. Only Beth goes to visit the Hummels, and after one of her visits, she contracts scarlet fever from the Hummel baby. Beth teeters on the brink of death until Marmee returns. Meanwhile, Amy spends time at Aunt March's house in order to escape the disease. Beth recovers, though not completely, and Mr. Brooke, Laurie's tutor, falls in love with Meg, much to Jo's dismay. Mr. Brooke and Meg are engaged by the end of Part One.

Three years pass before Part Two begins. Mr. March is home from the war, and Laurie is nearly done with school. Soon, Meg marries and moves into a new home with Mr. Brooke. One day, Amy decides to have a lunch for her art school classmates, but poor weather ruins the festivities. Jo gets a novel published, but she must cut it down in order to please her publishers. Meanwhile, Meg struggles with the duties of keeping house, and she soon gives birth to twins, Demi and Daisy. Amy gets to go to Paris instead of Jo, who counted on the trip, because their Aunt Carroll prefers Amy's ladylike behavior in a companion.

Jo begins to think that Beth loves Laurie. In order to escape Laurie's affections for her, Jo moves to New York so as to give Beth a chance to win his affections. There Jo meets Professor Bhaer, a poor German language instructor. Professor Bhaer discourages Jo from writing sensationalist stories, and she takes his advice and finds a simpler writing style. When Jo returns home, Laurie proposes to her, but she turns him down. Beth soon dies. Amy and Laurie reunite in France, and they fall in love. They marry and return home. Jo begins to hope that Professor Bhaer will come for her. He does, and they marry a year later. Amy and Laurie have a daughter named Beth, who is sickly. Jo inherits Plumfield, Aunt March's house, and decides to turn it into a boarding school for boys. The novel ends with the family happily gathered together, each sister thankful for her blessings and for each other.

CHARACTER LIST

Josephine March The protagonist of the novel, and the second-oldest March sister. Jo, who wants to be a writer, is based on Alcott herself, which makes the story semiautobiographical. Jo has a temper and a quick tongue, although she works hard to control both. She is a tomboy and reacts with impatience to the many limitations placed on women and girls. She hates romance in her real life and wants nothing more than to hold her family together.

Meg March The oldest March sister. Responsible and kind, Meg mothers her younger sisters. She has a small weakness for luxury and leisure, but the greater part of her is gentle, loving, and morally vigorous.

Beth March The third March daughter. Beth is very quiet and very virtuous, and she does nothing but try to please others. She adores music and plays the piano very well.

Amy March The youngest March girl. Amy is an artist who adores visual beauty and has a weakness for pretty possessions. She is given to pouting, fits of temper, and vanity; but she does attempt to improve herself.

Laurie Laurence The rich boy who lives next door to the Marches. Laurie, whose real name is Theodore Laurence, becomes like a son and brother to the Marches. He is charming, clever, and good-hearted.

Marmee The March girls' mother. Marmee is the moral role model for her girls. She counsels them through all of their problems and works hard but happily while her husband is at war.

Mr. March The March girls' father and Marmee's husband. Mr. March serves in the Union army as a chaplain. When he returns home, he continues acting as a minister to a nearby parish.

Mr. Brooke Laurie's tutor. Mr. Brooke is poor but virtuous.

Frederick Bhaer A respected professor in Germany who becomes an impoverished language instructor in America. Mr. Bhaer lives in New York, where he meets Jo. He is kind and fatherly.

Mr. Laurence Laurie's grandfather and the Marches' next-door neighbor. Mr. Laurence seems gruff, but he is loving and kind.

Hannah The Marches' loyal servant.

Aunt March A rich widow and one of the March girls' aunts. Although crotchety and difficult, Aunt March loves her nieces and wants the best for them.

Daisy Meg and Mr. Brooke's daughter. Daisy is the twin of Demi. Her real name is Margaret.

Demi Meg and Mr. Brooke's son and Daisy's twin. Demi's real name is John Laurence.

Mrs. Kirke The woman who runs the New York boarding house where Jo lives.

Kate Vaughn One of Laurie's British friends. At first, Kate turns up her nose at the bluntness and poverty of the Marches. She later decides that she likes them, however, showing that she is able to overcome her initial prejudice.

Sallie Gardiner Meg's rich friend. Sallie represents the good life to Meg, and Meg often covets Sallie's possessions.

Aunt Carrol One of the March girls' aunts. Aunt Carrol is ladylike, and she takes Amy with her to Europe.

Florence Aunt Carrol's daughter. Florence accompanies her aunt and Amy to Europe.

Fred Vaughn One of the Vaughn siblings. Fred is Laurie's friend, but he soon develops a romantic interest in Amy.

Esther Aunt March's servant. Esther is a French Catholic.

Annie Moffat Another wealthy friend of Meg's. Annie is fashionable and social, and she wears stylish clothing that Meg envies.

Ned Moffat The older brother of Meg's friend Annie Moffat.

Frank Vaughn One of the Vaughn siblings. Frank is sickly.

Grace Vaughn The youngest sister of the Vaughn family. Grace and Amy become friends on a picnic.

Dr. Bangs A doctor who tends to Beth when she is ailing.

The Hummels A family that lives near the Marches. The Hummels are poor and in bad health.

ANALYSIS OF MAJOR CHARACTERS

JO MARCH The main character of *Little Women*, Jo is an outspoken tomboy with a passion for writing. Her character is based in large part on herself. Jo refuses Laurie's offer of marriage, despite the fact that everyone assumes they will end up together. In the end, Jo gives up her writing and marries Professor Bhaer, which can be seen either as a domestic triumph or as a professional loss, since Jo loses her headstrong independence.

Because she displays good and bad traits in equal measure, Jo is a very unusual character for nineteenth-century didactic fiction. Jo's bad traits—her rebelliousness, anger, and outspoken ways—do not make her unappealing; rather, they suggest her humanity. Jo is a likely precursor to a whole slew of lovably flawed heroes and heroines of children's books, among them Mark Twain's Tom Sawyer.

BETH MARCH The third March sister, Beth is very shy and quiet. Like Meg, she always tries to please other people, and like Jo, she is concerned with keeping the family together. Beth struggles with minor faults, such as her resentment for the housework she must do. Beth resembles an old-fashioned heroine like those in the novels of the nineteenth-century English author Charles Dickens. Beth is a good person, but she is also a shade too angelic to survive in Alcott's more realistic fictional world. With Beth's death, Alcott lets an old type of heroine die off. The three surviving March sisters are strong enough to live in the changing real world.

Beth is close to Jo; outgoing Jo and quiet Beth both have antisocial tendencies. Neither of them wants to live in the world the way it is, with women forced to conform to social conventions of female behavior. Similarly, it is not surprising that Meg and Amy are particularly close to each other, since generous Meg and selfish Amy both find their places within a gendered world.

AMY MARCH The youngest March sister, Amy is an artistic beauty who is good at manipulating other people. Unlike Jo, Amy acts as a perfect lady because it pleases her and those around her. She gets what she wants in the end: popularity, the trip to Europe, and Laurie. Amy serves as a foil—a character whose attitudes or emotions contrast with, and thereby accentuate, those of another character—for Jo, who refuses to submit to the conventions of ladyhood. Both artists struggle to balance society's expectations with their own natural inclinations. The more genuine of the two and the more generous, Jo compares favorably to Amy. Both characters, however, are more lovable and real for their flaws.

MEG MARCH The oldest March sister, Meg battles her girlish weakness for luxury and money, and ends up marrying a poor man she loves. Meg represents the conventional and good; she is similar to her mother, for whom she was named. Meg sometimes tries to alter who she is in order to please other people, a trait that comes forth when she allows other girls to dress her up like a rich girl at her friend Annie Moffat's house. She becomes an agreeable housewife, pretending to like politics because her husband does, and forgoing luxury because her husband is poor.

LAURIE LAURENCE The Marches' charming, fun, and intelligent next-door neighbor, Laurie becomes particularly close to Jo but ends up marrying Amy. In between the publication of Part One and Part Two,

Alcott received many letters asking her to marry Jo to Laurie. Perhaps to simultaneously please her readers and teach them a lesson, Alcott had Jo get married, but not to Laurie.

Laurie struggles with his grandfather's expectations of him, in a similar manner to the way Jo struggles with becoming a lady. Laurie is not manly enough for his grandfather because he does not want to enter the business world. Likewise, Jo is not feminine enough for her sisters because she swears, soils her gloves, and speaks her mind at all times.

THEMES, MOTIFS, AND SYMBOLS

THEMES

WOMEN'S STRUGGLE BETWEEN FAMILIAL DUTY AND PERSONAL GROWTH While on the surface a simple story about the four March girls' journeys from childhood to adulthood, *Little Women* centers on the conflict between two emphases in a young woman's life—that which she places on herself, and that which she places on her family. In the novel, an emphasis on domestic duties and family detracts from various women's abilities to attend to their own personal growth. For Jo and, in some cases, Amy, the problem of being both a professional artist and a dutiful woman creates conflict and pushes the boundaries set by nineteenth-century American society.

At the time when Alcott composed the novel, women's status in society was slowly increasing. As with any change in social norms, however, progress toward gender equality was made slowly. Through the four different sisters, Alcott explores four possible ways to deal with being a woman bound by the constraints of nineteenth-century social expectations: marry young and create a new family, as Meg does; be subservient and dutiful to one's parents and immediate family, as Beth is; focus on one's art, pleasure, and person, as Amy does at first; or struggle to live both a dutiful family life and a meaningful professional life, as Jo does. While Meg and Beth conform to society's expectations of the role that women should play, Amy and Jo initially attempt to break free from these constraints and nurture their individuality. Eventually, however, both Amy and Jo marry and settle into a more customary life. While Alcott does not suggest that one model of womanhood is more desirable than the other, she does recognize that one is more realistic than the other.

THE DANGER OF GENDER STEREOTYPING *Little Women* questions the validity of gender stereotypes, both male and female. Jo, at times, does not want to be a conventional female. In her desires and her actions, she frustrates typical gender expectations. She wants to earn a living, for example—a duty conventionally reserved for men. Also, she wears a dress with a burn mark to a party, evidence that she does not possess tremendous social grace, a quality that nineteenth-century American society cultivated in women. Similarly, there are times when Laurie does not want to be a conventional man. He wants to pursue music, at that time a culturally feminine pursuit, instead of business, a culturally masculine pursuit. Even his nickname, Laurie, which he uses in favor of his much more masculine given name, Theodore, suggests his feminine side. Alcott bestows the highest esteem upon Jo and Laurie, who, in their refusal to embody gender stereotypes, willingly expose themselves to particular obstacles.

THE NECESSITY OF WORK Over the course of *Little Women*, the March sisters try to find happiness through daily activities, their dreams, and each other; but when they do not engage in any productive work, they end up guilty and remorseful. When they indulge in selfishness by dressing up in finery, hoarding limes, neglecting chores, or getting revenge, the girls end up unhappy. The only way they find meaningful happiness is when they are working, either for a living or for the benefit of their families. The novel demonstrates the importance of the Puritan work ethic, which dictates that it is holy to do work. This work ethic, in line with the transcendentalist teachings with which Alcott grew up, thrived in New England, where many Puritans lived and where the novel takes place. Alcott ultimately recommends work not as a means to a material end, but rather, as a means to the expression of inner goodness and creativity through productivity.

THE IMPORTANCE OF BEING GENUINE *Little Women* takes great pains to teach a lesson about the importance of being genuine. To make this point, Alcott contrasts the Marches with more well-to-do young women like Amy Moffat and Sally Gardiner. Transcendentalists emphasized the importance of paying more attention to the inner spiritual self than to temporary, earthly conditions like wealth and impressive appearances, and Alcott incorporates this philosophy into *Little Women.* For instance, Meg and Amy constantly struggle with vanity and eventually overcome it. Amy turns down Fred Vaughn's offer of marriage, even though he is rich, because she does not love him. The March sisters all learn to be happy with their respective lots in life and not to yearn for meaningless riches. The Marches' snug New England home is presented as more desirable than mansions in Paris. This theme is particularly American, especially distinctive of New England. Unlike their counterparts in Europe, many middle-class Americans at the time did not mind having come from humble origins and did not crave titles or other superficial trappings of wealth. These Americans wanted only what they deserved and believed that what they deserved depended on how hard they worked.

MOTIFS

MUSIC In *Little Women,* music has an interesting relationship to a character's degree of conformity. For the March girls, the more musically inclined a sister is, the more traditionally feminine and adherent to feminine duty she is. Marmee sings to the girls all the time, and she embodies the ideal dutiful and domestic mother. Beth, similarly, is both very musical and very passive. In contrast, Amy has a bad voice and Jo has the worst voice of all; both girls are independent and impatient with the limitations placed on women. Interestingly, Laurie also likes music and wants to be a professional musician, but this interest makes him ill-adapted to the role expected of him as a man.

TEACHING Many of the characters in *Little Women* are teachers, reinforcing the idea that the novel is didactic and that we are supposed to learn from the novel's lessons. Mr. March, for example, is a minister, and he instructs his congregation. Marmee, a good transcendentalist mother, reinforces the teaching of her husband. Mr. Brooke and Professor Bhaer, two men whom March girls marry, are teachers by profession. In the end, Jo inherits Plumfield, Aunt March's house, and she and Bhaer turn it into a school for boys. The frequent interaction that the novel's characters have with teaching—both giving and learning lessons—reflects the structured society in which they live.

DIFFERING USES OF LANGUAGE Language appears throughout the novel in an interesting inverse relationship with creativity: the more proper the language one of the March girls uses, the less creative and independent she is. Beth does not talk much, for example, and Meg uses proper language; both are typically feminine women, and their relationship to language reflects their alignment with what society expects of them. In contrast, Jo swears and Amy mispronounces words. These two, the independent artists of the family, resist conforming to the behavior that society expects of them, including the use of proper and delicate speech.

SYMBOLS

UMBRELLAS In *Little Women,* umbrellas symbolize the protection a man offers a woman. Before Meg and John Brooke marry, Jo gets angry at Mr. Brooke's umbrella. It seems Jo is angry that Mr. Brooke is going to take care of her sister. At the end of the novel, Professor Bhaer extends his umbrella over Jo, and her acceptance of its coverage symbolizes that she is ready to accept not only his love and protection, but also the idea that men are supposed to offer women love and protection.

BURNING *Little Women* is filled with images of burning that simultaneously represent writing, genius, and anger. At a party, Jo wears a dress with a burn mark on the back, which symbolizes her resistance to having to play a conventional female role. In anger, Amy burns Jo's manuscript after Jo will not let her come to a play. Whenever Jo writes, her family describes her inspiration as genius burning. At the end of the novel, Jo burns her sensationalist stories after Professor Bhaer criticizes that style of writing. This fire seems to destroy her earlier self as well, as it marks the end of the fiery Jo of the novel's beginning.

IMPORTANT QUOTATIONS EXPLAINED

1. *I'll try and be what he loves to call me, "a little woman," and not be rough and wild; but do my duty here instead of wanting to be somewhere else.*

Jo speaks these words in Chapter 1 after hearing the letter from Mr. March, who is serving in the Civil War. Jo says that she would like to be doing something exciting, such as being in the Civil War like her father, instead of sitting at home. Jo points out that women cannot fight in the Civil War, and generally lead less adventurous lives than do men. In this statement, Jo also demonstrates a wish to make her father happy by acting stereotypically female. Jo struggles throughout the novel because she wants both to lead an adventurous, independent life and to help and please her family. In other words, the struggle for individual success conflicts with the duty and affection she feels for her family and with the domestic sphere that most women of the time accept.

Mr. March's letter comes immediately after all the March girls say that they want more out of life than what they have. After hearing his letter, they each decide to be content with what they have, demonstrating that the renunciation of their material dreams is learned, rather than natural, behavior.

2. *I am angry nearly every day of my life.*

Marmee makes this statement in Chapter 8 when she tells Jo that she too struggles with a quick temper. Throughout the novel, however, Marmee seems serene and composed, which suggests that the appearance of a docile woman may hide turmoil underneath. Marmee's admission makes Jo feel better, because she realizes that she is not the only one with a temper. At the same time, though, Marmee's words suggest that there is no hope for Jo—Marmee is still angry after forty years, and perhaps Jo will be, too. Many feminist critics have noted this sentence as an expression of anger about nineteenth-century society's demand that women be domestic.

L

3. *Money is a needful and precious thing,—and, when well used, a noble thing,—but I never want you to think it is the first or only prize to strive for. I'd rather see you poor men's wives, if you were happy, beloved, contented, than queens on thrones, without self-respect and peace.*

Marmee speaks these words in Chapter 9, after Meg has returned from a two-week stay at the Moffats' home. Marmee tells Meg that she does not want any of her daughters to marry for material comforts, as was suggested by a guest at the Gardiners'. At a moment in history when women's futures hinged solely on their choice of a husband, Marmee's statement is very compassionate and unusual. After all, the other guests at the party easily assume that Meg must be intending to marry for money.

Alcott does not completely sanction Marmee's statement. *Little Women* depicts marrying poor as a serious burden for a nineteenth-century woman to bear. One should not marry for money, but at the same time, quarrels and stress come about from marrying a poor man. Alcott does not depict romantic love without mentioning the practical reality of living with little money. The daughter of an improvident father, she knew firsthand the worry of having to depend on someone else for a living.

4. *I'd have a stable full of Arabian steeds, rooms piled with books, and I'd write out of a magic inkstand, so that my works should be as famous as Laurie's music. I want to do something splendid before I go into my castle—something heroic, or wonderful—that won't be forgotten after I'm dead. I don't know what, but I'm on the watch for it, and mean to astonish you all, some day. I think I shall write books, and get rich and famous; that would suit me, so that is my favorite dream.*

Jo speaks these words in Chapter 13 when the March girls and Laurie are discussing their dreams. In contrast to the typical dreams of her sisters, Jo's dream is startlingly big and confidently expressed. The horses Jo wants, and with which she is constantly compared, represent the wild freedom for which she yearns. Significantly, Jo does not mention a husband or children in her dream, but says she wants books and ink. This powerful statement reaches well beyond the confines of a woman's small living room and demands lasting fame and independence in a man's world. Jo's sentences are very direct and begin commandingly with the word "I."

Jo also mentions the desire to have her work equal Laurie's. The pursuit of an art is represented as an idyllic field in which men's and women's work are considered equal. Also, Jo aligns going into a castle—getting married and having a house—with dying, for she wants to do something great before either event happens to her.

---

5. *Oh, my girls, however long you may live, I never can wish you a greater happiness than this!*

These words from Marmee conclude the novel, at the end of Chapter 47, and also sum up the novel's message. Through the four March sisters, Alcott presents many possible ways a woman can walk through life. Both the novel and Marmee finally decide that women must make some sacrifices for their families, in order to have the happiest life possible. Perhaps Alcott sometimes wished her life had turned out more traditionally and that she had married and had children. This ending is ambiguous at best, however, since the novel has called traditional values into question throughout.

Lucy: A Novel

Jamaica Kincaid (1949–)

CONTEXT

Jamaica Kincaid was born Elaine Potter Richardson on May 25, 1949, on the British-ruled Caribbean island of Antigua. She showed intelligence at an early age but received little encouragement from those around her. Raised by her mother, a homemaker, and her step-father, a carpenter, Kincaid attended government schools, where teachers chastised her for sass and disobedience. Kincaid's mother, a book lover, taught her to read at age three and gave her an Oxford Dictionary for her seventh birthday, but she discouraged Kincaid's goal of attending college and becoming a librarian or teacher. Kincaid spent the first nine years of her life as an only child and felt rejected when her mother gave birth to the first of her three brothers. She escaped her misery by immersing herself in the work of William Shakespeare, John Milton, the Brontë sisters, and other classic British scribes. Because she encountered literature only by white, long-dead authors, the young Kincaid never considered the possibility that she, too, could become a writer.

As Kincaid entered adolescence, her unhappiness turned into anger, and her relationship with her mother worsened. Strongly influenced by British colonial values, Kincaid's mother demanded pristine behavior from Kincaid yet deemed her unable to restrain her sexuality. At sixteen, Kincaid left her poor homeland to become an au pair for a wealthy New York family and pursue her education. She earned her G.E.D. and studied photography at the New School for Social Research and Franconia College, but she never completed her degree. In 1973, when she began writing magazine articles, she changed her name, both to protect her privacy and to signify her new start in life. She developed a friendship with *New Yorker* writer George Trow, who introduced her to the magazine's editor, William Shawn. Shawn encouraged her to submit work to him, and her writing career blossomed as she became a regular contributor to his pages. Shawn's importance in her life took a new turn in 1979, when she wed his son, Allen.

Kincaid's nonlinear, stream-of-consciousness *New Yorker* pieces bear the influence of modernists, such as James Joyce, Virginia Woolf, and Alain Robbe-Grillet. Kincaid builds on that style in her first fictional work, a short story called "Girl," which consists of a list of a mother's orders to her daughter. "Girl" showcases the poetic, chant-like, hallucinogenic prose that characterizes Kincaid's first short fiction collection, *At the Bottom of the River* (1983), and her debut novel, *Annie John* (1985). Both books display Kincaid's talent for evoking states of mind without sacrificing sharp external detail, as well as her ability to address social issues through the domestic realm. They also explore themes that figure into much of Kincaid's work, such as loss of innocence, betrayal by the mother, identity confusion caused by colonialism, and parallels between maternal and imperial authority. Kincaid's next publication, the nonfiction *A Small Place* (1988), poses a scathing comment on Antigua's tourism and postcolonial institutions and marks a new level of anger in her writing.

Lucy, published in 1990, retains the anger of *A Small Place* but simplifies the style of Kincaid's earlier work by using less repetition and surrealism. The first of her books set completely outside the Caribbean, *Lucy*, like most of Kincaid's writing, has a strong autobiographical basis. The novel's protagonist, Lucy Josephine Potter, shares one of Kincaid's given names and her birthday. Like Kincaid, Lucy leaves Antigua to become an *au pair* in a large American city. At nineteen, Lucy is older than previous Kincaid protagonists, which lends the book a more mature and cynical perspective than in her previous fiction. Still, Lucy has pangs of homesickness and unresolved feelings about her mother, and she has never lived on her own or seen much of the world. With plenty of room for growth, Lucy's journey takes the form of a bildungsroman, a novel in which a young protagonist makes the transition to adulthood.

Lucy also joins the tradition of American immigration literature, tales that recount a newcomer's experience in the United States, such as those seen in Anzia Yezierska's *Bread Givers*, Willa Cather's *My Antonia*, and Julia Alvaerez's *How the Garcia Girls Lost Their Accents*. Along with exploring immigration,

Lucy, as does much of Kincaid's work, grapples with tensions between mother and daughter. Colonial themes of identity confusion and the connection between maternal and imperial rule stand out less clearly in *Lucy* than in Kincaid's earlier books but have an underlying presence in Lucy's relationship with her white, affluent employers, her homeland, and her new surroundings.

Kincaid continues to publish acclaimed fiction and nonfiction, such as *The Autobiography of My Mother* (1995) and *Mr. Potter* (2002), both novels, *My Garden (Book)* (1999), a book-length essay, and *My Brother* (1997), a memoir concerning her brother's death from AIDS. While black, feminist, and postcolonial critics take much interest in Kincaid, her writing resists fitting into neat political categories. Unlike many Caribbean authors, who try to shake off the traditions of their colonizer to form independent modes of expression, Kincaid draws upon her colonial literary heritage to explore her experience. In the process, she critiques and redefines that heritage. Though her writing often explores issues of race, gender, and class, she rejects the idea of viewing her identity and work primarily in terms of social politics. Others might lump her together with other black woman writers, but she sees little connection between herself and African-American female authors such as Toni Morrison. Nonetheless, she believes in the importance of knowing one's history, as *Lucy* and her other books eloquently demonstrate.

PLOT OVERVIEW

At nineteen, Lucy Josephine Potter leaves her British-ruled Caribbean homeland with high hopes for the future, but she instantly grows disillusioned upon arriving in America to work as an *au pair* for an affluent family, whose lives, to her, seem incredibly charmed. After years of dreaming of escape from her birthplace, she finds her new surroundings cold and mundane and suffers intense homesickness. She dismisses her former dreams of a better existence as mere fantasies. Though she always felt out-of-place in her native land, she experiences extreme isolation in her new country, and while she likes her employers, Lewis and Mariah, and wants one day to emulate their happy family life, her initial attempt to reach out to them breeds only misunderstanding.

Lucy grows closer to Mariah but also marvels at the differences between her impoverished colonial background and Mariah's privileged circumstances. Despite Lucy's frequent memories of home, she speaks bitterly of those she left behind and focuses increasingly on thoughts of her mother, toward whom she feels great animosity and only occasional tenderness. As Lucy emerges from a hard winter, she gains confidence that she has truly begun her new life. When she, Mariah, and Mariah's four daughters take a trip to the Great Lakes, however, Lucy sees ways in which Mariah, like her mother, tries to control her. She and Mariah have disparate views on everything from dining cars and plowed fields to Indian heritages and fish, and Lucy regards Mariah's pampered perspective of the world with a mixture of rage and pity.

Summer brings another trip to the Great Lakes, this time with Lewis joining the family, and Lucy develops a deep affection for Lewis and Mariah's youngest daughter, Miriam, who reminds her of her childhood and happier times with her mother. Mariah, too, continues to resemble Lucy's mother in both good and bad ways. Noting something amiss in Lewis and Mariah's relationship, Lucy pledges her loyalty to Mariah and thinks back to her own sexual awakening, which involved much physical pleasure but little emotional investment. With her good friend, Peggy, back in the city, Lucy experiences loneliness but also enjoys the warm weather and the lakeside picnics with the children. The arrival of Dinah, Mariah's vain and envious best friend, puts Lucy on guard, but Lucy takes quickly to Hugh, Dinah's brother, developing a sexual relationship with him that pleases her enormously, but, she insists, arouses no love. Meanwhile, Mariah and Lewis's marriage deteriorates into frequent fighting, and Lucy catches Lewis nuzzling Dinah. By the end of the summer, Lucy feels little nostalgia about her time at the lake and easily says her goodbyes.

Upon returning to the city, Lucy, jaded from the summer's revelations about Lewis and Mariah, abandons her plans to attend school and become a nurse and despairs of her chances of eluding her mother's influence. Though she refuses to open her mother's letters, she doesn't discard them, and she increasingly believes she has become her mother's clone. Due to their differences, tensions between Peggy and Lucy grow, and when Lucy falls for Peggy's co-worker, Paul, Peggy disapproves, further harming their friendship. But because Peggy wants to escape her family and Lucy has tired of living under Lewis and Mariah's roof, they overlook their problems to discuss getting an apartment together. Paul and Lucy see a lot of each other, spending most of their time in bed, but when Lucy decides to buy a camera and take up photography, she follows the camera salesman home and sleeps with him. Soon after, Paul declares his love for Lucy, who doesn't share his feelings. Mariah and Lewis argue constantly, and not long after Mariah kicks Lewis out, Lucy discovers, from a fellow countrywoman, that her father has died, leaving her mother penniless. Overcome with emotion, Lucy sends her mother money, along with a vitriolic letter detailing her mother's many transgressions. She burns the letter she receives in return, along with the other letters from her mother that she's saved. During a discussion with Mariah, Lucy reveals how her mother neglected her once her brothers arrived. To help Lucy resolve her feelings for her mother, Mariah gives her some feminist tomes, but Lucy finds them useless in addressing the loss of the one great love of her life.

The death of her father intensifies Lucy's wish to move away from Mariah, and when she announces her impending departure, Mariah becomes angry, starts treating her less like a friend than a servant, and gives her a cool farewell. A year after Lucy's arrival in America, she once again finds herself embarking on a fresh start, and while she appreciates having her own place and belongings, her changed circumstances please her less than she'd hoped. Peggy proves an irritating roommate, her office job falls short of her expectations, and Paul's constant presence at her new home annoys her. Before Mariah moves away, Lucy and Mariah have a pleasant visit, but Lucy wonders if she'll ever see her again. Peggy and Paul appear to develop a secret relationship, but Lucy feels so disconnected from them that she hardly minds. Having finally achieved her independence, Lucy wishes she had the capacity to experience profound love.

CHARACTER LIST

Lucy Josephine Potter An *au pair* for a wealthy American family, and the novel's protagonist and narrator. More than anything, Lucy wants to escape the influence of her native land, a British-ruled Caribbean island, but her homesickness and difficult relationship with her mother stand in her way. Sharply observant and frequently critical, she grows close to her employers while remaining keenly aware of the disparate circumstances separating her from them. Lucy unapologetically enjoys her sexual encounters with men but reserves her deepest, most painful feelings for her relationships with women. Though she suffers persistent dissatisfaction and disillusion as her new existence fails to meet her expectations, she also experiences moments of hope and peace and demonstrates great strength and determination in her quest to live on her own terms.

Mariah The woman of the household in which Lucy works. Though Mariah holds liberal views, she inadvertently offends Lucy with the naïveté and arrogance of her privileged upbringing. Still, Mariah demonstrates more generosity and kindness than others in her class, and Lucy comes to view her as a mother figure. As Mariah's marriage declines, she becomes increasingly vulnerable, which leads Lucy to understand that even the wealthy have problems.

Lewis The man of the household in which Lucy works. Despite his friendliness and good humor, Lewis epitomizes Lucy's worst ideas about men when he cheats on Mariah. Handsome and rich, he has spent his life getting what he wants with little effort, and Lucy believes that he manipulates Mariah into ending their marriage so as to avoid taking blame for the relationship's demise.

Annie Potter Lucy's mother. Left behind in Lucy's homeland, Annie makes no physical appearance in the novel, but she nonetheless has an immense presence in Lucy's life. Often portrayed as godlike, Annie holds a place in Lucy's heart as her first, and possibly only, great love. However, she discouraged Lucy's educational and career aspirations while supporting her sons' goals, which infuriates Lucy. Annie's strained relationship with Lucy affects all aspects of Lucy's life and sparks fears that Lucy will never overcome her past.

The Maid A servant in Lewis and Mariah's household. One of the first people Lucy meets in America, the maid treats Lucy with hostility and increases her feelings of isolation.

Sylvie Lucy's mother's friend. Sylvie has had a difficult existence, which left her with a scar on her cheek that Lucy views as a symbol of real life.

Gus Mariah's family's hired hand. Gus brings out Lucy's sympathies when Mariah treats him imperiously, but Lucy, deciding his Swedish ancestry makes him too different from her, refrains from reaching out to him.

Lucy's Father The first important male figure in Lucy's life. A philanderer who kept his distance from Lucy, he set the stage for Lucy's dismissive attitude toward men. His death gives Lucy the resolve to leave Mariah and Lewis's apartment.

Tanner The boy with whom Lucy first explores her sexuality. Tanner and Lucy share a purely physical bond that arouses Lucy so much that she grows curious about the pleasures that other boys may have to offer.

Miriam Lewis and Mariah's youngest daughter. Miriam reminds Lucy of herself as a child and of her early experiences with her mother. Though her role in the novel is small, she bears the distinction of being the one person toward whom Lucy exhibits unconditional love.

Louisa Lewis and Mariah's oldest daughter. Entering adolescence, Louisa shows signs of rebellion against Mariah that recall Lucy's initial defiance of her mother.

May and Jane Lewis and Mariah's two other daughters. Though Lucy focuses little on their individual characteristics, May and Jane share the charming playfulness of all of Lewis and Mariah's brood. Lucy wishes her own mother had cultivated those traits in her and hopes one day to raise such happy, free-spirited children herself.

The Boy in the Library An acquaintance who abruptly kisses Lucy. The boy and Lucy meet regularly for wordless sexual encounters until Lucy grows tired of him.

Dinah Mariah's best friend. Dinah impresses Mariah with her generosity and zest for life, but Lucy finds her arrogant, envious, and vain, a view confirmed when Lucy catches her sexually involved with Lewis.

Peggy Lucy's best friend. Peggy impresses Lucy with her fun-loving, carefree attitude, but the differences between her and Lucy, as well as Lucy's association with Paul, eventually come between them. Lucy often compares their relationship to that of disgruntled lovers, and her inability to maintain closeness with Peggy shows Lucy's difficulty in sustaining her most intimate ties. Still, by renting an apartment with Lucy, Peggy serves an important role in Lucy's independence from Mariah and her mother.

Hugh Dinah's brother and Lucy's first North American boyfriend. Intelligent and well-traveled, Hugh wins over Lucy with his respectful attitude towards her homeland. He delights Lucy sexually, but she denies loving him and has no qualms about their parting.

L

The Nurse A friend of Lucy's mother. Poor and unloved, the nurse evokes Lucy's fears about compromising herself in an occupation that her mother encourages but that Lucy believes falls short of her potential.

Paul Peggy's coworker and Lucy's lover. Though Peggy deems him a pervert, Paul charms Lucy with his bright eyes and artistic sensibilities. He and Lucy embark on an intensely sexual relationship, which drives a wedge between Lucy and Peggy. He feels more strongly about Lucy than she does about him, and she tires of his constant presence at her new apartment.

Roland A camera salesman with whom Lucy has a fling. Though she quickly jumps into his bed, Roland means little to Lucy. Her romp with him also displays her lack of feeling for Paul.

Maude Quick The woman from Lucy's homeland who brings Lucy news of her father's death. Though Maude strikes Lucy's mother as a model of proper behavior, Maude serves as a bit of a foil for Lucy, who finds her sadistic and an inspiration, by negative example, to leave her mother's home by age nineteen. Despite Maude's unpleasantness, she provides Lucy some comfort when bringing news of Lucy's father's death, evoking Lucy's violently mixed feelings about her native land.

Myrna Lucy's childhood friend. Abnormally small, Myrna gladly takes money from a local fisherman, Mr. Thomas, to let him molest her, a revelation that provokes sexual jealousy in Lucy. Though Lucy desperately wants to know how Myrna's encounters with Mr. Thomas felt, she is too inhibited by social convention to ask.

Mr. Thomas A fisherman from Lucy's island who dies at sea. Mr. Thomas always behaved like a gentleman around Lucy, who wishes he had molested her instead of Myrna. Years later, Paul's hands cause Lucy to remember Mr. Thomas, whose hands, forever lost to her, represent the height of sexual mystery.

Mr. Simon A photographer and Lucy's employer. Mr. Simon is the first person Lucy has met who has compromised his art for money. He lets her use his darkroom, facilitating her artistic development.

ANALYSIS OF MAJOR CHARACTERS

LUCY JOSEPHINE POTTER Lucy, the novel's protagonist and narrator, seeks independence from the colonial and maternal forces that shaped her youth, but her journey to North America to serve as an *au pair* for a wealthy family only highlights many of the influences that have hindered her and reveals the ambivalence behind her apparent drive for freedom. For all her bitter remarks about her mother and her native land, she frequently experiences intense homesickness and longing for her mother's love. Though she no longer lives under British rule, she resents the upper-class privileges of her American employers. She replicates her difficult relationship with her mother in her dealings with Mariah and, to a lesser extent, Peggy. As she did at home, she embarks on sexual relationships with men who please her physically but leave her emotionally detached. Lucy realizes early on that her hopes of creating a glorious new life for herself bear little resemblance to reality, and with each new disappointment, Lucy develops a fatalism that at once strengthens her and makes her vulnerable. Though Lucy's harsh view of the world prepares her for the hardships of living on her own terms, it also, at times, drives her to despair.

Much of Lucy's quest for freedom results in isolation. She spends her first weeks as an immigrant without much human connection, and though she grows close to Mariah, Miriam, and Peggy, her most important relationships eventually unravel, and she finds herself, for the first time, truly living on her own. She has even further separated herself from her mother, and, by implication, her entire homeland, by giving a false report of her whereabouts. While Lucy, to some degree, has achieved her independence, it doesn't bring her the joy she imagines. On the contrary, the novel's conclusion finds her tearfully yearning for the capacity to love. Lucy's alienation is typical of the immigrant experience, but only some of her loneliness clearly relates to her new surroundings. Her estrangement goes back to her place of birth and follows her beyond her adjustment to America. For Lucy, isolation transcends immigration to form an essential part of her existence, regardless of location or circumstance.

MARIAH Mariah, Lucy's employer, represents both Lucy's past and her present. Though Mariah, an affluent North American white woman, is very different from Lucy's mother, Lucy comes to view her as a mother figure who to some extent embodies the best and worst of her mother. Like Lucy's mother, Mariah tries to mold Lucy in her own image, imposing her views on everything from daffodils to women to her Great Lakes home, but she also shares the warmth and tenderness that Lucy's mother exhibited during Lucy's childhood. In response, Lucy displays a similar ambivalence towards Mariah as she does toward her own mother, wavering between deep affection, pity, and resentment. The ways in which Mariah differs from Lucy's mother also shed light on Lucy's past. When Lucy appreciates Mariah's good humor and tolerance, she exposes the lack of such traits in her mother. Despite her rage toward her mother, however, she also betrays her admiration for her when she derides Mariah for lacking the strength her mother would show in dealing with Lewis.

Mariah epitomizes traits of the new world to which Lucy has fled. Her wealth and privilege initially strike Lucy as the keys to happiness, though Lucy often disdains the naïve arrogance that accompanies Mariah's good fortune. Mariah's liberal attitude toward her children impresses Lucy, who hopes to emulate Mariah when she has her own family. Yet as Lucy learns that Mariah's advantages fail to protect her from the unhappiness of a bad marriage, Mariah's way of life loses its charm, and Lucy comes to understand the universality of human dissatisfaction and suffering, a knowledge that both matures and embitters her. Mariah, for her part, shows her imperious side once Lucy decides to leave her behind, which calls her generous and egalitarian impulses into question and underscores the ultimate distinctions between Lucy and herself. Though Mariah aids in Lucy's journey to independence, Lucy must break with her in order to truly pursue her freedom.

ANNIE POTTER Annie Potter, Lucy's mother, constitutes a major force in the novel, despite her physical absence. Often referred to as godlike, she provides the motivation for much of Lucy's behavior, for Lucy has made escaping her mother's influence the supreme goal of her life. But as Lucy herself admits, she and her mother have much in common, so much so that as a child, Lucy thought of her mother as an extension of herself. Like Lucy, Annie possesses a sharp tongue and a strong mind, and she vacillates between nurture and withdrawal. Unlike Lucy, however, Annie has spent her life playing the part of the proper woman, attempting to instill in Lucy values of prudence and submission that Lucy believes go against both their natures. Whereas Lucy's mother has made little use of her intelligence and married a man who has a bevy of other women, Lucy takes pains to avoid following the same path.

Lucy's anger at her mother, however, goes beyond a disagreement about life choices and principles. Lucy calls her mother the great love of her life, and much of her rage is derived from what she sees as her mother's rejection of that love with the birth of her brothers. From the difficult relationships that Lucy builds with the other women to her lack of true intimacy with men, the specter of Lucy's lost love for her mother haunts her every move. Lucy's feelings for her mother replicate her attitude toward her colonized homeland, which she both longs for and spurns in her mission to honor her true self. Only when Lucy attempts to resolve those feelings, by at once showing compassion for her mother and removing her from her life, can she begin to move forward by leaving Mariah's home. Thus, Lucy's mother both inspires and undermines Lucy's quest for freedom, as Lucy attempts to flee the most important and persistent emotional bond of her existence.

THEMES, MOTIFS, AND SYMBOLS

THEMES

THE CYCLICAL NATURE OF EXISTENCE Upon arriving in America, Lucy follows a cyclical path, wherein her apparent progress leads her to the very condition she's tried to reject. Lucy abandons her native land with the expectation that her life will instantly become different and better. However, she exchanges her dissatisfaction with her country for the discontents of immigration, yearning for her island with the same intensity with which she once ached for escape. The isolation and longing she initially experiences parallel her condition at the novel's conclusion, when, alone in her new apartment, she laments her incapacity for true love. The novel's structure reinforces Lucy's cyclical journey, both starting and ending in January. Amid the larger cycle of Lucy's first year in America, Lucy experiences smaller cycles, vacillating between hope and despair in her aspirations and between closeness and distance in her relationships. This cyclical perspective contrasts with Western industrial society's linear notions of progress, in which individuals supposedly move increasingly beyond adversity through the systematic application of hard work and reason. Lucy, who lacks no determination or intelligence, shows a more complex reality.

THE DIFFICULTY OF MOTHER-DAUGHTER RELATIONSHIPS Despite her physical absence from Lucy's life, Lucy's mother continually occupies Lucy's thoughts, inspiring anger, contempt, longing, and regret. Lucy relates an enormous amount of her experiences to some memory or observation about her mother, which demonstrates the power of the mother-daughter bond. Yet that power has the ability to do as much harm as good. Lucy once saw her mother as an extension of herself and considered her the great love of her life. Because of the strength of their relationship, Lucy became devastated when the arrival of her brothers diverted her mother's attention and support. Adolescence furthered tensions between Lucy and her mother, as Lucy resented her mother's attempts to shape her in her own image. The very separation that Lucy hopes to complete with her journey to America, however, causes her sorrow, for she believes she'll never again experience the kind of love she shared with her mother. Though Lucy determines that she must break with her mother to achieve adulthood, she suffers intense feelings of loss in the process.

THE POWER OF CIRCUMSTANCE ON PERCEPTION Having grown up under colonial rule, Lucy views the world differently from those with backgrounds unlike hers. While Mariah's affluent North American upbringing prompts her to extol the beauty of daffodils and plowed fields, Lucy sees a symbol of colonial injustice and the labor of those who worked the soil. Lucy notices the racial breakdown of the train's dining car, but Mariah appears oblivious to the division between the white passengers and the black help. When the weather turns bad, Mariah laments the obstacle to her desires, whereas Lucy never expects that the conditions outside should accommodate her wants. To Mariah's wealthy friends, Lucy's Caribbean homeland, the origin of Lucy's disappointments and dreams, serves as little more than a site for their relaxation and recreation. As Paul, a white male artist, sings praises of the human quest for freedom, Lucy can think only of the cost that the disadvantaged members of society pay for that quest. Though Lucy relates to some people of circumstances vastly different from hers, she constantly encounters reminders that varied experiences lead to disparate perceptions.

MOTIFS

THE SEASONS As Lucy experiences her first year abroad, she shows a keen awareness of the changing seasons, which often parallel her emotional states. Beginning and ending with Lucy's lonely winters, Kincaid shows Lucy moving from renewal in springtime to contentment in summer and disillusionment in the fall. The link between Lucy's journey and the seasons promotes the notion that human existence follows a cyclical, rather than linear, path. The seasons also highlight differences between Lucy's old equatorial surroundings and her new northern climate. Lucy has an attitude toward the seasons that mirrors her mixed feelings about her native country. Though she appreciates the variety of weather and finds the summers less oppressive than at home, in the colder months, she misses the warm sun and vibrant colors of the island. The seasons, then, highlight both Lucy's inner and outer conditions and grant them larger meaning by connecting them to a natural phenomenon experienced by many.

LETTERS Lucy's letters from home illuminate her difficult relationship with her mother. As Lucy takes to piling her mother's unopened letters on her dresser, she shows a defiance that also betrays her daughterly attachment: she doesn't discard them and fears the longing she'd feel if she glimpsed her mother's words. When Lucy finally reads the letter detailing her father's death and her mother's misfortune, she comes to her mother's financial aid but also releases her fury in a letter home, once again demonstrating her mixed feelings. After burning the letters she's saved, Lucy finds herself able to move forward. She prepares to leave Lewis and Mariah's apartment and sends a letter home, expressing compassion for her mother but also breaking with her by giving a false address. Throughout the novel, letters serve as markers of Lucy's struggle to make a new life for herself by escaping her past.

FOOD Food appears in the novel as a source of comfort and, occasionally, dissension. Lucy's best memories of home often involve detailed descriptions of dishes, such as the mullet and figs cooked by her grandmother, the cow's tongue in lemon juice evoked by her thoughts of Tanner, or the exquisitely fried fish she pictures eating by a vibrantly blue sea. Lucy's attention to the food of her homeland illustrates that despite her bitterness about her past, her country has sustained her physically and emotionally. But food also elicits painful emotions. The food she remembers in the throes of homesickness may provide comfort, but it also taunts her with its absence. Mariah's baked fish reminds Lucy yet again of the distance between Mariah and herself and how far she is from home. And Lucy's mother ridicules her when she inquires about the preparation of fish in a Bible story that Lucy wishes more accurately reflected her island surroundings. For Lucy, food represents the finest moments of her upbringing but also recalls all she's lost.

SYMBOLS

"THE ISLANDS" Mariah's friends refer to the West Indies as "the islands," a phrase that reveals their presumptuously familiar attitude toward Lucy's homeland, a place they've vacationed but don't truly know. Because, as Lucy observes, many ranges of islands exist in the world, the failure to identify *which* islands implies a shared understanding among Mariah's white, affluent friends, which lies in their frequent jaunts to the Caribbean for rest and relaxation. By referring to "the islands" in Lucy's presence, they reduce her homeland to a tourist attraction, denying the presence of the everyday reality of an island where impoverished, colonized people live. Mariah's friends, though not the literal colonizers of Lucy's birthplace, show a colonial mentality by imposing their own experiences on the West Indies instead of recognizing the region's native characteristics. The short phrase "the islands" speaks volumes about the arrogance of those of wealth and privilege.

PHOTOGRAPHS The photographs Lucy takes with her new camera suggest Lucy's evolving sense of self. Initially, Lucy admires art and artists, but she believes that someone of her background is ill-equipped to pursue artistic endeavors. Eventually, however, a beloved book of photographs inspires her to take pictures herself. While the results don't resemble the work in the book, Lucy still finds beauty in her prints, which she posts on her wall as a validation of her personal vision. Lucy's journey toward selfhood has its drawbacks, and her photographs, too, illustrate her problems achieving self-fulfillment. Though she regularly develops photographs in her employer's darkroom, they fail to meet her expectations, just as Lucy's dreams fall short when they become realities. The photographs also represent Lucy's difficulty in achieving intimacy, for she produces them by hiding behind the camera, indulging in her view of others without turning the lens on herself.

DAFFODILS Daffodils suggest Lucy and Mariah's disparate perceptions of the world. For Mariah, daffodils, her favorite flower, mean beauty and the arrival of spring. Lucy, however, sees them as reminder of a colonial education that forced her to memorize a poem about a flower she'd never seen, while ignoring the features of her native land. As Mariah leads Lucy to a field of daffodils in an attempt to change Lucy's feelings about the flower, Lucy's animosity toward daffodils only increases. She wants to kill them: not only do they recall colonial injustice, but they also represent Mariah's colonial-like determination to make Lucy see the world as she does. While daffodils point to Lucy and Mariah's opposing perspectives, they also represent symbols themselves, by showing how the same object can have vastly divergent meanings for different people. Symbols, then, have no inherent import but derive their significance from the person who views them.

IMPORTANT QUOTATIONS EXPLAINED

---

1. *I wondered if ever in my whole life a day would go by when these people I had left behind, my own family, would not appear before me in one way or another.*

This comment appears in "Poor Visitor" after Lucy remembers an unpleasant childhood acquaintance, and it illustrates Lucy's ambivalence toward the community she has abandoned. Lucy's words may simply express her attachment to her origins, but the context of the quote renders it more complex. This thought emerges during an intense bout of homesickness that surprises her, since she has long craved escape from her native land. Given Lucy's bleak state of mind and her disdainful attitude toward the girl she has just remembered, the quote assumes a melancholy tone, suggesting that such constant appearances of those Lucy left behind would not be welcome. If Lucy will always mentally revisit her family and friends, then she has little chance of realizing her hope of achieving freedom from her past. Yet Lucy clearly misses her home, and the notion that she may never be without regular reveries about her community attests to the strength of her ties to it.

The quote's internal structure sheds further light on the complexity of Lucy's relationship with people back home. The phrase "these people I left behind, my own family," has an ambiguous meaning that further complicates Lucy's feelings. On one level, Lucy may simply consider her family a subgroup of those she left behind, as in "these people I left behind, *including* my own family." However, the absence of a word defining the relationship of her family to those she left behind gives the impression of interchangeability between "these people I left behind" and "my own family." Perhaps Lucy suggests here that everyone she left behind is like family to her, which, given Lucy's reluctant filial ties, implies a close but not especially welcome bond with her community. Or, alternatively, despite her recent reference to her childhood acquaintance, Lucy implies that of those she left behind, her family, above all, concerns and haunts her, and that ultimately her greatest fears and hopes derive from leaving her family. The ambiguous construction makes Lucy's final meaning difficult to pin down, but ambiguity seems fitting in light of the confused emotions about home that Lucy shows throughout the novel.

---

2. *It wasn't her fault. It wasn't my fault. But nothing could change the fact that where she saw beautiful flowers I saw sorrow and bitterness.*

This remark occurs in "Mariah" after Mariah leads Lucy to a field of daffodils in hopes of changing Lucy's hostility toward the flowers, and it encapsulates the vast differences in perception caused by Lucy and Mariah's disparate backgrounds. While privileged Mariah can appreciate daffodils for their aesthetic qualities, Lucy, whose British-run school forced her to memorize a poem about this species of flower, which is alien to her island, can't divorce daffodils from the injustices of colonialism, a system responsible for imposing foreign principles and interests on Lucy's native land. Though Lucy has resented Mariah's sheltered perspective of the world, she realizes that Mariah bears no more blame for loving daffodils than Lucy does for hating them, suggesting that perception derives not from choice but from circumstances beyond individual will. Yet by absolving herself and Mariah from holding their divisive views, Lucy also recognizes that she and Mariah can do nothing to bridge the perceptual gap between them, since they can't change what they can't control. This quote, by showing Lucy's ability for forgiveness and insight, demonstrates Lucy's conciliatory impulses while exposing just how much her colonial upbringing distances her from the white, affluent people in her midst.

---

3. *The times that I loved Mariah it was because she reminded me of my mother. The times that I did not love Mariah it was because she reminded me of my mother.*

These words appear in "The Tongue," as Lucy observes Mariah standing among enormous flowers in the Great Lakes house. It illustrates the close link, in Lucy's mind, between Mariah and her mother, and it also depicts Lucy's ambivalence about both women. Here, Lucy judges Mariah's behavior as a reflection of her mother's, for her love for Mariah depends on whether Mariah mimics her mother's good or bad traits, rather than on how Mariah performs on her own terms. The use of the plural, *times*, conveys that Lucy habitually identifies Mariah with her mother and possesses no feelings for Mariah outside the realm of that identification. Furthermore, rather than speaking of love as unconditional, Lucy reveals how frequently her love comes and goes, which demonstrates the wavering nature of her affections for both women. Though in other passages Lucy emphasizes ways in which Mariah and her mother differ, for much of the novel, Mariah serves as a mother figure to Lucy, through whom Lucy continues to play out the fierce, unresolved emotions she has for her real mother.

---

4. *I used to think that just a change in venue would banish forever from my life the things I most despised. But that was not to be so. As each day unfolded before me, I could see the sameness in everything; I could see the present take a shape—the shape of my past.*

This passage appears in "Cold Heart," as Lucy waits alone on a bleak Sunday for Peggy to call, and it illustrates Lucy's disillusion about making a new life for herself in North America. Despite her grand hopes of escaping her homeland, Lucy, in the months since her departure, has failed to realize her dreams. Though she has shed much of the homesickness that had previously besieged her, she experiences other forms of heartache, many of which parallel the bane of her island existence. At home, Sundays depressed her, and here, they depress her, too. She has fled her unhappy family only to witness the decline of Lewis and Mariah's marriage, in which Lewis, with his philandering, behaves much like her father. Most important, as the paragraph immediately following this quotation indicates, Lucy still finds herself caught in a battle for freedom from her mother, whose mocking voice rings in her head and whose letters she can neither bear to read nor discard. Lucy also continues to mirror her ambivalence toward her mother in her relationship with Mariah. As her problems follow her across a great distance, Lucy comes to see that her difficulties transcend her environment.

---

5. *I could write down only this: "I wish I could love someone so much that I would die from it." And then a great wave of shame came over me and I wept and wept so much that the tears fell on the page and caused all the words to become one great big blur.*

These are the final lines of the novel, and they demonstrate the despair and isolation that Lucy continues to feel despite the progress she's made. In many ways, Lucy has achieved the goals she set for herself upon leaving home. She lives in her own apartment, she has a decent job, and, by sending a letter with a false address, she has solidified the distance between herself and her mother. However, Lucy still lacks true intimacy with other people—though by the end of the novel she recognizes just how much she needs intense human connection. This acknowledgment reveals her maturation and suggests the possibility of future change. Lucy also admits that the dearth of love in her life results from her own shortcomings. By wishing she *could* deeply love someone, she implies that she *can't*, and the shame she feels also suggests her strong sense of blame for her own loneliness. While Lucy's assumption of responsibility for her own plight may mark a positive step for her, this quote ultimately casts a dark mood over the conclusion of Lucy's journey toward independence, with Lucy in tears that obliterate her mournful expression of growth.

A Medieval Life

Judith Bennett (1951–)

CONTEXT

Judith M. Bennett's lifelong passion for the Middle Ages has served her well in writing *A Medieval Life*, a speculative biography of a woman who lived during the thirteenth and fourteenth centuries. As a child, Bennett devoured historical novels at a rate that worried her parents. At the age of fifteen, she undertook her first independent research project, an inquiry into the real-life character of Richard III of England, after reading a pair of novels that held diametrically opposed views on the notoriously controversial king. Now, as a professor of history at the University of North Carolina at Chapel Hill, Bennett devotes her academic career to her two primary areas of expertise, medieval history and women's history, and most of her output sits at the junction of these two scholarly disciplines. In addition to *A Medieval Life*, Bennett has written several books and articles on the experiences of women in the Middle Ages, including *Medieval Women in Modern Perspective* (2000); *Ale, Beer, and Brewsters in England: Women's Work in a Changing World* (1996); and *Women in the Medieval English Countryside* (1987).

Whereas Bennett's love of the Middle Ages dates back to her adolescence, her intimate rapport with women's history began in young adulthood. When Bennett was a graduate student at the University of Toronto, she had to come to terms with the discovery that she was homosexual, and she became politically active in the lively lesbian community there. This experience sensitized her to women's issues, and soon, Bennett diversified her medieval studies to include women's history. Thus, from a relatively young age, Bennett has been concerned with the status, roles, and representations of women throughout history, as well as the ways in which historians have portrayed them. Not only does Bennett's academic output reflect this concern, but her commitment to teaching and public debate regarding gender, feminism, and sexuality also demonstrate her advocacy of women's issues in both an academic context and a larger social one. As she once said in an interview, "women's history . . . has to have its own internal coherence and integrity." As an historian, Bennett has taken it upon herself to reveal the structural inequalities throughout history that have left women at a disadvantage, in the hope of seeing her work lead to widespread modern structural change that puts women on a more equal footing with men.

M

Bennett used these feminist concerns as guiding principles when writing *A Medieval Life*. Dissatisfied with the male-focused nature of history, Bennett set out to write *A Medieval Life* with an aim to reconceptualize the typical patriarchal view of society—that in which the central figure is inherently male. The subject of her biography, Cecilia Penifader, had an exceptionally well-documented life, and though she was by no means a perfectly typical medieval peasant, her life was in many ways representative of medieval society. Bennett's biography of Cecilia gives form to the ways in which women fit into medieval society, the types of challenges they faced, and the joys and everyday activities they encountered. In addition, since Cecilia managed to prosper despite never having married, *A Medieval Life* shuns the commonly held notion that peasants, especially peasant women, had to marry in order to survive.

A Medieval Life is more than a feminist tract of medieval history. While Bennett does explore the female story in human history, she refuses to burden her objective historical analysis with a radical feminist viewpoint. Her evocation of peasant life is both sober and well-balanced, and her speculation of what Cecilia must have been thinking and feeling in reaction to certain historical and day-to-day events is remarkably well-disciplined. Ultimately, Bennett's book is not merely about Cecilia but about medieval peasant life in general. After all, as Bennett notes in the introduction to *A Medieval Life*, peasants comprised 90 percent of the medieval population, yet they are consistently underrepresented both by historians and historical documents in favor of warring kings, crusading knights, imposing bishops, and haggling merchants. In outlining Cecilia's life and rigorously describing the society around her, Bennett provides a case study from which we may discern what a typical life was like in the Middle Ages.

PLOT OVERVIEW

A *Medieval Life* contains ten chapters in which Bennett tells Cecilia's story and paints a thorough picture of the world around her. Bennett organizes these chapters topically rather than chronologically, illuminating in each one an aspect of medieval society and describing how Cecilia behaved (or might have behaved) in each context. After an introductory chapter in which she gives a short overview of medieval England, Bennett uses three chapters to explore the central institutions of Cecilia's life: the village and surrounding pastoral community of her native home; the manor under whose lord's authority she lived; and the church that tended her spiritual existence. Bennett then discusses the Great Famine of 1315–1322, a time of transition for both Cecilia and England. In Chapters Six through Nine, Bennett further delves into the various facets of Cecilia's life: her relationship with her family; how she fit into the medieval economy; her rapport with others in the community; and how her gender affected her experiences. Bennett's final chapter examines the implications of Cecilia's life in relation to the medieval world and the modern one.

Cecilia Penifader was born to Robert and Alice Penifader in the late thirteenth century in Brigstock, a manor in central England. She was the seventh of eight children, only two of whom died before reaching adulthood, an unusually high birthrate for the time. Relative to other peasants, Cecilia's family was wealthy. Their large house, built of rubble, twigs, mud, and moss, covered about 450 square feet. It had only one room, at the center of which was a fire for warmth and cooking. Cecilia probably spent most of her childhood in the farmyard around the house, playing and, later, helping out with gardening, cooking, and watching her little sister, Agnes.

Surrounding Cecilia's home was a large and diverse community. There were two main villages in Brigstock manor, Brigstock and Stanion, where many people built their houses right next to each other, sometimes sharing a wall. Most business and trade occurred in the villages, but the most important economic activity took place in the countryside. The Brigstock economy relied heavily upon two types of land: arable fields, which comprised a quarter of the manor's lands and were used to grow wheat, barley, rye, and oats; and meadows and pastures, which existed mainly for the sheep, horses, and oxen kept by farmers and villagers. Brigstockers used the three-field system, in which peasants rotated crops among three fields each year. When Cecilia left her own premises, she could have walked among a few lanes of tightly bunched homes and outbuildings, then out to surrounding arable fields and meadows, and beyond that, to Rockingham Forest, which the king used as a hunting preserve. Many peasants would leave Brigstock to travel to the nearby markets in Geddington, Kettering, and Corby. Here, peasants got their news about goings-on in the wider world.

Manorialism, or feudalism, is the system of estates in which the elite who owned land profited from peasants, who worked in the fields and paid taxes to their landlords. Brigstock was a royal manor, which was unusually fortunate for a landholding tenant such as Cecilia. Whereas peasants on other manors might have had to deal with vigilant landlords, Cecilia enjoyed some independence from manorial rule because her landlords were absent. Additionally, as a tenant of Brigstock, Cecilia benefited from special legal status: she and other tenants could lease the manor and manage its affairs as they saw fit. Though they paid dearly for this privilege, in addition to paying yearly taxes and doing work for the landowner during each year's harvest, Brigstock peasants achieved dignity and freedom through self-government.

Cecilia's world was divided into three interdependent orders: the clergy, the landed elite, and the peasantry. Cecilia would have considered the clergy most important because it addressed her chief concern: her eternal salvation. The second most important was the landed elite—the kings and noblemen who protected the peasants from foreign invaders. Last was Cecilia's class, the peasants, who sustained the country through work. Though in theory each of these orders benefited equally from the other two, the peasantry was clearly the lowliest order, and all peasants had to defer to their social superiors in all matters, whether it meant obeying capricious and unfair laws, bowing one's head in a lord's presence, or performing special work on request.

The Saint Peter and Saint Andrew churches at the center of Stanion and Brigstock were the focal point of Cecilia's life. The only real communal structures in Brigstock, they were central meeting places for markets, ball games, gambling, gossip, and manorial court meetings. As the centers for spiritual worship, they held masses nearly every day and were especially popular on Sundays. Like virtually every other English peasant, Cecilia was a devout Christian who, unable to read, learned about Catholicism mostly from pictures and the local clergy. Cecilia and her neighbors also engaged in folk practices, such as spell-casting, and believed in fairies. The Church generally condoned this behavior and in some ways even incorporated these folk rituals into religious life, sharing holy days with some pagan gods. In this sense, Christianity for Cecilia was an extension of everyday life and responded to the rhythms of the natural world around her. Holy days often coincided with equinoxes, solstices, and times of harvest.

Cecilia matured during a great famine that ravaged England and northern Europe from 1315 to 1322. Brought on by exceptionally cold, wet weather, and exacerbated by overpopulation, the famine killed approximately one-tenth of England's six million people. To survive, peasants, including Cecilia, resorted to crime. Even as famine tapered off, crime rates remained inflated, as peasants felt either lingering resentment toward wealthier neighbors or were simply accustomed to taking a little more to assuage their worries over an uncertain future. Cecilia's parents' deaths during this time signaled the end of a relatively untroubled childhood. But in some ways, the Great Famine worked to her benefit. Cecilia's parents left her a sizeable inheritance, which she used to embark on a highly profitable career in landholding. Exploiting the desperate circumstances that led some peasants to sell their land leases at reduced prices, Cecilia made acquisitions at least six different times between 1319 and 1325, emerging from the famine with nearly twenty-five acres in her name.

From a young age, Cecilia had a good sense of nuclear family. Her own family was twice the average size, and every day, they slept, worked, and ate together. As head of the household, Cecilia's father, Robert, was the public face of his family until his sons became old enough to join tithings (groups of men responsible for one another's behavior and for law enforcement) and the girls married and moved away. Robert had to account publicly for Cecilia when a neighbor accused her of stealing hay from him in 1316. Robert was also responsible for beating his children and having them perform hard labor in the fields and around the house, practices that were quite common in the Middle Ages. Robert and Alice seemed to be exceptionally caring parents, given their efforts to provide some form of inheritance for all of their children, which was uncommon practice in medieval England.

Cecilia remained close with her family into adulthood, but as her brothers and sisters married and moved away, the nature of family changed for her. When Cecilia's sisters Christina and Agnes married, they effectively joined their husbands' families, transferring all of their landholdings and assets to them. At this point, Cecilia relied more heavily on her brothers Robert and William, who remained nearby and had power in the community. In 1319, Cecilia's brother, William, who had left Brigstock for a time and returned as an educated, low-ranking member of the clergy, bought a house next door to her. Toward the end of Cecilia's life, she combined her resources and household with those of her brother Robert.

Cecilia's economic livelihood required her to be flexible, innovative, and accommodating. This economy, called an "economy of makeshifts," consisted of three main markets: the labor market, the commodity market, and the land market. With landholdings so large, Cecilia employed skilled and unskilled laborers and servants on daily basis. The labor force in Cecilia's day was made up of local men and vagrants, wealthy and indigent, landholding and landless. Closely connected to the labor market was the land market. Land was a source of wealth for landless peasants, who often worked it for money and food. It was also a great source of wealth for Cecilia, who could profit from subletting and selling what she produced. Cecilia excelled in the land market by concentrating on buying pastures for animals to graze, which limited the number of people she would need to hire. Finally, the commodity market took place in villages, where people from the surrounding area would sell and buy everything ranging from food, cloth, and animals to tools, leather, and smith work. These simple exchanges fed more complex regional and international markets, which helped lead to regional specialization.

In Cecilia's day, community was powerful. Land and farming decisions were made as a group, all were responsible for the local parish's upkeep, and as manorial tenants, people were expected to work together to raise money for the landlords who required taxes and rent. Though there were king's courts for serious crimes, people often handled their own affairs by taking responsibility for each other. Heads of the household answered for their dependents, and all men were required to join tithings by the age of twelve. In addition to tithings, there were also officials who enforced the law and managed the manor's day-to-day affairs. The men who served as officials were generally wealthy peasants or minor gentry whose positions gave them power. Several Penifader men were officials, and though Cecilia profited, she couldn't heedlessly flaunt her wealth. Cecilia sat atop a socioeconomically diverse peasant class, but acting humbly and equitably allowed her to avoid resentment from neighbors and laborers.

Cecilia's world was one in which there were clear-cut distinctions between men's and women's roles in society. As a woman, Cecilia was forbidden to hold any office or act in any official manner. Literacy, education, and lucrative trade work, such as blacksmithing or thatching, were unavailable to her. Though women were exclusively responsible for brewing ales, Cecilia could not hold the office of ale-taster. And because she could not participate in tithings, she was technically left outside community law.

These restrictions left Cecilia at a substantial social disadvantage because the ability to serve in court and perform more active functions on the manor made an individual powerful in the community. Cecilia's disadvantages also extended to the realm of criminal justice. The Brigstock court records indicate that men were responsible for eighty percent of violent crimes, but surprisingly few of these crimes were against women, a phenomenon that suggests that the law did not protect women as readily as it did men and property.

Cecilia died in late May or early June of 1344. Her will dictated that her property be divided into thirds and that William's illegitimate son, John, Agnes's daughter, Matilda, and Robert Malin, a man about whom little is known, each be given a twenty-four–year lease on them. This decision led to bitter argument in the family because it effectively barred Cecilia's closest heirs from inheriting the property. Cecilia's sister Christina and nephew Martin, the son of her brother Henry, challenged her will in court and were able to convince a jury to overturn it. Christina and Martin then battled for sole rights to Cecilia's landholdings. After a long and contentious debate, the jury awarded Cecilia's legacy to Christina, who promptly transferred half of all of the properties to Martin, an act that suggests that Christina and Martin negotiated a deal outside of court. No one knows the drama behind Cecilia's inheritance, only that her death probably made a number of her kin unhappy with her.

CHARACTER LIST

Cecilia Penifader The daughter of Robert and Alice Penifader, and the protagonist of the story. Cecilia was a peasant, and her actions were exceptionally well documented in the courts of Brigstock. She amassed a substantial amount of wealth and land. Unmarried and childless, she lived as a *singlewoman* in Brigstock and remained close to her brothers and sisters throughout her life.

Robert Penifader The father of Cecilia and husband of Alice. Robert was a prosperous landholder who served as a Brigstock court officer in several capacities. His wealth and celebrity in Brigstock made him an important man among peasants. He died in 1318 from a sickness caused by malnutrition during the Great Famine.

Alice Penifader The wife of Robert and mother of Cecilia. Alice bore eight children, six of whom lived to adulthood. She seems to have been a dedicated mother, given her high success rate of healthy children. After Robert died in 1318, Alice provided for her youngest daughter, Agnes, by marrying her off to Henry Kroyl.

Robert Penifader II Cecilia's oldest brother and a wealthy landholder. Robert never married, but he did father an illegitimate daughter, Alice III. In 1336, he combined resources and households with Cecilia. Prior to his death in 1340, he bequeathed his lands to Alice III.

William Penifader Cecilia's older brother and a wealthy and important landholder. Like Cecilia, William never married, though he did father an illegitimate son to whom he willed his lands upon his death. As an adult, William lived next door to Cecilia, sharing a wall of his house with her. Also, he was unique among peasants insofar as he was educated and served officially as a cleric in Brigstock.

King Edward I Ruler of England from 1272 to 1307. An unusually strong monarch, Edward I ruled during a crucial epoch in the development of English law, witnessing the institution of parliamentary custom, common law, and codified property laws. In his last thirteen years, however, the state of England worsened as Edward I harshly taxed and drafted his subjects for his campaigns against the French and his attempted subjugation of Scotland, whose resistance was led by William Wallace.

King Edward II The son of Edward I and ruler of England from 1307 to 1327. Historians generally agree that Edward II was an eccentric and perhaps the most inept king ever to sit on the throne. He was temporarily the owner of Brigstock manor.

King Edward III The son of Edward II and ruler of England from 1327 to 1377. An able king, Edward III began a series of campaigns against the French, which later became known as the Hundred Years' War. In order to finance this war, Edward III heavily taxed the country. For a time, he was the owner of Brigstock manor.

Christina (Penifader) Power One of Cecilia's older sisters. After receiving several pieces of land from her father, Christina married Richard Power in 1317.

Richard Power of Cranford A well-to-do peasant and the husband of Cecilia's sister Christina.

Agnes (Penifader) Kroyl Cecilia's younger sister. After Robert died, Agnes's mother, Alice, dedicated herself to providing for Agnes by marrying her off to Henry Kroyl.

Henry Kroyl A well-to-do peasant and the husband of Cecilia's sister Agnes. Henry married Agnes during the Great Famine just after Agnes's father, Robert, died.

Henry Penifader The brother of Cecilia. Henry was not as economically successful as his brothers, William and Robert II, and his sister, Cecilia.

Emma Penifader The sister of Cecilia who died in early childhood.

Alice Penifader II The sister of Cecilia who died in early childhood.

Isabella Penifader The wife of Henry Penifader and mother of Martin, Thomas, and John II.

Alice Penifader III The illegitimate daughter of Cecilia's brother, Robert II, and Joan de Lowyk. Alice inherited Robert II's land after he died in 1340.

John Penifader The illegitimate son of Cecilia's brother William. John inherited a twenty-four–year lease on some of Cecilia's lands, only to see a jury deem his inheritance invalid.

Robert Malin A peasant of Brigstock. Though his relationship to Cecilia is unknown, Robert inherited a twenty-four–year lease on some of Cecilia's lands. A jury promptly deemed his inheritance invalid.

Matilda Kroyl Cecilia's niece and the daughter of Agnes Penifader. Matilda inherited a twenty-four–year lease on some of Cecilia's lands, only to see a jury deem her inheritance invalid.

Martin Penifader Cecilia's nephew and the son of Henry Penifader. After Cecilia's death, Martin claimed inheritance for Cecilia's lands but was denied in favor of Cecilia's sister Christina. Promptly following this decision, Martin received half of the lands in dispute from Christina, which suggested that he and Christina reached an informal agreement.

M

Margaret of France The wife of Edward I and owner of the manor of Brigstock for a period of time.

Isabella of France The wife of Edward II and owner of the manor of Brigstock for a period of time.

Archbishop of Canterbury The highest-ranking church official in England. During the Great Famine of 1315–1322, the Archbishop organized special masses and processions and encouraged people to fast, pray, and give alms.

William de Clive The vicar (a priest who stands in for a rector and takes care of the everyday religious needs of the community) of Brigstock from 1275–1325.

Roger de Corndale The vicar of Brigstock from 1325–1340.

John de Seymour The vicar of Brigstock from 1340–1344.

Serfs (villeins) Peasants who were not free to move from place to place. Serfs were attached to the land in which they were born and were expected to work for their manor. Serfdom was determined by birth.

Free peasants Peasants who were free of the restrictions and liabilities of serfs. Free peasants could emigrate, work, marry without asking for the manorial lord's permission, and take grievances to the king's court.

Bailiff The chief administrative officer of a manor. Usually a minor member of the English gentry or a prosperous peasant, the bailiff was a literate man who represented the manor to the peasants, kept track of payments coming into the manor, and supervised the other officials of the manorial court.

Reeve A manorial officer. The reeve managed the day-to-day business of the manor, usually on a part-time basis.

Hayward A manorial officer. Hayward kept track of what happened in the manor's fields and flocks, and often reported infractions of the law.

Afeeror A manorial officer who determined the amount of money to be paid for each reported action or offense. Afeerors generally would make the penalty in accordance with the person's means.

Jurors A constantly changing assortment of peasants who were in charge of reporting wrongdoing and judging cases that were brought to court. Unlike modern jurors, medieval jurors were expected to be informed, knowledgeable, and opinionated.

Aletasters Manorial officers who regulated the selling and tasting of ale and sometimes bread.

Brewsters Females who were responsible for brewing ale. Brewing was an exclusively female activity.

ANALYSIS OF MAJOR CHARACTERS

CECILIA PENIFADER Though the court rolls and manorial records of Cecilia's time offer a wealth of information about her actions, there is virtually no documentation that offers an accurate glimpse into Cecilia's thoughts and feelings. We can assume, however, that Cecilia was a survivor and a striver and that she likely possessed characteristics that promoted the prosperity she enjoyed. At the core of Cecilia was her hardiness. Blessed with good health and a family that nurtured and provided for her into adulthood, Cecilia demonstrated a resilience that was the hallmark of peasant life. From a young age, she likely helped with chores, including watching animals, supervising her younger sister, cooking, gardening, brewing ales, tying bundles of grain at harvest, and foraging for nuts and berries. As she grew older and had several acres of land to manage, she probably did some of the harder work that men did, which indicates both hardiness and independence. Further evidence of both her hardiness and independence rests in Cecilia's choice of lifestyle. A *singlewoman* her entire life, Cecilia eschewed the economic security that marriage typically guaranteed in favor of living on her own.

In order to succeed as Cecilia did, she had to be flexible, intelligent, and even ruthless. Because she was a woman and could not reap the benefits of being an officer, Cecilia probably relied on her network of family and friends to protect her interests at court. With so much land, she had much at stake, and she walked a fine line between garnering either respect or resentment from her poorer peasant neighbors. This balance required a shrewdness that Cecilia likely employed in the management of her lands as well as in her social relationships. Perhaps inherent in Cecilia's shrewdness was a willingness to get ahead at the expense of others in the community. Bennett notes several instances of Cecilia's neighbors accusing her of stealing grain from them, an act that seems unusual and risky given Cecilia's relative affluence. Additionally, Cecilia's seminal land acquisitions occurred during the Great Famine, when lands could be purchased at a bargain, which suggests that she was profiteering. In this light, Cecilia's surname Penifader—derived from *Pennyfather*, or pennypincher—was perhaps well-deserved.

The most interesting mysteries about Cecilia are those that surface in the records just enough to titillate our curiosity before receding into darkness and uncertainty. One such aspect is Cecilia's appearance. Beside the court record detailing Cecilia's will and last testament, there is a scribble of a tall, thin, curly-haired, pointy-nosed woman that may very well be the clerk's rendition of the deceased Cecilia, drawn from memory. The most apparent question about Cecilia, though, is why she decided not to marry, a somewhat unusual life choice in the Middle Ages. Bennett offers a practical explanation: marrying would have required Cecilia to cede herself and all her lands to her husband, a concession she may have been unwilling to make. But there are other explanations as well. Cecilia came of age during the Great Famine and certainly saw many acquaintances die. While highly improbable, it is not implausible that the love of Cecilia's life numbered among the dead. Perhaps slightly more probable, Cecilia may have had a lover who was her social inferior and could not marry him for fear of losing her standing in the community. Bennett wonders what relationship Cecilia had to Robert Malin, to whom she bequeathed a third of all of her landholdings. Once again, it is improbable but not implausible that Cecilia may have had an intimate relationship with Malin.

THEMES, MOTIFS, AND SYMBOLS

THEMES

THE UNIVERSALITY OF WOMEN'S EXPERIENCES In choosing Cecilia Penifader as a biographical subject, Bennett proves that women can represent the common man, not just other women. In an interview, Bennett bemoaned the fact that most books about the medieval peasantry portray peasants as "inherently male." Elsewhere in literature, women represent women, as Jane Austen and Charlotte Brontë's protagonists

M

do, or women represent children, as Lewis Carroll's Alice does, but women never represent mankind. In writing *A Medieval Life*, Bennett sets out to show readers that women can indeed embody the universal human condition as well as men can. While Cecilia did have characteristics and partake in activities that were drastically different from those of men, her status as a peasant was far more significant in dictating the terms of her life than was her status as a woman. As a peasant, Cecilia numbered among a group that comprised over 90 percent of Europe's population and was subject to a lifestyle similar to other peasants around Europe, working in the fields to serve the ruling class's interests. Thus, Cecilia's gender has no effect on her ability to represent the common man's lot in the Middle Ages—that of the peasant.

THE DISENFRANCHISEMENT OF ALL MEDIEVAL WOMEN Aside from representing humanity in general, Cecilia embodied the unique experience of women in the Middle Ages, and, according to Bennett, many of the disadvantages to being a female peasant like Cecilia extended to women of every class. Though women in the gentry could expect deference from both male and female peasants, they, like their sisters in the peasantry, occupied what historians call a "fourth estate," separate from and beneath the three orders of male warriors, male clergy, and male peasants. The law forbade women from serving in politics and did not protect women in matters of inheritance. Also, both peasant women and noble women legally ceded their property and individual rights the moment they married. In domestic life, the great majority of women could expect to bear and raise children, serve as helpmates to their husbands, prepare food, and repair clothes. Thus, gender rules proved in many cases to be strong enough to bridge great distinctions of rank and status.

SOCIAL CLASS AS DESTINY Bennett's detailed depiction of Cecilia's life makes clear that Cecilia was born into a fixed society that did not allow for the possibility of social mobility. Unlike today, where society is somewhat fluid and allows individuals to move through its ranks, the medieval social system fixed the nobility and the peasantry in place. From a very early age, Cecilia knew that her station in life as a peasant woman was immutable and that efforts to rise above her caste would be both futile and unwelcome by her superiors. In a sense, her status at birth was her destiny. During the entire Middle Ages, a period of approximately 1,000 years, very few individuals were able to transcend the circumstances of their birth. Bennett's mention of Robert Grosseteste, a twelfth-century peasant whose unequaled brilliance made it possible for him to teach at Oxford and later become a bishop, is the exception to the rule. Besides Grosseteste, medieval life was static to the extent that Cecilia, who never even met a member of the gentry, probably didn't entertain the thought of what it would be like to live as a lady of the gentry. Instead, she likely limited her ambition to the peasant order, within which she was able to achieve relative prosperity and eminence.

MOTIFS

FAMILY Bennett's constant references to Cecilia in the context of her kin emphasize the central role that family played during the Middle Ages. Not only was family the basic unit of social organization, but it was also the most significant determinant of an individual's path in life. Since a person's social standing was primarily determined by birth, his or her destiny depended entirely on the family into which he or she was born. Cecilia's wealthy parents enabled her to succeed by providing her with the capital to purchase her first parcels of land; by nourishing her better than other families could nurture their own children; and by acquainting her with Brigstock and Stanion's more important citizens. Cecilia was especially fortunate to have the parents she did, since custom did not require peasants to provide for anyone but their first-born sons. In this light, family is an even more powerful force in an individual's life: it is the economic and social wellspring from which an individual emerges and the basic network through which an individual comes into contact with others.

THOSE WHO WORK, THOSE WHO PRAY, THOSE WHO FIGHT The mantra "those who work, those who pray, those who fight" appears in various forms throughout *A Medieval Life* and clearly shows the social order of the Middle Ages. From an early age, Cecilia put the people around her into three categories: the peasants, who labored for the benefit of others; the clergy, who tended to the salvation of others' souls; and the knights, who provided protection. This system of stratification was a solid, absolute law of existence, and people were expected to follow it as if God had ordained it. Indeed, in many cases the clergy did offer this tripartite scheme as divinely inspired, explaining that the three orders were interdependent and that each order worked for the other two orders' benefit. In practice, the social harmony engendered by this system of social organization was fallacious because peasants were deemed of lesser value than the other two orders. This inequality led to the exploitation of peasant labor by the ruling classes. This tripartite idea reinforced a peasant's understanding of him- or herself as one whom God put upon the earth to work.

THE NUMBER THREE Aspects of medieval life are often neatly divisible into three parts, and people probably considered the number three to have magical significance. Cecilia's world is nearly entirely divided in threes: the social order consisted of three parts; the main political establishments entailed three overlapping institutions (village, parish, and manor); and there were three main economic markets (land, labor, and trade). The root of this fascination with three probably comes from the Bible, in which the number three is fraught with special meaning. The clergy surely employed this reasoning when relaying the Three Orders to the peasants, perhaps arguing that the organization of clergy, elite, and peasants was as natural as Father, Son, and Holy Spirit. The peasants demonstrated that they absorbed the weight of this concept when they devised a three-field system of farming, in which peasants rotated crops among three fields each year. If anything, this phenomenon suggests that the people of the Middle Ages tended to live in keen observation of and conformity to ritual and religious teachings.

SYMBOLS

SURNAMES When Cecilia was born, surnames were beginning to grow popular as a way to furnish information about an individual or family. Cecilia's surname, Penifader, stems from the word *pennyfather* and perhaps indicates that Cecilia's paternal grandfather was miserly or greedy. Robert Grosseteste, a twelfth-century peasant who was so intelligent that he rose to the rank of bishop, probably earned his name as a result of being so clever ("Grosseteste" translates to "large head"). In both cases, these surnames symbolize the power that society has over the individual vis-à-vis labeling and influencing public perception of that individual.

THE GREAT FAMINE, THE BLACK DEATH Many peasants readily believed that these two catastrophes were manifestations of God's wrath. In response, the people prayed with renewed fervor, hoping that God would relent and end their suffering. Ironically, crime increased dramatically during the Great Famine, ushering in a new, less trusting era.

IMPORTANT QUOTATIONS EXPLAINED

---

1. *Most medieval people were not knights, kings, churchmen, or merchants. Most (more than nine out of ten) were peasants who eked out hard livings from the land. This book tells the story of one such peasant.*

This comment, located in the first paragraph of Chapter 1, "Introduction," redirects readers' focus from the traditional association of medieval history with noblemen, kings, and clergy, to a view of medieval history that accounts for the overwhelming majority of people who lived through those times: the peasantry. In this light, Bennett bluntly offers the mission statement of her book, a detailed picture of medieval rural society constructed around the life of one peasant. In a more subtle way, Bennett exposes the irony inherent in medieval history by drawing attention to the fact that the kings, knights, and clergy who reside in mainstream history are the very people who exist at the margins of medieval society, while the peasants, who comprise mainstream society, exist in the margins of history. Bennett's clear insight in this passage not only helps to prime the reader for her alternative view of peasant society but also lends credence to her focus on the subject of a female peasant, a substantially more marginalized historical figure than the male peasant.

2. *"When Adam delved and Eve span, / Who then was a gentleman?"*

Though this peasant refrain came during the Peasants' Revolt of 1381, decades after Cecilia's death, Bennett includes it in Chapter 3, "Lords, Ladies, and Peasants," in order to illustrate that peasants did in fact question the status quo that placed them at the bottom of the social hierarchy. By alluding to Adam and Eve, the peasants responsible for the 1381 rebellion challenged the biblical justification of the social order that the clergy gave them. Their song captured the argument that just as there was no pretense of aristocracy in God's first incarnation of man, so there should be no distinctions of class that left the many-numbered peasantry at a disadvantage to the lords and ladies in the minority. Unlike the grudging medieval peasants, Adam and Eve only for themselves, not for others. Thus, this quotation highlights the hypocrisy of a ruling class that exploited religion to keep the peasant class at bay.

This quotation also reveals that peasants were aware of the ruling class's strategy for controlling them and thus regarded themselves at odds with their supposed social superiors. Many peasants probably believed that the social order could be crudely divided into two, rather than three, classes: the haves and the have-nots. Many peasants must have chaffed at their perpetual suppression. Given the tenor of the peasants' disgruntlement only a few decades after Cecilia's death, we may assume that Cecilia herself felt at least some bitterness toward the landed elite.

3. *As Cecilia's kin argued over her lands, her mental health, and her last actions, they acted out the oldest and most enduring story in peasant communities: the story of inheritance, kinship, and land.*

This remark, which occurs at the end of Chapter 6, "Kin and Household," reveals the importance of birth and family as the chief determinants of a peasant's quality of life. Just as Cecilia and her siblings benefited greatly from the inheritance that their parents left them, Cecilia's family relied on taking over Cecilia's assets upon her death in order to improve their social standing and fatten their purses. Cecilia may have lived independently as a *singlewoman*, but her familial ties nonetheless became increasingly relevant and fraught with complication upon her death in 1344. Her sister Christina and nephew Martin clamored to be chosen as Cecilia's sole heir, a recognition that would have brought them Cecilia's total landholdings, while the inheritors named in Cecilia's will (Matilda Kroyl, Robert Malin, and John Penifader) attempted to defend their claims to Cecilia's lands. The imbroglio that ensued centered on the jury's opinion as to who was Cecilia's closest relation, revealing the connection between inheritance and kinship. As Martin and Christina both believed, their close blood ties to Cecilia entitled them to Cecilia's land. Ultimately, the jury agreed with them and awarded the land to Christina, who promptly transferred half of the holdings to Martin.

The argument that erupted over Cecilia's will also demonstrates the value of land both as a source of family pride and as a source of wealth. Land was so important that family members would fight bitterly over its bequest. Clearly, Cecilia's relative prosperity and high social standing in Brigstock were derived from her and her family's massive landholdings. The fact that she did not leave her own land and migrate to another manor indicates that she was wealthy enough to remain where she had been born. Cecilia may have taken pride in the land that she held and managed, seeing it as an important part of her life and legacy. In battling for Cecilia's landholdings, Cecilia's relatives may have been after Cecilia's wealth, but they also may have been motivated by their desire to uphold the Penifader legacy. Such familial pride with regard to land ownership was the impetus for innumerable territorial disputes throughout history.

4. *Some people imagine that a sense of community was better achieved in past times—that it was free of conflict, strengthened by homogeneity, and purified by isolation. This is a fantasy. Cecilia's experience of community was much like ours: powerful and compelling in conception, fractured and partial in reality.*

In this passage, which appears at the end of Chapter 8, "Community," Bennett dismisses the historical view of the Middle Ages that nostalgically whitewashes the contradictions, discrepancies, and differences of experience that were prevalent in medieval society. While medieval society was more uniform and peaceful and less frenetic than modern society in many ways, it nevertheless proved to be diverse. Though English peasants were all alike in their inability to own land and in their social inferiority to the clergy and gentry, they were always ready to differentiate themselves from one another. To do so, they exploited economic disparity within the peasant class, which led to wildly different standards of living from one peasant to the next. The Penifaders were successful in this enterprise. They obtained land and wealth and gained political power in the community. Many of their neighbors, however, were not as fortunate, and were seen as social inferiors. Resentment over economic disparity often undermined the strong sense of communal solidarity that the peasants generally felt. The Penifaders may have exhibited compassion and pity for the hopeless poor, but that did not relieve the desperation some peasants felt, a desperation that often led to anger and crime.

---

5. *In such cases, their desperate expedients were her timely opportunities.*

This statement, which appears at the end of Chapter 7, "An Economy of Makeshifts," fleshes out an important aspect of Cecilia's character: her hardheartedness in profiting from others' misfortunes. The economy in which Cecilia lived, especially during the Great Famine when she launched her career in landholding, was an economy of scarcity. The overabundance of people combined with the shortage of resources drove many peasants to sell their land in order to buy food they could not grow. Land prices decreased, but peasants were forced to sell out of desperation. At this time, Cecilia took advantage of her neighbors' hard luck in order to amass landholdings. In her land-grabbing endeavor, Cecilia may have shown herself to be somewhat callous and exploitative, which indicates that she was more concerned with ensuring her own economic security than with neighborly goodwill. Whether or not her actions caused resentment among her fellow villagers, Cecilia clearly did right by herself and her family and benefited by seizing the opportunities generated by her neighbors' "desperate expedients."

M

Meridian

Alice Walker
(1944–)

CONTEXT

Though Alice Walker has worked in a variety of genres, including children's literature, poetry, nonfiction, and screenwriting, she is best known for her novels, which give voice to the concerns of an often doubly oppressed group: African American women. She is best known for her Pulitzer Prize–winning novel *The Color Purple*, which extends and solidifies many of the themes she first touched upon in her early work, which includes *Meridian*. In many ways, *Meridian* anticipates and paves the way for Walker's future preoccupations: it focuses on women's lives and examines how the past and the present interconnect and construct the future. *Meridian*, Walker's second work of long fiction, is set against the turbulent backdrop of the civil rights movement, which gained force in the 1960s, triggering sit-ins, demonstrations, and protests against the racist and segregationist policies that controlled and shaped the lives of African Americans in the South.

Meridian is in some respects autobiographical, but Walker and Meridian Hill, the novel's protagonist, differ in many significant ways. Both Walker and Meridian were raised in rural Georgia and became pregnant as young students, though Walker, unlike Meridian, did not have the child. While Meridian's relationship with her mother was fraught with problems, Walker blossomed under the influence of her mother, Minnie. Minnie bought the young Walker three pivotal and symbolic gifts: a sewing machine to encourage self-sufficiency, a suitcase to nudge her curious and errant spirit, and a typewriter to nurture the gifted wordsmith and budding writer in her daughter. Additionally, *Meridian*'s Saxon College is loosely based on Spelman College, the all-black women's college in Atlanta where Walker started her formal education in 1961. At the time, Atlanta was a hotbed of civil rights activism, but like the young women of Saxon, Spelman's students were viewed as ladies in training, too refined and upstanding to throw themselves into the fray of social protest. Walker resisted such rigid control of her life and transferred to Sarah Lawrence College, north of New York City. Walker returned to Georgia during the summer of 1965 to canvass voters in Liberty County. When she sat down to write *Meridian* almost a decade later, she drew from these experiences walking the dusty roads and encouraging residents to register to vote.

A tireless crusader on behalf of women, Walker in her later career defended her work against censorship and continued to speak out against the horrors of domestic violence, sexual abuse, and genital mutilation, a ritualistic practice employed by several native African cultures. Not precisely aligned with broad feminist concerns, Walker has often labeled herself a "womanist," establishing her primary goal as a writer and individual to free women from oppression in all of its forms. Walker is also a student of history, and she strives to create a dialogue in her work between the past and the present in an attempt to elucidate eternal truths as well as eternal struggles and hardships. Like Meridian's father, Walker has an abiding love of and respect for Native Americans and sees their plight as instructive and an important correlative to the black experience in the United States throughout the centuries.

Walker's various aesthetic and social concerns are harmoniously combined in *Meridian*, an exploration of a young woman's coming of age and her journey from loneliness, guilt, and self-doubt, to self-acceptance, empowerment, and love. Like Walker once was, Meridian is set on a path to greater self-realization and endures the hardships of firmly and irrevocably establishing her identity amid the chaos of social upheaval, sexual alienation, and people who are not always approving or supportive of either the woman or the cause.

PLOT OVERVIEW

Truman Held arrives in Chicokema, Georgia, to meet up with his former lover, Meridian Hill. He first sees her staring down a manned tank as she escorts local schoolchildren to a sideshow attraction displaying a mummified woman, on a day the children, mostly poor and black, are forbidden to attend. After collapsing and being brought home unconscious, she and Truman catch up. The action then shifts, in a flashback, to New York City, where, ten years ago, Meridian is unwilling to assert that she will kill on behalf of a black revolutionary organization, to the dismay of the others assembled. Then, even further back in time, Meridian, at the age of thirteen, is unwilling to accept Jesus into her life, a decision that prompts her mother to withdraw her love. Meridian, back in the present, has decided to return to her roots as a former civil rights worker, and vows to live and work amongst the people. Truman does not understand the mysterious illness that grips her, causing her to experience fainting spells and paralysis. He admits his inability to let her go.

The action shifts to Saxon College, where Meridian and Anne-Marion first meet. While canvassing a local neighborhood for voters, Meridian meets the Wild Child, a pregnant, homeless teenager. Meridian captures her, then bathes and feeds her. When Meridian makes phone calls to find additional assistance for her, the Wild Child escapes, runs out into the street, is struck by a car, and dies. Meridian, Anne-Marion, and other students and neighborhood residents carry the Wild Child's casket, leading the funeral cortege onto the campus grounds. But the president of the college denies them access to the chapel for the services. That night the students riot and chop down the Sojourner, the school's iconic magnolia tree.

In another flashback, Meridian's father deeds sixty acres of his farmland back to the Cherokee who once owned it, specifically to Walter Longknife. He camps on the parcel for a brief period in the summer then cedes ownership back to Meridian's father. The area, with its serpent-shaped mound, is then made into a historical site that bars blacks. Meridian and her father are no longer allowed access to the pit in the serpent's tail where they experienced the swooning, paralysis, and strange manifestations that are part of their unique family condition.

As a teenager, uninformed about sex, Meridian becomes pregnant, marries, and drops out of school to have the baby boy, who makes her feel indifferent at best. Around the time her marriage to Eddie is dissolving, Meridian notices the presence of white civil rights workers in a black neighborhood. Later, the house in which they are staying is bombed. The incident spurs Meridian to volunteer for the cause. At the headquarters, she meets Truman. Soon they are demonstrating together and getting beaten, arrested, and jailed. Meridian's mother disapproves of Meridian's radical political activities. Unexpectedly, Meridian is offered a scholarship to Saxon College. Her friends attempt to convince her mother that it is a great opportunity for Meridian. Giving up Eddie Jr., Meridian starts school but is plagued with the guilt that always dogs her.

Meridian tries her best to battle loneliness and adjust to college life. After the Wild Child incident, she moves off campus, actively continuing her civil rights protests and demonstrations. She also falls in love with Truman. The two begin dating, but their newfound bliss as a couple is compromised by the arrival of college students—white women—from the North who volunteer to assist the movement. Many invoke a racial patronage or romantically fetishize the foreign, black culture that they are fully confronting for the first time. Truman is taken by one of the new arrivals, Lynne, and the two begin dating. Although Truman and Meridian briefly resume sexual relations, Truman continues to pursue his budding relationship with Lynne. Pregnant, Meridian has an abortion and gets her tubes tied. After Lynne leaves, Truman attempts to rekindle his former love for Meridian, asking her to have his children. Meridian, in response, strikes him with her bookbag, cutting his cheek.

With graduation approaching, Meridian again falls ill, losing her sight and lapsing into unconsciousness. She stays in bed for a month. Miss Winters, one of Saxon's few black instructors, nurses her back to health. Anne-Marion, who has also been at Meridian's side, eventually concludes that she is incapable of loving Meridian and turns her back on her friend. Truman and Lynne, now married, are living in Mississippi, where her whiteness begins to endanger them and the movement when a fellow rights worker, Tommy Odds, has the lower half of one of his arms shot off. Increasingly, Lynne is excluded from the marches and meetings. Despite having a daughter, Camara, Truman grows more and more distant from his wife. He drives to Alabama to visit Meridian. Newly obsessed with his former lover, he tries to win her back, but Meridian spurns his advances. After the death of Camara, Lynne visits Meridian, whose illness has advanced and claimed most of her hair. Lynne is bitter over the slow dissolve of her marriage and the way her once-idealistic life has turned out. She has come in search of Truman, whose visits to Meridian have become more frequent.

The action then shifts, in flashback, to Lynne's younger years, when she leaves her family for her new life with Truman and the movement. After the shooting, Tommy Odds rapes her. He returns with three friends and encourages them to do the same, but they refuse. Lynne, hysterical, entertains thoughts of leaving and tells Truman what happened, but he doesn't believe her. Tommy tells Truman that Lynne is with him solely to atone for her sins, out of guilt for the racism blacks had suffered for centuries. Lynne and Truman grow increasingly distant, as Lynne eventually seduces or succumbs to the sexual advances of his friends and other men in the community. Eventually, the men tire of her and, pregnant, she moves to New York and lives on welfare. Truman also moves to New York, where he becomes an artist. When Lynne comes to his apartment uptown to tell him that Camara has been attacked by a man and hospitalized, she discovers that he is living with a young blond woman. After Camara dies, Truman sends for Meridian, who arrives to comfort him and Lynne. Lynne recalls her impressions of southern Jews and the way they treated her. She eventually resolves she has no regrets for leaving her past, and its association with white oppressors, behind.

The novel's final section opens with the Atlanta funeral cortege of Martin Luther King, Jr. Eight years later, Meridian struggles with questions of radicalism and how the movement ultimately turned out. Truman finds it easier to leave such issues alone. Meridian remains in her small town, advocating for the black residents to vote and try to change their lot. She recalls the time she took to regularly attend church services. Once, an old man, whose radical son had been killed while working for the movement, addressed the congregation. Meridian regained her wavering desire to kill on behalf of the rights of blacks. She and Truman continue their voter-registration drives in earnest. Truman tells Lynne he loves her and will support her as a friend. Truman asks Meridian to love him as she once did. Meridian readily asserts that she does love him but that her feelings have changed. Cured of her illness, Meridian prepares to move on, leaving Truman behind to continue the work that she started in Chicokema. Reading the poems she has posted on the wall, Truman falls to the floor in a swoon. Upon awakening, he concludes that he must take up the internal struggle of which Meridian has finally freed herself.

CHARACTER LIST

Meridian Hill A young civil rights worker and the protagonist of the novel. Thin and slight, with deep brown skin, Meridian is a deeply sad and serious presence. Bold, defiant, and courageous, Meridian seems older than she is. Cynical and often pessimistic, she does not fill her life and perceptions with hope. Rather, a stubborn ambivalence often prevails. Later, a serene, detached calm settles on her life. Almost repulsed by sex and the physical aggressions of men, she ultimately prefers her own company. As her illness progresses and her hair falls out, she takes to wearing a knitted cap at all times.

M

Truman Held Meridian's former lover and an active participant in the civil rights movement. Truman is a handsome man whose intelligence borders on arrogance. His air of pretension and his desire to impress set him apart. He often lapses into French when he knows that the person he is addressing has little or no grasp of the language. Passionate and emotionally volatile, he is unable to resist the powerful pull of the women in his life. At the same time, he can be aloof and distant, an emotional coward who would rather run away from a problem than confront it directly.

Lynne Rabinowitz A white Jew from the North, and Truman's eventual wife. Lynne is an argumentative, slightly aggressive woman who is seduced by ideology and her own heightened sense of self-importance, but she is also a selfless and dedicated worker in the movement. Her involvement is rooted partially in guilt and an exaggerated sense of her own complicity in racial injustice and the racism meted out by legions of American whites. Later, her idealism turns to regret, defeat, and a steely resignation as she is plagued with jealousy—of Meridian, in particular—and dissatisfaction of the course her life has taken.

Anne-Marion Coles Meridian's friend at Saxon College and a radical member of the civil rights movement. Anne-Marion is judgmental, opinionated, and easily angered, and she has a strong desire to succeed. She is also radical and rebellious, and she brings an intensity to her contributions to the civil rights movement. She cuts off her hair and openly disavows any belief in the Christian faith. At her worst, she is self-centered and incapable of true friendship or emotional vulnerability in any form.

Gertrude Hill Meridian's mother. A former teacher, Gertrude is deeply religious and has a rigid and unyielding sense of morality and propriety. Despite her deep reserves of faith, she is a fragile spirit who is not up to the tasks and demands of being a wife and mother. At times bitter and spiteful, she feels trapped and short-changed by how her life has turned out and is resigned to self-sacrifice. There is a sense of martyrdom in her acceptance of her status as a second-class citizen. Her stalwart sense of self-denial and her single-minded pursuit of virtue and rightness intimidate Meridian and those around her, making them feel insufficient and weak.

Meridian's Father A former history teacher and farmer. Dreamy, quiet, and unambitious, Meridian's father prefers mostly his own company. He has an abiding interest in historical studies, and he feels a profound connection to the Native Americans who lived on and worked the land before him. Although he is a practicing Baptist, he acknowledges the credence and viability of Native American spirituality as an alternative to the deep Christian faith his wife subscribes to.

Tommy Odds A friend of Truman's who works on voter-registration drives in Mississippi. Tommy is dedicated and charismatic, and he is successful at getting more southern blacks to register and vote. Later, his less appealing qualities emerge, as his anger and resentment over losing part of his arm boil over into rape and other violence. His desire for revenge and his wish to blame Lynne for his troubles blind him to reason and mute his otherwise kind and generous nature.

Eddie Meridian's husband and the father of her son. Eddie is Meridian's high school boyfriend, a stereotypical high school sports hero who never outgrows the popularity and glory he achieved via his athletic prowess and charm. Eddie is smart and hardworking but lacks the ambition and the ability to pull himself and his family out of their current station. His immaturity is evident through his infidelity and lack of serious commitment to his new family.

The Wild Child A pregnant orphan who lives in the slums surrounding Saxon College. Believed to be about thirteen, the Wild Child is a tough survivor who lives in an abandoned building and survives through scavenging. Uncouth and untouched by any civilizing influences, she has smoked and cursed since an early age. She is also elusive and wary of other people until Meridian seizes her.

Louvinie A West-African slave girl on the Saxon plantation. Louvinie has a jutting chin and is commonly thought to be so unattractive that she is relegated to working in the kitchen garden. Louvinie always wears black headrags, and many people believe she is incapable of smiling. Children are drawn to her and her ability to tell frightening tales of the supernatural.

Miss Winters A music professor at Saxon College. Sallow, with bulging black eyes and a blue wig, Miss Winters is worldly and learned and one of only three black instructors at the college. She teaches whatever she pleases and always manages to skirt the disapproval or control of the administration. A kindly maternal presence, she offers Meridian the warmth and forgiveness that Meridian's own mother cannot give her.

Mr. Reynolds A professor at Saxon College and Meridian's employer. Mr. Reynolds is tall and bony, with short white hair, a drooping left eyelid, mostly false teeth, and sour breath. He is a predator who offers Meridian money and food in exchange for sexual favors.

ANALYSIS OF MAJOR CHARACTERS

MERIDIAN HILL The fraught relationship that Meridian has with her mother casts a shadow over much of her life, and she struggles to overcome this and other obstacles as she searches for self-awareness and self-acceptance. Her mother's emotional distance, disapproving nature, and moral superiority fill Meridian with guilt and sadness, which persist well into adulthood. Meridian longs for guidance and a sense of belonging. Unsure of the existence of God and her own relationship to the spiritual world, Meridian finds that traditional paths and explanations do not comfort her. Instead, she turns to the civil rights movement, which gains force and momentum during her young adult years. Ultimately, she struggles with her own sense of sacrifice and dedication to the cause. She questions her own revolutionary impulses after admitting her inability to kill on behalf of the movement. Feeling a gulf in her life between the ideals of the other civil rights activists and the ways by which they actually go about implementing change, Meridian returns to her roots, working and living in often-impoverished and rural communities.

Meridian selflessly helps others in order to compensate for the guidance she never received from her mother. The work, coupled with her bravery and determination, result in the emergence of a calm, sustaining, and growing self-awareness. At the beginning of the novel, she is a broken and damaged individual, mourning a love and loss she cannot verbalize. At the end, she emerges whole and healthy, thanks to her struggles and the hard-won wisdom she has acquired along the way. Meridian ultimately realizes that no one person, movement, or institution can offer her the assistance she seeks, and she finally turns to herself. Meridian's journey to self-discovery is marked by physical and sexual abuse, a broken marriage, and a child she decides to give away. Her strange illness is in some ways a manifestation of her instability and insecurity. Her bouts of lost consciousness and episodes of paralysis signal that she is a woman without an identity or a sustaining inner life. Ultimately, she realizes that her power lies in her unique and unwavering courage.

TRUMAN HELD Truman faces numerous influences and desires in his life, which ultimately conflict and scatter him, making his personality ambiguous and unresolved. His inner conflict is expressed mainly in his fixation on the women in his life and the grip that they have on him. Meridian and Lynne represent two extremes, and Truman is drawn to each but is unable to commit to either. Meridian ultimately frees herself of his mercurial affections and his confusing presence, which are obstacles to her physical and emotional recovery. Initially, in their student days, she believes that Truman is guilty of the same overly reductive and short-sighted racial patronage as Lynne, and that he fetishizes Lynne's whiteness just as Lynne lives vicariously through his blackness. Later, as an artist in Harlem, Truman can only objectify black women, casting them in mute marble or obsessively painting representations of Meridian that are far from the woman she actually is. Just as Lynne views blacks and black life aesthetically, Truman turns to artistic representation to confront and work out his conflicted sense of his role and identity as a black man and his understanding of race and race relations.

Truman subscribes to traditional notions of gender roles, in which the man is the dominant force in a relationship, and his assumptions of male dominance are the source of his arrogance and short-sightedness. He expects women to uphold a standard of purity that he does not apply to himself, and in this way, he is a victim of the sexual attitudes of his world and times. He is drawn to powerful, intelligent, and charismatic women who only reveal the conflicted and confused man who exists beneath the swagger and stereotypical male behavior. Truman also struggles with his relationship to black culture. His pretension and desire for worldliness have led him to study abroad in France, and his dialogue is peppered with rudimentary French phrases. His interest in the movement, to which he initially dedicates much time and interest, sours. Only when he is freed of the various confusing presences and influences that mark his life is he able to confront himself as an individual and fill his life with purpose and meaning.

LYNNE RABINOWITZ When Lynne first appears in *Meridian*, she is an idealistic student who has arrived at Saxon College to take part in the allure of the burgeoning civil rights movement. She and the other northern transplants adopt a patronizing attitude toward the black women of Saxon, exoticizing and romanticizing their "otherness." Lynne eventually confesses that she equates the often-gritty reality of black life in the South with "art," trivializing the institutionalized racism that controls and regulates most aspects of black life. Lynne uses the movement to transcend her sanitized upbringing, though her guilt at coming from a white, privileged background becomes all-consuming. Her idealism and personal agenda initially hinder her effectiveness as a civil rights worker. On a voter-registration drive, accompanied by Meridian, Lynne comes into contact with a variety of impoverished, rural communities. During one visit, Lynne is more interested in arguing with than helping a highly religious woman who trusts her faith, and not the state and federal government, to instigate change in her life.

The gulf between ideology and reality and between theory and practice eventually shrinks for Lynne as she learns to sympathize with the reality of racism as it affects individual lives. Lynne feels she must go to greater lengths to establish herself within the black community as well as in the movement. However, her whiteness will always set her apart, and she remains an outsider, ultimately pushed to the fringes of the movement. Lynne's racial guilt is unanswerable, and she sinks into a slovenly, stagnant state. Eventually, she feels she must be the sacrifice that atones for years of racial injustice, and she does not resist or fight Tommy Odds when his aggressive sexual advances turn to rape. Perversely, she feels that by allowing him to have his way, she'll be atoning for her guilt. After the death of the daughter she has with Truman, she is stricken and dispossessed, with no identifiable future.

THEMES, MOTIFS, AND SYMBOLS

THEMES

THE DIFFICULTY OF IDEALISM *Meridian* is energized by a younger generation coming into its full power and raising its voice in dissent against the institutional racism that prevailed through the 1960s. Through occasionally violent protests and demonstrations, Meridian and other activists attempt to institute change and alter perceptions. Idealistic as they are, they ultimately find various degrees of satisfaction with the goals and ideals of the civil rights movement. Meridian feels that she will always stand on the fringes of the movement since she is unprepared to take her dissent to a radical, if not murderous, level. Lynne struggles with adapting and applying her own idealism to meaningful change in the lives of southern blacks. Truman eventually sours to the movement, having lost sight of its intentions in his self-absorption. In the end, Meridian realizes the fatuousness of dying or killing for the movement, concluding that the battle is won in small ways, such as getting blacks registered to vote and improving the lives of people victimized by the unchecked expression of racism.

THE INTERCONNECTION OF PAST AND PRESENT In *Meridian*, young activists attempt to break with tradition by bringing an end to the racism and segregation that had overshadowed black Americans for centuries. Walker shifts her focus from the present to the past to explore the lives of people who helped pave the way to the present moment. The experiences of Louvinie and Feather Mae, for example, frame the issues that Meridian and her father face. The serpent mound also evokes this powerful historical precedent, serving as a vital connection between Meridian, her father, and the ancestors who came before her. Throughout *Meridian*, Walker stresses the universality of the human experience and suggests that no one has cornered the market on suffering. Rather, many individuals from a variety of groups and backgrounds share a common history of exploitation, guilt, suffering, violence, and, ultimately, freedom, triumph, and acceptance.

MOTIFS

PHYSICAL FRAILTY Meridian is plagued by a mysterious inherited illness, much like epilepsy, which parallels and triggers her spiritual and physical transformation. The sickness renders her unconscious, episodes she refers to as "falling down," and it subjects her to paralysis, blindness, and hair loss. On one hand, the condition connects her directly with her father and great-grandmother, who suffered the same burden. The illness is also the physical rendering of Meridian's deep emotional and spiritual angst, the grief and sadness that have marked and gripped her throughout her life. The illness becomes a means for Meridian to suffer, to perform penance for this ambiguous wrong she felt she has done. It also offers her atonement and, ultimately, self-acceptance. When she is well again, rising out of her sick bed and heading full force into the future, she can finally forgive herself and love and accept herself for who she is.

MERIDIAN Walker prefaces her novel with a lengthy list of definitions and traditional usages of the word *meridian*. A total of twelve different meanings are included for both the word's noun and adjectival form. This alone signifies the fact that Meridian resists easy definition or simple categorization. She is a complex and capacious character whose presence and identity cannot be reduced to a simple phrase or formulation. The term also sets up a comparison between Meridian and the growing civil rights movement. One of the most common definitions of the term is "zenith, the highest point of power, prosperity, splendor." Not only does the novel trace the rise and growing power of social activism, united in the face of racist and segregationist policies, but it also tracks the ascent of Meridian from her spiritual and physical pain to a newly whole being in full charge of her capacities and inner wealth. An alternate meaning, "distinctive character," applies just as well to the novel's protagonist and namesake.

SYMBOLS

THE WILD CHILD The Wild Child, who makes only a brief appearance in *Meridian*, represents the possibility of pursuing life independently, on one's own terms. The Wild Child is an iconic figure—Walker does not even give her a name. The residents of the slums surrounding Saxon College know little of this mysterious, almost-feral girl who rummages for food in garbage cans and has not fully acquired language. Meridian ultimately fails to help her and, in fact, plays a role in her death—the Wild Child cannot be tamed, and she died trying to escape that fate. Like the Wild Child, Meridian strips her life of external influences, material goods, and physical comforts as she moves from community to community, registering voters and fighting racism. Both women live on the fringes of society, away from the scrutiny and judgment of mainstream life. Meridian's great-grandmother, Feather Mae, suggests a similar presence, a free, radical, and unconventional spirit who, after her profound experience in the pit in the serpent mound, renounces all religion not based on physical ecstasy. Later in her life, she took to walking around naked and worshipping the sun. These unique women pursue their lives on their own terms, extolling their fiercely individualistic spirits.

THE TANK The tank sits in the town square in Chicokema, where Meridian is living when the novel opens. Painted white and decorated with red, white, and blue ribbons, it was bought in the 1960s to ward off "outside agitators," those who advocated the extension of civil rights to all of the town's residents, including blacks. Positioned near the tank is a statue of a Confederate soldier, whose leg was permanently crushed when the tank was being put into place. This gestures to the fact that the civil rights movement is like a new civil war, one that has come with great force to replace and supersede that earlier conflict. When Truman meets up with Meridian again after a considerable absence, he witnesses her leading the town's children, forbidden on that day from touring the traveling exhibit, across the square. Men positioned inside the tank move the muzzle and point it directly at her, but she is neither cowed nor deterred. The tank serves as an ironic presence, suggesting that freedom must be defended from those who do not match the tank's white coloring. It also symbolizes the violence and oppression that marked not only the history of slavery but the civil rights movement as well.

THE SOJOURNER The Sojourner is the name given to the largest magnolia tree in the country, which grows in the quadrangle of Saxon College. It is associated with Louvinie, a slave on the plantation whose property would eventually be turned into Saxon College. Louvinie buries her tongue, cut out in punishment for unintentionally causing the death of one of the Saxon children, beneath a scrawny magnolia tree, which eventually grows into the renowned, towering giant. Thus, the magnolia serves as a living reminder of the past, of growth in the face of oppression and the millions of slaves who were silenced, their tongues metaphorically removed, by the institution of slavery. The tree also serves as a source of comfort for the lonely Meridian, who initially has trouble adjusting to college life. At one point, Meridian even chains herself to it to prevent its removal, a task at which she ultimately fails. When the students, in revolt, chop down the tree, the Sojourner's symbolic import changes. Now its destruction represents an abrupt breaking with the past and the racist traditions that marked it.

THE SACRED SERPENT MOUND Like the Sojourner, the serpent mound—and the deep mysterious pit contained in the coil of its tail—is a powerful connection to the past. The ancient mound, built by the region's original Native American inhabitants, is located on a patch of land behind the Hill home. It is a reminder of the need to study, honor, and learn from the past. Meridian's father has a spiritual connection to the lives of people buried there, and he honors the native presence that preceded his own as tenants of the land. The mound, to him, symbolizes the interconnectedness and the universality of human experience. It helps him to contextualize and better understand the black experience by signifying the lives of another marginalized people who were forever altered by a racist white power base. However, just as the land was taken from the Cherokee, Meridian's father is similarly forced to give up ownership of the parcel. Thus, also like the Sojourner, the mound's symbolic meaning and significance change when the area is taken over by the government and turned into a historical park that initially bars blacks from entering. What had once been a powerful connection to the past becomes a radical disconnection from it, as the site is exploited and its deep spiritual, cultural, and historical significance is trivialized and commercialized.

IMPORTANT QUOTATIONS EXPLAINED

---

1. *They have a saying for people who fall down as I do: If a person is hit hard enough, even if she stands, she falls.*

Meridian speaks these words in the novel's opening chapter, "The Last Return." She is referring to her illness, which causes her to collapse and lapse into unconsciousness. Her words are prophetic, as they also reference the various physical beatings and torments she experiences while protesting on behalf of the civil rights movement. Both her condition and the violence meted out by policemen and others unsympathetic to the cause serve as powerful threats that unsettle Meridian, qualifying her identity and stability. Meridian's words probe the nature of strength and resistance and the challenges, both internal and social, with which she is saddled. No matter how strong she is in the face of adversity, hatred and violence leach away her dignity, resolve, and her belief in herself. Meridian learns that, like racism, her "peculiar madness" is a legacy, an affliction that affected her great-grandmother and her father as well. Meridian's life is overburdened with this overwhelming genetic inheritance, just as her daily life is affected by segregation, which dehumanize those who are subjected to it. No matter how strong her resolve, Meridian's body and psyche bear the scars of the physical and emotional assaults that she must constantly repel.

---

2. *Her father sighed. "I never said either side was innocent or guilty, just ignorant. They've been a part of it, we've been a part of it, everybody's been a part of it for a long time."*

Meridian's father makes this comment in the chapter entitled "Indians and Ecstasy." It comes as part of a quasi-argument he is having with his wife, Gertrude, occasioned by his decision to return the parcel of land containing the serpent mound to the Cherokee Walter Longknife. Gertrude believes that she and her family bear no responsibility to those who owned and tended the land before them, while her husband views returning the acreage as an attempt to set right a history of abuse and exploitation. Meridian's father gains perspective on the civil rights movement and the treatment of blacks by looking at them in the context of past wrongs and injustices. By referring to the hardship experienced by a different group of people, Native Americans forced to give up their land and relocate to reservations to the west, he attempts to look further than white/black issues and consider broader humanitarian abuses. He argues that it is dangerous to ignore or minimize the plight of others who have been the victims of racial hatred. At the same time, he acknowledges the role black settlers had in wresting control of Native American-held lands in the Southeast.

---

3. *It was just that they knew, as she knew about them. That they were transplanted, as they had always been, to a place where they fit like extra toes on a foot. Where they were trusted by no one, exploited, when possible, by anyone with political ambitions.*

M

This comment appears in the third "Lynne" chapter and refers to Lynne's evolving perceptions of race, religion, ethnic identity, and what it means to be a minority in the South. Lynne is musing on a Jewish-owned deli in the town where she lived with Truman and worked for the civil rights movement. Lynne feels she was given a cold reception each time she shopped there because she was in an interracial marriage. However, she realizes that the experience of many southern Jews, subjected to anti-Semitism, was similar to the racism faced by blacks. Lynne is an outsider in both the community and the movement because of her color and religious upbringing, and she feels this separation more pointedly as the novel progresses. In drawing these conclusions about the Jews she met in her town, Lynne acknowledges a common history of dislocation, loss of identity, struggle, and mourning, whether via slavery, segregation, racism, genocide, or anti-Semitism. One history of abuse is no more tragic than another, yet the ultimate irony is that Lynne has chosen to align herself with an oppressed people who fail to acknowledge their essential commonality. She is a figure forced to the fringes, a wanderer uprooted time and again, with no sense of belonging.

---

4. *"Your ambivalence will always be deplored by people who consider themselves revolutionists, and your unorthodox behavior will cause traditionalists to gnash their teeth," said Truman, who was not, himself, concerned about either group.*

This statement appears in the last chapter, "Release," and clarifies Meridian's elusive qualities and her mysterious, difficult-to-summarize nature. Meridian searches for meaning and acceptance in the civil rights movement, but she finds that even though her ardor comes naturally and she is able to make significant contributions, the group's sensibilities do little to resolve her struggle for self-acceptance. At a gathering in New York City, Meridian refuses to avow her willingness to kill for the cause, despite being taunted, and Truman affirms that the thought of Meridian killing someone is ludicrous. Meridian finds she must extricate herself from such radical factions and pursue her own brand of social activism, returning to her roots in rural communities in Alabama and Georgia. Her methods of resistance are still unconventional, and she garners a sort of cult following as people feed and care for her. Her social actions are eventually labeled as "performances," akin to a spiritual revival, in which Meridian concludes the event by collapsing from emotional and physical exhaustion, her illness once again sapping her strength. In the end, though, it is this unconventional and fiercely independent spirit that leads Meridian to self-salvation, health, and wholeness.

---

5. *He . . . wondered if Meridian knew that the sentence of bearing the conflict in her own soul which she had imposed on herself—and lived through—must now be borne in terror by all the rest of them.*

This is the final sentence in the novel. Meridian, like a phoenix, has emerged whole and restored after facing various trials, and her transformation is quiet yet triumphant. Now Meridian packs her meager belongings and moves on to the next town and the next challenge, armed with her newfound strength and resolve. In her stead, Truman is struck with her mysterious illness, falling to the ground after reading the words of Meridian's poem in which she finally forgives him. The poem goes on to say that she loves him and that their innocence and purity have given way to wisdom and healing. Regaining consciousness after his spell, Truman wakes to find his cheek resting on Meridian's cap, the covering she no longer needs since her hair has grown back in. She can now expose herself to the world, no longer oppressed by her shame and guilt. In her absence, Truman becomes Meridian's surrogate. She has gone before the others and paved the way to self-acceptance and self-knowledge. At the conclusion of the novel, it is Truman's turn to embark on a similar, albeit difficult, journey toward the same goal.

Middlemarch

George Eliot
(1819–1880)

CONTEXT

Mary Anne Evans, better known by her male penname, George Eliot, was born on November 22, 1819, in Warwickshire, England. Daughter of an estate agent, she was raised with a Low Church religious background, an approach to Christianity associated with reform of the rigid Church structure. This liberal environment influenced her writing from the beginning. After translating Strauss's *Life of Christ* in 1846, she began writing for the *Westminster Review* in 1850 and became assistant editor in 1851. The *Westminster Review*, founded by liberal pillars John Stuart Mill and Jeremy Bentham, was the leading journal for philosophical radicals. In 1857, Eliot published "Amos Barton," the first of the "Scenes of Clerical Life," in *Blackwood's Magazine*. The collection of these "Scenes" launched Eliot's career as a writer. Her most famous work, *Middlemarch*, was published in 1871. In the 1850s, Eliot began her affair with the married English philosopher and literary critic George Henry Lewes. Although Lewes's wife refused to get a divorce, Eliot and Lewes lived together until Lewes's death in 1878. Two years later, Eliot married John Cross, and American banker, who was twenty years her junior. She died in 1880 at the age of sixty-one of a kidney ailment.

Eliot scorned the stereotypical female novelist; rather than writing the silly, unrealistic romantic tales expected of women writers, she wrote according to her own tastes. Her first attempt to write *Middlemarch*, now her most famous novel, ended in failure and despair. Shortly after this initial failure, she began a short novella entitled *Miss Brooke*. The writing proceeded quickly, and she later integrated the novella into *Middlemarch*. The novel was published serially in eight parts.

Middlemarch is a novel of epic proportions, but it transforms the idea of an epic. Epics usually narrate the tale of one important hero who experiences grand adventure, and they usually interpret events according to a grand design of fate. Every event has immediate, grand consequences. Kings and dynasties are made and unmade in epic tales. The subtitle of *Middlemarch*, "A Study of Provincial Life," indicates how *Middlemarch* represents the lives of ordinary people, not the grand adventures of princes and kings. The novel represents the spirit of nineteenth-century England through the unknown, historically unremarkable common people. The small community of Middlemarch is thrown into relief against the background of larger social transformations, rather than the other way around.

Middlemarch takes place while England is in the process of rapid industrialization. Social mobility is increasing rapidly. With the rise of the merchant middle class, one's birth no longer necessarily determines one's social class for life, and chance occurrences can make or break a person's success. Moreover, there is no single coherent religious order. Evangelical Protestants, Catholics, and Anglicans live side by side. As a result, religious conflicts abound in the novel, particularly those centering on the rise of Evangelical Protestantism, a primarily middle-class religion that created heated doctrinal controversy.

Middlemarch readers will be astonished by the novel's amazingly complex social world. Eliot continually uses the metaphor of a web to describe the town's social relations, and she intricately weaves together the disparate life experiences of a large cast of characters. Many characters subscribe to a worldview while others want to find a worldview in order to organize their lives. This absence of a single, triumphant worldview to organize all life is the basic design of *Middlemarch*.

No one occupies the center of the novel as the most important or influential person. Middlemarch social relations are indeed like a web, but the web has no center. Each individual occupies a point in the web, affecting and affected by the other points. Eliot's admirable effort to represent this web in great detail makes her novel epic in length and scope. Unlike in an epic, however, no single point in the web and no single worldview reign triumphant.

PLOT OVERVIEW

PRELUDE AND BOOK I: CHAPTERS 1–6 Dorothea Brooke and her sister Celia are orphans in the care of their wealthy uncle, Mr. Brooke. Dorothea longs to live an ascetic life devoted to some great project for improving the world. During a small dinner party at Tipton Grange, Sir James informs Mr. Brooke and Dorothea of his plans to improve conditions for the tenants on his estate. Mr. Brooke declares that he spends far too much on such endeavors. Dorothea disagrees and points out with sharp wit that Mr. Brooke spends large sums on entertainment and little on socially responsible projects. Her well-spoken retort catches the attention of Mr. Casaubon, a middle-aged scholar and clergyman.

Dorothea wants to become Casaubon's wife. Sir James attempts to please Dorothea by showing interest in her "plan for cottages." Dorothea devotes her spare time to drawing plans for better housing for the tenants on Brooke's estate. Sir James admits that Brooke is unlikely to spend the money for the project, but he states that he himself would like to follow her plans at Freshitt, his own estate. Dorothea is delighted, and the two of them set to work on putting the plan into action.

Celia informs Dorothea that Sir James wishes to marry her; Dorothea, shocked, plans to discourage him. Mr. Brooke arrives to tell her that Casaubon has asked him for her hand in marriage. Dorothea is overjoyed and accepts the proposal right away.

BOOK I: CHAPTERS 7–12 Casaubon looks forward to the end of the courtship, as he is eager to return his energies to his work.

The Brookes visit Lowick manor, Casaubon's residence. During the tour of the grounds, they notice a young man drawing sketches. Casaubon informs them that he is Will Ladislaw, his second cousin and grandson of his ill-fated aunt.

At the engagement party, Dorothea meets Lydgate, the new, young surgeon. Lydgate prefers the company of Rosamond Vincy, the mayor's beautiful, feminine daughter. Rosamond becomes interested in Lydgate. She prefers to marry a man who is not from Middlemarch, and she believes Lydgate has aristocratic relatives.

Rosamond and her brother, Fred, visit their elderly uncle, Peter Featherstone. Featherstone accuses Fred of borrowing money for gambling debts, using his possible inheritance of Featherstone's wealth as security. Featherstone demands that Fred secure a letter from Mr. Bulstrode, a wealthy banker and Fred's uncle. Bulstrode could prove or disprove the rumor because he would know everything about the borrowing or lending of money.

Mary Garth, Featherstone's niece by his first marriage, is charged with the care of the sick old man. Fred is also madly in love with her.

BOOK II: CHAPTERS 13–16 Bulstrode plans to name Lydgate as superintendent of the new Fever Hospital. Farebrother warns Lydgate that he will incur professional jealousy among other Middlemarch medical men because he wants to reform their outdated treatments. The hospital lies within Mr. Farebrother's parish, but Bulstrode wishes to elect another clergyman because he doesn't like Farebrother's doctrine. He wishes to elect Mr. Tyke as chaplain for the hospital. Lydgate replies that he doesn't want to become involved in clerical disputes.

Lydgate is the orphan son of a military man, and he settled on the medical profession at a young age. His guardians paid for his education, but he is forced to earn his own living, and he doesn't plan to marry soon.

Bulstrode arrived in Middlemarch some twenty years ago, and no one knows his origins. He managed to marry Mr. Vincy's sister and ally himself with an important family.

Fred speaks with Mary. He doesn't want to be a clergyman, and he has failed his examination at college. Fred demands that she promise to marry him, but she refuses. She suggests that he pass his exam as proof that he is not an idler, even though she thinks he would be an unfit clergyman. He owes one hundred and sixty pounds for a gambling debt. His creditor holds a bill signed by Mary's father as security against the debt.

Lydgate admires Rosamond, but he doesn't plan to marry for some years. He doesn't know that Rosamond has other ideas. She believes she will live in aristocratic style as his wife.

BOOK II: CHAPTERS 17–22 Lydgate visits Farebrother and learns that he supports his mother, aunt, and sister on his meager income. Farebrother's mother states that he compares to the best of clergymen, so he should have the position at the hospital. Lydgate learns that Tyke is a zealous, strict type. He also learns that Farebrother smokes, gambles, and studies etymology as well. Farebrother warns Lydgate of Middlemarch's petty politics and prejudices. He tells Lydgate that he will offend Bulstrode if he votes for him, and he says there will be no hard feelings if Lydgate votes for Tyke.

Lydgate's liking for Farebrother increases with greater acquaintance. Lydgate is frustrated that his vote will damage his relationship with Bulstrode. He begins to feel the harness of petty Middlemarch politics. Lydgate votes for Tyke. Farebrother treats Lydgate no differently than before.

Naumann, a painter friend of Will Ladislaw, draws his attention to a beautiful woman on the streets of Rome. The woman is Dorothea. Ladislaw informs him of her identity, and Naumann asks him to persuade Dorothea to sit for a portrait. Meanwhile, Dorothea is sobbing. She has begun to realize that her marriage is not what she expected it to be.

Ladislaw visits the Casaubons, but only Dorothea is home. Casaubon arrives, interrupting the conversation. Ladislaw agrees to dine with them the next day.

Ladislaw intensely admires Dorothea and schemes to see her alone. He visits when he knows Casaubon will not be home. Ladislaw laments her sad fate in being locked away in Lowick manor, but Dorothea stresses that Lowick is her chosen home. Ladislaw declares that he will renounce Casaubon's charity because he wishes to be independent. He hopes to impress Dorothea. She admires his resolve, but, after he mocks Casaubon's work, she pleads that he never do so again.

BOOK III: CHAPTERS 23–27 Fred did not want to go to his father about his debt, because Mr. Vincy tends to rage about his expensive habits. He settled on Caleb Garth, Mary's father. He makes his living managing the estates of wealthy landowners. Mrs. Garth, a former schoolteacher, supplements their income by giving lessons. Garth did not tell his wife he co-signed a debt for Fred Vincy.

Unable to pay his debt, Fred visits the Garth home and tells Mrs. Garth. Mrs. Garth must part with all the money that she has saved to pay the fee to apprentice her fifteen-year-old son to a trade. They have to ask Mary to part with some of her own savings to cover the rest of the debt. Garth regrets having to ask Mary for money, because he suspects she loves Fred. Mary assures her father that she will not engage herself to Fred if he remains so irresponsible.

After Mr. Wench, the Vincy family doctor, fails to correctly diagnose and treat Fred correctly when he catches typhoid fever, Mr. Vincy names Lydgate as the new family doctor. Wrench is insulted, and Lydgate makes an enemy.

BOOK III: CHAPTERS 28–33 Dorothea returns home from Rome. Celia tells Dorothea that she is engaged to Sir James Chettam. Casaubon thought he had found everything he wanted and more in Dorothea; he wanted a wife who would admire him uncritically, but he doesn't experience the bliss he expected.

After Casaubon collapses from some kind of fit, Lydgate advises Casaubon to be satisfied with moderate work and frequent relaxation. Lydgate states that Casaubon could live another fifteen years only if he is careful to follow Lydgate's advice. Ladislaw wants to deliver Naumann's painting of Casaubon in person, but, before he collapsed, Casaubon has told Dorothea that he does not want Ladislaw to come to Lowick. She requests that Mr. Brooke write Ladislaw and tell him not to come because Casaubon is ill. Brooke invites Ladislaw to come and stay at Tipton Grange without telling Dorothea.

Mrs. Bulstrode hints to Lydgate that Rosamond has gotten the wrong idea about Lydgate's wealth. Lydgate resolves to stay away from the Vincy household. Rosamond becomes very unhappy. However, one day he has to go see Mr. Vincy because Featherstone's health is beginning to fail. Vincy is not home, but Lydgate sees Rosamond, whose obvious heartache touches him. He leaves the Vincy household as an engaged man.

The news of Featherstone's imminent demise brings all of his relatives to Stone Court. Featherstone refuses to see any of them. One night, Featherstone tells Mary that he has written two wills, and he plans to burn one of them. He asks her to open his iron chest and take out the will inside it. She refuses. He is too weak to do it himself, so he tries to bribe her. Mary says she won't compromise her reputation. Featherstone dies that night clasping his would-be bribe money and the key to his iron chest.

BOOK IV: CHAPTERS 34–37 There is a stranger in attendance at Featherstone's funeral. Celia informs Dorothea that Ladislaw is staying at Tipton Grange. The news displeases Casaubon. He believes that Dorothea asked Mr. Brooke to invite Ladislaw to Tipton Grange.

All of Featherstone's relatives attend the reading of the will, as does the stranger. His name is Mr. Rigg and he is Featherstone's illegitimate son. Featherstone's lawyer, Mr. Standish, reads the earlier will first. Featherstone leaves small bequests to his siblings, which causes a flurry of indignant outbursts. The first will leaves ten thousand pounds to Fred, but the land is left to Joshua Rigg, who is to take the name of Featherstone.

The second will revokes everything except some small bequests. Joshua Rigg receives everything else excepting some property to be used for the erection of some almshouses in Featherstone's name. Fred laments that he will have to become a clergyman after all.

Mr. Vincy resolves to revoke his consent to Rosamond's marriage. However, Rosamond is determined to have her way. Vincy makes it clear that he won't advance any money should he and Rosamond get into financial straits. Lydgate arranges to rent a nice home in preparation for married life. His savings begin disappearing rapidly, so he begins buying on credit. She begins planning to have Lydgate leave Middlemarch and find a practice elsewhere.

Meanwhile, Mr. Brooke hires Will Ladislaw as editor of the Pioneer, a newspaper he has purchased. Brooke wants to be a political man, so he hops onto the Liberal reform platform. Ladislaw believes Casaubon wronged Dorothea in marrying her, so he resolves to stay near her and watch over her. Ladislaw reveals that his grandmother's family disowned her because she married a poor Polish man. Ladislaw's own mother ran away from her family to marry someone not to their liking.

The news that Ladislaw is staying greatly distresses Casaubon. He believes that Ladislaw feels contempt for him. Without telling her, Casaubon writes Ladislaw requesting that he leave Middlemarch. Dorothea asks Casaubon to leave half his wealth to Ladislaw upon his death to make amends for the disinheritance of his grandmother. Casaubon orders her to cease interference in his relationship with Ladislaw. He suspects Ladislaw and Dorothea are conspiring against him. Meanwhile, Ladislaw writes to state that he will not leave Middlemarch. Casaubon forbids Ladislaw to come to Lowick again.

BOOK IV: CHAPTERS 38–42 *The Trumpet*, an opposing newspaper, criticizes Brooke's penchant for preaching in favor of charity for the poor while allowing his own tenants to live in relative squalor.

Despite all of her devoted care, Casaubon's speculations regarding Ladislaw and Dorothea are full of suspicion and jealousy. He believes that she was the cause of Ladislaw's return from Rome and his decision to live in Middlemarch. However, he believes Dorothea to be innocent of bad intentions. Rather, he believes she is vulnerable to Ladislaw's manipulation. He resolves to protect Dorothea.

BOOK V: CHAPTERS 43–48 Dorothea visits Lydgate's home to ask if Casaubon consulted him because of new health problems. Lydgate is not home, but she discovers that Ladislaw is there visiting with Rosamond.

Bulstrode gives Lydgate full authority over the patients' treatment. Other doctors can consult, but they cannot contravene Lydgate's decisions. Not only is public opinion of Lydgate's support of reform of the medical profession already extremely divided, but now every medical man in town refuses to visit the Fever Hospital.

Public opinion of Ladislaw generally conforms to Casaubon's. The rumor has gotten out that they are relatives, but that Casaubon will have nothing to do with him. He visits the Lydgates frequently and alleviates Rosamond's boredom. Lydgate is out of temper because he has been unable to pay the debt he owes on his furniture, and Rosamond is pregnant.

Casaubon suspects that Ladislaw plans to fool Dorothea into marrying him when she becomes a widow in order to get possession of his wealth. However, Ladislaw worships Dorothea for other reasons. Dorothea is upset that her husband continues in refusing to speak to Ladislaw. The next morning Casaubon takes a walk. Dorothea finds him seated on a bench and discovers that he has died.

BOOK V: CHAPTERS 49–53 Celia reveals to Dorothea the details of a codicil to Casaubon's will. Casaubon forbids Dorothea to marry Ladislaw. If Dorothea were to marry Ladislaw, she would be stripped of Casaubon's property. The knowledge that Casaubon viewed her with suspicion embitters Dorothea.

Lydgate tells Dorothea to consider allowing Farebrother to take over the parish at Lowick instead of Tyke. He mentions Farebrother's gambling and says that an additional income would relieve him of the need to engage in such an activity.

Brooke gives an election speech. He notices an effigy of himself held above the shoulders of the crowd. The hecklers befuddle him, and the speech ends in disaster. The hecklers pelt both the effigy and

Brooke himself with eggs until Brooke flees. Brooke informs Ladislaw that he is out of a job, because he is selling the Pioneer. Ladislaw suspects that Brooke's friends have urged Brooke to be rid of him.

Farebrother learns that he is to have the Lowick parish. His mother, aunt, and sister urge him to court Mary Garth now that he has sufficient income to marry. Farebrother asks Mary about her feelings for Fred. Mary states that she won't marry Fred if he becomes a clergyman and if he doesn't settle on a steady occupation. Farebrother hints that he himself loves her. Mary says that she loves Fred too much to give him up for another. Feeling pained for his loss and proud for having done his duty, Farebrother leaves to deliver the message.

Raffles learns that Bulstrode purchased Stone Court from his stepson, Rigg Featherstone. Bulstrode bribes Raffles to stay away from Middlemarch. Raffles could damage Bulstrode's reputation as an eminent Christian by revealing the fact that Bulstrode contrived to prevent his first wife from finding her missing daughter and grandchild. The missing daughter's married name was Ladislaw.

BOOK VI: CHAPTERS 54–57 Mrs. Cadwallader connives to marry Dorothea off as soon as her period of mourning ends. Everyone hopes that a speedy marriage will cut short any malicious gossip regarding her relationship with Ladislaw. Irritated at such meddling, Dorothea declares that she will never marry again.

Fred asks Garth if he would consider hiring him. He confesses his love for Mary and informs Garth that she has refused to marry him if he becomes a clergyman. Garth tells him to report to his office early the next morning. Mr. Vincy tells Fred that he has thrown away his education and gone down a step in life. However, he tells his son to stick to his chosen occupation, because he can no longer depend on him for support other than a rent-free room in the Vincy household. Fred's decision upsets Mrs. Vincy even more, because she rightly suspects that her son plans to marry Mary Garth.

After Fred hears that Farebrother loves Mary, too, Fred walks to Lowick to find Mary. Mary assures Fred that Farebrother has not tried to win her away from him and admonishes him for his unfair distrust of Farebrother. Fred is relieved, but he stills feels an intense jealousy.

BOOK VI: CHAPTERS 58–62 Captain Lydgate, Lydgate's cousin and son of Sir Godwin, comes to visit. The captain takes Rosamond out riding. She suffers an accident and miscarries.

Lydgate gives a bill of sale on his furniture to his creditor as security for his debt. Rosamond wants to ask her father for money, but Lydgate forbids it. She tries to persuade him to sell everything and leave Middlemarch, but he refuses. Rosamond is unhappy with her marriage and has already unsuccessfully tried to get money from her father.

Bulstrode hires Ladislaw to attend an auction and bid for a painting that Mrs. Bulstrode wants. Ladislaw meets John Raffles there. Raffles says he knew Ladislaw's mother and that her parents made a fortune by selling stolen goods.

In his youth, Bulstrode became a partner in a pawnbroking business and slowly discovered that they were selling stolen goods. He did not resign, however, and continued to behave publicly as a deeply religious man. Dunkirk, the owner of the business, died, leaving his wife a wealthy woman. Her son died. She wanted to marry Bulstrode, but she asked him to locate her missing daughter before she would consent. Bulstrode hired Raffles to find her. The daughter, Sarah Ladislaw, and her small child, Ladislaw, were found, but Bulstrode bribed Raffles to keep silent. He married Mrs. Dunkirk and received all of her wealth upon her death. Raffles continues to blackmail Bulstrode.

Bulstrode tells Ladislaw that he married his grandmother and that he became wealthy as a result. He says that he was unable to find Ladislaw's mother. He offers to give Ladislaw a fair share of the inheritance that would have come to him if Bulstrode had located Ladislaw's mother. Will states that he doesn't believe Bulstrode's assertion that he didn't find his mother. Bulstrode admits his guilt and says he wants to atone for it. Ladislaw asks if Bulstrode's wealth derives from the thievery Raffles hinted at. Bulstrode replies that he entered the business after it had already become established. Ladislaw refuses Bulstrode's tainted money, because he doesn't want to do something that would disappoint Dorothea.

Mrs. Cadwallader tells Sir James and Dorothea that Ladislaw lingers in Middlemarch, stirring a scandal with his frequent visits with Rosamond. Dorothea uneasily remembers her encounter with Ladislaw at the Lydgate home. Ladislaw visits her at Lowick and announces that there is malicious gossip against his character. He says that what he cares for most is forbidden to him because of the gossip, so he must leave Middlemarch to save his reputation. Ladislaw, disappointed that Dorothea does not beg him to stay, leaves Middlemarch the following day.

BOOK VII: CHAPTERS 63–67 Lydgate is so deeply in debt that he needs at least one thousand pounds. He tells Rosamond that he wishes to move to a smaller, cheaper house. Ned Plymdale and his new wife are looking for a suitable home. Lydgate plans to employ Trumbell to negotiate the deal with Plymdale. Rosamond pleads that Lydgate write Sir Godwin and ask for money. Lydgate refuses.

Rosamond secretly pays a visit to Trumbell and revokes Lydgate's order. She needles the information out of Lydgate that a thousand pounds is necessary to remain in their present home. She secretly writes Sir Godwin asking for that sum.

A letter from Sir Godwin arrives, but it is addressed to Lydgate. When he reads it, Lydgate pales with anger and castigates his wife for her habit of acting secretly. Sir Godwin writes to order Lydgate never again to set his wife to write him when he has something to ask.

Lydgate learns that Rosamond has twice asked her father for money and been refused. She presses him to leave Middlemarch and practice elsewhere. Bulstrode requests his medical services. Lydgate asks for a loan. Bulstrode refuses and tells Lydgate that he should declare bankruptcy.

BOOK VII: CHAPTERS 68–71 Bulstrode arranges to transfer the management of the bank and the hospital. He speaks to Caleb Garth and asks him to manage Stone Court in his absence.

Garth visits Bulstrode at the bank to report that he found Raffles at Stone Court. He advises Bulstrode to secure the services of a doctor because Raffles is very sick. Bulstrode knows that Raffles told Garth everything when he tells Bulstrode that he must decline to do business with him. However, Garth promises not to repeat Raffles's accusations.

Raffles suffers from the ravages of alcoholism. Lydgate prescribes bed rest and instructs Bulstrode to refuse Raffles' requests for alcohol. The case is serious, but Lydagte is optimistic that Raffles could live. Lydgate is bitter that Bulstrode aids a wretch like Raffles though he would not help him with his debts. The auction of his furniture has been published in the papers.

Anxious to earn Lydgate's goodwill, Bulstrode tells him that he has changed his mind and wants to loan Lydgate the money. Enormously relieved, Lydgate goes away with a check for a thousand pounds. The housekeeper knocks on his door and tells Bulstrode that Raffles is begging for brandy. Bulstrode gives her the key to the liquor cabinet. Lydgate returns in the morning to watch Raffles take his dying breath. Lydgate is puzzled at the change, but he is so happy to be saved from bankruptcy that he thinks nothing of it.

Bulstrode is doomed. Raffles met Bambridge at the horse-fair and told him everything. Everyone now knows that Raffles died at Stone Court while under Bulstrode's care. They also know that the auction of Lydgate's furniture was canceled suddenly.

Bulstrode attends a town meeting to discuss sanitation measures. A member of the board announces that there are scandalous accusations against Bulstrode. He demands that Bulstrode deny them or resign from all public positions. The other men request that Bulstrode leave the meeting. Shaken, he complies. Lydgate stands to help him leave the room, associating himself with Bulstrode's infamy. He suspects his orders for Raffles were disobeyed. He knows that the town believes he took the loan from Bulstrode as a bribe.

BOOK VIII: CHAPTERS 72–79 Lydgate deduces that Bulstrode loaned him the money to bind him through a strong obligation in the event that Raffles disclosed any damaging details about his past. The townspeople avoid him, and he begins losing clients.

Bulstrode perceives that his wife has heard everything. He prepares himself to hear her say that she is leaving him. She dresses herself in mourning clothing and goes to see him. A wave of compassion hits her when she sees his shrunken frame. He bursts into tears with her sitting by his side. His confession and her resolve to stick with him are unspoken.

BOOK VIII: CHAPTERS 80–FINALE Lydgate consents to allow Dorothea, who believes he is innocent, to take over his debt from Bulstrode. Dorothea tells Rosamond that she, Farebrother, Sir James, and Mr. Brooke all support Lydgate wholeheartedly. Rosamond bursts into hysterical crying. Dorothea comforts her and counsels her to cling to her husband. Rosamond tells Dorothea that she is wrong to think badly of Ladislaw. She tells her that Ladislaw has done nothing wrong.

Ladislaw tells Dorothea that people say that he is the grandson of a thieving Jewish pawnbroker. They kiss, but Ladislaw declares sorrowfully that they can never be married. Dorothea replies that she cares nothing for her wealth and that she has a sufficient income from her deceased parents and Mr. Brooke. They become engaged. Dorothea decides to go to London and live with Ladislaw.

Garth tells Mary of an offer he has received from Mrs. Bulstrode for Fred to manage Stone Court in agreement with Mrs. Bulstrode. Fred is delighted at the news. He and Mary plan to marry shortly after he settles into Stone Court.

Fred and Mary settle into a solid, happy marriage and have three sons. They never become rich, but they live comfortably. Lydgate leaves Middlemarch and sets up a successful practice elsewhere. He still considers himself a failure and dies at fifty. His marriage never becomes a peaceful or wholly happy arrangement. He never has anything but praise for Dorothea, which continually arouses Rosamond's jealousy. Rosamond later marries a wealthy physician. Will Ladislaw becomes an ardent public man working for reforms. Dorothea remains happy in her position as wife and mother. Dorothea's son inherits Tipton Grange.

CHARACTER LIST

Mr. Bambridge A Middlemarch horse dealer. Fred Vincy sinks into debt with Mr. Bambridge. Raffles meets him at a horse-fair and tells him everything about Bulstrode's past.

Dorothea Brooke A kind-hearted and honest woman. Dorothea longs to find some way to improve the world. She thinks Casaubon is a great intellectual, but after she marries him, she quickly discovers that he is not passionate enough to make her happy. She also learns that she is not as submissive and sacrificing as she had previously thought. She draws plans for comfortable cottages to replace the ramshackle buildings on large estates. She helps Lydgate when he suffers for his connections with Bulstrode. She falls in love with Casaubon's young cousin, Will Ladislaw. She defies Casaubon's machinations and marries Will even though it means losing her inheritance as Casaubon's widow.

Arthur Brooke Dorothea and Celia's bachelor uncle. Arthur is a bumbling man who can never stick to an opinion, always wanting to please everyone. He hires Will Ladislaw to write for his paper, the *Pioneer*. He runs for a seat in Parliament on the Reform platform, but he lets his own tenants live in poverty and squalor. The scandal resulting from his hypocrisy prompts him to improve conditions on his own estate, Tipton Grange.

Celia Brooke Dorothea's sister. Celia marries Sir James Chettam.

M

Nicholas Bulstrode A wealthy Middlemarch banker married to Walter Vincy's sister. Bulstrode professes to be a deeply religious Evangelical Protestant, but he has a dark past: he made his fortune as a pawnbroker selling stolen goods. He married Will Ladislaw's grandmother after her first husband died. Her daughter had run away years before, and she insisted that Bulstrode find her daughter before she remarried, because she wanted to leave her wealth to her only surviving child. Bulstrode located the daughter and her child, Will Ladislaw, but he kept her existence a secret. He bribed the man he hired to find her, John Raffles, to keep quiet. John Raffles blackmails him with this information. When Raffles becomes ill, Bulstrode cares for him. However, he disobeys Lydgate's medical advice, and Raffles dies as a result. When the scandal about his past and the circumstances of Raffles's death become known, Bulstrode leaves Middlemarch in shame. He purchases Stone Court from Joshua Rigg Featherstone.

Harriet Bulstrode Walter Vincy's sister. Harriet is a kind, honest, religious woman. No one in Middlemarch blames her for her husband's misdeeds. She resolves to stay with her husband even after she learns of his wrongdoing.

Elinor Cadwallader Wife of the Rector at Tipton Grange, Brooke's estate. Elinor was born to a good family, but she married down and angered her friends and family. She is a practical woman who is forever trying to play matchmaker to unmarried young people, including Dorothea, Celia, and Sir James.

Humphrey Cadwallader Rector at Tipton Grange, Brooke's estate. Unlike his wife, Cadwallader doesn't believe in meddling in other people's affairs.

Edward Casaubon A scholarly clergyman who owns a large estate called Lowick. Casaubon's lifelong ambition is to write the Key to all Mythologies, but he is insecure and uncertain about his own abilities. He marries Dorothea because he thinks she is completely submissive and worshipful. Her stubborn independence frustrates him, and he mistakenly believes that she is constantly criticizing him. Casaubon is Will Ladislaw's cousin. His mother's sister was disowned by her family for running away to marry a man they didn't like. Her own daughter, Will's mother, also ran away to marry. Casaubon offers financial support to Will because he feels obligated to make amends for his aunt's disinheritance. He becomes jealous of Will's relationship with Dorothea. He includes an addendum in his will stating that Dorothea will lose his wealth and property if she ever marries Will Ladislaw. He dies before finishing his Key.

Sir James Chettam A baronet who owns a large estate called Freshitt. Chettam courts Dorothea, but she chooses to marry Casaubon. He later marries her sister. He enacts Dorothea's cottage plans on his own estate.

Mr. Dagley One of Brooke's impoverished tenants. Dagley's son is caught poaching on Brooke's lands. He refuses Brooke's request that he chastise his son.

Camden Farebrother A vicar and friend of Lydgate. Farebrother does not consider himself to be a very good clergyman, though many people like his sensible sermons. He becomes fast friends with Lydgate and supports his mother, sister, and aunt on his small income. He must gamble to make ends meet and to pursue his scientific hobbies. He loses in the election for the chaplaincy at the New Hospital. He receives the Lowick parish after Casaubon's death. Fred Vincy enlists his help in courting Mary Garth. He himself loves Mary, but he does his duty.

Mrs. Farebrother Camden Farebrother's widowed mother.

Winifred Farebrother Camden Farebrother's unmarried sister.

Peter Featherstone A wealthy, manipulative old widower. Featherstone owns Stone Court. He married twice but had no legitimate children. His first wife was Caleb Garth's sister. His second wife was Lucy Vincy's sister. He hints for years that he plans to leave his entire estate to Fred Vincy, his nephew by marriage. He even writes two separate wills. Mary Garth refuses to burn one of them. He leaves his property to his illegitimate son, Joshua Rigg.

Caleb Garth A poor businessman. Garth earns his living managing large estates. He co-signs a debt for Fred Vincy. When Fred is unable to pay, Garth's family suffers. He receives new business, overcomes the loss, and hires Fred Vincy to work for him. He declines to manage Stone Court for Bulstrode after Raffles reveals Bulstrode's dark past.

M

Susan Garth Caleb Garth's wife. Susan is a former schoolteacher.

Mary Garth Daughter of Caleb and Susan Garth. Mary loves Fred, but she refuses to marry him if he becomes a clergyman and fails to find a steady occupation.

Will Ladislaw Grandson of Casaubon's disinherited aunt. Bulstrode tries to give Ladislaw money to atone for hiding his existence from his grandmother. He refuses the money because he knows it came through thievery. He worships Dorothea. He doesn't care for money and loves everything that is beautiful.

Tertius Lydgate Orphan son of a military man. Lydgate chose the medical profession at a young age, much to the chagrin of his wealthy, titled relatives. He comes to Middlemarch hoping to test new methods of treatment. He marries Rosamond Vincy, whose expensive habits get him into debt. He takes a loan from Bulstrode and becomes embroiled in Bulstrode's scandal. Dorothea aids him in his darkest hour. He hopes to find the tissue that is the most basic building block of life.

Sir Godwin Lydgate Tertius Lydgate's uncle.

Captain Lydgate Tertius Lydgate's foppish cousin. Captain Lydgate takes Rosamond out riding. She suffers a miscarriage as a result of an accident on horseback.

Naumann Ladislaw's painter friend in Rome. Naumann uses Casaubon as a model for Thomas Aquinas as a ruse to draw a sketch of Dorothea.

Miss Noble Mrs. Farebrother's sister. Miss Noble steals small items of food to give to the poor. She becomes fond of Will Ladislaw.

Selina Plymdale Good friend of Harriet Bulstrode. Selina's son courts Rosamond Vincy, but he is rejected.

Ned Plymdale Suitor of Rosamond. Plymdale courts Rosamond, but she refuses him.

John Raffles Old business partner of Bulstrode. Bulstrode bribed Raffles to keep the existence of the daughter and grandchild of his first wife secret. He comes back to blackmail Bulstrode. He is Joshua Rigg Featherstone's stepfather. He dies at Stone Court because Bulstrode interferes with Lydgate's medical treatment.

Joshua Rigg Featherstone Peter Featherstone's illegitimate son. John Raffles is Joshua Featherstone's stepfather. He inherits Stone Court. He sells it to Bulstrode because he wants to become a moneychanger.

Borthrop Trumbell Auctioneer in Middlemarch.

Walter Tyke Evangelical Protestant minister. Bulstrode is a supporter of Tyke's. Tyke wins the election for the chaplaincy at the New Hospital, beating out Farebrother.

Rosamond Vincy Daughter of Walter and Lucy Vincy. Rosamond grows up accustomed to an expensive lifestyle. She marries Lydgate because she thinks he is rich and because he has titled relatives. She dreams of leaving Middlemarch and living an exciting, aristocratic lifestyle, but her expensive tastes get Lydgate deeply into debt.

Fred Vincy Oldest son of Walter and Lucy Vincy. Fred Vincy's father sends him to college because he wants Fred to become a clergyman, but Fred doesn't want to work in the Church. He gets himself into debt by gambling. He is accustomed to a lavish lifestyle. He causes financial difficulty for the Garths because he cannot pay the debt on which Caleb Garth co-signed his name. He wants to marry Mary Garth, but she won't have him unless he finds a steady occupation other than the Church. He hopes to inherit Stone Court from his uncle, Peter Featherstone. These hopes are disappointed, so he works for Caleb Garth.

Walter Vincy A modestly well-off businessman in manufacturing and mayor of Middlemarch. Fred and Rosamond's expensive tastes infuriate Vincy. He refuses to lend Rosamond and Lydgate money to pay Lydgate's debt. He is Harriet Bulstrode's brother.

Lucy Vincy Walter Vincy's wife. Lucy is the daughter of an innkeeper, much to Rosamond's chagrin. She dotes on her son and doesn't want him to marry Mary Garth. She is the sister of Featherstone's second wife.

Mr. Wrench Middlemarch doctor and Lydgate's enemy. Mr. Wrench misdiagnoses Fred when Fred catches typhoid fever. Lydgate treats Fred's illness, and the Vincys fire Mr. Wrench. Mr. Wrench becomes Lydgate's enemy as a result.

M

ANALYSIS OF MAJOR CHARACTERS

DOROTHEA BROOKE Dorothea is an exceptional woman: she is smart, pious, and beautiful, and the governing principle of her character is her desire to help the needy, seen in her interest in redesigning the local farmers' cottages. By giving money to Lydgate's hospital, she is able to help the less fortunate, and by giving money directly Lydgate, she frees him from his debt to Bulstrode. Her philanthropic impulse indicates her essential goodness.

Dorothea is also stubborn and strong-willed, going against common advice to wed Casaubon, a much older man. Her marriage to him is driven by her desire to be taught by him, and she devotes herself to him entirely—and is appropriately devastated when he dies. Unfortunately, Casaubon doesn't trust her unmitigated devotion, either to his work or in loving him. When Dorothea learns of a clause in his will that forbids her to marry his cousin Will Ladislaw, Dorothea's devotion to her deceased husband shifts. She feels betrayed by his insinuation that she was unfaithful. In response, Dorothea refuses to finish Casaubon's work, an indication that she is returning to her independent, pre-marriage self. When Dorothea does marry Ladislaw, she reveals her growth as a person. This marriage is a mutual understanding and partnership, and both members are equals. This marriage required Dorothea to flout convention and forgo her inherited wealth, and her willingness to do so show that she has regained her earlier rebellious energy but with a newfound maturity.

TERTIUS LYDGATE Lydgate enters Middlemarch as the bright, cutting-edge handsome new doctor. Although he is of high birth, Lydgate wants to be a country doctor. Lydgate's desire is not entirely selfless, but he is genuinely interested in helping others. He is motivated by the desire to reform medical practices, and he symbolizes change and reform coming to Middlemarch. At first, things go well for Lydgate. His practice grows, he starts a new hospital, and he gains a reputation as a good doctor with patients of high social and financial standing. But when he abruptly falls in love with Rosamond, things begin to go downhill rapidly. Marriage ruins Lydgate, both financially and idealistically. As he gets further and further into debt, his personality changes, vacillating between coddling and soothing Rosamond and feeling intense bitterness toward her. The financial burden of marriage comes between him and his desire to reform the provincial medical practices of the neighborhood. In addition to his debts, the scandal of Raffles death marks him as an accomplice to murder.

ROSAMOND VINCY Rosamond is the most genteel character in *Middlemarch*. Her interests are not serious; she is concerned with social niceties, upward mobility, and living well. While Dorothea is beautiful, Rosamond is stunning and swanlike, a model of perfection. Although Rosamond comes from a middle-class background, her education lifts her to a higher social circle. She represents the ability to change social status through conduct, but in the end her education ruins her marriage and happiness.

Rosamond's primary motivation is social advancement, which fuels her desire to wed Dr. Lydgate. Initially Rosamond seems to genuinely love Lydgate, but when he loses his money, Rosamond loses interest in him. Their marriage fails as Rosamond struggles to keep her house and her possessions and becomes petulant and manipulative in the process.

THEMES, MOTIFS, AND SYMBOLS

THEMES

THE IMPERFECTION OF MARRIAGE Most characters in *Middlemarch* marry for love rather than obligation, yet marriage still appears negative and unromantic. Marriage and the pursuit of it are central concerns in *Middlemarch*, but unlike in many novels of the time, marriage is not considered the ultimate source of happiness. Two examples are the failed marriages of Dorothea and Lydgate. Dorothea's marriage fails because of her youth and of her disillusions about marrying a much older man, while Lydgate's marriage fails because of irreconcilable personalities. Mr. and Mrs. Bulstrode also face a marital crisis due to his inability to tell her about the past, and Fred Vincy and Mary Garth also face a great deal of hardship in making their union. As none of the marriages reach a perfect fairytale ending, *Middlemarch* offers a clear critique of the usual portrayal of marriage as romantic and unproblematic.

M

THE HARSHNESS OF SOCIAL EXPECTATIONS The ways in which people conduct themselves and how the community judges them are closely linked in *Middlemarch*. When the expectations of the social community are not met, individuals often receive harsh public criticism. For example, the community judges Ladislaw harshly because of his mixed pedigree. Fred Vincy is almost disowned because he chooses to go against his family's wishes and not join the clergy. It is only when Vincy goes against the wishes of the community by foregoing his education that he finds true love and happiness. Finally, Rosamond's need for gentility and the desire to live up to social standards becomes her downfall. In contrast, Dorothea's decision to act against the rules of society allows her to emerge as the most respectable character in the end.

SELF-DETERMINATION VS. CHANCE In *Middlemarch*, self-determination and chance are not opposing forces but, rather, a complicated balancing act. When characters strictly adhere to a belief in either chance or self-determination, bad things happen. When Rosamond goes against the wishes of her husband and writes a letter asking for money from his relative, her act of self-determination puts Lydgate in an unsavory and tense situation coupled with a refusal to help. On the flip side, when Fred Vincy gambles away his money, relying solely on chance, he falls into debt and drags with him the people who trust him. Only when he steps away from gambling and decides not to go into the clergy do good things begin to happen for him. In particular, the character of Farebrother demonstrates the balance between fate and self-determination. This balance is exemplified in his educated gamble in the game of whist. Through a combination of skill and chance, he is able to win more often than not. His character strikes a balance between chance and his role in determining that fate. The complexity of the tension between self-determination and chance is exemplary of the way in which the novel as a whole tends to look at events from many vantage points with no clear right or wrong, no clear enemy or hero.

MOTIFS

EPIGRAPHS Each chapter begins with a small quotation or a few lines of verse known as an epigraph.

These epigraphs work as a way of summarizing the following chapter and moving the plot forward. They also work to place *Middlemarch* into a larger canon of literary works, as Eliot chooses quotes a variety of writers such as Shakespeare, Dante, Chaucer, and William Blake. Eliot was charged with being too intellectual for a woman author in part because of the learned nature of her chosen quotations.

GOSSIP AND SPEAKING FOR OTHERS Often characters, especially characters of opposite genders, do not communicate to each other directly, instead using other characters to speak on their behalf. Carrying messages, sending "diplomats," and not speaking for themselves draws attention to the weblike community of Middlemarch. Part of this web functions to maintain an intricate social web, but it also works to avoid direct communication. Gossip, another form of speaking for another person, plays an important part in the novel as it is often how information is conveyed. Characters frequently use the fact that the information will eventually come around to avoid direct conversation.

DEBT AND BORROWING MONEY Debt appears throughout *Middlemarch*, and money often indicates elements of a character's personality. The plot is driven by characters worrying about money or asking others for money. Fred Vincy must ask several people for loans, Lydgate incurs serious debt due to his failure to manage money and his wife Rosamond's cultured tastes, and Raffles's constant begging and blackmailing for money indicates his threatening role. On the other hand, Mary Garth's refusal to take money from the dying Featherstone proves her good, honest nature. The exchange of money and the passing of debts ties the characters together in an economic subtext.

SYMBOLS

M

THE PORTRAIT OF LADISLAW'S GRANDMOTHER A miniature portrait of Ladislaw's grandmother appears several times in the text and is symbolic of Dorothea's future choice of giving up wealth for love. Ladislaw's grandmother also gave up wealth to be with the man she loved. The portrait hangs in Dorothea's bedroom at Casaubon's house, and Dorothea often recalls the portrait when she thinks of Ladislaw. When Ladislaw comes to say goodbye to Dorothea in a tense conversation filled with romantic subtext, Dorothea offers him the portrait as a parting gift. When Ladislaw refuses it saying he has no need for the past, he indicates that the chance they will end up together remains.

RAFFLES The character of Raffles symbolizes the ominous return of the past. Most often he appears as a lone black figure walking down the country roads and is described as a man of ill-repute and questionable background, associating the danger of the past with the unsavory lower class. His repeated appearance disrupts the sanctity of Middlemarch, for he ties together the dark pasts of Bulstrode and Ladislaw. His death fuels neighborhood gossip that almost forces Ladislaw from town, causes Bulstrode's downfall, and brings about the climax of the novel.

IMPORTANT QUOTATIONS EXPLAINED

---

1. *Not only young virgins of that town, but grey-bearded men also, were often in haste to conjecture how a new acquaintance might be wrought into their purposes, contented with very vague knowledge as to the way in which life had been shaping him for their instrumentality. Middlemarch, in fact, counted on swallowing Lydgate and assimilating him very comfortably.*

This passage, located at the end of Chapter 15 after Lydgate is introduced as the idealistic new doctor, introduces the neighborhood of Middlemarch as a sort of character. Middlemarch is not particularly interested in Lydgate as an individual and instead views him as an instrument and part of the greater community. This illustrates the pull between individual and community that drives the novel forward. In the novel *Middlemarch,* there cannot be individuals without community nor a community without individuals.

This passage also shows a contradiction between Middlemarch as an ominous force that swallows its inhabitants and a comfortable force that draws its inhabitants into its community that is part of the structure of the novel. It demonstrates the pluses and the minuses of living in a country community, much like the entire book does. It captures the realistic, contradictory nature of Eliot's realistic portrayal of country living.

---

2. *"It was wicked to let a young girl blindly decide her fate in that way, without any effort to save her."*

Sir James makes this remark in Chapter 29, when he learns that Mr. Casaubon has fallen ill. Sir James finds it morally deplorable that Dorothea was allowed to choose her own husband. While he is somewhat motivated by his own jealousy that Dorothea didn't marry him, he is more distressed that she was not better advised as to the ramifications of marrying an older and not very desirable man. That it was wicked to not interfere in the affairs of another shows how important community interference and interaction is to the novel.

This quotation also draws attention to the novel's tension between self-determination and chance. The contradiction in the phrase "decide her fate" shows that Sir James (and by extension the novel) believes that the individual has a part in deciding his or her own fate, even if, at times, a person's life seems to move forward of its own accord, for better or for worse.

---

3. *"I mean, marriage drinks up all of our power of giving or getting any blessedness in that sort of love. I know it may be very dear—but it murders our marriage—and then the marriage stays with us like a murder—and everything else is gone."*

Dorothea makes these comments to Rosamond at the end of Chapter 81. Dorothea believes that Rosamond is having an affair with Ladislaw, and this quotation shows how Dorothea believes romantic love and marriage are incompatible. By linking marriage and murder, Dorothea's quote supports the idea prevalent in the work that marriage isn't always perfect or always a guarantee of happiness. The choice of the metaphor of murder is particularly interesting because she is speaking of Lydgate being under suspicion of aiding in the Raffles's murder. Murder, in the literal sense, is already a part of Rosamond's married life.

---

4. *But we insignificant people with our daily words and acts are preparing the lives of many Dorotheas, some of which may present a far sadder sacrifice than that of the Dorothea whose story we know.*

In her final thoughts at the end of the novel, Eliot shifts from third person to first person plural in order present the moral of the story. The shift to the "we" breaks the rigidity of Dorothea's story being particular to the fictional world of *Middlemarch* and expands it to the greater real world. By calling attention to how the acts of common people create cultural norms, Eliot holds everyone who does not question the norms of social life responsible for the sadness of their fellow citizens. By focusing on the trials of Dorothea, Eliot calls particular attention to a woman's role in marriage. Ending on this thought makes Eliot's concern with conventional marriage the central theme of the story. This move points to a particularly feminist type of thought in a novel long before feminism was a common ideology.

A Midwife's Tale

Laurel Thatcher Ulrich (1938–)

CONTEXT

Laurel Thatcher Ulrich was born in 1938 and raised in Sugar City, Idaho. She received her B.A. from the University of Utah. Soon after, she moved to New England and received her Ph.D. from the University of New Hampshire. After graduating, she became a professor of American history at the same school, specializing in the histories of women in early America. During this time, she married fellow teacher Gael Ulrich and became the mother of three girls and two boys. Like the women whose lives she studied, Ulrich gained a firsthand experience of the struggles inherent in balancing the needs of a family with both at-home and office work. Despite this struggle, Ulrich remained dogged in her research, finding and bringing to light the lives of women who were so often ignored in the histories of men.

In 1982, Ulrich compiled these histories and used them as the material for her first book, *Good Wives: Image and Reality in the Lives of Women in Early New England, 1650–1750*. Around this time, Ulrich was doing research in Augusta, Maine, and decided to look up two diaries she had seen in a bibliography of women's history. Though the first was a disappointing ten-page typescript, the other diary belonged to a woman named Martha Ballard—two fat volumes bound in homemade linen covers. Because she had found so few documents written by women during her research for *Good Wives*, Ulrich was awed by the sheer bulk of it. The faded ink made reading difficult, but Ulrich transcribed several pages, planning to turn them into a grant application for a summer fellowship to study the historically vital book. Without documentation there is no history, and women in history had left very few documents behind. In the public histories and town records from the seventeenth and eighteenth centuries, women were either not mentioned at all or were mere names attached to the dealings of their husbands—and sometimes their names were not even correct. Other than Martha, few women had left private records of their lives, and none so faithfully kept as Martha's had been.

M

Ulrich formed the idea for *A Midwife's Tale* soon after she began her research. A mix of the journal itself and editorial commentary, the book would be written in a more accessible format than the original diary and would therefore reach a much wider audience. Though other historians had studied the diary, they had used only the more dramatic entries in their work and dismissed the bulk of the diary as pointless day-to-day trivia. This trivia, however, is what Ulrich found particularly gripping: only through these small details can the lives of women from the eighteenth century be fully revealed. Ulrich spent eight years transforming the life she discovered in the diary into *A Midwife's Tale*, which wound up being almost three times the length she had originally planned it to be. In a speech that she later gave at Bancroft University, Ulrich talked about how working with Martha's diary, begun when Martha was fifty years old, helped Ulrich comprehend ways in which the second half of a person's life could be seen as a new beginning.

Published in 1990, *A Midwife's Tale* debuted to highly positive critical response. Several critics commended it for the insight it offered into the lives of eighteenth-century women, and even more critics were impressed by the way it illuminated life in early New England as a whole. In the educational community, reaction to the book was even more effusive, and Ulrich earned the Bancroft Prize, the Joan Kelly and John H. Dunning prizes, and the Pulitzer Prize for History in 1991. Perhaps more important to Ulrich, the success of *A Midwife's Tale* brought greater attention to the life and diary of Martha Ballard. In 1992, a complete transcription of the diary, written by Robert and Cynthia McCauseland, was finally published.

During her tenure as a MacArthur Fellow, Ulrich collaborated with filmmaker Laurie Kahn-Leavitt on a documentary based on the book that would air on the PBS series "The American Experience." A simplification of *A Midwife's Tale*, the documentary offers a clearer look at Martha Ballard's life by suggesting many of its smaller moments and entirely omitting the bulk of the historical context. Several scenes were reenacted, bolstered by dialogue but narrated largely with voice-overs from the diary that occasionally were not included in Ulrich's book. Ulrich herself narrated as well. In voiceovers and interviews, she described both Martha's life and part of the process by which *A Midwife's Tale* came into being. Not included in the book, this latter discussion gave audiences a glimpse into the life of a historian as well as that of a midwife. The documentary aired on PBS in 1997. Currently a Phillips Professor of Early American History at Harvard University, Ulrich continues to write books that bring the forgotten lives of early American women to light.

PLOT OVERVIEW

Ulrich begins each chapter by transcribing a few entries from Martha's diary, from the month and year listed in the chapter title. Ulrich follows these entries with an essay that further explains the entries' details and relates the entries to what happened to Martha in the surrounding few years. Ulrich explains and builds on the entries with her own analysis, and she provides a wider historical context by drawing from documents such as town records and the diaries of Martha's New England contemporaries.

Martha Moore was born in 1735 in the small town of Oxford, Massachusetts, to a well-educated family. She married Ephraim Ballard in 1754 and had her first child, Cyrus, two years later. She quickly had five more children—four daughters and one more son—but lost three of the girls to a diphtheria epidemic in 1769. That same year, she gave birth to her fifth daughter, and her sixth followed two years later. In 1773, Ephraim traveled to Maine to find a new home for the family, finally settling in Hallowell and taking management of the mill and property owned by a British sympathizer who had fled to Canada. Martha and the children joined Ephraim there in October of 1777, and Martha officially delivered her first child as a midwife in July of 1778. Martha's oldest daughter, Lucy, married her cousin Ephraim Towne that same year, and in 1799, Martha gave birth to her youngest son. She begins writing in her diary on January 1, 1785.

In August of 1787, Martha describes several events that give an overview of the many medically related tasks she is called on to perform, including delivering babies, answering false alarms, preparing bodies for burial, making medical calls, dispensing pills, and harvesting and preparing healing herbs. Ulrich then gives an overview of homeopathic remedies of the time and the relationship between local healers and physicians. In September of 1788, Martha talks about the goods she and her daughters trade with local women and the help her daughters give her with the housework, particularly the weaving. Ulrich then discusses the gender-based division of duties, the female economic subsystem of the time period, and the importance of household help in a midwife's career. In October of the following year, Martha's family is forced to relocate when the mill's original owner returns, and she discusses the difficulties of living so much closer to her neighbors. She also talks about being questioned when one of these new neighbors accuses a public official of rape. Ulrich offers a fuller historical account of the case and its participants.

M

In November of 1792, Martha's niece, Parthenia Barton, who had been living with the family for some time, marries Shubael Pitts. Martha's daughter Hannah marries Moses Pollard, the son of an old friend, Merriam Pollard, who often worked as a town nurse. Ulrich then describes traditional marriage practices in those days, including simple, work-intensive weddings and the fact that couples lived apart until they were able to set up a household. Martha also talks about being summoned to Sally Pierce's delivery. Sally identified Martha's son Jonathan as the father of her illegitimate baby and sued him for support, which he fulfilled by marrying her. Ulrich then discusses the histories and results of other paternity suits from that time period. In November and December of 1793, Martha describes several complication-free deliveries she performs in the quiet period following the weddings. Ulrich expands upon this by explaining in more detail how these deliveries might have gone and comparing Martha's success rate to other historical rates.

Martha's youngest daughter, Dolly, marries Barnabas Lambard in May of 1795, and in Martha's entries for January of the following year, the problem of housework has become dramatically larger now that she has no one at home to help her with it. In November of that year, Martha recounts that a band of armed men had attacked her husband while he attempted to complete a survey job. Ulrich adds further explanation, saying that poor settlers often saw surveyors as agents of richer men who were trying to take away the land that the settlers felt they had won for themselves. Even in these more difficult times, Martha's medical involvement in the community still continues, and in February of 1801, Martha talks about tending to the death of her daughter-in-law's nephew and being asked by the doctor to be an attendant at his dissection. Ulrich follows this with a more detailed look at the little boy's history and offers a look at the changing relationship between doctors and midwives.

By March of 1804, Martha had grown weary, troubled by untrustworthy hired help, Jonathan's often alcohol-induced temper, and Ephraim's imprisonment for debt related to his job as a tax collector.

Ulrich gives a more detailed picture of what Ephraim's imprisonment would have been like, after which Martha describes the difficulties of being a woman on her own. Jonathan and his family move in with her, but due to her strained relationship with Jonathan, and Sally's insistence on being mistress of the house, the move only adds to Martha's troubles. In 1806, however, Martha's neighborhood faces even greater obstacles when they discover that a neighbor, Captain Purrinton, had slaughtered almost his entire family before committing suicide. Ulrich describes the entirety of the case and gives a few theories offered at the time as to Captain Purrinton's motives. Eight months later, another tragedy hits Martha's family when the husband of her niece, Betsy Barton, commits suicide.

By May of 1809, Martha's focus is mainly on her garden, the preparation that went into it, and what happened to the produce that came from it. Grandchildren are now old enough to help her with the housework, and the number of deliveries she attends has increased dramatically. Ulrich offers details on gardens of the time period but also describes the larger political turmoil of the area that is only offered in brief, family-related details in Martha's diary. Martha attends several deliveries early in 1812, but the stress makes her ill, and her last entry describes the family and preacher gathering at her house on May 7. She dies a few weeks later. The diary is passed down through Dolly's descendents until it reaches Martha's great-great-granddaughter, Mary Hobart, one of the country's early female physicians. Mary treasures the diary but gives it to the Maine State Library in 1930 so that it might be more accessible to historians.

CHARACTER LIST

Martha Moore Ballard A Hallowell midwife and the protagonist of *A Midwife's Tale*. A reserved woman, Martha deeply values her own autonomy and avoids passing judgment on others. However, she is very firm in her own opinions and finds ways of making her displeasure known when she or someone she likes is slighted. Though Martha rarely says so explicity, her actions show that she loves her family and has a comfortable, mutually helpful marriage with Ephraim. Martha takes her duties as a nurse and midwife very seriously, giving help to anyone who needs it, no matter what their position in society or her own life situation. Deeply religious, Martha is aware of God's power and influence in her life even when she doesn't attend meetings. Like all women, Martha occasionally feels very tired and sorry for herself, and during these times, the diary serves as an outlet for the feelings she can't share with her family.

M

Ephraim Ballard Martha's husband. A surveyor for most of his life, Ephraim is a well-respected man who holds several positions of authority and trust within the community. Ephraim is calm and independent and generally lets Martha have full authority over her duties and whereabouts. He angers Martha only when he feels she is complaining too much about the help. Finally sick of being attacked, Ephraim quits his surveying job and becomes a tax collector. Though the job leads him to being jailed for debt, Ephraim seems to see his confinement almost as a period of relaxation. When he is home, however, Ephraim is a great help around the house and generally a good friend to Martha.

Cyrus Ballard Martha's oldest son. Quiet and unmarried, Cyrus follows miller jobs wherever they become available and moves in and out of his parents' house until he is in his early forties. Having developed powerful shoulders through his years of re-chiseling mill stones, Cyrus is a great help to Martha whenever he is in town. Though no mention of it is made in the diary, Ulrich theorizes that Cyrus had great difficulty achieving independence due to some sort of mental impairment.

Jonathan Ballard Martha's middle son. Jonathan is brash and drinks too much, and his fits of temper are a source of contention between him and Martha for much of her life. On more than one occasion, Martha records fights that Jonathan has instigated with neighbors, and though the rest of the family learns to accept these brawls, Martha's descriptions indicate that she remains opposed to his behavior. Despite his temper, Jonathan is very aware of his responsibilities. He marries Sally when she gives birth to his child, and he makes sure his mother is taken care of even if it isn't in the way she might have wanted. Ephraim's declared heir, Jonathan has occasional problems with debt but works hard to raise the fortunes of himself and his children.

Hannah Ballard Pollard One of Martha's daughters. A quiet, dutiful girl who masters all of the domestic skills necessary to set up a good household of her own, Hannah is the only daughter living at home during the course of the diary who isn't mentioned in conjunction with directly helping with her mother's nursing duties. After her marriage to Moses Pollard, Hannah's focus seems to be on her own large family. Still, Hannah's birth so close to the death of her sisters may have led to a special relationship between her and Martha, as she is the only child listed at Martha's bedside in the diary's final entry.

Dolly Ballard Lambard Martha's youngest daughter. The only daughter to develop a specific career of her own, Dolly trains and begins working as a dressmaker for a period of time before her marriage to Barnabas Lambard. Dolly is a hard, uncomplaining worker, and she assists her mother during her midwiving and nursing duties, though she is not always sympathetic enough to Martha's needs. Dolly is left in charge of Martha's papers after she dies, and she passes the diary on to her daughters.

Parthenia Barton Pitts One of Martha's nieces. Sent by her mother, Dorothy Barton, to live with Martha as a teenager, Parthenia likes the arrangement so well that she stays with Martha until she marries Shubael Pitts and sets up a household of her own. A patient, uncomplaining worker, Parthenia assists Martha both through housework and by watching patients when Martha can't do so herself. Baptized during her final illness, Martha commends the niece she thinks of as a daughter on her patience and Christian meekness. Parthenia dies at a young age.

Sally Pierce Ballard Jonathan's wife and Martha's daughter-in-law. A strong woman who knows what she wants, Sally has no trouble claiming Jonathan as the father of her daughter and pressuring him until he agrees to marry her. This strength of will gives both her and Martha considerable difficulty when they live under the same roof, each fighting to be mistress of the same space. Though she often complains of Martha's inflexibility, the entries suggest that she behaves similarly when living as a widow under her own son's roof. Sally cares very much for her sister Hitty and occasionally fulfills nursing needs in the neighborhood.

Captain James Purrinton Martha's neighbor, who murders his family before committing suicide. Sober, industrious, taciturn James is a respected member of the local militia, and, before the murders, Martha bakes for James and often trades goods with the rest of the family. Early historians have theorized that James diverts from his original plan to only commit suicide because he needs to control his family's future. A Universalist, he believes that everyone will be saved regardless of their actions.

M

Rev. Isaac Foster A local preacher who Martha likes. Somewhat more radical in his religious beliefs than many town leaders, Foster is given to suing his enemies and is eventually dismissed from his position. Looking for work out of town at the time, Foster seems able to do little to defend his wife's safety or reputation from the abuse of town leaders. Eventually, he and his family are forced to flee Hallowell in disgrace and debt. The same traits that brought him and Rebecca such trouble in Hallowell also get them chased out of several other towns. Eventually, they find a town that accepts their eccentricities.

Henry Sewell Another Hallowell diarist often quoted by Ulrich. Martha's neighbor and occasional employer, Sewell is very conservative in his religious beliefs and is a major force behind driving the Fosters out of town. Sewell is highly patriotic and attuned to ceremony, and he disapproves of any activity that even hints of scandal. In his diary, he offers a very male perspective of the time—that is, he seems completely oblivious to the daily rhythms of life going on around him. Even the birth of one of his children is recorded only in Martha's diary, not in his.

Judge Joseph North Martha's neighbor who is accused of rape. A well-respected member of the community, North seems to feel sympathy for the woman he is accused of attacking. He is acquitted of Rebecca Foster's rape charges and seems to suffer no lasting effects on his career. Martha and her family, however, never forgive him, and her daughters go out of their way to have someone else officiate at their weddings.

Dr. Benjamin Page A Hallowell physician who sometimes works with Martha. Page is intent on developing an obstetrics practice rather than arriving during emergencies like most physicians, and Martha thinks him bumbling enough to record more than one of his mistakes for posterity. His skill improves with experience, however, and during the years when Martha delivers fewer babies, he is one of the main people whom the expectant mothers request.

Mary Hobart Martha's great-great-granddaughter, who inherited the diary. A practicing physician in the late 1800s, Mary is one of the first women allowed into the once exclusively male Massachusetts Medical Society. Mary cherishes Martha's diary, admiring her great-grandmother's skill and professionalism and feeling a deep kinship with her. She donates the diary to the Maine State Library to keep it safe and give others greater accessibility to it. Though highly disappointed by the deletions in the incomplete transcript they give her in return, Mary is gracious enough to thank the library for their efforts.

ANALYSIS OF MAJOR CHARACTERS

MARTHA BALLARD Though Martha seldom mentions deep friendships in her diary, she relies heavily upon her connections to people in her community. One of the most significant elements in her diary is her chronicle of neighbors she visits with and those who visit her. The interaction itself, not the reason for the visit, is what matters to Martha, and sometimes she makes no mention of why the visit takes place. Her midwifery is the greatest example and facilitator of these connections, giving a wide variety of people a reason to reach out to Martha and ask her for help. Martha is a popular midwife, and her delivering and nursing take her to most of the community. When the Purrinton murders strike the community, Martha focuses on the neighbors' actions instead of on the crime itself and describes how together they deal with the dead and help the survivor. When Martha becomes increasingly homebound, her isolation from the rest of the community bothers her a great deal, and she begins deliberately passing along the produce from her garden in an effort to reach out to the community once again.

Though contact with others is vital for Martha, she also needs to maintain authority over her own life. Midwifery gives Martha the chance to make her own decisions, spend considerable time away from home, and work with only the eyes of the community as supervision. Unlike most jobs available to women, midwifery provides a salary equal to her husband's and the chance to manage it independently, both of which help Martha gain a greater autonomy in her marriage. Martha clashes with the local doctors only when they try to deny her ability to make intelligent, skilled decisions on her own, and though she acknowledges their skills, she does her best to avoid working with them. Martha's need for autonomy also contributes to making the later years of her life difficult. Without the responsibility and constructive effort of midwifery, she feels she has lost the ability to control her own life.

HENRY SEWELL Though Martha and Sewell meet only rarely during their lifetimes, Sewell's diary is a perfect foil for Martha's. While Martha builds her life on the strength of the people she is connected to and on the worth of her daily accomplishments, Sewell's highest priority is clearly the philosophies and ideals he most supports. The funeral of a dead president, merely a local event for Martha, becomes for Sewell an opportunity to ruminate on the ideals of the new republic and how Washington had served as a symbol for those ideals. Sewell has a long and bitter feud going with Isaac Foster and contributes wholeheartedly to driving the family out of town, but in none of his entries on Foster does Sewell have anything bad to say about the man as a person. The entirety of Sewell's very strong dislike is a disagreement with Foster's religious beliefs. Ideas are Sewell's focus even when writing about the Purrinton murders. His entry about the funeral focuses less on the tragedy than on the fact that the preacher is a Methodist. For Sewell, people matter far less than what they believe in.

THEMES, MOTIFS, AND SYMBOLS

THEMES

ACTIONS SPEAK LOUDER THAN WORDS Though Martha is reluctant to write down her own opinion on certain matters, her actions always make her feelings about a topic clear. She never mentions her views of equality in her diary, but she does record that she goes out to deliver black children with the same speed and skill that she does the white ones. She never discusses her opinion of the Fosters, but she cares about the family enough to stay away from church for the four years that it is controlled by the people who chased them away. Martha is careful not to state her feelings about Judge North's acquittal, but she retains negative enough feelings about the man that when her daughters get married, they all go out of their way to make sure someone other than North marries them. Martha's opinion of local doctors comes through in her treatment toward them. She occasionally defers to their specialized skills but generally sees them as completely unnecessary.

THE IMPORTANCE OF SIMPLE MOMENTS Much of the significance of Martha's diary comes from the simple rhythms of her daily life rather than from the dramatic events she experiences and witnesses. Though Martha's descriptions of dangerous rides and crossing the frozen Kennbec River are exciting, it is the gentle practicality with which she treated the families she was attending that reveal most clearly what it meant to be a mother and social healer during that time period. Though Martha was a close neighbor to the Purrintons, her description of their murder-suicide is far more limited and less detailed then records from other sources. The simple, comprehensive records of the illegitimate babies she delivered as part of her regular workload, however, offer new insight into sexuality and marriage customs of early New England. Martha generally avoids the story of what Ephraim may have experienced in debtor's prison, but her slowly self-defeating struggle to survive winter without her husband there to offer assistance truly shows the damage that debtor's prison could cause to people's lives.

THE CONTENTMENT OF A WELL-ORDERED LIFE In the sections of the diary where Martha seems the most at peace, her life is functioning smoothly and efficiently. Early in the diary, when she still has daughters and nieces she trusts living at home to take on the responsibility of housework, the entries clip along with the activity-focused efficiency Martha prefers. After the girls marry and move out, leaving Martha to tackle a mountain of housework along with her usual load of deliveries, complaints and talk of weariness begin to appear ever-increasingly in her diary. Chaos now awaits her each time she returns home from a delivery, and her inability to predict the behavior of her now-independent children adds chaos to her personal life. Only in the last section of her diary does talk of Martha's difficult life slowly begin to disappear from the pages. Grandchildren appear to lessen the load of housework, and Martha decides not to dwell on her children's behavior, instead focusing on her garden, the part of the world she can order as she sees fit.

MOTIFS

BIRTHS Martha's diary is full of the records of births with which Martha assists on almost a daily basis. In certain sections, nearly every day contains the record of a birth, listing the mother, sex of the child, and payment later received as well as the basic facts of the delivery itself. When complications arise, Martha describes them as simply and clearly as possible, preferring to focus on what is being done to help the mother and any improvement that might be seen in her or her baby's condition. The entries rarely contain even a hint of the drama often shown in fictional representations of deliveries. Rather, these records are simple, straightforward accounts of the lives that Martha helps bring into the world. Added to this are the running tallies of births Martha assists, with a separate number for each year and a larger one that covers her entire career as a midwife. For Martha, these numbers are a way to quietly mark the value of her life. The effort she has put into helping her community is made clear in the tiny lives she helps bring into it.

COMMUNITY RELATIONS Martha devotes most of her diary to her interactions with other people in the community, including patients, assistants, economic partners, and neighbors. She carefully lists all of the women whose babies she delivers and the sick people she treats. Her nursing records also include doctors and other women who either assist Martha with her patients or take care of those she doesn't have the time or resources to help. She faithfully records all of the midwifery fees she receives and the people who pay them, and though her trade with her neighbors is much more complex, she records the specifics of those exchanges whenever she can. Even when she can't, however, the visits between Martha, her daughters, and her neighbors are always recorded. Such entries trace a map of connections within the community—the network of those in need and those offering assistance—that is such an integral part of Martha's life.

RESPONSIBILITY Martha's life is largely determined by her feeling of responsibility toward others, and she expects her family to live in a similar manner. She travels dangerous paths and spends a significant amount of time away from her home and family because she knows how much the women in the community need her, slackening only later in life when she becomes too ill to do her job effectively. Even when Martha isn't involved with a sick neighbor, she still keeps track of their progress. She helps and supports the Fosters because she feels responsible for maintaining the community web even when others will not. Though Martha knows that Sally has already sworn out a warrant on Jonathan, she still asks her who the father of her illegitimate child is because taking such testimony is part of Martha's responsibility as a midwife. Much of Martha's trouble with her children comes when she feels they aren't fulfilling their responsibility to her, not only leaving her without support but going against the example she has worked so hard to set for them.

SYMBOLS

MARTHA'S HOUSE To Martha, her house represents her increasing frustrations with her workload, her family, and her life in general. Martha struggles to balance a career with the responsibilities of her home life, and after her daughters marry and move out, Martha finds it impossible to stop her home from sliding into ever-greater chaos. Her daughters are no longer around to help, her son Jonathan interrupts the peace of her house with drunken rages, and Ephraim, who faces none of the responsibilities of housework, attempts to interfere when Martha berates a hired girl who is supposed to help her. When Ephraim is in debtor's prison and her sons are not willing to help, the demands of the house are almost more than she can deal with, and Martha is forced to nearly give up midwifery in order to cope. When Jonathan and his family move in, the house reflects her frustration over her stolen autonomy as she is forced to scale her life down from the entire spread of the house to what can fit in the back room.

MARTHA'S GARDEN To Martha, her garden is a microcosm of her life, her investment into the community, and her career as a midwife. All of the benefits she gleans from a garden are rewards for her effort, since vegetables will not grow without careful planting and tending. Like nursing the sick and delivering babies, gardening requires regular care and attention. In several entries, Martha describes the weeks and months of hard work with the simple comment that she has worked in her garden. Maintaining the garden is personal, but it is also a community effort, with Ephraim helping to dig and set hop poles and neighbors plowing the field. Near the end of Martha's life, her garden represents the order she wishes she could find in her own life, and in her diary, descriptions of planting pea and squash plants replace traumatic moments with children and neighbors that she doesn't wish to discuss.

PRAYER For Martha, prayer is less a religious observance than a symbol of the constant presence and support of God in her life. Though she seems to see church meetings as simply pleasant diversions and is absent from them for years with no noticeable effect, she regularly includes in her diary pleas to God for strength, comfort, and gratitude for receiving those things. When a difficult delivery turns out well, she thanks God for being by her side throughout the proceedings, and when a sickness worsens, she prays that God will watch out for the ill person as he has always watched out for her. When the Malta rebels threaten to attack the town, Martha says a simple prayer for the safety of her friends and neighbors. After the Purrinton murders, Martha realizes she is witnessing a sickness far out of her power to heal, and she prays to God that he will make something good out of the tragedy. God is also there during a more personal tragedy: the death of Martha's beloved niece, Parthenia. When Martha finally sees that all chances for physical healing have passed, she helps Parthenia find God in the hopes that she will receive the same comfort and strength that Martha has always had.

IMPORTANT QUOTATIONS EXPLAINED

---

1. *The mixing of governours in a household, or subordinating or uniting of two masters, or two dames under one roof, doth fall out most times, to be a matter of much unquietness to all parties.*

This observation is from an early English treatise on marriage, and Ulrich uses it in the March 1804 chapter to discuss the problems between Martha and her daughter-in-law Sally. These words offer a philosophy by which Martha seems to have lived her entire life. Though she never attempts to interfere with Ephraim's decisions and duties, Martha expects the same respect in return and assumes full authority over the responsibilities she considers hers. She alone decides what plants will be part of her garden and where each will go, and she alone manages all of the female workers who enter the house. One of the few times Martha records being truly upset with Ephraim is when he attempts to defend one of the hired girls whom Martha feels isn't fulfilling her duties as household help. He has no experience with housework and won't be held responsible if it isn't completed properly, so he therefore has no business defying Martha's authority in this area.

Martha even chose a profession that gives her complete authority over her own actions and business dealings, which was rare in early America. Though she is summoned to each birth by the family, it is her choice whether or not she will go. If a ride isn't provided for her by the husband or family of the expectant mother, it is her job to find one, and though Ephraim or one of her sons occasionally offers her a ride, she has enough horsemanship skills to not be dependent upon them. On all but a few occasions, payment for her services goes directly into her hands rather than her husband's, even though men are often the ones who settle the debts. If her work brings her in contact with the male doctors who also work in the area, she listens to their opinions but grows frustrated when she thinks they are interfering with her work. Her experience has proven her authority in this area, and she will not quietly accept it being questioned.

---

2. *In such circumstances it was comforting to have the women with her; they could witness her efforts to ensure a safe delivery and they could assist with the sorrowful task of preparing an infant for burial.*

Ulrich makes this observation in the December 1793 chapter as she discusses infant mortality rates, and her comment shows how important community opinion is to Martha's success as a midwife. At no time does Martha mention simply showing up at a birth that isn't family-related. Rather, the parents of the unborn baby must summon her to the mother's bedside and trust that she is the right one to successfully deliver their child. This trust is often developed through word-of-mouth of family, friends, and neighbors, and the people spreading the word are usually the women who have actually watched Martha perform successful deliveries and who have confidence that she can reproduce such success. Observers at the tragic deliveries also strengthen her reputation, since they can attest that insurmountable medical problems rather than incompetence led to the death. They can then relate to others that Martha had fought as hard as she could to prevent the loss of the child or mother.

These neighborhood witnesses to deliveries also help strengthen Martha's own opinion of her success as a midwife. She devotes much of her diary to marking the births she spends so much of her life successfully guiding, counting the worth of her days and years by how many mothers and children she attends to in their time of need. However, she allows herself to describe little more than the barest circumstances of the delivery and the results for the mother and child, rarely mentioning the effort involved in her part of the process. The women who observe and help in these deliveries, then, are living records of this effort. She feels no need to brag about her work to others or defend it to future generations, since she is secure in the knowledge that the people she helps know firsthand just how much of herself she gives to her profession.

---

3. *In her universe, 'Girls washt' was an important statement, something on the order of 'got across the river safely.'*

Ulrich makes this statement in the January 1796 chapter after Martha talks about losing the help of her daughters, and it offers insight into the way Martha structures her diary and her life as a whole. Some historians seem interested only in the dramatic events that the diary relates, such as the Purrinton murders and the trial of Martha's nephew Elijah Barton, but when Martha's diary is taken as a whole, these are relatively minor matters. Martha's diary is not a history but a life, and like all lives, it is filled mainly with work, household chores, and talks with friends and neighbors. To Martha, finishing the housework for the day and making it home safely are just as important as the shocking things that happen to her neighbors. Less important than either of these are the country's larger political troubles, which are included in the diary only when they personally touch Martha's life in some way. Martha's first priority is always her own little corner of the world.

Martha is also grateful for all of the blessings to be found in that little corner, and she makes sure to acknowledge those blessings alongside the records of her work. Whenever she describes a river crossing that was more dangerous than normal, she is sure to include a thank you to God for protecting her. Though this gratitude is not specifically recorded on the more mundane crossings, she makes sure to mention each one she makes safely so that she can better remember each and every time God has kept an eye on her. "Girls washt," for all its simplicity, holds much the same weight in her diary. Entries written after her daughters are married are filled with the stress and dislike that Martha feels toward household chores, so when she does have her daughters at home, she carefully notes each time they take that particular weight off her shoulders. Because her daughters wash, she doesn't have to, and she is grateful for it every day.

---

4. *There is little more to add, except that for almost four years after Isaac Foster's dismissal Martha neglected 'Public Worship'.*

Ulrich makes this observation in the October 1789 chapter as part of her description of Hallowell's treatment of the Fosters. Martha's statement of disapproval is much stronger than it appears, especially since her entries suggest a general unwillingness on her part to publicly question community leaders. She does not want her authority to be interfered with, so she tries not to interfere in the authority of others, and she does not comment on the unfairness of their decision to drive Isaac Foster and his wife out of town. However, Martha expresses her feelings by slowing her once regular church worship to a trickle. She continues to acknowledge God in her diary during the time period even though she is largely absent from meetings, and as soon as the church is divided and the extreme moderates take charge elsewhere, she once again begins attending regularly.

Martha feels such disapproval in part because the dismissal contradicts the neighborhood connections that she values so much. The community is connected by a web of mutual assistance, one that Martha carries out by delivering the babies even of freed blacks and the poor. If they need help, she offers it, because it is her responsibility as their neighbor. The community leaders' determination to drive out the Fosters because of a mere difference in religious opinion is in complete opposition to this philosophy. The action goes against everything she believes in, and it is impossible for her not to respond.

---

5. *Daughter Ballard and a Number of her Children here. Mrs Partridge & Smith allso. Revered Mr Tappin Came and Converst swetly and mad a prayer adapted to my Case.*

This is the last entry in Martha's diary, and it contains a mention of everything she values most in life. The family she devoted so much time and energy to raising and helping pays their final respects to her. Two of her neighbors are there, signifying her beloved community network and the medical cycle of which she was a part. Her lifelong faith is supported by the presence of Mr. Tappin. Throughout her life, she gathered by the deathbeds of others, and members of the community now gather by her deathbed to offer what assistance they can. The moment is a perfect summary of and homage to her seventy-seven years of life. Though Martha lives for a few more weeks, she ends her diary here as part of her effort to order the diary as she always wanted to order her life. If she had the strength to write this entry, odds are she could have had the strength to write more, but she chose not to do so. She wrote the diary so that people would know how she lived, not how she died, and she seems content with the way her recorded life ends.

Mrs. Dalloway

Virginia Woolf (1882–1941)

CONTEXT

Virginia Woolf, the English novelist, critic, and essayist, was born on January 25, 1882, to Leslie Stephen, a literary critic, and Julia Duckworth Stephen. Woolf grew up in an upper-middle-class, socially active, literary family in Victorian London. She had three full siblings, two half-brothers, and two half-sisters. She was educated at home, becoming a voracious reader of the books in her father's extensive library. Tragedy first afflicted the family when Woolf's mother died in 1895, then hit again two years later, when her half-sister, Stella, the caregiver in the Stephen family, died. Woolf experienced her first bout of mental illness after her mother's death, and she suffered from mania and severe depression for the rest of her life.

Patriarchal, repressive Victorian society did not encourage women to attend universities or to participate in intellectual debate. Nonetheless, Woolf began publishing her first essays and reviews after 1904, the year her father died and she and her siblings moved to the Bloomsbury area of London. Young students and artists, drawn to the vitality and intellectual curiosity of the Stephen clan, congregated on Thursday evenings to share their views about the world. The Bloomsbury group, as Woolf and her friends came to be called, disregarded the constricting taboos of the Victorian era, and such topics as religion, sex, and art fueled the talk at their weekly salons. They even discussed homosexuality, a subject that shocked many of the group's contemporaries. For Woolf, the group served as the undergraduate education that society had denied her.

The Voyage Out, Woolf's first novel, was published in 1915, three years after her marriage to Leonard Woolf, a member of the Bloomsbury group. Their partnership furthered the group's intellectual ideals. With Leonard, Woolf founded Hogarth Press, which published Sigmund Freud, Katherine Mansfield, T. S. Eliot, and other notable authors. She determinedly pursued her own writing as well: during the next few years, Woolf kept a diary and wrote several novels, a collection of short stories, and numerous essays. She struggled, as she wrote, to both deal with her bouts of bipolarity and to find her true voice as a writer. Before World War I, Woolf viewed the realistic Victorian novel, with its neat and linear plots, as an inadequate form of expression. Her opinion intensified after the war, and in the 1920s she began searching for the form that would reflect the violent contrasts and disjointed impressions of the world around her.

In *Mrs. Dalloway*, published in 1925, Woolf discovered a new literary form capable of expressing the new realities of postwar England. The novel depicts the subjective experiences and memories of its central characters over a single day in post–World War I London. Divided into parts, rather than chapters, the novel's structure highlights the finely interwoven texture of the characters' thoughts. Critics tend to agree that Woolf found her writer's voice with this novel. At forty-three, she knew her experimental style was unlikely to be a popular success but no longer felt compelled to seek critical praise. The novel did, however, gain a measure of commercial and critical success. This book, which focuses on commonplace tasks, such as shopping, throwing a party, and eating dinner, showed that no act was too small or too ordinary for a writer's attention. Ultimately, *Mrs. Dalloway* transformed the novel as an art form.

Woolf develops the book's protagonist, Clarissa Dalloway, and myriad other characters by chronicling their interior thoughts with little pause or explanation, a style referred to as stream of consciousness. Several central characters and more than one hundred minor characters appear in the text, and their thoughts spin out like spider webs. Sometimes the threads of thought cross—and people succeed in communicating. More often, however, the threads do not cross, leaving the characters isolated and alone. Woolf believed that behind the "cotton wool" of life, as she terms it in her autobiographical collection of essays *Moments of Being* (1941), and under the downpour of impressions saturating a mind during each moment, a pattern exists.

Characters in *Mrs. Dalloway* occasionally perceive life's pattern through a sudden shock, or what Woolf called a "moment of being." Suddenly the cotton wool parts, and a person sees reality, and his or her place in it, clearly. "In the vast catastrophe of the European war," wrote Woolf, "our emotions had to be broken up for us, and put at an angle from us, before we could allow ourselves to feel them in poetry or fiction." These words appear in her essay collection, *The Common Reader*, which was published just one month before *Mrs. Dalloway*. Her novel attempts to uncover fragmented emotions, such as desperation or love, in order to find, through "moments of being," a way to endure.

While writing *Mrs. Dalloway*, Woolf reread the Greek classics along with two new modernist writers, Marcel Proust and James Joyce. Woolf shared these writers' interest in time and psychology, and she incorporated these issues into her novel. She wanted to show characters in flux, rather than static, characters who think and emote as they move through space, who react to their surroundings in ways that mirrored actual human experience. Rapid political and social change marked the period between the two world wars: the British Empire, for which so many people had sacrificed their lives to protect and preserve, was in decline. Countries like India were beginning to question Britain's colonial rule. At home, the Labour Party, with its plans for economic reform, was beginning to challenge the Conservative Party, with its emphasis on imperial business interests. Women, who had flooded the workforce to replace the men who had gone to war, were demanding equal rights. Men, who had seen unspeakable atrocities in the first modern war, were questioning the usefulness of class-based sociopolitical institutions. Woolf lent her support to the feminist movement in her nonfiction book *A Room of One's Own* (1929), as well as in numerous essays, and she was briefly involved in the women's suffrage movement. Although *Mrs. Dalloway* portrays the shifting political atmosphere through the characters Peter Walsh, Richard Dalloway, and Hugh Whitbread, it focuses more deeply on the charged social mood through the characters Septimus Warren Smith and Clarissa Dalloway. Woolf delves into the consciousness of Clarissa, a woman who exists largely in the domestic sphere, to ensure that readers take her character seriously, rather than simply dismiss her as a vain and uneducated upper-class wife. In spite of her heroic and imperfect effort in life, Clarissa, like every human being and even the old social order itself, must face death.

Woolf's struggles with mental illness gave her an opportunity to witness firsthand how insensitive medical professionals could be, and she critiques their tactlessness in *Mrs. Dalloway*. One of Woolf's doctors suggested that plenty of rest and rich food would lead to a full recovery, a cure prescribed in the novel, and another removed several of her teeth. In the early twentieth century, mental health problems were too often considered imaginary, an embarrassment, or the product of moral weakness. During one bout of illness, Woolf heard birds sing like Greek choruses and King Edward use foul language among some azaleas. In 1941, as England entered a second world war, and at the onset of another breakdown she feared would be permanent, Woolf placed a large stone in her pocket to weigh herself down and drowned herself in the River Ouse.

PLOT OVERVIEW

Mrs. Dalloway covers one day from morning to night in one woman's life. Clarissa Dalloway, an upper-class housewife, walks through her London neighborhood to prepare for the party she will host that evening. When she returns from flower-shopping, an old suitor and friend, Peter Walsh, drops by her house unexpectedly. The two have always judged each other harshly, and their meeting in the present intertwines with their thoughts of the past. Years ago, Clarissa refused Peter's marriage proposal, and Peter has never quite gotten over it. Peter asks Clarissa if she is happy with her husband, Richard, but before she can answer, her daughter, Elizabeth, enters the room. Peter leaves and goes to Regent's Park. He thinks about Clarissa's refusal, which still obsesses him.

The point of view then shifts to Septimus, a veteran of World War I who was injured in trench warfare and now suffers from shell shock. Septimus and his Italian wife, Lucrezia, pass time in Regent's Park. They are waiting for Septimus's appointment with Sir William Bradshaw, a celebrated psychiatrist. Before the war, Septimus was a budding young poet and lover of Shakespeare; when the war broke out, he enlisted immediately for romantic patriotic reasons. He became numb to the horrors of war and its aftermath: when his friend Evans died, he felt little sadness. Now Septimus sees nothing of worth in the England he fought for, and he has lost the desire to preserve either his society or himself. Suicidal, he believes his lack of feeling is a crime. Clearly Septimus's experiences in the war have permanently scarred him, and he has serious mental problems. However, Sir William does not listen to what Septimus says and diagnoses "a lack of proportion." Sir William plans to separate Septimus from Lucrezia and send him to a mental institution in the country.

Richard Dalloway eats lunch with Hugh Whitbread and Lady Bruton, members of high society. The men help Lady Bruton write a letter to the *Times*, London's largest newspaper. After lunch, Richard returns home to Clarissa with a large bunch of roses. He intends to tell her that he loves her but finds that he cannot, because it has been so long since he last said it. Clarissa considers the void that exists between people, even between husband and wife. Even though she values the privacy she is able to maintain in her marriage, considering it vital to the success of the relationship, at the same time she finds slightly disturbing the fact that Richard doesn't know everything about her. Clarissa sees off Elizabeth and her history teacher, Miss Kilman, who are going shopping. The two older women despise one another passionately, each believing the other to be an oppressive force over Elizabeth. Meanwhile, Septimus and Lucrezia are in their apartment, enjoying a moment of happiness together before the men come to take Septimus to the asylum. One of Septimus's doctors, Dr. Holmes, arrives, and Septimus fears the doctor will destroy his soul. In order to avoid this fate, he jumps from a window to his death.

Peter hears the ambulance go by to pick up Septimus's body and marvels ironically at the level of London's civilization. He goes to Clarissa's party, where most of the novel's major characters are assembled. Clarissa works hard to make her party a success but feels dissatisfied by her own role and acutely conscious of Peter's critical eye. All the partygoers, but especially Peter and Sally Seton, have, to some degree, failed to accomplish the dreams of their youth. Though the social order is undoubtedly changing, Elizabeth and the members of her generation will probably repeat the errors of Clarissa's generation. Sir William Bradshaw arrives late, and his wife explains that one of his patients, the young veteran (Septimus), has committed suicide. Clarissa retreats to the privacy of a small room to consider Septimus's death. She understands that he was overwhelmed by life and that men like Sir William make life intolerable. She identifies with Septimus, admiring him for having taken the plunge and for not compromising his soul. She feels, with her comfortable position as a society hostess, responsible for his death. The party nears its close as guests begin to leave. Clarissa enters the room, and her presence fills Peter with a great excitement.

CHARACTER LIST

Clarissa Dalloway The eponymous protagonist. The novel begins with Clarissa's point of view and follows her perspective more closely than that of any other character. As Clarissa prepares for the party she will give that evening, we are privy to her meandering thoughts. Clarissa is vivacious and cares a great deal about what people think of her, but she is also self-reflective. She often questions life's true meaning, wondering whether happiness is truly possible. She feels both a great joy and a great dread about her life, both of which manifest in her struggles to strike a balance between her desire for privacy and her need to communicate with others. Throughout the day, Clarissa reflects on the crucial summer when she chose to marry her husband, Richard, instead of her friend Peter Walsh. Though she is happy with Richard, she is not entirely certain she made the wrong choice about Peter, and she also thinks frequently about her friend Sally Seton, whom she also once loved.

Septimus Warren Smith A World War I veteran suffering from shell shock, married to an Italian woman named Lucrezia. Though he is insane, Septimus views English society in much the same way as Clarissa does, and he struggles, as she does, to both maintain his privacy and fulfill his need to communicate with others. He shares so many traits with Clarissa that he could be her double. Septimus is pale, has a hawklike posture, and wears a shabby overcoat. Before the war, he was a young, idealistic, aspiring poet. After the war, he regards human nature as evil and believes he is guilty of not being able to feel. Rather than succumb to the society he abhors, he commits suicide.

Peter Walsh A close friend of Clarissa's, once desperately in love with her. Clarissa rejected Peter's marriage proposal when she was eighteen, and he moved to India. He has not been to London for five years. He is highly critical of others, is conflicted about nearly everything in his life, and has a habit of playing with his pocketknife. Often overcome with emotion, he cries easily. He frequently has romantic problems with women and is currently in love with Daisy, a married woman in India. He wears horn-rimmed glasses and a bow tie and used to be a Socialist.

Sally Seton A close friend of Clarissa and Peter in their youth. Sally was a wild, handsome ragamuffin who smoked cigars and would say anything. She and Clarissa were sexually attracted to one another as teenagers. Now Sally lives in Manchester and is married with five boys. Her married name is Lady Rosseter.

Richard Dalloway Clarissa's husband. A member of Parliament in the Conservative government, Richard plans to write a history of the great English military family, the Brutons, when the Labour Party comes to power. He is a sportsman and likes being in the country. He is a loving father and husband. While devoted to social reform, he appreciates English tradition. He has failed to make it into the Cabinet, or main governing body.

Hugh Whitbread Clarissa's old friend, married to Evelyn Whitbread. An impeccable Englishman and upholder of English tradition, Hugh writes letters to the *Times* about various causes. He never brushes beneath the surface of any subject and is rather vain. Many are critical of his pompousness and gluttony, but he remains oblivious. He is, as Clarissa thinks, almost too perfectly dressed. He makes Clarissa feel young and insecure.

Lucrezia Smith (Rezia) Septimus's wife, a twenty-four-year-old hat-maker from Milan. Rezia loves Septimus but is forced to bear the burden of his mental illness alone. Normally a lively and playful young woman, she has grown thin with worry. She feels isolated and continually wishes to share her unhappiness with somebody. She trims hats for the friends of her neighbor, Mrs. Filmer.

Elizabeth Dalloway Clarissa and Richard's only child. Gentle, considerate, and somewhat passive, seventeen-year-old Elizabeth does not have Clarissa's energy. She has a dark beauty that is beginning to attract attention. Not a fan of parties or clothes, she likes being in the country with her father and dogs. She spends a great deal of time praying with her history teacher, the religious Miss Kilman, and is considering career options.

Doris Kilman Elizabeth's history teacher, who has German ancestry. Miss Kilman has a history degree and was fired from a teaching job during the war because of society's anti-German prejudice. She is over forty and wears an unattractive mackintosh coat because she does not dress to please. She became a born-again Christian two years and three months ago. Poor, with a forehead like an egg, she is bitter and dislikes Clarissa intensely but adores Elizabeth.

Sir William Bradshaw A renowned London psychiatrist. When Lucrezia seeks help for her insane husband, Septimus, Septimus's doctor, Dr. Holmes, recommends Sir William. Sir William believes that most people who think they are mad suffer instead from a "lack of proportion." He determines that Septimus has suffered a complete nervous breakdown and recommends that Septimus spend time in the country, apart from Lucrezia. The hardworking son of a tradesman, Sir William craves power and has become respected in his field.

Dr. Holmes Septimus's general practitioner. When Septimus begins to suffer the delayed effects of shell shock, Lucrezia seeks his help. Dr. Holmes claims nothing is wrong with Septimus, but that Lucrezia should see Sir William if she doesn't believe him. Septimus despises Dr. Holmes and refers to him as "human nature." Dr. Holmes likes to go to the music hall and to play golf.

Lady (Millicent) Bruton A member of high society and a friend of the Dalloways. At sixty-two years old, Lady Bruton is devoted to promoting emigration to Canada for English families. Normally erect and magisterial, she panics when she has to write a letter to the editor and seeks help from Richard Dalloway and Hugh Whitbread. She has an assistant, Milly Brush, and a chow dog. She is a descendant of General Sir Talbot Moore.

Miss Helena Parry (Aunt Helena) Clarissa's aunt. Aunt Helena is a relic of the strict English society Clarissa finds so confining. A great botanist, she also enjoys talking about orchids and Burma. She is a formidable old lady, over eighty, who found Sally Seton's behavior as a youth shocking. She has one glass eye.

Ellie Henderson Clarissa's dowdy cousin. Ellie, in her early fifties, has thin hair, a meager profile, and bad eyesight. Not trained for any career and having only a small income, she wears an old black dress to Clarissa's party. She is self-effacing, subject to chills, and close to a woman named Edith. Clarissa finds her dull and does not want to invite her to the party, and Ellie stands alone nearly the whole time, aware that she does not really belong.

Evans Septimus's wartime officer and close friend. Evans died in Italy just before the armistice, but Septimus, in his deluded state, continues to see and hear him behind trees and sitting-room screens. During the war, Evans and Septimus were inseparable. Evans was a shy Englishman with red hair.

Mrs. Filmer The Smiths' neighbor. Mrs. Filmer finds Septimus odd. She has honest blue eyes and is Rezia's only friend in London. Her daughter is Mrs. Peters, who listens to the Smiths' gramophone when they are not at home. Mrs. Filmer's granddaughter delivers the newspaper to the Smiths' home each evening, and Rezia always makes the child's arrival into a momentous, joyous event.

Daisy Simmons Peter Walsh's lover in India, married to a major in the Indian army. Daisy is twenty-four years old and has two small children. Peter is in London to arrange her divorce.

Evelyn Whitbread Hugh Whitbread's wife. Evelyn suffers from an unspecified internal ailment and spends much of her time in nursing homes. We learn about her from others. Peter Walsh describes her as mousy and almost negligible, but he also points out that occasionally she says something sharp.

Mr. Brewer Septimus's boss at Sibleys and Arrowsmith. Mr. Brewer, the managing clerk, is paternal with his employees and foresees a promising career for Septimus, but Septimus volunteers for the war before he can reach any degree of success. Mr. Brewer promotes Septimus when he returns from the war, but Septimus is already losing his mind. Mr. Brewer has a waxed moustache and a coral tiepin.

Jim Hutton An awful poet at the Dalloways' party. Jim is badly dressed, with red socks and unruly hair, and he does not enjoy talking to another guest, Professor Brierly, who is a professor of Milton. Jim shares with Clarissa a love of Bach and thinks she is "the best of the great ladies who took an interest in art." He enjoys mimicking people.

ANALYSIS OF MAJOR CHARACTERS

CLARISSA DALLOWAY Clarissa Dalloway, the heroine of the novel, struggles constantly to balance her internal life with the external world. Her world consists of glittering surfaces, such as fine fashion, parties, and high society, but as she moves through that world she probes beneath those surfaces in search of deeper meaning. Yearning for privacy, Clarissa has a tendency toward introspection that gives her a profound capacity for emotion, which many other characters lack. However, she is always concerned with appearances and keeps herself tightly composed, seldom sharing her feelings with anyone. She uses a constant stream of convivial chatter and activity to keep her soul locked safely away, which can make her seem shallow even to those who know her well.

M

Constantly overlaying the past and the present, Clarissa strives to reconcile herself to life despite her potent memories. For most of the novel she considers aging and death with trepidation, even as she performs life-affirming actions, such as buying flowers. Though content, Clarissa never lets go of the doubt she feels about the decisions that have shaped her life, particularly her decision to marry Richard instead of Peter Walsh. She understands that life with Peter would have been difficult, but at the same time she is uneasily aware that she sacrificed passion for the security and tranquility of an upper-class life. At times she wishes for a chance to live life over again. She experiences a moment of clarity and peace when she watches her old neighbor through her window, and by the end of the day she has come to terms with the possibility of death. Like Septimus, Clarissa feels keenly the oppressive forces in life, and she accepts that the life she has is all she'll get. Her will to endure, however, prevails.

SEPTIMUS WARREN SMITH Septimus, a veteran of World War I, suffers from shell shock and is lost within his own mind. He feels guilty even as he despises himself for being made numb by the war. His doctor has ordered Lucrezia, Septimus's wife, to make Septimus notice things outside himself, but Septimus has removed himself from the physical world. Instead, he lives in an internal world, wherein he sees and hears things that aren't really there and he talks to his dead friend Evans. He is sometimes overcome with the beauty in the world, but he also fears that the people in it have no capacity for honesty or kindness. Woolf intended for Clarissa to speak the sane truth and Septimus the insane truth, and indeed Septimus's detachment enables him to judge other people more harshly than Clarissa is capable of. The world outside of Septimus is threatening, and the way Septimus sees that world offers little hope.

On the surface, Septimus seems quite dissimilar to Clarissa, but he embodies many characteristics that Clarissa shares, and thinks in much the same way she does. He could almost be her double in the novel. Septimus and Clarissa both have beak-noses, love Shakespeare, and fear oppression. More important, as Clarissa's double, Septimus offers a contrast between the conscious struggle of a working-class veteran and the blind opulence of the upper class. His troubles call into question the legitimacy of the English society he fought to preserve during the war. Because his thoughts often run parallel to Clarissa's and echo hers in many ways, the thin line between what is considered sanity and insanity gets thinner and thinner. Septimus chooses to escape his problems by killing himself, a dramatic and tragic gesture that ultimately helps Clarissa to accept her own choices, as well as the society in which she lives.

PETER WALSH Peter Walsh's most consistent character trait is ambivalence: he is middle-aged and fears he has wasted his life, but sometimes he also feels he is not yet old. He cannot commit to an identity, or even to a romantic partner. He cannot decide what he feels and tries often to talk himself into feeling or not feeling certain things. For example, he spends the day telling himself that he no longer loves Clarissa, but his grief at losing her rises painfully to the surface when he is in her presence, and his obsession with her suggests that he is still attracted to her and may even long for renewed romance. Even when he gathers his anger toward Clarissa and tells her about his new love, he cannot sustain the anger and ends up weeping. Peter acts as a foil for Richard, who is stable, generous, and rather simple. Unlike calm Richard, Peter is like a storm, thundering and crashing, unpredictable even to himself.

Peter's unhealed hurt and persistent insecurity make him severely critical of other characters, especially the Dalloways. He detests Clarissa's bourgeois lifestyle, though he blames Richard for making her into the kind of woman she is. Clarissa intuits even his most veiled criticisms, such as when he remarks on her green dress, and his judgments strongly affect her own assessments of her life and choices. Despite his sharp critiques of others, Peter cannot clearly see his own shortcomings. His self-obsession and neediness would have suffocated Clarissa, which is partly why she refused his marriage proposal as a young woman. Peter acquiesces to the very English society he criticizes, enjoying the false sense of order it offers, which he lacks in his life. Despite Peter's ambivalence and tendency toward analysis, he still feels life deeply. While Clarissa comes to terms with her own mortality, Peter becomes frantic at the thought of death. He follows a young woman through the London streets to smother his thoughts of death with a fantasy of life and adventure. His critical nature may distance him from others, but he values his life nonetheless.

SALLY SETON Sally Seton exists only as a figure in Clarissa's memory for most of the novel, and when she appears at Clarissa's party, she is older but still familiar. Though the women have not seen each other for years, Sally still puts Clarissa first when she counts her blessings, even before her husband or five sons. As a girl, Sally was without inhibitions, and as an adult at the party, she is still effusive and lacks Clarissa's restraint. Long ago, Sally and Clarissa plotted to reform the world together. Now, however, both are married, a fate they once considered a "catastrophe." Sally has changed and calmed down a great deal since the Bourton days, but she is still enough of a loose cannon to make Peter nervous and to kindle Clarissa's old warm feelings. Both Sally and Clarissa have yielded to the forces of English society to some degree, but Sally keeps more distance than Clarissa does. She often takes refuge in her garden, as she despairs over communicating with humans. However, she has not lost all hope of meaningful communication, and she still thinks saying what one feels is the most important contribution one can make to society.

Clarissa considers the moment when Sally kissed her on the lips and offered her a flower at Bourton the "most exquisite moment of her whole life." Society would never have allowed that love to flourish, since women of Clarissa's class were expected to marry and become society wives. Sally has always been more of a free spirit than Clarissa, and when she arrives at Clarissa's party, she feels rather distant from and confused by the life Clarissa has chosen. The women's kiss marked a true moment of passion that could have pushed both women outside of the English society they know, and it stands out in contrast to the confrontation Peter remembers between Sally and Hugh regarding women's rights. One morning at Bourton, Sally angrily told Hugh he represented the worst of the English middle-class and that he was to blame for the plight of the young girls in Piccadilly. Later, Hugh supposedly kissed her in the smoking-room. Hugh's is the forced kiss of traditional English society, while the kiss with Clarissa is a revelation. Ultimately, the society that spurs Hugh's kiss prevails for both women.

RICHARD DALLOWAY Richard's simplicity and steadfastness have enabled him to build a stable life for Clarissa, but these same qualities represent the compromise that marrying him required. Richard is a simple, hardworking, sensible husband who loves Clarissa and their daughter, Elizabeth. However, he will never share Clarissa's desire to truly and fully communicate, and he cannot appreciate the beauty of life in the same way she can. At one point, Richard tries to overcome his habitual stiffness and shyness by planning to tell Clarissa that he loves her, but he is ultimately too repressed to say the words, in part because it has been so long since he last said them. Just as he does not understand Clarissa's desires, he does not recognize Elizabeth's potential as a woman. If he had had a son, he would have encouraged him to work, but he does not offer the same encouragement to Elizabeth, even as she contemplates job options. His reticence on the matter increases the likelihood that she will eventually be in the same predicament as Clarissa, unable to support herself through a career and thus unable to gain the freedom to follow her passions.

Richard considers tradition of prime importance, rather than passion or open communication. He champions the traditions England went to war to preserve, in contrast to Septimus, and does not recognize their destructive power. Despite his occasional misgivings, Richard has close associations with members of English high society. He is critical of Hugh, but they revere many of the same symbols, including the figure of the grand old lady with money, who is helpless when it comes to surviving in a patriarchal society. Richard likes the fact that women need him, but sometimes he wrongly assumes they do. For example, he does not recognize that a female vagrant may not want his help but may instead enjoy living outside the rules of his society. For Richard, this sort of freedom is unimaginable.

THEMES, MOTIFS, AND SYMBOLS

THEMES

COMMUNICATION VS. PRIVACY Throughout *Mrs. Dalloway*, Clarissa, Septimus, Peter, and others struggle to find outlets for communication as well as adequate privacy, and the balance between the two is difficult for all to attain. Clarissa in particular struggles to open the pathway for communication and throws parties in an attempt to draw people together. At the same time, she feels shrouded within her own reflective soul and thinks the ultimate human mystery is how she can exist in one room while the old woman in the house across from hers exists in another. Even as Clarissa celebrates the old woman's independence, she knows it comes with an inevitable loneliness. Peter tries to explain the contradictory human impulses toward privacy and communication by comparing the soul to a fish that swims along in murky water, then rises quickly to the surface to frolic on the waves. The war has changed people's ideas of what English society should be, and understanding is difficult between those who support traditional English society and those who hope for continued change. Meaningful connections in this disjointed postwar world are not easy to make, no matter what efforts the characters put forth. Ultimately, Clarissa sees Septimus's death as a desperate, but legitimate, act of communication.

DISILLUSIONMENT WITH THE BRITISH EMPIRE Throughout the nineteenth century, the British Empire seemed invincible. It expanded into many other countries, such as India, Nigeria, and South Africa, becoming the largest empire the world had ever seen. World War I was a violent reality check. For the first time in nearly a century, the English were vulnerable on their own land. The Allies technically won the war, but the extent of devastation England suffered made it a victory in name only. Entire communities of young men were injured and killed. In 1916, at the Battle of the Somme, England suffered 60,000 casualties—the largest slaughter in England's history. Not surprisingly, English citizens lost much of their faith in the empire after the war. No longer could England claim to be invulnerable and all-powerful. Citizens were less inclined to willingly adhere to the rigid constraints imposed by England's class system, which benefited only a small margin of society but which all classes had fought to preserve.

In 1923, when *Mrs. Dalloway* takes place, the old establishment and its oppressive values are nearing their end. English citizens, including Clarissa, Peter, and Septimus, feel the failure of the empire as strongly as they feel their own personal failures. Those citizens who still champion English tradition, such as Aunt Helena and Lady Bruton, are old. Aunt Helena, with her glass eye (perhaps a symbol of her inability or unwillingness to see the empire's disintegration), is turning into an artifact. Anticipating the end of the Conservative Party's reign, Richard plans to write the history of the great British military family, the Brutons, who are already part of the past. The old empire faces an imminent demise, and the loss of the traditional and familiar social order leaves the English at loose ends.

THE FEAR OF DEATH Thoughts of death lurk constantly beneath the surface of everyday life in *Mrs. Dalloway*, especially for Clarissa, Septimus, and Peter, and this awareness makes even mundane events and interactions meaningful, sometimes even threatening. At the very start of her day, when she goes out to buy flowers for her party, Clarissa remembers a moment in her youth when she suspected a terrible event would occur. Big Ben tolls out the hour, and Clarissa repeats a line from Shakespeare's *Cymbeline* over and over as the day goes on: "Fear no more the heat o' the sun / Nor the furious winter's rages." The line is from a funeral song that celebrates death as a comfort after a difficult life. Middle-aged Clarissa has experienced the deaths of her father, mother, and sister and has lived through the calamity of war, and she has grown to believe that living even one day is dangerous. Death is very naturally in her thoughts, and the line from *Cymbeline*, along with Septimus's suicidal embrace of death, ultimately helps her to be at peace with her own mortality. Peter Walsh, so insecure in his identity, grows frantic at the idea of death and follows an anonymous young woman through London to forget about it. Septimus faces death most directly. Though he fears it, he finally chooses it over what seems to him a direr alternative—living another day.

THE THREAT OF OPPRESSION Oppression is a constant threat for Clarissa and Septimus in *Mrs. Dalloway*, and Septimus dies in order to escape what he perceives to be an oppressive social pressure to conform. It comes in many guises, including religion, science, or social convention. Miss Kilman and Sir William Bradshaw are two of the major oppressors in the novel: Miss Kilman dreams of felling Clarissa in the name of religion, and Sir William would like to subdue all those who challenge his conception of the world. Both wish to convert the world to their belief systems in order to gain power and dominate others, and their rigidity oppresses all who come into contact with them. More subtle oppressors, even those who do not intend to, do harm by supporting the repressive English social system. Though Clarissa herself lives under the weight of that system and often feels oppressed by it, her acceptance of patriarchal English society makes her, in part, responsible for Septimus's death. Thus she too is an oppressor of sorts. At the end of the novel, she reflects on his suicide: "Somehow it was her disaster—her disgrace." She accepts responsibility, though other characters are equally or more fully to blame, which suggests that everyone is in some way complicit in the oppression of others.

MOTIFS

TIME Time imparts order to the fluid thoughts, memories, and encounters that make up *Mrs. Dalloway*. Big Ben, a symbol of England and its might, sounds out the hour relentlessly, ensuring that the passage of time, and the awareness of eventual death, is always palpable. Clarissa, Septimus, Peter, and other characters are in the grip of time, and as they age they evaluate how they have spent their lives. Clarissa, in particular, senses the passage of time, and the appearance of Sally and Peter, friends from the past, emphasizes how much time has gone by since Clarissa was young. Once the hour chimes, however, the sound disappears—its "leaden circles dissolved in the air." This expression recurs many times throughout the novel, indicating how ephemeral time is, despite the pomp of Big Ben and despite people's wary obsession with it. "It is time," Rezia says to Septimus as they sit in the park waiting for the doctor's appointment on Harley Street. The ancient woman at the Regent's Park Tube station suggests that the human condition knows no boundaries of time, since she continues to sing the same song for what seems like eternity. She understands that life is circular, not merely the linear, which is the only sort of time that Big Ben tracks. Time is so important to the themes, structure, and characters of this novel that Woolf almost named her book *The Hours*.

SHAKESPEARE The many appearances of Shakespeare specifically and poetry in general suggest hopefulness, the possibility of finding comfort in art, and the survival of the soul in *Mrs. Dalloway*. Clarissa quotes Shakespeare plays many times throughout the day. When she shops for flowers at the beginning of the novel, she reads a few lines from a Shakespeare play, *Cymbeline*, in a book displayed in a shop window. The lines come from a funeral hymn in the play that suggests death should be embraced as a release from the constraints of life. Since Clarissa fears death for much of the novel, these lines suggest that an alternative, hopeful way of addressing the prospect of death exists. Clarissa also identifies with the title character in *Othello*, who loves his wife but kills her out of jealousy, then kills himself when he learns his jealousy was unwarranted. Clarissa shares with Othello the sense of having lost a love, especially when she thinks about Sally Seton. Before the war, Septimus appreciated Shakespeare as well, going so far as aspiring to be a poet. He no longer finds comfort in poetry after he returns..

The presence of an appreciation for poetry reveals much about Clarissa and Septimus, just as the absence of such appreciation reveals much about the characters who differ from them, such as Richard Dalloway and Lady Bruton. Richard finds Shakespeare's sonnets indecent, and he compares reading them to listening in at a keyhole. Not surprisingly, Richard himself has a difficult time voicing his emotions. Lady Bruton never reads poetry either, and her demeanor is so rigid and impersonal that she has a reputation of caring more for politics than for people. Traditional English society promotes a suppression of visible emotion, and since Shakespeare and poetry promote a discussion of feeling and emotion, they belong to sensitive people like Clarissa, who are in many ways antiestablishment.

TREES AND FLOWERS Tree and flower images abound in *Mrs. Dalloway*. The color, variety, and beauty of flowers suggest feeling and emotion, and those characters who are comfortable with flowers, such as Clarissa, have distinctly different personalities than those characters who are not, such as Richard and Lady Bruton. The first time we see Clarissa, a deep thinker, she is on her way to the flower shop, where she will revel in the flowers she sees. Richard and Hugh, more emotionally repressed representatives of the English establishment, offer traditional roses and carnations to Clarissa and Lady Bruton, respectively. Richard handles the bouquet of roses awkwardly, like a weapon. Lady Bruton accepts the flowers with a "grim smile" and lays them stiffly by her plate, also unsure of how to handle them. When she eventually stuffs them into her dress, the femininity and grace of the gesture are rare and unexpected. Trees, with their extensive root systems, suggest the vast reach of the human soul, and Clarissa and Septimus, who both struggle to protect their souls, revere them. Clarissa believes souls survive in trees after death, and Septimus, who has turned his back on patriarchal society, feels that cutting down a tree is the equivalent of committing murder.

WAVES AND WATER Waves and water regularly wash over events and thoughts in *Mrs. Dalloway* and nearly always suggest the possibility of extinction or death. While Clarissa mends her party dress, she thinks about the peaceful cycle of waves collecting and falling on a summer day, when the world itself seems to say "that is all." Time sometimes takes on waterlike qualities for Clarissa, such as when the chime from Big Ben "flood[s]" her room, marking another passing hour. Rezia, in a rare moment of happiness with Septimus after he has helped her construct a hat, lets her words trail off "like a contented tap left running." Even then, she knows that stream of contentedness will dry up eventually. The narrative structure of the novel itself also suggests fluidity. One character's thoughts appear, intensify, then fade into another's, much like waves that collect then fall.

Traditional English society itself is a kind of tide, pulling under those people not strong enough to stand on their own. Lady Bradshaw, for example, eventually succumbs to Sir William's bullying, overbearing presence. The narrator says "she had gone under," that her will became "water-logged" and eventually sank into his. Septimus is also sucked under society's pressures. Earlier in the day, before he kills himself, he looks out the window and sees everything as though it is underwater. Trees drag their branches through the air as though dragging them through water, the light outside is "watery gold," and his hand on the sofa reminds him of floating in seawater. While Septimus ultimately cannot accept or function in society, Clarissa manages to navigate it successfully. Peter sees Clarissa in a "silver-green mermaid's dress" at her party, "[l]olloping on the waves." Between her mermaid's dress and her ease in bobbing through her party guests, Clarissa succeeds in staying afloat. However, she identifies with Septimus's wish to fight the cycle and go under, even if she will not succumb to the temptation herself.

SYMBOLS

THE PRIME MINISTER The prime minister in *Mrs. Dalloway* embodies England's old values and hierarchical social system, which are in decline. When Peter Walsh wants to insult Clarissa and suggest she will sell out and become a society hostess, he says she will marry a prime minister. When Lady Bruton, a champion of English tradition, wants to compliment Hugh, she calls him "My Prime Minister." The prime minister is a figure from the old establishment, which Clarissa and Septimus are struggling against. *Mrs. Dalloway* takes place after World War I, a time when the English looked desperately for meaning in the old symbols but found the symbols hollow. When the conservative prime minister finally arrives at Clarissa's party, his appearance is unimpressive. The old pyramidal social system that benefited the very rich before the war is now decaying, and the symbols of its greatness have become pathetic.

PETER WALSH'S POCKETKNIFE AND OTHER WEAPONS Peter Walsh plays constantly with his pocketknife, and the opening, closing, and fiddling with the knife suggest his flightiness and inability to make decisions. He cannot decide what he feels and doesn't know whether he abhors English tradition and wants to fight it, or whether he accepts English civilization just as it is. The pocketknife reveals Peter's defensiveness. He is armed with the knife, in a sense, when he pays an unexpected visit to Clarissa, while she herself is armed with her sewing scissors. Their weapons make them equal competitors. Knives and weapons are also phallic symbols, hinting at sexuality and power. Peter cannot define his own identity, and his constant fidgeting with the knife suggests how uncomfortable he is with his masculinity. Characters fall into two groups: those who are armed and those who are not. Ellie Henderson, for example, is "weaponless," because she is poor and has not been trained for any career. Her ambiguous relationship with her friend Edith also puts her at a disadvantage in society, leaving her even less able to defend herself. Septimus, psychologically crippled by the literal weapons of war, commits suicide by impaling himself on a metal fence, showing the danger lurking behind manmade boundaries.

THE OLD WOMAN IN THE WINDOW The old woman in the window across from Clarissa's house represents the privacy of the soul and the loneliness that goes with it, both of which will increase as Clarissa grows older. Clarissa sees the future in the old woman: she herself will grow old and become more and more alone, since that is the nature of life. As Clarissa grows older, she reflects more but communicates less. Instead, she keeps her feelings locked inside the private rooms of her own soul, just as the old woman rattles alone around the rooms of her house. Nevertheless, the old woman also represents serenity and the purity of the soul. Clarissa respects the woman's private reflections and thinks beauty lies in this act of preserving one's interior life and independence. Before Septimus jumps out the window, he sees an old man descending the staircase outside, and this old man is a parallel figure to the old woman. Though Clarissa and Septimus ultimately choose to preserve their private lives in opposite ways, their view of loneliness, privacy, and communication resonates within these similar images.

THE OLD WOMAN SINGING AN ANCIENT SONG Opposite the Regent's Park Tube station, an old woman sings an ancient song that celebrates life, endurance, and continuity. She is oblivious to everyone around her as she sings, beyond caring what the world thinks. The narrator explains that no matter what happens in the world, the old woman will still be there, even in "ten million years," and that the song has soaked "through the knotted roots of infinite ages." Roots, intertwined and hidden beneath the earth, suggest the deepest parts of people's souls, and this woman's song touches everyone who hears it in some way. Peter hears the song first and compares the old woman to a rusty pump. He doesn't catch her triumphant message and feels only pity for her, giving her a coin before stepping into a taxi. Rezia, however, finds strength in the old woman's words, and the song makes her feel as though all will be okay in her life. Women in the novel, who have to view patriarchal English society from the outside, are generally more attuned to nature and the messages of voices outside the mainstream. Rezia, therefore, is able to see the old woman for the life force she is, instead of simply a nuisance or a tragic figure to be dealt with, ignored, or pitied.

IMPORTANT QUOTATIONS EXPLAINED

---

1. *For Heaven only knows why one loves it so, how one sees it so, making it up, building it round one, tumbling it, creating it every moment afresh; but the veriest frumps, the most dejected of miseries sitting on doorsteps (drink their downfall) do the same; can't be dealt with, she felt positive, by Acts of Parliament for that very reason: they love life.*

This passage, part of Clarissa's thoughts as she walks to the flower shop in the early morning and Big Ben chimes the hour, reveals her strong attachment to life and the concept of life as her own invention. The long, galloping sentence, full of commas and semicolons, mirrors her excitement at being alive on this June day. Clarissa is conscious that the impressions of the things around her do not necessarily hold beauty or meaning in themselves, but that humans act as architects, building the impressions into comprehensible and beautiful moments. She herself revels in this act, in the effort life requires, and she knows that even the most impoverished person living on the streets can derive the same wonder from living. She sees that happiness does not belong to a particular class, but to all who can build up a moment and see beauty around them. Later her husband Richard sees a vagrant woman on the street but classifies her only as a social problem that the government must deal with. Clarissa believes that every class of people has the ability to conceptualize beauty and enjoy life, and she therefore feels that government intervention has limited uses. She does not equate class with happiness.

2. *She had a perpetual sense, as she watched the taxi cabs, of being out, out, far out to sea and alone; she always had the feeling that it was very, very dangerous to live even one day.*

This observation, which occurs during Clarissa's shopping expedition when she pauses for a moment to look at the omnibuses in Piccadilly, emphasizes the contrast between the busyness of public life and the quiet privacy of the soul. Clarissa, even when she is walking in the crowded city streets, contemplates the essential loneliness of life. The image of water acts much like the image of the sun in the novel. The sun beats down constantly, sometimes creating a wonderful feeling of warmth, sometimes scorching unbearably. The rhythmic movement of the sea's waves is similar. Sometimes the cyclical movement is breathtaking, while sometimes it threatens to drown whoever is too weak to endure the pressure, such as Lady Bradshaw or Septimus. Each person faces these same elements, which seems to join humans in their struggle. However, everyone is ultimately alone in the sea of life and must try to stay afloat the best they can. Despite the perpetual movement and activity of a large city like London, loneliness is everywhere.

Clarissa's reflection occurs directly after she considers her old friend Peter, who has failed to fulfill the dreams of his youth. As Clarissa ages, she finds it more difficult to know anybody, which makes her feel solitary. She hesitates to define even herself. Failing, becoming overwhelmed by the pressures of life, and drowning are far too easy. Clarissa is fifty-two, she's lived through a war, and her experiences amplify the dangers of living and of facing the world and other people.

3. *This late age of the world's experience had bred in them all, all men and women, a well of tears. Tears and sorrows; courage and endurance; a perfectly upright and stoical bearing.*

This remark occurs directly after Clarissa reads lines from Shakespeare's play *Cymbeline* in a bookshop window. The lines, "Fear no more the heat o' the sun / Nor the furious winter's rages," come from a hymn sung at a funeral and suggest that death is a release from the hard struggle of life. The words speak very directly to Clarissa's own time period, the years after World War I. England is still in shock after having lost so many men in battle, the world now seems like a hostile place, and death seems like a welcome relief. After Clarissa reads the words from *Cymbeline*, she considers the great amount of sorrow every person now bears. Everyone, regardless of class, has to some degree been affected by the war.

Despite the upright and courageous attitudes many people maintain, they all carry a great sadness, and people cry constantly in *Mrs. Dalloway*. Peter Walsh bursts into tears at Clarissa's house. Clarissa's eyes fill with tears when she thinks of her mother walking in a garden. Septimus cries, and so does Rezia. Tears are never far from the surface, and sadness lurks beneath the busy activity of the day. Most people manage to contain their tears, according to the rules of society, or cry only in private. Septimus, the veteran, is the only character who does not hesitate to cry openly in the park, and he is considered mentally unstable. People are supposed to organize bazaars to help raise money for the veterans. People are supposed to maintain a stiff upper lip and carry on. Admitting to the horrors of the war by crying is not acceptable in English culture, though as Clarissa points out, a well of tears exists in each of them.

4. *Clarissa had a theory in those days . . . that since our apparitions, the part of us which appears, are so momentary compared with the other, the unseen part of us, which spreads wide, the unseen might survive, be recovered somehow attached to this person or that, or even haunting certain places after death . . . perhaps—perhaps.*

This passage occurs as Peter Walsh walks back to his hotel. He hears the ambulance go by to pick up Septimus's body and remembers Clarissa's passion during their youth. Clarissa was frustrated at how little one person could know another person, because she felt that so much of a person existed out of reach of others. A person's soul was like a plant or a tree, with a small part showing aboveground and a complex, unseen root system existing underneath. Although Clarissa had experienced death at a young age when her sister Sylvia died, she did not want to believe that death was the absolute end. Instead she believed that people survived, both in other people and in the natural world. To know someone beyond the surface, one had to seek out the people and places that completed that person. The structure of *Mrs. Dalloway* supports Clarissa's theory, since most of the novel concerns people's thoughts rather than surface actions. These thoughts connect to people and things far beyond the people and things that are ostensibly closest to them.

Clarissa told Peter of this transcendental theory while riding on an omnibus with him through London. The omnibus, an open-air bus that offers a view of everything around, symbolizes the ease with which the friends could once share their deepest thoughts. As adults, they are restricted by the repressive rules of English society, which is symbolized by great and somber automobiles with their blinds drawn. Clarissa still believes in the interconnectedness of humans and the natural world, and she thinks about it during her walk to the shops. However, Peter and Clarissa no longer feel so easy sharing their most deeply held ideas with one another, and Peter supposes Clarissa has hardened into a boring and shallow upper-class society wife who would no longer consider such ideas true or important.

---

5. *She felt somehow very like him—the young man who had killed himself. She felt glad that he had done it; thrown it away. The clock was striking. The leaden circles dissolved in the air. He made her feel the beauty; made her feel the fun. But she must go back. She must assemble.*

This phrase occurs at the day's end, when Clarissa is at her party and receives news of Septimus's death from Lady Bradshaw. Clarissa retreats to the small room where the prime minister sat to reflect on the young veteran. She had never met him and does not even know his name, but she experiences a moment of clarity, or "moment of being," in the small room when she identifies strongly with him and his dramatic action. Woolf created Septimus as Clarissa's double, and throughout the book he has echoed her thoughts and feelings. In this scene, Clarissa realizes how much she has in common with this working-class young man, who on the surface seems so unlike her.

Everything converges in this one moment, and this scene is the climax of the book. The narratives of Clarissa and Septimus finally meet. A wall separates the public sphere of the party from Clarissa's private space, where her soul feels connected to Septimus's soul. The clocks that have been relentlessly structuring the passing day continue to chime. Despite the sounding clocks and the pressures of the party outside, however, Clarissa manages to appreciate that Septimus has preserved his soul through death. Clarissa began her day by plunging metaphorically into the beautiful June morning, and Septimus has now literally plunged from his window. An effort and commitment to the soul is necessary to plunge into life or death, and Clarissa, who has reached middle age and is keenly aware of the compromises she has made in her own life, respects Septimus's unwillingness to be crushed by an oppressive power like the psychiatrist Sir William. Clarissa repeats the line from *Cymbeline*, "Fear no more," and she continues to endure. She will go back to her party and "assemble." In the postwar world, life is fragmented and does not contain easy routes to follow, but Clarissa will take the fragmented pieces and go on trying to make life up as best she can.

Throughout Virginia Woolf's *Mrs. Dalloway*, Clarissa reflects on her past and indulges in her memories. What effect, if any, does her nostalgia have on her present life and her relationships with others?

Clarissa Dalloway, the protagonist of Virginia Woolf's *Mrs. Dalloway*, has a successful life: she is married to a kindhearted man, has a beautiful daughter, and is a prominent figure in society. Yet Clarissa is not as engaged and happy with her life as she appears to be. She reserves her true passion for events and people from the past, which alienates her from the present and from the people she loves.

Clarissa's fixation on the past leads her to constantly reevaluate her marriage. She loves Richard, but she understands that her choice to marry him involved sacrificing the passion she once held for her former love, Peter Walsh. She vividly recalls her intense feelings for Peter, and both she and Peter hold secret, occasional regrets about her decision to spurn his advances. When Peter visits her on the morning of her party, both Peter and Clarissa question their respective lifestyles and happiness. Clarissa feels superficial in front of Peter because of her excitement about the party, while Peter feels excluded from the social world of the Dalloways. Peter's ambivalence about his life endears him to Clarissa, and she wonders whether she would have been happier married to him.

Though these feelings strengthen the bond between Clarissa and Peter, they separate Clarissa from her more immediate life with Richard in the present. Richard is dependable and provides Clarissa with security, and though this dependability is the reason Clarissa chose to marry him, it is also the reason that he cannot fully satisfy her. No passion exists between Clarissa and Richard—they even have separate bedrooms. When Richard does attempt to tell Clarissa how much he loves her, he can't find the words. No marriage is perfect, but Clarissa's memory of her passion for Peter puts this placid relationship into stark relief, bringing its flaws to the surface.

Student Essay

Clarissa's insistent memories of Sally Seton separate her even more dramatically from the present. In Clarissa's eyes, and now in her memory, Sally was tough, rebellious, and attractive, and Clarissa still regards the moment in which Sally picked her a flower and kissed her on the lips as the most exquisite of her life. When Sally unexpectedly arrives at Clarissa's party, they embrace again, in a less intense echo of their earlier interactions. As with Peter, Clarissa questions her current life in the face of her old friend. However, Clarissa quickly discovers that the real Sally is less perfect than the Sally in Clarissa's memory. Clarissa can't reconcile the past with the present, and though she is happy to see Sally, she feels, at the same time, distant from her.

The harm Clarissa's nostalgia has wrought on her present relationships becomes most clear at her party. Her shock at seeing Sally after so many years is compounded by Peter's presence in the same room. Suddenly, it is as though Clarissa is back at Bourton, finally reliving the past she's remembered so many times—but much has changed, and the moment is foreign, not familiar. Instead of sitting down to catch up with old friends, Clarissa retreats to another room, alone. Clarissa must take stock of her life as it is and finally let go of the past.

My Ántonia

Willa Cather
(1873–1947)

CONTEXT

Willa Cather was born on December 7, 1873, in rural Virginia. At the age of nine, she moved with her family to Red Cloud, Nebraska, where she spent the remainder of her childhood. After graduating from the University of Nebraska at Lincoln in 1895, she moved to Pittsburgh to begin a career in journalism. Cather spent five years in the Pittsburgh newspaper and magazine trade, working at *Home Monthly* and the *Pittsburgh Leader*. Between 1901 and 1906, she taught high school English and Latin in Pittsburgh and the Pittsburgh area. During this period, she began to publish her first short stories. These early successes led to a position in New York City with *McClure's*, a magazine that often featured investigative journalism, where Cather served as an editor for six years.

In 1912, Cather published her first novel, *Alexander's Bridge*, which received a lukewarm reception. The next year, Cather caught the attention of the literary world with the appearance of *O Pioneers!* (1913), a novel that explores and celebrates frontier life in the American West. In 1918, she made her most lasting contribution to her status as one of the most celebrated post–Civil War American authors with the publication of *My Ántonia*. Like many of Cather's novels, *My Ántonia* fictionalizes recollections of her youth in rural Nebraska.

Though the narrative of *My Ántonia* is fictional, there are many similarities between Cather's life and that of the novel's protagonist, Jim Burden. As Cather did, Jim moves from Virginia to Nebraska as a child to live with grandparents; the town of Black Hawk, to which Jim and his grandparents move, is a fictionalized version of the Red Cloud of Cather's youth. Jim attends the University of Nebraska at Lincoln and eventually moves from Nebraska to New York, both of which Cather did.

If certain of the situations in the novel derive from Cather's recollections of her youth, however, the novel's high stature in American literature results from Cather's ability as a writer. Her sensitivity to the prairie landscape and her elegantly uncomplicated prose style have earned her a spot among America's finest novelists, and *My Ántonia* continues to stand as the most lasting hallmark of her skill. *My Ántonia* is generally considered a modernist novel. In the early twentieth century, many authors were concerned with the alienation from society that resulted from ongoing processes of mechanization and industrialization. These writers responded to what they perceived as an increased fragmentation of the world by creating narratives and stories that were themselves fragmented. Cather participates in this tradition both by creating a novel whose plot does not have a highly structured form and by idealizing a preindustrial life far from the noise and speed of the city.

Cather was most prolific during the 1920s, when she published many of her finest works. After being awarded the Pulitzer Prize for *One of Ours* in 1922, she also enjoyed popular successes with *The Professor's House* (1925), *My Mortal Enemy* (1926), and *Death Comes for the Archbishop* (1927). In her final two decades, Cather continued to write short stories and novels, albeit with less frequency and refinement. Nevertheless, she enjoyed an extraordinary amount of attention and critical esteem in her lifetime. In 1930 she won the Howells Medal for Fiction, and in 1944 she was awarded the gold medal of the National Institute of Arts and Letters.

Cather died on April 24, 1947, in New York City, where she had lived for thirty-nine years with her companion, Edith Lewis. Her reputation equalled that of any published American female novelist of her day, and critical and popular attention to her work continues to expand. Many critics place her firmly among such lauded American authors as William Faulkner and Ernest Hemingway, and there are those who would argue that hers is the single finest craft of her generation.

PLOT OVERVIEW

Jim Burden, a successful New York City lawyer, gives an acquaintance a memoir of his Nebraska childhood in the form of a recollection of their mutual friend, Ántonia Shimerda. This memoir makes up the bulk of the novel.

Jim first arrives in Nebraska at the age of ten, when he makes the trip west to live with his grandparents after finding himself an orphan in Virginia. On the train out west, Jim gets his first glimpse of the Shimerdas, a Bohemian immigrant family traveling in the same direction. As fate would have it, the Shimerdas have taken up residence in a farm neighboring the Burdens'. Jim makes fast friends with the Shimerda children, especially Ántonia, who is nearest to him in age and eager to learn English. Jim tutors Ántonia, and the two of them spend much of the autumn exploring their new landscape together.

In late January, tragedy strikes with the suicide of Mr. Shimerda. After an emotional funeral, the Shimerdas retreat into despair, and the Burdens struggle to be as accommodating as possible. As a result of the hardships that the Shimerdas suffer, Ántonia and Jim find that a wedge has been driven between them.

A couple of years later, the Burdens decide to move into town, and shortly thereafter Ántonia takes a job as a housekeeper with a neighboring family, the Harlings. Jim begins to see more of Ántonia once again, especially when a dancing pavilion comes to town and enlivens the social scene.

Jim's high school years quickly come to a close, and he is offered a spot at the university in Lincoln. He makes a great success of his high school commencement speech and spends the summer hard at work in preparation for his course of study. Before leaving, he takes one last trip out to the countryside with Ántonia and her friends, where they gather to reminisce about old times together.

In Lincoln, Jim throws himself into his studies, which take up the majority of his time in the first year and a half of his course. In the spring of his second year, he begins to see a good deal of Lena Lingard, a mutual friend of his and Ántonia's who has always intrigued Jim. After a few months of theatergoing and dalliances about town, Jim decides that he needs to make a fresh start of things and prepares to transfer to Harvard University for his final two years of college.

While Jim is away, Ántonia gets engaged to a local boy and moves to Denver in order to be with him. Days before the wedding, the boy abandons Ántonia, and she returns to Nebraska heartbroken. She covers up an unexpected pregnancy throughout its term, but in giving birth to a daughter incurs the disapproval of her family. However, she resolves to take care of her baby and continues to work on the farm with her brother.

After graduating from college, during the summer before entering law school, Jim returns to Nebraska to be with his grandparents. Upon hearing of Ántonia's situation, he decides to drive out to the countryside and visit her. They spend a happy day together reliving old times, and Jim parts with a promise to visit her again very soon.

Twenty years pass before Jim is able to visit Ántonia again. In the intervening period, he establishes himself as a prosperous New York City lawyer, and Ántonia marries and has many children with a man named Cuzak, also of Bohemian origin. Jim's visit to the Cuzak farm is a happy one, with plenty of laughter and stories. Ántonia and Jim renew their old ties, and Jim resolves to be in closer contact with the Cuzaks in the coming years.

As he prepares to leave Nebraska and return to New York City, Jim walks along the outskirts of town, near the overgrown road that leads to his childhood home. At peace with himself in this familiar landscape, he feels that his life has come full circle, and he reflects in the moonlight on all that his past with Ántonia has meant to him.

CHARACTER LIST

Jim Burden The author of the youthful recollection that makes up the body of the novel. As a youth in Nebraska, Jim develops a close friendship with a Bohemian immigrant girl, Ántonia Shimerda. Jim is an intelligent, introspective young man who responds strongly to the land and the environment in which he lives. Unlike most other boys his age, Jim is more interested in academics and reflection than in roughhousing; in fact, he seems to prefer spending time alone or with girls such as Ántonia. At the time of the narrative's composition, Jim is married, but without children, and working as a legal counsel in New York City.

Ántonia Shimerda The focus of Jim's recollection and one of his closest childhood friends. Ántonia moves to Nebraska from Bohemia with the rest of her family in her early teenage years. Intelligent, optimistic, loyal, and kindhearted, the naturally gregarious Ántonia is forced to accept a difficult life after the death of her father. At the time Jim writes the narrative, she is raising her large family on the Nebraska prairie, not far from where she and Jim grew up.

Lena Lingard A Norwegian immigrant's daughter and a friend of Ántonia's. Lena has a brief liaison with Jim in Black Hawk and a more extended relationship with him in Lincoln, where she sets up her own dressmaker's shop. Lena is pretty and blonde, and craves independence and excitement. Men are always attracted to her, but she refuses to marry and give up her freedom.

Josiah Burden Jim's grandfather. Josiah is a strongly religious man, silent and given to hard work.

Emmaline Burden Jim's grandmother. Emmaline shows great concern and compassion for the Shimerdas and is a loving maternal figure for Jim.

Otto Fuchs The Burdens' hired hand, who looks like a cowboy out of one of Jim's books but is actually an Austrian immigrant. Good-natured despite his rough appearance, Otto decides to seek his fortune in the West after the Burdens move to Black Hawk.

Jake Marpole Another hired hand of the Burdens. Jake makes the trip from Virginia to Nebraska along with Jim and accompanies Otto out west after the Burdens move to Black Hawk. Jake has a powerful temper but generally displays a good-natured and even childlike innocence about the world.

M

Mr. Shimerda The patriarch of the Bohemian immigrant family. A melancholy man given to artistic and scholarly pursuits, Mr. Shimerda feels very much out of place in foreign land. His depression eventually leads to suicide, leaving his family members to pick up the pieces and struggle to make a living on their own.

Mrs. Shimerda The matriarch of the Bohemian immigrant family. Mrs. Shimerda is a brusque, bossy, and often curt woman. After the suicide of her husband, she is forced to make do with the little that she has in an attempt to provide for her family.

Yulka Shimerda The youngest of the Shimerda children. Yulka is a pretty, young girl who later helps Ántonia raise her baby.

Ambrosch Shimerda The Shimerdas' oldest son. Mrs. Shimerda and her daughters dote on Ambrosch, claiming that he is brilliant and the reason they came to America. Ambrosch shares his mother's curt and presumptuous attitude, but becomes the unquestioned head of the family after Mr. Shimerda's suicide.

Marek Shimerda The younger of the two Shimerda brothers. Marek's physical deformities are accompanied by a handful of psychological instabilities and mental deficiencies.

Tiny Soderball One of the hired girls in Black Hawk and a friend to Ántonia and Lena. After working with Mrs. Gardener in the Boys' Home, Tiny travels west and makes a small fortune during the Alaskan gold rush.

Russian Pavel A tall, gaunt, nervous immigrant who falls ill under the care of the Shimerdas. Pavel had been ostracized and forced to leave his native Russia after a frightful incident involving a wolf attack on a wedding party.

Russian Peter Pavel's housemate, and a fat, happy man. Like Pavel, Peter was forced into exile from his native Russia following a wolf attack on a wedding party. Peter eventually finds himself severely in debt and sells off his belongings, leaving America for a job as a cook in a Russian labor camp.

Mr. Harling The patriarch of the Harling family, neighbors to the Burdens in Black Hawk. A businessman of keen ability, Mr. Harling disapproves of Ántonia's frequent carousals at the dancing pavilion and eventually forces her to leave her post as their housekeeper because of her lifestyle.

Mrs. Harling The active, charismatic matriarch of the Harling family. Mrs. Harling develops a strong affection for Ántonia, and she provides myriad activities for her children, Ántonia, and Jim, to take part in.

Frances Harling The oldest of the Harling children. Frances has a sound business mind and manages her father's accounts with a great deal of skill.

Charley Harling The only Harling son. Charley is of a military persuasion and eventually goes on to a successful career at the Naval Academy in Annapolis.

Julia Harling The middle Harling daughter. Julia is Jim's age and has a penchant for music.

Sally Harling The youngest Harling daughter, and something of a tomboy.

Larry Donovan Ántonia's fiancé, and an arrogant and selfish young man. After being fired from his job as a railroad conductor, Donovan leaves Ántonia on the eve of their wedding, running away to Mexico in search of a quick fortune.

Mrs. Gardener The proprietress of the Boys' Home in Black Hawk.

Samson d'Arnault A blind, black pianist. D'Arnault comes to Black Hawk on a blustery March weekend and gives a concert at the Boys' Home that brings down the house.

Wick Cutter The leading moneylender in Black Hawk and a shady character.

Gaston Cleric Jim's tutor at the university in Lincoln. Cleric eventually moves on to a teaching position at Harvard University and brings Jim along with him. His premature death from pneumonia has a strong effect on Jim.

Widow Steavens The Burdens' tenant at their old farmhouse. Widow Steavens develops a close relationship with Ántonia in the time surrounding the breaking of Ántonia's engagement.

Anton Jelinek A Bohemian homesteader and friend of the Shimerdas who later moves to Black Hawk and becomes a saloon proprietor.

Peter Krajiek A Bohemian immigrant and neighbor to the Burdens who sells the Shimerdas their first farm in America and cheats them out of several comforts.

Cuzak A Bohemian immigrant to America who marries Ántonia and raises a large family with her.

ANALYSIS OF MAJOR CHARACTERS

JIM BURDEN Intelligent and introspective, Jim is well qualified to be the narrator of the story. His thoughtfulness gives him the ability to portray himself and others with consistency and sympathy and to convey the sense of a lost Nebraska with an evocative, poetic accuracy. Furthermore, his romantic nature and strong attachment to the people of his youth and to the Nebraska landscape give his narrative a sense of deep commitment and a longing, nostalgic quality that colors his story. The wistful nature of Jim's memoir highlights the novel's emphasis on the past as something personal to the individual who remembers it, which Jim acknowledges in choosing to call his memoir "My Ántonia" rather than "Ántonia." Jim is not claiming ownership of Ántonia; he is indicating that the story of Ántonia contained within his memoir is just as much a product of his own mind and heart as it is of the past.

Over the course of the novel, Jim ages from a ten-year-old boy into a middle-aged man and grows from a shy orphan into a successful lawyer for the railroad companies, acquiring an impressive education along the way at the University of Nebraska and Harvard. In spite of the great changes that he undergoes, Jim remains a consistent character. He always has interest in others but is content to spend time alone; he often assumes the role of the detached observer watching situations unfold. The word "I" appears in *My Ántonia* with surprising infrequency, given the fact that the novel is a first-person memoir. Only at the end of the novel, when Jim sets aside his reservations to reunite with the middle-aged Ántonia on the Cuzak farm, does he seem to move past his passive role and make an active attempt to connect with the past he cannot forget.

Jim's most important relationship in the novel is his friendship with Ántonia, and the fact that he allows Ántonia to recede in his mind as an abstract symbol of the past is itself a strong illustration of Jim's introspective mentality. Rather than remaining close to Ántonia through the years, Jim allows himself to drift apart from her, always preserving her special place in his heart by treating her memory with greater and greater nostalgia as the years go by. Though the final segment of the novel—Jim's reunion with Ántonia after twenty years apart—is not presented as a staggering breakthrough, it nevertheless seems to be a great step forward in Jim's growth and maturity. He can at last contemplate re-creating a real relationship with Ántonia, acknowledging that she still exists and is still herself even after the past that they shared has ended.

ÁNTONIA SHIMERDA Captured by Jim in his nostalgic memoir of his younger days, Ántonia gradually emerges from Jim's emotional presentation of her to become a believable, independent character in her own right. In fact, by the end of the novel, Ántonia has perhaps made more of an impression on many readers than Jim has. Many critics argue that Ántonia, despite the fact that she barely appears in the last quarter of the novel, is the real protagonist. Pretty, vivacious, and extremely generous, Ántonia fascinates Jim. He feels that Ántonia is unusually alive, a sentiment that he echoes even after meeting her as the mother of ten children at the end of the novel.

Throughout the novel, Ántonia is caught between her natural optimism and cheer and the extremely difficult circumstances that she faces after her emigration from Bohemia and her father's suicide in America. She is also trapped by the cultural differences that make her feel like a perpetual outsider in Nebraska and lead, in part, to her inability to love Jim as more than a brother: the Shimerdas go hungry, and their poverty forces Ántonia to work as a servant girl; certain members of the Black Hawk community judge her harshly for her love of dancing; her fiancé betrays her and leaves her to raise a child alone. Yet she never loses her quality of inner grace and self-sufficiency. Ántonia always tries to make the best of her circumstances, but she refuses to sacrifice her independence to improve her life. For example, she would rather work for the wretched Wick Cutter than follow Mr. Hartling's order to stop going to the dances.

Ántonia is based on an actual figure from Cather's childhood— a girl named Annie Pavelka, like Ántonia an immigrant and a hired girl in town whose father committed suicide. Cather admired Annie's inner radiance and her independence and sought to capture those qualities in Ántonia. In the process, she created a character from whom the heart of her novel developed: Ántonia symbolizes the past, possesses a deep rapport with her landscape, and embodies the experiences of both immigrants and the Nebraska pioneers.

LENA LINGARD While Jim and Ántonia are by far the most important figures in *My Ántonia*, one should not overlook Lena's importance to Jim's youth (the third book of the novel bears her name as the title, indicating the extent of her impact on his life). Cather conjures Lena to contrast sharply with Ántonia: while Ántonia possesses an independence that gives her quiet inner strength, Lena craves excitement and autonomy, refusing to marry any of the men who fall in love with her beauty and charisma. Her choice to live in San Francisco is nearly as extreme for someone from Black Hawk as Jim's decision to move to New York.

It is no coincidence that Lena becomes important in Jim's life at the moment he begins to transition out of childhood and into adulthood. Just as Ántonia comes to embody Jim's memories of childhood innocence and purity, Lena, with her desire for sophistication and her precocious sexuality, comes to represent Jim's emergence as a young adult. Tellingly, Jim fantasizes sexually about Lena in a way that he cannot about Ántonia. Even as a young man in Black Hawk, Jim already associates Ántonia with a lost past and invests her with an aura of emotional purity that precludes sex. Lena continues to become more important to Jim as he attends college when they are both in Lincoln together. Though Jim never grants Lena an exalted place in his memory as he does to Ántonia, she is still a pivotal figure in his growth from childhood to adulthood, and, given the importance he gives her in his story, she may continue to figure more largely in Jim's dream of the past than even Jim himself realizes.

THEMES, MOTIFS, AND SYMBOLS

THEMES

HUMANKIND'S RELATIONSHIP TO THE PAST The central narrative of *My Ántonia* is a look into the past, and though in his narration Jim rarely says anything directly about the idea of the past, the overall tone of the novel is highly nostalgic. Jim's motive for writing his story is to try to reestablish some connection between his present as a high-powered New York lawyer and his vanished past on the Nebraska prairie; in re-creating that past, the novel represents both Jim's memories and his feelings about his memories. Additionally, within the narrative itself, characters often look back longingly toward a past that they have lost, especially after the first book of the novel. Living in Black Hawk, Jim and Ántonia recall their days on the farms; Lena looks back toward her life with her family; the Shimerdas and the Russians reflect on their lives in their respective home countries before they immigrated to the United States.

M

The two principal qualities that the past seems to possess for most of the characters in the novel are that it is unrecoverable and that it is, in some way, preferable to the present. Ántonia misses life in Bohemia just as Jim misses life in Nebraska, but neither of them can ever go back. This impossibility of return accounts for the nostalgic, emotional tone of the story, which may have been autobiographical as well, informed by Cather's own longing for her Nebraska childhood. But if the past can never be recovered, it can never be escaped, either, and Jim is fated to go on thinking about Black Hawk long after he has left it.

The other important characteristic of the past in *My Ántonia* is that it is always personal: characters never look back toward bygone eras or large-scale historical conditions, but only toward the personal circumstances—places, people, things—that they remember from their own lives. As a result, a character's emotions are destined to color his or her memories for the rest of his or her life, a fact that is made thematically explicit in the novel by Jim's decision to call his memoir "My Ántonia" rather than simply "Ántonia." In thus laying claim to Ántonia, Jim acknowledges that what he is really writing is simply a chronicle of his own thoughts and feelings.

The novel ends on an optimistic note, with Jim's return to Nebraska twenty years after he last saw Ántonia and his mature decision to visit more often and to keep Ántonia in his life. This decision implies that, by revisiting his past, Jim has learned to incorporate it into his present, to seek a real relationship with Ántonia rather than transform her into a symbol of the past in his own mind. The past, the novel seems to suggest, is unrecoverable, but the people who shared one's past can be recovered, even after a separation of many years.

HUMANKIND'S RELATIONSHIP TO ITS ENVIRONMENT Related to the novel's nostalgic feeling for the past is its in-depth exploration of humankind's relationship to its environment. What characters in *My Ántonia* miss about the past is not simply lost time but a lost setting, a vanished world of people, places, and things, especially natural surroundings. The characters in *My Ántonia* respond powerfully to their environments—especially Jim, who develops a strong attachment to the Nebraska landscape that never really leaves him, even after two decades in New York.

As Cather portrays it, one's environment comes to symbolize one's psychology and may even shape one's emotional state by giving thoughts and feelings a physical form. The river, for example, makes Jim feel free, and he comes to prize freedom; the setting sun captures his introspective loneliness, and the wide-open melancholy of Nebraska's plains may play a role in forming his reflective, romantic personality—if it does not create Jim's personality, it at least comes to embody it physically. Thus, characters in *My Ántonia* often develop an extremely intense rapport with their surroundings, and it is the sense of loss engendered by moving beyond one's surroundings that occasions the novel's exploration of the meaning of the past.

THE IMMIGRANT EXPERIENCE IN THE UNITED STATES *My Ántonia* explores the lives of immigrants on the United States frontier in the second half of the nineteenth century. The Nebraska prairie of the novel is an ethnic hodgepodge combining American-born settlers with a wide range of European immigrants, especially eastern and northern Europeans such as the Bohemian Shimerdas, the Russians Peter and Pavel, and the Norwegian Lena. The novel creates a sympathetic portrait of the many hardships that immigrants faced, including intense homesickness (a form of longing for the past), inability to speak English, and a bewildering array of cultural and religious differences that the novel's immigrants must overcome if they wish to fit in with the often judgmental American settlers who make up the economic and cultural mainstream in Black Hawk. Because of the rigid (and, in Jim's eyes, preposterous) social hierarchy of Black Hawk, simply getting by can be very difficult for the immigrants, who lack the same opportunities as the Americans—Jim goes to school, for instance, while Ántonia must help her family eke out an existence after her father's suicide.

Though Cather's portrait of the immigrant experience is sympathetic, it never quite rises to the level of advocacy: Jim is describing a vanished past, not agitating for social change, and he himself shares many of the cultural assumptions of the American-born settlers. Thus, *My Ántonia* has little in common with more socially inflammatory works about the hardships faced by immigrants such as Upton Sinclair's *The Jungle* (1906), which was written to bring about social change. *My Ántonia* is a much more personal story and is more concerned with re-creating an emotional reality than with awakening the nation to a moral outrage.

THE TRADITIONAL NATURE OF FRONTIER VALUES *My Ántonia* evokes the living conditions and mindset of the nineteenth century, as well as the simple, hardworking, homespun ethic of that era's settlers, an ethic Cather approves of strongly even if she does not always approve of its application, such as the prejudicial treatment of the hired girls in town. The novel also explores the social assumptions of the frontier people on matters such as race (in the passage about Samson d'Arnault) and gender (in the passages about the hired girls, and in Jim's general desire to spend time with girls rather than with boys). These rigid traditional social assumptions require that Jim learn to fight and swear so that he will seem more like a boy. Nevertheless, despite their shortcomings, the settlers share values of family, community, and religion that make Black Hawk a close-knit and positive community, not unworthy of the nostalgia in which it is bathed throughout the novel.

MOTIFS

CHILDHOOD AND ADULTHOOD As the generation to which the main characters (Ántonia, Jim, and Lena) belong grows from young children into adults, the novel indirectly evokes many of the characteristics and feelings of children as they make the transition into adulthood. As a result, the vanished past for which many of the characters long is often associated with an innocent, childlike state that contrasts with the more worldly, grown-up present. But the motif of childhood and adulthood is propagated in the novel mostly by the feelings of the characters as they gradually begin to experience independence, responsibility, and sexuality, leading to a natural contrast between the before and after states of their lives. Once Jim begins to fantasize sexually about Lena, his earlier years become less relevant; once Ántonia begins to live for the town dances, she is never again the same simple farm girl. In marking these sorts of divisions, the novel charts the growth of its principal characters, who eventually gain the maturity to understand the relationship between their past and their present.

RELIGION Of all the cultural differences between the European immigrants and the American settlers (and there are many, often complicated differences, as we see when Jim's grandmother attempts to give the Shimerdas a gift of food), the one that recurs most interestingly is the difference in religion. Most of the Europeans are Catholic, as the Shimerdas are, and most of the Americans are Protestant, as the Burdens are. In addition to this dichotomy, there are smaller cultural differences, such as language and attitude, which the novel explores from time to time. The motif of religion is most visible during the novel's depictions of Christmas and the circumstances surrounding Mr. Shimerda's suicide.

SYMBOLS

THE NEBRASKA LANDSCAPE The most important and universal symbol in *My Ántonia* is the Nebraska landscape. Cather's poetic and moving depiction of it is perhaps the most famous and highly praised aspect of the novel. The landscape symbolizes the larger idea of a human environment, a setting in which a person lives and moves. Jim's relationship with the Nebraska landscape is important on its own terms, but it also comes to symbolize a great deal about Jim's relationship with the people and culture of Nebraska, as well as with his inner self. Throughout the novel, the landscape mirrors Jim's feelings—it looks desolate when he is lonely, for instance—and also awakens feelings within him. Finally, the landscape becomes the novel's most tangible symbol of the vanished past, as Jim, the lawyer in distant New York, thinks back longingly on the landscape of his childhood.

M

THE PLOW The plow, which Jim and Ántonia see silhouetted against the enormous setting sun, symbolizes the connection between human culture and the natural landscape. As the sun sets behind the plow, the two elements are combined in a single image of perfect harmony, suggesting that man and nature also coexist harmoniously. But as the sun sinks lower on the horizon, the plow seems to grow smaller and smaller, ultimately reflecting the dominance of the landscape over those who inhabit it.

IMPORTANT QUOTATIONS EXPLAINED

---

1. *During that burning day when we were crossing Iowa, our talk kept returning to a central figure, a Bohemian girl whom we had both known long ago. More than any other person we remembered, this girl seemed to mean to us the country, the conditions, the whole adventure of our childhood.*

This passage from the Introduction is the first time the reader hears of Ántonia. The narrator of the Introduction, who grew up with Jim and Ántonia in Nebraska, describes a train ride taken with Jim many years later and details their conversation about Ántonia. They agreed that Ántonia, more than any other person, seemed to represent the world they had grown up in, to the point that speaking her name evokes "people and places" and "a quiet drama . . . in one's brain." This quotation is important because it establishes that Ántonia will both evoke and symbolize the vanished past of Jim's childhood in Nebraska. It situates Ántonia as the central character in Jim's story and explains Jim's preoccupation with her by connecting her to his memories of the past. Finally, it establishes Jim's character with its implication that

Jim shares the unnamed narrator's romantic inclination to dwell on the past and to allow people and places to take on an extraordinarily emotional, nostalgic significance.

---

2. *"I never know you was so brave, Jim," she went on comfortingly. "You is just like big mans; you wait for him lift his head and then you go for him. Ain't you feel scared a bit? Now we take that snake home and show everybody. Nobody ain't seen in this kawn-tree so big snake like you kill."*

Ántonia speaks these lines in Book i, Chapter vii, praising Jim for having killed the rattlesnake. Jim is angry with Ántonia for failing to warn him about the snake (in a moment of panic, she screams out in her native language), and she quickly appeases him by gushing about his bravery and manliness. The quote captures Ántonia's way of speaking in the early part of the novel, as she is learning English; it also represents a moment of transition in Jim's relationship with her. Because she is older than Jim, Ántonia has had a tendency to treat him somewhat condescendingly, to Jim's increasing frustration. After he proves his strength by killing the rattlesnake, she regards him with a new respect and never talks down to him again. She may never love Jim romantically, but at this moment, she clearly comes to regard him as an equal and as someone very special to her.

---

3. *"Why aren't you always nice like this, Tony?" "How nice?" "Why, just like this; like yourself. Why do you all the time try to be like Ambrosch?" She put her arms under her head and lay back, looking up at the sky. "If I live here, like you, that is different. Things will be easy for you. But they will be hard for us."*

This dialogue from Book i, Chapter xix, occurs as Jim and Ántonia sit on the roof of the chicken house, watching the electrical storm. The two have grown apart somewhat following Mr. Shimerda's suicide, as Jim has begun to attend school and Ántonia has been forced to spend her time working on the farm. Jim has found himself dismayed by Ántonia's increasing coarseness and her pride in her own strength. As they sit watching the lightning storm, Jim feels his old intimacy returning, and he brings himself to ask Ántonia why she has changed. Ántonia understands Jim's question and, because she is four years older, understands better than he does why their lives have begun to move in separate directions. Jim has opportunities and a bright future ahead of him, but for Ántonia, life now means simply helping her family get by. Ántonia acknowledges this unalterable circumstance with her customarily wise simplicity: "Things will be easy for you. But they will be hard for us."

---

4. *On some upland farm, a plough had been left standing in the field. The sun was sinking just behind it. Magnified across the distance by the horizontal light, it stood out against the sun, was exactly contained within the circle of the disk; the handles, the tongue, the share—black against the molten red. . . . Even while we whispered about it, our vision disappeared; the ball dropped and dropped until the red tip went beneath the earth. The fields below us were dark, the sky was growing pale, and that forgotten plough had sunk back to its own littleness somewhere on the prairie.*

This passage from Book ii, Chapter xiv, recounts a sunset that Jim and Ántonia watch the summer after Jim graduates from high school. Gradually, the sun sinks behind a plow on the horizon, so the plow is superimposed on the red sun, "black against molten red." The passage is an excellent example of Cather's famous ability to evoke the landscape, creating a sensuous and poetic picture of a sunset on the Nebraska prairie. It also indicates the extraordinary psychological connection that Cather's characters feel with their landscape, as the setting sun perfectly captures the quiet, somewhat bittersweet moment the characters are experiencing—they care for one another and have had a wonderful day together, but they are growing up and will soon go their separate ways.

The image of the plow superimposed on the sun also suggests a symbolic connection between human culture (the plow) and the nature (the sun). As the plow fills up the disk of the sun, the two coexist in perfect harmony, just as Jim recalls the idyllic connection between the natural landscape and the settlements in Nebraska. But as the sun sinks beneath the horizon, the plow dwindles to insignificance ("its own littleness"), suggesting that, in the relationship between humankind and environment, environment is dominant.

5. *She lent herself to immemorial human attitudes which we recognize by instinct as universal and true. . . . She was a battered woman now, not a lovely girl; but she still had that something which fires the imagination, could still stop one's breath for a moment by a look or gesture that somehow revealed the meaning in common things. . . . She was a rich mine of life, like the founders of early races.*

This passage, which concludes Book v, Chapter i, finds the adult Jim still contemplating the fascination he feels for Ántonia. Here he attributes her significance to her nurturing and generous presence, which suggests an enviable fullness of life. Ántonia is full of love and loyalty, and, as Jim portrays it, Ántonia is a "rich mine of life," an inexhaustible source of love and will from which others draw strength and warmth. This portrayal explains why Ántonia lingers so prominently in the minds of so many people from Jim's childhood. In her presence they have been filled with the love and strength that she exudes, and they will never forget the way it made them feel.

Apart from standing as the novel's final important analysis of Ántonia, this quote is important because it reveals the psychological changes that the passage of time has wrought in Jim. Whereas before he avoided Ántonia for twenty years because he did not want to see the lovely girl he knew transformed into a hardened, overworked matron, he can now see beyond Ántonia's age to her essential inner quality, which he finds can still "stop one's breath." This newfound connection to the present indicates that Jim can finally move beyond his dreamlike preoccupation with his nostalgia for his youth and contemplate Ántonia as more than a symbol of the past.

In *My Ántonia*, in what ways does Willa Cather feminize the role of the narrator, Jim Burden?

An author's biography occasionally gives new insight into characters, motivations, and subtexts within a work. Willa Cather, author of *My Ántonia*, dressed for several years as a man, calling herself William Cather. Cather's experiences with gender-bending are mirrored in *My Ántonia*'s narrator, Jim Burden. Through his daily activities and moments of violence, Jim takes on a feminized role.

Jim Burden is clearly depicted as feminine at several places in the novel. He spends a great deal of time in the female domain of the kitchen and the home in the presence of women, while the men and other young boys are working outside. While his best friend Ántonia is considered "one of the boys" for her work in the fields, Jim is "one of the girls," helping his grandmother and doing chores such as collecting the eggs and sweeping the kitchen. This continues into his adulthood: he reads, studies, goes to school, and spends free evenings playing games with Ántonia and the younger neighbor girls instead of the boys his age. Even his adolescent rebellion, sneaking out to the dancing tent on Saturday nights, is done with his girlfriends.

Jim's femininity is crystallized through his struggle with various symbols of masculine domination. The clearest depiction of this conflict is young Jim's clash with a snake. Here Cather's language is heavy with sexual allusion: the serpent's "abominable muscularity,""loathsome, fluid motion,"and his tightened coils all make Jim sick. Echoing the life power associated with the phallus, the snake has a "disgusting vitality" as he lifts his "hideous little head" and prepares to penetrate his victim. Jim lashes out at the snake, striking not from fear, but from hate. Hate of the "ancient, eldest Evil" whose kind "have left horrible unconscious memories in all warm-blooded life" (Chapter VII). This line suggests passionate antimale feeling, a testimony against rape, abuse, domination, suppression, and oppression of female bodies, minds, and spirits. Clearly, the snake, a traditional phallic symbol, is the male domination and sexual power that threatens Jim Burden, William Cather, and the women they love.

Another major struggle between Jim and masculine domination is in the attempted rape scene. Ántonia is alone while her employers are away and is bothered by Wick Cutter's attitude. As a precaution, she asks Jim to sleep in her bed while she stays with his grandmother. Sure enough, Jim awakens to find someone on the end of the bed leaning over to kiss him. A violent fight breaks out, as Jim tries to escape the bigger, stronger, enraged Cutter. The description echoes the snake scene: Cutter is described as "hissing," and he sends Jim "sprawling to the floor." Jim finally escapes not by overpowering Cutter, but by "fighting like a girl" and bending Cutter's thumb backward, a tactic requiring little strength. Jim's breaking of Cutter's thumb, another phallic symbol, renders this scene a more intense version of the snake's earlier destruction.

Although he eventually escapes the house, Jim's reaction and recovery from his fight echoes that of a woman having been raped. Not only does he have bruises and cuts all over his body, but he hides from the world, not allowing anyone except his grandmother to see him or know what happened. Unlike the snake incident, where he was pleased that all the neighbors came to see his trophy and hear stories of his bravery, Jim fears his neighbors' knowing about his latest struggle. As a boy he could resist weaker opponents and challenges to his masculinity, but as an adult, he now must face the extent to which his flawed masculinity will affect his acceptance in society as a male figure.

Love for strong women and their company and struggles with figures who represent male power lead Jim into an antimale, highly feminized position that creates conflict with his biological gender. Jim Burden mirrors William Cather's struggles to find a true sense of gender and identity in his relationships with women and society.

Nectar in a Sieve

Kamala Markandaya (1924–2004)

CONTEXT

Kamala Markandaya was born in 1924 in Mysore, in southern India. She attended college at the University of Madras, where she studied history. Between 1940 and 1947, she worked as a journalist and published short stories in Indian newspapers. She married an Englishman and immigrated to England in 1948, where she had one daughter.

Markandaya published *Nectar in a Sieve*, her first novel, in 1954, to wide critical acclaim. In the United States, it was chosen as a Book of the Month Club Main Selection, and in 1955, the American Library Association named it a Notable Book. Remarkably, Markandaya was the only woman in a group of mid-century Indians writing in English, a group that included Mulk Raj Anand, R. K. Narayan, Raja Rao, and Khushwant Singh. Despite her success, Markandaya remained an intensely private writer who revealed little about her personal influences. She was so private, in fact, that she used a pen name—she was born Kamala Purnaiya. However, we can gain insight into her work by evaluating the religious, political, and social contexts in which she lived and wrote.

Raised in India as a Hindu-Brahmin, Markandaya addresses a fundamental question of Hindu belief in her work: what does it mean to be human? To a Hindu, *dharma* is a moral or virtuous way of living, characterized in part by devotion to truth, the practice of forgiveness, inner and outer purity, controlling anger, not coveting material goods, and reducing attachments to worldly things. *Karma* means "deed" or "action," and because all life is interrelated, every deed has consequences. Human beings have free will and can choose their own actions to produce joy or misery for themselves and others. Suffering is a form of purification. The soul's highest goal is liberation, and truth transcends all other moral values. Such Hindu beliefs are central to *Nectar in a Sieve*.

Hindu traditions are also important in Markandaya's writing. Rukmani, the main character in *Nectar in a Sieve*, worships the Mother Goddess, the Earth incarnate, who embodies creative energy, passion, and power. Echoes of the epic *Ramayana*, one of the best-loved Indian stories, are clear in this novel. *Ramayana* recounts the adventures of Prince Rama and his ideal Hindu wife, Sita, who must prove her faithfulness to her husband after her abduction. Years later, gossips question her fidelity. In despair, Sita cries out to her mother, the Earth Goddess, who opens the earth to take Sita home. Critics of Markandaya's work compare *Nectar*'s Rukmani to the legendary Sita. Markandaya shapes Rukmani's story around the traditional life stages of the Brahmin caste. Celibate studenthood is first, followed by the householder stage of marriage, procreation, work, and duty. After the first grandson, the forest-dweller stage begins, characterized by withdrawing from material concerns. The final stage, wandering beggar, marks the end of wanting and fearing and of being at peace with oneself and the gods. Rukmani passes through all of these traditional stages.

In addition to the beliefs and traditions of Hinduism, contemporary Indian politics contribute to an understanding of *Nectar in a Sieve*. When Markandaya was growing up and attending college, India was governed as a conquered colony of Great Britain. British law transformed Indian zamindars, traditional land-revenue collectors, into landowners and absentee landlords. British rule brought the Industrial Revolution to India, changing traditional rural life. Young men moved off the land to earn money in factories instead of by growing crops. The British also introduced English education and ideals to India's students, including the literature of revolution and freedom. During World War II, Mahatma Gandhi, the great figure of freedom and civil disobedience, began his "Quit India" campaign against British rule. India earned its independence in 1947. Britain partitioned the country into predominately Hindu India and predominately Muslim Pakistan. This partition created millions of refugees, and in the chaos and terror that followed, a million people died. In India's first general election in 1952, Nehru won the presidency with his goal of freedom from want for the masses. Two years later, Markandaya published *Nectar in a Sieve*, which draws upon the political concepts and turmoil of her age.

Markandaya was not yet twenty when the famine of 1943 in Bengal claimed over three million lives, and her detailed, realistic portrayal of human starvation comes from those desperate times. India's conflicts between Hindus and Muslims often erupted in violence during the years before independence, and she scrutinizes religious intolerance in her novel as well. The status of women in Indian society was a major issue of the day, and new laws regarding women's rights were not enacted until after independence. Traditionally, procreation was so important that if a bride failed to conceive, her husband could take another wife. The birth of a daughter was considered a liability, but the birth of a son was celebrated with festivities, and these events appear in the novel. Gandhi believed that the whole structure of urban, industrialized society was violent and repressive, crushing human souls and destroying the beauty of nature. *Nectar in a Sieve* captures the effects of such social upheaval on its characters.

Markandaya drew the title *Nectar in a Sieve* from a tragic poem by Samuel Taylor Coleridge called "Work Without Hope": "Work without Hope draws nectar in a sieve, / And Hope without an object cannot live." She went on to publish nine additional novels, and among these, *Some Inner Fury* (1958), about a young Indian woman in love with an Englishman, is perhaps her most autobiographical. She died in London in 2004.

PLOT OVERVIEW

Rukmani, an old woman, reflects on her life. The educated daughter of a village headman fallen on hard times, Rukmani is married at the age of twelve to Nathan, a tenant farmer. Nathan treats her with kindness and respect as she learns the chores her new life requires. Within a year they have a beautiful daughter, Ira, and good rice harvests. During the next six years, Rukmani does not conceive. Troubled that she cannot produce a son for Nathan, Rukmani visits her ill mother and there meets Kenny, a foreign doctor. He treats her infertility without Nathan's knowledge. In quick succession, Rukmani bears five sons. With each birth, however, the family has a little less to eat. When a tannery is built nearby, unpleasant changes come to village life. Rukmani's two oldest sons eventually go to work there. They help the family a great deal with their wages but are eventually dismissed for being ringleaders in a labor strike.

The year they arrange a good marriage for Ira, monsoon rains destroy all their crops. Rukmani sacrifices her savings to buy food for the family. Ira's husband returns Ira to her parents' home because she is barren. Again Rukmani turns to Kenny without her husband's knowledge, this time to help Ira conceive. His treatments are too late, however, since Ira's husband has taken another woman. Rukmani becomes pregnant again and bears her last son, Kuti. Caring for Kuti lifts Ira out of her depression and despair until the crops fail from drought and the family once again goes hungry. They sell most of their possessions just to pay half of what they owe the landowner for their lease. Reduced to foraging for roots and leaves, the family begins to weaken and starve. Kenny secures a servant's position in the city for Rukmani's third son. Rukmani's fourth son is killed stealing a calfskin from the tannery. Kuti suffers the most from hunger, and Ira prostitutes herself to feed him. Despite her efforts, he dies. A good rice harvest arrives too late to save Rukmani's sons.

Kenny returns from one of his long absences with money raised to build a hospital in the village. He offers to train Rukmani's remaining son, Selvam, as his assistant. Some villagers speculate that Kenny is kind to Rukmani because they have an illicit relationship. Kunthi, a neighborhood wife who became a prostitute, spreads this rumor out of spite. When they were both young, Nathan fathered Kunthi's two sons. Kunthi uses this as leverage over them until Rukmani learns the truth and forgives Nathan. Now, as Nathan nears fifty, he has no sons left to work the land. He suffers from rheumatism and debilitating fevers. Rukmani and Ira try to help, but they are not strong enough. Ira has a baby to care for, an albino boy conceived in prostitution but loved nonetheless. The family experiences its greatest loss when the land agent tells Nathan and Rukmani their land has been sold to the despised tannery. No one else will lease land to a man as old and ill as Nathan, and Rukmani and Nathan must leave their home of thirty years to go to their son Murugan in the city. They leave Ira and their grandchild under Selvam's care.

Their possessions reduced to the few bundles they carry, Nathan and Rukmani try to find Murugan in the city. They rest one night at a temple, where thieves steal their bundles and all their money. A leprous street urchin named Puli helps them find the home of Kenny's doctor friend. They learn that Murugan has not worked there for the past two years and that he left the position for better wages at the Collector's house. At the Collector's, Murugan's wife informs them that Murugan has deserted her. Her older boy, their grandson, is thin with hunger. Her starving baby is too little to be Murugan's son. Rukmani sees that she and Nathan cannot impose upon their daughter-in-law. They return to the temple, where food is distributed each night to the destitute.

Rukmani and Nathan dream of home but have no means to make the trip. Rukmani tries to get work as a letter reader but earns only enough to buy rice cakes. Puli takes them to a stone quarry where there is better-paying work. He helps them learn to break stones, and they come to rely on him. They entrust him with their earnings, and, as they save, they begin to hope. One evening, Rukmani splurges on extra food and toys for Puli and her grandson. When she returns to Nathan at the temple, she expects him to be angry, but instead he is violently ill. During a week of monsoon rains, Nathan continues to work in the quarry despite his fevers and chills. One evening, after she gets paid, Rukmani begins to plan for a cart to take them home. Hurrying to catch up with Nathan, she finds him collapsed in the mud in the street. Kind strangers help carry him to the temple, where he dies in her arms after reminding her of their happiness together. After his death, Rukmani rashly promises Puli his health if he returns to the country with her, a promise Kenny and Selvam will help her keep. She introduces Puli to Selvam and Ira as the son she and Nathan adopted while they were away. Demonstrating both hope and compassion, Ira hastens to prepare a meal for Puli, and Selvam promises his mother they will manage.

CHARACTER LIST

Rukmani The narrator and protagonist of the novel. Rukmani recalls with clarity and unflinching honesty the choices and decisions that have brought both joy and despair. Her father taught her to read and write, and she passes these valuable skills on to her children. She develops a great love for the beauty and the land. Though not outwardly beautiful, she is loving, hardworking, thrifty, and patient. She is also capable of violence when pushed too far.

Nathan Rukmani's husband, a tenant farmer who loves the land. Nathan is gentle and kind to his wife and becomes a true life partner to her over the years. None of his children show interest in working the land with him, which is both heartbreaking and a hardship for him. Nathan is upright and thoughtful, serious but also capable of joy. A tireless worker with a gift for farming, Nathan introduces hardships to his family through his infidelity with Kunthi.

Kenny A white doctor who ministers to the people in the village. When Kenny helps Rukmani overcome her infertility, she is forever grateful, and the two become friends. Kenny finds his Indian patients both endearing and frustrating. Their poverty appalls him, and he believes in fighting fate—a Western viewpoint he voices throughout the novel. Kenny is mysterious, private, moody, and occasionally sharp-tongued, yet he does what he can from time to time to help Rukmani's family. He is tall and gaunt and has eyes the color of a kingfisher's wing, neither blue nor green.

Kunthi The village beauty, pregnant when Rukmani first meets her. Kunthi is distant, reserved, and slightly contemptuous of Rukmani, but she is provocative with men. She rejoices when the tannery makes the village larger and more exciting, and she often goes to town for the admiring looks she receives from young men. People say she married beneath her, and when times are desperate, Kunthi turns to prostitution and extortion.

Ira Rukmani's daughter, her first child. Ira is named for the great Irawaddy River because water is so precious. Ira is more beautiful than either of her parents and has a sweet, obedient, uncomplaining nature. She sings like a bird. When her husband abandons her because she is barren, she falls into a depression lifted only by the birth of her youngest brother, Kuti. She devotes herself to him with great determination, as she later does to her own illegitimate albino son.

Puli A nine-year-old leper orphan from the city, and head of a gang of street children. When Puli begs, he assumes a pathetic, helpless demeanor, but he is strong and clever in the ways of the streets. Rukmani and Nathan survive with his assistance and trust him with their savings, turning to him as they could not to their own son.

Kali The wife of a neighboring farmer in the village. Kali is plump and jovial, and she introduces Rukmani to the neighbor women. Kali shows the young Rukmani how to perform the chores of a farm wife. She helps out at the birth of Rukmani's first child. Kali expresses the views of the villagers about events in the novel and is particularly disdainful of Rukmani's belief in the value of reading and writing.

Old Granny A woman without family who barely scrapes a living selling produce in the village. Old Granny remains friendly with Rukmani even after Rukmani stops selling garden produce to her.

At Rukmani's request, Old Granny arranges what all consider a good marriage for Ira. Old Granny never forgives herself for the failure of that marriage, and she brings a rupee as a gift when Ira's baby is born, when she herself is starving.

Arjun Rukmani and Nathan's first son. Though Arjun is a wonderful student, he goes to work in the tannery because he is tired of being hungry and of watching his siblings go hungry. He is generous with his earnings, giving them all to his mother for the family. He is idealistic and becomes a spokesman for the striking tannery workers.

Thambi Rukmani and Nathan's second son, who also goes to the tannery. Like his older brother, Arjun, Thambi is idealistic and generous until the tannery turns him bitter. He and Arjun become known in the tannery as troublemakers, and they must leave their village and their family in order to make lives in the tea plantations of Ceylon.

Murugan Rukmani and Nathan's third son. Kenny refers Murugan for work in the city and reports to Rukmani that he is doing well. However, Murugan stays away from his family. He marries without consulting his parents, then fails to let them know he has abandoned the city, his job, and his wife and child.

Raja Rukmani and Nathan's fourth son. Raja is killed by tannery watchmen for allegedly stealing a calfskin during a time of famine.

Selvam Rukmani and Nathan's fifth son. Selvam is conscientious and hardworking, but he does not take to farming. When Kenny offers him the job as assistant in his hospital, Selvam embraces the opportunity. Selvam is compassionate and shames the adults who criticize his sister Ira's albino baby, Sacrabani. Selvam has a special bond with Ira and promises his parents he will care for Ira and Sacrabani.

Kuti Rukmani and Nathan's sixth son, born to Rukmani late in life. Kuti is a happy baby who brings Ira out of her hopelessness, but he suffers the most when famine comes. His wailing is nearly impossible for the family, especially Ira, to bear.

Sacrabani Ira's albino son, considered a freak by the villagers. Sacrabani is conceived as a result of Ira's prostitution. His skin and hair are white, and his eyes are pink. He sunburns easily, and sunlight hurts his eyes. He suffers the ridicule of children and the stares of adults.

Sivaji The agent for the landowner. Unlike most go-betweens, Sivaji does not demand bribes from the tenant farmers. Kindly and compassionate, he allows Nathan and Rukmani extra time to pay their debts when the crops fail.

Biswas The moneylender who thrives on the misfortunes of others.

Janaki The village shopkeeper's homely wife who befriends Rukmani.

Das The kind servant of Murugan's former employer in the city.

Ammu Murugan's abandoned and unfaithful wife.

ANALYSIS OF MAJOR CHARACTERS

RUKMANI Born to the village headman, Rukmani is spoiled by her social station in the village. When she is twelve and ready to become a bride, she expects a grand wedding like her older sisters enjoyed. However, her family's circumstances have declined under British rule, and Rukmani is married to Nathan, a landless tenant farmer. When she first sees the mud hut Nathan prepared for her, she compares it in her mind to her father's fine house and sinks to the ground in fear and despair. Yet instead of ranting or pouting, Rukmani notices Nathan's pleading expression and reassures him. After this difficult beginning, Rukmani continues to call upon and develop her better nature. She learns the chores of a farmer's wife and soon improves upon them by growing a superlative vegetable garden. Rukmani is closely associated with the earth and draws spiritual strength from its fertility and beauty. She learns to help other women in childbirth, to adapt to and accept the unpleasant changes the tannery brings to the village, and to withstand seasons of want and hunger. Instead of petulance, Rukmani exhibits tenacious and life-affirming endurance.

Rukmani faces loss after loss over the years, and as her endurance is continuously tested, her capacity for anger intensifies—but her spirit also grows. Kunthi arouses her rage by suggesting several times that Rukmani is sexually involved with Kenny. The first time, Rukmani grabs her and shakes her so furiously her sari drops away. The second time, Rukmani's wrath so overpowers her that she longs to kill Kunthi. Finally, in a murderous rage, Rukmani attacks and almost kills Ira, mistaking her for Kunthi. After this near disaster, Rukmani finds peace by telling Nathan the truth, forgiving him for his transgressions, and learning to control her anger so she is never again tempted to injure another person. Rather, Rukmani grows in generosity and compassion. She gives up the strictures of caste when her sons go to work in the tannery, and she gives up the tradition of shame when her daughter turns to prostitution. Rukmani forgives her daughter-in-law for failing her duty to help them, and she learns to judge strangers not by their differences but by their deeds and their hearts. Finally, she extends her love and care to Puli, a child even more destitute than she is. By the end of the novel, Rukmani has conquered the hardships of her existence.

NATHAN Like Rukmani, Nathan identifies with the sustaining and replenishing earth. As a young husband, he thrives on the hope of one day owning land. However, with each passing year, the tannery gains ascendancy over the rural landscape, and his hope diminishes. Nathan is heartbroken when his sons repudiate a farmer's life and turn to other occupations, yet he refuses to ask any of them to sacrifice their hopes for a better future. Despite bitter times, Nathan is capable of great happiness and joy, and the prospect of a good harvest renews his spirit. He dances joyously with his sons at the Festival of Lights and loves Rukmani passionately. Often he praises her cleverness and calls her the best of wives. Like Rukmani, Nathan is not perfect. His secret infidelity with Kunthi early in his marriage fills him with shame and regret until he confesses to Rukmani and earns her forgiveness. Rukmani describes Nathan as an upright man. He will not eat the food his daughter procures from prostituting herself, nor will he fight like an animal for food at the temple as others do. At his death, the flame atop the temple goes out as his soul is liberated from his suffering body. Like the land he loves, Nathan exemplifies spiritual harmony.

KENNY Not only does Kenny cry out against injustice and poverty, he takes what actions he can to fight against them. He questions the status quo and exhorts the suffering to call for help. Sometimes his questions are naïve, such as when he remonstrates with Rukmani for taking dung out of the fields or for nursing her child past the age of weaning. Kenny does not always understand the severe marginality of the impoverished, yet Rukmani admires his gentle ways and tender heart. He brings western medicine to the village and helps both Rukmani and Ira conceive children, their greatest desire. Kenny sacrifices his wife and children to his calling in India and lives a lonely, isolated life. He helps others however he can, securing work in the city for Murugan and training Selvam as his assistant. He raises money by appealing to the humanity of the outside world and is tireless in building a hospital for the village. He is determined, says Rukmani, to find ways and means. In the novel, Kenny stands for hope.

KUNTHI Although Kunthi and Rukmani are neighbors in similar circumstances, Kunthi chooses a very different life path. Where Rukmani remains a faithful wife, Kunthi is unfaithful even as a young bride. She uses her beauty and her seductiveness first to lure Nathan and later to attract the attention of the young tannery workers. For Kunthi, the tannery means a town with excitement and luxuries, whereas for Rukmani, it represents the repudiation of beauty, health, and values. Kunthi transfers her own morality to Rukmani by assuming that Rukmani and Kenny are conducting an illicit affair. At first she merely threatens Rukmani with exposure, but as her conditions becomes more dire, Kunthi extorts food from both Rukmani and Nathan. Her power comes from their fear and is so strong and evil that Rukmani and Nathan risk their family's starvation to satisfy her. Rukmani and Nathan finally break her power with truth. Truth is the transcendent Hindu value, and Kunthi stands in opposition to it.

THEMES, MOTIFS, AND SYMBOLS

THEMES

HUNGER AS A THREAT TO DIGNITY In Rukmani's quest for dignity, hunger is a potent enemy. Fear of hunger, she says, torments the peace of every peasant who lives by the vagaries of the wind and rain. Tired of constant hunger, her elder sons break up the family to seek new lives in a new land. Another son resorts to theft and is killed for it, leaving Rukmani to grieve for his meaningless life. Her daughter chooses the degradation of prostitution over the degradation of starvation. Rukmani nearly becomes a murderer, thinking Kunthi has come to steal the last of their rice. In the city, Rukmani observes the supplicants at the temple pushing and shoving like animals to secure a share of food. Similarly, beggar children snarl and fight like beasts over a scrap dropped in the street. Rukmani indicts both the industrialization of the villages, represented by the tannery, and the laws of land ownership that impoverish and displace peasants like her and Nathan. In *Nectar in a Sieve,* hunger breeds thieves, prostitutes, murderers, and subhuman beasts. Not only nature's whims but also the choices of an unjust society produce the shameful misery of starvation.

KNOWLEDGE AS POWER The poor in Markandaya's novel often suffer at the hands of the strong, but some of them understand that knowledge is a powerful weapon for change. Rukmani insists on teaching all of her children to read and write, even though many in the village believe such knowledge leads to trouble. Her eldest sons are branded troublemakers because they dare to band the workers together in a strike for better wages. The tannery wins because the workers' coalition fails to hold. Arjun complains that the people will never learn, echoing Kenny's sentiments as an educated outsider. Rukmani turns to Kenny because, she says, white men have power. Kenny uses his power for good, treating the poor and raising funds to build a hospital. Kunthi uses her knowledge to exercise an evil power, but once Nathan and Rukmani share the truth with each other, Kunthi's power over them is broken. Puli shares his knowledge of the city to help Nathan and Rukmani save money for their fare home. Throughout the novel, the admirable characters are those who apply their knowledge to help people stand together in a display of moral power.

THE STRENGTH OF TRUTH Rukmani is a strong voice for the world's poor because she speaks with clarity and truth. She reveals a world the literate are seldom forced to examine, and her descriptions of the physical ravages of starvation are simple, powerful, and timeless. One of Rukmani's particular strengths lies in confronting her own misconceptions, as people and events often challenge her traditional views. Her sons repudiate their caste, her daughter redefines dishonor, and her grandson crosses the barrier of skin color. Kenny demands that she rethink her preconceptions about distrusting strangers, suffering passively, and taking action against injustice. In each case, Rukmani gets stronger because of her devotion to truth, and at the same time she exhibits the Hindu belief that truth transcends all other moral values.

THE IMPORTANCE OF FERTILITY Fertility is so precious to Rukmani that she takes risks to pursue it. When she is pregnant with Ira, she encounters a cobra in her pumpkin vine, and though it might have killed her and does induce early labor, she does not stop raising vegetables for fear of snakes. Her vegetables are a source of both food and beauty to Rukmani, and she compares their rounded shapes to fertile young women. She conquers her fear of a foreign doctor to seek treatment for barrenness, risking Nathan's disapproval. Because of Kunthi's blackmail, the risk extends to losing Nathan's love and support, without which she feels she cannot live. Ira's miseries also stem from infertility, and she loses her husband to another woman because she cannot give him sons. The fertility of the land is paramount, for when the land does not produce, the family starves. Images of grains of rice, sprouting paddy, and the harvest represent life itself.

MOTIFS

DRUMBEATS Great change is accompanied by drumbeats in Rukmani's life. Drummers first appear to call laborers into the village, and Rukmani loses her first two sons to Ceylon. Ira has a drummer and a fiddler for her wedding before she leaves her mother's home. Drumbeats announce the widespread devastation of the flood that destroys their crops. Drummers emphasize the passion and joy of Deepavali, the Festival of Lights, which marks a highlight for Rukmani as well as the conception of her last child. When Raja is killed by the tannery guards, Rukmani listens to the drumbeats at his funeral pyre until they die away. Just before Nathan dies, Rukmani buys Puli a dum-dum cart that plays a drum as it is pulled along. With their insistent rhythm, drumbeats announce and predict each change of circumstance.

CONFRONTING THE STRANGER Again and again, Rukmani confronts those who are different and learns from her encounters. From the Muslim wife of a tannery official she learns that possessions are less important than freedom. From the tannery official who visits after Raja's death, she learns that a cold and mercenary heart creates a chasm between people that cannot be crossed. From Kenny she learns that some strangers care enough about the suffering of others to contribute funds for a hospital. From Das, the servant in the city, she learns the value of kindness to the destitute. From a helpful stranger, she learns there is food for the poor at the temple. From Puli she learns that family can be created through generosity. Rukmani's life is enriched by the strangers who enter it.

SYMBOLS

RICE Rice is the overriding symbol for life itself in *Nectar in a Sieve*. Nathan presses grains from his harvest into Rukmani's hands to impress his bride with their prospects for prosperity. As Rukmani learns to plant, she is struck by the wonder of seeds that contain, for her, life itself. Mounds of rice tinted with saffron and fried in butter mark the birth feast for Rukmani's first son. The monsoon floods destroy the paddy and, with it, the family's chance to eat that season. They use their precious savings to buy rice at exorbitant prices, for without it they will not live. When the drought takes their harvest, Rukmani runs her fingers obsessively through the last of her hoarded rice. She loves the feeling of the rice because she loves life so fiercely.

BULLOCKS By their strong and patient work, bullocks are closely allied with the hardworking peasants who live on the land. The bullocks who carry Rukmani as a bride to her new home wear bells on their horns to tinkle a happy accompaniment to the song of birds and sweet smells of the land. Like Nathan and Rukmani, the bullocks underscore the harmony of nature. They provide the dung Rukmani uses to burn for fuel and waterproof her hut. But like the peasants, the bullocks suffer from the injustice of overwork. One of the bullocks pulling them to the city develops a festering sore. The carter explains that he has to continue to work the animal in order to make his living, just as Nathan and Rukmani must work to gather in their harvest even while they are starving to death. The bullock flinches when the yoke is put upon his raw neck, but he patiently accepts his fate. Rukmani's sympathy for the injured beast is indicative of her stand against the injustice of the peasant's lot.

THE SARI Rukmani's wedding sari is the material possession she most prizes, and she holds fast to it as a source of prestige, dignity, and pride. Made of rich cloth with wide borders in silver thread, it communicates that her father was a headman and that she comes from important people. For Ira's wedding, Rukmani brings forth hoarded stores of food and delicacies to make a fine showing for the feast, but, more important, she provides the wedding sari for Ira to wear. During their hard and hungry times, Rukmani holds on to the wedding sari to wear at her sons' future weddings so she will not shame them. When faced with destitution, Rukmani must choose between the sari and the land. She offers the sari for sale along with their bullocks and household possessions in order to hold on to the land they need to live. By relinquishing her most prized possession, Rukmani reduces her attachment to worldly goods as an important step toward achieving the Hindu virtue of dharma.

IMPORTANT QUOTATIONS EXPLAINED

---

1. *While the sun shines on you and the fields are green and beautiful to the eye, and your husband sees beauty in you which no has seen before, and you have a good store of grain laid away for hard times, a roof over you and a sweet stirring in your body, what more can a woman ask for?*

Reflecting in Chapter 1 upon the happy first year of her marriage, Rukmani succinctly touches on themes and motifs of significance throughout the novel. Nature and its beauty appear in the sun and the green fields as the first source of her well-being. Rukmani expresses her appreciation for Nathan, who has discovered a beauty in her that she did not know she possessed. At the same time, Rukmani conveys Nathan's appreciation for her and for a beauty that is more than skin-deep. The all-important grain represents life itself. A good store of grain means more than sustenance—it means freedom from fear and doubt about survival. Her mention of the shelter of a roof foreshadows a time when the roof is threatened by monsoon floods, but it also acknowledges that the hut Nathan built for her with his own hands is sufficient for her needs. Initially, she felt diminished by the mud hut with its thatched roof, but she has grown in understanding since her first days as a bride.

Since fertility is such an important concern for Rukmani, the sweet stirring of pregnancy to which she refers completes her catalog of happiness. Procreation is the critical role for a woman in Rukmani's society, and a woman who fails to conceive early in her marriage may be renounced by her husband, as Ira is. After Ira's birth, Rukmani's failure to produce a son for Nathan nearly destroys her happiness. When she first meets Kenny, the signs of grief in her face reveal her desperation to conceive. Fertility and procreation celebrate the precious quality of life for Rukmani. Her "sweet stirring" is linked to her awakening sexuality and the bond of desire and love she and Nathan share. In one sentence, Rukmani captures the elements of her happiness. By wondering what more any woman could ask, Rukmani is mindful that true joy comes from essentials rather than from luxuries.

---

2. *Privately I thought, Well, and what if we gave in to our troubles at every step! We would be pitiable creatures indeed to be so weak, for is not a man's spirit given to him to rise above his misfortunes?*

After Kenny offers Selvam a position as his assistant, Rukmani counters Kenny's philosophy on want and endurance in Chapter 19. Once again Kenny exhorts Rukmani to cry out when she needs help rather than suffer in silence. Yet even her argument against his position is silent, expressed only in her thoughts. In this passage, she highlights the contrast between Western and Indian traditions. Kenny stands for action, particularly to alleviate physical suffering, and as a doctor, he dedicates his life to this goal. In the chapter just preceding the quote, Kenny admits to Rukmani that he has lost his wife and children because of his work in India, another concept quite foreign to Rukmani, for whom family is critical. As a westerner, Kenny fights the appalling poverty of India with his will and his skills. He works among the people until he droops with fatigue. Kenny lives what he preaches, taking direct action against suffering by treating the villagers' illnesses and crying out for help through his fund-raising.

Rukmani, on the other hand, puts more emphasis on the spirit than on the flesh. She considers it a weakness to give in to trouble. As her losses mount, her endurance increases. When Raja dies at the hands of the tannery guards, Rukmani does not cry out for compensation, for she believes there is no compensation equal to a human life. When the monsoon flood ruins their crops and damages their shelter, Rukmani turns to her resources and savings rather than expecting help from outside. With her strong spirit, she refuses the role of "pitiable creature" even though she is poor. In Hindu belief, suffering is a form of purification, and Rukmani is willing to bear her suffering and rise above misfortunes. However, there is one exception: when she realizes she is barren, she cries out to Kenny for help. By consulting Western medicine, Rukmani reaches across the philosophical divide.

---

3. *It is not enough to cry out, not sufficient to lay bare your woes and catalogue your needs; people have only to close their eyes and their ears, you cannot force them to see and to hear—or to answer your cries if they cannot and will not.*

Two events in Chapter 21 lead Rukmani to continue her reflection on crying out for help: the death of Old Granny and setbacks in the hospital construction. Rukmani is devastated when Old Granny dies on the path to the well, starved and alone. She feels culpable, partly because she stopped selling her vegetables to Old Granny to earn her livelihood and partly because she accepted a rupee from her at Sacrabani's birth. Bitterly, she observes that the villagers provide the last decencies for Old Granny once she is beyond asking for further assistance from them. Rukmani feels that the villagers, herself included, closed their eyes and ears to Old Granny's plight though she lived within sight and sound of them. She speculates that Old Granny might have been saved by the hospital had it been finished, but Nathan points out that a hospital is not a soup kitchen, and even the tireless Kenny understands that the hospital will not be able to serve all those who need help. Although Rukmani is amazed that strangers do often give to the needy in her village and in soup kitchens elsewhere, in this passage she laments the extent of the need and the ease with which it can be ignored. She realizes that help requires two-way communication, dependent in part on the needy asking for help, but equally dependent upon a receptive humanity to answer those needs.

4. *For where shall a man turn who has no money? Where can he go? Wide, wide world, but as narrow as the coins in your hand. Like a tethered goat, so far and no farther. Only money can make the rope stretch, only money.*

By Chapter 27, Rukmani has lost everything, even the hope of turning to her son Murugan, who has abandoned the city and his family. She and Nathan return to the temple and unhappily subsist on the single daily meal the temple provides. Rukmani and Nathan consider the skills with which they might earn a living and find none of them suited to the city. Nathan can farm but has no land. Rukmani can spin and weave but has no money for materials. Despite all of the people and the commerce surrounding them in the city, they have no opportunities. This passage is Rukmani's lament. Her vivid image of the tethered goat describes both her constraint and her powerlessness. It evokes the gentleness of the goats at the temple whose grateful eyes thanked Rukmani for a mouthful of leaves. In the country, Rukmani and Nathan manage to survive without much money by living simply on the products of their own labor. In the city, with no work available, Rukmani rues the fact that only money counts. The city's insistence upon cash reduces a person to an animal state and deprives Rukmani of the free will that characterizes her as human. Just as city thieves rob Nathan and Rukmani of their last coins, the city's unjust structure robs them of liberty and choice, their birthrights as humans.

5. *"Would you hold me when my time is come? I am at peace. Do not grieve."*
   "If I grieve," I said, "it is not for you, but for myself, beloved, for how shall I endure to live without you, who are my love and my life?"
   "You are not alone," he said. "I live in my children. . . ."

This dialogue between Nathan and Rukmani as he is dying in Chapter 29 completes the circle of their life together. Reminiscent of a groom with his bride, Nathan asks Rukmani to hold him. On several occasions in the novel, Rukmani remembers the physicality of their love, reaffirmed in this request. In the first chapter, Rukmani recalls the sweetness of nights she went to her husband, not as a pained and awkward child bride, but as a woman. In Chapter 10, the Festival of Deepavali provides the setting for a night of joy and passion between them. In her reflection on married love in Chapter 20, Rukmani draws upon her life with Nathan to describe both the fire and the tenderness they shared. Now that Nathan prepares to leave his body, he seeks Rukmani's encircling arms one last time. For Nathan and Rukmani, their physical love provides one of the sweetest aspects of their human existence and underscores the precious quality of life itself.

As Rukmani begins to grieve for her impending loss, Nathan reminds her of their important contribution to the continuation of life. She will not be alone, he says, because he lives on in his children. Throughout Rukmani's story, she has celebrated life and its abundant fertility. The years of her barrenness were harder for her to bear than the years of privation and loss. While she endured hardship with quiet dignity, she cried out for help to conceive her sons. When Nathan assures Rukmani that he lives on in their children, he promises his continued care. She need not be alone or unloved because of the lives they created together from their separate selves. Nathan also assures his wife that he is at peace. His physical journey is over, but his enduring spirit has achieved the liberation and transcendence that are the great goals of a Hindu life.

Nervous Conditions

Tsitsi Dangarembga (1959–)

CONTEXT

Tsitsi Dangarembga finished writing *Nervous Conditions* when she was in her mid-twenties and, upon its publication in 1988, won widespread critical acclaim for its complex and nuanced portrayal of the challenges that a young Shona girl faces in her efforts to break free of her impoverished background and acquire an education. "Shona" is the name given to various tribal groupings living mostly in the eastern half of Zimbabwe, north of the Lundi River. In addition to writing plays and screenplays, Dangarembga became the first Zimbabwean to direct a feature-length film, releasing *Everyone's Child* in 1996. Despite her varied aesthetic interests and successes, it is her novel that has opened her voice and her unique vision to the widest audience.

Dangarembga was born in 1959 in a small town in Zimbabwe that was known as the colony of Rhodesia. She lived in England from the ages of two to six while her parents attended school there. Her initial education was conducted in the British school system, and the young Dangarembga became fluent in English at the expense of Shona, her native tongue. When she returned to her native land, she continued her education after relearning Shona at a mission school. Later, she attended a private American convent school in the city of Mutare.

In 1977, Dangarembga returned to England to study medicine. No longer a child living in a foreign culture, she witnessed and fully understood the often racist or racially stereotypical attitudes held by many members of English society. Returning to Zimbabwe in 1980, just before the nation became self-governing and independent, she began to develop in earnest as a writer. Despite years of rejection and lack of acknowledgment, *Nervous Conditions* was eventually published in England, four years after Dangarembga had completed it.

The events that shaped Dangarembga's early years loosely inform the life of Tambu, the protagonist in *Nervous Conditions*. In one sense, the novel is Dangarembga's attempt to analyze and better understand her emergence into adulthood through the lens of fictional creation. However, Dangarembga's talents lie in her ability to take the autobiographical details of her own life and transform them into a multifaceted and highly realistic novel peopled with psychologically rich and varied characters. This realism is the hallmark of Dangarembga's fiction. While other African novelists directly confront the effects of colonialism and gender discrimination, Dangarembga allows her characters to enact and dramatize the pressures these forces inflict on their lives. In *Nervous Conditions*, white characters make only the briefest of appearances. Repressive figures are not distant or symbolic presences but the individuals found within the same family unit. Rather than offering an epic sweep or grand historical scale with which to frame her contemporary investigation, Dangarembga looks instead to the effects and harm that foreign interference and sexism have on a single African family.

In *Nervous Conditions*, Dangarembga focuses in particular on a small group of women who struggle to be heard and to succeed in a world that often aggressively seeks to silence and control them. Though in a way these women are successful in their struggle, their victories are not grand. They do not openly challenge the status quo, topple repressive systems, or alter prevailing behaviors and ways of thinking. Instead, their victories lie in the strength they muster to navigate a world that is unsympathetic to their concerns, and their success is rooted in their unflinching desire to succeed where others have readily failed.

PLOT OVERVIEW

Tambu, the narrator, is unmoved by the death of her brother, Nhamo. The afternoon he is expected home at the end of his term at the mission school, he does not arrive. He dislikes taking the bus and then walking the rest of the way through the countryside to the family's homestead. Tambu is relieved at his absence, as she does not have to kill and prepare a chicken to celebrate his return.

Tambu then reflects on the events leading up to her brother's death. Despite the family's poverty, Tambu's parents were able to raise the fees to send Nhamo to school. There was not enough money to send Tambu as well, so she decided to grow and sell vegetables and raise the money herself. When she discovered that her brother was stealing food from her garden patch, she attempted to beat him up while the two were attending Sunday school. Tambu's teacher, Mr. Matimba, took her to Umtali, a local urban center, to sell green ears of corn. A white woman, Doris, and her husband pitied Tambu and gave Mr. Matimba ten pounds sterling to pay for her education.

The extended family gathered to celebrate the return of Babamukuru, his wife, Maiguru, and their two children, Chido and Nyasha, back from studying abroad in England. Chido and Nyasha, Tambu's cousins, had lost the ability to speak their native tongue, Shona. Maiguru did not want them participating in the dancing and other festive activities. At the end of the meal, Tambu was ordered to bring a bowl of water to each member of the extended family so they could wash their hands. Babamukuru's three siblings praised his success. He proposed educating a member of each family, focusing especially on the neediest branch, Tambu's clan. They chose Nhamo to go to the mission school, but after his sudden death, Tambu is selected to replace him.

Tambu, returning her focus to the present, is excited and awed by her new life in her aunt and uncle's house on the mission school grounds. Maiguru warmly welcomes Tambu into her new home. She serves Tambu tea and pastries and gives her an entirely new wardrobe, all in preparation for her first day of school. The coldness and emotional distance that once existed between Nyasha and Tambu quickly disappear. Tambu becomes absorbed in her studies. She soon learns the rhythms of the household, witnessing Nyasha and Babamukuru's frequent fights. She also learns that Maiguru is highly educated.

To mark the end of the term, Nyasha, Tambu, and the children of white missionaries attend a dance. Tambu reluctantly joins the festivities. At the end of the evening, Nyasha resists coming inside, still trying to master a new dance one of the boys is teaching her. When the young people finally enter the house, a violent argument erupts between Babamukuru and Nyasha, in which Babamukuru accuses Nyasha of lewd behavior. Nyasha strikes her father, who vows to kill her for performing the taboo act of assaulting her own parent. Nyasha grows more detached in the following weeks, and Tambu tries to help assuage her guilt.

During the school vacation, Tambu and her relatives head back to the homestead. Maiguru laments the fact that, as senior wife, she is expected to cook and clean for the extended family the entire time. Babamukuru is upset to find Lucia, Tambu's mother's sister, and Takesure, a relative of Tambu's father, still living at the homestead. To make matters worse, Lucia is pregnant with Takesure's child. A family meeting is held to decide what course of action should be taken. Ultimately the couple is allowed to remain, as Babamukuru shifts his focus to another moral issue that rankles him: his own brother's unsanctified domestic status. Babamukuru declares that Jeremiah and Ma'Shingayi must be married in a formal Christian ceremony as soon as possible.

Tambu's mother comes to the mission hospital and gives birth to a son. Lucia soon follows and asks Babamukuru to find her a job, which he does. She cooks at the school and begins taking classes. Preparations are being made for the impending nuptials. When it comes time to leave, Tambu, who is vehemently opposed to her parents' wedding, feigns illness. When Babamukuru tells her to be ready in thirty minutes, she refuses to attend. When he returns from the wedding, he punishes her by lashing her and forcing her to perform the maid's duties for two weeks. Maiguru argues with Babamukuru over the lack of respect that she gets and the fact that her economic contribution to the family is not recognized. She leaves the next day and stays with her son, Chido.

While the girls are preparing for final exams, nuns arrive at the mission and administer a test. Tambu is offered a scholarship to study at the esteemed mission school. At first, Babamukuru is opposed to her accepting the offer, but he eventually relents. Home for the holiday, Tambu finds her mother ill. Lucia arrives and nurses her sister back to health. When Tambu returns to the mission and prepares to leave for the convent school, she cannot find Nyasha anywhere. When she finally finds Nyasha, Nyasha is cold toward her, upset that her best friend will soon be leaving and she will be left alone with her unsympathetic father.

Tambu leaves for the convent school, where she shares a crowded room with other African girls. Busy with her studies, she soon falls out of touch with Nyasha. Tambu returns to the mission to find Nyasha changed, frightfully thin and suffering from a severe eating disorder. One night, Nyasha has what appears to be a psychotic episode. Nyasha sees a psychiatrist and slowly regains her health. Tambu fears she is succumbing to the negative, colonial influence that made Nyasha mentally ill. Her other cousin, Chido, has a white girlfriend, much to Maiguru's chagrin. Tambu declares her intention to begin questioning her world and the influences that it exerts on her.

CHARACTER LIST

Babamukuru Tambu's uncle. Babamukuru is the highly educated and successful headmaster of the mission school. A patriarchal and authoritarian figure, he uses his power and position to improve the lives of his extended family, but he does it out of duty, not love. He is a remote, cold, and distant father and takes no pains to hide his disappointment in and growing contempt for his daughter, Nyasha.

Chido Nyasha's brother, son of Babamukuru and Maiguru. Chido is tall, athletic, and handsome, as well as charismatic, intelligent, and highly educated. He has little interest in his family or in visiting either the homestead or the mission. Educated mostly among white colonists, he grows accustomed to a life of luxury and eventually takes a white girlfriend.

Jeremiah Tambu's father and Babamukuru's brother. Jeremiah is naïve, ignorant, and superstitious. He seems barely concerned with the future and success of his children and grows increasingly detached from his family. In Babamukuru's presence he is servile and fawning, lauding his siblings' accomplishments. With his immediate family, however, he is disdainful of education and does little to encourage his children's ambitions.

Lucia Ma'Shingayi's sister. Lucia is a mysterious, strong-willed woman who is feared by many and said to be a witch. Shrewd and sexually promiscuous, Lucia is the object of gossip and rumor and is said to have had many affairs with rich men. She is outspoken and pays no heed to the social code that requires woman to be silent and obedient. She emerges as an independent and ambitious woman, eager to educate herself and improve her lot in life.

Maiguru Tambu's aunt and Babamukuru's wife. Maiguru is a strong, educated, and successful professional woman and thus stands out from the rest of the women in her family. Life in England has changed her, and she wants her children to act more Western. She later fears they have become too Anglicized. Gentle, conscientious, and caring, she accepts her passive role in her marriage and the sacrifices she must make to keep Babamukuru happy. Though she rebels and leaves him, she returns out of her sense of duty and her love for her family.

Ma'Shingayi Tambu's mother. Initially, Ma'Shingayi is portrayed as a hardworking figure who has toiled and sacrificed so that her son can have an education. After Nhamo's death, she grows spiteful, angry, and jealous of those around her. Her hard life also makes her apathetic and accepting of the limitations with which life has saddled her.

Netsai Tambu's younger sister. Netsai is obedient and subservient, a kindhearted and hardworking girl who helps Nhamo and the rest of the family, not solely out of duty, but because she truly loves them.

Nhamo Tambu's brother. Nhamo takes advantage of his status as the eldest son in the family. He is spiteful and mean and goes out of his way to taunt Tambu and lord over her the fact that he is receiving an education. After he leaves for the mission, he grows superior, lazy, and condescending, offering no assistance to his family in their daily toils.

Nyasha Tambu's cousin, daughter of Babamukuru and Maiguru. Nyasha is silently observant with an often unsettling intensity. Though she can be precocious and charming, she does little to make the other girls at school like her. At times she is easily provoked, volatile, and strong-willed, and she likes to argue with and openly resist Babamukuru. She is a product of two worlds and grows increasingly confused of her identity and the hybrid influences of life in England and Rhodesia.

Takesure A cousin of Babamukuru and Jeremiah. After Nhamo's death, Takesure is enlisted to help Jeremiah with the labors on the homestead. Like Jeremiah, he is lazy, foolish, and superstitious and abuses his power as a man. He has many wives, whom he cannot support. He impregnates Lucia and tries to make her his concubine.

Tambu The novel's narrator and protagonist. An intelligent, hardworking, and curious fourteen-year-old girl, Tambu is hungry for an education and eager to escape life on the homestead. While she is sensitive

N

and kind, she is also often harsh and unyielding in her judgments. Tambu is sympathetic to the powerful pull of tradition, but at the same time, she wishes to break free of the limitations placed on her sex.

ANALYSIS OF MAJOR CHARACTERS

BABAMUKURU The central male presence in the novel, Babamukuru is a cold and enigmatic figure who is difficult to penetrate. While the book's point of view is decidedly female, Babamukuru enacts the pressures and duties placed on men attempting to raise their families' status and to shake off the specter of poverty. Babamukuru's intelligence, ambition, and accomplishments are often taken for granted by others, as it is the others who reap the benefits of his hard work without attaining a full understanding of the sacrifices involved. His dual roles as parent and administrator are often at odds. He uses his job as headmaster to avoid any form of emotional intimacy with the women who share his home with him. His relationship with Nyasha is especially fraught, since her general conduct and academic performance at the mission school reflect his abilities not only as a father but also as a leader.

From his earliest days, Babamukuru is the pawn of those who have offered him assistance and opportunity. He feels he has no choice but to accept the charity that the administrators at the mission school extend to him. After completing his education in South Africa, he does not want to pursue a higher degree in England, and he realizes that the hope of a brighter future for his extended family rests solely on his shoulders. Babamukuru stoically accepts his duty, even if he risks being viewed as a haughty authoritarian or unsympathetic bully by dictating what direction his family will take. He may not wish to be the leader, stern taskmaster, and voice of moral guidance in his family, but if he does not accept that role, his relatives will not be able to alter their circumstances on their own. Partly because of Babamukuru's story and life experiences, Tambu realizes there are multiple interpretations to the choices that individuals make and the motives behind those choices.

MAIGURU Maiguru is a complex, often contradictory, and multilayered character who grows increasingly concerned about the development of her children and their responses to the various cultural traditions, both Western and African, with which they have been raised. Her fears and anxieties are rooted in her own experience of trying to reconcile attitudes and behaviors that come from two very different worlds. Her conflicting attitudes suggest the deep divide that exists in her perception of herself as a woman and as an African. When the family returns to Rhodesia, Maiguru wishes her children to retain the mark of distinction and difference that they have achieved from living in a Western society. She defends the fact that they have lost their ability to communicate fluently in Shona, their native tongue. After the family has settled back into life in Rhodesia, Maiguru's reactions and attitudes change, and she grows concerned at how Anglicized her children have become. Only when her daughter is severely ailing in the final stages of the novel does she realize the dire consequences of these conflicting cultural pressures that have been placed on her children.

N

When the family returns to the homestead for the holidays, Maiguru, highly educated and accustomed to earning her own living as an educator, is reduced to a traditional role as domestic drudge. During subsequent holidays, Maiguru refuses to attend the celebrations. Even more boldly, Maiguru confronts her husband about her lack of respect and recognition in the family, an action that leads to the even bolder move of her leaving the house altogether. Although she returns to the family fold, Maiguru has evolved into a realistic model of modern womanhood for the young girls in her care. She represents a subtle but emerging voice of feminist dissent, a woman ahead of her time who attempts to enact change in gradual and realizable ways.

NYASHA Highly intelligent, perceptive, and inquisitive, Nyasha is old beyond her years. Like the other female characters in *Nervous Conditions*, she is complex and multifaceted, and her dual nature reflects her status as the product of two worlds, Africa and England. On one hand she is emotional, passionate, and provocative, while on the other she is rational and profound in her thinking. Nyasha is admired by Tambu for her ability to see conflict and disagreement not as threats but as opportunities to increase her understanding of herself and the world. She uses the various experiences life presents her with as a chance to grow, learn, and improve. Initially, she thrives in her state of unresolved and often warring emotions and feelings, and she sees any inconsistencies in her feelings or her world as opportunities for greater self-development.

Nyasha's precocious nature and volatile, ungrounded identity eventually take their toll, and isolation and loneliness are her reward for being unconventional and fiercely independent. She is unpopular at the mission school, but this unpopularity is due more to her willfulness than the fact she is the headmaster's daughter. Her inner resources and resolve are highly developed, but they can sustain her only so far. Over the course of the novel, the elements that define her and the aspects of her personality she most cherishes become the source of her unrest and ultimate breakdown. Nyasha begins to resent her outspoken nature and the constant spirit of resistance she displays, particularly to her father. The transformation leads to self-hatred, a dangerously negative body image that results in an eating disorder, and mental illness. Nyasha becomes a symbolic victim of the pressures to embrace modernity, change, enlightenment, and self-improvement.

TAMBU Throughout *Nervous Conditions*, the adult Tambu looks back on her adolescence and her struggle to emerge into adulthood and formulate the foundation on which her adult life would be built. There are essentially two Tambus in the novel, and the narrator Tambu successfully generates tension between them. Tambu is a crafty and feisty narrator. She explores her own conflicted perceptions not only as a teenager but as an adult reexamining those years, a dual perspective that gives the novel richness and complexity. Tambu introduces herself to the reader harshly, proclaiming the fact that she is not upset that her brother has died. As the presiding voice in the novel, she can manipulate how she is represented and perceived, but under the tough exterior is a hardworking girl who is eager to please and eager to advance herself. Her self-portrayal, with its unflattering as well as praiseworthy elements, represents the adult Tambu's effort to convey the challenges faced by impoverished yet talented women in central Africa in the 1970s. A figure of those tumultuous and ever-changing times, Tambu emerges not as a flat and one-dimensional symbol but ultimately as a fallible and triumphant human presence.

THEMES, MOTIFS, AND SYMBOLS

THEMES

THE PERVASIVENESS OF GENDER INEQUALITY Tambu was born a girl and thus faces a fundamental disadvantage, since traditional African social practice dictates that the oldest male child is deemed the future head of the family. All of the family's resources are poured into developing his abilities and preparing him to lead and provide for his clan. When Nhamo dies, the tragedy is all the more profound since no boy exists to take his place. Tambu steps into the role of future provider, yet she is saddled with the prejudices and limitations that shackled most African girls of her generation. Her fight for an education and a better life is compounded by her gender. Gender inequality and sexual discrimination form the backdrop of all of the female characters' lives. In the novel, inequality is as infectious as disease, a crippling attitude that kills ambition, crushes women's spirits, and discourages them from supporting and rallying future generations and other female relatives.

N

THE INFLUENCE OF COLONIALISM The essential action of the novel involves Tambu's experiences in a Western-style educational setting, and the mission school both provides and represents privileged opportunity and enlightenment. Despite Ma'Shingayi's strong objections, Tambu knows the only hope she has of lifting her family out of poverty lies in education. However, the mission school poses threats, as well: Western institutions and systems of thought may cruelly and irreversibly alter native Africans who are subjected to them. Nyasha, who has seen firsthand the effect of being immersed in a foreign culture, grows suspicious of an unquestioning acceptance of colonialism's benefits. She fears that the dominating culture may eventually stifle, limit, or eliminate the long-established native culture of Rhodesia—in other words, she fears that colonialism may force assimilation. The characters' lives are already entrenched in a national identity that reflects a synthesis of African and colonialist elements. The characters' struggle to confront and integrate the various social and political influences that shape their lives forms the backbone and central conflict of *Nervous Conditions*.

TRADITION VS. PROGRESS Underpinning *Nervous Conditions* are conflicts between those characters who endorse traditional ways and those who look to Western or so-called "modern" answers to problems they face. Dangarembga remains noncommittal in her portrayal of the divergent belief systems of Babamukuru and his brother Jeremiah, and she shows both men behaving rather irrationally. Jeremiah foolishly endorses a shaman's ritual cleansing of the homestead, while Babamukuru's belief in a Christian ceremony seems to be rooted in his rigid and unyielding confidence that he is always right. As Tambu becomes more fixed and established in her life at the mission school, she begins to embrace attitudes and beliefs different from those of her parents and her traditional upbringing. Nyasha, ever the voice of reasonable dissent, warns Tambu that a wholesale acceptance of supposedly progressive ideas represents a dangerous departure and too radical of a break with the past.

MOTIFS

GEOGRAPHY Physical spaces are at the heart of the tensions Tambu faces between life at the mission and the world of the homestead. At first, Tambu is isolated, relegated to toiling in the fields and tending to her brother's whims during his infrequent visits. When she attends the local school, she must walk a long way to her daily lessons, but she undertakes the journey willingly in order to receive an education. When the family cannot pay her school fees, Mr. Matimba takes Tambu to the first city she has ever seen, where she sells green corn. Tambu's increased awareness and knowledge of the world coincides with her growing physical distance from the homestead. The mission school is an important location in the novel, a bastion of possibility that becomes the centerpiece of Tambu's world and the source of many of the changes she undergoes. At the end of *Nervous Conditions*, Tambu's life has taken her even farther away from the homestead, to the convent school where she is without family or friends and must rely solely on herself.

EMANCIPATION Emancipation is a term that appears again and again in *Nervous Conditions*. Usually, the term is associated with being released from slavery or with a country finally freeing itself from the colonial power that once controlled it. These concepts figure into the broader scope of the novel, as Rhodesia's citizens struggle to amass and assert their identity as a people while still under British control. When the term *emancipation* is applied to Tambu and the women in her extended family, it takes on newer and richer associations. Tambu sees her life as a gradual process of being freed of the limitations that have previously beset her. When she first leaves for the mission school, she sees the move as a temporary emancipation. Her growing knowledge and evolving perceptions are a form of emancipation from her old ways of thinking. By the end of the novel, emancipation becomes more than simply a release from poverty or restriction. Emancipation is equated with freedom and an assertion of personal liberty.

DUAL PERSPECTIVES Dual perspectives and multiple interpretations appear throughout *Nervous Conditions*. When Babamukuru finds Lucia a job cooking at the mission, Tambu is in awe of her uncle's power and generosity, viewing it as a selfless act of kindness. Nyasha, however, believes there is nothing heroic in her father's gesture and that in assisting his sister-in-law he is merely fulfilling his duty as the head of the family. In addition to often wildly differing interpretations of behavior, characters share an unstable and conflicting sense of self. For Tambu, her two worlds, the homestead and the mission, are often opposed, forcing her to divide her loyalties and complicating her sense of who she is. When she wishes to avoid attending her parents' wedding, however, these dual selves offer her safety, protection, and an escape from the rigors of reality. As her uncle chides her, Tambu imagines another version of herself watching the scene safely from the foot of the bed.

SYMBOLS

TAMBU'S GARDEN PLOT Tambu's garden plot represents both tradition and escape from that tradition. On one hand, it is a direct link to her heritage, and the rich tradition has guided her people, representing the essential ability to live off the land. It is a direct connection to the legacy she inherits and the wisdom and skills that are passed down from generation to generation, and Tambu fondly remembers helping her grandmother work the garden. At the same time, the garden represents Tambu's means of escape, since she hopes to pay her school fees and further her education by growing and selling vegetables. In this sense, the garden represents the hopes of the future and a break with the past. With a new form of wisdom acquired at the mission school and the power and skills that come with it, Tambu will never have to toil and labor again. Her mother, however, must water the valuable and fertile garden patch despite being exhausted from a long day of work.

THE MISSION For Tambu, the mission stands as a bright and shining beacon, the repository of all of her hopes and ambitions. It represents a portal to a new world and a turning away from the enslaving poverty that has marked Tambu's past. The mission is an escape and an oasis, a whitewashed world where refinement and sophistication are the rule. It is also an exciting retreat for Tambu, where she is exposed to new ideas and new modes of thinking. The mission sets Tambu on the path to becoming the strong, articulate adult she is destined to become.

THE OX In the family's lengthy holiday celebration, the ox represents the opulence and status Babamukuru and his family have achieved. Meat, a rare commodity, is an infrequent treat for most families, and Tambu's parents and the rest of the extended clan willingly partake of the ox. At the same time, they secretly resent such an ostentatious display of wealth, since the ox is a symbol of the great gulf that exists between the educated branch of the family and those who have been left behind to struggle. Maiguru closely regulates the consumption of the ox and parcels out the meat over the several days of the family's gathering. Eventually the meat starts to go bad, and the other women chide Maiguru for her poor judgment and overly strict control of its distribution. At that point, the ox suggests Maiguru's shortcomings and how, in the eyes of the others, her education and comfortable life have made her an ineffective provider.

IMPORTANT QUOTATIONS EXPLAINED

---

1. *I was not sorry when my brother died.*

The novel begins with this shocking confession from Tambu. Tambu has had a murky, often ambivalent relationship with her brother, Nhamo. He represents everything she is denied and the principal failing of the social structure and family hierarchy into which she has been born. Simply because he is a male and the eldest, he is the sole repository of the family's hopes and ambitions. Tambu, regardless of her intelligence, talents, and abilities, must be satisfied with a secondary role, an understudy whose sole job it is to support and assist Nhamo as he makes his way in the world. With his sudden and unexpected death, Tambu's life takes a dramatic turn for the better. She is offered his place at the mission school, and because of his death, she is able to write the story she is beginning in the novel's opening paragraphs.

N

---

2. *And these days it is worse, with the poverty of blackness on one side and the weight of womanhood on the other. Aiwa! What will help you, my child, is to learn to carry your burdens with strength.*

These words are spoken by Ma'Shingayi, Tambu's mother, in Chapter 2. They underscore the harsh reality faced by many Africans, particularly African women. Ma'Shingayi is arguing that being black and female is a double burden and that the two obstacles are too considerable to surmount. What sets her apart from Tambu, however, is how she qualifies this statement. Rather than exhort her daughter to be strong and rally against the prevailing conditions that conspire to keep her down, Tambu's mother encourages her to passively accept the forces she feels are too powerful for her to control. This passage shows the differences not only between the two women but between the older, more traditional beliefs and the new attitudes emerging in a more contemporary Africa.

The passage also reveals the conflicting thoughts and attitudes of many of the novel's female characters. While Ma'Shingayi presents herself as the model of humble acquiescence, she rails against the laziness of men and grows increasingly jealous of her brother- and sister-in-law, whose educations have afforded them greater economic mobility and a more comfortable lifestyle. Ma'Shingayi is a prime example of how reality and ideology, or theory and practice, grow increasingly conflicted in the novel.

---

3. *"What it is," she sighed, "to have to choose between self and security."*

Maiguru speaks these words in Chapter 5, after Tambu has questioned her about her past, her education, and what happens to the money she earns at the mission. Maiguru's words succinctly summarize the sacrifices she has made in order to raise a family and subscribe to a more traditional notion of a woman's role in African society. Maiguru goes on to tell Tambu of the possibilities she witnessed while living in

England, glimpses of the things she could have become had she been free of restrictive gender roles and the expectation that she would play the part of the subservient provider. She feels there is no recognition or appreciation of the compromises she has made and, similar to Tambu's mother, stoically bears her burdens in silence.

Maiguru's sacrifices, of putting her husband and her family before her own needs and ambitions, are viewed by Nyasha as a costly compromise to her mother's dignity and honor. Tambu remains undecided and does not take sides in this debate, as she understands her own compromised and precarious position in her uncle's household. Later in the year, when Nyasha and her father have a violent argument, Tambu realizes firsthand her need to choose security over self and remains noncommittal. She stifles and censors any opinion she may have on the issue, hiding comfortably instead in the role of a "grateful, poor, female relative."

---

4. *It's bad enough . . . when a country gets colonized, but when the people do as well! That's the end, really, that's the end.*

Nyasha makes this pronouncement in Chapter 7 as part of her ongoing role in which she challenges and shapes Tambu's perceptions and modes of thought. Slowly, Tambu has become seduced by her exposure to the colonialist-influenced "new ways." Despite the fact that Tambu is opposed to the humiliation her parents will suffer by having to endure a Christian wedding ceremony, she agrees with Babamukuru's insistence that the ritual, and not the traditional cleansing rites, be performed. Nyasha quickly dismisses Babamukuru's position, warning Tambu of the dangers inherent in assuming that Christian ways are necessarily progressive ways.

Nyasha's words gesture to another preoccupation in Dangarembga's work. Rhodesia has been placed under British control, and the life of the nation has been clearly altered by this foreign influence. Without the opportunities colonialism has created for them, Babamukuru and his family, as well as Tambu, would not be in their positions of privilege and power. At the same time, the novel is narrated through the lens of African lives and the inner workings and struggles of one extended family. The African and the colonial cannot coexist without eventually influencing, even colliding, with each other. Slowly, the effects of colonialism has trickled down, infecting Tambu and Nyasha's family. Nyasha's observations foreshadow the nervous breakdown she will soon suffer as she feels colonialism infiltrating not only her nation and people but her own identity as well.

---

5. *Quietly, unobtrusively and extremely fitfully, something in my mind began to assert itself, to question things and refuse to be brainwashed, bringing me to this time when I can set down this story. It was a long and painful process for me, that process of expansion.*

Tambu closes her account, in Chapter 10, with these words. She has actively sought advancement, winning a scholarship to the convent school, but she begins to question what it has cost her sense of self and her ailing mother, heartsick at the thought of another of her children being altered by their desire for a Western education. Her school and the nuns who run it are no longer the sun on her horizon, as she puts it. Her use of the word *brainwashed* is telling, denoting a radical shift in her thinking. In this passage, Tambu seems to be speaking for Nyasha, who is also depressed and ailing, saying the words that Nyasha, in her compromised state, can no longer say for herself. Tambu exhorts herself to no longer be passively influenced by the people and institutions around her. She is firm in her resolve to question.

This evolution of perception and thought, which could be considered an epiphany, allows Tambu to write her own story. She is freed of the need to be dutiful and grateful and can become her own person and seize control of her own voice and destiny. Her education has been more than learning the rudiments of reading, writing, and mathematics—it has helped her refine her perceptions and recognize and embrace her personal liberty. This expansion and certitude have finally grounded her and helped her resolve the often contradictory forces that had buffeted and unsettled Tambu throughout her life.

Nisa: The Life and Words of a !Kung Woman

Marjorie Shostak (1947–1996)

CONTEXT

Marjorie Shostak was born in Brooklyn, New York, and majored in English literature as an undergraduate. She met her future husband, Melvin Konner, at Brooklyn College and followed him in 1969 to the Dobe region of Africa, where he was conducting doctoral research. Shostak did not train to become an anthropologist, but her move to Dobe was the first step in her creation of a text that is widely regarded as a classic in that field. Harnessing her considerable talents as a photographer and musician, Shostak began documenting the artistic output of the women of the !Kung tribe. (The *!* in *!Kung* signifies a tongue click in the !Kung language.) She painstakingly learned and practiced the !Kung language until she could speak it proficiently, and then set about conducting interviews with women of varying ages and experiences.

Nisa, a real woman to whom Shostak has given a pseudonym, was one of those women. She stood out in Shostak's eyes for her highly articulate stories, her emphatic methods of storytelling, and her profound and often tragic life experiences. Shostak conducted fifteen interviews with Nisa during that first trip to Dobe, then followed up during a second trip in 1975–1976, which enabled her to observe the increasingly sedentary and settled lifestyle of the once entirely independent !Kung people. These transcribed interviews, along with Shostak's own analyses and observations, constitute the bulk of *Nisa: The Life and Words of a !Kung Woman* (1981). Several years after publishing this book, Shostak was diagnosed with breast cancer. She returned to Africa in 1989 for follow-up interviews and had nearly completed *Return to Nisa* when she died in 1996. Her husband and two friends finished the manuscript, which was published in 2002.

N

Nisa is unusual among canonical anthropological texts in that its primary focus is a single person. Shostak sets Nisa against a vivid background of village life, domestic responsibilities, and family obligations, and she takes pains to show that Nisa, though in possession of superlative storytelling abilities and very much her own person, is representative of !Kung women in general. She has such a vivid personality, such profoundly tragic life experiences, and such a strong command of her own stories that the text takes on all the qualities of a classic work of fiction with a riveting and charismatic heroine or of a frank autobiography. Indeed, as Nisa's portions of the text are transcribed interviews, they are unaltered by Shostak save for her translation. Nisa is a natural storyteller, and her narrative unravels seamlessly, with little to no prompting or direction from Shostak (at least not that the readers can see).

Shostak knows, however, that a memoir alone cannot paint the big picture, and she grounds her readers by providing a section of scientific context and statistics before each of Nisa's fifteen interviews. The book is thus an alternating pattern of objective third-person analysis and Nisa's first-person narration. The entire structure of the text mimics the structure of Shostak's own interactions with Nisa, both in terms of the interview process, in which there is a continual give-and-take, and in terms of the space between each of the fifteen individual interviews. It also suggests Shostak's own experience of comparing Nisa's personal stories to her own objective observations about !Kung life.

Given her training in English literature, Shostak is perhaps an unlikely or even an amateur anthropologist, but she is nevertheless an effective one. She is finely attuned to the nuances of her new tongue and examines its cadences just as closely as she analyzes its content. She admits to being very much taken in by the expressiveness and beauty of the !Kung language, which is often repetitive in its phrasings and metaphorical in content. Nisa often speaks of extreme irritation or rage as "drinking anger," and distress is signaled by the words "her heart flew out." Shostak cites another favorite expression of hers, one that Nisa used to indicate when a story had come to an end: "The wind has taken that away." Shostak clearly enjoys these turns of phases, just as she enjoys the brazen sexual imagery that is used in women's banter as well as in jocular insults. This fascination with the patterns of language and the significance of particular emphasis or motifs gives Shostak's text a rich, rounded, aesthetic quality that might have been absent were it written by a more scientifically minded anthropologist.

Shostak's book is remarkable for many reasons, but it is not the sole text on !Kung life, nor were Shostak and her husband the first anthropologists to make contact with the !Kung people—Irven DeVore and Richard Lee, two anthropologists from Harvard University, had that honor in 1963. Previous visitors to the region had already laid some groundwork for Shostak in terms of the !Kung's dietary habits, mortality rates, child-rearing practices, life cycles, and so on. Shostak writes in *Nisa* that she read through a great many findings of prior expeditions before arriving in Dobe and that none of them satisfied her curiosity about the inner lives, emotions, hopes, and fears of the !Kung. She also confesses to being motivated in her desire to study !Kung women by her own feminist inclinations, specifically by the burgeoning women's movement in the West. *Nisa*, therefore, belongs not only to the canon of anthropological texts but also to the realm of feminist literature. It has been embraced by many feminists for its representation of a society in which women's labor is more important to the economy than men's, in which women freely discuss sex, and in which extramarital affairs are regularly conducted by both sexes. Though the !Kung men do dominate in many ways, Shostak positions Nisa and her fellow !Kung women as exceptions to Margaret Mead's famous pronouncement of the universality of male dominance.

PLOT OVERVIEW

Nisa opens with an introduction by Shostak, detailing her own preparations and expectations for her first trip to the Dobe region of Africa, in northwest Botswana and at the edge of the Kalahari Desert. Shostak describes Nisa's people, the Zhun/twasi ("real people"), bushmen who are hunter-gatherers and members of a racial group known as Khoisan. The Khoisan are considered by biologists to be distinct from black Africans, with fair skin, high cheekbones, and an average height of only about five feet.

Shostak narrates from a position in the present, reflecting back on her experiences in Africa. (Nisa, too, tells her stories in the past tense.) In the introduction, Shostak says that her motivation for coming to Africa was primarily to learn about the internal lives of the !Kung people, whose more easily discernable qualities (such as diet, life cycle, and demographics) had already been studied by other anthropologists for years. She and her husband join in the ongoing research, Shostak feeling particularly inclined to study the women of the !Kung tribe. She learns the language and interviews a number of women, but it is Nisa who captures her attention most. Nisa answers Shostak's questions with colorful language and vivid stories. After a few interviews, Nisa tells Shostak that her mother wanted to kill Nisa's younger brother right after he was born so that Nisa could continue to nurse. Shostak is taken aback and starts to doubt Nisa's truthfulness, but she eventually comes to trust her.

The rest of the book is divided into fifteen chapters, one for each of the interviews Shostak has with Nisa during her first Dobe visit, plus an epilogue. Each chapter opens with an overview by Shostak on the topic, theme, stage of life, or experience Nisa is about to narrate. In these introductions, Shostak draws from interviews with other !Kung men and women, work done by other anthropologists, her own observations and analyses, and historical and geographical contexts.

In Chapter 1, Nisa describes her early memories of accompanying her pregnant mother as she gives birth to Nisa's baby brother, Kumsa, and threatens to kill him, though she does not actually commit infanticide. In Chapter 2, Nisa recalls growing up with her brother, playing with him, experiencing sibling hatred, and protecting him from harm. She remembers her mother's pregnancy with her fourth child, Kxamshe, who dies young. In Chapter 3, Nisa describes the life of a hunter-gatherer, hunting prey, celebrating the arrival of meat in the village, gathering roots and bulbs, experiencing thirst in times of drought, and gorging on caterpillars in times of rain.

In Chapter 4, Nisa remembers what it was like to engage in sex play with other children in the village for the first time, and she recalls some of the boys' sexual aggression toward her and other girls. She notes that parents and children sleep in the same hut, so that the children become aware of what their parents are doing when they move under the blankets. In Chapter 5, Nisa tells Shostak about her first two marriages, one to a man named Bo, the other to a man named Tsaa. Both marriages end quickly, as is typical of early "trial" marriages in !Kung society. Nisa also describes her feelings of love for a man named Kantla, who is already married and who invites her to be a co-wife, an offer that Nisa refuses.

In Chapter 6, Nisa enters her first long marriage, to a man named Tashay. She and Tashay grow to love each other. Early in their marriage, Nisa experiences her first menstruation, and the women of the village enclose her in a hut and perform the ritual ceremonies that accompany that momentous event in a !Kung woman's life. Chapter 7 concerns the infrequent though not uncommon practice of adopting a co-wife. Nisa tells of her own brief experience with a co-wife Tashay brings to the hut. Before long, Nisa drives the co-wife away and the marriage resumes as normal.

Nisa takes on several lovers, as is common in !Kung society, and when she becomes pregnant, as recounted in Chapter 8, her husband gets very jealous. He accuses her of infidelity and questions the baby's paternity. Nisa gives birth to a baby girl, Chuko, who dies in infancy. In Chapter 9, Nisa describes her four subsequent pregnancies. She has a baby girl, Nai, then miscarries, then has another girl who dies young, and then has a son, Kxau.

Chapter 10 begins with Shostak's observations of the !Kung's changing environment and way of life, which have been increasingly influenced by neighboring cattle-herding groups, the Tswana and the Herero. Nisa then discusses her marriage to a Tswana man named Besa, as well as the complications of her several love affairs with other men. In Chapter 11, Nisa travels from the Tswana village back to her parents' village after learning her father has died. Soon after, her mother dies, and Nisa herself falls ill but is cured by her elder brother, Dau, who is a healer. Nisa begins working in the house of a European woman who lives near their village. She also becomes pregnant with Besa's child but miscarries. In Chapter 12, Nisa continues to tell Shostak about her many lovers and also recalls being a child and seeing her mother with her lover and telling her father about her mother's affair. She also explains to Shostak that the !Kung women talk freely with each other about sex, and she asks Shostak if that isn't the same with all women.

Chapter 13 deals with the !Kung belief in the spirit world and, in particular, with the role spirits are thought to play in illness and healing. Nisa describes her father's and older brother's healing abilities. She also tells Shostak about how her mother taught her to go into a trance and about her own once-potent capabilities as a healer. In Chapter 14, Nisa painfully recounts the deaths of her two last surviving children. Nai dies after being shoved by her husband, and Kxau succumbs to serious illness after eating honey that the spirits have designated for the honey badger. In Chapter 15, Nisa expresses hurt over the fact that her husband no longer wants to sleep with her very often, and she says she feels she has grown ugly. She mentions that she has been through menopause and asks Shostak for medicine to bring back her menses.

The epilogue briefly describes Shostak's return to Dobe in 1975, when she, her husband, and a graduate student conduct a research study on women's menstrual cycles. She also meets with Nisa and interviews her again. She finds Nisa to be calm and in good spirits, and Nisa agrees when Shostak asks if it would be all right to publish the interviews as a book.

N

CHARACTER LIST

Marjorie Shostak Nisa's interviewer. Shostak accompanies her anthropologist husband to Africa, where he is conducting his own studies, and sets out to understand !Kung life, particularly the lives of !Kung women, more deeply than previous researchers. She takes the tribal name Hwantla, although in the transcripts Nisa refers to her most often as "Marjorie" or "my niece."

Nisa The pseudonym Shostak gives to the !Kung woman whose interviews constitute the bulk of the book. Nisa is about fifty years old at the time of the interviews. She is a member of the !Kung San, or !Kung, a group of bushmen who live in Botswana, Namibia, and Angola. The !Kung are hunter-gatherers, although at the time of Nisa's interviews they are beginning to feel the influence of nearby cattle-herding groups and European settlements. Nisa has lived through many marriages, the deaths of all her children, and numerous other heartaches and happy memories, all of which she relates to Shostak.

Bau A !Kung woman Shostak interviews prior to Nisa. Bau tells Shostak particularly intimate details from her life, including incidents of childhood sex play, an extramarital affair, and domestic abuse.

Kxoma and Tuma Two !Kung men who accompany Shostak and her husband to their campsite after their arrival in Africa.

Gau Nisa's father. Gau sometimes exhibits a fiery temper, threatening to hit Nisa or his wife or actually hitting one or both of them. But he is also very protective of Nisa and his other children. Gau is a medical healer and is able to enter trance states and heal sick members of the village. In her storytelling, Nisa recalls her excitement at seeing Gau coming back into the village with meat for her to eat. Gau dies while Nisa is living near a Tswana village with her husband Besa, and she returns home to her parents' village to mourn.

Chuko Nisa's mother. As !Kung children are brought up in almost constant contact with their mothers in their early years, Chuko is an important presence in Nisa's life. Nisa vividly remembers Chuko's attempts to wean her, despite Nisa's distress at having to give up nursing at her mother's breast. Nisa accompanies her mother when Chuko gives birth to Nisa's younger brother, Kumsa, and is horrified when Chuko says she plans to bury Kumsa so that Nisa can drink the milk in her breasts. Many years later, after Chuko dies, Nisa goes into an intense period of mourning.

Dau Nisa's older brother. Dau is protective of Nisa and intervenes when their parents treat her too harshly. He also brings her mongongo nuts to eat because he knows they are her favorite. Later, after Dau's wife dies, Nisa takes care of their daughter as her own. Nisa says she loves Dau and looks up to him enormously, and she demonstrates this adoration again and again in her stories.

Kumsa Nisa's younger brother. Nisa is present at Kumsa's birth, and she is horrified when her mother tells her to get a digging stick so that she can bury the infant. Nisa is jealous of Kumsa and steals some of his milk from her mother's breasts, only to be scolded by her mother.

Kxamshe Nisa's sister who dies in childhood after a "trembling sickness."

Tikay Nisa's young boyfriend with whom she begins to learn about sex, as all young !Kung children do.

Tuma Nisa's cousin who wants to engage in sex play with her, though Nisa refuses.

Kantla Nisa's first real love and one of the "important men" in her life. Kantla is married to a woman named Bey, and they both want Nisa to be a co-wife. They have a trial marriage, but it fails. Later, Kantla continues to make overtures of marriage but Nisa continues to refuse him. Kantla remains in Nisa's life as her lover.

Dem Kantla's younger brother. Dem is Nisa's lover for a time, and he and Kantla get into a fight over her.

N

Bo Nisa's first husband. Bo sleeps with Nukha while they are in the marriage hut. Nisa hears them and tells her parents, who scold Nukha sternly and dissolve the marriage.

Tsaa Nisa's second husband. Nisa likes Tsaa a great deal more than Bo, but she is still young and refuses to have sex with him. Tsaa refuses to give Nisa and her father meat, and Nisa's father sends him away.

Tashay Nisa's third husband. Her marriage to Tashay is Nisa's first substantial marriage, and Tashay becomes the father of her children. Tashay is jealous of Nisa's lovers, and after Tashay dies, his relatives say that the spirit of Nisa's lovers killed him. "Tashay" is also the tribal name given to Shostak's husband.

Saglai Gau's co-wife, briefly. Gau brings Saglai home to be his co-wife, unbeknownst to his wife. However, Chuko flies into a rage and drives Saglai out of the village.

Tiknay Nisa's co-wife, briefly, during her marriage to Tashay.

Little Chuko Nisa's first daughter. Nisa conceives her first child out of wedlock, and she tries to conceal this fact from her husband at the time, Tashay. However, the child grows to look just like her lover, Twi. The !Kung believe in the power of spiritual forces to cause sickness and death, and when Little Chuko dies in infancy, Nisa blames the fact that Chuko was her lover's child and not her husband's.

Nai Nisa's second daughter and her only daughter to survive infancy. Nai dies when she is sixteen or seventeen, by Shostak's estimate, after a physical brawl with her husband that results in a broken neck. She lives for a few days after her injury, and Nisa goes to her side, but there is nothing the healers can do to help her. After Nai dies, Nisa attacks Nai's husband and the husband's older sister in retaliation.

Bau Nisa's fourth child, a daughter, who does not survive infancy.

Kxau Nisa's son and last born. Kxau dies as a teenager from a disease that strikes him as a result of eating some honey from a hive that has been partially consumed by a honey badger. When Dau performs a trance, he sees that God has made Kxau sick because he intended the honey for the badger.

Besa Nisa's fourth husband. Nisa comments several times on Besa's sexual demands, and she calls him "very bad." He leaves Nisa while she is pregnant with their child, and the marriage eventually dissolves.

Kashe One of Nisa's lovers. Besa chases him with a knife, and eventually Nisa's father drives Kashe away.

Bo Nisa's fifth husband. Nisa is married to Bo during the initial fifteen interviews, and she is still married to him four years later, when Shostak returns to Africa. Nisa admits that they have big fights and small fights but says that they love each other.

Debe Another of Nisa's lovers. When Bo finds out that Nisa and Debe have stolen away into the bush for a tryst, he kicks Nisa in the chest, almost killing her.

ANALYSIS OF MAJOR CHARACTERS

MARJORIE SHOSTAK Marjorie Shostak is the author and narrator of *Nisa* as well as Nisa's interviewer, but with an academic background in English literature, she is not your average anthropologist. She travels to Africa with her husband, who is conducting his own work in the Dobe region, and begins studying the !Kung as a means of occupying her time while she is there. Most of this backstory does not appear in *Nisa*, however, and Shostak does her best to prove her capability as an anthropologist. She thoroughly describes her research methods, from providing full disclosure about the kinds of payment she offers to her subjects to corroborating Nisa's stories independently to assess their truthfulness. Upon her arrival in Africa, she throws herself fully into the !Kung group. She learns the language, joins the hunts and gathering expeditions, listens to discussions around the fire, watches medicinal ceremonies, and observes food division, preparation, and consumption.

Despite her efforts to immerse herself in the group, she continues to feel dissatisfied with the depth of her knowledge of the !Kung, so she begins talking individually to the !Kung women. Shostak's willingness to show herself to the !Kung as a woman who is herself struggling with issues of sexuality, marriage, work, age, and love helps convince the women to be interviewed. Though Shostak does not become a confidante or a best friend to any of the women, even Nisa, she does break down many of the barriers between their two cultures, attaining a very vivid picture of women's roles in !Kung society.

NISA Nisa is a member of the !Kung San, or !Kung, a group of hunter-gatherers who live in the isolated bush areas of Botswana, Namibia, and Angola. Nisa's own tribe lives in the Dobe region in Botswana, at the edge of the Kalahari Desert. Though they live mainly off the land, the !Kung of Nisa's generation are beginning to feel the influence of nearby cattle-herding groups and European settlements. Nisa says that when she was young, she did not know about any way of life other than her own, but by the time Shostak meets her, her knowledge of the world has increased dramatically. Shostak is not the only anthropologist to travel to the !Kung of the Dobe region, and Nisa is savvy enough to understand what she stands to gain from these outsiders. She often mentions two previous researchers, Richard and Nancy, who were very generous to her, in an effort to goad Shostak into generous giving as well. In return, Nisa provides Shostak with hours of fascinating narration.

Nisa is about fifty years old at the time of her first fifteen interviews, and she uses her age as proof of her wisdom. She cultivates an authoritative and somewhat indulgent relationship with Shostak, calling her "my niece" and teasingly saying she will educate her about sexual relationships. Though Nisa is real, she exhibits some of the characteristics of a classic literary heroine. She experiences more than her fair share of tragedy, and at times her network of lovers and extramarital affairs can read like a soap opera. Above all, her narration is rich, engaging, and extremely colorful, captivating her listeners by using imagery and original turns of phrases.

CHUKO Since Shostak focuses her book mainly on the lives of the !Kung women, Nisa's mother, Chuko, plays an especially important role. Chuko's behavior sets an example for Nisa in many ways, from the expected (pregnancy, childbirth, child rearing) to the unexpected (the taking of lovers). Many of Nisa's early memories concern maternal events, such as when she witnesses her mother giving birth alone or when she sees her mother with a lover who is not her husband. Indeed, Chuko is inevitably an integral part of Nisa's own life story, particularly in its early stages, since !Kung children are brought up in almost constant contact with their mothers. While a small female !Kung child would not ordinarily be allowed to follow her father on a hunt, for example, she would certainly be able to accompany her mother on a gathering expedition, either walking on her own or carried by her mother. Nisa expresses poignantly her closeness to her mother in describing the intensity of her mourning following Chuko's death.

TASHAY Tashay, Nisa's third husband, is particularly significant in Nisa's life because he is the father of her children. Unlike Nisa's first two "trial" marriages, her marriage to Tashay contains a strong element of love. Nisa and Tashay actually build a life together, although it does start on somewhat rocky ground. With Tashay, Nisa has her first experience of intercourse, after which she feels such pain that she binds herself with a leather strap so Tashay can't have her. Eventually, she comes to enjoy their sexual relationship, and this sexual development corresponds with her growing understanding of her adult responsibilities and her own womanhood. Though Tashay is but one of Nisa's five husbands and only one of her numerous sexual partners, he occupies a special, central place in Nisa's storytelling, and she mourns his death deeply. Nisa's sadness over this death is complex, given Tashay's occasional physical aggression toward her. However, Shostak presents Nisa's marriage to Tashay as the epitome of !Kung marriage, in which the bride is much younger than the groom, intense fights occur and then get resolved, and both parties may have extramarital affairs.

THEMES, MOTIFS, AND SYMBOLS

THEMES

THE INTRUSION OF THE MODERN WORLD In *Nisa* in general, and the chapter called "Change" in particular, Nisa describes how the !Kung people and their traditional ways are increasingly faced with the modern world. The cattle-herding Tswana and Herero peoples intrude on the !Kung way of life when they establish settlements in the once-isolated Dobe region. Their cattle and goats pollute once pristine streams, cars and trucks occupy the region, and Tswana justice becomes the law of the land. Their growing influence on the !Kung is one of the central themes of *Nisa*, and the changes wrought effectively divide Nisa's life in two. In the first half of her life, Nisa does not know any way of life but her own. In the second half, she not only observes the new, agrarian lifestyle but also enters into it as the wife of a "village man" and the employee of a woman living on a European settlement. Nisa therefore embodies a tension between the old, traditional mode of subsistence, which involves hunting and gathering one's food, and the modern, agrarian method of food production, in which animals are herded and crops are planted.

The Western anthropologists themselves also introduce modern ideas into !Kung society, though this intrusion is much less overt that that of the Herero and Tswana groups. The anthropologists pay their subjects in tobacco or other goods, use tape recorders, cameras, and other gadgets, and drive their trucks near the villages. A striking example of the influence of Shostak's modern world on the traditional !Kung people is when Shostak catches a !Kung girl looking at herself in the side-view mirror of Shostak's truck—new self-perceptions and the possibility of a new focus on appearance are suddenly introduced. Such is the unavoidable confluence of modern and traditional in any anthropological study of bush societies like that of the !Kung.

THE UNIVERSALITY OF WOMEN'S EXPERIENCE Shostak aimed to observe women in an unfamiliar culture and determine what constants bind women in societies around the world. She also wanted to examine the !Kung women in light of the women's movement of the 1960s. Shostak pays particular attention to how !Kung women experience menstruation, sexuality, pregnancy, childbirth, and menopause, and she observes their stoic approach to pain associated with women's conditions. The work done by !Kung women, who gather the bulk of a village's food supply, puts them in a position of power and strength, and, as a result, a high degree of sexual equality exists. The condition of !Kung women is therefore not directly similar to the condition of American women, though Shostak posits that the !Kung women represent an archetypal experience of womanhood. She argues that the !Kung division of labor and relative sexual equality present a truer picture of the intrinsic role of women than what we see in western society, in which there is a more pronounced male bias. Shostak also uses her connection to

Nisa to suggest the power of sisterhood. She feels she is better able to reach across cultural boundaries to the !Kung women than to the men, with whom she has little in common.

THE IMPORTANCE OF SEXUALITY Nisa's narrative is full of sex in the form of sexual slang used as insults, descriptions of genitalia, accounts of sexual activities, and philosophical discussions about the nature of sex. The women of the !Kung tribe are eager to discuss their sexual relationships, and in !Kung marriages, infidelity is almost a given. Many of the people Nisa mentions are her former and/or current lovers. Nisa tells Shostak many of the liberated ideas the !Kung have about female sexuality, such as the belief that a woman who is having intercourse must finish her work (a euphemism for having an orgasm) or else risk falling ill. She also reveals the !Kung belief that a woman who does not satisfy her sexual desires will die. Despite the frankness of Nisa's narration and the bawdiness of her fellow !Kung women, jealousy over extramarital affairs and lovers is common, and, ideally, affairs are kept hidden. Still, the frequency with which men and women take lovers outside of their marriages points to the primacy in !Kung society of satisfying sexual desires and maintaining a fulfilling sexual life.

MOTIFS

FOOD AND HUNGER As hunters and gatherers, the !Kung people do not have a perfectly reliable source of food and water. During Nisa's childhood, before the influx of agrarian settlers to the area, drought and other weather conditions wreak havoc on the food and water supply. Moreover, even the best of !Kung hunters bring home meat only once every few days, and the young Nisa is constantly hungry. She gets very excited when her father or brother brings home meat or honey, a special treat, and she gorges herself on plant foods such as klaru and mongongo nuts. Periods of bounty alternate with periods of scarcity, and Nisa recalls a time of drought when the only water she had to drink was collected by mashing up bitter plant roots. The focus on food and hunger among the hunter-gatherer !Kung is contrasted later in the book to the agrarian lifestyle of cattle-herding groups. As these groups exert their influence on the !Kung, Nisa's people begin to keep cattle and goats and to plant gardens as ready food sources. Still, many of the !Kung continue to hunt and gather their food, citing an intrinsic appetite for foods of the bush.

VIOLENCE Nisa's narrative is shockingly violent, in terms of both her own assaults on others and the violence perpetrated against her, and this violence contradicts the popular Western view of bush tribes like Nisa's being very peaceful societies. Though the !Kung do not have any weapons developed specifically for harming other humans, and they have no ritualized notion of warfare, they often engage one another in verbal squabbles that tend to escalate into physical altercations and, sometimes, homicides. Tswana law sends convicted !Kung murderers to jail, but for much of the !Kung's long history, violence persisted, with only disapproval and occasional intervention to thwart it. Nisa's parents and husbands often hit her, and she occasionally lashes out and attacks others. She tells of some disturbing accounts of men attacking women, such as when Nisa's father kicks his pregnant wife in the stomach. Most notable is the fact that Nisa's daughter, Nai, is a victim of domestic abuse. Nai is killed when her husband pushes her down to the ground because she refuses to have sex with him. The fall breaks Nai's neck, and she dies. In retaliation, Nisa attacks Nai's husband and his sister.

TRAVEL The !Kung are essentially nomadic, though they frequently travel back and forth among the same villages. The !Kung may spontaneously get up and move to the bush for a few days, tracking prey, or may erect an entirely new village in the aftermath of a villager's death. Their huts are easily and quickly assembled, and they do not own very much in the way of material possessions beyond the essential equipment for hunting, gathering, and preparing food, as well as decorative objects such as jewelry and clothing. Traveling light is necessary since they travel so often. Nisa describes her journeys back and forth from village to village, moving from location to location. She attributes much of the journeying to her succession of husbands, each of whom takes her to live in a different place. On a smaller scale, daily hunts and gathering expeditions involve travel away from the village for much or all of the daylight hours, and this extremely active lifestyle is one of the reasons for the tribe members' generally good physical condition.

RITUALISTIC DANCING When a member of a village falls ill, it is up to a healer or healers to fall into a trance, harness his or her *n/um* (healing force), and make every effort to pull the sickness out of the body or converse with the spirits and convince them to let the victim live. *N/um* is typically activated during a ritual medicinal or trance dance, in which participants clap, sing, and dance around a campfire while the healer works himself into a trance state. Other than in times of serious illness, such dances may be spontaneous, and Nisa mentions several occasions when her father and brother, both healers, sing a ritual song or enter a trance in order to cure someone who is ill. Trance dances are core elements of village social life, and they continue to be even with the influence of Tswana and Herero settlers. The Tswana and Hereros often come to observe or participate in the dances, which are highly energetic and occasions for exuberant celebration.

SYMBOLS

THE MONGONGO NUT In a society that subsists on food that is hunted or gathered, a dietary staple, such as the mongongo nut, represents existence and nourishment, especially when other food sources are scarce. The mongongo nut, plentiful in the Dobe region, is a very hard nut that must be cracked with a stone in order to release the edible portion inside. Nisa loves mongongo nuts and talks often about eating them as a child. She fondly remembers the time when her brother Dau collected nuts for Nisa and forbade anybody else from eating them because he knew how much she liked them.

NAMES The !Kung have a limited number of names they give to infants as well as honorary members of the tribe, such as Shostak and her husband, and many members of a village or larger group have the same name. Rather than being considered an inconvenience or a lack of creativity, however, the repetition of names is thought to enhance the bonds between members of a group. Often, names are given specifically to create a special bond, as when Nisa names her first daughter Chuko, after her mother. Names are therefore imbued with the characteristics of the namesakes, those who already possess them.

IMPORTANT QUOTATIONS EXPLAINED

1. *Was my childhood a happy one? By the time I had grown and was a young girl, I knew that my heart was usually happy. But when I was a small child, I wasn't aware enough of things to be able to think about whether I was happy or sad.*

These are the last lines of Chapter 3, "Life in the Bush," and they emphasizes the division of Nisa's life into two parts: one made up of lived experience and the other of retrospective consideration of that experience. This passage reveals Nisa's intricate understanding of what it means to tell a story. She demonstrates her own innate awareness that a storyteller does not merely relate events but also layers them with significance and meaning. This understanding is one of the things that makes Nisa such a compelling narrator and sets her apart from the other women Shostak interviews.

This phrase also demonstrates Nisa's ability to structure her narration neatly and eloquently, in such a way that her transcribed interviews are compelling and effective as they stand. She knows what patterns can make a sentence or a passage moving and memorable. Here, beginning with a question signals a break from the previous section of narration and alerts the reader to a new idea or set of ideas. She follows this break with her answer, broken into two sections so as to provide the most specific and accurate answer possible. Moreover, she remembers her childhood well enough to be able to distinguish between different stages of it and to attach various emotional states to those stages. Specificity, precise language, attention to detail, and the ability to analyze events and feelings are all essential qualities of a good storyteller, and in this passage Nisa demonstrates her possession of each of these characteristics.

2. *I am an old woman and know about things, because whenever I hear people talking, I listen.*

This quotation comes at the beginning of Nisa's section of Chapter 4, "Discovering Sex." The beguilingly incantatory tone is indicative both of Nisa's particular brand of storytelling and of the patterns of the !Kung oral tradition, in which fables and morality tales are handed down from the older members of the tribe to the younger. Many of the elder speakers in Nisa's stories preface their words by emphasizing their age and sagacity. Nisa, too, frequently begins her interviews with a direct address. One of the intriguing messages of this particular quote is its idea that wisdom comes from listening to others, not only from firsthand experience. !Kung society is very verbal, and the !Kung do not have a written system of communication. Given the significance of speech, it makes sense that lessons are expressed in the form of conversation or lecture, as anecdotes or fables. Nisa herself actively participates in this tradition, teaching her own wisdom to Shostak using the traditional oral medium. This passage also emphasizes the value of the tribe's elder members. Though they may not be able to hunt or gather very much, they contribute in other ways, including the communication of traditional wisdoms.

3. *Here, in a society of ancient traditions, men and women live together in a nonexploitative manner, displaying a striking degree of equality between the sexes—perhaps a lesson for our own society.*

These lines come from Shostak's introduction to Nisa's narrative in Chapter 11, "Women and Men." Shostak's proposal that !Kung life is an example for our own society to follow is the thesis of her book. Though her overt mission is to provide the context for Nisa's stories, her more subtle goal is to use this example of a society in which men and women are largely equal as fuel for the women's movement, which brought to light many inadequacies in the treatment of women in Western society. American society had essentially promoted a culture in which women were exploited for their domestic labor while men reaped the economic advantages. Moreover, the activities and responsibilities usually carried out by women—caring for children, sewing, cooking—were regularly deemed less valuable than the labor done by men. By examining a culture in which men and women both contribute to the life of the village, Shostak aims to prove a point—namely, that there is no intrinsic reason why women's work should be less valuable than men's and that women's labor is just as critical to a society's functioning.

4. *Zhun/twa men say that women are the chiefs, the rich ones, the wise ones. Because women possess something very important, something that enables men to live: their genitals.*

At the end of her narrative in Chapter 12, "Taking Lovers," Nisa makes this profound statement about the role of women in !Kung society, as well as of the importance of sex. Women, as she says, are elevated to a high position of power by virtue of their sexuality, which both metaphorically and literally rejuvenates the men of the group. In a figurative sense, sex brings life back into a person's body, so that women can restore a man's vitality. Sex is also the method of procreation, and women rejuvenate the village by giving birth to new members. This masculine conception of female genitalia also helps to shed some light on the types of insults the !Kung women hurl at each other in Nisa's narrative ("Death to your genitals!"). The position of prominence that female genitalia occupy in the group's mind-set explains why cursing a woman's genitals would be considered particularly insulting.

5. *That's something that you, a woman, know about as well.*

Nisa says this to Shostak in Chapter 15, "Growing Older," following a description of how pregnancy follows on the heels of sexual activity. Nisa has been talking in general about sexual relationships between women and men, as well as her own sexual relationships with men. She voices her displeasure with her lack of lovemaking with Bo, her current husband, and says that if she had married someone more desirous of her, she might have gotten pregnant again. She explains that having frequent sex increases the chances of becoming pregnant, then addresses Shostak with the above words. This is one of several interjections in this section that Nisa aims directly at Shostak, and it reinforces the idea that Nisa is not simply recounting her life story for a field anthropologist but having an intimate conversation with another woman. She uses these addresses to enhance their bond.

This statement reveals Nisa's understanding of Shostak's mission to uncover the universal conditions of womanhood among diverse cultures. Nisa recognizes that she is not merely being asked to narrate her own history but also to explain the conditions of being a !Kung woman and of being a woman in general. She recognizes that biological similarities can establish a bond that transcends cultural barriers and that certain experiences are the same for women no matter where they live or what language they speak. In gesturing outward from her story to encompass Shostak's own experience, Nisa seeks to bridge the cultural divide between them. It does not matter that Shostak's experience as a woman is rooted in a culture that is completely unfamiliar to Nisa. Nisa still sees their womanhood as a basis for oneness of mind on issues that have to do with being female.

Oranges Are Not the Only Fruit

Jeanette Winterson (1959–)

CONTEXT

Jeanette Winterson was born on August 27, 1959 in Manchester, England. John and Constance Winterson adopted Jeanette in her infancy and raised her in Accrington, Lancashire. Her adoptive parents belonged to a Pentecostal Evangelical congregation. Winterson lived a very sheltered early life, reading the few books found in her house, which included the Bible, Charlotte Brontë's *Jane Eyre* (1847), and Malory's *Le Morte d'Arthur* (1485). Winterson trained to be a preacher at a young age and always desired to be a missionary. When she reached her teenage years, she found a Saturday job at the local library and started reading voraciously. Around the same time, her increasing romantic preference for members of her own sex caused conflicts within her congregation. Winterson's lesbianism led to an exorcism performed by church officials. Soon after, Winterson broke off her connection to her family and her church. She left home at the age of sixteen and began working in various temporary jobs, such as an ice cream truck driver, a makeup artist at a funeral parlor, and an employee at a mental home.

Winterson replicates most of these crucial events from her early life in *Oranges Are Not the Only Fruit* (1985), her first novel. The similarities between Winterson's life and that of her main character, also named Jeanette, suggests that *Oranges* contains autobiographical elements. Winterson started writing *Oranges* several years after she received a degree in English from St. Catherine's College at Oxford University. After working briefly in advertising and theater, Winterson sought a job in publishing. According to Winterson, the idea for her novel germinated during an interview for an editorial position at Pandora Press, the company that later published *Oranges*. When Winterson realized that the interview was going poorly, she started to entertain the interviewer with stories of her own life. The interviewer was so impressed that she encouraged Winterson to write down these accounts. Winterson followed this suggestion, and her novel was published two years later.

Oranges won the Whitbread Prize for a first novel in 1985, and a television adaptation, for which Winterson wrote the screenplay, followed in 1990. By that time, Winterson had published three more books: *Boating for Beginners* (1985), *The Passion* (1987), and *Sexing the Cherry* (1989). Since 1990, Winterson has published five more books: *Written on the Body* (1992); *Art & Lies: A Piece for Three Voices and a Bawd* (1994); *Gut Symmetries* (1997); and *Art Objects: Essays on Ecstasy and Effrontery* (1995). In the early 1990s, England celebrated Winterson as one of its hottest new writers. Gore Vidal called her one of the most exciting new writers he had seen in twenty years. Her attention to lesbian and feminist themes brought her to the forefront of many feminist scholarly groups.

Jeanette Winterson's work fits firmly in the postmodern tradition, as her techniques reflect the ideas of such theorists as Michel Foucault, Julia Kristeva, Roland Barthes, and Jean Lacan. Unlike the modernist period before it, postmodern art attempts to step beyond the mere presentation of a narrative in order to question the ability for a narrative to stand separate from reality at all. In many ways, *Oranges* appears to be an autobiography, and it could also be considered a classic novel about growing up, or bildungsroman. However, Winterson refutes the idea that the novel is simply an autobiography by placing not just stories about her narrator in her novel, but stories about other myths (some taken from Malory's *Le Morte D'Arthur*) and made-up fables that range from meaningful to highly comic. Winterson's placement of these stories in her novel creates a "metafiction," or a fictional novel that attempts to question the nature of fiction instead of just recounting a simple plot. By forcing her readers to question the nature of storytelling, Winterson pushes them toward another postmodern idea, which concerns the questioning of "objective reality." Since many of the stories in the novel are blatantly mythical and even farcical, the reader cannot accept any portion of the story as true, even those elements that appear to be Winterson's autobiography. As such, Winterson supports the postmodern idea that no truth can be true since the truth, our reality, can only exist in the way that we represent it—which will always be subjective.

The ultimate effect of Winterson's efforts is a narrative that might appear slightly confusing to some. Her story is not always told chronologically, and she frequently jumps to inserted tales that appear to have nothing to do with the life of the main character. This relative difficulty in reading, however, is intentional. The fragmented style helps demonstrate Winterson's desire to explore the relationship between the reader and the text.

PLOT OVERVIEW

Jeanette retells the story of her life, beginning when she is seven years old and living in England with her adoptive parents. Jeanette's mother is a fundamentalist Christian and dominates Jeanette's life. Jeanette's father is almost never present. Up until the age of seven, Jeanette's mother had educated her at home, mostly by teaching her to read the Bible. Jeanette's mother adopted Jeanette because she wanted to acquire a child in a sexless manner whom she could train to be a servant to God. Her mother has instilled in Jeanette the idea that she is unique and will eventually become a missionary to the world. Jeanette does not know anyone aside from the other members of the church until, at the age of the seven, her mother is ordered to send Jeanette to school.

Jeanette also loses her hearing at the age of seven. Her condition is misdiagnosed for a long time since her mother and the congregation believe that she is in a state of rapture. Another church member, Miss Jewsbury, discovers that Jeanette simply has a physical ailment, and Jeanette is treated at the hospital. Following her operation, Jeanette spends a lot of time with another church member, Elsie, who teaches Jeanette about poetry and other worldly phenomena, such as Wagner.

At school, Jeanette is always an outcast because of her evangelical beliefs. The teachers shun her essays that deal with missionary work. Her art projects that quote biblical text are equally disdained. Ultimately, one teacher, Mrs. Vole, informs Jeanette that she is obsessed with God and that she has been scaring the other students with her talk of hell. Mrs. Vole sends a letter to Jeanette's mother about this issue, but Jeanette's mother reacts with elation rather than anger. Eventually, Jeanette stops making projects that refer to biblical themes, but she still finds that she remains an outcast.

As she ages, Jeanette realizes that she sometimes disagrees with the teachings of her congregation. Jeanette particularly disagrees with one sermon about the nature of perfection. Although Jeanette begins to see some differences in her ideas and those of the church, she is still closely aligned with her mother, who is a motivating member of their Society for the Lost.

As Jeanette grows older she starts to think about romance. She worries about whether or not men are beasts, and she listens intently to other women's complaints and opinions about their husbands. One day Jeanette and her mother go downtown and Jeanette sees a compelling girl named Melanie working at a fish stall. Jeanette tries to talk to Melanie, but Melanie cannot talk on that day. Soon after, Jeanette is offered a job washing dishes in a nearby ice cream shop and spends her Saturdays working and looking at Melanie. Eventually, she and Melanie become friends.

Jeanette brings Melanie to their church, and on the first visit Melanie agrees to be saved by Jesus Christ. After this, Jeanette frequently visits Melanie's house for Bible study. As the two spend more time together, they start having a love affair. Jeanette eventually tells her mother how much she loves and needs Melanie because she makes her feel so happy. The following Sunday at church, the pastor publicly confronts them about their fallen state. Melanie repents immediately, but Jeanette argues and flees. She takes refuge in the house of Miss Jewsbury, who is herself a lesbian, and that evening Miss Jewsbury and Jeanette sleep together. The following day, the elders of the church attempt to exorcise the demons from Jeanette by laying hands on her for fourteen hours. When she still will not repent, her mother locks her in the parlor for thirty-six hours with no food. After this hungry spell, she pretends to repent, but maintains her conviction that she has not done anything wrong by loving both Melanie and God.

Melanie disappears and Jeanette becomes deeply involved in the church again. Her role in the church has grown and she now preaches her own sermons and teaches Sunday school. Soon Jeanette begins a new affair with Katy, a recent convert. When they are caught one weekend, Jeanette takes all of the blame, saying that she had been with Melanie. The church then decides that Jeanette has been given too much responsibility so that she now almost thinks that she is a man. They insist that she give up teaching and preaching. Instead, Jeanette quits the church. Jeanette's mother forces her to leave their home since her evilness will bring illness to them all.

With no home, friends, or money, Jeanette takes up various jobs. She works in a funeral parlor, as an ice cream truck driver, and eventually at a mental hospital. On occasion, she runs into her mother or members of her congregation, who treat Jeanette coldly and say she is possessed by demons. Eventually she moves to the city. After an unspecified time, Jeanette does return home one winter to see her mother. Her mother still faithfully believes, but her Society for the Lost has been shaken by corruption. Jeanette's mother does not discuss Jeanette's lifestyle with her, but her behavior indicates that she has softened in her beliefs. Jeanette's mother still listens to the missionary reports on the radio system with her usual fervor.

CHARACTER LIST

Jeanette The novel's narrator. Jeanette retells her life from when she is seven years old to an unspecified time after her teenage years. Jeanette is a sincerely devout child who earnestly believes in God and love. As Jeanette grows into her teenage years, she falls in love with another girl. Eventually, she realizes that her same-sex love is part of her nature that cannot be denied. Although others categorize Jeanette as evil, Jeanette maintains an impression of goodness and even sacrifice. Jeanette is the novel's mythic heroine. Her quest is for her true self. In her community of religious hypocrisy, Jeanette represents truth and spirit.

Jeanette's mother A fundamentalist Christian woman. Jeanette's mother adopted Jeanette because she wanted to train her daughter to be a servant to God. Jeanette's mother is combative and controlling. Jeanette's mother often appears to be hypocritical. She keeps a wine glass in her house for "medicinal purposes" yet criticizes the "Heathens" for drinking. She professes to be very religious but often acts in uncharitable ways. Jeanette's mother represents the rigid establishment of the church. Jeanette's mother also represents the hypocrisy inherent in members of the church.

Elsie Norris A member of the church. Elsie Norris is energetic, outgoing, and entertaining. Elsie is a very devout member of the church who testifies daily. Despite her genuine religiousness, she is also quite eccentric. Her past has involved traveling outside of England to such places as Saudi Arabia. She appears to be another live soul amid the congregation that is full of unthinking, spiritless practitioners. Elsie represents the possibility of the imagination and the world outside of Jeanette's small circle. Elsie also serves as a loving mother figure to Jeanette when Jeanette's own mother is neglectful.

Miss Jewsbury A member of Jeanette's church who plays the oboe. Miss Jewsbury represents the closeted lesbian that Jeanette refuses to become. Miss Jewsbury's character is awkward, slightly unfriendly, and generally disdained by others who deem her unholy because of her latent sexual desires. Still, Miss Jewsbury's inability to choose either her lesbianism or her religion leaves her as a character torn between two contradictory worlds. She can never live with a full identity. After Jeanette has liberated herself by choosing her sexuality over her community, she declines to visit Miss Jewsbury, who lacked the courage to make a similar choice.

Melanie Jeanette's first lover, whom she meets at a fish stand. Melanie is sweet, docile, and not too smart. Initially, she tells Jeanette she got her name because her head resembled a melon—a wry comment also upon Melanie's limited intellectual capacity. Melanie's docility leads her to later marry, have children, and deny that she ever had a lesbian love. Melanie represents another weak soul who refuses to follow her true desires and venture outside of the role society has placed upon her, unlike Jeanette.

Katy Jeanette's second long-term lover. Katy is confident, open, and unashamed. Katy's obviously sexual invitation to Jeanette demonstrates to Jeanette a new confidence about same-sex relations. Katy contrasts with the character of Melanie in that Katy understands what she is doing with Jeanette but lacks any shame about her behavior. Not surprisingly, their confidence and happiness lead to their being caught, but the capture differs greatly from the time that Melanie and Jeanette were found out. Katy has helped to instill Jeanette with confidence in herself and in her sexuality.

Jeanette's father A man who is almost never mentioned in the novel. Jeanette's father works in a factory and leaves for work at five in the morning. He and Jeanette's mother do not have sex. Jeanette father plays a nonexistent role in governing the household and dealing with Jeanette. His absence in the household is the most important thing about him. It demonstrates that Jeanette grew up in a primarily matriarchal household.

Mrs. White A very religious member of Jeanette's church. As her name indicates, Mrs. White appears to be of the utmost purity. With Jeanette's mother, she represents one of the church members who holds very unbending ideas about sin and goodness. The narrator frequently uses Mrs. White's alleged purity for comic effect. While Mrs. White is supposedly devout, she grabs a wine glass to better eavesdrop on the fornication at the next-door neighbors, an act of a gossip rather than a saint. Further, Mrs. White's eventual difficulty in breathing because of her proximity to a lesbian seems ludicrous.

Ida One of the lesbian women who owns the paper shop. Ida presence foreshadows Jeanette's eventual sexual identity. Ida also acts as one of the few people in the narrative who follows her own inclinations. Her presence helps Jeanette's latent feelings come to light. Significantly, Ida is present on the day that Jeanette meets Melanie.

Pastor Spratt The pastor who converted Jeanette's mother and whom she idolizes. Jeanette and her mother frequently discuss Pastor Spratt's crusades in the tropics. Pastor Spratt appears infrequently in the narrative, but his presence pervades Jeanette's mother's life. He symbolizes the extreme elements in the church.

Pierre An ex-lover of Jeanette's mother. Pierre's name evokes the passion that Jeanette's mother once had but since has lost. References to him frequently dot the text whenever the themes of romance or sin appear.

Pastor Finch A visiting minister to Jeanette's church. Pastor Finch's name suggests that he resembles a songbird who simply repeats the tunes taught to him. Pastor Finch is a comic character who unleashes a fiery sermon about the dangers of being seven to Jeanette. The seriousness of his sermon compared to Jeanette's innocence of age renders him ridiculous.

Mrs. Arkwright A woman who owns a shop for ridding vermin in Jeanette's town. Mrs. Arkwright tells Jeanette that Jeanette's mother is crazy. She buys Jeanette a drink after Jeanette revisits her home as a grownup.

May ("Auntie May") A member of Jeanette's church. Auntie May is generally seen as a kind friend to Jeanette and her mother.

Mrs. Rothwell A near-deaf member of Jeanette's church who almost drowns in Blackpool. Mrs. Rothwell is a comic character who interrupts fiery sermons because she cannot hear and who waved goodbye to the congregation when she was drowning instead of crying for help.

Alice ("Auntie Alice") A member of the church.

Mrs. Vole The head of Jeanette's school. Mrs. Vole sends a note home about Jeanette's religiosity.

Mrs. Virtue Jeanette's sewing teacher who does not like Jeanette's work.

O

ANALYSIS OF MAJOR CHARACTERS

JEANETTE Jeanette is the narrator of the novel, its heroine, and its primary star. She is a kind, questioning girl who has approached the world with seriousness from a young age. As a child, she deeply believes in her church. At school, she decorates her arts and crafts with biblical texts. Her church family makes her feel happy and warm. The strong ideas advocated by her mother initially form Jeanette's own ideology, but as she is exposed to more of the world, Jeanette begins to develop her own ideas. In time, her own intellect offers different interpretations from what she has been taught. In the end, Jeanette will even go so far as to embrace her lesbianism, which is a characteristic completely disdained by her society. Jeanette's relative fearlessness in embracing her true self shows her to be a heroine of considerable bravery.

Jeanette's behavior also is compassionate and kind. Although her church already has tortured her by starving her for thirty-six hours, Jeanette still takes pains to comfort some of its members in their distress. When the congregation fights with men in Blackpool, it is only Jeanette who has the ability to calmly defuse the situation. When women in the society cry because they have been kicked out of the Salvation Army band, Jeanette supports and cheers them. Jeanette's unwavering love for these members of her church makes her highly sympathetic. Although the church rejects her out of hand, Jeanette's behavior is never reactionary or angry. Because Jeanette is such a compassionate and thoughtful character, it is easy to take her side and believe that her lesbianism is not wrong. The church group and Jeanette's mother, on the other hand, appear to be thoughtless and simply follow regulations with no thoughts of their own. Jeanette stands, in contrast, as a symbol of spirit and life.

JEANETTE'S MOTHER Jeanette's mother is a woman characterized by hypocrisy. She is one of the most devout members of her congregation, but a close examination of her actions shows that her religiousness does not parallel her sincere goodwill toward others. The lack of charity in her heart can be seen in the way that she treats Jeanette. Jeanette's mother adopted her because she wanted to have Jeanette fight with her against the evil of the world. She plans to make her daughter a servant of God—his missionary. During the opening chapters, Jeanette's mother does appear to love her daughter, but this love is conditional upon the way that Jeanette fills her mother's expectations.

When Jeanette fails to be the servant of God that her mother envisions, Jeanette's mother loves her less. Jeanette's mother is elated when she thinks that Jeanette is in a state of rapture at the age of seven, but when it turns out that Jeanette has actually gone deaf, Jeanette's mother ignores her and tends to church affairs. A true believer in the teachings of Jesus likely would spend more time comforting her sick daughter than tending to bureaucratic matters. Jeanette's mother lacks the compassion characteristic of a truly religious person. In the opening chapter, Jeanette says that her mother is Old Testament through and through: the combative and even vengeful nature of Jeanette's mother follows the harsher God that is characteristic of that time. Jeanette's mother actively seeks out combat with others. She feels delighted when she is able to sing hymns to irritate the next-door neighbors. She spends much of her day tracking the missionary activities of Pastor Spratt, almost as if she is the map-keeper during a war.

ELSIE NORRIS Elsie Norris is one of the few characters in the novel, aside from Jeanette, whom Winterson regards favorably. Elsie supports Jeanette during all phases of her life, even after it is clear that Jeanette is a lesbian. Elsie probably is the kindest character within the novel. She also is one of the rare church members who truly seems to hold a pure form of religion in her heart. Goodness and compassion motivate Elsie's actions. Elsie becomes close friends with Jeanette when Jeanette is sick in the hospital. Perhaps since Jeanette's mother neglected her, Elsie took pains to visit the hospital every single day. The tales that Elsie told from literature and her own life expose Jeanette to an imaginative realm Jeanette had never seen.

Elsie is a respected and fervent member of the church, but she is quite different from the congregation. Elsie is a character who knows her true self. In other words, she represents what Jeanette will spend the novel trying to become—a realized being. Elsie also teaches Jeanette the tools that will help Jeanette on her quest—those found in the imagination. Elsie guides Jeanette onto the right path and, unlike Jeanette's mother, is a true helper. Even when Jeanette quits the church, Elsie meets with her and does not shun her. Elsie even suggests that it is best for Jeanette to go off and make her own way in the world and that her identity is not necessarily wrong. Unfortunately, Elsie is frequently sick during the novel and dies at its end. Her sickness may be a commentary on the difficulty this forceful woman had in remaining in such a deadened congregation and world. When she dies at the end of the novel, Jeanette feels deeply saddened because she has lost her kindly surrogate mother and friend. Elsie Norris stands out as one of the few truly noble characters in the novel.

THEMES, MOTIFS, AND SYMBOLS

THEMES

THE FICTIVENESS OF ALL STORIES *Oranges Are Not the Only Fruit* tells many stories but ultimately concerns itself with the very act of telling stories. By juxtaposing legends and myths with the life of the main character, Jeanette, Winterson questions the reality of the stories told by the narrators. None of the stories can be verified, so they must all equally be accepted as fictions. It is for this reason that Winterson would say that her novel is not an autobiography: the "truth" of the life of Jeanette is not true at all. As Winterson took pains to express in Chapter Five, no stories or histories are ever wholly true because subjective writers have written them. Winterson forces the realization that no objective reality exists anywhere. Whenever reality is represented by an art form, the realness of the reality must be called into question because it has been subjectively framed.

THE MYTHIC JOURNEY The idea that Jeanette is on a mythical journey thematically frames her narrative. Jeanette's birth and adoption are described with images from the story of Christ. From an early age, Jeanette believes that she will emerge as a Christlike figure who will help to save the world. As she ages, however, it becomes clear that her true quest is simply to find and accept herself. This task is not an easy. Jeanette's homosexual desires contradict the regulations that she has believed all of her life. To accept who she truly is, Jeanette must embark on a physical and spiritual adventure. She must both leave her home and leave her assumptions of how the world and herself are defined. Winterson borrows the standard techniques from a mythic story for Jeanette's adventure. Winterson also places other mythic characters in the novel, such as Sir Perceval, to place Jeanette's story in the mythic realm. Although Jeanette's adventure requires that she venture outside of the normative heterosexual sphere, her quest still takes the standard steps. From her birth Jeanette was destined for a mission and by the end of the novel it becomes clear that even though she has become a lesbian, her quest still continues. Even as a writer and a lesbian, Jeanette can still help to fight against the evil in the world as her mother originally intended.

THE ABSENCE OF BINARY OPPOSITIONS An overriding theme in the novel concerns the conflict between binary factors. Jeanette's mother can see the world only as good or evil, friend or foe. Yet Jeanette's homosexuality places her outside of that binary by showing that she is neither wholly good nor wholly evil. At the same time, Jeanette's lesbianism defies the binary gender roles that traditionally dominate society. Jeanette is a woman who does not act as a traditional woman because she does not love men. Winterson takes pains to illustrate the shifting nature of genders by switching some of gender roles in her mythical tales. She, like other postmodern feminists such as Julia Kristeva and Monique Wittig, proposes that the concept of gender is socially constructed, not biologically inherent. Overall, the construction of the world in binary systems limits and excludes those people and stories that fall outside of the definitions. By not seeing the world as a strict duality, a greater multiplicity of people can be seen as creating its essence. People are not simply black and white, but also line the many shades of gray in between.

MOTIFS

ORANGES The title *Oranges Are Not the Only Fruit* demands an explanation that can be offered only through analyzing the many appearance of oranges in the story. On the broadest level, these oranges represent the dominant ideology that pervades the world in which Jeanette lives. Whenever Jeanette feels uncertain about something, her mother offers her oranges. In some circumstances, these oranges appear to strictly represent heterosexuality. But generally they represent more than just the dominance of heterosexuality; they represent the entire repressive system that Jeanette's mother espouses. When Jeanette sees Melanie after their relationship has ended, Melanie offers her an orange, but Jeanette refuses to take it. Her refusal represents her refusal to succumb to the ideas of the status quo, as Melanie has. Jeanette wants to remain true to her own principles and decides to head out into the world, but she refuses to ever sell oranges. Throughout the novel, Jeanette's mother believes that oranges are the only fruit, but Jeanette can see that there are others. Heterosexuality is just one way of living life, but there are many others that should be equally valued.

THE DIFFERENCE BETWEEN GOD AND HIS SERVANTS The hypocrisy among the followers of God appears frequently in *Oranges*. Nowhere in the novel does the main character ever decide she is against God. What becomes clear to her as she grows, however, is that her church, like many others, often decides what God believes in ways that the narrator finds to be untrue. Jeanette initially observes that she disagrees the pastor's contention that man was "perfect" before the fall. Later, she will disagree when the church says that same sex love is incorrect and that women should not take responsibility in the church. By the end of the novel, Jeanette still feels closely aligned with God but decides that much of the church's rhetoric is false. In addition, she often observes that the church members broadly preach guidelines but do not follow them sincerely in their hearts. Winterson's commentary upon the subjective nature of stories additionally questions the notion of an accurate interpretation of God's will. In her "Deuteronomy" chapter, Winterson critiques blind adherence to biblical law by demonstrating that even the contents of a biblical book were shaped by its narrator. Just as the member of Jeanette's church have their own agendas, so too could have these biblical narrators—which affected the things that they wrote.

DEATH Images of death and dying appear frequently in *Oranges* and act as a commentary upon the lugubrious world surrounding Jeanette. Most members of the Society of the Lost live almost like the living dead. They worship ancient rhetoric about a dying martyr and refuse to let their living spirits guide them. Jeanette, on the other hand, nourishes her spirit and represents life. When heading to Melanie's house, she grabs flowers from cemetery graves for her love. The image of these fresh flowers in the midst of such decay points to the contrast between Jeanette's acceptance of her living, true self and the lifeless regime the Society for the Lost promotes. The contrast is revealed again when Jeanette and Katy stay at the guesthouse for the bereaved. The owner of the guesthouse, a Society member, discovers Jeanette and Katy's love affair during their stay. The subtext of this discovery is that the passion and life present in Katy and Jeanette stood out so much that it was noticed. Ultimately, Jeanette will come to be an attendant at a funeral parlor and will be charged with preparing the dead for their final placement. The irony of Jeanette's position is striking: she actually has been helping to care for the living dead all along. Jeanette appears to be one of the few people up to the task.

SYMBOLS

THE PINK MACKINTOSH A "mackintosh" is a British word for a raincoat. Jeanette's mother buys her one after Jeanette rips hers. The raincoat is too large and a brilliant pink, and Jeanette hates it. This raincoat symbolizes a final attempt by Jeanette's mother to force her into something she is not. The pink suggests the femininity or girliness that Jeanette's mother wants Jeanette to maintain. When Jeanette's mother forces it over Jeanette's head, Jeanette thinks of the Man in the Iron Mask. The main character in that story is confined in prison with a mask over his face for many years. For Jeanette, this pink raincoat symbolizes the ideological mask that her mother is trying to keep on her; it requires that Jeanette become a heterosexual and follow her mother's ideas. After Jeanette leaves the store, she feels nauseous. Her physical distress arises because Jeanette knows on an unconscious level how little this coat matches who she truly is. Ironically, it is Jeanette's sickness that leads her to look around the marketplace and see Melanie, her first love. Apparently, Jeanette is still able to peer out through her iron mask of a pink raincoat to liberate herself. Her mother's final attempt at symbolic imprisonment no longer works.

SHADRACH, MESHACH, AND ABEDNEGO The names Shadrach, Meshach, and Abednego are used twice in the novel, once for the three white mice that Elsie Norris places in the painted fiery box, and once for the sorcerer's three ravens. The names come from the biblical book of Daniel. Shadrach, Meshach, and Abednego worked for King Nebuccanezzar during the period that the Jews were in exile. One day, the King ordered them to pay homage to a golden religious idol, but the three men refused because they were devout Jews. For their disobedience, the King cast them into a fiery furnace. The three men, however, did not die because God rewarded their faithfulness. When the King looked in the furnace, he saw them alive with a creature that appeared to be an angel. The King freed the men, promoted them, and praised the greatness of their God.

The martyrdom and eventual success of these three men mirror that of Jeanette. Like Shadrach, Meshach, and Abednego, Jeanette refuses to pay homage to an idol, or actually an "ideal"—that of homosexuality. For her disobedience, her church members punish her in various ways. Despite these hardships, Jeanette does not die. It is her faith in her own interpretation of God that will save her. Jeanette's unwillingness to grovel beneath religious ideas that appear idolatrous to her, such as homophobic notions in the church, brings her final salvation. This metaphor contains a scathing commentary upon Jeanette's church by suggesting that through their misunderstanding of the word of God they are actually going against his ways. Nevertheless, the story of Shadrach, Meshach, and Abednego testifies to the way that the faithful will be protected in the midst of persecution. Just as it worked for these three men, so too will it work for Jeanette. She too will become free and promoted in society, with the greatness of her version religion recognized.

THE STONE PEBBLE The stone pebble has a dual meaning in the novel. At first, the pebble appears to be a possible weapon. The orange demon throws it to Jeanette after her fantasy about the Forbidden City, a location in which a stone could kill a person. Because of the power of a stone in Jeanette's fantasy, the pebble initially appears to be a tool that could help Jeanette conquer her enemies, whether they be her mother or her church members. When the pebble appears the second time, the raven Abednego coughs it up (it represents his heart) to keep Winnet Stonejar (Jeanette's mythical alter ego) safe. Here the pebble becomes a talisman that evokes the fable of Hansel and Gretel. Hansel and Gretel used pebbles when they went into the forest so that they could find their way home. The pebble from the raven also helps to guide Jeanette/Winnet toward her home—which ultimately is her true self. The pebble will stay with Winnet as she wanders through the forest and eventually makes it to the city. In the end, the pebble will become both a weapon and a way home. Jeanette finds her true self through her writing. In the act of creating her novel, she is liberating her self. In the act of writing a novel, Jeanette is also able to fight against the oppression that she suffered in her years. The pebble has both guided her home and allowed her to fight.

IMPORTANT QUOTATIONS EXPLAINED

---

1. *She had never heard of mixed feelings. There were friends and there were enemies.*

This quotation comes from the beginning of the first chapter of the book, "Genesis," when Jeanette is describing her mother's character. This character description lays the backdrop for the future conflict that Jeanette will have with her mother. Jeanette's mother sees the world only in black and white terms, with no layers in between. For her there are friends and there are enemies. A person is holy or evil. She does not allow room for people to be nonreligious but still good people. For Jeanette's mother, if you are not saved by Christ, then you are a heathen. Such dualistic views of the world have deeply been impressed upon Jeanette. Yet as she grows older and becomes a lesbian, she falls into a middle ground. Homosexuality falls outside of the assumed heterosexual binary. Winterson criticizes the mother's perspective and suggests in her novel that the world does not exist in a series of binaries.

---

2. *And so it was that on a particular day, some times later, she followed a star until it came to settle above an orphanage, and in that place was a crib, and in that crib, a child. A child with too much hair.*

This passage from the novel's first chapter, "Genesis," describes the adoption of Jeanette in terms that compare her to Jesus Christ. This imagery is important because throughout the plot Jeanette will embark on a mythic quest that in some ways resembles the quest of Christ. The imagery and style are also important because they mimic the Bible. The star over Jeanette's crib can be compared to the star of Bethlehem, and the long sentence starting with "And" replicates the Bible's narrative technique. The narrator twists this generally austere style by saying that the child that was found was "a child with too much hair." This comedic touch is not consistent with a true biblical tone, as its content gently pokes fun at the biblical style. This inconsistency is part of Winterson's questioning of the nature of narratives and fictions, and it also represents her attempt to rewrite a classic book in her own style. In the act of rewriting, Winterson suggests that no text, even ones considered sacred, actually represents truth. For Winterson, texts are representations of reality that necessarily subjective because they were created.

---

3. *The salt beef of civilization rumbling round in the gut. Constipation was a great problem after the Second World War. Not enough roughage in the diet, too much refine food.*

This phrase comes from the "Deuteronomy" chapter of the novel, in which the narrator comments on the nature of history. The narrator is speaking directly to the reader to make her point. She starts discussing beef because she suggests that the act of making history resembles the act of making a sandwich. This phrase demonstrates the comedic irony with which the narrator explains her position. The image of beef comes from her metaphor of history being like a sandwich, but after mentioning beef the narrator throws in images of constipation and roughage since they came to mind. This technique highlights the narrator's stream of consciousness, and this placement of images adds a comic light to a serious subject—historiography. The comedy may help facilitate the reader's understanding of the concept. The concrete images also manage to breakdown postmodern theory into physical terms. Ultimately, the quote might push the reader into laughter.

4. *I love you almost as much as I love the Lord.*

In the "Joshua" chapter, Jeanette says this to Melanie as they are heading to church. The quotation is important because it comes right before the church meeting where the pastor accuses the two girls of being sinful with their love. The quote shows Jeanette's sincere love and affection for Melanie, as well as her belief that she is not doing anything wrong by loving Melanie. It contrasts greatly with the subsequent scene in which the church members brutally condemn Jeanette for her impure thoughts and desires. Despite their criticism, Jeanette still sees no such fault. In fact, Jeanette's love for God, Melanie's love for God, and Jeanette's love for Melanie all seem to fit perfectly together in Jeanette's world. One reason that Jeanette feels so happy in her love for Melanie is because Melanie has joined her religious community, which basically has been her lifelong family. Jeanette sees Melanie as a gift from God, not as a temptation sent by the devil. Even after her condemnation, Jeanette will maintain her idea that she can love women and love God equally. Jeanette will never believe that she cannot love God simply because she is a lesbian. Jeanette's disagreement with the church on this matter starts her deep understanding of the religious misinterpretations of her church.

5. *Pillars hold things up, and salt keeps things clean, but it's a poor exchange for losing your self. People do go back, but they don't survive, because two realities are claiming them at the same time.*

This observation appears toward the end of the final chapter, "Ruth," when the Jeanette is thinking about whether or not she should revisit her past by going home to visit her mother. Jeanette is thinking but speaks directly to the readers as she does so. Jeanette's discussion of pillars refers to Lot's wife. According to the Bible, Lot's wife turned into a pillar of salt when she turned to look back at burning Sodom and Gomorrah. God had previously told Lot not to have his family look back, but Lot's wife still did. Jeanette parallels the wife's act of looking back to the act of looking backward over one's past. Jeanette proposes that it is impossible to live in your past while you are in your present. Your life always is changing and going forwarded, if you cling excessively to your past identity it will destroy you. For Winterson, the self is malleable and always in a process of being created and reinvented. Jeanette has been able to change as she has grown. If she were to have clung only to her childhood identity, her liberation would not have been possible. Eventually, Jeanette develops a profound understanding of her self where she can see who she was before and what she is now. By not defining herself only by her past, Jeanette will not become one of the living dead. This remark crucially relates to one of the main themes in the book: the need to find your own identity. Jeanette's lengthy philosophical thinking on the matter helps to inform the reader for his or her own life.

How do Jeanette's sexual relationships reflect her coming of age in *Oranges Are Not the Only Fruit*?

The character of Jeanette in *Oranges Are Not the Only Fruit* by Jeanette Winterson is strong-willed and confident. Initially, she derives her strength from her church and her domineering mother. In the first chapter, Jeanette says of her mother, "She had never heard of mixed feelings. There were friends and there were enemies" (Chapter 1). But when she reveals her unorthodox sexuality, Jeanette is rejected by the two constant forces in her life—her mother and her church. By the end of the novel, she has successfully established her own independent convictions about her life and her sexuality. Jeanette's forced separation from her mother and church leads to a cultivation of a distinct internal confidence, which is demonstrated in her role with her three romantic partners in the novel: Melanie, Miss Jewsbury, and Katy.

From the outset, Jeanette's relationship with Melanie is riddled with pain and miscommunication. In their first encounter, Jeanette's mother has just forced her to wear an ugly, oversized pink raincoat. Jeanette is mortified, especially when she glimpses an attractive girl—Melanie—at a nearby shop. Jeanette eventually befriends Melanie and even brings her to church. They sleep together and spend all their time together. Initially, Jeanette naïvely thinks that she can reconcile her faith and her sexuality, telling Melanie, "I love you almost as much as I love the Lord" (Chapter 6). She is sincere, but her proclamation proves ironic when her church immediately shuns her for her homosexuality. In front of the entire congregation, the pastor accuses Jeanette and Melanie of falling under Satan's web. Jeanette defends her love for Melanie and her love for the Lord, while Melanie immediately repents. From that point, the church keeps Jeanette and Melanie apart, and their relationship ends. Although Jeanette's affection for Melanie is sincere, she cannot reconcile it with the rest of her life; their relationship proves too weak to overcome the obstacles against it.

Student Essay

After the episode in church, Jeanette spends the night with Miss Jewsbury, a member of her congregation who is also a lesbian. Miss Jewsbury approaches her in the night and they make love, even though this disgusts Jeanette. Miss Jewsbury takes advantage of Jeanette's vulnerability, and this, coupled with Jeanette's lack of attraction to her, leaves Jeanette all the more uneasy about their sexual encounter. The next morning, at church, Jeanette denies spending the night at Miss Jewsbury's. There is nothing positive about their intimacy, and Jeanette feels even worse about her sexuality.

With Katy, Jeanette finally finds a healthy relationship. She says, "[Katy] was my most uncomplicated love affair, and I loved her for it" (Chapter 6). Katy joins Jeanette's church, and she and Jeanette are immediately drawn to each other. Unlike in Jeanette's relationship with Melanie, Katy initiates this relationship, and unlike her disgust at her encounter with Miss Jewsbury, Jeanette is equally interested in Katy. Jeanette's relationship with Katy further contrasts with her previous relationships in that Katy feels no shame about their relationship. Indeed, the women's lack of shame leads to their being caught, but because of Katy's love and support, this experience is far less traumatic than other similar incidents. Jeanette must leave her mother's house and the church, but Katy helps Jeanette find pride in her sexuality and enough confidence to begin a new life on her own.

Jeanette moves from trying to be loyal to her church, mother, and herself to realizing that her *first* priority must be herself. By the end of *Oranges Are Not the Only Fruit*, Jeanette has found a new foundation for herself. This break from her childhood influences traces through her relationships, ultimately resulting in a strong, independent, adult.

Pride and Prejudice

Jane Austen (1775–1817)

CONTEXT

Jane Austen was born in Steventon, England, in 1775, where she lived for the first twenty-five years of her life. Her father, George Austen, was the rector of the local parish and taught her largely at home. She began to write while in her teens and completed the original manuscript of *Pride and Prejudice*, titled *First Impressions*, between 1796 and 1797. A publisher rejected the manuscript, and it was not until 1809 that Austen began the revisions that would bring it to its final form. *Pride and Prejudice* was published in 1813, two years after *Sense and Sensibility* (1811), her first novel, and it achieved a popularity that has endured to this day. Austen published four more novels: *Mansfield Park* (1814), *Emma* (1815), *Northanger Abbey*, and *Persuasion*. The last two were published in 1818, a year after her death.

During Austen's life, only her immediate family knew of her authorship of these novels. At one point, she wrote behind a door that creaked when visitors approached; this warning allowed her to hide manuscripts before anyone could enter. Though publishing anonymously prevented her from acquiring an authorial reputation, it also enabled her to preserve her privacy at a time when English society associated a female's entrance into the public sphere with a reprehensible loss of femininity. Additionally, Austen may have sought anonymity because of the more general atmosphere of repression pervading her era. As the Napoleonic Wars (1800–1815) threatened the safety of monarchies throughout Europe, government censorship of literature proliferated.

The social milieu of Austen's Regency England was particularly stratified, and class divisions were rooted in family connections and wealth. In her work, Austen is often critical of the assumptions and prejudices of upper-class England. She distinguishes between internal merit (goodness of person) and external merit (rank and possessions). Though she frequently satirizes snobs, she also pokes fun at the poor breeding and misbehavior of those lower on the social scale. Nevertheless, Austen was in many ways a realist, and the England she depicts is one in which social mobility is limited and class-consciousness is strong.

Socially regimented ideas of appropriate behavior for each gender factored into Austen's work as well. While social advancement for young men lay in the military, church, or law, the chief method of self-improvement for women was the acquisition of wealth. Women could only accomplish this goal through successful marriage, which explains the ubiquity of matrimony as a goal and topic of conversation in Austen's writing. Though young women of Austen's day had more freedom to choose their husbands than in the early eighteenth century, practical considerations continued to limit their options.

Even so, critics often accuse Austen of portraying a limited world. As a clergyman's daughter, Austen would have done parish work and was certainly aware of the poor around her. However, she wrote about her own world, not theirs. The critiques she makes of class structure seem to include only the middle class and upper class; the lower classes, if they appear at all, are generally servants who seem perfectly pleased with their lot. This lack of interest in the lives of the poor may be a failure on Austen's part, but it should be understood as a failure shared by almost all of English society at the time.

In general, Austen occupies a curious position between the eighteenth and nineteenth centuries. Her favorite writer, whom she often quotes in her novels, was Dr. Samuel Johnson, the great model of eighteenth-century classicism and reason. Her plots, which often feature characters forging their respective ways through an established and rigid social hierarchy, bear similarities to such works of Johnson's contemporaries such as *Pamela* (1740), written by Samuel Richardson. Austen's novels also display an ambiguity about emotion and an appreciation for intelligence and natural beauty that align them with Romanticism. In their awareness of the conditions of modernity and city life and the consequences for family structure and individual characters, they prefigure much Victorian literature, as does Austen's usage of such elements as frequent formal social gatherings, sketchy characters, and scandal.

PLOT OVERVIEW

The news that a wealthy young gentleman named Charles Bingley has rented the manor of Netherfield Park causes a great stir in the nearby village of Longbourn, especially in the Bennet household. The Bennets have five unmarried daughters—from oldest to youngest, Jane, Elizabeth, Mary, Kitty, and Lydia—and Mrs. Bennet is desperate to see them all married. After Mr. Bennet pays a social visit to Mr. Bingley, the Bennets attend a ball at which Mr. Bingley is present. He is taken with Jane and spends much of the evening dancing with her. His close friend, Mr. Darcy, is less pleased with the evening and haughtily refuses to dance with Elizabeth, which makes everyone view him as arrogant and obnoxious.

At social functions over subsequent weeks, however, Mr. Darcy finds himself increasingly attracted to Elizabeth's charm and intelligence. Jane's friendship with Mr. Bingley also continues to burgeon, and Jane pays a visit to the Bingley mansion. On her journey to the house she is caught in a downpour and catches ill, forcing her to stay at Netherfield for several days. In order to tend to Jane, Elizabeth hikes through muddy fields and arrives with a spattered dress, much to the disdain of the snobbish Miss Bingley, Mr. Bingley's sister. Miss Bingley's spite only increases when she notices that Darcy, whom she is pursuing, pays quite a bit of attention to Elizabeth.

When Elizabeth and Jane return home, they find Mr. Collins visiting their household. Mr. Collins is a young clergyman who stands to inherit Mr. Bennet's property, which has been "entailed," meaning that it can only be passed down to male heirs. Mr. Collins is a pompous fool, though he is quite enthralled by the Bennet girls. Shortly after his arrival, he makes a proposal of marriage to Elizabeth. She turns him down, wounding his pride. Meanwhile, the Bennet girls have become friendly with militia officers stationed in a nearby town. Among them is Wickham, a handsome young soldier who is friendly toward Elizabeth and tells her how Darcy cruelly cheated him out of an inheritance.

At the beginning of winter, the Bingleys and Darcy leave Netherfield and return to London, much to Jane's dismay. A further shock arrives with the news that Mr. Collins has become engaged to Charlotte Lucas, Elizabeth's best friend and the poor daughter of a local knight. Charlotte explains to Elizabeth that she is getting older and needs the match for financial reasons. Charlotte and Mr. Collins get married and Elizabeth promises to visit them at their new home. As winter progresses, Jane visits the city to see friends (hoping also that she might see Mr. Bingley). However, Miss Bingley visits her and behaves rudely, while Mr. Bingley fails to visit her at all. The marriage prospects for the Bennet girls appear bleak.

That spring, Elizabeth visits Charlotte, who now lives near the home of Mr. Collins's patron, Lady Catherine de Bourgh, who is also Darcy's aunt. Darcy calls on Lady Catherine and encounters Elizabeth, whose presence leads him to make a number of visits to the Collins's home, where she is staying. One day, he makes a shocking proposal of marriage, which Elizabeth quickly refuses. She tells Darcy that she considers him arrogant and unpleasant, then scolds him for steering Bingley away from Jane and disinheriting Wickham. Darcy leaves her but shortly thereafter delivers a letter to her. In this letter, he admits that he urged Bingley to distance himself from Jane, but claims he did so only because he thought their romance was not serious. As for Wickham, he informs Elizabeth that the young officer is a liar and that the real cause of their disagreement was Wickham's attempt to elope with his young sister, Georgiana Darcy.

This letter causes Elizabeth to reevaluate her feelings about Darcy. She returns home and acts coldly toward Wickham. The militia is leaving town, which makes the younger, rather man-crazy Bennet girls distraught. Lydia manages to obtain permission from her father to spend the summer with an old colonel in Brighton, where Wickham's regiment will be stationed. With the arrival of June, Elizabeth goes on another journey, this time with the Gardiners, who are relatives of the Bennets. The trip takes her to the North and eventually to the neighborhood of Pemberley, Darcy's estate. She visits Pemberley, after making sure that Darcy is away, and delights in the building and grounds, while hearing from Darcy's servants that he is a wonderful, generous master. Suddenly, Darcy arrives and behaves cordially toward her. Making no mention of his proposal, he entertains the Gardiners and invites Elizabeth to meet his sister.

Shortly thereafter, however, a letter arrives from home, telling Elizabeth that Lydia has eloped with Wickham and that the couple is nowhere to be found, which suggests that they may be living together out of wedlock. Fearful of the disgrace such a situation would bring on her entire family, Elizabeth hastens home. Mr. Gardiner and Mr. Bennet go off to search for Lydia, but Mr. Bennet eventually returns home empty-handed. Just when all hope seems lost, a letter comes from Mr. Gardiner saying that the couple has been found and that Wickham has agreed to marry Lydia in exchange for an annual income. The Bennets are convinced that Mr. Gardiner has paid off Wickham, but Elizabeth learns that the source of the money, and of her family's salvation, was none other than Darcy.

Now married, Wickham and Lydia briefly return to Longbourn, where Mr. Bennet treats them coldly. They then depart for Wickham's new assignment in the North of England. Shortly thereafter, Bingley returns to Netherfield and resumes his courtship of Jane. Darcy goes to stay with him and pays visits to the Bennets but makes no mention of his desire to marry Elizabeth. Bingley, on the other hand, presses his suit and proposes to Jane, to the delight of everyone but Bingley's haughty sister. While the family celebrates, Lady Catherine de Bourgh pays a visit to Longbourn. She corners Elizabeth and says that she has heard that Darcy, her nephew, is planning to marry her. Since she considers a Bennet an unsuitable match for a Darcy, Lady Catherine demands that Elizabeth promise to refuse him. Elizabeth spiritedly refuses, saying she is not engaged to Darcy, but she will not promise anything against her own happiness. A little later, Elizabeth and Darcy go out walking together and he tells her that his feelings have not altered since the spring. She tenderly accepts his proposal, and both Jane and Elizabeth are married.

CHARACTER LIST

Elizabeth Bennet The novel's protagonist. The second daughter of Mr. Bennet, Elizabeth is the most intelligent and sensible of the five Bennet sisters. She is well read and quick-witted, with a tongue that occasionally proves too sharp for her own good. Her realization of Darcy's essential goodness eventually triumphs over her initial prejudice against him.

Fitzwilliam Darcy A wealthy gentleman, the master of Pemberley, and the nephew of Lady Catherine de Bourgh. Though Darcy is intelligent and honest, his excess of pride causes him to look down on his social inferiors. Over the course of the novel, he tempers his class-consciousness and learns to admire and love Elizabeth for her strong character.

Jane Bennet The eldest and most beautiful Bennet sister. Jane is more reserved and gentler than Elizabeth. The easy pleasantness with which she and Bingley interact contrasts starkly with the mutual distaste that marks the encounters between Elizabeth and Darcy.

Charles Bingley Darcy's considerably wealthy best friend. Bingley's purchase of Netherfield, an estate near the Bennets, serves as the impetus for the novel. He is a genial, well-intentioned gentleman, whose easygoing nature contrasts with Darcy's initially discourteous demeanor. He is blissfully uncaring about class differences.

P

Mr. Bennet The patriarch of the Bennet family, a gentleman of modest income with five unmarried daughters. Mr. Bennet has a sarcastic, cynical sense of humor that he uses to purposefully irritate his wife. Though he loves his daughters (Elizabeth in particular), he often fails as a parent, preferring to withdraw from the never-ending marriage concerns of the women around him rather than offer help.

Mrs. Bennet Mr. Bennet's wife, a foolish, noisy woman whose only goal in life is to see her daughters married. Because of her low breeding and often unbecoming behavior, Mrs. Bennet often repels the very suitors whom she tries to attract for her daughters.

George Wickham A handsome, fortune-hunting militia officer. Wickham's good looks and charm attract Elizabeth initially, but Darcy's revelation about Wickham's disreputable past clues her in to his true nature and simultaneously draws her closer to Darcy.

Lydia Bennet The youngest Bennet sister, gossipy, immature, and self-involved. Unlike Elizabeth, Lydia flings herself headlong into romance and ends up running off with Wickham.

Mr. Collins A pompous, generally idiotic clergyman who stands to inherit Mr. Bennet's property. Mr. Collins's own social status is nothing to brag about, but he takes great pains to let everyone and anyone know that Lady Catherine de Bourgh serves as his patroness. He is the worst combination of snobbish and obsequious.

Miss Bingley Bingley's snobbish sister. Miss Bingley bears inordinate disdain for Elizabeth's middle-class background. Her vain attempts to garner Darcy's attention cause Darcy to admire Elizabeth's self-possessed character even more.

Lady Catherine de Bourgh A rich, bossy noblewoman, Mr. Collins's patron, and Darcy's aunt. Lady Catherine epitomizes class snobbery, especially in her attempts to order the middle-class Elizabeth away from her well-bred nephew.

Mr. and Mrs. Gardiner Mrs. Bennet's brother and his wife. The Gardiners, caring, nurturing, and full of common sense, often prove to be better parents to the Bennet daughters than Mr. Bennet and his wife.

Charlotte Lucas Elizabeth's dear friend. Pragmatic where Elizabeth is romantic, and also six years older than Elizabeth, Charlotte does not view love as the most vital component of a marriage. She is more interested in having a comfortable home. Thus, when Mr. Collins proposes, she accepts.

Georgiana Darcy Darcy's sister. Georgiana is immensely pretty and just as shy. She has great skill at playing the pianoforte.

Mary Bennet The middle Bennet sister, bookish and pedantic.

Catherine Bennet The fourth Bennet sister. Like Lydia, Catherine is girlishly enthralled with the soldiers.

ANALYSIS OF MAJOR CHARACTERS

ELIZABETH BENNET The second daughter in the Bennet family, and the most intelligent and quick-witted, Elizabeth is the protagonist of *Pride and Prejudice* and one of the most well-known female characters in English literature. Her admirable qualities are numerous—she is lovely, clever, and, in a novel defined by dialogue, she converses as brilliantly as anyone. Her honesty, virtue, and lively wit enable her to rise above the nonsense and bad behavior that pervade her class-bound and often spiteful society. Nevertheless, her sharp tongue and tendency to make hasty judgments often lead her astray; *Pride and Prejudice* is essentially the story of how she (and her true love, Darcy) overcome all obstacles—including their own personal failings—to find romantic happiness. Elizabeth must not only cope with a hopeless mother, a distant father, two badly behaved younger siblings, and several snobbish, antagonizing females, she must also overcome her own mistaken impressions of Darcy, which initially lead her to reject his proposals of marriage. Her charms are sufficient to keep him interested, fortunately, while she navigates familial and social turmoil. As she gradually comes to recognize the nobility of Darcy's character, she realizes the error of her initial prejudice against him.

FITZWILLIAM DARCY The son of a wealthy, well-established family and the master of the great estate of Pemberley, Darcy is Elizabeth's male counterpart. The narrator relates Elizabeth's point of view of events more often than Darcy's, so Elizabeth often seems a more sympathetic figure. The reader eventually realizes, however, that Darcy is her ideal match. Intelligent and forthright, he too has a tendency to judge too hastily and harshly, and his high birth and wealth make him overly proud and overly conscious of his social status. Indeed, his haughtiness makes him initially bungle his courtship. When he proposes to her, for instance, he dwells more on how unsuitable a match she is than on her charms, beauty, or anything else complimentary. Her rejection of his advances builds a kind of humility in him. Darcy demonstrates his continued devotion to Elizabeth, in spite of his distaste for her low connections, when he rescues Lydia and the entire Bennet family from disgrace, and when he goes against the wishes of his haughty aunt, Lady Catherine de Bourgh, by continuing to pursue Elizabeth. Darcy proves himself worthy of Elizabeth, and she ends up repenting her earlier, overly harsh judgment of him.

JANE BENNET AND CHARLES BINGLEY Elizabeth's beautiful elder sister and Darcy's wealthy best friend, Jane and Bingley engage in a courtship that occupies a central place in the novel. They first meet at the ball in Meryton and enjoy an immediate mutual attraction. They are spoken of as a potential couple throughout the book, long before anyone imagines that Darcy and Elizabeth might marry. Despite their centrality to the narrative, they are vague characters, sketched by Austen rather than carefully drawn. Indeed, they are so similar in nature and behavior that they can be described together: both are cheerful, friendly, and good-natured, always ready to think the best of others; they lack entirely the prickly egotism of Elizabeth and Darcy. Jane's gentle spirit serves as a foil for her sister's fiery, contentious nature, while Bingley's eager friendliness contrasts with Darcy's stiff pride. Their principal characteristics are goodwill and compatibility, and the contrast of their romance with that of Darcy and Elizabeth is remarkable. Jane and Bingley exhibit to the reader true love unhampered by either pride or prejudice, though in their simple goodness, they also demonstrate that such a love is mildly dull.

MR. BENNET Mr. Bennet is the patriarch of the Bennet household, driven to exasperation by his ridiculous wife and difficult daughters. He reacts by withdrawing from his family and assuming a detached attitude punctuated by bursts of sarcastic humor. He is closest to Elizabeth because they are the two most intelligent Bennets. Initially, his dry wit and self-possession in the face of his wife's hysteria make him a sympathetic figure, but, though he remains likable throughout, the reader gradually loses respect for him as it becomes clear that the price of his detachment is considerable. Detached from his family, he is a weak father and, at critical moments, fails his family. In particular, his foolish indulgence of Lydia's immature behavior nearly leads to general disgrace when she elopes with Wickham. Further, upon her disappearance, he proves largely ineffective. It is left to Mr. Gardiner and Darcy to track Lydia down and rectify the situation. Ultimately, Mr. Bennet would rather withdraw from the world than cope with it.

MRS. BENNET Mrs. Bennet is a miraculously tiresome character. Noisy and foolish, she is a woman consumed by the desire to see her daughters married and seems to care for nothing else in the world. Ironically, her single-minded pursuit of this goal tends to backfire, as her lack of social graces alienates the very people (Darcy and Bingley) whom she tries desperately to attract. Austen uses her continually to highlight the necessity of marriage for young women. Mrs. Bennet also serves as a middle-class counterpoint to such upper-class snobs as Lady Catherine and Miss Bingley, demonstrating that foolishness can be found at every level of society. In the end, however, Mrs. Bennet proves such an unattractive figure, lacking redeeming characteristics of any kind, that some readers have accused Austen of unfairness in portraying her—as if Austen, like Mr. Bennet, took perverse pleasure in poking fun at a woman already scorned as a result of her ill-breeding.

THEMES, MOTIFS, AND SYMBOLS

THEMES

THE POWER OF LOVE *Pride and Prejudice* contains one of the most cherished love stories in English literature: the courtship between Darcy and Elizabeth. As in any good love story, the lovers must elude and overcome numerous stumbling blocks, beginning with the tensions caused by the lovers' own personal qualities. Elizabeth's pride makes her misjudge Darcy on the basis of a poor first impression, while Darcy's prejudice against Elizabeth's poor social standing blinds him, for a time, to her many virtues. (Of course, one could also say that Elizabeth is guilty of prejudice and Darcy of pride—the title cuts both ways.) Austen, meanwhile, poses countless smaller obstacles to the realization of the love between Elizabeth and Darcy, including Lady Catherine's attempt to control her nephew, Miss Bingley's snobbery, Mrs. Bennet's idiocy, and Wickham's deceit. In each case, anxieties about social connections, or the desire for better social connections, interfere with the workings of love. Darcy and Elizabeth's realization of a mutual and tender love seems to imply that Austen views love as something independent of these social forces, as something that can be captured if only an individual is able to escape the warping effects of hierarchical society. Austen does sound some more realist (or, one could say, cynical) notes about love, using the character of Charlotte Lucas, who marries the buffoon Mr. Collins for his money, to demonstrate that the heart does not always dictate marriage. Yet with her central characters, Austen suggests that true love is a force separate from society and one that can conquer even the most difficult of circumstances.

THE IMPORTANCE OF REPUTATION *Pride and Prejudice* depicts a society in which a woman's reputation is of the utmost importance. A woman is expected to behave in certain ways, and stepping outside the social norms makes her vulnerable to ostracism. This theme appears in the novel when Elizabeth walks to Netherfield and arrives with muddy skirts to the shock of the reputation-conscious Miss Bingley and her friends. At other points, the ill-mannered, ridiculous behavior of Mrs. Bennet gives her a bad reputation with the more refined (and snobbish) Darcys and Bingleys. Austen pokes gentle fun at the snobs in these examples, but later in the novel, when Lydia elopes with Wickham and lives with him out of wedlock, the author treats reputation as a very serious matter. By becoming Wickham's lover without benefit of marriage, Lydia clearly places herself outside the social pale, and her disgrace threatens the entire Bennet family.

The fact that Lydia's judgment, however terrible, would likely have condemned the other Bennet sisters to marriageless lives seems grossly unfair. Why should Elizabeth's reputation suffer along with Lydia's? Darcy's intervention on the Bennets' behalf thus becomes all the more generous, but some readers might resent that such an intervention was necessary at all. If Darcy's money had failed to convince Wickham to marry Lydia, would Darcy have still married Elizabeth? Does his transcendence of prejudice extend that far? The happy ending of *Pride and Prejudice* is certainly emotionally satisfying, but in many ways it leaves the theme of reputation, and the importance placed on reputation, unexplored. One can ask of *Pride and Prejudice*, "To what extent does it critique social structures, and to what extent does it simply accept their inevitability?"

THE BOUNDARIES IMPOSED BY CLASS Both reputation and class reflect the strictly regimented nature of life for the middle and upper classes in Regency England. The lines of class are strictly drawn. While the Bennets, who are middle class, may socialize with the upper-class Bingleys and Darcys, they are clearly their social inferiors and are treated as such. Austen satirizes this kind of class-consciousness, particularly in the character of Mr. Collins, who spends most of his time toadying to his upper-class patron, Lady Catherine de Bourgh. Though Mr. Collins offers an extreme example, he is not the only one to hold such views. His conception of the importance of class is shared, among others, by Mr. Darcy, who believes in the dignity of his lineage; Miss Bingley, who dislikes anyone not as socially accepted as she is; and Wickham, who will do anything he can to get enough money to raise himself into a higher station. Mr. Collins's views are merely the most extreme and obvious. The satire directed at Mr. Collins is therefore also more subtly directed at the entire social hierarchy and the conception of all those within it at its correctness, in complete disregard of other, more worthy virtues.

Through the Darcy-Elizabeth and Bingley-Jane marriages, Austen shows the power of love and happiness to overcome class boundaries and prejudices, thereby implying that such prejudices are hollow, unfeeling, and unproductive. Of course, this whole discussion of class must be made with the understanding that Austen herself is often criticized as being a classist: she doesn't really represent anyone from the lower classes; those servants she does portray are generally happy with their lot. Austen does criticize class structure but only a limited slice of that structure.

MOTIFS

COURTSHIP In a sense, *Pride and Prejudice* is the story of two courtships—between Darcy and Elizabeth and between Bingley and Jane. Within this broad structure appear other, smaller courtships: Mr. Collins's aborted wooing of Elizabeth, followed by his successful wooing of Charlotte Lucas; Miss Bingley's unsuccessful attempt to attract Darcy; Wickham's pursuit first of Elizabeth, then of the never-seen Miss King, and finally of Lydia. Courtship takes on a profound, if often unspoken, importance in the novel. Marriage is the ultimate goal, while courtship constitutes the real working-out of love. Courtship becomes a sort of forge of a person's personality, and each courtship becomes a microcosm for different sorts of love—or different ways to abuse love as a means to social advancement.

JOURNEYS Nearly every scene in *Pride and Prejudice* takes place indoors, and the action centers around the Bennet home in the small village of Longbourn. Nevertheless, journeys—even short ones—function repeatedly as catalysts for change in the novel. Elizabeth's first journey, by which she intends simply to visit Charlotte and Mr. Collins, brings her into contact with Mr. Darcy, and leads to his first proposal. Her second journey takes her to Derby and Pemberley, where she fans the growing flame of her affection for Darcy. The third journey, meanwhile, sends various people in pursuit of Wickham and Lydia, and the journey ends with Darcy tracking them down and saving the Bennet family honor, in the process demonstrating his continued devotion to Elizabeth.

SYMBOLS

PEMBERLEY *Pride and Prejudice* is remarkably free of explicit symbolism, which perhaps has something to do with the novel's reliance on dialogue over description. Nevertheless, Pemberley, Darcy's estate, sits at the center of the novel, literally and figuratively, as a geographic symbol of the man who owns it. Elizabeth visits it at a time when her feelings toward Darcy are beginning to warm; she is enchanted by its beauty and charm, and by the picturesque countryside, just as she will be charmed, increasingly, by the gifts of its owner. Austen makes the connection explicit when she describes the stream that flows beside the mansion. "In front," she writes, "a stream of some natural importance was swelled into greater, but without any artificial appearance." Darcy possesses a "natural importance" that is "swelled" by his arrogance, but which coexists with a genuine honesty and lack of "artificial appearance." Like the stream, he is neither "formal, nor falsely adorned." Pemberley even offers a symbol-within-a-symbol for their budding romance: when Elizabeth encounters Darcy on the estate, she is crossing a small bridge, suggesting the broad gulf of misunderstanding and class prejudice that lies between them—and the bridge that their love will build across it.

IMPORTANT QUOTATIONS EXPLAINED

---

1. *It is a truth universally acknowledged, that a single man in possession of a good fortune, must be in want of a wife.*

This is the first sentence of *Pride and Prejudice* and stands as one of the most famous first lines in literature. Even as it briskly introduces the arrival of Mr. Bingley at Netherfield, the event that sets the novel in motion, this sentence also offers a miniature sketch of the entire plot, which concerns itself with the pursuit of "single men in possession of a good fortune" by various female characters. The preoccupation with socially advantageous marriage in nineteenth-century English society manifests itself here, for in claiming that a single man "must be in want of a wife," the narrator reveals that the reverse is also true: a single woman, whose socially prescribed options are quite limited, is in (perhaps desperate) want of a husband.

---

2. *"Which do you mean?" and turning round, he looked for a moment at Elizabeth, till catching her eye, he withdrew his own and coldly said, "She is tolerable; but not handsome enough to tempt me; and I am in no humour at present to give consequence to young ladies who are slighted by other men. You had better return to your partner and enjoy her smiles, for you are wasting your time with me."*

These words describe Darcy's reaction at the Meryton ball in Chapter 3 to Bingley's suggestion that he dance with Elizabeth. Darcy, who sees the people of Meryton as his social inferiors, haughtily refuses to condescend to dancing with someone "not handsome enough" for him. Moreover, he does so within Elizabeth's hearing, thereby establishing a reputation among the entire community for pride and bad manners. His sense of social superiority, artfully exposed in this passing comment, later proves his chief difficulty in admitting his love for Elizabeth. The rudeness with which Darcy treats Elizabeth creates a negative impression of him in her mind, one that will linger for nearly half of the novel, until the underlying nobility of his character is gradually revealed to her.

---

3. *"In vain have I struggled. It will not do. My feelings will not be repressed. You must allow me to tell you how ardently I admire and love you." Elizabeth's astonishment was beyond expression. . . . He spoke well, but there were feelings besides those of the heart to be detailed, and he was not more eloquent on the subject of tenderness than of pride. His sense of her inferiority—of its being a degradation—of the family obstacles which judgment had always opposed to inclination, were dwelt on with a warmth which seemed due to the consequence he was wounding, but was very unlikely to recommend his suit.*

Darcy's proposal of marriage to Elizabeth in Chapter 34 demonstrates how his feelings toward her transformed since his earlier dismissal of her as "not handsome enough." While Elizabeth rejects his proposal, this event marks the turning point in the novel. Before Darcy asks Elizabeth to marry him, she feels only contempt for him; afterward, she begins to see him in a new light, as certain incidents help illustrate the essential goodness of his character. At this moment, however, Elizabeth's eventual change of heart remains unforeseen—all she thinks of is Darcy's arrogance, his attempts to interfere in Bingley's courtship of Jane, and his alleged mistreatment of Wickham. Her judgment of Darcy stems from her initial prejudice against his snobbishness, just as his pride about his high social status hampers his attempt to express his affection. As the above quote makes clear, he spends more time emphasizing her lower rank and unsuitability for marriage to him than he does complimenting her or pledging his love. "He was not more eloquent on the subject of tenderness than of pride," the narrator states; Darcy must prioritize love over his sense of superiority before he is worthy of Elizabeth's hand.

4. *It was a large, handsome, stone building, standing well on rising ground, and backed by a ridge of high woody hills;—and in front, a stream of some natural importance was swelled into greater, but without any artificial appearance. Its banks were neither formal, nor falsely adorned. Elizabeth was delighted. She had never seen a place where nature had done more, or where natural beauty had been so little counteracted by an awkward taste. They were all of them warm in her admiration; and at that moment she felt that to be mistress of Pemberley might be something!*

These lines open Chapter 43 and provide Elizabeth's introduction to Darcy's grand estate at Pemberley. Her visit to Darcy's home, which occupies a central place in the narrative, operates as a catalyst for her growing attraction toward its owner. In her conversations with the housekeeper, Mrs. Reynolds, Elizabeth hears testimonials of Darcy's wonderful generosity and his kindness as a master; when she encounters Darcy himself, while walking through Pemberley's grounds, he seems altogether changed and his previous arrogance has diminished remarkably. This initial description of the building and grounds at Pemberley serves as a symbol of Darcy's character. The "stream of some natural importance . . . swelled into greater" reminds the reader of his pride, but the fact that it lacks "any artificial appearance" indicates his basic honesty, as does the fact that the stream is neither "formal, nor falsely adorned." Elizabeth's delight, and her sudden epiphany about the pleasure that being mistress of Pemberley must hold, prefigure her later joy in Darcy's continued devotion.

5. *Elizabeth was much too embarrassed to say a word. . . . Elizabeth feeling all the more than common awkwardness and anxiety of his situation, now forced herself to speak; and immediately, though not very fluently, gave him to understand, that her sentiments had undergone so material a change, since the period to which he alluded, as to make her receive with gratitude and pleasure, his present assurances.*

This proposal and Elizabeth's acceptance mark the climax of the novel in Chapter 58. Austen famously prefers not to stage successful proposals in full, and the reader may be disappointed in the anticlimactic manner in which the narrator relates Elizabeth's acceptance. It is important to remember, however, that the proposal and acceptance are almost a foregone conclusion by this point. Darcy's intervention on behalf of Lydia makes obvious his continuing devotion to Elizabeth, and the shocking appearance of Lady Catherine de Bourgh in the previous chapter, with her haughty attempts to forestall the engagement, serves to suggest strongly that a second proposal from Darcy is imminent.

The clunky language with which the narrator summarizes Elizabeth's acceptance serves a specific purpose, as it captures the one moment of joyful incoherence for this supremely well-spoken character. She accepts Darcy's proposal "immediately," the narrator relates, but "not very fluently." As Elizabeth allows herself to admit that her love has supplanted her long-standing prejudice, her control of language breaks down. The reader is left to imagine, with some delight, the ever-clever Elizabeth fumbling for words to express her irrepressible happiness.

How do attitudes about social/economic class and marriage play out in *Pride and Prejudice*?

Jane Austen's most famous novel, *Pride and Prejudice*, tells the story of the Bennet sisters as they try to find husbands among the gentlemen of their rural English town. Class and economic status figure heavily in each potential relationship, and every character seems to have a different opinion on what is "right" when it comes to marriage. Austen makes clear her views on the importance of love in marriage through the ways in which she portrays various groups of characters.

One group of characters is extremely concerned with social class and wealth and believes the economic and class ties created by marriage to be more important than love or romance. These characters are caricatures—their strongest features are overexaggerated to absurdity, totally dominating their personality. The most obvious example is Mr. Darcy's aunt, Lady Catherine de Bourgh, a hard-hearted, overbearing, snobby noblewoman who does her best to prevent Darcy from marrying Elizabeth. She believes Elizabeth to be beneath her well-bred nephew and is only seen working to end their courtship. Although a very different personality, Elizabeth's close friend Charlotte Lucas also fits into this first group. While Elizabeth is romantic and outgoing, Charlotte is pragmatic and simple, almost overwhelmingly so. Her marriage to Mr. Collins is financially advantageous—and not out of her social class—and therefore she accepts him, despite not loving him. For these characters, the social and economic implications of a marriage far outweigh the relationship or emotions involved, and therefore they are characterized in an extreme and unrealistic form.

At the other end of the spectrum are the eldest Bennet sister, Jane, and her eventual fiancé, Charles Bingley. Bingley is considerably wealthy, and his purchase of a nearby estate opens the novel, while the Bennets live on a moderate, middle-class income. Jane Bennet and Mr. Bingley are totally unconcerned about social status, class, and economic motivations in getting married. They are portrayed as kind, calm, compatible, and even a bit boring. Bingley and Jane are so pleasantly perfect that they seem paler and less real than other characters. Austen merely sketches them, indicating the incompleteness of their characters, their thoughts, and their love.

Elizabeth Bennet and Fitzwilliam Darcy fall somewhere between these two groups. Initially spouting much of the same rhetoric as his aunt, Darcy must overcome his pride and class assumptions in facing his love for Elizabeth. Elizabeth, meanwhile, makes many similar assumptions, basing her initial impression of Darcy on prejudice and false rumor. Her feelings for Darcy force her to reexamine her attitudes and change the way she thinks about him and about marriage. Their relationship is a fiery, passionate, and tested love between two strong-willed individuals. It is also a marriage across economic and social class lines in which romance is the driving force. Both Elizabeth and Darcy are complex characters, sharing the narrative role and developing nuanced opinions on how marriage, love, and class should be mixed. These characters are brilliantly created, their experiences provoking real empathy in the reader.

The depth and detail in character development reflects the personal growth of the various characters, as well as the diverse attitudes regarding marriage and social class. In this way, Austen illustrates the difficulty surrounding marriage for women in the early 1800s and makes a case for romantic love as the most important ingredient in a marriage.

The Red Tent

Anita Diamant
(1951–)

CONTEXT

Anita Diamant, the daughter of two Holocaust survivors, was born on June 27, 1951, in New York City. She spent much of her early childhood in Newark, New Jersey, before moving to Denver, Colorado, at age twelve. She attended the University of Colorado for two years, then transferred to Washington University in St. Louis, Missouri, where she received a bachelor's degree in comparative literature in 1973. She went on to earn a master's degree in English from the State University of New York at Binghamton in 1975. She settled just outside of Boston, where she lives with her husband and teenage daughter, Emilia.

Diamant began her career as a freelance journalist in the Boston area in 1975. Over the years, she has written for local, regional, and national magazines and newspapers, including the *Boston Phoenix*, the *Boston Globe*, and *Boston Magazine*, as well as *New England Monthly*, *Yankee*, *Self*, *Parenting*, *Parents*, *McCalls*, and *Ms*. In 1985, she began writing about contemporary Jewish practice and the Jewish community, publishing articles in *Reform Judaism* magazine, in *Hadassah* magazine, and on the webzine www.jewishfamily.com. She has also written seven handbooks on contemporary Jewish life and lifecycle events.

In *The Red Tent* (1997), her first novel, Diamant transforms the brief but violent story found in Genesis 34 about Dinah, the only daughter of Jacob, into a full-length work. In an article from *Reform Judaism Magazine*, Diamant says "I did not set out to explain or rewrite the biblical text, but to use Dinah's silence to try to imagine what life was like for women in this historical period." One does not need to be familiar with the book of Genesis to appreciate *The Red Tent*; Diamant carefully carries readers who are not familiar with the backbone of the story. In fact, those who are familiar with the story are often surprised by Diamant's version: the author changes substantial portions of the Bible's narrative, which focuses primarily on men and their relationships with God, in order to make her novel a story of women and their relationships with one another.

The Red Tent has been quite controversial, because its narrative adapts the biblical story of Jacob's family. Some critics, mainly devout Jewish and Christian scholars, believe Diamant essentially blasphemes against the Bible in her version of Dinah's life, changing basic elements of the stories of Jacob and his wives and presenting Leah and Rachel as polytheistic—a representation that directly contradicts the Judeo-Christian belief that Leah and Rachel were the matriarchal founders of the Jewish people and pioneers of monotheism.

Less devoutly religious readers have sometimes categorized *The Red Tent* as a *midrash*, or a story that attempts to fill in gaps in the Bible. The term *midrash* is based on the Jewish word for "interpretation" or "exegesis." Classical *midrashim* (plural) are interpretive teachings, often used by ancient rabbis to more clearly illustrate the meanings behind the Bible's text. Modern *midrashim* attempt to make stories from the Bible more applicable to readers today. Biblical stories about women tend to be abbreviated and seemingly less important, and many contemporary female writers have turned to the art of *midrash*-making to cast new light on such figures as Lilith (Adam's first wife, who was created as his equal), Serah bat Asher (a descendant of Jacob who leads Moses to Joseph's coffin prior to the Exodus), and Miriam (a prophetess). According to Professor Howard Schwartz of the University of Missouri—quoted in the Bonny Fetterman article—this act of *midrash*-making is "a continuing process of the reintegration of the past into the present. Each time this takes place, the tradition is transformed and must be re-imagined. And it is this very process that keeps the tradition vital and perpetuates it."

The Red Tent goes beyond the traditional function of *midrashim*, because Diamant's novel fills in the gaps of the Genesis story and removes the story from its religious context entirely. In Genesis, the stories of Jacob and his offspring are part of an evolving relationship between God and the descendants of Abraham, and Diamant's narrative simply does not fit into this sequence of events. Diamant herself has stated emphatically that her novel is not a *midrash*, but simply a novel based on a biblical character. In a biography provided by Simon & Schuster, Diamant says: "*The Red Tent* is not a translation but a work of fiction. Its perspective and focus—by and about the female characters—distinguishes it from the biblical account, in which women are usually peripheral and often totally silent. By giving Dinah a voice and by providing texture and content to the sketchy biblical descriptions, my book is a radical departure from the historical text." Thus she acknowledges how her fictional text differs from the biblical text, and, as a fiction author, she does not expect her readers to accept her version of Dinah's life as the "true" version. Her intent in writing *The Red Tent* was to provide Dinah with an opportunity to speak, an opportunity not found in the Bible. Diamant seems interested in Dinah solely as a human character—not as a part of the Bible in need of exegesis or explanation.

Regardless of its label, the novel's success is impressive. *The Red Tent* was first printed in 1997 with no advertising budget. It received few reviews in major newspapers or magazines and instead found its success through word of mouth, the loyalty of its readers, the support of independent bookstores, and help from clergy, some of whom even preached about *The Red Tent* from the pulpit. The novel went on to become a *New York Times* best-seller and Booksense Book of the Year 2001. Since its publication, Diamant has written another novel, *Good Harbor* (2001).

PLOT OVERVIEW

Dinah, the narrator, opens *The Red Tent* by introducing herself and explaining that she is reciting the memories of her life and her mothers' lives—because without a daughter to tell the story, a woman's history does not live on. Dinah focuses initially on the stories of her mothers, the four wives of Jacob—Leah, Rachel, Zilpah, and Bilhah—and how they come to be married to the same man. Jacob is threatened with death by his twin brother, Esau, in their home of Canaan and goes to Haran to seek out his uncle Laban and marry one of his daughters. He meets Rachel and immediately loves her, for she is uncommonly beautiful. Leah, who is older, begins to love him. On Rachel and Jacob's wedding day, Zilpah convinces Rachel (who is afraid of the wedding night) to let Leah wear the bridal veil and marry Jacob. She does, and Leah and Jacob spend a blissful honeymoon week together. Then Rachel realizes she has been tricked and marries Jacob herself several months later. By then, Leah is pregnant. Laban offers his two illegitimate daughters, Zilpah and Bilhah, as part of his other daughters' dowries to serve as Jacob's concubines. One by one, they all bear sons—Leah bears six sons, and Zilpah and Bilhah bear two each—except Rachel, who miscarries for years and eventually becomes a midwife. At last, Leah bears the only daughter, Dinah. Shortly thereafter, Rachel gives birth to two healthy sons, Benjamin and Joseph.

Dinah recounts her childhood growing up as the only girl among eleven brothers. She spends most of her time at her mothers' knees, following them as they cook and run the family's camp. While Dinah plays most often with Joseph, she is adored by her mothers and can frequently be found in one of their tents having her hair braided. Because of her special status as the only female child, she is allowed to enter the red tent each month with her mothers as they begin their menstrual cycles and celebrate the new moon. There Dinah learns to sing the songs of women, eats their special foods, and hears the stories of her grandmother and the goddesses of her people. She is content to be wherever her mothers are.

After many years on Laban's lands, Jacob decides to return with his family to the land of his own people. They pack up their entire camp, and Jacob bargains with Laban for the flocks and possessions he sees as rightfully his, having been overseer of Laban's flocks for many years. Rachel steals Laban's household gods (which are icons or figurines), as they are hers by birthright (since she is the being youngest daughter). They set off for Canaan, and Dinah is awestruck by the excitement of travel: she sees slaves, jugglers, and strange animals. When they finally meet her uncle Esau and his family, the reunion is a happy one. Dinah meets her cousin Tabea, who is the first girl friend she makes of her own age. Esau offers to share his lands with Jacob, but he refuses, and the family moves on to find space enough to support Jacob's many sons. They make camp at last, and some of his sons take wives.

Several years later, Jacob moves the family again, to just outside the city of Shechem. Dinah gets her first period and is received with ceremony inside the red tent by her mothers. She begins traveling with Rachel as a midwife's apprentice and one day is called into Shechem to deliver the son of the king's concubine. There, she meets Shalem, the prince, and falls instantly in love. The queen takes a liking to Dinah and requests her presence again several weeks later, scheming to get her together with the prince. They end up in bed together, and Shalem calls her his wife. The king goes to Jacob to offer a handsome bride-price but is refused. Jacob's sons request that the entire city of Shechem be circumcised. The king agrees, and circumcisions are performed on all the men of Shechem. Several days later, two of Dinah's brothers, Simon and Levi, slaughter all of these men in their sleep and carry Dinah back home. Dinah curses her father and brothers and leaves Jacob's camp for the last time. She then flees to Egypt with her mother-in-law, Re-nefer.

In Egypt, Dinah gives birth to a son, Re-mose, who, against Dinah's will, is brought up as Re-nefer's son. Dinah lives in the gardens of Re-nefer's brother's home for many years, watching her son grow up and leave for school. She becomes good friends with the midwife Meryt and begins to practice midwifery again. One day at the market, she meets Benia, a master carpenter, and feels an instant attraction to him. Several months later, she and Meryt move to the Valley of the Kings to live with Meryt's son, and she is reunited with Benia. They marry, and Dinah becomes a renowned midwife in the town. Years later, she is called by a messenger (her son, Re-mose, who has become a scribe) to deliver the son of his master, the vizier, who turns out to be her brother Joseph. The brother and sister are reunited, but when Re-mose learns the story of his father's murder, he tries to kill his uncle, Joseph. Dinah convinces him to go away for his own safety and never sees him again.

One day, Joseph calls on Dinah and asks her to accompany him to bid their dying father farewell. She and Benia go, and she learns that her father no longer remembers her. She does not see him. She talks to one of her nieces and learns that the story of her tragedy and her name is very much alive in the family history, and she is satisfied. Then her brother Judah speaks to her and gives her a token left to her by Leah: Rachel's ring. She returns home, having accepted her past and feeling satisfied with her present. She spends the rest of her days happy in the company of Benia and Meryt. She dreams of her mothers and finds peace in the dream. She dies content.

CHARACTER LIST

Dinah The only surviving daughter of Jacob, and the protagonist of the novel. As the only daughter among twelve sons born to four mothers, Dinah grows up pampered and adored by her mothers. She spends her childhood in the women's tents, learning their private stories and rituals. Dinah is a thoughtful and intelligent girl, fascinated by the workings of her polygamous family. She vigilantly observes the relationships between each of her mothers and her father, as well as between the women themselves. She is largely disinterested in the ways of men in the fields and prefers the day-to-day activities of women in the family's camp. She also prefers the women's stories and songs to those of the men. She embraces the skill of midwifery, which she learns from her aunt Rachel, and uses it to continue to forge relationships with women throughout her life.

R

Jacob Son of Isaac and Rebecca. Though Jacob is the younger of two twins (his brother is Esau), he and his mother trick Isaac into giving him the blessing that is Esau's birthright. Jacob is a tall, charismatic, good-looking man. Because of his charm and kindness, all the sisters fall in love with him, except for Zilpah. He is a skilled herdsman and, under his care, Laban's flock grows and brings wealth to his family. He spreads the practice of circumcision, one of the tenets of Judaism, from Haran to Canaan to Shechem, converting followers to his father's religion. His obsession with growing his flock and his family's power indirectly leads to the slaughter of men at Shechem and the death of Dinah's husband.

Leah Eldest of the four daughters of Laban, and the first wife of Jacob. Leah is a strong, capable woman, extremely skilled in brewing and baking, as well as with the herds. She is the head of the women of her family, minding the children and the family's camp at the same time. She is often consulted by Jacob in regard to family affairs and is ultimately the one who saves Ruti, Laban's ill-treated wife, from being sold as a slave. Leah is the most fertile of the sisters, bearing seven sons and the only daughter, Dinah. While Leah's mismatched eyes—one blue and one green—are off-putting to some, Dinah finds them beautiful.

Rachel The most beautiful of Laban's daughters, and the second wife of Jacob. Rachel is the second youngest of the four sisters and the most beautiful woman in the region. Early in the novel, Rachel is petty and petulant, sniping at her sisters and keeping mostly to herself. As Leah steadily bears healthy sons and Rachel suffers miscarriage after miscarriage, her jealousy pushes them even further apart. She begins to apprentice as a midwife with Inna, proving that she too can bring life into the world. She finally gives birth to Joseph. Rachel's tent is often a retreat for Dinah as she grows up, and Rachel eventually teaches her the skill of midwifery. Rachel dies giving birth to her second son, Benjamin.

Bilhah The youngest of Laban's daughters, and the third wife of Jacob. The illegitimate daughter of Laban and a field hand, Bilhah grows up in the shadows of her more outgoing sisters. Dark, quiet, and introspective, Bilhah sees everything that happens but takes part in very little. She is considered the kindest and most nurturing of the sisters, and she teaches Dinah the art of spinning and tells her stories of the goddess Uttu. Although she is a dutiful and loving wife to Jacob, her true love is his son Reuben, and their union results in their disgrace. She bears one son, Dan.

Zilpah Second daughter of Laban, and the fourth and least important wife of Jacob. Zilpah is the most spiritual of the sisters and is happiest among the company of her goddesses. She dislikes and distrusts men, preferring to keep to herself. Leah is her favorite sister, and Zilpah arranges for Leah to marry Jacob first, out of spite for Rachel. She instills a love of storytelling in Dinah and bears twin sons, Gad and Asher.

Werenro Messenger and slave of Rebecca. Werenro invites Jacob's family to Rebecca's for the barley festival, and during their meeting, Dinah becomes entranced with her red hair and strange costume. Werenro is brutally attacked and raped while traveling one day and is nearly killed. She manages to live and ekes out a pitiful existence as a traveling singer. She and Dinah are reunited later in the novel when Dinah recognizes her song in Egypt. Werenro is the first person to whom Dinah relates her tragedy.

Meryt The Egyptian midwife who delivers Dinah's son. Meryt is a kind woman, twenty years older than Dinah, who becomes Dinah's closest friend and confidante in Egypt. Meryt is barren but has two adopted sons. As lonely years pass for Dinah after her son has gone off to school, it is Meryt who convinces her to renew her practice as a midwife. Their partnership results in Dinah's introduction to Benia and her reunion with her brother Joseph.

Benia Dinah's second husband. Benia is a master craftsman and carpenter in Egypt and a good and honest man. Dinah and Benia meet by chance in a market and feel an immediate connection to each other. Benia eventually seeks Dinah out when they've both moved to another town and asks her to marry him. His love gives Dinah the strength to count her blessings, forgive her family, and move on.

Re-nefer Wife of Hamor and Shalem's mother. Re-nefer is a doting mother and connives to bring Dinah and Shalem together. After Shalem is murdered, she smuggles Dinah out of Shechem to her brother's house in Egypt, where she then raises Dinah's son, Re-mose, as her own, and employs Dinah as his wet nurse.

Joseph Rachel's first son and the recipient of Jacob's blessing. Joseph and Dinah are nursed together, and, as the closest to each other in age, they spend much of their childhoods at each other's side. Joseph eventually outgrows Dinah's company and spends his time with his brothers in the field. He is good-looking and charismatic like his father. After he is sold into slavery by Simon and Levi, his cleverness and dream-interpreting abilities help him rise to the position of vizier in Egypt.

Inna Accomplished midwife and healer. Inna is present to deliver many of Jacob's children, and it is she who trains Rachel to be a midwife. They become lifelong friends, and Inna leaves Haran with Jacob's family. When Rachel dies, Inna stays at her grave and mourns her.

Tabea Dinah's cousin by Esau's wife Basemath. Tabea is Dinah's first girl friend of her own age. Tabea is callously banished by their grandmother Rebecca for not being initiated into womanhood properly and serves as an example of both Rebecca's cruelty and the importance within Dinah's family of respecting the rituals of women.

Shalem Dinah's first love and first husband, the prince of Shechem. Shalem's beauty and kindness instantly endear him to Dinah, and they quickly consummate their love. His passion for Dinah leads him to agree to Jacob's absurd bride-price, as well as the agreement to have himself and every man in Shechem circumcised.

Re-mose/Bar-Shalem Dinah's only child. Re-mose is born of Shalem and Dinah but raised in Egypt with Re-nefer and Nakht-re as his Egyptian parents and Dinah as his nurse. Re-mose is a strong and determined young man, and he unknowingly becomes the scribe for his uncle Joseph, the vizier.

Laban Cruel and selfish father of Leah, Rachel, Zilpah, Bilhah, Kemuel, and Beor. Laban is a worthless cheat who mistreats his wife and daughters and tries to bamboozle Jacob of his due as overseer of his lands. He eventually backs down in fear of Jacob's god.

Esau Jacob's twin brother and the other son of Isaac. Esau is a good son to Rebecca and Isaac and a kind and forgiving brother to Jacob. Their reconciliation brings Jacob's family to Canaan.

Rebecca Jacob's mother. Rebecca is the Oracle of Mamre: she can see the future and has healing powers. She is the matriarch of the family and schemes to give Isaac's blessing to Jacob, her favorite son. She appears cruel and heartless to Dinah, who spends three months waiting on her after Tabea is banished. She predicts unhappiness in Dinah's life.

Isaac Son of Abraham, father of Jacob and Esau. Abraham was told by God to sacrifice Isaac, his only son. Just before Abraham does so, God stops him and lets Isaac live because of Abraham's show of faith.

Reuben Eldest of Jacob's sons by Leah. Reuben is known for his kindness and good counsel and is among Dinah's favorite brothers. He eventually develops a deep love for his aunt, Bilhah, and their affair results in his banishment.

Simon and Levi Sons of Jacob by Leah. The cruelest of all of Jacob's children, Simon and Levi become his closest counselors in Canaan and Succoth. Concerned that their own legacies and power might diminish, they reject Dinah's marriage to Shalem and slaughter all of the men of Shechem in their sleep.

Judah Handsomest of Jacob's sons by Leah. Judah is beloved by Dinah and marries Shua. He eventually becomes the head of the clan when Reuben, Simon, and Levi die. He is the one who gives Dinah her mother's ring—and some closure—at the end of the novel.

Zebulun Fifth son of Jacob by Leah.

Naphtali and Issachar Twin sons of Jacob. Diamant describes them as twins born to Leah, even though Naphtali was born to Bilhah in the Bible.

Gad and Asher Twin sons of Jacob by Zilpah.

Benjamin The youngest of all of Jacob's sons. Benjamin's birth kills his mother, Rachel. At the end of the novel, Benjamin's daughter tells Dinah that her name and her story are remembered.

Dan Only son of Jacob and Bilhah. Dan is kind and true like his mother, and he is one of Dinah's favorite brothers.

Nakht-re Brother of Re-nefer and esteemed scribe in Egypt. Nakht-re acts as Re-mose's father and provides Dinah with a home for many years.

Ruti Laban's mistreated young wife, who produces his two male heirs. Ruti is treated pitifully, as little more than a slave, and her sons do not respect her any more than Laban does. Ruti's character is not found in the Bible—she is purely Diamant's invention.

Kiya One of Meryt's granddaughters. Dinah becomes close to Kiya when she moves to the Valley of the Kings and marries Benia. Her own son is far away and Kiya takes on the role of surrogate daughter. Kiya eventually learns the skill of midwifery from Dinah and remains close to her the rest of her life.

ANALYSIS OF MAJOR CHARACTERS

DINAH Dinah is the first daughter born to a polygamous family that includes four mothers and eleven sons. As the long-awaited daughter, she is spoiled, adored, and given special treatment and attention from her multiple mothers. She enjoys her special status and occasionally uses the jealousy between Leah and Rachel to her advantage: for example, she sleeps in Rachel's tent when Leah is short with her. Intelligent and lively, Dinah makes up games to play with her many brothers. Although most of her brothers are older, she often assumes the role of boss and chief storyteller. When the boys grow older and move out to the fields with their father, Dinah contentedly spends the majority of her time in the tents with the women, as she is a keen and diligent observer who takes pleasure in noting their family dynamics. As a narrator, she is careful to detail even the subtlest actions of her family members but rarely takes such care in describing herself. For the majority of Dinah's life, she describes herself as a passive observer, taking little responsibility for the events in her life. When Re-nefer takes Dinah's son as her own, Dinah is practically unresponsive, grieving quietly but not defending herself. This passiveness is a curious aspect of Dinah's personality, as her mother Leah had been a role model of the strong-minded and assertive woman.

Over the course of the novel, Dinah grows from being a lively but passive girl attached to her mothers to one who an independent, active agent in her own life. Although Dinah endures unspeakable grief and loss, she rebuilds herself—eventually finding a new home, a new husband, and a new family that fulfill her desire for a productive and peaceful life.

LEAH Leah is a determined, decisive, and capable woman. She marries Jacob, despite his love for her sister, and revels in the joy he finds in her arms. She's taller than most men and more talented than most women: she brews excellent beer and effortlessly produces fine spinning. While Leah is probably the least self-centered character in the novel, she is self-conscious about her mismatched eyes. She takes care to hide them as much as possible and rewards those who can look into them.

As a mother, Leah is formidable. Bearing eight healthy children and breastfeeding many of her nephews barely distracts her from her daily duties as the head of Jacob's household. She is surprisingly sexual, craving Jacob's body and enjoying the pleasures they find in each other. Leah proves herself to be a skilled herdsman, noting the mating patterns of their flocks and helping her husband to grow their meager beginnings into more prosperous holdings. She even proves herself to be cunning at times, cleverly outwitting her father by stitching herbs and spices into the women's clothes in order to smuggle them. Yet even with all of her talents and triumphs as a mother, Leah is a somewhat tragic figure. Her sister Rachel remains the true love of Jacob's life, and she loses her only daughter, Dinah, through circumstances beyond her control. She dies pining for the love and comfort of her only daughter.

RACHEL Among her sisters, Rachel stands out initially for her beauty, her magnetism, and her magical water smell. Their father, Laban, treats her most gently; as a result, she ends up somewhat spoiled and conniving. She is fully aware of the power her beauty has over others and is quite willing to use it. She insists on having Jacob when she meets him, though she is not yet marriageable and would embarrass her two older sisters by marrying first. Then she shows herself to be deceptive as well, agreeing to let Leah replace her under the bridal veil. Rachel's jealous nature flourishes when Leah conceives and bears several healthy sons in a row and Rachel remains barren. Rachel is not satisfied with being Jacob's favorite wife—she needs more. She compensates for Leah's fertility by seeking out the calling of midwife and finds that she is extremely talented. Her new skills help heal her relationship with her sister, though Rachel is not satisfied until she bears her own son.

Rachel changes significantly with the birth of her son and her growing success as a midwife. She finds a softer, more maternal side to her personality and begins to cultivate a more peaceful relationship with her sister. She takes delight in her niece, and, through Dinah, her relationship with Leah improves further. She acts as a midwife mentor to Dinah. Although Rachel improves significantly with age and is a talented midwife and healer, she remains primarily a jealous and unhappy woman.

JACOB At the start of the novel, Jacob is a confident and charismatic man, favored by his god. He is a good husband and a kind and gentle lover to each of his wives, giving and taking satisfaction in equal measure. He meticulously ministers his attentions to each of his wives, wanting to keep peace in his household and to do what is best for his family. He works diligently as a herdsman to grow Laban's flocks and honor his bargain of bride-prices for Leah and Rachel, while also increasing the prosperity and prospects of his family. As a father, he is attentive to his sons and brings them to the fields with him, teaching them the ways of good pasturage as well as the religion of his father's people. He is entirely devoted to his god and liberal with his sacrifices. When he leaves Laban's lands to return to his own people, his is fairer and more generous in his settlement with Laban than might be expected by a son-in-law who has been treated as poorly as he was.

As Jacob grows older and his properties multiply, he changes. He becomes less of the fair and honest man he was in his youth and relies more on the poor counsel of his sons Simon and Levi than the just counsel of his wife Leah and son Reuben. He grows greedy, seeking to move continuously to new lands to increase their property. Never attentive to Dinah as a child, he is callous and unfeeling when he hears the news of her union to Shalem. He allows his sons' suggestion of a hideous bride-price to be exacted and, in doing so, orchestrates his downfall. Full of regrets, Jacob dies cursing several of his sons.

THEMES, MOTIFS, AND SYMBOLS

THEMES

THE BURDEN OF MEMORY Dinah is consumed by the weight of her memories—the memories of her mothers, her childhood, and the loss of her husband—which renders her unable to move on with her life. What compels Dinah to narrate her story is the fear that her memories will not live on, that people will not remember her and that her tragedy will mean nothing. She would seem to have good cause to worry: her story is practically a footnote in the Bible, while the stories of Rebecca, Leah, and Rachel live on, although the Bible does not represent these women as Dinah knew them. She holds on so tightly throughout the novel to her memories that when faced with a fresh start and a new life, she is barely able to experience it, as she is still living in her past. As the narrator, she relays her ancient story to a modern reader, giving us her version of the past in order to release herself from the burden of her memories. According to Dinah, and contrary to the Bible, her mother Leah *was* beautiful, Jacob *did* love Leah, and, mostly important, Dinah's marriage to Shalem was truly a union of love, not a rape.

CHILDBIRTH AS A DEFINING EXPERIENCE With four central characters acting as midwives—Inna, Rachel, Dinah, and Meryt—childbearing is highlighted throughout the novel as a woman's unavoidable battle with life and death. *The Red Tent* vividly describes the frightening and painful conditions of childbirth in ancient times. Many of Dinah's would-be sisters and brothers die, and as a midwife she loses many children and their mothers. By narrating graphic scenes of women in labor, being clutched at by their sisters as they tear and bleed in the process of giving birth, Diamant portrays a world where women must fear for their lives at every moment during delivery. Dinah might have lost her own life in childbirth had she not the experience and presence of mind to ask for a knife and mirror. During many of the births described, either the baby or the mother almost dies at least once. The assistance of a midwife was a luxury to women, and even this assistance offered no assurance that woman or child would live out the day. Dinah's narrative as a midwife offers a startling portrayal of the real and bloody experience of childbirth in ancient times.

R

THE POWER OF THE MOON AND OF NATURE In *The Red Tent*, the moon provides more than just a way of marking months and seasons to Dinah's family: it also denotes the harmony between the women themselves and the women with the Earth. Diamant's descriptions of the monthly celebrations in the red tent illustrate the close relationship with land and nature cultivated by seminomadic women in ancient times. The women in Dinah's family menstruate at the same time, attributing their cycles to that of the moon, and thus allowing them to celebrate the lunar cycle together each month. Their dependence on the land for food, exposure to the elements, and close observations of the cycles of the sun and moon to mark time forged strong bonds between people and nature—bonds much stronger than those generally possessed by people today. The women's worship of the moon's power also signified the renewal of their bodies and the gifts of health and fertility they received from the goddess Innana.

MOTIFS

HEALING AND RENEWAL Allusions and images of healing and renewal occur throughout the novel. These images refer to the women's monthly rebirth in the red tent, to the ongoing struggles of childbirth, and to Dinah's luxuriating in the smell and feel of the river. This motif is most visible in Dinah's coming to terms with her own history in Part Three. She bottles up her story for years, unaware that healing can only begin when she faces her tragedy head on. When she first tells her story to Werenro, she stops focusing on her painful past and focuses for a moment instead on the present. The release she feels is tremendous, and as time passes she tells her story again and again—to Re-mose, Meryt, and Benia. Each time she feels a bit stronger, a bit freer, and in the final telling she does not cry. Although it takes her nearly twenty years, she slowly undergoes a process of healing and renewal, gaining the ability to talk about and accept her past, and at last finds peace.

MOTHERS Mothers play the roles of teacher, caregiver, protector, and best friend in *The Red Tent*. The men in the novel have little impact on the lives of the women, other than to father children, and the comfort of mothers is paramount in Dinah's life. She begins telling her own story by first telling the story of each of her mothers, explaining that without them she would have no story of her own. With no school to go to and no friends her age in the family camp, Dinah grows up in the small society of her mothers, learning their songs and their stories as her daily lessons in life. They carry Dinah through her pampered childhood, offering her every attention and protection. Her shocking entrance into adulthood—the murder of her husband—forces her, for the first time in her life, to find her way alone, without the comfort of female arms around her. She stumbles for years, lost, until she finds a new mother to guide her: Meryt. It is Meryt who resuscitates Dinah, working alongside her as a midwife. After many years, Dinah then passes the torch to Kiya, at last assuming her role as mother and teacher.

DREAMS Dreams are a powerful source of prophecy, premonition, and faith in the novel. Each of the main characters attaches great importance to his or her dreams—from Jacob wrestling with an angle of God to Zilpah's dream of giving birth to a fully grown daughter. Dinah finds both comfort and spiritual direction in her dreams. Even though she has not seen her mothers in many years, when Meryt dies, she dreams of each of them, and through her dreams alone they exchange forgiveness and goodbyes. She also dreams of the river goddess Taweret on the night her womb is opened but, despite feeling a deep connection to the water and despite her faith in her vision, never fulfills the prophecy of living by a river. By virtue of his similar power to interpret dreams, Joseph rises from a slave to the position of a great man. Dreams represent a personal spirituality and sense of power for the characters, in that they can foretell the future or determine the will of fate through them, rather than relying on the gods alone.

SYMBOLS

TERAPHIM The goddesses of Dinah's mothers are represented by the teraphim and symbolize the difference between the religion practiced by Jacob's wives and the religion practiced by Jacob. Jacob has received the word of the One God from his father and grandfather, and his religion recognizes only the one deity, with animal sacrifices and practices, such as the circumcision of baby boys. This new religion does not fit the lives of his wives, who have practiced their rituals for their goddesses under the moon for many years. They fulfill their religious duties to his god to his face, but under the cover of the red tent they consider holy only their teraphim and secret rites. They take care not to offend Jacob with their practice, keeping it out of sight, knowing that he cannot condone such practices by his wives. When he learns of Dinah's initiation into womanhood, he smashes the teraphim, in essence forcing his wives to end their practices and convert entirely to his religion. The loss of her beloved goddesses is too much, and Zilpah dies.

THE RED TENT As its title indicates, the red tent is one of the most important and recurring images of the novel and symbolizes the private and magical world of women. It is the red tent in which each of the children in Dinah's family are born, and it is the red tent in which each girl becomes a woman. But it is more than just a place of birth and maturity; it is also a sacred gathering place for women. In the red tent, the women sequester themselves for several days each month, taking time out from their daily duties as mothers and wives to spoil themselves with cakes and rest upon the straw. It is in the tent that they forge, break, and rebuild their bonds to one another, as occurs between Leah and Rachel. Outside of the tent, men rule society and the families. But inside the tent there are only women, and therefore women make the rules. They share special songs and rites that only the sisters of the tent are privy to. In a story that uncovers the bonds between women, it is fitting that so much of the action occurs in the red tent.

THE MIDWIVES' BRICKS The midwives' bricks, which women stand on as they are giving birth, represent the strength and endurance exhibited by women of ancient times while in labor. In Dinah's world, women were not attended to by physicians during childbirth and would consider themselves lucky to have a skilled midwife. Without epidurals, antibiotics, or antiseptics, as many babies died as lived, often taking their mothers with them. Leah, Bilhah, and Rachel all lose babies to miscarriage and stillbirth, despite having the benefits of Inna's midwifing skills. In each birthing scene, as the women prepare to push, they mount the bricks for support and positioning, symbolizing the gathering of their courage as they prepare to stare death in the face. Diamant chillingly details the strength of these women, portraying how they were able to consistently return to the red tent and stand on the bricks, not knowing if they would walk out.

IMPORTANT QUOTATIONS EXPLAINED

---

1. *It is terrible how much has been forgotten, which is why, I suppose, remembering seems a holy thing.*

This quotation is from the prologue, and it occurs after Dinah recounts how her life has been distilled down to a few lines in the Bible over time. She laments that the "chain connecting mother to daughter was broken," naming this chain as the reason that her true story, which is a love story, fell by the wayside. At the time when Dinah lived, only men's histories were committed to paper, and women's stories were transmitted orally from mother to daughter across generations. Her story would have been important only to her daughters. Since she did not have daughters, Dinah's story has faded from memory but for a few gruesome details. Dinah comments indirectly on the mistaken descriptions of her story and her mothers' stories in the Bible, proclaiming that her telling will truthfully amend the record. As a result, the memory of the women of her family will no longer be distorted and half-forgotten.

Dinah introduces herself as both the narrator and the protagonist of the novel in the prologue. By telling her story in the form of "remembering," as if from the distant past, she creates valuable psychological distance between herself as the narrator and her traumatic personal history. Dinah's detached narration gives the story the feeling of a legend—a story that should be heard, remembered, and then recounted over and over again through generations. In the prologue, Dinah also alludes to a promise she made to her mothers to keep their stories alive. She says that they held her face between their hands and made her swear to remember their secrets and stories. In telling her story, Dinah fulfills an oath to her mothers to remember and honor them.

---

2. *They do not celebrate the first blood of those who will bear life, nor do they return it to the earth. They have set aside the Opening, which is the sacred business of women, and permit men to display their daughters' bloody sheets, as though even the pettiest baal would require such a degradation in tribute.*

Leah speaks these lines in Part Two, Chapter Five, as she explains to Dinah why Rebecca has cast out her cousin Tabea. The women in her family have always honored the goddess Innana and her gift of monthly blood. When each young girl becomes part of their circle, they induct her with a ritual to give her blood back to the earth and the goddess by opening her womb (breaking her hymen). In this way, a girl's "first blood" belongs to the female goddess Innana, rather than to the man who first sleeps with her. The women of Tabea's family are from Canaan, where women are expected to prove their virginity and worth with the bloody sheets from their wedding night. By displaying the bloody sheets, the husband validates his "purchase" of a bride. The Canaanite custom gives the power of a woman's blood to her husband. Diamant sets up an archetype in which women of a pre-modern age refuse to validate their worth by giving their virginity to their husbands and instead claim power over their own bodies. This passage is important because it helps Dinah realize how lucky she is to be a part of the traditions of the women of her family. Diamant has stated that she wrote novel to empower the female characters of the Bible. She endows them with this power by making women claim their virginity as part of this sacred women's ritual, rather than giving it to their husbands on the wedding night.

---

3. *Jacob shall never know peace again. He will lose what he treasures and repudiate those he should embrace. He will never again find rest, and his prayers will not find the favor of his father's god.*

Dinah speaks these lines in Part Two, Chapter Eight, as she verbally attacks and curses her father, Jacob, for his hand in the slaughter of Shechem. Dinah has just been carried out of her murdered husband's bed by her brothers Levi and Simon and forcibly returned to her family's camp. In an uncharacteristic move, Dinah acts blindly and authoritatively, going to Jacob to accuse him of his responsibility in the mass murder of Shechem's men. Though he denies participation in the massacre, she glimpses the guilt in his eyes. As the only daughter of her family, Dinah has had very little contact with Jacob up until this point. In fact, in one passage in the previous chapter, Jacob muses that he cannot quite conjure up the image of Dinah's face, since he only has a vague impression of her appearance. Dinah is the first person in the novel to stand up to Jacob.

This remark is the first real interaction Dinah has with her father as an adult. Dinah's marriage and skills as a midwife have made her a woman in the eyes of her community, even though she is probably just fourteen years old. She stands before her guilty father and finds that she looks at him with the clear eyes of an equal. She draws upon a well of power within herself as she curses Jacob and leaves the camp immediately after, planning never to return. Her words find their mark: after this time, Jacob's luck does indeed change. He changes his name to Isra'El so that he will not be recognized as the "butcher of Shechem." This moment marks the beginning of Dinah's own adventure in the novel, and from now on she acts not as a child of her mothers but as her own woman, leaving behind everything she has ever known to travel to a new land and begin a new life.

---

4. *Why had no one told me that my body would become a battlefield, a sacrifice, a test? Why did I not know that birth is the pinnacle where women discover the courage to become mothers?*

This thought is from Dinah's narration in Part Three, Chapter One, as she gives birth to her son. As soon as Dinah goes into labor, her first thought is to cry out for her mothers. In the tradition of her people, women in childbirth are always surrounded by their mothers and sisters. She feels very alone without the familiar faces of Leah and Rachel and without anyone to speak to her in her native tongue. Dinah has served as a midwife and seen the terror and pain on women's faces, but she had always assumed she would do better when her time came. However, during her own experience of childbirth, she learns the reason why delivery is so difficult: it prepares women for a lifetime of sacrifice and selfless giving as mothers. She experiences firsthand both the fear of death and the power of another woman in the room as she calls her name and encourages her. Dinah finds a source of strength from her mothers in her labor, remembering the teachings of Inna and Rachel. Armed with this knowledge, she instructs the midwife to cut her and pull the baby out. With the memory of her mothers, she finds the courage within her to become a mother herself.

---

5. *My husband's words found their mark, and I recalled something that Zilpah had told me when I was a child in the red tent, and far too young to understand her meaning. "We are all born of the same mother," she said. After a lifetime, I knew that to be true.*

This quotation is from Dinah's narration at the very end of the novel in Part Three, Chapter Five. Dinah has just returned home from visiting her family's camp with Joseph after many years away. There she encountered Judah, who gave her Rachel's ring, a gift passed on from Leah. Ever since she received the ring, Dinah has tried to understand why Leah would leave her a token of Jacob's love for Rachel. Benia believes it is because Leah found peace with sharing her husband. Leah wanted Dinah to know that, despite the conflicts between the sisters, they loved one another and especially loved Dinah. Dinah understands that as women they are connected to one another as derivations of the great goddess, a fact that supersedes individual wants and needs. Dinah is as much Rachel's daughter as she is Leah's and Zilpah's and Bilhah's, because they all share the same relationship with the goddesses and the Earth. In Meryt, Dinah has been lucky enough to find yet another mother during her life. Dinah realizes that their love indeed unites them and makes them all one.

A Room of One's Own

Virginia Woolf
(1882–1941)

CONTEXT

Virginia Woolf was born Virginia Stephen in 1882 into a prominent and intellectually well-connected family. Her formal education was limited, but she grew up reading voraciously from the vast library of her father, the critic Leslie Stephen. Her youth was traumatic, including the early deaths of her mother and brother, a history of sexual abuse, and the beginnings of a depressive mental illness that plagued her intermittently throughout her life and eventually led to her suicide in 1941.

After her father's death in 1904, Woolf and her sister (the painter Vanessa Bell) set up residence in a neighborhood of London called Bloomsbury, where they fell into association with a circle of intellectuals that included such figures as Lytton Strachey, Clive Bell, Roger Fry, and, later, E. M. Forster. In 1912, Woolf married Leonard Woolf, with whom she ran a small but influential printing press. The highly experimental character of her novels, and their brilliant formal innovations, established Woolf as a major figure of British modernism. Her novels, which include *To the Lighthouse* (1927), *Mrs. Dalloway* (1925), and *The Waves* (1931), are particularly concerned with the lives and experiences of women.

In October of 1928, Woolf was invited to deliver lectures at Newnham College and Girton College, which at that time were the only women's colleges at Cambridge. These talks, on the topic "women and fiction," were expanded and revised into *A Room of One's Own*, which was printed in 1929. The title has become a virtual cliché in our culture, which testifies to the book's importance and its enduring influence. Perhaps the single most important work of feminist literary criticism, *A Room of One's Own* explores the historical and contextual contingencies of literary achievement.

PLOT OVERVIEW

The dramatic setting of *A Room of One's Own* is that Woolf has been invited to lecture on the topic "women and fiction." She advances the thesis that "a woman must have money and a room of her own if she is to write fiction." Her essay is constructed as a partly fictionalized narrative of the thinking that led her to adopt this thesis. She dramatizes that mental process in the character of an imaginary narrator ("call me Mary Beton, Mary Seton, Mary Carmichael or by any name you please—it is not a matter of any importance") who is in her same position, wrestling with the same topic.

The narrator begins her investigation at Oxbridge College, where she reflects on the different educational experiences available to men and women as well as on more material differences in their lives. She then spends a day in the British Library, perusing the scholarship on women, all of which has been written by men and all of which has been written in anger. Turning to history, she finds so little data about the everyday lives of women that she decides to reconstruct their existence imaginatively. The figure of Judith Shakespeare is generated as an example of the tragic fate a highly intelligent woman would have met with under those circumstances. In light of this background, she considers the achievements of the major women novelists of the nineteenth century and reflects on the importance of tradition to an aspiring writer. A survey of the current state of literature follows, conducted through a reading of the first novel of one of the narrator's contemporaries. Woolf closes the essay with an exhortation to her audience of women to take up the tradition that has been so hardly bequeathed to them, and to increase the endowment for their own daughters.

CHARACTER LIST

"I" The fictionalized narrator. The fictionalized author-surrogate's ("call me Mary Beton, Mary Seton, Mary Carmichael or by any name you please—it is not a matter of any importance") process of reflection on the topic "women and fiction" forms the substance of the essay.

The Beadle An Oxbridge security official. The beadle reminds the narrator that only "Fellows and Scholars" are permitted on the grass; women must remain on the gravel path.

Mary Seton A student at Fernham College and a friend of the narrator.

Mary Beton The narrator's aunt. Mary Beton's legacy of five hundred pounds a year secures her niece's financial independence. Mary Beton is also one of the names Woolf assigns to her narrator, whose identity, she says, is irrelevant.

Judith Shakespeare The imagined sister of William Shakespeare. Judith suffers greatly and eventually commits suicide because she can find no socially acceptable outlets for her genius.

Mary Carmichael A fictitious novelist, contemporary with the narrator of Woolf's essay. In her first novel, Mary Carmichael has "broken the sentence, broken the sequence" and forever changed the course of women's writing.

Mr. A An imagined male author. Mr. A's work is overshadowed by a looming self-consciousness and petulant self-assertiveness.

ANALYSIS OF MAJOR CHARACTERS

THE NARRATOR The unnamed female narrator is the only major character in *A Room of One's Own*. She refers to herself only as "I"; in chapter one of the text, she tells the reader to call her "Mary Beton, Mary Seton, Mary Carmichael or any other name you please . . . " The narrator assumes each of these names at various points throughout the text. The constantly shifting nature of her identity complicates her narrative even more, since we must consider carefully who she is at any given moment. However, her shifting identity also gives her a more universal voice: by taking on different names and identities, the narrator emphasizes that her words apply to all women, not just herself.

The dramatic setting for *A Room of One's Own* is Woolf's thought process in preparation for giving a lecture on the topic "women and fiction." But the fictionalized narrator is distinct from the author Woolf. The narrator lends a storylike quality to the text, and she often blends fact and fiction to prove her points. Her liberty with factuality suggests that no irrefutable truth exists in the world—all truth is relative and subjective.

The narrator is an erudite and engaging storyteller, and she uses the book to explore the multifaceted and rather complicated history of literary achievement. Her provocative inquiries into the status quo of literature force readers to question the widely held assumption that women are inferior writers, compared to men, and this is why there is a dearth of memorable literary works by women. This literary journey is highlighted by numerous actual journeys, such as the journey around Oxbridge College and her tour of the British library. She interweaves her journeys with her own theories about the world—including the principle of "incandescence." Woolf defines incandescence as the state in which everything is personal burns away and what is left is the "nugget of pure truth" in the art. This is the ideal state in which everything is consumed in the intensity and truth of one's art. The narrator skillfully leads the reader through one of the most important works of feminist literary history to date.

R

THEMES, MOTIFS, AND SYMBOLS

THEMES

THE IMPORTANCE OF MONEY For the narrator of *A Room of One's Own*, money is the primary element that prevents women from having a room of their own, and thus, having money is of the utmost importance. Because women do not have power, their creativity has been systematically stifled throughout the ages. The narrator writes, "Intellectual freedom depends upon material things. Poetry depends upon intellectual freedom. And women have always been poor, not for two hundred years merely, but from the beginning of time . . ." She uses this quotation to explain why so few women have written successful poetry. She believes that the writing of novels lends itself more easily to frequent starts and stops, so women are more likely to write novels than poetry: women must contend with frequent interruptions because they are so often deprived of a room of their own in which to write. Without money, the narrator implies, women will remain in second place to their creative male counterparts. The financial discrepancy between men and women at the time of Woolf's writing perpetuated the myth that women were less successful writers.

THE SUBJECTIVITY OF TRUTH In *A Room of One's Own*, the narrator argues that even history is subjective. What she seeks is nothing less than "the essential oil of truth," but this eludes her, and she eventually concludes that no such thing exists. The narrator later writes, "When a subject is highly controversial, one cannot hope to tell the truth. One can only show how one came to hold whatever opinion one does hold." To demonstrate the idea that opinion is the only thing that a person can actually "prove," she fictionalizes her lecture, claiming, "Fiction is likely to contain more truth than fact." Reality is not objective: rather, it is contingent upon the circumstances of one's world. This argument complicates her narrative: Woolf forces her reader to question the veracity of everything she has presented as truth so far, and yet she also tells them that the fictional parts of any story contain more essential truth than the factual parts. With this observation she recasts the accepted truths and opinions of countless literary works.

MOTIFS

INTERRUPTIONS When the narrator is interrupted in *A Room of One's Own*, she generally fails to regain her original concentration, suggesting that women without private spaces of their own, free of interruptions, are doomed to difficulty and even failure in their work. While the narrator is describing Oxbridge University in chapter one, her attention is drawn to a cat without a tail. The narrator finds this cat to be out of place, and she uses the sight of this cat to take her text in a different direction. The oddly jarring and incongruous sight of a cat without a tail—which causes the narrator to completely lose her train of thought—is an exercise in allowing the reader to experience what it might feel like to be a woman writer. Although the narrator goes on to make an interesting and valuable point about the atmosphere at her luncheon, she has lost her original point. This shift underscores her claim that women, who so often lack a room of their own and the time to write, cannot compete against the men who are not forced to struggle for such basic necessities.

GENDER INEQUALITY Throughout *A Room of One's Own*, the narrator emphasizes the fact that women are treated unequally in her society and that this is why they have produced less impressive works of writing than men. To illustrate her point, the narrator creates a woman named Judith Shakespeare, the imaginary twin sister of William Shakespeare. The narrator uses Judith to show how society systematically discriminates against women. Judith is just as talented as her brother William, but while his talents are recognized and encouraged by their family and the rest of their society, Judith's are underestimated and explicitly deemphasized. Judith writes, but she is secretive and ashamed of it. She is engaged at a fairly young age; when she begs not to have to marry, her beloved father beats her. She eventually commits suicide. The narrator invents the tragic figure of Judith to prove that a woman as talented as Shakespeare could never have achieved such success. Talent is an essential component of Shakespeare's success, but because women are treated so differently, a female Shakespeare would have fared quite differently even if she'd had as much talent as Shakespeare did.

SYMBOLS

A ROOM OF ONE'S OWN The central point of *A Room of One's Own* is that every woman needs a room of her own—something men are able to enjoy without question. A room of her own would provide a woman with the time and the space to engage in uninterrupted writing time. During Woolf's time, women rarely enjoyed these luxuries. They remained elusive to women, and, as a result, their art suffered. But Woolf is concerned with more than just the room itself. She uses the room as a symbol for many larger issues, such as privacy, leisure time, and financial independence, each of which is an essential component of the countless inequalities between men and women. Woolf predicts that until these inequalities are rectified, women will remain second-class citizens and their literary achievements will also be branded as such.

IMPORTANT QUOTATIONS EXPLAINED

1. *Call me Mary Beton, Mary Seton, Mary Carmichael or any other name you please—it is not a matter of importance.*

This line comes from Chapter One, and its enigmatic and elusive tone regarding the true identity of the narrator is maintained throughout the text. Woolf and the narrator both struggle with the same issues, but they are two distinct entities. The narrator is a fictionalized character—an invention of Virginia Woolf—and she remains vague about her true identity. In this quotation she even instructs the reader to refer to her by different names. This lack of one "true" identity for the narrator gives *A Room of One's Own* a sense of being universal: the ideas apply to all women, not just one. The lack of one identity also makes the narrator more convincing. By taking on different identities, the narrator transcends one single voice, and consequently she makes herself a force to be reckoned with. Her blasé attitude about something that is considered fixed and important by most people—identity—makes her all the more intriguing.

2. *A woman must have money and a room of her own if she is to write fiction.*

This phrase from Chapter One is perhaps the most famous line from *A Room of One's Own*, and it functions as the thesis of the work. The phrase "a room of one's own" has gained such a stronghold in our culture that it has almost become a cliché. With this line, and the entire book, Woolf has touched off one of the most important assertions of feminist literary criticisms. The oft-held argument that women produce inferior works of literature must necessarily be qualified by the fact of the circumstances of women. Unlike their male counterparts, they are routinely denied the time and the space to produce creative works. Instead, they are saddled with household duties and are financially and legally bound to their husbands. By being deprived of rooms of their own, there is little possibility for women to rectify the situation. Even though this is clearly a historical truth, Woolf's assertion was revolutionary at its time. It recast the accomplishments of women in a new and far more favorable light, and it also forced people to realize the harsh truths about their society.

3. *One must strain off what was personal and accidental in all these impressions and so reach the pure fluid, the essential oil of truth.*

R

This assertion, presented in Chapter Two, characterizes the narrator's initial mission in *A Room of One's Own*. She endeavors to find the absolutely essential truth and expose it, but over the course of the text, the narrator comes to realize that no absolute truth exists. She sees that the experience of each person and his or her life is inextricable from his or her perceptions of reality. In other words, we cannot remove the self, the historical period, or any other inherent biases from someone's opinion. Everything depends on everything else, and the kind of person someone is absolutely influences everything he or she does—even the kind of art he or she creates. This idea is connected to her argument that the plight of women has influenced the dearth of good literature that they have produced. The narrator fictionalizes *A Room of One's Own*, demonstrating this synthesis of fact and fiction.

4. *It would have been impossible, completely and entirely, for any woman to have written the plays of Shakespeare in the age of Shakespeare.*

This passage in Chapter Three is one of the most significant conclusions of *A Room of One's Own*. While the more common argument is that the lack of important, impressive literary works by women proves that they are less capable than men, the narrator takes the opposite approach. She chooses to examine her historical period and question the context in which women are judged. What she realizes is that the playing field is incredibly unequal. Given the circumstances of the treatment of women of her time, there is no way they could have rivaled men in literary achievements. The narrator invents the figure of

Judith Shakespeare to illustrate this point. She tells a story of a fictional twin sister of Shakespeare, who is just as talented as her famous brother but, because she is a woman, her talent leads to a very different end.

---

5. *Life for both sexes—and I look at them, shouldering their way along the pavement—is arduous, difficult, a perpetual struggle. It calls for gigantic courage and strength. More than anything, perhaps, creatures of illusion that we are, it calls for confidence in oneself.*

Woolf presents this claim in Chapter Two. She asserts this point amidst a discussion about the unequal treatment of women by men. In this discussion, she cites men as the reason for this—she believes that men have systematically subordinated women in order to reinforce their own confidence as the more capable sex—but she does not blame men for this. Rather, she sympathizes with men in their quest for confidence, and she speaks of the importance of confidence in creating art. The lack of confidence amongst women has led to the generally inferior quality of their art. To Woolf, the anger in women about their plight as second-class citizens is reflected in their writing. And yet, they persist. She relates the fact that women continue to write even though they are actually lacking in confidence to the way that people continue living their lives even when wracked by doubt about their relevance in society. In this way, she depicts women as valiant.

Rubyfruit Jungle

Rita Mae Brown
(1944–)

CONTEXT

Rubyfruit Jungle, a story of a woman who comes of age as a lesbian and aspiring artist in the mid-twentieth century, is very much a book of its time. Author Rita Mae Brown grew up in the segregated South of the 1950s and 1960s, and she experienced firsthand the prejudice that sought to prevent her and others from attaining personal and professional freedom. Like *Rubyfruit Jungle*'s protagonist and narrator, Molly Bolt, Brown is a lesbian who was born in southern Pennsylvania and moved to Florida during her adolescence. Indeed, Molly is in many ways the fictional version of Brown, and she shares several details of Brown's own life. Both Brown and Molly were adopted as infants and taunted as bastard children in their early childhood. Both were attractive, intelligent, and athletic teenagers who saw their beloved adoptive fathers die while in high school. Both were forced to leave the University of Florida after their scholarships were revoked, in part because they were lesbians. And both hitchhiked to New York City, where they were forced to share an abandoned car with a gay black man before finding work at a publishing company and attending New York University.

When Brown was in her twenties in the late 1960s, she became politically active, and her experience during this time plays a large role in the lesbian and feminist tracts of the novel. Brown formed the Student Homophile League while attending NYU and served as the administrative coordinator for the National Organization for Women's main office. However, she soon became disenchanted with feminist groups because she felt they were not accepting of her lesbianism. She turned to the radical Gay Liberation Front but quickly became disheartened by its disregard for political awareness and its latent sexism. Brown's frustration during this period surfaces in *Rubyfruit Jungle,* when Molly discovers that several subcultures within the gay and feminist community in New York exist and frequently clash.

Brown continued to be involved in politics through the 1970s, publishing numerous essays for feminist journals that advocated radical grass-roots social change. But though she infused *Rubyfruit Jungle* with much of what she learned about feminist social criticism, Brown ultimately decided her fiction should concern itself principally with the personal. To Brown, politics and activism were the province of essayists and academics—novels were different, requiring a sustained focus on the individual lives that society affects. At heart, *Rubyfruit Jungle* is a book about one woman's quest for personal fulfillment, facing the obstacles that come from being a female in a man's world, a lesbian in a fervidly heterosexual world, a budding artist with a story to tell, and an individual who longs to be accepted for herself.

As a prose stylist, Brown draws on a variety of literary traditions to enrich Molly's journey through life. Like Mark Twain, Brown's literary hero and obvious forebear, Brown makes use of the humorist tradition to satirize society from the margins. Brown's writing also resembles Twain's in its identification with the South and southern values, including the importance of roots, honest labor, and hard work; a deep reverence for the land as a source of life; a strong sense of individualism; and a personal code of honor. These values are apparent in Molly's father, Carl, whom Brown portrays with respect and love. The work of both Brown and Twain falls into the picaresque genre, which uses the story of a roguish individual who travels through society as a way to criticize that society. Like Molly's story, picaresque novels are structured around a loosely organized series of episodes featuring the hero that tell something either about the hero or about the society in which he or she lives. *Rubyfruit Jungle* is also a bildungsroman, a novel that charts a protagonist's coming of age in society. In Molly's case, however, the bildungsroman does not apply completely, because Molly ultimately resists integrating into society in favor of living in defiance of it.

Rubyfruit Jungle was initially rejected by several major publishers because its subject matter was thought too controversial for mass market appeal. However, in 1973, a small, independent, feminist publishing house called Daughters Press agreed to print it. Over the next four years, it sold an astonishing 70,000 copies and was bought and reprinted by Bantam Publishing in 1977. The novel began to receive wide critical praise, and Brown decided to use the proceeds from her deal with Bantam to launch a full-time writing career. Since then, Brown has published a great number of books and has written for television and film, listing among her credits such diverse works as *The Long Hot Summer* and *Slumber Party Massacre*, though none of her fiction has garnered the accolades that her first novel did. *Rubyfruit Jungle* continues to sell today, reflecting the growing acceptance of lesbian subject matter in America, as well as the strides made toward gender equality.

PLOT OVERVIEW

Molly Bolt first learns she is a bastard when she is seven years old, living with her adoptive parents in poor, rural Coffee Hollow, Pennsylvania. A sharp child, she devises a moneymaking scheme one day after finding out that her friend Broccoli Detwiler has an odd-looking penis. Molly charges a nickel to look at Broccoli's penis and a dime to touch it. The business thrives among Molly's schoolmates until Earl Stambach, another classmate, tattles on her to their teacher, Miss Martin. Miss Martin tells Carrie, Molly's adoptive mother, who explodes with rage when Molly comes home from school. Among insults and rebukes, Carrie tells Molly she is a bastard, the daughter of a slut named Ruby Drollinger.

Molly spends much of her early childhood playing with her slow-witted cousin, Leroy. Together, they work on the family farm, picking bugs from the potato patch and devising schemes to torment Earl. Even at this point in her life, Molly knows she is different from others. She is dark-featured, whereas others are fair, and she is more intelligent and athletic. Carrie urges her to be more ladylike, but Molly runs around with the boys, feeling unrestricted by the conventional rules of gender that dictate she should like playing with dolls or playing nurse.

Shortly after the incident with Broccoli, Leroy's mother, Jenna, has a baby and names him after Molly's kind adoptive father, Carl. The baby dies after only two days, however, and Jenna dies a few weeks later of cancer. She'd known about the cancer for a while but kept it secret from her husband, Ep, because she knew the family couldn't afford a doctor. The night of Jenna's funeral, Molly wants to sleep next to Leroy to comfort him, but Carrie tells her that boys and girls aren't allowed to sleep with each other.

In sixth grade, Molly develops a crush on a female classmate named Leota B. Bisland. They become friends, and through Molly's urging, they begin to kiss in the woods after school every day. When Molly finds out her family is moving to Florida to look for work, she and Leota make love before separating.

Molly and Leroy's families move to the Fort Lauderdale area, where Carl and Ep find jobs that split up Molly and Leroy. At school, Molly quickly learns the differences between the posh, bright-eyed rich students and the poor, who seem slovenly in spirit as well as in appearance. As the years pass, Molly uses her intelligence and sense of humor to become popular among the wealthier children, while Leroy becomes more like a redneck. Tension develops between them, but they try to remain close. Molly has her first heterosexual experience with Leroy after he tells her one day that he's had repeated sexual experiences with an older man named Craig.

By the time Molly is a high-school upperclassman, she and Leroy have grown apart and do not have sex anymore. Molly belongs to the ruling clique at school, complete with social club membership and football-player boyfriend. She also obtains financial support from the school administration for a successful bid as class president after catching her principal in an adulterous affair with another teacher. The only snag in Molly's junior year comes from Carrie and Carrie's sister, Florence, who frequently criticize Molly for her arrogance, obstinacy, and apparent lack of feeling when Carl dies. Though their unjustified antagonism upsets her, Molly remains unapologetic about how she lives her life.

When Molly is a senior, she has an affair with Carolyn, one of her two best friends and captain of the cheerleading squad. Carolyn becomes so enraptured with Molly that she becomes jealous when Molly spends time with her other best friend, Connie. Carolyn accuses Molly of sleeping with Connie, which Connie overhears, forcing Molly to explain to Connie that she and Carolyn have been lovers. Connie says she can no longer be Molly's friend, and Carolyn, upset with being called a lesbian, says Molly is the real lesbian because she isn't feminine. The girls stop talking to each other.

The following fall, Molly attends the University of Florida on a full scholarship. She befriends her roommate, Faye Raider, a rich freshman who wants only to drink and carouse. When they begin an affair midway through the first semester, they ignore their social obligations in favor of spending time together in bed. Other girls notice and tell the dean of female students, Dean Marne. Dean Marne offers to help Molly with her problem, but Molly accuses her of hypocrisy and calls her a closet fairy. Angered by Molly's insolence and concerned about her own reputation, Dean Marne commits Molly to a sanitarium for a few days. When Molly emerges, she gets a letter revoking her scholarship for "moral" reasons and finds Faye gone from school.

Unable to stay in school and unwelcome in Carrie's house, Molly hitches a ride to New York City, where she believes she can make a better life for herself. Penniless, she spends her first nights in an abandoned car with Calvin, a young black man who fled from his parents because they found out he is gay. Calvin introduces Molly to his friends, shows her where she can get free meals, helps her make money, and brings her to a lesbian bar. When he leaves abruptly for San Francisco, Molly finds a ramshackle apartment in the West Village and a waitress job at the Flick, a burger joint where the waitresses dress like *Playboy* bunnies. There, she meets Holly, a voluptuous black lesbian.

Before meeting Holly, Molly unhappily fritters away her days at the Flick and her nights at truck-driver-filled lesbian bars where butch lesbians accost her for easy sex. But with Holly, Molly begins to see the more glamorous side of lesbian New York. Holly is a "kept" woman, receiving an allowance to be another woman's lover. She encourages Molly to do the same and brings her to a party to meet Chryssa Hart, an eminent lesbian archaeologist. Chryssa offers to support Molly in exchange for her sexual companionship, but Molly refuses, even though she knows she could use the money to enroll in film school—her great passion. Instead, Molly labors to win a scholarship from New York University and works nights to pay the rest. This decision causes tension between Holly and Molly, and they argue the night Holly gets both herself and Molly fired from the Flick. Unable to reconcile her insecurity about the shallow life she leads with Molly's industriousness, Holly leaves Molly.

Molly finds a job at Silver Publishing Company, reducing her class load to work during the day. She is promoted to the editorial staff and meets Polina Bellantoni, a lovely middle-aged professor writing a book about the Middle Ages. Molly immediately determines to have a relationship with her, but Polina has a husband, daughter, and male lover, and she is uncomfortable with Molly's sexuality. She eventually relents, eager to explore her bisexual side, but her sexual fantasies of being a man repulse Molly. Trapped in a relationship with Polina, Molly begins an affair with Polina's teenage daughter, Alice. Alice and Molly keep their tryst a secret until one day, in a tantrum, Alice tells Polina she and Molly are lovers. Polina sends Molly away, forbidding Alice to fraternize with her.

Demoralized by her experiences in New York, Molly escapes to her hometown in Pennsylvania. She meets Leota again, who now has two children and looks unnaturally aged. Leota is harsh with Molly about their shared sexual experience and thinks Molly is mentally disturbed for being a lesbian. Molly leaves Leota and never sees her again.

Back in New York, Molly decides to journey to Florida to film Carrie for her senior project, a documentary on Carrie's life. Carrie is now completely alone and dying of cancer. She is overjoyed to see Molly, though she still disapproves of Molly's sexuality. Carrie lets herself be filmed for a week, all that time telling Molly her thoughts, feelings, and dreams. Now, she thinks of Molly as her daughter and denies ever having said Molly is not hers. She tells Molly about her biological mother, Ruby, and her biological father, a French athlete from whom Molly seems to have received all of her physical traits. Molly leaves at the end of the week, having shot all her footage and made peace with Carrie.

Molly's film does not impress her class, and the entire department is against her because she's a woman. She graduates summa cum laude and Phi Beta Kappa but has trouble finding a job in the movie industry. She knows that many forces will prevent her from fulfilling her dreams of making films, but she resolves to continue striving.

CHARACTER LIST

Molly Bolt The sharp-witted lesbian protagonist. Molly is beautiful, athletic, and highly intelligent, and she has a very strong will. She rarely backs down from a dispute, is honest to the point of painfulness, and is driven to succeed beyond society's expectations. Molly's determination often gets her into trouble, but she always exudes self-esteem and remains unapologetic for being who she is.

Carrie Bolt Molly's adoptive mother. Carrie is strong-willed and often stubborn and bitter. Though she loves Molly, she seems resentful of her achievements and tends to criticize her for being arrogant and unladylike. She was rebellious when she was younger, just as Molly is.

Leroy Denman Molly's cousin. The tubby, slow-witted son of Ep and Jenna, Leroy is Molly's main childhood playmate. As an adolescent, Leroy thins out and becomes more of a redneck, spending most of his free time at the motorcycle shop. Though he seems unsure of his sexuality in his teens, he marries and has children by his twenties.

Carl Bolt Molly's adoptive father. Gentle and good-natured, Carl shows Molly that men can be sensitive as well as strong. Unlike Carrie, Carl encourages Molly to follow her ambitions and use her mental and physical advantages to achieve success.

Holly A beautiful, black lesbian Molly meets in New York City. Holly comes from a middle-class family, but in New York she lives a ritzy life by being a "kept" woman. Though she seems to love her lifestyle of hobnobbing with the rich and famous, she harbors insecurities about her lack of ambition and questionable ethics.

Polina Bellantoni A middle-aged history professor who becomes one of Molly's lovers. Polina is attractive, learned, and sophisticated, and she understands and fights against the challenges women face in the working world. Her sexual fantasies of being a man repulse Molly.

Faye Raider Molly's freshman-year roommate at the University of Florida. Because she is wealthy and popular, Faye has a cavalier attitude toward life. She drinks and carouses, leaving no time to study. She is also generous with her money. After sleeping with Molly, she becomes more conscientious and works hard to stay in school so they can be together.

Florence Carrie's loud-mouthed, opinionated sister. Florence often behaves self-righteously and officiously toward her family, neighbors, and friends. In emergency situations, she proves capable of taking charge and helping effectively.

Carolyn Simpson One of Molly's two best friends in high school and captain of the cheerleading team. Unlike Connie and Molly, Carolyn is prudish and innocent. She doesn't swear and expresses surprise when Connie and Molly confess they've had sex with their boyfriends. When she has sex with Molly, she becomes obsessed with her.

Connie Pen One of Molly's two best friends in high school and editor of the school newspaper. Though Connie is not as pretty as Carolyn and Molly, her irreverent wit and intelligence make her popular. She is boy-crazy and uncomfortable with Molly's sexuality.

Leota B. Bisland Molly's best girlfriend in sixth grade. Cat-eyed and quiet, Leota provides Molly with her first homosexual experience. Though reluctant at first, Leota becomes the more sexually adventurous of the two. As a woman, Leota renounces her affinity for Molly and stubbornly believes she has no time for thinking and no opportunity for improving her own life.

Ruby Drollinger Molly's biological mother. According to Carrie, Ruby was promiscuous. Molly's voice is exactly like Ruby's.

Jean-Pierre Bullette Molly's biological, French father. According to Carrie, Jean-Pierre was a handsome Olympic athlete who jilted Ruby when he found out she was pregnant. Carrie suspects that Molly has inherited his looks, athleticism, and yearning to be an artist.

Calvin A black homosexual streetwalker who befriends Molly in New York. Young and handsome, Calvin peddles his body each night so he can find a place to sleep. He is both courteous and helpful toward Molly when she arrives in town.

Dean Marne The heiferlike, red-haired dean of girls at the University of Florida. Dean Marne lives uncomfortably in a state of denial of her sexuality, despite having a female lover Molly knows about.

Jenna Denman Leroy and Ted's mother and Ep's wife. Jenna is an angel among women. Realizing Ep cannot afford a doctor for her, she keeps her cancer a secret until the last week of her life. The entire town grieves her death.

Ep Denman Leroy and Ted's father and Jenna's husband. Though poor and unable to give his family much, Ep works hard and loves his children and wife. He is beside himself when his wife Jenna dies and depends on Carl to comfort him.

Alice Bellantoni Polina's sixteen-year-old daughter and one of Molly's lovers. Alice is beautiful and intelligent like Polina. She harbors incestuous feelings toward Polina and demonstrates little self-control when she fights with her.

Kim Wilson A famous, aging screen actress who "keeps" Holly. Rather than regaling Molly with tales of Hollywood, Kim talks humbly about philosophy and her poor upbringing in Chicago. She is surprisingly down-to-earth and friendly.

Chryssa Hart An older, famous archaeologist who offers to finance Molly's life and school plans in return for a sexual relationship. Slender and tan with very short hair, Chryssa is direct, predatory, and arrogant about her profession.

Brockhurst (Broccoli) Detwiler Molly's elementary school friend. Broccoli is at first reluctant to go along with Molly's plan to show his uncircumcised penis to the other kids at school, but he soon grows to enjoy it.

Ralph An MIT student who takes Molly to New York City. A perfect gentleman, Ralph talks with Molly the entire way to New York. He expresses no romantic interest in her, only polite, human consideration.

Paul Digita Polina's extramarital lover. Paul teaches English at NYU, specializing in the use of punctuation in poetry. His lectures are incredibly boring, but his sexual fantasies while making love are undeniably strange. Just before he thinks he's going to have sex with Molly, he imagines himself a woman with large, luscious breasts.

Mr. Bellantoni Polina's husband. Old-looking and paunchy, Mr. Bellantoni lives the life of an effete and vapid intellectual. He pompously lectures about his lifelong study of cows in Western art, never taking his pipe out of his mouth.

Mr. Beers Molly's high school principal. Mr. Beers appears friendly and supportive of Molly, especially after she catches him having an affair with Mrs. Silver, an administrator at the high school.

Professor Walgren The head of the film department at NYU. Professor Walgren is almost openly contemptuous of Molly, simply because she is a woman. He is patronizing and unaccommodating.

Cheryl Spiegelglass A dainty and disliked playmate of Molly's. Cheryl's prissy, feminine behavior endears her to Carrie and other adults.

Earl Stambach Molly's tattling nemesis in elementary school. Slow and stupid, Earl gets by at school by telling on people, especially Molly.

ANALYSIS OF MAJOR CHARACTERS

MOLLY BOLT At the very beginning of *Rubyfruit Jungle*, Molly declares that she is a "bastard," and her status as an outsider of sorts affects and influences nearly every aspect of her life: economically because she is poor; politically because she is a female in a man's world; legally because she has no father; spiritually because she is a bastard child; and emotionally because she is eventually rejected by her adoptive mother, Carrie. Despite being born at a disadvantage, however, Molly never blames herself for her troubles and rarely becomes despondent, even as she encounters hatred, betrayal, and exclusion from society. Instead, she draws on her belief that she is innocent of wrongdoing in order to call up the spiritual defiance, ambition, and courage that help her accomplish her goals. These qualities give Molly a strong sense of self, perhaps her most distinctive characteristic. Her unwavering honesty, pride in being poor, and rejection of Chryssa's offer to "keep" her all demonstrate her unwillingness to compromise this sense of self. Her refusal or inability to hold on to a lover is most likely a symptom of this ardent sense of independence.

As a woman and individual, Molly is a quadruple threat to those around her: she is beautiful, athletic, highly intelligent, and fiercely funny, and she uses these advantages to pursue her personal goals. She believes in equality for women and for all people, and she distrusts those who seem to condone or endorse the system of inequality she sees around her. This belief sets up many of the conflicts Molly faces as she develops into an adult and aspiring filmmaker. Throughout the novel, Molly must struggle against the institutional and personal prejudices of traditional society in order to fulfill her dreams. Yet she remains optimistic about her eventual success, if not about the rectification of society. Her pluckiness in the face of adversity distinguishes her from the other characters in the novel, and the novel ends on a high note, despite Molly's professional and personal troubles.

CARRIE BOLT Like Molly, Carrie is stubborn and strong-willed and has a well-defined sense of values and an aversion to class pretense. In other words, she is proud and poor. Molly reveals that even though Carrie is well below the poverty line, she assiduously refuses handouts, and Carrie is pleased that Molly is intellectually superior to the rich northerners who are her classmates in New York. Even when she is emotionally destroyed by Carl's death, Carrie notes with caustic humor that they never could have ridden in a Lincoln Continental if Carl hadn't died. Carrie's observation in this scene points to her astute awareness of how class differences are played out in everyday life.

Unlike Molly, Carrie is firmly rooted in the patriarchal social system that prescribes secondary, supporting, and, above all, "ladylike" roles for women. This difference constitutes much of the tension between Carrie and Molly, especially when Carrie learns of Molly's lesbianism and throws her out of the house. Carrie's resentment of Molly ultimately stems from the fact that she couldn't have a child of her own. Because she believes genuine maternity consists of giving birth to one's own child, Carrie cannot accept Molly as her daughter or as an individual. She frequently rebukes Molly for arrogance and unladylike behavior, revealing how threatened she is by Molly's brazen illegitimacy and how deeply she believes in traditional gender roles. At heart, Carrie wants Molly to inherit the shame she feels as an illegitimate mother. As an older woman, alone and dying of cancer, Carrie asserts that she never disowned Molly and that she's always seen herself as Molly's true mother, but whether she actually believes this is unclear.

LEROY As a child, Leroy is slow and chubby, physical characteristics that also represent his malleable personality. He relies on Molly for all of his behavioral cues, because she is as boyish as the rest of the boys in town. When Carrie forces Molly to stay inside and learn domestic chores, Leroy volunteers to learn them as well. He can't maintain his resolve, however, and Carrie bullies him into leaving by telling him the rest of the neighborhood will think he's queer if he stays in the house. This scene highlights Leroy's major weakness, which significantly separates him from Molly: he fears what others will think of him, especially in matters of sexuality. As an adolescent, Leroy confides to Molly that he's had a homosexual experience. However, even as he considers the possibility that he is gay, he clings to the dictums of society. His rabid fear of social deviance shines through when he says, "I may be queer but I ain't kissing no man." Ultimately, Leroy is a slave to what others think. Without Molly's constant reassurance and influence, he falls into the modes of behavior prescribed by the indigent greasers and rednecks who make up his society, where intelligence is suspiciously regarded and homosexuality is punished with violence. Not surprisingly, when Leroy marries and has children, he remains unfulfilled, having made everyone happy but himself.

THEMES, MOTIFS, AND SYMBOLS

THEMES

THE ROLE OF SEXUALITY IN THE SEARCH FOR THE SELF *Rubyfruit Jungle* chronicles Molly's homosexual odyssey in lurid detail, but it does more than just dramatize one woman's life as a lesbian. More important, it shows that the search for individual identity is not limited to defining oneself sexually. Molly's homosexuality may be a fundamental part of her identity, but it is still just one facet of a more complex self. She often repeats "I'm me" and "I'm here," which suggests her desire to be regarded in her totality, not just as a type or as a part of her past. In this sense, Molly seems to embody an idea of humanity in which sexual identity is subordinate to broader considerations of selfhood. Her journey in the novel ultimately leads her to realize that her identity already exists within her and that she'll have to fight society to be true to herself.

THE EXPLOITATIVE NATURE OF CAPITALISM Throughout the novel, Brown criticizes American society by illuminating how the capitalist system exploits individuals in order to generate commerce. Molly unwittingly demonstrates this principle when she creates a lucrative business parading Broccoli's penis around the forest. As Molly grows up, she becomes acutely aware of this phenomenon, often finding herself the object of exploitation. Her first two legitimate jobs in New York, as a bunny-suited waitress and a dancer, involve the crass use of sexual enticement to attract customers. Calvin and Holly's occupations as hustler and "kept" woman literally embody the idea that sex sells. In each of these cases, Brown criticizes the dehumanizing effects this kind of capitalism has on individuals. As both Holly and Molly experience firsthand, sexual exploitation promotes gender inequality by pitting women as objects that men can purchase.

THE OPPRESSIVE NATURE OF THE PATRIARCHAL SYSTEM In the American society of *Rubyfruit Jungle*, the patriarchal system, where men rule, threatens women's selfhood and precludes the possibility of gender equality. In every sphere of her life, including public, personal, sexual, and professional, Molly encounters obstacles and resistance, which seem to be ingrained in the social fabric of the world around her. As a child, she is discouraged from playing doctor because only men are doctors, and as a teenager, she faces Carrie's criticism for serving as student council president instead of running for prom queen. As an adult, Molly loses jobs in the film industry to her male classmates, despite her stronger performance in school. For both Brown and Molly, being a woman in a patriarchal world means being at a social disadvantage. Worse, the patriarchal system also creates a climate of hostility among women. Carrie and Dean Marne butt heads with Molly, whom they think improper for challenging the status quo, instead of standing together in solidarity. As long as the patriarchal social structures are in place, Molly and other women cannot have the total freedom needed to lead fulfilling lives.

NATURE AS A SOURCE OF STRENGTH Molly's embrace of rural Pennsylvania and her antipathy for the urban North reflect her feelings about the natural world. Mired in New York, Molly longs to return to Pennsylvania, not only because it was her home during a more innocent period of her life but also because New York City's manmade ugliness distresses her. Molly returns to rural Pennsylvania just before completing her degree at NYU and joining the professional urban world, and the trip rejuvenates her. Molly has a vivid, unburdened narrative style in this scene, as she finds strength in the nature around her. Her love of nature may stem from the fact that women are freer to forge their own roles and identities there than they are in actual human society, where being in the world requires a woman to subordinate her personal agenda to the patriarchal system's needs.

MOTIFS

HUMOR Partly as a result of her disadvantaged beginnings, Molly learns the importance of humor both as a survival mechanism and as a device for self-advancement. She employs it in elementary school to become best friends with her first crush, Leota. She uses it in middle and high school to become popular among her wealthier classmates, managing to avoid their resentment even though she is smarter, more beautiful, and more athletic than they are. As Molly grows older, she uses humor to make her controversial opinions and behavior more palatable. Her amusing social observations to Polina about how sex sells not only bring Polina around to her point of view but also make Polina feel more comfortable about having sex with her. Throughout the novel, Brown uses humor as a method of inclusion and persuasion. The constant joking wins readers' loyalty, even as Brown casts a critical eye at how society mistreats women, gays, minorities, and the poor.

NAMES AND NAMING Brown gives many of her characters names that reveal something significant about their personalities. Molly's surname, Bolt, suggests that Molly surges with energy, much like a bolt of lightning. It also suggests that Molly anchors her convictions with steadfast stubbornness, just as a bolt that fastens two things together. In both senses, Bolt aptly characterizes Molly's plucky resolve. The similarity of Paul and Polina's names implies that they are facsimiles of each other, an idea that gains credence as they both reveal their penchant for academic debate and transsexual fantasies. Likewise, the similarity of the names Holly and Molly suggests that despite their frequent airing of differences, the two women are more alike than they think. Molly criticizes Holly for her social climbing, but she is just as guilty of it when she is a teenager—she is thrilled to have sex with Carolyn because she is the head cheerleader. And though Molly disapproves of Holly's idea to go to Paris to clear her head, Molly herself makes a ritual of escaping her problems by leaving New York.

VERB TENSE CHANGE Molly narrates the story in the past tense, from a time just after the novel's final events. However, she occasionally shifts into the present tense when depicting a particularly remarkable scene or strongly felt emotion in order to signify that her impressions during that specific moment are still very much with her. This narrative trick helps reveal particularly vulnerable aspects of Molly's life and puts us right in the moment with her. In these sections, Molly's feelings take on an immediacy that distinguishes them from the rest of the text. This technique works particularly well when Molly recreates her reaction to Carrie's calling her a bastard in Chapter 1. Her lapse into the present tense demonstrates

R

how strongly Molly feels her illegitimacy as a seven-year-old girl—and continues to feel it even as a twenty-something relating the story.

ROLE-PLAYING/ACTING Brown often uses roles and role-playing to highlight Molly's struggle to define her identity. Strangely, the role-playing that occurs during scenes of actual stage acting tend to have a stronger basis in reality than do the scenes in which Molly is forced to play roles in real life. Cast as the Virgin Mary in her sixth-grade production of the Nativity, Molly finds herself in a position like Carrie's: a mother caring for an illegitimate child. Molly's fight in this scene with her school rival Cheryl, who plays Joseph, and the subsequent breakdown of the play dramatize the effect that Molly believes she has at home, where she witnesses Carl and Carrie fight over her. Molly's casting as one of the Weird Sisters in her high school production of *Macbeth*, along with her best friends Carolyn and Connie, also seems revealing, given Molly's homosexual relations with Carolyn.

Molly's sexual identity as a lesbian forces her to play various phony roles in her real life. The greatest acting Molly undertakes involves convincing the university psychiatrists that she is normal enough to rejoin society after being hospitalized for her lesbianism and aggression toward Dean Marne. Similarly, Molly finds that in the trashier gay bars in New York, lesbians typically take on gender roles in matters of behavior and sex. For example, there are "butch" lesbians, who assume a man's role and become the active, aggressive partner in a sexual encounter. There are also "femme" lesbians, who assume a woman's role and become the more passive partner. Molly is femme, but she lies that she is butch to a butch lesbian named Mighty Moe in order to avoid her advances. Through these experiences, Molly comes to distrust the idea of roles in real life because they limit one's individuality by dictating behavior.

SYMBOLS

THE FOREST The forest is where Molly's early childhood business with Broccoli and sexual adventures with Leota take place, and it represents a wilderness of possibility for Molly, a setting in which she may experiment with impunity. In this light, the forest suggests Molly's spiritual freedom. At the same time, it also suggests the dark and frightening feelings of loneliness Molly experiences when she runs away from home in the first chapter. Frightened by the chilly dark of the woods, Molly realizes she cannot support herself alone in the world and decides to return to her house.

THE CITY In the South, Molly fails to find tolerance for her sexuality, and from a distance, the city suggests the hope and possibility of success and freedom. Faye's final letter to Molly after they have been broken up exhorts Molly to find a city so that she may live freely. Molly takes Faye's advice, realizing she'll succeed only in a place where she can find acceptance for her lesbianism. When Molly finally arrives in the city, however, it winds up representing something entirely different: the false promise of the American dream. Instead of finding unbridled opportunities and a network of friends, Molly encounters a legion of impediments to her goals. The city itself becomes one of the forces Molly must strive against in order to achieve success.

DRAINPIPES The drainpipes in *Rubyfruit Jungle* suggest the birth canal leading back to the womb of Molly's childhood, when she led a more innocent, idyllic life. Molly mentions drainpipes the first time when she dreams of leaving the hell of New York by sewer to return to warm and peaceful Fort Lauderdale. She mentions them again when she crawls through an old drainpipe during her trip back to her Pennsylvania hometown. In each reference, Molly reveals her metaphoric desire to move back in time to the places where she has felt most secure.

POLINA, PAUL, AND MR. BELLANTONI Through their areas of professional specialization, Polina, Paul, and Mr. Bellantoni suggest the intellectual bankruptcy of modern life and academics. As university professors, they are highly educated and in positions to contribute to the discussion of meaningful themes of existence. Instead, they fritter away their considerable talents on minutia, such as Polina's study of Babylonian underpants and Mr. Bellantoni's study of the representation of cows in Western art.

IMPORTANT QUOTATIONS EXPLAINED

---

1. *No one remembers her beginnings. Mothers and aunts tell us about infancy and early childhood, hoping we won't forget the past when they had total control over our lives and secretly praying that because of it, we'll include them in our future.*

This passage, which comprises the opening paragraph of the novel, establishes Molly's stance on the importance of origins in a person's character. Her insight into the secret hopes that mothers and aunts harbor implies that Molly sees a selfish motive in family members' constant reminders of childhood. Molly seems to understand that parents need children as much as children need parents. Because parents inevitably see their children as versions of themselves, they will hold the past over their children in order to imprint themselves onto the next generation, just as Carrie does to Molly at the end of the novel. As an orphan and a bastard, Molly obviously feels disconnected from her predecessors. Her orphan status highlights the fact that, though she has no control over her past, she also is not beholden to it as she goes about creating her own character. However, Molly's point in this quotation is that we all create and are responsible for our own characters, regardless of our origins. Whether or not she feels a need to defend her orphan status, Molly demonstrates that she believes wholly in the present and its extension into the future, the two things over which she has some control.

In addition to establishing Molly's belief in herself, this passage also helps to illuminate the origins of Molly's sexuality. Molly believes that our origins not only have little to do with the decisions we make, but they also have little to do with who we are as people. Accordingly, Molly's lesbianism exists independent of external factors and circumstances of birth. Molly's lesbianism is merely a part of who she is and thus requires no psychological explanation. In this light, we may view Molly's early childhood experience with Broccoli as a joke that toys with the idea that Molly's lesbianism is related to her revulsion at his wrinkly penis.

---

2. *Well, if it makes a difference to them, the hell with them, too. I can't see why it's such a big deal. Who cares how you get here? I don't care. I really don't care. I got myself born, that's what counts. I'm here.*

This thought occurs at the end of Chapter 1, when Molly considers how others will react to the knowledge that she's an illegitimate child. Molly's fierce dismissal of all those who would dare disapprove of her marks a turning point in her own self-development, as in the novel. Though she has always been brazen and strong-willed as a child, Molly definitively decides at this point that she will remain forever unapologetic in the face of social disapprobation. In choosing this course of action, she defines the pattern of conflict she'll face for the rest of her life. Those who would disavow and ostracize Molly, whom she refers to as "them," are her antagonists. Molly is admirably fearless in making this declaration, especially when we consider her willingness to forswear Carrie, the only mother she has known. However, her "me-versus-them" mentality faces its ultimate test when the main point of contention in Molly's life shifts from her bastard status to her lesbian one. She soon discovers that lesbianism is a vastly more polarizing issue than bastardization.

The second half of the phrase again underlines Molly's resistance to being defined by her past. Both a declaration and a challenge, her final sentence—"I'm here"—establishes and affirms her place in the world and demands that she be taken at face value. On a subtler note, Molly's "I'm here" also refers to the novel as a whole. The story Molly narrates is her coming-out story, in which she charts the personal problems she confronts as she attempts to integrate herself into society while growing up. But whereas most coming-out stories are accompanied by the anxiety and frustration of going public as a lesbian, Molly arrives fully formed and boldly demands to be dealt with on the basis of her character and actions, not her origins or sexual preferences.

3. *Why does everyone have to put you in a box and nail the lid on it? I don't know what I am—polymorphous and perverse. Shit. I don't even know if I'm white. I'm me. That's all I am and all I want to be. Do I have to be something?*

When Connie asks Molly in Chapter 9 if she's a "queer," Molly responds with an impassioned diatribe against the use of labels and roles to define a person and dictate behavior. To Molly, Connie's question lays bare the conventional, small-minded thinking that threatens to break down relationships and communication between people. Once Connie knows that Molly is in fact a "queer," she disregards the perfectly normal friendship they have. Her irrational fear that Molly might try to rape her displays the potency of the labeling mentality: even an individual as intelligent as Connie accepts the premise that Molly's lesbian status prescribes her actions toward all women. In this passage, Molly exposes and rebels against society's need to define and compartmentalize rigidly all aspects of life. Her description of herself as "polymorphous and perverse," terminology used to describe someone who exhibits sexual tendencies in which the genitals are not the sole or principal sexual organs, places Molly outside Connie's conventional classification. As she does in Chapter 1 with the phrase "I'm here," Molly insists "I'm me" and that she should be viewed on the basis of her character rather than on labels or her past.

Though little is made of it in the text, Molly's reference to uncertainty about her being white exposes the prevailing attitude in America toward race during the pre–civil rights era. As a child, Molly experiences the effects of segregation firsthand when she accidentally uses a bathroom reserved for blacks and is punished by Carrie. Even Carl, Molly's model of fairness and compassion, falls in with the conventional behavior that separates whites from blacks. In this passage, Molly seems to taunt Connie by equating the taboo of being lesbian with that of being partly black. By grouping them together, Molly suggests that Connie and other small-minded people think these traits are equally reprehensible and do not belong in the social mainstream. Molly herself, however, pays no attention to these prejudices as she meets different kinds of people in the book. Her failure to reveal explicitly that Holly and Calvin are black points to her lack of racial bias.

4. *People have no selves anymore (maybe they never had them in the first place) so their home base is their sex—their genitals, who they fuck.*

R

This phrase from Molly, which occurs in Chapter 15 in conversation with Polina, constitutes one of Molly's major criticisms of society: that people depend on their gender in order to express their most fundamental identity. Molly fears that this frame of mind leads people to view all other aspects of their lives through their gender and sexuality, and thus as secondary to those traits. Molly resists being defined by her sexuality alone, because she believes that selfhood is infinitely more complex and varied than the simple distinctions between man and woman. She notes that such simple distinctions have led to some of the greatest injustices in history and will continue to do so until society rejects such crude divisions. In her assertions, Molly moves toward a new and more humanistic understanding of people, where considerations of sex are secondary to the multiple possibilities of the self.

Molly is well aware that social institutions such as advertisers manipulate individuals by exploiting their preoccupation with sex. If considerations of sex are central to motivating human behavior, then advertisers succeed most in getting their messages across to the public by appealing to basic instincts. Molly sees this practice as a manifestation of patriarchal rule: big corporate institutions, which are governed by men, use images of scantily clad women or promises of liaisons with scantily clad women to sell their products to men, who have most of the money in the American economy. In this sense, advertising preserves patriarchal rule by objectifying women and promoting inequality.

5. *I wished I could be that frog back at Ep's old pond. I wished I could get up in the morning and look at the day the way I used to when I was a child. I wished I could walk down the streets and not hear those constant, abrasive sounds from the mouths of the opposite sex. Damn, I wished the world would let me be myself. But I knew better on all counts. I wish I could make my films. That wish I can work for.*

In this passage at the end of *Rubyfruit Jungle*, Molly's shift from past to present tense marks a transition from childhood to adulthood. As she has grown and changed, Molly has acquired a past of her own. Against her better judgment, she often finds herself yearning for the relative comfort and safety of her earlier years to insulate her from the painful present, where she has few job prospects and even fewer friends. However, Molly's resolve to turn away from the past and the impracticality of wishing for things that cannot come true signifies that she is ready to meet the challenges of the present and fight through hardship by concentrating on the outcomes of her life that she can control. Though it may be improbable, Molly's final wish to make films is one she can work to fulfill. Having closed the chapter on her early life, Molly sets out on a new course of adulthood.

The distinction between the wishes Molly discards and the one to which she ultimately clings suggests Brown's final attitude toward feminism and society. Whereas most coming-of-age stories end with the integration of the protagonist into society, Molly's story continues in the direction of personal fulfillment. Perhaps realizing that it will take generations of activism for the world to let Molly be herself, Molly focuses on advancing her personal agenda. She and Brown seem to believe that wider social change can occur only after individual change takes place, and Molly as an individual withdraws into the achievement of her artistic career.

R

A Small Place

Jamaica Kincaid
(1949–)

CONTEXT

Elaine Potter Richardson, who later became the novelist and essayist Jamaica Kincaid, was born in 1949 in St. John's, the capital city of the Caribbean island of Antigua. By Kincaid's own account, she was a highly intelligent but often moody child, and she became increasingly distant from her mother as the family grew in number—an estrangement that would later become a central theme in her fiction. As she matured, Kincaid also became estranged from the social and cultural milieu in which she found herself. Too ambitious and intellectually curious to be satisfied with her career prospects in her tiny island home, she was also becoming alienated from the mostly white, European tradition handed down to her through her colonial education. At seventeen, Kincaid moved to New York to work as an *au pair* while continuing her studies, eventually earning a scholarship to Franconia College in New Hampshire. Dissatisfied, she left school after a year and moved back to Manhattan, where she began working as a magazine and newspaper features journalist. During this period, Elaine Richardson changed her name to Jamaica Kincaid in a symbolic act of self-definition and freedom from the "weights" of personal and political history. As Kincaid herself put it in an interview with the *New York Times Magazine*, the new name represented "a way for me to do things without being the same person who couldn't do them—the same person who had all these weights."

Kincaid's big break came when she was hired as a staff writer by *The New Yorker*, and the magazine's editor, William Shawn (famous as a judge of talent and an exacting critic of prose) became her mentor. Kincaid's first book of short stories, *At the Bottom of the River*, was published in 1983, and her first novel, *Annie John*, followed two years later. Kincaid's early fiction, such as the much-anthologized story "Girl," often focuses on the mental world of a young girl much like the young Kincaid, with particular attention to the nuances and rhythms of Caribbean English. This evocation of the speech of the islands is reminiscent of the poetry of Derek Walcott (of St. Lucia) and Edward Kamau Brathwaite (of Barbados), and the stories of *At the Bottom of the River* have often been compared to prose poems. Kincaid's treatment of the lingering effects of slavery and colonialism on the minds of those descended from slaves and from the once-colonized Caribbean "natives" places her in the company of the Trinidadian novelist V. S. Naipaul and the Dominican novelist Jean Rhys, as well as the poets just mentioned. However, Kincaid's primary allegiance in her fiction—more than any affinity she might have to a movement or school of writing—is to her own vision and voice.

In addition to her fiction, Kincaid has produced a steady stream of nonfiction, beginning with her brief "Talk of the Town" pieces for *The New Yorker* and continuing more recently with her essays on gardening for the same magazine. *A Small Place* was, in fact, first meant for *The New Yorker*, but it was rejected as too harsh and angry in tone. The essay has been controversial since it first appeared in book form in 1988. Since then, it has gradually found its place within the English tradition of anticolonial travel writing, a tradition stretching back to Jonathan Swift's mercilessly satirical writings on Ireland in the eighteenth century and including George Orwell's classic essay "Shooting an Elephant," as well as works by such writers as Graham Greene and the American Paul Theroux. Kincaid's essay has also been important to "postcolonial" theory, a branch of literary studies that is concerned with understanding how a colonized people both internalizes and resists the colonizing culture. *A Small Place* has come to be seen as a perfect example of a postcolonial text: in it, a former colonial subject turns the greatest tools of empire, culture, and language into weapons directed against imperialism itself.

PLOT OVERVIEW

A Small Place is divided into four loosely structured, untitled sections. The first section begins with Kincaid's narration of the reader's experiences and thoughts as a hypothetical tourist in Antigua. The reader, through Kincaid's description, witnesses the great natural beauty of the island, while being sheltered from the harsher realities of the lives of those who must live there. Kincaid weaves into her narrative the sort of information that only an "insider" would know, such as the reason why the majority of the automobiles on the island are poorly running, expensive Japanese cars. Included in her guided tour are brief views of the mansions on the island, mostly gained through corruption or outright criminality. She also mentions the now-dilapidated library, still awaiting repairs after an earthquake ten years earlier. The tour continues at the hotel, and Kincaid concludes the section with a discussion of her view of the moral ugliness of being a tourist.

The second section deals with Kincaid's memories of the "old" Antigua, the colonial possession of Great Britain. Kincaid recalls the casual racism of the times, and the subservience of Antigua to England and, especially, to English culture. She delves briefly into the history of Barclay's Bank and discusses the Mill Reef Club, an elite, all-white enclave built by wealthy foreigners. She describes and deplores the great hoopla made over the visit of Princess Margaret to the island when Kincaid was a child. Much of the section is concerned with the distortions that colonialism has created in the minds of the Antiguans; Antiguans do not tend to recognize racism as such, says Kincaid, and the bad behavior of individual English people never seems to affect the general reverence for English culture. For Kincaid, the problem is compounded by the fact that the people of Antigua can express themselves only in the language of those who enslaved and oppressed them. She then discusses the connection she sees between the colonial past of the island and its impoverished, corrupt present.

The third section, the longest, deals with Antigua's present and begins with Kincaid asking herself the disturbing question of whether, considering the state of the island today, things weren't, in fact, better in the old days. As an example, she takes the state of the library, awaiting repairs after all these years and forced to reside in "temporary" quarters above a dry goods store. Kincaid has fond, if ambivalent, feelings toward the old library, which was a haven of beauty and an escape into reading for her as a child. She recalls the imperious ways of the head librarian (who suspected Kincaid, rightly, of stealing books), who is now sadly reduced to campaigning, mostly unsuccessfully, for funds to build a new library, while the collection decomposes in cardboard boxes. The rich members of the Mill Reef Club have the funds to help, but will do so only if the old library is rebuilt—a demand that Kincaid sees as having more to do with nostalgia for the colonial regime than with a true desire to help. Kincaid mentions the ironies involved in Antigua having a Minister of Culture without having a culture to administer. She also mentions her politically active mother's run-in with the current Minister of Culture, who has allowed the library to languish. Education has clearly suffered on Antigua in the years since independence, and Kincaid ruefully notes the poor speech habits of the younger Antiguans.

Kincaid discusses the way Antiguans experience the passage of time, and connects this to their oddly detached view of the corruption of their government. She then goes into a litany of the many abuses of power on the island, including misappropriation of funds, kickbacks, drug smuggling, and even political violence—all of which are known by the average Antiguan. Kincaid then discusses the political history of Antigua since independence, showing how power has rested in the same hands for most of the period, with one brief, unimpressive exception. Kincaid sees corruption as an ingrained element of political life on the island, so much so that government officials who do not steal are held in contempt as fools rather than admired for their honesty. She tells of the fears that many Antiguans have for the future and hints that open dictatorship or political upheaval may lie ahead.

The fourth, and final, section is a sort of coda to the piece, starting with an evocation of the intense physical beauty of the island. She describes the beauty as so extreme as to appear "unreal," almost like an illustration or a stage-set. Kincaid says that the beauty of their surroundings is a mixed blessing to the Antiguans, who are trapped in an unchanging setting in which their poverty is part of the scenery. The slaves who were brought to Antigua by force were victims, and therefore noble—but their descendants, today's Antiguans, are simple human beings, with all the problems and contradictions of human beings anywhere.

CHARACTER LIST

V. C. Bird The first postindependence Prime Minister of Antigua, and, with the exception of one five-year term, the only one. The Antigua airport is named for V. C. Bird. He is the head of an extremely corrupt government, and his sons are poised to take his place once he dies. This, along with the facts that Antigua has a standing army with nothing to do and that the government controls the media, leads Kincaid to worry about the long-term viability of democracy on the island.

The Head Librarian An imposing figure in the life of the young Jamaica Kincaid. The head librarian holds a culturally prestigious post, though a diminished one now. At one time, she worked in the beautiful old library in the central part of town. After an earthquake destroyed the library, the collection moved to "temporary" quarters—for over ten years. The head librarian's struggles to raise money for a new library, and her makeshift bookroom above a dry goods store, render her a sad figure of the decline of the already meager cultural institutions on Antigua.

The Irish Headmistress A twenty-six-year-old woman recruited by the Colonial Office in England to run the girl's school in Antigua. The headmistress often rebuked the girls by telling them to stop behaving "as if they were monkeys just out of the trees." Her thoughtless racism is emblematic of the callousness of colonial rule and of the passivity of the Antiguans when faced with it.

Jamaica Kincaid The author and narrator of *A Small Place*. Kincaid makes use of personal experience and history in the essay, and the entire work is permeated with her anger and intelligence. Kincaid emerges as a character both as a young girl, desperate for knowledge and a wider world, and as an adult, looking at her birthplace with a ruthlessly penetrating eye.

Kincaid's Mother The author's mother. Kincaid's mother appears briefly in an anecdote that Kincaid tells about her political activity. Her brash opinions and loud mouth earn her a reputation as a troublemaker, and the Minister of Culture is not pleased to find her posting signs for the opposition party in front of his house. When he tries to snub her, Kincaid's mother implies that he is a crook and that she knows all about it; the Minister retreats. Even in this brief scene, Kincaid's admiration for and ambivalence toward her formidable mother are clear.

The "Other Prime Minister" The man, unnamed by Kincaid, who supplants Bird for one term. This Prime Minister campaigns as an enlightened democrat and promises to fight corruption. There are stories of dishonesty in his own past, including one that he destroyed the accounting books of one of his employers to hide his embezzlement. The great optimism that greets his election is soon quenched by the incompetence of his administration, and he is jailed after losing the next election.

Princess Margaret The younger sister of the future queen of England, Elizabeth II. Margaret makes a state visit to Antigua when Kincaid is a child. The entire island is spruced up for her arrival, and the princess is greeted by crowds who regard the visit as one of the great events in Antigua's history. Years later, Kincaid learns that, far from being motivated by any particular interest in Antigua or the Antiguans, Margaret had simply been trying to escape a sticky personal situation back in England—she had fallen in love with a married man.

The Syrians Foreigners who have moved to Antigua to make their fortunes in business speculation. To the Antiguans, the Syrians are involved in most of the corruption on the island. Kincaid points out that they have connections high in the government and that they have become fabulously wealthy by renting properties to the government at exorbitant prices. She also implies that the Syrians may be involved in politically and economically motivated violence, such as the strange deaths-by-electrocution that befall certain officials.

The Woman from the Mill Reef Club A wealthy woman Kincaid speaks to regarding the rebuilding effort for the library. This unnamed woman is well-known for her dislike of the Antiguans in any role except that of a servant. She encourages "her girls" (employees) to use the library and wants to rebuild it just as it was before the earthquake. Kincaid sees her as motivated by nostalgia for the days of colonial rule and resents the woman's smirking at the corruption of the post-independence government, though she also resents the accuracy of the charge.

"You" The personified reader whom Kincaid addresses throughout the essay. Especially in the first section, "you," the reader, is characterized as a basically ordinary, middle-class American or European, mostly ignorant of Antigua's history and of the lives of its inhabitants. "You" becomes the main focus of Kincaid's attack on what she sees as the moral ugliness of tourism.

ANALYSIS OF MAJOR CHARACTERS

JAMAICA KINCAID As a child, Kincaid is a close, critical observer of the behavior of the adults around her. Her attitude toward the visiting Princess Margaret is reminiscent of the child in the story of the Emperor's New Clothes: while everyone else is happy—even excited—to stand around for hours in the sun to catch a glimpse of the royal guest, the seven-year-old Kincaid is unimpressed. A voracious reader, the young Kincaid exhausted the children's books in the library, and Kincaid explains that reading was a kind of escape from the frustration and boredom of her daily life. So passionate is the young Kincaid about reading that she steals books from the library.

As an adult, the same critical eye with which Kincaid saw through the pomp of the royal visit is turned on the island at large. She speaks bitterly of the corruption of the government and the passivity of the people, but the main force of her anger is directed toward the English who colonized Antigua. Kincaid lays the present predicament of the Antiguans at the feet of the English, for populating the island with their slaves in the first place and for educating descendents of those slaves to admire the country that enslaved them. Kincaid describes herself as so angry about England's crimes that she cannot bear to hear England praised—she even speaks about her resentment at dinner parties. Her anger toward tourists is slightly less intense and is focused on the willful ignorance required of people to enjoy themselves in a desperately poor place. Unlike the average Antiguans she describes, Kincaid cannot resign herself to the past oppression and present corruption. She is mystified that more Antiguans don't share her outrage, and is frustrated by their apparent acceptance of their status as bit players in the vacation videos of others. As the anger of the adult Kincaid reveals, she remains deeply attached to her home and to her people. However, Kincaid has no illusions about the future of the island and seems glad to have made her partial escape.

Although *A Small Place* is not a conventional memoir, Kincaid is very present in her memories and perceptions. It is important to remember that even in a memoir or nonfiction essay, the voice in the work who speaks to the reader as "I" is first and foremost a literary creation—a representation of the author within the work, rather than the author herself. In other words, the "Jamaica Kincaid" who appears in *A Small Place* is a character—a highly edited version of the real Jamaica Kincaid—created by Kincaid to speak to the reader on her behalf. Kincaid appears in the essay both in memory as a child, and in the present day as a grown-up who is trying to assess Antigua's history and current situation, and to explain it all.

"YOU" Kincaid address the reader, "you," throughout *A Small Place*, especially in the opening section, in which she describes the vacation experience that a "typical" tourist would have in Antigua as well as what this person doesn't understand about this place. Kincaid's "typical" tourist is a white, middle-class person from Europe, the United States, or Canada, with the attitudes and assumptions Kincaid thinks are common to those with this background. The details of Antigua that Kincaid chooses to describe or emphasize are those that, to her, would be most striking to a comfortable, bourgeois, Western tourist. Kincaid characterizes "you" as basically well-meaning but ignorant and somewhat callous. "You" have an ordinary life at home, with people who love you. Your travels are motivated by boredom, and you want to observe the lives of others in a beautiful place.

For "you," everything about the lives of the Antiguans, from their clothes to their personal habits, seems interesting and picturesque. What Kincaid wants to emphasize is that the lives of these others will always be opaque to an outsider, for whom they are part of the scenery of the "small place" they have chosen to visit. "You" are bound to miss the significance of such things as the noisy Japanese cars and the giant mansions. "You" are pleased that "your" trip is unlikely to be ruined by rain—but don't understand the difficulties caused for the residents by a lack of fresh water. For Kincaid, however nice "you" may be at home, "you" are ugly as long as "you" are a tourist—someone for whom the poverty and labor of others are merely distractions from the boredom and emptiness of "your" own existence.

THEMES, MOTIFS, AND SYMBOLS

THEMES

THE UGLINESS OF TOURISM For Kincaid, tourists are morally ugly, though in her description of fat, "pastrylike-fleshed" people on the beach, she shows that physical ugliness is part of tourism as well. The moral ugliness of tourism is inherent in the way tourists make use of other, usually much poorer, people for their pleasure. Kincaid is not referring to direct exploitation of others (though she does mention one government minister who runs a brothel); rather, she refers to a more spiritual form of exploitation. According to Kincaid, a tourist travels to escape the boredom of ordinary life—they want to see new things and people in a lovely setting. Kincaid points out that the loveliness of the places that tend to attract tourists is often a source of difficulty for those who live there. For example, the sunny, clear sky of Antigua, which indicates a lack of rainfall, makes fresh water a scarce and precious commodity. For tourists, however, the beauty is all that matters—the drought is someone else's problem.

Others' problems can even add to the attraction of a place for tourists. Kincaid notes that tourists tend to romanticize poverty. The locals' humble homes and clothing seem picturesque, and even open latrines can seem pleasingly "close to nature," unlike the modern plumbing at home. Kincaid believes that this attitude is the essence of tourism. The lives of others, no matter how poor and sad, are part of the scenery tourists have come to enjoy, a perspective that negatively affects both tourists and locals. The exotic and often absurd misunderstanding that tourists have of a strange culture ultimately prevents them from really knowing the place they have come to see.

ADMIRATION VS. RESENTMENT OF THE COLONIZER Kincaid observes the quality of education on Antigua, as well as the minds of its inhabitants, and remains deeply ambivalent about both. She herself is the product of a colonial education, and she believes that Antiguan young people today are not as well-educated as they were in her day. Kincaid was raised on the classics of English literature, and she thinks today's young Antiguans are poorly spoken, ignorant, and devoted to American pop culture. However, one of the things Kincaid despises most about the old Antigua was its cultural subservience to England. If young Antiguans today are obsessed with American trash, in the old days they were obsessed with British trash. One of the insidious effects of Antiguans being schooled in the British system is that all of their models of excellence in literature and history are British. In other words, Antiguans have been taught to admire the very people who once enslaved them. Kincaid is horrified by the genuine excitement the Antiguans have regarding royal visits to the island: the living embodiment of British imperialism is joyously greeted by the former victims of that imperialism.

Antiguans' minds have been shaped from the bottom up by the experience of being enslaved and, later, colonized. This intimate shaping determines the contours of daily life and even private thoughts. For example, the young Kincaid's greatest pleasure is in reading, but everything she reads is tainted by bitterness, since she is learning the dominant culture from the position of a dominated people. English is her first language, and Kincaid complains that even her critique of colonialism must be expressed in the words she learned from the colonialists themselves. Kincaid doesn't feel at home in either world. She will never be truly English because of race and history, yet her intimacy with English culture expands her horizons far beyond the small boundaries of Antigua. Thanks to slavery and to being ruled from afar for so long, the Antiguans have become accustomed to being passive objects of history, rather than active makers of it. The experiences of the colonized are therefore always secondary in some sense; it is the people from the "large places" who determine events, control history, and even control language.

THE PREVALENCE OF CORRUPTION For Kincaid, corruption is related to colonization in that it is a continuation of the oppression of colonialism—except that corruption turns the once-colonized people against themselves. Kincaid insists that corruption pervades every aspect of public life in Antigua, that everyone knows about it, and that no one seems to know what to do about it. Government ministers run brothels, steal public funds, and broker shady deals, but there is a conspicuous lack of outrage on the part of the public. Kincaid attributes this lack of anger to the Antiguans' general passivity, but she also sees their attitude as a logical reaction to the "lessons" of Antiguan history. The British claimed to be bringing civilization to the colonized territories while actually exploiting them and taking from them as much as they could. Naturally, when the Antiguans themselves came to power, they followed the example they had been given: under the motto "A People to Mold, A Nation to Build," their ministers claim to be working for the greater good while lining their own pockets.

MOTIFS

DIRECT ADDRESS TO THE READER Kincaid speaks directly to the reader throughout *A Small Place*, even accusing the reader of taking part in the moral ugliness of tourism. Kincaid begins by describing what the reader might see and think as a visitor to Antigua, and she refers to what "you" are probably thinking as "you" read. This direct address has two effects. First, it emphasizes that, from the Antiguans' point of view, the reader is just as much a part of a generalized group as they are, and that he or she will not be seen as an individual but as a stereotype. Second, it forces the reader to consider the ways in which he or she does, in fact, fit Kincaid's stereotype of a tourist. Anyone who has traveled to the tropics in search of a relaxing "getaway" is likely to find reading *A Small Place* uncomfortable due to Kincaid's accusing, sarcastic tone. By addressing the reader this way, Kincaid hopes to intensify her angry denunciation of the state of things in Antigua by pointing her finger directly at the reader and anticipating the reader's criticism. For Kincaid, any alienation that the reader feels is part of the plan.

"UNREAL" BEAUTY Throughout *A Small Place*, especially in the final section, Kincaid pauses to illustrate Antigua's natural beauty. She describes the intense colors, the unrelenting sunlight, and the sea. She frequently uses the word "unreal" to describe the scenery, as though everything looks too perfect to be believable. This idea of unreality is part of what Kincaid sees as the effect of the island's beauty on those who live or travel there. For tourists, everything, including the Antiguans themselves, is a kind of movie backdrop, a stage set up for their own enjoyment. The history and the sufferings of others are incidental, forgettable. For the Antiguans, the unchanging quality of the beauty suggests that their own lives are peripheral to a larger plan. When nothing changes, there is no sense of history or hope of development to motivate people. For Kincaid, the landscape is a determining factor in life on the island, but something morally neutral—the Antiguans' daily blessing and their historical curse.

SYMBOLS

THE LIBRARY'S SIGN The sign on the old colonial library in Antigua's capital reads, "THIS BUILDING WAS DAMAGED IN THE EARTHQUAKE OF 1974. REPAIRS ARE PENDING." As Kincaid points out, both the sign and the damage to which it refers date back to the colonial period in Antigua. When Kincaid wrote *A Small Place*, the repairs had been "pending" for more than ten years. Clearly, says Kincaid, people who can wait for something that has been pending for so long must have an unusual sense of time. The library stands on both a literal and a metaphorical fault line: just as the earthquake shook the ground under the building, so did the shift from colonial- to self-rule cause a seismic disruption in the culture that the building was meant to serve. For Kincaid, the status of the library is emblematic of the status of the island as a whole: damaged remnants of a colonial structure remain, but the Antiguans are unable either to repair it or to move on to a new structure. The sign on the library becomes a sign of the stasis in which the Antiguans are trapped and of the inescapability of the colonial past.

JAPANESE CARS The Japanese cars, ubiquitous on the island, are an example of the kind of detail a tourist might observe without truly understanding its significance. A tourist might assume that the Antiguans simply prefer Japanese cars, even though they seem oddly out of place amid the general poverty. Kincaid says that only a local would see the significance: the car dealerships are partly owned by government officials who have made sure that low-cost car loans are available to everyone. In other words, the popularity of Japanese cars on the island is part of a moneymaking scheme that has nothing to do with either the common good or the preferences of individual consumers. The unleaded gasoline required to run the cars properly is not even available, though the drivers seem unaware of this. For Kincaid, the Japanese cars throughout Antigua are a potent symbol both of the pervasive corruption endemic in even the most mundane exchanges on the island, and of the way in which the true significance of the details of daily life are invisible to the tourist's oblivious eye.

IMPORTANT QUOTATIONS EXPLAINED

---

1. *[A]nd so you needn't let that slightly funny feeling you have from time to time about exploitation, oppression, domination develop into full-fledged unease, discomfort; you could ruin your holiday.*

Taken from the first section of *A Small Place*, this passage is an example of Kincaid's direct address to the reader, as well as her sarcastic tone. The kind of reader Kincaid has in mind is likely to be well-educated enough to have some idea of the colonial history, and present difficulties, of a place like Antigua, but is just as likely to suppress such knowledge for comfort's sake, in order not to "ruin their holiday." One of Kincaid's primary intentions is to make such complacency impossible. An important weapon in her arsenal is the kind of classic rhetorical device she uses here: an anticlimax. In comparison to the grand political and moral issues she references—"exploitation, oppression, domination"—the reader's concern for an unspoiled tropical vacation is bound to seem petty and rather squalid. The "funny feeling" she wants to gain access to is the reader's conscience.

---

2. *Do you ever try to understand why people like me cannot get over the past, cannot forgive and cannot forget? There is the Barclay's Bank. The Barclay brothers are dead. The human beings they traded, the human beings who to them were only commodities, are dead. . . . So do you see the queer thing about people like me? Sometimes we hold your retribution.*

In the second section of *A Small Place*, Kincaid indicts the British colonial system and, by extension, the entire enterprise of European colonialism. She condemns the early capitalist system that traded in humans, turning them into a commodity no different from sugar or rum. The Barclay Brothers illustrate how historical acts of exploitation are never really over, despite our desire to pretend otherwise. After making their fortunes in the slave trade, the Barclays went into banking, and the financial institution they set up continues to operate worldwide. Ironically, Barclay's Bank is the major banking company on Antigua, issuing loans and managing the meager funds of the descendents of the very slaves who were the source of the Barclay fortune. The Barclays are, in a sense, still profiting from those they exploited long after their deaths, which suggests the unending ramifications of actions that seem safely ensconced in history. Kincaid "cannot forgive and cannot forget," because there is no way to undo the injustice of slavery, and, in a way, the injustice continues. The Barclays are beyond punishment, and their victims are beyond help. Kincaid can only keep the thought of them alive as a sort of "retribution."

---

3. *I[I]f you could hear the sound of [the old library's] quietness . . . , the smell of the sea . . . , the heat of the sun . . . , the beauty of us sitting there like communicants at an altar . . . , the fairy tale of how we met you, your right to do the things you did . . . you would see why my heart would break at the dung heap that now passes for a library in Antigua.*

This passage, from the beginning of the third section, is part of Kincaid's attempt to answer the question of whether Antigua was better off under colonial rule. The library perfectly captures the dilemma, as well as Kincaid's ambiguous feelings about it. Kincaid's loving, lyrical description of the library is one of the most tender moments in the book. The old library is like a church in Kincaid's memory, and the current library above the dry goods store is a mockery of the old, now-damaged building. Kincaid's nostalgia is undercut by a wary realization that the library served a political function in the old Antigua. To Kincaid, the library was part of the "fairy tale" of Empire—the story of how the British brought culture and civilization to the so-called savage parts of the world. Kincaid emphasizes that the ultimate purpose of the education she received under the colonial system was to teach her that the British were right to do what they did to win their empire and that her own status as a subject of a foreign crown was just. Kincaid's emotional ambivalence is crucial to her portrayal of the library, which is itself ambivalent: formerly a lovely place and now a liberated "dung heap."

---

4. *Antigua is a small place. Antigua is a very small place. In Antigua, not only is the event turned into everyday, but the everyday is turned into an event.*

Toward the middle of the third section, Kincaid discusses how Antiguans experience the passage of time, and, by extension, how they think of history. Antiguans have a distorted perspective of their lives: small things loom large, and major events are reduced to an "ordinary" occurance. For example, Antiguans think daily about their history as slaves, and they think of emancipation as if it has just occurred. Turning this extraordinary event into an everyday occurrence weakens the uniqueness of the moment and obscures the importance of any subsequent event, such as Antigua's rampant corruption. At the same time, ordinary events take on an exaggerated importance, such as when two men turn an inconsequential accident into a years-long feud. By repeatedly asserting that Antigua is "a small place," Kincaid emphasizes the overwhelming physical constraints placed on life by Antigua's physical environment and positions it as the perfect example of a colonized society. In this sense, Antigua is the ultimate "small place," and its struggles are like those of all such places as they try to define themselves against the "large" places and forces of the world.

---

5. *It is as if, then, the beauty—the beauty of the sea, the land, the air, the trees, the market, the people, the sounds they make—were a prison, and as if everything and everybody inside it were locked in and everything and everybody that is not inside it were locked out. And what might it do to ordinary people to live in this way every day? What might it do to them to live in such heightened, intense surroundings every day?*

In this passage from the final section, Kincaid addresses the mixed blessing of Antigua's beauty. Once again, she does so by considering the difference between the Antiguan point of view and that of anyone not from the island. The landscape cannot make Antigua wealthy in a material sense—there is no oil, timber, or great fertile prairie to be developed. Instead, the landscape's beauty is Antigua's great natural resource, which means it is also one of the great determining factors of Antiguans' lives. Tourists are drawn to the island because of this beauty, and, for them, the inhabitants are part of the scenery. In this sense, outsiders are "locked out" of understanding what the lives of the insiders are truly like. The insiders are "locked in" in a similar way—they belong to the landscape more than it can ever belong to them. The surroundings are so "heightened" and "intense" that they seem to negate some of the intensity of people's actual existences. As Kincaid says, the beauty of the island is so perfect and unchanging that change itself seems impossible. When everything is extraordinary, making judgments about what needs to change is difficult, and the fate of becoming simply a passive observer of a beautiful cage seems unavoidable.

S

The Sovereignty and Goodness of God

Mary Rowlandson (~1637–1711)

CONTEXT

After the arrival of the *Mayflower* in 1620, relations between the newly arrived British settlers and long-established native peoples were uneasy at best. A major source of tension between the two groups was their differing approaches to the land. The Native Americans who lived in what is now New England hunted and gathered nuts to eat, but they also farmed, with corn as their principal crop. When the settlers arrived, the Native Americans focused on the land's resources, assuming the resources would still be at their disposal even if the new settlers used the land as well. The colonists, in contrast, came from Britain, where plots of land separate from common land were individually fenced off as areas for livestock to graze. Livestock suddenly appeared on land the Native Americans had planned to use for resources, a conflict that became one of the causes of King Philip's War (also called Metacom's War), named for the leader of the Wampanoag Indians.

The Native Americans and the colonists had lived peacefully together for nearly fifty years before the war broke out in 1675, but their calm coexistence ended as the colonists demanded more land from the Native Americans, who felt their culture was being threatened. Deep-seated resentment bubbled to the surface, and neighbors became enemies. The war, marked by Native American raids on the colonists' settlements and the colonists' retaliation, didn't end until Philip's death in 1676. Chaos and violence characterized the raids on British towns: in Lancaster, for example, a number of Native Americans arrived at sunrise and opened fire on the town, using guns they had acquired in trade or in warfare with other settlers.

In addition to killing some colonists, the attackers took captives, not only in Lancaster but elsewhere. By taking settlers captive, King Philip (also known as Metacom, though not mentioned by that name in *The Sovereignty and Goodness of God*) and his tribesmen gained an effective bargaining tool: the Native Americans could trade their captives for ransom in the form of money, weapons, or provisions. The attack on Lancaster in 1675 was one of the earliest raids, but it did not come entirely without warning. Prior to the attack, rumors had circulated that the Wampanoag tribes were planning violent raids on the frontier settlements of what is now western Massachusetts, with Lancaster named as the first target. Some settlers, including the Reverend Joseph Rowlandson, took these rumors and warnings seriously and traveled to Boston to ask the government there for military aid. Help did not come soon enough, however, and the attack was devastating. Many settlers in the town were killed or wounded, and others, including Mary Rowlandson and several of her family members, were taken captive.

Though born in England, Mary Rowlandson, whose maiden name was White, moved with her parents to the Massachusetts Bay Colony sometime before 1638. Fifteen years later, the family moved to Lancaster, where they were considered wealthy. Though Lancaster was then on the far western frontier of British settlements, life was relatively peaceful. In 1656, Mary married the Reverend Joseph Rowlandson. By 1675, she had had four children, the eldest of whom had died as a young boy. Lancaster was a close-knit community. Members of Rowlandson's extended family, including her sisters and their husbands and children, lived nearby, and neighbors were friends and acquaintances. This closeness no doubt made the attack all the more devastating: what had been a happy and comfortable extended family was torn apart, with some family members dead and others taken captive and then separated from one another in the wilderness. Such was the situation for Rowlandson's family and for other families in the village.

Faced with the chaos of the attack and the trials of an experience in captivity, Rowlandson turned to Puritan theology to make sense of it all. Her devotion was not surprising, since her husband was a minister and Christian thought and practice were central in Puritans' lives. The Puritans were known for their

S

piety, and they saw themselves as a "community of saints." At the same time, however, their society felt scared and guilty. They worried they were not pious enough and feared, perhaps unconsciously, that leaving England had been the wrong choice. Their worldview, meanwhile, was marked by a belief that everything happened for a reason, which suggested that a lesson could be learned from every experience. Rowlandson did not, therefore, see her captivity as an act of random or undeserved violence. Rather, she struggled to come to terms with her experiences and to understand why God had chosen to punish and then save her. She documented her struggle in her narrative, *The Sovereignty and Goodness of God*, the true story of her captivity and return to civilization.

Rowlandson's book, first printed in 1682, is the first of a genre that then began to flourish: the captivity narrative. Some of these narratives, such as Rowlandson's, were told from the first-person point of view. Other narratives, such as that of Mary Jemison (who was taken captive in the 1750s, three-quarters of a century after Rowlandson's captivity), were told in the first person but were written down by writers or interviewers rather than by the captives themselves. Still others were delivered as sermons, such as the 1697 sermon by the famous Boston preacher Cotton Mather, which concerns the separate captivities of two young women, Hannah Swarton and Hannah Dustan. Significantly, while both men and women were taken captive by Native Americans, the captivity narrative as a genre consists primarily of the captivity experiences of women, perhaps because of their perceived helplessness and innocence. The narratives also share a common religious framework: they use the same vocabulary of suffering, exile in the wilderness, and ultimate redemption. Rowlandson's narrative served as an example for later imitators, but later narratives were not mere mimicry. Rather, the persistence of the genre for well over a century suggests that the captivity narrative was a way to express some of the deepest tensions present in colonial and early American society.

PLOT OVERVIEW

On the morning of February 10, 1675, the British settlement of Lancaster, in the Massachusetts Bay Colony, is besieged by Native Americans. The attackers burn down houses and open fire on the settlers, wounding and killing several of them, and take a number of the survivors captive. Mary Rowlandson is one of the wounded, as is her youngest child, Sarah. Other members of Rowlandson's family are killed outright. As the melee dies down, the Native Americans begin to lead their captives, including Rowlandson and her three children, from the settlement into the surrounding wilderness. At this point, Rowlandson and her two elder children are separated, but she and the youngest are allowed to remain together.

After a night spent in an abandoned town nearby, from which colonists had fled in fear of Indian attack, the captors and their captives begin to trek westward, farther into the forest. As Rowlandson and her daughter are both wounded, the journey is difficult and painful. After another day of travel, they reach an Indian settlement called Wenimesset. Here, Rowlandson meets another British captive, Robert Pepper, who wants to offer the new captives comfort. The Indians and their captives remain in Wenimesset for over a week, and during this time, Rowlandson's wounded child becomes more ill, finally dying on February 18. By this time, Rowlandson's original captor has sold her to a Saggamore Indian named Quannopin, who is related by marriage to King Philip. Quannopin oversees the burial of Rowlandson's dead child, and a grieving Rowlandson visits her elder daughter (also named Mary), who she learns is also being held in Wenimesset. As she despairs over the fate of her family, her son visits her—he has been allowed to come from the nearby Indian settlement where he is being held in captivity. Meanwhile, the Indians continue to attack British towns, including Medfield, killing and looting as they go. Her captors give Rowlandson a Bible, part of the spoils of Medfield, and in it she finds comfort and hope.

After the fighting at Medfield, the Indians decide again to "remove" westward, now heading north as well. Rowlandson is again separated from her family and acquaintances. After a four-day rest in the forest, the band of Indians with whom Rowlandson is traveling begins to travel more swiftly. Rowlandson suspects that the British army must be close. They reach the Baquaug River and cross it, and the English arrive close behind. The British soldiers, however, are unable to ford the river, and the Indians and Rowlandson continue to the northwest. Rowlandson and her captors soon reach the Connecticut River, which they plan to cross in order to meet with King Philip. Here, however, are English scouts, and the Indians and Rowlandson are forced to scatter in the forest to remain undetected. Rowlandson again meets up with her son and his captors, though they must soon part ways.

After this detour, Rowlandson and the Indians cross the river, and on the other side, she meets with King Philip as planned. For some time, she remains at this settlement, sewing clothes for the Indians in return for food. The Indians, meanwhile, raid Northampton and return with spoils, including horses.

Rowlandson asks to be taken to Albany on horseback, hoping that there she will be "sold" in exchange for gunpowder, but instead, the Indians prepare to take her northward and over the river once more.

After a brief sojourn at a settlement five miles north of King Philip's abode, Rowlandson's captors once again bring her north but then turn south again. Rowlandson hopes she'll be returned home, but the Indians delay the journey, continuing south down the Connecticut River rather than turning east toward civilization. Indian attacks on British towns continue, and another captive, Thomas Read, joins Rowlandson's group. From Read, Rowlandson learns that her husband is alive and well, which heartens her. Rowlandson also sees her son again, briefly. Rowlandson and her captors finally begin to move east.

They again cross the Baquaug River. Messengers meet them and report that Rowlandson must go to Wachuset, where the Indians will meet to discuss her possible return to freedom. More hopeful than she has been in some time, Rowlandson eagerly sets off toward the council's meeting place. But the journey tires her, and she is disheartened by the sight of an injured colonist, wounded in still another Indian attack. At Wachuset, she speaks with King Philip, who promises her she'll be free in two weeks. Nonetheless, the council continues to deliberate, asking Rowlandson how much her husband would be willing to pay them as ransom. The Indians then send a letter to Boston, stating that Rowlandson can be redeemed for twenty pounds. Meanwhile, attacks on British settlements continue, including an attack on Sudbury, after which Rowlandson must travel with her captors back into the forest.

As the Indians celebrate their victories, messengers arrive from the council, along with an Englishman named John Hoar. Rowlandson hopes she'll be allowed to leave with Hoar, but negotiations continue for several more days. Rowlandson is finally allowed to travel back to now-abandoned Lancaster, then on to Concord, and finally to Boston. After nearly twelve weeks in the wilderness, Rowlandson is reunited with her husband. The two stay with a friend in Concord for eleven weeks, during which time Rowlandson's sister is also released from her captivity. Rowlandson's son and daughter are eventually returned as well. The family, together again at last, sets up a new household in Boston, where they continue to live until 1677.

CHARACTER LIST

Mary Rowlandson The narrator and protagonist. Mary Rowlandson is a wife and mother who finds her life disrupted when Indians take her captive after the attack on Lancaster. Rowlandson finds solace in the Bible during her captivity, and her charity and kindness prompt her to help others when she is able, often by helping them find solace in the Bible as well. As her time with the Indians progresses, however, Rowlandson becomes less sure of her own moral high ground and less certain of the savagery of her captors. She begins to realize the capacity for savagery that lies within all people, even Christians, and this knowledge haunts her even after her return to civilization. But she is grateful to God for her redemption and writes her story as a way of teaching other settlers about God's power and grace.

Reverend Joseph Rowlandson Mary Rowlandson's husband. Joseph Rowlandson is away in Boston when the attack on Lancaster takes place. He is a faithful husband who uses his ties to the church to help free his family and other captives.

Joseph Rowlandson (son) The only living son of Joseph and Mary Rowlandson. Joseph is only thirteen years old when he is taken captive in the attack on Lancaster. Pious, responsible Joseph visits his mother whenever he can, and the two of them pray and read the Bible together.

Mary Rowlandson (daughter) The eldest daughter of Joseph and Mary Rowlandson. Mary is ten years old when she is taken captive and separated from her family. Like Joseph, she is brave and pious and visits her mother whenever she can.

Sarah Rowlandson The youngest daughter of the Rowlandsons. Sarah is taken captive along with her mother when she is only six years old. She is badly wounded in the attack on Lancaster and dies relatively early into Rowlandson's captivity.

King Philip The unstable, unreliable leader of the Wampanoag Indians. At times, King Philip reassures Rowlandson that she'll soon be free. But when her redemption is near, he tries to bypass the structure of the council, refusing to meet with the rest of the Indians in their General Court and promising Rowlandson her freedom in exchange for food and goods. Philip may be unreliable, but he is not unkind, and the ambivalence of Rowlandson's attitude toward Philip suggests the larger uncertainty Rowlandson has about her captors' savageness and her own civilized nature.

Robert Pepper A captive colonist who proves helpful to Rowlandson. Pepper meets Rowlandson after he has already been traveling with the Indians for some time. Like Rowlandson, he had a wound to tend to when he was first taken captive. He shares with Rowlandson the folk knowledge he learned from the Indians, teaching her how oak leaves can help to heal her. Pepper, who has learned how to use nature to his advantage, is a positive example of a settler negotiating the world of the wilderness.

John Gilbert A young settler from Springfield whom the Indians hold captive. John is ill and suffering when Rowlandson visits him in a settlement near Hadley. Underclothed and left outside, along with an orphaned Indian baby, John moves Rowlandson to pity. His predicament exemplifies the Indians' cruelty and the extent to which all captives are reduced to dependence on the kindness of strangers.

John Hoar An English settler who is friendly with the "praying Indians" of Massachusetts. Kind, diplomatic Hoar acts as a messenger and helps to negotiate Rowlandson's release. He arrives at Wachuset with letters to King Philip from the council in Boston, and when Rowlandson is freed, he travels back to Boston with her. Well-connected in both Indian and British circles, Hoar provides a means for settlers to interact with Indians without losing any of their own civility.

Thomas Read Another captive Rowlandson meets in the middle of her captivity. Read tells Rowlandson her husband is alive and well. As a settler, Read is a reliable and trustworthy source of information, unlike the Indians.

Mary Thurston Another captive Rowlandson meets near the end of her captivity. Mary lends Rowlandson her hat when Rowlandson is bothered by the sun's glare. This act of charity and kindness marks Thurston as a good Christian.

Tom and Peter "Praying Indians" and acquaintances of John Hoar. Tom and Peter act as messengers between the council of the colonists and the General Court of the Indians, helping to negotiate freedom for the captives.

Wettimore One of Quannopin's three wives. Wettimore is proud and vain, concerned primarily with wealth, status, and her own appearance. She is generally unkind to Rowlandson, and only when Rowlandson's freedom approaches does she begin treating her better, possibly because she wants some of the ransom money the settlers will offer. Wettimore serves as a foil to Rowlandson: her negative qualities contrast strongly with Rowlandson's positive characteristics.

Onux The oldest of Quannopin's three wives. Onux is kind to Rowlandson, unlike Wettimore, another of Quannopin's wives. When Rowlandson arrives in Wachuset, Quannopin asks Onux to tend to Rowlandson's needs, and Onux feeds her a meal of beans, meat, and ground-nut cake. As an Indian who is willing to treat a captive decently, Onux demonstrates the kindness and compassion that can exist even among people who are presumed to be savages and who are, in wartime, the enemy.

Quannopin A Saggamore Indian who is related to King Philip by virtue of being married to Philip's wife's sister. Quannopin is Rowlandson's master when she is among the Indians. Having purchased Rowlandson from the Indian who originally took her captive, Quannopin is generally kind and decent to her. He is not always present to make sure Rowlandson is well-treated, however. For several weeks of Rowlandson's captivity, Quannopin travels elsewhere among the Indian settlements, leaving Rowlandson in the care of one of his three wives.

Thomas Shepard A kind settler who lives in Charlestown. Shepard shelters the Rowlandsons in his home for eleven weeks after Mary Rowlandson's release from captivity.

ANALYSIS OF MAJOR CHARACTERS

MARY ROWLANDSON The protagonist and narrator of *The Sovereignty and Goodness of God* is a middle-aged wife and mother of three children. Though she was born in England, she has lived in the American colonies for nearly four decades and has lived in the frontier settlement of Lancaster for more than twenty years. Married to a minister, she is pious, and her Christian faith, like that of other Puritans, plays a central role in her life. Rowlandson believes God plays an active role in people's lives, showing his grace in the form of safety and well-being and expressing his disapproval by plaguing people with misfortunes or tragedy. When confronted with a disastrous Indian attack, Rowlandson questions her conception of herself and her society. She is certain that such an attack must have happened for a reason, and, taken captive and unsure if she will survive, she seeks to uncover that reason.

In her search for understanding, she turns to Christianity and finds meaning and comfort in the Bible. Like other Puritans, she projects the struggles that occur in the Bible and in her own psyche onto the landscape around her. America often seems to be a new Eden, but the landscape and its native inhabitants also seem connected to hell and the devil. Rowlandson casts herself alternately as Job (whose suffering is a test of his faith) and as one of the Israelites fated to wander in the wilderness (whose trials are brought upon them as punishment for their own failings). Rowlandson has a great fear of devolving to savagery—of "backsliding" religiously and socially—a fear that appears in other Puritan writings as well.

KING PHILIP The leader of the Wampanoags, known as King Philip by the British, plays a large but ambiguous role in Mary Rowlandson's narrative. Though as a leader he has power and status, Philip often seems removed from the politics and violence of his people and seems distant even from the war that bears his name. When he first meets Rowlandson, he is courteous, offering her some of his tobacco in a gesture of friendship. Far from being a demanding ruler with a sense of entitlement, Philip engages Rowlandson in his culture on an economic level by offering her money or food for her services as a seamstress. This exchange, however small it may be, suggests Philip's decency and humanity. Rowlandson may be a captive of his tribe, but she is still a person, and she is not a slave.

Despite this basic decency and kindness, Philip does not set Rowlandson free, though as a leader, he might have had the power to do so. When the General Court of the Indians meets to discuss freeing her, Philip refuses to attend, prolonging Rowlandson's captivity through his petty, immature action. He offers Rowlandson her freedom in exchange for clothing, money, and food, but Rowlandson distrusts him, fearing he'll go back on his word. This mention of Philip's possibly false offer, and his childish sulking, is the last Rowlandson says of him in her story.

WETTIMORE One of Quannopin's three wives, Wettimore is one of the Indians with whom Rowlandson has the most contact. Unfortunately for Rowlandson, Wettimore is proud and vain, with a strong streak of cruelty. Wettimore's greatest concerns are image and status. She sometimes does not feed Rowlandson well or let her warm herself by the fire, but she complains that she and Quannopin look bad when Rowlandson begs for food or a warm place to sleep at other wigwams. Wettimore is angered by Rowlandson's faith and piety and her ability to find comfort in the Bible. When Wettimore's child has died and she returns from its burial to find Rowlandson reading the Bible, she is enraged and throws her Bible to the ground. Wettimore's short-temperedness appears at other times as well. On the same day, she slaps Rowlandson across the face and tells her to get out of her sight. Though both Rowlandson and Wettimore have lost young children, this does not become a point of sympathy or bonding for them.

Rowlandson casts Wettimore as something of a foil of herself: the two are opposites, and by listing Wettimore's bad qualities, Rowlandson subtly emphasizes her own positive traits. When describing Wettimore's daily routine, Rowlandson compares her to wealthy white nobles: Wettimore spends as much time arranging her hair, clothing, and jewelry as the richest of the settlers. Her shallowness shows that savagery and violence are not the Indians' only negative qualities—vanity in such rugged conditions is ridiculous. Wettimore's values are opposite to those Christian values that Rowlandson espouses. While Rowlandson learns that worldly treasures have little use or meaning, Wettimore focuses on the superficial trappings of clothing and status.

THEMES, MOTIFS, AND SYMBOLS

THEMES

THE BLURRED LINE BETWEEN CIVILIZATION AND SAVAGERY Even though Rowlandson's forced journey from civilization into the wilderness culminates in a triumphant return to civilization, her once-clear conception of what is and is not "civilized" undergoes a radical and permanent shift. Initially, Rowlandson views civilization as that which is not savage or not wilderness, and at times she implies that the Indians' savagery is actually connected to the natural world around them. The Indians eat coarse food such as horse meat and bear, they live in wigwams, and they spend their days traveling through forests and swamps. As a result, she speculates, they are violent savages. Later, however, similarities between the Indians and the settlers become more apparent. Wettimore is as vain as a rich white woman, "praying

Indians" claim to have converted to Christianity, and Indians sometimes wear the colonists' clothing. Rowlandson also recognizes her own capacity for uncivilized behavior. She finds herself eating and enjoying the Indians' food, and at times she behaves with a callousness comparable to that of her captors. No longer are civilization and savagery so distinct. Rowlandson's initial vision of the world as a place defined by opposites (good and evil, civilization and savagery, Puritans and Indians) eventually gives way to a worldview that contains more ambiguity.

LIFE IS UNCERTAIN The attack on Lancaster and Rowlandson's subsequent captivity teach Rowlandson that life is short and nothing is certain. All of the seeming stability of life, including material possessions, can disappear without warning, even during a single day. Rowlandson's descriptions of her time with the Indians reinforce this lesson: nothing, during her captivity, is consistent. One day, her captors treat her well, while the next day they give her no food or reprimand her without reason. One day, they tell her she'll soon be sold to her husband; the next day, she is forced to travel farther into the wilderness. In her captive state, Rowlandson can take nothing for granted. She does not even know for sure if she'll survive the experience.

THE CENTRALITY OF GOD'S WILL As a Puritan, Rowlandson believes that God's grace and providence shape the events of the world. She and other Puritans also believe that God arranges things for a purpose. Throughout her narrative, Rowlandson argues that humans have no choice but to accept God's will and attempt to make sense of it. Rowlandson's attempt to understand involves drawing parallels between her own situation and biblical verses. She compares herself to Job, to the Israelites, and to Daniel in the lion's den, among others. Like these biblical figures, she is at the mercy of God's will and grace. Everything in her narrative, she believes, happens for a reason, and the reason British troops do not defeat the Indians sooner is that the Puritans have not yet learned their lesson. They are not humble and pious enough for the reward of victory.

THE FEAR OF THE NEW WORLD In her narrative, Rowlandson explores the fearful hesitation white settlers feel in the face of new environments and experiences. Rowlandson, like other Puritans, is unsure how far the colonists should forge into the wilds. Lancaster is a frontier settlement, and the attack serves as a sign that perhaps the settlers are pushing too far west, too far from their established towns. However, Rowlandson goes still farther inland when she is taken captive, and her experience brings her even further from what she knows. She and other captives, such as Robert Pepper, are able to amass practical knowledge about the natural world during their time with the Indians. Rowlandson learns to gather food for herself and to tolerate meats that would formerly have repulsed her. Though this practical knowledge is positive, it also brings anxiety and guilt because Rowlandson fears leaving "civilization" behind.

MOTIFS

THE THREATENING LANDSCAPE The threatening wilderness through which Rowlandson moves characterizes the dangers and threats of the New World as a whole. Rowlandson's journey begins with an uphill trek, which suggests the difficulties to come. From the summit, Rowlandson gets the last glimpse of civilization she'll have for some time. The next day, the travelers set off down a steep hill, and Rowlandson and her daughter tumble off their horse: their descent into the hell of the wilderness has begun. The landscape grows increasingly bleak, and Rowlandson crosses desolate swamps, dark thickets, and icy streams. As she travels, Rowlandson sees farmlands gone to waste and slaughtered farm animals, and she fears the triumph of the Indians and the dark, unknown wilderness over the order and reason of civilization.

CHRISTIAN IMAGERY AND THE BIBLE Rowlandson frequently quotes the Bible and alludes to biblical tales, which emphasizes her own faith, her own knowledge of the scriptures, and their centrality in her life. She also uses the Bible to reinforce her descriptions of a world of dichotomies: punishment and retribution, darkness and light, and evil and good. By casting the Indians as children of the devil, Rowlandson depicts them as a large, permanent enemy. That is, the Indians are not just the enemy of the colonists in this war, in a specific time and a place, but rather represent the enemies of Christianity, goodness, and light throughout all time. By alluding to the Bible so frequently, Rowlandson turns her own story into an epic and allegorical tale that is broader than the story of one woman's captivity.

SYMBOLS

THE ATTACK ON LANCASTER The attack on Lancaster, described as a fiery inferno, represents God's wrath and the strife and chaos of King Philip's War as a whole. When Rowlandson describes the start of the attack, she writes that "several houses were burning, and the smoke ascending to heaven." This image of smoke rising to heaven suggests ritual sacrifice and emphasizes that this attack has religious meaning and is more than just a random or political attack.

ROBERT PEPPER'S OAK LEAVES The oak leaves, which Robert Pepper helps Rowlandson use to heal her wound, suggest the positive potential of nature. In addition to being a dangerous temptation, the natural world can also be a means of curing a person's ills. One must be taught, however, how to use nature's bounty, and God must be willing to provide assistance as well. That the natural world proves to be a source of healing is also a threat to Rowlandson, since she has always linked the wilderness with savagery, not civilization. These healing leaves help Rowlandson develop a different, more ambiguous perspective on the world.

THE INDIANS' CLOTHING The Indians Rowlandson encounters often dress in the colonists' clothes. Sometimes this is a sign that the Indians are converts to Christianity, but at other times it signifies their savagery, since the clothes are from enemies they have killed and towns they have ransacked. The Indian in British clothes, then, suggests the unreliability of outward appearances. Though the Indians may look civilized, Rowlandson suspects—though she is not certain—that they are still savages underneath.

IMPORTANT QUOTATIONS EXPLAINED

---

1. *It was a solemn sight to see so many Christians lying in their blood, some here and some there, like a company of sheep torn by wolves.*

Rowlandson uses these words in the opening section of her narrative when she describes the chaos and devastation of the Indian attack on Lancaster. In one sentence, she conveys the gravity and seriousness of the situation. More important, however, is the simile Rowlandson chooses to describe the scene. In Christian imagery, Jesus is traditionally compared to a shepherd, and his followers are a flock of innocent sheep. By drawing from this imagery, Rowlandson situates her narrative in a biblical framework. By then comparing the Indians to wolves, Rowlandson introduces opposition and dichotomy into her text. The Puritans are innocent, civilized, and domesticated, while the Indians are wild animals.

---

2. *Yet the Lord still shewed mercy to me, and helped me; and as he wounded me with one hand, so he healed me with the other.*

As she narrates the story of the Third Remove, Rowlandson uses these words to refer to her immediate situation. She is wounded and captive, but she has just met Robert Pepper, another captive, who teaches her to use oak leaves to cure her wound. This passage summarizes Rowlandson's entire time in captivity and also encapsulates the broader Puritan worldview. Here, Rowlandson expresses a belief in the centrality of God's will: everything that happens, she says, happens for a reason, and both good things and bad occur because God arranges them.

---

3. *When I came I asked them what they had done with it? then they told me it was upon the hill: then they went and shewed me where it was, where I saw the ground was newly digged, and there they told me they had buried it: There I left that Child in the Wilderness, and must commit it, and myself also in this Wilderness-condition, to him who is above all.*

The Third Remove also brings about the death and burial of Rowlandson's youngest daughter, which Rowlandson speaks of in the quotation above. Rowlandson's daughter has been suffering for over a week from the wound she received on the morning of the attack. Now God has put the child out of her misery, but Rowlandson, understandably, grieves for her. Also troubling is the fact that the girl does not receive a proper Christian burial in a Puritan churchyard. For family members and loved ones, a funeral and burial provide important closure, and without them, Rowlandson lacks this sense of finality.

When Rowlandson emphasizes having to leave her daughter "in the wilderness," she explicitly compares her daughter's state to her own, and the quotation above can be applied to all of Puritan society. All the settlers are far from home, far from the country where their ancestors were born. They are building a civilization on the edge of the wilderness, but they fear that their settlements will not be enough to keep the wilderness out. The future of every individual is uncertain, as is the future of the society as a whole. This uncertainty exists for every human society, but the geographic and psychological isolation of the Puritan settlers intensifies it. In the face of this terrifying ignorance of the future, Rowlandson claims, the only thing to do is to have faith in God.

---

4. *The first week of my being among them, I hardly eat any thing; the second week, I found my stomach grow very faint for want of something; and yet it was very hard to get down their filthy trash; but the third week, though I could think how formerly my stomach would turn against this or that, and I could starve and die before I could eat such things, yet they were sweet and savory to my taste.*

This passage, which appears in the Fifth Remove, reveals how Rowlandson's thoughts and actions have changed in her time among the Indians. On a practical and logical level, it is not surprising that Rowlandson finds herself willing to eat foods that previously disgusted her. Three weeks of little food and strenuous travel have taken a physical toll on Rowlandson, and her body's need for nourishment is strong enough to overcome any squeamishness she previously felt about eating the Indians' food. On a psychological level, however, Rowlandson finds her increased appetite worrisome. She wants to survive in order to be reunited with her family and to teach others the lessons she has learned during captivity, so being able to eat her captors' food without feeling nausea or disgust is a blessing from God, a sign of divine favor. At the same time, Rowlandson worries about her own capacity for savagery and fears she may devolve to the barbarism of the Indians. A willingness to eat horse liver and bear meat, therefore, brings anxiety. It proves Rowlandson's ever-increasing distance from civilization and suggests her growing similarity to her captors.

---

5. *When the Lord had brought his people to this, that they saw no help in any thing but himself, then he takes the quarrel into his own hand; and tho' they had made a pit, as deep as hell for the Christians that summer, yet the Lord hurled themselves into it.*

In the final pages of her narrative, Rowlandson summarizes the situation of the past several months. This statement is important because it again emphasizes Rowlandson's belief in the centrality of God's will. Far from believing in a distant or absent God, Rowlandson and the Puritans have faith in an active God who determines the course of daily events on earth. This God is an angry and punishing God, but he is also forgiving. He has plagued the colonists with Indian attacks and the violence of King Philip's War in order to teach them a lesson. Once they have learned their lesson and understand the insignificance of outward appearances and wealth and the powerlessness of humans in the face of the divine, God is willing once again to embrace the Christians as his chosen people. Though the Indians have had a string of victories and though it had seemed that they might win the war altogether, it is now their turn to learn a lesson. Pride comes before a fall, the saying goes, and now God is turning things in the Puritans' favor. This quotation expresses confidence in God's capacity for mercy and forgiveness, as well as knowledge of his power and capacity for wrath.

Surfacing

Margaret Atwood (1939–)

CONTEXT

Margaret Atwood was born in 1939 in Ottawa, Canada. She went on to study at Victoria College at the University of Toronto and eventually received a master's degree from Radcliffe College. *Surfacing* is Margaret Atwood's second novel, which was published in 1972, only three years after her first novel *The Edible Woman* was published. Though one of Atwood's early novels, *Surfacing* is not one of Atwood's earliest publications. By the time *Surfacing* was published, she had already published several books of poetry. Atwood's writing has been published in more than thirty languages.

Surfacing takes place in Quebec, and the unique identity of Quebec's population comes into play in the novel. Quebec is the only Canadian province populated by residents of French (rather than British) descent. Atwood wrote *Surfacing* at a time when the cultural differences between Quebec and the rest of Canada were manifesting themselves in terms of rising Quebec nationalism. The 1960s saw the Quiet Revolution in Quebec: a series of economic and educational reforms coupled with a secularization of society. The Quiet Revolution afforded Quebec greater political and economic autonomy, giving Quebec's French citizens a sense of nationalism and a desire to separate from Canada. Atwood marks this political change in *Surfacing*.

Surfacing is a postcolonial novel, though not in the traditional sense. Most postcolonial novels are written by authors from countries that have gained bloody independence from empires such as Britain, France, Spain, or America. These novels usually mark the effects of upheaval and bloody revolution, documenting a search for an independent national identity coupled with a reaction to the political scarring left by imperialism. Since Canadian independence from Britain occurred so gradually, *Surfacing* does not fall into the traditional postcolonial categorization. *Surfacing* does, however, explore an emerging Canadian national identity. Atwood includes a passage about the Canadian national flag, which had only been adopted in 1965. More important, *Surfacing* exists as a postcolonial novel in its consideration of Americans and the way that America exerts its cultural influence over Canada. Atwood claims that America's subtle cultural infiltration of Canada is actually a form of colonialism.

Through *Surfacing*, Atwood questions a woman's conventional social and sexual role. *Surfacing* touches on the health risks associated with hormonal contraception, the idea of contraception as a male invention, the power inherent in pregnancy, the social implications of makeup, the potentially false ideal of marriage, the notion of a natural woman, and the psychological mechanisms that men use to exert control over women. Atwood creates a narrator who feels alienated by social pressures that cast her in a specific gender role, and the narrator's response to those pressures is complete withdrawal. As such, Atwood presents a frank condemnation of the sexual and social norms forced upon women. Surfacing can therefore be seen as a proto-feminist novel.

Surfacing marks a social period of growing secularization and of widening generational gaps. Atwood deems religion as more of a social regulatory force than a truth. For example, the town priest abuses his religious authority on the village by enforcing a strict dress code for women. The narrator also labels Christianity as a social control mechanism that is learned at a young age and stays potent throughout adulthood. Religion in *Surfacing* becomes a false ideal, and Atwood's condemnation of Christianity marks a larger social tendency toward secularization. At the same time, Atwood explores a growing rift between generations. The narrator of the book casts the older generation as crippled by a rigid sense of morality. In this way, Atwood documents a split between the conservative older generation and the liberal younger generation.

A minor undercurrent in *Surfacing* is the novel's existence as a post–World War II novel. The narrator recalls growing up in the wake of World War II and documents small effects of the war on her childhood. She believes that the war served as an outlet for men's inherent violence, and she tries to trace the effects of pent-up violence in a society devoid of war. The narrator sees the American infiltration of Canada as a direct result of American restlessness during the post-war period. *Surfacing* examines the ambiguous moral landscape left in the wake of World War II. The narrator's childhood recollection of Hitler as the embodiment of all evil depicts the World War II era as morally simplistic. The post-war world is more ambiguous, and the narrator challenges herself to discover the roots of evil now that humans no longer have a single scapegoat.

Surfacing predates the environmentalist movement, but the narrator's reverence for the Canadian wilderness is a pro-environmentalist one. The narrator feels protective of nature and reacts with hostility to the American tourists who overfish, kill for sport, and litter the ground. *Surfacing* is full of tourists, urban outgrowth, and technology that directly encroach upon the unspoiled land. These environmental concerns still resonate today given continuing trends toward overconsumption and the prevalence of technology that relies upon natural resources.

PLOT OVERVIEW

The unnamed narrator returns to Quebec after years of absence to search for her missing father. She brings her boyfriend, Joe, and a married couple, Anna and David. On the way to a village near her father's island, the narrator visits her father's friend Paul. Paul can provide no new information on how to locate the narrator's father. A guide named Evans takes the narrator and her companions to her father's island, where the narrator searches for clues regarding her father's disappearance. She becomes convinced that her father has gone mad and is still alive.

The narrator works in spurts on her freelance job illustrating a book of fairy tales, but her worries prevent her from accomplishing any real work. David proposes staying on the island for a week. The narrator agrees, though she secretly fears her crazed father's reemergence. During their stay, David launches constant insults at Anna, couching them as jokes. Anna confesses to the narrator that David is a womanizer. She complains that David constantly demands that Anna wear makeup. The four go on a blueberry-picking expedition. They canoe to a nearby island, where Joe unexpectedly proposes to the narrator. The narrator refuses Joe, telling him how she left her last husband and child.

Back on the island, Paul arrives with an American named Malmstrom. Malmstrom claims to be from a Detroit wildlife agency. He offers to purchase the island, but the narrator refuses. She pulls Paul aside and tells him that her father is still alive. Paul seems skeptical. After the visitors leave, David offhandedly accuses Malmstrom of being a C.I.A. operative who is organizing an American invasion of Canada. The narrator looks through her father's records and consequently believes that he is likely dead. She sees that he had been researching Indian wall paintings and that he had marked several sites on a map. She decides to visit a site.

The narrator convinces her friends to accompany her on a camping trip to see the wall paintings. On their way to the campsite, they see a decomposing blue heron that has been hanged from a tree. David insists on filming the dead heron for a movie he is making called *Random Samples*. The heron's death haunts the narrator. She sees evidence of two campers entering the area beforehand, and she quickly assumes that they are Americans and to blame for the crime. Meanwhile, the four companions set up camp. Anna tells the narrator she has forgotten her makeup and David will punish her. The narrator goes fishing with David and Joe. They encounter the Americans, and the narrator notices an American flag on their boat. The narrator brings her companions to a site from her father's map, but there are no wall paintings. Frustrated and confused, they return to camp. On the way, they again encounter the American campers. The narrator is surprised to discover that the campers are actually Canadian; what she had thought was an American flag is actually a sticker. However, the narrator claims the campers are still Americans because their slaughter of the heron is a distinctly American action.

The four return to the cabin. The narrator locates another site on her father's map but realizes that the government has raised the water level in this part of the lake. She will have to dive to see the paintings. Outside, the narrator observes David tormenting Anna by insisting she take off her clothes for *Random Samples*. Anna eventually relents but then feels humiliated. The narrator asks David why he tortures Anna, and David claims he does so because Anna cheats on him. The narrator canoes to a site from her father's map. She dives repeatedly in search of the paintings. On a particularly deep dive, she sees a disturbing object and screams and swims for the surface. Joe has followed her onto the lake and demands to know what she's doing. She ignores Joe and realizes that what she saw was a dead child. She believes it to be her aborted baby. She changes her story from leaving her husband and child to having an affair with her art professor and being forced to abort their baby.

S

The narrator's vision throws her into a psychosis. She believes that her father had found sacred Indian sites and resolves to thank the gods for granting her "the power." Joe tries to speak to the narrator, but she remains impenetrable. He tries to rape her, but he leaves her alone once she warns him that she will get pregnant. Later, David tries to seduce the narrator, telling her that Joe and Anna are having sex. The narrator nevertheless resists David's advances. A police boat comes to the island, and David tells the narrator that the police have found her father's body. Deep in her madness, the narrator refuses to believe David. That night, she seduces Joe so she can get pregnant. She feels that a new child will replace her lost baby. Joe falsely believes that the narrator has forgiven him for cheating on her.

On their last day on the island, the narrator abandons her friends. She destroys David's film and escapes in a canoe. The narrator's companions search in vain for her, eventually leaving the island. Alone on the island, the narrator falls deeper into madness. She destroys the art from her job and nearly everything inside the cabin. She becomes an animal, running around naked, eating unwashed plants, and living in a burrow. She imagines raising her baby outdoors and never teaching it language. She also has visions of her parents. Eventually, hunger and exhaustion bring the narrator to sanity. She looks at herself in the mirror and sees just a natural woman. She resolves not to feel powerless anymore. Paul arrives at the island with Joe. The narrator realizes she loves Joe and resolves to reunite with him. She pauses in the cabin, looking out at Joe, waiting.

CHARACTER LIST

The Narrator The unnamed protagonist of *Surfacing*. The narrator is reverential toward nature, intensely private, anti-American, and introspective. She works as a freelance artist. She searches for her missing father on a remote island in Quebec along with her boyfriend, Joe, and her friends, David and Anna. Socially alienated and distrustful of love, the narrator suffers a debilitating emotional numbness that eventually fixes itself through a grand psychological transformation. She eventually goes mad on the island. For a time she lives like an animal, but she eventually emerges as a more enlightened being. *Surfacing* is composed entirely of the narrator's unfiltered thoughts and observations.

Joe The quiet, shy, well-meaning boyfriend of the narrator. Joe is an unsuccessful artist who makes ugly pottery and teaches pottery classes. Joe remains too simple-minded to understand the narrator's complexities. He insists on marrying the narrator, which she resists. Joe is a good man, but he is also potentially violent.

David The psychologically abusive and womanizing husband of Anna. David is a communications teacher who loves baseball. He is an amateur filmmaker composing a film with Joe called *Random Samples*. David's constant joking and imitation of cartoon characters serves as a poor cover for his selfish and sexist behavior, and the manner in which he communicates with Anna is deeply cruel. David is staunchly anti-American, yet he possesses all of the awful qualities that the narrator associates with Americans.

S

Anna The vulnerable yet sly wife of David. Anna puts on a veneer of sweetness in order to please her husband. She constantly sings and applies makeup. She believes her marriage is a war that she fights using her body; Anna uses sex with her husband and with other men to curb David's behavior. She is more talkative and social than the narrator but far less introspective or self-aware.

Paul The compassionate yet reserved best friend of the narrator's father. Paul is the first one to inform the narrator of her father's disappearance. He is a poor man who lives a modest life, and he operates by traditional morals and codes of courtesy and provides as much help as he can in locating the narrator's father. Paul was the model of "the simple life" to the narrator's father, though the narrator observes that he is a model through financial necessity and not choice.

The Narrator's Mother An aloof and secretive woman. The narrator's mother died from a brain tumor before the novel begins, and the narrator constantly tries to remember her. Her mother serves as the narrator's image of inner strength. The narrator continually remembers the image of her mother in a leather jacket feeding blue jays.

The Narrator's Father A stern man who disappears, forcing the narrator to search for him on his island. The narrator's father is an atheist and a fan of the eighteenth-century rationalists. Self-reliant and rugged, he built the cabin on his own and had used the island as respite from city life. He dies accidentally on a trip researching local Indian wall paintings.

The Narrator's Brother A character who never appears in person. The narrator's brother fled from his parents years before the novel takes place. The narrator finds it difficult to imagine him as an adult. He nearly drowned as a child, and the narrator constantly reflects on the image of his drowning. He was loving toward his sister, but he had a rather dark childhood. He kept a laboratory on the island, running experiments on animals in jars.

The "Fake Husband" The narrator's ex-lover. The fake husband is eventually revealed to be the narrator's art professor, a married man with whom she had an affair. He forced the narrator into having an abortion. He is emotionally callous in nature and tries to avoid letting his affair with the narrator influence his actions.

Bill Malmstrom A shady and wealthy American whom the narrator immediately distrusts. Malmstrom claims to be a representative of a Detroit-based wildlife preservation agency. He offers to purchase the narrator's father's island. David suspects that Malmstrom is an undercover C.I.A. operative.

The "Americans" Two Canadian campers whom the narrator initially mistakes for American tourists. They are avid fishers, and they befriend David. They are also responsible for killing and hanging a heron, and for their senseless violence the narrator believes them to be Americans.

Claude A young boy working at a generic bar attached to a new motel in the village. Claude gives fishing licenses to David and to other tourists and also guides American tourists on fishing expeditions. He speaks in a yokel dialect.

Evans The seasoned American guide who takes the narrator, Joe, Anna, and David to and from the narrator's father's island. Evans is gruff and minds his own business; he is aware that the narrator's father has disappeared, but he never asks the narrator about it.

Madame Paul's wife. Madame is a French woman living in the village close to the narrator's father's island. Simple and polite, she speaks only French. Because they only speak English, the narrator and the narrator's mother both experience long, awkward conversations with Madame.

The Town Priest The local priest whom the narrator remembers from childhood. The town priest forbade women in the narrator's village from wearing slacks. Instead, he forced them to wear long, concealing skirts. The narrator reflects that he is likely dead by now.

The Old Shopkeeper One-armed French woman whom the narrator remembers simply as "Madame." The old shopkeeper operated from a storefront attached to her house. The narrator remembers how the shopkeeper used to tie packages with her stump arm and how she used to sell candies that the narrator was never allowed to buy.

The New Shopkeeper A French woman who works in a small village near the narrator's father's island. The new shopkeeper is a rude, snide woman who humiliates the narrator for speaking broken French. The shopkeeper wears slacks, which would have been forbidden in the village years ago.

S

ANALYSIS OF MAJOR CHARACTERS

THE NARRATOR Atwood avoids naming the narrator of *Surfacing* in order to emphasize the universality of the narrator's feeling of alienation from society. The causes and effects of the narrator's psychological transformation remain somewhat mysterious. The narrator feels emotionally numb, isolated by the numerous roles she is supposed to play in her life. Part of the cause is grief, and part of it is due to spending too much time in the wilderness. But the narrator's madness also stems in large part from systematic social alienation. Atwood explores a woman's place in all of its facets: as a human, a wife, a religious person, a mother, and a sexual being. The narrator's madness seems to arise from her anger at all of the standard roles forced upon women. Her response to this alienation is to become an animal. She sees animals not as beasts without reason, but as graceful creatures that are better than humans at peacefully coexisting with nature. The result of the narrator's transformation is a greater understanding of her place in society. This understanding comes out of necessity, because the narrator realizes that complete withdrawal from society will result in her death. However, the narrator also reaches new conclusions about how she will cope with society's ills. She resolves to rejoin society without succumbing to the pressures that once subdued her.

JOE At first, the narrator depicts Joe as simple-minded and agreeable, but as *Surfacing* progresses, Joe's personality undergoes changes. Where once he seemed content, he becomes irritable and sullen when the narrator refuses his marriage proposal. Also, Joe's actions become less predictable. His proposal is unexpected, and the narrator becomes less able to discern Joe's intentions. When David asks Anna to be filmed naked and Joe defends her, the narrator has trouble discerning whether Joe is helping a friend or seeking a way to become sexually aroused. The narrator shows herself to be unreliable in depicting Joe objectively. For example, she keeps bracing herself for a hit from Joe that never comes.

As her impressions of Joe fluctuate, the narrator's impression of their love also shifts. Initially, the narrator downplays Joe's love for her. She believes that Joe wants to marry her out of a conceptual ideal and not out of affection. The narrator also downplays her love for Joe, claiming she only enjoys Joe for his physical qualities. However, *Surfacing* ends with legitimate love between the two, and Joe displays his sincere affection for the narrator when he searches for her on the island. Despite this love, the narrator filters Joe's actions through her own biases, making his true character unknowable.

DAVID David is the model of male dominance in *Surfacing*. David initially appears to be an ideal husband, as he jokes and flirts with Anna. However, Atwood twists her portrayal of David by revealing the cruelty that underscores his jokes and the emptiness of his flirtation. Under the guise of joking, David constantly tries to control Anna's behavior. As the week progresses, he becomes overtly antagonistic toward her, calling her fat and snubbing her ideas, and eventually uses psychological cruelty to dominate her. He also objectifies Anna by referring to her body in front of Joe. The narrator recognizes that David's flirtation serves as a display. She calls his banter with Anna a "skit," noticing that both David and Anna drop their flirtation once they lose their audience.

David spews generic anti-American sentiment, calling the Americans pigs and proposing that they be thrown out of Canada. However, these anti-American politics lack substance. The best justification that David can muster for hating Americans is a ridiculous prediction of an American invasion of Canada. David possesses nearly all of the despicable characteristics the narrator comes to associate with Americans. Additionally, his own life seems at odds with his anti-American sentiments. David loves the distinctly American pastime of baseball, and he constantly laughs like the American cartoon character Woody Woodpecker. David's political standing illustrates that Americans are marked by behaviors and not by nationality.

ANNA Anna's primary role in *Surfacing* is to crystallize the narrator's opinions about love, sex, and marriage. Anna's constant chatter helps the narrator to better understand relationships. She asks whether the narrator takes birth control, mentioning the blood clot she developed in her leg as a result of taking the pill. Anna's frankness about contraception allows the narrator to identify contraception as a male invention that puts females at risk. When the narrator asks Anna about marriage, Anna's comparison of marriage to skiing blindly down a hill helps solidify the narrator's fear of marriage. Also, Anna's admission that David either withholds sex or hurts her during sex helps the narrator to see the way men use sex as a weapon.

The narrator also observes the psychological cruelty that men inflict on women through the way that Anna crumbles in the face of David's cruel jokes. The degradation of Anna's marriage confirms the narrator's suspicions about marriage in general. At first, the narrator seems to envy Anna's love for her husband, and she marvels at the way Anna keeps her marriage together. However, the narrator eventually comes to understand Anna's marriage as one balanced by hate rather than love, and David's cynicism allows her to reject marriage altogether. Anna's life as a whole becomes a cautionary tale for the narrator. The narrator learns through Anna the pitfalls of unhappy marriage, empty sex, and fractured love.

THEMES, MOTIFS, AND SYMBOLS

THEMES

LANGUAGE AS CONNECTION TO SOCIETY Throughout *Surfacing*, the narrator's feeling of powerlessness is coupled with an inability to use language. When she goes mad, she cannot understand David's words or speak out against his advances. Similarly, when the search party comes for her, she cannot understand their speech, and her only defense from them is flight. Words betray her, as it is by yelling that the search party discovers her. The narrator maintains the false hope that she can reject human language just as she imagines she can reject human society. She admires how animals know the types of plants without naming them. When she goes mad, she vows not to teach her child language—yet eventually she conquers her alienation by embracing language.

THE TOTAL ALIENATION OF WOMEN Atwood uses the narrator's near-constant feeling of alienation to comment on the alienation of all women. The narrator feels abandoned by her parents because of the disappearance of her father and the detachment of her mother. She finds men especially alienating because of the way they control women through religion, marriage, birth control, sex, language, and birth. She depicts the way that men view relationships as a war, with women as the spoils. The narrator also describes her alienation as systematic, highlighting the way that children learn gender roles early on in life. The result of the narrator's alienation is madness and complete withdrawal. The narrator remains unnamed, making her a universal figure and suggesting that all women are in some way alienated.

MOTIFS

AMERICAN EXPANSION Atwood packs *Surfacing* with images of Americans invading and ruining Canada. The Americans install missile silos, pepper the village with tourist cabins, leave trash everywhere, and kill for sport. David even goes so far as to theorize an American invasion of Canada for Canadian fresh water. Atwood depicts American expansion as a result of psychological and cultural infiltration. The narrator calls Americans a brain disease, linking American identity to behaviors rather than nationality. To the narrator, an American is anyone who commits senseless violence, loves technology, or overconsumes. David claims he hates Americans, yet he loves baseball and imitates Woody Woodpecker. Atwood depicts American expansion as destructive and a corruptive psychological influence.

THE POWER The narrator mentions power several times before going mad and actively seeking "the power." In Chapter 4, she remembers thinking that seeds from a certain plant will make her all-powerful. In Chapter 9, she says that doctors pretend childbirth is their power and not the mother's. In Chapter 15, she remembers alternately pretending to be a helpless animal and an animal with power. The narrator's later quest for "the power" emphasizes her response to alienation. Ever since childhood, she has been isolated and emotionally numb, crippled by unsuitable religious ideals and gender roles. The narrator's psychotic search for "the power" represents the false hope that by withdrawing from society she can regain her humanity. Ultimately, the narrator gains power by resolving not to be powerless. She acknowledges that in order to function in society, she must learn to love and communicate. The narrator's quest for "the power" is similar to her anxiety over social alienation.

SYMBOLS

THE BAROMETER Paul's wooden barometer, which features a wooden man and woman inside, becomes an unfortunately accurate emblem of marriage for the narrator. The narrator's shifting assessment of the barometer traces her shifting attitudes toward marriage. Initially, the narrator views the barometer couple as representative of a simplistic and even empty marriage, and she compares them to Paul and Madame. She mentions how Paul and Madame even look wooden. The narrator later compares the barometer couple to Anna and David in that the wooden couple, like Anna and David's happiness, is not real. The narrator also thinks of the barometer in relation to her parents. She compares the image of the barometer with the image of her mother and father sawing a piece of birch. The image of the birch is evocative because the narrator associates birches with unspoiled nature. The implication is that the barometer represents an unattainable, unrealistic version of love, whereas her parents possess true love.

THE HANGED HERON The hanged heron at the portage represents the American destruction of nature. The narrator obsesses over the senselessness of its slaughter, especially that it was hanged and not buried. The heron's death emphasizes that the narrator defines someone as American based on his or her actions. She condemns any act of senseless violence or waste as distinctly American. That the bird is killed with a bullet and hanged using a nylon rope emphasizes the subversion of nature to technology.

Also, the narrator thinks of the hanged bird as a Christ-like sacrifice, which reflects Christian ideology. By using Christian ideas to describe nature, the narrator emphasizes her near-religious reverence for nature. The narrator also compares herself to the heron during her madness, when she worries that the search party will hang her by the feet. By associating the narrator with the hanged heron, Atwood associates the way Americans destroy nature with the way men control women.

MAKEUP Anna's makeup, which David demands she wear at all times, represents the large-scale subjugation of women. The narrator compares Anna to a doll when she sees her putting on makeup, because Anna becomes David's sexual plaything. At the same time, makeup represents female deception. Anna uses makeup as a veneer of beauty, and the behavior is representative of the way she acts virtuous (but sleeps with other men) and happy (but feels miserable). Makeup goes completely against the narrator's ideal of a natural woman. The narrator calls herself a natural woman directly after her madness, when she looks in a mirror and sees herself naked and completely disheveled. The narrator comments that Anna uses makeup to emulate a corrupt womanly ideal.

THE RING The narrator's ring symbolizes marriage and its entrapping effects. The narrator describes wearing both her boyfriend's and her fake husband's rings around her neck. She compares her rings to a crucifix or a military decoration. The crucifix suggests that marriage is not only a sacrifice but a sacrifice toward a false ideal. The image of a military decoration implies that marriage forces women into becoming the spoils of war. Atwood uses the narrator's ring to foreshadow Joe's demand for marriage, as she mentions in Chapter 1 that Joe fiddles with the narrator's ring.

IMPORTANT QUOTATIONS EXPLAINED

---

1. *He's enjoying himself, he thinks this is reality . . . He spent four years in New York and became political, he was studying something; it was during the sixties, I'm not sure when. My friends' pasts are vague to me and to each other also, any one of us could have amnesia for a year and the others wouldn't notice.*

The narrator observes David and comments on his past just before taking her friends to the island in Chapter 3. The narrator's disdain for David's enjoyment of Greenwich Village reflects her intolerance for tourists who come to Quebec seeking an authentic outdoor experience. David is a city-dweller, and the narrator feels perturbed by his casual enjoyment of the trappings of outdoor life, such as fishing or chopping firewood. She inherits this disdain in part from her father, who used to size up men for their ability to live outdoors on their own. Another part of her resents the American tourists who seek out the wilderness only to spoil it.

The flippancy with which the narrator describes David's political conscience is in fact justified. David knows politics only superficially, and his nondescript anti-American sentiment comes across as a weak substitute for true political knowledge. Also, his background in New York seems ironic given his anti-American leanings. The narrator continually juxtaposes David's anti-American statements against his clear adoption of American culture. Though he says he hates America, David imitates American cartoons and loves baseball. David's years in New York help build a picture of a hypocrite who claims to hate Americans and yet is dominated by American culture.

The narrator's admission that she knows little about her friends' backgrounds emphasizes the superficiality of nearly all of her relationships. The narrator remains unable to commit to people emotionally. She retains only insubstantial friendships, which she recognizes. The same message comes across when she comments that Anna is her best friend, and then admits they have known each other for only two months. The narrator's withdrawal from her friends points to her role as a social outcast. An intensely private and introspective woman, this passage emphasizes the gap between the narrator's thoughts and her outward appearance to the other characters.

2. *I have to be more careful about my memories. I have to be sure they're my own and not the memories of other people telling me what I felt, how I acted, what I said: if the events are wrong the feelings I remember about them will be wrong too, I'll start inventing them . . . .*

The narrator makes this statement in Chapter 8, when she holes herself up in an outhouse, waiting for David and Joe to explain to Evans that they want to stay on the island. While hiding in the outhouse, the narrator remembers facets of her childhood and contrasts the time she spent on the island with the time she spent in the city. She decides she has always felt safer in the wilderness than in the city. She then retracts that notion once she remembers all of the times she felt scared on the island. The narrator begins to worry here that her memories are unwittingly changing, and this quotation points out the frightening notion that memories are subjective. She panics at this realization, worrying that if she changes her memories she will have no way of checking herself. She worries she will act irrationally by relying on information that is not accurate.

Though here the narrator worries about others' opinions affecting her memory, it is actually the narrator's own subconscious that corrupts her memory. This passage foreshadows the narrator's later exposure of a repressed memory. She recants the memory of her wedding, replacing it with the memory of having an affair with her art professor and aborting their baby. Interestingly, the false memory contains multiple true facts lifted from other sources. For example, she remembers a fountain from the company town near the village, but inserts the fountain into the memory of her wedding. She remembers what her lover said to her after the abortion, but instead remembers him saying it after her wedding. She even goes on to create a new false memory just as she exposes the repressed one. She remembers her brother keeping frogs in jars and inserts that memory into her abortion, falsely claiming that the doctors gave her the fetus in a jar. The narrator's memories change themselves to fit with her desires and emotions, effectively erasing her abortion. Atwood's audience becomes subject to the same difficulty as the narrator, unwittingly relying on false information.

3. *It wasn't the city that was wrong, the inquisitors in the schoolyard, we weren't better than they were; we just had different victims. To become like a little child again, a barbarian, a vandal: it was in us too, it was innate. A thing closed in my head, hand, synapse, cutting off my escape . . .*

In Chapter 15, the narrator compares the cruelty she exhibited toward animals on the island with the cruelty that school children inflicted upon her in the city. Her rumination on cruelty occurs after she sees the hanged heron at the portage. The narrator recalls throwing leeches into fires and also claims responsibility for killing the animals that her brother had kept in jars in his laboratory. She also recounts how she killed a doll, remembering how she pretended to be a swarm of bees and had ripped up the doll and thrown it into the lake. She calls the instance a killing because, as a child, the doll had been alive to her. By weighing her own cruelty against that of the schoolchildren who used to torment her, the narrator concludes that all children have an innate capacity for violence. For a while, she had entertained the hope that the island would be a haven for her. This passage disavows the narrator of that notion, because violence seems to follow humans regardless of environment.

4. *Joe is not there. He appears then at the top of the sand cliff, running, halting. He yells my name, furiously: if he had a rock he would throw it.*

   The canoe glides, carrying the two of us, around past the leaning trees . . . The direction is clear, I see I've been planning this, for how long I can't tell.

The narrator's description of Joe casts him as a caveman. The detail of throwing a rock paints him as a sort of frustrated and helpless primeval man. The narrator's description contains a seed of truth, in that Joe's simplicity repeatedly prevents him from grasping the narrator's complex and sophisticated private world. Joe's insistence on marriage and his one-sided conception of love fail to match the intricacies of the narrator's conceptions of love and relationships. This passage contains specific words that reflect the narrator's deepest concerns. She mentions that the canoe carries two people, which is a reference to her pregnancy. After remembering a past abortion, the narrator maintains constant awareness of her current pregnancy. Her new baby becomes a means for salvation from her guilt, and she thinks of the child as a potential solution to the social ailments she sees all around her. Her mention of the sand cliff points to her awareness that the island is eroding. The narrator remains concerned about the impermanence of the cabin, perhaps because she fears that the erosion of the island will erase her childhood. However, the narrator eventually embraces the erosion of the cabin because it signifies the triumph of nature over human development.

---

5. *This above all, to refuse to be a victim. Unless I can do that I can do nothing. I have to recant, give up the old belief that I am powerless and because of it nothing I can do will ever hurt anyone . . . withdrawing is no longer possible and the alternative is death.*

The narrator makes this remark in Chapter 27, after coming out of her madness. The phrase punctuates her attempt to completely withdraw from society and live like a natural animal, and it contains her cathartic conclusion to rejoin society. When she refers to being a victim, she refers to mental stumbling blocks that had once made her believe she was being oppressed by forces beyond her control, including religion, men, and marital conventions. Here, the narrator decides not to be a victim. The narrator's mention of powerlessness echoes her earlier search for "the power" during her madness. The narrator had searched for "the power" in her dead parents, the Indian gods, and in nature. Here, her resolution not to feel powerless marks the moment when she finally seeks refuge from her social isolation by internal (rather than external) means.

In this passage, the narrator comes to the conclusion that she possesses agency, and that her actions have consequences. Previously, emotional numbness had prevented her from believing that anything she did could affect others. She believed that her friends looked at her as a mirror of themselves, and that therefore she played no part in their lives. This opinion comes about when she asserts that Joe wants to marry an idea rather than a person. Here, the narrator concedes that because she will become an active member of society, her actions will have consequences. She relinquishes her emotional numbness by acknowledging that in possessing emotions, she will affect others' emotions.

S

Their Eyes Were Watching God

Zora Neale Hurston (1891–1960)

CONTEXT

Zora Neale Hurston was born on January 7, 1891, in Notasulga, Alabama, to John Hurston, a carpenter and Baptist preacher, and Lucy Potts Hurston, a former schoolteacher. Hurston was the fifth of eight children, and while she was still a toddler, her family moved to Eatonville, Florida, the first all-black incorporated town in the United States, where John Hurston served several terms as mayor. In 1917, Hurston enrolled in Morgan Academy in Baltimore, where she completed her high school education.

Three years later, she enrolled at Howard University and began her writing career. She took classes there intermittently for several years and eventually earned an associate's degree. The university's literary magazine published her first story in 1921. In 1925, she moved to New York and became a significant figure in the Harlem Renaissance. A year later, she, Langston Hughes, and Wallace Thurman organized the journal *Fire!*, considered one of the defining publications of the era. Meanwhile, she enrolled in Barnard College and studied anthropology with arguably the greatest anthropologist of the twentieth century, Franz Boas. Hurston's life in Eatonville and her extensive anthropological research on rural black folklore greatly influenced her writing.

Their Eyes Were Watching God was published in 1937, long after the heyday of the Harlem Renaissance. The literature of the 1920s, a period of postwar prosperity, was marked by a sense of freedom and experimentation, but the 1930s brought the Great Depression and an end to the cultural openness that had allowed the Harlem Renaissance to flourish. As the Great Depression worsened, political tension increased within the United States; cultural production came to be dominated by "social realism," a gritty, political style associated with left-wing radicalism. The movement's proponents felt that art should be primarily political and expose social injustice in the world. This new crop of writers and artists dismissed much of the Harlem Renaissance as bourgeois, devoid of important political content and thus devoid of any artistic merit. The influential and highly political black novelist Richard Wright, then an ardent Communist, wrote a scathing review of *Their Eyes Were Watching God* upon its publication, claiming that it was not "serious fiction" and that it "carries no theme, no message, no thought."

Hurston was also criticized for her comportment: she refused to bow to gender conventions, and her behavior often seemed shocking, if not outrageous. Although she won a Guggenheim Fellowship and had published prolifically (both works of fiction and anthropological works), Hurston fell into obscurity for a number of years. By the late 1940s, she began to have increasing difficulty getting her work published. By the early 1950s, she was forced to work as a maid. In the 1960s, the counterculture revolution continued to show disdain for any literature that was not overtly political, and Hurston's writing was further ignored.

A stroke in the late 1950s forced Hurston to enter a welfare home in Florida. After she died penniless on January 28, 1960, she was buried in an unmarked grave. Alice Walker, another prominent African-American writer, rediscovered her work in the late 1960s. In 1973, Walker traveled to Florida to place a marker on Hurston's grave, containing the phrase, "A Genius of the South." Walker's 1975 essay "In Search of Zora Neale Hurston," published in *Ms.* magazine, propelled Hurston's work back into vogue. Since then, Hurston's opus has been published and republished many times; it has even been adapted for the cinema: Spike Lee's first feature film, *She's Gotta Have It* (1986), parallels *Their Eyes Were Watching God* and is an interesting modern adaptation of the novel.

One of the strengths of Hurston's work is that it can be studied in the context of a number of different American literary traditions. Most often, *Their Eyes Were Watching God* is associated with Harlem Renaissance literature, even though it was published in a later era, because of Hurston's connection to that scene. Certain aspects of the book make it possible to discuss it in other literary contexts. For example, some critics argue that the novel should be read in the context of American southern literature: with its rural southern setting and its focus on the relationship between man and nature, the dynamics of human relationships, and a hero's quest for independence, *Their Eyes Were Watching God* fits well into the tradition that includes such works as Mark Twain's *The Adventures of Huckleberry Finn* (1885) and William Faulkner's *The Sound and the Fury* (1929). The novel is also important in the continuum of American feminist literature, comparing well to Kate Chopin's *The Awakening* (1899). More specifically, and due in large part to Walker's essay, Hurston is often viewed as the first in a succession of great American black women writers that includes Walker, Toni Morrison, and Gloria Naylor.

But *Their Eyes Were Watching God* resists reduction to a single movement, either literary or political. Wright's criticism from 1937 is, to a certain extent, true: the book is not a political treatise—it carries no single, overwhelming message or moral. Far from being a weakness, however, this resistance is the secret of the novel's strength: it is a profoundly rich, multifaceted work that can be read in a number of ways.

PLOT OVERVIEW

Janie Crawford, an attractive, confident, middle-aged black woman, returns to Eatonville, Florida, after a long absence. The black townspeople gossip about her and speculate about where she has been and what has happened to her young husband, Tea Cake. They take her confidence as aloofness, but Janie's friend Pheoby Watson sticks up for her. Pheoby visits her to find out what has happened. Their conversation frames the story that Janie relates.

Janie explains that her grandmother raised her after her mother ran off. Nanny loves her granddaughter and is dedicated to her, but her life as a slave and experience with her own daughter, Janie's mother, has warped her worldview. Her primary desire is to marry Janie as soon as possible to a husband who can provide security and social status for her. She finds a much older farmer named Logan Killicks and insists that Janie marry him.

After moving in with Logan, Janie is miserable. Logan is pragmatic and unromantic and, in general, treats her like a pack mule. One day, Joe Starks, a smooth-tongued and ambitious man, ambles down the road in front of the farm. He and Janie flirt in secret for a couple of weeks before she runs off and marries him. Janie and Jody, as she calls him, travel to all-black Eatonville, where Jody hopes to have a "big voice." A consummate politician, Jody soon succeeds in becoming the mayor, postmaster, storekeeper, and the biggest landlord in town. But Janie seeks something more than a man with a big voice. She soon becomes disenchanted with the monotonous, stifling life she shares with Jody. She wishes that she could be a part of the rich social life in town, but Jody doesn't allow her to interact with "common" people. Jody sees Janie as the fitting ornament to his wealth and power, and he tries to shape her into his vision of what a mayor's wife should be. On the surface, Janie silently submits to Jody; inside, however, she remains passionate and full of dreams.

After almost two decades of marriage, Janie finally asserts herself. When Jody insults her appearance, Janie rips him to shreds in front of the townspeople, telling them all how ugly and impotent he is. In retaliation, he savagely beats her. Their marriage breaks down, and Jody becomes quite ill. After months without interacting, Janie goes in to visit him on his deathbed. Refusing to be silenced, she once again chastises him for the way he treated her. As she berates him, he dies.

After Jody's funeral, Janie feels free for the first time in years. She rebuffs various suitors who come to court her because she loves her newfound independence. But when Tea Cake, a man twelve years her junior, enters her life, Janie immediately senses a spark of mutual attraction. She begins dating Tea Cake despite critical gossip within the town. To everyone's shock, Janie then marries Tea Cake nine months after Jody's death, sells Jody's store, and leaves town to go with Tea Cake to Jacksonville.

During the first week of their marriage, Tea Cake and Janie encounter difficulties. He steals her money and leaves her alone one night, making her think that he married her only for her money. But he returns, explaining that he never meant to leave her and that his theft occurred in a moment of weakness. Afterward, they promise to share all their experiences and opinions with each other. They move to the Everglades, where they work during the harvest season and socialize during the summer off-season. Tea Cake's quick wit and friendliness make their shack the center of entertainment and social life.

A terrible hurricane bursts into the Everglades two years after Janie and Tea Cake's marriage. As they desperately flee the rising waters, a rabid dog bites Tea Cake. At the time, Tea Cake doesn't realize the dog's condition; three weeks later, however, he falls ill. During a rabies-induced bout of madness, Tea Cake becomes convinced that Janie is cheating on him. He starts firing a pistol at her and Janie is forced to kill him to save her life. She is immediately put on trial for murder, but the all-white, all-male jury finds her not guilty. She returns to Eatonville where her former neighbors are ready to spin malicious gossip about her circumstances, assuming that Tea Cake has left her and taken her money. Janie wraps up her recounting to Pheoby, who is greatly impressed by Janie's experiences. Back in her room that night, Janie feels at one with Tea Cake and at peace with herself.

CHARACTER LIST

Janie Mae Crawford The protagonist of the novel. Janie defies categorization: she is black but flaunts her Caucasian-like straight hair, which comes from her mixed ancestry; she is a woman but defies gender stereotypes by insisting on her independence and wearing overalls. Behind her defiance are a curiosity and confidence that drive her to experience the world and become conscious of her relation to it. Part of Janie's maturity rests in her ability to realize that others' cruelty toward her or their inability to understand her stems not from malice but from their upbringing or limited perspective.

Tea Cake Janie's third husband and first real love. Twelve years younger than Janie, Tea Cake impresses her with his quick wit and zest for living. But behind the flash, he has a real affection for, and understanding of, Janie. He doesn't try to force Janie to be anything other than herself, and he treats her with respect. He is not without faults, however; he steals from her once and beats her. These reprehensible incidents, though, make him a more real character than one who possesses only idealized positive qualities.

Jody Starks Janie's second husband. Jody travels from Georgia to Eatonville to satisfy his ambition and hunger for power. A consummate politician and businessman, he becomes the postmaster, mayor, storekeeper, and biggest landlord in Eatonville. But he treats Janie as an object rather than a person, and their marriage deteriorates.

Logan Killicks Janie's first husband. Nanny arranges Janie's marriage to Logan because she values financial security and respectability over love. Logan pampers Janie for a year before he tries to make her help him with the farming work. Feeling used and unloved, Janie leaves him for Jody Starks.

Pheoby Watson Janie's best friend in Eatonville. Pheoby gives Janie the benefit of the doubt when the townspeople gossip viciously about Janie. She is the audience for Janie's story and her presence is occasionally felt in the colloquial speech that the narrator mixes in with a more sophisticated narrative style.

Nanny Crawford Janie's grandmother. Nanny's experience as a slave stamped her worldview with a strong concern for financial security, respectability, and upward mobility. These values clash with Janie's independence and desire to experience the world, though Janie comes to respect Nanny's values and decisions as well intended.

Mr. and Mrs. Turner Everglades residents who run a small restaurant. Mrs. Turner prides herself on her Caucasian features and disdains anyone with a more African appearance. She worships Janie because of her Caucasian features. She cannot understand why a woman like Janie would marry a man as dark as Tea Cake, and she wants to introduce Janie to her brother.

Sam Watson Pheoby's husband. Sam is a source of great humor and wisdom during the conversations on Jody's porch. When a few Eatonville residents begin to express their resentment toward Jody, Sam acknowledges that Jody can be overbearing and commanding but points out that Jody is responsible for many improvements in the town.

Leafy Crawford Janie's mother. Leafy was born shortly before the end of the Civil War and ran away after giving birth to Janie.

Amos Hicks A resident of Eatonville. Hicks is one of the first people to meet Janie and Jody. He tries unsuccessfully to lure Janie away from Jody.

Motor Boat One of Tea Cake and Janie's friends in the Everglades. Motor Boat flees the hurricane with them and weathers the storm in an abandoned house.

Hezekiah Potts The delivery boy and assistant shopkeeper at Jody's store. After Jody's death, Hezekiah begins to mimic Jody's affectations.

Dr. Simmons A friendly white doctor who is well known in the muck.

Johnny Taylor A young man whom Janie kisses when she starts to feel sexual desires at age sixteen. This incident prompts Nanny to force Janie to marry the more socially respectable Logan Killicks.

Annie Tyler and Who Flung A wealthy widow who lived in Eatonville, and her much younger fiancé, who took her money and fled at the first opportunity. Early in her marriage to Tea Cake, Janie fears that he will turn out to be like Who Flung and that she will end up like Annie Tyler.

Mr. and Mrs. Washburn Nanny's employers after she became a free woman. Nanny lived in a house in the Washburns' backyard, and they helped raise Janie with their own children.

Nunkie A girl in the Everglades who flirts relentlessly with Tea Cake. Janie grows extremely jealous of Nunkie, but after Tea Cake reassures her that Nunkie means nothing to him, Nunkie disappears from the novel.

ANALYSIS OF MAJOR CHARACTERS

JANIE Although *Their Eyes Were Watching God* revolves around Janie's relationships with other people, it is first and foremost a story of Janie's search for spiritual enlightenment and a strong sense of her own identity. Janie's development along the way can be charted by studying her use of language and her relationship to her own voice. At the beginning of her story, she is unsure of who she is or how she wants to live. When she tells her story to Pheoby, she begins with her revelation under the blossoming pear tree, which initiates her quest. Under the pear tree, she witnesses a perfect union of harmony within nature. She knows she wants to achieve this type of love, a reciprocity that produces oneness with the world, but is unsure how to proceed. At this point, she is unable to articulate even to herself exactly what she wants.

Men both help and hinder Janie's progress in figuring out who she is. When Jody Starks enters her life, he seems to offer the ideal alternative to the dull and pragmatic Logan Killicks. With his ambitious talk, Jody convinces Janie that he'll use his thirst for conquest to help her realize her dreams, whatever they may be. Janie learns that Jody's exertion of power only stifles her. But just before Jody's death, Janie's repressed power breaks through in a torrent of verbal retaliation. Her somewhat cruel tirade at the dying Jody measures the depth of Jody's suppression of her inner life. Having begun to find her voice, Janie blows through social niceties to express herself.

Janie flourishes in her relationship with Tea Cake, as he "teaches her the maiden language all over." Her control of speech reaches a new level as she learns to be silent when she chooses. This idea of silence as strength rather than passivity comes to the forefront during Janie's trial, when the narrator glosses over her testimony. Dialogue has been pivotally important up to this point, and one might expect Hurston to use the courtroom scene to showcase Janie's hard-won, mature voice. The absence of dialogue here, as Mary Ellen Washington argues in the foreword present in most editions of the novel, reflects Hurston's discomfort with rhetoric for its own sake; Hurston doesn't want Janie's voice to be confused with that of the lawyer or politician. Janie's development of her voice is inseparable from her inner growth, and the drama of the courtroom may be too contrived to draw out the nuances of her inner life. Janie summarizes the novel's attitude toward language when she tells Pheoby that talking "don't amount tuh uh hill uh beans" if it isn't connected to actual experience.

TEA CAKE Like all of the other men in Janie's life, Tea Cake plays only a supporting role. Before she meets Tea Cake, Janie has already begun to find her own voice, as is demonstrated when she finally stands up to Jody. Tea Cake accelerates her spiritual growth. Ever since her moment under the pear tree, Janie has known that she will find what she is searching for only through love. In Tea Cake she finds a creative and vivacious personality who enjoys probing the world around him and respects Janie's need to develop. Whereas Logan treats her like a farm animal and Jody silences her, Tea Cake converses and plays with her. Instead of stifling her personality, he encourages it, introducing her to new experiences and skills.

While Tea Cake is vital to Janie's development, he is not an indispensable part of her life, a crucial truth that is revealed when Janie shoots him. He plays a role in her life, helping her to better understand herself. By teaching her how to shoot a gun, ironically, he provides her with the tools that ultimately kill him. Janie's decision to save herself rather than yield her life up to the crazy Tea Cake points to her increasing sense of self and demonstrates that Tea Cake's ultimate function in the novel is not to make Janie dependent on him for happiness but to help her find happiness and security within herself.

JODY STARKS Jody is cruel, conceited, and disinterested in Janie as a person, but his cruelty is not a result of any specific animosity toward Janie. Rather, it is a reflection of the values he holds and the way he understands his relationship to the world. Jody depends on the exertion of power for his sense of himself; he is happy and secure when he feels he holds power over those around him. In Janie's words, he needs to "have [his] way all [his] life, trample and mash down and then die ruther than tuh let [him]self heah 'bout it." He needs to feel like a "big voice," a force of "irresistible maleness" before whom the whole world bows.

In order to maintain this illusion of irresistible power, Jody tries to dominate everyone and everything around him. His entire existence is based on purchasing, building, bullying, and political planning. He marries Janie not because he loves her as a person but because he views her as an object that will serve a useful purpose in his schemes. She is young, beautiful, and stately, and thus fits his ideal of what a mayor's wife should be. Jody is obsessed with notions of power, and Janie remains unfulfilled by their relationship because these notions require her to be a mute, static object and prevent her from growing. He forces her to tie her hair up because its phallic quality threatens his male dominance and because its feminine beauty makes him worry that he will lose her. Janie ultimately rebels against Jody's suppression of her, and by toppling his secure sense of his own power, she destroys his will to live.

THEMES, MOTIFS, AND SYMBOLS

THEMES

THE IMPORTANCE OF LANGUAGE AND SILENCE *Their Eyes Were Watching God* is most often celebrated for Hurston's unique use of language, particularly her mastery of rural southern black dialect. Throughout the novel, she utilizes an interesting narrative structure, splitting the presentation of the story between high literary narration and idiomatic discourse. The long passages of discourse celebrate the culturally rich voices of Janie's world; these characters speak as do few others in American literature, and their distinctive grammar, vocabulary, and tone mark their individuality. Hurston's use of language parallels Janie's quest to find her voice. As Henry Louis Gates Jr. writes in the afterword to most modern editions of the book, *Their Eyes Were Watching God* is primarily concerned "with the project of finding a voice, with language as an instrument of injury and salvation, of selfhood and empowerment." Jody stifles Janie's speech, as when he prevents her from talking after he is named mayor; her hatred of him stems from this suppression of her individuality. Tea Cake, on the other hand, engages her speech, conversing with her and putting himself on equal terms with her; her love for him stems from his respect for her individuality.

After Janie discovers her ability to define herself by her speech interactions with others, she learns that silence too can be a source of empowerment; having found her voice, she learns to control it. Similarly, the narrator is silent in conspicuous places, neither revealing why Janie isn't upset with Tea Cake's beating nor disclosing her words at the trial. In terms of both the form of the novel and its thematic content, Hurston places great emphasis on the control of language as the source of identity and empowerment.

POWER AND CONQUEST AS MEANS TO FULFILLMENT Whereas Janie struggles to assert a place for herself by undertaking a spiritual journey toward love and self-awareness, Jody attempts to achieve fulfillment through the exertion of power. He tries to purchase and control everyone and everything around him; he exercises his authority hoping to subordinate his environment to his will. He labors under the illusion that he can control the world around him and that, by doing so, he will achieve some sense of profound fulfillment. Others exhibit a similar attitude toward power and control; even Tea Cake, for example, is filled with hubris as the hurricane whips up, certain that he can survive the storm through his mastery of the muck. For both Jody and Tea Cake, the natural world reveals the limits of human power. In Jody's case, as disease sets in, he begins to lose the illusion that he can control his world; the loss of authority over Janie as she talks back to him furthers this disillusionment. In Tea Cake's case, he is forced to flee the hurricane and struggles to survive the ensuing floods. This limit to the scope of one's power proves the central problem with Jody's power-oriented approach toward achieving fulfillment: ultimately, Jody can neither stop his deterioration nor silence Janie's strong will.

RELATIONSHIPS VS. INDEPENDENCE *Their Eyes Were Watching God* is the story of how Janie achieves a strong sense of self and comes to appreciate her independence. But her journey toward enlightenment is not undertaken alone. The gender differences that Hurston espouses require that men and women provide each other things that they need but do not possess. Janie views fulfilling relationships as reciprocal and based on mutual respect, as demonstrated in her relationship with Tea Cake, which elevates Janie into an equality noticeably absent from her marriages to Logan and Jody.

Although relationships are implied to be necessary to a fulfilling life, Janie's quest for spiritual fulfillment is fundamentally a self-centered one. She is alone at the end yet seems content. She liberates herself from her unpleasant and unfulfilling relationships with Logan and Jody, who hinder her personal journey. Through her relationship with Tea Cake, Janie experiences true fulfillment and enlightenment and becomes secure in her independence. She feels a deep connection to the world around her and even feels that the spirit of Tea Cake is with her. Thus, even though she is alone, she doesn't feel alone.

MOTIFS

COMMUNITY As Janie returns to Eatonville, the novel focuses on the porch-sitters who gossip and speculate about her situation. In Eatonville and the Everglades, particularly, the two most significant settings in the novel, Janie constantly interacts with the community around her. At certain times, she longs to be a part of this vibrant social life, which, at its best, offers warmth, safety, connection, and interaction. In Chapter 18, when Tea Cake, Janie, and Motor Boat seek shelter from the storm, the narrator notes that they "sat in company with the others in other shanties"; of course, they are not literally sitting in the same room as these others, but all of those affected by the hurricane share a communal bond, united against the overwhelming, impersonal force of the hurricane.

At other times, Janie scorns the pettiness of the gossip and rumors that flourish in these communities, which often criticize her out of jealousy for her independence and strong will. These communities, exemplifying a negative aspect of unity, demand the sacrifice of individuality. Janie refuses to make this sacrifice, but even near the end of the novel, during the court trial, "it [i]s not death she fear[s]. It [i]s misunderstanding." In other words, Janie still cares what people in the community think because she still longs to understand herself.

RACE AND RACISM Because Hurston was a famous black author who was associated with the Harlem Renaissance, many readers assume that *Their Eyes Were Watching God* is concerned primarily with issues of race. Although race is a significant motif in the book, it is not a central theme. As Alice Walker writes in her dedication to *I Love Myself When I Am Laughing . . . and Then Again When I Am Looking Mean and Impressive: A Zora Neale Hurston Reader*, "I think we are better off if we think of Zora Neale Hurston as an artist, period—rather than as the artist/politician most black writers have been required to be." Along the same lines, it is far more fulfilling to read Janie's story as a profoundly human quest than as a distinctly black one.

T

But issues of race are nonetheless present. Janie and Tea Cake experience prejudice from both blacks and whites at significant moments in the book. Two moments in particular stand out: Janie's interactions, in Chapter 16, with Mrs. Turner, a black woman with racist views against blacks, and the courtroom scene, in Chapter 19, after which Janie is comforted by white women but scorned by her black friends. In these moments, we see that racism in the novel operates as a cultural construct, a free-floating force that affects anyone, white or black, weak enough to succumb to it. Hurston's perspective on racism was undoubtedly influenced by her study with influential anthropologist Franz Boas, who argued that ideas of race are culturally constructed and that skin color indicates little, if anything, about innate difference. In other words, racism is a cultural force that individuals can either struggle against or yield to rather than a mindset rooted in demonstrable facts. In this way, racism operates in the novel just like the hurricane and the doctrine to which Jody adheres; it is an environmental force that challenges Janie in her quest to achieve harmony with the world around her.

THE FOLKLORE QUALITY OF RELIGION As the title indicates, God plays a huge role in the novel, but this God is not really the Judeo-Christian god. The book maintains an almost Gnostic perspective on the universe: God is not a single entity but a diffuse force. This outlook is particularly evident in the mystical way that Hurston describes nature. At various times, the sun, moon, sky, sea, horizon, and other aspects of the natural world appear imbued with divinity. The God in the title refers to these divine forces throughout the world, both beautiful and threatening, that Janie encounters. Her quest is a spiritual one because her ultimate goal is to find her place in the world, understand who she is, and be at peace with her environment.

Except for one brief reference to church in Chapter 12, organized religion never appears in the novel. The idea of spirituality, on the other hand, is always present, as the novel espouses a worldview rooted in folklore and mythology. As an anthropologist, Hurston collected rural mythology and folklore of blacks in America and the Caribbean. Many visions of mysticism that she presents in the novel—her haunting personification of death, the idea of a sun-god, the horizon as a boundary at the end of the world—are likely culled directly from these sources. Like her use of dialogue, Hurston's presentation of folklore and non-Christian spirituality celebrates the black rural culture.

SYMBOLS

JANIE'S HAIR Janie's hair is a symbol of her power and unconventional identity, and it represents her strength and individuality in three ways. First, it represents her independence and defiance of petty community standards. The town's critique at the very beginning of the novel demonstrates that it is considered undignified for a woman of Janie's age to wear her hair down. Her refusal to bow down to their norms clearly reflects her strong, rebellious spirit. Second, her hair functions as a phallic symbol; her braid is constantly described in phallic terms and functions as a symbol of a typically masculine power and potency, which blurs gender lines and thus threatens Jody. Third, her hair, because of its straightness, functions as a symbol of whiteness; Mrs. Turner worships Janie because of her straight hair and other Caucasian characteristics. Her hair contributes to the normally white male power that she wields, which helps her disrupt traditional power relationships (male over female, white over black) throughout the novel.

THE PEAR TREE AND THE HORIZON The pear tree and the horizon represent Janie's idealized views of nature. In the bees' interaction with the pear tree flowers, Janie witnesses a perfect moment in nature, full of erotic energy, passionate interaction, and blissful harmony. She chases after this ideal throughout the rest of the book. Similarly, the horizon represents the far-off mystery of the natural world, with which she longs to connect. Janie's hauling in of her horizon "like a great fish-net" at the end of the novel indicates that she has achieved the harmony with nature that she has sought since the moment under the pear tree.

THE HURRICANE The hurricane represents the destructive fury of nature. As such, it functions as the opposite of the pear tree and horizon imagery: whereas the pear tree and horizon stand for beauty and pleasure, the hurricane demonstrates how chaotic and capricious the world can be. The hurricane makes the characters question who they are and what their place in the universe is. Its impersonal nature—it is simply a force of pure destruction, lacking consciousness and conscience—makes the characters wonder what sort of world they live in, whether God cares about them at all, and whether they are fundamentally in conflict with the world around them. In the face of the hurricane, Janie and the other characters wonder how they can possibly survive in a world filled with such chaos and pain.

IMPORTANT QUOTATIONS EXPLAINED

---

1. *Ships at a distance have every man's wish on board. For some they come in with the tide. For others they sail forever on the horizon, never out of sight, never landing until the Watcher turns his eyes away in resignation, his dreams mocked to death by Time. That is the life of men. Now, women forget all those things they don't want to remember, and remember everything they don't want to forget. The dream is the truth. Then they act and do things accordingly.*

This passage, which opens *Their Eyes Were Watching God*, establishes the novel's unusual perspective on gender difference. Because it is the story of a woman and because it was the first major novel published by a black woman, *Their Eyes* is often classified as a feminist novel. But feminism is often associated with the idea that men and women are absolutely equal; here, the narrator immediately establishes a fundamental difference between men and women. The idea that men and women need certain things from each other recurs many times throughout the novel, as Janie searches for the man who can complement her and give her those things that she doesn't have, and Logan, Jody, and Tea Cake attempt to fill their respective needs in their respective relationships with Janie. The passage also foreshadows the novel's thematic concerns: the statement about women is proud and defiant, saying that while men never really reach for their dreams, women can control their wills and chase their dreams. As the novel unfolds, Janie acts according to this notion, battling and struggling in the direction of her dreams.

---

2. *She saw a dust-bearing bee sink into the sanctum of a bloom; the thousand sister-calyxes arch to meet the love embrace and the ecstatic shiver of the tree from root to tiniest branch creaming in every blossom and frothing with delight. So this was a marriage! She had been summoned to behold a revelation.*

This passage from Chapter 2 marks the beginning of Janie's spiritual and sexual awakening. She is a young girl under the care of her grandmother, and this incident propels her upon her quest to reach her horizon. The embrace between the bee and the flowers imprints itself upon Janie as an idealized vision of love—a moment of mutual, reciprocal fulfillment. The flowers arch to meet the arriving bee, and the consequent union of the two provides each partner something desired. Janie searches for such a give-and-take love throughout the novel.

The passage also relates to an even deeper desire, which is the ultimate goal of the love that Janie seeks: a sense of enlightenment, of oneness with the world around her. The language of this passage is evocative of the erotic, naturalistic romanticism of Walt Whitman. Like Whitman's poetry, Hurston's prose here finds divinity and spirituality in the fertile lushness of the natural world ("the ecstatic shiver of the tree . . . frothing with delight"). Janie sees nature as she wants it to be: a world full of beauty and fulfillment. She chases after this ideal because she wants to experience a harmonization with the beautiful and wild forces that she witnesses under the pear tree. Later events—particularly the hurricane of Chapter 18—introduce a very different vision of nature, but the pear tree continues to serve as her vision of ideal love, of a perfect union with another person.

---

3. *"Listen, Sam, if it was nature, nobody wouldn't have tuh look out for babies touchin' stoves, would they? 'Cause dey just naturally wouldn't touch it. But dey sho will. So it's caution." "Naw it ain't, it's nature, cause nature makes caution. It's de strongest thing dat God ever made, now. Fact is it's de onliest thing God every made. He made nature and nature made everything else."*

T

This interchange, which occurs in Chapter 6, is an excerpt from a lively debate between Lige Moss and Sam Watson on the porch of Jody's store. In addition to being an excellent example of Hurston's use of dialect and idiomatic English, this dialogue speaks to Janie's developing understanding of herself in relation to the world. Here, Sam and Lige argue about the relationship between mankind and God and between themselves and the world around them. In modern terms, it is a discussion of nature versus nurture. Lige argues that humans are taught everything that they know; such a perspective implies a fundamental antagonism between humanity and the natural world. In Lige's terms, there are hot stoves everywhere, and humans must learn and be vigilant to survive. Sam, on the other hand, argues that humans are naturally cautious; such a perspective implies a fundamental harmony between humanity and the natural world. According to Sam, humans, as creatures made by God, are inherently part of nature. Over the course of the novel, Janie progresses through the obstacles that the world presents her until she finally, harmoniously, reaches the horizon that she has long sought.

4. *It was inevitable that she should accept any inconsistency and cruelty from her deity as all good worshippers do from theirs. All gods who receive homage are cruel. All gods dispense suffering without reason. Otherwise they would not be worshipped. Through indiscriminate suffering men know fear and fear is the most divine emotion. It is the stones for altars and the beginning of wisdom. Half gods are worshipped in wine and flowers. Real gods require blood.*

In this passage from Chapter 16, Hurston carves out an exception to the gender dichotomy that she presents in the opening sentences of the novel. Mrs. Turner's worship of qualities that she will never possess groups her with the men whose ships "sail forever on the horizon." What is most strange about the passage, though, is the implicit comparison between Mrs. Turner and Janie. The "indiscriminate suffering" and "real blood" that may lead to wisdom could equally well belong to Janie. Janie's trip to the horizon requires her to suffer at the hands of two husbands, shoot her third, and brave a ferocious hurricane. Yet for Janie, suffering is not an end in itself. She endures it so that she may experience the fullness of life and the good that comes with the bad. Mrs. Turner, however, worships her false gods because they give her a sense of superiority over her peers and because, something of a masochist, she enjoys the pain that these gods dole out. When she is mocked for her views by others, she feels like a victim and a martyr, a feeling she finds pleasurable. The narrator's stylized description, in the paragraph just below the above quote, of her wish for "an army, terrible with banners and swords," illustrates the fantastic vengefulness and inflated sense of self-importance that Mrs. Turner's ostracism gives her. It is this pleasure in pain that motivates her to worship "gods who dispense suffering without reason."

5. *The wind came back with triple fury, and put out the light for the last time. They sat in company with the others in other shanties, their eyes straining against crude walls and their souls asking if He meant to measure their puny might against His. They seemed to be staring at the dark, but their eyes were watching God.*

These lines from Chapter 18 neatly summarize the central conflict of the novel, as Janie, Tea Cake, and Motor Boat seek refuge from the raging hurricane outside. The struggle at the heart of the novel is set forth in the starkest terms: humans against God, Janie and the others against nature. It is significant that Motor Boat joins Janie and Tea Cake in their house and that the narrator notes that everybody is united in the same struggle. We see here that the bonds of human interaction and intimacy provide refuge against the forces of nature. Tea Cake and Janie share an intimacy that allows them to struggle and survive these forces. The sense of self that Janie gains from the love that she shares with Tea Cake enables her subsequently to endure another hostile force—the mean-spirited scorn of the black women of Eatonville—and maintain her inner peace.

Compare and contrast Janie's three marriages in *Their Eyes Were Watching God*. What initially draws her to each of the three men? How do they differ from one another? What does she learn from each experience?

Their Eyes Were Watching God by Zora Neale Hurston revolves around Janie Crawford and her relationships with three men: Logan Killicks, Jody Starks, and Tea Cake. Each of these relationships is unique, and each provides Janie with bits of self-knowledge that eventually result in her becoming stronger, smarter, and more independent.

Janie marries Logan because her grandmother insists she marry someone who can provide her with financial stability. Janie feels no romantic attraction to Logan—in fact, it is when Nanny catches her kissing another local boy that she coerces her into marrying Logan. Nanny admits her motives: "'Tain't Logan Killicks Ah wants you to have, baby. It's protection" (Chapter 1). Janie consents, hoping she will grow to love Logan after they are married, but this does not happen. As time goes on, Logan begins to treat Janie like a possession, which makes her even more miserable. Her relationship with Logan is more like a business arrangement than a marriage; consequently, the passionate Jody Starks easily woos Janie from Logan.

While Logan is dull, predictable, and boring to Janie, Jody is aggressive and free-spirited, which she finds exciting. Jody whisks Janie away to the town of Eatonville, where they set up a new life for themselves and he quickly becomes the town's mayor. Although she is proud of him, Janie feels overshadowed by her increasingly domineering husband. The more established Jody becomes, the more he controls Janie. He stops her from socializing with other townspeople and insists that she hide her beautiful hair in a head wrap. Outwardly, Janie cowers to him, but she resents him and falls out of love. When Jody falls ill, Janie tries to take care of him, but he grows increasingly hostile. They quarrel even on the day of his death. With Jody gone, Janie feels a sense of freedom and relief, which she expresses by releasing her hair from the wrap that had confined it for seven years. Jody's healthy ego, which was initially so attractive to Janie, becomes the reason that she is desperate to get away from him.

Tea Cake, Janie's third husband, comes closest to truly understanding her. Janie is happy to be unmarried after Jody's death and has no intention of attaching herself to a man again. But Tea Cake is unlike any man she has ever met, and because she has become stronger living alone, she feels confident in choosing to be with the much younger and free-spirited Tea Cake. Whereas Logan and Jody overshadowed Janie, Tea Cake engages Janie and fosters her personal growth. Although she loves him, when Tea Cake's mental health deteriorates, Janie prioritizes herself over him by shooting him when he becomes threatening to her. Ironically, it is Tea Cake who teaches Janie to shoot a gun and also Tea Cake who reinforces the idea that Janie must take care of herself. In this way, he provides her with a method of escape when her life is at risk.

Though her three husbands differ in many ways, each supports Janie's continual quest for her own identity. *Their Eyes Were Watching God* is Janie's story; her husbands each play important supporting roles. She explores different aspects of her personality with each of them, and ultimately arrives at a stronger, more independent state because of these relationships.

To the Lighthouse

Virginia Woolf
(1882–1941)

CONTEXT

Virginia Woolf was born on January 25, 1882, into one of Victorian England's most prestigious literary families. Her father, Sir Leslie Stephen, was the editor of the *Dictionary of National Biography* and was married to the daughter of the writer William Thackeray. Woolf grew up among the most important and influential British intellectuals of her time and received free rein to explore her father's library. Her personal connections and abundant talent soon opened doors for her. Woolf wrote that she found herself in "a position where it was easier on the whole to be eminent than obscure." Almost from the beginning, her life was a precarious balance of extraordinary success and mental instability.

As a young woman, Woolf wrote for the prestigious *Times Literary Supplement*, and as an adult she quickly found herself at the center of England's most important literary community. Known as the "Bloomsbury Group" after the section of London in which its members lived, this group of writers, artists, and philosophers emphasized nonconformity, aesthetic pleasure, and intellectual freedom and included such luminaries as the painter Lytton Strachey, the novelist E. M. Forster, the composer Benjamin Britten, and the economist John Maynard Keynes. Working among such an inspirational group of peers and possessing an incredible talent in her own right, Woolf published her most famous novels by the mid-1920s, including *The Voyage Out*, *Mrs. Dalloway*, *Orlando*, and *To the Lighthouse*. With these works she reached the pinnacle of her profession.

Woolf's life was equally dominated by mental illness. Her parents died when she was young—her mother in 1895 and her father in 1904—and she was prone to intense, terrible headaches and emotional breakdowns. After her father's death, she attempted suicide, throwing herself out a window. Though she married Leonard Woolf in 1912 and loved him deeply, she was not entirely satisfied romantically or sexually. For years she sustained an intimate relationship with the novelist Vita Sackville-West. Late in life, Woolf became terrified by the idea that another nervous breakdown was close at hand, one from which she would not recover. On March 28, 1941, she wrote her husband a note stating that she did not wish to spoil his life by going mad. She then drowned herself in the River Ouse.

Woolf's writing bears the mark of her literary pedigree as well as her struggle to find meaning in her own unsteady existence. Written in a poised, understated, and elegant style, her work examines the structures of human life, from the nature of relationships to the experience of time. Yet her writing also addresses issues relevant to her era and literary circle. Throughout her work she celebrates and analyzes the Bloomsbury values of aestheticism, feminism, and independence. Moreover, her stream-of-consciousness style was influenced by, and a response to, the work of the French thinker Henri Bergson and the novelists Marcel Proust and James Joyce.

This style allows the subjective mental processes of Woolf's characters to determine the objective content of her narrative. In *To the Lighthouse* (1927), one of her most experimental works, the passage of time, for example, is modulated by the consciousness of the characters rather than by the clock. The events of a single afternoon constitute over half the book, while the events of the following ten years are compressed into a few dozen pages. Many readers of *To the Lighthouse*, especially those who are not versed in the traditions of modernist fiction, find the novel strange and difficult. Its language is dense and the structure amorphous. Compared with the plot-driven Victorian novels that came before it, *To the Lighthouse* seems to have little in the way of action. Indeed, almost all of the events take place in the characters' minds.

Although *To the Lighthouse* is a radical departure from the nineteenth-century novel, it is, like its more traditional counterparts, intimately interested in developing characters and advancing both plot and themes. Woolf's experimentation has much to do with the time in which she lived: the turn of the century was marked by bold scientific developments. Charles Darwin's theory of evolution undermined an unquestioned faith in God that was, until that point, nearly universal, while the rise of psychoanalysis, a movement led by Sigmund Freud, introduced the idea of an unconscious mind. Such innovation in ways of scientific thinking had great influence on the styles and concerns of contemporary artists and writers like those in the Bloomsbury Group. *To the Lighthouse* exemplifies Woolf's style and many of her concerns as a novelist. With its characters based on her own parents and siblings, it is certainly her most autobiographical fictional statement, and in the characters of Mr. Ramsay, Mrs. Ramsay, and Lily Briscoe, Woolf offers some of her most penetrating explorations of the workings of the human consciousness as it perceives and analyzes, feels and interacts.

PLOT OVERVIEW

To the Lighthouse is divided into three sections: "The Window," "Time Passes," and "The Lighthouse." Each section is fragmented into stream-of-consciousness contributions from various narrators.

"The Window" opens just before the start of World War I. Mr. Ramsay and Mrs. Ramsay bring their eight children to their summer home in the Hebrides (a group of islands west of Scotland). Across the bay from their house stands a large lighthouse. Six-year-old James Ramsay wants desperately to go to the lighthouse, and Mrs. Ramsay tells him that they will go the next day if the weather permits. James reacts gleefully, but Mr. Ramsay tells him coldly that the weather looks to be foul. James resents his father and believes that he enjoys being cruel to James and his siblings.

The Ramsays host a number of guests, including the dour Charles Tansley, who admires Mr. Ramsay's work as a metaphysical philosopher. Also at the house is Lily Briscoe, a young painter who begins a portrait of Mrs. Ramsay. Mrs. Ramsay wants Lily to marry William Bankes, an old friend of the Ramsays, but Lily resolves to remain single. Mrs. Ramsay does manage to arrange another marriage, however, between Paul Rayley and Minta Doyle, two of their acquaintances.

During the course of the afternoon, Paul proposes to Minta, Lily begins her painting, Mrs. Ramsay soothes the resentful James, and Mr. Ramsay frets over his shortcomings as a philosopher, periodically turning to Mrs. Ramsay for comfort. That evening, the Ramsays host a seemingly ill-fated dinner party. Paul and Minta are late returning from their walk on the beach with two of the Ramsays' children. Lily bristles at outspoken comments made by Charles Tansley, who suggests that women can neither paint nor write. Mr. Ramsay reacts rudely when Augustus Carmichael, a poet, asks for a second plate of soup. As the night draws on, however, these missteps right themselves, and the guests come together to make a memorable evening.

The joy, however, like the party itself, cannot last, and as Mrs. Ramsay leaves her guests in the dining room, she reflects that the event has already slipped into the past. Later, she joins her husband in the parlor. The couple sit quietly together, until Mr. Ramsay's characteristic insecurities interrupt their peace. He wants his wife to tell him that she loves him. Mrs. Ramsay is not one to make such pronouncements, but she concedes to his point made earlier in the day that the weather will be too rough for a trip to the lighthouse the next day. Mr. Ramsay thus knows that Mrs. Ramsay loves him. Night falls, and one night quickly becomes another.

Time passes more quickly as the novel enters the "Time Passes" segment. War breaks out across Europe. Mrs. Ramsay dies suddenly one night. Andrew Ramsay, her oldest son, is killed in battle, and his sister Prue dies from an illness related to childbirth. The family no longer vacations at its summerhouse, which falls into a state of disrepair: weeds take over the garden and spiders nest in the house. Ten years pass before the family returns. Mrs. McNab, the housekeeper, employs a few other women to help set the house in order. They rescue the house from oblivion and decay, and everything is in order when Lily Briscoe returns.

In "The Lighthouse" section, time returns to the slow detail of shifting points of view, similar in style to "The Window." Mr. Ramsay declares that he and James and Cam, one of his daughters, will journey to the lighthouse. On the morning of the voyage, delays throw him into a fit of temper. He appeals to Lily for sympathy, but, unlike Mrs. Ramsay, she is unable to provide him with what he needs. The Ramsays set off, and Lily takes her place on the lawn, determined to complete a painting she started but abandoned on her last visit. James and Cam bristle at their father's blustery behavior and are embarrassed by his constant self-pity. Still, as the boat reaches its destination, the children feel a fondness for him. Even James, whose skill as a sailor Mr. Ramsay praises, experiences a moment of connection with his father, though James so willfully resents him. Across the bay, Lily puts the finishing touch on her painting. She makes a definitive stroke on the canvas and puts her brush down, finally having achieved her vision.

CHARACTER LIST

Mrs. Ramsay Mr. Ramsay's wife. A beautiful and loving woman, Mrs. Ramsay is a wonderful hostess who takes pride in making memorable experiences for the guests at the family's summer home on the Isle of Skye. Affirming traditional gender roles wholeheartedly, she lavishes particular attention on her male guests, who she believes have delicate egos and need constant support and sympathy. She is a dutiful and loving wife but often struggles with her husband's difficult moods and selfishness. Without fail, however, she triumphs through these difficult times and demonstrates an ability to make something significant and lasting from the most ephemeral of circumstances, such as a dinner party.

Mr. Ramsay Mrs. Ramsay's husband, and a prominent metaphysical philosopher. Mr. Ramsay loves his family but often acts like something of a tyrant. He tends to be selfish and harsh due to his persistent personal and professional anxieties. He fears, more than anything, that his work is insignificant in the grand scheme of things and that he will not be remembered by future generations. Well aware of how blessed he is to have such a wonderful family, he nevertheless tends to punish his wife, children, and guests by demanding their constant sympathy, attention, and support.

Lily Briscoe A young, single painter who befriends the Ramsays on the Isle of Skye. Like Mr. Ramsay, Lily is plagued by fears that her work lacks worth. She begins a portrait of Mrs. Ramsay at the beginning of the novel but has trouble finishing it. The opinions of men like Charles Tansley, who insists that women cannot paint or write, threaten to undermine her confidence.

James Ramsay The Ramsays' youngest son. James loves his mother deeply and feels a murderous antipathy toward his father, with whom he must compete for Mrs. Ramsay's love and affection. At the beginning of the novel, Mr. Ramsay refuses the six-year-old James's request to go to the lighthouse, saying that the weather will be foul and not permit it; ten years later, James finally makes the journey with his father and his sister Cam. By this time, he has grown into a willful and moody young man who has much in common with his father, whom he detests.

Paul Rayley A young friend of the Ramsays who visits them on the Isle of Skye. Paul is a kind, impressionable young man who follows Mrs. Ramsay's wishes in marrying Minta Doyle.

Minta Doyle A flighty young woman who visits the Ramsays on the Isle of Skye. Minta marries Paul Rayley at Mrs. Ramsay's wishes.

Charles Tansley A young philosopher and pupil of Mr. Ramsay who stays with the Ramsays on the Isle of Skye. Tansley is a prickly and unpleasant man who harbors deep insecurities regarding his humble background. He often insults other people, particularly women such as Lily, whose talent and accomplishments he constantly calls into question. His bad behavior, like Mr. Ramsay's, is motivated by his need for reassurance.

T

William Bankes A botanist and old friend of the Ramsays who stays on the Isle of Skye. Bankes is a kind and mellow man whom Mrs. Ramsay hopes will marry Lily Briscoe. Although he never marries her, Bankes and Lily remain close friends.

Augustus Carmichael An opium-using poet who visits the Ramsays on the Isle of Skye. Carmichael languishes in literary obscurity until his verse becomes popular during the war.

Andrew Ramsay The oldest of the Ramsays' sons. Andrew is a competent, independent young man, and he looks forward to a career as a mathematician.

Jasper Ramsay One of the Ramsays' sons. Jasper, to his mother's chagrin, enjoys shooting birds.

Roger Ramsay One of the Ramsays' sons. Roger is wild and adventurous, like his sister Nancy.

Prue Ramsay The oldest Ramsay girl, a beautiful young woman. Mrs. Ramsay delights in contemplating Prue's marriage, which she believes will be blissful.

Rose Ramsay One of the Ramsays' daughters. Rose has a talent for making things beautiful. She arranges the fruit for her mother's dinner party and picks out her mother's jewelry.

Nancy Ramsay One of the Ramsays' daughters. Nancy accompanies Paul Rayley and Minta Doyle on their trip to the beach. Like her brother Roger, she is a wild adventurer.

Cam Ramsay One of the Ramsays' daughters. As a young girl, Cam is mischievous. She sails with James and Mr. Ramsay to the lighthouse in the novel's final section.

Mrs. McNab An elderly woman who takes care of the Ramsays' house on the Isle of Skye, restoring it after ten years of abandonment during and after World War I.

Macalister The fisherman who accompanies the Ramsays to the lighthouse. Macalister relates stories of shipwreck and maritime adventure to Mr. Ramsay and compliments James on his handling of the boat while James lands it at the lighthouse.

Macalister's Boy The fisherman's boy. He rows James, Cam, and Mr. Ramsay to the lighthouse.

ANALYSIS OF MAJOR CHARACTERS

MRS. RAMSAY Mrs. Ramsay emerges from the novel's opening pages not only as a woman of great kindness and tolerance but also as a protector. Indeed, her primary goal is to preserve her youngest son James's sense of hope and wonder surrounding the lighthouse. Though she realizes (as James himself does) that Mr. Ramsay is correct in declaring that foul weather will ruin the next day's voyage, she persists in assuring James that the trip is a possibility. She does so not to raise expectations that will inevitably be dashed, but rather because she realizes that the beauties and pleasures of this world are ephemeral and should be preserved, protected, and cultivated as much as possible. So deep is this commitment that she behaves similarly to each of her guests, even those who do not deserve or appreciate her kindness. Before heading into town, for example, she insists on asking Augustus Carmichael, whom she senses does not like her, if she can bring him anything to make his stay more comfortable. Similarly, she tolerates the insufferable behavior of Charles Tansley, whose bitter attitude and awkward manners threaten to undo the delicate work she has done toward making a pleasant and inviting home.

As Lily Briscoe notes in the novel's final section, Mrs. Ramsay feels the need to play this role primarily in the company of men. Indeed, Mrs. Ramsay feels obliged to protect the entire opposite sex. According to her, men shoulder the burden of ruling countries and managing economies. Their important work, she believes, leaves them vulnerable and in need of constant reassurance, a service that women can and should provide. Although this dynamic fits squarely into traditional gender boundaries, it is important to note the strength that Mrs. Ramsay feels. At several points, she is aware of her own power, and her posture is far from that of a submissive woman. At the same time, interjections of domesticated anxiety, such as her refrain of "the bill for the greenhouse would be fifty pounds," undercut this power.

Ultimately, as is evident from her meeting with Mr. Ramsay at the close of "The Window," Mrs. Ramsay never compromises herself. Here, she is able—masterfully—to satisfy her husband's desire for her to tell him she loves him without saying the words she finds so difficult to say. This scene displays Mrs. Ramsay's ability to bring together disparate things into a whole. In a world marked by the ravages of time and war, in which everything must and will fall apart, there is perhaps no greater gift than a sense of unity, even if it is only temporary. Lily and other characters find themselves grasping for this unity after Mrs. Ramsay's death.

MR. RAMSAY Mr. Ramsay stands, in many respects, as Mrs. Ramsay's opposite. Whereas she acts patient, kind, and diplomatic toward others, he tends to be short-tempered, selfish, and rude. Woolf fittingly describes him as "lean as a knife, narrow as the blade of one," which conjures both his physical presence and suggests the sharpness (and violence) of his personality. An accomplished metaphysician who made an invaluable contribution to his field as a young man, Mr. Ramsay bears out his wife's philosophy regarding gender: men, burdened by the importance of their own work, need to seek out the comforts and assurances of women. Throughout the novel, Mr. Ramsay implores his wife and even his guests for sympathy. Mr. Ramsay is uncertain about the fate of his work and its legacy, and his insecurity manifests itself either as a weapon or a weakness. His keen awareness of death's inevitability motivates him to dash the hopes of young James and to bully Mrs. Ramsay into declaring her love for him. This hyperawareness also forces him to confront his own mortality and face the possibility that he, like the forgotten books and plates that litter the second part of the novel, might sink into oblivion.

LILY BRISCOE Lily is a passionate artist, and, like Mr. Ramsay, she worries over the fate of her work, fearing that her paintings will be hung in attics or tossed absentmindedly under a couch. Conventional femininity, represented by Mrs. Ramsay in the form of marriage and family, confounds Lily, and she rejects it. The recurring memory of Charles Tansley insisting that women can neither paint nor write deepens her anxiety. It is with these self-doubts that she begins her portrait of Mrs. Ramsay at the beginning of the novel, a portrait riddled with problems that she is unable to solve. But Lily undergoes a drastic transformation over the course of the novel, evolving from a woman who cannot make sense of the shapes and colors that she tries to reproduce into an artist who achieves her vision and, more important, overcomes the anxieties that have kept her from it. By the end of the novel, Lily, a serious and diligent worker, puts into practice all that she has learned from Mrs. Ramsay. Much like the woman she so greatly admires, she is able to craft something beautiful and lasting from the ephemeral materials around her—the changing light, the view of the bay. Her artistic achievement suggests a larger sense of completeness in that she finally feels united with Mr. Ramsay and the rational, intellectual sphere that he represents.

JAMES RAMSAY A sensitive child, James is gripped by a love for his mother that is as overpowering and complete as his hatred for his father. He feels a murderous rage against Mr. Ramsay, who, he believes, delights in delivering the news that there will be no trip to the lighthouse. But James grows into a young man who shares many of his father's characteristics, the same ones that incited such anger in him as a child. When he eventually sails to the lighthouse with his father, James, like Mr. Ramsay, is withdrawn, moody, and easily offended. His need to be praised, as noted by his sister Cam, mirrors his father's incessant need for sympathy, reassurance, and love. Indeed, as they approach the lighthouse, James considers his father's profile and recognizes the profound loneliness that stamps both of their personalities. By the time the boat lands, James's attitude toward his father has changed considerably. As he softens toward Mr. Ramsay and comes to accept him as he is, James, like Lily, who finishes her painting on shore at that very moment, achieves a rare, fleeting moment in which the world seems blissfully whole and complete.

THEMES, MOTIFS, AND SYMBOLS

THEMES

THE TRANSIENCE OF LIFE AND WORK Mr. Ramsay and Mrs. Ramsay take completely different approaches to life: he relies on his intellect, while she depends on her emotions. But they share the knowledge that the world around them is transient—that nothing lasts forever. Mr. Ramsay reflects that even the most enduring of reputations, such as Shakespeare's, are doomed to eventual oblivion. This realization accounts for the bitter aspect of his character. Frustrated by the inevitable demise of his own body of work and envious of the few geniuses who will outlast him, he plots to found a school of philosophy that argues that the world is designed for the average, unadorned man, for the "liftman in the Tube" rather than for the rare immortal writer.

Mrs. Ramsay is as keenly aware as her husband of the passage of time and of mortality. She recoils, for instance, at the notion of James growing into an adult, registers the world's many dangers, and knows that no one, not even her husband, can protect her from them. Her reaction to this knowledge is markedly different from her husband's. Whereas Mr. Ramsay is bowed by the weight of his own demise, Mrs. Ramsay is fueled with the need to make precious and memorable whatever time she has on earth. Such crafted moments, she reflects, offer the only hope of something that endures.

ART AS A MEANS OF PRESERVATION In the face of an existence that is inherently without order or meaning, Mr. and Mrs. Ramsay employ different strategies for making their lives significant. Mr. Ramsay devotes himself to his progression through the course of human thought, while Mrs. Ramsay cultivates memorable experiences from social interactions. Neither of these strategies, however, proves an adequate means of preserving one's experience. After all, Mr. Ramsay fails to obtain the philosophical understanding he so desperately desires, and Mrs. Ramsay's life, though filled with moments that have the shine and resilience of rubies, ends. Only Lily Briscoe finds a way to preserve her experience, and that way is through her art. As Lily begins her portrait of Mrs. Ramsay at the beginning of the novel, Woolf notes the scope of the project: Lily means to order and connect elements that have no necessary relation in the world—"hedges and houses and mothers and children." By the end of the novel, ten years later, Lily finishes the painting she started, which stands as a moment of clarity wrested from confusion. Art is, perhaps, the only hope of surety in a world destined and determined to change: for, while mourning Mrs. Ramsay's death and painting on the lawn, Lily reflects that "nothing stays, all changes; but not words, not paint."

THE SUBJECTIVE NATURE OF REALITY Toward the end of the novel, Lily reflects that in order to see Mrs. Ramsay clearly—to understand her character completely—she would need at least fifty pairs of eyes; only then would she be privy to every possible angle and nuance. The truth, according to this assertion, rests in the accumulation of different, even opposing, vantage points. Woolf's technique in structuring the story mirrors Lily's assertion. She is committed to creating a sense of the world that not only depends upon the private perceptions of her characters but is also *nothing more than* the accumulation of those perceptions. To try to reimagine the story as told from a single character's perspective or—in the tradition of the Victorian novelists—from the author's perspective is to realize the radical scope and difficulty of Woolf's project.

THE RESTORATIVE EFFECTS OF BEAUTY At the beginning of the novel, both Mr. Ramsay and Lily Briscoe are drawn out of moments of irritation by an image of extreme beauty. The image, in both cases, is a vision of Mrs. Ramsay, who, as she sits reading with James, is a sight powerful enough to incite "rapture" in William Bankes. Beauty retains this soothing effect throughout the novel: something as trifling as a large but very beautiful arrangement of fruit can, for a moment, assuage the discomfort of the guests at Mrs. Ramsay's dinner party.

Lily later complicates the notion of beauty as restorative by suggesting that beauty has the unfortunate consequence of simplifying the truth. Her impression of Mrs. Ramsay, she believes, is compromised by a determination to view her as beautiful and to smooth over her complexities and faults. Nevertheless, Lily continues on her quest to "still" or "freeze" a moment from life and make it beautiful. Although the vision of an isolated moment is necessarily incomplete, it is lasting and, as such, endlessly seductive to her.

MOTIFS

THE DIFFERING BEHAVIORS OF MEN AND WOMEN As Lily Briscoe suffers through Charles Tansley's boorish opinions about women and art, she reflects that human relations are worst between men and women. Indeed, given the extremely opposite ways in which men and women behave throughout the novel, this difficulty is no wonder. The dynamic between the sexes is best understood by considering the behavior of Mr. and Mrs. Ramsay. Their constant conflict has less to do with divergent philosophies—indeed, they both acknowledge and are motivated by the same fear of mortality—than with the way they process that fear. Men, Mrs. Ramsay reflects in the opening pages of the novel, bow to it. Given her rather traditional notions of gender roles, she excuses her husband's behavior as inevitable, asking how men can be expected to settle the political and economic business of nations and not suffer doubts. This understanding attitude places on women the responsibility for soothing men's damaged egos and achieving some kind of harmony (even if temporary) with them. Lily Briscoe, who as a single woman represents a social order more radial and lenient than Mrs. Ramsay's, resists this duty but ultimately caves in to it.

T

BRACKETS In "Time Passes," brackets surround the few sentences recounting the deaths of Prue and Andrew Ramsay, while in "The Lighthouse," brackets surround the sentences comprising Chapter VI. Each set of sentences in brackets in the earlier section contains violence, death, and the destruction of potential; the short, stabbing accounts accentuate the brutality of these events. But in Chapter VI of "The Lighthouse," the purpose of the brackets changes from indicating violence and death to violence and potential survival. Whereas in "Time Passes," the brackets surround Prue's death in childbirth and Andrew's perishing in war, in "The Lighthouse" they surround the "mutilated" but "alive still" body of a fish.

SYMBOLS

THE LIGHTHOUSE Lying across the bay and meaning something different and intimately personal to each character, the lighthouse is at once inaccessible, illuminating, and infinitely interpretable. As the destination from which the novel takes its title, the lighthouse suggests that the destinations that seem surest are most unobtainable. Just as Mr. Ramsay is certain of his wife's love for him and aims to hear her speak words to that end in "The Window," Mrs. Ramsay finds these words impossible to say. These failed attempts to arrive at some sort of solid ground, like Lily's first try at painting Mrs. Ramsay or Mrs. Ramsay's attempt to see Paul and Minta married, result only in more attempts, further excursions rather than rest. The lighthouse stands as a potent symbol of this lack of attainability. James arrives only to realize that it is not at all the mist-shrouded destination of his childhood. Instead, he is made to reconcile two competing and contradictory images of the tower—how it appeared to him when he was a boy and how it appears to him now that he is a man. He decides that both of these images contribute to the essence of the lighthouse—that nothing is ever only one thing—a sentiment that echoes the novel's determination to arrive at truth through varied and contradictory vantage points.

LILY'S PAINTING Lily's painting represents a struggle against gender convention, represented by Charles Tansley's statement that women can't paint or write. Lily's desire to express Mrs. Ramsay's essence as a wife and mother in the painting mimics the impulse among modern women to know and understand intimately the gendered experiences of the women who came before them. Lily's composition attempts to discover and comprehend Mrs. Ramsay's beauty just as Woolf's construction of Mrs. Ramsay's character reflects her attempts to access and portray her own mother.

The painting also represents dedication to a feminine artistic vision, expressed through Lily's anxiety over showing it to William Bankes. In deciding that completing the painting regardless of what happens to it is the most important thing, Lily makes the choice to establish her own artistic voice. In the end, she decides that her vision depends on balance and synthesis: how to bring together disparate things in harmony. In this respect, her project mirrors Woolf's writing, which synthesizes the perceptions of her many characters to come to a balanced and truthful portrait of the world.

THE RAMSAYS' HOUSE The Ramsays' house is a stage where Woolf and her characters explain their beliefs and observations. During her dinner party, Mrs. Ramsay sees her house display her own inner notions of shabbiness and her inability to preserve beauty. In the "Time Passes" section, the ravages of war and destruction and the passage of time are reflected in the condition of the house rather than in the emotional development or observable aging of the characters. The house stands in for the collective consciousness of those who stay in it. At times the characters long to escape it, while at other times it serves as a refuge. From the dinner party to the journey to the lighthouse, Woolf shows the house from every angle, and its structure and contents mirror the interior of the characters who inhabit it.

THE SEA References to the sea appear throughout the novel. Broadly, the ever-changing, ever-moving waves parallel the constant forward movement of time and the changes it brings. Woolf describes the sea lovingly and beautifully, but her most evocative depictions of it point to its violence. As a force that brings destruction, has the power to decimate islands, and, as Mr. Ramsay reflects, "eats away the ground we stand on," the sea is a powerful reminder of the impermanence and delicacy of human life and accomplishments.

THE BOAR'S SKULL After her dinner party, Mrs. Ramsay retires upstairs to find the children wide-awake, bothered by the boar's skull that hangs on the nursery wall. The presence of the skull acts as a disturbing reminder that death is always at hand, even (or perhaps especially) during life's most blissful moments.

THE FRUIT BASKET Rose arranges a fruit basket for her mother's dinner party that serves to draw the partygoers out of their private suffering and unite them. Although Augustus Carmichael and Mrs. Ramsay appreciate the arrangement differently—he rips a bloom from it; she refuses to disturb it—the pair is brought harmoniously, if briefly, together. The basket testifies both to the "frozen" quality of beauty that Lily describes and to beauty's seductive and soothing quality.

IMPORTANT QUOTATIONS EXPLAINED

1. *Who shall blame him? Who will not secretly rejoice when the hero puts his armour off, and halts by the window and gazes at his wife and son, who, very distant at first, gradually come closer and closer, till lips and book and head are clearly before him, though still lovely and unfamiliar from the intensity of his isolation and the waste of ages and the perishing of the stars, and finally putting his pipe in his pocket and bending his magnificent head before her—who will blame him if he does homage to the beauty of the world?*

As Mr. Ramsay strolls across the lawn in Chapter VI of "The Window," he catches sight of Mrs. Ramsay and James in the window. His reaction comes as something of a surprise given the troubled ruminations of his mind described just pages before. He, like nearly every character in the novel, is keenly aware of the inevitability of death and the likelihood of its casting his existence into absolute oblivion. Mr. Ramsay knows that few men achieve intellectual immortality. The above passage testifies to his knowledge that all things, from the stars in the sky to the fruits of his career, are doomed to perish. Here, rather than cave in to the anxieties brought on by that knowledge, punish James for dreaming of the lighthouse, or demand that Mrs. Ramsay or Lily lavish him with sympathy, Mr. Ramsay satisfies himself by appreciating the beauty that surrounds him. The tableau of his wife and child cannot last—after all, they will eventually move and break the pose—but it has the power, nevertheless, to assuage his troubled mind. These moments integrate the random fragments of experience and interaction in the world. As Mr. Ramsay brings his wife and son visually "closer and closer," the distance among the three shortens, buoying Mr. Ramsay up from the depths of despair.

2. *Could loving, as people called it, make her and Mrs. Ramsay one? for it was not knowledge but unity that she desired, not inscriptions on tablets, nothing that could be written in any language known to men, but intimacy itself, which is knowledge, she had thought, leaning her head on Mrs. Ramsay's knee.*

These musings come from Lily in Chapter IX of "The Window," as she and William Bankes stand on the lawn watching the Ramsays. Bankes criticizes Mr. Ramsay for his hypocrisy in being narrow-minded, and Lily is about to respond with a criticism of Mrs. Ramsay when she notices the look of rapture on Bankes's face. She realizes that he loves Mrs. Ramsay, and she feels that this emotion is a contribution to the good of humanity. Overwhelmed with love herself, Lily approaches Mrs. Ramsay and sits beside her. Her thoughts here are noteworthy because they point to the distinction between ways of acquiring knowledge: instinct, on the one hand, and intelligence, on the other. Mrs. Ramsay knows what she does of the world by the former method, while Mr. Ramsay depends upon "inscriptions on tablets." Here, as she wonders how one person comes to truly know another, Lily straddles the line that separates emotions from intellect, and that separates Mrs. Ramsay from her husband. This position anticipates Lily's role at the end of the novel, when she stands watching Mr. Ramsay's boat and indulges in powerful remembrances of Mrs. Ramsay. At that moment, Lily arrives at her elusive vision, completes her painting, and achieves the unity she craves in the above passage.

3. *It partook . . . of eternity . . . there is a coherence in things, a stability; something, she meant, is immune from change, and shines out (she glanced at the window with its ripple of reflected lights) in the face of the flowing, the fleeting, the spectral, like a ruby; so that again tonight she had the feeling she had had once today, already, of peace, of rest. Of such moments, she thought, the thing is made that endures.*

Chapter XVII of "The Window" is, in many respects, the heart of the novel. In Mrs. Ramsay's dinner party, we see the rhythmic movement from chaos to order, from obscurity to clarity of vision, through which the novel progresses. The dinner party begins, to Mrs. Ramsay's mind, as something of a disaster. Not all of the guests have arrived (Paul and Minta, for instance, have yet to return from the beach with Andrew and Nancy); Charles Tansley makes hostile comments to Lily; Augustus Carmichael offends his host by asking for a second plate of soup. Soon enough, however, as darkness descends outside and the candles are lit, the evening rights itself. Everyone is content, as Mrs. Ramsay intends, and everyone will remember the evening as beautiful and right. This passage describes these rare, priceless moments, which take on a kind of psychological permanence. The guests will remember this evening and will experience, with inexorable nostalgia, peace and rest. In a world in which struggle and destruction are inevitable, the possibility for such domestic respite provides great comfort.

---

4. *[S]he could not say it. . . . [A]s she looked at him she began to smile, for though she had not said a word, he knew, of course he knew, that she loved him. He could not deny it. And smiling she looked out of the window and said (thinking to herself, Nothing on earth can equal this happiness)—*

   "Yes, you were right. It's going to be wet tomorrow. You won't be able to go." And she looked at him smiling. For she had triumphed again. She had not said it: yet he knew.

This passage, taken from Chapter XIX of "The Window," is a lyrical demonstration of how disjointed people and their fragmented emotions can come together. Mr. and Mrs. Ramsay represent opposite approaches to life. Possessed of a stolidly rational and scientific mind, Mr. Ramsay relies on what can be studied, proven, and spoken. Hence, at the end of "The Window," he wants to hear Mrs. Ramsay declare her love for him. Mrs. Ramsay, however, navigates life on a less predictable course. She is led by her emotions rather than her mind. This approach provides her a greater range and freedom of expression. For instance, she can express her affection for her guests by orchestrating a lovely and memorable evening rather than forcing herself to articulate (or, like Mr. Ramsay, punish herself for not being able to articulate) these feelings. In Woolf's estimation, these traits are gender-specific. She argues that men are most often satisfied by direct declarations, as when, in the novel's final pages, James is mollified only by his father's praise of his sailing skills. Women, on the other hand, often convey their meaning by what they choose *not* to say. Like Mrs. Ramsay in her triumph at the end of "The Window," Lily is able to convey her sympathy for Mr. Ramsay without pronouncing it: she lets him tie her shoe.

---

5. *The Lighthouse was then a silvery, misty-looking tower with a yellow eye, that opened suddenly, and softly in the evening. Now—*

   James looked at the Lighthouse. He could see the white-washed rocks; the tower, stark and straight; he could see that it was barred with black and white; he could see windows in it; he could even see washing spread on the rocks to dry. So that was the Lighthouse, was it?

   No, the other was also the Lighthouse. For nothing was simply one thing. The other Lighthouse was true too.

As the Ramsays' boat approaches the lighthouse in Chapter VIII of "The Lighthouse," James reflects on images of the edifice that are competing in his mind. The first is from his childhood, when the lighthouse, seen from a distance, was a "silvery, misty-looking tower." The second image, formed as he sails closer, is stripped of its shadows and romance. The structure appears hard, plain, and real. Its barred windows and the laundry drying on the rocks present nothing magical. James's first inclination is to banish one of these pictures from his mind and grant the other sovereignty, but he corrects himself, realizing that the lighthouse is both what it was then and what it is now. The task that James faces is a reconciliation of these competing images into a whole truth. This challenge is the same one that Lily faces at the end of the novel, for she must reconcile her romantic vision of, and disappointment with, Mrs. Ramsay. To do so and to admit the complex, even contradictory, nature of all things, the novel suggests, is to possess a greater (and more artful) understanding of life.

Uncle Tom's Cabin

Harriet Beecher Stowe (1811–1896)

CONTEXT

Upon meeting Harriet Beecher Stowe for the first time, Abraham Lincoln reportedly said, "So this is the little lady who made this big war." Stowe was little—under five feet tall—but what she lacked in height, she made up for in influence and success. *Uncle Tom's Cabin* became one of the most widely read and deeply penetrating books of its time. It sold hundreds of thousands of copies and was translated into numerous languages. Many historians have credited the novel with contributing to the outbreak of the Civil War.

The daughter of an eminent New England preacher, Stowe was born into a family of eccentric, intelligent people. As a child, she learned Latin and wrote a children's geography book, both before she was ten years old. Throughout her life, she remained deeply involved in religious movements, feminist causes, and the most divisive political and moral issue of her time: the abolition of slavery.

Stowe grew up in the Northeast but lived for a time in Cincinnati, which enabled her to see both sides of the slavery debate without losing her abolitionist's perspective. Cincinnati was evenly split for and against abolition, and Stowe wrote satirical pieces on the subject for several local papers there. She often wrote pieces under pseudonyms and with contrasting styles, and one can see a similar attention to voice in *Uncle Tom's Cabin*, in which dialects and patterns of speech contrast among characters. Though Stowe absorbed a great deal of information about slavery during her Cincinnati years, she nonetheless conducted extensive research before writing *Uncle Tom's Cabin*. She wrote to Frederick Douglass and others for help in creating a realistic picture of slavery in the Deep South. Her black cook and household servants also helped by telling her stories of their slave days.

Stowe's main goal with *Uncle Tom's Cabin* was to convince her large northern readership of the necessity of ending slavery. Most immediately, the novel served as a response to the passage of the Fugitive Slave Act of 1850, which made it illegal to give aid or assistance to a runaway slave. Under this legislation, Southern slaves who escaped to the North had to flee to Canada in order to find real freedom. With her book, Stowe created a sort of exposé that revealed the horrors of Southern slavery to people in the North. Her radical position on race relations, though, was informed by a deep religiosity. Stowe continually emphasizes the importance of Christian love in eradicating oppression. She also works in her feminist beliefs, showing women as equals to men in intelligence, bravery, and spiritual strength. Indeed, women dominate the book's moral code, proving vital advisors to their husbands, who often need help in seeing through convention and popular opinion.

Uncle Tom's Cabin was published in episodes in the *National Era* in 1851 and 1852, then published in its entirety on March 20, 1852. It sold 10,000 copies in its first week and 300,000 by the end of the year, astronomical numbers for the mid-nineteenth century. Today, analysis of both the book's conception and reception proves helpful in our understanding of the Civil War era. Within the text itself are insights into the mind of a Christian, feminist abolitionist. For example, the arguments Stowe uses give a glimpse into the details of the slavery debate. Looking beyond the text to its impact on its society, we gain an understanding of the historical forces contributing to the outbreak of war.

PLOT OVERVIEW

Having run up large debts, a Kentucky farmer named Arthur Shelby faces the prospect of losing everything he owns. Though he and his wife, Emily Shelby, have a kindhearted and affectionate relationship with their slaves, Shelby decides to raise money by selling two of his slaves to Mr. Haley, a coarse slave trader. The slaves in question are Uncle Tom, a middle-aged man with a wife and children on the farm, and Harry, the young son of Mrs. Shelby's maid Eliza. When Shelby tells his wife about his agreement with Haley, she is appalled because she has promised Eliza that Shelby would not sell her son.

However, Eliza overhears the conversation between Haley and his wife and, after warning Uncle Tom and his wife, Aunt Chloe, she takes Harry and flees to the North, hoping to find freedom with her husband George in Canada. Haley pursues her, but two other Shelby slaves alert Eliza to the danger. She miraculously evades capture by crossing the half-frozen Ohio River, the boundary separating Kentucky from the North. Haley hires a slave hunter named Loker and his gang to bring Eliza and Harry back to Kentucky. Eliza and Harry make their way to a Quaker settlement, where the Quakers agree to help transport them to safety. They are joined at the settlement by George, who reunites joyously with his family for the trip to Canada.

Meanwhile, Uncle Tom sadly leaves his family and Mas'r George, Shelby's young son and Tom's friend, as Haley takes him to a boat on the Mississippi to be transported to a slave market. On the boat, Tom meets an angelic little white girl named Eva, who quickly befriends him. When Eva falls into the river, Tom dives in to save her, and her father, Augustine St. Clare, gratefully agrees to buy Tom from Haley. Tom travels with the St. Clares to their home in New Orleans, where he grows increasingly invaluable to the St. Clare household and increasingly close to Eva, with whom he shares a devout Christianity.

Up North, George and Eliza remain in flight from Loker and his men. When Loker attempts to capture them, George shoots him in the side, and the other slave hunters retreat. Eliza convinces George and the Quakers to bring Loker to the next settlement, where he can be healed. Meanwhile, in New Orleans, St. Clare discusses slavery with his cousin Ophelia, who opposes slavery as an institution but harbors deep prejudices against blacks. St. Clare, by contrast, feels no hostility toward blacks but tolerates slavery because he feels powerless to change it. To help Ophelia overcome her bigotry, he buys Topsy, a young black girl who was abused by her past master, and arranges for Ophelia to begin educating her.

After Tom has lived with the St. Clares for two years, Eva grows very ill. She slowly weakens, then dies, with a vision of heaven before her. Her death has a profound effect on everyone who knew her: Ophelia resolves to love the slaves, Topsy learns to trust and feel attached to others, and St. Clare decides to set Tom free. However, before he can act on his decision, St. Clare is stabbed to death while trying to settle a brawl. As he dies, he at last finds God and goes to be reunited with his mother in heaven.

St. Clare's cruel wife, Marie, sells Tom to a vicious plantation owner named Simon Legree. Tom is taken to rural Louisiana with a group of new slaves, including Emmeline, whom the demonic Legree has purchased to use as a sex slave, replacing his previous sex slave, Cassy. Legree takes a strong dislike to Tom when Tom refuses to whip a fellow slave as ordered. Tom receives a severe beating, and Legree resolves to crush his faith in God. Tom meets Cassy and hears her story. Separated from her daughter by slavery, she became pregnant again but killed the child because she could not stand to have another child taken from her.

Around this time, with the help of Tom Loker—now a changed man after being healed by the Quakers—George, Eliza, and Harry at last cross over into Canada from Lake Erie and obtain their freedom. In Louisiana, Tom's faith is sorely tested by his hardships, and he nearly ceases to believe. He has two visions, however—one of Christ and one of Eva—which renew his spiritual strength and give him the courage to withstand Legree's torments. He encourages Cassy to escape. She does so, taking Emmeline with her, after she devises a ruse in which she and Emmeline pretend to be ghosts. When Tom refuses to tell Legree where Cassy and Emmeline have gone, Legree orders his overseers to beat him. When Tom is near death, he forgives Legree and the overseers. George Shelby arrives with money in hand to buy Tom's freedom, but he is too late. He can only watch as Tom dies a martyr's death.

Taking a boat toward freedom, Cassy and Emmeline meet George Harris's sister and travel with her to Canada, where Cassy realizes that Eliza is her long-lost daughter. The newly reunited family travels to France and decides to move to Liberia, the African nation created for former American slaves. George Shelby returns to the Kentucky farm, where, after his father's death, he sets all of the slaves free in honor of Tom's memory. He urges them to think on Tom's sacrifice every time they look at his cabin and to lead a pious Christian life, just as Tom did.

CHARACTER LIST

Uncle Tom A good and pious man, Uncle Tom is the protagonist of *Uncle Tom's Cabin*. Even under the worst conditions, Uncle Tom always prays to God and finds a way to keep his faith. As the novel progresses, the cruel treatment Tom suffers at the hands of Simon Legree threatens his belief in God, but Tom withstands his doubts and dies the death of a Christian martyr.

Aunt Chloe Uncle Tom's wife and the Shelbys' cook. Chloe often acts like a jovial simpleton around the Shelbys to mask her more complex feelings.

Arthur Shelby The owner of Uncle Tom in Kentucky. Shelby sells Tom to the cruel Mr. Haley to pay off his debts. An educated, kind, and basically good-hearted man, Shelby nonetheless tolerates and perpetuates slavery. Stowe uses him to illustrate that the immorality inherent in slavery makes villains of all its practitioners—not just the most cruel masters.

Emily Shelby Mr. Shelby's wife. Emily is a loving, Christian woman who does not believe in slavery. She uses her influence with her husband to try to help the Shelbys' slaves and is one of the novel's many morally virtuous and insightful female characters.

George Shelby The Shelbys' good-hearted son, called "Mas'r George" by Uncle Tom. George loves Tom and promises to rescue him from the cruelty into which his father sold him. After Tom dies, he resolves to free all the slaves on the family farm in Kentucky. More morally committed than his father, George not only possesses a kind heart but acts on his principles.

George Harris Eliza's husband and an intellectually curious and talented mulatto. George loves his family deeply and willingly fights for his freedom. He confronts the slave hunter Tom Loker and does not hesitate to shoot him when he imperils the family.

Eliza Harris Mrs. Shelby's maid, George's wife, and Harry's mother. Eliza is an intelligent, beautiful, and brave young slave. After Mr. Shelby makes known his plans to sell Eliza's son to Mr. Haley, she proves the power of her motherly love as well as her strength of spirit by making a spectacular escape. Her crossing of the Ohio River on patches of ice is the novel's most famous scene.

Harry Harris Eliza and George's young son.

Augustine St. Clare Tom's master in New Orleans and Eva's father. St. Clare is a flighty and romantic man, dedicated to pleasure. St. Clare does not believe in God, and he carouses and drinks every night. Although he dotes on his daughter and treats his slaves with compassion, St. Clare shares the hypocrisy of Mr. Shelby in that he sees the evil of slavery but nonetheless tolerates and practices it.

Eva St. Clare and Marie's angelic daughter. Eva, also referred to in the book as Little Eva (her given name is Evangeline) is presented as an absolutely perfect child—a completely moral being and an unimpeachable Christian. She laments the existence of slavery and sees no difference between blacks and whites. After befriending Tom while still a young girl, Eva becomes one of the most important figures in his life. In death, Eva becomes one of the text's central Christ figures.

Miss Ophelia St. Clare's cousin from the North (Vermont) who comes to help him manage the household. Ophelia opposes slavery in the abstract, but she finds actual slaves somewhat distasteful and harbors considerable prejudice against them. After Eva's death, and through her relationship with Topsy, Ophelia realizes her failings and learns to see slaves as human beings. Stowe hoped that much of her northern audience might recognize themselves in Ophelia and reconsider their views on slavery.

Marie St. Clare's self-centered wife. Petty, whining, and foolish, she is the very opposite of the idealized woman figure that appears repeatedly throughout the novel.

The Quakers A Christian group that arose in mid-seventeenth-century England and dedicated themselves to achieving an inner understanding of God, without the use of creeds, clergy, or outward rites. The Quakers have a long history of contributing to social reform and peace efforts. In *Uncle Tom's Cabin*, many Quaker characters appear who help George and Eliza, as well as many other slaves. Stowe uses them to portray a Christianity free of hypocrisy, self-righteous display, or bigoted conventions. This kind of Christianity, she implies, can play a crucial role in the abolition of slavery.

Senator and Mrs. Bird Mrs. Bird is a virtuous woman who tries to exert influence through her husband, and Senator Bird exemplifies the well-meaning man who is sympathetic to the abolitionist cause but who nonetheless remains complacent or resigned to the status quo.

Tom Loker A slave hunter hired by Mr. Haley to bring back Eliza, Harry, and George. Loker first appears as a gruff, violent man. George shoots him when he tries to capture them, and, after he is healed by the Quakers, Loker experiences a transformation and chooses to join the Quakers rather than return to his old life.

Mr. Haley The slave trader who buys Uncle Tom and Harry from Mr. Shelby. Gruff and coarse, Haley presents himself as a kind individual who treats his slaves well. Haley, however, mistreats his slaves, often violently.

Topsy A wild and uncivilized slave girl whom Miss Ophelia tries to reform. Topsy gradually learns to love and respect others by following the example of Eva.

Simon Legree Tom's ruthlessly evil master on the Louisiana plantation. Vicious, barbaric, and loathsome, Legree fosters violence and hatred among his slaves.

Cassy Legree's (slave) mistress and Eliza's mother. Cassy proves a proud and intelligent woman and devises a clever way to escape Legree's plantation.

Emmeline A young and beautiful slave girl whom Legree buys for himself, perhaps to replace Cassy as his mistress. Emmeline has been raised as a pious Christian.

ANALYSIS OF MAJOR CHARACTERS

UNCLE TOM History has not been kind to Uncle Tom, the hero of *Uncle Tom's Cabin* and one of the most popular figures of nineteenth-century American fiction. After its initial burst of sensational popularity and influence, *Uncle Tom's Cabin* fell into neglect. Its circulation declined following the end of the Civil War and Stowe's death, and by the mid-1900s, the book was virtually out of print. Not until the early 1960s, when the Civil Rights Movement reawakened an interest in anti-slavery fiction, did the novel again become widely read. More than a hundred years after its initial publication, however, *Uncle Tom's Cabin* stood as a testament to a past set of standards and expectations. The values and attributes that seemed admirable in its characters in 1852 frequently appeared incomprehensible and even contemptible to twentieth-century readers. In particular, the passive acceptance of slavery practiced by Uncle Tom seemed horrendously out of line with the resolve and strength of modern black Civil Rights crusaders. The term "Uncle Tom" became an insult, conjuring an image of an old black man eager to please his white masters and happy to accept his own position of inferiority.

Although modern readers' criticisms hold some validity, the notion of an "Uncle Tom" contains generalizations not found within the actual character in the novel. First, Tom is not an old man. The novel states that he is eight years older than Shelby, which probably places him in his late forties at the start of the novel. Moreover, Tom does not accept his position of inferiority with happiness. Tom's passivity owes not to stupidity or to contentment with his position, but to his deep religious values, which impel him to love everyone and selflessly endure his trials. Indeed, Tom's central characteristic in the novel is this religiosity, his strength of faith. Everywhere Tom goes in the novel, he manages to spread some of the love and goodwill of his religious beliefs, helping to alleviate the pain of slavery and enhance the hope of salvation. And while this religiosity translates into a selfless passivity on Tom's part, it also translates into a policy of warm encouragement of others' attempts at freedom. Thus, he supports Eliza's escape, as well as that of Cassy and Emmeline from the Legree plantation. Moreover, while Tom may not actively seek his own freedom, he practices a kind of resistance in his passivity. When Legree orders him to beat the slave girl in Chapter XXXIII, he refuses, standing firm in his values. He will submit to being beaten for his beliefs, but he will not capitulate or run away.

Even in recognizing Tom's passivity in the novel and Stowe's approving treatment of it, we should note that Stowe does not present this behavior as a model of *black* behavior but as a heroic model of behavior that should be practiced by everyone, black and white. Stowe makes it very clear that if the villainous white slaveholders of the novel were to achieve Tom's selfless Christian love for others, slavery would be impossible, and Tom's death never would have happened. Because Stowe believes that a transformation through Christian love must occur before slavery can be abolished successfully, she holds up Tom's death as nobler than any escape, in that it provides an example for others and offers the hope of a more generalized salvation. Through this death, Tom becomes a Christ figure, a radical role for a black character to play in American fiction in 1852. Tom's death proves Legree's fundamental moral and personal inferiority and provides the motivating force behind George Shelby's decision to free all the slaves. By practicing selflessness and loving his enemy, Tom becomes a martyr and effects social change.

Although contemporary society finds its heroes in active agents of social change and tends to discourage submissiveness, Stowe meant for Tom to embody noble heroic tendencies of his own. She portrayed his passivity as a virtue unconnected to his minority status. Within the world of *Uncle Tom's Cabin*, Tom is presented as more than a black hero—he is presented as a hero transcending race.

OPHELIA ST. CLARE Probably the most complex female character in the novel, Ophelia deserves special attention because she is treated as a surrogate for Stowe's intended audience. It is as if Stowe conceived an imaginary picture of her intended reader, then brought that reader into the book as a character. Ophelia embodies what Stowe considered a widespread northern problem: the white person who opposes slavery on a theoretical level but feels racial prejudice and hatred in the presence of an actual black slave. Ophelia detests slavery, but she considers it almost necessary for blacks, against whom she harbors a deep-seated prejudice—she does not want them to touch her. Stowe emphasizes that much of Ophelia's racial prejudice stems from unfamiliarity and ignorance rather than from actual experience-based hatred. Because Ophelia has seldom spent time in the presence of slaves, she finds them uncomfortably alien.

Ophelia is one of the only characters in *Uncle Tom's Cabin* who develops as the story progresses. Once St. Clare puts Topsy in her care, Ophelia begins to have increased contact with a slave. At first she tries to teach Topsy out of a sense of mere duty. But Stowe suggests that duty alone will not eradicate slavery—abolitionists must act out of love. Eva's death proves the crucial catalyst in Ophelia's transformation, and she comes to love Topsy as a human being, overcoming her racial prejudice and offering a model to Stowe's northern readers.

SIMON LEGREE Although largely a uniformly evil villain, Simon Legree does possess some psychological depth as a character. He has been deeply affected by the death of his angelic mother and seems to show some legitimate affection for Cassy. Nonetheless, Legree's main purpose in the book is as a foil to Uncle Tom, and as an effective picture of slavery at its worst. Often associated with firelight and flames, Legree demonstrates literally infernal qualities, and his devilishness provides an effective contrast with the angelic qualities of his passive slave. Legree's demoniacally evil ways also play an important role in shaping the end of the book along the lines of the traditional Christian narrative. Above all, Legree desires to break Tom's religious faith and to see him capitulate to doubt and sin. In the end, although Tom dies and Legree survives, the evil that Legree stands for has been destroyed. Tom dies loving the men who kill him, proving that his faith prevails over Legree's evil.

THEMES, MOTIFS, AND SYMBOLS

THEMES

THE EVIL OF SLAVERY Stowe wrote *Uncle Tom's Cabin* after the passage of the Fugitive Slave Act of 1850, which made it illegal for anyone in the United States to offer aid or assistance to a runaway slave. Stowe seeks to attack this law and the institution it protected, ceaselessly advocating the immediate emancipation of the slaves and freedom for all people. Each of Stowe's scenes, while serving to further character and plot, also serves, without exception, to persuade the reader—especially the Northern reader of Stowe's time—that slavery is evil, un-Christian, and intolerable in a civil society.

For most of the novel, Stowe explores the question of slavery in a fairly mild setting, in which slaves and masters have seemingly positive relationships. At the Shelbys' house, and again at the St. Clares', the slaves have kind masters who do not abuse or mistreat them. Stowe does not offer these settings in order to show slavery's evil as conditional. She seeks to expose the vices of slavery even in its best-case scenario. Though Shelby and St. Clare possess kindness and intelligence, their ability to tolerate slavery renders them hypocritical and morally weak. Even under kind masters, slaves suffer, as we see when a financially struggling Shelby guiltily destroys Tom's family by selling Tom, and when the fiercely selfish Marie, by demanding attention be given to herself, prevents the St. Clare slaves from mourning the death of her own angelic daughter, Eva. A common contemporary defense of slavery claimed that the institution benefited the slaves because most masters acted in their slaves' best interests. Stowe refutes this argument with her biting portrayals, insisting that the slave's best interest can lie only in obtaining freedom.

In the final third of the book, Stowe leaves behind the pleasant veneer of life at the Shelby and St. Clare houses and takes her reader into the Legree plantation, where the evil of slavery appears in its most naked and hideous form. This harsh and barbaric setting, in which slaves suffer beatings, sexual abuse, and even murder, introduces the power of shock into Stowe's argument. If slavery is wrong in the best of cases, in the worst of cases it is nightmarish and inhuman. In the book's structural progression between "pleasant" and hellish plantations, we can detect Stowe's rhetorical methods. First she deflates the defense of the pro-slavery reader by showing the evil of the "best" kind of slavery. She then presents her own case against slavery by showing the shocking wickedness of slavery at its worst.

THE INCOMPATIBILITY OF SLAVERY AND CHRISTIAN VALUES Writing for a predominantly religious, predominantly Protestant audience, Stowe takes great pains to illustrate the fact that the system of slavery and the moral code of Christianity oppose each other. No Christian, she insists, should be able to tolerate slavery. Throughout the novel, the more religious a character is, the more he or she objects to slavery. Eva, the most morally perfect white character in the novel, fails to understand why anyone would see a difference between blacks and whites. In contrast, the morally revolting, nonreligious Legree practices slavery almost as a policy of deliberate blasphemy and evil. Christianity, in Stowe's novel, rests on a principle of universal love. If all people were to put this principle into practice, Stowe insists, it would be impossible for one segment of humanity to oppress and enslave another. Thus, not only are Christianity and slavery incompatible, but Christianity can actually be used to fight slavery.

The slave hunter Tom Loker learns this lesson after his life is spared by the slaves he tried to capture and after being healed by the generous-hearted and deeply religious Quakers. He becomes a changed man. Moreover, Uncle Tom ultimately triumphs over slavery in his adherence to Christ's command to "love thine enemy." He refuses to compromise his Christian faith in the face of the many trials he undergoes at Legree's plantation. When he is beaten to death by Legree and his men, he dies forgiving them. In this way, Tom becomes a Christian martyr, a model for the behavior of both whites and blacks. The story of his life both exposes the evil of slavery—its incompatibility with Christian virtue—and points the way to its transformation through Christian love.

THE MORAL POWER OF WOMEN Although Stowe wrote *Uncle Tom's Cabin* before the widespread growth of the women's rights movement of the late 1800s, the reader can nevertheless regard the book as a specimen of early feminism. The text portrays women as morally conscientious, committed, and courageous—indeed, often as *more* morally conscientious, committed, and courageous than men. Stowe implies a parallel between the oppression of blacks and the oppression of women, yet she expresses hope for the oppressed in her presentation of women as effectively influencing their husbands. Moreover, she shows how this show of strength by one oppressed group can help to alleviate the oppression of the other. White women can use their influence to convince their husbands—the people with voting rights—of the evil of slavery.

Throughout the novel are many examples of idealized womanhood, of perfect mothers and wives who attempt to find salvation for their morally inferior husbands or sons. Examples include Mrs. Bird, St. Clare's mother, Legree's mother, and, to a lesser extent, Mrs. Shelby. The text also portrays black women in a very positive light. Black women generally prove strong, brave, and capable, as seen especially in the character of Eliza. In the cases where women do not act morally—such as Prue in her drunkenness or Cassy with her infanticide—the women's sins are presented as illustrating slavery's evil influence rather than the women's own immorality. Not all women appear as bolsters to the book's moral code: Marie acts petty and mean, and Ophelia begins the novel with many prejudices. Nonetheless, the book seems to argue the existence of a natural female sense of good and evil, pointing to an inherent moral wisdom in the gender as a whole and encouraging the use of this wisdom as a force for social change.

MOTIFS

CHRIST FIGURES As befits its religious preoccupation, the novel presents two instances of a sacrificial death linked to Christ's. Eva and Tom, the two most morally perfect characters in the novel, both die in atmospheres of charged religious belief, and, in a sense, they both die to achieve salvation for others. Eva's death leads to St. Clare's deathbed conversion to Christianity and to Ophelia's recognition and denunciation of her own racial prejudice. Tom's death leads to Emmeline and Cassy's escape and to the freedom of all the slaves on the Shelby farm in Kentucky. Both Tom and Eva are explicitly compared to Christ: Ophelia says that Eva resembles Jesus, and the narrator depicts Tom carrying his cross behind Jesus. This motif of Christlike sacrifice and death enables Stowe to underscore her basic point about

Christian goodness while holding up models of moral perfection for her reader to emulate. It also enables her to create the emotionally charged, sentimental death scenes that were popular in nineteenth-century literature.

THE SUPERNATURAL Several supernatural instances of divine intervention in the novel suggest that a higher order exists to oppose slavery. For instance, when Eliza leaps over the Ohio river, jumping rapidly between blocks of ice without fear or pain, the text tells us that she has been endowed with a "strength such as God gives only to the desperate," facilitating her escape from oppression. Similarly, when Tom's faith begins to lapse at the Legree plantation, he is visited by religious visions that restore it, thus sustaining him in his passive resistance of Legree. Before Eva dies, she glimpses a view of heaven and experiences a miraculous presentiment of her own death; these occurrences reinforce Eva's purity and add moral authority to her antislavery stance.

Instances of supernaturalism thus support various characters in their efforts to resist or fight slavery. But they also serve to thwart other characters in their efforts to practice slavery. As Legree pursues his oppression of Tom, he has an upsetting vision of his dead mother and becomes temporarily paralyzed by an apparition of a ghost in the fog. The fear caused by this apparition weakens Legree to the point that Cassy and Emmeline can trick him into believing that ghosts haunt the garret. This ploy enables them to escape.

SYMBOLS

UNCLE TOM'S CABIN Near the end of the novel, after George Shelby frees his slaves, he tells them that, when they look at Uncle Tom's cabin, they should remember their freedom and dedicate themselves to leading a Christian life like Uncle Tom's. The sight of Uncle Tom's cabin on George Shelby's property serves as a persistent reminder to him of the sufferings Tom experienced as a slave. The cabin also becomes a metaphor for Uncle Tom's willingness to be beaten and even killed rather than harm or betray his fellow slaves—his willingness to suffer and die rather than go against Christian values of love and loyalty. The image of the cabin thus neatly encapsulates the main themes of the book, signifying both the destructive power of slavery and the ability of Christian love to overcome it.

ELIZA'S LEAP The scene of Eliza's leap across the half-frozen Ohio river constitutes the most famous episode in *Uncle Tom's Cabin*. The scene also serves as an important metaphor. The leap from the southern to the northern bank of the river symbolizes in one dramatic moment the process of leaving slavery for freedom. Indeed, Eliza's leap from one bank to the next literally constitutes a leap from the slave-holding states to the nonslave-holding states, as the Ohio River served as the legally recognized divide between the South and the North. The dangers Eliza faces in her leap, and the courage she requires to execute it successfully, represent the more general instances of peril and heroism involved in any slave's journey to freedom.

GEOGRAPHY *Uncle Tom's Cabin* uses the North to represent freedom and the South to represent slavery and oppression. The opposition is obviously rooted in history, but Stowe embellishes the opposition so as to transform it from literal to literary. Two main stories dominate the novel—the story of Eliza and George and the story of Uncle Tom. One story serves as an escape narrative, chronicling Eliza and George's flight to freedom. The other story is a slavery narrative, chronicling Uncle Tom's descent into increasingly worse states of oppression. Not surprisingly, the action in the escape narrative moves increasingly northward, with Canada representing its endpoint and the attainment of freedom by the escaped slaves. The action in the slavery narrative moves increasingly southward, with Tom's death occurring on Legree's plantation in rural Louisiana, far into the Deep South. This geographical split represents the wide gulf between freedom and slavery and plays into Stowe's general use of parallelism and contrast in making her political points.

IMPORTANT QUOTATIONS EXPLAINED

---

1. *"You ought to be ashamed, John! Poor, homeless, houseless creatures! It's a shameful, wicked, abominable law, and I'll break it, for one, the first time I get a chance; and I hope I shall have a chance, I do! . . . Now, John, I don't know anything about politics, but I can read my Bible; and there I see that I must feed the hungry, clothe the naked, and comfort the desolate; and that Bible I mean to follow."*

This is Mrs. Bird's side of an exchange between Senator Bird and Mrs. Bird that occurs in Chapter IX, just before Eliza arrives at their doorstep. The quote crystallizes some of the main themes of the novel, condemning slavery as contrary to Christianity and portraying a woman as more morally trustworthy than her male counterpart. More specifically, this passage bears witness to Stowe's attack on a common claim of her time—that slavery, and laws such as the Fugitive Slave Act, should be tolerated in the interest of greater public interest or civic order. Arguing against a law that basically paraphrases the historical Fugitive Slave Act, Mrs. Bird routs Senator Bird by insisting that she will follow her conscience and her Bible rather than an immoral law. She thus asserts that inner conscience should take precedence over law as a guide to virtue. This idea receives reiteration throughout *Uncle Tom's Cabin*. In Chapter XLV, Stowe writes, "There is only one thing that every individual can do—they can see to it that *they feel right*."

---

2. *"I looks like gwine to heaven," said the woman; "an't thar where white folks is gwine? S'pose they'd have me thar? I'd rather go to torment, and get away from Mas'r and Missis."*

The horribly abused slave Prue speaks these words in Chapter XVIII, when Tom tries to convince her to find God and lead a Christian life, which he tells her will assure her an eternal reward in heaven. With this one line, Prue dramatically illustrates the extent to which racial politics and slavery were impressed upon slaves as unalterable, universal facts of existence. She assumes that if white people are going to heaven, she will be required to work as a slave to them in the afterlife. She unwittingly offers a devastating commentary on the horror of life as a slave when she says that she would rather go to hell ("torment") to escape her master and his wife than go to paradise with them. Stowe intended her novel for a largely Christian audience, and with these lines she meant to shock the reader into an awareness of the extreme misery slaves endured.

---

3. *"Mas'r, if you was sick, or in trouble, or dying, and I could save ye, I'd give ye my heart's blood; and, if taking every drop of blood in this poor old body would save your precious soul, I'd give 'em freely, as the Lord gave his for me. Oh, Mas'r! don't bring this great sin on your soul! It will hurt you more than't will me! Do the worst you can, my troubles'll be over soon; but, if ye don't repent, yours won't never end!"*

Tom speaks these words to Legree in Chapter XL as he pleads not to be beaten for refusing to divulge information about Cassy's escape. Tom urges Legree to reconsider, not for Tom's sake, but for Legree's. Tom explains that his own "troubles" will soon end (i.e., he will die and go to paradise), but the damage Legree does to his own soul will lead to his eternal damnation. The quote reveals the extent of Tom's piety and selflessness. Threatened with pain and death by a man who oppresses and torments him, Tom's first thought is for his oppressor's soul. He even tells Legree that he would give his "heart's blood" to save him. In these lines and elsewhere, Tom seems to prove the validity of the Christian injunction to "love thy enemy." Because he continues to love Legree, Tom ultimately defeats him, even in death.

---

4. *"Witness, eternal God! Oh, witness that, from this hour, I will do what one man can to drive out this curse of slavery from my land!"*

George Shelby makes this dramatic vow after Tom's death in Chapter XLI, when he decides to work against slavery. The quote showcases Stowe's most sentimental, melodramatic style, but it also brings a note of moral conclusion to the problem of how a person should undertake to stop slavery. Men like George's father and St. Clare can see the evil of slavery but continue to tolerate and practice it. St. Clare says that he does so because there is nothing one man can do to change an entire system. But Stowe advocates acting on one's own conscience, in accordance with one's personal relationship to God. When George declares that he will do "what one man can," he essentially overrides all concerns about "the system." Every individual should work against oppression to the extent that he or she can, in his or her own life. If all people did this, Stowe implies, following their consciences and practicing Christian love, then slavery would cease to exist.

---

5. *"It was on his grave, my friends, that I resolved, before God, that I would never own another slave, while it is possible to free him; that nobody, through me, should ever run the risk of being parted from home and friends, and dying on a lonely plantation, as he died. . . . Think of your freedom, every time you see Uncle Tom's Cabin; and let it be a memorial to put you all in mind to follow in his steps, and be as honest and faithful and Christian as he was."*

This quotation from Chapter XLIV is George Shelby's speech to his slaves as he sets them all free, fulfilling the dramatic vow he made two chapters earlier. The speech explains the novel's title and establishes the image of Uncle Tom's cabin as the central metaphor of the novel. When George Shelby sees the house, he remembers that Uncle Tom was taken from it, separating him from his wife and children and tearing apart his family. He therefore tells his former slaves to think of their freedom when they see the cabin and to resolve to lead lives of Christian piety, following Tom's example. In this way, the cabin becomes a metaphor for the destructive power of slavery, which can split apart a family and break a home. It also comes to stand for the redemptive power of Christianity and love—for Tom's enactment of these at his death motivated Shelby to set his slaves free. Thus the cabin comes to embody two of the novel's central themes, uniting the idea of slavery's vice and Christianity's redemption in a single image.

Warriors Don't Cry

Melba Patillo Beals
(1941–)

CONTEXT

Melba Patillo Beals was born on December 7, 1941, in Little Rock, Arkansas, on the same day that Japanese troops bombed the U.S. fleet at Pearl Harbor (now called Pearl Harbor Day). The first-born child of Lois and Will Patillo, Beals was born with a scalp infection, which caused significant complications. Her health was further compromised by the fact that she was African American; white nurses and doctors did very little to help her. Luckily, Beals's mother spoke to a janitor who had overheard a doctor recommending Epsom salts to clean the infection. Beals's mother got the Epsom salts, and Beals survived.

At the time that Beals was born, black and white people in many parts of America (especially the southern states) lived in a legally segregated society. After the Civil War, the "Jim Crow" Laws were put into place to thwart the advancement of black people, and during the time that Beals was a child, these laws severely restricted the rights of black people. Beals's mother was a teacher, and her father worked for the railroad. Though they were better off than many other blacks in Arkansas, they were still subject to the same injustices as the rest of their community. As Beals describes in this book, most black people lived in constant fear of making white people angry and facing brutal, violent retaliation for even the smallest offense. For example, Beals witnessed her father stand powerless as the milkman sexually harassed her mother. Yet Beals's mother, Lois, fought through the prejudices at the University of Arkansas and managed to obtain a master's degree in education. Though Lois encouraged her husband, Will, to finish his degree as well, he felt unable to do so. By the time Beals was eleven, Will had moved out of the house.

Aside from her parents, the strongest influence in Beals's life was her grandma, India. India was deeply religious, and she taught Beals to look to the Bible for guidance. She also taught Beals to rely on God for strength, a lesson that would help her later when she became one of the first black students to enter Little Rock's all-white high school in the fall of 1957.

In 1954, when Beals was twelve, the Supreme Court made a momentous decision in the lawsuit Brown v. the Board of Education of Topeka, Kansas. The lawyer, Thurgood Marshall, who would later become the first black justice on the Supreme Court, argued on behalf of a young African-American girl named Linda Brown, who was prevented from attending a nearby all-white elementary school. Marshall was also the chief counsel for the National Association for the Advancement of Colored People (NAACP), and he argued that segregation, the idea validated by the "separate but equal" finding in Plessy vs. Ferguson, was a violation of the Fourteenth Amendment to the Constitution. The Fourteenth Amendment, passed after the abolition of slavery, stated that all citizens of the United States were guaranteed the same rights, including the same rights to public education and protection under the law.

The Supreme Court found that segregation was indeed unconstitutional, and civil rights activists began to work toward integration and equal rights for white and black people. Their largest battle was the effort to integrate the schools in southern communities. Three years later, in Little Rock, Arkansas, nine black students were sent to the all-white Central High School to force integration. This group was known as the Little Rock Nine, and Beals was one of them.

Beals spent one terrible year at Central High School, facing death threats, violence, and hatred. The governor of Arkansas at the time, Orval Faubus, sent troops to prevent the Little Rock Nine from entering the school. President Eisenhower decreed that Faubus was defying federal law and sent federal troops down to force the integration. Their battle continued throughout the school year. The next year, Faubus shut down the Little Rock schools so that he would not have to allow desegregation, and Beals was eventually sent to live with a family of white Quakers in California. Two more years passed before black students were allowed back in Central High School. After graduating from high school, Beals relocated to California, where she went to college and married a white man named John. Beals dreamed of becoming a journalist, and John wanted a housewife, so they eventually divorced. They had one child, Kelli.

Beals got a master's degree in journalism from Columbia University; she later became a reporter for NBC, and then a communications consultant and an author.

PLOT OVERVIEW

Warriors Don't Cry begins when Melba and eight other black men and women in their forties return to their home state of Arkansas to meet the then-governor, Bill Clinton. Melba, the narrator and author, explains that the group, called the Little Rock Nine, is visiting Central High School in Little Rock. As teenagers in 1957, the nine of them were the first African-American students to be integrated into the school.

When Melba is twelve years old, the Supreme Court rules that separate schools for whites are illegal, a ruling called Brown v. the Board of Education of Topeka, Kansas. In the year after the ruling, Melba sees very little change in segregation. She is still at an all-black high school, but she and sixteen other black students sign up to attend the white school.

Because of the threat of violence, the number of black students who will participate in the integration is decreased from seventeen to nine. Several times in the few days before school is supposed to start, lawsuits are filed that threaten to stop the nine students. Governor Faubus declares that he is going to send the Arkansas National Guard to the high school, though he does not say whether they are there to protect the nine or to stop them from entering the school. Grandma India begins to stay awake at night with a shotgun near her. Finally, a few days after school has started, federal court judge Ronald Davies orders that the students be allowed to attend.

On September 3, 1957, Melba and her mother drive to Central High School for Melba's first day of class. A huge white mob has gathered, and the Arkansas National Guard encircles the school. Luckily, both Melba and her mother make it to the car and escape unharmed. Melba is not allowed to leave her house or answer the door or the phone. She tells her grandmother that she wants to go back to Horace Mann, her old high school, but her grandmother insists that Melba is not a quitter.

President Eisenhower and Governor Faubus meet and attempt to resolve the problem of integration in Arkansas, but the meeting is unsuccessful, and on September 20, 1957, the State of Arkansas goes to federal court before Judge Davies. Judge Davies rules that the Arkansas National Guard must be removed and that the Little Rock Nine must be allowed into Central High School. Governor Faubus removes the guard and predicts that blood will run in the streets of Little Rock if the schools are integrated.

On Monday, September 23, 1957, Melba and the other black students go to school. They are again greeted by a mob of angry white people. In the middle of one class, Melba is forced to flee to the principal's office, as the mob has broken the barricades and is headed for the school. Someone in the principal's office proposes that they give the crowd one of the children to kill so the others can escape. Gene Smith, the assistant chief of police, smuggles the nine students out of the school. The day after the mob attack, Melba stays home and reads that President Eisenhower has announced he will use force to prevent this kind of mob rule and to enforce federal law. The next day, the 101st Airborne Division (a division of war heroes) arrives in Little Rock.

Each black student has his or her own escort from the 101st Airborne Division. Melba's solider, Danny, protects her when someone attempts to throw acid in her eyes. In October, Melba, Ernie, and Minnijean meet with some of Central High's white students under the guidance of a Norwegian reporter, Mrs. Jorumn Rickets, who hopes to foster some sort of understanding between the two groups. The meeting is a failure. Eisenhower withdraws the 101st Airborne, and the nine students are forced to rely on the Arkansas National Guard for protection. The Nine continue to be terrorized: one day, white girls attack Melba in the showers and hold her under scalding water. At the same time, the newspaper that Mrs. Bates (the President of the NAACP in Little Rock) runs is being financially ruined by white businesspeople, and the State Attorney is threatening NAACP officials across the state.

On December 17th, white boys surround Minnijean in the school cafeteria. Minnijean throws hot chili on two of the boys. Minnijean is suspended. The segregationists start a new chant: "One nigger down and eight to go." Minnijean is allowed to return to school, and a short while later, a white boy pours a bucket of soup on her head. Later, the boy who poured soup on Minnijean attacks her, and a fight ensues. Nobody knows exactly what happened, but the white students allege that Minnijean fought back. Minnijean is expelled from Central High School, and three white students are suspended. The NAACP arranges for a scholarship for Minnijean at a high school in New York.

One day, Melba is almost surrounded by a group of white boys led by Andy, her main tormentor. She is saved by a white boy named Link, who gives her the keys to his car. That night, Melba returns Link's car to him, and he begins to warn her of the plans that the segregationists have made for her. Melba and Link become friends. On April 16, Judge Davies is removed from the Little Rock integration lawsuits and replaced by an Arkansas judge named Harry Lemley.

One Saturday morning, Link and Melba visit Nana Healey, Link's black nanny. Link thinks that Nana Healey has tuberculosis. Melba finds a doctor in the black community to tend to her. Nana Healey is dying, and Melba has to tell Link. Meanwhile, the integration case is reopened, with Judge Lemley presiding, and the school board once again asks for a postponement of integration at Central High School. Melba's mother, Lois, is nearly fired from her teaching job of fourteen years because Melba won't withdraw from Central High School. The end of the school year is approaching, and the segregationists are desperate to keep Ernie, the oldest of the nine, from graduating. Yet, on May 27, Ernie graduates. The next day, Link calls in tears. Nana Healey has died. Link asks Melba to leave Little Rock with him. Melba agrees to go, knowing she will not follow through with her promise.

By May 29, the Nine (including Minnijean) have begun a tour of the northern states, where they are treated like heroes and celebrities. Meanwhile, the integration effort in Little Rock is disintegrating. Judge Lemley grants the school board's plea to delay integration for three years. The NAACP sets up a round of appeals, and by September of 1958, the students are gearing up for their second year at Central. Rather than allow that to happen, Governor Faubus shuts down all of Little Rock's high schools. While Melba is waiting to return to school, Grandma India is diagnosed with leukemia and dies in October of 1958. By September of 1959, the NAACP has decided that the strain on the families is too great. They ask people in NAACP chapters across the country to take in the students. Melba is sent to Santa Rosa, California, to the home of the McCabes, a white Quaker family. The McCabes nurture and care for Melba and convince her to go to college in January of 1960.

In September of 1960, Central is again open to integration, but only two of the nine students are readmitted. They eventually graduate. Melba begins to attend San Francisco State University with predominantly white students. One night in 1962, while she is at school, a white soldier named John comes to her room to meet her roommate. There is mutual attraction, and soon they are engaged to be married. Melba relates how she keeps in touch with Link during this time. But when Link hears that she is getting married, and to a white man, he is furious, as Melba had always maintained she could not date a white man. They never speak again. Six months later, Melba and John are married. They have a daughter named Kelli. Seven years after their daughter's birth, they split up because Melba wants to be a reporter and work, and John wants a housewife. Melba goes to journalism school at Columbia and becomes a reporter. She ends the book by saying that if her experience at Central High School has taught her anything, it is that we are all one.

CHARACTER LIST

Melba Patillo Beals The main character and narrator of *Warriors Don't Cry*. Melba is one of the Little Rock Nine (i.e., the first black students in the United States to attend a previously all-white high school). She fights racism in its many forms throughout her life.

W

Grandma India Melba's grandmother. Grandma India is one of the most influential figures in Melba's life. She is a deeply religious woman who provides Melba with a deep sense of purpose. It is Grandma India who tells Melba that warriors don't cry, thus providing her with the title of her memoir.

Link A white student who befriends Melba. Link has a close relationship with his Nanny, who is black, which leads him to empathize with Melba. Though Link helps Melba in her fight against the segregationists, he never publicly declares his friendship with her.

Conrad Patillo Melba's younger brother. As an adult, Conrad becomes the first and only black captain of the Arkansas State Troopers.

Lois Patillo Melba's mother, also called Mother Lois. Lois teaches English at a Little Rock high school, and, at the time of the book's events, is separated from Melba's father, Will.

Will Patillo Also called "Papa Will." Will is Melba's father. He leaves the family before the events of the book unfold. Will objects to the integration effort.

Kelli Beals Melba's daughter.

Virgil Blossom The superintendent of Little Rock's schools. He supports the plan for integration, but he does little to enforce it or protect the students.

Minnijean Brown One of the Little Rock Nine. Minnijean is Melba's closest friend in the group. She is eventually expelled from Central for "fighting" and is sent to New York to attend school. Minnijean eventually becomes a Canadian citizen and lives on a farm as a writer and a mother.

Nana Healey Link's nanny from childhood. Nana Healey is black, and Link has a very close relationship with her.

Mrs. Higgenbottom Grandma India's shotgun.

Andy A white Central High student who is especially vicious toward Melba.

Mrs. C. Daisy Bates The president of the NAACP (National Association for the Advancement of Colored People) in Little Rock. Mrs. Bates also runs a local newspaper, the *Arkansas State Press*, which champions integration.

General Clinger The general in charge of the Arkansas National Guardsmen who are supposed to be guarding the Nine.

Vince Melba's boyfriend. He and Melba break up as a result of her transfer to Central.

Bill Clinton A governor of Arkansas, later the president of the United States. When Melba returns to Arkansas to be honored with the rest of the Little Rock Nine, Governor Clinton treats them with kindness and respect, in stark contrast to former Governor Faubus.

Ronald Davies A federal judge from Nebraska who orders Governor Faubus of Arkansas to allow integration to continue.

Danny A white soldier with the 101st Airborne Division (the elite fighting force that President Eisenhower assigned to protect the African-American students at Central High School). Danny is assigned to protect Melba—at one point saving her from acid that is thrown toward her eyes.

Elizabeth Eckford One of the "Little Rock Nine," the nine African-American students who participated in the 1957 integration of Little Rock's Central High School. On the first day that Elizabeth attempts to enter the school, she is confronted by the Arkansas National Guard and almost attacked by an angry white mob. She is escorted away from the crowd by two white people, Grace Lorch and Benjamin Fine. As an adult, Elizabeth is the only one of the nine to remain in Little Rock. She holds a job as a social worker.

Dwight D. Eisenhower The then-president of the United States, Eisenhower proclaims that Governor Faubus is not allowed to defy the federal order to desegregate schools. When Faubus sends in the Arkansas National Guard to keep the African-American students out of Central High School, President Eisenhower responds by sending the elite 101st Airborne Division to escort the Little Rock Nine into Central High School.

Orval Faubus Governor of Arkansas in 1957. Faubus gives the order to keep the African-American students out of Central High School, and orders armed Arkansas National Guardsmen to prevent Melba and her friends from entering the school.

Benjamin Fine A white reporter for the *New York Times* who protects Elizabeth Eckford from a mob of segregationists on her first day at Central High School.

Joseph Fox A "moderate" Central High School student who attends the meeting with Mrs. Jorumn Rickets. He is called moderate because he does not advocate violence to keep the Nine out of Central.

Goggles A three-hundred–pound soldier with the 101st Airborne Division. Goggles is called in whenever any of the nine is facing major problems with the kids at school.

Ernest Green One of the Little Rock Nine, and the oldest of the group. Ernest is the first African-American student to graduate from Central High School. After his graduation, integration is halted for three years. Ernest eventually becomes vice president of a company called Shearson Lehman Hutton.

J. Edgar Hoover The director of the FBI. He dismisses Faubus's outrageous claims that the FBI is holding white students for questioning.

Elizabeth Huckaby The vice principal of Central High School. Mrs. Huckaby can't protect the African-American students, but she does her best to control some of their attackers. Toward the end of the year, she essentially gives up.

Judge Harry Lemley An Arkansas judge who is assigned to the Little Rock integration case after Judge Davies is removed.

Grace Lorch A white woman who protects Elizabeth Eckford from a mob of segregationists on her first day at Central High School.

Woodrow Mann The mayor of Little Rock, who opposes Governor Faubus and supports integration.

Marissa A crazy young girl in Melba's community. Marissa saves Melba from a white man who tries to rape her when the announcement of Brown v. the Board of Education is made in 1954.

Marsha Melba's good friend—not one of the Little Rock Nine—who eventually begins to avoid Melba's company, as she fears violence.

Thurgood Marshall The lawyer who argues on behalf of Linda Brown in the historic Brown v. the Board of Education of Topeka, Kansas. As chief counsel for the NAACP (the National Association for the Advancement of Colored People), Marshall supports the Little Rock Nine's efforts to integrate their school. Marshall goes on to become the first black justice on the Supreme Court of the United States.

Jess Matthews The principal of Central High School in Little Rock.

Carol McCabe A white Quaker woman from Santa Rosa, California. The McCabe family takes Melba in after Governor Faubus shuts down the Little Rock high schools.

Dr. George McCabe A white Quaker man from Santa Rosa, California, whose family takes Melba in after Governor Faubus shuts down the Little Rock high schools. His wife is Carol.

Thelma Mothershed One of the Little Rock Nine. Thelma has a heart problem that sometimes makes her breathless and weak. Thelma later becomes a teacher in Illinois.

Sammy Dean Parker A staunch segregationist and one of the main white troublemakers at Central High School. She is one of the white students who meet with the black students at the request of a Norwegian reporter named Mrs. Jorumn Rickets.

Mrs. Pickwick Melba's shorthand teacher, and one of the few teachers at Central who disciplines the unruly segregationists.

W

Gloria Ray One of the Little Rock Nine. She later becomes a magazine publisher.

Mrs. Jorumn Rickets A Norwegian reporter who arranges for a meeting between some of Central High School's staunchest segregationists and some of the Nine.

Terrence Roberts One of the Little Rock Nine, Terry is a junior like Melba. Terry eventually becomes a professor at UCLA.

Sarge The driver of the station wagon that Melba takes to school under the supervision of the 101st Airborne. Sarge is friendly and efficient.

Bishop O.J. Sherman A powerful cleric in the black community. He gets Melba's mother her job back.

Gene Smith The Little Rock assistant chief of police. Smith rescues Melba and the other African-American students from the mob that surrounds Central High School on their first day of class.

Jefferson Thomas One of the Little Rock Nine, Jefferson is an athlete and a top student. He eventually becomes an accountant for the Defense Department in California.

Carlotta Walls One of the Little Rock Nine. Carlotta eventually becomes a realtor in Denver, Colorado.

ANALYSIS OF MAJOR CHARACTERS

MELBA PATILLO BEALS Over the course of *Warriors Don't Cry*, Melba transitions from a normal teenage girl to a hardened warrior. When she starts school at Central High School, she has no idea of the hardships she will face. With Grandma India's help, Melba learns to give up all of the things that other teenagers care about—friends, free time, boyfriends and girlfriends, and extracurricular activities—and instead focuses on the larger issue of integration. Melba quickly learns that she will not have a normal high school experience. What she will have is the knowledge that she has fought on the right side, and that she has, according to Grandma India, fought God's fight.

By the end of her time at Central, Melba has given up on friends and has broken up with her boyfriend, Vince. She has a single purpose: to survive to the end of the year, and to prove to the segregationists that she can't be beaten. When Melba is at Central, she has to assume an almost superhuman demeanor. When people slap her or spit on her, she learns to say "thank you" and not fight back. The religion Melba relies on so heavily makes her seem even more saintlike, which alienates many people who want to be friends with her. But by the end of her year at Central, it is quite clear that Melba is an entirely different person than the pretty young girl who started there. She has replaced her innocence with a sense of purpose. This experience is why she eventually goes into journalism: she feels that were it not for the attention of the press, she would never have been admitted to Central High School. She sees her work as a journalist as an extension of that fight. Because of her experience at Central, the adult Melba finds she can't back away from a fight.

GRANDMA INDIA Grandma India acts as Melba's steely backbone during her struggle to integrate Central High School. Every time Melba considers abandoning the struggle, Grandma India encourages her to persist. Grandma India fortifies Melba with faith and stubbornness, and it is Grandma India who tells Melba that God's warriors don't cry. This is the first introduction that Melba has to the idea that in order to successfully integrate into the school, she will need to become more than a regular teenager. Because Grandma India is deeply religious, she is able to provide Melba with a sense of purpose. She reminds Melba that she is a child of God and that the opinion of her fellow teenagers doesn't matter as long as God loves her. Grandma India always assures Melba that God approves of what she is doing.

Grandma India repeatedly shows Melba that she is not afraid to stand up to white people when they are doing something wrong. She also shows Melba that there are peaceful, respectful ways of standing up to the white people. Melba is thus able to avoid the provocations of Andy and his friend and avoid the temptation to fight back. When Grandma India dies during what would have been Melba's second year at Central (had Faubus not shut down the schools), it is as though Melba has lost her will to fight. Melba moves to California to live in a more accepting community. Grandma India is the living embodiment of Melba's strength; when she dies, Melba has to learn how to find that strength inside herself.

LINK The son of a prominent white family, Link is the white student who helps Melba escape time and time again from the violent segregationists who want to kill her. His father is pro-segregation but appalled by the attacks on black teenagers and children. Though Link is popular and bound for success in the white world, he helps Melba. In spite of his racist family, Link has a different perspective on black people because of his close relationship with Nana Healey. Nana Healey is black, and Link loves her and resents the treatment she receives from his parents now that she no longer works for them. Because he knows that Nana Healey is a good and loving person, he can imagine that other black people might be good and loving as well. Link is the only white student who shows Melba any kindness, and he is the only white person she comes to trust during her time at Central High School.

Though Link undermines the efforts of the violent segregationists, he is never able to openly defy them and declare his friendship with Melba. Link wants to help Melba, but he is fearful of becoming an outsider. While Melba puts aside those fears in order to do something for the greater good, Link hides behind them. He still helps Melba, but he does it in secret. His secretive attitude about their relationship is in part why Melba never seems to return Link's romantic feelings. When he asks her to flee to the North and escape the angry white people, Melba feels he is asking her to give up. What is most important to Melba at this time is proving that she cannot be defeated by the anger and hatred of the segregationists. Because Link is just a normal teenager, and because everything has come relatively easy for him, he will never understand this.

THEMES, MOTIFS, AND SYMBOLS

THEMES

THE SHIFTING OF POWER THROUGH RESISTANCE Melba's year at Central High School centers around maturation, race relations, and challenging the power dynamic in the United States. In the segregated South, white people had power and black people did not. The small act of defiance of nine black children entering an all-white school took on such significance because it threatened to change the way white segregationists wielded their power. With this and many other acts, integrationists such as Melba showed that the power of the white segregationists was a fragile illusion. Melba's story makes clear that the power of whites lie, to some extent, in the consent of the black people. Once blacks—even just a few of them—stopped consenting, the power structure began to fail.

Grandma India teaches Melba about passive resistance. Melba learns to smile and meet every outrageous abuse with a polite "thank you." For Grandma India, power lies not in displays of physical strength or firepower, but in inner strength and faith. The mobs of white people who rely on numbers to overwhelm a tiny black teenager are only showing that they don't have the power they say they do. Grandma India tells Melba she is only a victim if she lets herself be one. Melba learns that nobody has any power to hurt her unless she gives it to them. This simple act of refusing to be afraid when people threaten her changes not just the way Melba sees herself but also the way other people see her.

THE PROMINENCE OF RACE RELATIONS People's perceptions of race cloud the way they behave throughout *Warriors Don't Cry*. Melba is born into a segregated society, in which black people lack the basic rights afforded to white people. In Melba's narrative, this is a system more or less acknowledged by both white and black people. And though the black people suffer much more in the system, they also help to enforce it out of fear of retribution from the white people. The white people are afraid that the black people will rise up and take over their lives, and the black people are afraid of being punished by the white people for rising up. This mutual fear often turns into mistrust and hatred. Even those within the white community who try to reach out to blacks are called traitors and are threatened with violence.

Though Melba has a valid reason to mistrust many white people throughout the course of the book, she learns that people can make decisions based more on honor, trust, and love than race. Link, the white boy whose love for his nanny humanizes black people for him, proves to Melba that she can trust some white people. The two white people who save Elizabeth Eckford from the white mob and the Quaker family that takes her in after she leaves Arkansas are other trustworthy whites. Eventually, she falls in love with John, the white soldier who woos her in college. Outside of the tangle of racial conflict set up by the history in Little Rock, Melba can learn to relate to people as people rather than as members of a race.

W

MOTIFS

SELF-RELIANCE While for most teenagers, high school involves building social skills and a community, for Melba and the other black students it is primarily about self-reliance. Not only are they entering a school in which almost every person is hostile toward them but they are also slowly losing friends from their old lives. Melba's friends from Horace Mann begin to avoid her because they fear for their own safety and because she becomes so serious while undergoing the abuse at Central. Melba does begin to date Vince, but because he cannot understand what she is going through, they gradually drift apart. Melba is close to her family, but she learns that even they cannot protect her from the people in her school.

Melba has to face each challenge and attack by herself. Danny sees Melba through some difficult times, but eventually he disappears when the 101st Airborne is withdrawn. Though Link helps her, he does not openly declare himself her friend. While other teenagers around her travel in packs of friends, Melba is isolated and rarely allowed out in public. Grandma India gives her strength and purpose, but eventually, Grandma India dies. In the process of becoming an adult, Melba has to learn to rely more and more on herself instead of on the people around her.

THE LOSS OF INNOCENCE The transformation from being innocent, idealistic teenagers to warriors is a recurring motif throughout *Warriors Don't Cry*. Battered by the hatred and violence at Central High

School, each of the Nine has to learn how to live without friends and rely solely on themselves. They also learn that they cannot rely on the protection of their parents or any of the authority figures in the school to protect them. Each of the Little Rock Nine has to learn to survive in hostile conditions. Each of them has to give up a youthful dream, whether it is seeing Elvis perform, playing on the school basketball team, or singing in the school talent show. All of the black students have to recognize that their lives are about much more than their own petty concerns: their pain contributes to some greater good. If they are unable to recognize this, they will not last very long. Because Minnijean cannot accept that it may be impossible for her to make friends and have a normal teenage life, it becomes harder and harder for her to stifle her natural emotions. She is expelled.

The story in *Warriors Don't Cry* is not just about the black students' loss of innocence. It is the story of how Little Rock lost its innocence, as well. The segregationists in Little Rock fight so hard against the integration of the schools because, in some part, integration would mean admitting they had been mistreating black people all these years. Link loses his innocence by watching not just how Melba and her friends are treated but also how his own family treats his beloved Nana Healey. Seeing them turn an ailing old woman away makes him realize he doesn't really trust his family. It becomes difficult to reconcile the image of the parents he loves with their treatment of someone who had always loved and cared for him. The images that appear in the newspaper after Elizabeth Eckford is turned away from Central the first time, in which a tiny black girl is surrounded by a howling mob of white people, shame some white adults. The reason segregationists talk about black people "making trouble" is that the lives they live have hitherto been innocent of the suffering of the black people around them. Being forced to recognize the pain of others requires a loss of innocence, for which they're not prepared.

SYMBOLS

CENTRAL HIGH SCHOOL Central High School comes to symbolize not just a good education but also the barriers to education that Melba and the other black students have to face. Its forbidding, fortress-like exterior represents the barriers put up by society against black people. The quest to conquer Central High School concerns more than just getting nine black children into an all-white high school: it also concerns the large scale dismantling of barriers in all aspects of American life and ensuring that black people are afforded the same opportunities as white people.

The luxury and wealth of the school also symbolize all that Melba's people do not have. When Melba is able to observe the school around her, she sees lovely things, such as the preparations for the school play and the new textbooks. All of this is vastly different from Melba's old high school, Horace Mann. Because the Central High students are surrounded by other white people but served in the cafeteria by black people, the school is also a microcosm of the white world, in which white people are rarely forced to confront the realities of racism. But Melba's interactions with Central High School also represent the curiosity and spirit that make it possible for her to survive her first year there. The drive to know what goes on in the white world pushes Melba to overcome her fears.

MELBA'S EASTER DRESS Every year, Melba's family chooses fabric from Grandma India's trunk to make their special Easter clothing. This event has always been a high point of the year, and Grandma India's trunk is filled with treasures. Though Melba's family is not wealthy, they have real dignity in their traditions. The tradition of making the dress each year accentuates the pride that Melba's family takes in their clothing, their religion, and their lives. But in this particular year, Melba insists on an adult dress made of adult fabric. Her mother and grandmother agree that it is time for Melba to have a lady-like dress. The dress symbolizes Melba's difficult passage from a high-school girl to an adult warrior for justice and is a reward for her work.

When Melba wears the dress to school, one of the segregationist students sprays the dress with black ink and ruins it. Thus, the dress becomes a symbol of all that Melba cannot escape. Though Melba had hoped to use her adult dress as a kind of protection against the cruelty and solitude she experiences at Central High School, it does not work. Melba cannot escape the realities that await her every day at Central.

JOURNALISTS Journalists are omnipresent in Melba's story. She often uses newspaper headlines to begin chapters of her book, and in the story itself, reporters frequently pepper Melba and her friends with questions. She credits them with having kept attention on the crisis at Central High School. Had newspapers not been running stories regularly, says Melba, Governor Faubus and the segregationists might have been allowed to triumph. One of the two white people who save Elizabeth Eckford is a journalist, and several black journalists are beaten by the savage crowd that surrounds Central High School on the first day of school that the Little Rock Nine attend. Journalists recognize Melba's talent with words and encourage her to write. But what means the most to Melba is the kind of fraternity they create for themselves, in which black and white reporters work together. For journalists, finding the truth seems more important than discussing superficialities, such as the color of someone's skin.

The journalists who visit Melba's town give her a glimpse of something larger than Little Rock and its segregated society. By observing these people who serve truth before social convention, Melba realizes that there is a better life out there. This is the first time she understands that she could have such a future. In her rushed maturation during her time at Central High School, Melba interacts with journalists and realizes she could continue to fight for truth and justice as a career and that she could do it with words.

IMPORTANT QUOTATIONS EXPLAINED

---

1. *"God's warriors don't cry."*

Grandma India says this to Melba in Chapter 6 after Melba cries in front of her. Melba is crying because her family, fearing that she will be the target of an attack, has forbidden her from attending a wrestling match. But Melba had planned to meet Vince, the boy she has a crush on, at the wrestling match. When her grandmother tells her she can't come to the matches, Melba feels like every part of her life has been taken away from her. Grandma India lets Melba cry for a bit and then tells her she can never cry again. Grandma India explains to Melba, for the first time, that what she is doing is greater than just going to high school for a year. Melba is fighting a battle, and the battle is for the future of black people in the United States. She is fighting God's war. Grandma India sounds cruel when she tells Melba to stop crying, but her point is that Melba has to learn to accept pain. If Melba is going to have any chance of surviving her year at Central, she is going to have to learn how to be tougher than the average teenager.

This quotation also reflects the war that is being waged all across the country, not just at Central High School. Melba and similar individuals are soldiers at the front of a very dangerous battle. Yet in spite of these dangers, Melba and the other black students at Little Rock persist. The struggle entails more than one person's desire to go to a better high school or eat at a better diner or ride in the front of the bus. Melba's struggle is a quest to improve the lives of black people all over the country. Melba's participation in this quest is why her grandmother calls her one of God's warriors.

---

2. *"One nigger down, eight to go."*

This is the chant recited by the segregationists at Central High School after a handful of them managed to drive Minnijean out in Chapter 23. The Little Rock Nine have been warned time and time again not to retaliate. A few students push Minnijean too far one day, and she dumps soup on them. She is suspended, and when she returns to school, she becomes a target for all of the fury of the segregationist students. They have learned that they can provoke her, and they do. Minnijean eventually fights back again, and she is expelled. Overjoyed at their success, the segregationists begin taunting the other black students with this chant. For the segregationists, it is proof that they can get rid of the black students. To the remaining members of the Little Rock Nine, it is a reminder of how strong they have to be and how harsh the consequences will be if they falter.

---

3. *"Please, God, let me learn how to stop being a warrior. Sometimes I just need to be a girl."*

Melba writes this in her diary on her sixteenth birthday, in Chapter 20. All her life, Melba has dreamt of her "sweet sixteen," imagining it down to the last detail. Her real sixteenth birthday, however, turns out to be very different from her daydreams. Though she has planned a party with all of her friends from her old high school, only Vince shows up. Everyone else has decided not to come because they are too afraid to be seen with Melba. They all go to another party, and they don't want Melba to come because they want to have a good, safe evening. Eventually, even Vince leaves for the other party, and Melba cries herself to sleep.

This party is Melba's last effort to prove that the fight at Central High School is not her whole life. She tries to surround herself with friends who know nothing about the battle for integration. When Melba writes that she sometimes needs to just be a girl, she is trying desperately to cling to the innocence that's been slipping away throughout the year. Sadly, her dream of a sweet sixteen is crushed. When nobody shows up, Melba is forced to confront the fact that she has changed. Having accepted the role of a warrior for integration, Melba finds that she can't put it aside so easily. She learns that being a warrior means more than just venturing into new and hostile territory. It also means leaving behind old pleasures and friends. It means that she can no longer indulge in just being a girl.

---

4. *"Change the rules of the game, girl, and they might not like it so much."*
   "They'd think I was crazy."
   "They'd think you were no longer their victim."

In Chapter 23, this exchange between Melba and her grandmother comes after Minnijean has been attacked in school and suspended for the second time. Attacks on the other black students have been stepped up as well, and Melba and her grandmother have this conversation while attempting to remove spoiled eggs from her hair and dress—eggs that were thrown on Melba by a segregationist. Throughout Melba's time at Central, her grandmother has advised her to follow the teachings of Jesus and to draw her strength from the Bible and God. Here, she advises Melba to model her behavior in school after Mahatma Gandhi's methods in India. Gandhi practiced a form of protest called "passive resistance," in which protestors were strictly nonviolent and preached peace and love instead of violence and anger. Melba's grandmother is advising Melba to approach her attackers with love and kindness as a way of empowering herself.

Grandma India tells Melba to thank the segregationists when they attack and to smile sweetly, as though they've done something kind. She tells Melba that the segregationists at school have no power over Melba other than the power that Melba gives them. And the power she gives them consists of reacting the way they want her to react. If Melba isn't affected (or at least pretends to be unaffected) by their taunts and cruelty, then they have no power over her. Because Melba acts a representative of millions of other people, she has to change the power dynamic between her and her oppressors. The segregationists hope to teach her that they can control her, but Melba defies this. By refusing to be a victim, Melba shows segregationists that they do not, in fact, have such power over her.

---

5. "Namasté" *(The God in me sees and honors the God in you).*

Melba ends her book with this quotation, a Sanskrit prayer of acceptance and peace in Chapter 28. *Namasté* literally means, "I bow to you." A form of greeting in India, it supposes that there is a divine spark (or God) in every human being. When a person bows with his hands in a prayer position at his heart, he recognizes that the divine spark within him is also in every other person around him. Because Melba has lived through so much anger and hatred, the prayer with which she closes her story of struggle and hatred is a profoundly respectful one. It is a message to her readers that, more than anything else, she's learned that all people have divinity in them, regardless of their color. By extending this gesture of peace and acceptance to her readers, she extends her message to the world.

For Melba, this prayer is a means of understanding the trauma of her year at Central High School. She is no longer a girl who simply wants people to like her. She has become an adult, toughened by life and her experiences at Central but also able to forgive the world for its cruelty towards her. Because of her time at Central, Melba knows the significance of her closing prayer. Until people learn to recognize both human and divine attributes in themselves and others, peace will be impossible. The prayer is not just for forgiveness; it is also Melba's hope for the world.

The Waves

Virginia Woolf (1882–1941)

CONTEXT

Virginia Woolf was one of the great literary figures of the twentieth century, and *The Waves* (1931) represents, in a career filled with bold experiments, her most audacious exploration of the possibilities of the novel form. *The Waves* abandons traditional structure and plot as practiced in the English novel since the days of the writer Henry Fielding, in favor of a lyrical, almost dreamlike evocation of character. Instead of narrating her characters' outward actions, Woolf enters their minds and reports their thoughts and perceptions as they occur, with few external clues to provide shape or context. Woolf builds her characters from the inside out, and one of the concerns of the novel is the way individual personalities and sensibilities are shaped by relationships with others. The resulting work still presents unique challenges and rewards for the reader, even more than fifty years since its publication. Woolf herself, however, worked hard in her lifetime to create an intellectual and critical environment in which such formally adventurous works as *The Waves* could be understood and appreciated.

Woolf was born in 1882 into an already distinguished literary and artistic family. Her father, Sir Leslie Stephen, was one of the most notable intellectuals of his day, and her sister, Vanessa, went on to become a well-regarded painter. Along with her husband, the publisher Leonard Woolf, whom she married in 1912, Woolf became one of the leading figures in the Bloomsbury Group of artists and writers. Named for the London district in which the Woolfs lived, the Bloomsbury Group was an informal circle of writers, artists, and thinkers who formed one of the most well-known branches of the literary avant-garde of the early twentieth century. Not so much a "movement" as a collection of like-minded friends, Bloomsbury stood for a moderately leftist political stance, a commitment to formal innovation in the arts, a refined critical and aesthetic sensibility, and an intensely inward focus on the way the mind translates experience into language and meaning. The Bloomsbury Group also tended to define itself in opposition to the Victorian period, the era of their parents and grandparents. As avowed modernists, they turned their backs on what they saw as the stuffy formality and hypocritical morality of the Victorians. Through their experiments in art and literature, they hoped to discover a new artistic method to match the new century.

Woolf was at the forefront of these efforts. In her critical writing, she championed the work of such contemporaries as James Joyce, whose novel *Ulysses* (1922) set the standard for modernist writing and is—apart from Woolf's own work—the most obvious forerunner of *The Waves*. She also pioneered efforts to establish a canon of women writers. Her influential readings of such authors as Jane Austen and George Eliot help to locate her own work within a tradition of female novelists.

In her famous essay "Modern Fiction," Woolf distinguishes between those writers she labels "materialists," who focus on the surface of things and events at the expense of inner meaning, and those such as Joyce and herself, who are "spiritual" and want to convey "that innermost flame" of people and events, even if this concern leads them away from what we are used to thinking of as realistic writing. For Woolf, capturing the "innermost flame" is the most important task of the modern novelist, who tries to reveal the extraordinary quality of "an ordinary mind on an ordinary day." In her greatest works, such as *Mrs. Dalloway* (1925), *To the Lighthouse* (1927), and *The Waves*, Woolf epitomizes such a modern writer, leaving behind the conventional structures of the novel in order to pursue the fleeting impressions within the minds of her characters, capturing them in flight within a net of language and imagery.

PLOT OVERVIEW

The Waves is a portrait of the intertwined lives of six friends: Bernard, Neville, Louis, Jinny, Susan, and Rhoda. The novel is divided into nine sections, each of which corresponds to a time of day, and, symbolically, to a period in the lives of the characters. Each section begins with a detailed description of the course of this symbolic day.

The first section deals with early morning, or childhood, when the six main characters are attending a day-school together. As each of the children awakens, he or she begins an internal monologue composed of thoughts, feelings, and impressions. The children interact in various ways throughout the day, and each begins to take shape as an individual in response to the stimulus provided by the world and by the presence of one another. Although their thoughts are somewhat incoherent and mostly fixated on immediate experience, their distinct personalities begin to emerge: Bernard's loquacity and obsession with language; Neville's desire for order and beauty; Louis's insecurity and ambition; Jinny's physicality; Susan's intensity and attachment to nature; and Rhoda's dreamlike abstraction from ordinary life.

The second section deals with adolescence, after the boys and girls have been sent off to their separate boarding schools. Bernard, Louis, and Neville differ in their reactions to the school's authority and traditions, and they all form friendships with Percival, a popular, handsome boy who is to become a central figure in the lives of the six main characters. All three boys develop literary ambitions of some sort, though they differ markedly in their goals and expressions. The girls mostly want school to be over and done with: Jinny desires to begin her real life in society, Susan longs to return home to her father and her farm, and Rhoda wants an escape from the disruptions to her mental solitude caused by school. At the close of the section, each character sets out, whether for college, work, or otherwise, on a more solitary track.

The third section traces the characters through young adulthood. Bernard and Neville are at college together and remain close friends. They both admire Percival, but Neville has fallen in love with him. Percival has become the focus of Neville's desire for beauty and perfection. Bernard is concerned with his own gregarious nature and thinks deeply about the way his personality is constructed out of his relationships with others. Neville shares one of his poems with Bernard, and the moment is important for both of them. Louis is working as a mid-level clerk at a shipping firm in London. He spends his lunch hour reading at a diner and people-watching, hoping to make poetry out of his observations of everyday life. Susan is at home on her farm and communes with the rhythm of natural life. She walks across the fields before dawn and senses growth all around her, though she begins to submerge her own active will. Back in London, Jinny and Rhoda attend the same party, though their experiences are very different. Jinny comes fully alive in the social setting, and she takes a great, sensual pleasure in the beauty of her surroundings and in her own personal attractiveness. Rhoda, on the other hand, feels negated by the others around her and longs to disappear.

The fourth section is set later in adulthood and centers on a dinner party, meant to honor Percival, who is leaving for a position in the colonial government in India. At the party, the six characters are united again. At first, the group is tense and uneasy in one another's company, and they primarily notice their differences. When Percival arrives, however, these tensions are relaxed and the group comes together. Briefly, the friends are united in a moment of true communion, and their individual voices seem to blend. All too soon, however, the moment ends and the group dissolves back into its singular parts.

The fifth section takes place not long after the dinner party, when the friends have learned that Percival has been killed in India. Neville is devastated by the news, overwhelmed by a sense of death and the fragility of life. Bernard is torn between joy and sorrow: his child has just been born and his friend has just died. Bernard goes to a museum to look at paintings and finds a kind of solace, even as he is aware that his memories of Percival must inevitably fade. Rhoda finds a similar solace in music when she attends an opera soon after she learns of Percival's death, and she finds the strength to go on for a time.

In the sixth section, the characters have entered full maturity. Louis is rising in his firm and leads a sort of double life. Although he is a respectable businessman, he is drawn to the seamier side of life and spends his time roaming around poorer neighborhoods. Louis and Rhoda have become lovers. Susan is a mother now, both deeply gratified and stifled by her chosen life. On one hand, she is fully a part of the cycle of natural life; on the other, her own life has become subordinate to the lives of her children and the ongoing life of the farm. Jinny continues her purely physical existence, taking lovers but never settling down, content to revel in her own being. Neville also moves from lover to lover, but in his case, he is trying to keep the intensity of first desire alive—it is the source of his creativity.

The seventh section deals with midlife, as the characters begin to age. Bernard has traveled to Rome, where he observes the ruins and tries to come to terms with his own sense of failure, as he has begun to doubt both his own abilities and the ability of stories to capture reality. As Susan sinks deeper into her rural and domestic life, she regrets what she has lost even as she finds a measure of contentment in what she has gained. Jinny has a moment of dread in which she sees that she is aging and her beauty is fading. She reconciles herself to the inevitable passage of time, however, and resolves to make the most of her remaining years. Neville is becoming a successful writer. He is mellowing a bit, but he continues to shift the focus of his desire from lover to lover. Louis rises ever higher in his firm but still returns to his attic room to write. Literature seems to him an idealized realm even as his eye is continually drawn to the street. Rhoda has left Louis and travels to Spain, where she too has a moment in which she comes face to face with death—here in the form of the vast sea seen from the cliffs.

In the eighth section, the friends once again gather for a dinner, though this time the meeting is shadowed by death, thanks both to their increasing age and to the absence of Percival. Although there is tension among the friends, as at the earlier meeting, this tension is resolved as they begin to share their common experiences. The characters have lived long enough to know that this meeting is one such common experience, and they have another moment of silent communion, though the moment is elegiac rather than triumphant. Rhoda and Louis have a quiet moment together as the others walk into the park, but it inevitably comes to an end.

The ninth and final section is told entirely from Bernard's point of view. Bernard speaks to a casual acquaintance over dinner, and tries to give a "summing up" of his life. Bernard is still doubtful about the accuracy of any representation of reality through language. He tries to give a sense of the texture of his life, rather than making sweeping statements about it. Bernard discusses the others and how things have turned out for them, including the fact that Rhoda has killed herself. The most profound moment Bernard describes is one in which he himself seems to move beyond language into a direct perception of reality. In the end, however, Bernard sees his life as an attempt to use language to fight against death, and he sees how the others have, in their individual ways, been part of the same struggle. Bernard vows to keep fighting until the end.

CHARACTER LIST

Bernard One of the narrators. Bernard is friendly, garrulous, and in many ways the glue that holds the group of friends together. He is the least snobbish of the group, willing to talk to anyone as an equal. Bernard wants to become a novelist, though his hopes go unfulfilled. By the end of the novel, however, he achieves the greatest insight into the lives of the other characters.

Dr. Crane The headmaster at the private boarding school the boys attend. Dr. Crane represents both traditional authority and religion, and the boys' individual responses to him are telling. Neville despises him as a repressive, pompous, insincere figure, while Louis admires him as the representative of the English society he so much wants to be a part of. Bernard sees the headmaster primarily as a character about whom he can spin a story.

Jinny One of the narrators. Jinny is a beautiful, upper-class woman who leads the life of a glamorous socialite. She is grounded in the here-and-now, rarely wondering about the deeper significance of events or the symbolic value of things—a marked contrast to her friends. She is intensely physical, seeing her body and her sexuality as her primary means of interacting with the world. Jinny is perhaps the most static of the main characters, though she does come to terms with her own aging.

Louis One of the narrators. Louis's father is an Australian banker, and Louis is painfully aware of his own accent and his lower-class status in comparison with his friends. He is driven by a desire to escape his position as an outsider and to prove the superiority of his own intellect. Louis becomes a successful businessman, but he also wants to become a poet in order to make something permanent out of the passing disorder of everyday life. Louis is attracted to both the concrete reality of life in London and the ideal realm of art. He and Rhoda are lovers for a time, but she eventually leaves him.

Neville One of the narrators. Neville is refined, intellectual, and upper class, with a deep appreciation of beauty. Neville loves Percival from afar, admiring him for being everything Neville is not—athletic, charismatic, and grounded in practical reality. After Percival's death, Neville pursues many different lovers, devoting himself intensely to each for a time and then moving on. Neville desires order and beauty, and he tries to exclude much of the disorder and ugliness of the world from his life by isolating himself with his books and his lovers. Neville becomes a famous poet.

Percival A friend of each of the main characters. The boys meet Percival at school, where he is one of the most popular students. Percival is handsome and charismatic, a natural leader. He is killed when he is thrown from a horse in India, where he has gone to work in the colonial government. Percival is in love with Susan, though he does not act on it, and Neville is in love with him, though Percival has no idea. Percival is an idealized figure for the other characters, and they each respond deeply to his death, though in different ways.

Rhoda One of the narrators. Rhoda is introverted, highly sensitive, and almost phobic when it comes to interacting with others. She tends to drift off into her imagination as a means of escaping from social situations, and she comes to feel that her own personality is insubstantial and illusory. Rhoda and Louis become lovers, but Rhoda is terrified of intimacy and leaves him. Eventually Rhoda's sense of the transience of life and her own desire for unconsciousness lead her to take her own life.

Susan One of the narrators. Susan hates city life and cannot wait to return home from school to her family farm, where she wants to tend the land and raise children. Susan is an earthy, passionate woman who is highly compelling to men, though not as classically beautiful as Jinny. Susan has an intense relationship with the land and with nature, but her cultivation of this natural bond leads to the suppression of many of her other desires. Susan loves Bernard, for example, but sacrifices any passion of her own for the sake of her family and her place in the cycle of rural life.

ANALYSIS OF MAJOR CHARACTERS

BERNARD Bernard is deeply concerned with language, and one of his first apparent traits is his obsession with "making phrases." This activity is a means of both impressing and helping others, as in the case of Susan early in the novel. As a child, Bernard sees language as a way to mediate and control reality, to turn random events into a chain of meaning. When he leaves for school, for example, Bernard makes phrases as a way to remain in control of his emotions. Later, he begins to turn his phrases into stories, transforming language into a tool for understanding others. Here he begins to run into a problem, however. Bernard has trouble capturing the lives of others (such as Dr. Crane) in his stories, and he is nagged by a sense that some element of the truth always escapes him.

Over time, Bernard comes to think that the problem with his stories is inherent in language itself. Reality, Bernard comes to think, is always more complex than our words can grasp. Part of the reason this is so is related to Bernard's concept of identity as fluid and changing. Bernard sees himself as a compound being, influenced by and even composed of the people who surround him. Bernard spends much time trying to break down the barriers between different selves. His dissatisfaction with language and traditional narrative echoes many of Woolf's own concerns and gives a clue as to why she felt the need to try bold experiments with the nature of fiction, such as *The Waves* itself. In her memoirs, Woolf tells of certain moments, which she calls "moments of being," in which she gains a direct perception of reality, apart from the distortions and omissions of language. Bernard has such a moment toward the end of the novel, and the moment is a kind of culmination for his character.

JINNY Jinny lives her life utterly apart from concerns about the soul. She thinks of herself as a body, first and foremost, interacting with other bodies. From the first moment we see Jinny, kissing Louis among the bushes, she is a creature of motion, surface, and physicality. More than once, Jinny compares herself to an animal and the social world in which she moves to a jungle, in which she is a huntress. She is aware of her own physical beauty, and her greatest pleasure is in being able to pick a man from the crowd and summon him with a gesture. It might sound from this description as though Woolf is being critical of Jinny, but Woolf presents Jinny's perspective as radically honest and admirably direct. She is not an intellectual and prefers to relate to a world of physical objects rather than ideas, but she is neither stupid nor insensitive.

In her own way, Jinny is just as devoted to beauty and to her ideal of life as someone more obviously idealistic, such as Neville. On the dance floor, swept up in the communal whirl of bodies and music, Jinny feels unified with something larger than herself, something like the flow of life. The problem with Jinny's ideal is that it cannot be sustained: music ends, beauty fades, and attractiveness withers with it. Neville, Louis, and Susan are each deeply concerned with making something that will last, and this, of course, Jinny cannot do—this is the great failing of Jinny's way of life. Catching a glimpse of herself in a mirror, she sees that her hedonistic time is drawing to a close, but she does not despair. Death is simply part of the bargain, and her attitude is *carpe diem*—seize the day, and live while you can.

LOUIS Louis's deepest sense of himself is that he does not fit in. Embarrassed as a child by his Australian accent and by his poorer background, Louis becomes an ambitious striver, eager to make his mark and to shed his status as an outsider. He becomes keenly aware of social distinctions and is drawn to Rhoda from the beginning, seeing her as a fellow misfit. At school, Louis discovers poetry and sees the tradition of literature as a kind of society open to those with enough genius and drive to gain admittance. From that point, his ambitions include becoming a great poet. But Louis does not go to college along with Neville and Bernard. Instead, he takes a job with a shipping firm in London, and from that time on, he leads a sort of double life. As he sits in a greasy-spoon diner, Louis's attention is split between the book of poems he reads and the gossiping crowd around him. Later, he rises in the company and become a distinguished businessman, while still retaining his poetic ambition and his attraction to the seamy side of life.

Louis wants to unify the ideal realm of poetry with the hurly-burly of daily life—his idea of a poetic image is a mangy cat rubbing its side against a chimney. What Louis hopes to do by writing poems about such things is to reveal the permanent existence beneath the random flow of ordinary events. Louis's project is somewhere between Jinny's (submerging the self in life's flow, without imposing concepts on it) and Neville's (living a life of artistic isolation from everyday life). Woolf seems to be sympathetic to this plan, which has a certain resemblance to her own, but it remains unclear how well Louis is able to realize it. He seems compromised by his materialistic desire for success in business and his attraction to the tawdry. Louis and Rhoda become lovers for a time, but Louis is unable to forge a lasting connection there as well.

NEVILLE At first, Neville might seem to be a rather clichéd portrait of a homosexual aesthete: he is physically weak, overly refined, obsessed with male beauty, and somewhat promiscuous. But Neville is also a great artist—the most successful artist in the novel. Unlike Louis and Bernard, who also harbor literary ambitions, Neville centers his life on his relationship to his art, to the exclusion of most other relationships. This intense purity of focus seems to make the difference in his success as a poet. From the start, Neville is disturbed by mess and disorder, continually noticing Bernard's sloppiness of dress. But Neville's desire for order goes beyond the material realm. For Neville, life itself is a chaotic mess, and only in art and literature is perfection attainable. Neville understands this fact clearly after the death of Percival, whom Neville loves and idealizes. Once Percival is gone, Neville looks to a series of lovers for a temporary replacement for the intense feelings he once got from merely watching Percival. In each case, Neville uses his concentrated if fleeting devotion to the new lover as a source of energy for writing his poetry. In the end, Neville sees that he has spent an entire lifetime devoted to the study of love itself.

If Bernard's problem with language is that it is not large enough to contain reality, Neville's problem is that it is not focused enough to serve his particular needs. Neville's life is one of concentration and exclusion. He shuts the world out from his book-lined room, awaiting only the approach of his latest "one." Neville's need for a focused, polished language to express his meaning is part of the reason for his disdain for Dr. Crane and for conventional religion. For Neville, the headmaster is a pompous fool, mouthing empty phrases, and most religion is little more than a collection of such insincere words. Beyond the platitudes of the sermons he hears, Neville also sees Christianity as a sad, death-obsessed religion and prefers the pagan Greeks and Romans for what he sees as their love of life and pleasure in this world.

RHODA Rhoda is an eternal outsider, even more so than Louis, to whom she is drawn for a time. Our first glimpse of Rhoda is as a child, staring into a basin of water that she imagines is her own private ocean. For Rhoda, the world inside her head is a refuge from the external world of other people. She is terrified of human contact, terrified of being criticized and judged. Her deep sense of alienation from others eventually turns into a desire to abandon consciousness altogether, rather than risk losing her perfect solitude through intimacy with others. Her most characteristic gesture, even among friends, is to stare out the window, lost in imagination. Nothing comes easily to Rhoda, and everything seems foreign—she has to carefully copy the way Jinny and Susan dress to avoid making mistakes. She comes to see herself as a ghostlike, faceless figure, drifting through life without affecting others. She ultimately commits suicide, though it is unclear exactly what occurs. Some of Bernard's comments in the concluding section seem to imply that she leaps from a cliff, perhaps the same one she looks down from earlier in the novel.

Before her tragic end, Rhoda finds some measure of consolation from two sources, the first of which is music. In the wake of Percival's death, Rhoda enters an opera house and is moved by what she hears. Death is both the ultimate disruption of solitude and its ultimate expression, and the music seems, to

Rhoda, like a kind of structure in which she can find temporary shelter. Rhoda is briefly able to find similar solace in her relationship with Louis, but she is unable to maintain the state of intimacy and breaks it off. In the end, Rhoda's greatest desire is simply to cease desiring and existing. She is drawn away from the basin-ocean, in which she has imaginative control, and into the ocean she sees from the cliffs in Spain, which she thinks of in symbolic terms as death itself—a vast ocean of emptiness and stillness that swallows her up.

SUSAN Like Jinny, Susan is a strongly physical presence, and like Rhoda, Susan is at least partially motivated by a desire to lose herself within a larger force. But Susan wishes to engage with life through her body at the primal level of generation and reproduction, and through this process to become one with the growth of the land and of her home. From Susan's perspective, Jinny's life is one of sterile—literally fruitless—activity, while Rhoda tragically resists her body's own desires. Susan walks her fields in the early morning, sensing the awakening life all around her, and Woolf's appreciation of the value and reward of Susan's choice is clear. Susan wants a productive, work-filled life that fosters the land and nurtures others. Through her life on the farm, Susan is seeking to find meaning in ordinary life.

Woolf acknowledges that sacrifice is involved in Susan's life choice. Susan has always been emotional and passionate, either hating or loving (or both at once) most people she meets. As a mother, however, Susan must put others first, and she thinks to herself that her greatest emotions will be for and through her children, and most of her work will be on their behalf. At a certain point, Susan realizes that the price of the fulfillment she has found has been to lose herself within the role of wife and mother, becoming a generic, de-individualized person even in her own eyes. Susan looks back longingly at her youth and her first love, Bernard, whose phrases had always seemed too complex and subtle for her. She thinks continually of Jinny and her comparatively free existence. By the end of the novel, Susan's life is shot through with regret, and she even speaks, to Bernard, of her life as a ruined, wasted thing.

THEMES, MOTIFS, AND SYMBOLS

THEMES

THE INFLUENCE OF THE OTHER ON THE SELF Throughout *The Waves*, the characters struggle to define themselves, which they do through their relationships with others. Bernard articulates this struggle most clearly. He realizes that who he is depends on who surrounds him—his words and thoughts change in relation to his companions. Bernard sees the mind and the self as fluid, with permeable boundaries that enable people to "flow" into one another and essentially create one another. Bernard's understanding of reality connects to this idea of "flow": he sees reality as a product of consciousness. He rejects the idea of an "outer" world of unchanging objects and an "inner" world of the mind and ideas. Rather, our minds are part of the world, and vice versa. For Bernard, if there were no minds to perceive the world and bring it into being, the world would be empty. He applies this idea to the flower on the table during the first dinner party. Since seven people perceive the flower at once, it is a "seven-sided flower." Later, after Percival's death, Bernard thinks that reality itself is diminished by the loss of a consciousness—the flower is now only "six-sided."

All the characters grapple with self-definition in different ways. Neville defines himself in opposition to society's conventions and insincerity and tries to reduce his relationships to intense, pure devotion. Louis is deeply concerned with what others think and tries, with varying success, to shed his provincial self and to create a new, "insider" self. Jinny has a stronger sense of self than the others, and she happily takes her place in London's social world. However, the physical self is for her the most real self, and all interaction is essentially physical. For Susan, a sense of self is rooted in a sense of place as well as in her relations with others, and she submerges her personal identity within the larger "self" of family and nature. Rhoda's sense of self is the most fragile and oppressive. Unlike Jinny, who sees herself as all body, Rhoda feels phantomlike, unable to interact with others without losing all substance. She feels an intolerable pressure from contact with others, which, for Bernard, is the essence of selfhood. In the end, Bernard, who has always worked to overcome the false boundaries we create between selves, has the last word.

THE DESIRE FOR ORDER AND MEANING As the characters struggle to define themselves, they must learn to make sense of the impressions that flash before them and sweep them along. Each character longs for a sense of order and wants to find something lasting in a world of constant change. Louis, Neville, and Bernard have literary ambitions. For Woolf, one of the functions of literature and art in general is to bring order and meaning to the confusion of life. Life itself, as depicted in *The Waves*, is a constant stream of sense-impressions and random events. Art can be a place outside of the flow of time, where our fleeting perceptions can be made permanent and beautiful. Neville approaches his poetry with this goal in mind, and Louis also thinks of his writing as a way to forge an unbreakable link out of the chaos of daily life.

Rhoda's response to the music of the opera hall and Bernard's response to the paintings in the museum suggest that one of the functions of creativity is to bring a sense of peace and solace to life, especially when one is confronted with meaninglessness and death. But Bernard presents a critique of this function of art. He is dissatisfied with the way language and, by extension, all creativity must simplify life in order to give it shape. He rejects the traditional shape of stories, with a beginning, middle, and end, because he believes that such a shape is untrue to the way life is actually lived. In his final "summing up," Bernard says he will not try to fit his life into any kind of overarching plotline. Rather, he will simply trace the events and try to highlight those that are significant as they arise. Meaning will then emerge out of the process of life in its full development, without the imposition of one person's limited point of view. Bernard's method is an obvious reference to Woolf's own method in *The Waves*, and the novel can be seen as her attempt to address Bernard's struggles with language and narrative.

THE ACKNOWLEDGMENT OF DEATH Much of the characters' self-knowledge begins in recognizing their own mortality. Louis and Rhoda, in particular, are aware of loss and emptiness from the beginning, but they all must confront death when Percival is killed in India. Each of the characters must then struggle to incorporate knowledge of death into the structure of their lives, and each follows an individual path with differing success. Death functions as a kind of reality principle in the novel, reminding the characters that their time is not limitless—death is the "enemy" that Bernard sees facing them all by the end. Five of the six characters, in some way or other, make a commitment to life in the face of death: Neville and Louis through art, Susan through the natural world, Jinny through her own physicality, and Bernard through language. Rhoda is the only one who does not commit to life. Bernard is at one pole of the awareness of death, vowing to fight for consciousness and meaning until the end, while Rhoda is at the other, surrendering at last to the pull of oblivion and joining the world of inanimate things.

MOTIFS

STREAM-OF-CONSCIOUSNESS NARRATION In her essay "Modern Fiction," Woolf describes life as "an incessant shower of innumerable atoms," and she says that a modern writer must "record the atoms as they fall upon the mind in the order in which they fall." This idea helps explain the stream-of-consciousness method Woolf uses in *The Waves*. Rather than summarizing for us what the characters see, think, and do, reporting from the outside, or tidying up a character's thoughts into standard, clear sentences, Woolf tries to give the reader an impression of what it is like to be inside the characters' heads. She forces us to sift through a flow of sense impressions, inchoate emotions, and memories, just as the characters themselves are forced to do. In each section from each narrator, we get a combination of thought, sensation, memory, description, action, and speech, and we must separate for ourselves what is purely "internal" and what is a combination of "internal" and "external." Woolf is trying to give a more realistic picture of psychology than had ever before been presented in fiction. Whether she succeeded in presenting accurate psychological portraits through this method, or whether consciousness is in fact anything like "stream-of-consciousness" fiction, is a common point of debate when approaching Woolf's work.

LEITMOTIFS In opera, a leitmotif is a musical phrase or melody that is associated with a particular character—when a character appears or is mentioned, the leitmotif is heard. Woolf makes use of a similar device in *The Waves* to differentiate the characters from one another and to provide an insight into their values and desires. She gives each narrator a set of characteristic phrases or gestures, and the appearance of these "leitmotifs" in various contexts helps us to understand a given character's situation. One example is Jinny's act of lifting her arm in summons to a man. For Jinny, this gesture is the sign of the power she wields by virtue of her beauty. As long as the gesture works, her identity is stable. Another example is the use of the term "making phrases" in relation to Bernard. The term has a different tone depending on who uses it, but it is always meant to evoke the constant stream of language Bernard is capable of pouring forth. Woolf also uses certain types of imagery around certain characters. Water is a leitmotif of Rhoda, history is a leitmotif of Louis, and leaves and growing things are leitmotifs of Susan.

SYMBOLS

THE WAVES When the narrators are children, the first thing they hear in the morning is the sound of waves crashing on the shore. Each of them tries to make sense of the rhythmic pounding—Louis, for example, hears the stamping of a chained beast—and the sound becomes a background noise to their day. As the novel proceeds, the rhythm of the waves becomes associated with the passage of time. Certain characters are more aware of the passage of time than others. Louis is always sensitive to it, and Rhoda saturates her narration with water and wave imagery. Each of the characters has a moment in which he or she is reminded of the passage of time, and the effect is similar to someone who has become used to the sound of the waves at the beach and suddenly hears again the sound that has never ceased and that will continue long after he or she is gone. The novel itself demonstrates this idea of continuity, as it ends just as it begins—with an image of the breaking waves.

"FIN IN A WASTE OF WATERS" On his trip to Rome, Bernard catches a glimpse of the sea from a parapet and sees a porpoise turn quickly in the water. He immediately turns this sense-impression into language: "Fin in a waste of waters" is the phrase he makes. At the time, Bernard simply files the phrase among all the others he has made, but the fin breaking the surface eventually comes to symbolize the way meaning and reality can break the surface of life with no warning. The majority of our waking lives, Bernard comes to feel, is made up of routine, boredom, and automatic actions and words—getting a haircut, traveling to work, and so on make up the "waste of waters." Every now and again, we get a brief glimpse of what is real and lasting, a glimpse of being in and of itself—a hidden purpose in the emptiness of our daily lives. Neville uses a similar image when reading his modernist poem: he compares the poem to a searchlight trained on the waves at night, catching a glimpse of some creature just surfacing. This image clearly works together with the symbolic waves and indicates the understanding Bernard is able to achieve in the face of time and death.

THE APPLE TREE The apple tree Neville is looking at as he overhears the servants at the school discussing a local murder becomes inextricably linked to his knowledge of death. Neville finds himself unable to pass the tree, seeing it as glimmering and lovely, yet sinister and "implacable." When he learns that Percival is dead, he feels he is face to face once again with "the tree which I cannot pass." Eventually, Neville turns away from the natural world to art, which exists outside of time and can therefore transcend death. The fruit of the tree appears only in Neville's room on his embroidered curtain, a symbol itself of nature turned into artifice. The apple tree image also echoes the apple tree from the Book of Genesis in the Bible, the fruit of which led Adam and Eve to knowledge and, therefore, expulsion from Eden. Though Woolf doesn't dwell on this particular connection, the idea of knowing "too much" makes sense in the context of *The Waves*. In a way, Neville yearns for knowledge—of his own self as well as the world—but is uncomfortable with the difficult reality of death.

IMPORTANT QUOTATIONS EXPLAINED

---

1. *I oppose to what is passing this ramrod of beaten steel. I will not submit to this aimless passing of billycock hats and Homburg hats and all the plumed and variegated head-dresses of women . . . and the words that trail drearily without human meaning; I will reduce you to order.*

As Louis sits in the eating-shop in the third section, he watches the people around him, contrasting their lives with the idealized world of the poems he reads. His own poetic project is conceived in terms of resistance, order, and rigidity. He thinks of poetry as a steel ramrod that he will use to straighten out the crookedness of reality. Louis's tone is defiant, almost angry. He refuses to "submit" to the chaos around him and will "reduce" it to order. However, he still desires to include the details of modern life in his art. In contrast, Bernard becomes dissatisfied with stories precisely because they "reduce" life too much, while "reduction," in the sense of the elimination of the ugly or mundane, is the secret of Neville's creativity. Louis, meanwhile, intends to take a ramrod to reality. The human activity he is so captivated with seems like an ocean of chaos; the people are "aimless," and their "dreary" words lack meaning. Louis wants to state the meaning these passersby will never see for themselves.

---

2. *Should I seek out some tree? Should I desert these form rooms and libraries, and the broad yellow page in which I read Catullus, for woods and fields? Should I walk under beech trees, or saunter along the river bank, where the trees meet united like lovers in the water? But nature is too vegetable, too vapid. She has only sublimities and vastitudes and water and leaves. I begin to wish for firelight, privacy, and the limbs of one person.*

Neville asks these questions in the second section, while he is at school. Neville is distancing himself from the natural world and turning toward his own private domain. The problem Neville has with nature is similar to what Louis sees in the city—it is full of disorder and emptiness. Neville longs for both human warmth and for an ideal state of perfection. These two desires are contradictory, of course, but at this point in the novel, Percival is still alive and Neville has yet to learn of the incompatibility of perfection and temporal existence. Another problem Neville sees with nature is simply that it is too big. Neville wants beauty, including harmony, grace, and proportion, rather than sublimity, which is awe-inspiring, forceful, and huge. The perfection Neville seeks is by definition to be found on a smaller, more intimate scale. In Neville's desire for form and organization, we can see the beginnings of his future life of books and seclusion with a chosen lover, as well as his fondness for classical poets and orderliness.

---

3. *Beneath us lie the lights of the herring fleet. The cliffs vanish. Rippling small, rippling grey, innumerable waves spread beneath us. I touch nothing. I see nothing. We may sink and settle on the waves. The sea will drum in my ears. The white petals will be darkened with sea water. They will float for a moment and then sink. Rolling me over the waves will shoulder me under. Everything falls in a tremendous shower, dissolving me.*

In the seventh section, Rhoda travels to Spain, where she has this vision of the ocean from high atop a cliff. The scene is beautiful but ominous, and there is a double meaning to Rhoda's statements about touching and seeing "nothing." That is, what she is seeing and touching in this scene is *nothingness*, non-existence. Rhoda is imagining the dissolution of her body into the larger body of the sea. The symbolic value of the "waves" is clearly active here as well—Rhoda knows she is constantly being dissolved by the passage of time anyway, and she is strongly tempted to give in to the process. As it happens, Rhoda does not give in to the temptation here, but this scene is a kind of harbinger of future events and a portrait of the drift of Rhoda's mind. It also serves as a kind of counterpoint to the scene in which Bernard, also looking down upon the ocean, sees the porpoise break the surface. In his case, meaning and life come welling up from below, while Rhoda imagines herself being sucked under by meaninglessness and death.

---

4. *How tired I am of stories, how tired I am of phrases that come down beautifully with all their feet on the ground! Also, how I distrust neat designs of life that are drawn upon half sheets of notepaper. . . . What delights me . . . is the confusion, the height, the indifference, and the fury. Great clouds always changing, and movement; something sulphurous and sinister, bowled up, helter-skelter; towering, trailing, broken off, lost, and I forgotten, minute, in a ditch. Of story, of design, I do not see a trace then.*

As Bernard begins his "summing up," he expresses again his distrust of stories. As he says, the problem with stories is that they try to squeeze reality into a kind of straightjacket, forcing it into a predetermined shape. Bernard is always interested in what gets left out of the "neat designs of life." For Bernard, stories have trouble accommodating the wild, formless nature of reality—illustrated by the roiling, shifting mass of clouds he sees overhead from his ditch. Bernard's last sentence, which links the words "story" and "design," suggests that he sees neither narrative meaning nor pattern in nature. Implicitly, Bernard is denying the presence of God in the world and saying that whatever meaning is found in the universe has been made by us in the act of trying to comprehend it. Woolf is clearly explaining her own procedure in *The Waves* in this passage. The novel tries to find meaning in human lives while staying true to the shifting, formless nature of reality.

5. *Our friends, how seldom visited, how little known—it is true; and yet, when I meet an unknown person, and try to break off, here at this table, what I call 'my life,' it is not one life that I look back upon; I am not one person; I am many people; I do not altogether know who I am—Jinny, Susan, Neville, Rhoda, or Louis: or how to distinguish my life from theirs.*

Late in the last section, Bernard returns to his idea of the fluidity of identity. For Bernard, all personalities are multiple: we are not self-sufficient, self-created entities. Bernard seems to suggest that we should be both humbled and comforted by the extent to which we have been shaped by others. This idea is key to a kind of ethical dimension in Woolf's writing. If we can see others as connected to ourselves, as part of ourselves, we will be less likely to objectify or exploit others to suit our own desires. By the end of the novel, Bernard is able to put his own desires, and even his own thoughts, to the side and to look upon others with a compassionate detachment born of the certainty that we all share in the same life, and are all journeying toward the same end.

When Heaven and Earth Changed Places

Le Ly Hayslip
(1949–)

CONTEXT

The American-Vietnam War was one of the bloodiest and most unpopular wars in Western history. During World War II, Japan invaded and occupied the then-French colony Vietnam, leading to a period of brutality and unrelenting warfare. The Viet Minh was formed to defend the country against the invading Japanese. After the withdrawal of the Japanese troops at the end of WWII, the Viet Minh turned their fight for an independent nation toward their colonial rulers. From 1946 until 1954, Ho Chi Minh waged a resistance movement with the Viet Minh against the French. After fighting for almost eight years, France decided to leave Vietnam, on the condition that it would be split it into North and South Vietnam at the 17th parallel.

The division of the country worked well in theory: South Vietnam was pro-Western, Catholic like the French, and led by the Western puppet president Diem; in contrast, North Vietnam was communist, Buddhist, and led by Ho Chi Minh. However, the situation was, in fact, much more complex. Much of the country was politically split, and many people changed affiliations during the war.

Starting in the early 1960s, the United States sent troops, money, and supplies to assist South Vietnam. After refusing to hold free elections, the United States removed President Diem from office. During this time, political dissent in the South started to move underground, creating military support in troops known as the Vietnamese Liberation Front, or Viet Cong. The United States sent more troops over the next decade; at one point, over 500,000 troops were present. Despite its military strength, though, the United States was unable to defeat the North Vietnamese forces and Viet Cong. Fighting in an unfamiliar and dense jungle against guerrilla warfare, the military might of the United States was insufficient. The war faced strong opposition at home as well. Although peace talks began in 1968 between North Vietnam and the United States, they were stalled numerous times. In 1973, the United States finally pulled troops out of Vietnam, leaving the country to the Vietnamese Communist Party.

The losses of the war—physical, emotional, financial, and psychological—were enormous. Over 50,000 U.S. troops died, and more than 300,000 were wounded; more than 5 million Vietnamese are estimated to have lost their lives. The war cost the United States over 100 billion dollars and left Vietnam nearly destroyed. During the war, many Vietnamese left the country for other Asian or Western countries, mainly the United States and France. These Vietnamese expatriates, or Viet Ku, were a displaced population. In the 1980s, the North Vietnamese Communist Party allowed Viet Ku back on special visas, hoping to better international opinion of their failing and impoverished nation. Le Ly Hayslip was one of these Viet Ku and documented her experience in the first book of her memoirs, *When Heaven and Earth Changed Places*.

W

Born Phung Thi Le Ly in 1949, Hayslip was the youngest of six children. She spent her childhood and adolescence struggling through two wars. In 1970, she left for the United States with her two children and her American husband. They settled in San Diego. When he died a few years later, she briefly remarried, but her second husband died shortly after their wedding. She was left to raise her three boys alone. Hayslip started The East Meets West Foundation in 1988, a humanitarian relief organization that aims to heal some of the war wounds of all sides involved. The foundation has established health centers and schools in Vietnam and provides emotional treatment for American GIs who were scarred by their experiences in the war.

In 1989, Hayslip began to write *When Heaven and Earth Changed Places* with Jay Wurts. Her book was the culmination of her journey back to her homeland after an absence of seventeen years. The book chronicles her life growing up as a peasant on the central coast of Vietnam, a region geographically and politically torn between North and South Vietnam. Hayslip experienced the war from every side, as a member of the Viet Cong, a war profiteer, and a friend and ally of the American GIs. Her book contained her own personal experiences as well as lessons learned from war—that tolerance and forgiveness are the ways to heal the horrors inflicted from war and can lead to peace. *When Heaven and Earth Changed Places* enjoyed both critical and popular success.

The second book of her memoirs, *Child of War, Woman of Peace,* chronicles her experiences once she arrived in the United States. Hayslip's literary work and humanitarian foundation have attracted the attention of many supporters, including Senator John Kerry, a highly decorated Vietnam veteran turned peace advocate, with whom she built Peace Village, a medical center for children in Vietnam; and filmmaker Oliver Stone, also a Vietnam veteran, who produced and directed a film based on Hayslip's two autobiographies, titled *Heaven and Earth* (1993).

In addition to the East Meets West foundation, Hayslip also founded The Global Village in 1999, which focuses on improving schools and the quality of education for children in Vietnam. Hayslip currently lives in San Diego and continues her humanitarian work related to Vietnam.

PLOT OVERVIEW

The narrator, Le Ly, is the youngest of six children born to peasant farmers in Ka Ly, a town on the central coast of Vietnam. She has a close relationship with her parents, who teach her valuable lessons she carries through her life. From her father, Trong, she learns important Buddhist philosophies that help her make sense of the war; from her mother, Huyen, she learns the love and bonds of family.

Villagers of Ka Ly fight for both sides of the war. Le Ly's own brothers are split between North and South, and many families change sides during the war. By day, the village is under the rule of the Republicans, and at night, under that of the Viet Cong. At first, the Viet Cong's motives for war correspond more closely to the villagers own beliefs and values then those of the South, and consequently, the villagers, including Le Ly, help the Viet Cong. However, Le Ly soon learns the severity of the Viet Cong when she is raped and exiled from the village. Her mother joins her, and they leave to find work in Saigon, while her father remains there to tend to the land of their ancestors.

The bustling city of Saigon is overwhelming and intimidating to Le Ly and her mother. They eventually find employment from a wealthy businessman, Anh, and his family. Le Ly is a governess to his children and a personal maid to his sickly wife; Huyen is a second housekeeper. Le Ly falls in love with Anh and soon becomes pregnant with his child. When she discovers her pregnancy, Le Ly and her mother are thrown out of the house. She returns to Danang, homeless, unemployed, and pregnant. The pregnancy is hard for Le Ly because she lives with her sister Lan and Lan's abusive American boyfriends. When he hears about his daughter's unwed pregnancy, Trong disowns her, but after her son Huang's birth, Trong forgives his beloved daughter. After the birth of her son, Le Ly supports her family by selling souvenirs on the black market. She also secretly visits and cares for her father, who remains in the village. In spite of Le Ly's diligent care, Trong becomes inconsolably disillusioned with the war. He also grows depressed because he is separated from his family. He commits suicide by drinking acid.

Through her positive dealings with Americans—her relationship with her first husband, Ed, and her subsequent boyfriends—and negative experience with the Viet Cong, Le Ly's opinion of "the enemy" changes. After her father's death, Le Ly is no longer confused about where her loyalty should lie. She decides that she will leave Vietnam as soon as possible. Over the next few years, Le Ly works at a hospital and at GI bars. She has many American boyfriends: Red, a nerdy Navy medic who changes her appearance; Jimmy, a Chinese-American civilian contractor becomes a violent drunk; Paul, a U.S. Air Force officer; and Ed Monroe, an elderly civilian contractor. Ed, lonely for companionship, asks Le Ly to marry him. Taken with his kindness and the opportunity to leave Vietnam for the United States, Le Ly accepts. After months of preparation and the birth of her second son, Le Ly leaves her homeland, unsure if she will ever return.

In the 1980s, the Communist Party of Vietnam starts to allow Viet Ku—Vietnamese expatriates—to return to the country. Le Ly is anxious about returning and wary of how her family will receive her. When she arrives in Saigon, Anh greets her warmly. Together they travel to Danang for the reunion with her family. Le Ly realizes that she has returned to a country controlled by fear, more so than when she left. She also realizes that she may be putting her family in danger by returning.

Le Ly is most anxious about her reunion with her eldest brother, Bon Ngh, and her mother. Bon Ngh left for Hanoi when Le Ly was only five, so he is like a stranger to her. He is very suspicious of her motivations for returning and suspects that she is a spy. Over the next few days of her visit, Le Ly slowly convinces her brother that she has returned only to see her family and that she is eager to mend the wounds of the war. Huyen is also cold toward Le Ly at first but gradually warms up to her. During their time together, Huyen shares many stories with Le Ly and gladly accepts all of her gifts.

Le Ly speaks to her brother about setting up a medical center and improving the relationship between the government and the Viet Ku and the rest of the world. She exposes her family to the important lessons that she learned. From her teaching, Huyen mends the strained relationship with her daughter and reunites the whole family. After a tearful goodbye to her mother and sisters, Le Ly leaves Danang with a renewed desire to help her country. On the flight back to Saigon, she catches a glimmer of Ka Ly out the window.

CHARACTER LIST

Le Ly (Hayslip) The narrator. Le Ly is a Vietnamese peasant who grows up on the central coast of Vietnam. She leaves Vietnam in 1970 for the United States with her American husband and two children. In 1986, she returns to Vietnam for the first time to visit her family. The memoir recounts important events of her childhood and adolescence in Vietnam and her experiences on her return journey.

Tran Thi Huyen The mother of six children, including Le Ly. Huyen teaches Le Ly about her duties as a woman in Vietnamese society. Beautiful and hard-working, Huyen marries Trong because they are in love. She is expelled from the village by the Viet Cong and moves with Le Ly to Saigon and Danang. When her daughter returns to Vietnam in 1986, Huyen is the embodiment of the resilient strength of her homeland.

Phong Trong Le Ly's father, with whom she shares a special bond. Trong works as a subsistence rice farmer and is also a devout Buddhist. When all of his children and his wife are forced to leave the village, he remains at their home to tend to their ancestral shrine. Lonely and depressed without his family and broken by war, he commits suicide by drinking acid. His Buddhist philosophies about the nature of war and forgiveness govern Le Ly throughout her life.

Hai Le Ly's eldest sister. Hai's husband leaves to fight with the Viet Cong early in their marriage and is never seen again. She lives in Saigon with her daughter Tinh until her father's death, when she returns to the family home to tend to the land and the family shrine.

Ba Huyen and Phong's second daughter. After Ba's husband leaves for the North, his cousin Chin, a local Republican official, bullies her into marrying him. Ba hoards all of the gifts that Le Ly sends from the United States, causing a rift with the rest of the family. She is accepted back only after Le Ly convinces her mother of the importance of forgiveness.

Bon Nghe Le Ly's eldest brother. Bon Nghe is Huyen's favorite child. He spends the duration of the war fighting with the Viet Cong and becomes a Communist Party official after the war. He later settles with his wife and son in Danang. Bon Nghe has the greatest number of reservations about Le Ly's return visit to Vietnam, but after discussing her intentions, they are able to find a common ground.

W

Lan The fourth child in the family. Lan moves to Danang, where she works in bars as a tea girl and has many American boyfriends. Le Ly lives with her while pregnant with her first child, and Lan treats her poorly until Le Ly saves her from a boyfriend's drunken attack. Lan immigrates to the United States after Le Ly does.

Sau Ban The second youngest child. Sau Ban is artistic and caring, and he is Le Ly's closest friend and playmate when they are young. Soon after his marriage, he is drafted into the Republican forces, despite numerous attempts to join the Viet Cong. After months of no contact with his family, he is presumed dead, although Le Ly never gives up hope of finding him.

Bac Lac Hai's husband. Bac Lac goes to Hanoi at the beginning of the war and never returns.

Tinh Daughter of Hai and Bac Lac, Tinh is Le Ly's niece. Tinh warmly accepts her into her home for her homecoming.

Bien Tinh's husband. Bien is a kind man who helps Le Ly reunite with her family in Danang.

Anh A wealthy businessman for whom Le Ly and her mother work in Saigon. Anh and Le Ly fall in love and have a child. He keeps in touch with her after her move to the United States and acts as her guide when she returns to Vietnam. His relationship with Le Ly is one of deep, familial love, and he seems to regret not being more of a part of her life.

Lien Anh's first wife. Lien is wealthy but in very poor health. Le Ly acts as her personal maid but Lien throws Le Ly out when she discovers that Le Ly is carrying Anh's child.

Yen Anh's second wife. Yen warmly welcomes Le Ly to their home when she returns to Saigon.

Jimmy (Huang) Le Ly's oldest son, fathered by Anh. Jimmy is raised by his grandmother while Le Ly works in the souvenir trade business in Danang. When Le Ly returns to Vietnam, Jimmy is attending college. Jimmy and his brothers do not want their mother to return to her homeland.

Tommy Le Ly's middle child, fathered by Ed Monroe. Tommy is born in Danang a few months before Le Ly leaves for the United States.

Alan Le Ly's youngest child. Alan is born in the United States. Being the youngest of the brothers, Alan is the most worried about his mother's journey to Vietnam.

Per The Norwegian in the UN employ. Per helps Le Ly by giving her information and support on her way from the Philippines to Vietnam on her return journey.

Uncle Luc A relative of Le Ly's family. Uncle Luc lives in Ka Ly and is an original supporter of the Viet Cong. He helps Le Ly and her family out of trouble many times.

Aunt Thu Huyen's aunt, who helps raise her after Huyen's parents dies. Thu dies during a French-led bomb attack.

Loi A member of the local Viet Cong. Loi tortures and rapes Le Ly instead of killing her as he had been instructed.

Mau A member of the local Viet Cong. Mau also tortures and rapes Le Ly.

Greg (Red) Le Ly's first American boyfriend. Red is a nerdy medical technician in the hospital where Le Ly works. He convinces Le Ly to change her peasant appearance into a sexier city one, quit her job, and work as a dancer in a club. However, after discovering that the club is topless, Le Ly walks out on Red and his job offer.

Jimmy A half-Chinese, half-Irish-American civilian contractor who dates and lives with Le Ly. An angry and abusive drunk, Jimmy is removed from Saigon after Le Ly places a complaint with the local MPs.

Paul The Air force officer who dates and lives with Le Ly. Paul is a Texan, and he and Le Ly share similar views about the importance of land and family. He leaves without notice and is reassigned to the United States.

Big Mike A GI who works on one of the bases. Mike is friendly toward Le Ly. One day, he pimps her to two GIs for $400.

Ed Monroe An older American who approaches Le Ly, looking for companionship. Ed is sweet and caring and asks Le Ly to marry him and accompany him to the United States. They emigrate shortly thereafter.

Sister Hoa A black-market profiteer whom Le Ly pays to get her birth certificate and other papers in order to leave the country.

Cou Loi A wealthy man from Bai Gian. Cou Loi is a family friend. After the attacks on his village, Cou Loi and his family are made homeless beggars. Cou Loi is representative of many who lost everything in the war.

Thien Cou Loi's daughter and Le Ly's friend. Thien is tortured incessantly by the Viet Cong and eventually disappears.

Bich A Ka Ly village girl who is one of the first to go to Saigon and report back on the wonders of the city. Bich teaches Le Ly about make-up, high heels, and electricity.

Nham Sau Ban's wife. Nham and Sau Ban are married shortly before Sau Ban is forced into the Republican guard. When he is presumed dead, she returns to her family. Nham is representative of many young Vietnamese women left without husbands due to the war.

Tuan The chauffeur during Le Ly's state-sponsored tour of the countryside. At first he is reserved toward Le Ly, but eventually he opens up and shares his real thoughts on the situation in Vietnam.

ANALYSIS OF MAJOR CHARACTERS

LE LY HAYSLIP Having been a Viet Cong spy, a servant, a black marketer, a teenage single mother, and an expatriate, Le Ly is, above all, a survivor. She does whatever necessary to survive through the war and its atrocities. In this way, she is an embodiment of her country: forced by war into extreme and unusual circumstances, she perseveres in any way she can. The war has left her with a mix of traditions and thoughts; she values her father's Buddhism, as well as his emphasis on family, but she has left her ancestral home for a better life abroad. On her return to Vietnam, she quenches her homesickness for Vietnamese food but continues to dress in Western style. This combination of East and West in Le Ly is representative of how the war altered many people, displacing their values and changing their perspectives.

In addition to being representative of the generation affected by the war, Le Ly is also a messenger of peace. Throughout her memoir, Le Ly conveys the most important lessons she has learned from the war: forgiveness is the way to mend the hurt that was inflicted on all sides involved in the war, family is the most important thing in life, and all sides, the Vietnamese and the Western world, need to work together to bring life and hope back into her homeland. She wants these lessons to be a prescriptive to all of those affected by and hurt from the war. Le Ly returns to Vietnam in part to help mend what the war had destroyed in her country and in her family. Her memoirs are an extension of this healing journey, administering peace as an antidote to war and forgiveness as an antidote to hate.

HUYEN (MOTHER) Huyen, Le Ly's mother, represents the Vietnamese peasantry, closely adhering to its traditions and social code. Throughout her life, she works hard raising her family and caring for their land. She embraces the Viet Cong, even after her own near-execution and subsequent exile. When Le Ly returns from the United States, she is greeted rather coldly by her mother, who gradually accepts her again, as Vietnam gradually re-embraces the West. Huyen remains suspicious of Le Ly and her Western ways, and Huyen chooses to sleep on the floor at the hotel and generally to continue her traditional peasant way of life. Yet she does not reject Le Ly and what she has come to stand for; in fact, she eagerly accepts gifts from Le Ly on numerous occasions. Huyen is centered between the two ideological poles of her children—a Communist official son and an Americanized daughter. She still believes in the idea of a Communist and independent Vietnam but eagerly accepts the benefits of the Western world. Most Vietnamese, like Huyen, remain somewhere in the middle.

W

Huyen also represents the Vietnamese people in her slow but eventual ability to learn to forgive. From Le Ly, Huyen is reminded of the healing power and goodness of forgiveness, and is thus able to forgive her daughter, Ba, which reunites the family one last time. In a broader sense, Le Ly aims to convey this lesson to the Vietnamese in general. Through forgiveness, healing and much-needed reunification are possible.

TRONG (FATHER) A kind and gentle man and devout Buddhist, Trong is a stable and spiritual presence in Le Ly's life. Trong represents the disappearing Vietnamese culture based on the importance of family, land, and peace. In this tradition, he imparts three important lessons on Le Ly. First, he advises his daughter that the best way in which she can fight and be a woman warrior is by being a mother and creating her own family. Second, he teachers her that war is the enemy—not a particular side or ideology. Throughout the atrocities, Trong continues to try to believe in the goodness of his fellow man. Men do terrible things because of the terrible situation of war. Third is the power of forgiveness. His philosophy on war enables Le Ly to forgive those who have wronged her because of the war. Although he advocates the power of forgiveness, Trong ultimately is not as strong as his daughter. Unable to cope with the war and its ramifications on the Vietnamese way of life, Trong kills himself. His suicide is symbolic of the larger death of the traditional way of life of the Vietnamese people, destroyed by war and the modern ideologies of capitalism and communism. Yet, the important parts of this tradition survive in Le Ly, and in turn to all the people she is able to reach through her book.

ANH A wealthy businessman with a large household, Anh represents the capitalist class in Vietnam; the change in him represents the change in this class due to the war. Although Anh was not initially as affected by the war as the peasant villagers, the war finally bankrupted him, and the Communists repossessed his home and business. After the war, he divorced his wife and remarried, changing from an elegant and expensive wife to a more communist and proletariat one. Le Ly returns to Saigon to find him no longer living in a palatial estate but in an impoverished neighborhood, no longer owning his own business, but working for a government factory. Although Anh never fully embraces Communism, he accepts it and lives with it, but like Le Ly, he does what he needs to do in order to survive.

The relationship between Anh and Le Ly is also symbolic of the relationship between Vietnam and the United States. Starting as a dangerous yet passionate affair, they grew apart, yet they are always connected by what they share: their son and their common suffering from the war. Over the years, their relationship changes from lovers to siblings. Just as all those involved—Anh and Le Ly, Americans and Vietnamese, businessmen, and village girls—are forever connected by common experience, so are the two countries as siblings of war.

THEMES, MOTIFS, AND SYMBOLS

THEMES

THE ENEMY IN WAR IS WAR ITSELF From the beginning of the hostilities, Le Ly's father tells her that the only true enemy is the war itself. During her experience in the war, Le Ly fights and befriends both the Americans and the Viet Cong. She suffers brutalities from many different fronts: cruel punishment from Republican guards, rape and near death from the Viet Cong, and brutality and degradation from American GIs. She also has positive experiences with all sides, making it difficult for her to determine who was the enemy. With her father's death, Le Ly begins to truly understand this. By comprehending that war is the enemy, Le Ly is able to forgive those who wrong her and to heal her own war wounds. Her perspective of the war leaves her hopeful and strong, and although she never forgets the atrocities that took place, she is able to forgive and find peace in her own life.

THE IMPORTANCE OF FAMILY BONDS Le Ly's relationships with her family—especially her mother and father—inform her beliefs throughout the war and beyond. She and her sisters take care of each other in many ways. Even though there are problems between family members—Ba and Huyen have differences over the gifts, Le Ly and Sau Ban over ideology—the family remains connected. Seeking to reestablish this connection with her family, Le Ly returns to her homeland after an absence of seventeen years. The result of her journey is her discovery that despite war wounds and different life paths, the strength and bond of family is unshakable. The war separates and displaces many families and disconnects people from their ancestors, but at the end, Le Ly finds a deeper connection with her family and draws strength from it.

WAR'S EFFECT ON IDENTITY Le Ly's identity transforms numerous times due to the war: from daughter to mother, dependent to provider, country to city girl, Viet Cong spy to black market profiteer. Her father changes from a strong father of six to a single man living alone. Ultimately, he kills himself because he cannot handle this change. Rich men become beggars in the village. Many lose their homes, their farms, their children, and their lives. Farmers become soldiers and children become spies. On her return to Vietnam, Le Ly sees the continuation of the changes: Anh transforms from a rich business man to an impoverished worker, her sisters changes from proud farmers into market vendors, and her brother changes from a friend into a suspicious stranger.

MOTIFS

MISTREATMENT BY MEN The mistreatment of women by men is one of the byproducts of the total abuse of war. Throughout her life, Le Ly is abused by men. As a teenager, she is tortured and raped by two former friends and Viet Cong members. In Saigon, she is assaulted by a family friend and some boys on the street. During her time in Danang, Le Ly has many American boyfriends, all of whom treat her poorly. Even her loving relationship with Anh becomes bitter when he abandons her. Le Ly is not alone in such abuse, as there are many other examples of rape, forced prostitution, and abuse toward women.

Single mothers are left to care for families, and young girls are forced into prostitution, all versions of the woman warrior fighting in her own way. Yet Le Ly is able to forgive those who abused and harmed her, believing that the war forced people to do horrible things.

BUDDHIST TRADITION At the beginning of the war, Le Ly notes that the Communists told the villagers that they are fighting in order to preserve their Buddhist traditions from the Catholic republicans and foreigners. These traditions—respecting the land and worshipping one's ancestors—are cornerstones to the villagers' way of life. Trong best represents the connection of the villagers to the Buddhist tradition. However, as the war progresses, the Viet Cong makes it harder for the villagers to practice their traditions. The reasons for fighting change and people desert traditions. Despite this, Le Ly returns again and again to her Buddhist traditions, mainly through the advice and teachings of her father. The rituals and rites of Buddhism continue throughout Le Ly's life and help support her during the war, as well as show her a way to cope with the horrors around her.

FAMILY NETWORK Throughout her life in Vietnam, Le Ly is connected to and supported by her family. Relatives connected to either the Republican or Communist side help her out of jail; her sisters find her jobs and give her a place to live; her parents provide and care for her. In turn, she cares for and supports her family members when she can. However, the war erodes these familial networks, making family members unable or unwilling to help each other, and infusing fear and mistrust in the family unit. When Le Ly returns to Vietnam, she sees how this mistrust had found a place in her family between herself and her brother, and between her mother and Ba. Still, Le Ly promotes building trust where it had been destroyed. On a small scale, she rebuilds the trust within her own family. On a larger scale, she hopes to re-establish the trust between Vietnam and the United States so that everyone can finally heal from the war.

SYMBOLS

THE ELEPHANT AND THE ANT Le Ly often compares the brute strength and sheer force of the American military to an elephant, and the stealthier, more secretive Viet Cong to ants. While the elephant may stamp about on the ground, destroying everything, the ants will hide underground and wait to attack. The ants, although small, are able to defeat the elephant. Despite its technological advancements and brute strength, the United States was unable to defeat the North Vietnamese forces and the Viet Cong. One reason for this is because the Viet Cong were using guerrilla tactics. They built intricate underground hideouts and used a network of villagers and children to supply them. The symbols of the elephant and ant represent the United States's misunderstanding of the type of war In which they were involved, similar to an elephant using the wrong tactics. This symbol also represents the sense of unity of the Vietnamese. Alone, they feel small and defenseless, but together—as promised by the Viet Cong—they feel strong. This mentality of community strength is important in unifying a nation under a Communist ideology.

RICE Rice is an essential crop for the Vietnamese people. Rice connects the people to the land and to the past, but during the war, the rice paddies became war zones. They no longer produced life-giving rice but instead death and destruction, symbolic of the Vietnamese people and their way of life. Le Ly explains the difficult nature of rice through a legend in which God intended rice to grow easily everywhere and grass to need a lot of care and planning. However, the messenger who brought rice and grass to Earth mistakenly switched the two, making rice a labor-intensive crop and grass a ubiquitous plant. As punishment, the messenger is turned into a beetle and made to crawl through grass for eternity. Le Ly's whole family helps in the planting, growing, harvesting and preparation of rice. From a young age, Le Ly helps her mother in their rice paddies and it was in these paddies that many important events in her life take place. In the rice paddies, her mother and father both teach her important life lessons and stories of their ancestors.

WOMAN WARRIOR As a young girl, Le Ly idolizes the legendary female warrior in the stories her father told her. She professes that she too would like to be a warrior, fighting for her country. This desire leads to her involvement with the Viet Cong and, after her exile from the village, her anger and unrest at being unable to fight. The image of the strong female warrior stays with Le Ly through her experiences in

Saigon and Danang; in fact, memories of this image encourage her to become involved with the war. However, from the moment that he tells his young daughter the fable of the woman warrior, Trong laughs at Le Ly's insistence that she can be a woman warrior. Trong tells her that her purpose in this life is not to fight: it is to have a family and raise children to carry on the family traditions.

Trong later reiterates this idea when Le Ly again feels anxious to fight. Trong reminds her that Vietnam does not need more people who are ready to fight; rather, it needs people who are willing to live, to find peace and continue the traditions of land and family. Le Ly eventually comes to understand her father's words. However, she does not give up the image of the woman warrior, but rather, becomes a woman warrior in her own way: instead of fighting with guns and bombs, she fights war with ideas of peace, hate with forgiveness, death of too many civilians and soldiers with the lives of her children. Le Ly reinvents the image of the woman warrior and transforms herself into one.

IMPORTANT QUOTATIONS EXPLAINED

---

1. *The special gift of suffering, I have learned, is how to be strong while we are weak, how to be brave when we are afraid, how to be wise in the midst of confusion, and how to let go of that which we can no longer hold. In this way, anger can teach us forgiveness, hate can teach us love, and war can teach us peace.*

In the Prologue, Le Ly outlines her intention of writing a memoir about growing up in Vietnam during the war. Through her experience in Vietnam, she sees that the war and its atrocities wound people physically and emotionally. The war leaves many people in Vietnam and the United States angry, confused, and at a loss for meaning. Her experience and world view help her create meaning from the awful atrocities she endured. This outlook enables Le Ly to find a positive outcome from the negative experiences of war. Her pregnancy, although difficult because she is young and alone, makes her realize that family is more important than fighting. She loses many things during the war—her home, her beloved brother, the father of her child, and her childhood— but she learns to live for the future and for her children. In doing so, she is able to avoid growing burdened by the past. She is able to find a new life in the homeland of the aggressors who attack her village, and find a friendship with her brother, who works for the government that tried to kill her.

Not all of the characters are able to extract such meaning from the war. Upon returning to Vietnam, Le Ly is amazed to see the transformation of her countrymen from generous to petty, and even more shocked to see such behavior in her own family. Leading by her own example of forgiveness, Le Ly is able to influence her mother to forgive Ba. This is a small start to the larger project of mending the hurt inflicted by the war. Her perspective on war is a prescription for others who suffer from the war; it is a recipe for peace and healing.

---

2. "*No,*" *my father replied sadly,* "*don't hate Chin - and don't hate Ba for marrying him. Hate the war for doing what it did to them both.*"

This quotation occurs in Chapter 6, when Trong comforts an enraged Le Ly with these words. The husband of Le Ly's older sister, Ba, leaves for Hanoi to train and enlist with the Viet Cong. During his absence, his cousin Chin starts to make inappropriate advances toward Ba. Chin, being a Republican official, is able to abuse his office and position as a way to spend time with Ba. After threatening her with imprisonment, Ba agrees to marry him and forget her first husband.

Although he is explicitly discussing his daughter's unfortunate situation, Trong's words apply to all of the people affected by the war. For Trong, there is no right side and no wrong side; the enemy is not the Americans or the Republicans or the Viet Cong. The enemy is always war. His perception of the war is rooted in his strong Buddhist beliefs that the purpose of life is to care for your family, your land, and the memories of your ancestors. War is antagonistic to this way of life. This is one of the most valuable lessons that Le Ly's father taught her. War is the villain that made neighbors report on each other, made soldiers kill children, made wives abandon their husbands and children their parents. By understanding that wars—not people—are the enemy, Le Ly is able to forgive those who wronged her and to find peace in her life.

3. *"My little peach blossom - haven't you learned yet that fate or luck or god works in its own way, and reveals its secrets in its own time? When has it ever paid you to turn your face from life? Keep your faith, Bay Ly: Look those deepest, darkest, most terrible fears in the face and learn the lessons they've come to teach -"*

In Chapter 6, upon arriving in Danang, Le Ly settles into her hotel and her thoughts turn to the worst. She imagines that her mother had already died, that her brother and sisters will not see her, and that the Communist government is waiting to imprison her. She then hears her father's voice, which soothes her. Le Ly often returns to her father's words and philosophy for support and guidance. Trong is the most devoutly religious Buddhist in Le Ly's life and his belief system—that wars, not people, are the enemy—is what she ultimately accepts as her own way to deal with living through hardships. Her father's words give Le Ly strength when she is unsure and help her look at her own life and realize her own strength. Having already survived years of war, escape, and life in a new country, she knows that she would be able to face her family and whatever was in store for her in her homeland. Her father's words also imply that she should let fate guide her if she is open to it.

Le Ly is soothed by these words that she attributes to her father, but they have also become her own words. She has already taken the advice of learning from her hardships and difficult experiences and turning those lessons into something positive. She has put this advice into practice: returning to her homeland to mend her internal pain and that of her family, writing a memoir in order to explain and illuminate her and other's experiences of war, and planning to become more involved in rebuilding the ties between Vietnam and the United States.

---

4. *Vietnam already had too many people who were ready to die for their beliefs. What it needed was men and women - brothers and sisters - who refused to accept either death or death-dealing as a solution to their problems. If you keep compassion in your heart, I discovered, I discovered, you never long for death yourself. From my father's death, I had finally learned how to live.*

This passage appears in Chapter 7. Trong tells Le Ly legends of famous Vietnamese women warriors when she is a young girl. As a child, Le Ly wants to be a warrior, to fight like men, giving up their lives for a cause. However, her father tells her that her role is far greater: to have children and care for them as a mother, teaching them about their ancestors, the land, and peace. Despite her father's philosophy, Le Ly feels that her role is to fight alongside the Viet Cong. After her expulsion from her village and from the Viet Cong, she is confused about her purpose. The entire country, including her family and friends, is caught up in war and she believed that it is her duty to fight.

Yet her father's death brings her an inner peace and understanding about her role in life; it marks a turning point for Le Ly. She starts appreciating what she has and works hard to get out of Vietnam. Her outlook shifts from feeling hopeless to feeling like a warrior who would overcome the hardships, protect her children, and survive. Fighting, politics, and honor were no longer important. Her duty is to her son, to her family, and to preserving them for the future. Her anger toward the Viet Cong and the village that expelled her, toward her rapists, toward the man she loved who abandoned her, and toward the drunken GIs, all dissipate. Her father's philosophy helps her see that these people were not the enemy: their fear and hatred brought on by war was the enemy. When she comes understand her father's view of humanity, she is able to forgive all sides for their atrocities during the war. This philosophy—war, not people, is the enemy—is the backbone for her mission to heal the wounds caused by the war to all involved. Her memoir is her forgiveness in action, a return to the war-torn country in an attempt to start to mend some of the damage done.

5. *Like they say, Mot cau mhin, chin car lanh (One word of forgiveness brings back nine gentle favors).*

This passage, from Chapter 14, is a village saying that is rooted in Buddhism. Le Ly, despite the places that she traveled and the roles in life that she fulfilled, remained at heart a peasant girl from a rich Buddhist tradition. Her roots in this tradition help her find the guidance and methods in order to make sense of the war and what the war does to her family. This saying is anchored in Buddhist thought. It demonstrates the central and ongoing importance of family and ancestral tradition to Le Ly's life and work. Forgiveness, an important theme in her life, is a lesson learned from the war. For Le Ly, the only way in which to overcome the horrors of the war and to find peace is through forgiveness. She demonstrates this adage in her own life. When she is touring the countryside with the icy Communist Party inspectors, Le Ly forgives them their treatment of her and buys them a special lunch. In return for this act of forgiveness and kindness, the officers share with her many anecdotes and real stories of what happened to her homeland in her absence. Another example is her forgiveness of Anh for his abandonment of her and their child. In return, he becomes a trusted and true friend, helping her many years later. Her examples and attitude of forgiveness prompt her mother to act in kind, and she forgives Ba for hoarding all of the gifts that Le Ly sent from the United States. In addition, her goal in writing her memoir of the war is to teach to a larger audience the lessons of forgiveness and, by doing so, help mend the war wounds of two nations.

Wide Sargasso Sea

Jean Rhys
(1890–1979)

CONTEXT

Jean Rhys was born in Dominica, one of the Windward Islands in the Caribbean, in 1890. The daughter of a Welsh doctor and a white Creole mother, Rhys grew up in the final days of England's colonial heyday, a time that witnessed the waning of an aristocratic and exploitative Creole culture. Her parents' heritage situated Rhys between two competing ideologies—one that sought to exoticize Caribbean life and one that incorporated the racial pluralism of West Indian values. Rhys was further influenced by the black servants who raised her and introduced her to the language, customs, and religious beliefs of the native Caribbeans.

While *Wide Sargasso Sea* reflects the distinct sensibilities of a West Indian writer, it also bears the stamp of European modernism. At sixteen, Rhys left her home in Dominica and moved to England, aligning herself more closely with her father's Welsh heritage. A feeling of displacement that characterizes both Rhys's own life and the lives of her characters left her unable to root herself to her ancestors' home.

Throughout the 1920s, Rhys traveled in Europe as a bohemian artist, living sporadically in Paris, where she became familiar with the innovative works of modern artists and writers. This period of wandering placed Rhys on the outskirts of conventional society. Thus marginalized, she began to question the codes and traditions of the male-dominated urban environment. Plagued by poverty, illness, and alcoholism, she felt firsthand the psychological and physical toll of being a single woman in a patriarchal culture—a theme she explores in much of her writing.

Rhys's first four novels—*Postures or Quartet* (1928), *After Leaving Mr. Mackenzie* (1930), *Voyage in the Dark* (1934), and *Good Morning Midnight* (1939)—mirror her own life, with heroines who lead drifting, alienated lives as stigmatized outsiders. While these early novels met with some success, they never went far in establishing Rhys as a leading European modernist.

With some reluctance, Rhys settled down in England, a country for which she felt little fondness. She more or less disappeared from the literary scene until the 1960s, when her work was rescued from obscurity. The 1966 publication of *Wide Sargasso Sea*, twenty-seven years after the appearance of her last novel, reflects the culmination of her earlier heroine sketches, while shifting focus away from an industrial European context and back to a nineteenth-century Caribbean landscape.

W

When Rhys read Charlotte Brontë's *Jane Eyre* as a young girl, she began to imagine the Caribbean upbringing of the character Rochester's infamous Creole wife, Bertha Mason. Years later, Rhys recalled, "I thought I'd try to write her a life." The result is one of literature's most famous prequels, a novel that seeks to humanize the racially pejorative characterization of a West Indian madwoman. An aesthetic experiment in modernist techniques and a powerful example of feminist rewriting, *Wide Sargasso Sea* gives voice to a marginalized character and transforms her original tragic demise into a kind of triumphant heroism.

As a West Indian writer, Rhys seeks to uncover an alternate truth, exposing the limits of a literary canon that assumes a shared white heritage in its audience. She writes this conflict into the very dialogue of her novel, creating, in the characterization of Mr. Mason, an unflattering picture of patriarchal entitlement. When Annette describes her sister's marital problems—specifically her husband's tyrannical behavior—Mr. Mason responds coldly "That's her story. I don't believe it." He effectively silences the Creole woman's voice. Rhys aims to restore this voice with her text. She intended *Wide Sargasso Sea* to stand on its own, apart from Brontë's novel, as a challenge to the canon.

If Rhys's novel breaks thematic conventions by foregrounding the story of Antoinette/Bertha, it also innovates stylistically, adopting narrative, temporal, and aesthetic schemes that reflect a cultural and racial pluralism. Entrenched in the literary concerns of the mid-twentieth century, *Wide Sargasso Sea* features a web of symbols and images that underlies its dreamlike plot and informs its feverish snatches of dialogue. Delving into the psyche of her principal characters, Rhys examines their fragmented identities and unconscious fears, focusing on an inner world that mirrors the impressions of an evocative physical landscape. The tripartite structure of the novel, with its shifts in narrative voice and jumps through time and space, affords the book a complex, porous surface that differs markedly from the linear progression found in its nineteenth-century counterpart. Championed by postcolonial, feminist, and modernist critics alike, *Wide Sargasso Sea* struggles against dominant traditions and espouses the cause of the underrepresented.

Wide Sargasso Sea has generated heated debate among these literary critics, resisting easy categorization within the context of twentieth-century fiction. As a postcolonial work, the novel indicts England's exploitative colonial empire, aligning its sympathies with the plight of the black Caribbeans. However, Rhys's narrator—a white Creole—remains a step removed from racial oppression and struggles primarily against the dictates of patriarchy. For this reason, the character is a touchstone for feminist theorists. That *Wide Sargasso Sea* is a rewriting of *Jane Eyre*—a text long upheld as a triumph of feminist liberalism—complicates the feminist debate. Rhys's text also invites psychoanalytic readings, through its experimentation with narrative and exploration of the unconscious. In its formal techniques and thematic sources, Rhys's novel incorporates modern and postmodern devices of fragmentation, while drawing, at times, on Romantic notions of sublimity, passion, and the supernatural.

PLOT OVERVIEW

Antoinette's story begins when she is a young girl in early nineteenth-century Jamaica. The white daughter of ex-slave owners, she lives on a run-down plantation called Coulibri Estate. Five years have passed since her father, Mr. Cosway, reportedly drank himself to death, his finances in ruins after the passage of the Emancipation Act of 1833, which freed black slaves and led to the demise of many white slave owners. Throughout Antoinette's childhood, hostility flares between the crumbling white aristocracy and the impoverished servants they employ.

As a young girl, Antoinette lives at Coulibri Estate with her widowed mother, Annette, her sickly younger brother, Pierre, and gossiping servants who seem particularly attuned to their employers' misfortune and social disrepute. Antoinette spends her days in isolation. Her mother, a beautiful young woman who is ostracized by the Jamaican elite, spends little time with her, choosing to pace listlessly on the house's glacis (the covered balcony) instead of nurturing her child. Antoinette's only companion, Tia, the daughter of a servant, turns against her unexpectedly.

One day, Antoinette is surprised to find a group of elegant visitors calling on her mother from Spanish Town, the island's version of a sophisticated metropolis. Among them is an English man named Mr. Mason who, after a short courtship, asks for Annette's hand in marriage. When Mr. Mason and Annette honeymoon in Trinidad, Antoinette and Pierre stay with their Aunt Cora in Spanish Town. In the interim, Mr. Mason has had the estate repaired and restored to it to its former grandeur, and has bought new servants. Discontent, however, is rising among the freed blacks, who protest one night outside the house. Bearing torches, they accidentally set the house on fire, and Pierre is badly hurt. As the family flees the house, Antoinette runs desperately towards Tia and her mother. Tia throws a jagged rock at Antoinette, cutting her forehead and drawing blood.

The events of the night leave Antoinette dangerously ill for six weeks. She wakes to find herself in Aunt Cora's care. Pierre has died. Annette's madness, which has revealed itself gradually over the years, has fully surfaced after the trauma of the fire. When Antoinette visits her mother, who has been placed in the care of a black couple, she hardly recognizes the ghostlike figure she encounters. When Antoinette approaches, Annette violently flings her away.

Antoinette then enrolls in convent school along with other young Creole girls. For several years, she lives at the school with the nuns, learning everything from proper ladylike deportment to the tortured histories of female saints. Antoinette's family has all but deserted her: Aunt Cora has moved to England for a year, while Mr. Mason travels for months away from Jamaica, visiting only occasionally.

When Antoinette is seventeen, Mr. Mason announces on his visit that friends from England will be coming the following winter. He means to present Antoinette into society as a cultivated woman, fit for marriage. At this point, the end of Part One, Antoinette's narration becomes increasingly muddled, jumping from present-tense descriptions of her life in the convent to muddled recollections of past events.

Antoinette's husband, an Englishman who remains nameless, narrates Part Two. After a wedding ceremony in Spanish Town, he and Antoinette honeymoon on one of the Windward Islands, at an estate that once belonged to Antoinette's mother. He begins to have misgivings about the marriage as they approach a town ominously called Massacre. He knows little of his new wife, having agreed to marry her days before, when Mr. Mason's son, Richard Mason, offered him £30,000 if he proposed. Desperate for money, he agreed to the marriage.

When the couple arrives at Granbois, Antoinette's inherited estate, the man feels increasingly uncomfortable around the servants and his strange young wife. Hostility grows between the man and Christophine, Antoinette's surrogate mother and a servant who wields great power in the house. The man soon receives a menacing letter from Daniel Cosway, one of old Cosway's illegitimate children. Venomous in tone, letter warns of Antoinette's depravity, saying that she comes from a family of derelicts and has madness in her blood. After reading this letter, the man begins to detect signs of Antoinette's insanity.

Antoinette, sensing that her husband hates her, asks Christophine for a magic love potion. Christophine grudgingly agrees. That night, when the man confronts Antoinette about her past, they argue passionately. He awakes the next morning believing he has been poisoned, and he later sleeps with the servant girl, Amelie, who helps him recover. Sitting in the next room, Antoinette hears everything. The next morning, Antoinette leaves for Christophine's. When she returns, she seems to be totally mad. Drunk and raving, she pleads with the man to stop calling her "Bertha," a name he has given her without explanation. Antoinette then bites her husband's arm, drawing blood. After she collapses and falls in bed, Christophine rails at him for his cruelty. That night, he decides to leave Jamaica with Antoinette.

Antoinette narrates Part Three from England, where she is locked away in a garret room in her husband's house, under the watch of a servant, Grace Poole. A hidden captive, Antoinette has no sense of time or place; she does not even believe she is in England when Grace tells her so. Violent and frenzied, Antoinette draws a knife on her stepbrother, Richard Mason, when he visits her. Later she has no memory of the incident. Antoinette has a recurring dream about taking Grace's keys and exploring the house's downstairs quarters. In this dream, she lights candles and sets the house ablaze. One night, she wakes from this dream and feels she must act on it. The novel ends with Antoinette holding a candle and walking down from her upstairs prison.

CHARACTER LIST

Antoinette The daughter of ex-slave owners and the story's principal character, based on the madwoman Bertha from Charlotte Brontë's gothic novel *Jane Eyre*. Antoinette is a sensitive and lonely young Creole girl who grows up with neither her mother's love nor her peers' companionship. In a convent school as a young woman, Antoinette becomes increasingly introspective and isolated, showing the early signs of her inherited emotional fragility. Her arranged marriage to an unsympathetic and controlling English gentleman exacerbates her condition and pushes her to fits of violence. Eventually her husband brings her to England and locks her in his attic, assigning a servant woman to watch over her. Delusional and paranoid, Antoinette awakes from a vivid dream and sets out to burn down the house.

Annette Antoinette's young and beautiful mother. Annette is the second wife first to Alexander Cosway and later to Mr. Mason. The white Jamaican women ostracize Annette because of her beauty and outsider status—she is originally from Martinique. A disembodied presence throughout the book, Annette shows signs of madness and melancholy in her daughter's earliest recollections. Often the subject of gossip, she feels abandoned, scared, and persecuted. After the fire, Mr. Mason leaves Annette in the care of a black couple who reportedly humiliate her and mock her condition. Annette dies when Antoinette is at the convent school.

Rochester Antoinette's English husband who, though never named in the novel, narrates at least a third of the story. Rochester, the youngest son of a wealthy Englishman, travels to the West Indies for financial independence, as his older brother will inherit his father's estate. When Rochester arrives in Spanish Town he comes down with a fever almost immediately. He is pressured into marrying Antoinette, although he has only just met her and knows nothing of her family. He soon realizes the mistake he has made when he and Antoinette honeymoon on one of the Windward Islands. Eventually, they abandon the Caribbean lifestyle Rochester has come to abhor. They move back to England, where he locks his deranged wife in an upstairs garret.

Christophine A servant given to Annette as a wedding present by her first husband, Alexander Cosway. Christophine, like her mistress, comes from Martinique and is therefore treated as an outsider by the Jamaican servant women. A wise and ageless figure, Christophine is loyal to both Annette and her daughter, and she exercises an unspoken authority within the household. Christophine practices obeah, a Caribbean black magic, with which she tries to help Antoinette regain first her husband's love and then her sanity.

Mr. Mason One of the elegant English visitors who visits Antoinette's mother at Coulibri Estate. Mr. Mason is a wealthy Englishman who comes to the West Indies to make money. Captivated by his second wife's beauty, he intends to become even more prosperous by restoring Coulibri. He is confident in his authority to control the servants, believing them harmless and lazy and dismissing his wife's fears of revolt. Mr. Mason effectively abandons Annette and her daughter after the fire.

Aunt Cora The widow of a prosperous slave owner. Aunt Cora lives alone in Spanish Town. Unlike Antoinette's own mother Annette, Cora nurtures and cares for Antoinette, and eventually enrolls her in a convent school. But eventually Cora, too, abandons Antoinette when she moves to England for a year. On her return, Cora tries to ensure Antoinette's financial independence by giving her a silk pouch and two of her treasured rings. Ill and in bed, Cora tells her niece that she does not trust Richard and that she fears that the Lord has forsaken them.

Alexander Cosway Antoinette's deceased father. Alexander Cosway was a debased ex-slave owner known for fathering illegitimate children, squandering the family's money, and drinking himself into a stupor. His family lived on Jamaica for several generations as detested plantation owners; according to his bastard child, Daniel, madness ran in their genes. By the time Mr. Cosway died, leaving his second wife and their two children on their own, the Emancipation Act had led to the ruin of his sugar plantation and the end of his fortune.

Amelie A young half-caste servant who accompanies Antoinette and her husband to Granbois. The lovely and cunning Amelie snickers at her newlywed employers with a sort of knowing contempt, using her thinly veiled amusement to unsettle them. When Antoinette slaps Amelie for an impudent comment, Amelie slaps Antoinette back, calling her a "white cockroach" and smiling suggestively at her husband. Later, Amelie feeds and comforts Antoinette's husband, then sleeps with him. When he offers Amelie a gift of money the following morning, she refuses it and announces that she is going to leave Massacre and go to Rio, where she will find rich, generous men.

Sandi Cosway One of Alexander Cosway's bastard children. Sandi helps his half-sister, Antoinette, when she is harassed on her way to school. Although Antoinette would like to call him "Cousin Sandi," Mr. Mason scolds her for acknowledging her black relatives. According to Daniel Cosway, Sandi is "more handsome than any white man" and is well-received by polite white society. Daniel also suggests that Sandi and Antoinette were sexually involved as young children. Indeed, Antoinette's fragmented memory of a goodbye kiss with Sandi supports this possibility that the two may have been intimate at some point.

Daniel Cosway Another of Alexander Cosway's bastard chidren. Daniel writes a letter to Rochester that informs him of the madness that runs in Antoinette's family. The half-white, half-black Daniel is a racially split counterpart to the culturally split Antoinette.

Richard Mason Mr. Mason's son by his first marriage. After studying for several years in the Barbados, Richard moves to Spanish Town, where he negotiates Antoinette's marriage arrangements after his father's death. He persuades the nameless English gentleman to marry his stepsister, offering him £30,000 and rights to the girl's inheritance. Later, Richard visits the couple in England and hardly recognizes Antoinette as the madwoman locked in the attic. She flies at him in a delusional rage, cutting him with a secretly obtained knife.

Tia Maillotte's daughter and Antoinette's only childhood friend. At the water pool, Tia betrays Antoinette by taking her pennies and stealing her clothes. Tia's disloyalty manifests the allure and corrupting power of money in the text. Like Mr. Mason and Mr. Rochester, she appears to covet money more than a loving relationship, whether it be a childhood friendship or a marriage.

Pierre Antoinette's mentally and physically disabled younger brother. While not explicitly stated, it is suggested that Pierre's illness is a result of inbreeding and physical decline in the Cosway family. When the house at Coulibri is set on fire, Pierre is trapped in his burning room for some time, and he dies soon after.

Mr. Luttrell One of Annette Cosway's only friends after the death of her husband. Mr. Luttrell lives at Nelson's Rest, the estate that neighbors the Cosway home. Suffering financial hardship in the wake of the Emancipation Act, in sudden desperation he shoots his dog and swims out to sea, never to be seen again. Distant relatives finally reclaim Mr. Luttrell's abandoned estate.

Baptiste One of servants at Granbois, and the overseer of the mansion. Baptiste is a dignified man of advanced age.

Godfrey One of the old Cosway servants who stays on after the master's death. Godfrey is considered a greedy and untrustworthy "rascal," at least in Annette's view. He makes constant allusions to death and damnation.

Sass One of the servants who has been at Coulibri for several years, ever since his mother abandoned him there as a child. Sass leaves the estate when Annette's money runs out, but he returns when Mr. Mason arrives. Annette distrusts Sass, believing him to be greedy and self-serving.

Grace Poole A woman who answers an advertisement placed by Mrs. Eff for a servant to look after the deranged Antoinette. Grace is promised twice as much as the other household servants as long as she keeps her mouth shut and guards Antoinette well. Sharing the same garret space with Antoinette, Grace drinks frequently, often falling asleep with the garret key in plain view of her captor and charge.

Leah The cook employed by Antoinette's husband. Leah is one of only three servants who know about the woman in the attic.

Mrs. Eff An incarnation of Mrs. Fairfax and the head housekeeper at Thornfield Hall. While Mrs. Eff never appears in the novel, Grace mentions her in her conversation with Leah.

Mother St. Justine The head instructor at the convent school. Mother St. Justine tells the girls about the lives of female saints, instructs them on manners and cleanliness, and teaches them how to be proper Christian ladies.

Mannie A groom. Mannie is one of the new servants who Mr. Mason brings to Coulibri.

Maillotte Like Christophine, a black servant who distinguishes herself by not being Jamaican. Maillotte is Tia's mother and Christophine's only friend.

ANALYSIS OF MAJOR CHARACTERS

ANTOINETTE The character of Antoinette derives from Charlotte Brontë's poignant and powerful depiction of a deranged Creole outcast in her gothic novel *Jane Eyre*. Rhys creates a prehistory for Brontë's character, tracing her development from a young solitary girl in Jamaica to a love-depraved lunatic in an English garret. By fleshing out Brontë's one-dimensional madwoman, Rhys enables us to sympathize with the mental and emotional decline of a human being. Antoinette is a far cry from the conventional female heroines of nineteenth- and even twentieth-century novels, who are often more rational and self-restrained (as is Jane Eyre herself). In Antoinette, by contrast, we see the potential dangers of a wild imagination and an acute sensitivity. Her restlessness and instability seem to stem, in some part, from her inability to belong to any particular community. As a white Creole, she straddles the European world of her ancestors and the Caribbean culture into which she is born.

Left mainly to her own devices as a child, Antoinette turns inward, finding a world that can be both peaceful and terrifying. In the first part of the novel, we witness the development of a delicate child—one who finds refuge in the closed, isolated life of the convent. Her arranged marriage distresses her, and she tries to call it off, instinctively feeling that she will be hurt. Indeed, the marriage is a mismatch of culture and custom. She and her English husband, Mr. Rochester, fail to relate to one another; and her past deeds, specifically her childhood relationship with a half-caste brother, sullies her husband's view of her. An exile within her own family, a "white cockroach" to her disdainful servants, and an oddity in the eyes of her own husband, Antoinette cannot find a peaceful place for herself. Going far beyond the pitying stance taken by Brontë, Rhys humanizes "Bertha's" tragic condition, inviting the reader to explore Antoinette's terror and anguish.

CHRISTOPHINE As a surrogate mother, Christophine introduces Antoinette to the black culture of the Caribbean and instills in her a sensitivity to nature and belief in the practices of obeah. Significantly, it is Christophine's voice that opens the novel, as she explains Annette's exclusion from Spanish Town society; Christophine is the voice of authority, the one who explains the world to Antoinette and explains Antoinette to the readers. With her words gliding from a French patois to a Jamaican dialect and back into English, her command of language corresponds with the power of her words and her ability to invoke magic. She seems omniscient, intimately linked with the natural and tropical world and attuned to animal and human behavior.

Christophine, much like Antoinette and her mother, is an outsider. Coming from Martinique, she dresses and speaks differently from the Jamaican blacks. She is a servant, but, unlike the other black servants who live at Coulibri, she remains loyal to the Cosway women when the family's fortunes dwindle—an alliance at which the other servants sneer. Like Antoinette and her mother, Christophine becomes the subject of cruel household gossip, although she still commands some household respect because of her knowledge of magic.

A wedding present from the old Mr. Cosway to Annette, Christophine is a commodified woman, but is still fiercely self-willed. She provides a contrast to Annette in that she exercises complete independence from men and implicitly distrusts their motives. When Mr. Rochester arrives at Granbois, he immediately senses Christophine's contempt, and he associates her with all that is perverse and foreign about his new Caribbean home and his indecipherable Creole wife. A threat to Rochester's English privilege and male authority, Christophine calmly monitors his attempts to assert dominance. She instructs Antoinette that "woman must have spunks to live in this wicked world." Christophine adopts an increasingly assertive role in protecting Antoinette when Rochester begins to challenge his wife's sanity. Ultimately, Christophine advises Antoinette to leave her increasingly cruel husband, citing her own independence as an example to emulate. Having had three children by three different fathers, Christophine remains unmarried, saying "I thank my God. I keep my money. I don't give it to no worthless man." Christophine's final confrontation with Rochester establishes her as Antoinette's more lucid spokeswoman.

MR. ROCHESTER Mr. Rochester, Antoinette's young husband, narrates more than a third of the novel, telling, in his own words, the story of Antoinette's mental downfall. His arrival in Jamaica and his arranged marriage to Antoinette is prefigured in the first part of the novel by the appearance of Mr. Mason, another English aristocrat seeking his fortune through a Creole heiress. However, unlike Mason, Rochester remains nameless throughout the novel, referred to only as "that man" or "my husband." In a novel in which naming is so important, Rochester's anonymity underscores the implied authority of his account. He is the nameless creator and, as a white man, his authority and privilege allow him to confer identity on others. For instance, he decides to rename his wife, calling her "Bertha" in an attempt to distance her from her lunatic mother, whose full name was Antoinette. Later, he takes away Antoinette's voice along with her name, refusing to listen to her side of the story. As he continues to fragment her identity, he creates the new name of "Marionetta," a cruel joke that reflects Antoinette's doll-like pliability. He ultimately refashions Antoinette into a raving madwoman and treats her as a ghost. Having totally rejected his Creole wife and her native customs, Rochester exaggerates his own cool, logical, and distinctly English rationale; he asserts his total English control over the Caribbean landscape and people.

Rochester's narration in Part Two reveals that he and his estranged wife are actually more similar than dissimilar. Both characters are essentially orphans, abandoned by their family members to fend for themselves. As the youngest son, Rochester legally inherits nothing from his father, who already favors the older child. Antoinette, who was persistently neglected by her mother in favor of her brother, Pierre, receives an inheritance that is tainted, at best. She is left with the burdens of a divided cultural identity, the hatred of the blacks, the contempt of the whites, and the responsibility of a dilapidated estate. Both Rochester and Antoinette struggle for some sense of place and identity, and enter the arranged marriage with apprehension and anxiety. Rhys creates further parallels between her two antagonists in their bouts with fever and their twinned experiences with dreamed or actual forests.

THEMES, MOTIFS, AND SYMBOLS

THEMES

THE OPPRESSION OF SLAVERY AND ENTRAPMENT The specter of slavery and entrapment pervades *Wide Sargasso Sea*. The ex-slaves who worked on the sugar plantations of wealthy Creoles figure prominently in Part One of the novel, which is set in the West Indies in the early nineteenth century. Although the Emancipation Act has freed the slaves by the time of Antoinette's childhood, compensation has not been granted to the island's black population, breeding hostility and resentment between servants and their white employers. Annette, Antoinette's mother, is particularly attuned to the animosity that colors many employer-employee interactions.

Enslavement shapes many of the relationships in Rhys's novel—not just those between blacks and whites. Annette feels helplessly imprisoned at Coulibri Estate after the death of her husband, repeating the word "marooned" over and over again. Likewise, Antoinette is doomed to a form of enslavement in her love for and dependency upon her husband. Women's childlike dependence on fathers and husbands represents a figurative slavery that is made literal in Antoinette's ultimate physical captivity.

THE COMPLEXITY OF RACIAL IDENTITY Subtleties of race and the intricacies of Jamaica's social hierarchy play an important role in the development of the novel's main themes. Whites born in England are distinguished from the white Creoles, descendants of Europeans who have lived in the West Indies for one or more generations. Further complicating the social structure is the population of black ex-slaves who maintain their own kinds of stratification. Christophine, for instance, stands apart from the Jamaican servants because she is originally from the French Caribbean island of Martinique. Furthermore, there is a large mixed-race population, as white slave owners throughout the Caribbean and the Americas were notorious for raping and impregnating female slaves. Sandi and Daniel Cosway, two of Alexander Cosway's illegitimate children, both occupy this middle ground between black and white society.

Interaction between these racial groups is often antagonistic. Antoinette and her mother, however, do not share the purely racist views of other whites on the island. Both women recognize their dependence on the black servants who care for them, feeling a respect that often borders on fear and resentment. In this manner, power structures based on race always appear to be on the brink of reversal.

THE LINK BETWEEN WOMANHOOD, ENSLAVEMENT, AND MADNESS Womanhood intertwines with issues of enslavement and madness in Rhys's novel. Ideals of proper feminine deportment are presented to Antoinette when she is a girl at the convent school. Two of the other Creole girls, Miss Germaine and Helene de Plana, embody the feminine virtues that Antoinette is to learn and emulate: namely, beauty, chastity and mild, even-tempered manners. Mother St. Justine's praises of the "poised" and "imperturbable" sisters suggest an ideal of womanhood that is at odds with Antoinette's own hot and fiery nature. Indeed, it is Antoinette's passion that contributes to her melancholy and implied madness.

Rhys also explores her female characters' legal and financial dependence on the men around them. After the death of her first husband, Antoinette's mother sees her second marriage as an opportunity to escape from her life at Coulibri and regain status among her peers. For the men in the novel, marriage increases their wealth by granting them access to their wives' inheritance. In both cases, womanhood is synonymous with a kind of childlike dependence on the nearest man. Indeed, it is this dependence that precipitates the demise of both Antoinette and Annette. Both women marry white Englishmen in the hopes of assuaging their fears as vulnerable outsiders, but the men betray and abandon them.

MOTIFS

MADNESS Madness in *Wide Sargasso Sea* is intricately linked with images of heat, fire, and female sexuality. Madness is Antoinette's inheritance: her father was mad, according to his bastard son Daniel, as was her mother, Annette. Antoinette's upbringing and environment exacerbate her inherited condition, as she feels rejected and displaced, with no one to love her. She becomes paranoid and solitary, prone to vivid dreams and violent outbursts. It is significant that women like Antoinette and her mother are the most susceptible to madness, pushed as they are into childlike servitude and feminine docility. Their madness consigns them to live invisible, shameful lives. The predominance of insanity in the novel forces us to question whose recollections are trustworthy. The fragmented memory of a madwoman like Antoinette opens up the possibility for alternate stories and imagined realities.

DISEASE AND DECLINE In the Caribbean portrayed in the novel, an atmosphere of sickness reflects the perverse and unnatural subjugation of blacks by whites and of women by men. Repression explodes into fevers, fits, and madness, so that the body says what the mouth cannot. Both Antoinette and Rochester suffer near-fatal fevers, as if to mark their feelings of persecution and fear of the outside world.

Images of disease, rot, and illness also suggest the moral and financial decline of Antoinette's family. Disease works as a kind of moral retribution, in that the Cosway family, after generations of abuse, inherits a legacy of alcoholism, madness, and deformity (the young boy Pierre is degenerate). Antoinette naïvely believes her family's cure lies abroad, in England. On the night of the fire, she leans over the crib of her sleeping brother to assure him that, once Mr. Mason takes them to England, he will "be cured, made like other people." However, England offers no cure, as Antoinette herself further deteriorates when she is there.

DEATH Death seemingly hovers over Antoinette's every moment. One of the first memories she recounts from her childhood is that of her mother's poisoned horse, lying dead in the heat and swarming with flies. This image creates a mood of sinister anticipation and points to an evil undercurrent haunting Coulibri. The death of the horse also foreshadows the deaths of Pierre, Antoinette's mother, Aunt Cora, and Mr. Mason, all of which leave Antoinette without a family. So attuned to death's presence in her childhood tale, Antoinette foreshadows her own violent end.

At Coulibri, allusions to zombies and ghosts further contribute to the eerie mood. Christophine's supernatural tales, drawn from voodoo legends, share Antoinette's fascination with death. Antoinette incorporates these superstitions, using a stick as a protective talisman and believing that her mother has become a zombie—a body without a soul. It is Antoinette's faith in an invisible world that accounts for her peculiar preoccupation with death.

MAGIC AND INCANTATION In his decision to take Antoinette away from Jamaica, Rochester bitterly thinks to himself, "No more false heavens. No more damned magic." The Windward Islands, where Granbois is located, are home to the magical, syncretic religions of their black inhabitants. Christophine's unique powers, which command respect from her peers, derive from her expertise in obeah practices and her knowledge in casting spells. Antoinette incorporates Christophine's superstitious beliefs, leading her to read signs and symbols in the natural world. On the night of the fire, for instance, Antoinette shrinks in horror when she sees her mother's parrot burn alive, believing it is bad luck to kill a parrot or watch one die. This knowledge of magic is Antoinette's one source of power and independence.

FIRE Fires recur throughout the novel, representing destruction, damnation, and smoldering passions. In Part One, Antoinette describes the fire that burned down Coulibri Estate and triggered her mother's collapse into madness. In Part Two, Rochester describes the use of candles at night, paying particular attention to the moths that burn themselves in the flames. These descriptions not only recall the grotesque death of Annette's bird, but they also mirror Antoinette's perverse fascination with fire and foreshadow her own tragic end.

SYMBOLS

BIRDS Coco, Annette's pet parrot, enacts Antoinette's own doom. With his wings clipped by Mr. Mason—notably, an Englishman—the bird is shackled and maimed, mirroring Antoinette's own flightless dependency. As Antoinette recalls, "[Coco] made an effort to fly down but his clipped wings failed him and he fell screeching. He was all on fire." This passage presages the apocalyptic dream that ends the novel, including Antoinette's fiery fall from the attic. As omens and warnings, birds invite Antoinette to invest meaning and significance in the natural world. When she sees a cock crowing alongside Christophine's house, Antoinette thinks, "That is for betrayal, but who is the traitor?" As with the parrot, the appearance of the cock portends danger.

FORESTS AND TREES Antoinette's recurring forest dream introduces a cool, dark, unknown landscape that contrasts sharply with Jamaica's colorful brightness. A nightmare that is also a premonition, the dream takes place among "tall dark trees" that lead to an enclosed stone garden. Following a sinister and faceless man, Antoinette finds herself in a foreign place that portends her future captivity in England. Another forest omen resides in the name of the honeymoon estate, Granbois, which translates into "great forest." Like Antoinette's dream, this name foretells her move to the cold forests of England. It is here at Granbois that her husband loses himself in the woods, stumbling upon the haunting ruins of a stone house. Rochester's eerie experience in the forest echoes his wife's dream; in fact, it provides the second half of her nightmarish prediction. In the forest, he seems to be gazing upon the consequences of his own actions: a ruined house in the woods, a clear image of his English estate that will be burned and abandoned.

THE GARDEN Antoinette compares the garden at Coulibri Estate to the biblical Garden of Eden, with its luxurious excess and lost innocence. In her own words, the garden has "gone wild," assaulting the senses with its brilliant colors, pungent odors, and tangling overgrowth. The flowers look vaguely sinister; Antoinette describes one orchid as being "snaky looking," recalling the biblical fall and man's decline into greed and sensuality. The decadent Creole lifestyle as portrayed in the novel—predicated upon exploitation, wealth, and ease—finds its natural counterpart in the fallen garden.

IMPORTANT QUOTATIONS EXPLAINED

---

1. *There is no looking glass here and I don't know what I am like now. I remember watching myself brush my hair and how my eyes looked back at me. The girl I saw was myself yet not quite myself. Long ago when I was a child and very lonely I tried to kiss her. But the glass was between us—hard, cold and misted over with my breath. Now they have taken everything away. What am I doing in this place and who am I?*

This passage, narrated by Antoinette in Part Three, reflects several significant themes regarding her captivity in Thornfield Hall. Delivered in the present tense, these lines suggest the immediacy of Antoinette's situation and place us within the attic alongside Rhys's heroine. While Antoniette is unable to follow the passage of time, she remains acutely perceptive about her immediate surroundings, maintaining a lucidity that often breaks the surface of her madness. For instance, she notices the absence of a mirror, as it would provide her with a reflection of herself and a reassurance of her existence. Mirrors underscore the important questions of identity that pull at Rhys's central characters.

Annette, Antoinette's mother, constantly looked for her own reflection—a habit adopted by her daughter, and one that indicates their shared need to be visible in a world that neither accepts nor invites them.

By putting Antoinette in a mirrorless prison, alone save for a taciturn guard, Rochester exacerbates her feeling of disconnection. He has already deprived her of her name, calling her Bertha and effectively erasing her existence as Antoinette. Without a name, she does not know what to call herself; without a face, she becomes a ghost. As a child, Antoinette tried to kiss her reflected image, uniting the two halves of her split cultural identity, but she came up against the hard, separating glass. Antoinette's lifelong desire to close this gap—to become a visible, accepted member of any community—informs this passage and accounts for her inability to grasp and master reality.

---

2. *I hated the mountains and the hills, the rivers and the rain. I hated the sunsets of whatever colour, I hated its beauty and its magic and the secret I would never know. I hated its indifference and the cruelty which was part of its loveliness. Above all I hated her. For she belonged to the magic and the loveliness. She had left me thirsty and all my life would be thirst and longing for what I had lost before I found it.*

Spoken by Rochester, these lines appear at the close of Part Two, at the point when he prepares to leave the Caribbean and decides to bring Antoinette with him. His sudden and largely unexplained decision to render his wife lifeless and mad—to "force the hatred out of her eyes"—makes Rhys's Rochester a more complex and psychologically interesting character than his Brontë prototype. Rochester's willingness to believe Daniel Cosway's sensational stories and his need to confirm his misgivings prompt him to reflect, on receipt of the first incriminating letter, that "I felt no surprise. It was as if I'd expected it, been waiting for it." Like Antoinette, Rochester suffers from paranoia, suspecting that everyone, including his father,

Richard Mason, and his own young bride, are laughing at him. The nagging suspicion that he stands on the outside of a well-kept conspiracy drives Rochester to self-contempt, hatred, and an irrational need to regain control. Turning this anger on Antoinette, he seeks to assert his power by becoming her puppeteer, a godlike tyrant who can kill her with his words alone. Rochester symbolically enacts her death at the end of this section of the novel, covering her with a sheet "as if [he] covered a dead girl."

Rochester's hatred of the natural landscape stems from his inability to read it or commune with it. While his servants and his wife find an abundance of meaning in their surroundings, Rochester sees it as an alien, feeling bombarded by its beauty and excess. Rejecting its elaborate contours and intricate meanings, he speaks of the "mountains, and the hills, the river and the rain," refusing to color these nouns with adjectives and descriptions. He reverts to simple nouns, adopting a sparer language and holding the landscape's secret at a safe, controllable distance. His wife's beauty, like that of her home, threatens to bewitch and ensnare Rochester. This passage, more palpably than elsewhere, exposes the logic, however despicable, of his cruel need to gain dominance.

---

3. *Our parrot was called Coco, a green parrot. He didn't talk very well, he could say Qui est la? Qui est la? And answer himself Che Coco, Che Coco. After Mr. Mason clipped his wings he grew very bad tempered. . . . .*

   I opened my eyes, everybody was looking up and pointing at Coco on the glacis railings with his feathers alight. He made an effort to fly down but his clipped wings failed him and he fell screeching. He was all on fire.

These two passages act as premonitions and serve to draw parallels between a highly symbolic natural world and the characters who inhabit it. Eerie and grotesque, descriptions of dead, rotten, and dying animals litter the first and second parts of the novel. Annette's poisoned horse, left to rot and swarming with flies, provides the first in a series of images that prefigure Antoinette's tragic abandonment and violent death. Coco, Annette's beloved parrot and the only possession that she attempts to rescue from the fire, emerges as a key symbol of women's captivity within the novel. Unable to "talk very well," the parrot mirrors the inability of women to gain voice in a patriarchal society. When he does speak, the parrot uses a French patois that aligns it with a female world embodied by Christophine, Martinique, and natural magic. His repeated question, "Qui est là," translates to "Who is there?" and underscores the paranoia, persecution, and issues of identity that trouble both Antoinette and her mother. Responding to itself, "I am Coco," the parrot repeatedly asserts its own name and fixes it own identity, reciting a mantra that, like an incantation, works as protection. Mr. Mason's unexplained impulse to clip the bird's wings indicates the white, male, English need to control.

Describing the events of the Coulibri fire, Antoinette recalls Coco's gruesome death in vivid detail. She experiences, perhaps, an unconscious presentiment of her own final moments, falling from the burning battlements of Thornfield Hall. In the dream that precedes and inspires her death, Antoinette thinks back to Coco, imagining herself as a wild incarnation of the tropical bird: "The wind caught my hair and it streamed out like wings. It might bear me up, I thought, if I jumped to those hard stones." Just as the gathered servants point and stare at the flaming bird, generations of readers have imagined the ghoulish image of a Creole madwoman and watched her death with a voyeuristic complacency.

---

4. *"He has no right to that name," she said quickly. "His real name, if he has one, is Daniel Boyd. He hates all white people, but he hates me the most. He tells lies about us and he is sure that you will believe him and not listen to the other side."*

   "Is there another side?" I said.

   "There is always the other side, always."

When Rochester approaches his wife with Daniel Cosway's sensational reports, Antoinette attempts to plead her case, arguing that she and her family have been unfairly persecuted and unjustly defamed. She responds to Rochester's unflattering insinuations by debunking Daniel's dubious credibility and exposing his ulterior motivations. Urging her husband to weigh the evidence with objective fairness, Antoinette points to Daniel's half-caste status and illegitimate birth as cause for his venomous accusations. Claiming that her half-brother has "no right to that name," Antoinette raises the important issue of naming and identity—an issue that pervades her story and spells out her tragedy. As Antoinette seeks to define herself, to find her "real name," she discovers that she is, in a sense, nameless—a girl whose mother rejects her and whose peers deride her. In the convent, the young Antoinette was preoccupied with the appearance of her own name and sought to make herself visible when she stitched on a cloth, "Antoinette Mason, nee Cosway." Given by men, her father and stepfather, Antoinette's names signal patriarchy and a changing of hands. As she searches for her own "real name," Antoinette suffers the indignity of others' naming: she is called, in turn, "the white cockroach," "Bertha," and "Marionette."

Confronted with Rochester's accusations, Antoinette reminds him to consider "the other side," asking him to listen to her own story, though he refuses. She offers to tell Rochester the truth about her mother, but he clings obstinately to Daniel's exaggerated tales and to the belief that he has been intentionally deceived. When Antoinette assures her husband that there is always another side, she speaks to the very cause of Rhys's feminist and postcolonial rewriting. As a book that adopts the perspective of a marginalized and exoticized literary figure, *Wide Sargasso Sea* promotes an awareness of other versions.

---

5. *How can one discover the truth, I thought, and that thought led me nowhere. No one would tell me the truth. Not my father nor Richard Mason, certainly not the girl I had married. I stood still, so sure I was being watched that I looked over my shoulder. Nothing but the trees and the green light under the trees. A track was just visible and I went on, glancing from side to side and sometimes quickly behind me. This was why I stubbed my foot on a stone and nearly fell. The stone I had tripped on was not a boulder but part of a paved road. There had been a paved road through this forest. The track led to a large clear space. Here were the ruins of a stone house and round the ruins rose trees that had grown to an incredible height. At the back of the ruins a wild orange tree covered with fruit, the leaves a dark green. A beautiful place.*

Almost immediately upon his arrival at Granbois, Rochester begins to question his hastily conceived and financially motivated marriage to Antoinette. Feeling painfully alone and shamefully duped, the young man follows a path from the dilapidated house into the woods, encountering an abandoned old house and losing himself in the overgrowth. Bathed in an eerie green light, the forest surrounds him but withholds its secret. Rochester comes no closer to discovering "the truth," to understanding his wife, or to finding his place on the island. Suffering from paranoia—a feeling that he shares with Antoinette—Rochester senses he is being watched, and the forest becomes a metaphor for his psychological wanderings. Invested with symbols and meanings, the hushed scene projects Rochester's inner world and mysteriously replicates Antoinette's recurring forest nightmare. In both her unconscious mind and his conscious act, a feeling of inevitability and fated doom colors the landscape and pulls them onward. In Rochester's case, the ruins of a stone house prefigure the burned remains of Thornfield Hall, as he unwittingly gazes upon a tragic fate that he himself will engineer. Rhys is thus even-handed in exposing the psychological sufferings of both characters. Rather than focusing primarily on Antoinette's victimhood, Rhys shows the parallel fears and struggles both Antoinette and Rochester face.

Woman at Point Zero

Nawal El Saadawi (1931–)

CONTEXT

Nawal El Saadawi was born in the Egyptian village of Kafr Tahla in 1931. Her father was a civil servant, and her mother came from an upper-class Egyptian family. At the age of six, and at the insistence of her mother, El Saadawi underwent a clitoridectomy (also known as female genital mutilation), a procedure in which a young girl's clitoris is removed. El Saadawi was one of nine children, and her parents made the unusual decision to send all of their children—boys and girls—to school. El Saadawi excelled in school, and in 1949 she entered medical school at the University of Cairo. There, El Saadawi met and eventually married Ahmed Helmi, a fellow medical student and an Egyptian freedom fighter who opposed Britain's presence in Egypt. They were soon divorced. Despite the limitations placed on women by governmental and religious rule at the time, El Saadawi became a doctor in 1955.

After her divorce from her first husband, El Saadawi was pressured by her family into marrying Dr. Rashad Bey, who disapproved of El Saadawi's writing and her feminist viewpoints. El Saadawi in turn disliked Bey, and they, too, divorced. She then moved to New York to attend Columbia University, where she obtained her master's degree in public health in 1966. By this time, El Saadawi had married her third husband, Sherif Hetata. Like El Saadawi, Hetata is both a doctor and a novelist, and so was supportive of both of El Saadawi's passions. Hetata has since translated several of El Saadawi's works into English. Upon their return to Egypt, El Saadawi rose to become Egypt's Director of Public Health. She also worked as the editor-in-chief of *Health* magazine and assistant general secretary for Egypt's Medical Association.

In 1972, El Saadawi published her first nonfiction work, *Women and Sex*, which dealt with religion, sex, and clitoridectomy. Infuriated, the Egyptian government and religious establishment pressured the Ministry of Health into dismissing El Saadawi. She simultaneously lost her jobs as editor-in-chief of *Health* and as assistant general secretary in the Medical Association in Egypt.

From 1973 to 1976, El Saadawi researched women and neuroses at the Medical School of Ain Shams University. During this time, she did extensive research on women in prisons, traveling often to Qanatir Women's Prison. It was there that she met the woman who inspired the character of Firdaus in *Woman at Point Zero*—a prostitute condemned to death for killing the man who would have been her pimp.

From 1979 to 1980, El Saadawi worked for the United Nations as the advisor for the Women's Program in Africa and the Middle East. By this time, she had established a formidable bibliography and had published numerous works of fiction and non-fiction, including *Memoirs of a Woman Doctor* (1958), *Two Women in One* (1968), *She Has No Place in Paradise* (1972), *God Dies by the Nile* (1976), *The Circling Song* (1977), and *The Hidden Face of Eve: Women in the Arab World* (1977). All of her works have a feminist point of view, and El Saadawi was threatened by various Islamic fundamentalist groups throughout her life.

In 1981, El Saadawi was imprisoned by the regime of Egyptian President Anwar Sadat for criticizing his one-party rule. She spent two months in Qanatir Women's Prison—the same prison in which she visited Firdaus, the protagonist of *Woman at Point Zero*—under the Egyptian "Law for the Protection of Values from Shame." She was released one month after President Sadat's assassination in 1981. In 1982, El Saadawi founded the Arab Women's Solidarity Association, a feminist organization that was subsequently banned in 1991. Not long after, El Saadawi's name began to appear on "death lists" issued by Islamic fundamentalist groups who objected to her outspoken feminism and her unapologetic criticism of some aspects of Islam. El Saadawi and Hetata fled to the United States, where she taught at Duke University in North Carolina and Washington State University in Seattle. Finally, in 1996, she returned to Egypt.

But her troubles weren't over. In 2001, the seventy-three-year-old El Saadawi suggested in an interview that the pilgrimage that Muslims make to Mecca has its roots in a pagan tradition. In the same interview, she suggested that Islamic laws of inheritance were discriminatory toward women. Consequently, El Saadawi was accused of "straying from the circle of Islam." A famous Egyptian lawyer invoked an old and out-of-use law that allows one Muslim to accuse another of "apostasy," or renunciation of the Islamic faith. Because under Sharia, or Islamic law, a non-Muslim is not allowed to be married to a Muslim, the lawyer, Nabih al-Wahsh, tried to force El Saadawi to divorce Hetata, her husband of 40 years. The case was overturned in July of 2001, and El Saadawi and Hetata remain married. El Saadawi continues to be a provocateur.

PLOT OVERVIEW

In *Woman at Point Zero*, Nawal El Saadawi describes her experiences as a psychiatrist in Egypt, studying the psychological effects of prison on female prisoners. She states in her introduction that when she was conducting these studies, she had no idea that one day she would be imprisoned by the government. On one visit to Qanatir prison, Nawal meets a doctor who tells her that there is a prisoner there who is truly remarkable. She is awaiting the death penalty for killing a man, but the doctor cannot believe that this woman is capable of killing anyone. He wrote out a request for a pardon, but the condemned woman refused to sign it. Nawal desperately wants to meet with this woman, named Firdaus, but Firdaus keeps refusing to meet with her. Finally, the day before she is to be put to death, Firdaus agrees to meet with Nawal.

Nawal goes to Firdaus's cell, and Firdaus commands her to sit on the ground. Firdaus begins to tell her life story. She was born into an extremely poor family in the countryside. Her father often beat her mother; sometimes he beat her as well. Firdaus used to play in the fields with other children. A boy named Mohammadain was her special playmate, and when they were young, they used to play "bride and bridegroom." Firdaus got pleasure from her sexual experiments with Mohammadain. One day, her mother performed a clitoridectomy on her, and after that, Firdaus is no longer allowed to play with Mohammadain, nor does she ever feel sexual pleasure in the same way. Soon, Firdaus's mother and father die, and Firdaus is sent to live with her uncle, a sometime scholar, who lives in Cairo.

At first, everything goes well for Firdaus in Cairo. She and her uncle get along well, and she is allowed to go to school, which she loves. She and her uncle share a bed and are close. Her uncle gets married and the new wife does not like Firdaus, so Firdaus is sent to a boarding school. Firdaus is an excellent student and works hard. Unlike the other girls, she does not fantasize about boys and marriage. She spends most of her time at the library and in the courtyard, where she encounters a teacher named Miss Iqbal, with whom she forms a friendship. When Firdaus graduates, she is given an award, but she and her family are not at the ceremony, so Miss Iqbal accepts it for Firdaus. When school is over, Firdaus's uncle comes to get her.

Back at her uncle's house, Firdaus is miserable. One night, she overhears her aunt and uncle discussing whether they will marry Firdaus to her aunt's old uncle, Sheikh Mahmoud. He is sixty and has a facial deformity. Firdaus runs away, but while she is on the streets, she is terrified by the strange men who approach her, so she returns home. They marry her to Sheikh Mahmoud. He is selfish and stingy and beats Firdaus. His facial deformity is a large swelling on his chin with a hole in the middle that leaks pus. After one bad beating, Firdaus runs away. She ends up in a coffee shop, where she meets Bayoumi, the coffee shop owner. She goes with him to his apartment. At first Bayoumi is kind to Firdaus. Then Firdaus announces that she wants to get a job, and Bayoumi is enraged. He beats her and begins to lock her in the apartment when he leaves. He brings his friends home and allows them to have sex with her. Firdaus escapes with the help of a neighbor and flees Bayoumi's apartment for the city.

Resting by the Nile, Firdaus feels hopeless until an wealthy-looking woman approaches her. Her name is Sharifa, and she is a prostitute. She takes Firdaus in and teaches her to become a high-class prostitute. Sharifa makes money from Firdaus's body until one night when her friend Fawzy comes over. Firdaus overhears Sharifa and Fawzy fighting over who will get to keep her, so she runs away again. Still a prostitute, Firdaus becomes her own boss and eventually has a beautiful home and expensive things. One night, a client named Di'aa tells her that she is not a respectable woman, and Firdaus is devastated. She gives up her nice apartment and beautiful things, moves into a shack, and begins working as an office assistant. There, she realizes that the life of an assistant is in many ways worse than the life of a prostitute. She meets a man named Ibrahim, and falls in love with him. They have a relationship, and Firdaus begins to feel that the world is not so horrible, until she discovers that Ibrahim has become engaged to the boss's daughter.

Firdaus leaves the company and becomes a prostitute again. She is very expensive and very popular. Many powerful men come to her, and she turns some of them away to prove that she has power over her own body, and because she despises them. Ibrahim comes to her, and she realizes he never loved her;

rather, he just wanted free sex. A pimp tries to take over Firdaus's life, and for a little while, she lets him. Then they fight and she kills him. Shortly after that, Firdaus meets an Arab prince who takes her home and offers her $3,000. She sleeps with him, rips up the money, and slaps him. Terrified, the man calls the police. They come and arrest Firdaus. Firdaus is tried and sentenced to death.

She is, she tells Nawal, just waiting to die, because she is excited to go somewhere new. She knows that the men who sentenced her want to kill her because they're afraid of the truth she has to tell, not because they're afraid she'll kill again. After she finishes her story, police come to her cell and take her away to be executed. Nawal leaves the cell and is ashamed of the world. Everywhere she looks, she sees lies and unhappiness. As Nawal drives away from the prison, she thinks about running people over with her car, but she doesn't. She realizes that Firdaus is braver than she is.

CHARACTER LIST

Nawal El Saadawi The author and narrator of the book. Nawal is a psychiatrist who interviews women in prison. She meets one prisoner, Firdaus, and decides to tell her the sad story of her life.

Firdaus The narrator of most of the book. Firdaus is a young woman who flees her abusive husband and becomes a prostitute, then an office worker, and then a prostitute again. She finally kills a man who forces her to accept him as her pimp. When Nawal El Saadawi meets Firdaus, she is in prison waiting to be executed.

Firdaus's Uncle The man who takes Firdaus in after her parents die.

Bayoumi The coffee shop owner Firdaus meets after she flees her husband's beatings. Bayoumi is kind to Firdaus at first, but then he begins to beat her. Eventually, he locks her in the apartment and allows his friends to have their way with her.

Di'aa The journalist and onetime client of Firdaus. Di'aa becomes her friend, and then tells her she is not respectable, prompting Firdaus to give up prostitution and begin working at an office.

Fatheya Firdaus's friend from work. Fatheya suspects that Firdaus is in love with Ibrahim.

Fawzy A male friend of Sharifa's. Fawzy wants to take Firdaus with him and become her pimp, but Sharifa is already making money off of Firdaus and won't let him. When Firdaus hears them discussing this, she flees and sets up her own prostitution business.

Hala A toddler. Hala is the youngest of Firdaus's uncle's children, and the only one who is kind to Firdaus.

Ibrahim One of Firdaus's colleagues at her office, and a "revolutionary." Ibrahim joins Firdaus in the courtyard of the office compound one night, where they cry together. Firdaus falls in love with him, and they have a relationship that ends when she overhears that he is engaged to be married.

Iqbal Firdaus's teacher at secondary school. Iqbal joins Firdaus at the school playground one night, and they cry together.

Mohammadain The little boy from Firdaus's childhood, with whom she used to play "bride and bridegroom." This is the first time that Mohammadain and Firdaus experience sexual pleasure.

The Prison Doctor The doctor at Firdaus's prison. The doctor filled out an appeal for Firdaus (to commute her sentence from death to life imprisonment), but she refused to sign it.

Saadia Firdaus's uncle's servant girl.

Sharifa Salah el Dine A high-class prostitute who takes Firdaus in and turns her into a prostitute. Sharifa makes a profit off of Firdaus's body until Firdaus runs away.

Sheikh Mahmoud Firdaus's husband for a brief period of time. Sheikh Mahmoud beats Firdaus and she flees to Bayoumi's home.

Wafeya Firdaus's friend at school. Wafeya suspects that Firdaus is in love with Miss Iqbal.

ANALYSIS OF MAJOR CHARACTERS

NAWAL EL SADAAWI Nawal El Sadaawi is both the author and the narrator of *Woman at Point Zero*. As the author, she presents a fictionalized version of two real people: Firdaus and herself. Though the fictional characters closely resemble the two real people, they are distinct. The fictional El Sadaawi struggles with feelings of insignificance, and by the end of the book she is consumed with helpless rage over the condition of women, including herself, in her country. Undoubtedly, the author El Sadaawi also has these feelings, but by the time she wrote *Woman at Point Zero*, she had long been a significant figure in her country's consciousness, as well as a crusader for women's rights.

The fictional El Sadaawi is first introduced when she visits the prison in which Firdaus is awaiting her execution. El Sadaawi approaches her meetings with Firdaus with desperation. Firdaus is an imprisoned prostitute, and El Sadaawi, an educated and wealthy doctor, occupies a much higher social position. Still, El Sadaawi is devastated by Firdaus's initial refusal to be interviewed; it makes her feel insignificant. When Firdaus finally agrees to meet El Sadaawi, El Sadaawi approaches her like a petitioner. This is because El Sadaawi, despite her education and status, is still subject to discrimination and feels insignificant most of the time. Because the imprisoned Firdaus refuses to be "put in her place," El Sadaawi suspects that Firdaus might have some sort of strength or knowledge for which El Sadaawi is desperate. The doctor therefore approaches the prisoner for wisdom and guidance.

El Sadaawi's reaction to the end of Firdaus's tale—the helpless fury and sorrow she feels after Firdaus goes to her execution—further demonstrates her feelings of insignificance. The truth of Firdaus's story, which shows so starkly the position of women in El Sadaawi's society, is such that El Sadaawi feels her own lack of power all the more keenly. She has spoken to someone who had been oppressed for much of her life before finally seizing power. Yet El Sadaawi does not act on violent impulses to destroy the oppressive forces in her society after Firdaus is killed, and she is disappointed in herself. The book ends with character El Sadaawi's realization that Firdaus has more courage than she, El Sadaawi, has. Here, again, it is important to separate the fictional character from the figure of the revolutionary author. The real El Sadaawi was galvanized by her encounters with the woman who inspired the character of Firdaus. Among other things, the encounter inspired her to write the book, *Woman at Point Zero*, to illuminate the sufferings of Egyptian women for a larger audience.

FIRDAUS Firdaus is a woman struggling to live a dignified life in a society in which women have limited options. Throughout the book, Firdaus fights not just to be in control of her own destiny but also to figure out who she is. But she has little time to devote to self-exploration. The scene in Bayoumi's coffee shop is an example of this. Bayoumi asks Firdaus whether she wants oranges or tangerines, and Firdaus is unable to answer him, having never considered whether she might like one thing more than another. For most of her life, it has never been important what she wanted. What *was* important was what the men around her wanted. And as Firdaus tells it, all of the men around her are brutes who exult in the power that they have over women. To some extent, Firdaus's life becomes about living in opposition to the men in her life. Taking pleasure from a relationship with men is never really an option for her. This is partially because she needs to be treated like an equal, which never happens, but also because of her clitoridectomy. This procedure robs her of pleasure during sex.

W

By the time Firdaus becomes a prostitute, she has discovered that she can exploit the desire that many men have for her by getting money for it. She learns that people with money can also command respect. But having money and commanding respect do not make Firdaus feel respectable. To someone who dreamed of studying and becoming a scholar, the life of a prostitute is disappointing and demeaning, yet Firdaus also suggests that the life of a prostitute might be a surer path to dignity and self-determination than the "respectable" life of an office assistant. At least as a prostitute Firdaus need not show deference toward even the most powerful of men.

UNCLE Firdaus's uncle is a complicated figure in her life, and in many ways her relationship with him forms a template for her relationships with the other men in the story. When Firdaus is a young girl living with her mother and father, her uncle represents a kind of freedom. He is a scholar, and he lives in Cairo, far away from the rural world of Firdaus's immediate family. Yet he also sexualizes young Firdaus, as shown in the way he caresses her thighs. Though Firdaus is uncomfortable with the way in which he touches her, she does not object because it doesn't occur to her to do so. As a result of this and her father's behavior toward her mother, Firdaus learns to think that men own women's bodies. Despite this, her uncle is still her savior. After Firdaus's parents die, her uncle brings her to Cairo, where they sleep in the same bed and live like a married couple, though it isn't clear whether they have a sexual relationship. Firdaus's uncle sends her to school and consequently provides her with a much better life than the one she lived with her parents.

However, her uncle soon abandons the life of a scholar to become a civil servant. At this point, Firdaus learns that men value power above all else. She also learns how insignificant she is to her uncle when compared to his thirst for power. In order to advance, Firdaus's uncle marries above his station. Because his new wife does not care for Firdaus, Firdaus is sent to boarding school. Firdaus's uncle turns out to be just as selfish as all of the other men in her life. When he eventually marries Firdaus off to his wife's old and disfigured uncle for a large sum of money, he confirms Firdaus's belief that she is alone in the world, and that men are horrible hypocrites who will do anything for money and power.

SHARIFA Sharifa is the high-class prostitute who finds Firdaus sitting by the Nile after her escape from Bayoumi's house. Sharifa takes Firdaus to her luxurious home, and it occurs to Firdaus for the first time that she could one day have a home of her own and be surrounded by nice things. Sharifa, through her confidence and the skillful application of makeup, helps Firdaus see that she has beauty and strength. Unfortunately, Sharifa shows her these things in order to make her more appealing to the men to whom Sharifa hopes to sell Firdaus's body. Though she takes Firdaus under her wing in order to earn more money, Sharifa does act as a mother figure to Firdaus, and it is under Sharifa's care that it first occurs to Firdaus that she might be able to live without the protection of a man. Like Firdaus's own mother, Sharifa both supports and undermines Firdaus. Under Sharifa, Firdaus is reborn as an attractive woman aware of the power that she has over men. But like Firdaus's mother, Sharifa is jealous of the attention men give to Firdaus, and seeks to control her.

Eventually, Firdaus realizes that she has to leave Sharifa. This realization comes because she needs to make her own money and determine the course of her own destiny. In addition, Sharifa's imagination is constrained by a patriarchal society in a way in which Firdaus's is not. Sharifa only wants money and a comfortable life, and is willing to play the game that powerful men have set up in order to attain these things. Sharifa is more charming with the men who come to visit, and more eager to please. This is because she still believes herself to be, in some respect, a supplicant, lucky to get whatever money men throw her way. Firdaus wants to be comfortable, but she also wants power of her own. Firdaus begins by emulating Sharifa, but it is only after Firdaus leaves Sharifa that she realizes that as a prostitute, she commands power over men, not the other way around.

THEMES, MOTIFS, AND SYMBOLS

THEMES

THE CONNECTION BETWEEN SURVEILLANCE AND OWNERSHIP Throughout the telling of her story, Firdaus describes the act of seeing as akin to an act of possession. One of Firdaus's earliest memories as a child is the memory of her mother's eyes watching her, holding her up when she struggled to learn how to walk and negotiate the world. For the young Firdaus, this sense of belonging to her mother and being watched over by her is very comforting. She feels that being a possession of her mother is what protects her. Later, though, the act of being surveyed takes on a very different meaning. When Firdaus grows older, she no longer feels her mother's eyes supporting her. From then on, whenever Firdaus senses someone's eyes watching her, she feels threatened. When Firdaus first runs away from her uncle's house, she encounters a terrifying man who runs his eyes up and down her body, making Firdaus feel invaded, and as if her body were not her own.

Firdaus's life-long struggle is to claim her body as her own. When Firdaus marries Sheikh Mahmoud, his eyes never leave her dish at mealtimes, and he watches every morsel of food she eats with jealous intensity. Firdaus becomes self-conscious about eating. Firdaus describes almost all of the men she encounters in the same way—they rake their eyes over her body and, in doing so, act as though her body exists only for them. It is not until she is in prison that Firdaus learns to feel at ease during other people's examinations of her. This is because Firdaus has proven to herself that she owns herself and that she is in control of her own destiny.

THE NATURE OF POWER For the young Firdaus, the nature of power seems at first to be very simple: men have it and women do not. Her father has power over her mother. Her uncle has power over her. When she is married, Sheikh Mahmoud has power over her. Even men on the street have power over the women they pass, merely by turning them into objects with their eyes. Bayoumi, who locks Firdaus in his apartment and lets his friends have sex with her, has power over her. It isn't until Firdaus meets Sharifa that her ideas of power begin to change. Sharifa is a wealthy, independent woman. Rather than allowing men free use of her body, as married women do, Sharifa uses the power of the desires that men have for her to her advantage. She teaches Firdaus how to command the power of her physical appearance. Still, Firdaus doesn't know what it means to possess power of her own. She learns that women can have power, too, but she cannot fully wield her own power while living under Sharifa's control.

When she sets out on her own as a prostitute, Firdaus finally learns what it means to have something that other people desire. This is power. She learns that she can command higher and higher prices simply by denying people what they want, or exercising the power that she has over them. Because of this, she feels that money is power. When she possesses money of her own, she has power over the people who slander her, and she can give herself a respectable name by hiring a lawyer and suing. Her brief stint as an office worker only serves to reinforce this idea, and when she goes back to prostitution, she charges more money than ever and uses her money to mingle with more powerful people. Firdaus comes to believe that she has attained real power. But the pimp who claims her proves that this is not the case. He threatens to defame her or kill her, proving that no matter how much money she has, Firdaus is still vulnerable to men because she has something to lose. When she kills the pimp and later tears up the prince's money, Firdaus finally proves that she has control over herself.

THE IMPORTANCE OF ATTAINING RESPECT Attaining respect does not become one of Firdaus's goals until Di'aa, who has engaged her services as a prostitute, points out to her that in spite of her financial security, she is not respectable. Until Firdaus has money of her own, the way that the world views her never really enters into her consideration. This is in part because the world has never paid her much attention before. She was just an invisible person occupying the role of daughter or wife. When she finally accumulates some wealth and power, the world takes notice. Men take notice because, in Firdaus's world, men don't want women to have power over them. By condemning her work as a prostitute as shameful, they try to minimize her power, though they are also involved in the exchange of sex and money. For the men in Firdaus's story, respectable women are women who are submissive and live under the protection of a powerful man.

When Di'aa tells Firdaus that she is not respectable because the work she does is shameful, she is deeply hurt. In an effort to become a more respectable woman, she gives up her nice apartment and prostitution in order to work in an office. Indeed, she becomes a "respectable" woman by placing herself under the power of men again. Firdaus's relationship with Ibrahim is a part of this quest for respectability. She's playing by the rules and, for the first time, she feels as though she's met a man she can trust. The sacrifices she's made to become respectable seem worthwhile. However, when Firdaus discovers that Ibrahim was using her for sex, she once again realizes that "respectability" is a trap that is designed to put women at the mercy of men. By quitting her job and taking up prostitution again, Firdaus rejects the pursuit of a "respectable" life in favor of a life of power and self-determination. Firdaus has come to see that respectability in her world means playing by someone else's rules.

MOTIFS

SEXUAL PLEASURE During her childhood, Firdaus experiments sexually with a local boy named Mohammadain. They play "bride and bridegroom," meaning that they take off their clothes and rub against one another. Firdaus describes the sensation of pleasure she gets from her encounters with Mohammadain, which end when her mother forces her to undergo a strange surgery. It is not fully explained in the book, but Firdaus undergoes a clitoridectomy (the removal of her clitoris). After this procedure, Firdaus never again experiences sexual pleasure the way she once did. Though her mother forces her to undergo the procedure as a matter of tradition and doesn't seem to think about it politically, Firdaus considers the tradition another attempt to suppress women. By removing the clitoris, sex has become an act in which only men take pleasure. Firdaus believes that if women were equal to men, then both would find pleasure in sex.

Pleasure is out of the question in her sexual encounters with her old, deformed husband. To Firdaus, these encounters are horrific, and she describes the stench of his open wound and the lack of joy she feels during sex. She also describes with contempt the way men who come to her as clients will demand, during sex, to know whether or not she is taking pleasure in the act. For these men, the act is not about two people enjoying each other, but instead about proving their physical prowess. They are determined to wring pleasure from Firdaus, whether she wants it or not. Firdaus tells the men that she enjoys sex (though she does not), which stops them from asking. When Firdaus overhears her uncle and his wife having sex, the idea of it warms her, but she is unable to take pleasure in it herself.

CHOICE As a woman from a poor family, Firdaus has never had to make many choices. Her clitoris is removed and she is married to a tyrannical older husband without anyone ever asking her opinion. The first real choice she has ever had to make comes when she flees her husband's home. When Bayoumi asks her whether she prefers oranges or tangerines, Firdaus is struck by the fact that nobody has ever asked her to make a decision like that before. She realizes she does not even know which fruit she prefers, because she has never had to think about what she wanted. Other people always told her what would happen. After this, choice becomes an obsession for Firdaus.

As a prostitute, Firdaus has the money and the power to make choices for herself. She chooses her own apartment and clothing and also begins to choose which men she will and will not sleep with. Because of this, she begins to believe in her own independence. The power to choose for herself is intoxicating. And soon, the fact that she has rejected powerful men makes her even more alluring to them. By exercising choice, Firdaus commands more and more money and gets an increasingly prestigious clientele. However, the pimp who moves in and demands control over her shatters the illusion of choice for Firdaus. Firdaus realizes that no matter how powerful she might seem, she is still a woman, and men will still attempt to exercise control over her. In Firdaus's world, there is no way for her to make real choices. Though it seems to some that a female prisoner has less power than even the lowliest wife, Firdaus feels that waiting on death row is the most liberating thing that has ever happened to her. She chooses not to appeal her sentence; she would prefer to die in order to escape the control that other people have over her. Only when dead will Firdaus be free.

CAPTIVITY Firdaus explains that all of her life *until* the time she spends in prison has been spent in captivity. Though as a child, a wife, and a prostitute, she had some degree of physical freedom, she did not attain mental freedom until she got to prison. Captivity, for Firdaus, means living under someone else's power. It means not making choices for oneself and agreeing to be deceived by those in power (whether those in power are presidents or fathers or husbands). Though Firdaus is waiting to die in prison, she considers herself freer than anyone else in the world. She certainly feels freer than Nawal El Saadawi, who hopes to interview her. Nawal senses this, and it is for this reason that she is so devastated when Firdaus refuses, time and time again, to be interviewed.

Firdaus looks forward to death because it means that she will have a chance to start over. Though she is enclosed in a cell, she feels free. She refuses to work with the system, sign an appeal, or visit with the doctor because she does not want to feel like a captive. Signing appeals would only serve to entrap her again, as she would have to appeal to, and thereby recognize, the power of men. When she finally agrees to meet with Nawal, it is only in order to spread a message of truth and to do further damage to the world that abused her before she dies.

SYMBOLS

MONEY Firdaus grows up in a poor family in a community of poor families, and she further recognizes the power of money when she moves to Cairo. As Firdaus tells it, she never really had money of her own until she started prostituting herself. Before this, she was at the mercy of her stingy father, uncle, husband, and Sharifa—because they had money and she did not. All of them recognized this fact, and they were careful not to give her any money of her own, lest she escape their grasp. When Firdaus first ventures out on her own—after leaving Sharifa's house—and learns that her body has a monetary value to men, she also learns that she can command more money from them because she has something they want. To men, her body is a commodity, just as food and clothing are a commodity: the more difficult it is for them to obtain, the more money they will pay. In this way, Firdaus begins to amass money of her own. She despises her work, and she loathes the men who come to see her, but she greatly values her newfound power. She is not at the mercy of men anymore.

When she is slandered in public, Firdaus uses her "shameful" money to pay a lawyer to clear her name. At this point, money is everything to Firdaus. It even has the ability to cleanse her public image. But by the time Firdaus kills the pimp and demands $2,000 from the prince, money has come to mean something very different. It becomes just another symbol of the hypocrisy of her society. It gives power to the unworthy and makes the despicable seem respectable. It allows men to rule over women, and makes the prince think that he can buy Firdaus. When Firdaus tears up the $2,000, she demonstrates to the prince that his money has no power over her. Because of this demonstration, the prince declares that she must really be a princess—i.e., one outside the reach of money's power. Because of Firdaus's newfound understanding of the treachery of money, the prince is right. Firdaus is truly outside the reach of money's power.

BOOKS Firdaus's uncle gives Firdaus her first taste of the power of books when he secretly teaches her how to read. Books become a symbol of the kindness of her uncle, who takes an interest in young Firdaus and tries to teach her. Through reading, Firdaus comes to realize that there is more in the world than her poor village and humble family. Even before her uncle teaches her to read, she views the books he brings with him from Cairo as a kind of passport to a life in which she, too, could be a scholar. When she moves to Cairo and goes to school, Firdaus spends the few happy years of her life immersed in books and learning. The time that they spend reading together is a time of bonding between Firdaus and her uncle.

When her uncle gives up the life of a scholar and marries his boss's daughter, he sends Firdaus to boarding school. Essentially, her uncle gives up books in exchange for wealth and status. This feels like a betrayal to Firdaus, but boarding school proves more advantageous for her than living with her uncle and aunt. She soon develops a reputation as a bookworm, and often spends long evenings in the library. She becomes an excellent student and wins many academic prizes. Books become more important to Firdaus than people. Yet when Firdaus is married off to Sheikh Mahmoud, books virtually disappear from her life. Firdaus has to fit herself into the role of submissive wife, and there is no room for her to be a prize pupil or a reader. Books, which represented her uncle's kindness and the potential for a better life, disappear.

IMPORTANT QUOTATIONS EXPLAINED

---

1. *The woman sitting on the ground in front of me was a real woman, and the voice filling my ears with its sound, echoing in a cell where the window and door were tightly shut, could only be her voice, the voice of Firdaus.*

Nawal writes this after she has finally met Firdaus, on the day that Firdaus is scheduled to die. Nawal immediately senses that there is something about Firdaus that is different from everyone she has ever met. When she says that Firdaus is a "real woman," she means that there is something painfully real about Firdaus and her experience in jail. Firdaus becomes more than just a case study for Nawal. She becomes a symbol of truth: a living demonstration of all that is wrong with their shared society. Firdaus is undeniably an individual.

Because she has always had to fight for the right to be herself, and because she is in prison for killing a man in order to achieve self-determination, Firdaus seems more real than anyone Nawal has ever met. When Nawal describes Firdaus's voice echoing in a sealed cell, she reminds her audience that prison has not lessened Firdaus's personality. Because choosing imprisonment has made Firdaus more free than at any other time in her life, the force of her personality has grown. The cell is a symbol of how the world thinks it can contain and control Firdaus, but to Nawal that is absurd. Prison and the threat of death have no power over Firdaus. She has finally gotten control of her own life, and has undeniably become an individual.

2. *"All my life I have been searching for something that would fill me with pride, make me feel superior to everyone else, including kings, princes and rulers."*

When Nawal first meets Firdaus, Nawal marvels at how cool and collected Firdaus seems. She wonders why Firdaus has decided not to appeal her sentence and try to live longer, and why Firdaus remains so calm in the face of impending death. Firdaus explains that she doesn't fear death. In fact, she's looking forward to it. Since her whole life has been spent under someone else's control, and because that life has never really brought her any happiness, she is looking forward to ending it. She says that her whole life has been a quest to prove to herself that she was as good as, if not better than, the men who control her world. She has nothing but contempt for these rulers. All she sees of them is hypocrisy and deceit. They deceive their subjects and abuse their power, and yet are terrified of being less powerful than they think they are.

Firdaus discovers how vulnerable these men are when, as a prostitute, she refuses to sleep with some of them. They panic and offer her ever-increasing sums of money, simply because it terrifies them to think that their power might not have the reach they think it does. Still, though Firdaus proves in this way that their power is incomplete, she knows full well that her own is even more precarious. Only in death will she be free from them. Choosing to die is one of the first real choices that Firdaus has ever made, and in doing so, she challenges the power of those who think they are punishing her. Also, Firdaus explains, she will die before these powerful men die. She will be a pioneer, no longer afraid of the thing that all of these powerful, hypocritical men fear most. Only in this way can she finally feel superior to them.

3. *"Do you prefer oranges or tangerines?"*

Bayoumi asks Firdaus this when she is coming to his house for the first time. The question is striking because Firdaus realizes she has never been asked whether she had a preference for anything before. It has never mattered what she preferred. If her father wanted lamb for dinner, the whole family would eat lamb. If Firdaus's husband wanted to eat at 6:00, Firdaus would also eat at 6:00. Because she's never been offered a choice before, Firdaus does not know what she prefers. Only after she stammers out an answer does she realize that she's answered incorrectly. She says tangerines and realizes that she in fact prefers oranges, but she was ashamed to say so because oranges are more expensive. This is the first conscious choice that Firdaus has ever had to make. Though she leaves her husband, she does so unthinkingly, simply fleeing his violence. Though she stays with Bayoumi, she does so mainly because he tells her to. But in asking her this simple question, Bayoumi forces Firdaus to realize that she is capable of making her own choices.

Firdaus's departure from Bayoumi much more deliberate than her departure from her husband. In order to leave Bayoumi, she has to beg for help from a neighbor woman and break out of the apartment. Bayoumi has created in Firdaus an obsession with the ability to choose for herself and determine the course of her own life, and she uses it to escape him. The simple question about citrus fruits changes the way Firdaus sees her life. When Firdaus becomes an independent prostitute, she finally has the money and the power to make choices for herself. This gives her a false sense of independence and self-determination. It is not until the pimp demands control over Firdaus that the illusion of choice is shattered. Firdaus realizes that she's still a woman, even if she has money and power, and she is still under the control of men. Even with the newfound freedom of a prostitute, what men want matters more.

4. *"My work is not worthy of respect. Why then do you join in it with me?"*

Firdaus asks this of Di'aa, a client of hers who tells her that she is not respectable. Di'aa has been stung by Firdaus's professional attitude about prostitution, and tells her that she should hang out a list of prices, as a doctor would do. Firdaus asks him if he's being sarcastic, and he says yes. He says that a doctor charges by the minute as well, but a doctor feels he is worthy of respect. Prostitutes, according to Di'aa, deserve no respect. Firdaus responds with the quote above. For Firdaus, this exchange is typical of the hypocrisy of men. She and her clients are both having illicit sex, and yet only Firdaus is considered shameful. Di'aa's comments only reinforce her idea that men and women live in separate worlds with separate rules, and that there can be no reconciling them. Still, she tries to point out to him that though he considers himself respectable, he is also engaging in an activity not worthy of respect. Di'aa is unfazed, and tries to kiss her. Firdaus kicks Di'aa out, but his words haunt her. This is the first time it has occurred to Firdaus that she might be unworthy of respect. Because of this, she stops prostituting, and goes to work in an office, trying to learn what it means to be respectable.

---

5. *Her voice continued to echo in my ears, vibrating in my head, in the cell, in the prison, in the streets, in the whole world, shaking everything, spreading fear wherever it went, the fear of the truth which kills, the power of truth, as savage, and as simple, and as awesome as death, yet as simple and as gentle as a child that has not yet learnt to lie.*

Nawal writes this after hearing Firdaus's story and watching Firdaus be escorted to her execution. Nawal leaves Firdaus's cell feeling light-headed. She gets in her car and begins to drive home, still hearing Firdaus's voice and its undeniable truths echoing in her ears. She considers accelerating the car into people in the street, but does not. Firdaus's story and personality have convinced Nawal that their society is a lie, and that the destruction of it wouldn't be so bad. Nawal's conversation with Firdaus seems to lift a veil from Nawal's eyes. It is as if Nawal had spent her entire life believing in an illusion, and that simply speaking with Firdaus had made her realize that her whole life, and the lives of those around her, was based on lies. The simple facts of Firdaus's life, and her apparent joy at her approaching death, reveals this.

Nawal also realizes at this point that Firdaus is not really in prison because authorities fear that she will kill again if released, but because they fear the truth that she now possesses. Because she dared to seize control of her own life and deny the power of those around her to control her, she threw into question a fundamental truth of their society. Women, and especially women like Firdaus, are not supposed to have the kind of freedom and power Firdaus aspired to have, nor are women supposed to fight back when men try to put them in their place, as the pimp tried to do. When she fights back, and later refuses to beg for mercy from the powerful men, Firdaus becomes incredibly threatening to them and to everyone else who works to ensure that the illusion of their power is sustained. Killing a pimp is not Firdaus's real crime. Her true crime is in exposing the hypocrisy and powerlessness of the leaders and princes she so despises.

The Woman Warrior

Maxine Hong Kingston (1940–)

CONTEXT

Maxine Hong Kingston was born in 1940 in Stockton, California, where her parents, Tom and Ying Lan Hong, operated a laundry. Kingston graduated from Berkeley in 1962 and married actor Earll Kingston the same year. After becoming involved in the antiwar protests of the late sixties, the Kingstons moved to Hawaii, where Kingston taught English and began composing her two memoirs, *The Woman Warrior* (1976) and *China Men* (1980). She published her first novel, *Tripmaster Monkey: His Fake Book* (1988), after returning to California with her husband. In 1990, Kingston began teaching at Berkeley.

The Woman Warrior received praise from critics and won the National Book Critics Circle Award for nonfiction. Its appeal cut across a wide variety academic disciplines, attracting both those interested in postmodern techniques of autobiography and those interested in stories of cultural displacement and alienation. For scholars of autobiography, Kingston's story represents an important break from past writings; her complex, multilayered and quasifictional narrative flies in the face of traditional autobiographies, which tend to follow a linear-chronological pattern and maintain a stable narrator—an "I"—throughout. Kingston's memoir, on the other hand, is a blending of voices and styles, often contradictory, that use many of the techniques of postmodernism: ambiguity, incoherence, pluralism, and irony.

Kingston has received some criticism for purporting to represent the "typical" experience of Chinese-Americans and, in other cases, for taking traditional material and changing it to suit her own needs. One source of the latter criticism is the story of Fa Mu Lan, a traditional Chinese myth about a girl who took the place of her father in battle. In the "White Tigers" section of *The Woman Warrior*, Kingston adds and incorporates elements from other myths to create an entirely new fantasy from the story of Fa Mu Lan. For her part, Kingston claims that she never intended such stories to be either representative or accurate. Furthermore, we must keep in mind that *The Woman Warrior* is not a chronicle of Chinese culture or traditions but simply a reflection of the experience of one Chinese-American far removed from the culture and traditions about which she is writing.

Though Kingston's work may not be universally representative, it does offer a glimpse into the realities of life for many Chinese emigrants to America and their children. As early as the 1840s, Chinese immigrants had been arriving in America in search of better lives, driven from their home country by widespread poverty and attracted by possibilities in the new American West. However, like many other ethnic groups entering America at the time, the immigrants faced social, economic, and legal discrimination that limited their rights and opportunities, keeping most of them living together in pockets of Chinese communities such as the area in Stockton where Kingston grew up. Women such as Brave Orchid, who had once been a doctor in her own country, were forced to toil in sweatshops or become laundry workers—some of the few jobs available to Chinese-Americans well into the twentieth century.

Kingston's memoir finds its way onto the syllabi of many women's studies courses for the gender issues it raises, especially regarding the role of women in traditional Chinese society. Brave Orchid embodies an archetypal Chinese attitude of self-denial and self-abnegation for the good of the community—the very qualities that "No-Name Woman" lacks. Kingston's memoir is further peppered with references to the subjugation of women in Chinese culture and tradition, such as the oft-repeated phrase "better to have geese than girls."

The Woman Warrior is as much about Kingston's finding voice and strength as an independent woman within this tradition, and how to reconcile the notion of Chinese wife-slave with the talk-stories about swordswomen and shamans. Though *The Woman Warrior* easily stands on its own, Kingston did intend it to be read in conjunction with *China Men*, her companion piece published four years later. While the first work tells the stories of the important women in Kingston's life, with the men relegated to the background, the second focuses on Kingston's father, thus completing the picture of Kingston's childhood. Kingston also believes that she finds more of a voice in *China Men* and that, in order to appreciate

The Woman Warrior, it is helpful to read what she feels is her more accomplished text. Still, it is the first memoir that usually appears on high school and college syllabi or in anthologies. The most popular chapters in anthologies tend to be the first two, "No-Name Woman" and "White Tigers."

PLOT OVERVIEW

The Woman Warrior focuses on the stories of five women—Kingston's long-dead aunt, "No-Name Woman"; a mythical female warrior, Fa Mu Lan; Kingston's mother, Brave Orchid; Kingston's aunt, Moon Orchid; and finally, Kingston herself—told in five chapters. The chapters integrate Kingston's lived experience with a series of talk-stories—spoken stories that combine Chinese history, myths, and beliefs—that her mother tells her.

The first chapter, "No-Name Woman," begins with one such talk-story, about an aunt Kingston never knew she had. Because this aunt had brought disgrace upon her family by having an illegitimate child, she killed herself and her baby by jumping into the family well in China. After hearing the story, which is told to her as a warning, Kingston is never allowed to mention her aunt aloud again, so she decides to create a history of her aunt in her memoir. She imagines the ways that her aunt attracted a suitor, comparing her aunt's actions of quiet rebellion against the community to her own rebellion. Kingston also recreates her aunt's horrible experience of giving birth in a pigsty and imagines her aunt's ghost walking around with no one to give it gifts, as was Chinese custom. In the end, Kingston is unsure whether she is doing justice to her aunt's memory or just serving her own needs.

"White Tigers" is based on another talk-story, one about the mythical female warrior Fa Mu Lan. Fa Mu Lan, whose story is told through Kingston's first-person narrative, trains to become a warrior from the time she is seven years old, then leads an army of men—even pretending to be a man herself—against the forces of a corrupt baron and emperor. After her battles are over, she returns to be a wife and mother. The story of Fa Mu Lan is contrasted sharply with Kingston's own life in America, in which she can barely stand up to her racist bosses. Kingston realizes, however, that her weapons are her words.

"Shaman" focuses on Kingston's mother, Brave Orchid, and her old life back in China. Brave Orchid was a powerful doctor, midwife, and, according to the talk-story, destroyer of ghosts back in her village. To a young Kingston, Brave Orchid's past is as astounding as it is terrifying, and many of the images from her mother's talk-story—Chinese babies left to die, slave girls being bought and sold, a woman stoned to death by her villagers—haunt Kingston's dreams for years to come. At the end of the chapter, Maxine visits her mother after being away for many years. The two arrive at some kind of understanding after many years of disagreement and conflict, and Brave Orchid is warm and affectionate toward her daughter for the first time in the memoir.

The title "At the Western Palace" refers to another of Brave Orchid's talk-stories, about an emperor who had four wives. It is an analogy for her sister Moon Orchid's situation: Moon Orchid's husband, now a successful Los Angeles doctor, left her behind in China and remarried in America. Brave Orchid urges her sister into a disastrous confrontation with the man to demand her due as his wife. As a result, Moon Orchid, who does not speak a word of English, is left to fend for herself in America. She eventually goes crazy and dies in a California state mental asylum.

The final chapter of the memoir, "A Song for a Barbarian Reed Pipe," is about Kingston herself. This section focuses mainly on her childhood and teenage years, depicting her anger and frustration in trying to express herself and attempting to please an unappreciative mother. There are a number of characters whose personalities highlight many of Kingston's own characteristics, including a silent Chinese girl whom Kingston torments as a little girl. In a pivotal moment in the chapter, Kingston, after unsuccessfully trying to express her feelings one at a time, erupts at her mother with a torrent of complaints and criticisms. Later in her life, however, Kingston comes to appreciate her mother's talk-stories. At the end of the chapter, she even tells one herself: the story of Ts'ai Yen, a warrior poetess captured by barbarians who returns to the Chinese with songs from another land. It is a fitting conclusion to a text in which Kingston combines very different worlds and cultures and creates a harmony of her own.

CHARACTER LIST

Maxine Hong Kingston The author and narrator of *The Woman Warrior*. Kingston relates both her own memoir and the stories of women related or linked to her in some way: her mother, her aunt (Moon Orchid), No-Name Woman, and mythical characters such as Fa Mu Lan. Though Kingston is the narrator, she shares the protagonist role with her mother. Her memories of own life do not figure prominently until the final chapter, "A Song for a Barbarian Reed Pipe," in which she grows out of the frustrations of her childhood and finds her own voice.

Brave Orchid Kingston's mother, whose "talk-stories" about Chinese life and traditions haunt Kingston like ghosts from another world. Brave Orchid is a proud and intelligent woman who comes off as both gentle and cruel in the memoir. She appears throughout the book but figures most prominently in "Shaman," which depicts her life in China as a doctor and a woman of almost magical powers. Along with her sister, Moon Orchid, Brave Orchid is a main focus of "At the Western Palace."

Moon Orchid Brave Orchid's sister, who comes to America in her 1960s. Moon Orchid emigrates—at Brave Orchid's encouragement—in an attempt to find her estranged husband, who left China thirty years earlier. Whereas Brave Orchid is forceful and capable and determined, Moon Orchid is timid and incapable of completing even the easiest tasks. She is largely unable to adjust to life in America.

No-Name Woman Kingston's unnamed aunt, who kills herself and her illegitimate child in China by jumping into the family well. Kingston knows nothing about her aunt and must make up stories in "No-Name Woman." Kingston portrays her aunt as a timid woman who gave in to a forbidden passion and was then driven to suicide when she was cast out from the village.

Fa Mu Lan A heroic female warrior from a traditional Chinese legend, whom Brave Orchid originally describes to Kingston in a talk-story. Fa Mu Lan represents both the Chinese female ideal—as a loving mother and wife—and a source of great power and independence. Kingston feels a kinship with the woman warrior and, in "White Tigers," reimagines her story in the first person, as if she were the warrior herself. Kingston also contrasts Fa Mu Lan's great accomplishments and victories with the disappointments of her own life.

The Silent Girl A classmate whom Kingston torments when she is young, as related in "A Song for a Barbarian Reed Pipe." Both Kingston and the girl are quiet and unpopular, so Kingston hates the girl for reminding her of her own weaknesses.

Moon Orchid's Husband A successful doctor in Los Angeles. He had not seen Moon Orchid in thirty years before the confrontation described in "At the Western Palace." He is typical of many emigrant Chinese who find new lives in America and try to forget their old responsibilities.

The Old Couple An elderly couple who, in "White Tigers," train Fa Mu Lan in martial arts and survival skills on top of the mountain. The old couple are quasideities—Fa Mu Lan sees that they are hundreds of years old—and, significantly, are more like parents to the woman warrior than her own parents are.

Ts'ai Yen A Chinese poetess born in 175 A.D., the source of the title of the final chapter. Ts'ai Yen was captured by barbarians and forced to fight their battles, and she brought back to her people, the Han, a song called "Eighteen Stanzas for a Barbarian Reed Pipe." She serves a metaphor for both Kingston's own project in writing her memoir—bringing her songs back to her people from "savage lands"—and for the act of talk-story in general.

Kingston's Father A man who runs the laundry in America with Brave Orchid and appears in the memoir only rarely. In both "No-Name Woman" and "Shaman," Kingston's father has already left for America, and in "At the Western Palace," he disappears quickly after Moon Orchid's arrival. Kingston's father is the main character of her second memoir, *China Men*.

ANALYSIS OF MAJOR CHARACTERS

MAXINE HONG KINGSTON Kingston is an elusive, multifaceted narrator in *The Woman Warrior*. Sometimes she disappears entirely into the story of someone else, as in the mythical story of Fa Mu Lan in "White Tigers." At other times she disappears completely, as in the story of her aunt Moon Orchid in "At the Western Palace," a chapter that does not contain a single instance of the word "I"—very unusual for an autobiographical work. It is worth noting that when Kingston discusses *The Woman Warrior* elsewhere, she puts quotes around the "I." This underscores the fact that the narrator is in many ways just as made-up as a character in a work of fiction.

The Woman Warrior is very different from traditional memoirs and autobiographies, in which we can count on the stability and reliability of the "I" as a guide to the text. Because the "I" changes in *The Woman Warrior*, we cannot rely on the author to provide a truthful account in the strictest sense of the word. We learn, for instance, that the entire confrontation episode in "At the Western Palace" was told to Kingston second- or even third-hand. We wonder, therefore, just how much of this episode is true. At the end of the text, Kingston admits that even she cannot tell what is fact from fiction. Her point, however, is that the truth does not really matter. What is important are Kingston's memories and how she comes to terms with them.

Kingston takes on so many voices and personas that it is difficult to pin down a list of character traits. She is at times rebellious, verbally lashing out against her mother as a teenager; she is curious and imaginative, inventing scenarios about her unnamed aunt in "No-Name Woman"; she is meek, allowing her racist bosses to walk all over her in "White Tigers"; and she is cruel, tormenting a poor silent girl in her school. We do see broad changes in Kingston's character—personal growth that makes the text seem, at times, more like a traditional autobiography. Kingston grows from a girl who can barely speak to a woman who finds outlet for her words on paper. She grows from someone scared by the ghosts of her mother's talk-stories to a person who can peer into the dark corners of her past. Perhaps most important, she grows from a frustrated and anguished daughter to an independent adult who can compose a poetic memoir about her heritage.

BRAVE ORCHID Brave Orchid is as much the protagonist of *The Woman Warrior* as Kingston is, and her character is nearly as elusive. Brave Orchid is a bundle of contradictions: fiercely intelligent but rarely perceptive, misguided about Moon Orchid's husband; proud of her heritage but also guarded about much of her past, such as the suicide of No-Name Woman; and gentle at times to her family but also capable of incredible coldness and cruelty, as in her constant demeaning of her daughter's achievements. In many ways, Brave Orchid is representative of the emigrant Chinese, who fiercely guard the customs and traditions of their people and consider all Americans to be "ghosts" on the outside. The emigrant Chinese attitude to the American-born Chinese—their own sons and daughters—comes across as a mixture of fear, resentment, and disappointment.

Brave Orchid has suffered considerable culture shock coming to America, particularly in making the transition from being an independent and well-respected doctor in China to slaving at a laundry and picking tomatoes in California. Throughout most of the memoir she seems to harbor the notion that the family will one day return to China, and she is often quite ignorant—perhaps purposefully so—of the killings that are going on in her home country during the Communist revolution. In one of the more poignant moments of the book, Brave Orchid tells Kingston—after they have been in America for more than thirty years—that they have finally given away the land back in China and that she must resign herself to living in America.

For all of the frustration and anguish behind Kingston's portrayal of her mother, it is also comic. Brave Orchid is a fish out of water in America, and a number of her culture clashes are hilarious. She takes Kingston's cold pill, thinking that it is LSD; she invents wild scenarios in which she helps Moon Orchid reclaim her lost husband; she makes Kingston demand free candy from the pharmacist when he delivers a wrong prescription; she cuts—or so she claims—part of Kingston's tongue in order to loosen up her speech. There is something ridiculous to the extremes of Brave Orchid's behavior, and Kingston seems to realize this in hindsight. The humor of the situation thus allows Kingston to take a much kinder view of her mother as an adult than perhaps she could have as a child.

MOON ORCHID Besides Kingston and Brave Orchid, Moon Orchid is the only other fully realized character in *The Woman Warrior*, although she appears in only one chapter. Pretty, weak, and uncoordinated—in her sister's words, "useless"—Moon Orchid plays foil to Brave Orchid's force of personality, determination, and ability. Moon Orchid is also an effective contrast to her Chinese-American nieces and nephews, whom she follows around the house, observing their everyday actions and foibles. She and the children are so different from each other in language, age, and culture that they almost appear to one another like different species.

Like her sister, Moon Orchid represents the ridiculousness of clinging to Chinese customs and traditions in California. The scene in which she and Brave Orchid hatch plans to surprise her husband is as funny as it is sad, and the outcome of the encounter is disastrous. Afterward, when Moon Orchid tries to live on her own in Los Angeles, she proves wholly unable to adjust to American life and slowly goes insane, having paranoid delusions about Mexicans trying to kill her. Moon Orchid's disintegration in America is partly a function of her age, but it is also clear that she is inherently not as strong as her sister. Moon Orchid's story reminds us that the cultural clash can have terrible effects on those who are not equipped to deal with it.

THEMES, MOTIFS, AND SYMBOLS

THEMES

THE ROLE OF WOMEN IN CHINESE SOCIETY Men are conspicuously, intentionally absent from *The Woman Warrior*. Each chapter focuses on a woman who affects Kingston's life and in most cases depicts how that woman relates to the male-dominated society around her. However, it is often not the men themselves who are most oppressive in the memoir, but rather the power of tradition as carried through women. It is women who utter phrases like "better to have geese than girls" to Kingston, women who are pictured destroying the house of No-Name Woman, and girls who torment each other on the playground in the final chapter. The subtext of Kingston's relationship with her mother—and her mother's talk-stories in particular—is both empowerment and disempowerment. Her mother tells her stories of female swordswomen and shamans and is herself an accomplished, intelligent doctor, but she also reinforces the notion that girls are disappointments to their parents, despite what they may accomplish. As a young girl, Kingston feels haunted by the images or ghosts of little Chinese girls whose parents left them to die because they wanted sons instead. Given such conflicting messages, it is no surprise that in Kingston's fantasy retelling of the story of Fa Mu Lan, the warrior manages to be everything to everyone, able to satisfy the role of wife and mother while still leading her people to victory in battle. It is the only way—besides leaving home—that Kingston is able to reconcile what she has been taught.

THE SEARCH FOR A VOICE From the first words of Kingston's memoir—"You must not tell anyone"—Kingston must struggle to find her voice. This opening is both ironic and paradoxical; the former because Kingston is in effect telling everyone, the latter because so much of what Brave Orchid teaches Kingston is based on telling, giving voice to Chinese customs, traditions, and the lives of the past. As a whole, however, the Chinese emigrants are so guarded of their community that they keep silent about anything that could disrupt it. It is often their children, as Chinese-Americans, who bear the burden of the community's silence. Kingston is naturally quiet and socially awkward, and much of her memoir, especially "A Song for a Barbarian Reed Pipe," is about the process of finding her own voice. Kingston's mother is clearly both a help and a hindrance: note how she says she cut Kingston's tongue in order to help her talk more, while Kingston believes her mother did it for exactly the opposite reason. It is with some pride, however, that Kingston eventually begins to tell talk-stories herself. In the end, the very act of writing her story becomes her way of finding a voice.

THE DIFFICULTIES OF GROWING UP CHINESE-AMERICAN Though Kingston claims elsewhere that she does not want her memoir to be "representative," it is clear that she is also reaching out to other Chinese-Americans who share her feelings of displacement and frustration. For the first generation born in America, it is especially difficult to reconcile the heavy-handed and often restrictive traditions of the emigrants with the relative freedom of life in America. Being Chinese-American often means that one is torn between both worlds without really being part of either. Indeed, Kingston feels as different from her American classmates as she does from her own relatives. For a woman, this frustration is heightened because many of the typical traits of Chinese women, such as a loud speaking voice, are not considered "American-feminine." Another difficulty in being Chinese-American is that one's cultural heritage is always second-hand, filtered through the lens—or talk-story—of someone else. At the time Kingston wrote her memoir she had never even been to China. Much of the memoir is about the attempt to sort out the difference between what is Chinese and what is peculiar to her family, what is real and what is just "the movies."

W

MOTIFS

GHOSTS Ghosts are the most frequently recurring motif in *The Woman Warrior* and also the most difficult to pin down. Ghosts refer to both American and Chinese, humans and animals, the living and the dead. There are malevolent ghosts that do harm, such as the "sitting ghost"; ancestral ghosts that look after the living; and everyday ghosts that do what everyday ghosts do, such as the "newsboy ghost." The elusiveness of ghosts is what makes them so powerful in the memoir. Kingston grew up listening to so many of her mother's talk-stories that in writing the memoir, she can no longer tell what is real from what is imagined. Did she really have a mentally retarded boy follow her around, or is he just another ghost, a creation of her memory? Kinston must shine lights into the corners of her past to determine what is real.

An important facet of ghosts in the story is that they change depending on the point of view. To Brave Orchid, everyone in America who is not Chinese is a ghost; the most important world is the world of emigrant Chinese around her. But to Americans or Chinese-Americans, it is often the Chinese who are ghosts. After hearing Brave Orchid talk about ghosts for so long, it is a shocking role reversal when Brave Orchid and Moon Orchid confront Moon Orchid's husband and find that he wants nothing to do with any of them; it is they who have suddenly become the ghosts.

THE WARRIOR The warrior motif is an extremely important part of Kingston's memoir, referring as it does to Fa Mu Lan, Brave Orchid, and Kingston herself. Much of *The Woman Warrior* is a struggle—between mother and daughter, daughter and society, and so on—making the warrior motif especially appropriate. Fa Mu Lan, the true warrior, becomes the standard by which Kingston measures herself. Though in some ways Kingston comes up wanting comparing herself to the mythical female warrior, she discovers that the very act of writing is both a battle and a victory. Brave Orchid is at times a warrior, at times an inspiration to her daughter, and at times a bitter enemy. She is clearly the most forceful and free-willed woman in the memoir, especially in comparison to her sister, Moon Orchid. There are a number of instances, fictional or otherwise, when Brave Orchid fights battles, such as when she destroys the "sitting ghost" and when she threatens to hit Moon Orchid's husband. Much of Kingston's memoir is about trying to find a way to fight back: in "A Song for a Barbarian Reed Pipe," she actually shows some fighting spirit herself in a vitriolic outburst against her mother. It is significant, however, that the chapter ends with Ts'ai Yen, who is both a warrior and a poetess. As much as Kingston might want to be a fierce warrior, she knows that her true power is in her word and song.

TALK-STORIES Talk-stories, which draw on both Chinese myths and lived experience, give structure to *The Woman Warrior*. There is at least one talk-story in every chapter, most often told by Brave Orchid to Kingston when she is a little girl. Furthermore, the memoir begins and ends with important talk-stories, one about No-Name Woman and another about Ts'ai Yen. Most often, Brave Orchid tells talk-stories in order to teach her family about important life lessons or Chinese traditions or to make them behave in a certain way. As such, the stories are both stifling and liberating to Kingston, responsible for many of her fears and insecurities but also providing her with inspiration. Though she is frequently upset by her mother's talk-stories, at the end of the memoir she tells Brave Orchid with pride that she tells talk-stories too. In a symbolic gesture of reconciliation, the memoir ends with a talk-story that is half Kingston's and half her mother's.

SYMBOLS

BIRDS Birds are important symbols in "White Tigers" and "Shaman." In "White Tigers," a bird guides Kingston, as seven-year-old Fa Mu Lan, up the mountain to meet her mentors. The bird represents the bravery of a child who would be willing to climb a mountain in pursuit, and also represents the fantastical possibility of a girl literally rising above her station in life and growing to become a great leader. The bird is such an auspicious symbol in the legend of Fa Mu Lan, in fact, that Kingston is especially disturbed that a bird represents death in another story, that of her Fourth Uncle's death—he is killed by Communists while he is trying to capture birds as food for his family. To Kingston, it is almost as if the talk-stories are contradicting themselves.

Birds are an auspicious symbol in the talk-stories of "Shaman." A sea bird is painted on the side of Brave Orchid's boat to Canton. To Kingston, the bird represents luck because the very next ship is boarded by pirates. It might also be said to represent fortune in the literal sense; when Brave Orchid goes to the market to shop, her wallet unfolds "like wings."

MOUNTAINS Mountains represent isolation, safety, fortune and possibility in *The Woman Warrior*. The mountain in "White Tigers" is a magical place where Fa Mu Lan learns wisdom and martial arts. In

"Shaman," the mountain near Brave Orchid's village is a place of refuge during the Japanese bombing of China. Throughout the memoir, the "Gold Mountain" is a powerful symbol of the fortune and promise of America.

The mountain is also, however, an illusory symbol. It hardly proves a refuge from the horrors of war in "Shaman," as the villagers stone to death a crazy woman whom they believe a spy. Moreover, the "Gold Mountain" does not turn out to be such a blessing for Kingston's parents, who must toil in laundries and tomato fields to earn a living. Like the bird, the mountain is a symbol that Kingston finds alternately promising and disturbing.

BOUND FEET Bound feet are the most literal symbol in the memoir, representing the restrictions placed upon women in traditional Chinese society. Bound feet make only brief appearances in the text, most likely because the practice had died out before most of the women in Kingston's family lived (there is a brief mention of her grandmother's having bound feet at the end of "A Song for a Barbarian Reed Pipe"). There is an important section of "White Tigers" where Kingston writes about China wrapping metaphorical "double binds" around her feet. Just as the binding of feet represents both restriction and—in the most one-sided of ways—love and support, so is Kingston both frustrated by Chinese customs envious of women "loved enough to be supported."

CIRCLES The circle appears in "No-Name Woman" as a literal symbol, or "talisman," to represent the Chinese belief in community, family kinship, and law. The Chinese family—that is, the community of kin—is like a circle: people have children to look after them when they get old, and then the dead continue to look after the family. It is also a closed circle—shut off to everyone outside the community, like Americans—and any interruption in the circle has profound effects. Thus, even a private action, such as No-Name Woman's transgression, affects the rest of the village, and be punished with dire consequences.

IMPORTANT QUOTATIONS EXPLAINED

---

1. *"You must not tell anyone," my mother said, "what I am about to tell you."*

The opening words of *The Woman Warrior*, spoken by Brave Orchid, set the tone for much of the rest of the memoir. Much of the memoir is either directly or indirectly dominated by Brave Orchid's talk-stories, and it is up to Kingston to make sense of them. It is especially notable and ironic that the memoir begins with the phrase "You must not tell anyone." Kingston's struggle in "No-Name Woman" and in the memoir as a whole is to write about that which is never said: her unnamed dead aunt, the atrocities in her mother's Chinese village, and another aunt, Moon Orchid, who is unable to adapt to life in America. Kingston's struggle is also about finding a voice, as both a Chinese-American and a woman, after she has been silenced all her life. Writing a memoir therefore becomes a rebellion of sorts, from the first sentence—she is in fact telling everyone. She displays a willingness to break the silence and asserts power over those who have held her back.

W

---

2. *The swordswoman and I are not so dissimilar. May my people understand the resemblance soon so that I can return to them. What we have in common are the words at our backs. The idioms for revenge are "report a crime" and "report to five families." The reporting is the vengeance—not the beheading, not the gutting, but the words. And I have so many words—"chink" words and "gook" words too—that they do not fit on my skin.*

At the end of "White Tigers," Kingston draws a sharp contrast between her fantasy about Fa Mu Lan, the woman warrior, and the defining moments of her real "American life." Whereas Fa Mu Lan vanquishes entire armies and defeats evil barons and giants, Kingston cannot even stand up to her petty racist bosses. However, in this quotation, the closing thoughts of the chapter, she makes an important comparison between herself and the warrior: they both are burdened with words. Fa Mu Lan had her village's grievances tattooed on her back; Kingston has Chinese stories practically drilled into her brain and is labeled with racial epithets. Her personal struggle and vengeance lie in making sense of the stories through writing, in depicting through words the struggles of growing up Chinese-American. There is an important difference, though: Fa Mu Lan could achieve her vengeance and then return home, but Kingston's vengeance seems to be a never-ending struggle. She has so many words to deal with that "they do not fit on my skin." *The Woman Warrior* is just the beginning of Kingston's attempt to articulate her experience, and her journey as a writer is far from over.

---

3. *To make my waking life American-normal, I turn on the lights before anything untoward makes an appearance. I push the deformed into my dreams, which are in Chinese, the language of impossible stories. Before we can leave our parents, they stuff our heads like the suitcases which they jam-pack with homemade underwear.*

This passage, from "Shaman," emphasizes the anguish and fear Kingston so often feels as a result of Brave Orchid's talk-stories and the difficulty in mixing Chinese and American cultures. Ghosts are everywhere in Brave Orchid's world of Chinese talk-stories, bothering and threatening human beings at all times. In America, however, ghosts do not fit in with Kingston's idea of a normal life; they are simply "impossible stories." In her waking hours, then, Kingston maintains an "American-normal" life, while in her dreams, the ghosts crammed in her head by her mother's talk-stories come back: deformed babies, women driven crazy and killed, strange animals and creatures. The suitcase, packed as it is with "homemade underwear," is especially appropriate, given that Kingston is living among emigrants who have picked up their lives and moved to another country. It is as if Kingston's mother, through her talk-stories, will not let her carve out a new life in America without carrying her cultural baggage of ghosts.

---

4. *"He's living in Los Angeles with his second wife, and they have three children. Claim your rights. Those are your children. He's got two sons, you have two sons. You take them away from her. You become their mother."*

   "Do you really think I can be a mother of sons? Don't you think they'll be loyal to her, since she gave birth to them?"

   "The children will go to their true mother—you," said Brave Orchid. "That's the way it is with mothers and children."

This exchange between Brave Orchid and Moon Orchid precedes their trip to Los Angeles to find Moon Orchid's husband, who had come to America thirty years before and left Moon Orchid back in China. Brave Orchid has grand illusions of her sister confronting her estranged husband and being welcomed into his new home. In fact, Brave Orchid has orchestrated it so that Moon Orchid has practically no other choice, as she has sold her apartment and has moved to America for good. Most important, this quotation illustrates the extent of Brave Orchid's delusions about how emigrant Chinese behave in America. She assumes that the old traditions will carry over in the new country and asserts without hesitation the absurd notion that children would renounce their own biological mother. Ironically, Moon Orchid, who is much closer to Chinese traditions than her sister, is the voice of reason in this exchange. She points out what just about everyone else besides Brave Orchid is thinking, foreshadowing the disaster of the eventual confrontation. The fact that Brave Orchid is so misguided raises questions about just how much she misinterprets Chinese traditions. If Brave Orchid can be so wrong in her beliefs, how is Kingston to interpret her talk-stories?

---

5. *Be careful what you say. It comes true. It comes true. I had to leave home in order to see the world logically, logic the new way of seeing. I learned to think that mysteries are for explanation. I enjoy the simplicity. Concrete pours out of my mouth to cover the forests with freeways and sidewalks. Give me plastics, periodical tables, TV dinners with vegetables no more complex than peas mixed with diced carrots. Shine floodlights into dark corners: no ghosts.*

This passage appears in "A Song for a Barbarian Reed Pipe," shortly after the episode in which Kingston yells at her mother. It encapsulates some of the clarity Kingston begins to have once she leaves home—her ability to tell what is real from what is not, to make sense where before there was only confusion. It points to what we might call an "Americanization" of her life, a life filled with simple things like plastics and TV dinners. At the same time, it also points to a sadness that Kingston feels for having renounced some important aspects of her heritage. Note the regretful, almost gloomy repetition of the phrase "It comes true." Whereas her mother tells talk-stories about mythical places and peoples, Kingston says that she pours concrete out of her mouth—not exactly a poetic skill—as if she were turning the mazes and mysteries of her past into an ordered American city. The ordering of life may be useful to Kingston in some ways, but it can also deny the richness of her heritage. In fact, perhaps this quotation is most useful as a reminder of what *The Woman Warrior* is not: a traditional linear autobiography. Rather, living in a world with "no ghosts" is only one phase of Kingston's life; her memoir is more notable—and interesting—for the complexity and confusion of her recollection than it is for its clarity.

The Women of Brewster Place

Gloria Naylor (1950–)

CONTEXT

Gloria Naylor was born in New York City on January 25, 1950. She was raised in a comfortable middle-class community in Queens, but her family's roots were in Mississippi. Naylor's parents migrated from the South during the Great Migration of African-Americans from rural southern communities to large, industrial northern cities. Naylor's first novel, *The Women of Brewster Place*, reflects this dual cultural inheritance. Almost all of the characters are transplanted from their home community in the South to the unnamed northern city that is the context for this novel.

After receiving a bachelor's degree in literature from Brooklyn College, Naylor began to seriously write fiction. Although she was raised to respect and love the classics of English literature, Naylor was acutely aware of the fact that missing from the narratives of Faulkner, Dickens, Baldwin, and Ellison were the stories that reflected her own experiences as an African-American woman. Before she could break from the tradition in which she had been raised, however, she needed a model through which she could begin to filter her own narratives. Around the same time that Naylor began to write fiction, Toni Morrison published her first novel, *The Bluest Eye* (1965). Morrison's novel, which received widespread critical acclaim and marked the start of Morrison's Nobel Prize-winning writing career, had a profound effect on Naylor. The novel not only revealed literature's unique ability represent Naylor's own stories but it also gave her the confidence and authority she needed to write about the places and people she knew.

Naylor published *The Women of Brewster Place* in 1982 after completing a master's degree in African-American studies at Yale. The novel was well-received by critics and authors alike for its lyrical prose style and its frank yet hopeful portrayal of an African-American community struggling to survive in a depressed landscape. In *The Women of Brewster Place*, Naylor draws on many ideas critical to her own personal and intellectual development, including class, gender, sexuality, and general reflections on the African-American experience in the United States, from the legacy of the Civil Rights Era to the importance of faith and religion.

Following the success of *The Women of Brewster Place*, Naylor published her second novel, *Linden Hills* (1985). If *The Women of Brewster Place* is the first half of Naylor's attempt to chronicle the experiences of African-Americans, then *Linden Hills* is its faithful counterpart: the community of affluent African-Americans that it treats is mentioned several times in *The Women of Brewster Place*. The spiritual and moral concern that Naylor brought to her first novel are recast onto a different strata of African-Americans. Regardless of class distinction, however, Naylor's primary concerns remain consistent throughout her work. In her next three novels, *Mama Day* (1993), *Bailey's Café* (1993), and *The Men of Brewster of Place* (1998), Naylor continued to present the ideas that compromise the experiences of African-Americans, especially those of black women.

PLOT OVERVIEW

The Women of Brewster Place is a novel told in seven stories. Of the seven stories, six are centered on individual characters, while the final story is about the entire community. The primary characters and the title characters of each chapter are all women and residents of Brewster Place.

Brewster Place is a housing development in an unnamed city. It seems destined to be an unfortunate place since the people linked to its creation are all corrupt. Despite the secretive circumstances surrounding its development, Brewster Place survives for decades, offering a home to one new wave of migrants after another. The life history of Brewster Place comes to resemble the history of the country as the community changes with each new historical shift. Following the Civil Rights Era, Brewster Place inherits its last inhabitants, African-Americans, many of whom are migrants from the southern half of the United States. The stories within the novel are the stories of these residents.

The first and longest narrative within the novel is Mattie Michael's. Mattie, along with several other characters, arrives in Brewster Place from her parents' home in the South. Mattie leaves her parents' home because she is pregnant by a disreputable man named Butch Fuller. Mattie decides to move to the North at approximately the same time in history as the Great Migration. Living away from home with a new baby, Mattie takes a job working in an assembly line. She works long hours and is forced to live in a dilapidated building. After a rat bites her child, Mattie decides to find a new home. While walking with her baby, she runs into Ms. Eva Turner, an old, kind, light-skinned African-American woman who takes her into her home and refuses to charge her rent. After Ms. Eva dies, Mattie purchases the house and remains there to raise her son, Basil.

Basil grows up to be a troubled young man who is unable to claim responsibility for his actions. One night, he kills a man in a bar fight and is arrested. Mattie uses her house for collateral, which Basil forfeits once he disappears. Mattie, after thirty years, is forced to give up her home and move to Brewster Place.

Mattie's childhood friend, Etta Johnson, joins Mattie at Brewster Place. After a long life of running from one man to the next, she has arrived at Mattie's, hoping to find some stability. Mattie takes her to church, where Etta meets Reverend Woods. She is taken by his looks, wealth, and status, but after sleeping with him, she realizes it was all just a fantasy and that he wanted only sex. Etta leaves feeling broken, but her spirit is restored once she finds out that Mattie has stayed up all night waiting for her.

Kiswana Browne is different from all of Brewster Place's other residents in that she has chosen to live there voluntarily. Raised in the affluent community, Linden Hills, Kiswana dropped out of college to live in Brewster Place, where she believes she can effect real social change in the black community. Kiswana is nervously waiting her mother's first visit to her rundown studio apartment. Once her mother arrives, the two women have several short arguments that culminate in Kiswana calling her mother a "white-man's nigger." Kiswana's mother responds by explaining the origin of Kiswana's real name, Melanie, and the pride she has in her heritage. Before leaving, she secretly gives Kiswana enough money to have a phone line installed.

Lucielia Louis Turner, also known as Ciel, is the granddaughter of Ms. Eva. Lucielia grew up with Mattie and her son, Basil. Now grown, Lucielia has a daughter, Serafina, with a man named Eugene. Eugene, in addition to constantly leaving Lucielia, also treats her and their daughter terribly. After complaining about his lack of opportunities, Eugene indirectly gets Lucielia to abort what would have been their second child. Shortly afterward, however, he comes home to say that he's found a new job in Maine and must leave right away. His lying is obvious; he's simply determined to leave. While Lucielia and Eugene are fighting, Serafina chases a roach into an electric socket with a fork. She is electrocuted and dies, leaving Lucielia nearly lifeless with grief. Following the funeral, Mattie is the one who begins to release Lucielia's enormous grief by rocking and bathing her until she falls asleep crying.

As a child, Cora Lee was obsessed with babies, and this obsession continues when she is an adult. Beginning in her sophomore year of high school, she has one child after another, almost all with different men. She lives in a filthy apartment, and her children are terribly neglected, since she can only care for them while they're infants. One day, Kiswana finds one of Cora Lee's children eating out of a garbage can. She tries to help Cora Lee by inviting her to a production of a Shakespeare play being staged in the park. Cora Lee is so moved by Kiswana's brief appearance that she takes interest in her children. She cleans them and the house in preparation for the play. At the play, the children and Cora Lee are all touched by the performance. By the end, Cora Lee begins to imagine a better future for her children. She kisses them all goodnight. However, when she goes to her own bed, there's a nameless man waiting for her. She drops her clothes and goes to bed with him.

Lorraine and Theresa are the only lesbian residents of Brewster Place. The residents fear Lorraine and Theresa, even though they are a loving and considerate couple. One resident in particular, Sophie, watches their every move and spreads rumors about their behavior. Lorraine is hurt by the judgmental responses of her neighbors. Theresa, however, claims not to care what people think or say. Lorraine tries to incorporate herself into the community by attending Kiswana's tenants' association meeting, but there, Sophie attacks her for her sexuality. She leaves in tears, and Ben, the oldest resident and the janitor of the complex, consoles her by taking her to his apartment and telling her the story of his daughter and wife. Ben's daughter was indirectly led into prostitution by her parents, who refused to do anything about the fact that she was being forced to sleep with their white landlord.

Lorraine gains confidence from her burgeoning relationship with Ben. After a fight with Theresa, Lorraine goes to a party on her own. Afterward, instead of coming straight home, she goes down a dark alley. She is confronted by a group of young men who had earlier insulted her because of her sexuality. They gang rape her and leave her for dead. Lorraine manages to get up just as the sun is rising. She stumbles down the alley and sees Ben. She grabs a brick and crushes his skull with it.

Following Ben's death, Mattie has a dream that the rain that has drenched Brewster Place since Ben's murder has suddenly stopped in time for the block party planned by the tenants' association. The rain eventually returns during the party, and everyone except the women run for shelter. The women believe that the wall in front of which Ben died still has blood on it, so they begin to frantically tear it apart, brick by brick. Mattie wakes to a beautiful sunny day. In the end, all of the residents of Brewster Place are forced out, and the block is condemned. Brewster Place, abandoned, lives on only in the hopes and memories of the women who once lived there.

CHARACTER LIST

Brewster Place The name of the housing development in which the novel is set. Although Brewster Place is a physical structure, it is personified and endowed with a spirit that brings it to life. Brewster Place is at once a warm, loving community and a desolate and blighted neighborhood on the verge of collapsing.

Mattie Michael The most important character in the novel. Mattie moves to Brewster Place late in life, after her son abandons her and forces her to lose her home. Mattie quickly becomes a surrogate mother to several of the women in the housing complex, offering love and support to women who, like her, have only one another to rely on.

Etta Mae Johnson Mattie's childhood friend and a resident of Brewster Place. Etta has spent her life bouncing from one city and man to the next, constantly in search of the fulfillment of some unnamed desire. Etta moves into Brewster Place late in life. When she arrives, she feels that her spirit has broken. Eventually, she comes to understand the value of her relationship with Mattie.

Kiswana Browne One of the six women portrayed in the novel. Kiswana, whose real name is Melanie, was born and raised in an affluent black suburb, Linden Hills. Kiswana, however, drops out of college, changes her name, and moves into Brewster Place in order to fight for the cultural and class revolution she so ardently believes in. Kiswana is young and naïve but full of optimism and ideals.

Eva Turner The woman who provides Mattie and her son with a home. Eva has a brief but important role in the novel. Her act of kindness provides Mattie with a home in which to raise her child. In addition, Eva's keen insight into Mattie's relationship with her son foreshadows the problems Mattie will have with him as an adult.

Basil Michael Mattie's only son. Basil is the center of Mattie's life from the moment of his birth and grows up under her watchful and loving eye. He is unable to accept any responsibility for his actions, and, as an adult, he kills a man in a fight. While out on bail, he selfishly decides to flee and forfeit his mother's house rather than risk even the slim chance of going to jail.

Butch Fuller Mattie's one-time lover and Basil's father. Butch lives his life only for the moment. He moves from one woman to the next, always leaving before any problems or trouble can arise. He indirectly passes his life philosophy on to Basil.

Cora Lee One of the women of Brewster Place. Cora, from a young girl, is obsessed with new baby dolls, demanding a new one every Christmas of her childhood. She grows up to have a number of different children by different men and is unable to care for any of them.

Lorraine One half of the lesbian couple portrayed in "The Two." Lorraine is skinny, light-skinned, and sensitive. She is overly concerned with the way people treat and judge her for her sexuality. She tries to fit in with the other women of Brewster Place but is rejected. She eventually finds comfort in Ben, whom she murders after being gang raped in an alley.

Theresa One half of the lesbian couple portrayed in "The Two." Theresa is the opposite of her partner, Lorraine. She is shorter, darker, and more attractive. Theresa is a strong-willed, commanding woman who tries not to care what anyone says about her, but she is obviously disturbed by the prejudice she and Lorraine encounter.

Ben The oldest resident of Brewster Place and a drunk. Ben is the first African-American to move into Brewster Place. He arrives from the South after his wife and daughter abandon him. He is tormented by his memories and is constantly seeking solace in alcohol. Ben becomes a brief father figure for Lorraine, and reveals the depths of his compassion and emotion. He is killed by Lorraine.

C. C. Baker The leader of a group of boys who do drugs and rob people. C. C. is a young African-American male who terrorizes his community with drugs and violence. He is the primary figure responsible for Lorraine's rape. He takes out on her, and the other residents of Brewster Place, his frustrated desires.

Lucielia Turner One of the women of Brewster Place. Lucielia is Eva's granddaughter. She appears again in the novel as a young woman with a daughter, Serafina, and a worthless boyfriend, Eugene, whom she loves desperately despite his shortcomings. Lucielia is heartbroken and devastated after Serafina dies.

Eugene Lucielia's boyfriend and the father of her daughter, Serafina. Eugene, like many of the other men in the novel, is irresponsible and too self-absorbed to be concerned with the consequences of his actions. While fighting with Lucielia over his decision to leave her and Serafina, Serafina accidentally kills herself.

Sophie A resident of Brewster Place. Sophie is responsible for leading the campaign against Lorraine and Theresa. She is petty and vindictive, and her attacks on Lorraine are rooted in her own insecurities.

Ms. Browne Kiswana Browne's mother. Ms. Browne is a prosperous, middle-aged black woman who lives in affluent Linden Hills. Despite her daughter's claim that she is divorced from the black community, Ms. Browne reveals herself to be a thoughtful and proud woman who wants only what's best for her daughter.

ANALYSIS OF MAJOR CHARACTERS

MATTIE MICHAEL Mattie Michael is the most consistent and prominent character in *The Women of Brewster Place*. As an older woman who has already raised and lost a child, she is a surrogate mother figure to several of the other women. She has endured her share of hardships—losing a child, fleeing her parents' home, and losing her own home—yet she continues to persevere. Her constant strength is a source of support for women such as Etta Mae Johnson and Lucielia Turner. Her generous heart and deep faith represent the best elements not only of Brewster Place but also of African-American women in general. In many ways, Mattie is the bedrock of the Brewster Place community. When she arrives, she does so knowing that it may very well be the last place she ever lives. However, she is determined not to be broken by that knowledge. She continues to live her life the best way she knows how, and, in doing so, she is able to add a measure of comfort to almost everyone she encounters.

ETTA MAE JOHNSON Etta spends the bulk of her life after fleeing the South searching to fulfill some unnamed desire, a mixture of a desire for love, stability, and someone with whom to share her life. She moves from one man to the next, hoping to find in each of them at least a part of what she's seeking. Like the old blues songs she carries in her head, Etta sees herself as a tragic and lonely figure. Her name, in fact, could even be taken as an invocation of Etta James, the famous jazz singer whose mournful songs have clearly played an important role in defining Etta's identity. After a long life of disappointments, Etta settles into Brewster Place, hoping that perhaps she can find that long-sought-after security. Instead, she finds more disappointment and failure. Only at the end of her chapter in the novel does Etta realize that she has already found in Mattie at least some of what she's searching for. Etta is Mattie's childhood friend, and she is, in almost every regard, Mattie's exact opposite. While Etta is sexually adventurous and bold with no true religious devotion, Mattie is solitary and devout. In Mattie she finds a true friend, someone who can help make her life matter.

BEN Ben is the first African-American to live in Brewster Place, and he is the most consistent figure in the community. Known mainly for being a drunk, Ben remains a mystery for most of the novel. When he does appear, he is almost always in a drunken stupor. He keeps the source of his sorrow secret until just before his death. Ben's life, like the lives of many of the women of Brewster Place, has been steeped in loss. Abandoned by both his wife and his daughter, Ben has spent his life trying to run from the ghosts of his past. On the surface, he appears to represent some of the worst elements of life in Brewster Place: he is disheveled and drunk and spends his early morning hours perched on a garbage can in an alley. However, Ben is actually an incredibly compassionate and giving man whose death proves to be an important and tragic loss to the community. Before dying, Ben is able to at least temporarily play the role of a father to Lorraine, providing her with the strength she has needed to stand up for herself. Shortly after Ben's murder, Brewster Place is shut down, suggesting the significance of both his life and his death.

LORRAINE Lorraine is the primary character in the "The Two." A thin, light-skinned woman, Lorraine is much more sensitive to the prejudices and judgments passed on her than is her partner, Theresa. Lorraine is the ideal resident in every regard. A kind neighbor and schoolteacher, Lorraine embodies the best ideals of domestic stability. She is a faithful and loving spouse to Theresa, and, despite the obvious bias against her, she still tries to be a part of Brewster Place's tenants' association. Regardless of Lorraine's qualities as an individual, the women of Brewster Place, Sophie in particular, treat her harshly. She is viewed as a threat to her community, not because of any real threat that she may pose but because of her sexuality. Lorraine's mere presence is able to draw out the deep-seated insecurities the other women of Brewster Place keep buried within themselves. The irony surrounding Lorraine is that her relationship with a woman is more stable and loving than any of the other relationships explored in the narrative.

CORA LEE As a young girl, Cora Lee was obsessed with the newness and freshness of baby dolls, and every year she demanded a new one from her family for Christmas. Cora's fascination with dolls gradually becomes a fascination and obsession with babies of her own. As an adult, Cora is the mother of several children, all of whom she neglects when they are no longer infants. Cora's obsession with babies, and her inability to care for them as children, speaks to a larger idea: Cora is unable to face the reality and hardship that comes with children growing up. She wants only the dependency, need, and affection a baby can offer. The harder relationships in life, the ones that demand patience, sacrifice, and compromise, are beyond her capabilities. In this regard, Cora bears a striking resemblance to Butch Fuller, who had a similar perspective toward women, and Eugene, who, when faced with the difficulties of having a family, chooses immediately to leave.

THEMES, MOTIFS, AND SYMBOLS

THEMES

THE SEARCH FOR A HOME The residents of Brewster Place are constantly searching for a home, both as a literal place to live and as a metaphorical state of mind. For Mattie, her search for a home other than the one in which she was raised takes her from a rundown apartment in the city to a wonderful home in which she raises her child, and finally, to Brewster Place. The journey from one home to another is repeated with every character in the novel. Just as important as any physical location is the security and comfort attached to the idea of home. Brewster Place, though it's falling apart, offers Etta a form of security and comfort she has long lived without. It offers Kiswana the opportunity to live out her ideals, and it offers Mattie the opportunity to become a surrogate mother to a host of women. In every search for a home, what ultimately defines the idea of "home" isn't the condition of the walls but the strength of the relationships within those walls.

THE HOPEFULNESS OF MIGRATION The residents of Brewster Place have migrated to Brewster Place from their parents' home in the South, from the Mediterranean, from the middle-class suburbs ringing the city, or from more secure lives and homes. Regardless of where they come from, they have ended up here, and they have chosen, or been forced, to call it home. Migration, in addition to being a central theme of the novel, is also a central theme in African-American history. From the slave migration to the North prior to the Civil War, to the Great Migration of millions of African-Americans following the post-World War II industrial boom, the idea of escaping to the North has always held hope and promise of a better future.

For most of the residents of Brewster Place, however, migration isn't the fulfillment of a dream but the culmination of a long, frustrating life. Mattie loses her home and ends up in Brewster Place, while Etta arrives after a series of failed relationships. Ben comes to Brewster Place after being abandoned by his wife and daughter, while Lorraine and Theresa are forced out of their more comfortable middle-class existence because of their sexuality. Despite the frustrations and difficulties of life in Brewster Place, it brings all of its residents hope: a light is left on all night; a late-night conversation brings comfort; and many of those searching for meaning find some version of it here.

THE POWER OF PERSONAL CONNECTIONS Throughout the novel, characters reach out to one another across generational, cultural, and gender lines. They reach out to one another and, in doing so, are able to ease the loneliness and hardship that surround their lives. One example of a powerful personal connection is Mattie's relationship with Eva. The women are separated by class, skin tone, and age, yet they find each other and make each other's lives more bearable. Similar benefits arise from other connections, including Mattie's relationship with Etta, Mattie's relationship with Lucielia, Kiswana's relationship with Cora, and Ben's relationship with Lorraine. Each relationship shows how personal connections can sustain and offer hope in even the direst circumstances. The relationships show individuals at their best, and they serve as a necessary counterweight to the abandonment, prejudice, and brutality that comprise much of the novel.

MOTIFS

ILLEGITIMATE BIRTHS In Brewster Place, births are nearly always illegitimate. Every child we hear about is missing a father, from Mattie's son to all of Cora's children. These children are missing half their identities, and their fates seem dire—just as the fate of Brewster Place itself seems dire. Brewster Place's conception is even referred to as a bastard birth. From the moment of Brewster Place's creation, its fate is sealed, the buildings and their inhabitants destined to live in ever-worsening conditions.

FLIGHT The men in *The Women of Brewster Place* are masters at disappearing. Faced with any hardship or difficulty, men such as Basil, Eugene, and Butch run from any responsibility. Their flight is in direct response to any perceived threat to their freedom. Basil disappears when faced with the remote possibility of going to jail. Eugene disappears once his responsibilities as a father and husband become too demanding, and Butch Fuller lives a philosophy dedicated to living in the moment. While the men in the novel are constantly running away, the women are constantly returning home to one another.

BLENDING OF LIVES In *The Women of Brewster Place*, Naylor portrays a broad spectrum of women to show the similarities and differences between the experiences of each generation. In every encounter between an older and younger woman, past and present blend together, and the connection between generations adds perspective and historical depth to the experiences of each. For example, despite Kiswana's dramatic differences of opinion with her mother, she comes to recognize that her life, in fact, is not so different after all. She is merely living her own slightly altered version of the life her mother lived. That realization restores the connection that had previously been threatened when Kiswana insulted her mother.

SYMBOLS

BREWSTER PLACE'S WALL The wall separating Brewster Place from the main avenues of the city serves several important purposes. Following its initial creation, the wall comes to symbolize the indifference with which Brewster Place is treated by the men responsible for its creation. Because of the wall, Brewster Place is economically and culturally isolated from the rest of the city. The wall has forced Brewster Place to fend for itself. For the residents of Brewster Place, the wall symbolizes the fact that for most of them, Brewster Place will be the end of the road. Their lives will go no further, regardless of how much they may hope or dream. The wall, for them, represents the wall that has been built around their lives, either by failed opportunities or by a series of misfortunes. The true disastrousness of the wall becomes evident at the end of the novel. Along this wall, Lorraine drags her nearly lifeless body after she is gang raped, and it is from this wall that she grabs the brick she uses to kill Ben.

SUGAR CANE Butch Fuller uses sugar cane not only to lure Mattie into the fields with him but also to espouse a whole philosophy on life. From the start of Mattie and Butch's trip to the sugar cane field, there is an ominous overtone cast by the large machetes that each of them wields. There is something dangerous about Butch, and that danger is encapsulated perfectly in his attitude toward the world. When preparing to eat the sugar cane, Butch tells Mattie to spit it out while it's still sweet. In telling her this, he not only reveals something about his perspective toward life but also prepares her for what's about to come. Following their brief encounter, Mattie winds up pregnant while Butch becomes nothing more than a ghost. He stays just long enough to enjoy the pleasures of Mattie's body, while refusing to stay around to experience any of the complications or hardships that come about as a result.

COLOR Brewster Place is full of color, from the clothes the children wear on a summer afternoon to the color of its residents. Naylor describes the color of nearly every character that appears in the novel. Characters are described as caramel, honey, light-skinned, dark-skinned, and blue-eyed. In describing characters this way, Naylor shows the spectrum of shades and experiences that have defined African-American culture. There is a diversity of experiences, evident not only in the lives of the characters but in the characters' very skin. In addition, the color of the residents also occasionally serves as a contrast to the drab colors that otherwise characterize Brewster Place. The sky may be gray and the walls "ashen," but the residents of Brewster Place, full of life, are vibrant and rich.

IMPORTANT QUOTATIONS EXPLAINED

---

1. *If she had seen Ben, nothing would have made her believe that practically every apartment contained a family, a Bible, and a dream that one day enough could be scraped from those meager Friday night paychecks to make Brewster Place a distant memory.*

The third-person narrator of the novel expresses this thought in the "Kiswana Browne" chapter, as Kiswana's mother is approaching Brewster Place for the first time. The thought exemplifies the combination of hope and frustration that defines the lives of Brewster Place's residents. Ben has lived in Brewster Place longer that any other resident, and he is also the first African-American to have lived in the community. As such, Ben, whose life has deteriorated into a series of drunken stupors, embodies Brewster Place's deteriorated condition perhaps better than any other resident. His story, like the story of Brewster Place, is more complicated than what is evident on the surface. Despite his alcoholism, Ben is a decent man who has endured more than his fair share of tragedy.

---

2. *She stopped straining when it suddenly came to her that it wasn't important what song it was—someone was waiting up for her.*

As Etta James returns home at the end of her chapter, she finds that Mattie Johnson, her best friend, has waited up all night for her. Etta, who has spent her life running from one home and man to another, is filled with a sense of being loved and being at home in at least one place in the world. Just a few moments earlier, Etta had begun to walk toward Brewster Place, feeling utterly alone and broken. Another man had disappointed her, and yet another dream of finding that long-sought-after sense of security had vanished with him. Fortunately, a different form of security and comfort is waiting for her: it's the comfort and support that come from decades of friendship and love, and, in the end, that is what will support her.

---

3. *They were now sung with the frantic determination of a people who realized that the world was swiftly changing, but for some mystic, complex reason their burden had not.*

This quotation appears in Etta James's chapter during a church service that Etta and Mattie attend together. The crowd has begun to sing an old gospel hymn, clearly moved by the words that have been sung by one generation after another. The words connect the past with the present. They connect the African-American struggle for freedom from slavery to the current struggle of the present generation to make their way in a world that, on the surface, has changed rapidly, but that in reality remains all too similar to the world their parents and their grandparents inherited. Although the African-American experience has changed drastically over the years, there is still so much that remains the same. Yet another generation remains disenfranchised and burdened by poverty. They sing the same hymns, hoping for the same relief and finding the same solace.

---

4. *The young black woman and the old yellow woman sat in the kitchen for hours, blending their lives so that what lay behind one and ahead of the other became indistinguishable.*

Shortly after Mattie Michael and Eva Turner meet for the first time in Mattie's chapter, they begin to share their life stories with each other. They are separated not only by age but by experience. The content of their lives varies in almost every regard, from the fact that Eva has had a number of different husbands while Mattie has had only one brief lover, to the differences in the quality of their lives. Eva is a relatively prosperous woman with a large, beautiful house, while Mattie is poor and homeless. Their differences are highlighted even more by the contrast in their skin tone and age. Yet as the passage stresses, these differences are only superficial. The women are connected to each other by their gender and color. The quote also foreshadows what lies ahead for Mattie. After Eva dies, Mattie inherits her house, and just as Eva's children eventually abandoned her, so too will Mattie's son Basil abandon Mattie. The hardship and joy that Eva has experienced during her life will come to mirror Mattie's own experiences.

The ability to connect to another human being is an essential idea throughout the novel, touched upon again and again in every story that unfolds. Mattie and Eva's connection is the first in a series of life-altering relationships that have the power to restore hope to an otherwise hopeless situation. Mattie finds Eva shortly after she flees her rundown apartment, Etta finds Mattie waiting up for her when she is her lowest point, and Lorraine finds Ben when it seems as if no one else in the world understands her.

---

5. *Ya know, you can't keep him runnin' away from things that hurt him. Sometimes, you just gotta stay there and teach him how to go through the bad and good of whatever comes.*

Eva, upon first meeting Mattie in Mattie's chapter, offers Mattie this simple piece of advice on how to raise her son, Basil. Mattie is ferociously protective of her son. He's all she has, she wants to be there to comfort and protect him from any injustice. Eva's words are prophetic. As Basil grows older, he never learns to deal with life's hardships. He is unable to accept any responsibility for his actions, and when finally called on to do so, he selfishly runs away, forfeiting his mother's house as a result. In this regard, Basil is exactly like his father and many of the other men who appear in the novel. In the face of adversity or challenge, they run away. Butch Fuller is the first male character in the novel to openly maintain that running away is his life philosophy. He indirectly passes this legacy on to Basil.

Wuthering Heights

Emily Brontë (1818–1848)

CONTEXT

Wuthering Heights, which has long been one of the most popular and highly regarded novels in English literature, seemed to hold little promise when it was published in 1847, selling very poorly and receiving only a few mixed reviews. Victorian readers found the book shocking and inappropriate in its depiction of passionate, ungoverned love and cruelty (despite the fact that the novel portrays no sex or bloodshed), and the work was virtually ignored. Even Emily Brontë's sister Charlotte—an author whose works contained similar motifs of Gothic love and desolate landscapes—remained ambivalent toward the unapologetic intensity of her sister's novel. In a preface to the book, which she wrote shortly after Emily Brontë's death, Charlotte Brontë stated, "Whether it is right or advisable to create beings like Heathcliff, I do not know. I scarcely think it is."

Emily Brontë lived an eccentric, closely guarded life. She was born in 1818, two years after Charlotte and a year and a half before her sister Anne, who also became an author. Her father worked as a church rector, and her aunt, who raised the Brontë children after their mother died, was deeply religious. Emily Brontë did not take to her aunt's Christian fervor; the character of Joseph, a caricature of an evangelical, may have been inspired by her aunt's religiosity. The Brontës lived in Haworth, a Yorkshire village in the midst of the moors. These wild, desolate expanses—later the setting of *Wuthering Heights*—made up the Brontës' daily environment, and Emily lived among them her entire life. She died in 1848 at the age of thirty.

As witnessed by their extraordinary literary accomplishments, the Brontë children were a highly creative group, writing stories, plays, and poems for their own amusement. Largely left to their own devices, the children created imaginary worlds in which to play. Yet the sisters knew that the outside world would not respond favorably to their creative expression; female authors were often treated less seriously than their male counterparts in the nineteenth century. Thus the Brontë sisters thought it best to publish their adult works under assumed names. Charlotte wrote as Currer Bell, Emily as Ellis Bell, and Anne as Acton Bell. Their real identities remained secret until after Emily and Anne had died, when Charlotte at last revealed the truth of their novels' authorship.

Today, *Wuthering Heights* has a secure position in the canon of world literature, and Emily Brontë is revered as one of the finest writers—male or female—of the nineteenth century. Like Charlotte Brontë's Jane Eyre, *Wuthering Heights* is based partly on the Gothic tradition of the late eighteenth century, a style of literature that featured supernatural encounters, crumbling ruins, moonless nights, and grotesque imagery, seeking to create effects of mystery and fear. But *Wuthering Heights* transcends its genre in its sophisticated observation and artistic subtlety. The novel has been studied, analyzed, dissected, and discussed from every imaginable critical perspective, yet it remains unexhausted. And while the novel's symbolism, themes, structure, and language may all spark fertile exploration, the bulk of its popularity may rest on its unforgettable characters. As a shattering presentation of the doomed love affair between the fiercely passionate Catherine and Heathcliff, it remains one of the most haunting love stories in all of literature.

PLOT OVERVIEW

In the late winter months of 1801, a man named Lockwood rents a manor house called Thrushcross Grange in the isolated moor country of England. Here, he meets his dour landlord, Heathcliff, a wealthy man who lives in the ancient manor of Wuthering Heights, four miles away from the Grange. In this wild, stormy countryside, Lockwood asks his housekeeper, Nelly Dean, to tell him the story of Heathcliff and the strange denizens of Wuthering Heights. Nelly consents, and Lockwood writes down his recollections of her tale in his diary; these written recollections form the main part of *Wuthering Heights*.

Nelly remembers her childhood. As a young girl, she works as a servant at Wuthering Heights for the owner of the manor, Mr. Earnshaw, and his family. One day, Mr. Earnshaw goes to Liverpool and returns home with an orphan boy whom he will raise with his own children. At first, the Earnshaw children—a boy named Hindley and his younger sister Catherine—detest the dark-skinned Heathcliff. But Catherine quickly comes to love him, and the two soon grow inseparable, spending their days playing on the moors. After his wife's death, Mr. Earnshaw grows to prefer Heathcliff to his own son, and when Hindley continues his cruelty to Heathcliff, Mr. Earnshaw sends Hindley away to college, keeping Heathcliff nearby.

Three years later, Mr. Earnshaw dies, and Hindley inherits Wuthering Heights. He returns with a wife, Frances, and immediately seeks revenge on Heathcliff. Once an orphan, later a pampered and favored son, Heathcliff now finds himself treated as a common laborer, forced to work in the fields. Heathcliff continues his close relationship with Catherine, however. One night they wander to Thrushcross Grange, hoping to tease Edgar and Isabella Linton, the cowardly, snobbish children who live there. Catherine is bitten by a dog and is forced to stay at the Grange to recuperate for five weeks, during which time Mrs. Linton works to make her a proper young lady. By the time Catherine returns, she has become infatuated with Edgar, and her relationship with Heathcliff grows more complicated.

When Frances dies after giving birth to a baby boy named Hareton, Hindley descends into the depths of alcoholism, and behaves even more cruelly and abusively toward Heathcliff. Eventually, Catherine's desire for social advancement prompts her to become engaged to Edgar Linton, despite her overpowering love for Heathcliff. Heathcliff runs away from Wuthering Heights, staying away for three years, and returning shortly after Catherine and Edgar's marriage.

When Heathcliff returns, he immediately sets about seeking revenge on all who have wronged him. Having come into a vast and mysterious wealth, he deviously lends money to the drunken Hindley, knowing that Hindley will increase his debts and fall into deeper despondency. When Hindley dies, Heathcliff inherits the manor. He also places himself in line to inherit Thrushcross Grange by marrying Isabella Linton, whom he treats very cruelly. Catherine becomes ill, gives birth to a daughter, and dies. Heathcliff begs her spirit to remain on Earth—she may take whatever form she will, she may haunt him, drive him mad—just as long as she does not leave him alone. Shortly thereafter, Isabella flees to London and gives birth to Heathcliff's son, named Linton after her family. She keeps the boy with her there.

Thirteen years pass, during which Nelly Dean serves as Catherine's daughter's nursemaid at Thrushcross Grange. Young Catherine is beautiful and headstrong like her mother, but her temperament is modified by her father's gentler influence. Young Catherine grows up at the Grange with no knowledge of Wuthering Heights; one day, however, wandering through the moors, she discovers the manor, meets Hareton, and plays together with him. Soon afterward, Isabella dies, and Linton comes to live with Heathcliff. Heathcliff treats his sickly, whining son even more cruelly than he treated the boy's mother.

Three years later, Catherine meets Heathcliff on the moors and makes a visit to Wuthering Heights to meet Linton. She and Linton begin a secret romance conducted entirely through letters. When Nelly destroys Catherine's collection of letters, the girl begins sneaking out at night to spend time with her frail young lover, who asks her to come back and nurse him back to health. However, it quickly becomes apparent that Linton is pursuing Catherine only because Heathcliff is forcing him to; Heathcliff hopes that if Catherine marries Linton, his legal claim upon Thrushcross Grange—and his revenge upon Edgar Linton—will be complete. One day, as Edgar Linton grows ill and nears death, Heathcliff lures Nelly and Catherine back to Wuthering Heights and holds them prisoner until Catherine marries Linton. Soon after the marriage, Edgar dies, and his death is quickly followed by the death of the sickly Linton. Heathcliff now controls both Wuthering Heights and Thrushcross Grange. He forces Catherine to live at Wuthering Heights and act as a common servant, while he rents Thrushcross Grange to Lockwood.

Nelly's story ends as she reaches the present. Lockwood, appalled, ends his tenancy at Thrushcross Grange and returns to London. However, six months later, he pays a visit to Nelly, and learns of further developments in the story. Although Catherine originally mocked Hareton's ignorance and illiteracy (in an act of retribution, Heathcliff ended Hareton's education after Hindley died), Catherine grows to love Hareton as they live together at Wuthering Heights. Heathcliff becomes more and more obsessed with the memory of the elder Catherine, to the extent that he begins speaking to her ghost.

Everything he sees reminds him of her. Shortly after a night spent walking on the moors, Heathcliff dies. Hareton and young Catherine inherit Wuthering Heights and Thrushcross Grange, and they plan to be married on the next New Year's Day. After hearing the end of the story, Lockwood goes to visit the graves of Catherine and Heathcliff.

CHRONOLOGY

The story of *Wuthering Heights* is told through flashbacks recorded in diary entries, and events are often presented out of chronological order—Lockwood's narrative takes place after Nelly's narrative, for instance, but is interspersed with Nelly's story in his journal. Nevertheless, the novel contains enough clues to enable an approximate reconstruction of its chronology, which was elaborately designed by Emily Brontë. For instance, Lockwood's diary entries are recorded in the late months of 1801 and in September 1802; in 1801, Nelly tells Lockwood that she has lived at Thrushcross Grange for eighteen years, since Catherine's marriage to Edgar, which must then have occurred in 1783. We know that Catherine was engaged to Edgar for three years, and that Nelly was twenty-two when they were engaged, so the engagement must have taken place in 1780, and Nelly must have been born in 1758. Since Nelly is a few years older than Catherine, and since Lockwood comments that Heathcliff is about forty years old in 1801, it stands to reason that Heathcliff and Catherine were born around 1761, three years after Nelly. There are several other clues like this in the novel (such as Hareton's birth, which occurs in June, 1778). The following chronology is based on those clues and should closely approximate the timing of the novel's important events. A "~" before a date indicates that it cannot be precisely determined from the evidence in the novel but only closely estimated.

1500 The stone above the front door of Wuthering Heights, bearing the name of Hareton Earnshaw, is inscribed, possibly to mark the completion of the house.

1758 Nelly is born.

~1761 Heathcliff and Catherine are born.

~1767 Mr. Earnshaw brings Heathcliff to live at Wuthering Heights.

1774 Mr. Earnshaw sends Hindley away to college.

1777 Mr. Earnshaw dies; Hindley and Frances take possession of Wuthering Heights; Catherine first visits Thrushcross Grange around Christmastime.

1778 Hareton is born in June; Frances dies; Hindley begins his slide into alcoholism.

1780 Catherine becomes engaged to Edgar Linton; Heathcliff leaves Wuthering Heights.

1783 Catherine and Edgar are married; Heathcliff arrives at Thrushcross Grange in September.

1784 Heathcliff and Isabella elope in the early part of the year; Catherine becomes ill with brain fever; young Catherine is born late in the year; Catherine dies.

1785 Early in the year, Isabella flees Wuthering Heights and settles in London; Linton is born.

~1785 Hindley dies; Heathcliff inherits Wuthering Heights.

~1797 Young Catherine meets Hareton and visits Wuthering Heights for the first time; Linton comes from London after Isabella dies (in late 1797 or early 1798).

1800 Young Catherine stages her romance with Linton in the winter.

1801 Early in the year, young Catherine is imprisoned by Heathcliff and forced to marry Linton; Edgar Linton dies; Linton dies; Heathcliff assumes control of Thrushcross Grange. Late in the year, Lockwood rents the Grange from Heathcliff and begins his tenancy. In a winter storm, Lockwood takes ill and begins conversing with Nelly Dean.

1801–1802 During the winter, Nelly narrates her story for Lockwood.

1802 In spring, Lockwood returns to London; Catherine and Hareton fall in love; Heathcliff dies; Lockwood returns in September and hears the end of the story from Nelly.

1803 On New Year's Day, young Catherine and Hareton plan to be married.

W

CHARACTER LIST

Heathcliff An orphan brought to live at Wuthering Heights by Mr. Earnshaw who falls into an intense, unbreakable love with Mr. Earnshaw's daughter, Catherine. After Mr. Earnshaw dies, his resentful son Hindley abuses Heathcliff and treats him as a servant. Because of her desire for social prominence, Catherine marries Edgar Linton instead of Heathcliff. Heathcliff's humiliation and misery prompt him to spend most of the rest of his life seeking revenge on Hindley, his beloved Catherine, and their respective children (Hareton and young Catherine). A powerful, fierce, and often cruel man, Heathcliff acquires a fortune and uses his extraordinary powers of will to acquire both Wuthering Heights and Thrushcross Grange, the estate of Edgar Linton.

Catherine The daughter of Mr. Earnshaw and his wife. Catherine falls powerfully in love with Heathcliff, the orphan Mr. Earnshaw brings home from Liverpool. Catherine loves Heathcliff so intensely that she claims they are the same person. However, her desire for social advancement motivates her to marry Edgar Linton instead. Catherine is free-spirited, beautiful, spoiled, and often arrogant. She is given to fits of temper, and she is torn between her wild passion for Heathcliff and her social ambition. She brings misery to both of the men who love her.

Edgar Linton A well-bred but rather spoiled boy who grows into a tender, constant, but cowardly man. Edgar is almost the ideal gentleman: Catherine describes him as "handsome," "pleasant to be with," "cheerful," and "rich." However, this full assortment of gentlemanly characteristics, along with his civilized virtues, proves useless in Edgar's clashes with his foil, Heathcliff, who gains power over his wife, sister, and daughter.

Ellen "Nelly" Dean The chief narrator of *Wuthering Heights*. A sensible, intelligent, and compassionate woman, Nelly grew up essentially alongside Hindley and Catherine Earnshaw and is deeply involved in the story she tells. She has strong feelings for the characters in her story, and these feelings complicate her narration.

Lockwood An intermediary between Nelly and the reader, whose narration forms a frame around Nelly's. A somewhat vain and presumptuous gentleman, Lockwood deals very clumsily with the inhabitants of Wuthering Heights. Lockwood comes from a more domesticated region of England, and he finds himself at a loss when he witnesses the strange household's disregard for the social conventions that have always structured his world. As a narrator, his vanity and unfamiliarity with the story occasionally lead him to misunderstand events.

Young Catherine The daughter of Edgar Linton and the first Catherine. The first Catherine begins her life as Catherine Earnshaw and ends it as Catherine Linton; her daughter begins as Catherine Linton and, assuming that she marries Hareton after the end of the story, goes on to become Catherine Earnshaw. The mother and the daughter share not only a name but also a tendency toward headstrong behavior, impetuousness, and occasional arrogance. However, Edgar's influence seems to have tempered young Catherine's character, and she is a gentler and more compassionate woman than her mother.

Hareton Earnshaw The son of Hindley and Frances Earnshaw, and Catherine's nephew. After Hindley's death, Heathcliff assumes custody of Hareton and raises him as an uneducated field worker, just as Hindley had done to Heathcliff himself. Thus Heathcliff uses Hareton to seek revenge on Hindley. Illiterate and quick-tempered, Hareton is easily humiliated, but shows a good heart and a deep desire to improve himself. At the end of the novel, he marries young Catherine.

Linton Heathcliff Heathcliff's son by Isabella. Weak, sniveling, demanding, and constantly ill, Linton is raised in London by his mother and does not meet his father until he is thirteen years old, when he goes to live with him after his mother's death. Heathcliff despises Linton, treats him contemptuously, and, by forcing him to marry the young Catherine, uses him to cement his control over Thrushcross Grange after Edgar Linton's death. Linton dies not long after this marriage.

Hindley Earnshaw Catherine's brother and Mr. Earnshaw's son. Hindley resents Heathcliff's at Wuthering Heights. After his father dies and he inherits the estate, Hindley begins to abuse the young Heathcliff, terminating his education and forcing him to work in the fields. When Hindley's wife Frances dies shortly after giving birth to their son Hareton, he lapses into alcoholism and dissipation.

Isabella Linton Edgar Linton's sister, who falls in love with Heathcliff and marries him. Isabella sees Heathcliff as a romantic figure, like a character in a novel. Ultimately, she ruins her life by falling in love with him. He never returns her feelings and treats her as a mere tool in his quest for revenge on the Linton family.

Mr. Earnshaw Catherine and Hindley's father. Mr. Earnshaw adopts Heathcliff and brings him to live at Wuthering Heights. Mr. Earnshaw prefers Heathcliff to Hindley but nevertheless bequeaths Wuthering Heights to Hindley when he dies.

Mrs. Earnshaw Catherine and Hindley's mother, who neither likes nor trusts the orphan Heathcliff when he is brought to live at her house. Mrs. Earnshaw dies shortly after Heathcliff's arrival at Wuthering Heights.

Joseph A long-winded, fanatically religious, elderly servant at Wuthering Heights. Joseph is strange, stubborn, and unkind, and he speaks with a thick Yorkshire accent.

Frances Earnshaw Hindley's simpering, silly wife, who treats Heathcliff cruelly. Frances dies shortly after giving birth to Hareton.

Mr. Linton Edgar and Isabella's father and the proprietor of Thrushcross Grange when Heathcliff and Catherine are children. An established member of the gentry, Mr. Linton raises his son and daughter to be well-mannered young people.

Mrs. Linton Mr. Linton's somewhat snobbish wife, who does not like Heathcliff to be allowed near her children, Edgar and Isabella. Mrs. Linton teaches Catherine to act like a gentle-woman, thereby instilling her with social ambitions.

Zillah The housekeeper at Wuthering Heights during the latter stages of the narrative.

Mr. Green Edgar Linton's lawyer, who arrives too late to hear Edgar's final instruction to change his will, which would have prevented Heathcliff from obtaining control over Thrushcross Grange.

ANALYSIS OF MAJOR CHARACTERS

HEATHCLIFF Though *Wuthering Heights* centers around the story of Heathcliff, Heathcliff defies being understood. Brontë teases the reader with the possibility that Heathcliff's cruelty is merely an expression of his frustrated love for Catherine, or that his sinister behaviors serve to conceal the heart of a romantic hero—expectations we fall prey to. Traditionally, romance novel heroes initially appear dangerous, brooding, and cold, only later to emerge as fiercely devoted and loving. One hundred years before Emily Brontë wrote *Wuthering Heights*, the notion that "a reformed rake makes the best husband" was already a cliché of romantic literature, and contemporary romance novels center around the same cliché. However, Heathcliff does not reform, and his malevolence proves so great and long-lasting that it cannot be adequately explained even as a desire for revenge against Hindley, Catherine, Edgar, and others. As he himself points out, his abuse of Isabella is purely sadistic, as he amuses himself by seeing how much abuse she can take and still come cringing back for more.

The fact that Heathcliff begins his life as a homeless orphan on the streets of Liverpool is significant. When Brontë wrote her book, in the 1840s, the English economy was severely depressed, and the conditions of the factory workers in industrial areas like Liverpool were so appalling that the upper and middle classes feared violent revolt. Thus, many of the more affluent members of society beheld these workers with a mixture of sympathy and fear. In literature, the smoky, threatening, miserable factory-towns were often represented in religious terms and compared to hell. The poet William Blake, writing near the turn of the nineteenth century, speaks of England's "dark Satanic Mills." Heathcliff, of course, is frequently compared to a demon by the other characters in the novel.

Considering this historical context, Heathcliff seems to embody the anxieties that the book's upper- and middle-class audience had about the working classes. The reader may easily sympathize with him when he is powerless, as a child tyrannized by Hindley Earnshaw, but he becomes a villain when he acquires power and returns to Wuthering Heights with money and the trappings of a gentleman. This change corresponds with the ambivalence the upper classes felt toward the lower classes—the upper classes had charitable impulses toward lower-class citizens when they were miserable, but they feared the prospect of the lower classes trying to escape their miserable circumstances by acquiring political, social, cultural, or economic power.

CATHERINE The location of Catherine's coffin symbolizes the conflict that tears apart her short life. She is not buried in the chapel with the Lintons, nor is her coffin placed among the tombs of the Earnshaws. Instead, as Nelly describes in Chapter XVI, Catherine is buried "in a corner of the kirkyard, where the wall is so low that heath and bilberry plants have climbed over it from the moor." Moreover, she is buried with Edgar on one side and Heathcliff on the other, suggesting her conflicted loyalties. Her actions are driven in part by her social ambitions, which initially are awakened during her first stay at the Lintons' and which eventually compel her to marry Edgar. However, she is also motivated by impulses that prompt her to violate social conventions—to love Heathcliff, throw temper tantrums, and run around on the moor.

Isabella Linton—Catherine's sister-in-law and Heathcliff's wife, who was born in the same year that Catherine was—serves as Catherine's foil. The two women's parallel positions allow us to see their differences with greater clarity. Catherine represents wild nature, in both her high, lively spirits and her occasional cruelty, whereas Isabella represents culture and civilization, both in her refinement and in her weakness.

EDGAR Just as Isabella Linton serves as Catherine's foil, Edgar Linton serves as Heathcliff's. Edgar is born and raised a gentleman. He is graceful, well-mannered, and instilled with civilized virtues. These qualities cause Catherine to choose Edgar over Heathcliff and thus to initiate the contention between the men. Nevertheless, Edgar's gentlemanly qualities ultimately prove useless in his ensuing rivalry with Heathcliff. Edgar is particularly humiliated by his confrontation with Heathcliff in Chapter XI, in which he openly shows his fear of fighting Heathcliff. Catherine, having witnessed the scene, taunts him, saying, "Heathcliff would as soon lift a finger at you as the king would march his army against a colony of mice." As the reader can see from the earliest descriptions of Edgar as a spoiled child, his refinement is tied to his helplessness and impotence.

Charlotte Brontë, in her preface to the 1850 edition of *Wuthering Heights*, refers to Edgar as "an example of constancy and tenderness" and goes on to suggest that her sister Emily was using Edgar to point out that such characteristics constitute true virtues in all human beings, not just in women, as society tended to believe. However, Charlotte's reading seems influenced by her own feminist agenda. Edgar's inability to counter Heathcliff's vengeance, and his naïve belief on his deathbed in his daughter's safety and happiness, make him a weak, if sympathetic, character.

THEMES, MOTIFS, AND SYMBOLS

THEMES

W

THE DESTRUCTIVENESS OF UNCHANGING LOVE Catherine and Heathcliff's passion for one another is stronger and longer lasting than any other emotion displayed in the novel, and it is the source of most of the major conflicts. As Nelly tells Catherine and Heathcliff's story, she criticizes them harshly, condemning their passion as immoral, but this passion is one of the most compelling aspects of the novel. Brontë is unclear about whether she intends the reader to condemn these lovers as blameworthy or to idealize them as romantic heroes whose love transcends social norms and conventional morality. The novel is actually structured around two parallel love stories: the love between Catherine and Heathcliff in the first half; the developing love between young Catherine and Hareton in the less dramatic second half. In contrast to the first, the latter tale ends happily, restoring peace and order to Wuthering Heights and Thrushcross Grange. The differences between the two love stories contribute to the reader's understanding of why each ends the way it does.

The most important feature of young Catherine and Hareton's love story is that it involves growth and change. Early in the novel, Hareton seems irredeemably brutal, savage, and illiterate, but over time he becomes a loyal friend to young Catherine and learns to read. When young Catherine first meets Hareton, he seems completely alien to her world, yet her attitude also evolves from contempt to love. Catherine and Heathcliff's love, on the other hand, is rooted in their childhood and is marked by the refusal to change. In choosing to marry Edgar, Catherine seeks a more genteel life, but she refuses to adapt to her role as wife, either by sacrificing Heathcliff or embracing Edgar. In Chapter XII she suggests to Nelly that the years since she was twelve years old and her father died have been like a blank to her, and she longs to return to the moors of her childhood. Heathcliff, for his part, possesses a seemingly superhuman ability to maintain the same attitude and to nurse the same grudges over many years.

Catherine and Heathcliff's love is based on their shared perception that they are identical. Catherine declares, famously, "I *am* Heathcliff," while Heathcliff, upon Catherine's death, wails that he cannot live without his "soul," meaning Catherine. Their love denies difference and is strangely asexual. The two do not kiss in dark corners or arrange secret trysts, as adulterers do. Given that Catherine and Heathcliff's love is based upon their refusal to change over time or embrace difference in others, it is fitting that the disastrous problems of their generation are overcome not by some climactic reversal but simply by the inexorable passage of time and the rise of a new and distinct generation. Ultimately, *Wuthering Heights* presents a vision of life as a process of change and celebrates this process over and against the romantic intensity of its principal characters.

THE PRECARIOUSNESS OF SOCIAL CLASS As members of the gentry, the Earnshaws and the Lintons occupy a somewhat precarious place within the hierarchy of late eighteenth- and early nineteenth-century British society. At the top of British society was the royalty, followed by the aristocracy, the gentry, and the lower classes, who made up the vast majority of the population. Although the gentry, or upper-middle class, possessed servants and often large estates, they held a fragile social position. The social status of aristocrats was a formal and settled matter because aristocrats had official titles. Members of the gentry, however, held no titles, and their status was thus subject to change. A man might see himself as a gentleman but find, to his embarrassment, that his neighbors did not share this view. A discussion of whether or not a man was really a gentleman would consider such questions as how much land he owned, how many tenants and servants he had, how he spoke, whether he kept horses and a carriage, and whether his money came from land or "trade"—gentlemen scorned banking and commercial activities.

Considerations of class status often crucially inform the characters' motivations in *Wuthering Heights*. Catherine's decision to marry Edgar so that she will be "the greatest woman of the neighborhood" is the most obvious example. The Lintons are relatively firm in their gentry status but nonetheless take great pains to prove this status through their behaviors. The Earnshaws, on the other hand, rest on much shakier ground socially. They do not have a carriage, they have less land, and their house, as Lockwood remarks with great puzzlement, resembles that of a "homely, northern farmer" and not that of a gentleman. The shifting nature of social status is demonstrated most strikingly in Heathcliff's trajectory from homeless waif to young gentleman-by-adoption to common laborer to gentleman again (although the status-conscious Lockwood remarks that Heathcliff is only a gentleman in "dress and manners").

MOTIFS

DOUBLES Brontë organizes her novel by arranging its elements—characters, places, and themes—into pairs. Catherine and Heathcliff are closely matched in many ways and see themselves as identical. Catherine's character is divided into two warring sides: the side that wants Edgar and the side that wants Heathcliff. Catherine and young Catherine are both remarkably similar and strikingly different. The two houses, Wuthering Heights and Thrushcross Grange, represent opposing worlds and values. The novel has not one but two distinct narrators, Nelly and Mr. Lockwood. The relation between such paired elements is usually quite complicated, with the members of each pair being neither exactly alike nor diametrically opposed. For instance, the Lintons and the Earnshaws may at first seem to represent opposing sets of values, but, by the end of the novel, so many intermarriages have taken place that one can no longer distinguish between the two families.

REPETITION Repetition is another tactic Brontë employs in organizing *Wuthering Heights*. It seems that nothing ever ends in the world of this novel. Instead, time seems to run in cycles, and the horrors of the past repeat themselves in the present. The way that the names of the characters are recycled, so that the names of the characters of the younger generation seem only to be rescramblings of the names of their parents, leads the reader to consider how plot elements also repeat themselves. For instance, Heathcliff's degradation of Hareton repeats Hindley's degradation of Heathcliff. Also, the young Catherine's mockery of Joseph's earnest evangelical zealousness repeats her mother's. Even Heathcliff's second try at opening Catherine's grave repeats his first.

THE CONFLICT BETWEEN NATURE AND CULTURE In *Wuthering Heights,* Brontë constantly plays nature and culture against each other. Nature is represented by the Earnshaw family, and by Catherine and Heathcliff in particular. These characters are governed by their passions, not by reflection or ideals of civility. Correspondingly, the house where they live—Wuthering Heights—comes to symbolize a similar wildness. On the other hand, Thrushcross Grange and the Linton family represent culture, refinement, convention, and cultivation.

When, in Chapter VI, Catherine is bitten by the Lintons' dog and brought into Thrushcross Grange, the two sides are brought onto the collision course that structures the majority of the plot. At the time of that first meeting between the Linton and Earnshaw households, chaos has already begun to erupt at Wuthering Heights, where Hindley's cruelty and injustice reign, whereas all seems to be fine and peaceful at Thrushcross Grange. However, the influence of Wuthering Heights soon proves overpowering, and the inhabitants of Thrushcross Grange are drawn into Catherine, Hindley, and Heathcliff's drama. Thus the reader almost may interpret Wuthering Heights's impact on the Linton family as an allegory for the corruption of culture by nature, creating a curious reversal of the more traditional story of the corruption of nature by culture. However, Brontë tells her story in such a way as to prevent our interest and sympathy from straying too far from the wilder characters and often portrays the more civilized characters as despicably weak and silly. This method of characterization prevents the novel from flattening out into a simple privileging of culture over nature, or vice versa. Thus, in the end, the reader must acknowledge that the novel is no mere allegory.

SYMBOLS

MOORS The constant emphasis on landscape within the text of *Wuthering Heights* endows the setting with symbolic importance. This landscape is comprised primarily of moors: wide, wild expanses, high but somewhat soggy, and thus infertile. Moorland cannot be cultivated, and its uniformity makes navigation difficult. It features particularly waterlogged patches in which people could potentially drown. (This possibility is mentioned several times in *Wuthering Heights.*) Thus, the moors serve very well as symbols of the wild threat posed by nature. As the setting for the beginnings of Catherine and Heathcliff's bond (the two play on the moors during childhood), the moorland transfers its symbolic associations onto the love affair.

GHOSTS Ghosts appear throughout *Wuthering Heights,* as they do in most other works of Gothic fiction, yet Brontë always presents them in such a way that whether they really exist remains ambiguous. Thus the world of the novel can always be interpreted as a realistic one. Certain ghosts—such as Catherine's spirit when it appears to Lockwood in Chapter III—may be explained as nightmares. The villagers' alleged sightings of Heathcliff's ghost in Chapter XXXIV could be dismissed as unverified superstition. Whether or not the ghosts are "real," they symbolize the manifestation of the past within the present, and the way memory stays with people, permeating their day-to-day lives.

IMPORTANT QUOTATIONS EXPLAINED

---

1. *But Mr. Heathcliff forms a singular contrast to his abode and style of living. He is a dark-skinned gypsy in aspect, in dress and manners a gentleman, that is, as much a gentleman as many a country squire . . . I know, by instinct, his reserve springs from an aversion to showy displays of feeling—to manifestations of mutual kindliness. He'll love and hate, equally under cover, and esteem it a species of impertinence to be loved or hated again—No, I'm running on too fast—I bestow my own attributes over-liberally on him.*

This passage, from the first chapter and spoken in the voice of Lockwood, constitutes the first of many attempts to explain the mysterious figure of Heathcliff. Critics and readers face the same questions as Lockwood: how is Heathcliff best understood? Is he a gentleman or a gypsy? We enter the novel as Lockwood enters the house, and are immediately confronted with all sorts of strange scenes and characters—Heathcliff the strangest of all—and must venture interpretations of them. Later illuminations of Heathcliff's personality show this first interpretation to be a laughable failure, indicating little beyond Lockwood's vanity. Lockwood, in claiming to recognize in Heathcliff a kindred soul, whom he can understand "by instinct," makes assumptions that appear absurd once Heathcliff's history is revealed.

Lockwood, while he rather proudly styles himself a great misanthrope and hermit, in fact resembles Heathcliff very little. In the many misjudgments and blunders Lockwood makes in his early visits to Wuthering Heights, we see how easy it is to misinterpret Heathcliff's complex character, and the similarity between our own position and Lockwood's becomes a warning to us as readers. We, too, should question our instincts.

---

2. *The ledge . . . was covered with writing scratched on the paint. . . . nothing but a name repeated in all kinds of characters, large and small—Catherine Earnshaw, here and there varied to Catherine Heathcliff, and then again to Catherine Linton. In vapid listlessness I leant my head against the window, and continued spelling over Catherine Earnshaw—Heathcliff—Linton, till my eyes closed; but they had not rested five minutes when a glare of white letters started from the dark, as vivid as spectres—the air swarmed with Catherines . . .*

In this passage from Chapter III, Lockwood relates the first of the troubling dreams he has in Catherine's old bed. The statement testifies to Lockwood's role as a reader within the novel, representing the external reader—the perplexed outsider determined to discover the secrets of Wuthering Heights. Upon Lockwood's first arrival at the house, no one answers his knocks on the door, and he cries, "I don't care—I will get in!" The same blend of frustration and determination has marked the responses of many readers and critics when facing the enigmas of *Wuthering Heights*.

The connection between Lockwood and readers is particularly clear in this passage. Catherine first appears to Lockwood, as she does to readers, as a written word—her name, scratched into the paint. When Lockwood reads over the scraped letters, they seem to take on a ghostly power. Ghosts are a key image throughout the novel. In this instance, it is crucial to note that what comes back, in this first dream, is not a dead person but a name, and that what brings the name back is the act of reading it. Brontë, by using Lockwood as a stand-in for her readers, indicates how she wants her readers to react to her book: she wants her words to come vividly before them, to haunt them.

This passage is also an example of *Wuthering Heights*'s ambiguous genre. The work is often compared to the Gothic novels popular in the late eighteenth century, which dealt in ghosts and gloom, demonic heroes with dark glints in their eyes, and so on. But Brontë wrote her book in the 1840s, when the fashion for the Gothic novel was past and that genre was quickly being replaced as the dominant form by the socially conscious realistic novel, as represented by the work of Dickens and Thackeray. *Wuthering Heights* often seems to straddle the two genres, containing many Gothic elements but also obeying most of the conventions of Victorian realism. The question of genre comes to a head in the appearances of ghosts in the novel. Readers cannot be sure whether they are meant to understand the ghosts as nightmares, to explain them in terms of the psychology of the characters who claim to see them, or to take them, as in a Gothic novel, as no less substantial than the other characters. Brontë establishes this ambiguity carefully. The "spectres" here are introduced within a simile, and in a context that would support their interpretation as a nightmare. Similarly subtle ambiguities lace Lockwood's account, a few pages later, of his encounter with the ghost of Catherine.

---

3. *It would degrade me to marry Heathcliff now; so he shall never know how I love him; and that, not because he's handsome, Nelly, but because he's more myself than I am. Whatever our souls are made of, his and mine are the same, and [Edgar's] is as different as a moonbeam from lightning, or frost from fire.*

Catherine's speech to Nelly about her acceptance of Edgar's proposal, in Chapter IX, is the turning point of the plot. At this point, Heathcliff leaves Wuthering Heights, after he has overheard Catherine say that it would "degrade" her to marry him. Although the action of *Wuthering Heights* takes place so far from the bustle of society, where most of Brontë's contemporaries set their scenes, social ambition motivates many of the actions of these characters, however isolated they are among the moors. Catherine's decision to marry Edgar Linton out of a desire to be "the greatest woman of the neighbourhood" exemplifies the effect of social considerations on the characters' actions.

In Catherine's paradoxical statement that Heathcliff is "more myself than I am," we can see how the relation between Catherine and Heathcliff often transcends a dynamic of desire and becomes one of unity. Heterosexual love is often described in literature in terms of complementary opposites—like moonbeam and lightning, or frost and fire—but the love between Catherine and Heathcliff opposes this convention. Catherine says not, "I love Heathcliff" but "I *am* Heathcliff." In following the relationship through to its painful end, the novel ultimately may attest to the destructiveness of a love that denies difference.

---

4. *". . . I got the sexton, who was digging Linton's grave, to remove the earth off her coffin lid, and I opened it. I thought, once, I would have stayed there, when I saw her face again— it is hers yet—he had hard work to stir me; but he said it would change, if the air blew on it, and so I struck one side of the coffin loose, and covered it up . . ."*

When Heathcliff narrates this ghoulish scene to Nelly in Chapter XXIX, the book enters into one of its most Gothic moments. Heathcliff, trying to recapture Catherine herself, constantly comes upon mere reminders of her. However, far from satisfying him, these reminders only lead him to further attempts. Heathcliff's desire to rejoin Catherine might indeed explain the majority of Heathcliff's actions, from his acquisition of Thrushcross Grange and Wuthering Heights, to his seizure of power over everyone associated with Catherine.

He tries to break through what reminds him of his beloved to his beloved herself by destroying the reminder, the intermediary. The language he uses here reveals this difference between the objects that refer to Catherine and Catherine herself. When he opens her coffin, he does not say that he sees her again. Instead, he says, "I saw her face again," showing that her corpse, like her daughter or her portrait, is a thing she possessed, a thing that refers to her, but not the woman herself. It seems that, in this extreme scene, he realizes at last that he will never get through to her real presence by acquiring and ruining the people and possessions associated with her. This understanding brings Heathcliff a new tranquility, and from this point on he begins to lose interest in destruction.

---

5. *I cannot look down to this floor, but her features are shaped on the flags! In every cloud, in every tree—filling the air at night, and caught by glimpses in every object by day, I am surrounded with her image! . . . The entire world is a dreadful collection of memoranda that she did exist, and that I have lost her!*

In this passage from Chapter XXXIII, Heathcliff confesses to Nelly his inner state. What Nelly calls Heathcliff's "monomania on the subject of his departed idol" has now reached its final stage of development. In the passage in which Heathcliff describes his excavation of Catherine's grave, the reader gains insight into Heathcliff's frustration regarding the double nature of all of Catherine's "memoranda." While Catherine's corpse recalls her presence, it fails to substitute fully for it, and thus recalls her absence. Heathcliff's perception of this doubling comes through in his language. The many signs of Catherine show that "she did exist" but that "I have lost her." In the end, because his whole being is bound up with Catherine, Heathcliff's total set of perceptions of the world is permeated by her presence. Consequently, he finds signs of Catherine in "[t]he entire world," and not just in localized figures such as her daughter or a portrait of Catherine.

The Yellow Wallpaper

Charlotte Perkins Gilman (1860–1935)

CONTEXT

Charlotte Perkins Gilman was best known in her time as a crusading journalist and feminist intellectual, a follower of such pioneering women's rights advocates as Susan B. Anthony, Elizabeth Cady Stanton, and Harriet Beecher Stowe, Gilman's great-aunt. Gilman was concerned with political inequality and social justice in general, but the primary focus of her writing was the unequal status of women within the institution of marriage. In such works as *Concerning Children* (1900), *The Home* (1904), and *Human Work* (1904), Gilman argued that women's obligation to remain in the domestic sphere robbed them of the expression of their full powers of creativity and intelligence, while simultaneously robbing society of women whose abilities suited them for professional and public life. An essential part of her analysis was that the traditional power structure of the family made *no one* happy—not the woman who was made into an unpaid servant, not the husband who was made into a master, and not the children who were subject to both. Her most ambitious work, *Women and Economics* (1898), analyzed the hidden value of women's labor within the capitalist economy and argued, as Gilman did throughout her works, that financial independence for women could only benefit society as a whole.

Today, Gilman is primarily known for one remarkable story, "The Yellow Wallpaper," which was considered almost unprintably shocking in its time and which unnerves readers to this day. This short work of fiction, which deals with an unequal marriage and a woman destroyed by her unfulfilled desire for self-expression, deals with the same concerns and ideas as Gilman's nonfiction but in a much more personal mode. Indeed, "The Yellow Wallpaper" draws heavily on a particularly painful episode in Gilman's own life.

In 1886, early in her first marriage and not long after the birth of her daughter, Charlotte Perkins Stetson (as she was then known) was stricken with a severe case of depression. In her 1935 autobiography, *The Living of Charlotte Perkins Gilman*, she describes her "utter prostration" by "unbearable inner misery" and "ceaseless tears," a condition only made worse by the presence of her husband and her baby. She was referred to Dr. S. Weir Mitchell, then the country's leading specialist in nervous disorders, whose treatment in such cases was a "rest cure" of forced inactivity. Especially in the case of his female patients, Mitchell believed that depression was brought on by too much mental activity and not enough attention to domestic affairs. For Gilman, this course of treatment was a disaster. Prevented from working, she soon had a nervous breakdown. At her worst, she was reduced to crawling into closets and under beds, clutching a rag doll.

Once she abandoned Mitchell's rest cure, Gilman's condition improved, though she claimed to feel the effects of the ordeal for the rest of her life. Leaving behind her husband and child, a scandalous decision, Charlotte Perkins Stetson (she took the name Gilman after a second marriage, to her cousin) embarked on a successful career as a journalist, lecturer, and publisher. She wrote "The Yellow Wallpaper" soon after her move to California, and in it she uses her personal experience to create a tale that is both a chilling description of one woman's fall into madness and a potent symbolic narrative of the fate of creative women stifled by a paternalistic culture.

In purely literary terms, "The Yellow Wallpaper" looks back to the tradition of the psychological horror tale as practiced by Edgar Allan Poe. For example, Poe's "The Tell-Tale Heart" is also told from the point of view of an insane narrator. Going further back, Gilman also draws on the tradition of the Gothic romances of the late eighteenth century, which often featured spooky old mansions and young heroines determined to uncover their secrets. Gilman's story is also forward-looking, however, and her moment-by-moment reporting of the narrator's thoughts is clearly a move in the direction of the sort of stream-of-consciousness narration used by such twentieth-century writers as Virginia Woolf, James Joyce, and William Faulkner.

PLOT OVERVIEW

The narrator begins her journal by marveling at the grandeur of the house and grounds her husband has taken for their summer vacation. She describes it in romantic terms as an aristocratic estate or even a haunted house and wonders how they were able to afford it, and why the house had been empty for so long. Her feeling that there is "something queer" about the situation leads her into a discussion of her illness—she is suffering from "nervous depression"—and of her marriage. She complains that her husband John, who is also her doctor, belittles both her illness and her thoughts and concerns in general. She contrasts his practical, rationalistic manner with her own imaginative, sensitive ways. Her treatment requires that she do almost nothing active, and she is especially forbidden from working and writing. She feels that activity, freedom, and interesting work would help her condition and reveals that she has begun her secret journal in order to "relieve her mind." In an attempt to do so, the narrator begins describing the house. Her description is mostly positive, but disturbing elements such as the "rings and things" in the bedroom walls, and the bars on the windows, keep showing up. She is particularly disturbed by the yellow wallpaper in the bedroom, with its strange, formless pattern, and describes it as "revolting." Soon, however, her thoughts are interrupted by John's approach, and she is forced to stop writing.

As the first few weeks of the summer pass, the narrator becomes good at hiding her journal, and thus hiding her true thoughts from John. She continues to long for more stimulating company and activity, and she complains again about John's patronizing, controlling ways—although she immediately returns to the wallpaper, which begins to seem not only ugly, but oddly menacing. She mentions that John is worried about her becoming fixated on it, and that he has even refused to repaper the room so as not to give in to her neurotic worries. The narrator's imagination, however, has been aroused. She mentions that she enjoys picturing people on the walkways around the house and that John always discourages such fantasies. She also thinks back to her childhood, when she was able to work herself into a terror by imagining things in the dark. As she describes the bedroom, which she says must have been a nursery for young children, she points out that the paper is torn off the wall in spots, there are scratches and gouges in the floor, and the furniture is heavy and fixed in place. Just as she begins to see a strange sub-pattern behind the main design of the wallpaper, her writing is interrupted again, this time by John's sister, Jennie, who is acting as housekeeper and nurse for the narrator.

As the Fourth of July passes, the narrator reports that her family has just visited, leaving her more tired than ever. John threatens to send her to Weir Mitchell, the real-life physician under whose care Gilman had a nervous breakdown. The narrator is alone most of the time and says that she has become almost fond of the wallpaper and that attempting to figure out its pattern has become her primary entertainment. As her obsession grows, the sub-pattern of the wallpaper becomes clearer. It begins to resemble a woman "stooping down and creeping" behind the main pattern, which looks like the bars of a cage. Whenever the narrator tries to discuss leaving the house, John makes light of her concerns, effectively silencing her. Each time he does so, her disgusted fascination with the paper grows.

Soon the wallpaper dominates the narrator's imagination. She becomes possessive and secretive, hiding her interest in the paper and making sure no one else examines it so that she can "find it out" on her own. At one point, she startles Jennie, who had been touching the wallpaper and who mentions that she had found yellow stains on their clothes. Mistaking the narrator's fixation for tranquility, John thinks she is improving. But she sleeps less and less and is convinced that she can smell the paper all over the house, even outside. She discovers a strange smudge mark on the paper, running all around the room, as if it had been rubbed by someone crawling against the wall.

The sub-pattern now clearly resembles a woman who is trying to get out from behind the main pattern. The narrator sees her shaking the bars at night and creeping around during the day, when the woman is able to escape briefly. The narrator mentions that she, too, creeps around at times. She suspects that John and Jennie are aware of her obsession, and she resolves to destroy the paper once and for all, peeling much of it off during the night. The next day she manages to be alone and goes into something of a frenzy, biting and tearing at the paper in order to free the trapped woman, whom she sees struggling from inside the pattern.

By the end, the narrator is hopelessly insane, convinced that there are many creeping women around and that she herself has come out of the wallpaper—that she herself is the trapped woman. She creeps endlessly around the room, smudging the wallpaper as she goes. When John breaks into the locked room and sees the full horror of the situation, he faints in the doorway, so that the narrator has "to creep over him every time!"

CHARACTER LIST

The Narrator A young, upper-middle-class woman, newly married and a mother, who is undergoing care for depression. The narrator—whose name may or may not be Jane—is highly imaginative and a natural storyteller, though her doctors believe she has a "slight hysterical tendency." The story is told in the form of her secret diary, in which she records her thoughts as her obsession with the wallpaper grows.

John The narrator's husband and her physician. John restricts her behavior as part of her treatment. Unlike his imaginative wife, John is extremely practical, preferring facts and figures to "fancy," at which he "scoffs openly." He seems to love his wife, but he does not understand the negative effect his treatment has on her.

Jennie John's sister. Jennie acts as housekeeper for the couple. Her presence and her contentment with a domestic role intensify the narrator's feelings of guilt over her own inability to act as a traditional wife and mother. Jennie seems, at times, to suspect that the narrator is more troubled than she lets on.

ANALYSIS OF MAJOR CHARACTERS

THE NARRATOR The narrator of "The Yellow Wallpaper" is a paradox: as she loses touch with the outer world, she comes to a greater understanding of the inner reality of her life. This inner/outer split is crucial to understanding the nature of the narrator's suffering. At every point, she is faced with relationships, objects, and situations that seem innocent and natural but that are actually quite bizarre and even oppressive. In a sense, the plot of "The Yellow Wallpaper" is the narrator's attempt to *avoid* acknowledging the extent to which her external situation stifles her inner impulses. From the beginning, we see that the narrator is an imaginative, highly expressive woman. She remembers terrifying herself with imaginary nighttime monsters as a child, and she enjoys the notion that the house they have taken is haunted. Yet as part of her "cure," her husband forbids her to exercise her imagination in any way. Both her reason and her emotions rebel at this treatment, and she turns her imagination onto seemingly neutral objects—the house and the wallpaper—in an attempt to ignore her growing frustration. Her negative feelings color her description of her surroundings, making them seem uncanny and sinister, and she becomes fixated on the wallpaper.

As the narrator sinks further into her inner fascination with the wallpaper, she becomes progressively more dissociated from her day-to-day life. This process of dissociation begins when the story does, at the very moment she decides to keep a secret diary as "a relief to her mind." From that point, her true thoughts are hidden from the outer world, and the narrator begins to slip into a fantasy world in which the nature of "her situation" is made clear in symbolic terms. Gilman shows us this division in the narrator's consciousness by having the narrator puzzle over effects in the world that she herself has caused. For example, the narrator doesn't immediately understand that the yellow stains on her clothing and the long "smootch" on the wallpaper are connected. Similarly, the narrator fights the realization that the predicament of the woman in the wallpaper is a symbolic version of her own situation. At first she even disapproves of the woman's efforts to escape and intends to "tie her up."

When the narrator finally identifies herself with the woman trapped in the wallpaper, she is able to see that other women are forced to creep and hide behind the domestic "patterns" of their lives, and that she herself is the one in need of rescue. The horror of this story is that the narrator must lose herself to understand herself. She has untangled the pattern of her life, but she has torn herself apart in getting free of it. An odd detail at the end of the story reveals how much the narrator has sacrificed. During her final split from reality, the narrator says, "I've got out at last, in spite of you and Jane." Who is this Jane? Some critics claim "Jane" is a misprint for "Jennie," the sister-in-law. It is more likely, however, that "Jane" is the name of the unnamed narrator, who has been a stranger to herself and her jailers. Now she is horribly "free" of the constraints of her marriage, her society, and her own efforts to repress her mind.

JOHN Though John seems like the obvious villain of "The Yellow Wallpaper," the story does not allow us to see him as wholly evil. John's treatment of the narrator's depression goes terribly wrong, but in all likelihood he was trying to help her, not make her worse. The real problem with John is the all-encompassing authority he has in his combined role as the narrator's husband and doctor. John is so sure that he knows what's best for his wife that he disregards her own opinion of the matter, forcing her to hide her true feelings. He consistently patronizes her. He calls her "a blessed little goose" and vetoes her smallest wishes, such as when he refuses to switch bedrooms so as not to overindulge her "fancies." Further, his dry, clinical rationality renders him uniquely unsuited to understand his imaginative wife. He does not intend to harm her, but his ignorance about what she really needs ultimately proves dangerous.

John knows his wife only superficially. He sees the "outer pattern" but misses the trapped, struggling woman inside. This ignorance is why John is no mere cardboard villain. He cares for his wife, but the unequal relationship in which they find themselves prevents him from truly understanding her and her problems. By treating her as a "case" or a "wife" and not as a person with a will of her own, he helps destroy her, which is the last thing he wants. That John has been destroyed by this imprisoning relationship is made clear by the story's chilling finale. After breaking in on his insane wife, John faints in shock and goes unrecognized by his wife, who calls him "that man" and complains about having to "creep over him" as she makes her way along the wall.

THEMES, MOTIFS, AND SYMBOLS

THEMES

THE SUBORDINATION OF WOMEN IN MARRIAGE In "The Yellow Wallpaper," Gilman uses the conventions of the psychological horror tale to critique the position of women within the institution of marriage, especially as practiced by the "respectable" classes of her time. When the story was first published, most readers took it as a scary tale about a woman in an extreme state of consciousness—a gripping, disturbing entertainment, but little more. After its rediscovery in the twentieth century, however, readings of the story have become more complex. For Gilman, the conventional nineteenth-century middle-class marriage, with its rigid distinction between the "domestic" functions of the female and the "active" work of the male, ensured that women remained second-class citizens. The story reveals that this gender division had the effect of keeping women in a childish state of ignorance and preventing their full development. John's assumption of his own superior wisdom and maturity leads him to misjudge, patronize, and dominate his wife, all in the name of "helping" her. The narrator is reduced to acting like a cross, petulant child, unable to stand up for herself without seeming unreasonable or disloyal. The narrator has no say in even the smallest details of her life, and she retreats into her obsessive fantasy, the only place she can retain some control and exercise the power of her mind.

THE IMPORTANCE OF SELF-EXPRESSION The mental constraints placed upon the narrator, even more so than the physical ones, are what ultimately drive her insane. She is forced to hide her anxieties and fears in order to preserve the façade of a happy marriage and to make it seem as though she is winning the fight against her depression. From the beginning, the most intolerable aspect of her treatment is the compulsory silence and idleness of the "resting cure." She is forced to become completely passive, forbidden from exercising her mind in any way. Writing is especially off limits, and John warns her several times that she must use her self-control to rein in her imagination, which he fears will run away with her. Of course, the narrator's eventual insanity is a product of the *repression* of her imaginative power, not the expression of it. She is constantly longing for an emotional and intellectual outlet, even going so far as to keep a secret journal, which she describes more than once as a "relief" to her mind. For Gilman, a mind that is kept in a state of forced inactivity is doomed to self-destruction.

Y

THE EVILS OF THE "RESTING CURE" As someone who almost was destroyed by S. Weir Mitchell's "resting cure" for depression, it is not surprising that Gilman structured her story as an attack on this ineffective and cruel course of treatment. "The Yellow Wallpaper" is an illustration of the way a mind that is already plagued with anxiety can deteriorate and begin to prey on itself when it is forced into inactivity and kept from healthy work. To his credit, Mitchell, who is mentioned by name in the story, took Gilman's criticism to heart and abandoned the "resting cure." Beyond the specific technique described in the story, Gilman means to criticize any form of medical care that ignores the concerns of the patient, considering her only as a passive object of treatment. The connection between a woman's subordination in the home and her subordination in a doctor/patient relationship is clear—John is, after all, the narrator's husband and doctor. Gilman implies that both forms of authority can be easily abused, even when the husband or doctor means to help. All too often, the women who are the silent subjects of this authority are infantilized, or worse.

MOTIFS

IRONY Almost every aspect of "The Yellow Wallpaper" is ironic in some way. *Irony* is a way of using words to convey multiple levels of meaning that contrast with or complicate one another. In *verbal irony*, words are frequently used to convey the exact opposite of their literal meaning, such as when one person responds to another's mistake by saying "nice work." (Sarcasm—which this example embodies—is a form of verbal irony.) In her journal, the narrator uses verbal irony often, especially in reference to her husband: "John laughs at me, of course, but one expects that in marriage." Obviously, one expects no such thing, at least not in a healthy marriage. Later, she says, "I am glad my case is not serious," at a point when it is clear that she is concerned that her case is very serious indeed.

Dramatic irony occurs when there is a contrast between the reader's knowledge and the knowledge of the characters in the work. Dramatic irony is used extensively in "The Yellow Wallpaper." For example, when the narrator first describes the bedroom John has chosen for them, she attributes the room's bizarre features—the "rings and things" in the walls, the nailed-down furniture, the bars on the windows, and the torn wallpaper—to the fact that it must have once been used as a nursery. Even this early in the story, the reader sees that there is an equally plausible explanation for these details: the room had been used to house an insane person. Another example is when the narrator assumes that Jennie shares her interest in the wallpaper, while it is clear that Jennie is only now noticing the source of the yellow stains on their clothing. The effect intensifies toward the end of the story, as the narrator sinks further into her fantasy and the reader remains able to see her actions from the "outside." By the time the narrator fully identifies with the trapped woman she sees in the wallpaper, the reader can appreciate the narrator's experience from her point of view as well as John's shock at what he sees when he breaks down the door to the bedroom.

Situational irony refers to moments when a character's actions have the opposite of their intended effect. For example, John's course of treatment backfires, worsening the depression he was trying to cure and actually driving his wife insane. Similarly, there is a deep irony in the way the narrator's fate develops. She gains a kind of power and insight only by losing what we would call her self-control and reason.

THE JOURNAL An "epistolary" work of fiction takes the form of letters between characters. "The Yellow Wallpaper" is a kind of epistolary story, in which the narrator writes to herself. Gilman uses this technique to show the narrator's descent into madness both subjectively and objectively—that is, from both the inside and the outside. Had Gilman told her story in traditional first-person narration, reporting events from inside the narrator's head, the reader would never know exactly what to think: a woman inside the wallpaper might seem to actually exist. Had Gilman told the story from an objective, third-person point of view, without revealing the narrator's thoughts, the social and political symbolism of the story would have been obscured. As it is, the reader must decipher the ambiguity of the story, just as the narrator must attempt to decipher the bewildering story of her life and the bizarre patterns of the wallpaper. Gilman also uses the journal to give the story an intense intimacy and immediacy, especially in those moments when the narrative is interrupted by the approach of John or Jennie. These interruptions perfectly illustrate the constraints placed on the narrator by authority figures who urge her not to think about her "condition."

SYMBOLS

THE WALLPAPER "The Yellow Wallpaper" is driven by the narrator's sense that the wallpaper is a text she must interpret, that it symbolizes something that affects her directly. Accordingly, the wallpaper develops its symbolism throughout the story. At first it seems merely unpleasant: it is ripped, soiled, and an "unclean yellow." The worst part is the ostensibly formless pattern, which fascinates the narrator as she attempts to figure out how it is organized. After staring at the paper for hours, she sees a ghostly sub-pattern behind the main pattern, visible only in certain light. Eventually, the sub-pattern comes into focus as a desperate woman, constantly crawling and stooping, looking for an escape from behind the main pattern, which has come to resemble the bars of a cage. The narrator sees this cage as festooned with the heads of many women, all of whom were strangled as they tried to escape. Clearly, the wallpaper represents the structure of family, medicine, and tradition in which the narrator finds herself trapped. Wallpaper is domestic and humble, and Gilman skillfully uses this nightmarish, hideous paper as a symbol of the domestic life that traps so many women.

IMPORTANT QUOTATIONS EXPLAINED

---

1. *If a physician of high standing, and one's own husband, assures friends and relatives that there is really nothing the matter with one but temporary nervous depression—a slight hysterical tendency—what is one to do? . . .*

   So I take phosphates or phosphites—whichever it is, and tonics, and journeys, and air, and exercise, and am absolutely forbidden to "work" until I am well again.

   Personally, I disagree with their ideas . . .

In this passage, which appears near the beginning of the story, the main elements of the narrator's dilemma are present. The powerful, authoritative voices of her husband, her family, and the medical establishment urge her to be passive. Her own conviction, however, is that what she needs is precisely the opposite—activity and stimulation. From the outset, her opinions carry little weight. "Personally," she disagrees with her treatment, but she has no power to change the situation. Gilman also begins to characterize the narrator here. The confusion over "phosphates or phosphites" is in character for someone who is not particularly interested in factual accuracy. And the choppy rhythm of the sentences, often broken into one-line paragraphs, helps evoke the hurried writing of the narrator in her secret journal, as well as the agitated state of her mind.

---

2. *I sometimes fancy that in my condition if I had less opposition and more society and stimulus—but John says the very worst thing I can do is think about my condition, and I confess it always makes me feel bad. So I will let it alone and talk about the house.*

This section appears near the beginning of the story, and it helps characterize both the narrator's dilemma and the narrator herself. Notably, the narrator interrupts her own train of thought by recalling John's instructions. Gilman shows how the narrator has internalized her husband's authority to the point that she practically hears his voice in her head, telling her what to think. Even so, she cannot help but feel the way she does, and so the move she makes at the end—focusing on the house instead of her situation—marks the beginning of her slide into obsession and madness. This mental struggle, this desperate attempt not to think about her unhappiness, makes her project her feelings onto her surroundings, especially the wallpaper, which becomes a symbolic image of "her condition." The play on words here is typical of Gilman's consistent use of irony throughout the story. She feels bad whenever she thinks about her "condition," that is, about both her depression and her condition in general within her oppressive marriage.

---

3. *There are things in that paper which nobody knows but me, or ever will.*

   Behind that outside pattern the dim shapes get clearer every day.

   It is always the same shape, only very numerous.

   And it is like a woman stooping down and creeping about behind that pattern. I don't like it a bit. I wonder—I begin to think—I wish John would take me away from here!

About halfway through the story, the sub-pattern of the wallpaper finally comes into focus. The narrator is being drawn further and further into her fantasy, which contains a disturbing truth about her life. Gilman's irony is actively at work here: the "things" in the paper are both the ghostly women the narrator sees and the disturbing ideas she is coming to understand. She is simultaneously jealous of the secret ("nobody knows but me") and frightened of what it seems to imply. Again the narrator tries to deny her growing insight ("the dim shapes get clearer every day"), but she is powerless to extricate herself. Small wonder that the woman she sees is always "stooping down and creeping about." Like the narrator herself, she is trapped within a suffocating domestic "pattern" from which no escape is possible.

Y

4. *Life is very much more exciting now than it used to be.*

This comment comes just after the scene in which the narrator catches Jennie touching the paper and resolves that no one else is allowed to figure out the pattern. It captures one of the most distinctive qualities of "The Yellow Wallpaper": Gilman's bitter, sarcastic sense of humor. Now that the narrator has become hopelessly obsessed with the pattern, spending all day and all night thinking about it, life has become more interesting and she is no longer bored. Gilman manages to combine humor and dread in such moments. The comment is funny, but the reader knows that someone who would make such a joke is not well. Indeed, in the section that follows, the narrator casually mentions that she considered burning the house down in order to eliminate the smell of the wallpaper.

---

5. *I don't like to* look *out of the windows even—there are so many of those creeping women, and they creep so fast. I wonder if they all come out of that wall-paper as I did?*

In the story's final scene, just before John finally breaks into her room, the narrator has finished tearing off enough of the wallpaper that the woman she saw inside is now free—and the two women have become one. This passage is the exact moment of full identification, when the narrator finally makes the connection she has been avoiding, a connection that the reader has made already. The woman behind the pattern was an image of herself—she has been the one "stooping and creeping." Further, she knows that there are many women just like her, so many that she is afraid to look at them. The question she asks is poignant and complex: did they all have to struggle the way I did? Were they trapped within homes that were really prisons? Did they all have to tear their lives up at the roots in order to be free? The narrator, unable to answer these questions, leaves them for another woman—or the reader—to ponder.

Appendix: Titles Listed by Author

Author	Title
Ahmed, Leila	*A Border Passage*
Aidoo, Ama Ata	*Changes: A Love Story*
Alcott, Louisa May	*Little Women*
Allende, Isabel	*The House of the Spirits*
Alvarez, Julia	*How the Garcia Girls Lost Their Accents*
Angelou, Maya	*I Know Why the Caged Bird Sings*
Atwood, Margaret	*The Handmaid's Tale*
	Surfacing
Austen, Jane	*Emma*
	Pride and Prejudice
Beals, Melba Patillo	*Warriors Don't Cry*
Bennett, Judith	*A Medieval Life*
Brontë, Charlotte	*Jane Eyre*
Brontë, Emily	*Wuthering Heights*
Brown, Rita Mae	*Rubyfruit Jungle*
Burgos-Debray, Elisabeth	*I, Rigoberta Menchu*
Cather, Willa	*My Ántonia*
Chopin, Kate	*The Awakening*
Cisneros, Sandra	*The House on Mango Street*
Dangarembga, Tsitsi	*Nervous Conditions*
Danticat, Edwidge	*Krik? Krak!*
de Erauso, Cataline	*Lieutenant Nun*
de Jesus, Carolina Maria	*Child of the Dark*
de Pizan, Christine	*The Book of the City of Ladies*
Diamant, Anita	*The Red Tent*
Eliot, George	*Middlemarch*
El-Saadawi, Nawal	*Woman at Point Zero*
Emecheta, Buchi	*Joys of Motherhood*
Gilman, Charlotte Perkins	*Herland*
	The Yellow Wallpaper
Ginzburg, Eugenia	*Journey Into the Whirlwind*
Harper, Francis Ellen Watkins	*Iola Leory*
Hayslip, Le Ly	*When Heaven and Earth Changed Places*
Hurston, Zora Neale	*Their Eyes Were Watching God*
Jacobs, Harriet	*Incidents in the Life of a Slave Girl*
Kempe, Margery	*The Book of Margery Kempe*
Kincaid, Jamaica	*Annie John*
	Lucy: A Novel
	A Small Place
Kingston, Maxine Hong	*The Woman Warrior*
Klein, Gerda Weissman	*All But My Life*
Markandaya, Kamala	*Nectar in a Sieve*
Moody, Annie	*Coming of Age in Mississippi*
Morrison, Toni	*Beloved*
	The Bluest Eye
Naylor, Gloria	*The Women of Brewster Place*

Plath, Sylvia	*The Bell Jar*
Rhys, Jean	*Wide Sargasso Sea*
Rifaat, Alifa	*Distant View of a Minaret*
Rowlandson, Mary	*True History of the Captivity*
Shelley, Mary	*Frankenstein*
Shostak, Marjorie	*Nisa: The Life and Words of a !Kung Woman*
Silko, Leslie Marmon	*Ceremony*
Stowe, Harriet Beecher	*Uncle Tom's Cabin*
Tan, Amy	*The Joy Luck Club*
Ulrich, Laurel Thatcher	*A Midwife's Tale*
Walker, Alice	*Meridian*
	The Color Purple
Wharton, Edith	*The House of Mirth*
Winterson, Jeanette	*Oranges Are Not the Only Fruit*
Woolf, Virginia	*A Room of One's Own*
	Mrs. Dalloway
	The Waves
	To the Lighthouse
Yezierska, Anzia	*Bread Givers*